The Development of Children

The Development of Children

EIGHTH EDITION

Cynthia Lightfoot
Pennsylvania State University, Brandywine

Michael Cole
University of California, San Diego

Sheila R. Cole

worth publishers
Macmillan Learning
New York

Vice President, Social Sciences: *Charles Linsmeier*
Executive Program Manager: *Carlise Stembridge*
Development Editor: *Elaine Epstein*
Editorial Assistant: *Un Hye Kim*
Senior Marketing Manager: *Lindsay Johnson*
Marketing Assistant: *Chelsea Simens*
Director of Media Editorial, Social Sciences: *Noel Hohnstine*
Senior Media Editor: *Laura Burden*
Assistant Media Editor: *Nik Toner*
Media Project Manager: *Joseph Tomasso*
Director, Content Management Enhancement: *Tracey Kuehn*
Managing Editor: *Lisa Kinne*
Senior Workflow Project Supervisor: *Paul Rohloff*
Production Supervisor: *Jose Olivera*
Content Project Manager: *Louis C. Bruno Jr.*
Photo Editor: *Cecilia Varas*
Director of Design, Content Management: *Diana Blume*
Designer: *Lumina Datamatics, Inc.*
Art Manager: *Matthew McAdams*
Illustrations: *Matthew McAdams, Kim Martens, Chris Notarile, Northeastern Graphic, Inc.*
Project Management: *Misbah Ansari/Lumina Datamatics, Inc.*
Composition: *Lumina Datamatics, Inc.*
Printing and Binding: *King Printing Co., Inc.*
Cover Photo: *Martin Puddy/Getty Images*

Library of Congress Control Number: 2017936739

ISBN-13: 978-1-4641-7886-3
ISBN-10: 1-4641-7886-0

©2018 by Worth Publishers
©2013, 2009 by Cynthia Lightfoot, Michael Cole, Sheila R. Cole
©2001 by Michael Cole and Sheila R. Cole
All rights reserved.

Printed in the United States of America

Second printing

Worth Publishers
One New York Plaza
Suite 4500
New York, NY 10004-1562
www.macmillanlearning.com

To our families, to whom we owe a debt of gratitude for our own development

ABOUT THE AUTHORS

Courtesy Richard Lightfoot

CYNTHIA LIGHTFOOT is Professor of Human Development and Director of Academic Affairs at the Pennsylvania State University, Brandywine. Her published works focus on the sociocultural contexts of child and adolescent development, including teen pregnancy, risk-taking, identity development, and youth culture. Recent and ongoing projects address issues of diversity and inclusion in higher education. Lightfoot currently serves on the editorial board of *Culture and Psychology* and is the immediate Past-President of the Jean Piaget Society. Her interest in developmental psychology began during her undergraduate years, when she worked with emotionally troubled and autistic children in school settings and became engaged in research focused on language development, communication, and culture.

Courtesy Michael Cole

MICHAEL COLE is a Professor Emeritus at the University of California, San Diego, where he is the Director of the Laboratory of Comparative Human Cognition. For many years he spent his afternoons participating with children and undergraduates in development-enhancing after-school programs. He is an editor of the journal *Mind, Culture and Activity*. He has published widely on the role of culture and schooling in development, for which he has been awarded honorary degrees at Copenhagen University and the University of Helsinki. He is a member of the American Academy of Arts and Sciences and the National Academies of Education (of the United States and Russia).

Courtesy Sheila Cole, photo by Merideth French

SHEILA COLE is a former journalist who specialized in writing about families, children, development, and education. She also writes books for children. Her most recent book offers a history of American childhood and is written for young people. She has also authored picture books, historical fiction, and novels for young adults. She participates in literacy programs for homeless adolescents.

The Coles have three grandchildren, with whom they like to spend their summers.

BRIEF CONTENTS

CONTENTS

Alex Treadway/Getty Images

Martin Puddy/Getty Images

CHAPTER 3 BOXES

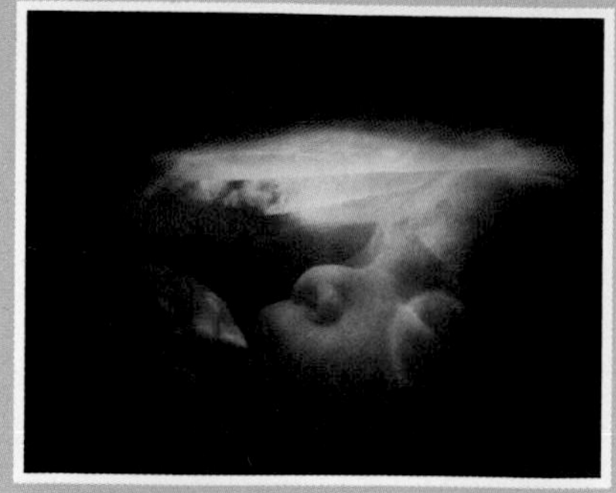

NEIL BROMHALL/SCIENCE PHOTO LIBRARY/Getty Images

CHAPTER 4 BOXES

Karin Dreyer/Getty Images

Tetra Images/Getty Images

Jessica Lia/Getty Images

CHAPTER 7 BOXES

Andy Andrews/Getty Images

PART THREE | Early Childhood 224

CHAPTER 8 BOXES

Daniel Grill/Getty Images

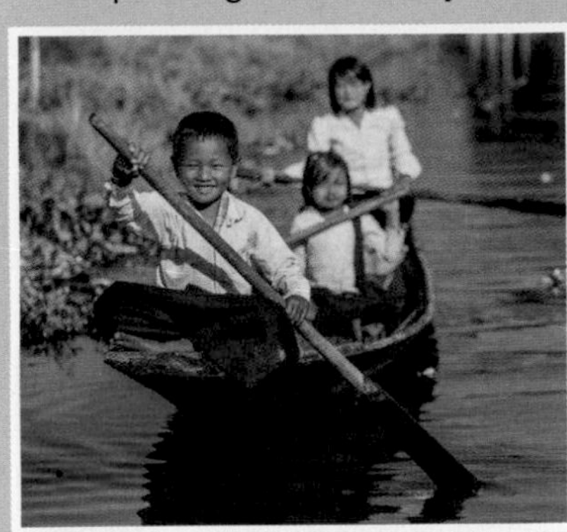
Bartosz Hadyniak/Getty Images

Lew Robertson/Getty Images

PART **FOUR** | Middle Childhood 368

CHAPTER 11 BOX

In The Field: Let's Move! A National Campaign to Battle Childhood Obesity 376

Floresco productions/Getty Images

CHAPTER 12 BOX

Now Trending in Practice: Educating Naturally in Forest Schools 423

Stuart Fox/Getty Images

SM Rafiq Photography./Getty Images

Alistair Berg/Getty Images

CHAPTER 15 BOXES

wundervisuals/Getty Images

PREFACE

Welcome to the eighth edition of *The Development of Children*. If you are new to the book, we hope you will find it a thorough yet lively review of developmental theory, research, and practice that focuses on countries and cultures from around the world as it engages the interest and intellect of today's students. If you have used previous editions, we think you will be pleased with how we have continued to integrate recent advances in developmental science with central themes that have characterized *The Development of Children* since its debut in 1989: the interaction of cultural and biological processes throughout development; the integration of theory, research, and practice; and the child as situated within a dynamically changing set of contexts.

Our interest in children's development is the result of years of personal and professional experience. My own interest was sparked during my undergraduate years, when I worked in classrooms and programs for autistic and developmentally delayed children. Later, between graduate degrees, I worked in a program for teen mothers and their children, many of whom were Vietnamese and Cambodian refugees. Having spent my adolescence in Japan, I had developed an early interest in the relationship between culture and behavior. Over time, my professional interests focused on development, culture, and issues affecting minority and immigrant children and families.

LOUISA GOULIAMAKI/Getty Images

Recent decades have seen a surge in refugee children and families who are forced to flee their native countries because of oppression and political violence. The pathways of development for the refugee children pictured here will hopefully be smoother because of programs provided by volunteers running a refugee center on the Greek island of Chios.

Similarly, Michael and Sheila Cole's personal interest in children's development extends back to their youth, when they worked together as camp counselors. Their years of experience first as parents raising children and now as grandparents have deepened their appreciation for children's development and the changing contexts in which it occurs. Both have also committed their professional lives to children's development: Michael Cole specializes in the study of the role of culture in children's learning and cognitive development; Sheila Cole is a journalist who has written articles about children and books for children.

Beyond our interest in children's development, the Coles and I share a longstanding devotion to undergraduate education. Michael Cole has spent most of his professional life at a "research 1" university; I have spent most of mine at a small college that is part of a large state university system. He and I alike see our book as a tool for promoting cultural literacy and critical thinking as well as an appreciation for how research can improve the lives of children by leading to evidence-based programs and policies. Sweeping sociocultural changes animated by globalization, the reach of technology, and the migration and displacement of people across the planet make developmental science more relevant than ever. The goal of making a positive contribution to our students' development, as well as to the development of the children that they will someday go on to educate, counsel, study, and/or parent, was a high priority for us as we worked on this book. In the sections that follow, we explain how we have pursued this goal through the book's central themes and by strengthening these themes and making other changes in this new edition.

Theoretical Orientation

A Biocultural Approach

As mentioned, culture and biology have been focuses of this book from the first edition. Integrating some of the most influential and respected work in contemporary developmental sciences, the *biocultural approach*, which was introduced in the sixth edition and further emphasized in the seventh edition and now in this, the eighth edition, is true both to the direction of the field and to our general pedagogical priorities. Regarding the direction of the field, it is clear that the theories and methods of developmental science are expanding to embrace more synthetic conceptions of how culture and biology are intertwined in ontogenetic development. In contrast to past paradigms that asked, for example, "What part nature, what part nurture?" contemporary work increasingly recognizes that universality and variation are inherent to both cultural and biological processes, which are jointly manifested over the course of development for children and adolescents throughout the world. Regarding our pedagogical priorities, the biocultural approach reflects our conviction that students' understanding of diversity—of culture, gender, ethnicity, class, religion, sexual orientation—is essential to their own development in a rapidly globalizing world. In Chapter 2, we formally present the biocultural approach as a conceptual framework for learning about how cultural processes and the biological processes of inheritance relate to each other and to the development of individual children. Biocultural foundations are underscored throughout the book in numerous discussions and illustrations, further advancing students' understanding of their relevance to developmental pathways. For highlights of the book's thoroughgoing coverage of culture as a mediator of development, please see Table 1 (p. xxi).

Danita Delimont/Alamy

These Burundi children, displaced by genocidal violence, engage in the traditional practice of beating drums.

In addition to its relevance for students' understanding of the world around them, the diversity focus inherent to the biocultural approach speaks directly to our students' personal lives and histories. It is obvious that, like our neighborhoods, places of work, and society in general, our student populations are multiethnic and multilingual. It is equally clear that students naturally seek connections between course material and their own life experience. The diversity focus of our book encourages and rewards such relevance-seeking exploration. As our many years in the classroom have shown us, when students succeed in anchoring course content to their own experience, they are more likely to understand and remember.

Roberto E. Rosales/Albuquerque Journal/ZUMAPRESS.com/Alamy

Illustrating culturally responsive education, a professional artist works with school children to create a mural, "El Ritmo de la Agua" ("The Rhythm of the Water"), to represent the region's agricultural and Hispanic heritages.

Integrating Practice, Theory, and Research

As part of challenging students to look at information critically, we promote the understanding that information arises in the context of particular

TABLE 1

Highlights of the Coverage of Culture in the Eighth Edition

Culture as a context of development, pp. 3, 4–5
Cultural variations about managing fussiness in children, p. 5
Refugee families, p. 6
Culture and development of walking, pp. 12–13
Japanese and American understandings of aggression in children, p. 16
Vygotsky and sociocultural theory, pp. 22–23
Ecological systems theory and cultural values, pp. 28–29
Cultural differences and academics, pp. 30–31
Ethnography, p. 34
Symbolic cultural tools, pp. 52–53
Cultural inheritance, pp. 53–55
Cumulative cultural evolution, pp. 55–56
Coevolution of culture and biology, pp. 72–74
Cultural variations in maternal conditions and prenatal care, pp. 90–94
Cultural variations in childbirth, pp. 105–107
Midwifery and Inuit culture, p. 108
Newborn functioning in different cultures, p. 112
Factors related to prematurity, p. 114
Parental responses to infants by culture, pp. 116–117
Cultural factors and taste preferences, p. 139
Variations in temperament in different cultures, p. 151
Sleeping arrangements around the world, including back-to-sleep practice, pp. 152–154, 155
Newborn feeding and cultural factors, p. 154
Crying and cultural factors, p. 156
Practice and motor development and cultural factors, pp. 173–174
Representation and cultural influence on infant timetables, p. 178
Cultural and universal emotional expressions, pp. 200–202
Imitative games across culture, p. 205
Emotional connections and cultural context, p. 206
Cultural variations in attachment, pp. 214–216
Learning two languages, pp. 236–239
Cultural context for the sentence and pragmatic development, pp. 239, 249
Developing narratives and cultural modeling, p. 251
Cultural explanations for language acquisition, pp. 252–255
Culture and sustained processing of spatial relations, p. 267
The role of language in culture, pp. 280, 285–286
Cultural scripts, pp. 286–288
Culturally organized contexts of children's developing competence, pp. 288–289
The cultural view and gender identity, pp. 300–301
Ethnic identity in childhood, pp. 301–302
Autobiographical memories and culture, p. 304
Cultures and moral, social, and personal rules, p. 306
The influence of culture on emotional regulation, pp. 309, 314–316
Cultural contributions to aggression, pp. 319–320
Family and culture, pp. 331, 332–333
Parenting goals and styles, pp. 334–335, 337
Siblings across cultures, pp. 337, 338–339
Immigrant families in the United States, pp. 339–341
Abusive families among cultures around the world, pp. 346–347

(Continued on next page)

TABLE 1

(Continued)

Neighborhoods and communities, and culture, pp. 352–353
Cultural traditions to help children cope with war, p. 355
Children's media and culture beliefs, pp. 356, 357
Social stereotypes, p. 360
Culture and athleticism in girls and boys, p. 378
Cultural influences on the acquisition of conservation, pp. 395–397
Cultural factors in the development of memory and attention, pp. 390, 397–398
Cultural variations in children's planning, p. 398
Cultural factors in cognitive development, pp. 398–399
Are IQ tests culturally biased? pp. 403–404
Cultural variations in school, pp. 409–411
Cultural variations in preschools, pp. 418–419
Contemporary challenges in a globalizing world, pp. 431–432
The culture of school, pp. 432–434
Culturally responsive classroom strategies, pp. 436–437
Cultural differences and popularity, p. 454
Bullying in cultures around the world, p. 456
The role of culture in competitive versus cooperative play, pp. 458–460
Culture and gender segregation, pp. 460–461
Cultural variations in parent expectations of children, pp. 467–468
Divorce rates in cultures around the world, pp. 469, 470
Cultural issues in adolescence and emerging adulthood, pp. 479–480
Cultural issues and continuous versus discontinuous societies, p. 482
Culture, physical development, and pubertal onset among the Pumé foragers, p. 485
Cultural variations and the timing of puberty, pp. 491–492, 494
Cultural influences on epistemic development, p. 502
Cultural variations in moral reasoning of adolescents, pp. 507–508, 509–510
Cultural variations in support for adolescent dating, the transmission of sexual knowledge and values, the sexual debut, teen pregnancy, and child marriage, pp. 515–516, 529, 532–533, 535
Cultural variations in parent–adolescent conflicts, pp. 537–538, 539
Cultural variations on adolescent self-determination and agency, pp. 540–541
Ethnic identity in adolescence, pp. 544–550

theories, and particular research questions and methods of inquiry, and that it should be held to standards of science. However, along with wanting students to understand the connections among information, theory, and research, we want them to understand that child development research—its questions and methods—is significantly tied to meaningful matters of practice—that is, to the issues, problems, plans, and concerns of the day. To give practice its proper place, as well as for pedagogical reasons, we make certain not to allow the story of development to be overwhelmed and obscured by seemingly disconnected facts and figures and by theoretical disputes of interest only to people in the field. Our goal is to provide students with the essential information they need to acquire meaningful, connected, and relevant *knowledge* of development and to present that information in a way that is accessible, transparent, and engaging from beginning to end.

The focus on practice—especially in the context of increasing globalization—is also apparent in the ways we have engaged our students in the enterprise of developmental science. Undergraduate students are heavily involved in Michael Cole's Fifth Dimension after-school program, which has sites across the globe. My own students have conducted projects involving immigrant families, nutrition education programs for inner-city children, and teen mothers' identity development. They have also explored peer culture and graffiti in Philadelphia and Paris in order to understand the developmental challenges of immigrant youths. In all cases, our students are actively involved in the research process, carrying knowledge from the classroom to the contexts in which children around the world live and develop.

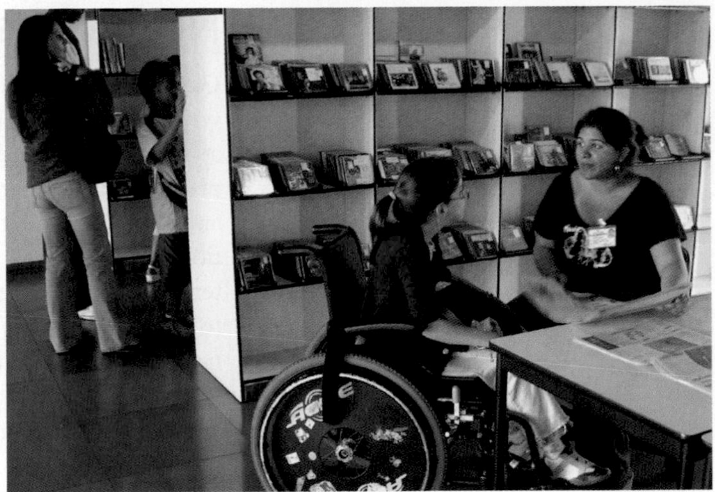
SARAH Network of Rehabilitation Hospitals

Research supports the idea that learning is effective when teachers link lessons to real-world issues and problems, as suggested here by the teacher's use of a newspaper in working with her student.

Our belief in the importance of linking practical, theoretical, and research orientations in studying development comes not only from our own experience but also as a response to the increasingly global focus of developmental science, as well as to the increasing interest in practice, service, and diversity that we see in our students. It is therefore natural that our book should focus on research as an ethical enterprise, underscoring its implications for defining and creating healthy contexts of development and preventing or solving problems that threaten children's well-being. Among the many issues we discuss are the effects of aligning cultural beliefs and birthing practices, bullying prevention strategies, culturally responsive classrooms, classroom climate and academic performance, evidence-based programs for refugee children and families, best practices for sexual education, and factors that contribute to positive youth development. Indeed, "In The Field" boxes, a special feature of the book, showcase developmentalists whose applied work is being recognized for its important impact on developmental and child-welfare and social justice issues. And, new to this edition, special feature boxes "Now Trending in Practice" and "Now Trending in Research" further support the integration of practice, theory, and research. We also include many examples drawn from the everyday lives of children to show how a society's beliefs influence its children's development by shaping both the laws and the social norms that govern child-rearing practices.

A Focus on Dynamic Interaction

The Development of Children combines traditional chronological and topical approaches to the study of development in a deliberate attempt to make as clear as possible the idea that development is a process involving the whole child situated within dynamic, interacting contexts. Although the book is chronological in its overall structure and adopts traditional age boundaries for each of its major sections, its organization is topical in two important respects. First, within the traditionally defined age periods, it describes development in physical, cognitive, social, and emotional domains, emphasizing the interaction among domains. Second, it includes several chapters devoted to underscoring the role of dynamic contexts in general and of the special context of school in particular in shaping developmental pathways.

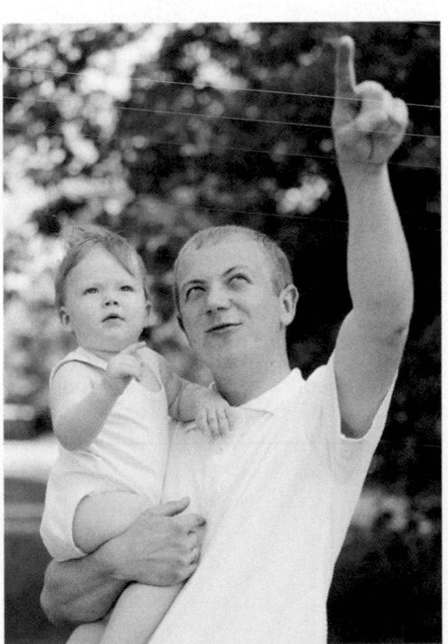
Olesya Turchuk/Shutterstock

For children just beginning to acquire language, the problem of learning what words refer to is particularly acute. This father may be telling his daughter to look at a squirrel—or a bird, tree, cloud, or any number of other objects in the direction of his pointing finger.

Our emphasis on development in context is meant to inspire students to look more closely at children in order to understand their developmental needs and how they experience the world—their peers and parents, their schools and playgrounds, their toys and games, and the monsters under their beds. After all, in their personal, professional, and civic lives, our students will influence the contexts of children's development, potentially on a global scale, thereby affecting children's potential for success and happiness. Our goal as teachers is to ensure that they do so mindfully and with purpose.

New to the Eighth Edition

Our principal goal for this edition of *The Development of Children* is to provide students with an overview of children's development that is as thought provoking and inspiring as it is comprehensive and rigorous. We take a decidedly student-centered approach, placing student learning front and center, intentionally yoking developmental theory and research to the daily lives and experiences of an increasingly diverse student population. The new coverage and thorough updating throughout enhance the book's characteristic focus on research and culture, while micro-level, sentence-by-sentence revisions to facilitate students' interest in and command of every discussion make this edition the most lively and student-friendly yet. We have also retained several highly praised pedagogical features, including compelling vignettes that open each chapter and focus on children from a range of regions, countries, and cultures, and "In The Field" boxes, which introduce students to developmentalists who apply developmental research in real-world settings. Another well-received pedagogical feature is the "Apply>Connect>Discuss" exercises at the end of each major chapter section. These exercises ask students, individually or in groups, to reflect and draw on what they have just read—for example, by comparing and contrasting theoretical viewpoints, creating an experiment or intervention, conducting online research, or applying what they have learned to a scenario or their own personal experience. New pedagogical features are included at the beginning and end of each chapter: "Warming Up" exercises ask students to reflect on issues and questions to be addressed in the chapter, and "Insight and Integration" exercises at the end of each chapter ask students to connect ideas across chapters and, in some instances, to consider new knowledge in light of their responses to the "Warming Up" exercises. Each chapter now begins with a set of "Learning Outcomes" to focus students and instructors on material to come and provide a resource for studying and preparing study guides. Each chapter ends with a "Looking Ahead" section, which summarizes the chapter in ways that promote links with the chapter to follow. We have also developed new special feature boxes—"Now Trending in Research," which highlights emerging developments in child development research, and "Now Trending in Practice," which highlights emerging applications of developmental research, with both features having a global reach.

High points of the revision include several improvements, which we describe below.

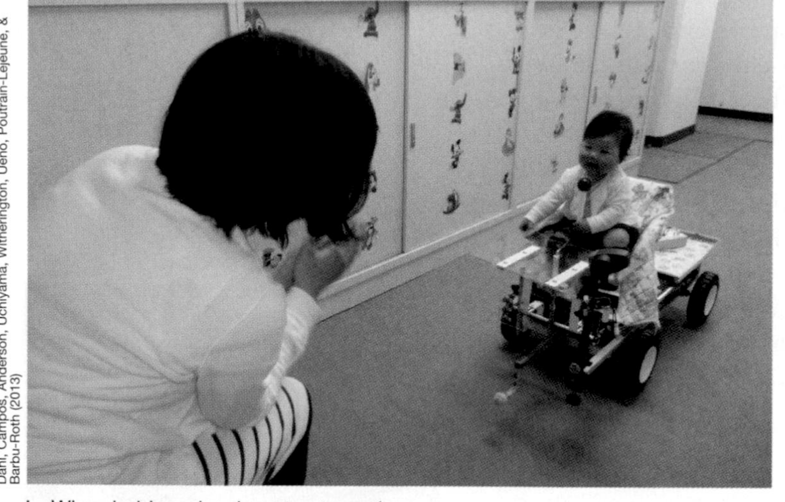

Dahl, Campos, Anderson, Uchiyama, Witherington, Ueno, Poutrain-Lejeune, & Barbu-Roth (2013)

When babies who do not yet crawl get experience moving around their environments in self-controlled go-carts, they develop wariness of heights. This suggests that wariness is due to visual proprioception, rather than experiences falling in the course of learning to crawl.

Stronger Focus on Developmental Plasticity and Diversity in Dynamic Contexts

New and expanded material underscores the interrelationship between children and the multiple, interacting contexts of their development, with increased emphasis on the diversity of children and their developmental pathways. For instance, we have expanded coverage of children growing up in multilingual and multicultural contexts and the impact of these contexts on children's social, cognitive, and identity development. We also emphasize throughout the myriad ways that development is affected by globalization, including electronic communications, media, and migration. Our diversity focus extends to culture, ethnicity, class, gender, and sexual orientation, placing developmental science within the lived experience of our students, enriching students' understanding of how basic processes of development interact with sociocultural practices, beliefs, values, and traditions, while increasing students' cultural literacy and inquisitiveness about the larger global landscape in which they live.

Updated Coverage of the Brain

Expanded coverage of the brain reflects the burgeoning of developmental neuroscience—from prenatal and infant brain development and the emergence of executive function in middle childhood to the role of various brain structures in the triggering of puberty and the significance of the prefrontal cortex in adolescent risk-taking and decision making. Engaging examples and illustrations help students make sense of recent research on brain development and its effects on other developmental domains. For highlights of the coverage of the brain in the eighth edition, see Table 2 (below).

TABLE 2

Highlights of the Coverage of the Brain in the Eighth Edition
High-tech research on brain function, development, and disorders, p. 33
The brain and biological inheritance, pp. 55, 56, 57, 58
The brain and genetic disorders, pp. 63–64, 66
Female embryos and rate of brain growth, p. 85
Brain activity and maturation during prenatal development, pp. 88–89
Fetal brain development and cortisol levels, p. 91
Impact of prenatal nutrition on brain development, p. 92
Impact of teratogens, including marijuana, on brain development, pp. 95, 97–98, 100, 102
Relationship between low birth weight and brain development, p. 113
Neonatal brain development, pp. 126–131
Experience and development of the brain, pp. 129–131
Language areas of the brain and babies ability to distinguish phonemes of native language, p. 134
Brain maturation and blurry vision in infants, p. 134
Infant reflexes and neural processing as babies reach and grasp, pp. 142, 143, 144
Neural development and preterm babies, p. 145
Brain activity and sleep, as well as SIDS, pp. 152–153, 155
Brain activity and infant crying, p. 156
Infant brain development, including early life deprivation, pp. 164–168
Motor development and infant brain activity, pp. 171, 182
Infant brain activation and understanding of number (counting) and categorization, pp. 187, 189
Brain development and emotion regulation, p. 201
Intersubjectivity and the brain, pp. 205–206
Relationship between attachment and brain development, p. 214
Brain development and self-conscious emotions, p. 221
Language development and the developing brain, including in language-deprived environments, pp. 230, 233–235, 236
Bilingualism and brain development, p. 238
Brain function and fast mapping, p. 245
Undernutrition and brain development during early childhood, p. 266
Brain development and scale errors during early childhood, pp. 266–267
Information processing and neural development, pp. 273, 276
Brain development in middle childhood, pp. 379–381
Increased speed and capacity of working memory during middle childhood, p. 390
Executive function and brain development, p. 394
Brain development and test performance, p. 404
Brain involvement in specific learning disabilities, pp. 424–425
Brain circuitry, brain-wave activity, and expanded influence of frontal lobes by adolescence, p. 471
Brain development in adolescence and its role in of puberty and on behavior, pp. 487–491
Executive function and maturation of the brain in middle childhood and adolescence, pp. 503–504
Mindfulness education and brain development, p. 519
Significant brain changes during adolescence, p. 520

Increased Focus on Health, Resilience, and Well-Being

Responding to a groundswell of research seeking to elaborate an alternative to traditional "deficit models" of child health, we have included new material on the resilience of families and children in the face of stress and challenges, research on the effectiveness of preventive programs, and expanded coverage of positive youth development.

Detailed Chapter Additions

Chapter 1: The Study of Human Development

- Introduction of technologies and social media as significant influences on development
- New special feature, "Now Trending in Practice: Helping Refugee Families in Transition"
- Revised focus for special feature, "Now Trending in Research: Observing the Living Brain"

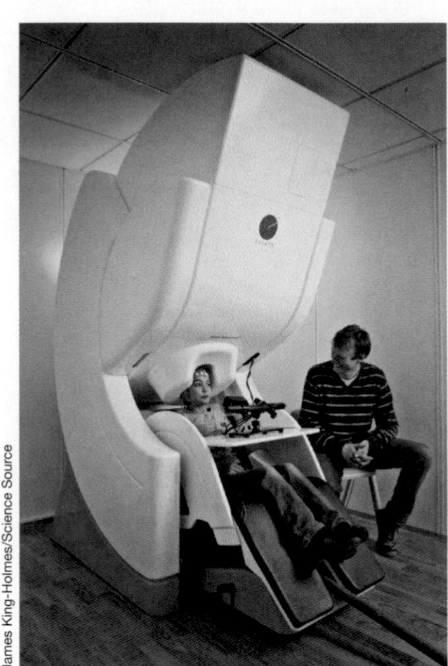

James King-Holmes/Science Source

New technologies have expanded opportunities for studying children's development. This 8-year-old girl, accompanied by her father, is sitting in a magnetoencephalograph (MEG), which can detect extremely small magnetic fields generated by neural activity in her brain. Data provided by the MEG can be used in conjunction with other tests to investigate neurological disorders such as ADHD, epilepsy, and autism spectrum disorder (ASD).

Chapter 2: Biocultural Foundations

- New discussion of how advances in technology and medical science impact prenatal assessment
- New special feature, "In The Field: Penatal Genetic Counseling"

Chapter 3: Prenatal Development and Birth

- New table on fetal behavioral states (Table 3.1)
- Discussion of new research about "fetal learning"
- New material on maternal stress and fetal development
- New discussion of microbiome
- Updated research on teratogens

Chapter 4: The First 3 Months

- New discussion of perceptual narrowing
- New discussion of new technologies to track infant gaze
- New discussion of impact of bilingual environment on perceptual narrowing and development
- Discussion of new methodologies for exploring the development of reaching
- Expanded discussion of relationship between culture and temperament
- Presentation of new research on co-sleeping

Chapter 5: Physical and Cognitive Development in Infancy

- Discussion of infant growth and interpretation of growth norms in light of challenging environments in developed and developing countries
- Expanded discussion of brain development and early-life adversity
- New special feature, "Now Trending in Practice: Bringing Up Babies in the Digital Age"
- Expanded discussion of cascade effects between motor development and other developmental domains
- Updated discussion of developing understanding of cause–effect relationships
- Revised presentation of developing memory, including the relationship to "exuberant learning"

Chapter 6: Social and Emotional Development in Infancy

- Introduction of etic and emic approaches for understanding infant emotions and emotional development in cultural contexts
- New discussion of cultural influences on maternal sensitivity and developing attachment relationships
- New tables summarizing the four phases of attachment (Table 6.1) and components of the Strange Situation procedure (Table 6.2)
- Expanded discussion of stability of attachment across development, including intergenerational transmission
- Expanded discussion of the connection between attachment relationships and later psychological adjustment
- Expanded discussion of cultural differences in networks of attachment relationships
- Revised focus for special feature, "Now Trending in Research: The Moral Life of Babies"

Odua Images/Shutterstock

Various emotional intensities are clearly apparent in the different smiles shown by this baby.

Chapter 7: Language Acquisition

- New research presented on perceptual scaffolding as it relates to how the sounds of familiar words serve as anchors for learning new words
- Revised focus for special feature, "Now Trending in Research: Creating a Language"
- New research on how multilingual environments affect babbling
- New table summarizing common first words across language environments (Table 7.2)
- New research on the acquisition of a signed language
- New research on the language environments and language development of children with cochlear implants
- Expanded discussion of language development in multilingual environments

Chapter 8: Physical and Cognitive Development in Early Childhood

- Updated discussion of sleep and how it is affected by the use of digital devices
- New research presented on precausal thinking
- Revised presentation of cognitive development in privileged domains, with new research on the animate–inanimate distinction (biology) and the "gravity error" (physics)

Chapter 9: Social and Emotional Development in Early Childhood

- Expanded discussion of gender identity and gender role development, including cultural influences
- Expanded discussion of ethnic identity development
- New research on effortful control, including its measurement by "hot" versus "cool" tasks, and how cultural beliefs, values, and practices, as well as socioeconomic status, affect its development
- Expanded discussion of the influence of culture on emotion expression and aggressive behavior

Rolf Bruderer/Getty Images

Despite an early awareness that White Americans are more likely than Black Americans to have wealth and power, African American children generally display positive self-esteem. The traditional dress of his young girl and her grandmother express their sense of ethnic pride.

Chapter 10: Contexts of Development

- Revised discussion of Bronfenbrenner's model to place more emphasis on the chronosystem
- Greater emphasis on the relationship between ethnicity and parenting practices
- Updated research on sibling relationships
- Expanded discussion of family diversity, including introduction of familism of Hispanic families
- Revised focus for special feature, "Now Trending in Practice: Children and War"
- Expanded discussion of electronic media and their impact on aggression
- New table summarizing the United Nations Convention on the Rights of the Child (Table 10.4)

Chapter 11: Physical and Cognitive Development in Middle Childhood

- Expanded discussion of gender differences in motor development and physical activity
- Thoroughly revised section on the developing brain, including expanded discussion of the limbic system and developing connections between brain regions
- New research presented on the development and control of attention
- Expanded coverage of cultural variations in memory and attention
- Introduction of meta-analysis as a research tool for documenting the Flynn effect across different types of intelligence quotient (IQ) scores (fluid, crystalized, spatial)

Chapter 12: School as a Context for Development

- New discussion of how different language environments affect mapping number words onto specific quantities
- Updated research on national differences in academic performance
- Thoroughly revised section on specific learning disabilities (SLDs) and their assessment
- Expanded discussion on the relationship between literacy and cognitive development, including metalinguistic skills
- Expanded discussion of the relationship between family culture and school culture
- New special feature, "Now Trending in Practice: Educating Naturally in Forest Schools"

Chapter 13: Social and Emotional Development in Middle Childhood

- Expanded discussion of "self" development in relation to use of electronic media, including functions of social media for social comparison and effects on developing self-esteem
- Expanded discussion of self-esteem and parenting practices
- Revised discussion of the relationship between theory of mind and moral reasoning
- Greater emphasis on the role of culture in children's popularity and social status

Hero Images/Getty Images

Schools are important sources of cooperative and competitive experiences with peers.

- New section on bully–victim relationships and peer victimization and their impacts on development
- New special feature on educating middle schoolers about bullying, "Now Trending in Practice: Katy Butler Takes on Hollywood"
- Increased emphasis on cultural influence on developing gender differences
- New section addressing gender-variant children and cultural belief systems, including the "gender binary"

Chapter 14: Physical and Cognitive Development in Adolescence

- New section highlighting Margaret Mead's contributions to understanding adolescence, including her distinction between continuous and discontinuous societies
- Major reorganization and expansion of the section "Brain Development," including discussion of limbic system changes associated with the reward system and association with adolescent exploration and risk-taking
- New discussion of normal and variants of pubertal timing
- New table overviewing normal variants of puberty (Table 14.1)
- New special feature, "Now Trending in Research: Family Stress and Pubertal Timing"
- New discussion of multitasking and effects on executive function and task performance

Chapter 15: Social and Emotional Development in Adolescence

- Increased emphasis on cultural differences in responses to sexual development
- New special feature, "Now Trending in Research: Neuroscience Meets Buddhist Philosophy in Mindfulness Education"
- New table summarizing ethnic identity statuses (Table 15.2)
- Expanded discussion of gender differences in friendships and peer relationships
- New section on how digital media impacts adolescents' relationships
- Updated discussion of peer relationships, peer culture, and delinquency
- Thoroughly revised section on the development of sexuality and sexual behaviors
- New special feature, "In The Field: Sex and . . . Pizza?"
- New section on family sexual culture
- New discussion on cyberporn and its impact on sexuality development
- New special feature, "Now Trending in Practice: Exposing and Ending Child Marriage"
- New section on parent–adolescent attachment and adjustment
- New section on the development of self-determination and agency and their relationship to resilience
- New section on the sexual self, healthy sexual development, and culture

Juice Images/Alamy Stock Photo

Romantic relationships become increasingly important during the adolescent years. In addition to providing opportunities for exploring intimacy and identity, romantic relationships are important to adolescents' sense of belonging and group status.

- Expanded coverage of ethnic identity development, including the notion of "White privilege"
- Thoroughly revised and expanded section on bicultural identity development
- Expanded discussion of racial/ethnic socialization
- Thoroughly revised and expanded section on sexual identity development, including introduction of sexual-orientation mobility

Pedagogy

This edition includes a number of pedagogical features, several of which are new. We begin each chapter with two new features: "Warming Up" exercises invite students to begin engaging with upcoming material by reflecting on their personal experiences and/or general knowledge; "Learning Outcomes" provide a key to chapter concepts and serve as a an excellent resource for studying as well as for preparing study guides. We continue the "Apply>Connect>Discuss" activities at the end of each major section to help students reflect on material and consider implications. Each chapter ends with "Insight and Integration," which encourages students to think more deeply about the material, oftentimes in light of what has been presented in the "Warming Up" exercise as well as the previous chapters; a summary; and a list of key terms designed to help students review what they've learned.

As in the previous edition, each major book part begins with a prose introduction accompanied by "Major Milestones," which is a table that presents relevant milestones in physical, cognitive, and social and emotional domains as they relate to development and sociocultural factors. Along with the milestones table, each part opener now includes a table that introduces the relevant module in the *Developing Lives* simulation (see below) and presents questions that might arise for parents about decisions they will make related to their child's physical, cognitive, and social and emotional development.

Media and Supplements

The eighth edition of *The Development of Children* is accompanied by a number of supplementary materials designed to amplify the themes of the text.

LaunchPad with *Developing Lives*, LearningCurve Quizzing, and More

Built to solve key challenges in the course, LaunchPad (LaunchPadWorks.com) gives students what they need to prepare for class and gives instructors what they need to set up a course, shape the content, craft presentations and lectures, assign and assess homework, and guide the learning of every student.

NEW! *Developing Lives:* An Interactive Simulation

Developing Lives is a sophisticated interactive experience in which each student "raises" a virtual child from sperm-and-egg to teenager. With *Developing Lives*, each student provides a personal profile, selects a virtual partner (or chooses to be a single parent) and marks the arrival for their newborn (represented by a unique avatar based on the parents' characteristics). As the child grows, the student responds to events both planned and unforeseen, making important decisions (nutrition choices, doctor visits, sleeping location) and facing uncertain moments (illness, divorce, a new baby), with each choice affecting how a child grows. Throughout, *Developing Lives* deepens each student's attachment and understanding of key concepts with immediate, customized feedback based on child development research. *Developing Lives* is fully integrated into LaunchPad and includes more than 200 videos and animations along with quizzes and essay questions that are easy to assign and assess.

Interactive e-Book

The full e-Book is available in LaunchPad and integrates the full text with the student resources. LearningCurve adaptive quizzing is designed to get students into the e-Book and enhance learning.

LearningCurve Adaptive Quizzing

LearningCurve gives individualized question sets and feedback based on each student's correct and incorrect responses. All the questions are tied back to the e-Book to encourage students to read the book in preparation for class and exams.

Video Collection for Human Development

This collection covers the full range of the course, from classic experiments to investigations of children's play to adolescent risk-taking. Instructors can assign these videos through LaunchPad and also choose activities that combine videos with short-answer and multiple-choice questions.

Instructor's Resources

The *Instructor's Resource Manual* features chapter-by-chapter previews, learning objectives, topics for discussion and debate, handouts for student projects, and supplementary readings from journals. Course planning suggestions and ideas for term projects are also included.

The editable *Lecture Slides* for every chapter provide instructors with a dynamic starting place to engage students during classroom presentations of core topics.

The thoroughly revised *Test Bank* includes multiple-choice, true/false, and essay questions for every chapter. Each question is keyed to the textbook by topic, page number, and level of difficulty.

Acknowledgments

A book of this scope and complexity could not be produced without the help of others. A great many people gave generously of their time and experience to deepen our treatment of various areas of development, particularly the many scholars who consented to review drafts of our manuscript and make suggestions for improvement. The remaining imperfections exist despite their best efforts.

For this edition, we thank **Brandy Moore**, Texas A&M University; **Catherine Caldwell Harris**, Boston University; **Dana Donohue**, Northern Arizona University; **Etta Caver**, Miami University; **Kimberly Rhoades**, Washington State University; **Jana McCurdy**, College of Western Idaho; **Jennifer Weaver**, Boise State University; **Meenal Rana**, Humboldt State University; **Marlene Bumgarner**, Gavilan College; **Mary Ann Siderits**, Marquette University; **Myra-Beth Bundy**, Eastern Kentucky University; **Nadine Agosta**, San Francisco State University; and **Rachel Romero**, Central New Mexico Community College.

We are grateful to Elaine Epstein, Carlise Stembridge, Un Hye Kim, Lou Bruno, Matthew McAdams, Cecilia Varas, Laura Burden, Diana Blume, Tracey Kuehn, and Lisa Kinne from Worth Publishers; and also Misbah Ansari from Lumina Datamatics.

Cynthia Lightfoot
Glen Mills, Pennsylvania
October, 2017

Alex Treadway/Getty Images

CHAPTER 1

The Study of Human Development

Early one morning during the cold winter of 1800, a dirty, naked boy wandered into a hut at the edge of a tiny village in the French province of Aveyron, in search of food. In the months before this appearance, some of the people in the area had caught glimpses of the boy digging for roots, climbing trees, swimming in a stream, and running rapidly on all fours. They thought he was inhuman, perhaps a wild beast. When the boy appeared in the village, word spread quickly, and everyone went to see him.

Among the curious was a government commissioner, who took the boy home and fed him. The child, who appeared to be about 12 years old, seemed ignorant of the civilized comforts that the people offered to him. When clothes were put on him, he tore them off. He refused meat and would eat only raw potatoes, roots, and nuts. He rarely made a sound and seemed indifferent to human voices. In his report to the government, the commissioner concluded that the boy had lived alone since early childhood, "a stranger to social needs and practices. . . . [T]here is . . . something extraordinary in his behavior, which makes him seem close to the state of wild animals" (quoted in Lane, 1976, pp. 8–9).

The commissioner's report caused a public sensation when it reached Paris. Newspapers hailed the child as the "Wild Boy of Aveyron." In the climate that prevailed following the French Revolution, many hoped that, with instruction, the boy could rapidly develop intellectually and socially to demonstrate that even the poor and outcast of a society could be as capable as the wealthy if they were provided a proper education. The Wild Boy seemed a perfect test case because his life had been so devoid of supportive human contact.

Unfortunately, plans to help the Wild Boy soon ran into trouble. The first physicians to examine him concluded that he was mentally deficient and speculated that he had been put out to die by his parents for that reason. (In France in the late eighteenth century, as many as one in three normal children, and a greater percentage of abnormal children, were abandoned by their parents, usually because the family was too poor to support another child [Heywood, 2001].)

Most of the doctors recommended that the boy be placed in an asylum, but one young physician, Jean-Marc Itard (1774–1838), disputed the diagnosis of retardation. Itard proposed that the boy appeared to be mentally deficient only because he had been isolated from society and thereby prevented from developing normally. In support of his view, Itard argued that if the boy had been mentally retarded, he certainly could not have survived on his own in the forest.

Itard took personal charge of the boy, with the goal of teaching him to become fully competent, to master the French language, and to acquire the best of civilized knowledge. To test

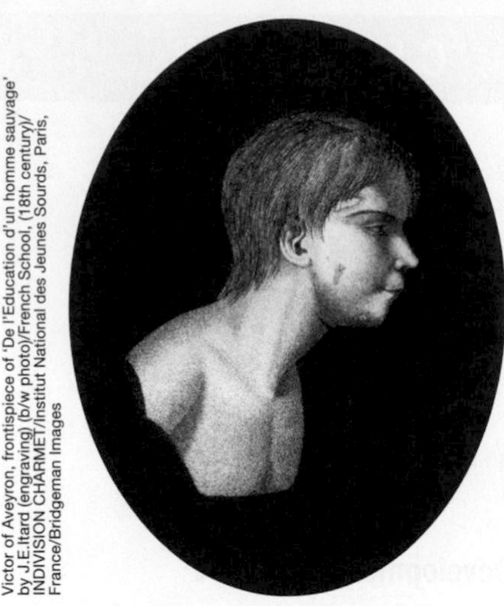

Victor of Aveyron, frontispiece of 'De l'Education d'un homme sauvage' by J.E.Itard (engraving) (b/w photo)/French School, (18th century)/INDIVISION CHARMET/Institut National des Jeunes Sourds, Paris, France/Bridgeman Images

Victor, the Wild Boy of Aveyron.

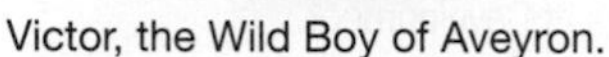

Jean-Marc-Gaspard Itard (1775-1838) 1879 (oil on canvas)/French School, (19th century)/INDIVISION CHARMET/Institut National des Jeunes Sourds, Paris, France/Bridgeman Images

Jean-Marc Itard, who tried to transform the Wild Boy into a civilized Frenchman.

his theory that the social environment has the power to shape children's development, Itard devised an elaborate set of experimental training procedures to teach the Wild Boy how to categorize objects, to reason, and to communicate (Itard, 1801/1982).

At first, Victor, as Itard had named the Wild Boy, made rapid progress. He learned to communicate simple needs as well as to recognize and write a few words. He learned to use a chamber pot. He also developed affection for the people who took care of him. But Victor never learned to speak or interact with other people normally.

After 5 years of intense work, Victor had not made enough progress to satisfy Itard's superiors, and Itard was forced to abandon his experiment. Victor was sent to live with a woman who was paid to care for him. Still referred to as the Wild Boy of Aveyron, he died in 1828, leaving unanswered the question of what factors prevented him from developing normally. Some modern scholars believe that Victor suffered from what is now defined as autism spectrum disorder, whose symptoms include a deficit in language and an inability to interact normally with others (American Psychiatric Association, 2013; Frith, 1989; see Chapter 8 for a detailed discussion of autism spectrum disorder). Others think that Itard may have been correct in his belief that Victor was normal at birth but was permanently stunted in his development as a result of his social isolation (Lane, 1976). It is also possible that Itard's teaching methods failed where different approaches might have succeeded. We cannot be sure.

Victor's case became a focal point for debating fundamental questions about human nature and development: To what extent is development determined from birth? To what extent is it influenced by the surrounding environment? What is the role of early experience in shaping later development? Can the effects of negative experience be undone? Although more than 200 years have passed since the Wild Boy wandered into the village of Aveyron, these questions remain at the forefront of research on children's development.

WARMING **UP**

1. Adults throughout the world hold ideas and beliefs about how children should be raised and what they need to develop properly. What are some of your ideas and beliefs about what is important to raising happy and healthy children? Where do you think your ideas and beliefs come from?
2. Describe some ways in which you have developed like all other individuals and some ways in which your development has been relatively unique. Why do you suppose that some developments are universal and common to all, whereas others are more variable?
3. What are three major questions that you have about children's development? Save your answer because you'll need to review it at the end of the chapter.

Developmental Science

This book will introduce you to **developmental science**, a field of study that focuses on the range of children's physical, intellectual, social, and emotional development. It is a rich and varied field, encompassing a wide array of theories and methods of study, and covering a broad range of children's characteristics. However, as Victor's story makes clear, the study of children's development has always been driven by two overarching goals. One goal is to understand the basic biological and cultural processes that account for the remarkable complexities of human development. The second goal is to devise effective methods for safeguarding children's health and well-being. These two goals come together in the popular idea, held by developmentalists and the public alike, that scientific research can make the world a better place by shedding light on the nature and conditions of children's development.

LEARNING OUTCOMES

Explain the goals of developmental science.

Identify periods of development in childhood.

Examine the interrelationship of domains and context in the study of development.

developmental science The field of study that focuses on the range of children's physical, intellectual, social, and emotional developments.

The field of developmental science has advanced and broadened considerably since Itard's day. As we discuss below, for much of its history, psychologists have dominated the study of children's development. In recent decades, however, the study of development has become increasingly *interdisciplinary*, profiting from the insights of a wide range of disciplines, including psychology, anthropology, biology, linguistics, neuroscience, and sociology. The study of development has also become increasingly *international*, reflecting a growing appreciation of the many ways developmental processes are influenced by cultural contexts. In recognition of the broad scope of modern studies of development, we use the term *developmentalist* to refer to someone who contributes to a growing knowledge of children's development, regardless of the person's specific discipline or area of expertise.

As the scope of developmental science widened, the pace and complexity of research increased. New technologies played an important role in these advances. The ability to record children's behaviors with video cameras, to obtain images of their brain activity, and to analyze data with powerful computers have revolutionized the way developmentalists do research. Concerns about the welfare of children have also fueled the pace and complexity of research. These concerns have created new questions for researchers—questions on such wide-ranging topics as the influence of maternal stress and nutrition on fetal brain growth, the effects of neighborhoods on family dynamics, how "screen time" and the use of digital devices affects development, and the special challenges facing children of immigrant and refugee families in their attempts to deal with an alien culture and an unfamiliar language. For many, especially refugee children, these challenges are compounded by recent traumas associated with their exposure to violence, war, and the loss of friends and family (Boss & Ishii, 2015; Daiute, 2016; Lucić, 2016).

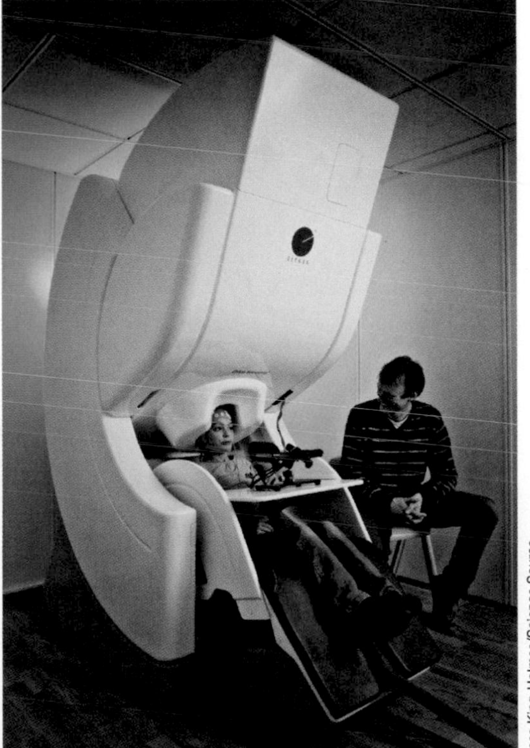

James King-Holmes/Science Source

New technologies have expanded opportunities for studying children's development. This 8-year-old girl, accompanied by her father, is sitting in a magnetoencephalograph (MEG), which can detect extremely small magnetic fields generated by neural activity in her brain. Data provided by the MEG can be used in conjunction with other tests to investigate neurological disorders such as ADHD, epilepsy, and autism spectrum disorder (ASD).

In addition to their roles as researchers looking for answers to such complex questions, developmentalists are often practitioners who strive to promote the healthy development of children. Developmentalists work in hospitals, child-care centers, schools, recreational facilities, and clinics. They assess children's development and make suggestions for helping children who are in difficulty. They design special environments, such as high-tech incubators that allow premature babies to develop normally outside the womb. They devise therapies for children who have trouble controlling their tempers, and they develop techniques to help children learn more effectively (Lerner, Almerigi, Theokas, & Lerner, 2005). Developmentalists also promote children's healthy development by working with government agencies and nongovernment organizations (NGOs) on health and education policies.

Periods of Development

In their research, theorizing, and practice, developmentalists divide the time between conception and the start of adulthood into five broad periods: the prenatal period, infancy, early childhood, middle childhood, and adolescence. Each period is marked by major changes in children's bodies and in how children think, feel, and interact with others. Each is also marked by significant changes in how children are treated by members of their society as a consequence of cultural assumptions and expectations about what children can and should be doing at different ages. Despite broad cultural differences in the particular tasks that children are expected to master, the institutions (such as school) that they are required to attend, and the rituals that they are made to undergo, most cultures organize the course of childhood in ways that recognize these five general developmental periods.

Domains of Development

As individuals move through each period of development, they undergo remarkable changes in several *domains*, or major areas of development: social, emotional, cognitive (intellectual), and physical. Although developmentalists are interested in the changes that take place within each of these four domains, they also recognize that development in any one of these domains is influenced by, and influences, development in the others. Consider, for example, how physical and cognitive developments influence each other. Physical changes in the body—including size, strength, and coordination—permit increasingly efficient ways for a child to move around, explore, and learn about the world. At the same time, the child's developing knowledge and interest in objects and people in the environment encourage even more exploration, providing additional opportunities for the body to develop greater strength and better coordination.

Contexts of Development

Those who work in the developmental sciences have never been more aware of the relationships between children's development and the *contexts* in which children live. As you will learn throughout this book, contexts of development, including physical environments, cultural beliefs and practices, families and peers, neighborhoods and communities, and institutions such as schools and governments, present children with both resources and risks that profoundly shape the course of their development. Does a child live with a single parent or in a large group of siblings, parents, grandparents, and other kin? Is the neighborhood clean and orderly, or is it impoverished, disorganized, and dangerous? Will the child attend school, or will he or she master skills through apprenticeship? Is it acceptable within a particular culture to spank or treat children harshly when they misbehave, or is physical punishment considered a form of violence that can result in severe psychological and emotional injury to both child and parent? Answers to such questions begin to define the contexts of the child's development.

To help get at the answers, researchers often compare children who experience or grow up under different conditions—in different types of families, neighborhoods, countries, cultures, and so on. This research contributes to our understanding of the risks and resources provided by various contexts and how those contexts affect children's development. It also helps us tease apart how different factors interact to influence development. For example, harsh physical discipline has been associated with children's aggression and anxiety in nine different countries (Lansford et al., 2016). However, the degree to which children are negatively affected seems to depend on the extent to which such punishment is considered "normal."

sanneke fisser / Alamy

Werner Van Steen/Getty Images

Children's development is profoundly affected by the contexts in which they live and grow. The contexts shown here illustrate significant differences in children's physical environments, daily activities, and social relationships.

In countries where harsh discipline is deemed an appropriate response to misbehavior, children are less affected compared to those in countries where such discipline is frowned upon. This suggests that children generally suffer harm when they are treated very harshly, but the harmful effects may be softened or aggravated by other factors in the broader context of the child's environment.

The effects of context are also apparent when children experience radical changes of context, as when divorce leads to family reorganization and a move to a new neighborhood and school or when war, poverty, or oppression leads to emigration to an entirely new country with a new language, culture, and lifestyle (see the box "Now Trending in Therapy: Helping Refugee Families in Transition," p. 6). Thus, although developmentalists remain interested in the fundamental questions raised in Itard's day, it is clear that contemporary researchers, teachers, counselors, and other developmental practitioners are also responding to questions and concerns raised by social forces of our time.

Children, Society, and Science

LEARNING OUTCOMES

Summarize the influence of historical beliefs about children on the emergence of developmental science.

Explain the influence of Preyer and Darwin on developmental science.

In order to appreciate contemporary developmental science fully, it is important to understand the cultural and historical forces that have shaped it (Cox, in press; Valsiner, van Oers, Wardekker, Elbers, & van der Veer, 2009). We begin our discussion by exploring beliefs about children and the way these beliefs have changed over the course of time, setting the stage for the emergence of developmental science. We then trace the history of developmental science from its early stages to its current state. Much of our discussion focuses on the history of childhood in the United States and Europe because these histories have been most fully explored. As historians of childhood broaden their scope to include places such as China, Japan, African countries, and India, they find evidence for both similarities and differences across time and nations in how childhood is understood and children are treated (Stearns, 2010).

Historical Beliefs About Children and Childhood

Societies abound with different beliefs about the nature of children and their development. Such beliefs affect every aspect of children's lives, from what behaviors are expected of them at different ages to how they are disciplined, what skills and values they are taught, how they spend their time each day, and with whom they are allowed to socialize (Apple, 2006; Mintz, 2004). Beliefs about children and childhood also differ from one historical era to another. Even within the relatively short span of decades, the pendulum can swing from one view to another about what is good or bad for children, what they should or should not do, and how adults should treat them. For example, not long ago in North America, it was thought that picking up crying or fussy babies would make them "spoiled" and demanding, whereas today this practice is considered as a sign of positive and responsive caregiving. Likewise, until fairly recently, children's play was thought to be important mostly because it promoted physical development. Consequently, children's playgrounds featured gymnastic equipment, such as ladders, climbing bars, swings. Now, however, play is believed to have much broader implications

Now TRENDING in PRACTICE Helping Refugee Families in Transition

In the early 1990s, ethnic hostilities of monstrous proportions tore apart the former Socialist Federal Republic of Yugoslavia. Armed conflicts and genocidal massacres across the six constituent regions that made up the republic claimed the lives of tens of thousands of men, women, and children. Thousands of families fled for safety and became refugees in foreign lands. Sadly, the number of refugee families fleeing conflicts and natural disasters worldwide has continued to rise over the past few decades (Lucić, 2016; Zuilkowski, et al., 2016). In 2015, a record 65.3 million people, or 1 person in 113, were forced from their homes because of conflict and persecution (United Nations High Commission for Refugees, 2016).

The needs of refugee families are great and often immediate—for food, shelter, and medical care, as well as for work and education. There are also needs of a more psychological and emotional nature—to impose some meaning on past experiences and current circumstances and to develop a sense of a healthy, hopeful, and productive future. Some families have directly experienced the serious injury or rape of family members; others have witnessed the killing of loved ones (Daiute, 2016). All have been forced by the threat of violence to leave their homes, schools, places of worship, jobs, friends, and extended families for uncertain futures in new countries where people may speak different languages and hold different values and beliefs.

Researchers have found that traumatic events experienced by refugee families before their exile in new countries can lead to significant psychological problems (Sullivan & Simonson, 2016). Children's attachment relationships with parents may be disrupted by insecurities, and mothers often feel challenged in meeting their children's needs while coping with their family's vastly changed lives (see Chapter 6 for a discussion of attachment theory; Montgomery, 2011; Robertson & Duckett, 2007; Stauffer, 2008). Children may suffer from anxiety, sleep disturbance, depressed mood, or other psychological problems (Montgomery, 2011). Two factors seem important for healthy adjustment: the quality of life in the new country and the quality of family relationships.

LOUISA GOULIAMAKI/Getty Images

Recent decades have seen a surge in refugee children and families who are forced to flee their native countries because of oppression and political violence. The pathways of development for the refugee children pictured here will hopefully be smoother because of programs provided by volunteers running a refugee center on the Greek island of Chios.

Family therapists in Sweden have been working with refugee families from Bosnia-Herzegovina, a war-torn region of the former Yugoslavia from which thousands of families were forced to flee for their lives (Bjorn, Gustafsson, Sydsjö, & Berterö, 2013). The therapists focused on helping family members communicate with each other about their fears and hopes and develop a meaningful story of their experiences. The stories told by the families had much in common. First, they tended to emphasize the good lives they lived before the war. They spoke of birthday celebrations with extended family and friends or of going to the seaside for vacations. Parents spoke of the good jobs they had in their home countries and of having enough money to care for their children and enjoy life. The war changed their lives dramatically; both parents and children spoke of bombings and the confusion in the aftermath, of the sadness and loss associated with their escape, of leaving nearly everything behind except each other and what could be packed into a few suitcases. Finally, the families discussed their new lives, including the challenges of finding jobs and schools, learning a new language, and acquiring medical care for everyday ailments such as colds and infections, as well as for the physical and mental traumas of the war. Most parents were very much focused on the here-and-now, with limited thought about the future. Children, however, seemed more future oriented and hopeful.

The goal of the therapists involved in this particular project was to help the refugee families develop coherent, meaningful stories of their family lives and experiences (Dalgaard & Montgomery, 2015). In a follow-up session conducted a year later, parents indicated that the sessions had been helpful and that their children were feeling better. In light of the ever-increasing numbers of families around the globe who are escaping violence and terrorism in their native lands and seeking refuge in other countries, it is important to understand their unique challenges and needs in order to assist their transitions to new lives.

Alfred Eisenstaedt / Getty Images

(a)

Agencja Fotograficzna Caro / Alamy

(b)

Although merry-go-rounds, slides, seesaws, and swings remain popular, early playgrounds (a) emphasized physical play and motor development to the exclusion of all other developmental domains. In contrast, modern playgrounds such as the one shown here in Germany (b) often include design features intended to foster creativity and social interaction.

for development, and playgrounds are built to stimulate the mind and imagination as well as the body (Carr & Luken, 2014; Refshauge, Stigsdotter, Lamm, & Thorleifsdottir, 2015).

For historians interested in how social beliefs about children have changed in recent centuries, there is a wealth of information to be found in child-care manuals, books, parent magazines, and all sorts of child-rearing paraphernalia (clothing, cradles, toys, feeding utensils, baby-carrying devices, and the like). But such information is much more difficult to come by when it involves reaching back into bygone centuries before social beliefs could be easily preserved in print and before the mass production of child-related objects.

Historians seeking to unearth beliefs about childhood during medieval times, for example, have had to rely largely on two unlikely kinds of sources: art and coroners' reports. Each yields a somewhat different picture of how people viewed children and childhood.

In general, portraiture and other art suggest that before the sixteenth century, people did not give much thought to children or their special needs. Many historians have concluded that during medieval times, there was a limited understanding of childhood as a unique period of the life course. Indeed, some historians have suggested that beyond the first few years of infancy and early childhood, children were considered miniature adults (Ariès, 1965). Accordingly, children were not provided with special toys or clothes and were not educated or cared for in ways that took into account their intellectual abilities and limitations. As illustrated in Figure 1.1, the miniature-adult view was expressed in the typical depiction of children as having adultlike body proportions, wearing elegant and fine, adultlike clothing, and engaging in serious-minded activities. In *Centuries of*

Erich Lessing / Art Resource, NY

FIGURE 1.1 Artwork before the sixteenth century depicts children with adultlike body proportions and clothing, rarely engaged in play or youthful activities. Because age differences between adults and children, and even between younger and older children, are represented simply in terms of relative size, historians describe the period as embracing a "miniature adult" view of childhood.

Childhood, one of the best-known books on the history of childhood, Philippe Ariès notes that artists of the time seemed "unable to depict a child except as a man on a smaller scale" (1965, p. 33). The belief that adultlike capacities, desires, interests, and emotions are present in early childhood is known as **preformationism**. You will see in our discussion below that this belief persisted for hundreds of years, influencing scientists as well as the general public.

preformationism The belief that adultlike capacities, desires, interests, and emotions are present in early childhood.

Coroners' reports about the circumstances of children's deaths are a rare exception to the dearth of written documents hinting at social beliefs about children. Using them as part of her research, Barbara Hanawalt, an expert on family life in medieval England, found that it was not uncommon for little babies to be entrusted to the care of children as young as 3 (Hanawalt & Kobialka, 2000). Needless to say, 3-year-olds make poor caregivers, and infants in their charge sometimes died due to their inattention or inability to intervene appropriately when problems arose. It was also relatively common for parents to leave infants and young children entirely alone and unsupervised for extended periods of time while they themselves did chores or worked in their fields. Although reflecting the miniature-adult cultural belief, these common practices drew criticism in coroners' reports that described young children as "bad custodians" of infants and explained the accidental deaths of unsupervised toddlers as caused by "being left without a caretaker" or being without "anyone looking after" them (p. 177). Interestingly, legal scholars of medieval England have found evidence of law codes clearly intended to protect children. So both coroners' reports and legal documents of the time cast doubt of the pervasiveness of cultural notions that children were simply little adults, suggesting instead considerable complexity in beliefs about the status of childhood and children's needs (Stearns, 2010).

A major turning point in the history of Western beliefs about children and childhood came in the sixteenth century, with the Protestant Reformation, a religious movement of considerable scope. This movement swept through Europe and crossed the ocean to the "New World," beginning with the Puritans' voyage on the *Mayflower* in 1620. It was associated with harsher child-rearing practices, which followed from the belief that children are born in original sin. In contrast to the medieval Catholic Church, Protestant denominations generally held that original sin could not be washed away by baptism and that salvation would be possible only through obedience and submission to authority—first to one's elders and then to God. Because obedience naturally requires the suppression of individual goals and desires, parents were advised to adopt practices that would hold children's innate sinfulness in check and replace their willful impulses with humility and compliance.

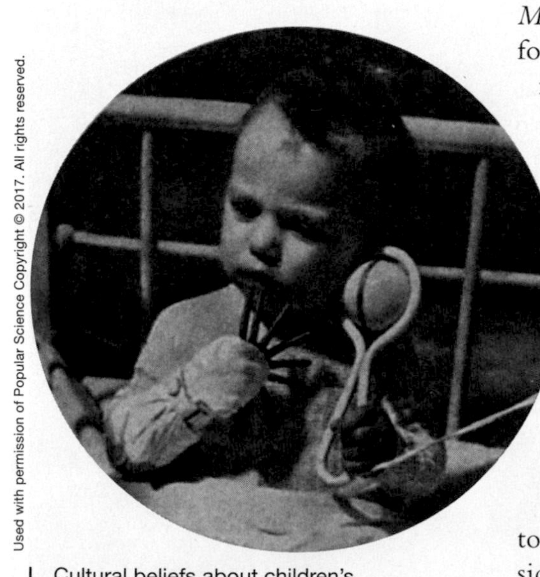

Used with permission of Popular Science Copyright © 2017. All rights reserved.

Cultural beliefs about children's development influence whether certain activities are encouraged. This child is wearing a special glove manufactured to prevent thumb-sucking, which once was thought to be overly arousing and harmful to children's development.

The legacy of Puritan ideas about children persisted for hundreds of years, as Martha Wolfenstein (1953) discovered when she analyzed manuals on infant care written in the early 1900s. The manuals urged mothers to wage war on their children's sinful and rebellious nature. Masturbation and thumb-sucking were of special concern because they involved "dangerous pleasures" that "could easily grow beyond control." Mothers were encouraged to use a variety of physical restraints, such as tying their children's feet to opposite sides of the crib to prevent their thighs from rubbing together and pinning the sleeves of their nightshirts to the bed to prevent them from touching themselves. Stiff arm cuffs were sold through stores and catalogues for the purpose of eliminating thumb-sucking. It was even recommended that rocking cradles be replaced by stationary cribs in order to further reduce experiences that might be stimulating or pleasurable.

Although evidence indicates that the idea of childhood as a unique period in development was already taking root in many societies, most historians agree that the modern notion of childhood emerged on a large scale in the late eighteenth and early nineteenth centuries, as a consequence of the Industrial Revolution (Stearns, 2010). Taking shape initially in Western Europe and the United States, industrialization transformed the contexts in which children developed in three major ways. First, consistent with a shift from predominantly rural to more urban living conditions, schooling and/or factory work (depending on the family's social and economic status) came to replace family farm work as the child's primary social obligation. Second, the birthrate dropped significantly, altering family relationships both between parents and their children and between siblings. Finally, the child death rate plummeted, also with impacts on family relationships.

As historian Peter Stearns points out, these three changes were interconnected and had considerable implications for children's lives and experience. With increased schooling, for example, children were removed from the workforce and became economic burdens rather than assets, so family size began to shrink. Increased schooling for girls, by helping to make possible new opportunities for women to work outside the home, played a special role in reducing family size. Beyond reducing the birthrate, girls' education contributed to declining child death rates because it resulted in mothers being more knowledgeable about how to ensure the healthy development of their infants and children. The schooling of all children reduced the authority of home and family, bringing children into more contact with other children and increasingly under the influence of peers and nonfamilial adults.

By the late nineteenth century, the industrial age was well under way throughout the world, and children and childhood had begun to receive considerable attention from parents, educators, and scientists.

The Emergence of Developmental Science

An effect of industrialization was to drive millions of children to labor in textile factories. The conditions under which they worked became a matter of social concern and soon sparked the attention of the scientific community. The Factories Inquiries Committee in England, for instance, conducted a study in 1833 to discover whether children could work 12 hours a day without being harmed. The majority of the committee members decided that 12 hours was an acceptable workday for children. Others who thought a 10-hour workday would be preferable were concerned less with children's physical, intellectual, or emotional well-being than with their morals. They recommended that the remaining 2 hours be devoted to the children's religious and moral education (Hindman, 2002). Despite its dismal conclusion, this early committee was a start, and concern for children's welfare increased throughout the century as children became ever more visible to both the social and scientific communities.

Also crucial to the rise of scientific interest in children was the work of Charles Darwin. The publication of Darwin's *The Origin of Species* in 1859 set the scientific community on fire and ultimately led to fundamental changes in beliefs about children's development. If human beings had evolved from earlier species, then might not the different stages of children's behavior offer clues to stages of human evolution? It became fashionable, for example, to compare the behavior of children with the behavior of higher nonhuman primates to see if children went through a "chimpanzee stage" similar to the one through which the human species was

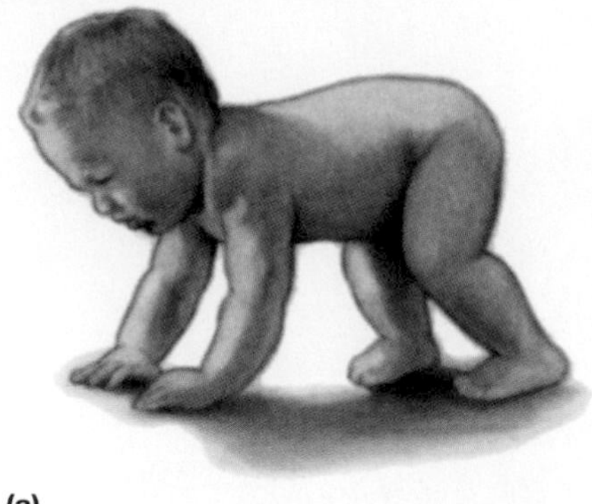

(a)

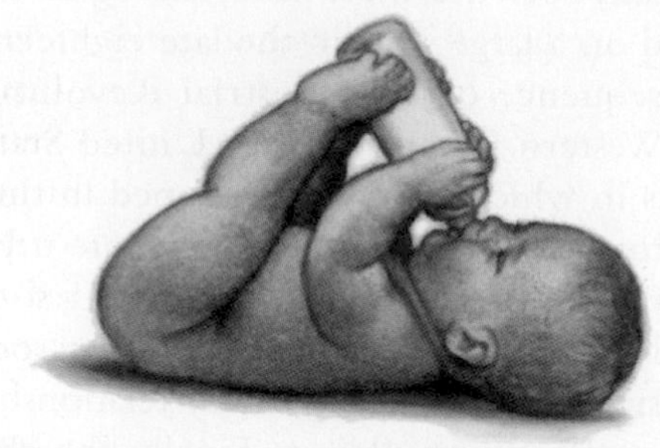

(b)

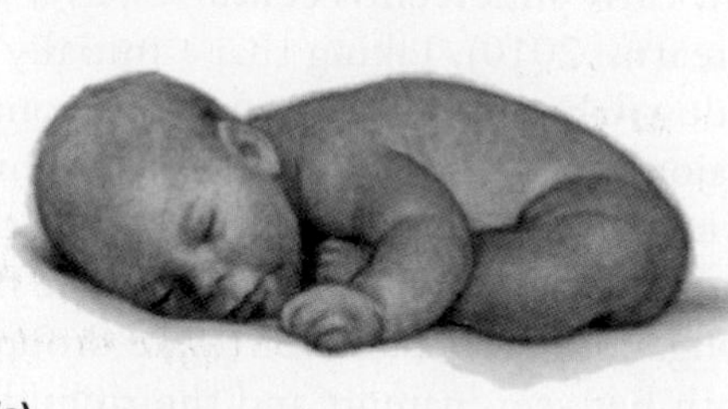

(c)

FIGURE 1.2 Early evolutionists scrutinized the motor development of children for evidence that it recapitulated evolutionary stages. Here an infant (a) crawls about on all fours like many animals, (b) uses its feet for grasping as primates do, and (c) sleeps in an animal-like crouch. This line of research was found to be overly simplistic.

thought to have evolved (see Figure 1.2). Although such parallels proved oversimplified, the idea that the study of human development is crucial to an understanding of human evolution won general acceptance (Bjorklund & Pellegrini, 2002). Because Darwin's theory of evolution continues to have far-reaching consequences for the way children's development is thought about and studied, we devote considerable attention to it in Chapter 2.

In the exciting aftermath of the publication of *The Origin of Species*, the study of child development grew by leaps and bounds. Some early developmentalists emphasized the importance of using scientific methods of observation to understand fully how the human mind changes over time. William Preyer (1841–1897), for example, wrote the first textbook on child development (Preyer, 1888), proposing that the development of emotion, intention, mind, and language could be studied scientifically by applying strict rules of observation (see Table 1.1). He was particularly eager to identify *sequences of behavior* because he believed that they would show how new forms of behavior emerge from earlier forms—for example, how walking emerges from crawling. Preyer was also interested in understanding how biological and environmental factors influence a child's development.

TABLE 1.1 Preyer's Rules of Observation

- Rely only on direct observations; avoid the reports of "persons not practiced in scientific observing."
- Record observations immediately so that details are not forgotten.
- Make every effort to be unobtrusive, to "observe without the child's noticing the observer at all."
- Avoid any "training" of the young child in order to observe "unadulterated mental development."
- If regular observations are interrupted for more than 1 day, another observer must be substituted, and his or her observations should be checked for accuracy. (Preyer observed and recorded his child's behavior two to three times every day!)
- Everything should be recorded, even behaviors that seem uninteresting at the time.

Source: Preyer, 1890, pp. 187–188.

Whereas Preyer's greatest contributions to developmental science were his *methods of study*, other developmentalists focused directly on the *nature of development*. James Mark Baldwin (1861–1934), for example, challenged scientists who believed in the preformationist view that adult abilities are present and fully formed in the child, just waiting "off stage" for their cue to emerge. In a striking reversal of this notion, Baldwin argued that children's abilities progress through a series of specific stages, taking on different forms and undergoing systematic changes before reaching their mature state. Baldwin's proposal represented the first of many *stage theories* of development that would emerge over the next century.

Still other developmentalists directed their efforts to practical applications. One such effort was Alfred Binet's (1857–1911) devising of methods of "mental testing" that eventually resulted in the first widely used intelligence test—the Stanford-Binet. Binet firmly believed that careful testing could reveal individual differences in children's mental abilities and identify schoolchildren who could benefit from special instruction. His work clearly established the role of developmental science in addressing practical problems and issues.

The New Field of Developmental Science

By the early twentieth century, owing in no small measure to the efforts of these pioneers, the study of development had become a recognized field of scientific inquiry. Special institutes and departments devoted to the study of development began to spring up in major universities in the United States. Much of this work focused on exploring basic developmental changes over the course of infancy and childhood. But some research involved "special mission" projects on a wide range of topics, including highly gifted children and the effects that watching motion pictures might have on children.

To this day, research on children's development continues to be motivated by the twin goals that were present at the discipline's origins: the scientific and philosophic goal of understanding how our biological and cultural heritages combine to shape our development as humans and the practical goal of understanding how best to promote the health and well-being of children. We now turn to the central issues that continue to guide and inspire developmental science.

APPLY > CONNECT > DISCUSS

Thumb through some magazines containing images of children (you will likely find a lot of such images in magazines focused on parenting and infant care). How are the children depicted? Describe their clothing, the activities in which they are engaged, and the people and objects they are shown with. What do the images suggest regarding current conceptions of children and childhood?

The Central Issues of Developmental Science

LEARNING OUTCOME

Distinguish the four fundamental issues of interest to developmentalists.

Despite great variety in the work they do, developmentalists share an interest in four fundamental issues concerning the process of development:

1. *Sources of development.* How do the forces of biology, the environment, and the child's own activities interact to produce new ways of thinking, feeling, and behaving?

2. *Plasticity.* To what extent and under what conditions is the course of development plastic—that is, malleable and subject to change as a result of either deliberate intervention or chance experience?
3. *Continuity/discontinuity.* Is development a gradual, continuous process of change, or is it punctuated by periods of rapid change and the sudden emergence of new ways of thinking and behaving?
4. *Individual differences.* No two human beings are exactly alike. How does a person come to have characteristics that make him or her different from all other people, and how stable are these characteristics over time?

Developmentalists' answers to these questions provide insight into principles of development as well as guidelines for promoting adaptive developmental outcomes.

Questions About the Sources of Development

What drives development? What, for instance, ensures that virtually every human infant will develop the ability to walk on two feet? To use language to communicate with others? To form emotional bonds? These are not easy accomplishments, and they often involve considerable effort, frustration, and even tears, as you know if you have watched a child struggle while learning to walk. While our shared biological heritage certainly plays a part in these universal human developments, human beings share more than genes. All human beings grow up in physical, social, and cultural environments that interact with each other and with our biological makeup to produce developmental change. For instance, in many cultures the development of walking is actively encouraged by family members eager to see their little one reach this major milestone. But in certain physical environments that are unsafe for toddlers, carrying the child around during its first years of life is common and may result in independent walking beginning at a substantially later age.

As you will learn throughout this book, the quest for knowledge about the sources of development include fascinating discoveries about how developments in some areas interact with and produce developments in other areas. Keeping to our example of walking, researchers have found in several countries that the onset

Even walking, which all typically developing children acquire, is influenced by physical, social, and cultural backgrounds. Some cultural traditions encourage early independent walking, whereas others promote extended carrying of toddler-aged children. And some physical environments are relatively safe in the event of falls, whereas others are less forgiving.

ArtisticCaptures/Getty Images

Bartosz Hadyniak/Getty Images

of walking may stimulate vocabulary development (He, Walle, & Campos, 2015). Although the exact nature of the interaction requires further study, one possibility is that because their hands are free, walkers produce substantially more gestures than crawlers, inviting responses from others that enrich the child's communication environment. This stands as an example (you will learn of many more) of how one of the most powerful sources of development is development itself.

Questions About Plasticity

The second major question about development concerns **plasticity**, the degree to which, and the conditions under which, development is open to change and intervention. Plasticity enables individuals to adapt to a wide range of different environments (Bjorklund & Ellis, 2014). An important question for developmentalists concerns the limits of plasticity in children's responses to different environments and experiences: For different aspects of development, does our experience influence our development significantly or not much at all?

plasticity The degree to which, and the conditions under which, development is open to change and intervention.

The limits of plasticity are influenced by *sensitive periods* in development. **Sensitive periods** are defined as times in an organism's development during which a particular experience (or lack of it) has a more pronounced effect on the organism than does exposure to that same experience at another time (Hartley & Lee, 2015; Lickliter, 2007). For example, children seem to be most sensitive to learning language in the first few years of life, easily acquiring any language to which they are regularly exposed. But even if they are not regularly exposed to language until the age of 6 or 7, it appears that they are still capable of acquiring it. Thereafter, however, the risk of failing to acquire language increases (Newport, Bavelier, & Neville, 2001).

sensitive period A time in an organism's development when a particular experience has an especially profound effect.

Questions about plasticity have important real-world implications. The answers are essential to understanding whether and how a child's development can be modified through deliberate intervention, such as therapy or education, or dramatically affected by particular experiences, from the everyday to the traumatic.

Questions About Continuity/Discontinuity

Questions about **continuity/discontinuity** have to do with the extent to which development tends to be *continuous*, consisting of the gradual accumulation of small changes, and the extent to which it is *discontinuous*, involving a series of abrupt, radical transformations.

continuity/discontinuity A fundamental issue concerning the process of development that addresses the extent to which development tends to be *continuous*, consisting of the gradual accumulation of small changes, and the extent to which it is *discontinuous*, involving a series of abrupt, radical transformations.

As a rule, developmentalists who believe that development is primarily a process of continuous, gradual accumulation of small changes emphasize *quantitative* change, such as growth in the number of connections among brain cells, the amount of information that can be stored in memory, or the number of words in one's vocabulary. Those who view development as a process punctuated by abrupt, discontinuous changes emphasize *qualitative* change, or new patterns of behavior emerging at specific points in development, such as the change from babbling to talking or from crawling to walking, or from the ability to reason only in terms of one's own experience to the ability to reason hypothetically. Qualitatively new patterns that emerge during development are referred to as **developmental stages**. The contrast between the continuity and discontinuity views is illustrated in Figure 1.3 (p.14).

developmental stage A qualitatively distinctive, coherent pattern of behavior that emerges during the course of development.

Supporters of discontinuity and the stage concept argue that the qualitative changes the child undergoes in each new stage alter the way the child

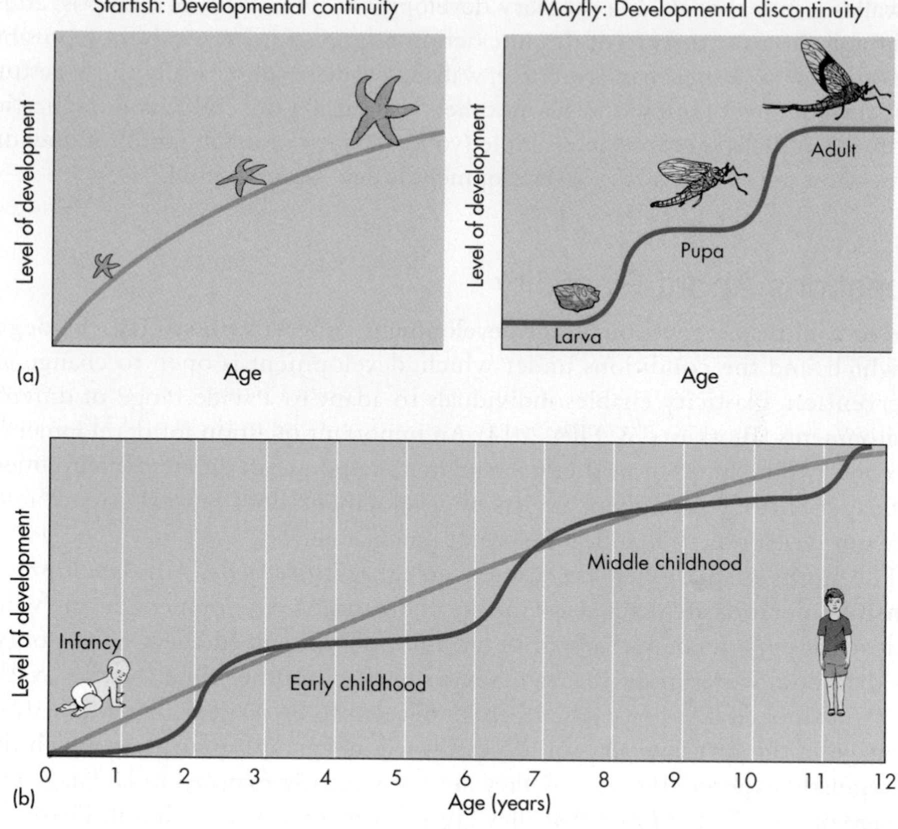

FIGURE 1.3 (a) The contrasting courses of development of starfish and insects provide idealized examples of continuous and discontinuous development. In the continuity view, development is a process of gradual growth (small starfish, medium-size starfish, large starfish). In the discontinuity view, development is a series of stagelike transformations (larva, pupa, adult). (b) Human development includes elements of both continuity and discontinuity.

experiences the world and the way the world influences the child. For example, before infants have any understanding of language, their learning about the world comes primarily through their actions on it. Once they begin to understand and produce language themselves, the way they learn about the world appears to change fundamentally, and so does the nature of their interaction with others. The discontinuity represented by the child's active participation in conversation is so notable that in many societies it marks the boundary between infancy and early childhood.

Supporters of the continuity view maintain that even when development appears to make an abrupt shift, continuity prevails in the underlying processes. For example, although very young children and adults appear to reason about the world in radically different ways, there still may be considerable continuity in reasoning between early childhood and adulthood. In particular, research conducted by Alison Gopnik (2012) suggests that, regardless of age, individuals reason much the way scientists do; that is, they have *theories* that allow them to explain, predict, and understand events and behavior, and they modify their theories when their predictions prove incorrect.

One major problem for supporters of the stage concept is that, contrary to their depiction of qualitatively consistent, across-the-board shifts in behavior and thinking, children often appear to be in one stage on one occasion and in a different stage on another. According to one influential stage theory of cognitive development, for example, 4-year-olds are in a stage in which their thinking is largely egocentric, making it difficult for them to see anything from a point of view other than their own. Consider 4-year-old Nyia, who wanted to give her mother a Bitty Kitty for her birthday. Nyia's birthday present choice indicates that she is, in this case, limited to her own perspective: She wants to give her mother what she herself would enjoy as a present, failing to see that her mother might rather have breakfast in bed. Yet when Nyia talks to her 2-year-old brother, she simplifies her speech, apparently taking the younger child's perspective and realizing that he might otherwise have difficulty in understanding her. The fact that at a given point in development a child can exhibit behaviors associated with different stages seems to undercut the idea that being in a particular stage defines the child's capabilities and psychological makeup.

Questions About Individual Differences

Although in some respects you are like all other human beings, in many ways you are psychologically and physically unique, like no one else in the world. What makes you different from everyone else? And will the features that make you different endure throughout your life? When we try to understand the nature of development, we must take into account these two questions about individual differences: (1) What makes individuals different from one another? and (2) To what extent are individual characteristics stable over time?

The question of what makes individuals different from one another is really another form of the question about the plasticity of development (Forsman, 2015). The ways in which you are like all other human beings reflect how certain developmental traits—the ability to walk, talk, and form close attachments to others—are highly constrained by evolution and have little plasticity. In contrast, the features that make you unique from everyone else reflect the capacity of certain traits to be more easily modified by experience.

The question of stability over time involves the extent to which the features that make you special endure throughout your life. Parents often remark that their children have been friendly or shy since infancy, but scientifically demonstrating the stability of psychological characteristics like these—at least from an early age—has proved difficult. One problem is that measures that seem appropriate for assessing psychological traits during infancy are not likely to be appropriate for assessing the same traits in an 8-year-old or in a teenager. Perhaps for this reason, many studies have found only moderate stability of individual characteristics in childhood (Bleidorn, Kandler, & Caspi, 2014). There is evidence that, for example, children who were shy and uncertain at 21 months of age still tend to be so at age 12 or later. Similarly, infants who rapidly processed visual information at 7 months of age still tend to be rapid visual processors at age 11 (Emde & Hewitt, 2001).

The extent of the stability of children's psychological characteristics over time depends in part on the extent of stability in their environment. Studies have found, for example, that children who are raised in an orphanage that provides adequate physical care but little emotional and intellectual stimulation tend to be lethargic and low in intelligence quotient (IQ). But if their environment changes—for example, if they are adopted into caring families in their early years—their condition improves markedly, and many of them become intellectually normal adults (Clarke & Clarke, 2000; Julian, 2013).

The four major issues of developmental sources, plasticity, continuity/discontinuity, and individual differences have endured for decades and continue to focus the research efforts of developmentalists. In the next section, we explore the major theories that developmentalists have used to help address these issues.

APPLY > CONNECT > DISCUSS

The central questions of developmental science are reflected in the ways parents and practitioners (teachers, counselors, and doctors) interpret children's behavior. Identify the central question (sources of development, continuity/discontinuity, individual differences, or plasticity) associated with each of the following common phrases.

"Oh, those terrible twos!"

"Don't worry. It's just a phase. She'll grow out of it."

"He's 2 going on 20" or "He's 20 going on 2."

"She's her own little person."

"Of course he's having trouble—his parents work all day and are never home."

"He's been moody since he hit puberty."

Now, drawing on your own experience, think of one or more similar phrases for each of the central questions.

LEARNING OUTCOMES

Point out the role of theories in development science.

Differentiate the four grand theories in developmental science.

Differentiate the four influential modern theories in developmental science.

Theories of Development

theory A broad framework or set of principles that can be used to guide the collection and interpretation of a set of facts.

Many students roll their eyes at the idea that theories are needed to understand children's development. "What's so complicated?" they wonder. "Just watch what children do and let the facts speak for themselves." But, contrary to popular belief, facts do not speak for themselves. The facts that developmentalists collect add to our understanding of development only when they are brought together and interpreted in terms of a **theory**, a framework of ideas or body of principles that can be used to guide the collection and interpretation of a set of facts. Without the lens of theory through which to observe, we would not know what we were looking at, much less how to characterize it or what to make of it.

To appreciate the role of theory, consider a hypothetical example: You are a developmentalist observing a little boy who is running around a preschool classroom, pushing the other children and grabbing toys away from them. How would you interpret this instance of misbehavior? If you were framing your explanation with a theory focused on antisocial behavior, you might see the child's actions as uncontrolled aggression, whereas if you were framing it with a theory focused on the interdependency of group members, you might see those same actions as a symptom of the child's having failed to develop a sense of his dependency on others for his well-being. (In fact, for cultural reasons, many Americans might tend toward the first interpretation, whereas Japanese people might tend toward the second.) Not only would your specific observations be likely to be influenced by the theory you used, but your prescriptions for dealing with the child's behavior would be as well.

The preceding example also illustrates a point made by Albert Einstein, namely, that theory is present even when we think that we are "objectively observing" the world. We think of our theories as being founded on observations, when "[i]n reality the very opposite occurs. It is the theory which decides what we can observe" (quoted in Sameroff, 1983, p. 243).

Einstein's point underscores the importance of theory. A deeper understanding of human development will not automatically come from the continuous accumulation of facts. Rather, it will come through new attempts to make sense of this accumulating evidence in the light of relevant theories. It also raises a caution: Developmental scientists, like all other scientists, need to keep in mind that theories can bias, or distort, their observations. Throughout this book, you will see examples of both the power and potential problems of theories.

Theory in Developmental Science

There is no single broad theoretical perspective that unifies the entire body of relevant scientific knowledge on human development. Instead, development is approached from several theoretical perspectives that differ in a number of important ways:

1. *Domains of development under investigation.* A theory may be most appropriate for understanding the ways in which children develop cognitively, socially, emotionally, or physically, or it may explore some combination of these domains.
2. *Research methods used.* As you will learn in the next section, particular theories are often associated with particular research methods—observational, experimental, and so forth.
3. *Central issues addressed.* The major theories also differ in their approach to the four central issues we discussed above—the sources of development, the degree of plasticity and openness to change, the extent of continuity or discontinuity, and the stability of individual differences.

We will begin our discussion of developmental theories by reviewing the "grand theories" that were developed when the field was relatively young. We will then examine several modern theoretical perspectives that the grand theories inspired.

Grand Theories

Most developmentalists would consider four theoretical perspectives to fall into the category of "grand theories"—the psychodynamic, behaviorist, constructivist, and sociocultural perspectives. These perspectives are "grand" not only because they laid the foundation for the modern theories of development that followed them but also because they are "grand" in scope, each presenting a sweeping view of various domains of development.

psychodynamic theories Theories, such as those of Freud and Erikson, that explore the influence on development and developmental stages of universal biological drives and the life experiences of individuals.

Psychodynamic Theories

Psychodynamic theories claim a significant place in the history of developmental science, having shown how universal developmental processes and stages can be understood by exploring the specific life experiences of particular individuals. Sigmund Freud was the first to develop a psychodynamic theory. Over the years, his theory has been adopted and modified by numerous developmentalists, the most prominent of them being Erik Erikson, who, as you will see, combined the primarily biological approach taken by Freud with the view that culture plays a leading role in shaping the path of development.

Sigmund Freud

Photo by Time Life Pictures/Mansell/The LIFE Picture Collection/Getty Images

Sigmund Freud. Trained as a neurologist, Freud (1856–1939) sought to create a theory of personality that would enable him to cure the patients who came to him with such symptoms as extreme fears and anxiety, hysteria, and inability to cope with everyday life. Although many of these symptoms initially appeared similar to those of neurological disorders, Freud believed that they were rooted in unresolved traumatic experiences in early childhood.

On the basis of the clinical data he gathered from his patients, including their recollections of the past and their current dreams, Freud constructed a general theory of psychological development that gave primacy to the ways in which children satisfy their basic biological drives. The theory also gave rise to the method of treatment known as *psychoanalysis*. Influenced by Darwin's theory of evolution, Freud reasoned that, whatever their significance for the individual, all biological drives have but a single goal: the survival and propagation of the species. Since

TABLE 1.2 Freud's Psychosexual Stages and Erikson's Psychosocial Stages Compared

Approximate Age	Freud (Psychosexual)	Erikson (Psychosocial)
First year	*Oral stage* The mouth is the focus of pleasurable sensations as the baby sucks and bites.	*Trust versus mistrust* Infants learn to trust others to care for their basic needs, or to mistrust them.
Second year	*Anal stage* The anus is the focus of pleasurable sensations as the baby learns to control elimination.	*Autonomy versus shame and doubt* Children learn to exercise their will and to control themselves, or they become uncertain and doubt that they can do things by themselves.
Third to sixth year	*Phallic stage* Children develop sexual curiosity and obtain gratification when they masturbate. They have sexual fantasies about the parent of the opposite sex and feel guilt about their fantasies.	*Initiative versus guilt* Children learn to initiate their own activities, enjoy their accomplishments, and become purposeful. If they are not allowed to follow their own initiative, they feel guilty for their attempts to become independent.
Seventh year through puberty	*Latency* Sexual urges are submerged. Children focus on mastery of skills valued by adults.	*Industry versus inferiority* Children learn to be competent and effective at activities valued by adults and peers, or they feel inferior.
Adolescence	*Genital stage* Adolescents have adult sexual desires, and they seek to satisfy them.	*Identity versus role confusion* Adolescents establish a sense of personal identity as part of their social group, or they become confused about who they are and what they want to do in life.
Early adulthood		*Intimacy versus isolation* Young adults find an intimate life companion, or they risk loneliness and isolation.
Middle age		*Generativity versus stagnation* Adults must be productive in their work and willing to raise a next generation, or they risk stagnation.
Old age		*Integrity versus despair* People try to make sense of their prior experience and to assure themselves that their lives have been meaningful, or they despair over their unachieved goals and ill-spent lives.

reproduction, the necessary condition for the continuation of the species, is accomplished through sexual intercourse, it followed for Freud that all biological drives must ultimately serve the fundamental sex drive.

Freud shocked his contemporaries by arguing that the behavior of children—even infants—is motivated by a need to satisfy the fundamental sex drive. Freud proposed that, beginning in infancy and moving through adolescence and the advent of adult sexuality, the form of sexual gratification changes, passing through an orderly series of *psychosexual stages* related to the parts of the body through which gratification is achieved. According to Freud (1920/1955), and as indicated in Table 1.2, each stage is associated with conflicts between the child's desires and social prohibitions and expectations that militate against the expression of those desires. The way children experience the conflicts at each stage, and whether or not children successfully resolve them, affects their later personality. Freud maintained, for example, that failure to resolve the conflicts of any given stage could result in the individual's becoming fixated with the issues related to that stage. Perhaps the best known of such conflicts occurs during the anal stage, when the child is socially required to control elimination. Unresolved conflicts related to overly strict toilet training can, in the Freudian view, lead to an "anal retentive" fixation and a personality marked by emotional rigidity and an extreme need for cleanliness and order.

Another important contribution to understanding development was Freud's belief that the personality is made up of three mental structures: (1) the primitive *id*, which is present from birth and consists of biological drives that demand immediate gratification; (2) the *ego*, which begins to emerge in early childhood and is the rational component of the personality that attempts to mediate a practical reconciliation between the demands of the id and the constraints imposed on those demands by the outside world; and (3) the *superego*, which emerges last and, acting as one's conscience, attempts to suppress the forbidden demands of the id and force the ego to make choices that are morally acceptable. (We will return to a discussion of these structures in Chapter 9; see p. 305.) According to Freud, these three structures are rarely, if ever, in perfect balance. The constant battle among them is the engine of developmental change, which Freud spoke of as *ego development*.

Erik Erikson. Whereas Freud's training was in medicine, Erik Erikson's (1902–1994) was eclectic, combining his experience in psychoanalysis with a background in art, teaching, and anthropology. Erikson built on many of Freud's basic ideas of development but departed from them in two significant ways. First, Erikson emphasized social and cultural factors, rather than biological drives, as the major force behind development. Second, he viewed the developmental process as continuing throughout the life span rather than ending in adolescence (the age of sexual maturity).

Erik Erikson

Bettmann/Getty Images

Erikson believed that the main challenge of life is the quest for identity. Throughout their lives, people ask themselves "Who am I?" and at each stage of life they arrive at a different answer (Erikson, 1963a, 1968b). For Erikson, each *psychosocial stage* is associated with a particular main task, as shown in Table 1.2. Erikson referred to these tasks as "crises" because they are sources of conflict within the person. The person must in some way accomplish the task, or resolve the conflict, in order to move on to the next stage. The resolution may be more on the positive side or more on the negative side—for example, for the first stage, more toward trust or more toward mistrust. A person's personality and sense of identity are formed in the resolution of these crises.

According to Erikson, each individual's life cycle unfolds in the context of a specific culture. While physical maturation determines the general timetable according to which the components of our personality develop, our culture provides us with the contexts in which we must resolve the crises and the tools with which we can resolve them.

Behaviorism

Behaviorism promotes the basic idea that personality and behavior are gradually and continuously shaped by the individual's learning experiences. This learning process involves modifying behavior by forming associations between observable behavior and its consequences, favorable and unfavorable. In this respect, behaviorism is radically different from psychodynamic theories and their focus on universal biological drives, the development of internal personality structures, and the resolution of inner conflicts. Indeed, according to John B. Watson (1878–1958), behaviorism entirely transformed how human behavior should be understood and studied because it shifted the focus from the inner workings of the mind and personality to external, observable behaviors and their consequences (Watson, 1930). This shift in focus, according to Watson and other behaviorists, made the science of human behavior and development more "objective" than it had been in the past.

An early proponent of behaviorism, Edward Thorndike (1874–1949), captured the general principle of the theory in his *law of effect*. In essence, the **law of effect**

behaviorism Theories that focus on development as a result of learning and on changes in behavior as a result of forming associations between behavior and its consequences.

law of effect Thorndike's notion that behaviors that produce a satisfying effect in a given situation are likely to be repeated in the same or similar situations, whereas behaviors that produce an uncomfortable effect are less likely to be repeated.

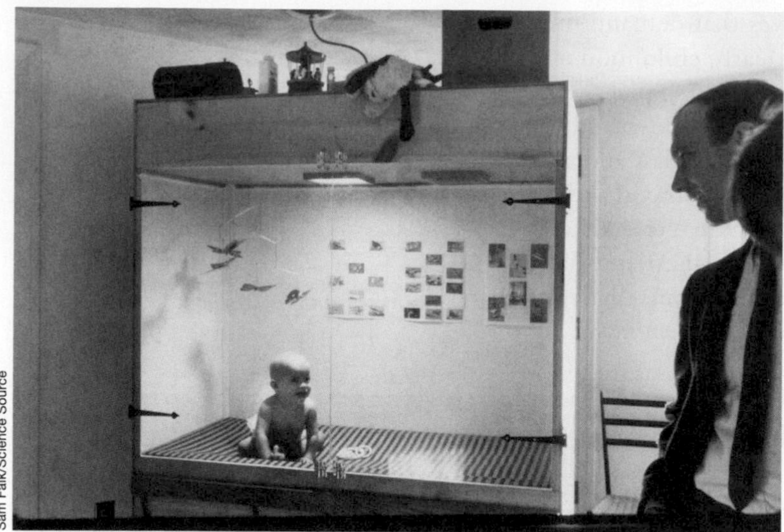
Sam Falk/Science Source

Behaviorist B.F. Skinner designed his famous and controversial "baby box" to make infancy easier for parents and infants by providing a soundproof, climate-controlled environment in which clothes were not necessary. He used the box with his own daughter during the first 2 years of her life.

states that behaviors that produce a satisfying effect in a given situation are likely to be repeated in the same or a similar situation, whereas behaviors that produce an uncomfortable effect are less likely to be repeated.

Thorndike's law of effect is readily apparent in efforts to explore how certain experiences, such as rewards, punishments, and other reinforcers, change the likelihood of a child's engaging in a particular behavior. According to behaviorism, rewards and punishments gradually shape children to become walkers, talkers, readers, and friends. Indeed, some theorists held the extreme position that development is overwhelmingly the product of learning alone. John B. Watson, for example, was so certain of the primary role of learning in human development, and of the insignificance of other factors, that he boasted that he could use learning principles to train any infant, regardless of talents, abilities, or family history, to become whatever she wished—doctor or lawyer, even beggar-woman or thief (1930, p. 104)!

Piaget's Constructivist Theory One of the most influential theories in the history of developmental science is Jean Piaget's theory of children's cognitive, or intellectual, development. Piaget (1896–1980) asserted that cognitive development is driven by the interaction of children's biologically driven motivation to learn and explore, the maturation of their brain and body, and all the experiences that they learn from their actions in the world. The hallmark of Piaget's theory is its emphasis on children's active role in shaping their own cognitive development. He argued in particular that children do not *discover* the world and the way it works but, rather, *actively construct* an understanding of the world on the basis of their experiences with it. In Piaget's **constructivist theory**, children construct successively higher levels of knowledge by actively striving to master their environments.

constructivist theory Piaget's theory, in which cognitive development results from children's active construction of reality, based on their experiences with the world.

Piaget believed that children progress through a series of stages of cognitive development (see Table 1.3), and he supported this idea through observation of, and interviews and experiments with, children of all ages. Each stage reflects a unique age-related way of understanding or organizing reality. Imagine, for instance, a 6-month-old baby playing with a set of wooden blocks. She may attempt to chew

TABLE 1.3 Piaget's Stages of Cognitive Development

Age (years)	Stage	Description
Birth to 2	Sensorimotor	Infants' achievements consist largely of coordinating their sensory perceptions and simple motor behaviors. As they move through the six substages of this period, infants come to recognize the existence of a world outside themselves and begin to interact with it in deliberate ways.
2 to 6	Preoperational	Young children can represent reality to themselves through the use of symbols, including mental images, words, and gestures. Still, children often fail to distinguish their point of view from that of others, become easily captured by surface appearances, and are often confused about causal relations.
6 to 12	Concrete operational	As they enter middle childhood, children become capable of mental operations, internalized actions that fit into a logical system. Operational thinking allows children to mentally combine, separate, order, and transform objects and actions. Such operations are considered concrete because they are carried out in the presence of the objects and events being thought about.
12 to 19	Formal operational	In adolescence, the developing person acquires the ability to think systematically about all logical relations within a problem. Adolescents display keen interest in abstract ideas and in the process of thinking itself.

on some and bang them on the floor. The knowledge she constructs about the blocks—that they are better for banging than for chewing—is entirely different from the knowledge she will construct about them when she is 6 years old and can arrange them into buildings and towns or throw them at her brother. Another example of how children's stage of cognitive development affects their understanding involves age-related differences in how they tend to explain their parents' divorce. Younger children who, as noted, have a difficult time understanding the perspectives of others, may believe that they themselves were somehow at fault. Older children, in contrast, have reached a stage of development that allows them to understand the divorce from their parents' perspective—that is, in terms of their parents' relationship with each other. As you will learn in later chapters, the ability to detach ourselves from our personal, idiosyncratic points of view in order to understand other perspectives takes place throughout childhood and adolescence and is key to the development of objectivity and advanced forms of reasoning. Indeed, believing that scientific reasoning is the pinnacle of cognitive development, Piaget devoted much of his work to understanding how less mature forms of objectivity and reasoning are transformed over time to become more scientific.

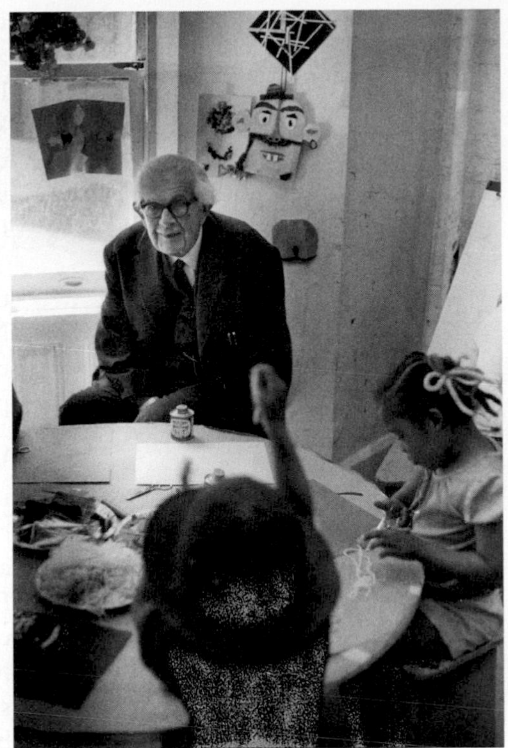
Bill Anderson/Science Source

Jean Piaget, whose work has had a profound influence on developmental psychology.

On the basis of data from various cultures, Piaget (1966/1974) believed that development can be speeded up or slowed down by variations in the environment (such as the presence or absence of formal schooling) but that all children go through the same basic stages. In this important sense, a constructivist approach assumes that the processes of developmental change are universal, the same in all human groups.

In Piaget's view, the most basic unit of cognitive functioning is the *schema*, a general framework that provides a model for understanding some aspect of the world (Piaget & Inhelder, 1969). Over time, as children interact with their environment, they change—strengthen or transform—their schemas through *adaptation* to new information, which involves processes Piaget termed *assimilation* and *accommodation*.

In *assimilation*, individuals incorporate new experiences into their existing schemas, strengthening those schemas. For example, in Piaget's view, infants have a primitive schema of sucking that enables them to draw milk from a nipple. However, sucking does not remain strictly bound to milk-yielding nipples. Soon, babies are likely to find, say, a pacifier, instead of a nipple, touching their lips, and to start sucking on the pacifier—and in much the same way, since a pacifier is designed to be similar to a nipple. In other words, they assimilate the pacifier, a new object, into their existing sucking schema, which is thereby strengthened.

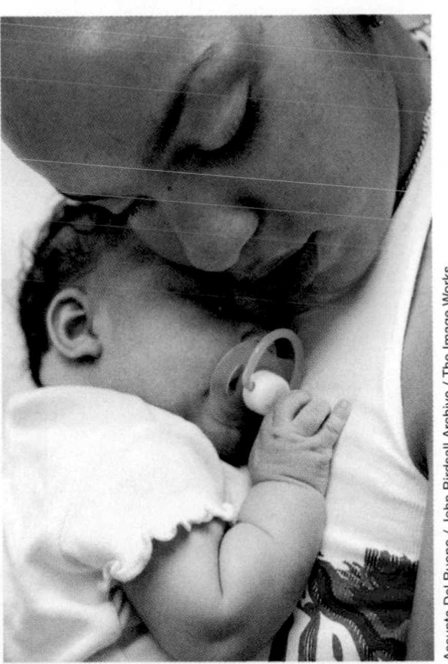
Assunta Del Buono / John Birdsall Archive / The Image Works

According to Piaget, as a consequence of experience mouthing variously shaped objects, the infant's inborn sucking reflex is transformed into a more general schema. This results in more efficient nursing and allows the baby to suck happily and well on other objects, such as pacifiers.

But pacifiers are not the only objects besides nipples that infants are likely to encounter. And many of these other objects cannot be assimilated into the infant's existing sucking schema. At this point, accommodation becomes relevant. In *accommodation*, individuals modify a schema so it can be applied to both old and new experiences. If an infant encounters her father's shoulder while she is being held, for instance, she may try to suck on it. However, because the qualities of Dad's shoulder are so unlike the qualities of a nipple or a pacifier, she is unable to assimilate the shoulder into her sucking schema and must make some accommodation to this new object. That is, she must modify the way she sucks, perhaps by choosing a bit of his shirt and sucking on that, using approximately but not exactly the same schema she had used to suck on a nipple. This transformation of her sucking schema makes it more effective, expanding the universe of suckable objects.

To summarize Piaget's theory, development occurs as the child acts on the world and searches for a fit between new experiences and existing schemas. A lack of fit leads to an imbalance, or disequilibrium, which is corrected through assimilation and accommodation. Piaget believed that this back-and-forth process of the child's search for a fit between existing schemas and new experiences creates a new balance

equilibration The main source of development, consisting of a process of achieving a balance between the child's present understanding and the child's new experiences.

in the child's understanding, which he referred to as **equilibration**. This process of achieving equilibrium between the child's present understanding of the world and his or her new experiences of it creates a more inclusive, more complicated form of knowledge, eventually bringing the child to a new stage of development. Of course, this new balance cannot last long because the process of biological maturation and the accumulation of experience/knowledge lead to new imbalances and to a search for a new equilibrium and a still higher, more inclusive level of adaptation.

As you will see in later chapters, contemporary developmentalists who follow in the tradition established by Piaget have refined or amended a number of his ideas. Nevertheless, these investigators agree with Piaget's belief that children's active engagement with the world interacts with human biology and environments to produce developmental change.

sociocultural theory The theory associated with Vygotsky that emphasizes the influence of culture on development.

Vygotsky's Sociocultural Theory

At the same time that Piaget was building the foundation of constructivism, Lev Vygotsky (1896–1934), a Russian psychologist, was at work developing a sociocultural theory of development. Vygotsky agreed that biological and social factors both play a role in development and, like Piaget, believed that children construct their own development through active engagement with the world. But Vygotsky differed from other theorists by claiming that a third force—culture—is part of the mixture. According to Vygotsky's **sociocultural theory**, human biology and environments shape development not by interacting directly but by interacting indirectly through culture (Greenfield, Keller, Fuligni, & Maynard, 2003; Rogoff, 2003; Valsiner, 2015; Vygotsky, 1978).

The influence of culture on development can be seen in children's acquisition of mathematical understanding. For example, children growing up among the Oksapmin, a group living in the jungles of New Guinea, appear to have the same universal ability to grasp basic number concepts as do children growing up in Boston or Berlin or Beijing. However, instead of using a formal number system to count, the Oksapmin use a system that refers to 27 specific parts of their bodies. To indicate given amounts, they point to their wrist, their elbow, their ear, and so on. This system would obviously be unwieldy if the Oksapmin had to solve arithmetic problems in school and later in a money economy like those of modern cultures, but it is perfectly adequate for dealing with the tasks of everyday life in traditional Oksapmin culture (Saxe, 2014). Thus, culture contributes to the course of development because it is through culture that biological and environmental factors interact.

Sovfoto/Getty Images

Lev Vygotsky, a prominent theorist of the role of culture in development.

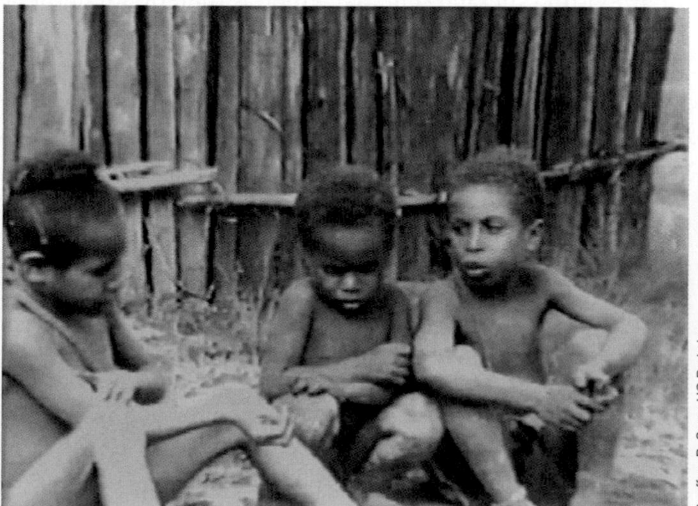

Geoffrey B. Saxe, UC Berkeley

Consistent with the mathematical system of his culture, the Oksapmin child on the left is indicating a number by pointing to a specific place on his body.

One of Vygotsky's most important contributions to understanding children's development is his concept of the **zone of proximal development (ZPD)**, defined as the gap between what children can accomplish independently and what they can accomplish when they are interacting with others who are more competent. The term "proximal" (nearby) indicates that the assistance provided goes just slightly beyond the child's current competence, complementing and building on the child's existing abilities. Consider the following scenario:

zone of proximal development (ZPD) For Vygotsky, the gap between what children can accomplish independently and what they can accomplish when interacting with others who are more competent.

> Amy, almost 4 months old, is sitting [o]n her father's lap in a booth at the coffee shop. He is talking to a friend, and she is teething on a hard rubber ring. The father holds Amy with his left arm, keeping his right hand free. Twice he uses that hand to catch the ring when it falls from her grasp. When Amy dropped the ring for the third time, her father interrupts his conversation, rolls his eyes and says, "Good grief; not again." He retrieves the ring, puts it on the table, and resumes his conversation. Amy leans forward, reaching excitedly, but both her hands and the ring are covered in drool, and her baby hands and fingers are not yet well coordinated. Her father, still talking to his friend while watching Amy's lack of progress, tilts the ring upward so Amy can get her thumb under it. She grasps the ring, pulls it away from her father, and returns to her enthusiastic chewing. (Adapted from Kaye, 1982, pp. 1–2.)

Here you see that, even with an infant, adults can provide help that enables children to function effectively and learn. Notice that, in keeping with Vygotsky's notion of the zone of proximal development, Amy's father did not put the teething ring in her hand or hold it up to her mouth but, instead, tilted it upward so that she could grasp it herself. To help a child appropriately, the adult must know what the child is trying to do and be sensitive to the child's abilities and signals. Vygotsky attributed great significance to such finely tuned child–adult interactions throughout development. Indeed, as shown in Table 1.4, Vygotsky's theory is unique in its emphasis on social interaction as the primary source of development.

Modern Theories

The grand theories just described continue to exert tremendous influence on thinking about children and their development. At the same time, modern theories of development have generated new and distinctive insights into the

TABLE 1.4 Thumbnail Sketch of Grand Theories

	Psychodynamic Theories	Behaviorism	Piaget's Constructivism
What develops	Freud: Personality structures of id, ego, superego Erikson: Personality, sense of identity	Patterns of behavior	Knowledge structures (schema)
Source of development	Freud: Biological drives Erikson: Social and cultural factors; tasks, or "crises"	Learning through social consequences (rewards, punishments)	Lack of fit between existing schemas and new experience (disequilibration)
Goal of development	Freud: Survival through sexual reproduction Erikson: Identity; moving through psychosocial stages	Socially appropriate patterns of behavior	Adaptation through balancing schemas and experience (equilibration)
Main developmental domains addressed	Physical, social, emotional	Cognitive, social	Cognitive
Main research methods used	Clinical interview	Experimental	Clinical interview
Main research designs used	Longitudinal	Microgenetic	Longitudinal, cross-sectional
Special topics and applications	Sexuality, aggression, identity	Self-efficacy, gender roles, behavior-modification therapies	Reasoning and scientific thinking

fundamental issues that have concerned developmentalists since the field was established. Although the number of developmental theories has expanded significantly in recent decades, four kinds of theories have been particularly influential: evolutionary, social learning, information processing, and systems. Because we will explore these theories in greater detail later in the book, we provide only brief sketches of them here.

evolutionary theories Theories that explain human behavior in terms of how it contributes to the survival of the species and that look at how our evolutionary past influences individual development.

Evolutionary Theories **Evolutionary theories** attempt both to explain human behavior in terms of how it contributes to the survival of the species and to address the ways in which our evolutionary past continues to influence individual

In The Field: Probing the Mysteries of Learning

Name: ELIZABETH VINSON LONSDORF

Education: Undergraduate degrees at Duke University, including summer internships in Hawaii and Florida to study whales and dolphins; Ph.D. at the Jane Goodall Institute Center for Primate Studies at the University of Minnesota

Current Position: Director of the Lester E. Fisher Center for the Study and Conservation of Apes, Lincoln Park Zoo in Chicago

Career Objectives: Participate in and support worldwide animal conservation projects

VIDEO CAMERA IN HAND, Elizabeth Vinson Lonsdorf crouches in a clearing of the Gombe National Park in Tanzania. The target of her attention is a mother–daughter pair of wild chimpanzees working to extract termites—a delicacy—from a termite mound. Chimpanzees use tools to gather their food—something that is exceedingly rare among animal species. From vegetation found nearby, they fashion a long tool that can be inserted into the depths of the mound. When the termites attack and cling to the "intruder," the chimpanzees carefully withdraw the tool and feast on the clinging insects. Primatologists refer to this process of foraging as "termite-fishing."

It has been known for some time that chimpanzees engage in tool-assisted foraging. What Elizabeth Lonsdorf and her colleagues want to know is how chimpanzees learn to use tools in this distinctive way (Musgrave et al., 2016). Her interest is motivated by the understanding that, because chimpanzees are our closest genetic kin, their behavior may shed light on the activities of our earliest evolutionary ancestors (Lonsdorf, 2007). In her words:

> ... it's ... easy to see the link between humans and the rest of the animal kingdom. They make and use tools, conduct warfare, and have very similar mother–child relationships as humans. By studying chimpanzees, we can gain insight into what the activities of our earliest ancestors might have been like.

Her studies of chimpanzee behavior in natural environments suggest that young chimps learn termite-fishing by watching their mothers, much as an apprentice acquires skills by observing a master. Although chimp mothers model successfully fishing for termites, and seem remarkably tolerant when youngsters interrupt their foraging with awkward efforts of their own, at no time were the mothers observed to deliberately teach their children how to fish. According to many evolutionary theorists, the deliberate teaching of the young may be a distinctively human trait (see Chapter 2).

mark higgins/Shutterstock

(a)

Courtesy of Lincoln Park Zoo, Chicago

(b)

(a) This chimpanzee is carrying a stick used to "fish" insects out of termite mounds.
(b) Elizabeth Lonsdorf is interested in learning how this tool-using practice, exceedingly rare in the animal kingdom, is transmitted to the young.

development (Bjorklund & Ellis, 2014; Jablonka & Lamb, 2015). As you will see in Chapter 2, according to evolutionary theory, species develop as they do because individuals with characteristics that favor survival in a particular environment are more likely to reproduce and pass those characteristics on to their offspring. Thus, human characteristics—physical, behavioral, and other—can be understood in terms of their role in contributing to the survival of individuals and, in turn, to the survival and evolution of the species. Of course, evolutionary theorizing about children's development has been around since Darwin. But it has recently emerged as a dominant perspective in the discipline, due in part to advances in sophisticated technologies and research methods that permit more direct measurements of biological processes (see the box "Now Trending in Research: Observing the Living Brain," p. 33).

An evolutionary approach is central in **ethology**, a field of study that explores animal (including human) behavior in natural environments (see the box "In the Field: Probing the Mysteries of Learning"). In its evolutionary approach, ethology focuses on how behaviors of various species are adapted to the environment in ways that increase the likelihood that individuals will reach reproductive maturity to have offspring of their own. Ethologists look both at the adaptive behaviors of the young and at the behaviors they elicit in others, and they ask how both types of behaviors contribute to survival.

ethology An interdisciplinary science that studies the biological and evolutionary foundations of behavior.

To illustrate how adaptive behaviors may have implications for the survival of the species, consider how infants and children elicit care from their parents. Clearly, human infants and children require considerable parental care and investment if they are to survive to maturity. From an evolutionary perspective, it makes good sense that caregiving should have a strong biological component. A question raised by ethologists is, "What products of evolution do children possess that ensure they will be cared for?" One answer to this question (you will learn of others in later chapters) is found in the infant's appearance. Babies, as we all know, are cute. This cuteness applies not only to our own babies but to those of many other species as well: kittens, puppies, and baby lions and tigers and bears are all cute. What we consider cute, however, boils down to several highly specific physical characteristics that distinguish newborns of many animal species from mature individuals and that seem key to eliciting care. These characteristics include a relatively large head; large eyes set low on the forehead; short, heavy limbs; big, round cheeks; and a button nose (Estren, 2012; Gould, 1980; see Figure 1.4).

carlos cardetas / Alamy

FIGURE 1.4 Betty Boop's large head, big eyes set low on her forehead, big round cheeks, and button nose embody the features of "babyness." Konrad Lorenz, a famous German ethologist, used the 1930s cartoon character to argue that babyness traits elicit the care and attention of adults.

Evidence in support of the idea that babyness evokes positive adult responses comes from a classic study by Willian Fullard and Ann Reiling (1976). These researchers asked people ranging in age from 7 years to young adulthood which of matched pairs of pictures—one depicting an adult and the other depicting an infant—they preferred. Some of the pictures were of human beings; others were of nonhuman animals. They found that adults, especially women, were most likely to choose the pictures of infants. Children between the ages of 7 and 12 preferred the pictures of adults. Between the ages of 12 and 14, the preference of girls shifted quite markedly from adults to infants. A similar shift was found among boys when they were between ages 14 and 16. These shifts in preference coincide with the average age at which girls and boys undergo the physiological changes that make them capable of reproducing.

Social Learning Theories Rooted in behaviorism, social learning theories explain development in terms of the associations that children make between behaviors and their consequences. However, unlike behaviorism, **social learning theories** emphasize the behavior–consequence associations that children learn by observing and interacting with others in social situations. Social learning theories have made a number of important contributions to the study of human

social learning theories Theories that emphasize the behavior–consequences associations that children learn by observing and interacting with others in social situations.

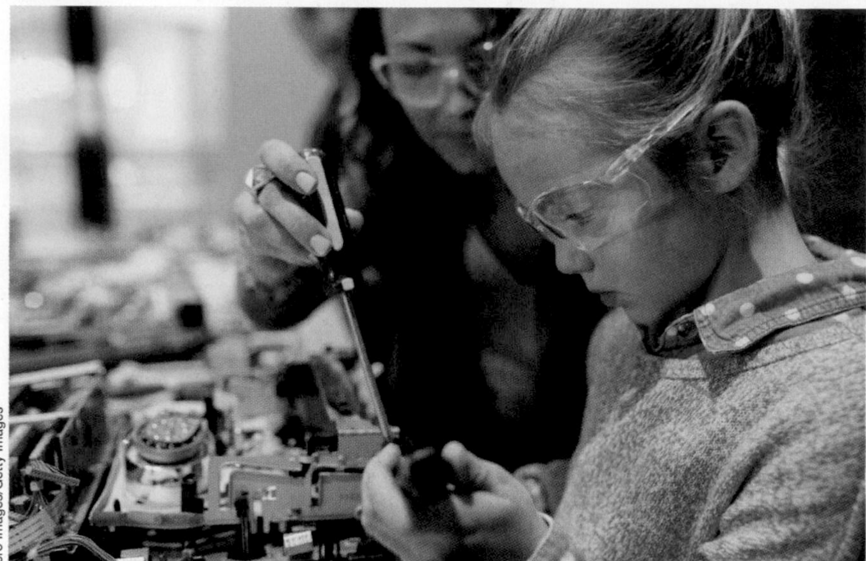

Hero Images/Getty Images

Many schools have science programs for girls that expose the girls to women engaged in math, science, and engineering. The hope is that girls will model these women's behavior and develop interest in science courses, majors, and professions.

development, two of which are generally associated with the work of Albert Bandura. One contribution is the concept of *modeling*, the process by which children observe and imitate others. As you will see in later chapters, the concept of modeling has proven to be particularly valuable for understanding children's gender-role development. Another key concept proposed by Bandura is *self-efficacy*, people's beliefs about their abilities to effectively meet standards and achieve goals (Bandura, 1974/2012). You probably know people who avoid taking on difficult tasks because they don't believe they are capable of doing them well. Or maybe you know people who have a huge amount of faith in their ability to master just about any challenge. Bandura would describe the first group of people as having low self-efficacy and the second group as having high self-efficacy. As we will discuss in Chapter 9, a child's self-efficacy can have a dramatic effect on learning.

Social learning theorists maintain that many aspects of personality, including personality problems such as aggression and dependency, are learned and therefore can be unlearned. This idea led to the development of *behavior modification*, a technique for breaking the associations between the behaviors and the environmental consequences that maintain them. For example, if a child engages in overly aggressive behavior in the home, a therapist might look into whether the parents are inadvertently rewarding the aggression, perhaps by giving the child a lot of attention. In order to break the association between the behavior and its rewarding consequences, the therapist might then set up a behavior-modification program in which the child's aggression results in being isolated in a "time out," thereby taking away the reward and substituting a punishment.

Information-Processing Theories The enormous magnitude of data processed through high-speed computer technologies and communications systems leaves no doubt that we live in an information age. In addition to introducing significant changes in the ways that people work, live, and learn, the information age has inspired changes in how developmentalists think about the mind. In particular, some developmentalists describe mental functioning in terms of the workings of a digital computer—that is, they take an information-processing approach to cognition and its development. **Information-processing theories** are concerned with how information flows through a child's developing mental system—how the child comes to perceive, remember, organize, and manipulate information in increasingly efficient ways.

information-processing theories Theories that look at cognitive development in terms of how children come to perceive, remember, organize, and manipulate information in increasingly efficient ways.

Information-processing approaches have been useful in understanding such topics as how attention and memory develop, how children build information into more complex systems of knowledge, and how children develop and use strategies to help remember things and solve problems. Some research focuses on the development of largely unconscious information-processing skills, such as how quickly information is processed or the amount of information that can be processed at one time. Other research, in contrast, examines children's developing abilities to consciously and purposefully manage information, as when you try to remember something by rehearsing it over and over or by skimming through a textbook to look for boldfaced key terms that might be useful to include in a term paper. In both instances, you are engaged in intentional behaviors that manipulate information in order to achieve specific goals.

systems theories Theories that envision development in terms of complex wholes made up of parts and that explore how these wholes and their parts are organized and interact and change over time.

Systems Theories

As the name suggests, **systems theories** envision development in terms of complex wholes made up of parts—that is, *systems*—and look at how these wholes and their parts are organized, as well as how they interact and change over time. The particular systems of interest vary. Some systems theorists focus on how specific behaviors of the child, such as walking, become organized and coordinated over time; for these theorists, the behaviors are the systems. Other theorists focus on more general systems, such as systems made up of the contexts in which children live (the family, the community, and so on) and of interrelationships among these contexts. Two types of systems theories have been particularly influential in the past few decades—*dynamic systems theory* and *bioecological systems theory*. Despite the considerable differences between them, they share the view that development is best understood as a complex and unified system that is organized and reorganized over time. In the words of Esther Thelen, who devoted her career to exploring the application of systems theory to children's development, a complete understanding of development requires recognizing "the multiple, mutual, and continuous interaction of all levels of the developing system, from the molecular to the cultural" (Thelen & Smith, 1998, p. 563).

dynamic systems theory A theory that addresses how new, complex systems of behavior develop from the interaction of less complex parts.

Dynamic Systems Theory. **Dynamic systems theory** addresses how new complex systems of behavior develop from the interaction of less complex parts. Consider, for example, baby Ryan's ability to reach and grasp a toy that his older brother dangles in front of him. Ryan's reaching-and-grasping system emerged from the development and interaction of several visual and motor (movement) components. First, the visual component of the system had to have developed such that Ryan's eyes can follow and fix the toy in his field of vision. In addition, his perceptual system had to have been sufficiently honed by experience for Ryan to accurately judge whether the toy is reachable and graspable. Further, his motor system must have developed the muscle coordination that allows him to engage in smooth reaching movements with his arms and effective grasping movements with his hands. Finally, all these components must interact in a unified system so that what Ryan *sees* (the toy) is successfully coordinated with what he *does* (reaches and grasps).

With development and experience, the components of Ryan's reaching and grasping will be coordinated into a stable and balanced system, and his reaching and grasping will become second nature, as it is for most of us. However, as you will learn in Chapter 4, reaching and grasping, as well as many other systems, are initially disorganized and sloppy approximations of what they will become. Dynamic systems theorists are interested in what sparks the beginnings of new systems and in how these new systems develop from initial disorganization and instability to become smoothly functioning and stable.

ecological systems theory A theory focusing on the organization and interactions of the multiple environmental contexts within which children develop.

bioecological model A model that sees children in the context of five interrelated systems: microsystem, mesosystem, exosystem, macrosystem, and chronosystem.

Ecological Systems Theory. The field of biology has been an important source of inspiration to ecological systems theory. *Ecology* is the subfield of biology that studies the relationship between organisms (plants and animals) and their environments. In developmental science, **ecological systems theory** focuses on the organization of the multiple environmental contexts within which children develop.

One of the most influential models of ecological systems is Uri Bronfenbrenner's **bioecological model**, which posits that the developing child is at the center of

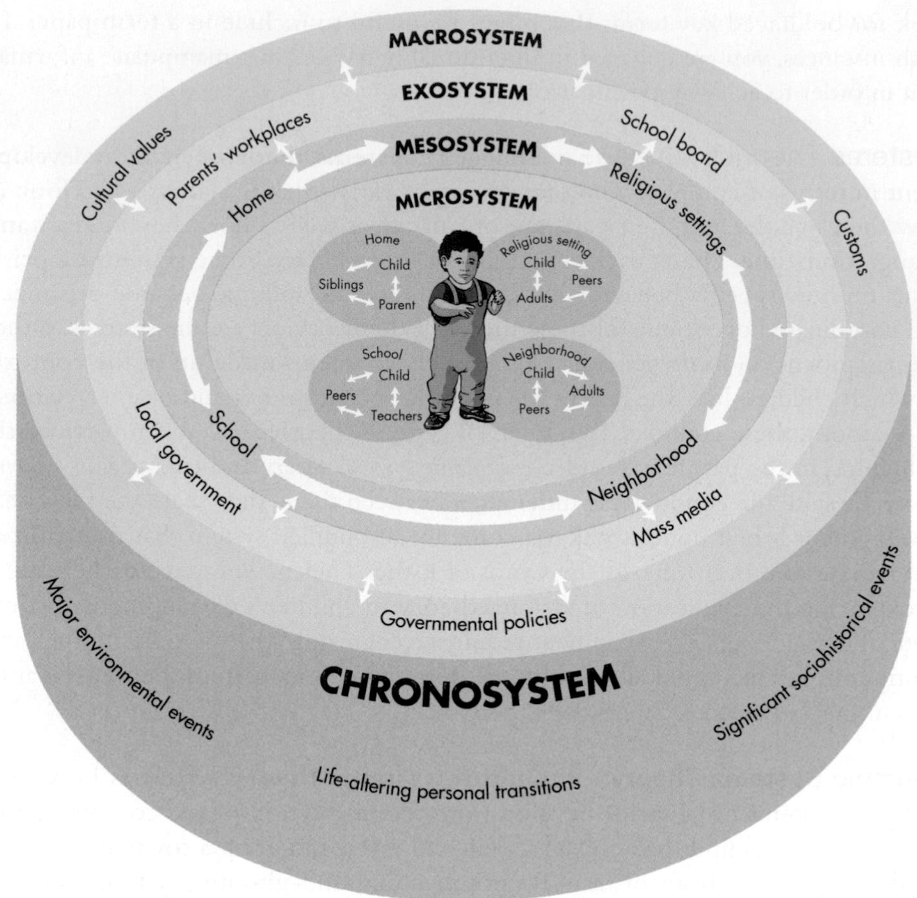

FIGURE 1.5 The bioecological model sees children in the context of all the various settings they inhabit on a daily basis (microsystems). These settings are related to one another in a variety of ways (mesosystems), which are in turn linked to settings and social institutions where the children are not present but which have an important influence on their development (exosystems). All these systems are organized in terms of the culture's dominant beliefs and ideologies (the macrosystem) and affected by the pattern of major personal transitions, environmental events, and sociocultural circumstances of the child (chronosystem).

five nested, interacting systems: microsystem, mesosystem, exosystem, macrosystem, and chronosystem (2005; Figure 1.5):

1. The innermost system, the *microsystem*, includes all the various settings that the child inhabits on a daily basis—the "face-to-face" settings of home, school, and peer groups.
2. The *mesosystem* is the connective tissue that links the face-to-face settings to one another, such as parents' involvement in their child's school. The strength and nature of these connections are important to children's development. For example, parents, teachers, and peers might be consistent with one another in supporting the child's academic success—or might be in conflict, as would be the case if the parents and teachers were pushing the child toward college but the peers wanted to form an indie-rock band and move to L.A. to play music full time.
3. Part three of Bronfenbrenner's model is the *exosystem*, which consists of settings that affect but do not usually include the child. An example would be the parent's workplace. If a parent's workplace provides a decent wage, security, satisfaction, and good benefits, including good medical benefits and paid leave when children are born or are ill, the parent may be more likely to provide quality care. If, on the other hand, a parent's workplace is one of stress, frustration, anxiety, and poor pay and benefits, quality of care may suffer.
4. The fourth part of the model is the *macrosystem*—the values, customs, hazards, and resources of the larger culture that shape what happens in all the settings of the systems nested within. The macrosystems of some cultures

are very supportive of children's needs, and this may be evident from, for example, child-protection laws and resources devoted to providing quality educational and child-care facilities and to ensuring access to health care. As we will see, values regarding such characteristics as race and ethnicity, socioeconomic status, and gender may seriously diminish the quality of care, nurturing, and interaction that children experience.

5. The *chronosystem* includes the timing of life-altering personal transitions, major environmental events, and significant sociohistorical circumstances that occur over the life span of the individual. Common personal transitions include divorce, deaths of family members or friends, and births of children. Environmental events typically include natural disasters such as hurricanes and earthquakes. Sociohistorical circumstances include events and experiences with broad societal and cultural impact, such as *Black Lives Matter*, which began in 2012 as a social media movement—#BlackLivesMatter—responding to the acquittal of George Zimmerman in the shooting death of the black teenager Trayvon Martin. The timing and sequencing of such significant events have pronounced effects on development.

As in all other systems theories, the five systems here are understood to interact and influence one another. For example, a famous study of the Great Depression in the 1930s found that when the unemployment rate in the United States sky-rocketed and parents lost jobs, relationships among family members deteriorated, parenting skills declined, and children's development and well-being were placed at considerable risk (Elder, 1998; Modell & Elder, 2002).

None of the theories outlined above is sufficiently comprehensive to provide a full picture of all the complexities of human development. But each provides an important and unique frame for looking at certain aspects of development and for formulating **hypotheses**, or possible explanations precise enough to be shown true or false, regarding why children behave as they do, why they change over time, and what practitioners can do to support their health and well-being. In the next section, we explore the research methods typically used to test theoretical hypotheses.

hypothesis A statement about expected research results that is precise enough to be shown to be true or false.

APPLY > CONNECT > DISCUSS

Little Parminder is playing intently with wooden blocks. She puts one on top of another and looks at her mother, who smiles, claps her hands, and exclaims, "Oh, aren't you clever? You got it on top! Are you a proud little girl?!" Parminder grasps another block and repeats her performance. She smiles broadly at her mother, who again responds with happy excitement. On the third try, however, Parminder topples her tower and bursts into tears and scatters the blocks. "Poor baby! They fell down, and now you're angry," says her mother. "Here, let me help you make the tower."

This scenario can be explored from several different theoretical perspectives. Considering the theories of Erikson, Vygotksy, and Piaget, what would you focus on? How would you interpret the scenario?

Methods for Studying Development

LEARNING OUTCOMES

Compare the goals of basic, applied, and action research.

Distinguish among the four criteria used to judge scientific research.

Contrast research data collection methods used in development research.

Point out the elements in each of four research designs used in developmental studies.

We mentioned previously that different theories tend to rely on different research methods for addressing questions and collecting information about human development. Indeed, the relationship between theory and method is of fundamental importance, and developmentalists take great care to ensure that one follows from the other (Valsiner, 2005). For example, it makes little sense to research children's memory development by collecting only quantitative information (e.g., changes in the number of words remembered from a long list) if, according to your theory, memory development proceeds through a sequence of qualitative stage transitions that are reflected in how memories are organized. Individual research methods, like the theories with which they are associated, provide only limited views that are often specific to particular developmental periods or domains. In the sections below, we examine the various goals of conducting research and the different methods by which those goals are accomplished.

The Goals of Developmental Research

Like any other scientists, developmentalists begin their research with particular goals in mind. The goals can range widely, from the "purely scientific" to the practical, often with a good deal of overlap. It is therefore helpful to consider three categories of research—*basic*, *applied*, and *action*—that differ according to the particular goals that motivate the researcher.

The goal of *basic research* is to advance scientific knowledge of human development—for example, to determine whether the ability to perceive depth is inborn or learned or to determine whether basic emotions develop universally in all children or emerge differently for children in different cultures. Although its results might be used to help solve practical problems, basic research is undertaken for the simple goal of gaining new knowledge, and it often explores major theoretical issues, such as questions of developmental continuity, plasticity, and sources of development.

In contrast to basic research, *applied research* is designed to answer practical questions related to improving children's lives and experiences—for example, assessing the effectiveness of different kinds of violence-prevention programs in schools or determining whether immigrant children learn better if they are instructed in their native language or in the language of their adopted country. In many cases, applied research also extends basic scientific knowledge. Its primary goal, however, is to benefit society by generating knowledge that can be used in solving specific problems.

Action research is a close cousin of applied research. Also known as "mission-oriented research," action research is designed primarily to provide data that can be used in making social-policy decisions (Coghlan & Jacobs, 2005). For example, action research has played an instrumental role in programs and policies ranging from the Head Start school-readiness program for disadvantaged children to federal regulations regarding the education of children with special needs; toy safety standards; requirements for foster care; and legislation concerning the prosecution of minors who have committed crimes. In contrast to basic and applied research, whose intended audience usually includes scientists and other developmental practitioners, action research is aimed at legislators and government officials and is often meant to sway their opinions.

In recent years, developmentalists have been increasingly drawn to action research. To some extent, this is the result of a growing commitment and sense of social obligation on the part of universities to recognize and serve the needs of their communities better (Coller & Kuo, 2014). Universities and communities across the United States and other nations are forging *university–community partnerships* around specific local issues. For example, cultural differences likely play a significant role in the poor academic test performance of many children from indigenous communities in the United States. In order to better prepare teachers to understand and serve the needs of indigenous students living in the Chicago area, a partnership was formed between Loyola University's teacher education program and an urban community organization of indigenous peoples from several tribal nations (Lees, 2016). In-depth interviews with members of the indigenous community organization produced several recommendations for teacher training. One recommendation was that student teachers spend considerable time interacting with indigenous families and community members in order to learn about their students' cultural values and beliefs. Another recommendation is that teachers understand and communicate to students that knowledge and education reside not only in schools but also in cultural communities and that community leaders, as well as teachers, are important sources of education.

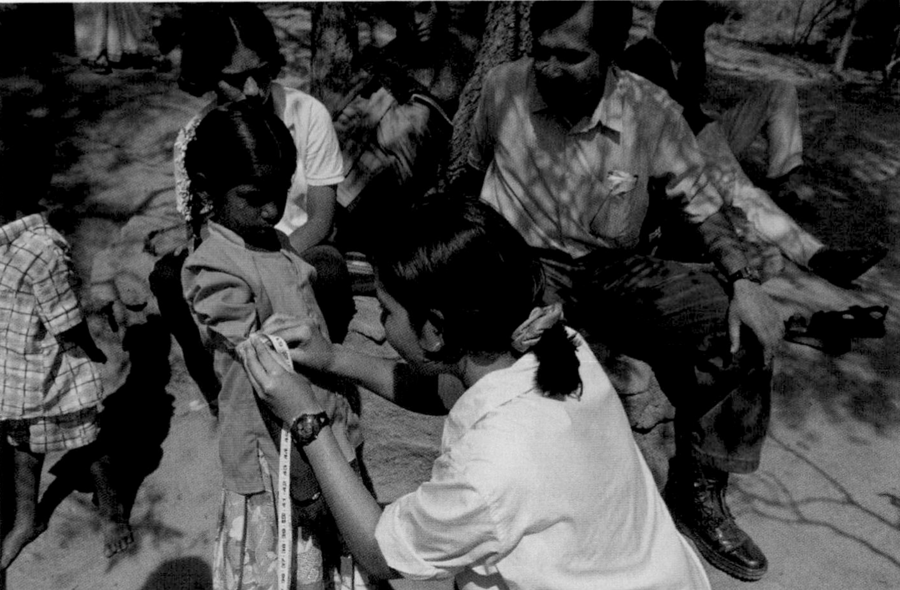

UniversalImagesGroup/Getty Images

Action- or mission-oriented research provides information that can be used to set governmental policies to improve children's health and well-being. For example, data on children's growth can be used to influence policies related to nutrition and health care.

Although categorizing research can be helpful, it is important to remember that basic, applied, and action research often overlap in their goals. For example, a research study on the effectiveness of Head Start programs is *basic* in the sense of addressing questions of plasticity, such as whether intervention with disadvantaged preschoolers can have lasting effects on IQ, *applied* in the sense of seeking knowledge to improve the lives of socially disadvantaged children, and *action*-oriented in that its data may influence social-policy decisions on program funding and development.

Criteria for Developmental Research

Whether engaged in basic, applied, or action research, developmentalists usually begin their work with commonsense observation and speculation. In this respect, they are like anyone else who might be trying to understand some interesting or puzzling aspect of children's behavior. The difference is that developmental researchers go beyond commonsense observation and speculation; as researchers, their approach to understanding children's behavior must meet certain specific criteria that have been determined by the scientific and scholarly community to which they belong. The criteria will vary to some extent, depending on the researcher's theory and method of data collection, as we discuss below. Four of the most commonly used criteria for judging scientific research are *objectivity*, *reliability*, *replicability*, and *validity*. Let us look at each in turn.

In a research study, data should be collected and analyzed with **objectivity**; that is, the gathering and analyzing of data should not be biased by the investigators' preconceptions. Total objectivity is impossible to achieve in practice because developmentalists, like everyone else, have beliefs that influence how they interpret what they see. But objectivity remains an important ideal to strive for.

objectivity The requirement that scientific knowledge not be distorted by the investigator's preconceptions.

Reliability refers to the consistency of the research findings. Research data should be reliable in two senses. First, investigators should get the same results each time they collect data under the same set of conditions. Second, the descriptions of independent observers' results should be in agreement with each other. Suppose, for example, that investigators want to determine how upset infants become when a pacifier is taken from them while they are sucking on it (Goldsmith & Campos, 1982). The findings about the degree of an infant's distress are considered reliable in the first sense if the level of distress (measured in terms of crying or thrashing about) is found to be the same when the baby's sucking is interrupted under the

reliability The scientific requirement that when the same behavior is measured on two or more occasions by the same or different observers, the measurements must be consistent with each other.

same conditions on successive occasions. The findings are considered reliable in the second sense if independent observers agree on how distressed the baby becomes each time the pacifier is taken away.

replicability The scientific requirement that other researchers be able to use the same procedures as an initial investigator did and obtain the same results.

Replicability, the third criterion, means that if other researchers independently create the same procedures as an initial investigator did, they will obtain the same results. In studies of newborns' ability to imitate, for example, some researchers report that newborns will imitate certain exaggerated facial expressions that they see another person making directly in front of them. However, using the same methods, other investigators have failed to find evidence of such imitation in newborns (see Chapter 6, p. 205). If investigators repeatedly obtain the same finding under the same conditions, the scientific community will likely regard the finding as firmly established.

validity The scientific requirement that the data being collected must actually reflect the phenomenon being studied.

Of the criteria of scientific evidence, validity is in certain respects the most important. **Validity** means that the data being collected actually reflect the phenomenon that the researcher is attempting to study. A study may meet all the other criteria—it may be objective, reliable, and replicable—but still may not meet the criterion of validity, in which case it is of no value. Imagine, for example, a study of infant intelligence. The researchers may be using a particular scale to measure intelligence that is not biased by the researcher's preconceptions (it is objective), that produces the same results when given under similar conditions or when scored by different raters (it is reliable), and that can be used by other researchers to yield the same results (it is replicable). However, imagine that the scale used to measure intelligence is based on hair color. Obviously, hair color has no bearing on intelligence, so the study lacks validity and has no meaning, even though the other criteria have been met. Our example is extreme for purposes of illustration. A vast array of other examples that developmental scientists deal with regularly are much more subtle and controversial. There are, for example, researchers who claim that many laboratory studies of development lack validity because laboratory conditions are artificial and foreign to children's experience. Memory development, they might argue, is best studied in the everyday contexts in which memory is used—contexts in which, for example, children remember their phone number or their friends' birthdays or their favorite team's vital statistics—not in sterile laboratory conditions in which they are required to memorize lists of random digits.

Methods of Data Collection

Over the past century, developmentalists have refined a variety of methods for gathering information about the development of children. Among the most widely used have been *naturalistic observations*, *experiments*, and *clinical interviews*. (For a research method that has come to the fore more recently, see the box "Now Trending in Research: Observing the Living Brain.") No single method can answer every question about human development. Each has a strategic role to play, depending on the topic and the goal of the researcher, and each has advantages and disadvantages (Table 1.5). Often researchers use a process called *triangulation*, in which two or more methods are combined to confirm their conclusions.

naturalistic observation Observation of the actual behavior of people in the course of their everyday lives.

Naturalistic Observation

The most direct way to gather objective information about children is to study them through **naturalistic observation**—that is, to watch them in the course of their everyday lives and record what happens.

For example, a team of researchers used naturalistic observation to explore whether shy Chinese children differ from their non-shy peers in adjusting to the transition from preschool to kindergarten (Feng, Harkness, Super, & Jia, 2014). The children were videotaped in their interactions with peers during play and with

TABLE 1.5 Methods of Data Collection

Method	Description	Advantages	Disadvantages
Naturalistic observation	Observing and recording the behavior of people in the course of their everyday lives	Direct way to gather objective information revealing the full complexity of behavior	People might behave differently under observation; expectations may shape observations; information may be lost or time-consuming to analyze
Experiment	Introducing a change in a group's experience and measuring the effects of the change	Best method of testing causal hypotheses	People may behave differently in the experimental setting, distorting the validity of the results
Clinical interview	Asking questions tailored to the individual	Possible to probe the child's way of thinking in order to discover patterns	Reliance on verbal expression makes the method inappropriate with very young children

teachers during class. Compared to non-shy children, the shy children were more socially withdrawn and less likely to initiate interactions with peers and teachers. However, in contrast to results from studies conducted in Western countries such as the United States, there were no differences between shy and non-shy children on measures of peer acceptance and invitations to join play. This is likely because Western cultures tend to value independent, assertive, and adventurous behavior, whereas

Now TRENDING in RESEARCH Observing the Living Brain

In the not-so-distant past, the only way to examine the brain was to surgically remove it from the skull. Neuroscientists, who study the brain and the rest of the nervous system, have been conducting postmortem research for more than a century in an effort to discover how the brain is designed, how it changes as we grow and age, and how it responds to injury. Although this research has generated a wealth of information on the anatomy of the brain, it has not revealed much about the functions of the living brain and their links to behavior. The recent development of brain-imaging technologies has begun to supply scientists with that information (Man, Kaplan, Damasio, & Damasio, 2013).

One such technology is functional magnetic resonance imaging (fMRI), which allows scientists to see brain activity in living patients by measuring blood flow through brain structures. A scan using magnetic fields and radio waves provides input to a computer that converts the data into a three-dimensional image of the brain. The fMRI has led to important advances in understanding the development and functions of various structures of the brain and has enabled neuroscientists to track the ebb and flow of brain activity under different experimental or disease conditions. For example, fMRI technology has led to fascinating insights into brain development during adolescence, particularly with regard to how changes in the frontal cortex, which is associated with higher levels of reasoning and decision making, may affect a number of behaviors, including risk taking (Silverman, Jedd, & Luciana, 2015). In addition, fMRIs have aided in the understanding of certain disorders, ranging from depression to attention-deficit/hyperactivity disorder (ADHD) and autism spectrum disorder (Bradley et al., 2016; Hernandez et al., 2015; Rhein et al., 2016).

New brain imaging technologies have elevated the role of neuroscience in understanding the sources of development. For example, Helen Neville (2005) studied the brains of deaf children and found that areas of the brain typically devoted to processing auditory information gradually shift their function to the processing of visual information. Likewise, in blind children, areas of the brain that would normally process visual information shift their function to auditory processing. Neville's work demonstrates how the brain responds and adapts to different forms of sensory experience.

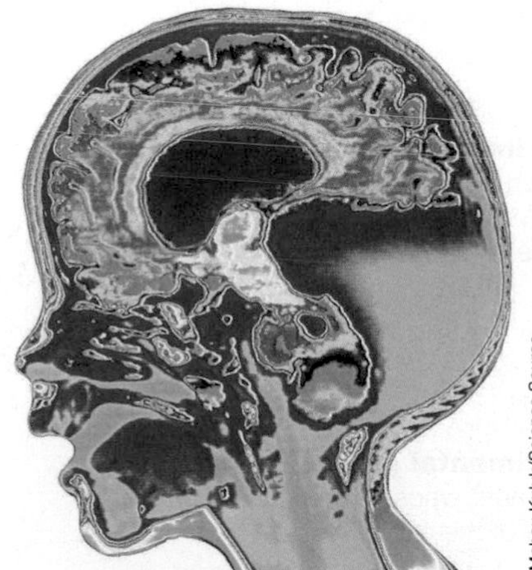

Mehau Kulyk/Science Source

This brain scan of an 11-month-old child clearly reveals a large kidney-shaped cyst (the large red area) in the center of the baby's cerebral cortex. Seeing the cyst helps developmentalists pinpoint its location and size and determine whether surrounding brain structures are injured. Developmentalists then use this information to devise a plan for treating the child.

Carlos Ciudad Photos/Getty Images

Naturalistic observation of children in the course of their everyday lives has been used to study the peer interactions of shy children. Research indicates that shy children in Western countries are less likely to be accepted by peers than are shy children in China.

Chinese culture typically values more cautious approaches to new situations (such as a new school), and behaviors that preserve interpersonal harmony, as the behaviors of shy children tend to do.

A special form of naturalistic observation is **ethnography**, which attempts to go beyond children's naturally occurring behaviors to explain the *meanings* of those behaviors in light of the customs, beliefs, and values of their culture. For example, researchers have documented how young infants born to the Efe foragers of the Congo's Ituri forest are routinely cared for by many people and are likely to be nursed by several women (Ivey, 2000). This pattern, which seems so at odds with Western ideas about child-rearing, is essential to the Efe's foraging way of life and is accepted by Efe children as natural (Ivey, 2000). For the Efe, as well as all other cultural groups, nursing is not just a behavior that feeds an infant; it is a meaningful activity that expresses cultural customs and patterns of life. (See Chapter 4 for a more detailed discussion of the relationship between culture and infant feeding practices.)

ethnography The study of the cultural organization of behavior.

Like all other methods of data collection, observational research has limitations. It has been demonstrated, for example, that when people know they are being watched, they often behave differently than they normally would (Hoff-Ginsberg & Tardiff, 1995). In addition, despite their best intentions to be objective, research observers often have expectations about what they are going to see and may observe selectively in accordance with those expectations. Another limitation is that an observer cannot write down everything, so information is inevitably lost. Some studies therefore use prearranged note-taking schemes to specify what to look for and how to report it. Recordings of behavior on videotape or film can help preserve information, but analyzing recordings is extremely time-consuming. Despite their limitations, observational studies are a keystone of child development research and a crucial source of data about children's development.

experiment In psychology, research in which a change is introduced into a person's experience and the effect of that change is measured.

Experiments A psychological **experiment** is used to study cause–effect relationships—that is, how changing one factor or variable (the *independent variable*) causes a change in another factor or variable (the *dependent variable*). Often the independent variable takes the form of a treatment condition or intervention, and the dependent variable takes the form of some behavioral change. To ensure that the change in the dependent variable is in fact caused by a change in the independent variable, and not some other extraneous factor, researchers randomly assign individuals to two different groups. One group, called the **experimental group**, is exposed to the treatment condition; the other, called the **control group**, is not. The two groups are then compared on the dependent variable(s) of interest to determine the effects of the independent variable. An experiment is designed to test a specific hypothesis—a statement of an expected research outcome that is precise enough to be proven true or false.

experimental group The group in an experiment whose experience is changed as part of the experiment.

control group The group in an experiment that is treated as much as possible like the experimental group except that it does not participate in the experimental manipulation.

An example of how developmentalists can apply the experimental method is provided by a study that tested the hypothesis that premature babies kept in skin-to-skin contact with their mothers—a practice dubbed "kangaroo care"—develop more successfully than premature babies kept in bassinets. The latter practice is currently the most common way of caring for premature newborns in locales where sophisticated incubators and highly trained nursing are scarce.

In this study, Charpak, Ruiz-Pelaez, Figueroa de Calume, and Charpak (2001) worked with 764 low-birth-weight infants in a Colombian hospital serving primarily poor and working-class mothers. The infants had weighed 4.5 pounds (2,000 grams) or less at birth and by definition were at risk for a variety of developmental problems. Half of the infants were randomly assigned to the experimental group, which received kangaroo care. The other half were assigned to the control group, which received the traditional care of being placed in a bassinet in warm, sanitary conditions.

In the short term, the babies assigned to the experimental group showed more regular breathing and quicker mastery of breast-feeding compared with babies in the control group. In the long term, the experimental-group babies showed significantly shorter hospital stays, less likelihood of illness or death, and faster growth rates. They were also quicker than the control group to reach important developmental milestones, such as raising their head spontaneously while lying on their stomach. These results help confirm the benefits of kangaroo care, which is being used increasingly in many countries around the world, including the United States (Cho et al., 2016).

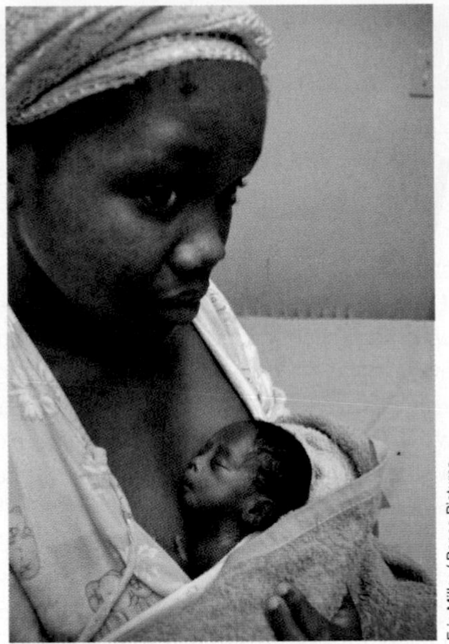

Eric Miller / Panos Pictures

This South African mother is practicing kangaroo care, which, according to experimental research, increases the likelihood that her premature infant will develop normally.

The clear strength of the experimental method is its unique ability to isolate causal factors. (For a discussion of the challenges to determining causation, see the box "Understanding Causes and Correlations," p. 36.) However, experiments also have limitations. One major drawback is that the very control of the environment that the experiments require may distort the validity of the results obtained. As we noted earlier, people sometimes behave differently in an artificial, experimental situation than they would normally. Children are particularly likely to behave unnaturally in an unfamiliar laboratory setting with researchers they have never met before. This, of course, raises doubts about the value of experimental results. When an experimental setting diverges so completely from children's natural environment that children behave differently than they would ordinarily, the experiment is said to lack **ecological validity**, and the results cannot be put to proper use.

ecological validity The extent to which behavior studied in one environment (such as a psychological test) is characteristic of behavior exhibited by the same person in a range of other environments.

Clinical Interviews

Whereas the experimental method is designed to apply uniform procedures of data collection to every person in a study, the essence of the **clinical interview** is to tailor procedures to each individual. For example, each question the researcher asks the participant depends on the answer to the one that precedes it, allowing the researcher to follow up on any given issue or insight that emerges, verify his or her understanding of the participant's responses, and probe more deeply into the participant's thoughts and feelings.

clinical interview A research method in which questions are tailored to the individual, with each question depending on the answer to the preceding one.

The advantages of the clinical interview are particularly evident in the work of Jean Piaget, whose use of the procedure laid a foundation for an entirely new way of understanding the intellectual development of the child. Piaget's goal was to provide an account of how children's thinking becomes organized over time. In one of his early studies, he used the clinical method to focus on how children's understanding of internal mental processes, such as "thinking" and "dreaming," changes as they grow older. In the examples that follow, note how Piaget adapted his questions to the flow of the conversation:

5-YEAR-OLD

Piaget: When you are in bed and you dream, where is the dream?
Child: In my bed, under the blanket.
Piaget: Is the dream there when you sleep?
Child: Yes, it is in my bed beside me.
[Piaget writes: "We tried suggestion:"] Is the dream in your head?
[The child forcefully rejects the possibility:] It is I that am in the dream: it isn't in my head.

(From Piaget, 1929/1979, p. 97)

Understanding Causes and Correlations

When a window shatters after we have thrown a rock at it, we say that the rock caused the window to break. When a light comes on after we have flipped a switch on the wall, we say that the switch (or the electric current it activates) caused the light. **Causation** refers to a relationship in which one event (or factor) depends upon the occurrence of a prior event (or factor). In the physical and mechanical worlds of rocks and windows, switches and lights, causal relationships can be identified with relative ease and certainty. In the developmental and behavioral worlds of children, in contrast, identifying causal relationships presents real challenges.

To see the problem, suppose that children who get good grades (do well on a measure of school performance) also have high intelligence quotient (IQ) scores (do well on a measure of intelligence). It might be tempting to conclude that there is a causal relationship between children's intelligence and their school performance—that is, that high intelligence is the prior factor that causes the exceptional school performance. However, another possibility is the opposite causal relationship—that is, working hard to get good grades might cause children's intelligence to rise. Yet another possibility is that some third factor—say, parents providing an intellectually stimulating home environment and setting high expectations for academic performance—is causing both children's high intelligence and their school achievement.

As you can see, identifying the causes of behavior and development is not as straightforward as one might expect. Just because two factors occur together does not mean that one caused the other. Indeed, causation is often confused with **correlation**, a relationship in which differences in one factor (intelligence, for example) are associated with differences in another factor (school performance). Although experiments designed specifically to identify causal relationships are used to study children's development (see p. 34), the most frequent type of study by far is one that makes use of correlational methods.

Correlational methods involve measuring two or more factors and then analyzing whether variations in one factor are linked systematically to variations in another factor. If, for example, we are able to measure the quality of a child's relationship with his or her parents, as well as the quality of the child's relationship with peers, we would be able to analyze whether variations (from high to low) in the quality of parent and peer relationships correlate with each other—that is, whether having good (or bad) relationships with parents correlates with having good (or bad) relationships with peers. The degree of association between factors is represented as a **correlation coefficient** (symbolized as r), a number that ranges from -1.0 to $+1.0$ and expresses both the strength (strong or weak) and direction (positive or negative) of the relationship. When $r = 1.00$, there is a perfect positive correlation between the two factors; that is, when one factor changes, the other factor changes in the same direction. In our example, a perfect positive correlation would exist when children who have good relationships with their parents also always have good relationships with their peers, and children who have bad relationships with their parents also always have bad relationships with peers. When $r = -1.00$, in contrast, there is a perfect negative correlation between the two factors, meaning that as one factor changes in one direction, the other factor always changes in the opposite direction. Thus, a perfect negative correlation between parent and peer relationships would mean that when the parent relationship is good, the peer relationship is inevitably poor, and vice versa. When two factors are uncorrelated, $r = 0$. Correlations, like people, are rarely perfect, and most correlation coefficients fall somewhere between 0 and $+1.0$ or -1.0, with weak associations producing coefficients that are close to 0 and strong associations producing coefficients closer to $+1$ or to -1.

Although correlational methods do not identify causal relationships, they do permit predictions, and for this reason they are highly valuable. For instance, correlational methods have generated a wealth of information regarding relationships between infant development and maternal behavior during pregnancy (diet, stress, smoking, etc.). The ability to predict developmental outcomes accurately from knowledge of maternal behavior makes it possible to identify "at-risk" infants and thus to initiate appropriate interventions early on.

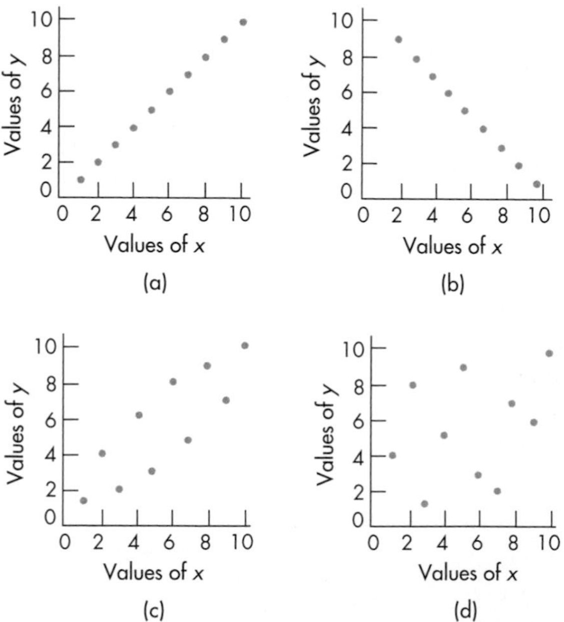

Four possible relationships between two variables: (a) As values of x increase, values of y increase, producing a correlation of 1.00. (b) As values of x increase, values of y decrease, producing a correlation of -1.00. (c) As values of x increase, values of y often increase, but there are some exceptions, producing a correlation of .84. (d) As values of x increase, values of y show a weak but noticeable tendency to increase, producing a correlation of .33.

causation When the occurrence of one event depends upon the occurrence of a prior event.

correlation The condition that exists between two factors when changes in one factor are associated with changes in the other.

correlation coefficient The degree of association between factors, symbolized as r and ranging between -1.0 and $+1.0$.

11-YEAR OLD
Piaget: What is a dream?
Child: It's a thought.
Piaget: What do you dream with?
Child: With the head.
Piaget: Are the eyes open or shut?
Child: Shut.
Piaget: Where is the dream whilst you are dreaming?
Child: In the head.
Piaget: Not in front of you?
Child: It's as if (!) you could see it.
(Adapted from Piaget, 1929/1979, pp. 39, 54)

Piaget's probing interviews of these and other children revealed two age-related patterns of understanding thinking and dreaming. For the younger child, dreams are objective, concrete things. You can see them happening—they are in the bed, under the blanket (no wonder they can be so scary!). In contrast, the older child conceives of thinking and dreaming as internal, mental processes that are invisible and unobservable; they happen "in the head." Piaget used such data to support his contention that children go through stagelike changes in the way they understand and experience the world. He believed that not until the age of 10 or 11 are children able to understand thinking as an internal mental process. Younger children, even when given explicit hints and leading suggestions, are not able to express such an understanding.

The strength of clinical interviews is that they allow the researcher to follow, probe, and challenge the child's way of thinking in order to discover developmental patterns. But the clinical interview method has its limitations, most notably its reliance on verbal expression, which makes it inappropriate for use with very young children. This is especially the case in trying to assess children's cognitive abilities, since young children often understand things well before they can explain or even express their understanding.

Research Designs

Before conducting research, developmentalists must not only select a method of data collection but also develop an overall plan. This plan, referred to as the **research design**, describes how the study is put together—who will be included in the study, how and when data will be gathered from them, and how the data will be analyzed. A wide range of designs is used in the social sciences, although developmentalists tend to favor those that are best suited to the complexities of studying age-related change over time.

research design The overall plan that describes how a study is put together; it is developed before conducting research.

Here we will describe the four most basic designs that developmentalists use—*longitudinal*, *cross-sectional*, *cohort sequential*, and *microgenetic*. (In later chapters you will be introduced to a few other designs.) As illustrated in Table 1.6 (p. 38) each design takes into account the passage of time in a different way, and accordingly, each has certain advantages and disadvantages.

The Longitudinal Design

The **longitudinal design** collects information about a group of people as they grow older. For example, in a study of the stability of shyness, Jerome Kagan (2001) led a research team at Harvard University that traced the behavior of a group of children from shortly after birth into early adolescence. This study provided evidence that children who are shy and uncertain at 21 months are likely to show similar traits in their behavior at 12 to 14 years of age. Without such longitudinal measurements, it would be impossible to discover whether there is continuity in behavior patterns and personality traits as children grow older. Other longitudinal studies have dealt with such varied topics as

longitudinal design A research design in which data are gathered about the same group of people as they grow older over an extended period of time.

TABLE 1.6 Research Designs

Design	Description	Advantages	Disadvantages
Longitudinal	Collects information about a group of people over time	Possible to discover patterns of continuity and change over time	Expense; long-term commitment may lead to selective dropout; risk of confounding age differences with cohort differences
Cross-sectional	Collects information about groups of various ages at one time	Relatively less time-consuming and expensive	Disconnected snapshots, requiring inferences about processes of change; if groups differ other than in age, risk of confounding age differences with those differences
Cohort sequential	Combines longitudinal and cross-sectional approaches by studying several cohorts over time	Age-related factors in change can be separated from cohort factors	To a lesser extent, disadvantages of the longitudinal and cross-sectional designs
Microgenetic	Focuses on development over short periods, especially when children are on the threshold of a change	Provides a record of change, revealing change processes	Limited to changes occurring over short periods of time

personality, mental health, temperament, intelligence, language development, and social adjustment (DuPaul et al., 2016; Laible, Carlo, Davis, & Karahuta, 2016; Spinath, Bleidorn, Briley, & Tucker-Drob, 2017).

Because it examines development over time, the longitudinal design would seem to be an ideal way to study development. Unfortunately, several drawbacks of the longitudinal design restrict its use. To begin with, carrying out longitudinal studies is expensive. These studies also require the researcher's long-term commitment to ventures that can be highly uncertain: Some parents, for example, decide that they do not want their children to continue in a lengthy study, or they may relocate, making it difficult for the researchers to stay in touch with the children for later assessments. Such difficulties may be more common with one social, economic, or ethnic group than with others, resulting in *selective dropout*, which creates a biased sample that can greatly reduce the validity of longitudinal work.

Longitudinal designs follow the same persons through the years as they age.

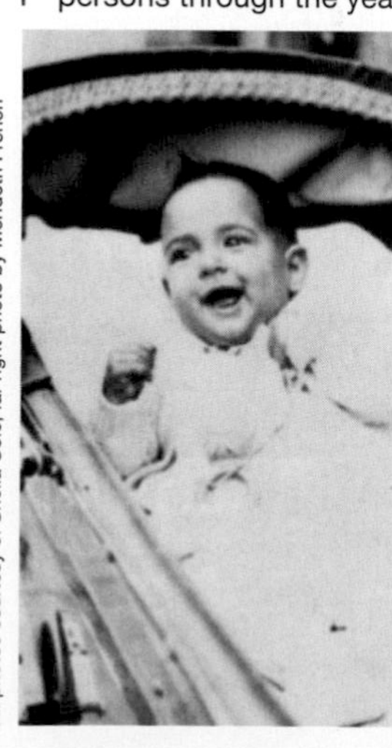

All photos courtesy of Sheila Cole; far right photo by Merideth French

Another weakness of longitudinal designs is that they are at risk of confusing differences related to age with differences related to cohort. A **cohort** is a group of persons who were born about the same time and who are therefore likely to share certain experiences that differ from those of people born earlier or later. In longitudinal research, these shared experiences may actually underlie differences that appear to be related to age. Suppose, for example, that a longitudinal study of the development of children's fears from birth onward began in London in 1932. In their early years, the children in this study would have been living through the economic hardships of the Great Depression. At the age of 9 or 10, many of these children would have lost one or both parents in World War II, and many others would have been sent away from their parents to the countryside in an effort to keep them safe from nightly air-raid bombings of the city. Suppose this study found that the children feared mainly hunger in their early years and later, at around age 9, began to fear losing their parents. In these circumstances, it would be impossible to determine whether these age trends reflected general laws of development, true at any time and in any place, or were the result of these particular children's experiences in this particular time and place, or both (Elder, 1998).

cohort A group of persons born about the same time who are therefore likely to share certain experiences.

The Cross-Sectional Design The most widely used method for studying development is the **cross-sectional design**, which collects information about people of various ages at one time. (Figure 1.6 highlights the basic differences between the cross-sectional and longitudinal designs.) To study the development of memory, for example, a researcher might test 4-year-olds, 10-year-olds, 20-year-olds, and 60-year-olds to see how well they remember a list of familiar words. By comparing how people in the four age groups go about the task and what the results of their efforts are, the researcher could then make inferences about developmental

cross-sectional design A research design in which individuals of various ages are studied at the same time.

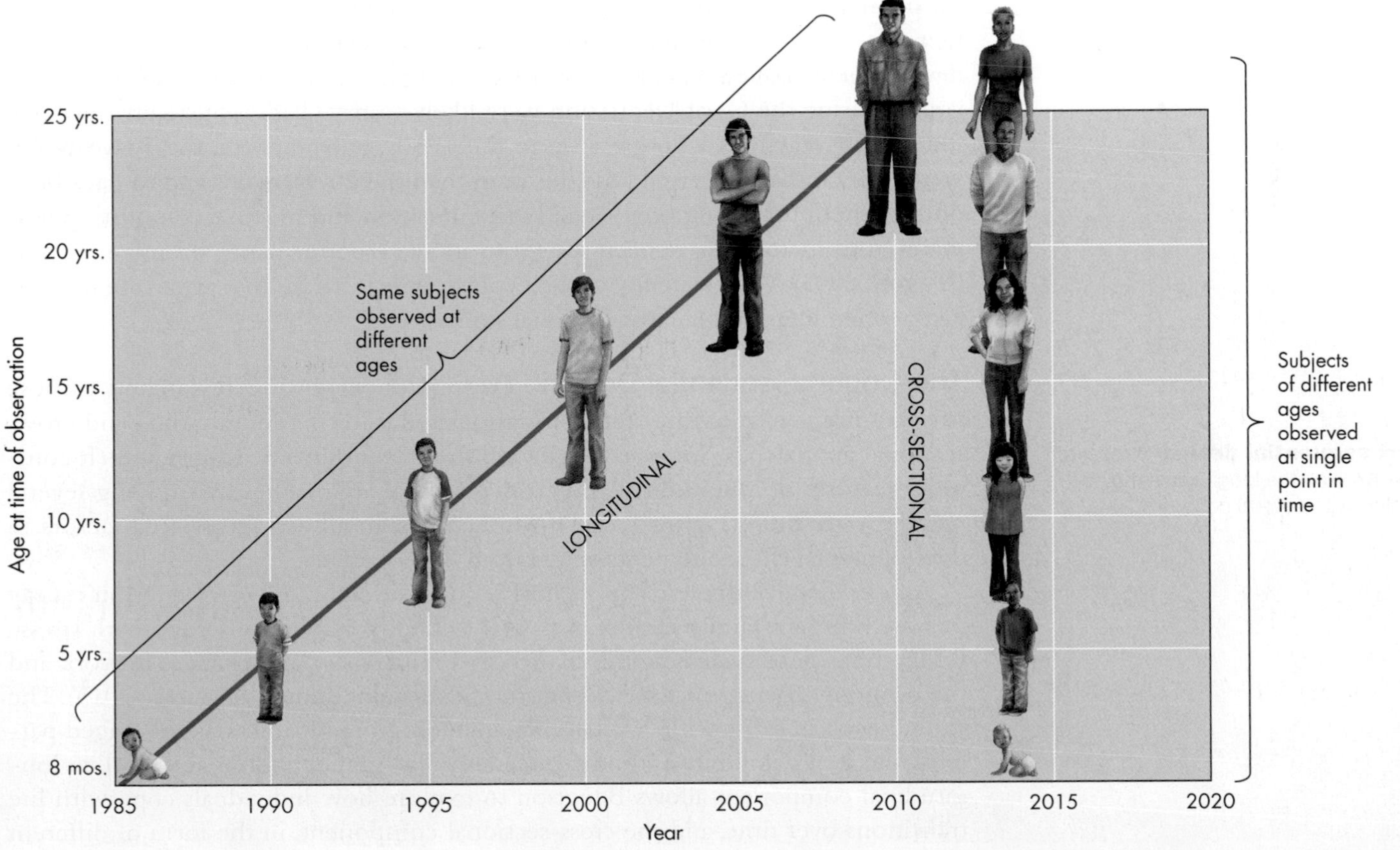

FIGURE 1.6 The difference between longitudinal and cross-sectional research designs.

changes in memory processes. In fact, researchers have carried out a great many cross-sectional studies of memory development demonstrating both quantitative and qualitative developmental changes that we will examine in later chapters.

Because it gathers data on several different ages at once, the cross-sectional design is less time-consuming and less expensive than the longitudinal design. The short time commitment required of the participants also makes it more likely that a representative sample will be recruited and that few participants will drop out of the study.

Despite these advantages, cross-sectional studies also have drawbacks. First, by looking at the behavior of different-age people at one time, cross-sectional studies slice up the ongoing process of development into a series of disconnected snapshots, and this is limiting. For example, although researchers can contrast the general ways in which 4- and 10-year-olds remember a list of words, they cannot gain direct insights into the developmental process by which memory abilities and strategies change over time because their study is not following the same children over time. Consequently, when theorists make inferences about development on the basis of cross-sectional designs, they must engage in a good deal of extrapolation and guesswork about processes of change.

A second drawback to the cross-sectional design is that, for studies to be properly conducted, all relevant factors other than age must be kept constant. That is, the makeup of all the age groups should be the same in terms of sex, ethnicity, amount of education, socioeconomic status, and so on. If the groups are not the same, findings may reflect these differences rather than age-related change.

In addition, as with longitudinal studies, cohort effects are possible in the cross-sectional design, with differences between the age groups reflecting the groups' different experiences rather than age-related changes. Suppose that, in a study of memory development conducted in 2000, 70-year-olds performed significantly more poorly than did 20-year-olds. These results might reflect a universal tendency for memory to decline with age, but they also might reflect differences in the participants' childhood nutrition. Early nutrition has been shown to affect intellectual development (Bailey, West, Keith, & Black, 2015), and the 70-year-olds who were young during the Great Depression were likely to have had poorer nutrition than did the 20-year-olds who grew up in the 1980s. Furthermore, the 70-year-olds were likely to have received less education than the 20-year-olds and to have been out of school for a long time—and both education and practice committing new material to memory have been shown to increase performance on memory tests (Rogoff, 2003). The possibility of such cohort effects means that great care must be taken when interpreting cross-sectional studies.

cohort sequential design A research design in which the longitudinal method is replicated with several cohorts.

The Cohort Sequential Design

Resources permitting, researchers can use various means to minimize problems associated with the longitudinal and cross-sectional approaches. Some have used a **cohort sequential design**, which combines features of longitudinal and cross-sectional approaches by studying several cohorts over time (Figure 1.7). This mixed design allows age-related factors in developmental change to be separated from cohort effects.

An excellent example of the cohort sequential design is Vern Bengtson's study of how different family members as well as family generations cope with stressful life transitions such as aging, divorce, and remarriage, and changes in work and the economy (Bengtson, 2005; Bengtson, Silverstein, Putney, & Harris, 2015). The study began in 1971 with 300 families, including grandparents, middle-aged parents, and grandchildren, and now includes great-grandchildren as well. The longitudinal component allows Bengtson to explore how individuals cope with life transitions over time, and the cross-sectional component, in the form of different

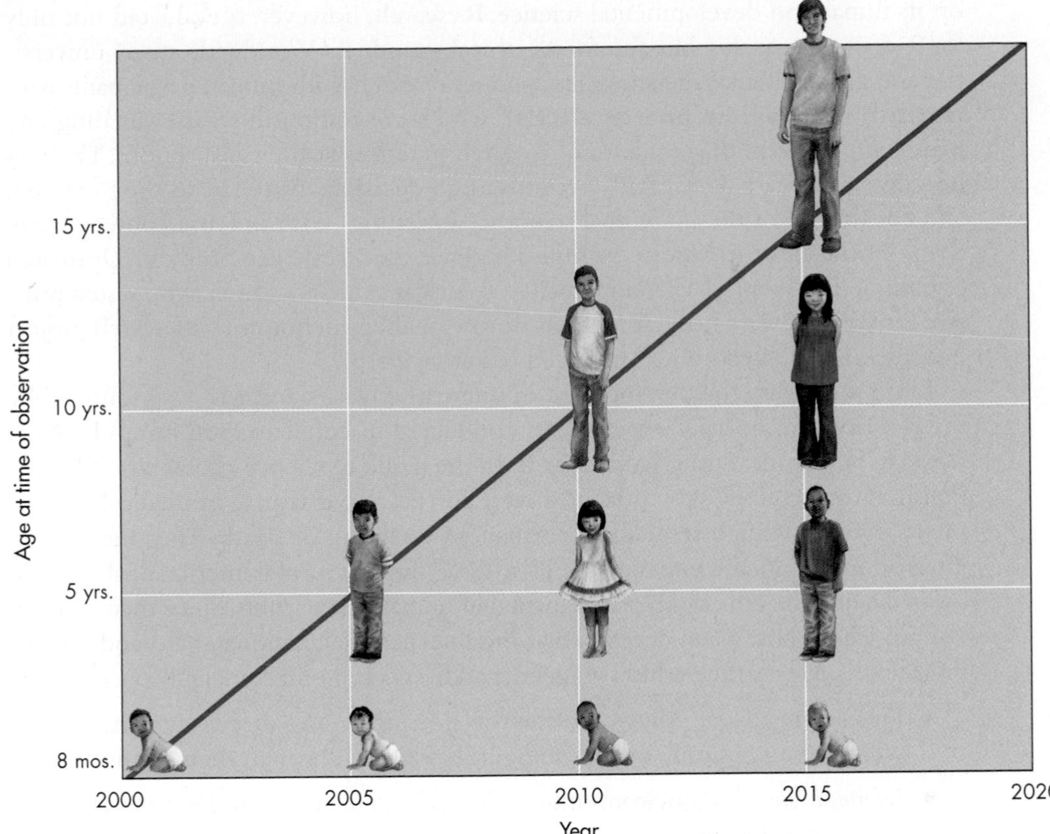

FIGURE 1.7 By combining features of longitudinal and cross-sectional approaches, the cohort sequential design allows researchers to distinguish between developmental effects and cohort effects.

generations, allows him to examine how these different cohorts adjust to the various transitions.

The Microgenetic Design To try to get closer to observing change processes, developmentalists sometimes use the **microgenetic design**, which focuses on children's development over relatively short periods of time, sometimes only a few hours or days (Flynn & Siegler, 2007; Lawrence & Valsiner, 2003; Vygotsky, 1978). As a rule, the microgenetic design is used to study children on the threshold of a significant developmental change, such as being able to use a new memory strategy or a new adding strategy (e.g., calculating 6 + 2 by counting up from 6 instead of starting at 1 and counting all the way to 8; Laski & Siegler, 2014). If researchers give the children concentrated experience in activities that are thought to facilitate the developmental change in question (such as playing games that involve simple addition), they are sometimes able to observe the change as it actually occurs, thereby learning what factors contributed to it.

microgenetic design A research method in which individuals' development is studied intensively over a relatively short period of time.

Robert Siegler (2005) offers a useful analogy for understanding the advantage of the microgenetic design. Whereas cross-sectional designs provide us with discontinuous snapshots of development, microgenetic designs provide us with a movie, a more or less continuous record of change. In later chapters, we will encounter specific examples of what can be learned about children's development through microgenetic designs.

Ethical Standards

You can see from our discussion above that, in conducting research, developmentalists make a number of important decisions regarding theory, method, and design. The decisions they make have a bearing on the quality and value of their work and

institutional review boards (IRBs) Groups responsible for evaluating and overseeing the ethical soundness of research practices at an institution.

on its impact on developmental science. Research, however, is evaluated not only for its scientific quality but also for its ethical soundness. Worldwide, many universities and governmental agencies that conduct research with human participants have **institutional review boards (IRBs)**, which are responsible for evaluating and overseeing the ethical soundness of research practices at their institutions. This was not always the case. Until fairly recently, such decisions were left to the judgment and conscience of the individual scientist, sometimes with horrific consequences. Some of the most infamous examples include the "Tuskegee Study of Untreated Syphilis in the Negro Male," in which 400 African American men, who tested positive for syphilis, were not told of their disease or their inclusion in a research project investigating its effects if left untreated (Capron, 2016).

In no small part, the development of uniform ethical standards was prompted by the revelation of horrific experiments conducted in concentration camps by Nazi German physicians during World War II. In the name of science, thousands of Jewish, Polish, Russian, and Gypsy prisoners were forced to participate in medical experiments, most of which resulted in permanent disability or death. After the war, an international council wrote the *Nuremberg Code*, the first formal international standard for evaluating the ethics of research involving human participants. Since then, numerous guidelines have been developed at the international, national, state, and institutional levels. Most of the ethical guidelines address certain fundamental concerns:

- *Freedom from harm.* Above all, scientists need to ensure that study participants will not be physically or psychologically harmed through their involvement.
- *Informed consent.* Participants must voluntarily agree to be in the study. This means that they must be given a reasonable understanding of what their participation entails, and it means their participation must not have been forced, coerced, or based on inappropriate incentives (e.g., the offer of money to low-income participants or higher grades to students). With children, "informed" consent becomes more difficult because young children cannot really understand what their participation entails. Usually, parental consent is required, as well as consent from other child advocates, such as school officials.
- *Confidentiality.* Personal information obtained in the course of research must be kept confidential—that is, confined to scientific uses and not made publicly available in a way that might embarrass or harm the participant. Often, investigators will assign code numbers to the participants to ensure the participants' anonymity. However, investigators sometimes uncover a serious problem that threatens the well-being of the participant, as when a child reports abuse or seems suicidal. Under such circumstances, the higher ethic of the participant's welfare requires that the researcher break confidentiality and inform authorities who are in a position to intervene and protect the child.

Freedom from harm, informed consent, and confidentiality are not accomplished easily. This is particularly true in the case of children. For example, what may be psychologically harmful for a 2-year-old is quite different from what might be harmful for a 12-year-old. In recognition of the unique issues involved in conducting research with child participants, a special set of ethical standards has been devised by the Society for Research in Child Development (see www.srcd.org). Institutional review boards in the United States use these guidelines to determine the ethical soundness of all research on children conducted at their universities or agencies.

APPLY > CONNECT > DISCUSS

Your little brother brought home the following letter from school. Evaluate the scientific and ethical merits of the study described. Propose an alternative study that will address the issues.

Dear Parent or Guardian:

In response to the mayor's proposal to re-route a major highway past our elementary school, we will conduct a study of the relationship between road noise and learning in our students. With the assistance of Dr. Heezrite of Baloney University, your child, *Jonathan*, has been randomly assigned to the following group:

- [x] During a lesson in mathematics, your child will be exposed to unexpected loud noises, similar to truck horn blasts, after which he/she will be given a test covering the content of the lesson.
- [ ] After a lesson in mathematics, your child will be given a test covering the content of the lesson.

Thank you for your cooperation in our effort to provide the best learning environment for our children.

Sincerely,

The Principal

Looking Ahead

LEARNING OUTCOMES

Recall the different periods of development and domains covered in the chapters of this book.

Explain the purpose of organizing this book around a biocultural approach.

In the chapters ahead, you will encounter many of the basic theories, methods, questions, and issues that we have outlined in this chapter. Across the five broad periods of child development—the prenatal period, infancy, early childhood, middle childhood, and adolescence—we will trace development in the physical, social, emotional, and cognitive domains. You will also come to understand how development throughout each period and within each domain is shaped by the child's interactions in a range of physical, family, neighborhood, and institutional contexts. To help organize the vast diversity of children's development, we will take a *biocultural approach*, emphasizing how biological and cultural processes intertwine over the course of childhood. Through it all, we will remain true to the two goals that have inspired developmentalists for centuries: the quest for knowledge and the desire to improve children's lives and well-being.

INSIGHT AND INTEGRATION

1. Return to the opening scenario about the Wild Boy of Aveyron. Explain the boy's development in terms of concepts presented in this chapter: *sources of development, plasticity, continuity and discontinuity*, and *individual differences*.
2. Developmentalists typically favor some theories of development over others. Of the theories described in this chapter, which one do you think provides the most interesting perspective on development? Why? Which one do you find least interesting? Why?
3. Review your answer to Warming Up question 3, regarding three major questions that you have about children's development. Can any of them be answered by research? If not, can you modify them into a form or hypothesis that allows for a scientific approach?

Summary

- One of the earliest efforts in the study of child development involved Jean-Marc Itard's work with the Wild Boy of Aveyron. This unusual case posed fundamental questions: To what extent is development determined from birth, and to what extent is it influenced by the environment? What is the role of early experience in shaping development, and can the effects of negative experiences be undone?

Developmental Science

- Developmental science is an interdisciplinary field of study that focuses on the changes that children undergo from conception onward. Its two goals are to understand the basic biological and cultural processes that account for the complexities of development and to devise ways of safeguarding children's health and well-being.
- Developmentalists divide the time between conception and adulthood into five periods: the prenatal period, infancy, early childhood, middle childhood, and adolescence.
- Developmentalists look at the changes children undergo in several closely interrelated domains—social, emotional, cognitive (intellectual), and physical.
- Children's development is profoundly shaped by the contexts in which they live, including physical environments, cultural beliefs and practices, families and peers, neighborhoods and communities, and institutions such as schools and governments.

Children, Society, and Science

- Developmental science emerged and developed within historical and cultural contexts, including that of changing beliefs about children. In medieval Europe, children evidently were considered miniature adults. In the sixteenth century, the Protestant Reformation led to the view of children as willful, sinful creatures whose disobedient acts called for harsh treatment. Nineteenth-century industrialization fundamentally altered family life, education, and work, and these changed conditions contributed to a protectionist view of children and to the rise of developmental science.
- Darwin's theory of evolution sparked scientific interest in children; by the early twentieth century, developmental science had become a recognized field.

The Central Issues of Developmental Science

- Developmentalists' research is focused on four fundamental issues:
  1. *Sources of development*. How do biological, physical, social, and cultural factors interact to produce development?
  2. *Plasticity*. To what degree, and under what conditions, is development open to change and intervention? Plasticity is greatest during sensitive periods.
  3. *Continuity/discontinuity*. To what extent does development consist of the gradual accumulation of small changes, and to what extent does it involve abrupt transformations, or stages?
  4. *Individual differences*. How do some developmental traits, affected by various environments, result in individual differences among people? To what extent are individual characteristics stable?

Theories of Development

- Theory plays an important role in developmental science by providing a broad conceptual framework to guide the collection and interpretation of facts.
- The grand theories laid the foundation for developmental science, and each covers various domains. The grand theories include:
  - Psychodynamic theories—Freud's theory, in which psychosexual stages are associated with the changing focus of the sex drive, and Erikson's theory, in which psychosocial stages are associated with tasks or crises shaped by social and cultural factors.
  - Behaviorist theories, which focus on development through learning, emphasize behavioral changes resulting from the individual's forming associations between behavior and its consequences.
  - Piaget's constructivist theory, in which children, by striving to master their environments and searching for fits between their existing schemas and new experiences, progress through universal stages of cognitive development.
  - Vygotsky's sociocultural theory, which focuses on the role of culture in development and on children learning through finely tuned interactions with others who are more competent.
- Influential modern theories of development include:
  - Evolutionary theories, which look at how human characteristics contribute to the survival of the species and at how our evolutionary past influences individual development.
  - Social learning theories, which, like behaviorist theories, focus on the learning of associations between behaviors and their consequences but emphasize learning that occurs through the observation of, and interaction with, others.
  - Information-processing theories, which, using computer analogies, look at how children process, store, organize, retrieve, and manipulate information in increasingly efficient ways.
- Systems theories—dynamic systems theory, which focuses on the development of new systems of behavior from the interaction of less complex parts, and ecological systems theory, which focuses on the organization of the environmental contexts within which children develop.

Methods for Studying Development

- Research—whether basic, applied, or action research—must be designed to meet the criteria of objectivity, reliability, replicability, and validity. Research must also be ethically sound.
- Depending on their topic and goal, researchers use one or more methods of data collection, each with advantages and disadvantages:
  - Naturalistic observation involves watching children in the course of their everyday lives and recording what happens.
  - Experiments consist of introducing some change into a group's experience and measuring the effects of the change on the group's members, who are compared with a similar group that did not undergo the experience.
  - Clinical interviews allow researchers to tailor data collection to each research participant.
- Researchers also use several designs, or overall plans, intended to capture the complexities of age-related change:
  - The longitudinal design studies the same children repeatedly over a period of time.
  - The cross-sectional design studies children of different ages at a single time.
  - The cohort sequential design combines the longitudinal and cross-sectional approaches by studying several cohorts over time.
  - The microgenetic design studies the same children over a short period, often one of rapid change.

Looking Ahead

- Taking a biocultural approach, which emphasizes how biological and cultural processes intertwine, the book will trace development in the physical, social, emotional, and cognitive domains across the periods of childhood.

Key Terms

developmental science, p. 3
preformationism, p. 8
plasticity, p. 13
sensitive period, p. 13
continuity/discontinuity, p. 13
developmental stage, p. 13
theory, p. 16
psychodynamic theories, p. 17
behaviorism, p. 19
law of effect, p. 19
constructivist theory, p. 20
equilibration, p. 22
sociocultural theory, p. 22
zone of proximal development (ZPD), p. 23
evolutionary theories, p. 24
ethology, p. 25
social learning theory, p. 25
information-processing theories, p. 26
systems theories, p. 27
dynamic systems theory, p. 27
ecological systems theory, p. 27
bioecological model, p. 27
hypothesis, p. 29
objectivity, p. 31
reliability, p. 31
replicability, p. 32
validity, p. 32
naturalistic observation, p. 32
ethnography, p. 34
experiment, p. 34
experimental group, p. 34
control group, p. 34
ecological validity, p. 35
clinical interview, p. 35
causation, p. 36
correlation, p. 36
correlation coefficient, p. 36
research design, p. 37
longitudinal design, p. 37
cohort, p. 39
cross-sectional design, p. 39
cohort sequential design, p. 40
microgenetic design, p. 41
institutional review boards (IRBs), p. 42

PART ONE

In the Beginning

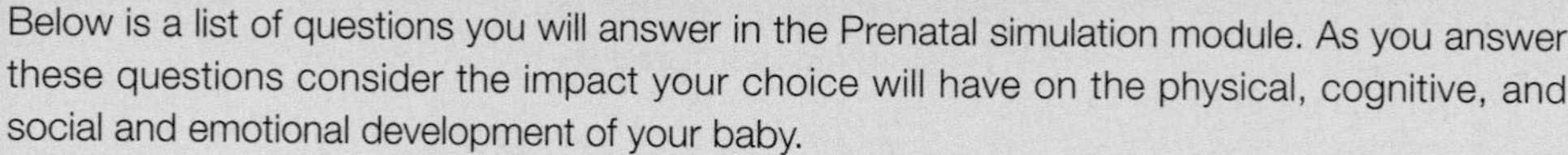

PRENATAL APPLICATION TO DEVELOPING LIVES PARENTING SIMULATION

Below is a list of questions you will answer in the Prenatal simulation module. As you answer these questions consider the impact your choice will have on the physical, cognitive, and social and emotional development of your baby.

	Physical	Cognitive	Social and Emotional
	• Will you modify your behaviors and diet during pregnancy? • Will you find out the gender of your baby prior to delivery? • What kind of delivery will you and your partner plan for (in the hospital with medication, at home with a doula etc.)?	• Are you going to talk to your baby while he or she is in the womb? • How much does your baby understand during prenatal development?	• How will you and your partner's relationship change as a result of the pregnancy? • Will you begin bonding with your baby prior to birth?

The table below lists some of the major developments you will learn about in the chapters of this book section.

MAJOR MILESTONES

	Physical Domain	Cognitive Domain	Social and Emotional Domains
What Develops . . .	• These milestones relate to the physical body: how it grows, moves, and functions. • Examples: Growth and development of the bones, muscles, and brain; nutrition and sleep requirements of the changing body; hormonal changes and maturation of the reproductive organs; emergence of motor skills such as grasping and walking.	• These milestones relate to intellectual functioning. • Examples: Changes in attention, memory, and problem solving; development of scientific reasoning, reasoning about moral issues, and language.	• These milestones relate to the child's social and emotional life. • Examples: Changing relationships with parents and peers; emotions and their expression; changes in how the child understands and feels about himself or herself as a person and as a member of a social group.
Sociocultural Contributions and Consequences . . .	• Here we highlight aspects of the child's social or cultural context that either contribute to specific developments in the physical domain or are significantly affected by those developments. • Examples: How cultural institutions and practices, including school, impact cognitive development; how cultural values support forms of moral reasoning.	• Here we highlight aspects of the child's social or cultural context that either contribute to specific developments in the cognitive domain or are significantly affected by those developments. • Examples: How cultural institutions and practices, including school, impact cognitive development; how cultural values support forms of moral reasoning.	• Here we highlight aspects of the child's social or cultural context that either contribute to or are significantly affected by developments within the social and emotional domains. • Examples: Cultural values and stereotypes for how boys and girls should behave; conditions believed to be appropriate or not appropriate to express particular emotions; cultural support for developing an ethnic or sexual minority identity.

The development of every human being starts with the formation of a single cell at the time of conception, a cell that carries genetic information stretching across millennia. At the same time, every individual is part of a vast stream of human social life that reaches back through thousands of generations. As a result, every human being is a product of the evolutionary past of our species—a past that includes both biological and cultural aspects.

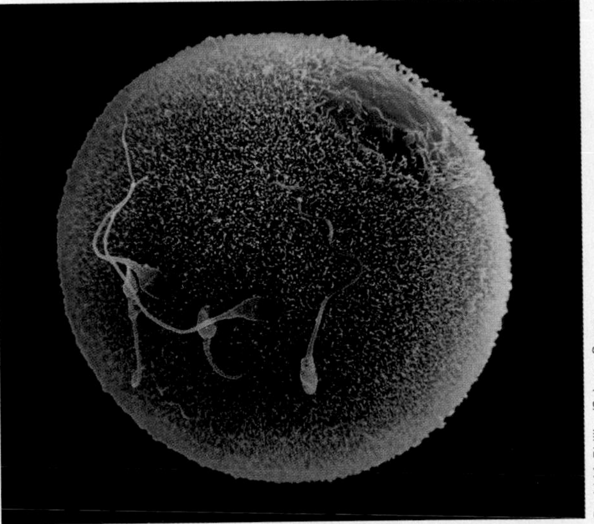
David M. Phillips/Science Source

Science views life as a process involving the constant interplay of forces that create order and pattern on the one hand and forces that create diversity and variation on the other. The interaction of these competing forces is the engine of developmental change for the species.

What forces create order and diversity in human development? In Chapter 2, you will see that part of the answer to this question can be found in our biological and cultural heritages. Order arises, on the biological side, from the fact that all human beings share a finite pool of genetic possibilities, and, on the cultural side, from the fact that we all share general ways of learning, communicating, and forming social relationships. Diversity is ever present in the fact that each human being is genetically unique (except in the case of identical twins) and in the fact that each human develops through a unique sequence of experiences associated with the specific features of the individual's family life, peer relationships, local environments, such as neighborhoods, and cultural values and traditions.

Whereas Chapter 2 focuses on the basic mechanisms of genetic and cultural transmission that enable both order and diversity in the ongoing evolution of our species, Chapter 3 narrows the focus to individual development from conception to birth. The process of prenatal development illustrates many of the basic questions about development discussed in Chapter 1. For example, gene–environment interaction in prenatal development relates to questions about sources of development; changes that distinguish the developing organism 5 months following conception from the organism at 5 weeks or 5 days following conception relate to questions about developmental continuity and discontinuity; sensitive periods of development, in which the organism is highly sensitive to hormonal secretions and to such external agents as drugs and toxins, relate to questions about plasticity.

After 9 months, during which the organism has grown and been nurtured within the mother's body, chemical changes initiate birth—and a radical transformation of the context of development. From the warm, dark womb, the baby crosses into a much richer and more varied environment, filled with new and constantly changing sights, sounds, and smells, and requiring new ways of moving, sensing, and behaving. Thus the cultural and biological forces that have shaped our species begin to orchestrate the development of a single individual, assuring that the newly born infant, while becoming like all other members of the species, will also be unique.

Martin Puddy/Getty Images

CHAPTER

2

Biocultural Foundations

The volcano to the east was active. Its fires dominated the night sky and held the African savannah woodland in an eerie twilight. By day, the sun barely penetrated the thick fog of smoke and ash, and the details of the landscape were muted by inches of ash that had settled on everything. Then a light rain fell, turning the ash underfoot into firm, moist clay. Across this surface moved several figures—short, sturdy gray ghosts, their fur caked with ash, surveying the world through dark eyes set deeply under thick, protruding brows. The footprints the passersby left behind hardened and were preserved and obscured by the falling ash of the volcano's continuing eruptions. They remained hidden for 3.5 million years, until they were uncovered by natural erosion and then discovered by a paleontologist named Andrew Hill (Leakey & Hay, 1979).

The discovery of these footprints at the Laetoli site in Tanzania is one of archeology's most fascinating finds (Figure 2.1, p. 50). As any criminologist will tell you, footprints can provide crucial information about the people who left them. Here is what we know about those who left the famous Laetoli prints. Two individuals walked side by side at an unhurried pace. One was about 4 feet tall (1.2 meters) and weighed about 62 pounds (28 kilograms); the other was about 4 feet 8 inches (1.4 meters) and weighed approximately 100 pounds (45 kilograms). Perhaps they were adults, or perhaps an adult and a child. The smaller of the two apparently was burdened on one side by a small load (an infant?). At one point, the larger individual turned east, toward the volcano, and then continued on with his or her companion. According to some analysts, there are traces of what may have been a child walking in the prints of the larger two. The most striking feature of the footprints is their resemblance to those of humans: They reveal a forward-pointing great toe, a well-rounded heel, a pronounced arch, and a striding bipedal gait. In short, the makers of these footprints walked upright, much as we do.

Although it is impossible to determine exactly *who* the walkers were, there is little controversy about *what* they were—members of the small-brained, apelike hominid species *Australopithecus afarensis*, the same species that produced Lucy, the celebrity skeleton discovered in Ethiopia that has helped scientists piece together our human evolutionary past. *A. afarensis* lived from about 4 million years ago until about 3 million years ago and may be one of the most ancient ancestors of our species. Recently, a team of Ethiopian scientists undertook a painstaking process of unearthing another remarkable find—a nearly complete fossil of an *A. afarensis* infant that confirms what scientists have inferred from the Laetoli footprints and from bone fragments: *A. afarensis* had lower limbs much like ours and were capable of walking upright. Their upper body and upper limbs, however, had many apelike characteristics, including broad shoulders and long curving fingers that would have made them effective tree climbers.

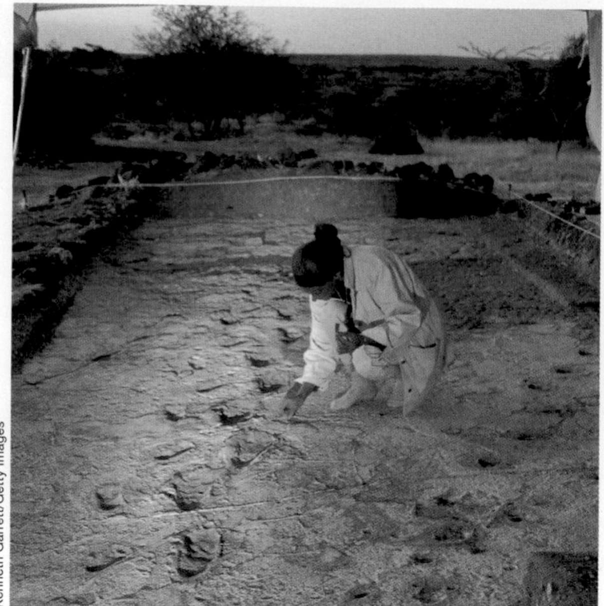

Kenneth Garrett/Getty Images

FIGURE 2.1 Scientists piece together the biocultural history of our species by examining footprints, skeletal fragments, and tools that have endured for millions of years. The famous Laetoli footprints of Tanzania provide evidence that the uniquely human trait of upright walking emerged 3 to 4 million years ago.

Thinking about the baby fossil and the individuals who left their footprints in volcanic ash 3.5 million years ago raises a host of questions that extend well beyond an interest in their physical bodies. Were these ancestors of humans generally peaceful or aggressive, solitary or sociable? If sociable, did they live in extended or nuclear family groups? How did they communicate with each other? How did they care for their young? How did they acquire and prepare their food? What risks did they face, and how did they protect themselves? How did they think? What emotions did they feel? And how, from these early beginnings, did biological and cultural processes lead to modern humans and to the developmental path we take from childhood to adulthood?

This chapter will focus on the biocultural foundations of children's development—foundations that were laid in distant times and have left little but bone fragments, cave paintings, primitive tools, and an occasional footprint from which we try to piece together the cultural and biological history of our species and how it is contained within each one of us. As you will discover, understanding these foundations can tell us a great deal about how and why all children tend to follow similar paths of physical, intellectual, social, and emotional development. Indeed, the fact that they do so is something of a miracle when you consider the wildly different and fluctuating environments in which children grow up. Pierre lives in Paris, France; Apatite lives in a Pygmy hunter-gatherer group in the Ituri forest of South Africa. These two children move through their worlds in similar bodies, use language and tools, solve complex problems, and develop social relationships and strong, lasting emotional attachments. Notwithstanding these commonalities, Apatite and Pierre also are different from each other in notable ways—from their height and skin color to the languages they speak, the specific skills they learn, the cultural values and beliefs they adopt, and the types of knowledge about the world they acquire. As you will learn in this chapter, in addition to giving us insight into those aspects of development that all children share, an understanding of the biocultural foundations of children's development sheds light on the sources and significance of developmental diversity.

We begin this chapter by defining and discussing human culture and how it is inherited by each child. We then address the child's genetic heritage and its expression in the particular traits and behaviors the child develops over time. Throughout our discussion, you will see how culture and biology interact in the life of the child, contributing both to the universal pathways of development shared by all children and to the diverse developmental patterns that unfold in relation to the particular circumstances and life experiences of each individual child.

The illustration of a female *Australopithecus afarensis* carrying an infant is consistent with archeological evidence provided by the Laetoli footprints and skeletal remains of this ancient hominid species.

Pascal Deloche/Getty Images

Randy Olson/Getty Images

These two photographs record dramatically different cultural rituals in vastly different parts of the world: Holy Communion in France and a Mbuti pygmy initiation ceremony in the Congo's Ituri forest. The biocultural foundations of children's development include aspects of diversity as well as features that are universal to all members of our species.

WARMING UP

1. Think about a particular family member that you grew up with—a parent or sibling, for example. What are some of the physical, social, and psychological characteristics that you share with that person? What accounts for these similarities?
2. The human species has a remarkable capacity to intentionally alter and manipulate its environments. What contributes to this capacity?
3. Reflecting on your own childhood, how did your parents or the adults who raised you alter or manipulate the environment to promote your health and well-being?

Inheriting Culture

LEARNING OUTCOMES

Distinguish between material tools and symbolic tools in cultures.

Explain the social processes by which children inherit cultural tools.

Point out examples of material and symbolic tools in the process of cumulative cultural evolution.

Years ago, a team of researchers traveled to a small island in Japan to study macaque monkeys. Their work was difficult because the monkeys spent much time in the forest, where they were hard to observe. In order to lure the macaques into open space, the researchers scattered sweet potatoes on the beach. The bribe worked well, but more remarkably, this seemingly innocent ploy initiated a cascade of new behaviors that entirely changed the monkeys' patterns of daily life. First, a young female named Imo began to wash her potatoes in a nearby stream (apparently, she objected to the dirt that clung to them). Before long, other individuals in the group picked up on her potato-washing behavior. As more time passed, the monkeys began washing the potatoes in the sea rather than carrying them to the stream, and they would even bite the potatoes first, presumably so the salt would penetrate and season them better (Figure 2.2).

There were other effects as well, and this is where the story gets really interesting. Mothers would carry their babies with them when they went to the sea to collect and wash the food. The babies began to play in the water—swimming, jumping, and diving. The males tended to hang out at the beach but did not participate much in the food preparation activities. They did, however, begin to eat fish discarded by the local fishermen and later began to collect fish and octopi from pools. Thus, the simple act of washing dirt from a sweet potato led to an entirely new pattern of life—a pattern that persists to this day. And while baby macaques from this small Japanese island learn how to wash their food and play in water, human observers of their activities are learning much about the meaning of culture and how it influences development.

Miles Barton/Nature Picture Library

FIGURE 2.2 This Japanese macaque is washing sand from a sweet potato, a practice that has become part of the culture of everyday life for macaques on Koshima Island.

In simple fashion, the story of the macaques highlights the fact that culture is rooted in everyday activities such as acquiring and preparing food, caring for children, and children's play. It also shows that these activities are interconnected and organized over time, forming complex networks: Once the macaques were drawn out of the forest where they had previously spent most of their time, a whole range of activities gradually emerged related to the beach and the water. But while many developmentalists are willing to grant that nonhuman primate species, including macaques, have evolved some of the rudiments of culture, it is clear that the human species is highly distinctive in how it has developed culture and the means by which it passes culture on to subsequent generations. Although there is a lot of debate about how to best define **culture**, most developmentalists agree that it consists of *material and symbolic tools that accumulate through time, are passed on through social processes, and provide resources for the developing child* (Cole, 2005; Rogoff, Najafi, & Mejía-Arauz, 2014; Valsiner, 2015). In the following sections, we will explain the meaning of this complex definition.

culture Material and symbolic tools that accumulate through time, are passed on through social processes, and provide resources for the developing child.

The Tools of Culture

Several nonhuman primate species are known to use tools of various sorts to reach food, for grooming, or to wield as weapons, and it has even been reported that some have *made* tools (Roffman et al., 2015). However, no other species even remotely compares to humans in the complexity of their tools and the extensiveness of their tool use. We are indeed a remarkable species in the extent to which tools and technology organize our behavior and modify our relationship to the environment. The briefest reflection should enable you to realize how tools and machines permeate your life. In fact, there is probably not a moment in the day when you are not using or being affected by them.

material tools Cultural tools, including physical objects and observable patterns of behavior such as family routines and social practices.

Developmentalists recognize that all cultural tools include two principal features: the *material* and the *symbolic* (Cole, 2005) (Table 2.1). Although all tools contain both features, developmentalists may refer to **material tools** when the focus is on *physical objects* (everything from abacuses and Androids to zithers and Zipcars) or on *observable patterns of behavior*, such as family routines (how children are "put to bed," how the family organizes dinnertime) and social practices (how children are educated, how they celebrate their birthdays). The environment of each and every child is saturated with material tools, which vary from one culture to the next. Born in the countryside of Japan, Kojima lives in a small house with paper walls (shoji screens) separating the rooms. As an infant, he is tightly wrapped in swaddling clothes and sleeps on a mat with his parents; he will never be placed in a crib. During mealtimes, he will not be put in a high chair or use a "sippy cup" but will sit in his mother's or older sister's lap and be helped to use "adult" eating utensils. His mother will never use an electronic baby monitor to keep tabs on him during his naptime but will carry him on her back most of the day while she works in the house and the garden. Clearly, the material tools of Kojima's culture influence his behavior and how he interacts with others (Enfield & Levinson, 2006; Jenkins, 1998).

symbolic tools Cultural tools, such as abstract knowledge, beliefs, and values.

In contrast to focusing on the concrete, material aspects of tools, developmentalists may refer to **symbolic tools** when they want to explore how abstract knowledge, beliefs, and values affect development. For example, Kojima will spend much of his time in school learning mathematics, a symbol system that he ultimately will use in a variety of ways—from measuring the wood for a new tool shed to eventually

TABLE 2.1 Examples of Cultural Tools

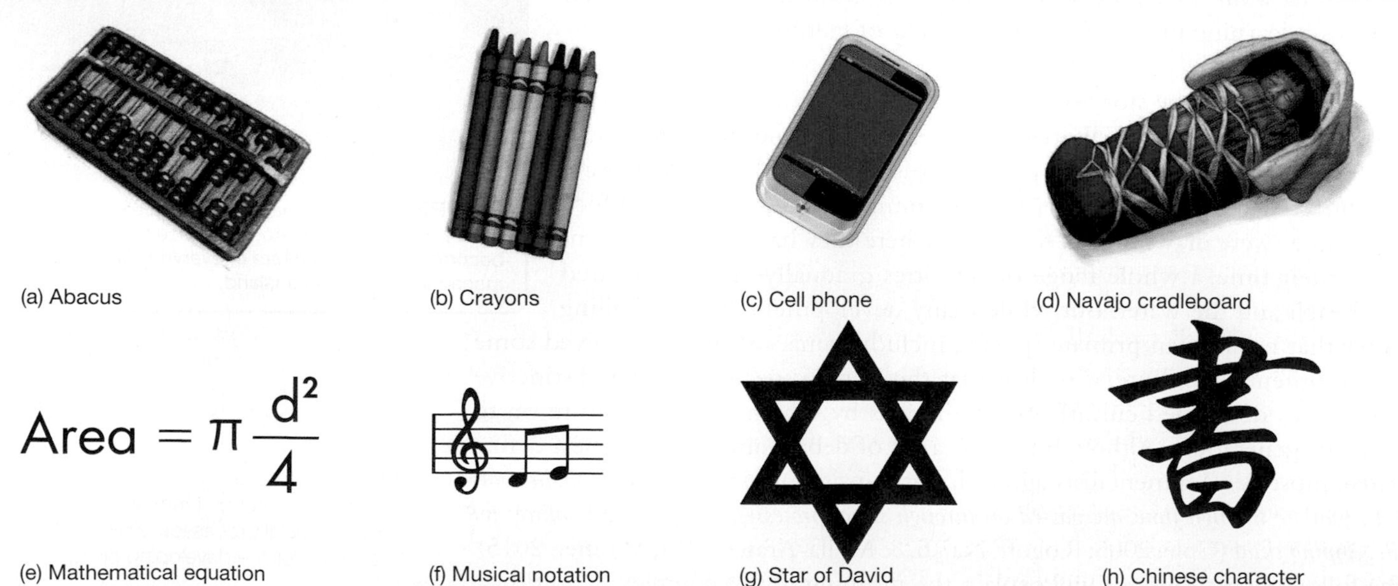

(a) Abacus (b) Crayons (c) Cell phone (d) Navajo cradleboard

(e) Mathematical equation (f) Musical notation (g) Star of David (h) Chinese character keeping the books for his family's business. Kojima will also learn his culture's expectations for masculinity and sexuality, including how certain ways of acting and speaking symbolize that he is "male." Raised within the Shinto spiritual tradition, he will come to believe that nature is sacred, that family should be honored, and that physical cleanliness is essential to the purity of spirit. All of these symbolic tools of Kojima's culture—mathematics, gender expectations, religious belief systems—will affect his intellectual, social, and emotional development. As should now be clear, all tools of culture are material and symbolic at the same time. For example, when Kojima accompanies his family to bathe in the river several times a week, he is both engaging in an observable pattern of behavior (an aspect of material culture) and expressing his belief that, as he cleanses his body, he is purifying his spirit (an aspect of symbolic culture).

Brown/EPA/REX/Shutterstock

This father and son are participating in a Shinto festival. One of the rituals involved in the day-long festival requires fathers to carry their 1- to 3-year-old sons over a steep and difficult mountain pass. It is said that as they participate in the rituals, the boys will become messengers of the local mountain deity.

The material and symbolic tools of a culture have pronounced effects on development because they *organize children's activities and the way they relate to their environments*. Developmentalists call the organization of activity through the use of tools **mediation**. The idea that material and symbolic tools mediate children's behavior and affect their development is at the heart of debates that range from whether violent video games promote aggressive behavior and Barbie dolls promote poor body image to whether the increase in students' disruptive classroom behavior is a symptom of a culture's collapsing educational values.

mediation The process through which tools organize people's activities and ways of relating to their environments.

Processes of Cultural Inheritance

When developmentalists say that material and symbolic tools accumulate over time and are passed on through social processes, thus providing resources for the developing child, they are making claims about how culture is transmitted and transformed from one generation to the next (Rogoff et al., 2007).

Social Processes of Cultural Inheritance

Children inherit culture—that is, they learn to use their culture's material and symbolic resources—through several *social processes*. The most basic of these processes is **social enhancement**, in which children use cultural resources simply because the activities of others have "enhanced" the immediate environment by making these resources available (Boyd, Richerson, & Henrich, 2011; Franz & Matthews, 2010). For example, when 18-month-old Tahira, who has never seen a crayon before, finds one on the family room floor and rubs it on the wall, she is learning through social enhancement that crayons are tools for marking surfaces. The other two processes through which children inherit culture are more complex forms of learning. When children learn by observing and copying the behaviors of others, they are using the social process of **imitation**, which we will describe in more detail in later chapters. When children are purposefully taught to use the material and symbolic resources of their culture, they are learning by **explicit instruction**.

social enhancement The most basic social process of learning to use cultural resources, in which resources are used simply because others' activities have made them available in the immediate environment.

imitation The social process through which children learn to use their culture's resources by observing and copying the behaviors of others.

explicit instruction The social process in which children are purposefully taught to use the resources of their culture.

Explicit instruction is the most complex way of inheriting culture, for two related reasons. First, unlike social enhancement and imitation, explicit instruction uses *symbolic communication*. The most obvious examples of symbolic communication are written and spoken language, but it also includes drawing, art, and music. Second, because it uses symbolic communication, explicit instruction makes it possible to teach children about things that are not present in their immediate environments. We use history books to teach children about the past; we use stories to teach them moral lessons to apply in the future; we use math to teach children calculations that they later can use to figure out everything from how to find the area of geometric shapes to the amount of data remaining in their smart phone accounts. Without the ability to use explicit instruction, our human culture might not be a great deal different than that of Imo and her clan.

The Special Role of Symbols and Language In addition to making it possible to teach children about things that are not immediately present in the environment, symbolic communication permits the expression of abstract ideas, desires, ambitions, and emotions. With astronomical diagrams, for example, we can chart the locations and movement of planets; through music, art, and poetry, we can express an infinite range of thoughts and feelings, both real and imagined; and through our stories and myths, we can learn and convey cultural values and beliefs and an understanding of our relationships to one another and the worlds in which we live. Clearly, symbols and symbolic systems are of tremendous importance to the culture-acquiring child. Symbols in the form of diagrams and stories, no less than video games and pencils, are cultural tools. Like all other cultural tools, they mediate children's activities and relationships in ways that are central to the process of development (Sterelny, 2016; Wells, 2007).

Studies of young children's self-control provide striking examples of how symbols mediate children's activities (Carlson, Davis, & Leach, 2005; White & Carlson, 2016). Three-year-olds are famous for acting on impulse rather than thinking things through. Consider the following example: Maria, a typical 3-year-old, is presented with two trays of candy, one of which plainly has more pieces of candy than the other. She is told to pick one tray, with the caution that the tray she chooses will be given away and that it is the other tray that she can keep for herself. According to a fascinating study conducted by Stephanie Carlson and her colleagues (2005), Maria is very likely to impulsively choose the tray with more candy—and she will continue to do so again and again, even though she sees that her choices leave her with fewer candies. However, Carlson's research suggests that Maria's behavior can be mediated by the use of symbols. In her experiment, the candies were presented in closed boxes instead of on trays (Figure 2.3), with a picture of a mouse placed on top of the box with fewer candies and a picture of an elephant placed on the box with more candies. After being told what the mouse and elephant symbolized (fewer and more candies, respectively), 3-year-olds had little trouble choosing

(a)

(b)

FIGURE 2.3 (a) When asked to choose a tray of candy that will be given away, 3-year-olds impulsively choose the tray with more candies. (b) However, when the task is modified so the candies are hidden in boxes, one box with a mouse indicating fewer candies, the other with an elephant indicating many candies, children will choose the box with fewer candies, suggesting that their behavior can be symbolically mediated.

the box with fewer candies. The symbols helped them control their impulses and organize their behavior to get what they wanted.

Carlson's research illustrates how symbols mediate young children's behavior in the carefully controlled environment of an experiment. In the real world, symbols and symbolic systems are a pervasive and complex part of children's lives and development.

The Complexity of Culture

There is often a tendency to think about culture as a thing of the past that is simply handed from one generation to the next. As we discussed above, it is certainly the case that culture is transmitted through specific social processes and shapes the development of individuals. However, it is also the case that individuals modify their cultures as they become users of cultural tools in the course of ongoing interactions with the people in their communities. In the words of Barbara Rogoff:

> . . . people of each generation, as they engage in sociocultural endeavors with other people, make use of and extend cultural tools and practices inherited from previous generations. As people develop through their shared use of cultural tools and practices, they simultaneously contribute to the transformation of cultural tools, practices, and institutions. (Rogoff, 2003, p. 52)

In short, cultures continue to evolve because individuals produce *variations* in the material and symbolic cultural tools they use. This dynamic process of cultural change through variation is known as **cumulative cultural evolution** (Mesoudi, 2016; Tomasello & Herrmann, 2010).

cumulative cultural evolution The dynamic ongoing process of cultural change that is a consequence of variation that individuals have produced in the cultural tools they use.

Developing technologies provide straightforward examples of how cultural resources—in this case, material resources—are modified and accumulate over time. For example, 150 years ago, personal communication was limited to either talking face-to-face or writing and reading letters. The harnessing of electricity in the nineteenth century led to the telegraph and the telephone, and then to the age of computers, smart phones, and video conferencing.

In the same way that variations in the material resources of a culture accumulate over time, so too do variations in its symbolic resources—its systems of knowledge, beliefs, and values. In many cultures, social beliefs and values about women, marriage, and family have undergone significant changes over time, as has the scientific understanding of everything from the movement of planets and the nature of light to how the brain works and affects behavior.

The nature of cumulative cultural evolution is an intriguing puzzle for developmentalists. If cultural evolution is all about accumulating new ideas, skills, technologies, and so on, where do these new things come from? According to anthropologists who study both ancient and modern cultures, a key ingredient is the shared knowledge that humans construct in groups (Caldwell, Atkinson, & Renner, 2016; Kline & Boyd, 2010). In particular, when groups are relatively large, complex, and connected to other groups, new ideas and technologies are more easily sparked, and culture is likely to thrive. On the other hand, when groups are small and isolated, variation is more limited, and culture is likely to stagnate or deteriorate. Michelle Kline and Robert Boyd found evidence supporting this argument when they studied several traditional societies from the islands in Oceania. All of these societies use a variety of tools to gather food from the ocean. Kline and Boyd analyzed the number and complexity of the tools and found that larger societies had a greater variety of tools compared with the smaller societies.

Significantly, other research has indicated that aspects of culture can be lost when societies become isolated from other groups. Such was the case for Tasmanian societies (Henrich, 2004; Henrich & Henrich, 2006) that once inhabited a region on the southern coast of Australia. According to archeologists, at least 18,000 years ago, Tasmanians interacted with other Australian Aborigine groups and crafted tools from bones and made special clothing to protect them from the winter cold. Then, 10,000 to 12,000 years ago, glaciers caused the sea level to rise, cutting off Tasmania from the rest of Australia. Across the next several thousand years, the Tasmanian cultural toolkit eroded and became less complex: Coarse stone tools replaced finely made bone tools, impeding the Tasmanians' ability to hunt, fish, and make cold-weather clothing. Joseph Henrich, who conducted the study, argued that the erosion of Tasmanian culture was a direct result of the dramatic reduction in the "pool of social learners" that would have otherwise transformed and transmitted the cultural toolkit to the next generation.

From the rather simple cases of Tasmanian societies and the Oceania islanders, you can imagine the vast possibilities for creative innovation available in large, technologically advanced societies in which the flow of ideas and opportunities for learning new skills are facilitated by modern communications and the ease of travel. Through variations, culture is, in the words of Patricia Greenfield, "constantly reinventing itself through the addition of new ethnic groups to multicultural societies, through changes in educational practices, through widening effects of the mass media, and through transformations in economy and technology" (Greenfield, Suzuki, & Rothstein-Fisch, 2006, p. 655). As you will see below, variation, inherent in culture and essential to cumulative cultural evolution, is also inherent in the child's biological inheritance and is an essential ingredient of biological evolution.

APPLY > CONNECT > DISCUSS

As usual, 3-year-old Star is the first in her family to awaken on this Saturday morning. She grabs her teddy bear, kicks off her Barbie-print covers, climbs out of bed, and pads down the hallway to the kitchen. She puts Teddy on a chair, instructing, "You wait right here, honey, and be quiet." Next, she moves a stepstool to the food cupboard, climbs up, and retrieves a box of cereal. She takes the cereal and the bear to the family room, where she settles on the sofa and hits the TV remote. *Sesame Street* fills the screen. Star watches intently, crunching cereal, snuggled up with her bear.

What are some of the material and symbolic tools described in this scene? How do they organize—that is, mediate—Star's behavior? What cultural beliefs, values, and practices might she be learning by using these cultural tools? How might her environment be organized differently to reflect a different set of cultural values and beliefs?

Biological Inheritance

LEARNING OUTCOMES

- Explain the relationship between genes and traits.
- Point out examples in the evolutionary process of natural selection.
- Summarize the process of genetic inheritance, including mutations and genetic abnormalities in sexual reproduction.
- Distinguish how kinship studies, family studies, twin studies, adoption studies, and studies about niche construction address issues related to heritability.

In the preceding sections, we made the point that cultural activities are interconnected and organized over time, forming complex networks. The tradition of washing potatoes in the ocean, for instance, emerged as a thread in a complex web of related cultural changes that involved such things as infant play (swimming) and foraging for food (scavenging from fishers, collecting octopi from pools). Like cultural evolution, biological evolution produces amazing networks in which things often, although not always, go together. As an example, think back to the story of our upright-walking *A. afarensis* ancestors. Walking upright was associated with a pelvic structure and a birth canal that were narrower than those of the knuckle-walking primates that preceded them. Over the several million years following the emergence of upright walking, however, the brain size of hominid species tripled and the skull enlarged considerably (Saveliev, 2010; Wittman & Wall, 2007). Consistent with this interlocking network of changes in locomotion, pelvic structure, birth canal, brain size, and skull size was a change in the length of pregnancy such that infants were born earlier, in a less developed state.

In order to appreciate how this worked, and its implications for modern children's development and behavior, you need to understand two fundamental issues. The first issue concerns how an individual's genetic endowment is actually expressed in all the physical and psychological traits that he or she displays. The second fundamental issue concerns the way that an individual's genetic endowment and corresponding traits enter into the process of evolution. We will address each of these issues in the following sections.

Genes and Traits

Evolution is made possible by **heredity**, the transmission of biological characteristics from one generation to the next. **Genes**—the basic units of heredity—contain instructions that guide the formation of all the individual's traits—both physical traits (sex, skin and eye color, susceptibility to certain diseases, and so on) and behavioral and psychological traits, including how the individual attends to and responds to the environment, communicates with others, and expresses needs and desires.

heredity The biological transmission of characteristics from one generation to the next.

genes The segments on a DNA molecule that act as hereditary blueprints for the organism's development.

The fundamental question for developmentalists is how these instructions become expressed. In addressing this question, developmentalists begin by distinguishing between the individual's *genotype* and his or her *phenotype*. An individual's **genotype** is the exact genetic makeup—the particular set of genes—that the individual has inherited. The **phenotype** represents all the observable physical, behavioral, and psychological traits that the individual actually develops. The distinction between the genotype and the phenotype is important for three reasons. First, knowledge of an individual's genotype and phenotype comes from different sources of information. Knowledge of the genotype comes from studying the individual's genetic material, whereas knowledge of the phenotype comes from studying the individual's body and behavior. Second, although an individual's genotype and phenotype are related, they do not necessarily coincide. Identical twins, for example, have precisely the same genotype, but their phenotypes—even their fingerprints—are never completely identical, and indeed they become increasingly different as the twins age (see p. 60). This is because the phenotype is influenced by the individual's environment, in addition to being influenced by the individual's genotype. Third and finally, the genotype and phenotype enter the process of evolution in distinctive ways, as we discuss below.

genotype The genetic endowment of an individual.

phenotype An organism's observable characteristics that result from the interaction of the genotype with the environment.

Evolution's Process of Natural Selection

Across vast tracts of time, the survival of species, including our own, has been continually threatened by shifting climates and food supplies, natural disasters such as earthquakes and floods, and attacks by other species ranging from microscopic viruses to mighty predators. According to Charles Darwin's famous argument, species survive because of the process of **natural selection**. Through this process, individuals with phenotypes that are adaptive to their particular environmental conditions (that is, whose traits are well fitted to the environment) have an increased chance of surviving and reproducing. In contrast, individuals whose phenotypes are not adaptive either do not survive or are less reproductively successful. (The fact that the odds of survival are greater for species better fitted to their environment gave rise to the well-known phrase "survival of the fittest.") Thus, those who are phenotypically well adapted to their environment are "selected" by natural conditions to survive and reproduce, and they pass on to the next generation the genotypes that contribute to the development of adaptive phenotypes.

natural selection The process through which species survive and evolve, in which individuals with phenotypes that are more adaptive to the environmental conditions survive and reproduce with greater success than do individuals with phenotypes that are less adaptive.

As Darwin described the process, natural selection requires *phenotypic variation*—that is, heritable variations of particular phenotypic traits that have survival value for the individual and the species.

The Emergence of Shorter Pregnancies The phenotypic trait of pregnancy duration provides an excellent example of how this process works. In our species, shorter pregnancies evolved as part of an integrated network of changes related to bipedalism, a smaller birth canal, a larger brain, and increased skull size. The natural selection process resulting in shorter pregnancies probably went something like this: Genotypic variations among females contributed to phenotypic variations in the length of their pregnancies. Females with longer pregnancies, who consequently gave birth to larger infants, were more likely to be damaged during the birth process, less likely to survive, and therefore less likely to have additional offspring than were females with shorter pregnancies. Likewise, the infants of those with longer pregnancies were more likely to be harmed during difficult deliveries, reducing their chances for reaching reproductive maturity. And those that did live to reproduce were likely to have inherited their mothers' genetic tendency for longer pregnancies, placing both themselves and their offspring at greater risk. In contrast, females whose genotypes favored the development of "shorter pregnancy" phenotypes would have given birth earlier to smaller infants. The mothers would have been more likely to survive and have additional offspring who would inherit the genetic tendency for shorter pregnancies. You can see that over the course of thousands of years, even tens of thousands of years, the average length of pregnancy for the entire species would have shortened as natural selection favored this adaptive phenotypic trait from one generation to the next.

In addition to affecting the evolution of physiological processes such as the length of pregnancy, natural selection works on phenotypic traits that are more behavioral in nature. For example, evolutionary theorists argue that our species' behavioral capacities for learning and socialization are due to the natural selection of adaptive phenotypes. It is important to note, however, that arguments regarding the selection of adaptive phenotypes are always tentative, especially in instances involving behavioral phenotypes (Witherington & Lickliter, 2016). In all instances, scientists make inferences about how particular behavioral phenotypes affect the survival of species, inferences that are based on the best available fossil evidence and on the survival value of comparable behaviors in species that are highly similar to humans, such as chimpanzees and bonobos.

In the sections below, we explore in more detail the processes that determine the formation of individual genotypes and the development of specific phenotypes.

Jezper/Shutterstock

FIGURE 2.4 DNA molecules include two long strands that spiral around each other in a double helix. DNA is a vast database containing all the genetic information a cell will need to develop.

Genetic Inheritance Through Sexual Reproduction

The *genotype*, you remember, refers to the individual's genetic endowment, which remains constant over the individual's lifetime. An individual's genotype contains information that defines the individual's membership in the human species, as well as information unique to that individual. All of this information is transmitted in the course of sexual reproduction, through the combination of the mother's egg and the father's sperm.

You may remember from your high school biology class that every human sperm and ovum (egg) contains 23 chromosomes and that a **chromosome** is a single molecule of **DNA (deoxyribonucleic acid)**. The DNA molecule takes the form of two long, connected strands that spiral around each other—the famous double helix (Figure 2.4). Every chromosome contains thousands of genes, each of which is a small segment of DNA.

chromosome A threadlike structure made up of genes. In humans, there are 46 chromosomes in every cell except sperm and ova.

DNA (deoxyribonucleic acid) A long, double-stranded molecule that makes up chromosomes.

Each gene carries a particular set of instructions for manufacturing the proteins that are used to create the body's cells and that control how the cells function. The 23 chromosomes in the ovum carry half the genes necessary for the development of a new individual. The chromosomes in the man's sperm carry the other half. When conception occurs, the ovum and sperm fuse to form a **zygote**, a single cell containing 46 chromosomes—23 from the mother and 23 from the father—that are arranged in 23 corresponding pairs. This single cell, with its 23 pairs of chromosomes, is the foundation for all the cells that will ever develop in the individual.

zygote The single cell formed at conception from the union of the sperm and the ovum.

germ cells The sperm and ova, which are specialized for sexual reproduction and have half the number of chromosomes normal for a species.

somatic cells All the cells in the body except for the germ cells (the ova and sperm).

mitosis The process of cell duplication and division that generates all of an individual's cells except sperm and ova.

meiosis The process that produces sperm and ova, each of which contains only half of the parent cell's original complement of 46 chromosomes.

Creating New Cells

Our cells are of two types: germ and somatic. **Germ cells** are the sperm and ova, which contain 23 unpaired chromosomes, as described above. **Somatic cells** (or *body cells*) are all the other cells of the body (skin cells, blood cells, bone cells, nerve cells, and so on). Each somatic cell contains 46 chromosomes in 23 pairs, identical to the chromosomes in the zygote. New somatic cells are created through a process called **mitosis**. The process of creating germ cells is called **meiosis**.

Mitosis: A Process of Making New Somatic Cells.

The process of mitosis begins with the 46 chromosomes in a cell replicating—that is, producing exact copies of themselves (Figure 2.5). These chromosomes then move to the middle of the cell, where they separate into two identical sets, which migrate to opposite sides of the cell. The cell then divides in the middle to form two daughter cells, each of which contains a set of 46 chromosomes. These two daughter cells go through the same process of replication and division to create two new cells each, which themselves replicate and divide as the process repeats itself again and again.

This process continues throughout the life of the individual, constantly creating new somatic cells and replacing those that die off. Each new somatic cell contains an exact copy of the original 46 chromosomes inherited by the zygote at conception. Thus, under the ordinary conditions of life, our chromosomes and the genes they carry are not altered by the passage of time or by the experiences that shape our minds and bodies; that is, as mentioned earlier, our genotype remains constant.

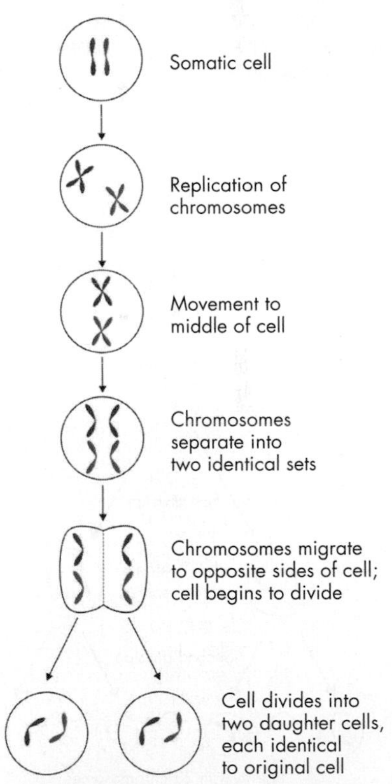

FIGURE 2.5 Mitosis is the process of cell division that generates new somatic cells. First, all the chromosomes in the cell replicate, producing a new set of chromosomes identical to the first. The two sets then separate and the cell divides, producing two daughter cells. Mitosis ensures that identical genetic information is maintained in the somatic cells over the life of the organism.

Meiosis: A Process of Making Germ Cells.

Mitosis works very well as a process of creating new somatic cells, each with 46 chromosomes identical to those inherited by the zygote. Germ cells, however, must have only 23 chromosomes each, so that when an ovum and sperm fuse, they create a zygote with 46 chromosomes. This is accomplished through the special cell-division process of meiosis.

In the first phase of this process, the 23 pairs of chromosomes in the cells that produce sperm or ova duplicate themselves, just as in mitosis. But then the cell divides not once, as in mitosis, but twice, creating four daughter cells (Figure 2.6, p. 60). Each of these daughter cells contains only 23 unpaired chromosomes—half the original set from the parent cell. Thus, when the ovum and sperm fuse at conception, the zygote receives a full complement of 46 chromosomes (23 pairs).

Meiosis represents the initial stage of shuffling genetic material from the parent generation to produce new genetic variations in the offspring. Although we receive 23 chromosomes from each of our parents, it is a matter of chance which member of any pair of chromosomes ends up in a given germ cell during meiosis. According to the laws of probability, there are 2^{23}, or about 8 million, possible genetic combinations for each sperm and ovum. Consequently, the probability that siblings will inherit exactly the same genes from both parents is, at best, 1 chance in 64 trillion! This extreme improbability shows the importance of meiosis as a source of variation, a means of introducing new genetic combinations in the species.

There is one exception to the odds of genetic variability—the special case of **monozygotic (MZ) twins**, who come from a single fertilized egg that, for reasons still not understood, divides and develops into two separate individuals. Because they originate from the same zygote, monozygotic twins have identical genetic material, so they potentially could have the same physical and psychological makeup. However, as a result of their encounters with their environments, "identical twins" are never exactly alike in every detail and may even appear far from identical. (Twins who come from two ova that were fertilized at the same time are referred to as **dizygotic [DZ] twins**, or "fraternal twins," and are no more likely to resemble each other than are any other two siblings.)

monozygotic (MZ) twins Twins who come from one zygote and therefore have identical genotypes.

dizygotic (DZ) twins Twins who come from two zygotes.

Sex Determination Like many other species on the planet, the human species has evolved two sexes—male and female. But what determines whether a given individual is one or the other? In 22 of the 23 pairs of chromosomes found in a human cell, the two chromosomes are of the same size and shape and carry corresponding genes. For chromosomes of the 23rd pair, however, this is not necessarily the case. This pair of chromosomes determines a person's genetic sex. In females, both members of the 23rd pair of chromosomes are of the same type, called an **X chromosome** (Figure 2.7). Males, however, have just one X chromosome, which is paired with a different, much smaller chromosome, called a **Y chromosome**. Since a female is XX, each of her eggs contains an X chromosome. Since a male is XY, half of his sperm carry an X chromosome and half carry a Y chromosome. If a sperm containing an X chromosome fertilizes an egg, the resulting child will be

X chromosome One of the two chromosomes that determine sex; in females, both members of the 23rd pair of chromosomes are X, and in males, one member of the 23rd pair is X.

Y chromosome One of the two chromosomes that determine sex; in males, one member of the 23rd pair of chromosomes is Y.

Somatic cell that produces sperm (contains 46 chromosomes)

Replication of chromosomes

Cell with 92 chromosomes

First division

Cells with 46 chromosomes

Second division

Sperm with 23 chromosomes

FIGURE 2.6 Meiosis is the process of cell division that generates new germ cells (in this case, sperm). Like mitosis, meiosis begins with replication of the cell's chromosomes, but the cell then divides twice. The result is sperm cells, each with just 23 chromosomes.

IAN BODDY/Getty Images

Despite apparently similar environments and identical genetic material, these monozygotic twin boys have distinguishably different facial features. This suggests that an individual's phenotype can be influenced by subtle variations in the environment.

Lawrence Migdale/Science Source

Because they developed from two separate ova, these dizygotic, or fraternal, twins look no more alike than nontwin siblings.

XX, a female. If the sperm contains a Y chromosome, the child will be XY, a male. A single chromosome determines a person's sex; however, other aspects of biology and behavior have more complex origins.

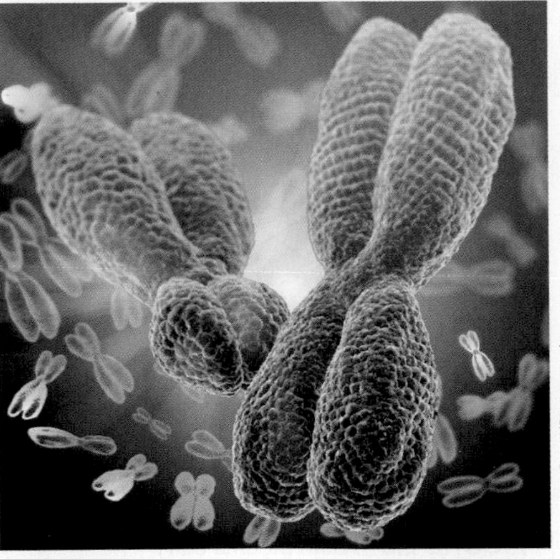

FIGURE 2.7 Human X (foreground) and Y (be hind the X) chromosomes. Note how much larger the X chromosome is. Males have both an X and a Y chromosome; females have two X chromosomes.

Iaremenko Sergii/Shutterstock

Laws of Genetic Inheritance

The laws of genetic inheritance describe several different ways in which genetic material transmitted by parents can be expressed in the child. In the simplest form, a single pair of corresponding genes, one from each parent, contributes to a particular inherited characteristic. A gene that influences a specific trait (for example, the presence or absence of a cleft in the chin) can have different forms. The specific form of a gene is called an **allele**. When the corresponding genes inherited from the two parents are the same allele (both "cleft" or both "uncleft"), the person is said to be **homozygous** for the trait. When the alleles are different (one "cleft" and one "uncleft"), the person is said to be **heterozygous** for the trait.

Whether the allele pairings are homozygous or heterozygous affects the characteristics of the phenotype. If a child is homozygous for a trait that is affected by a single pair of alleles, only one outcome is possible: The child will display the particular characteristics associated with that allele. If a child is heterozygous for such a trait, one of three outcomes is possible:

- The child will display the characteristics associated with only one of the two alleles. In such cases, the allele whose associated characteristics are expressed is referred to as a **dominant allele**, and the allele whose associated characteristics are not expressed is referred to as a **recessive allele**. Even though individuals who are heterozygous for a recessive trait do not express that trait, they are nevertheless **carriers** of the recessive allele, meaning that they can pass the allele on to their offspring. When a child inherits a recessive allele for a recessive trait from both parents, the child will exhibit the trait.
- The child will be affected by both alleles and will display characteristics that are intermediate between those associated with the two alleles. Thus, with skin color, for example, the offspring of a dark-skinned parent and a light-skinned parent may have skin tones in between those of the parents.
- Rather than displaying intermediate characteristics, the child will fully express the characteristics associated with each of the two alleles, an outcome that is called **codominance** For example, children with type AB blood may have a type-A mother and a type-B father. The blood type of each parent is fully expressed in the AB blood type of the child.

It is important to note that although most recessive traits are of little consequence for the health and development of the child (e.g., cleft chin, attached earlobes, straight hairline), there are a number of recessive disorders that can occur when a child inherits a recessive allele for the disorder from both parents. Among these *recessive disorders* are phenylketonuria and sickle-cell anemia, both of which we discuss below (see Table 2.2, p. 63, for other examples).

It is also important to reiterate that the patterns we have just outlined represent the simplest form of genetic inheritance. Most traits, especially behavioral traits—from empathy and intelligence to aggression and risk-taking—involve **polygenic inheritance**, in which a variety of genes—sometimes a great many—contribute to

allele The specific form of a gene that influences a particular trait.

homozygous Having inherited two genes of the same allelic form for a trait.

heterozygous Having inherited two genes of different allelic forms for a trait.

dominant allele The allele that is expressed when an individual possesses two different alleles for the same trait.

recessive allele The allele that is not expressed when an individual possesses two different alleles for the same trait.

carriers Individuals who are heterozygous for a trait with a dominant and recessive allele and thus express only the characteristics associated with the dominant allele but may pass the recessive allele, including one for a recessive disorder, on to their offspring.

codominance An outcome in which a trait that is determined by two alleles is different from the trait produced by either of the contributing alleles alone.

polygenic inheritance Refers to the contribution of a variety of genes—sometimes very many—to a particular trait.

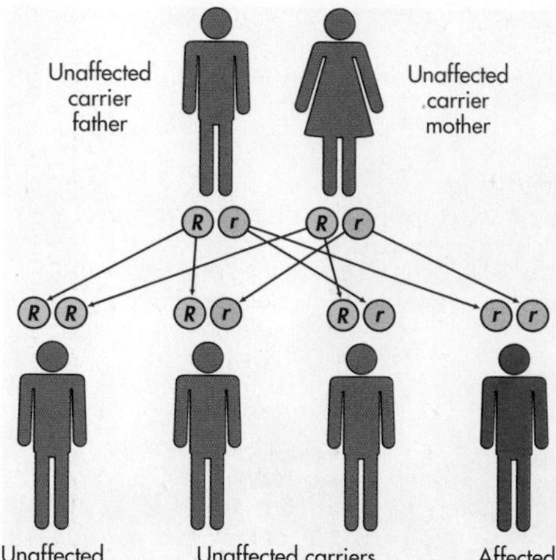

FIGURE 2.8 If both parents carry the recessive allele (*r*) for a disorder, a child who receives that allele from both parents (*rr*) will have the disorder; alternatively, a child may receive the dominant allele (*R*) from both parents (*RR*) and be unaffected or may receive a dominant and recessive allele (*Rr*) and be unaffected but be a carrier.

the development of the phenotype. In addition, some genes can influence a number of traits (Figure 2.8).

Mutations and Genetic Abnormalities

Sexual reproduction is a fantastic source of genetic diversity in human beings, but it is not the only one. Diversity also arises from **mutation**, which involves an alteration in the structure of an individual's DNA. Mutations can occur for a variety of reasons, including errors in chromosome replication during either meiosis or mitosis and exposure to external agents such as certain chemicals and certain forms of radiation.

mutation An alteration in the molecular structure of an individual's DNA.

When mutations occur in germ cells, the changed genetic information may be passed on to the next generation and, over time, to the human **gene pool**, the total variety of genetic information possessed by a sexually reproducing population. Geneticists assume that spontaneous mutations have been occurring in germ cells constantly and randomly for millions upon millions of years, introducing new genes into the gene pool of every species and providing a source of variation for the process of natural selection.

gene pool The total variety of genetic information possessed by a sexually reproducing population.

The fact that mutations are a natural and fundamental part of life does not, however, mean that they usually benefit the individual organisms in which they occur. Most mutations are lethal, rather than adaptive, and in humans and other mammalian species, result in early miscarriage (Biancotti et al., 2010).

Every year, nearly 8 million children—6 percent of total births worldwide—are born with some kind of genetic abnormality, resulting in approximately 303,000 newborn deaths within 4 weeks of delivery (Christianson, Howson, & Modell, 2006; Turnpenny & Ellard, 2012; World Health Organization, 2016). Some of the most commonly occurring disorders related to genetic abnormalities are listed in Table 2.2. These disorders are of two main types. Some are a consequence of the specific genetic material inherited by the individual by means of normal processes of inheritance. For example, recessive disorders such as phenylketonuria and sickle-cell anemia, as mentioned above, occur through ordinary processes when both parents transmit the relevant allele. The second type of disorder occurs as a result of a breakdown in the process of genetic transmission, such as the normal process of meiosis being disrupted for some reason, affecting the structure of chromosomes in the germ cell. Various abnormalities can result, such as Down syndrome and Klinefelter syndrome.

Thanks to advances in technology and medical science, doctors have a number of tools at their disposal to help determine whether a pregnancy may involve a genetic disorder: preconception tests, prenatal tests, and newborn tests. **Preconception tests**, which are conducted even before a pregnancy occurs, involve analyzing the parents' DNA using samples of their blood or saliva. Risk for sickle-cell anemia and Tay-Sachs diseases, among others, can be determined through preconception testing (see the discussion below for details on these and other genetic disorders). **Prenatal tests**, which are conducted during the pregnancy itself, involve taking DNA samples of the embryo or fetus. One of these tests is **amniocentesis**, in which a needle is inserted through the mother's abdomen and uterine wall and then into the amniotic sac, from which it withdraws amniotic fluid. The fluid contains fetal cells that can be analyzed for a number of genetic disorders, including Down syndrome. Amniocentesis is typically done during weeks 14 through 16 of pregnancy, and in conjunction with ultrasound. The ultrasound provides visual information about the location and movement of the fetus and is used to guide the insertion of the needle away from the fetus. Another prenatal test—one that can be done as early as week 8 of

preconception tests Analysis of parents' DNA using blood or saliva samples to determine the risk of genetic disorders in offspring.

prenatal tests Tests such as amniocentesis and chorionic villus sampling (CVS) that are used to analyze the DNA of an embryo or a fetus to determine genetic disorders.

amniocentesis A prenatal test that involves inserting a needle into the uterus and withdrawing amniotic fluid containing fetal cells that can be analyzed for genetic disorders.

TABLE 2.2 Research Designs

Common Genetic Disorders

	Disorder	Description	Incidence	Prenatal/Carrier Detection?	Treatment and Prognosis
Recessive disorders	Cystic fibrosis	Lack of an enzyme causes mucus obstruction, especially in lungs and digestive tract	1 in 3,000 Caucasian births in U.S.; 1 in 17,000 African American births	Yes/Yes	Medications, treatments, diet used to clear airways, loosen mucus, aid digestion. In U.S., most survive into 30s.
	Phenylketonuria (PKU)	Inability to metabolize phenylalanine, an amino acid, leads to its buildup in the bloodstream, retarding brain-cell development	1 in 10,000–15,000 U.S. infants	Yes/Yes	Treatment by diet beginning in infancy and continuing throughout life can reduce severity of brain damage and mental retardation.
	Sickle-cell anemia	Abnormally shaped blood cells cause circulatory problems and severe anemia	8–9% of African Americans; more than 20% of West Africans	Yes/Yes	Organ damage and severe pain can result. Treatment by medication can reduce symptoms and complications.
	Tay-Sachs disease	Lack of an enzyme causes buildup of waste in brain	1 in 3,600 among Ashkenazi Jews in U.S.	Yes/Yes	Neurological degeneration leads to death before age 4.
	Thalassemia (Cooley's anemia)	Abnormal red blood cells	1 in 500 births in populations from subtropical areas of Europe, Africa, and Asia	Yes/Yes	Listlessness, enlarged liver and spleen, occasionally death; treatable by blood transfusions.
X-linked recessive disorders	Duchenne muscular dystrophy	Weakening and wasting away of muscles	1 in 3,500 males under age 20	Yes/Yes	Crippling, often fatal by age 20.
	Hemophilia	Blood does not clot readily. Although usually the result of X-linked gene, also occurs by spontaneous mutation	1 in 10,000 live births of males	Yes/Yes, if not spontaneous mutation	Possible crippling and death from internal bleeding. Transfusions ameliorate effects.
Dominant disorders	Neurofibromatosis	Nervous system disorder, causing tumors on nerves and other abnormalities. Usually inherited, but 30–50% of cases arise through spontaneous mutation	1 in 3,000 births	Yes/Yes, if not spontaneous mutation	Symptoms are highly variable and may include café au lait spots, benign tumors on peripheral nerves, optic nerve tumors, learning disabilities. Treatment by surgery may be possible.
Chromosomal disorders	Down syndrome	Extra copy of chromosome 21 results in mental and physical retardation, distinctive physical characteristics, and susceptibility to certain medical conditions	1 in 1,000 live births in U.S.	Yes/N.A.	Medical conditions monitored and treated; special education to develop skills and independence. Depending on severity and complications, survival into 60s is possible.
	Klinefelter syndrome	Extra X chromosome in males (XXY) results in incomplete development of sex organs and secondary sex characteristics	1 in every 500–1,000 males born in U.S.	Yes/N.A.	Treatment by testosterone replacement therapy at puberty can be beneficial. Most lead normal lives, although with increased risk for certain cancers and heart disease.
	Turner syndrome	Lack of an X chromosome (XO) in females. Common symptoms include short stature, failure to develop secondary sex characteristics	1 in 2,500 females	Yes/N.A.	Growth hormone and estrogen therapies can facilitate growth and development. Most women lead normal lives but are infertile.

chorionic villus sampling (CVS) A prenatal test that samples tissue from the placenta to analyze for genetic disorders.

noninvasive prenatal diagnosis (NIPD) A prenatal test that samples blood from the mother and extracts fetal blood cells to analyze for genetic disorders.

pregnancy—is **chorionic villus sampling (CVS)**, which samples tissue from the placenta, the complex organ that attaches to the mother's uterine wall and connects to the embryo through the umbilical cord (see Chapter 3).

Amniocentesis and CVS are invasive tests that include a slight risk of causing fetal death or complications. Until recently, they were the only means of diagnosing genetic disorders prenatally. But now, a new, noninvasive test is available. Taking advantage of the fact that a very small amount of the fetus's DNA is present in the mothers' blood, **noninvasive prenatal diagnosis (NIPD)** involves taking a sample of the mother's blood, at no risk to either the mother or the fetus, to screen for genetic disorders such as Down syndrome, cystic fibrosis, and hemophilia.

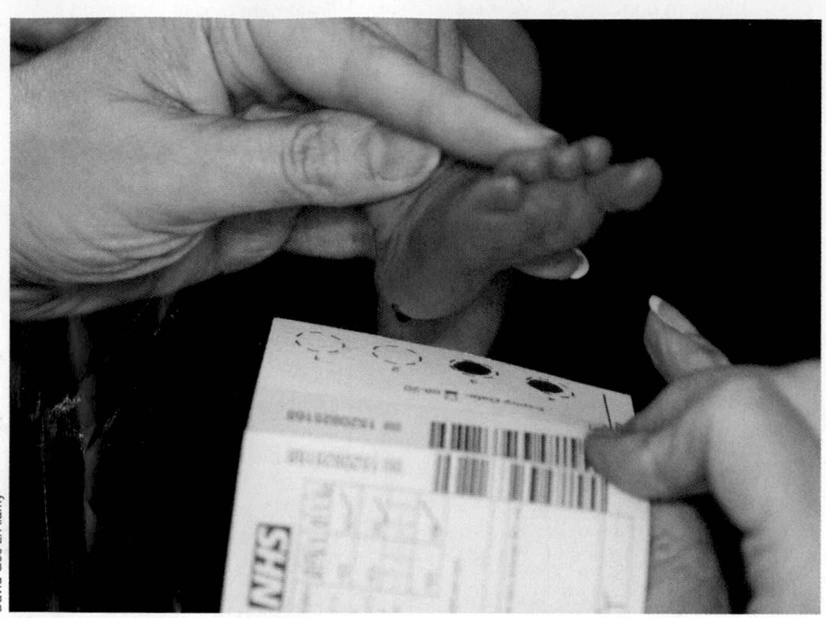

David Gee 2/Alamy

Blood drops taken from the newborn's heel will be used to screen for genetic disorders, including phenylketonuria, sickle-cell anemia, and cystic fibrosis.

Finally, genetic testing can be conducted after the baby is born. A common procedure is to draw blood by pricking the newborn's foot with a heel stick as seen in the photo. This simple test is used routinely to screen for a number of genetic disorders, including phenylketonuria, sickle-cell anemia, and cystic fibrosis.

Regardless of the timing of the genetic testing, parents often benefit from working with genetic counselors who can help them understand the testing procedures, the outcomes of the analyses, and the implications for their families (see the box "In the Field: Prenatal Genetic Counseling," p. 66).

Phenylketonuria: A Recessive Disorder

Phenylketonuria (*PKU*) is an example of a recessive disorder caused by specific genetic material inherited by the individual through the normal process of genetic transmission. PKU is a particularly debilitating condition that leads to severe intellectual disability if it is not treated. It is caused by a defective recessive allele that, when inherited from both parents, reduces the body's ability to metabolize phenylalanine, an amino acid that is highly concentrated in foods such as milk, eggs, bread, and fish. When too much phenylalanine builds up in a baby's bloodstream, brain-cell development is retarded (Camp et al., 2014). About 1 in every 10,000 to 15,000 infants born each year in the United States, Europe, China, and Korea has PKU, and about 1 in 100 people of European descent is a carrier of the recessive allele (Hardelid et al., 2008). The incidence of PKU is lower among Blacks than among Whites, and it is lower among people with sub-Saharan African and South Asian ancestry compared to those with other genetic backgrounds (Connor & Ferguson-Smith, 1993; Hardelid, et al., 2008).

PKU can be tested for prenatally, and most states in the United States require that all newborns be tested for the disorder. Infants who test positive are treated with diets that are low in phenylalanine. While such treatment significantly reduces the severity of intellectual disabilities, it does not prevent the effects of PKU entirely (Bilder et al., 2016). The timing of the treatment is crucial. If phenylalanine intake is not restricted by the time an infant with PKU is 1 to 3 months of age, the brain will already have suffered irreversible damage. Genetic testing can identify people who carry the recessive PKU allele, allowing prospective parents who are both carriers to decide whether they want to risk having a child with the disease.

Down Syndrome: A Chromosomal Disorder In contrast to disorders, such as PKU, that are caused by the inheritance of specific genetic material, Down syndrome is a consequence of a disruption in the normal process of genetic transmission. In the vast majority of cases, it results from an error during meiosis that creates extra genetic material on chromosome 21. Indeed, more than 95 percent of the children born with Down syndrome have three copies of chromosome 21 instead of two. (For this reason, the disorder is sometimes called *trisomy 21*.) The effects of this disorder, which occurs at the rate of about 1 of every 1,000 births in the United States, include varying degrees of mental and physical retardation, as well as several distinctive physical characteristics: slanting eyes and a fold on the eyelids; a rather flat facial profile; ears located lower than normal; a short neck; a protruding tongue; dental irregularities; short, broad hands; a crease running all the way across the palm; small curved fingers; and unusually wide-spaced toes. Children with this disorder are more likely than other children to suffer from heart, ear, and eye problems, and they are more susceptible to leukemia and to respiratory infections (Steiner et al., 2005). Although the trigger for the meiotic error that causes Down syndrome is unknown, the disorder is strongly associated with conceptions involving older parents, particularly older mothers (Rychtarikova, Gourbin, Sipek, & Wunsch, 2013; see Figure 2.9).

How effectively children with Down syndrome function as they grow up depends not only on the severity of their disorder but also on the environment in which they are raised. Supportive intervention that includes special education by concerned adults can markedly improve the intellectual functioning of some children with Down syndrome, especially when it is begun at an early age (Guralnick, 2005). As you will learn, even in the case of serious genetic abnormalities such as Down syndrome, variations in the environment can lead to a range of possible phenotypic outcomes.

Klinefelter Syndrome: A Disorder of the Sex Chromosomes Half of all chromosomal abnormalities in newborns involve the X and Y chromosomes. Occasionally, a boy is born with an extra X or Y chromosome—that is, with an

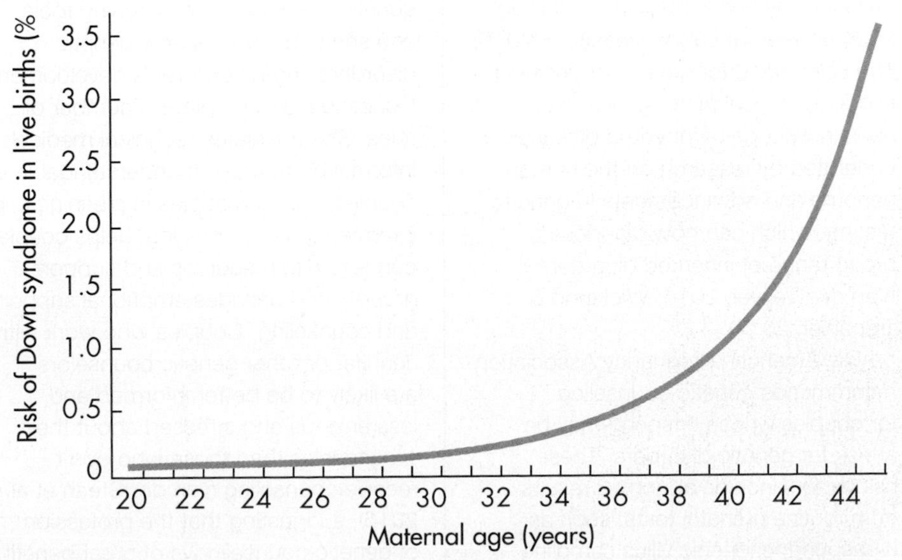

FIGURE 2.9 The risk of Down syndrome is closely associated with maternal age. As shown here, babies born to women in their 20s are highly unlikely to have the chromosomal disorder, whereas the risk rises dramatically for those born to women in their 40s. (Chaudhury & Mukherjee, 2016; data from Newberger, 2000.)

XXY or XYY genotype. Girls are sometimes born with only one X chromosome (XO genotype) or with three X chromosomes (XXX genotype). Both males and females can be affected by a condition in which the X chromosome, which carries many genes, is brittle and breaks into two or more pieces. Each of these chromosomal abnormalities has different implications for development.

The most common sex-linked chromosomal abnormality is *Klinefelter syndrome*, the condition in which males are born with at least one extra X chromosome (XXY). This abnormality occurs in about 1 of every 500 males born in the United States (Visootsak & Graham, 2006). Males who have Klinefelter syndrome appear to

In the Field: Prenatal Genetic Counseling

Name: JENNIFER HOSKOVEC MS, CGC

Education: Undergraduate degree in biology from Truman State University; Masters Degree in Genetic Counseling from University of Texas Graduate School of Biomedical Sciences, Houston, TX

Current Position: Director, Prenatal Genetic Counseling Services at McGovern Medical School, UTHealth, Houston, TX

Career Objectives: Counsel women and families about options for genetic testing and screening during pregnancy; teach graduate students in the UT genetic counseling training program

Jennifer Hoskovec

As a genetic counselor, Jennifer Hoskovec is part of a growing profession dedicated to helping people make decisions associated with their genetic health. Genetic counselors typically work in medical clinics or hospitals, as a part of a healthcare team including obstetricians, neurologists, and other doctors. Often, genetic counselors specialize in a particular area—such as cancer, heart disease, or brain and neurological disorders—which are known to have genetic underpinnings. Because of Jennifer's special focus on prenatal and preconception genetic counseling, she works with women and their families who are pregnant or thinking about becoming pregnant and whose pregnancies may be at risk for genetic diseases.

According to the National Society of Genetic Counselors, there are more than 4,000 certified genetic counselors today (National Society of Genetic Counselors, 2017). The need for genetic counselors is projected to grow at a fast clip—by nearly 30 percent through 2024 (Bureau of Labor Statistics, (2015). The rising need for genetic counseling is due to several factors, including new knowledge of inherited diseases generated by research on the human genome and advancements in genetic testing, which can now diagnose a broad range of inherited disorders (Van den Veyver, 2016; Wicklund & Trepanier, 2014).

The American Pregnancy Association recommends genetic counseling for couples whose offspring may be at risk for genetic disorders. These risk factors include abnormal results from routine prenatal tests, such as ultrasound; chorionic villus sampling (CVS) or amniocentesis results that indicate genetic abnormalities; having a close relative with a genetic disorder; or the age of the mother being greater than 35 years (American Pregnancy Association, 2017). Naturally, the diagnosis of a fetal genetic abnormality may be shocking, and it may arouse fear and anxiety in parents (van der Steen et al., 2016). As a prenatal genetic counselor, Jennifer is well versed in genetic medicine and screening tools, and she understands how genetic disorders impact children's development. Consequently, she plays a number of roles: She translates technical medical information to make it understandable to couples, assists couples in planning and informed decision making, helps couples connect with resources and support groups, and provides emotional support and counseling. Couples who work with Jennifer or other genetic counselors are likely to be better informed and less anxious and stressed about their pregnancies than those who don't receive counseling (van der Steen et al., 2016), suggesting that the profession of genetic counseling is of great benefit to families facing the uncertainties of genetic disorders.

develop normally until adolescence, when they fail to show the typical signs of sexual maturation because they have low levels of testosterone, the hormone that is key to sexual development in males. They do not acquire facial hair, their voices do not deepen, and their sex organs do not develop, making them sterile. In addition, most have speech, language, and cognitive deficits and, as a result, have problems in school and at work (Chang, Skakkebaek, & Gravholt, 2015; Temple & Sanfilippo, 2003).

The most prevalent treatment for Klinefelter syndrome is to begin testosterone replacement therapy at age 11 or 12, when testosterone levels normally begin to rise in males. The syndrome is not often diagnosed that early, but even if therapy is started later, it can have positive effects. The benefits include increased facial and pubic hair, a more masculine distribution of body fat, increased strength and bone density, and increased sexual functioning (Herlihy & McLachlan, 2015).

The Phenotype: From Genes to Traits

Notwithstanding the enormous power of the genotype to influence human development, the genotype does not account for how development actually takes place for each individual—that is, how all the phenotypic traits and characteristics that together define the individual emerge over time. For example, although Down syndrome substantially affects development, the care and support of family members, as well as educational and vocational services provided in schools and communities, can have an enormous impact on the skills and abilities the individual will acquire.

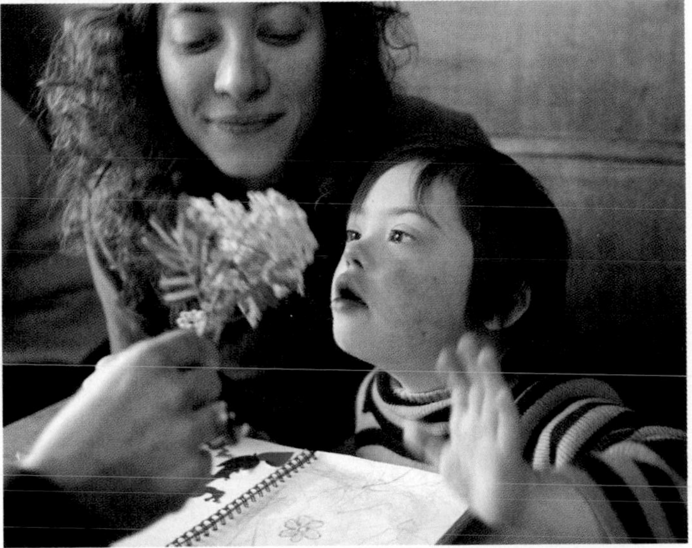

BL/AGE Fotostock

Although this young girl's intellectual development will be limited by Down syndrome, the enriched environment provided at home and school will have a significant impact on what she is able to accomplish as she grows up.

The most important question that developmentalists ask about the development of phenotypic traits concerns **phenotypic plasticity**—that is, the extent to which traits are determined by the genotype or are open to influence by the environment. In traits with *low plasticity*, such as eye color, the genotype is strongly influential, and the phenotype develops in a highly predictable manner, regardless of environmental factors. In contrast, in traits with *high plasticity*, the genotype exerts less pressure, so the phenotype is easily influenced by the environment and develops less predictably, as in the case of intellectual skills and abilities.

phenotypic plasticity The degree to which the phenotype is open to influence by the environment rather than determined by the genotype.

Conrad Waddington, a British geneticist, brilliantly captured the basic principles of phenotypic plasticity in his famous landscape of phenotypic development (Figure 2.10). He imagined the development of a phenotypic trait as a journey across a vast landscape of hills and intersecting valleys flowing downward from a high plateau. As shown in the figure, the ball that is rolling down from the top of the plateau represents the particular phenotypic trait in its "infancy"; the valleys represent the possible developmental pathways that lead to various

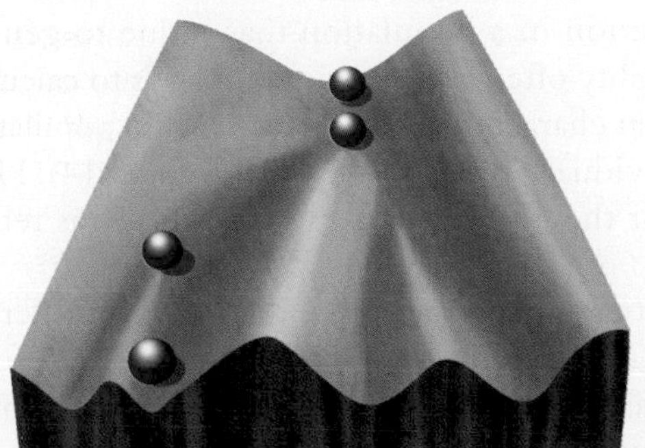

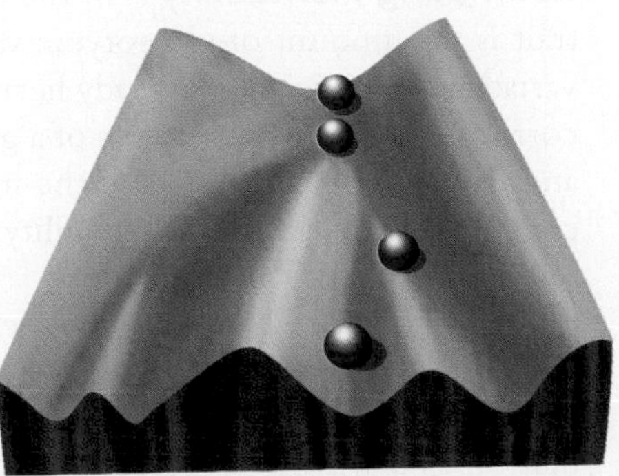

FIGURE 2.10 Waddington's landscape. The rolling ball represents a trait of the developing organism. At each fork in the road, development of the trait can proceed along one of several diverging pathways. (Research from Waddington, 1957.)

phenotypic outcomes. You can see from the figure that as the ball rolls downward, it sometimes encounters "forks in the road" where more than one valley is available for continuing the journey, as is the case for traits with high plasticity. You can also see that some valleys are narrow and deep, as is the case for low-plasticity traits. Waddington referred to these latter traits, which follow confined courses, as being **canalized**.

canalized Refers to a trait that follows a strictly defined path, regardless of most environmental and genetic variations.

The particular shape of the landscape—the forks, the hills, the depth of the valleys—is the result of a complex system of interactions between genes and the environment. And because the gene–environment system of interaction changes over the course of a lifetime, *the landscape is not stable over the life course of the individual.* Rather, it changes its shape, sometimes dramatically, according to the individual's particular experiences. Exposure to toxins during the prenatal period, for example, can substantially alter the landscape in ways that change the course of developing phenotypes, resulting in physical deformities, mental retardation, and other disorders (see Chapter 3).

We noted earlier in this chapter that development is astonishing in its capacity to generate common developmental outcomes in children despite vast differences in how and where they grow up. In part, this similarity is due to the tight control that the genotype exerts over the developing phenotype. Indeed, canalization ensures that the development of certain essential traits—walking, speaking, and forming friendships, for example—is not easily diverted by environmental variations. On the other hand, the high plasticity of some traits ensures that each individual is able to adapt to changes in the environment. Together, high plasticity and canalization are tremendously powerful forces in organizing children's development.

In the next section, we will continue to explore the genotype–phenotype relationship by considering whether and how certain phenotypic traits of parents are likely to occur in the development of their offspring.

Heritability

You have no doubt often seen news reports announcing the discovery of links between certain genes and this or that physical or psychological trait. Although it is tempting to look for genetic causes to explain human characteristics—from physical traits such as height and weight to behavioral traits such as aggressiveness, thrill-seeking, musical talent, intelligence, and so on—developmentalists know that the gene–behavior relationship is usually more complex. In particular, they know that any trait that shows a large range of individual differences—shyness, say—is almost certainly influenced by multiple genes, as well as by characteristics of the environment. Consequently, their conclusions about the role of genes with respect to phenotypic traits are likely to use the phrase "genetically influenced" rather than "genetically caused."

heritability A measure of the degree to which a variation in a particular trait among individuals in a specific population is related to genetic differences among those individuals.

Estimating Heritability

In the broadest sense, the **heritability** of a particular trait is the amount of phenotypic variation in a population that is due to genetic variation. Geneticists who study heritability often use statistical methods to calculate correlations between measures of a given characteristic among a specific population and the genetic relatedness of the individuals being studied (Plomin, 2014). High correlations reflect high heritability for the characteristic; low correlations reflect low heritability.

Using this method, behavioral geneticists have calculated estimations of heritability for a number of characteristics. Consider the example of height. For North Americans, height has a heritability of about 90 percent, meaning that for the population as a whole, 90 percent of the variation in height is the result of genetic factors. Keep in mind that heritability estimates are for populations; in another population, the heritability of height might be considerably lower. The reason for the high heritability of height in the United States is the relative lack of environmental diversity: Most of the population has access to adequate nutrition and health care, so environmental differences play relatively less of a role in height differences, and genetic differences play a relatively greater role (Tanner, 1990).

Studying Heritability To study the heritability of a given trait, developmentalists use **kinship studies** to determine the extent to which relatives of varying degrees of genetic closeness are similar on the trait in question (Krapohl & Plomin, 2016). Children share 50 percent of their genes with each parent, siblings (except for identical twins) share 50 percent of their genes with each other, half-siblings share 25 percent of their genes, and so on. As noted, if the extent of similarity on a particular trait correlates strongly with the degree of genetic closeness, it can be inferred that the trait is highly heritable, while weaker correlations indicate lower heritability. The three main types of research designs used in kinship studies are family studies, twin studies, and adoption studies.

kinship studies Studies that use naturally occurring conditions provided by kinship relations to estimate genetic and environmental contributions to a phenotypic trait.

In the typical **family study**, relatives who live together in a household—parents, children, stepchildren, half-siblings—are compared with one another to determine how similar they are on a given trait. The shortcoming of family studies for estimating the degree of genetic influence is the obvious fact that relatives who live together not only share genes but also, to a large degree, participate in the same family environment. Thus, whatever similarities are found among them could be attributable to environmental influences as well as to hereditary ones.

family study A study that compares members of the same family to determine how similar they are on a given trait.

In order to obtain more precise estimates of genetic and environmental contributions to individual differences, researchers capitalize on two other designs. In a **twin study**, monozygotic twins and dizygotic twins of the same sex are compared with each other and with other family members for similarity on a given trait (Lester et al., 2016; Uzefovsky, Döring, & Knafo-Noam, 2016). Because MZ twins have 100 percent of their genes in common, MZ twins raised together should, to the degree that the trait in question is genetically influenced, show greater similarity on the trait than do DZ twins or other siblings. By the same logic, DZ twins and siblings should be more similar than half siblings.

twin study A study in which groups of monozygotic (identical) and dizygotic (fraternal) twins of the same sex are compared to each other and to other family members for similarity on a given trait.

adoption study A study that focuses on children who have been reared apart from their biological parents.

In an **adoption study**, researchers compare children who have been reared apart from their biological parents. Some adoption studies compare twins or other siblings who have been adopted into different families; others compare children and their adoptive and biological parents. The basic purpose of this strategy is to determine whether adopted children are more similar to their biological parents and siblings, who share their genes, or to their adoptive parents and siblings, with whom they share a family environment.

Many family, twin, and adoption studies have shown that the degree of similarity among kin correlates with the degree of genetic similarity. This pattern has been shown for such varied characteristics as attention deficit/hyperactivity disorder (Chen et al., 2016), intelligence (Engelhardt, Mann, Briley, Church, Harden, & Tucker-Drob., 2016), personality traits (Macare et al., 2012), antisocial behavior (Viding et al., 2008), and susceptibility to schizophrenia (Edvardsen et al., 2008). Like family studies, twin and adoption studies are not without problems (Richardson & Norgate, 2006). It is possible, for example, that MZ twins may receive more similar treatment from parents and others than do DZ twins or other siblings, and to the extent that they do, MZ twins may be more alike than

blue jean images/Getty Images

These Japanese teenagers are clearly enjoying this interactive video game. Research suggests that their enthusiasm may be due to both genetic and environmental factors. Genetic factors may contribute to good eye–hand coordination, enhancing their enjoyment of and leading them to seek out experiences requiring such skill. At the same time, repeated exposure to such experiences results in even greater skill and, consequently, greater pleasure in challenging experiences.

DZ twins for environmental rather than genetic reasons. In addition, when siblings are adopted by different families and raised apart, it is not at all clear that the rearing environments are significantly different. Thus, the extent to which adopted children are similar to their biological families might not be entirely attributable to the similarity of their genes but may also be due to environmental similarities.

A further complication for kinship studies is that children within a family do not share the same family environment. Age, birth order, and gender can all affect how children within the same family experience family life, and differences in family-linked experiences may create differences between the siblings (Segal & Johnson, 2009). For example, not only do parents treat each of their children differently, siblings also offer different environments for each other. In addition, siblings are likely to have different teachers at school, different friends, and different experiences outside the home. The fact that the distinctive environments experienced by different children in the same family can lead to differences in their development in no way minimizes the importance of genetic factors. Rather, it affirms the principle that genes and the environment make essential contributions to phenotypic development.

An excellent illustration of this principle comes from studies of identical twins, conducted by Manel Esteller and his colleagues at the Spanish National Cancer Center in Madrid (Poulsen, Esteller, Vaag, & Fraga, 2007; Heyn et al., 2013). At birth, identical twins are on their way to developing identical phenotypes. However, as you already know, even genetically identical individuals develop phenotypic differences. Focusing largely on cellular processes associated with the development of particular diseases, Esteller found that the phenotypic traits of identical twins become increasingly different as the twins grow older, and they become greater still as the twins live apart in adulthood (Poulsen et al., 2007). The increasing divergence of their phenotypic characteristics is due in part to increasing differences in the twins' exposure to environmental and social factors assumed to influence phenotypic development, such as toxins, stress, and nutrition.

Genotypes, Phenotypes, and Human Behavior

At this point, you should have a fairly good idea about how phenotypes develop in relation to genetic and environmental factors. But Waddington's image of a ball rolling down a landscape, drifting across valleys, and falling into canals is limited in two ways, both of which relate to how the landscape is formed and re-formed over the course of development. First, Waddington's account can suggest that developing individuals themselves play but a small role in the process of their own development, when this is far from the case. Second, Waddington's ideas fail to adequately capture how the individual's cultural and social environments form and transform the landscape over the lifetime of the individual. We will now explore these issues in more detail.

niche construction The active shaping and modification of individuals' environments by the individuals' own behaviors, activities, and choices.

Niche Construction

Developmentalists are becoming increasingly aware of how children actively contribute to their own development. **Niche construction** is the term that developmentalists use to refer to how the behaviors, activities, and choices of individuals actively shape the environments (*niches*) in which they live. Take the example of an unusually quiet and nondemanding infant girl who may receive little social interaction and stimulation from her busy family simply because she seems content to be by herself. When she enters school, her social and communication skills may be lacking, making it hard for her to join group play and contributing to her further social withdrawal and isolation. Or think about a 10-year-old boy who wants to be just like his big brother—a gang member. He follows his brother around and hangs out on the fringe of the group, trying to talk, dress, and act in ways that would please them. Naturally, because his time and attention are spent in this way, he is not exposed to alternate contexts that may provide other, healthier avenues for his development.

In different ways, the behaviors of both these children dramatically affect the very environments in which they are developing. In this respect, the children play active roles in the process of niche construction (Lewontin, 2001; Parker, 2005; Torday & Miller, 2016). It is important to note, however, that niche construction is a social, not an individual, process. The quiet baby, for example, may have fared quite differently in a less busy family, in which a parent, grandparent, or other caregiver took a great deal of pleasure and time interacting with the quiet, companionable baby. Developmentalists use the term **co-construction** to capture the way that environments are shaped and reshaped through interactions between developing individuals and their caregivers, siblings, neighbors, and playmates.

co-construction The shaping of environments through interactions between children and their caregivers, siblings, neighbors, and friends.

Ecological Inheritance

You know from Chapter 1 that the term *ecology* refers to the relationship between individuals and their environments and that Bronfenbrenner proposed a *bioecological model* to explain how children develop at the center of nested, interacting social systems. Developmentalists interested in the foundations of human development have found it useful to return to a more expansive definition of ecology, one that includes not only children's social environments but their physical environments as well. This broader definition has encouraged scientists to explore the complex relationships between children and the environments in which they develop.

The term **ecological inheritance** refers to how niche construction can result in environmental modifications that affect the development of offspring and descendants. Such modifications take place when individuals or families elect to move to new places or when large groups of people migrate from one area to another—a behavior that ecologists refer to as *selection of habitat*. For example, if a young couple moves from a rural to an urban environment (habitat), they reconstruct the niche in which their children, and perhaps many future generations, will live and develop. This reconstruction occurs on a larger level when groups of people migrate to a new land in order to escape environmental disaster, oppression, or violence or to seek economic, educational, or political opportunities.

ecological inheritance Environmental modifications, as a result of niche construction, that affect the development of offspring and descendants.

The modifications that descendants inherit may also come about through *changes to the existing habitat*. Some examples include structural changes, such as building homes, subway systems, or schools. Other examples include depleting resources or introducing toxins—frequent consequences of human activity (for example, cutting down forests for building materials or polluting water sources with industrial waste).

Whether through selection of habitat or changes to the existing habitat, it is the niche-constructing behaviors and lifestyles of individuals that bring about the modified environments that are passed on to offspring and descendants through the process of ecological inheritance. Recent research undertaken from an ecological perspective has demonstrated the remarkable and sensitive connections between human behavior and the developing individual's genotype and phenotype. These connections become especially apparent in light of arguments regarding how our biological and cultural inheritances have coevolved.

APPLY > CONNECT > DISCUSS

If you could clone a child from your own exact genes and thereby create a genetic twin, how would this twin be the same as or different from you? Why?

In what ways does your own behavior shape your environment? How might this affect your children?

In human beings, language is a highly canalized trait, whereas intelligence appears to have greater plasticity. Why does this make sense from an evolutionary standpoint?

LEARNING OUTCOMES

Explain how culture and biology interact in the process of evolution.

Point out how lactose tolerance and sickle-cell anemia are examples of the coevolution of biology and culture.

The Coevolution of Culture and Biology

For many years it was believed that the biological and cultural characteristics of humans developed in a strict sequence: The biological capacities we associate with humanity evolved to a critical point at which humans became capable of developing language and generating culture. Now, however, the situation is believed to have been far more complicated. Contemporary studies of human origins have found evidence that rudimentary forms of culture were already present during early phases of human evolution. *Australopithecus* relatives of those who left the famous Laetoli footprints domesticated fire, built shelters, engaged in organized hunting, and used tools—flint knives, cooking utensils, and notation systems.

coevolution The combined process that emerges from the interaction of biological evolution and cultural evolution.

Baldwin effect The role of cultural factors in determining which phenotypes are adaptive.

Developmentalists are becoming increasingly aware of how culture and biology interact in a process of **coevolution** (Cousins, 2014; Lansing & Cox, 2011; Richerson & Boyd, 2005). Interestingly, the idea is a rather old one in the developmental sciences. James Mark Baldwin, whom we introduced in Chapter 1, proposed that cultural factors might influence the likelihood that people with various mental and physical qualities will survive and reproduce. His idea has been recently resurrected and dubbed the **Baldwin effect** (Cousins, 2014; DeJager, 2016). Cultural evolution and transmission of information about how to obtain and preserve food, how to make shelters, and how to heal the sick and injured are obvious examples of how cultural practices contribute to reproductive success. Individuals who have access to these types of cultural tools are more likely to live to reproductive maturity and to pass on both their genes and their cultural knowledge to the next generation. Insofar as the capacity to engage in cultural activities and make use of culture's material and symbolic tools confers a selective reproductive advantage, it is probable that the more effective users of culture have been more successful in passing on their genes to succeeding generations. In short, the two forms of evolution, biological and cultural, have interacted and coevolved, as we illustrate below with two famous examples.

Lactose Tolerance

Our first example of the coevolution of biology and culture comes from a study of *lactose tolerance*—that is, the ability to digest fresh milk (Heyer et al., 2011; Jablonka & Lamb, 2005). Following the domestication of cattle some 6,000 years ago, humans began to use milk, cheese, and other dairy products for food. However, despite the popular notion that milk is the "perfect food," most adults in the world are unable to profit from its nutritional content and get indigestion and diarrhea if they drink it. This is because they cannot produce a sufficient amount of lactase, an enzyme that is needed to break down the milk sugar lactose. The ability to produce lactase is present in virtually all newborn mammals, including humans, but it normally declines after weaning. Nevertheless, some adults can digest milk because they have a variant allele of the gene responsible for producing lactase, and this allele overrides the normal postweaning shutdown of lactase production. The variant allele occurs commonly among those of European descent, as well as those from cultures in which there is a selection pressure for adults to benefit from milk consumption. Pastoral nomads of the Middle East and Africa are an example. Hunger and thirst were probably very common among these groups, so animals that had been originally domesticated for meat became a source of food and drink in the form of fresh milk. In these "dairying cultures," those with the variant lactase allele were more likely to survive and have children, thus passing on the genetic capacity for digesting milk.

Art Wolfe/Science Source

Quechua child-care practices illustrate the coevolution of culture and biology. In their extremely cold environment, parents who use the cultural practices of infant swaddling and carrying are more likely to have surviving offspring and thus are more likely to pass both their genes and their cultural knowledge to the next generation.

In Scandinavian countries, more than 90 percent of the adult population has the variant lactase allele. But in this case, the selective advantage is related to the fact that lactose, like vitamin D, aids in the absorption of calcium. In sunny regions, exposure to the sun produces enough vitamin D to ensure that people absorb sufficient calcium to avoid rickets and other bone diseases. However, in the northern climes of Scandinavia, where the hours of sunlight are scant during the winter and people are well-bundled against the cold, lactose enables people to absorb vitamin D without much exposure to the sun. Interestingly, many Scandinavian myths and legends feature cows as sacred creatures and milk as a food of the gods and a source of strength.

Sickle-Cell Anemia

Another example of the coevolution of biology and culture involves the recessive-gene disorder known as *sickle-cell anemia*. People who inherit the recessive gene for this disorder from both parents, and thus are homozygous for it, have seriously abnormal red blood cells. Normally, red blood cells are disc-shaped, smooth, and flexible, but in people with sickle-cell anemia, they are more rigid and sticky, with a curved, sickle shape (Figure 2.11). Particularly when the supply of oxygen

extender_01/Shutterstock

FIGURE 2.11 Normal, round, red blood cells, and sickle-shaped red blood cells associated with sickle-cell anemia.

to the blood is reduced, as it may be at high altitudes, after heavy physical exertion, during a fever, or while under anesthesia, these abnormal blood cells tend to clump together and clog the body's smaller blood vessels, damaging affected organs and causing severe pain (National Heart, Lung, and Blood Institute, 2016). Because of their characteristics, sickle cells are prone to rupturing and die off much more quickly than normal red blood cells do, often resulting in chronic anemia. Complications of sickle-cell anemia may also lead to early death. People who are heterozygous for the sickle-cell gene are said to have the *sickle-cell trait* and usually do not suffer symptoms.

Sickle-cell anemia is found most prominently among people of African descent. In the United States, the incidence of the sickle-cell trait among African Americans is about 8 to 9 percent. But in West Africa, the incidence of the sickle-cell trait is greater than 20 percent (Oyeku, Raphael, Cassell, & Hulihan, 2016). This difference is explained in large part by the fact that carriers of the sickle-cell trait are highly resistant to the parasite that causes malaria. Much of the West African coast is infested with malaria-carrying mosquitoes because the cultural practice of cutting down vast forests has radically increased their habitat and reproductive success. Needless to say, West Africans who carry the sickle-cell gene are at a selective advantage because they are less likely to suffer from malaria, which can be deadly, and are more likely to survive to reproduce. Because of this selective advantage, the frequency of the sickle-cell gene has been maintained in the West African population despite the losses caused by the deaths of homozygous carriers. In the United States, where the sickle-cell trait confers no advantage, it is gradually being eliminated from the gene pool.

APPLY > CONNECT > DISCUSS

Think of some examples from your own cultural practices that may contribute to our species' evolution.

LEARNING OUTCOMES

Appraise the Laetoli footprints as an example of a human biocultural foundation.

Looking Ahead

We began this chapter by piecing together a scene from an ancient world. We asked how our evolutionary forebears experienced that world and how their lives and experiences were similar to yet different from our own. An understanding of our biocultural foundations, we argued, provides insight into both why all children follow a common path of biological and cultural development and why each child is nevertheless distinct from all others. Indeed, as we explained throughout the chapter, the complex interplay between commonality and distinctiveness, similarity and diversity assures that our biological and cultural heritages are passed on to subsequent generations but continue to evolve through time.

Although we have no way of knowing what happened to the individuals whose footprints on the world would survive for 3 million years, it is interesting to speculate about their fate in light of contemporary knowledge of the coevolution of our biological and cultural inheritances. The thick ash that recorded their steps suggests that volcanic activity was affecting their physical habitat, probably limiting food and water resources. So why was their pace so unhurried? Perhaps they, and others like them, were used to volcanic eruptions, and were able, for a time at least, to eke out a life with the food and water resources available to them. We know, however, that under such circumstances, their reproductive success would have been more restricted than it would have been in resource-rich environments, and their contributions to the human gene pool and cultural toolkit would have been more limited. But perhaps they were in the process of migrating to a new habitat with better resources and more opportunities to reproduce—biologically and culturally. If so, was this because the particular individuals were phenotypically uncommonly intelligent or had personality traits that encouraged their migration in the face of environmental destruction?

We may never know the answers to these questions. However, the accumulating knowledge of the ways in which biology and culture interact inspires us to consider ourselves in light of our biocultural foundations. The complex interactions between biology and culture are present at the very beginning of each life, when genes in the zygote start to express themselves and guide the creation of new cells that will ultimately result in a unique human being. Chapter 3 follows the course of this development from the moment the genetic material of the mother and father come together. In later chapters, as we follow the general patterns of the development of children, you will encounter many instances of the elegant dance between biology and culture.

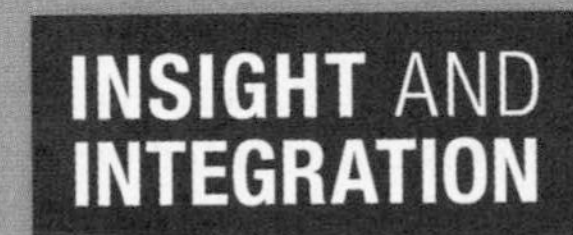

1. Explain how global changes in climate, the migration of people, and access to technologies such as the Internet may be influencing biological and cultural diversity. What are some of the pros and cons associated with these effects?
2. Scientific study has led to astonishing advances in genetic testing and prenatal diagnosis. What are some issues that cannot be solved by science? How would you go about addressing them?

Summary

Inheriting Culture

- Culture is defined by the use of material and symbolic tools that accumulate over time, are passed on through social processes, and provide resources for the developing child. Material tools are observable and include manufactured objects and patterns of behavior. Symbolic tools are more abstract and include systems of knowledge, beliefs, and values. Both types of tools provide resources for development by mediating children's behavior—that is, by organizing children's activities, including how children relate to their environment.
- Culture is inherited through social processes whereby children learn to use their culture's tools. These processes include social enhancement, in which children make use of tools simply because they are available; imitation, in which children copy the tool-using behaviors of others; and explicit instruction, which involves language and other symbolic communication. The use of symbolic communication, which is claimed to be uniquely human, allows children to learn about things not immediately present in the environment and about abstractions such as spiritual belief systems.
- Cultures change through the process of cumulative cultural evolution, as individuals produce variations in both material tools (e.g., the production of new technologies) and symbolic tools (e.g., modification of belief systems and the introduction of new knowledge). This process of change is complex and messy, not a harmonious pattern of progress.

Biological Inheritance

- Biological evolution is made possible by heredity—the transmission of genes from parents to offspring. Genes contain instructions that guide the formation of the individual's traits. The genotype (the individual's particular set of genes) strongly influences the phenotype (the individual's actual traits) but does not completely determine the phenotype, which is also strongly influenced by the individual's environment.
- Natural selection is the process whereby individuals with phenotypes well adapted to the local environment survive and reproduce to a greater extent than do individuals with less well-adapted phenotypes, preferentially passing on the genotypes associated with the better-adapted phenotypes. Over many generations, the more adaptive variations of phenotypic traits increase in the species as a whole, while the less adaptive variations decrease. The emergence of shorter pregnancies in our prehuman ancestors is an example of the process of natural selection.
- Humans reproduce through sexual reproduction: The 23 chromosomes in the mother's ovum and the 23 chromosomes

in the father's sperm are combined at conception, when ovum and sperm fuse to form a zygote with 23 pairs of corresponding chromosomes, 46 in all. A chromosome is a molecule of DNA; a gene is a segment of a chromosome, a working subunit of DNA.

- The sperm and ova are called germ cells; all the other cells of the body are called somatic cells. New somatic cells, each with 46 chromosomes in 23 pairs identical to those in the zygote, are constantly formed through mitosis. New germ cells, each with only 23 chromosomes, are formed through meiosis.
- A child's sex is determined by the chromosomes of the 23rd pair: A female has two X chromosomes, and a male has an X and a Y chromosome.
- A person who inherits the same form of a gene (the same allele) from both parents is homozygous for the trait influenced by that gene; a person who inherits different alleles is heterozygous. When a person is heterozygous for a particular trait, three outcomes are possible:
    - One allele is dominant (the person fully expresses the characteristics associated with that allele), and the other is recessive (the person does not express the characteristics associated with the allele but can pass the allele on to offspring).
    - The person expresses characteristics intermediate between those associated with each allele.
    - The alleles are codominant (the person fully expresses the characteristics associated with each allele).
- Mutations—alterations in the structure of an individual's DNA—can be passed on to the next generation if they occur in germ cells. Mutation is the only process that can add new genes to the gene pool and thus is an important source of variation of genotypes. However, most mutations are harmful or even lethal, not adaptive.
- A number of tests are available to screen for or diagnose genetic disorders, including amniocentesis, chorionic villus sampling (CVS), and tests using blood samples from the mother or the infant. Genetic counselors can help parents understand testing procedures, interpret test results, and make informed plans and decisions if a genetic abnormality is diagnosed.
- Disorders related to genetic abnormalities may result from genes inherited through normal processes of inheritance (for example, phenylketonuria) or from a breakdown in the process of genetic transmission affecting the chromosomes in a germ cell (for example, Down syndrome, Klinefelter syndrome).
- The extent to which the genotype determines any specific phenotypic trait depends on the plasticity of the trait: Traits with high plasticity are easily influenced by the environment, whereas traits with little plasticity always develop in much the same way, regardless of the environment. Traits, such as language acquisition, that are extremely resistant to environmental influences are said to be canalized.
- The heritability of a trait is the amount of phenotypic variation on the trait in a given population that is due to genetic differences. Statistical methods are used to estimate heritability, which is assessed through several types of kinship studies—namely, family, twin, and adoption studies.
- Traits are also influenced by the individual's own activities, as can be seen in the phenomena of niche construction, in which individuals actively shape their environments, and ecological inheritance, in which niche construction results in modified environments that affect the development of subsequent generations.

The Coevolution of Culture and Biology

- Culture and biology interact in the process of coevolution, whereby cultural factors influence the likelihood that people with certain genetically influenced mental and physical traits will survive and reproduce. For example, in certain populations, coevolution has favored the survival of individuals with the genes responsible for lactose tolerance and for sickle-cell anemia, which are advantageous because of cultural and environmental factors.

Looking Ahead

- The complex interplay of culture and biology ensures that both heritages of a child are passed on to subsequent generations and that both continue to evolve.

Key Terms

culture, p. 51
material tools, p. 52
symbolic tools, p. 52
mediation, p. 53
social enhancement, p. 53
imitation, p. 53
explicit instruction, p. 53
cumulative cultural evolution, p. 55
heredity, p. 57
genes, p. 57
genotype, p. 57
phenotype, p. 57
natural selection, p. 57
chromosome, p. 58
DNA (deoxyribonucleic acid), p. 58
zygote, p. 59
germ cells, p. 59
somatic cells, p. 59
mitosis, p. 59
meiosis, p. 59
monozygotic (MZ) twins, p. 60
dizygotic (DZ) twins, p. 60
X chromosome, p. 60
Y chromosome, p. 60
allele, p. 61
homozygous, p. 61
heterozygous, p. 61
dominant allele, p. 61
recessive allele, p. 61
carriers, p. 61
codominance, p. 61
polygenic inheritance, p. 61
mutation, p. 62
gene pool, p. 62
preconception tests, p. 62
prenatal tests, p. 62
amniocentesis, p. 62
chorionic villus sampling (CVS), p. 64
noninvasive prenatal diagnosis (NIPD), p. 64
phenotypic plasticity, p. 67
canalized, p. 68
heritability, p. 68
kinship studies, p. 69
family study, p. 69
twin study, p. 69
adoption study, p. 69
niche construction, p. 70
co-construction, p. 71
ecological inheritance, p. 71
coevolution, p. 72
Baldwin effect, p. 72

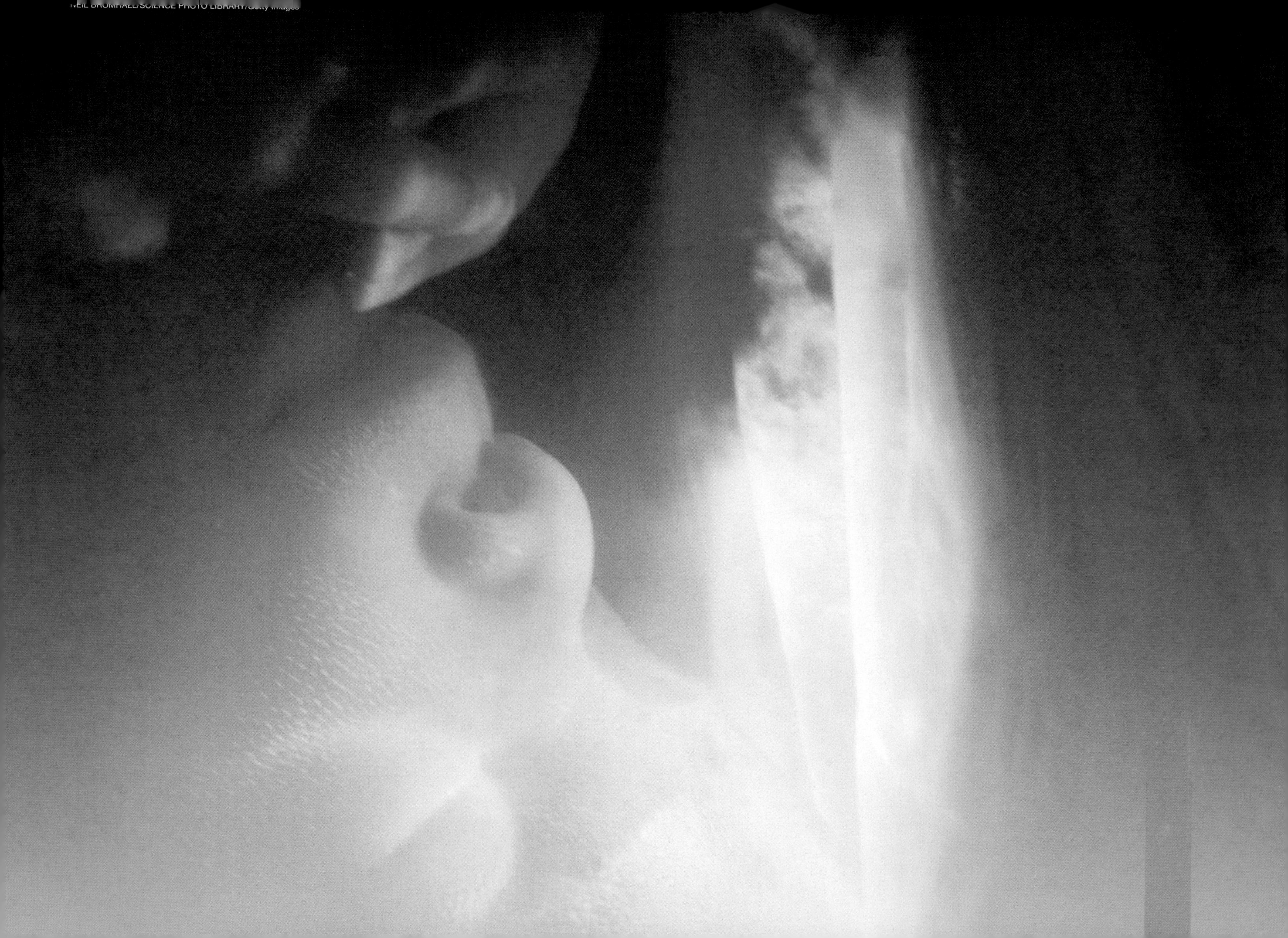

NEIL BROMHALL/SCIENCE PHOTO LIBRARY/Getty Images

CHAPTER

3

Prenatal Development and Birth

Raised in the Hmong community of Laos, Foua Lee is pregnant for the 10th time. According to her culture's beliefs, the health of her unborn child is critically dependent on the satisfaction of her food cravings. Unmet cravings for ginger, for example, can result in the baby being born with an extra finger or toe; unmet cravings for chicken flesh may cause the baby to have a blemish near its ear; and if Foua craves but does not eat eggs, the baby's head may be lumpy. At the first pangs of labor, Foua will hurry to her house, or to the house of her husband's cousins to avoid being attacked and hurt by an evil spirit. There will be no one with Foua when the baby is born. She will deliver the baby by reaching between her legs to ease out the head and then letting the rest of the body slip out onto her arms. After the birth, the father, Nao Kao, will bury the placenta in a hole that he digs in the dirt floor of their home. According to the Hmong, the placenta is a "jacket" for the soul. When a Hmong person dies, his or her soul travels back to the burial place of the placenta, puts on the jacket in which it was born and, thus protected, continues a dangerous journey to the land of ancestors. There it will wait until it is summoned to be reborn as the soul of a new baby. Indeed, a few days after their child is born, Foua and Nao Kao arrange a soul-calling ritual; they sacrifice a pig and invite family and friends to help them entice an ancestral spirit to be reborn in their infant's body.

(Information from Fadiman, 2012.)

Foua's beliefs about how to ensure a healthy pregnancy and successful delivery, and her experiences giving birth to her children, sound both foreign and familiar to those of us who have been raised in technologically advanced societies. Foua worries that unmet food cravings may result in particular malformations; we worry that nutritional deficiencies or environmental toxins may harm the developing fetus. Foua gives birth at home, where she feels protected from malevolent spirits; we give birth in hospitals or birthing centers, where we feel protected from potential medical problems. Foua and her family engage in ritual practices that link her newborn to a spiritual ancestral world; we participate in a variety of ritual practices (circumcision, baptism) to welcome, celebrate, and proclaim our babies as members of specific religious communities.

However they may differ in terms of particular beliefs and practices, these examples make clear that, around the globe, bringing children into the world is regarded as a matter of enormous weight and is approached with great care. The special consideration given to pregnancy and childbirth is understandable in light of the fact that some of the most eventful and vulnerable periods of human growth and development occur during the prenatal months and

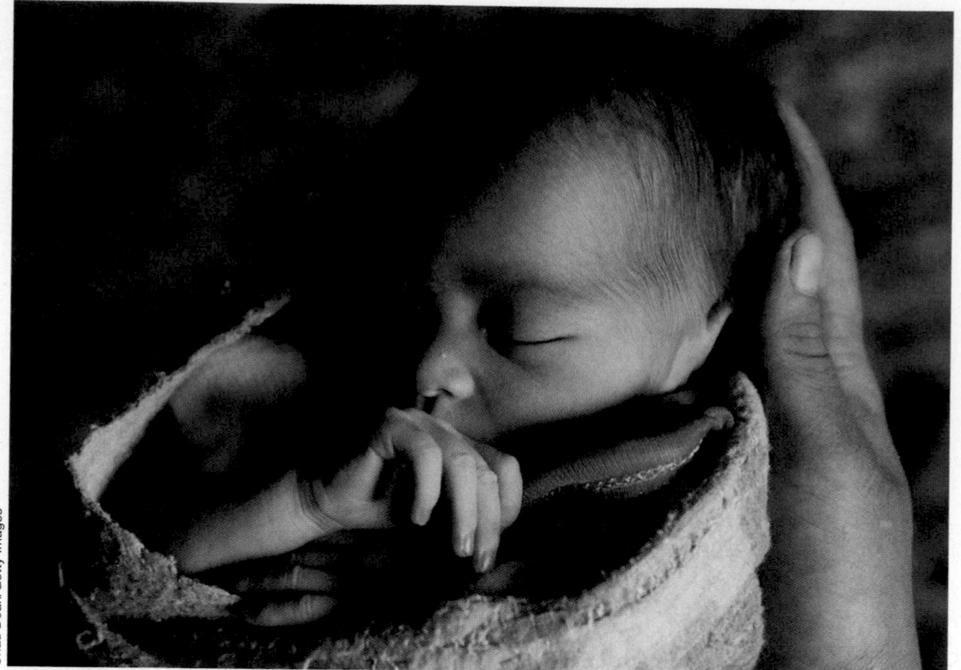

Chau Doan/Getty Images

A newborn Hmong baby boy rests in his mother's arms.

the hours of transition between the womb and the outside world.

As humans, we begin our development as a zygote, a single cell the size of a period on this page, weighing approximately 15 millionths of a gram. At birth only 9 months later, we consist of at least a trillion cells and weigh, on average, 7 pounds (3.2 kilograms). Along with these remarkable changes in size are truly astonishing changes in form (Figure 3.1) and behavior. The first few cells to develop from the zygote are all identical, but within a few weeks, many different kinds of cells will be arranged in intricately structured, interdependent organs. Within a few months, the baby-to-be will move and respond actively to its environment.

The study of prenatal development seeks to explain how these changes in size, form, and behavior take place. This goal is important for both theoretical and practical reasons. On the theoretical side, many scholars believe that development in the prenatal period reflects principles of development that apply in all subsequent periods, from birth to death. For example, development throughout life is characterized by changes both in the form of the organism and in the kinds of interactions the changing organism has with its environment. Following our discussion of prenatal development, we will outline these principles in Table 3.4 (see p. 100).

On the practical side, understanding the prenatal period is important because the developing organism can be positively or adversely affected by the mother-to-be's nutritional status, health, and habits, including whether she uses drugs or alcohol. Considerable research is devoted to promoting healthy prenatal development and preventing damage to the growing organism.

In order to make clear the relationship of development in the womb to later development in the world, we first must trace the changes that take place as the organism progresses from zygote to newborn and examine the environmental factors that support or threaten development. Then we can consider the circumstances surrounding the newborn's entrance into the world.

FIGURE 3.1 Changes in the size and form of the human body from 14 days to 15 weeks after conception. (Research from Arey, 1974.)

1. The fetus develops enclosed in the mother's womb and is born into a radically different environment. Think about some of the behaviors and experiences that newborns need immediately — those associated with feeding, breathing, paying attention to other members of their species, and so forth. What do you suppose might be going on during prenatal development that prepares the newborn to engage in these behaviors and have these experiences? Hold on to your answer to this question; we will return to it at the end of the chapter.
2. As many people know, women should avoid drugs and alcohol during pregnancy because these substances can adversely affect the fetus. In general, the effects can be especially disastrous during the first several months of pregnancy, resulting in serious defects or even fetal death. Why might this be so?

The Periods of Prenatal Development

LEARNING OUTCOMES

Identify the three periods of prenatal development.

Outline the main events in each of the three periods of prenatal development.

The transformations that occur during prenatal development are nothing short of amazing. Through a microscope, the fertilized ovum, or zygote, appears to be made up of small particles inside larger ones. The chromosomes bearing the genes are contained within the nucleus at the center of the cell. Surrounding the nucleus is the cell matter, which serves as the raw material for the first few cell divisions. Within the first few weeks after conception, this single cell subdivides many times to form many kinds of cells with vastly different destinies. In approximately 266 days, these cells will have been transformed into a wriggling, crying infant.

Developmental scientists often divide prenatal development into three broad periods, or trimesters, each characterized by distinctive patterns of growth and interaction between the organism and its environment:

1. The **germinal period** begins at conception and lasts until the developing organism becomes attached to the wall of the uterus, about 8 to 10 days later.
2. The **embryonic period** extends from the time the organism becomes attached to the uterus until the end of the 8th week, when all the major organs have taken primitive shape.
3. The **fetal period** begins the 9th week after conception, with the first signs of the hardening of the bones, and continues until birth. During this period, the primitive organ systems develop to the point where the baby can exist outside the mother without medical support.

germinal period The period that begins at conception and lasts until the developing organism becomes attached to the wall of the uterus about 8 to 10 days later.

embryonic period The period that extends from the time the organism becomes attached to the uterus until the end of the 8th week of pregnancy, when all the major organs have taken primitive shape.

fetal period The period that begins in the 9th week after conception, with the first signs of the hardening of the bones, and continues until birth.

At any step in these prenatal periods, the process of development may stop. One study estimates that approximately 25 percent of all pregnancies end before the woman even recognizes that she is pregnant (Wilcox, Baird, & Weinberg, 1999). If all goes well, however, the creation of a new human being is under way.

The Germinal Period

During the first 8 to 10 days after conception, the zygote moves slowly through the fallopian tube, where fertilization occurred, and into the uterus. The timing of this journey is crucial. If the zygote enters the uterus too soon or too late, the uterine environment will not be hormonally prepared, and the organism will be destroyed.

cleavage A series of mitotic cell divisions that transform a zygote into a blastocyst.

heterochrony Variability in the rates of development of different parts of an organism.

heterogeneity Variability in the levels of development of different parts of an organism at a given time.

totipotent stem cells Cells that have the potential to grow into a complete embryo and, ultimately, to become a normal, healthy infant.

implantation The process by which a developing organism becomes attached to the uterus.

The First Cells of Life

Recall from Chapter 2 (p. 59) that all body cells reproduce through the process of duplication and cell division known as *mitosis*. About 24 hours after conception, as the zygote travels down the fallopian tube, **cleavage** begins: The zygote divides by mitosis into two cells, which then divide into four, and those four divide into eight, and so on (see Figure 3.2). Thanks to this repeated duplication, the developing organism will already consist of hundreds of cells by the time it reaches the uterus. An important characteristic of cleavage is that the cells existing at any given moment do not all divide at the same time. Instead of proceeding in an orderly fashion from a two-cell stage to a four-cell stage, and so on, cells divide at different rates (Tills, Rundle, & Spicer, 2013). This is the first instance of developmental **heterochrony**, whereby different parts of the organism develop at different rates. (*Heterochrony* literally means "variability in time.") This unevenness in rates of development gives rise to **heterogeneity**—variability in the levels of development of different parts of the organism at a given time. The fact that a newborn's sense of hearing is more advanced than his ability to see, for example, means that he will recognize his mother more readily by the sound of her voice than by the way she looks. Both kinds of variability play an important role in the process of development throughout the life of the child.

As illustrated in Figure 3.2, cells formed during the first several cleavages resemble Ping-Pong balls crowded into a balloon. At this very early stage of development, all these cells are **totipotent** ("totally potent") **stem cells**, meaning that each has the potential to grow into an embryo and, ultimately, to become a normal, healthy baby (Altamura et al., 2016). In fact, identical twins develop when this single mass of totipotent cells separates into two cell masses, which then develop into two individual, genetically identical human beings. Such developmental freedom at the cellular level—the ability to develop into virtually any type of human cell and, consequently, into an entirely distinct human being—is unique to this very early period of cell division. Thereafter, the development potential of stem cells becomes limited. Stem cells are harbored in various tissues and organs for making repairs, and they can only develop into cells related to the specific tissues and organs they are part of. A stem cell in the brain, for instance, can become different sorts of neural cells (a neuron or glial cell) but not a bone or liver cell. Because they are capable of becoming different types of cells only within a closely related family of cells, adult stem cells are referred to as *multipotent stem cells*. As you are probably aware, many scientists believe that stem cells (both totipotent and multipotent) have the potential to be used therapeutically to replace damaged cells associated with myriad diseases, including heart disease, leukemia and other cancers, Parkinson's disease, and type 1 diabetes.

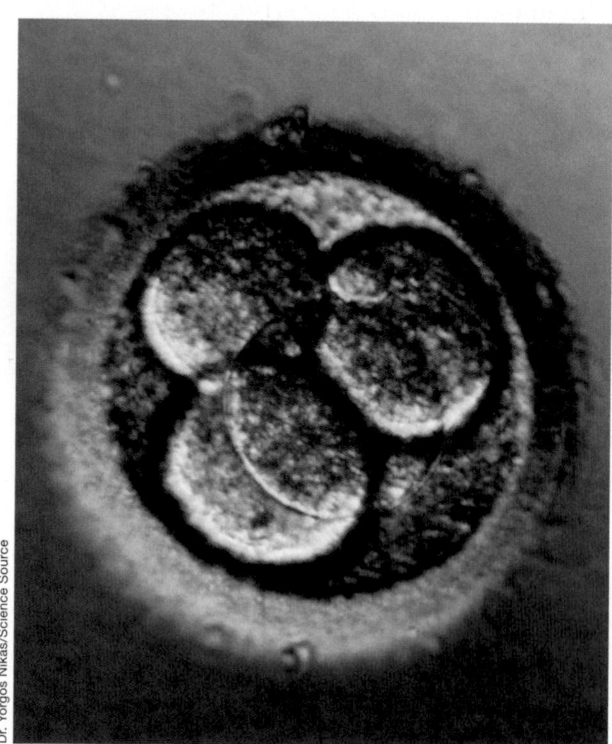
Dr. Yorgos Nikas/Science Source

FIGURE 3.2 A zygote after two cleavages, resulting in four cells of equal size and appearance.

Implantation

As the developing cell mass moves farther into the uterus, the outer cells put out tiny branches that burrow into the spongy wall of the uterus until they come into contact with the mother's blood vessels. This is the beginning of **implantation**, the process by which the developing organism becomes attached to the uterus. Implantation marks the transition between the germinal and embryonic periods. Like many other transitions, such as birth itself, implantation is hazardous for the organism, and the spontaneous termination of pregnancy during this process is common.

The Embryonic Period

If the developing organism is successfully implanted, it enters the embryonic period, which lasts for about 6 weeks. During this time, all the basic organs of the body take shape, and the embryo begins to respond to direct stimulation. The organism's rapid growth during this period is facilitated by the efficient way in which the mother now supplies nutrition and protects the organism from harmful environmental influences.

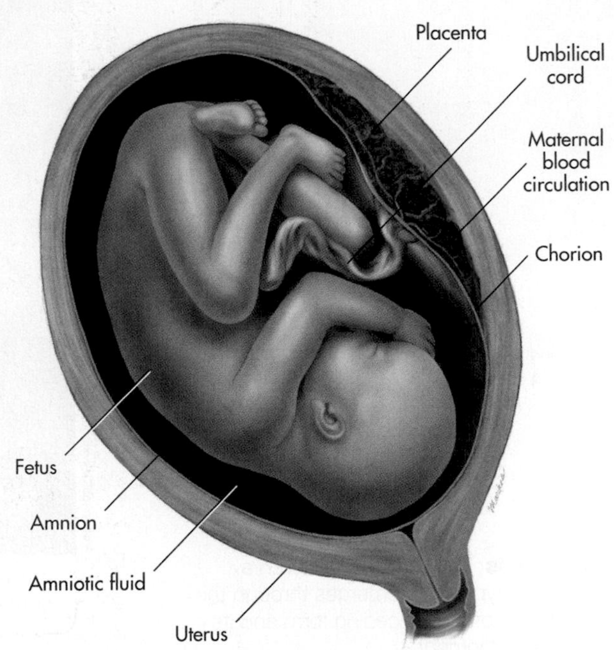

FIGURE 3.3 The fetus in its protective environment. (Research from Curtis, 1979.)

Sources of Nutrition and Protection

Early in the embryonic period, the **amnion**, a thin, tough, transparent membrane that holds the *amniotic fluid*, surrounds the embryo. (The amnion and the fluid are often called the "bag of waters.") The amniotic fluid cushions the organism as the mother moves about, provides liquid support for its weak muscles and soft bones, and gives it a medium in which it can move and change position.

Surrounding the amnion is another membrane, the **chorion**, which later becomes the fetal component of the **placenta**, a complex organ made up of tissue from both the mother and the embryo (Figure 3.3). Attached to the uterine wall, the placenta acts simultaneously as a barrier and a filter, preventing the bloodstreams of the mother and the embryo (and later the fetus) from coming into direct contact with each other, while at the same time allowing critical exchanges to occur between them. By means of this barrier/filter system, the placenta provides the embryo with nutrients and oxygen carried by the mother's blood and also enables the embryo's waste products to be absorbed by the mother's bloodstream, from which they are eventually extracted by her kidneys. These exchanges take place through the **umbilical cord**, a flexible, helical structure with a vein for carrying oxygen- and nutrient-rich blood from the placenta to the embryo and two main arteries for carrying depleted blood from the embryo back to the placenta (Heifetz, 1996). The umbilical cord is approximately 20 inches (51 centimeters) long and is filled with a gelatinous substance called *Wharton's jelly*, which contributes to its flexibility, allowing it to twist and turn as the fetus moves and grows.

amnion A thin, tough, transparent membrane that holds the amniotic fluid and surrounds the embryo.

chorion A membrane that surrounds the amnion and becomes the fetal component of the placenta.

placenta An organ made up of tissue from both the mother and the fetus that serves as a barrier and filter between their bloodstreams.

umbilical cord A flexible helical structure containing blood vessels that connects the developing organism to the placenta.

ectoderm Cells of the inner cell mass of the embryo that develop into the outer surface of the skin, the nails, part of the teeth, the lens of the eye, the inner ear, and the central nervous system.

endoderm Cells of the inner cell mass of the embryo that develop into the digestive system and the lungs.

mesoderm Cells of the inner cell mass of the embryo that give rise to the muscles, the bones, the circulatory system, and the inner layers of the skin.

Embryonic Growth

While the outer cells of the developing organism are forming the placenta and the other membranes that will supply and protect the embryo, the growing number of cells in the inner cell mass begin to differentiate into the various kinds of cells that eventually become all the organs of the body. The first step in this process is the separation of the inner cell mass into two layers. The **ectoderm**, the outer layer, gives rise to the outer surface of the skin, the nails, part of the teeth, the lens of the eye, the inner ear, and the central nervous system (the brain, the spinal cord, and the nerves). The **endoderm**, the inner layer, develops into the digestive system and the lungs. Shortly after these two layers form, a middle layer, the **mesoderm**, appears; it eventually becomes the muscles, the bones, the circulatory system, and the inner layers of the skin (Rivera-Mulia et al., 2015).

One of nature's greatest mysteries is the process through which a few identical stem cells with unlimited developmental capacity evolve into a highly differentiated cell community composed of specialized parts. What causes a cell to act like part of the endoderm rather than the exoderm or mesoderm and, later, to form liver tissue rather than pancreas or colon tissue? Scientists estimate that each cell contains something on the order of 25,000 genes, the vast majority of which remain inactive as the cell develops into its specialized phenotypic role—as part of the pancreas,

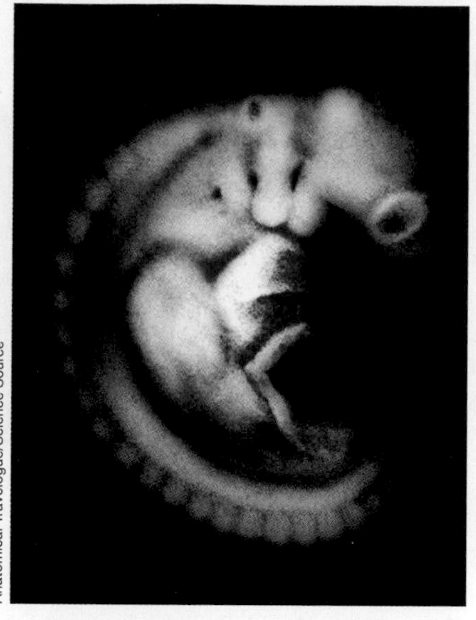

The human embryo at 3 weeks after conception.

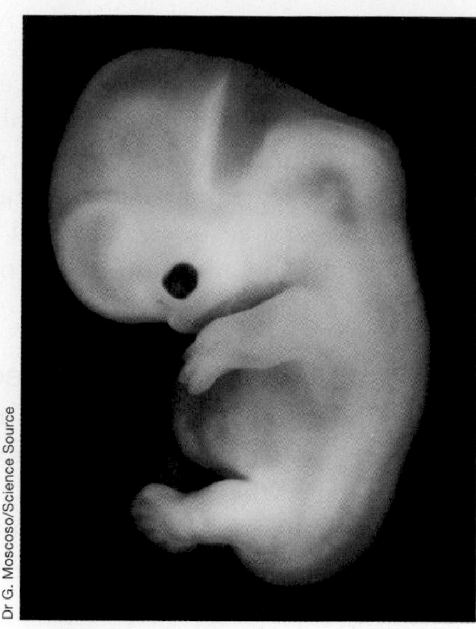

The human embryo at 5 weeks after conception.

epigenesis The process by which a new phenotypic form emerges through the interactions of the preceding form and its current environment.

cephalocaudal pattern The pattern of development that proceeds from the head down.

proximodistal pattern The pattern of development that proceeds from the middle of the organism out to the periphery.

liver, or colon, for example. Current explanations emphasize the idea that each new phenotypic form emerges as a result of the interactions that take place between the preceding form and its environment, a process called **epigenesis** (from the Greek, meaning "at the time of generation") (Lickliter, 2013). And what is the environment of a cell? In part, a cell's environment consists of surrounding cells, which exchange information and regulate each other's gene activities. Thus, a stem cell "knows" it should act like part of the endoderm because surrounding endoderm cells have "told" it to do so through the release of special signaling proteins. Interestingly, the signals from the surrounding cells do not appear to communicate which genes should be turned on; rather, they indicate which genes—those relevant to forming liver or pancreas tissue, for instance—should remain inactive (Boyer et al., 2005). According to the epigenetic explanation of embryonic development, the different interactions that cells have with their environmental conditions (including each other) is what leads to the creation of new kinds of cells and subsequent new forms of interactions between the organism and the environment (Lickliter, 2017) (Figure 3.4).

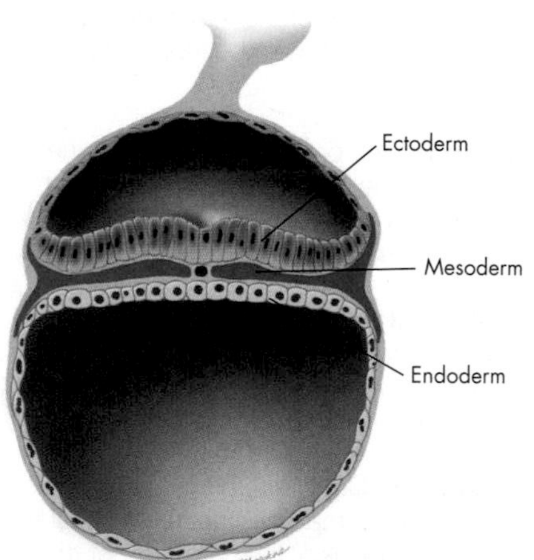

FIGURE 3.4 Within days of fertilization, a highly organized cell community develops. Distinct parts of the community are identified according to their location and the specialized functions they will take on. The ectoderm (outer layer) will develop functions associated with the growth of the skin, nails, and nervous system. The endoderm (inner layer) will develop functions associated with the digestive system and lungs. The mesoderm (middle layer) will develop functions associated with the growth of the muscles, bones, the circulatory system, and the inner layers of the skin.

The embryo develops at a breathtaking pace, as you can see in Table 3.1. The table also reflects two patterns of body development that are maintained until the organism reaches adolescence. In the first, the **cephalocaudal pattern**, development proceeds from the head down. The arm buds, for instance, appear before the leg buds. In the second, the **proximodistal pattern**, development proceeds from the middle of the organism out to the periphery. Thus, the spinal cord develops before the arm buds; the upper arm develops before the forearm; and so on. In general, the process of organ formation is the same for all human embryos, but in one major respect—sexual differentiation—it varies.

Sexual Differentiation As described in Chapter 2 (pp. 60–61), the genes that influence sexual determination are located on the X and Y chromosomes inherited at conception. Zygotes with one X and one Y chromosome are genetically

TABLE 3.1 Growth and Development of the Embryo

Days 10–13

Cells separate into ectoderm, endoderm, and mesoderm layers. The neural plate, which eventually will become the brain and the spinal cord, forms out of the ectoderm.

3rd Week

The three major divisions of the brain — the hindbrain, the midbrain, and the forebrain — begin to differentiate by the end of the third week. Primitive blood cells and blood vessels are present. The heart comes into being, and by the end of the week it is beating.

4th Week

Limb buds are visible. Eyes, ears, and a digestive system begin to take form. The major veins and arteries are completed. Vertebrae are present, and nerves begin to take primitive form.

5th Week

The umbilical cord takes shape. Bronchial buds, which eventually will become the lungs, take form. Premuscle masses are present in the head, trunk, and limbs. The hand plates are formed.

6th Week

The head becomes dominant in size. The halves of the lower jawbone meet and fuse, and the components of the upper jaw are present. The external ear makes its appearance. The three main parts of the brain are distinct.

7th Week

The face and neck are beginning to take form. Eyelids take shape. The stomach is taking its final shape and position. Muscles are rapidly differentiating throughout the body and are assuming their final shapes and relationships. The brain is developing thousands of nerve cells per minute.

8th Week

The growth of the gut makes the body evenly round. The head is elevated, and the neck is distinct. The external, middle, and inner ears assume their final forms. By the end of this week, the fetus is capable of some movement and responds to stimulation around the mouth.

male, and zygotes with two X chromosomes are genetically female. For the first 6 weeks after conception, there is no structural difference between genetically male and genetically female embryos. Both males and females have two ridges of tissue, called *gonadal ridges*, from which the male and female sex organs (*gonads*) will develop. Initially, these ridges give no clue to the sex of the embryo. Then in the 7th week, if the embryo is genetically male (XY), the process of sexual differentiation begins with the gonadal ridges beginning to form testes (Schoenwolf, Bleyl, Brauer, & Francis-West, 2015). If the embryo is genetically female (XX), no changes are apparent in the gonadal ridges until several weeks later, when ovaries begin to form.

It is not genes, however, but hormones that determine whether the embryo subsequently develops male or female external genitalia. The male gonads produce high levels of hormones called *androgens*, chief among which is *testosterone*. (Females also produce testosterone but in much smaller quantities.) If enough testosterone is present, a penis and scrotum develop; otherwise, female external genitalia are formed. Very rarely, errors in sex development (for example, too little testosterone in males or too much in females) result in a baby having sex organs that show characteristics of both sexes.

Interestingly, the influence of prenatal androgens is not limited to the gonads and the genital tract, nor is it limited to the prenatal period. For example, female embryos that produce higher levels of testosterone tend to have slower brain growth, as measured by head circumference at birth, compared with

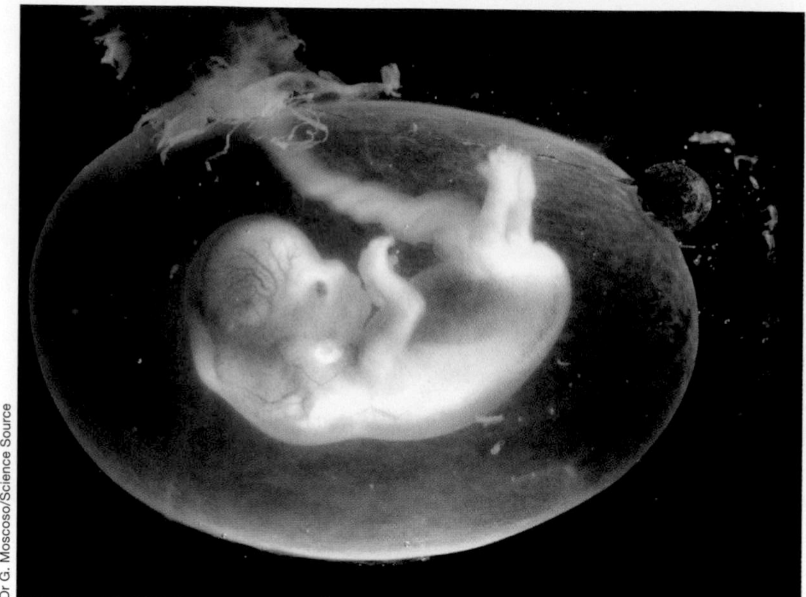

Dr G. Moscoso/Science Source

FIGURE 3.5 This fetus is approximately 9 weeks old. It is attached to the placenta and the mother's blood circulation by the umbilical cord and floating in an amniotic sac filled with fluid. The round, red structure is the remnant of the yolk sac. The embryo's eye and limbs are visible, as is its male sex.

those that produce lower levels (Whitehouse, Maybery, Hart, & Sloboda, 2010). Moreover, some studies have suggested that the effects of prenatal androgens can extend well into childhood to affect sex-typed play (Auyeung, Baron-Cohen, Ashwin, & Knickmeyer, 2009; Pasterski et al., 2015). For example, one longitudinal study found that 3- to 4-year-old boys who had been prenatally exposed to higher levels of androgen had stronger preferences for boy-type toys and activities — playing with cars rather than dolls, for instance — compared to boys with lower levels of prenatal androgen exposure (Pasterski et al., 2015). Nevertheless, it is important to note that the relationship between fetal testosterone exposure and later "masculinized" play preferences is far from clear and very likely includes substantial input from the child's social environment (Jordan-Young, 2010).

The Fetal Period

The fetal period begins once all the basic tissues and organs exist in rudimentary form and the tissue that will become the skeleton begins to harden, or *ossify* (Moore, Persaud, & Torchia, 2015; Figure 3.5). During the fetal period, which lasts from the 8th or 9th week of pregnancy until birth, the fetus increases in length from approximately 1½ inches to 20 inches (4 centimeters to 51 centimeters) and in weight from approximately 0.02 to 7.1 pounds (0.09 kilograms to 3.2 kilograms).

age of viability The age at which the fetus is able to survive outside the uterus.

Over the course of the fetal period, each of the organ systems increases in complexity. By the 10th week after conception, the intestines have assumed their characteristic position in the body. Two weeks later, the fetus's external sexual characteristics are clearly visible, and its neck is well defined. By the end of 16 weeks, the head is erect, the lower limbs are well developed, and the ears, which began to take form in the 4th week, migrate from the neck to the sides of the head. By the end of the 5th month, the fetus has almost as many nerve cells as it will ever have as a person. By the end of the 7th month, the lungs are capable of breathing air, and the eyes, which have been closed, open and can respond to light. Consequently, the 7th month is often described as the **age of viability** — that is, the age at which the fetus is able to survive outside the uterus. By the end of the 8th month, many folds of the brain are present, enabling brain cells to be packed more efficiently within the skull, and during the 9th month, the brain becomes considerably more wrinkled. In the final weeks before birth, the fetus doubles in weight.

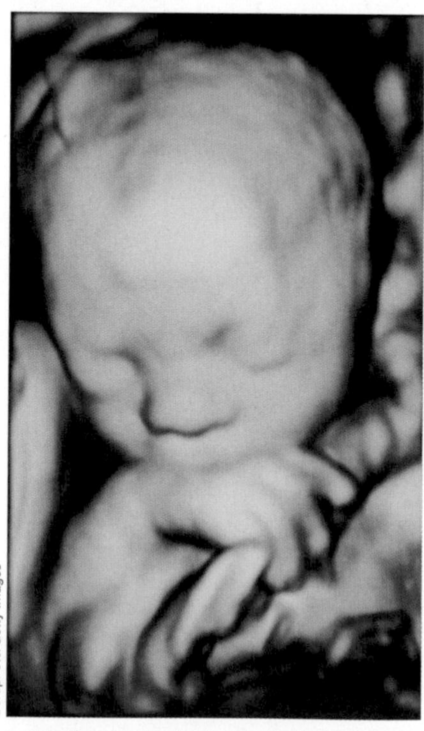

BorupFoto/Getty Images

Modern technologies, including the fetal ultrasound used here, produce such high-quality images of the fetus that a variety of disorders can be identified and, in some cases, surgically corrected long before birth.

The fetal period marks a critical stage during which the baby-to-be becomes responsive to its environment in new ways and is developmentally influenced by factors both inside and outside the uterus. We will now take a look at some of the events that affect fetal development and experience.

Sensory Capacities

Using modern techniques of measurement and recording, researchers have produced a relatively detailed picture of the development of sensory capacities before birth (Hepper, 2015). This information is essential for determining how the uterine environment influences the fetus; it suggests considerable continuity and stability in behavior between the last weeks of gestation and early infancy (Brakke, 2015). Scientists have discovered the following about the fetus's sensory capacities:

- *Touch.* As early as 8 weeks following conception, the fetus begins to respond to tactile contact from itself, the womb and umbilical cord, and, in the case of a multiple pregnancy, from other fetuses (Reissland et al., 2014).
- *Sensing motion.* The vestibular system of the middle ear, which controls the sense of balance, begins to function in the human fetus about 5 months after conception and is fully mature at birth (Lecanuet & Jacquet, 2002). This early maturity means that the fetus is capable of sensing changes in the mother's posture and orienting itself as it floats inside the fluid-filled amniotic sac.
- *Seeing.* Little is known for certain about the extent of the fetus's visual experience. At 26 weeks following conception, if a bright light is held against the mother's abdomen, the fetus may respond with changes in heart rate and movement (Lecanuet & Schaal, 1996). Aidan Macfarlane (1977) suggested that the fetus's visual experience of light that has penetrated the mother's stretched stomach wall may be similar to the glow seen when the palm of the hand covers the lens of a flashlight.
- *Hearing.* The fetus responds to sound at 5 to 6 months after conception (Abrams, Gerhardt, & Antonelli, 1998). Studies in which tiny microphones have been inserted into the uterus adjacent to the fetus's head reveal that the average sound level inside the womb is approximately 75 decibels, about the level at which we hear the outside world when we ride in a car with the windows up. When sounds of moderate or loud intensity are presented in laboratory situations, it is possible to detect changes in the fetus's heart rate (Kisilevsky & Hains, 2010; Morokuma et al., 2008). Background noise from the outside world is punctuated by the sound of air passing through the mother's stomach and, every second or so, by the more intense sound of the mother's heartbeat. Of all such sounds, the mother's voice is heard best because it is also transmitted as vibrations through her body. In what will prove essential to language acquisition, the fetus recognizes *changes* in sound between 6 and 7 months after conception (Draganova et al., 2007).

Fetal Activity Just about any woman who has been pregnant will tell you that the fetus does not float passively in its amniotic fluid. By the end of the 4th month, the mother-to-be can feel her fetus moving around, bumping and rolling against the uterus and sometimes kicking and elbowing—in later weeks, with enough force to make her uncomfortable. By midpregnancy, the movements of the fetus can be felt by placing a hand on the pregnant woman's belly, enchanting expectant parents, as well as brothers- and sisters-to-be.

Actually, movement in the womb occurs long before the mother can detect it. Modern technologies, such as ultrasound, have revealed that embryos become active within 8 weeks following conception. As the embryo enters the fetal stage, its body movements become increasingly varied and coordinated (Table 3.2 on page 88; Robinson & Kleven, 2005). At 15 weeks of age, the fetus is capable of all the movements observable in newborn infants, such as head turning and leg flexing; in fact, the behaviors of newborns are remarkably similar to those of fetuses during the last trimester of pregnancy (Einspieler, Marschik, & Prechtl, 2008; James, Pillai, & Smoleniec, 1995). Evidence indicates that spontaneous fetal activity plays a significant role in development (Hepper, 2015; Reissland et al., 2014). Fetal movements are believed to play

TABLE 3.2 Emergence of Movements in Fetal Development

Movements	Gestational Age (weeks)
Any movement	7
Startle	8
General body movements	8
Hiccups	8
Arm movements	9
Contact between hand and face	10
Breathing	10
Mouth opening	10
Stretching	10
Yawning	11
Sucking and swallowing	12

Data from De Vries, Hay, & Prechtl, 1982.

a similar role in establishing basic neuronal connections in humans (Robinson & Kleven, 2005).

Other prenatal activities that are important to later development include breathing, swallowing, and sucking. The fetus, of course, does not breathe in utero; as noted, it obtains oxygen through the placenta. But it makes certain "breathing" movements with its chest and lungs that help develop the muscles necessary for respiration after birth (Wilson, Olver, & Walters, 2007). It also engages in sucking behaviors, including thumb-sucking (Hepper, Wells, Dornan, & Lynch, 2013). Sucking and swallowing, which will be needed for feeding after birth, begin to occur by 15 weeks and become well coordinated with each other by the third trimester (Miller, Macedonia, & Sonies, 2006). In fact, shortly before birth, the fetus may be swallowing as much as 2 to 4 cups (0.5 to 1 liters) of amniotic fluid per day (Ross & Nyland, 1998). The extensive "practice" of breathing, sucking, and swallowing that occurs in the womb is vital, given that without these behaviors, the newborn cannot survive.

The coordination of fetal breathing, sucking, and swallowing is but one example of how even the earliest behaviors become organized over time into increasingly complex systems (Brakke, 2015). As we discussed in Chapter 1 (p. 27), *dynamic systems theory* helps explain how complex systems of behavior emerge from the interaction of less complex parts — in this instance, how breathing, sucking, and swallowing are coordinated into a system that will be essential to the infant's feeding. Research has also shown that fetal *inactivity* provides important clues to development. From 24 to 32 weeks after conception, the relatively high rate of fetal activity begins to alternate with quiet periods, and there is a gradual overall decrease in the fetus's movements (Kisilevsky & Low, 1998). This shift is believed to reflect the development of neural pathways that inhibit movement. The appearance of these inhibitory pathways is related to maturation in the higher regions of the brain (Figure 3.6). By 38 to 40 weeks after conception, four behavioral states can be identified: quiet and active sleep and quiet and active awake (see Table 3.3; Nijhuis, Prechtl, Martin, & Bots, 1982; Gingras, Mitchell, & Grattan, 2005).

The clearest evidence of these effects comes from studies of sudden periods of famine. In September 1941, during World War II, for example, the German army encircled Leningrad (now St. Petersburg, Russia), and no supplies reached the city until February 1942. The standard daily food ration in late November 1941 was 250 grams of bread (four slices) for factory workers and 125 grams (two slices) for everybody else. The bread was 25 percent sawdust. The number of infants born in the first half of 1942 was much lower than normal, and stillbirths doubled. Very few infants were born in the second half of 1942, all of them to couples who had better access to food than did the rest of the population. These newborns were, on average, more than a pound lighter than babies born before the siege, and they were much more likely to be premature. They were also in very poor condition at birth; they had little vitality and were unable to maintain body temperature adequately (Antonov, 1947). The sudden onset and duration of the famine provided an easy link to the timing of severe prenatal malnutrition and its consequences. Severe nutritional deprivation during the first 3 months of pregnancy was most likely to result in abnormalities of the central nervous system, premature birth, and death. Deprivation during the last 3 months of pregnancy was more likely to retard fetal growth and result in low birth weight.

Studies of the relationships between maternal nutrition, prenatal development, and neonatal health suggest that lesser degrees of undernourishment and malnourishment also increase risks to the fetus. Poor maternal nutrition can lead to low birth weight and even miscarriage (Acharya et al., 2016; Morton, 2006). Research conducted in a number of countries, including Nepal, Finland, Norway, Sweden, the United Kingdom, and the United States, provides ample evidence that poor prenatal nutrition can also have long-term effects, such as increased risk for heart disease, diabetes, strokes, and other illnesses in later life. This association is thought to result from the fetus's adaptation to an inadequate supply of nutrients during a sensitive period in early prenatal life that leads to permanent changes in physiology and metabolism and makes the body extremely efficient in processing nutrients. The body is thus prepared for surviving in a calorie-poor environment. When it instead encounters a persistently normal or rich dietary environment, its fetally reset metabolism becomes a liability that can lead to the aforementioned diseases, which are typically associated with obesity and overweight (Lawlor, Davey Smith, Clark, & Leon, 2006; Mennitti et al., 2015; Thompson & Einstein, 2010; Yajnik, 2014).

However, it is often difficult to isolate the effects of poor nutrition because undernourished and malnourished mothers frequently live in impoverished environments where housing, sanitation, education, and medical care, including prenatal care, are also inadequate. Expectant mothers with low incomes are also more likely to suffer from diseases or simply to be in a weakened state than are women who live in better material circumstances. Their babies are more likely to suffer from a wide variety of birth defects and illnesses and to be born prematurely (Padula et al., 2015). According to a variety of studies conducted in many parts of the world, including the United States, low-income mothers are also more likely to have babies who die at birth or soon after birth (UNICEF, 2015).

Several studies demonstrate that it is possible to prevent or reduce the damaging effects of malnutrition and an impoverished environment. In 1972, the U.S. government initiated one of the largest intervention programs — dubbed WIC (Women, Infants, Children) — to assess the effects of a massive supplemental food program on health and development. Today, low-income women in the program are given nutritious supplemental foods; nutrition education; counseling, including support for breast-feeding; and referrals to agencies providing

large for gestational age Babies whose weight at birth is above the 90th percentile of babies of the same sex who are the same gestational age.

gestational age The amount of time between conception and birth. The normal gestational age is between 37 and 43 weeks.

resources for pregnant and postpartum women and infants and children up to age 5 years (Thorn et al., 2015). In April 2014, 9.3 million women, infants, and children participated in WIC. Extensive research on the impact of WIC regularly shows benefits to participants. Using nationally representative, longitudinal data, one study found that when pregnant women get involved in WIC early in their pregnancies, their children tend to score higher on a test of intellectual development at 2 years of age and on tests of reading and math at 11 years of age (Jackson, 2015).

Although developmentalists have focused most of their attention on how babies' health suffers when their mothers do not get enough nutrients during their pregnancies, they have recently begun to emphasize that fetuses are also at risk when pregnant mothers are *overnourished*, usually as a result of their consuming a high-fat diet (Muhlhausler, S., Gugusheff, Ong, & Vithayathil, 2013). At birth, these babies are often **large for gestational age**; that is, their weight is above the 90th percentile of babies of the same sex who are the same **gestational age** (the amount of time since conception). Usually born to mothers who are diabetic and obese, overweight babies are likely to develop diabetes and obesity themselves.

You may well be thinking that the development of these diseases could be due not to the mother's diet during pregnancy but rather to the child's diet after birth. If so, you would be partially correct: Research has demonstrated that a mother's postnatal eating behavior can affect how much food her child consumes (Gluck et al., 2009). However, other research suggests that the uterine environment is at least partly implicated. Studies of nonhuman mammals (rats, mostly) find that mothers who are fed diets high in fat during pregnancy have offspring at risk for overweight, diabetes, and high blood pressure, as well as anxietylike behavior (Sasaki et al., 2013; Taylor, et al., 2005; Wu et al., 2016).

Developmentalists have expressed concern about the problem of overweight babies in future generations (Lenoir-Wijnkoop et al., 2015). In particular, while the rate of underweight babies has been generally stable, the rate of overweight babies has increased substantially. In the United States, for example, the number of large-for-gestational-age babies increased from 9.3 percent to 11.7 percent between 2000 and 2006. This is a distressing change that foreshadows a number of health problems as these individuals mature (Martin et al., 2008).

These conclusions concerning poor maternal and fetal nutrition must be considered with some caution because they are correlational. However, the overall evidence strongly suggests that millions of children throughout the world are damaged by undernourishment, malnutrition, or overnourishment before birth. Moreover, many of the children who are undernourished or malnourished prenatally also have nutritional and other deprivations in childhood: Most of them do not receive food supplements, and even fewer receive high-quality medical and educational help. Thus, they tend to have a cascade of risk factors in addition to poor maternal and fetal nutrition. Together, such conditions lead to high rates of infant mortality and shorter life expectancies (Pollitt, 2001).

APPLY > CONNECT > DISCUSS

Along with the famine in Leningrad during World War II, the famous Dutch famine of 1944 has provided a wealth of information for scientists interested in the effects of fetal malnourishment on subsequent development. Conduct some online research and explore some of the projects associated with the Dutch Famine Birth Cohort Study. What are some of the questions currently addressed by the study? What are some of the most recent findings?

Teratogens: Environmental Sources of Birth Defects

LEARNING OUTCOMES

Identify six general principles that apply to all teratogens.

Outline some common teratogens that may influence development during the prenatal periods.

Describe potential effects of various teratogens on the well-being of a child.

Other threats to the prenatal organism come from **teratogens**—environmental agents such as toxins, disease, drugs, and alcohol that increase the risk of deviations in normal development and can lead to serious abnormalities or death. Although the effects of teratogens on the developing organism vary with the specific agent involved, six general principles apply to all of them (Moore et al., 2015):

teratogens Environmental agents that can cause deviations from normal development and can lead to abnormalities or death.

1. A developing organism's susceptibility to a teratogenic agent depends on its developmental stage at the time of exposure. Overall, the gravest danger to life comes during the first 2 weeks, before the cells of the organism have undergone extensive differentiation and before most women are even aware that they are pregnant (Figure 3.8). During this sensitive period, a teratogenic agent may completely destroy the organism. Thereafter, the various body systems are most vulnerable during the initial stages of their formation and development. The most vulnerable period for the central nervous system is from 15 to 36 days after conception, whereas the upper and lower limbs are most vulnerable from 24 to 49 days after conception.
2. A teratogenic agent's effects are likely to be specific to a particular organ. Therefore, each teratogen causes a particular pattern of abnormal development. The drug thalidomide, for example, causes deformation of the legs and arms, and exposure to alcohol can result in abnormalities of the brain, eye, and heart.
3. Individual organisms vary in their susceptibility to teratogens. The way a developing organism responds to teratogenic agents depends to some degree

FIGURE 3.8 The sensitive periods in human prenatal development occur when the organs and other body parts are forming and therefore are most vulnerable to teratogens. Before implantation, teratogens either damage all or most of the cells of the organism, causing its death, or damage only a few cells, allowing the organism to recover without developing defects. In the figure, the blue portions of the bars represent periods of highest risk of major structural abnormalities; the peach portions represent periods of reduced sensitivity to teratogens. (Research from Moore & Persaud, 1993.)

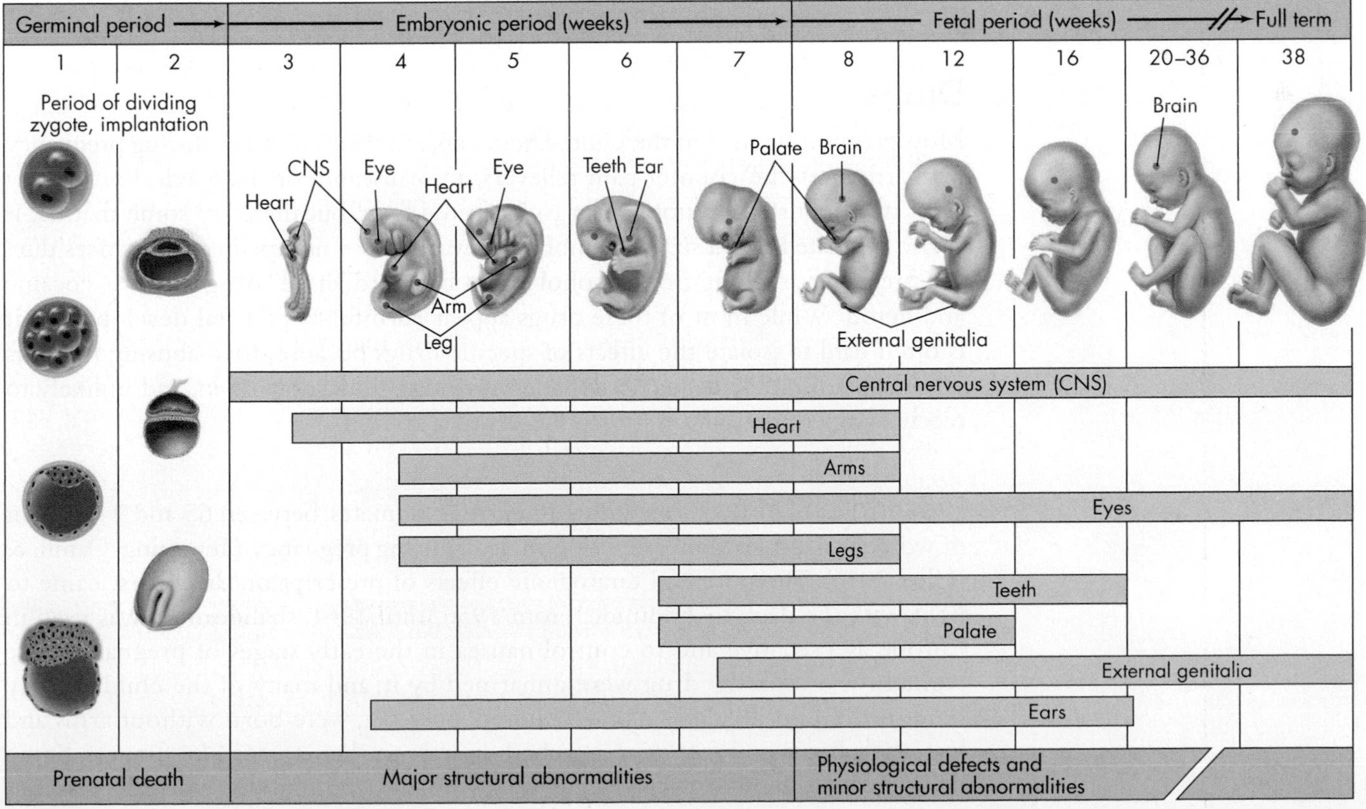

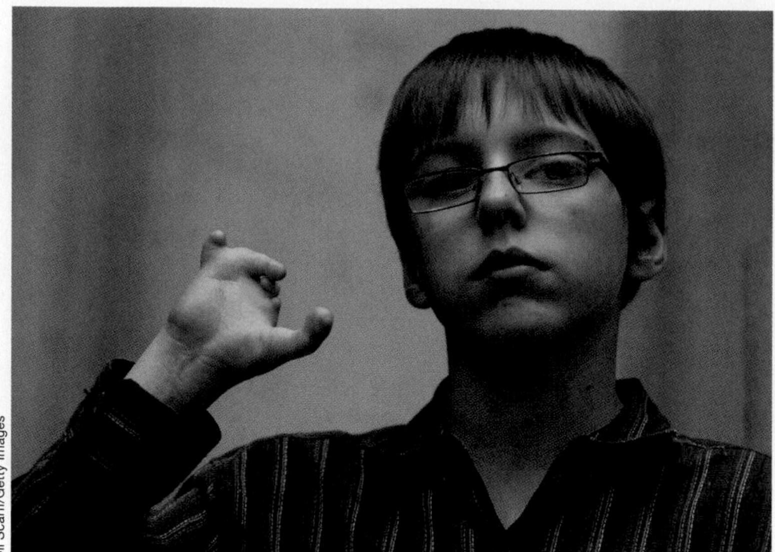
Oli Scarff/Getty Images

FIGURE 3.9 The deformed hand of this 13-year-old boy may have been caused by toxic materials released by a steel plant and inhaled and ingested by his mother when she was pregnant with him. A number of other children born around the same time to mothers in his London community were similarly affected with serious birth defects.

on its genetic vulnerability to these agents. For example, while maternal exposure to air pollution *increases the risk* of malformations in all fetuses, among fetuses equally exposed to a given air pollutant, some will be severely affected, others will be only slightly affected, and some will develop normally.

4. Susceptibility to teratogenic agents also depends on the mother's physiological state. The mother's age, nutrition, uterine condition, and hormonal balance all influence the effects that teratogens can have on the developing organism. The risk of malformation is highest, for example, when the mother is younger than 20 or older than 40; the precise reasons for this are not known. Nutritional deficiency in the mother intensifies the adverse effects of some teratogens. The impact of teratogens also appears to increase if the mother suffers from diabetes, a metabolic imbalance, or liver dysfunction, among other disorders.
5. In general, the greater the exposure to teratogenic agents, the greater the risk of abnormal development.
6. Some teratogens, such as rubella ("German measles"), that have little or only a temporary effect on the mother can lead to serious abnormalities during prenatal development. The most common such teratogens include certain drugs and infections, radiation, and pollution (Figure 3.9).

Drugs

Most pregnant women in the United States take some medication during pregnancy, primarily over-the-counter pain relievers, antinauseants, or sleep aids. Fortunately, most of these drugs do not appear to harm the fetus, but there are some that do. It is also estimated that a sizable minority of women use nonmedical substances during pregnancy, ranging from alcohol and tobacco to "hard" drugs such as cocaine and heroin. While most of these drugs appear harmful to prenatal development, it is often hard to isolate the effects of specific drugs because drug-abusing mothers often abuse multiple drugs or are generally poor, undernourished, and unlikely to receive proper prenatal care (Orioli & Castilla, 2000).

Prescription Drugs According to current estimates, between 65 and 94 percent of women take at least one prescription drug during pregnancy (Temming, Cahill, & Riley, 2016). The potential teratogenic effects of prescription drugs first came to light with the drug thalidomide. From 1956 until 1961, thalidomide was used in Europe as a sedative and to control nausea in the early stages of pregnancy. The women who took the drug were unharmed by it, and many of the children they bore suffered no ill effects. Some children, however, were born without arms and legs; their hands and feet were attached directly to their torsos like flippers. Some had defects of sight and hearing as well. About 8,000 children with deformities were born before their problems were traced to the drug and it was removed from the market (Vargesson, 2015).

Since the disastrous effects of thalidomide were discovered, other prescription drugs have been found to cause abnormalities in the developing organism, including the antibiotics streptomycin and tetracycline; anticoagulants; anticonvulsants; most artificial hormones; Thorazine (used in the treatment of schizophrenia); Valium (a tranquilizer); and Accutane (used to treat difficult cases of acne).

Tobacco Smoking tobacco has been found to harm the fetus in a variety of ways. Smoking is related to an increase in the rate of spontaneous abortion, stillbirth, and neonatal death (Marufu, Ahankari, Coleman, & Lewis, 2015). It also may contribute to the development of certain birth defects, including abnormal formation of arms, legs, fingers, or toes (Caspers et al., 2013). Nicotine, the addictive substance in tobacco, causes abnormal growth of the placenta, resulting in a reduction in the transfer of nutrients to the fetus. It also reduces the oxygen and increases the carbon monoxide in the bloodstream of both the mother and the fetus. As a result, mothers who smoke usually have babies whose birth weights are lower than those of infants born to women who do not smoke. The effects of cigarette smoke seem to be dose related: Pregnant women who smoke more have babies at greater risk for problems compared to those born to women who smoke less (Hindmarsh et al., 2008; Marufu et al., 2015). Research suggests that even if a pregnant woman does not smoke, the health of her baby can be significantly affected by the cigarette smoke of others (Caspers et al., 2013; Hoyt et al., 2016). Fortunately, nicotine replacement therapies in the form of patches or gum appear to substantially reduce the likelihood of developmental problems (Coleman et al., 2015).

fetal alcohol spectrum disorder (FASD) A range of problems, such as abnormal appearance and low intelligence, found in babies whose mothers consumed alcohol while pregnant.

fetal alcohol syndrome (FAS) A syndrome found in babies whose mothers were heavy consumers of alcohol while pregnant. Symptoms include an abnormally small head and underdeveloped brain, eye abnormalities, congenital heart disease, joint anomalies, and malformations of the face.

Alcohol Throughout the world, many women of childbearing age suffer from alcoholism, and many more are "social drinkers" who consume alcohol on a regular basis. In the United States 13 percent of women between the ages of 18 and 25 are dependent on or abuse alcohol (Center for Behavioral Health Statistics and Quality [CBHSQ], 2015). Pregnant women who drink substantial amounts of alcohol, especially during the first trimester, are in danger of having a baby with serious birth defects (Harris et al., 2017).

Many studies have found that a large proportion of infants born to mothers who were heavy drinkers during pregnancy—that is, who drank at least 14 standard drinks per week on average or engaged in binge drinking (4 or more drinks on a single occasion)—were abnormal in some way (see Molina et al., 2007, for a review). Many of these babies suffered from **fetal alcohol spectrum disorder (FASD)**, a range of problems that may include abnormal appearance, low intelligence, and problems with hearing or vision. The most severe form of FASD is **fetal alcohol syndrome (FAS)**, which can include an abnormally small head and underdeveloped brain, eye abnormalities, congenital heart disease, joint anomalies, and malformations of the face (Williams, Smith, & Committee on Substance Abuse, 2015; Figure 3.10). The physical growth and mental development of children with this syndrome are likely to be retarded. Women who drink heavily during the first trimester of pregnancy and then reduce their consumption of alcohol during the next 3 months do not reduce the risk of having children with this affliction. Binge drinking early in pregnancy has

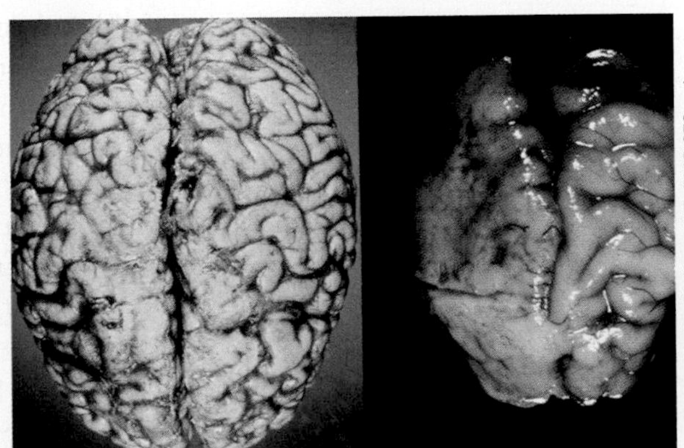

Courtesy Dr. Sterling K. Clarren, MD, FAAP CEO and Scientific Director Canada Northwest FASD Research Network

FIGURE 3.10 Children who suffer from fetal alcohol syndrome have underdeveloped brains and often severe retardation. When severely affected by alcohol, the brain (above right) lacks the convolutions characteristic of the brain of a normal child (above left). Such an affected brain will result in the death of the fetus.

St Petersburg Times/Newscom/ZUMA Press/UNKNOWN/Florida/USA

Heather was born with fetal alcohol syndrome. At 22 years of age, she is autistic, has cerebral palsy, a seizure disorder, and the intellectual capacities of a 3-year-old.

been associated with a subtle impairment of learning and behavior in adolescence (Kesmodel, 2001). As adults, individuals who were exposed to excessive amounts of alcohol prenatally (that is, whose mothers consumed more than 20 drinks per week, on average) perform more poorly on measures of learning and memory and have significantly smaller brains than do nonexposed individuals (Coles et al., 2011).

The effects of alcohol consumption on development can be profound and lifelong, leading most health-care experts to advise women to avoid alcohol in any amount throughout the course of their pregnancies (Williams et al., 2015).

Marijuana Recent changes in U.S. laws that legalize marijuana for medical and/or recreational purposes indicate that marijuana use is more socially acceptable than it has been in the past. It is the most commonly used illicit drug in general as well as among pregnant women (CBHSQ, 2015). Marijuana has not been definitively found to cause birth defects or to contribute to low birth weight or premature delivery independently of tobacco or other substance use. (Mothers who use marijuana are more likely to also smoke cigarettes and use other illegal drugs, compared to those who do not use marijuana; Conner et al., 2016; Mark, Desai, & Terplan, 2016.) Nonetheless, since it is estimated that approximately one-third of the psychoactive compound present in the marijuana-smoking mother's bloodstream crosses the placenta to the fetus, there is obvious cause for concern about possible short-term and long-term effects on development (Hurd et al., 2005). Marijuana use during pregnancy may also affect the placenta, causing it to grow larger than usual—a condition that has been associated with neurological deficits (Carter et al., 2016).

Cocaine A stimulant that rapidly produces addiction in the user, cocaine may result in numerous medical complications for the mother-to-be, including seizures, premature rupture of the amnion, and separation of the placenta from the uterus (Wendell, 2013). Babies of cocaine-addicted mothers are at elevated risk for a variety of problems, including stillbirth or premature birth, low birth weight, strokes, and birth defects (Cain, Bornick, & Whiteman, 2013). They are also described as being irritable, excessively reactive to environmental stimulation, uncoordinated, and slow to learn (Schuetze, Eiden, & Edwards, 2009).

Residual effects of cocaine exposure during the prenatal period may last for several years. For example, preschool-age children prenatally exposed to cocaine exhibit subtle delays in language development and are likely to experience difficulty regulating their emotions when frustrated (Lambert & Bauer, 2012; Schuetze, Eiden, & Danielewicz, 2009).

Despite the justified concern about the effects of prenatal exposure to cocaine, some researchers have been critical of claims that cocaine itself is the cause of the problems just described (Cain et al., 2013). These researchers note that, as we saw with marijuana, many mothers who use cocaine also are likely to drink alcohol and use other drugs. In addition, many of the mothers are poor and live in stressful circumstances. All these factors are known to contribute to symptoms such as those attributed to prenatal cocaine exposure. Consequently, while more recent research on prenatal cocaine exposure continues to show negative impacts on later development, a causal link between such exposure and later behavior is still not considered ironclad (Hurt et al., 2009; Morrow et al., 2003).

Methamphetamine Methamphetamines (also known as "meth" or "crystal") are among the most commonly abused illicit drugs during pregnancy, with the rate of hospital admissions of expectant mothers for methamphetamine-related problems tripling between 1994 and 2006 (Terplan, Smith, Kozloski, & Pollack, 2009; Wright, Schuetter, & Sauvage, 2014). A longitudinal study found that babies whose mothers had used the drug during their pregnancy were significantly smaller than babies whose mothers were nonusers (Nguyen et al., 2010). The study included nearly 4,000 women and statistically controlled for (that is, took into account) a number of other factors associated with deficient fetal growth, including prenatal care, maternal age, maternal weight gain, family income, and other drug use. Although this study provides strong evidence that methamphetamine exposure interferes with normal fetal growth, the precise mechanism of fetal growth retardation is not clear. One possibility is that the drug restricts the mother's blood flow, consequently restricting the nutrition that reaches the fetus. Regardless of the specific mechanism involved, fetuses exposed to methamphetamine very likely are at risk for problems known to affect other babies who are unusually small, as we discuss later in the chapter.

Heroin and Methadone Babies of mothers who are addicted to the opium derivatives heroin or methadone are born addicted themselves and must be given heroin or methadone shortly after birth to avoid the often life-threatening ordeal of withdrawal. These babies are at risk of being premature, underweight, and vulnerable to respiratory illnesses (Jones et al., 2010; Lund et al., 2013).

While these babies are being weaned from the drugs to which they were born addicted, they are irritable and have tremors, their cries are abnormal, their sleep is disturbed, and their motor control is diminished. The effects of the addiction are still apparent in their motor control 4 months later, and even after a year, their ability to pay attention is impaired (Yanai et al., 2000).

Several studies have also reported long-term developmental problems in children exposed in utero to heroin, methadone, or other opium derivatives. But as with marijuana and cocaine, whether these problems can be solely attributed to the mother's drug use is still open to question (Desai et al., 2015; Jones, 2006).

Infections and Other Health Conditions

A variety of infection-causing microorganisms can endanger the embryo, the fetus, and the newborn. Most infections spread from the mother to the unborn child across the placental barrier. In a few instances, however, the baby may become infected during the passage through the birth canal. Some of the infections and other maternal conditions that commonly affect the developing human organism are summarized below; Table 3.4 (p. 100) summarizes others.

Rubella Rubella (sometimes called the 3-day measles) is a mild condition with symptoms that include a rash, swollen lymph glands, and a low fever. If contracted by a mother-to-be early in pregnancy, however, the consequences can be devastating for her baby. Research has found that half of all children born to women who had the disease during the first 16 weeks of pregnancy exhibit a syndrome of congenital heart disease, cataracts, deafness, and mental retardation (Centers for Disease Control and Prevention [CDC], 2010). (Exposure to rubella infections after 16 weeks of pregnancy is less likely to have these effects.) The development of a vaccine for rubella in 1969 has greatly reduced the incidence of the disease, but rubella has not been eradicated, and several U.S. states require a blood test of

TABLE 3.4 Some Maternal Diseases and Conditions That May Affect Prenatal Development

Sexually Transmitted Diseases	
Genital herpes	Infection usually occurs at birth as the baby comes in contact with herpes lesions on the mother's genitals, although the virus may also cross the placental barrier to infect the fetus. Infection can lead to blindness and serious brain damage. There is no cure for the disease. Mothers with active genital herpes often have a cesarean delivery to avoid infecting their babies.
Gonorrhea	The gonococcus organism may attack the eyes while the baby is passing through the infected birth canal. Silver nitrate or erythromycin eyedrops are administered immediately after birth to prevent blindness.
Syphilis	The effects of syphilis on the fetus can be devastating. An estimated 25% of infected fetuses are born dead. Those who survive may be deaf, mentally retarded, or deformed. Syphilis can be diagnosed using a blood test and can be cured before the fetus is affected, since the syphilis spirochete cannot penetrate the placental membrane before the 21st week of gestation.
Other Diseases and Maternal Conditions	
Chicken pox	Chicken pox may lead to spontaneous abortion or premature delivery, but it does not appear to cause malformations.
Cytomegalovirus	The most common source of prenatal infection, cytomegalovirus produces no symptoms in adults, but it may be fatal to the embryo. Infection later in intrauterine life has been related to brain damage, deafness, blindness, and cerebral palsy (a defect of motor coordination caused by brain damage).
Diabetes	Diabetic mothers face a greater risk of having a stillborn child or one who dies shortly after birth. Babies of diabetics are often very large because of the accumulation of fat during the third trimester. Diabetic mothers require special care to prevent these problems.
Hepatitis	Mothers who have hepatitis are likely to pass it on to their infants during birth.
Hypertension	Hypertension (chronic high blood pressure) increases the probability of miscarriage and infant death.
Influenza	The more virulent forms of influenza may lead to spontaneous abortion or may cause abnormalities during the early stages of pregnancy.
Mumps	Mumps is suspected of causing spontaneous abortion in the first trimester of pregnancy.
Toxemia	About 5% of pregnant women in the United States are affected during the third trimester by this disorder of unknown origin. The condition occurs most often during first pregnancies. Symptoms are water retention, high blood pressure, rapid weight gain, and protein in the urine. If untreated, toxemia may cause convulsions, coma, and even death for the mother. Death of the fetus is not uncommon.
Toxoplasmosis	A mild disease in adults with symptoms similar to those of the common cold, toxoplasmosis is caused by a parasite that is present in raw meat and cat feces. It may cause spontaneous abortion or death. Babies who survive may have serious eye or brain damage.

Information from Moore & Persaud, 1993; Stevenson, 1977.

immunity to rubella before issuing a marriage license. Women are advised to avoid becoming pregnant for at least 6 months after they receive the vaccine.

HIV and AIDS In 2015, approximately 1.8 million children were living with HIV, most having been infected by their HIV-positive mothers (United Nations AIDS, 2016). The virus, which can lead to *acquired immune deficiency syndrome (AIDS)*, may be transmitted from the mother to her baby by passing through the placental barrier, by the baby's exposure to the mother's infected blood during delivery, or through breast-feeding. Children infected with HIV from their mothers are at significant risk for dying in the first few years of life, usually from complications associated with respiratory infections or severe diarrhea (Newell et al., 2004; Zash et al., 2016). The risk of transmission increases with the length of time the mother has been infected.

There is no known cure for AIDS. However, if HIV-positive women receive HIV-inhibiting antiretroviral drugs during pregnancy and at the time of delivery,

Gideon Mendel/Getty Images

This mother with AIDS, living in Lusikisiki, South Africa, has been taking antiretroviral drugs for three years. Her health has improved dramatically, as has her confidence in taking care of her children.

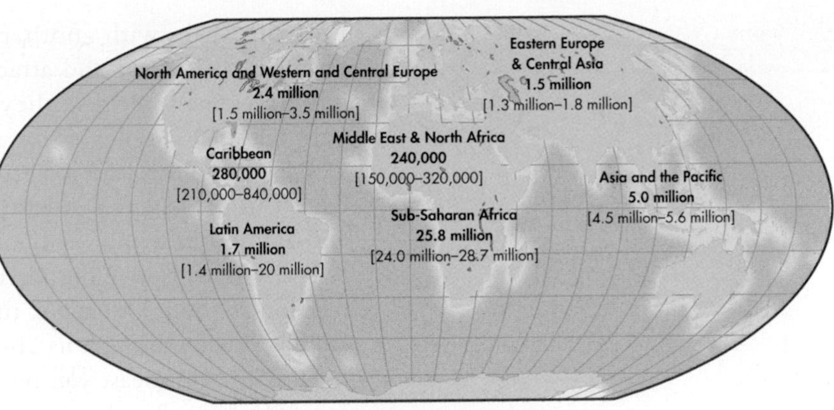

A total of 36.9 million adults and children were estimated to be living with HIV/AIDS at the end of 2014.

and their baby receives treatment immediately after birth, the chances of the baby's contracting the virus are substantially reduced (World Health Organization/UNAIDS/UNICEF, 2016). Therefore, there are two challenges to preventing mother-to-child transmission of HIV. The first is to identify HIV-infected mothers through testing; the second is to provide them, and their newborns, with antiretroviral drugs and infant-feeding alternatives. Global efforts to address these challenges have resulted in several promising signs. In the past decade especially, HIV prevalence rates appear to have been declining in a growing number of countries (see Figure 3.11; UNAIDS, 2016). There has also been progress in preventing mother-to-child transmission of the virus. Since 2010, new HIV infections among children have decreased by half, largely because infected pregnant women have been provided with access to antiretroviral medicines that prevent transmission of HIV to their babies.

Rh Incompatibility Rh is a complex substance on the surface of the red blood cells. One of its components is determined by a dominant gene, and people who have this component are said to be Rh-positive. Fewer than 1 in 10 people inherit the two recessive genes that make them Rh-negative (de Vrijer et al., 1999).

When an Rh-negative woman conceives a child with an Rh-positive man, the child is likely to be Rh-positive. During the birth of the baby, some of the baby's blood cells usually pass into the mother's bloodstream while the placenta is separating from the uterine wall. To fight this foreign substance, the mother's immune system creates antibodies, which remain in her bloodstream. If she becomes

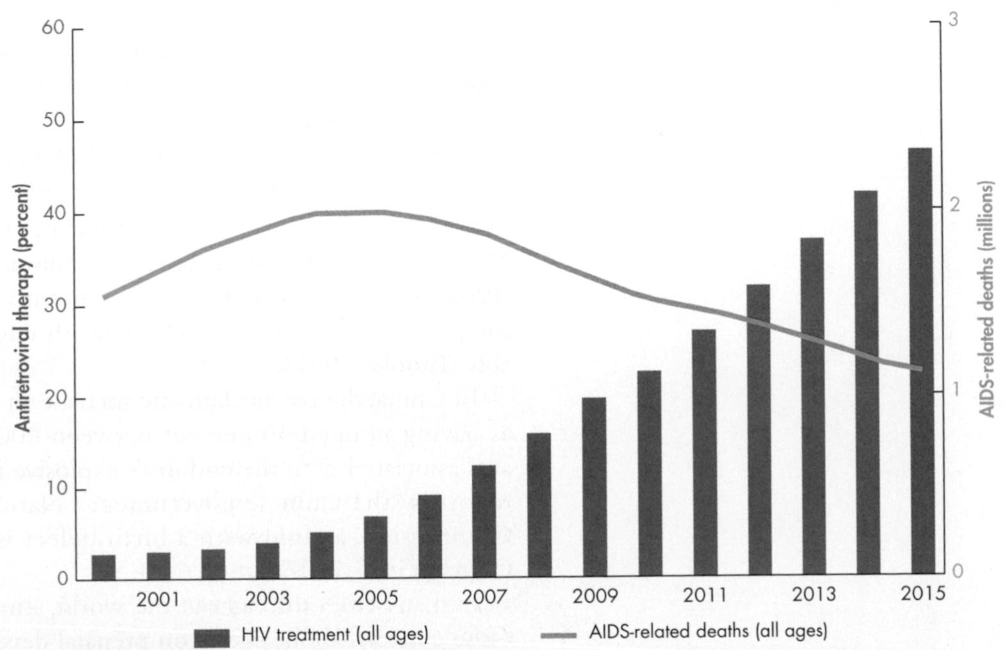

FIGURE 3.11 The number of individuals receiving antiretrovirals has increased significantly since 2001, resulting in declining rates of mother-to-child transmission of HIV and a substantial drop in the number of AIDS-related deaths. (Data from World Health Organization, UNAIDS, 2016.)

pregnant again with another Rh-positive child, these antibodies will enter the fetus's bloodstream and attack its red blood cells. (Firstborn children are usually unharmed because they are born before the mother has produced many antibodies.)

Rh disease can lead to serious birth defects and even death. Fortunately, physicians can prevent Rh disease by giving the Rh-negative mother an injection of anti-Rh serum within 72 hours of the delivery of an Rh-positive child. The serum kills any Rh-positive blood cells in the mother's bloodstream so that she will not develop antibodies to attack them. Alternatively, the fetus can be given blood transfusions, usually through its umbilical cord (Somerset et al., 2006). Children who are born with Rh disease can be treated with periodic blood transfusions (Hendrickson & Delaney, 2016).

Pollution Most of the thousands of chemicals that are present in our environments — in our homes, in the air we breathe, in the food and water we consume — have never been tested to see if they are harmful to prenatal development, even though some of these substances reach the embryo or fetus through the placenta (Heyer & Meredith, 2017). Many environmental toxins that have been studied, however, are associated with dramatic disruptions and disorders in fetal development, including birth defects, growth retardation, premature birth, and fetal death (Korten, Ramsey, & Latzin, 2017; Liang, Wu, Fan, & Zhao, 2014).

In 1956, the consumption of large quantities of fish from Minamata Bay in Japan was discovered to be associated with a series of neurological and other symptoms, which have come to be known as Minamata disease (Yorifuji et al., 2011). It was later determined that mercury waste discharged from an industrial plant had polluted the bay and that the mercury had passed, in increasingly concentrated amounts, through the bay's food chain to fish eaten by humans. Pregnant women who ate the contaminated fish passed the mercury on to their unborn babies. Symptoms in these babies included cerebral palsy (a disorder of the central nervous system), deformation of the skull, and sometimes an abnormally small head (Tuchmann-Duplessis, 1975).

The incidence of birth defects is also known to be abnormally high in areas of heavy atmospheric pollution (Deng et al., 2016). In the Brazilian industrial city of Cubatão, for instance, the air pollution from petrochemical and steel plants alone once exceeded that generated by all the combined industries in the Los Angeles basin of California. During the 1970s, 65 of every 1,000 babies born in Cubatão died shortly after birth because their brains had failed to develop — double the rate of this defect in neighboring communities that were not so heavily polluted (Freed, 1983). Fortunately, strong environmental safety efforts have greatly reduced the pollution in Cubatão, and the death rate of infants there has declined remarkably (Brooke, 1991).

In China, the recent dramatic increase in birth defects, which has been reported as having jumped 40 percent between 2001 and 2006, is largely due to pollutants associated with the country's explosive industrial growth. According to a 2007 report by the Chinese government's National Population and Family Planning Commission, a child with a birth defect is born every 30 seconds in mainland China (Yinan, 2007).

In many cities throughout the world, atmospheric pollution is severe enough to cause concern about effects on prenatal development. One study conducted in the United States found a strong relationship between rates of air pollution and infant death rates (Ritz, Wilhelm, & Zhao, 2006). A study conducted in Japan found that children born to mothers exposed to high levels of air pollution during their pregnancies scored lower on tests of verbal and motor development at 2½ years and had more difficulty controlling their behavior at 5½ years compared to children whose mothers were exposed to lower levels of pollution (Yorifuji et al., 2016). There is also a good deal of concern about the risk chemical dumps pose to the fetuses of pregnant women who live nearby. Unfortunately, much more research is required before the risks that these and other such environmental hazards pose for prenatal development can be accurately assessed.

Recently, developmentalists have identified yet another source of pollution that results in serious consequences for the developing fetus: toxins released into the environment by the explosions of bombs and other ammunition. Researchers have discovered high levels of lead in the teeth of children with birth defects born in war-torn areas of the Middle East (Savabieasfahani et al., 2016).

We have now come to the end of our survey of prenatal development. As we noted, many developmentalists view the prenatal period as a model for all subsequent development because certain principles that apply to prenatal development also appear to explain development after birth. Before moving on to our discussion of birth, you might find it helpful to review these principles, summarized in Table 3.5. Because the principles have been found useful for characterizing development during other periods, you will see them recur throughout our study of child development.

TABLE 3.5 Principles of Prenatal Development

Sequence is fundamental. One cell must exist before there can be two. Muscles and bones must be present before nerves can coordinate movement. Gonads must secrete testosterone before further sexual differentiation can occur.
Timing is crucial to development. If the ovum moves too rapidly or too slowly down the fallopian tube, pregnancy is terminated. If exposure to a particular teratogen occurs during a particular stage of development, the impact on the organism may be devastating, whereas if it occurs before or after this stage, there may be little or no impact – a difference that implies the existence of sensitive periods for the formation of organ systems.
Development consists of a process of differentiation and integration. From the single cell of the zygote, division leads to many identical cells, which eventually differentiate into the distinct kinds of cells of all the organs of the body, with the specifics likely the result of cells' interactions with surrounding cells. Arm buds differentiate to form fingers, which will differ from each other in ways that make possible the finely articulated movements of the human hand.
Development proceeds unevenly. From the earliest steps of cleavage, the various subsystems that make up the organism develop at their own rates. An important special case of such unevenness is physical development, which follows cephalocaudal (from the head down) and proximodistal (from the center to the periphery) sequences.
Development is characterized by changes both in the form of the organism and in the ways it interacts with its environment. The embryo not only looks altogether different from the fetus but also interacts with its environment in a qualitatively different way.
Development is epigenetic. Although the development of new phenotypic forms is constrained by genetic materials coded in the zygote, the phenotypic forms emerge out of the ongoing organism–environment interactions that sustain and propel development.

APPLY > CONNECT > DISCUSS

Visit the Web site of the Centers for Disease Control and Prevention. Explore the "One Test. Two Lives." initiative. What is the goal of the initiative? How does the CDC hope to implement the initiative? What materials and tools has the CDC developed to move the initiative forward?

LEARNING OUTCOMES

Summarize the events in each of the stages of birth.

Describe some cultural variations in childbirth.

Explain the connection between medical interventions in U.S. births and a rising interest in alternatives to these interventions.

Describe the effects of stress hormones on a newborn.

Birth

DELLA'S STORY

everything out of sync
lights on and off
contractions on top of each other . . .
nurse never really there—and when she was, she wasn't, reprimanding . . .
everybody talked to me while I'm blind—increasingly frozen with pain. Even

Dr. A trying to extricate himself from my grasp: "you're breaking my hand and if you don't let go I won't be able to deliver your baby. . . ."

then the order to move my legs "square up your knees" the giant operating lights suddenly descending from the ceiling behind Dr. A's head. where am I? my head won't talk to my legs—can't make them move—can't breathe for the pain. . . .

blue rubbery wet doll on my chest—I wish this gown was off. much to my amazement you are blond! (From Pollock, 1999.)

NISA'S STORY

Mother's stomach grew very large. The first labor pains came at night and stayed with her until dawn. That morning, everyone went gathering. Mother and I stayed behind. We sat together for a while, then I went and played with the other children. Later, I came back and ate the nuts she had cracked for me. She got up and started to get ready. I said, "Mommy, let's go to the water well, I'm thirsty." She said, "Uhn, uhn, I'm going to gather some mongongo nuts." I told the children that I was going and we left; there were no other adults around. We walked a short way, then she sat down by the base of a large nehn tree, leaned back against it, and little Kumsa was born. (From Shostak, 1981.)

These two descriptions of giving birth are from two vastly different cultures. The first describes the experience of Della, a highly educated, middle-class, urban American woman. The second is provided by Nisa, a woman of the !Kung, a hunting-and-gathering society in the Kalahari Desert of southern Africa. Each story is unusual in its own way, but neither is unique. In some societies, giving birth unassisted is treated as a cultural ideal that displays the mother's fearlessness and self-confidence. In other societies, birthing has become highly medicalized, while in still others, members of the community—particularly the women in the family of the mother-to-be—support the process.

Of all of life's transitions, birth may be the most radical. Before birth, the amniotic fluid provides a wet, warm environment, and the fetus receives continuous oxygen and nourishment through the umbilical cord. At birth, the lungs inflate to take in oxygen and exhale carbon dioxide for the first time. The first breath of oxygen acts to shut off the bypass that shunts blood away from the lungs to the placenta. It also causes the umbilical arteries to close down, cutting off fetal circulation to the placenta. Now the baby must obtain oxygen through the lungs, must work for nourishment by sucking, and no longer has the placenta to provide protection against disease-causing organisms.

The social and behavioral changes that occur at birth are no less pronounced than the biological ones. The newborn encounters other human beings directly for the first time, and the parents get their first glimpse of their child. From the moment of birth, infants and parents begin to construct a social relationship.

The Stages of Labor

The biological process of birth begins with a series of changes in the mother's body that force the fetus through the birth canal. It ends when the mother expels the placenta after the baby has emerged. Labor normally begins approximately 280 days after the first day of a woman's last menstrual period, or 266 days after conception. It is customarily divided into three overlapping stages (Figure 3.12).

The first stage of labor begins when uterine contractions of sufficient frequency, intensity, and duration begin to cause the cervix (the narrow outer end of the uterus) to dilate. This initial stage continues until the opening of the uterus into the vagina is fully dilated and the connections between the bones of the mother's pelvis become more flexible (Macones, 2015). The length of this stage varies from woman to woman and from pregnancy to pregnancy: It may last anywhere from less than an hour to several days. The norm for first births is about 14 hours. At the beginning of labor, contractions come 15 to 20 minutes apart and last anywhere from 15 to 60 seconds. As labor proceeds, the contractions become more frequent, more intense, and longer in duration.

The second stage of labor begins as the baby is pushed headfirst through the fully dilated cervix into the vagina. (This passage is facilitated by the fact that the baby's head is comparatively soft because the bones of the skull have not yet fused.) The contractions now usually come no more than a minute apart and last about a minute. The pressure of the baby in the birth canal and the powerful contractions of the uterus typically cause the mother to bear down and push the baby out.

Usually the top of the baby's head and the brow are the first to emerge. Occasionally, babies emerge in other positions, such as the breech position, with the feet or buttocks emerging first. In cases in which the baby is born in a breech position, which occurs in 3 to 4 percent of single births, both mother and fetus are at considerably increased risk of serious complications or death (Zsirai et al., 2016).

The third stage of labor, the final one, occurs when the baby has emerged from the vagina and the contractions of the uterus cause the placenta to buckle and separate from the uterine wall, pulling the other fetal membranes with it. Contractions quickly expel them, and they are delivered as the afterbirth.

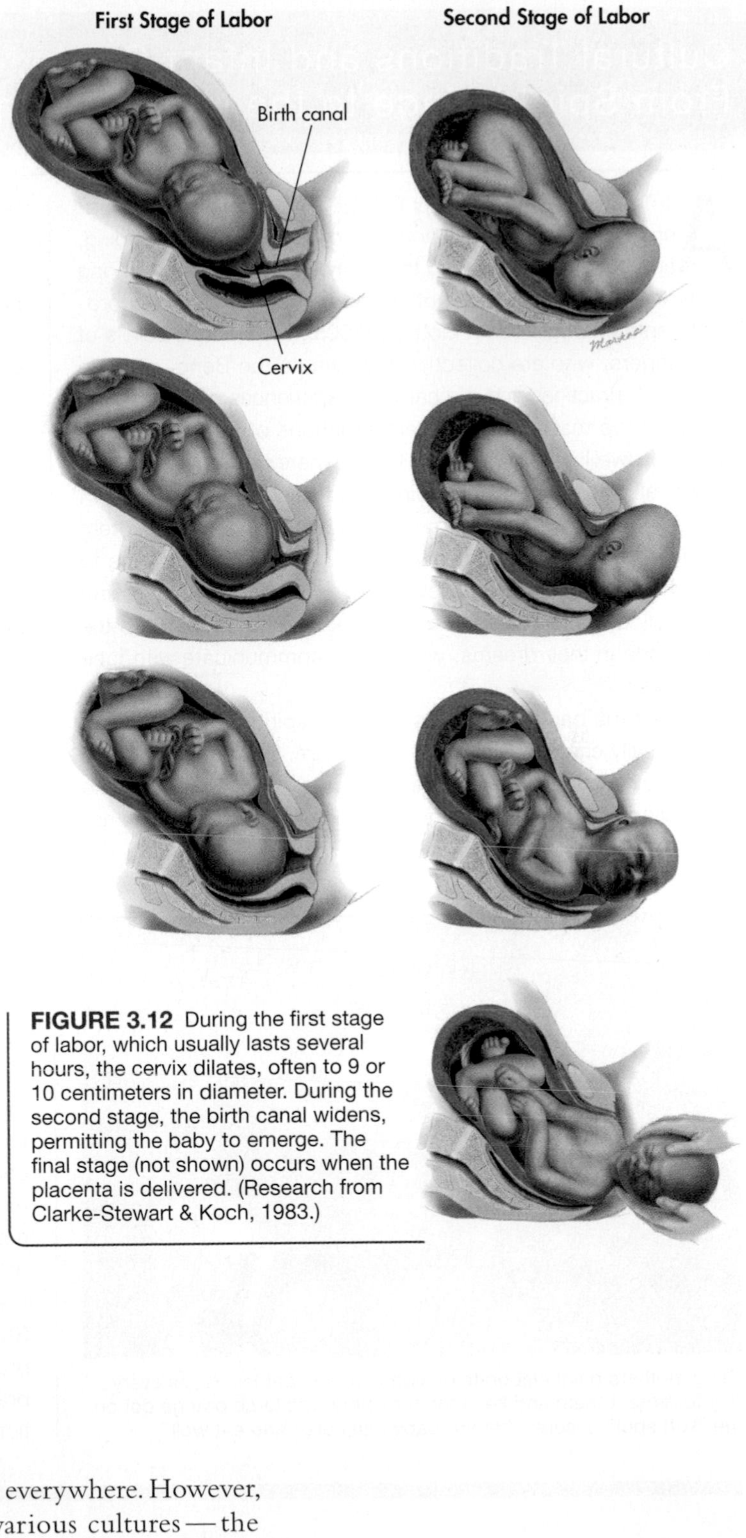

First Stage of Labor

Second Stage of Labor

Birth canal

Cervix

FIGURE 3.12 During the first stage of labor, which usually lasts several hours, the cervix dilates, often to 9 or 10 centimeters in diameter. During the second stage, the birth canal widens, permitting the baby to emerge. The final stage (not shown) occurs when the placenta is delivered. (Research from Clarke-Stewart & Koch, 1983.)

Cultural Variations in Childbirth

As a biological process, labor occurs in roughly the same way everywhere. However, as you encountered in our descriptions of childbirth in various cultures—the !Kung, the Hmong, and Western cultures such as the United States—there are wide cultural variations in childbirth practices. (For a detailed account of the intertwining of beliefs and practices surrounding childbirth, see the box "Cultural Traditions and Infant Care: From Spirit Village to the Land of Beng," p. 106.) One striking example concerns the presence of birth attendants who assist the mother as she labors. Although relatively rare, women in some cultures are expected to give birth unassisted. During childbirth, women in the remote Bajura district of eastern Nepal stay alone in an animal shed that is separate from the main home and is usually small and dirty. This isolation is based on the traditional Nepalese view that the blood and

Cultural Traditions and Infant Care: From Spirit Village to the Land of Beng

At the edge of a rain forest in West Africa, villagers engage in the daily activities of farming, housekeeping, and communicating with the many spirits that dwell among them and are the source of both good and bad fortune. According to anthropologist Alma Gottlieb (2005), the spiritual beliefs of the villagers, who are collectively known as the Beng, pervade infant care practices and the early life experiences of babies. The Beng believe that babies are reincarnations of dead ancestors currently dwelling in the "spirit village," where they enjoy rich and full social lives. The invisible spirit world exists side by side with the earthly world of the living, and the boundary between them is fluid and permeable, permitting easy movement from one to the other. Ancestors are believed to visit the world of the living on a daily basis, and some adults are known to have visited the spirit world in their dreams, where they communicate with their ancestors.

Against the backdrop of this complex spiritual belief system is an equally complex system of infant care. Babies are believed to occupy a precarious and risky place as they pass from the spirit village to the world of the living — a journey that does not begin until the umbilical stump drops off (a special drying salve is applied frequently to the stump to hurry the process along) and can take up to 7 years to complete. During this time, it is believed, there is a possibility that the infants will return permanently to the spirit village, usually because they miss the wealth, comforts, and friends they had there. Much of Beng infant care is therefore focused on convincing babies to stay by showering them with symbols of wealth. Because cowry shells are believed to be the primary form of wealth in the ancestral village, infants are adorned with cowry shell jewelry as a symbol of their wealth in the land of the living and are promised that they are valued and will be well cared for. They may also be provided with special jewelry or elaborate face paint to combat diseases and disabilities inflicted by ancestral spirits. Gottlieb noted that some babies wear "so many necklaces, bracelets, anklets, knee bands and waist bands that an outside observer might well wonder how the weighed-down infant ever manages to crawl" (p. 113). Infant bathing is highly ritualized, involving symbolic objects and washes, and lasts about an hour. Newborns are bathed four times a day; toddlers, twice daily. The purpose is to cleanse the residue of "dirt" from the spirit world. Special care is taken to keep infants and young children away from corpses, which might entice them to join their journey back to the spirit world. Beng infant care illustrates some of the same aspects of culture that are referred to in our discussion of the macaques (see Chapter 2), including the way that it is rooted in daily life and behavior and the way it forms a complex network of interconnected activities. But it also leads us to recognize that human culture involves other layers of complexity arising from a vast network of beliefs, values, and practices that reflect common human concerns and problems. Like many other communities in developing nations, the Beng suffer from high infant mortality rates; about 11 percent of all infants die before the age of 1 year, and about 17 percent die before age 5. (In contrast, the infant mortality rate for infants under 1 year in the United States is about 0.64.) It makes sense, then, that Beng child-care practices are oriented toward infant survival through cultural practices that follow from their beliefs about the spiritual relationship between life and death.

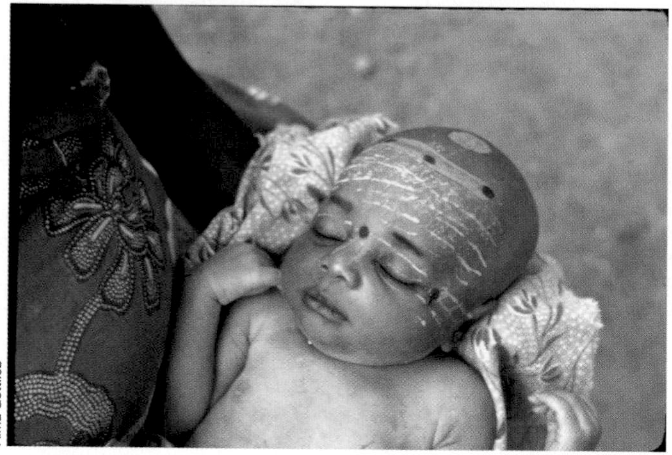
Alma Gottlieb

Beng mothers paint elaborate designs on their babies' faces every day to protect them and keep them healthy. The large orange dot on the "soft spot" ensures that the baby can nurse and eat well.

body fluids associated with childbirth are pollutants. During the delivery, no one helps or touches the mother, who must cut and tie the umbilical cord and then care for the baby herself. The villagers further believe that if a woman gives birth to a baby inside her home, God will be displeased and will cause family members and cattle to be become sick and die (Sreeramareddy et al., 2006). Similar childbirth practices and beliefs that divine will dictated birth outcomes were common in rural France as late as the end of the nineteenth century (Gelis, 1991).

Far more common is the practice of having several people attend the mother during labor and delivery, although there is cultural variation in who is expected to do the attending. Among the Ngoni of East Africa, for example, women regard men as "little children" in matters related to pregnancy and totally exclude them from the birth process. (Read, 1960/1968, p. 20). When a woman learns that her daughter-in-law's labor has begun, she and other female kin move into the woman's hut, banish the husband, and take charge of the preparations. They remove everything that belongs to the husband—clothes, tools, and weapons—and all household articles except old mats and pots to be used during labor. Men are not allowed back into the hut until after the baby is born. By contrast, among the Maya of the Yucatán peninsula, a trained midwife is present, and the husband is expected to be present as well, both to help his wife and to bear witness to the pain she feels (Jordan, 1993). If the husband is absent and the child dies, the death is likely to be attributed to his failure to participate.

In all developed countries, a large proportion of births take place in hospitals, where a physician or a trained midwife assists in the process—approximately 99 percent in the United States (MacDorman, Declercq, & Mathews, 2013). However, there are wide cultural variations in the place of delivery, in the extent to which midwives rather than physicians assist, and in such matters as the use of medication. For example, in Holland, roughly one-third of births take place at home, and the rate of infant mortality is actually lower for home births than for hospital births (Jordan, 1993). Moreover, practices are changing, not least in the areas where traditional practices had once been replaced by a more medical model (see the box "In the Field: Midwifery in the Inuit Villages of Northern Canada," p. 108).

Childbirth in the United States

The vast majority of all babies in the United States are born in hospitals and delivered by a physician (MacDorman, Mathews, & Declercq, 2014). Nevertheless, the United States ranks 26th in the world in infant mortality, with 6.1 deaths per 1,000 live births in 2010 (MacDorman et al., 2014). In the late 1960s and 1970s, when nurse-midwives became more common in U.S. hospital birth centers, several studies compared physician-assisted with nurse-midwife-assisted deliveries (MacDorman & Singh, 1998; Levy, Wilkinson, & Marine, 1971). In general, the studies found that nurse-midwife-assisted deliveries were much less likely to involve babies who had low birth weights or who died at birth or within the first weeks of life. Differences in outcomes between births attended by physicians and those attended by nurse-midwives may be due in part to labor and delivery practices, as well as to differences in prenatal care. Compared with physicians, nurse-midwives typically spend more time with women during their prenatal appointments and place more emphasis on education and counseling. They are also more likely to view themselves as an important source of emotional support during the labor and delivery process.

Given the relative success rates of home births and deliveries by nurse-practitioners, one might wonder why these practices aren't more common in the United States. Despite a dramatic increase in planned out-of-hospital births in the past decade, fully 99 percent of all U.S. births are planned to take place in hospitals (Snowden et al., 2015). Three major factors may contribute to the high rates of physician-assisted hospital birth. First, hospitals staffed by trained physicians and nurses are better equipped to provide both antiseptic surroundings and specialized help to deal with any complications that might arise during labor and delivery.

In The Field

Midwifery in the Inuit Villages of Northern Canada

Name: AKINISIE QUMALUK

Education: Trained in both traditional and scientific approaches to pregnancy, childbirth, and infant care

Current Position: Inuit elder and midwife

Career Objectives: Preserve and integrate traditional knowledge of health care for the purpose of increasing infant, family, and community well-being.

AKINISIE QUMALUK IS AN INUIT MIDWIFE WHO LIVES in a remote community in the far north of Quebec, Canada. Her craft of assisting women while they are pregnant, delivering their babies, and caring for their newborns draws from modern medical approaches as well as traditional Inuit knowledge. The blending of medical science with Inuit birthing and newborn care traditions is a major innovation in the education and practice of Inuit midwives. But what may be most remarkable is the fact that Akinisie is allowed to practice her craft in the local community. Although midwifery once was an integral part of traditional Inuit culture, in the 1970s the Canadian government began to insist that at 36 weeks' gestation, women be flown to a major city in the south in order to deliver their babies in modern medical facilities. As described by a member of the Inuit community, "This intimate, integral part of our life was taken from us and replaced by a medical model that separated our families, stole the power of the birthing experience from our women, and weakened the health, strength, and spirit of our communities" (Van Wagner et al., 2007).

Inuit women did not allow this invasion of their cultural heritage to go unchallenged. A community organization was formed for the purpose of reviving cultural practices, including midwifery, and establishing self-government. As a result of the organization's efforts, the first community birthing center was opened in 1986. The philosophy of the center was to provide care for pregnant Inuit women by educating health-care workers in the community in ways that integrated traditional midwifery skills and knowledge with modern approaches to care. Today, future midwives are recruited from the local villages to participate in an apprenticeship-style educational program rooted in Inuit teaching methods such as observation and storytelling.

Throughout the process of "returning childbirth to the villages," there was much discussion by women's groups, leaders, elders, and local health-care providers about the capacity and limitations of care in remote village locations and the potential for adverse outcomes should medical complications arise so far from emergency medical services. In response to such concerns, an Inuit elder explained that the danger of giving birth in remote areas is far outweighed by the danger of a "life without meaning." Indeed, taking birth out of the community is generally understood as disrespectful of Inuit culture and knowledge and harmful to women and families.

Interestingly, when pregnant Inuit women undergo "risk screening" to determine whether they might need to be evacuated to southern medical facilities equipped to deal with complications, the screening includes not only biomedical assessments but social, cultural, and community considerations as well. Conceptualizing risk within this broader context is consistent with Inuit beliefs that good health is not simply an absence of disease but also includes positive mental, emotional, and spiritual features and is related to health in the family and community as a whole.

Analyses indicate that the policy of allowing Inuit women to give birth in their own communities, assisted by midwives trained in both modern and traditional approaches, results in fewer labor and delivery complications than did the past practice of automatic evacuation. It is, of course, more difficult to gauge additional benefits such as mental, emotional, and spiritual well-being. But according to Inuit midwife Nellie Tukalak, midwives have become an important voice for families and the Inuit way of life.

Developmentalists are exploring traditional birthing practices of various native peoples in different parts of the world and how they might be integrated with medical practices in order to provide safe and meaningful birth experiences for women, families and communities (O'Driscoll et al., 2011).

(Information from Van Wagner, Epoo, Nastapoka, & Harney, 2007.)

Second, many drugs have been developed to relieve the pain of childbirth, and by law such drugs can be prescribed only by physicians. Third, most health insurance policies will not pay for services performed outside hospital settings.

There is no doubt that the lives of thousands of babies and mothers are saved each year by the intervention of doctors and nurses using modern drugs and special medical procedures; indeed, there may be a slightly greater risk of newborn death and seizures for babies born outside hospitals (Snowden et al., 2015). However, research indicates that typical labor and delivery practices in the United States may lean too heavily on medical procedures and actually place mothers and babies at risk for health problems, especially when medical interventions are used during normal, uncomplicated births (CDC, 2007; Snowden et al., 2015). In general, concerns center on two questions: What is the safest method for dealing with pain during childbirth? What precautions are necessary to ensure the health of the mother and the baby?

Childbirth Pain and Its Medication In developed nations, three types of drugs are primarily used to lessen the pain of labor and delivery during hospital births: *anesthetics* (which dull overall feeling), *analgesics* (which reduce the perception of pain), and *sedatives* (which reduce anxiety). In the United States, of all the available childbirth pain management drugs, epidural analgesia, which involves injecting a pain-relieving drug into a space in the spinal column, is among the most common, being used by more than half of all women (Osterman & Martin, 2011).

Although epidural anesthesia is highly effective in reducing pain, it is associated with complications, including increased risk of instrumental delivery (use of forceps or vacuum to assist delivering the baby), longer labor, and fetal distress. Because of their concern about the possible adverse effects of drugs on the newborn, many women use alternative methods of controlling the pain of labor. Typically, these methods include educational classes that give the mother-to-be an idea of what to expect during labor and delivery and teach her relaxation and breathing exercises to help counteract pain. Often they also involve having someone—the baby's father or a sympathetic friend—be at the woman's side during labor to provide comfort and emotional support.

Medical Interventions In addition to administering drugs to ease the pain of labor, doctors may use medical procedures to safeguard the well-being of the mother and child. For example, when the baby is significantly overdue or when the mother is confronted with some life-threatening situation, physicians commonly induce labor, either by rupturing the membranes of the amniotic sac or by giving the mother some form of the hormone oxytocin, which initiates contractions. However, between 1990 and 2010, the rate of induced labors more than doubled, rising from 9.5 percent in 1990 to 22 percent in 2006, with much of the increase due not to medical or obstetric conditions that threaten the baby or mother but to physician practice patterns or maternal choice (American College of Obstetricians and Gynecologists, 2009; CDC, 2006). Of special concern is the fact that induced labors are associated with higher rates of cesarean delivery (surgical removal of the baby from the uterus through an incision in the mother's belly), exposing both mother and child to increased health risks. The most recent trends indicate that rates of induced labor have declined somewhat from a high in 2010 of 23.8 percent (Osterman & Martin, 2014).

The cesarean procedure is typically used in cases of difficult labor, when the baby is deemed to be in distress during delivery or is not in the headfirst position. Starting in the 1970s, the number of cesarean sections performed in the United States began to increase significantly. By 2008, nearly one-third of all births were by cesarean section, an increase of 56 percent since 1996; the rate in 2015 was 32 percent (Martin, Hamilton, & Osterman, 2015). Critics argue that many of the cesarean operations performed in the United States not only are unnecessary (for example, cesarean sections that are initiated at the first sign of complications to avoid malpractice suits or to comply with the mother's wishes) but also raise the cost of childbirth, expose the mother to the risk of postoperative infection, cause mothers to be separated from their infants while they heal from surgery, and may be detrimental to the babies' well-being. For example, Herbert Renz-Polster and his colleagues report increased susceptibility of children delivered by cesarean section to hay fever and asthma (Renz-Polster & Buist, 2002), while others report increased chances of maternal death (Kusiako, Ronsmans, & Van der Paal, 2000).

Concerns about unnecessary medical intervention extend to other procedures, such as highly sensitive electronic monitoring of the vital signs of the fetus during labor, which has been associated with an increase in cesarean sections, perhaps because it overestimates potential problems (Wood, 2003). In part because of such concerns, there has been more interest in alternative ways of giving birth that range from birthing at home with the assistance of a midwife to the use of special birthing centers where family members can also be present (Akileswaran & Hutchison, 2016; Janssen, 2009). Such centers are often located in or near a hospital in case serious complications arise. Alternative measures are especially popular when prenatal examinations find no indications that the birth will be especially complicated. Moreover, in such cases, the involvement of midwives does in fact appear to reduce the use of medical interventions such as those we have mentioned. For example, a study carried out in the state of Oregon, which has among the highest rates of home births nationwide, found that certified nurse-midwives were less likely to use fetal monitoring or induce labor than were physicians. Their patients also were less likely to have spinal injections of anesthesia and cesarean sections than were the patients of family physicians and obstetricians (Snowden et al., 2015).

The Baby's Experience of Birth There is no doubt that the process of being born is stressful for babies, even if all proceeds normally. The baby must squeeze through a very narrow opening, placing a great deal of pressure on the head and body; and if the umbilical cord becomes constricted in the process, the baby's supply of oxygen is reduced. A number of studies document a surge in the fetus's production of stress hormones around the time of birth, which may be vitally important to survival outside the womb (Wynne-Edwards, Edwards, & Hancock, 2013; Yektaei-Karin, et al., 2007). For instance, high levels of the stress hormones in the hours before birth facilitate the absorption of

In many countries, families have choices regarding the context in which their babies will be born. Some prefer highly medical contexts, believing them "safer" in the event of trouble. Other families choose the intimacy of home birth. Still others choose alternatives such as water births, believing that they will relieve some of the stress typically associated with the birth process.

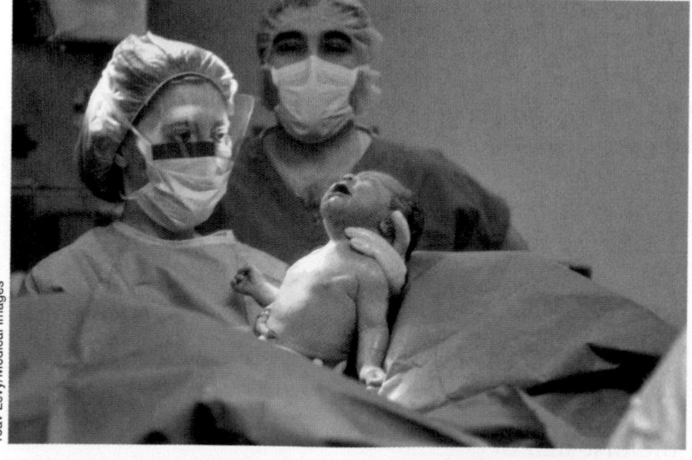

Yoav Levy/Medical Images

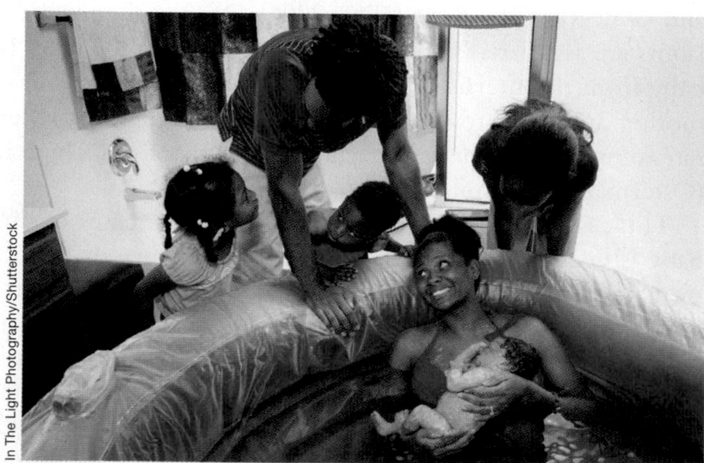

In The Light Photography/Shutterstock

liquid from the lungs, which allows the lungs to function well. The pressure of the birth canal also helps in this process; indeed, breathing difficulties are much more common among infants delivered by cesarean section compared to those delivered vaginally (Brüske et al., 2015).

The mode of delivery—vaginal or surgical—has other significant health implications for babies. For instance, passing through the vagina exposes the baby to more of the mother's microbiome (Yang et al., 2016). The **microbiome** consists of the millions of microorganisms that live on and in our bodies. Although some microorganisms are pathogenic and can contribute to sickness and disease, many of them are essential to the healthy functioning of critical systems—immune, hormonal, and metabolic systems, in particular. Babies who are delivered vaginally have microbiomes that more closely resemble that of their mother's, compared to babies delivered surgically. Moreover, vaginally delivered babies have higher concentrations of "good" microorganisms, whereas babies delivered by caesarean section have higher concentrations of pathogenic ones—differences that may persist through at least the first 7 years of childhood and may explain why children born through caesarean section are at greater risk for developing asthma (Azad et al., 2013; Lavin, Franklin, & Preen, 2016; Yang et al., 2016).

microbiome The millions of microorganisms that live on and in our bodies, some of which are pathogenic but many of which are essential to the healthy functioning of critical systems.

APPLY > CONNECT > DISCUSS

When it comes to prenatal care, labor, delivery, and newborn care, technologically advanced societies rely heavily on medical science. How would you characterize the culture of medical science? (You may want to review the definition of culture presented in Chapter 2, p. 51.) What are some of the costs and benefits of medical science for pregnant women and newborns?

The Newborn's Condition

LEARNING OUTCOMES

Explain how the Apgar scale is used to assess the physical condition of a newborn.

Compare the Apgar scale to the Brazelton Neonatal Assessment Scale.

Delineate risks and consequences associated with premature birth and/or low birth weight.

To first-time parents, especially those who imagine that newborns look like the infants pictured on jars of baby food, their neonate's actual appearance may cause disappointment or even alarm. A newborn's head is overly large in proportion to the rest of the body, and the limbs are relatively small and tightly flexed. Unless the baby has been delivered by cesarean section, the head may be misshapen because of the tight squeeze through the birth canal. (The head usually regains its symmetry by the end of the 1st week after birth.) Adding to this less-than-ideal appearance, the baby's skin may be covered with *vernix caseosa*, a white, cheesy substance that protects against bacterial infections, and it may be spotted with blood.

In the United States, neonates weigh an average of 7 to 7.5 pounds (3.2 to 3.4 kilograms), although babies weighing anywhere from 5.5 to 10 pounds (2.5 to 4.5 kilograms) are within the normal range. During their first days of life, most babies lose about 7 percent of their initial weight, primarily because of loss of fluid. They usually gain the weight back by the time they are 10 days old.

The average U.S. neonate is 20 inches (51 centimeters) long. To a large extent, the length of the newborn is determined by the size of the mother's uterus and thus does not reflect the baby's genetic inheritance for height. The genes that regulate height begin to express themselves shortly after birth (Tanner, 1990).

Assessing a Baby's Viability

In professionally assisted births, health-care practitioners (midwives, doctors, or nurses) check the neonate for indications of danger so that immediate action can be taken if something is wrong. They check the baby's size and vital signs and look for evidence of normal capacities. A variety of scales and tests are used to assess the neonate's physical state and behavioral condition (Gabbe et al., 2016).

Apgar scale A quick, simple test used to diagnose the physical state of a newborn infant.

Physical Condition

In the 1950s, Virginia Apgar (1953), an anesthesiologist who worked in the delivery room of a large metropolitan hospital, developed a quick and simple method of determining whether a baby requires emergency care. The **Apgar scale**, which is now widely employed throughout the United States, is used to rate babies at 1 minute and again at 5 minutes after birth, using five vital signs: heart rate, respiratory effort, muscle tone, reflex responsivity, and color. The individual scores are totaled to give a measure of the baby's overall physical condition. A baby with a score of less than 4 is considered to be in poor condition and requires immediate medical attention. According to a nationwide study, the proportion of newborns with Apgar scores indicating excellent health declined from 91.1 percent in 2003 to 88.6 percent in 2006, with non-Hispanic Black infants accounting for the highest percentage of very low Apgar scores (0–3 points), more than twice the level of Hispanic and non-Hispanic White infants (Martin et al., 2009).

Brazelton Neonatal Assessment Scale A scale used to assess a newborn's neurological condition.

Behavioral Condition

During the past half century, many scales have been constructed to assess the more subtle behavioral aspects of the newborn's condition (Gabbe et al., 2016). One of the most widely used is the **Brazelton Neonatal Assessment Scale**, developed by pediatrician T. Berry Brazelton and his colleagues in the late 1970s (Brazelton, 1984). A major purpose of this scale is to assess the neurological condition of newborns who are suspected of being at risk for developmental difficulties. It is also used to assess the developmental progress of infants, to compare the functioning of newborns of different cultures, and to evaluate the effectiveness of interventions designed to alleviate developmental difficulties (Lundqvist & Sabel, 2000).

The Brazelton scale includes tests of infants' reflexes, motor capacities, muscle tone, capacity for responding to objects and people, and capacity to control their own behavior (such as turning away when overstimulated) and attention. When scoring a newborn on such tests, the examiner must take note of the degree of the infant's alertness and, if necessary, repeat the tests when the baby is wide awake and calm. Here are some typical items on the Brazelton scale:

- *Orientation to animate objects—visual and auditory.* The examiner calls the baby's name repeatedly in a high-pitched voice while making up-and-down and side-to-side head movements in front of the baby. The goal is to see if the baby focuses on the examiner and follows the examiner's movements with smooth eye movements.
- *Pull to sit.* The examiner puts a forefinger in each of the infant's palms and pulls the infant to a sitting position, testing to see if the baby tries to adjust the posture of his or her head when in a seated position, and if so, how well the baby succeeds.
- *Cuddliness.* The examiner holds the baby in a cuddling position, checking to see whether the baby resists being held, is passive, or cuddles up.

- *Defensive movements.* The examiner places a cloth over the baby's face to see if the baby tries to remove it, either by turning away from it or by swiping at it.
- *Self-quieting activity.* The examiner notes whether the baby exhibits self-quieting behavior (such as thumb-sucking or looking around) during an episode of fussing.

In addition to their primary function of screening for infants at risk, neonatal assessment scales are used to predict aspects of newborns' future development, such as their temperament or their typical rate of learning. Research with neonates thought to be at risk has shown that these scales are, in fact, satisfactory guides for determining when medical intervention is necessary and that they are also fairly good at characterizing whether the baby is developing normally in the period following birth (Hart et al., 1999; Schuler & Nair, 1999). They are less useful when it comes to predicting later intelligence or personality, however.

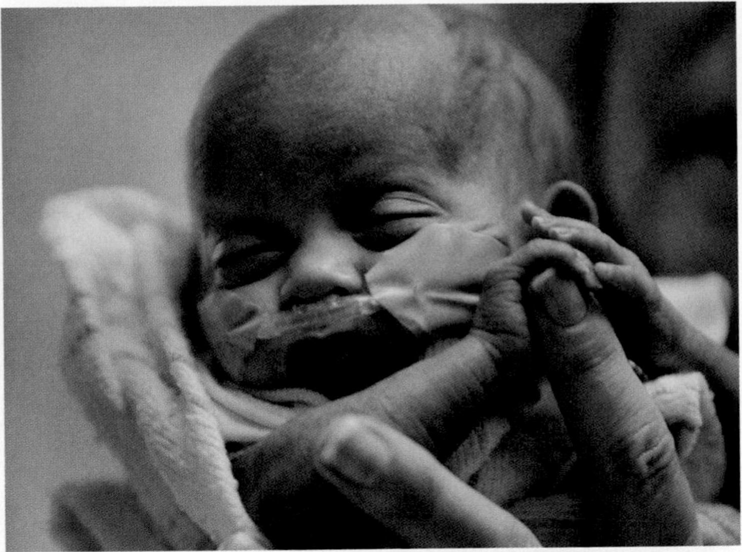

Scott Olson/Getty Images

FIGURE 3.13 At the time of her birth in 2004, Rumaisa Rahman (whose first name means "white as milk" in her native language) weighed 8.6 ounces (0.24 kilograms), making her the smallest known surviving baby in the world. After nearly 5 months of extensive medical care at the Loyola University Medical Center in Illinois (U.S.), Rumaisa, then weighing 5.5 pounds (2.5 kilograms), was discharged with a prognosis of normal development.

Problems and Complications

Though most babies are born without any serious problems, some are in such poor physical condition that they soon die. Others are at risk for later developmental problems. Newborns are considered to be at risk if they suffer from any of a variety of problems, including brain damage resulting from asphyxiation or a head injury during delivery, acute difficulty breathing after birth, or difficulty digesting food because of an immature digestive system (Korner & Constantinou, 2001). These are the kinds of problems that are likely to result in low scores on the Apgar scale. Most of the newborns who are at risk are premature, abnormally underweight, or both (Gabbe et al., 2016).

Prematurity

Prematurity is measured in terms of gestational age—in this case, the time that has passed between conception and birth. The normal gestational age is 37 to 43 weeks. Babies born before the 37th week are considered to be **preterm**, or premature (Figure 3.13). In the United States, after climbing 18 percent between 1990 and 2004, the rate of preterm births dropped to approximately 10 percent of all births in 2015, due in part to the decline in the number of births to teens and young mothers (CDC, 2017). Disorders related to premature birth are the fourth-leading cause of infant mortality. However, with the expert care and technology now available in modern hospitals, mortality rates for premature infants are declining in the United States.

preterm The term for babies born before the 37th week of pregnancy.

The leading cause of death among preterm infants is immaturity of the lungs (Lee et al., 2010). The other main obstacle to the survival of preterm infants is immaturity of their digestive and immune systems. Even babies of normal gestational age sometimes have difficulty coordinating sucking, swallowing, and breathing during the first few days after birth. The difficulty is likely to be more serious for preterm infants, who may need additional help with all of these functions. Their coordination may be so poor that they cannot be fed directly from breast or bottle, and special equipment must be used to feed them (Figure 3.14, p. 114). Moreover, their immature digestive systems often cannot handle normal baby formulas, and they must be fed special formulas.

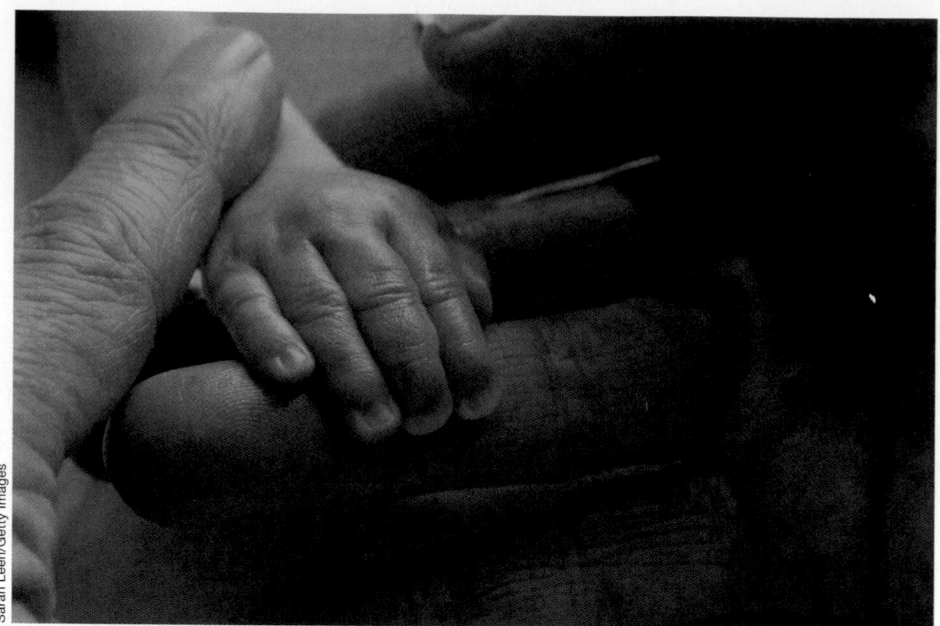
Sarah Leen/Getty Images

FIGURE 3.14 The care provided for premature infants in modern hospitals now includes gentle massage in addition to sophisticated medical technologies.

There are many potential contributors to prematurity, some of them known. Twins are likely to be born about 3 weeks early; triplets and quadruplets even earlier. Very young women whose reproductive systems are immature and women who have had many pregnancies close together are more likely to have premature babies. So are women who smoke, who are in poor health, or who have infections of the uterus. The chances of giving birth to a premature infant also vary with socioeconomic status (Joseph et al., 2007; Wood et al., 2014). Even in countries with universal health coverage, such as Canada, poor women are significantly more likely than affluent women to give birth to small or preterm infants or to infants who die in the first months of life. This disparity can be explained in part by the fact that poor women are more likely to be undernourished or chronically ill, to smoke, to be overweight, and to experience complications during pregnancy. Cultural factors such as the use of fertility drugs and fasting can also play a role.

Many other causes of prematurity are still not well understood. At least half of all premature births are not associated with any of the identified risk factors and occur after otherwise normal pregnancies to healthy women who are in their prime childbearing years and have had good medical care.

low birth weight The term used to describe babies weighing 5 pounds, 8 ounces (2,500 grams) or less at birth, whether or not they are premature.

small for gestational age Newborns whose birth weight falls in the lowest 10 percent for their gestational age because they have not grown at the normal rate.

Low Birth Weight

Newborns weighing less than 5 pounds, 8 ounces (2,500 grams) are said to have **low birth weight**. Often, low-birth-weight babies are preterm, but this is not necessarily the case. They may also be **small for gestational age**, meaning that their birth weight falls in the lowest 10 percent for their gestational age. Small-for-gestational-age infants have usually experienced intrauterine growth restriction; in other words, they have not grown at the normal rate. Multiple births, intrauterine infections, chromosomal abnormalities, maternal smoking or use of narcotics, maternal malnutrition, and abnormalities of the placenta or umbilical cord have all been identified as probable causes of intrauterine growth restriction (Figueras & Gardosi, 2011).

Interestingly, it seems that birth weight may also be affected by social factors such as maternal education and the family environment. Fetal growth, for example, especially growth of the head, tends to be significantly slower when mothers are less educated, probably because less educated women tend to receive poor health care and have less knowledge regarding what is required for healthy prenatal development (Silva, Jansen, et al., 2010). Regarding family environment, in rural South Africa, where multigenerational households are common, pregnant women who live with other family members but without a husband or nonmarital partner are more likely to give birth to small babies than are women who reside with a husband or partner (Cunningham, Elo, Herbst, & Hosegood, 2010). The researchers who studied this population controlled for a number of factors, including family income, and speculated that the social and emotional support provided by a husband or partner made a significant contribution to successful pregnancy outcomes.

Developmental Consequences

Intensive research has been conducted on the developmental consequences of prematurity and low birth weight. Both put babies at risk for later developmental problems, including delays and disorders in intellectual and language development, attention, and neurological functioning (Gardella et al., 2015; Johnson & Wolke, 2013; Yanuarti, Rusmil, & Effendi, 2014).

Low-birth-weight infants are at increased risk for developmental difficulty, even if they are full term. Two-thirds of the deaths that occur in the period immediately following birth are among low-birth-weight infants. In addition, low-birth-weight infants are three times more likely to have neurologically based developmental disabilities than are other babies, and the smaller the baby, the greater the risk (Holcroft, Blakemore, Allen, & Graham, 2003.

Common outcomes for low-birth-weight babies are a decrease in coordination and intellectual capacities. For example, one study that compared 7- to 11-year-olds who had very low birth weights with children born at a normal weight found that the low-birth-weight children performed more poorly on tests of motor coordination, intelligence, and arithmetic (Holsti, Grunau, & Whitfield, 2002).

The long-term outcome of prematurity appears to be influenced by various factors. Premature babies who are small for gestational age and have medical complications are most likely to have future developmental difficulties (Billimoria & Kamat, 2014). Premature babies who are of normal size for their gestational age may stand a much better chance of catching up with full-term babies (Lorenz, 2001). However, there is some evidence that even in the absence of any clinically detectable disability, compared with full-term children, children born prematurely are more likely to have problems with attention and in school (Alqahtani, 2016). They also tend to be shorter in stature and have elevated blood pressure, placing them at risk for developing cardiovascular diseases (Inomata et al., 2015).

Research on the social ecology of premature and low-birth-weight infants underscores the importance of a supportive environment in overcoming these potential risks. Babies who are raised in comfortable socioeconomic circumstances with an intact family and a mother who has had a good education are less likely to suffer negative effects from their condition at birth than are children who are raised without these benefits (Potijk et al., 2013). Low-birth-weight or premature babies who live in impoverished homes or have neglectful parents are more likely to suffer serious developmental problems in later years (Strathearn, Gray, O'Callaghan, & Wood, 2001).

APPLY > CONNECT > DISCUSS

Low birth weight is one of the leading causes of infant mortality. According to Dr. Alan Brann, a professor of pediatrics at Emory University, birth weight is an important indicator of a community's overall health status. In particular, Dr. Brann and his colleagues argue that low birth weight signals an unhealthy community (Dunlop, Salihu, Freymann, Smith, & Brann, 2011). In recent years, many Southern states have seen a shocking rise in the number of infant deaths. Have birth weights and infant deaths in your community/state/province/nation changed in recent years? How does your community/state/province/nation compare with others on measures of infant birth weight and mortality? What community/state/provincial/national efforts are under way to increase birth weight and/or decrease infant death?

Beginning the Parent–Child Relationship

Because human infants are dependent on the active support and protection of their caregivers for their very survival, the development of a close relationship between infants and their parents is crucial to infants' well-being. However, love and caring between parent and child is neither inevitable nor automatic. The large numbers of infants who are neglected, abused, abandoned, or murdered each year should convince even the most sentimental and optimistic observer of this harsh fact. In 2007, for example, approximately 5.8 million children in the United States were involved in child abuse reports and allegations (U.S. Department of Health & Human Services, 2009). How, then, is the bond between parent and child formed? And when no strong attachment develops, what has gone wrong? These are broad questions that you will encounter again and again in subsequent chapters because a close parent–child relationship is not formed in an instant; it develops over many years. Here we will examine two factors that come into play immediately after birth and help set the stage for future parent–child relations: parents' initial reaction to their newborn's appearance and the expectations they have for their babies.

LEARNING OUTCOMES

Explain the role of a newborn's appearance in the parents' response to their baby.

Point out how parents' social and cultural expectations help to shape a child's development.

The Baby's Appearance

In their search for the sources of attachment between mother and infant, some developmentalists have turned to *ethology*—the study of animal behavior and its evolutionary bases. These developmentalists believe that examination of what causes nonhuman mothers to protect or reject their young can shed light on the factors that influence human mothers. As noted in Chapter 1 (p. 25), one important factor that seems to influence animals' responses to their young is their offsprings' appearance (Koyama, Takahashi, & Mori, 2006). Parents tend to pay more attention to and respond more positively to "cute" infants, perhaps because their attractiveness signals physical fitness and a good prospect for survival. As we discussed in Chapter 1, ethologist Konrad Lorenz referred to the unique physical features of newborns—large head and eyes, full cheeks, and so forth—as "babyness."

Desires and expectations for their children's futures affect parenting practices and children's experiences from the first days of life. This mother is having her newborn blessed by a leader in her religious community.

James Estrin/The New York Times

Appearance may also be an explanation for parental rejection of offspring. Mothers in certain species, including dogs, cats, and guinea pigs, will kill malformed offspring. Though human parents usually do not kill their malformed babies, they do interact less frequently and less lovingly with infants they consider unattractive than they do with those they consider attractive. They also attribute less competence to unattractive babies (Langlois et al., 2000). This pattern is particularly noticeable for baby girls. While still in the hospital with their newborn girls, mothers of less attractive babies directed their attention to people other than their babies more often than did mothers of attractive babies (Langlois, Ritter, Casey, & Sawin, 1995).

Social Expectations

During pregnancy, most parents-to-be develop specific expectations about what their babies will be like, and no sooner does a baby emerge from the womb than the parents begin to examine the neonate's looks and behaviors for hints of his or her future. Will she have her grandmother's high, round forehead? Does his lusty cry mean that he will have his father's quick temper?

One of the most significant characteristics affecting parents' expectations is the sex of the baby (Basow, 2006). Children's sex determines what they are named, how they are dressed, how they are treated, and what will be expected of them in later life. Many of these expectations are based on cultural ideas about the experiences that males and females are likely to encounter as they grow from infancy to adulthood. In turn, these expectations shape the way parents perceive infants and the way they construct the contexts within which children develop. Thus, when differences are found in how boys and girls are treated, they occur not just because parents think that infant boys and girls are different to begin with but also, perhaps more significantly, because they believe that their infants will develop into men and women with different roles to play in their society.

Within the context of culture, then, parents organize their infants' activities and environments with an eye to the future (Lyra, 2007). This orientation is expressed in clear symbolic form by the Zincantecos of south-central Mexico (Greenfield, Brazelton, & Childs, 1989). When a son is born, he is given, in expectation of his adult role, a digging stick, an ax, and a strip of palm used in weaving mats. When a daughter is born, she is given a weaving stick. Such future orientation is not only present in ritual, it is coded in a Zincantecan saying: "For in the newborn baby is the future of our world."

Looking Ahead

LEARNING OUTCOMES

Point out genetic and environmental factors, starting at birth, that create a foundation for the development of infants.

Ultimately, parents' organization of the present in terms of the future contributes to the powerful role of culture in development (Valsiner & van der Veer, 2014). Just as infants are born with a set of genetically built-in capacities to learn about and act upon the world, parents come to this moment with their tendencies to respond in certain ways that have developed through their experience as members of their culture. These tendencies help shape the relationship between child and parents that begins at birth—itself an essential part of the foundation upon which development builds.

The next chapter focuses on the newborn period—the first three months after birth. You will learn about the remarkable ways that infants engage with an entirely new environment, and how the organization of their actions and experiences reflect the joint effects of biology and culture.

APPLY > CONNECT > DISCUSS

Provide some examples of how the relationship between the newborn's characteristics and the care he or she receives is mediated by cultural beliefs and values (see Chapter 2, p. 53).

1. Review the discussion of *ecological inheritance* in Chapter 2 (p. 71). Consider how it might influence the fetus's exposure to teratogens and implications across generations.
2. At the beginning of this chapter, you considered how prenatal development prepares the newborn for the radical transition from the uterine environment. Now that you have read the chapter, what have you learned about this preparation in terms of the fetus's sensory experiences and behavior?

Summary

The Periods of Prenatal Development

- Prenatal development is often divided into three broad periods:
  1. The germinal period begins at conception and lasts until the zygote enters the uterus and becomes implanted there about 8 to 10 days later. Through repeated division, the organism has grown from a single cell into hundreds of cells by the time it reaches the uterus.
  2. The embryonic period extends from implantation to the end of the 8th week. With cell differentiation, by the end of this period, all major organs have taken primitive shape, and sexual differentiation has begun. This rapid growth is facilitated by the efficient way the placenta allows the exchange of nutrients and waste products between the mother and the embryo.
  3. The fetal period goes from the 9th week, with the beginning of ossification, until birth. The fetus grows dramatically in size, and the brain and all organ systems increase in complexity to the point where the baby can exist outside the mother. The fetus is subject to environmental influences originating from outside as well as inside the mother. Basic sensory capacities (for sensing motion, light, and sound) develop during this period, enabling fetal learning. By 15 weeks, the fetus exhibits all movements observable at birth; fetal activity is crucial to neuronal development.

Maternal Conditions and Prenatal Development

- A mother's negative attitudes toward a pregnancy or stress during pregnancy may be associated with problems such as low birth weight and certain longer-term developmental risks. The problems may stem from the mother's elevated levels of the hormone cortisol during pregnancy.
- A mother's nutrition is an important factor in fetal development. Pregnant women are advised to consume 2,000–2,800 calories a day in a well-balanced diet and to increase their intake of folic acid, calcium, and iron. Extreme maternal undernourishment and malnutrition are associated with low birth weight, prematurity, abnormalities, and death. Lesser degrees also increase risk, although the effects can be difficult to isolate. Maternal overnutrition is also associated with negative outcomes, including overweight in babies, who may be at later risk for health problems such as obesity and diabetes.

Teratogens: Environmental Sources of Birth Defects

- Teratogens (environmental agents that can cause deviations from normal fetal development) take many forms. Six general principles apply to all of them:
  1. The susceptibility of the organism depends on its developmental stage.
  2. A teratogen's effects are likely to be specific to a particular organ.
  3. Individual organisms vary in their susceptibility to teratogens.
  4. The mother's physiological state influences susceptibility to teratogens.
  5. The greater the concentration of a teratogenic agent, the greater the risk.
  6. Teratogens that have little or no effect on the mother can seriously affect the developing organism.
- Among the common teratogens are drugs, including prescription drugs, tobacco, alcohol, marijuana, cocaine, and heroin and methadone. Their effects vary considerably; heavy drinking, for example, is associated with fetal alcohol syndrome. Other teratogenic agents are infections, including rubella and HIV, and high levels of pollution.

Birth

- Labor begins approximately 266 days after conception and proceeds through three stages, in which contractions cause the cervix to dilate, the baby is pushed through the birth canal and is delivered, and the afterbirth is delivered.
- There are marked cultural variations in childbirth, such that a woman may give birth unassisted, be assisted by a midwife and/or others at home, or be assisted by a physician or midwife in a hospital.

- In the United States, concern about the possible adverse effects of pain medication on the newborn and about the overuse of medical interventions (induced labor and cesarean sections, for example) has led to interest in alternatives, such as the use of midwives and birthing centers.
- Birth is a stressful experience for the baby, but research suggests that a surge of stress hormones as the process begins protects the baby from the adverse conditions and prepares the baby for survival outside the womb.

The Newborn's Condition

- The Apgar scale is used to assess a newborn's physical condition by measuring heart rate, respiratory effort, reflex responsivity, muscle tone, and color. Babies with a low Apgar score require immediate medical attention. Other scales have been developed to assess behavioral aspects of the newborn's condition.
- Risks are associated with prematurity (birth before the 37th week) and low birth weight (less than 5 pounds, 8 ounces [2,500 grams]). They are especially great for premature infants who are small for their gestational age and have medical complications.

Beginning the Parent–Child Relationship

- A newborn's appearance plays a significant role in the parents' response to the baby, with "babyness" evidently evoking caregiving behaviors.
- From birth, parents' expectations, influenced by the culture, influence the child's environment in ways that shape the child's development.

In the newborn period – the first three months after birth – the baby's behavior becomes organized in ways that reflect the interaction of biology and culture.

Looking Ahead

- Infants are born with biologically endowed capacities that impact their actions and how they learn about the world, and their parents nurture these capacities according their cultural experiences.

Key Terms

germinal period, p. 81
embryonic period, p. 81
fetal period, p. 81
cleavage, p. 82
heterochrony, p. 82
heterogeneity, p. 82
totipotent stem cells, p. 82
implantation, p. 82
amnion, p. 83
chorion, p. 83
placenta, p. 83
umbilical cord, p. 83
ectoderm, p. 83
endoderm, p. 83
mesoderm, p. 83
epigenesis, p. 84
cephalocaudal pattern, p. 84
proximodistal pattern, p. 84
age of viability, p. 86
neural tube, p. 92
large for gestational age, p. 94
gestational age, p. 94
teratogens, p. 95
fetal alcohol spectrum disorder (FASD), p. 97
fetal alcohol syndrome (FAS), p. 97
microbiome, p. 111
Apgar scale, p. 112
Brazelton Neonatal Assessment Scale, p. 112
preterm, p. 113
low birth weight, p. 114
small for gestational age, p. 114

PART TWO

Infancy

BABIES AND TODDLERS APPLICATION TO DEVELOPING LIVES PARENTING SIMULATION

Below is a list of questions you will answer in the Babies and Toddlers simulation module. As you answer these questions consider the impact your choice will have on the physical, cognitive, and social and emotional development of your child.

	Physical	Cognitive	Social and Emotional
	• Will you get your baby vaccinated? • Will you breast-feed your baby? If so, for how long? • What kind of foods will you feed your baby during the first year? • How will you encourage motor development? • How does your baby's height and weight compare to national norms?	• What kind of activities are you going to expose your baby to (music class, reading, educational videos)? • What kind of activities will you do to promote language development? • What stage of Piaget's Cognitive Stage of Development is your child in?	• How will you soothe your baby when he or she is crying? • Can you identify your baby's temperament style? • Can you identify your baby's attachment style? • What kind of discipline will you use with your child?

MAJOR MILESTONES OF INFANCY

	Physical Domain	Cognitive Domain	Social and Emotional Domain
What Develops . . .	• Growth is rapid to about 30–34 inches (76–86 centimeters) and 22–27 pounds (10–12 kilograms) by end of second year. • Ossification of bones occurs; ongoing changes in proportions begin; muscle strength increases. • Cerebral cortex areas develop, including prefrontal cortex and language-related areas. • Myelination of neurons occurs, including neurons of language-related areas and neurons linking areas of the brain. • Gross motor developments include crawling (around 8–9 months) and walking (around 1 year). • Fine motor developments include perfecting reaching and grasping and, by 2 years, performing movements needed to feed and dress self, etc.	• Behavior becomes increasingly intentional and goal directed. • Object permanence and representational thinking emerges. • Problem solving, symbolic play, deferred imitation, and language use increase. • Understanding of cause–effect relationships develop. • Ability to categorize objects according to common features develops. • Ability to control and sustain attention increases; speed of processing information increases. • Memory improves.	• Basic emotions are present at birth soon after. • Primary intersubjectivity emerges. • Ability to regulate emotions increase • Attachment to caregivers (7–9 mont develops; fear of strangers emerges with attachment. • Secondary intersubjectivity emerges • Language comprehension and spee emerge. • Ability to share and communicate knowledge, desires, and interests becomes greater. • Sense of self and associated sense independence emerge.
Sociocultural Contributions and Consequences . . .	• Factors such as socioeconomic status and diet can contribute to variations in growth. • Cultures vary in how they restrict or encourage specific motor actions, affecting the sequence and timing of attainment of gross motor milestones.	• Motor development coupled with interest in exploring can be risky; parents respond by "baby-proofing" the environment.	• Basic emotions facilitate ties to members of the community and, in this way, acquisition of culture occur • Cultures differ in ideas about what constitutes sensitive caregiving. • Emotionally warm and responsive interactions generate a sense of trus and exploration.

Passing from the birth canal into the hands of the mother or her birth attendant marks the transition from fetal life to infancy. Preparations for this event—perhaps the most radical in the life course of the individual—have been under way for 9 months or for millennia, depending on whether they are viewed through the lens of ontogeny (the individual's development) or in terms of the evolution of human species and culture. In either case, the transition from the intrauterine to the extrauterine environment takes place in the context of a facilitating or supportive environment. The birth canal, for example, the channel formed by the mother's cervix, vagina, and vulva, is not simply a physical structure through which the baby passes; it also plays a dynamic role in the transition by exerting pressure on the fetus's chest, forcing fluid from airways in preparation for the drawing of the first breath of life. Then the umbilical cord is cut, often with great ceremony, and the infant enters into a fundamentally new relationship with the environment.

E+/Getty Images

The chapters in Part II are organized to highlight the nature of this new relationship and how it continues to change over the course of infancy. Chapter 4 traces development from birth to about 3 months of age, exploring infants' earliest capacities for perceiving and acting on the world and highlighting the ways in which infants' behavior becomes increasingly organized and integrated. The most obvious requirement of this earliest postnatal period is that infants receive enough nourishment and protection to support their continued growth. This requirement is met through a wide variety of cultural systems of infant care that call upon and promote infants' basic capacities to signal their needs and learn from experience. A key element in this process is infants' increasing ability to coordinate their actions with those of their caregivers, helping to ensure that their basic needs are met.

Chapter 5 examines the marked changes in physical and cognitive development that take place between 3 months and 2 years of age. Increases in infants' physical size and strength are accompanied by increases in their motor coordination and control, opening up entirely new opportunities for exploring the world. Both memory and problem-solving abilities improve, providing infants with a finer sense of their environment and how to act upon it. The emergence of imitation and symbol use lays a foundation for new ways of communicating and connecting with others.

The processes through which infants are drawn into the lives of others are the focus of Chapter 6, where we examine the developmental course of infant emotions and emotional expressions, infants' attachments to their caregivers, and the beginnings of language. We discuss why infants become wary of strangers and become upset when left alone. We also explore the budding sense of self, the first glimmer of independence (sometimes described as the "terrible twos"), and the dawning ability to distinguish between "good" and "bad."

Throughout Part II, we underscore how interacting domains of development (physical, cognitive, social, and emotional) and the sociocultural contexts in which development occurs jointly contribute to the increasing organization and coordination of the infant's behavior.

Karin Dreyer/Getty Images

CHAPTER

4

The First 3 Months

On the second day: *M'ama Afwe is dozing on her bed with her 2-day-old daughter. As a 16-year-old first-time mother, she has much to learn about caring for her infant. But she knows already about a number of her West African cultural practices that will ensure her baby's well-being. She knows, for intance, that it is unsafe to take the infant outside until the umbilical cord falls off. Afwe also receives considerable help from older, experienced women in her family. When her daughter becomes hungry and starts to cry, Afwe leans over her, trying to breast-feed. But her breasts are large and full of milk, and this leaning-over position makes it difficult for the baby to latch onto the nipple. The hungry baby cries all the more. Afwe's grandmother observes the scene and suggests that Afwe lie down beside the baby so the nipple can more easily fit into the little mouth. Afwe tries out the new position. It works: The baby nurses eagerly.*

In the second week: *After some hours of cycling between fussing and nursing, Afwe's baby girl is sleeping in her grandmother's arms while Afwe naps, tired in the way that new mothers often are. A neighbor comes in to admire the latest addition to the community. When she takes the baby from the grandmother, the baby wakes and begins to fuss again. When the baby is returned to her grandmother's arms, she begins to cry vigorously. The grandmother speaks softly, hoping to soothe her, but the infant is inconsolable, and cries all the more, so the grandmother, who has a nursing toddler of her own, offers the baby her breast. Her granddaughter eagerly accepts it, nurses for a few moments, and then drops off to sleep.*

(Information from Gottlieb, 2000.)

Compared with other animals, many of which are fairly able to take care of themselves at birth, human beings are born in a state of marked immaturity and dependence. As Afwe quickly learned, she must help her baby to accomplish even such an elementary act as feeding. The relative helplessness of human babies at birth has several obvious consequences. Babies require extensive care and attention. This limits the mother's ability to provide for herself and her other children and, consequently, increases the importance of child-care assistance from her mate and others in her community. In Afwe's West African culture, extended kin, such as Afwe's grandmother, provide help with infant care. In other cultures or communities, babysitters or day-care providers may give comparable levels of assistance. Moreover, the survival of human offspring depends on the efforts of their parents and other adults for many years. As we discussed in Chapter 2, in order to survive on their own and become integrated into the activities of their community, human children must learn a vast repertoire of knowledge, skills, traditions, and patterns of living that they do not possess at birth.

In this chapter, we describe the initial phase of this integrative learning process, which begins immediately after birth and ends approximately 3 months later. Examining capacities and characteristics that babies bring with them into the world, we will see the ways in which newborns' brains and sensory systems allow them to experience the world, the ways in which their specific reflexes and temperamental styles influence how they respond to their experiences, and the ways in which certain innate learning capacities come to affect their early behavior.

In addition to exploring what babies bring with them into the world, we will examine how the world interacts with the newly born through the contexts of family, community, and cultural traditions and how these contexts and traditions affect the young infant's development. The story of early infancy, as you will see, is a story about organization and coordination: how the brain becomes organized into a highly efficient communication network, how newborn reflexes and sensory systems become organized into more complex systems of behavior, and how these brain and behavioral developments are coordinated with the particular social and cultural environment into which the child is born.

WARMING UP

1. Each newly born individual is genetically unique from all others, except in the case of identical twins. Do you think the behavior of newborns expresses this uniqueness? Do newborns have different "personalities"? How are such personalities apparent in the newborn's behavior?
2. Similarly to many other species, humans rely on others of their kind for care and survival. How might this need of humans for other human beings figures into the behavior of newborns?

LEARNING OUTCOMES

Describe the purpose of growth charts.

Explain how an infant's skull accommodates the growing brain.

Physical Growth

During the infant's first 3 months, physical growth progresses at an astonishing pace. In just 12 short weeks, the baby will gain approximately 6 pounds and grow more than 4 inches in length. As a consequence of the rapid development of the brain, the circumference of the head will increase by more than an inch. Keeping in mind that the average baby weighs a bit more than 7 pounds (3 kilograms) at birth, is just 19.5 or so inches (50 centimeters) long, and has a head circumference of about 14 inches (36 centimeters), these changes to the physical body are truly remarkable!

Measuring Body Growth

growth charts Charts that show average values of height, weight, and other measures of growth, based on large samples of normally developing infants; the charts are used to evaluate an infant's development.

Pediatricians and other health-care providers for infants closely monitor infants' early physical growth for reassuring signs of normal development—or for early warnings that a problem might exist. Typically, the baby's development is evaluated by using **growth charts**, which depict average values of height, weight, and other measures of growth that have been compiled by studying large samples of normally developing infants. Growth charts, such as those in Figure 4.1, indicate the average values as well as various degrees of deviation from the average.

Because growth charts are an integral tool for assessing a baby's health status, developmentalists are highly invested in assuring their validity. The problems that otherwise can ensue became apparent in recent years when many pediatricians became concerned that some breast-fed babies were malnourished because, according to growth chart averages, they were gaining weight relatively slowly. To compensate for what they believed was inadequate nutrition, some doctors advised mothers to supplement their infants' diets with formula and solid foods. Such advice goes against the recommendation of many infant-health organizations that babies be exclusively breast-fed throughout the first year to optimize healthy development (World Health Organization, 2016). Among other long-term benefits, breast-feeding is associated with decreased risk for immune-related diseases, childhood cancers, and obesity; improved cognitive functioning; and higher income in adult life (Hopkins, Steer, Northstone, & Emmett, 2015; WHO, 2016). Some of the benefits of breast milk, particularly those associated with the infant's immune function, may be due to the abundance of essential microorganisms that breast milk introduces to the infant's microbiome (see Chapter 3, p. 111; Andreas, Kampmann, & Le-Doare, 2015).

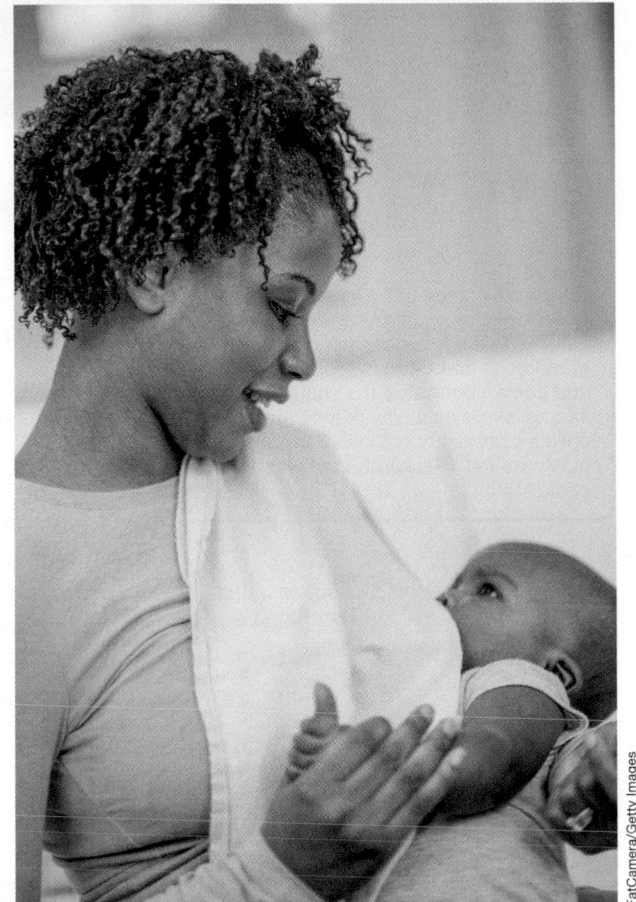

Perhaps because they have greater control over the amount of milk they drink, breast-fed babies tend to gain less weight during the first year compared with their bottle-fed counterparts.

As you can appreciate, the pediatricians faced a conflict. On one hand, many breast-fed babies appeared underweight; on the other hand, a trove of evidence indicates that breast-fed babies are generally healthier than their formula-fed peers. The conflict was resolved when it was realized that breast-fed babies typically gain less weight during the first year because, compared with formula-fed babies, they voluntarily take in less milk, due to the fact that it is easier to control the flow of milk from a breast than from a bottle (WHO, 2006). However, the growth charts were calculated with data from both breast- and formula-fed babies, so the heavier, faster-growing (but not necessarily healthier) formula-fed babies raised the averages.

Faced with mounting evidence that breast-fed and formula-fed babies grow differently during the first year, the World Health Organization (WHO) launched a massive international study to determine optimal standards of physical growth when children are being breast-fed through the first year of infancy and raised in a healthy environment (for example, with adequate health care and with mothers who do not smoke). Nearly 8,500 children growing up in such healthy environments in Brazil, Ghana, India, Norway, Oman, and the United States participated in the study, which resulted in new international standards for evaluating the physical growth of infants and young children. The study indicates that when raised in a healthy environment, babies everywhere, regardless of ethnicity or socioeconomic status, show comparable patterns of physical growth (WHO, 2006).

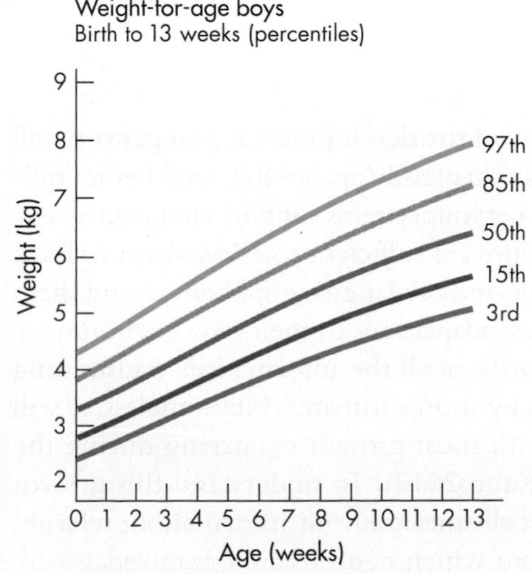

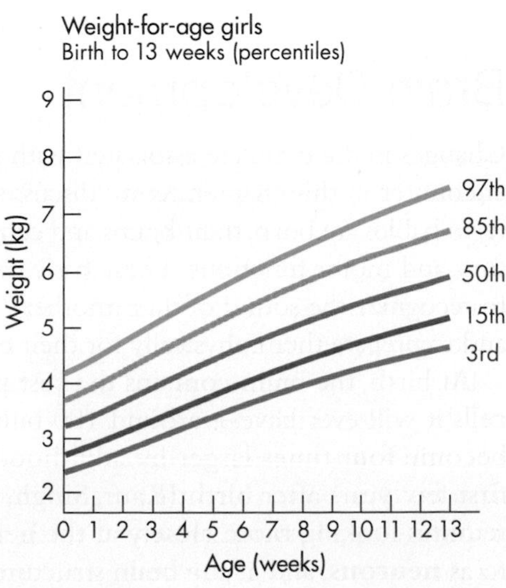

FIGURE 4.1 Growth charts show age-specific averages as well as variations from averages, helping health-care providers assess whether a child's development is on track or is a cause for concern. The figures to the left illustrate changes in weight averages for boys and girls between birth and 13 weeks of age. As shown in the chart for boys, at 8 weeks of age, 50 percent of all boys weigh more than 5.5 kilograms (12.1 pounds), and 50 percent weigh less (purple line). An 8-week-old boy weighing 4 kilograms (8.8 pounds) would be in the 3rd percentile (blue line), suggesting possible malnutrition and health problems. (Data from WHO, 2006.)

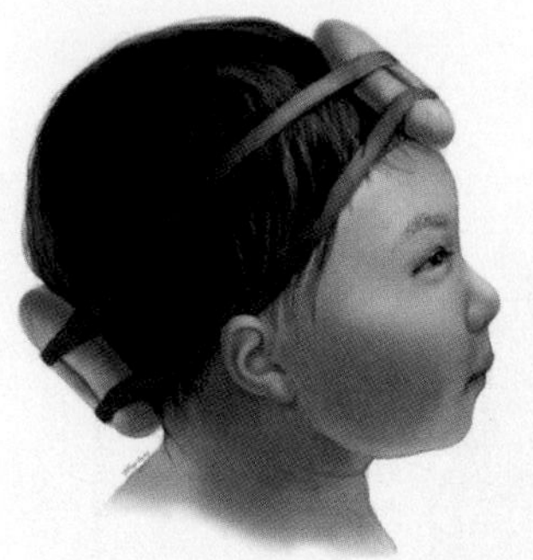

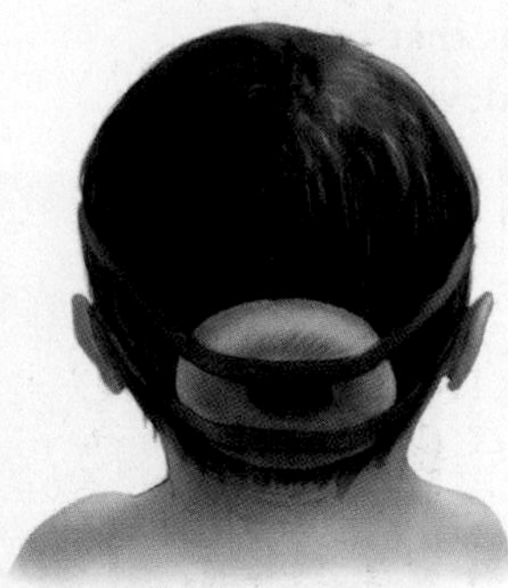

Emmanuel LATTES / Alamy

Taking advantage of how flexible the skull is in infancy, certain indigenous cultures in the Americas used a variety of methods and devices to intentionally and permanently alter the shape of their infants' skulls as a way of indicating the child's community or kinship ties and family wealth. (Research from Hoshower et al., 1995.)

fontanels "Soft spots," or spaces, that separate the bones of the skull prenatally and in early infancy.

Growth of the Skull

Health-care providers for infants track changes to the baby's head circumference because the primary determinant of the growth and shape of the head is the development of the brain. If you have ever stroked a baby's head, you know that a newborn's skull is considerably different than that of an older child or an adult. The infant's skull is composed of seven flat, membranous bones that are relatively soft and elastic (Jin et al., 2014). Early in development, the bones are separated by **fontanels**, also known as the "soft spots." Because the bones of the skull are separated, rather than fused together, they are capable of moving in response to external or internal pressure. This allows the skull to "mold" during birth in response to external pressure exerted by the relatively narrow birth canal and to expand in response to internal pressure exerted by a rapidly developing brain—an illustration of evolution's marvelous web of adaptations. During the first months of infancy, the growing brain pushes against the bones of the skull, expanding the infant's head circumference and contributing to its relatively round shape.

APPLY > CONNECT > DISCUSS

In societies in which mothers have the option of breast- or bottle-feeding their newborns, their choice is often influenced by cultural norms and expectations. Interview your mother and your grandmother about newborn feeding practices common in their generation. (If your mother or grandmother is not available, find another mother of the same generation.) Ask about how newborns were fed, why women might have chosen one method over another, what their own choices were, and so forth. Compare the two women's experiences and assess them in light of what is now known regarding feeding practices and infants' physical development.

Brain Development

LEARNING OUTCOMES

Identify the purpose for each part of a neuron involved in a neural network.

Describe the parts of the central nervous system and brain as presented in the text.

Explain the relationship between experience and the development of the brain.

Changes in the brain are associated with many of the developmental changes you will encounter in this chapter. As we discussed in Chapter 3 (pp. 86–87), well before full-term babies are born, their brains and central nervous systems support elementary sensory and motor functions. These basic capacities are sufficient to allow them to learn to recognize the sound of their mother's voice and the language spoken around them and to prepare them physically for their earliest adaptations to their new environment.

At birth, the brain contains the vast majority of all the information-transmitting cells it will ever have—around 100 billion, by most estimates. Nevertheless, it will become four times larger by adulthood, with most growth occurring during the first few years after birth (Kaur, Singh, & Kaur, 2017). To understand this growth requires looking more closely at the nerve cells that transmit information, referred to as **neurons**, and at the brain structures into which neurons are organized.

neuron A nerve cell.

Neurons and Networks of Neurons

The brain is an enormously complex communication system of neuron networks. Its complexity begins with how neurons transmit information. A neuron accomplishes its basic communication task in two ways: (1) by sending information via small electrical impulses along its **axon**, a branch that reaches out to connect with other brain cells, and (2) by receiving information from the axons of other cells through spiky protrusions called **dendrites** (Figure 4.2).

axon The main protruding branch of a neuron; it carries messages to other cells in the form of electrical impulses.

dendrites The protruding parts of a neuron that receive messages from the axons of other cells.

Between the axons and dendrites of communicating neurons is a tiny gap called a **synapse**. When an electrical impulse from the axon of the sending neuron arrives at the synapse, the sending neuron secretes a chemical called a **neurotransmitter** that carries the impulse across the synaptic gap, setting off a reaction in the receiving neuron.

synapse The tiny gap between the axon of one neuron and the dendrite of another.

neurotransmitter A chemical secreted by a neuron sending a message that carries the impulse across the synaptic gap to the receiving cell.

The combination of a sending neuron and a receiving neuron is the simplest form of a neuronal network. More complex networks are formed as multiple dendrites and axons interconnect. Many networks are established initially during the second half of gestation, although after birth they may change considerably in size and organization as a result of biological growth processes and the baby's experiences (Keunen, Counsell, & Benders, 2017; Smyser et al., 2010). Such multiple forms of connectivity—and the fact that there are billions and billions of neurons—make possible a virtually infinite variety of patterns of brain activity and behavior.

The basic architecture of neurons and neuronal networks suggests two of the reasons for the astonishing growth in brain size that occurs during infancy. Brain size is typically measured in terms of volume, which is estimated from brain scans (see the box "Observing the Living Brain" in Chapter 1, p. 33). Some of the growth in brain volume is due to an increase in the size and complexity of *gray matter*—that is, the information-receiving dendrites, which develop new branches, and the information-transmitting axons, which become longer. As a result of this increase, many new synapses are formed, in a process called **synaptogenesis**, which we discuss in more detail below. In addition to the increase in gray matter, brain volume grows as a result of increases in *white matter*, which includes **myelin**, an insulating material that forms a sheath around certain axons, speeding the transfer of information from one neuron to the next. Myelinated axons transmit signals anywhere from 10 to 100 times faster than unmyelinated axons, making possible more effective interconnections and communication among various parts of the brain, as well as more complicated forms of thought and action (Schmitt et al., 2014). Using magnetic imaging technology,

synaptogenesis The process of synapse formation.

myelin An insulating material that forms a sheath around certain axons and speeds the transmission of nerve impulses from one neuron to the next.

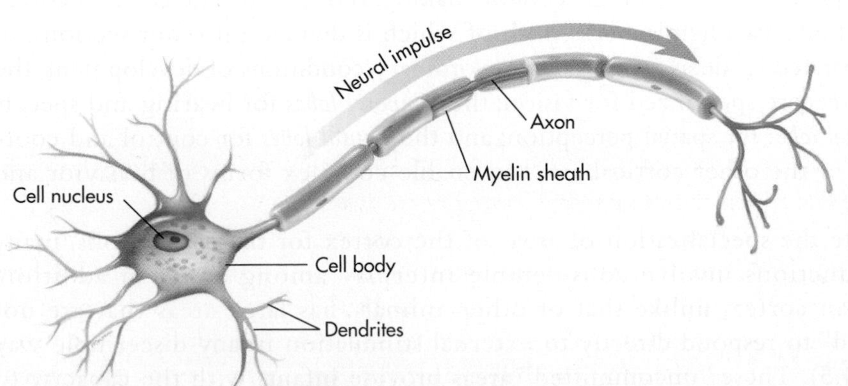

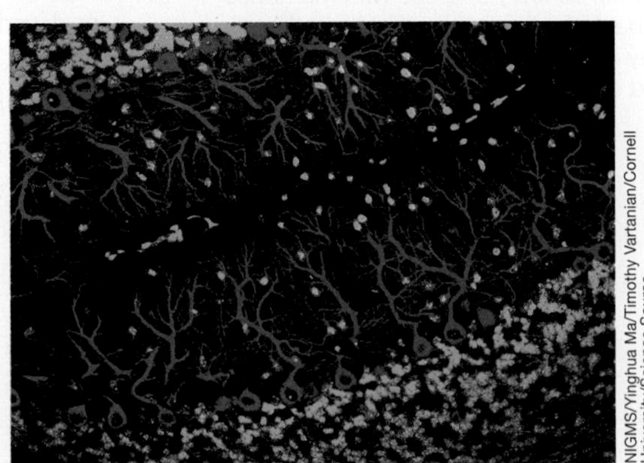

FIGURE 4.2 The neuron receives information from other neurons through its dendrites and feeds that information to other neurons through its axon. The photograph shows neurons in the cerebellum, a part of the brain that plays an important role in motor control.

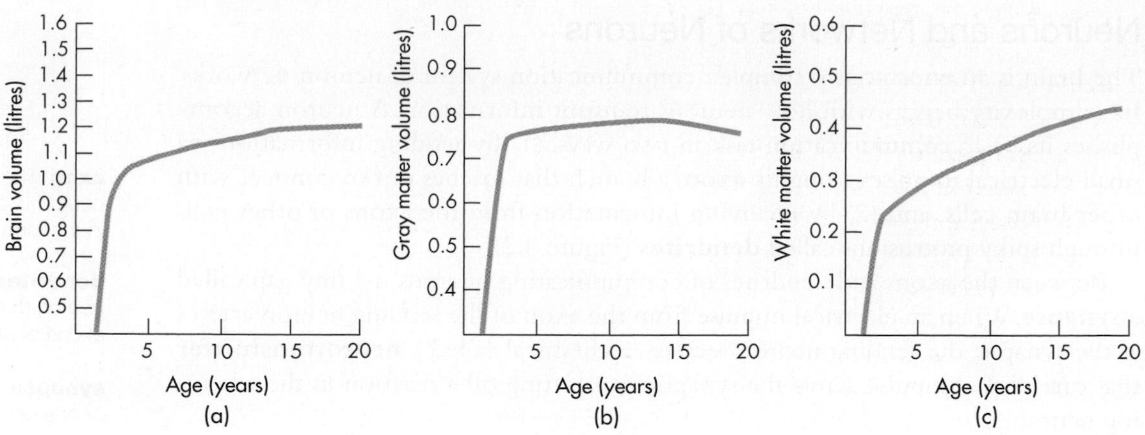

FIGURE 4.3 Magnetic imaging technology reveals substantial growth in brain volume during the early years of childhood (a). Much of this growth is a consequence of rapidly increasing gray matter, or *synaptogenesis* (b). White matter, or *myelin*, also increases rapidly during infancy and more gradually throughout childhood and adolescence (c). (Data from Schmitt et al., 2014.)

a team of developmental neuroscientists was able to chart changes in overall brain volume, gray matter, and white matter from birth to adulthood (Groeschel, Vollmer, King, & Connelly, 2010). As you can see in Figure 4.3, there is substantial growth during the first years of life, with gray matter making a particularly significant contribution to total brain volume.

The Structure of the Central Nervous System

Because of its association with the most complex behaviors of our species, the system of neural connections of greatest interest to developmentalists is the central nervous system. The central nervous system is conventionally divided into three major sections—the spinal cord, the brain stem, and the cerebral cortex. The **spinal cord**, a tubelike bundle of nerves, is encased in the spinal bones that extend from the base of the brain to below the waist. The nerves of the spinal cord carry messages back and forth from the brain to the spinal nerves that branch out from the spinal cord and communicate with specific areas of the body.

spinal cord The part of the central nervous system that extends from below the waist to the base of the brain.

The brain itself grows out of the top of the spinal cord (Figure 4.4). At its base is the **brain stem**, which controls such vital functions as breathing and sleeping, as well as such elementary reactions as reflexive blinking and sucking. All these capacities are established in at least rudimentary form during the later stages of prenatal development. At birth, the brain stem is one of the most highly developed areas of the central nervous system.

brain stem The base of the brain, which controls such elementary reactions as blinking and sucking, as well as such vital functions as breathing and sleeping.

The **cerebral cortex** is the brain's outermost layer and most complex system, the processing center for the perception of patterns, the execution of complex motor sequences, and planning, decision-making, and speech. The cerebral cortex is divided into two hemispheres, each of which is divided into four sections, or lobes, separated by deep grooves. Under ordinary conditions of development, the *occipital lobes* are specialized for vision; the *temporal lobes* for hearing and speech; the *parietal lobes* for spatial perception; and the *frontal lobes* for control and coordination of the other cortical areas to enable complex forms of behavior and thought.

cerebral cortex The brain's outermost layer. The networks of neurons in the cerebral cortex integrate information from several sensory sources with memories of past experiences, processing them in a way that results in human forms of thought and action.

Despite the specialization of areas of the cortex for these functions, many of the functions involve considerable interplay among areas. In addition, the human cortex, unlike that of other animals, has large areas that are not "prewired" to respond directly to external stimulation in any discernible way (Figure 4.5). These "uncommitted" areas provide infants with the capacity to develop brain circuits that grow and change depending on the experiences they have as they develop, a capacity we referred to in Chapter 1 (p. 13) as *plasticity*.

At birth, the circuitry of the cerebral cortex is less mature than that of the spinal cord and brain stem (that is, it has fewer dendritic branches and is less myelinated),

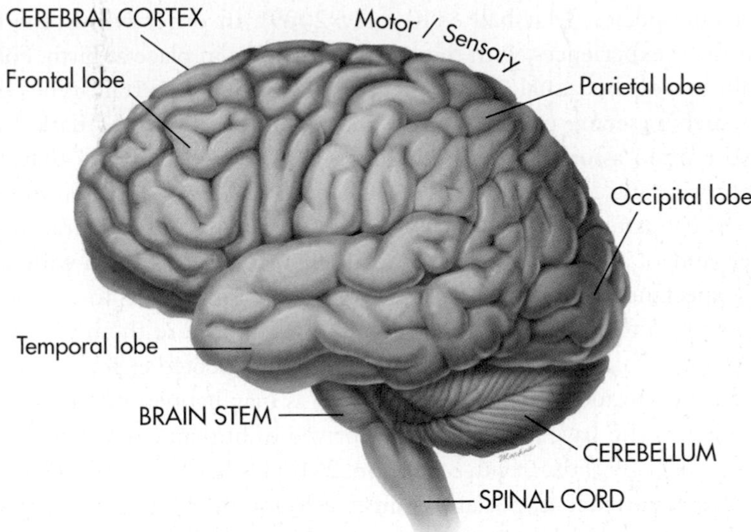

FIGURE 4.4 This schematic view of the brain shows the major lobes, or divisions, of the cerebral cortex (including the areas where some functions are localized); the brain stem, the cerebellum; and the spinal cord. (Research from Tanner, 1978.)

and it is poorly connected to the lower-lying parts of the nervous system that receive stimulation from the environment. Because of their relative maturity, the spinal cord and brain stem enable movement, responses to visual stimuli, and even elementary forms of learning without cortical involvement (Kennard, Brown, & Woodruff-Pak, 2013). As the nerve fibers connecting the cortex with the brain stem and spinal cord become myelinated, the infant's abilities expand.

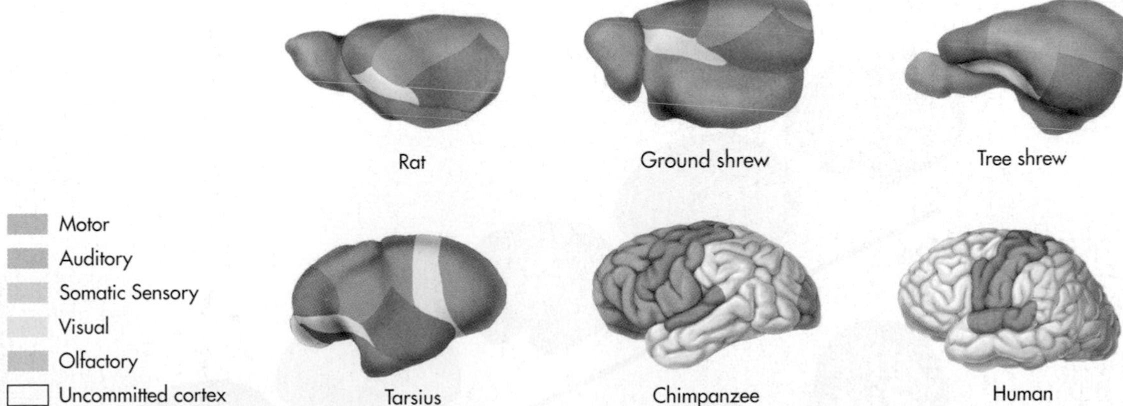

FIGURE 4.5 In these six mammalian species, the proportions of the brain mass that are devoted to different functions vary widely. The areas designated "uncommitted cortex" are not dedicated to any particular sensory or motor functions and are available for integrating information of many kinds. (Research from Fishbein, 1976.)

Experience and Development of the Brain

Although brain development in large measure takes place according to strictly internal biological processes, the environment also plays a major role in shaping the brain's structures. Developmentalists distinguish two major classes of brain development, which they refer to as *experience-expectant* and *experience-dependent* (Marshall & Kenney, 2009; Roembke, Wasserman, & McMurray, 2016).

As the name implies, **experience-expectant** processes of brain development are those that seem to *anticipate* experiences that are universal in all normally developing

experience-expectant Processes of brain development that seem to *anticipate* experiences that are universal in all normally developing members of our species.

members of our species (Marshall & Kenney, 2009). In other words, the brain is prewired for these experiences, with the relevant synapses in place at birth. For example, the evolution of the visual cortex prepares the baby for certain types of visual experiences such as seeing patterns and borders between light and dark. Likewise, the part of the brain associated with language has evolved in a way that prepares the baby to process and learn language (see Chapter 7). All human environments are infused with visual patterns and light–dark borders that help us distinguish one object from another. And, of course, virtually all human environments are rich with language. Experience-expectant processes of brain development allow infants to take advantage of their exposure to these features of the environment and use them to acquire the related basic human behaviors and abilities. When such expected experiences are lacking during sensitive periods of brain development, as may happen in the case of blind infants or of babies who have been severely deprived of human contact, the brain will fail to develop normally (Fox, Levitt, & Nelson, 2010; Hubel & Wiesel, 2004).

exuberant synaptogenesis A rapid growth in synaptic density that prepares the brain for a vast range of possible experiences.

synaptic pruning The process of selective dying-off of nonfunctional synapses.

Evidence for experience-expectant brain development is found in an interesting pattern of synaptic proliferation and elimination. At several points during development (including adolescence), different portions of the brain undergo an explosive increase in synapse formation, called **exuberant synaptogenesis**, which produces far more synapses than would be required by the particular experiences the growing organism is likely to encounter. In other words, the profusion of synapses, at different points in development, seem to prepare the brain for a range of possible experiences. Over time, in something like a "use it or lose it" process, synapses that are not used atrophy and die off, a phenomenon referred to as **synaptic pruning** (Piochon, Kano, & Hansel, 2016). It has been estimated that fully 70 percent of the neurons in the human cortex are pruned between the 28th week after conception and birth. Other intensive periods of synaptic pruning have been found in infancy, middle childhood, and adolescence (Giedd & Rapoport, 2010; Mah & Ford-Jones, 2012; Selemon, 2013) (see Figure 4.6).

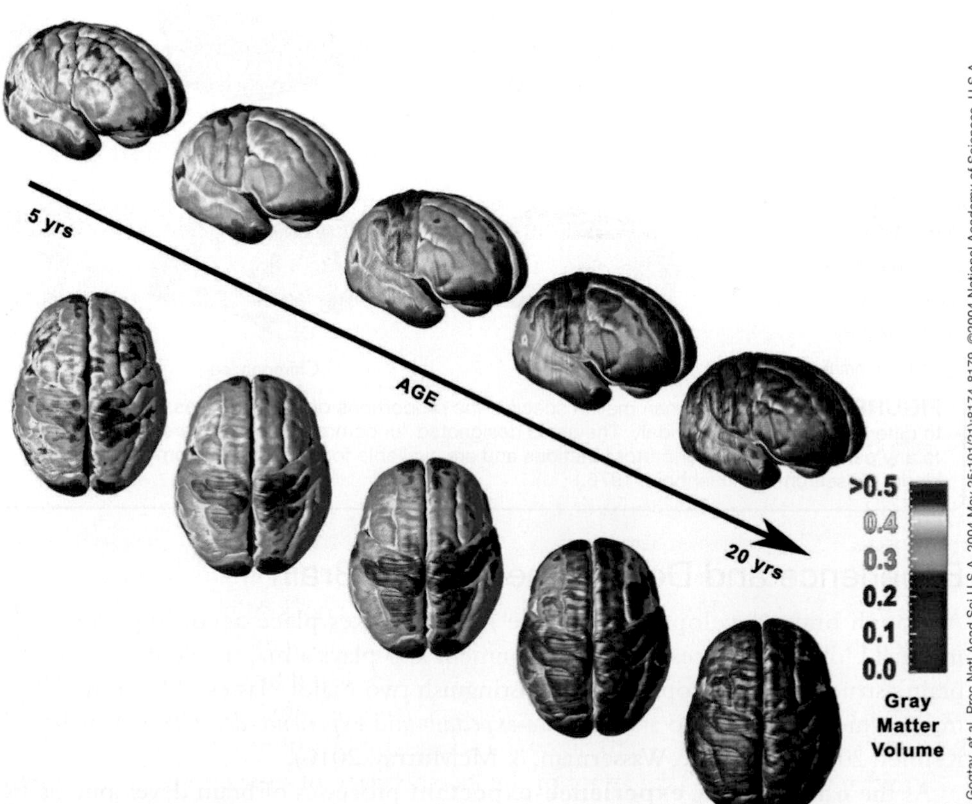

Nitin Gogtay, et al. Proc Natl Acad Sci U S A. 2004 May 25;101(21):8174-8179. ©2004 National Academy of Sciences, U.S.A.

FIGURE 4.6 Decreases in the amount of gray matter reflect a process of *synaptic pruning* in which synapses that are not used by the developing brain atrophy and die off. (Data from Gogtay et al., 2004.)

In contrast to the synapses involved in universal experience-expectant brain development, those involved in **experience-dependent** brain development are not created in advance of species-universal experiences; instead, they are generated in response to the specific experiences of specific individuals. Experience-dependent processes have evolved to allow the organism to take advantage of new and changing information in the environment. It is this experience-dependent brain–environment relationship that allows humans to learn from experience (Bialystok, 2017).

experience-dependent Development of neural connections that is initiated in response to experience.

An example of experience-dependent brain development comes from pioneering studies by Mark Rosenzweig and his colleagues (Rosenzweig, 1984), in which groups of young male laboratory rats from the same litter were raised in three different environments. Rats in the first two groups were housed individually or together in standard laboratory cages equipped with only food and water dispensers. In contrast, rats in the third group were provided with enriched conditions. They lived together in a large cage furnished with a variety of playthings that were changed daily to keep their lives interesting. They were also given formal training in running a maze or were sometimes placed in an open field filled with toys.

At the end of the experimental period, which lasted anywhere from a few weeks to several months, behavioral tests and examinations of the animals' brains revealed superior development in the animals raised in enriched conditions. Compared with the other two groups, these rats demonstrated:

- Increased rates of learning in standard laboratory tasks, such as learning a maze
- Increased overall weight of the cerebral cortex, the part of the brain that integrates sensory information
- Increased amounts of acetylcholinesterase, a brain enzyme that enhances learning
- Larger neuronal cell bodies and larger glial cells (cells that provide insulation, support, and nutrients to neuronal cells)
- More synaptic connections

These findings have been replicated and extended in numerous experiments (Cheng et al., 2014). As you will see in Chapter 6, they are also consistent with what is known about how the quality of the environment of human infants can affect their brain development as well as their development in other domains.

APPLY > CONNECT > DISCUSS

It is widely believed that the developing brain benefits from an enriched environment and suffers in an environment of deprivation. Using the language and concepts presented in this section, explain what it means for an environment to be "enriched" or "deprived."

Sensing the Environment

LEARNING OUTCOMES

Describe the state of various senses in newborns.

Illustrate some relationships between various senses and an infant's environment.

Explain the process of perceptual narrowing.

Describe some methods for evaluating the sensory capacities of infants.

Explain how infants use multimodal perception.

Baba is Qalandar, born to a nomadic tribe of entertainers who travel from town to town in Pakistan, exhibiting their dancing bears and monkeys, singing, juggling, and performing magic. As a newborn, when Baba wasn't in the arms of his mother or another tent member, he was placed in a *jhula*, a patchwork cloth hammock suspended a few feet off the ground from the tent ridgepole. Swinging gently in his *jhula*, he would be exposed to the smiling faces of other tent members as they kissed and tickled him, the smells of food and animals, and the sounds of language and laughter, music and chattering monkeys, and the jingling bells tied to his own ankles and wrists (Berland, 1982).

To what extent was Baba aware of the kaleidoscope of sights, sounds, and smells that surrounded his *jhula*? Did he perceive his surroundings as a "buzzing confusion,"

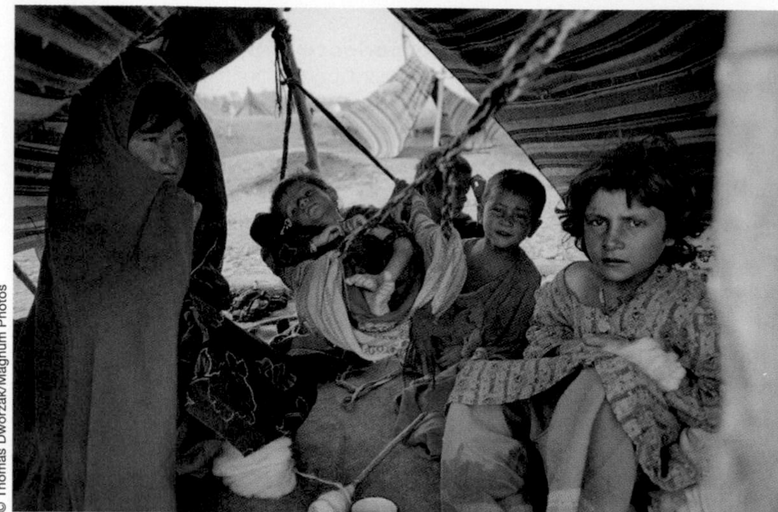

© Thomas Dworzak/Magnum Photos

As Qalandar custom dictates, this infant lies in a cloth hammock called a *jhula*, safe from snakes and insects and close to the faces of older siblings.

as the philosopher-psychologist William James (1890) believed all infants do—a perceptual jumble that would only gradually become clear with time and experience? Or was Baba born with fairly sophisticated, even adultlike, capacities that allowed him to perceive order and consistency in the world? Did he understand, for example, the connection between the jingling sounds he heard and the movement of his arms and legs?

Developmentalists are divided on how to answer such questions (Scott, Richman, & Baillargeon, 2015). This difference of opinion about what perceptual abilities and understandings infants start out with strongly influences the kind of theory needed to explain subsequent processes of developmental change. The idea that infants' perceptions initially amount to total confusion suggests that the world becomes an ordered and predictable place to infants only as they gain experience and learn about the environment. In contrast, the idea that infants are highly competent suggests that biology may play a critical role, endowing infants with special abilities that allow them to tune in to specific features of the environment—visual patterns or the sound of the human voice, for example. As you will see, most developmentalists take a middle ground, maintaining that initial sensory capacities are biologically determined, but only to the extent that they guide how experience shapes later development. This middle ground is consistent with **perceptual narrowing**, a process in which infants lose their apparently innate abilities to detect certain sensory features because those features do not occur very often in their environments. (We discuss perceptual narrowing in more detail in the section "Hearing.")

perceptual narrowing A process in which infants lose their apparently innate abilities to detect certain sensory features because those features do not occur very often in their environments.

Methods of Evaluating Infant Sensory Capacities

You do not have to spend much time with a newborn to understand the difficulties researchers face in assessing infants' initial capacities. Babies sleep a lot—about three-quarters of every day in the first month. When they are awake, they may be drowsy or upset. Even when they appear to be alert and calm, they often do not seem to be paying attention to anything in particular; occasionally something seems to catch their interest, but only fleetingly. These constant fluctuations in newborn states make it difficult for developmentalists to provide reliable and replicable evidence regarding particular newborn capacities.

Normal full-term newborns enter the world with all sensory systems functioning. However, not all of these systems have developed to the same level. For example, newborns' senses of touch and smell are considerably more advanced than their sharpness of vision. This is not surprising, given the relative importance of touch and odor for finding a food source—the breast—and the relative unimportance of vision to the newborn's survival. In addition, this unevenness illustrates the general rules of development of heterochrony and heterogeneity that we remarked on in Chapter 3 (p. 82). Different parts of an organism develop at different rates and are therefore at different levels of development at a given time.

The basic method developmentalists use to evaluate infant sensory capacities is to present infants with a stimulus and observe their overt behavioral or physiological responses to it. For example, an investigator might sound a tone or flash a light and watch for an indication—a turn of the head, a variation in brain waves, a change in heart rate—that the newborn has sensed it. One of the most common physiological methods used in this type of procedure is **electroencephalography (EEG)**,

electroencephalography (EEG) A common physiological method used to evaluate infant sensory capacities, which involves attaching sensors to the baby's head and measuring changes in brain waves in response to the presentation of different stimuli.

which involves attaching sensors to the baby's head and measuring changes in brain waves in response to the presentation of different stimuli (Marshall, Saby, & Meltzoff, 2013; Piazza et al., 2016). A widely used behavioral method, the **visual preference technique**, involves presenting two different stimuli at once to determine if the baby displays a preference by looking at one longer than the other (Griffey & Little, 2014). If so, the baby must be able to tell the stimuli apart. New technologies provide sophisticated devices for tracking infants' eye movements and computer software that analyzes the eye-movement data.

visual preference technique A common behavioral method used to evaluate infant sensory capacities, which involves presenting two different stimuli at once to determine if the baby displays a preference by looking at one longer than the other.

habituation The process in which attention to novelty decreases with repeated exposure.

dishabituation The term used to describe the process in which an infant's interest is renewed after a change in the stimulus.

Yet another technique for assessing sensory capacities exploits a process known as **habituation**, in which an infant's attention to a novel stimulus decreases following continued exposure to it. Using this technique, an investigator presents an infant with a novel stimulus that captures the infant's attention, such as a musical tone or a pictorial arrangement of simple geometric figures, and then continues presenting it until the infant gets bored and stops paying attention to it. The next step is to change some aspect of the stimulus, such as the pitch of the musical tone or the arrangement of the geometric figures, for example. If the infant shows renewed interest after the change in the stimulus, the infant is said to exhibit **dishabituation**, and the investigator can conclude that the infant perceived the change. The use of such subtle indicators of infants' attention to sensory stimuli provides developmentalists with essential tools for understanding developmental processes at a time when infants are still too immature to make their experiences known through coordinated movement or speech.

Image rights: Tobii AB

Which puppet is more appealing, the yellow one with the big smile, or the blue one with the googly eyes? This baby's preference for one or the other is determined by the amount of time spent looking at each. The black box on the table is a sophisticated eye-tracking device that measures the baby's visual fixation on the two objects. The device can also measure eye movements as the baby visually explores different objects.

Hearing

Fetuses respond to sounds outside the mother's womb, so it is not surprising that newborns respond to sound immediately after birth. Make a loud noise, and infants only minutes old will startle and may even cry. They will also turn their head toward the source of the noise, an indication that they perceive sound as roughly localized in space (Freigang, Richter, Rübsamen, & Ludwig, 2015; Morrongiello, Fenwick, Hillier, & Chance, 1994). Significantly, newborns can distinguish the sound of the human voice from other kinds of sounds, and they seem to prefer it to any other. They are especially attuned to the sounds of language. Newborns all over the world are particularly interested in speech directed to them that has a high pitch and slow, exaggerated pronunciation—speech known as "motherese," "baby talk," or "infant-directed speech" (Narayan & McDermott, 2016; Schachner & Hannon, 2011). The baby's attunement to speech with these characteristics may account for the finding that infants prefer to hear the vocalizations of other infants to those of adults (Masapollo, Polka, & Ménard, 2016).

One of the most striking discoveries about the hearing of very young infants is that it is sensitive to the smallest sound categories in human speech that distinguish meanings (Sato, Sogabe, & Mazuka, 2010). These basic language sounds are called **phonemes**, and they vary from language to language. In Spanish, for example, /r/ and /rr/ are different phonemes (linguists use slashes to denote phonemes); thus, "pero" and "perro," for example, which sound different—"perro" has a rolling *r*—have different meanings. In English, however, there is no such distinction. Similarly, /r/ and /l/ are different phonemes in English but not in Japanese.

phonemes The smallest sound categories in human speech that distinguish meanings. Phonemes vary from language to language.

In a pioneering study, Peter Eimas and his colleagues demonstrated that 2-month-olds distinguish among a variety of phonemes (Eimas, 1985). The researchers began by having the infants suck on a nipple attached to a recording device similar to the

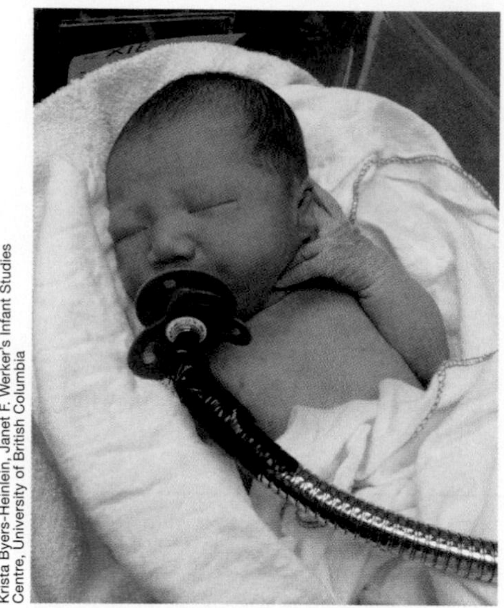

Krista Byers-Heinlein, Janet F. Werker's Infant Studies Centre, University of British Columbia

FIGURE 4.7 This photo shows an apparatus used to register young infants' responses to artificially manipulated speech sounds. The baby sucks on a pacifier connected to recording instruments as speechlike sounds are presented. The recording instruments register changes in the baby's rate of sucking as different sounds are presented.

one shown in Figure 4.7. After establishing a baseline rate of sucking for each baby, they presented the speech sound /pa/ to the babies each time they sucked. At first, the babies' rate of sucking increased, as if they were excited by each presentation of the sound, but after a while they settled back to their baseline rates of sucking. When the infants had become thoroughly habituated to the sound of /pa/, some of them heard a new sound, /ba/, which differed from the original sound in its initial phoneme—/b/ versus /p/. Others were presented with a sound that was different but remained within the /p/ phoneme category. The babies began sucking rapidly again only when they heard a sound that belonged to a different phoneme category, an indication that they were especially sensitive to the kinds of differences that languages use to distinguish phonemes (Figure 4.8).

Follow-up studies have shown that very young infants are able to perceive all the categorical sound distinctions used in all the world's languages. Adults, in contrast, perceive only those of their native language. Japanese babies, for example, can perceive the difference between /r/ and /l/; adult speakers of Japanese cannot (Yoshida et al., 2010). In one of the most well-known examples of perceptual narrowing, at around 6 to 8 months of age, and corresponding to specific changes taking place in language areas of the brain, infants' ability to make phonemic distinctions narrows to just those distinctions that are present in their native language (Altvater-Mackensen & Grossmann, 2016; Martin, Peperkamp, & Dupoux, 2013; Werker, Yeung, & Yoshida, 2012) (Figure 4.9). Interestingly, perceptual narrowing may develop differently for infants in bilingual environments. These babies may remain sensitive to nonnative phonemic contrasts for a longer period of time than do babies in monolingual environments (Byers-Heinlein & Fennell, 2014). Given the pattern of infant brain growth during this time, some developmentalists have speculated that the narrowing of the ability to make phonemic distinctions is an example of how cultural experience interacts with the biological process of synaptogenesis and pruning that we discussed earlier (see p. 130; Munakata, Casey, & Diamond, 2004).

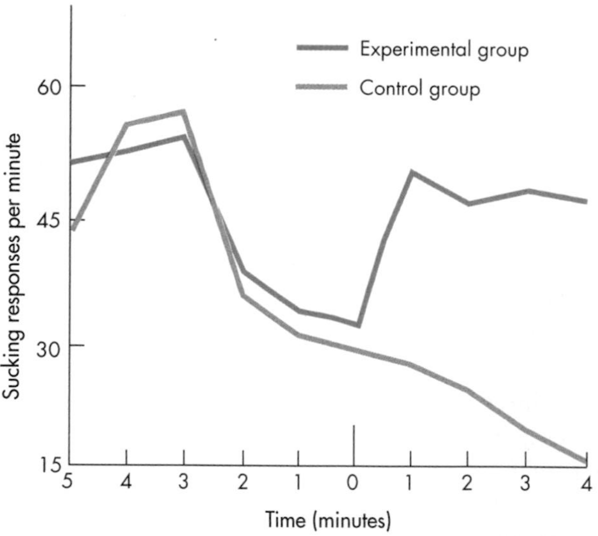

FIGURE 4.8 When two groups of infants were repeatedly presented with a single consonant over a 5-minute period, their rates of sucking decreased to just over 30 sucks per minute. For half of the infants (the experimental group), the consonant was changed at the time marked 0. Note that their rate of sucking increased sharply. For the remaining infants (the control group), who continued to hear the same consonant, the rate of sucking continued to decrease. (Data from Eimas, 1985.)

Vision

The basic anatomical components of the visual system are present at birth, but they are not fully developed. The lens of the eye and the cells of the retina are somewhat immature, limiting visual sharpness. In addition, the movements of the baby's eyes are not coordinated well enough to align the images on the two retinas to form a clear composite image. The result is that the baby's vision is blurry. The immaturity of some of the neural pathways that relay information from the retina to the brain further limits the newborn's visual capacities (Atkinson, 1998). Numerous studies have been conducted to determine exactly what, and how well, infants can see, as well as how the visual system changes over time (Braddick & Atkinson, 2011).

Visual Acuity

A basic question about infants' vision concerns their **visual acuity**—that is, their sharpness of vision. Estimates of newborns' visual acuity differ somewhat, depending on the particular measure used, but all suggest that newborns are very nearsighted, with a visual acuity in the neighborhood of 20/300 to 20/600. In other words, their visual acuity is about 60 times worse than that of adults (Maurer, 2016). (Figure 4.10 roughly indicates what infants can see at different ages.)

visual acuity Sharpness of vision.

Poor visual acuity is probably less troublesome to newborns than to older children and adults. After all, newborns are unable to move around on their own, and they cannot hold their heads erect without support. Still, their visual system is tuned well enough to allow them to see objects about 1 foot (30 centimeters) away—roughly the distance of the mother's face during nursing. This level of acuity allows them to make eye contact, which is important in establishing the social relationship between mother and child (Stern, 2002). Between 2 and 3 months of age, infants can coordinate the vision of both their eyes (Braddick & Atkinson, 2011). By 7 or 8 months of age, their visual acuity increases dramatically, but it doesn't approach adult levels until 7 years of age. Interestingly, the infant's visual experiences are key to developing greater levels of acuity. This has been demonstrated in studies of babies born with congenital cataracts that block all patterned visual input (Maurer, 2016). When the cataracts are removed—regardless of whether the treatment has occurred at 1 or 9 months of age—the baby's visual acuity is similar to that of a normally sighted newborn. Although there is a "catch-up effect" resulting in vision within normal limits by the first birthday, the gains do not persist, and babies born with cataracts typically develop poor vision as children and adults.

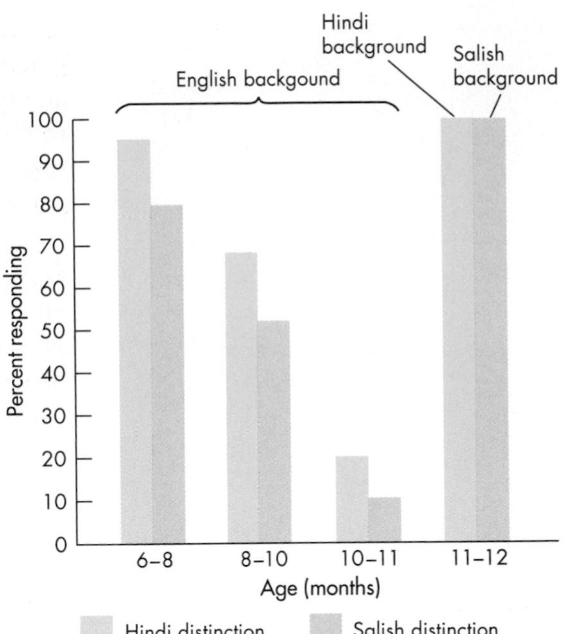

FIGURE 4.9 Infants can distinguish among language sounds that do not occur in their native language, but this capacity diminishes during the first year of life. Note the decrease in the proportion of infants from an English-speaking background who respond to consonants in Hindi and Salish (a Native American Indian language). In contrast, at 1 year, Hindi and Salish infants retain the capacity to distinguish sounds in their native languages. (Data from Eimas, 1985.)

Visual Scanning Despite their nearsightedness and their difficulty focusing, newborns actively scan their surroundings from the earliest days of life, and they even respond to certain visual stimuli; for example, they will open their mouths in response to a researcher moving his or her fingertip toward the mouth (Futagi et al., 2016; Maurer, 2016). Over the course of decades of research, developmentalists have devised increasingly sophisticated recording techniques that allow them to monitor infants' eye movements (see the photo of modern infant scanning technology on page 133). Early research discovered that even in a completely darkened room, neonates scan with short eye movements (Haith, 1980). Since no light is entering their eyes, the visual environment cannot cause this kind of scanning. It must therefore be *endogenous*, originating in the neural activity of the central nervous system. Endogenous eye movements seem to be an initial, primitive basis for looking behavior.

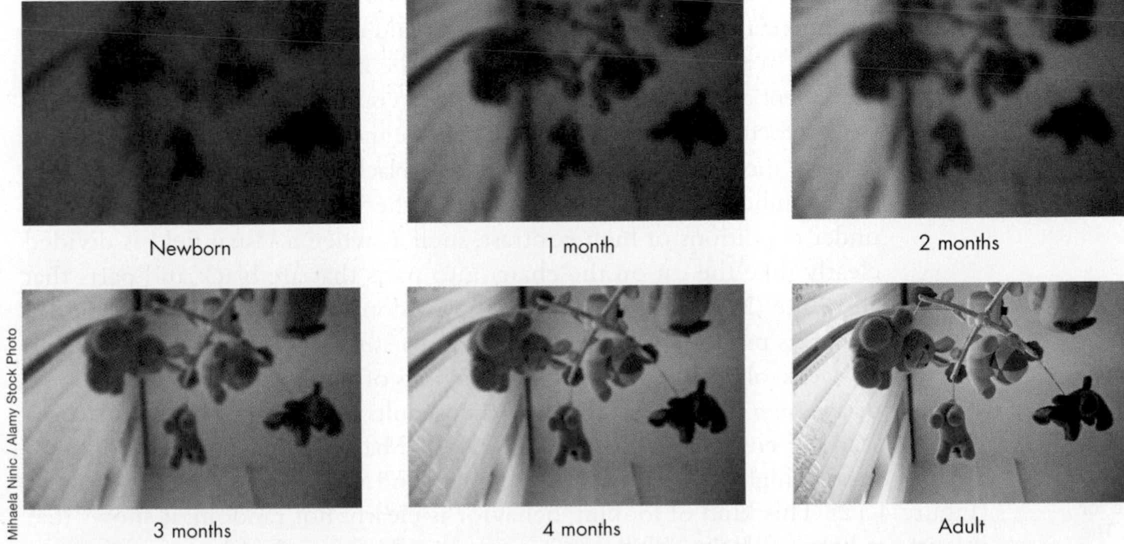

Mihaela Ninic / Alamy Stock Photo

FIGURE 4.10 Infants' visual acuity increases dramatically over the first few months of life. By the age of 4 months, a baby can see nearly as distinctly as an adult, as illustrated by this photographic conception of the appearance of a visual scene for infants of different ages.

Neonates also exhibit *exogenous* looking—that is, looking stimulated by the external environment. Exogenous looking occurs when the infant's gaze encounters an object or some change of brightness in the visual field. This very early sensitivity to changes in brightness, which is usually associated with the edges and angles of objects, appears to be an important component of the baby's developing ability to perceive visual forms (Haith, 1980).

Color Perceptions Newborns seem to possess all, or nearly all, of the physiological prerequisites for seeing color in a rudimentary form. When two colors are equally bright, however, they do not discriminate between them. By 2 months of age, infants' ability to perceive different colors appears to approach adult levels (Kellman & Banks, 1998).

Perception of Patterns and Objects What do babies see when their eyes encounter an object? Until the early 1960s, it was widely believed that neonates perceive only a formless play of light. In a classic series of studies, Robert Fantz (1961, 1963) disproved this assumption by demonstrating that babies less than 2 days old can distinguish between visual forms. The technique he used was very simple. He showed babies pairs of various forms and measured how much time they spent looking at them. Because the infants spent more time looking at some forms than at others, presumably they could tell the forms apart and looked longest at the ones they preferred. Fantz found that neonates would rather look at patterned figures, such as faces and concentric circles, than at plain ones (Figure 4.11). Fantz's findings set off a search to determine the extent of newborns' capacity to perceive objects and the reasons they prefer some forms to others. That research has confirmed that infants visually perceive the world as more than random confusion, as well as that infants' ability to perceive objects is far from adultlike and continues to develop over the first months of life (Bremner et al., 2016).

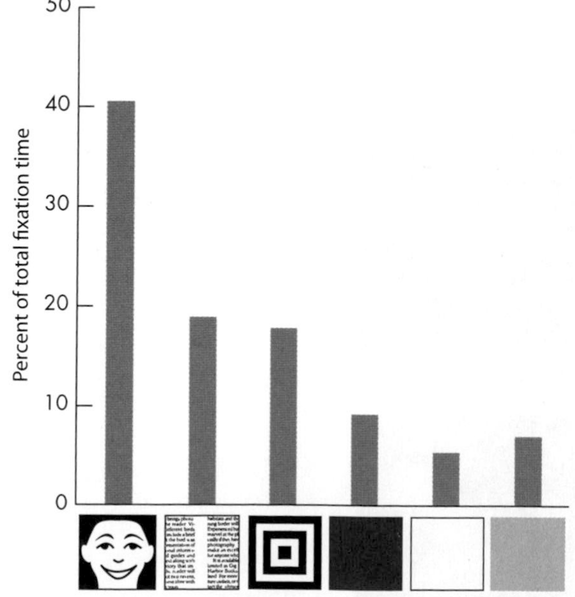

FIGURE 4.11 Infants tested during the first weeks of life show a preference for patterned stimuli over plain stimuli. The length of each bar indicates the relative amount of time the babies spent looking at the corresponding stimulus. (Research from Fantz, 1961.)

By 2 months of age, infants begin to show that in some circumstances they see the boundaries between objects and recognize that objects are three-dimensional (Taylor et al., 2014). These abilities are by no means as elementary as you might think. How, for example, does a newborn who is staring at a cat on a chair know that the cat is not part of the chair? Is it easier for the infant to distinguish between cat and chair if the cat meows or licks its paw? In a later section we will address the importance of vocalization and movement as important cues in the baby's visual perception of objects. Here we will focus on another important cue, contrast: The baby's ability to tell the cat from the chair is enhanced if the cat is black and the chair is white.

A number of studies have shown that the vision of young infants is best under conditions of high contrast, such as when a visual field is divided clearly (like the cat on the chair) into parts that are black and parts that are white (Kellman & Banks, 1998). Gordon Bronson (1991, 1994, 1997) used this property of newborn vision to study the way 2-week-old and 12-week-old babies scan outline drawings of simple figures, such as a cross or a V, on a lighted visual field. When adults are shown such figures, they scan the entire boundary. Two-week-old babies appear to focus only on areas of high contrast, such as black lines and angles on a white background (Figure 4.12). This kind of looking behavior is clearly not random; it shows that infants are born with the ability to perceive basic patterns. At 12 weeks of age, as Figure 4.12 indicates, infants scan more of the figure than at 2 weeks, although their scanning movements are sometimes off the mark and may still be arrested by areas of high contrast. In one of his studies, Bronson (1994) found that

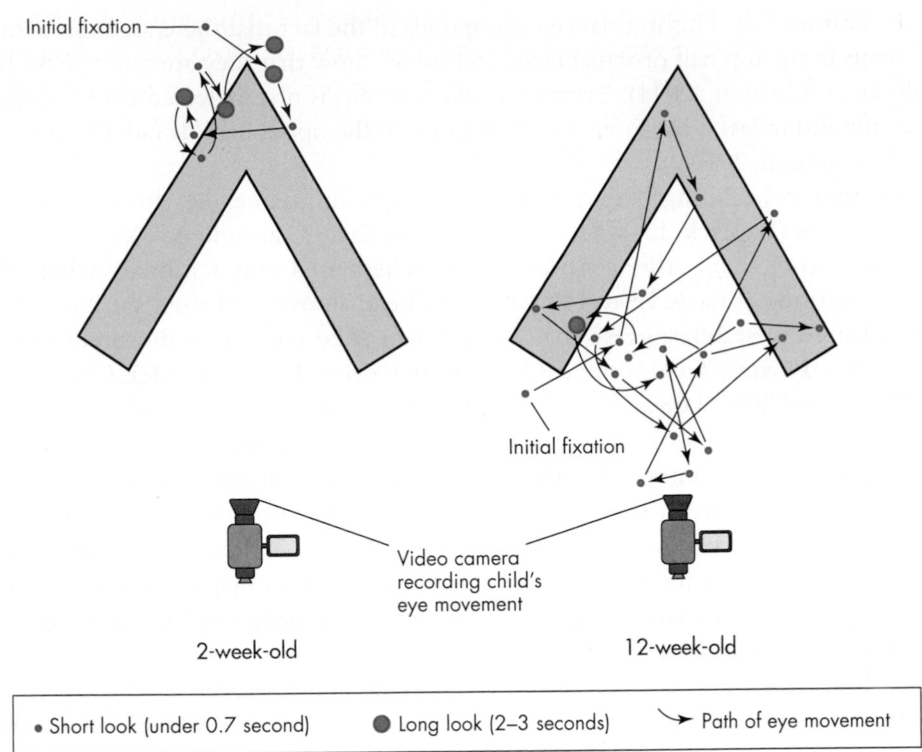

FIGURE 4.12 The diagram depicts the visual scanning of a triangle by young infants. The triangle was mounted on a wall. A video camera was mounted just beneath it, positioned to record the eye movements of infants as they gazed at the triangle. Note that the 2-week-olds concentrated their gaze on only one part of the figure, whereas the 12-week-olds visually explored the figure more fully. Large dots indicate long fixation times; small dots represent short ones. (Research from Bronson, 1991.)

13-week-old infants scanned more rapidly and extensively than did infants 10 weeks of age and under. The developmental change was so marked that Bronson concluded, "by 3 months of age [the] infants appear[ed] to be quite different organisms, at least with respect to their scanning characteristics" (p. 1260). He suggested that as the nervous system matures, it becomes more sophisticated and can begin to control visual scanning. However, research suggests that the ability to detect the contours of objects continues to develop throughout childhood and even into adolescence (Taylor et al., 2014).

Perception of Faces Because of babies' nearsightedness and the sheer amount of time they are held for feeding and comforting, the human face is one of the most common features of the newborn's visual world (Jayaraman, Fausey, & Smith, 2015). In some of his early studies, Fantz presented newborns with a schematic diagram of a human face and a diagram of a facelike form in which facial elements had been scrambled (Figure 4.13; Fantz, 1961, 1963). He found that the infants could distinguish the normal face from the jumbled face, and they preferred the normal one. Although the preference was small, the possibility that newborns have an unlearned preference for a biologically significant form like a face naturally attracted developmentalists' interest (Wilkinson et al., 2014).

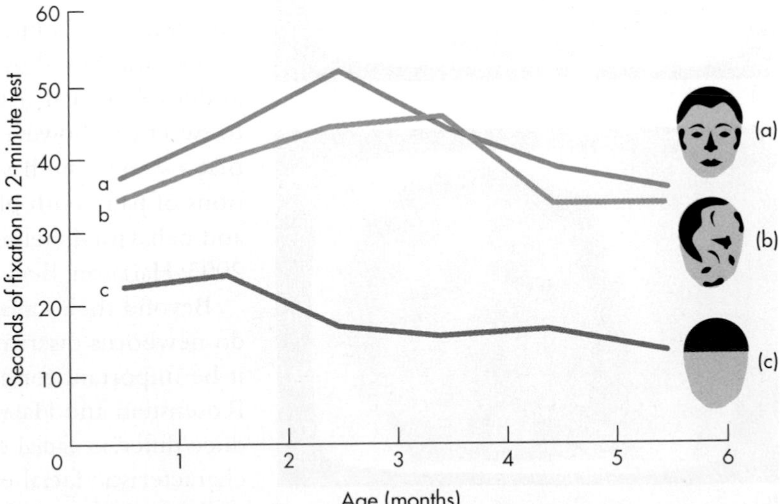

FIGURE 4.13 Visual preferences of infants for (a) a schematic face, (b) a scrambled schematic face, and (c) a nonfacelike figure, all having equal amounts of light and dark area. The infants preferred both facelike forms over the nonfacelike form, and they paid slightly more attention to the "real" than to the scrambled face. (Research from Fantz, 1961.)

Recent work has shown that a crucial factor in newborns' preference for faces is the presence of more elements in the upper part of the configuration than in the bottom half. This imbalance corresponds to the fact that there are more visual elements in the top half of actual faces, and babies show that they are sensitive to this imbalance (Liu et al., 2011). Even a facelike stimulus is not preferred over a scrambled stimulus unless it has more visual elements in the upper half (Turati, Di Giorgio, Bardi, & Simion, 2010).

Another key finding is that motion critically influences newborns' perception of faces (Bahrick, Lickliter, & Castellanos, 2013; Lalonde & Werner, 2016). In Fantz's studies and other early work, researchers used only stationary schematic representations of faces. In real life, people's heads move, and their facial expressions change. Research suggests that young infants, like adults, may discriminate and remember dynamic faces more easily than they do still faces (Lander, Chuang, & Wickham, 2006; Lewkowicz, 2010). This may help account for why newborns only 2 to 7 hours old recognize, and show a preference for, their mother's face when it is contrasted with that of a stranger, even after a delay as long as 15 minutes between the time that the infant sees the mother's face and the time the test is begun (Bushnell, 2001). In addition, infants' expectations that facial movements and speech should "go together" may help them discriminate speech from other background noise, which likely facilitates language learning (Lalonde & Werner, 2016).

Indeed, as we learned in the case of the auditory system, the developing visual system is highly sensitive to the baby's individual experiences, and it is subject to a similar process of perceptual narrowing (Mondloch & Desjarlais, 2010). Thus, by 3 months of age, babies tend to look more at faces with ethnic features (for example, Asian, Caucasian, African) similar to those with which they are most familiar (Liu et al., 2010). Likewise, over the course of the first year, infants become able to discriminate between faces of their own ethnicity better than they can discriminate between faces of some other ethnic group (Balas, 2012). Chinese babies, for example, become better at discriminating between faces with Asian features than between faces with African or Caucasian features (Kelly et al., 2009).

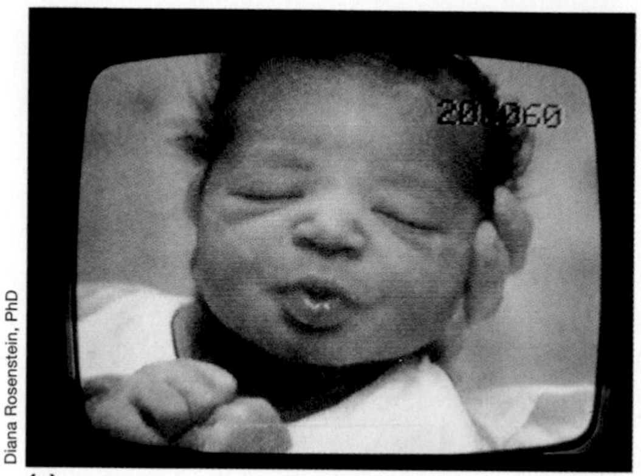
Diana Rosenstein, PhD

(a)

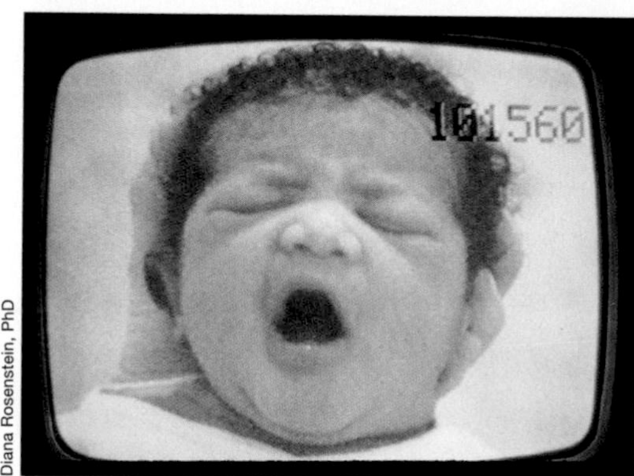
Diana Rosenstein, PhD

(b)

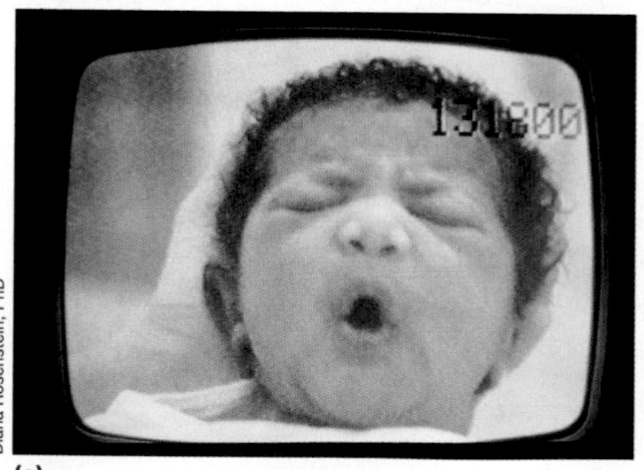
Diana Rosenstein, PhD

(c)

FIGURE 4.14 Newborns respond to different tastes with distinctive facial expressions that have significant adaptive value. In these photographs, newborns react to tastes that are (a) sweet, (b) bitter, (c) and sour.

Taste and Smell

Neonates have a built-in capacity to discriminate between different tastes and odors, and they show strong preferences for things that taste and smell sweet, as does their first natural source of food, breast milk. The newborn's reaction to sweetness, however, extends well beyond simple preference. Research shows that a sweet taste has a calming effect on crying babies and diminishes indications of pain, both physiological (for example, heart rate and brain excitation) and behavioral, helping babies cope with aversive situations (Fernandez et al., 2003; Harrison, Beggs, & Stevens, 2012).

Beyond their capacity to distinguish sweet from not-sweet, to what extent do newborns discriminate between different tastes and odors, and why might it be important for them to do so? An influential study conducted by Diana Rosenstein and Harriet Oster (1988) found that babies only 2 hours old produce different facial expressions in response to bitter, sour, and salty tastes. The characteristic facial expressions they make in response to specific tastes, especially those that are bitter and sour, look remarkably like the expressions made by adults when they encounter the same tastes, evidence that these expressions are innate and may have important evolutionary implications (Figure 4.14). Oster, who has done extensive studies of infant facial expressions, suggests that when the face puckers in response to a sour taste (see Figure 4.14c), it stimulates the production of saliva, which has the effect of diluting the pungency of a potentially edible substance. In contrast, in response to bitter tastes (see Figure 4.14b), newborns' mouths (like adults') tend to "gape," or open widely, as though in readiness to eject the food, an adaptive response given that bitter substances are more likely than others to be inedible and potentially harmful (Oster, 2005).

Infants' taste responses go beyond the innate capacity to make general distinctions among edible and inedible foods. They also involve cultural factors. For example, it has been known for some time that the flavors of the mother's diet during pregnancy are transmitted to the fetus by way of the amniotic fluid it swallows (Nehring, Kostka, von Kries, & Rehfuess, 2015). Similarly, flavors from the mother's diet are transmitted to her newborn by way of her breast milk (Birch, 2015; Mennella, 2014). A carefully controlled study suggests that these forms of indirect exposure to the flavors of food common in the mother's culture affect the newborn's taste preferences (Mennella, Jagnow, & Beauchamp, 2001).

In this study, pregnant women who planned on breast-feeding their infants were randomly assigned to experimental and control groups. Those in the experimental group drank a specified amount of carrot juice several times a week in their last trimester of pregnancy and/or during the period in which they breast-fed their newborns. Those in the control group drank water instead. The babies' taste preferences were tested several weeks after they began to eat cereal but before they had any direct exposure to the flavor of carrots. The test involved comparing the babies' reactions to cereal mixed with water and to cereal mixed with carrot juice. Compared with infants in the control group, the infants who had been exposed to carrot-flavored amniotic fluid or breast milk exhibited fewer negative facial expressions when being fed carrot-flavored cereal than when being fed cereal mixed with water, and they tended to eat more of the flavored cereal. The babies in the control group showed no such preferences.

This research is consistent with that conducted with nonhuman species (rabbits, for example) and suggests that the mother's prenatal diet prepares offspring for the particulars of the nutritional environment into which they will be born (Jablonka & Lamb, 2005). Interestingly, studies have shown that young children's food preferences can be influenced even by the flavors of the specific formulas they were fed as infants. More specifically, when 4-year-olds were exposed to an array of tastes, they preferred the tastes that were reminiscent of the formula they had been fed as infants, even when the formula tasted a bit like overcooked broccoli (Mennella & Beauchamp, 2005)!

In addition to reacting differently to various tastes, newborns are known to discriminate between different odors. Within just minutes of being born, infants will turn their head preferentially toward maternal breast odors, which help guide them toward the nipple (Porter & Winberg, 1999). In addition, the smell of mothers' breast odors has a calming effect on both full-term and premature newborns during the painful heel-stick procedure used to draw blood (see Chapter 2, p. 64; Badiee, Asghari, & Mohammadizadeh, 2013; Rattaz, Goubet, & Bullinger, 2005). One test of the newborn's capacities for odor discrimination involved holding either an odorless cotton swab or a swab soaked in one of various aromatic solutions under the baby's nose. The infants showed no reaction to the odorless swab but reacted to unpleasant odors, such as garlic or vinegar, by pursing their lips or wrinkling their nose; and when they smelled something sugary, they smiled. Like gaping and puckering in response to bitter and sour tastes, newborn (and adult) facial reactions to foul odors have the adaptive consequence of reducing the individual's contact with the unpleasant and potentially unhealthy stimulus. The common reaction of wrinkling the nose is a case in point. Take a deep breath through your nose and notice how freely the air flows into your lungs. Now do it again, but with your nose wrinkled up as though you smell something foul. See how the airflow is restricted? Pursing the lips has the same general effect of inhibiting airflow (try it!).

Multimodal Perception

multimodal perception The ability to perceive an object or event by more than one sensory system simultaneously.

One of the most intriguing areas of research on infants' perceptual capacities focuses on their **multimodal perception**—that is, their ability to simultaneously process various kinds of sensory information from an object or event and perceive them as interconnected. When seeing the mother's face while feeling her warmth, smelling her, and hearing her voice, for example, to what degree does the infant perceive these stimuli in a unitary way? Recent research suggests that infants may be born prepared to perceive certain stimuli as inherently connected to each other but that multimodal perception continues to develop according to the infant's experience (Johnson, Amso, Frank, & Shuwairi, 2008; Streri, Coulon, Marie, & Yeung, 2016).

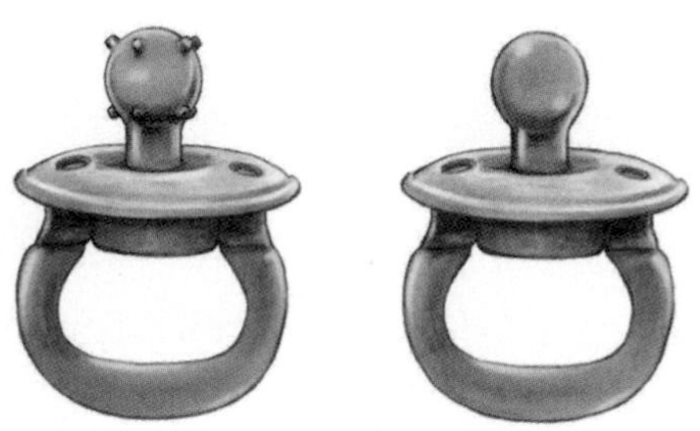

FIGURE 4.15 In a study of multimodal perception, infants were given one of two rubber shapes, like those depicted here, to feel with their mouth. When they were later shown the pair of shapes, the infants spent more time looking at the shape that matched the one they had felt in their mouth.

An early demonstration of multimodal perception was provided by a study in which, in a series of trials, 29-day-old infants were given a tiny rubber shape to feel with their mouth (Meltzoff & Borton, 1979). After they had "explored" the shape for 90 seconds, the shape was removed carefully so the babies could not see it. When the infants were then shown a pair of shapes (Figure 4.15), they looked longer at the one that they had felt in their mouth, suggesting that they had made a connection between what they had felt and what they were seeing.

Further research has examined how multimodal perception may be a vehicle for learning in the first hours of life (Sai, 2005). You know from our previous discussion that within hours of birth, babies learn the features of their mother's face and prefer looking at their mother's face to looking at a stranger's. However, because in the first few hours of interacting with the mother, the baby not only sees her face but also hears her voice, developmentalists have wondered whether hearing the mother's voice somehow contributes to the baby's ability to learn about the visual features of her face. To tackle this question, researchers compared preferences for the mother's face in two groups of babies 2 to 12 hours after birth. In one group, the infants did not hear their mother's voice prior to the preference tests (a condition ensured by a researcher who stayed with the mother from the birth of the baby until the experimental test). Mothers in the second group interacted with their newborns normally, including talking and cooing to them. A standard preference test, in which the infant is presented with the mother and a female stranger, was used to determine whether the babies recognized their mother. It was discovered that the babies who had been prevented from hearing their mother's voice were unable to recognize their mother's face in the experimental test, suggesting that the multimodal perception of the maternal face and voice is essential for newborns to learn the unique visual features of their mother's face.

Overall, there is extensive evidence that babies come into the world with sensory capacities in good working order and far more organized than were once thought. (Infants' sensory capacities are summarized in Table 4.1.) The next question is: What capacities do infants have for acting on the world? This is a crucial question because over the first 3 months of life, infants' growing ability to act in an organized way toward the people and objects in their environment fundamentally changes the nature of their interactions in the world and marks the starting point of postnatal psychological development.

TABLE 4.1 Early Sensory Capacities

Sense	Capacity
Hearing	Ability to distinguish phonemes Preference for native language
Vision	Slightly blurred, slight double vision at birth Color vision by 2 months of age Ability to distinguish patterned stimuli from plain Preference for moving, facelike stimuli
Smell	Ability to differentiate odors well at birth
Taste	Ability to differentiate tastes well at birth
Touch	Responsive to touch at birth
Temperature	Sensitivity to changes in temperature at birth
Position	Sensitivity to changes in position at birth

APPLY > CONNECT > DISCUSS

This section has introduced you to several different research methods that developmentalists use to answer questions about the newborn's sensory systems. Identify and briefly describe four of these methods. Choose one or two of them to design a study addressing some facet of infant sensory capacity.

The Organization of Behavior

LEARNING OUTCOMES

- Distinguish among various newborn reflexes presented in the text.
- Describe reflexes as building blocks for more complicated, coordinated forms of behavior organization.
- Summarize Piaget's sensorimotor stage, including each of its substages.
- Explain how infants learn through classical conditioning.
- Explain how infants learn through operant conditioning.

As a midwife in a small, rural Turkish village, Fulya is highly knowledgeable about and experienced in newborn care. In addition to giving advice on feeding, cleaning, and protecting infants from the evil eye, Fulya tells new mothers how important it is to keep their babies wrapped tightly in cloth:

> Swaddling makes the baby feel protected and helps it to sleep. I was shocked when ... told ... how Americans dress their babies—... almost naked, wearing little more than a tiny shirt and diaper. Poor little things with their arms and legs flailing around, they must feel quite unprotected. (Delaney, 2000, pp. 131–132.)

The practice of swaddling is very common across cultures and is thought to have a number of benefits, including reducing pain and stress. For instance, babies who are swaddled during the routine heel-stick procedure score lower than unswaddled newborns on a measure of pain expression (Morrow, Hidinger, & Wilkinson-Faulk, 2010). Consistent with Fulya's observation that swaddling helps infants sleep, research indicates that newborns who are swaddled tend to be calmer than those who are not swaddled (Nelson, 2017). Although it is hard to know whether swaddled babies "feel protected," as Fulya believes, it is clear that swaddling reduces opportunities for "arms and legs flailing around," a sign that the baby's behavior has become disorganized, as it does in states of fussiness and agitation.

Developing and maintaining behavioral organization is important for infants because it allows them to interact more effectively and adaptively with the world around them. At birth, babies possess a number of inborn behaviors (reflexes) that provide highly organized ways of responding adaptively to the environment. As development progresses during the early months of infancy, new forms of behavioral organization emerge, expanding infants' capacities for engagement with people and objects in their world. By the age of 3 months, for example, infants' physical control and coordination enable them to raise their head to look around, smile in response to the smiles of others, and perform deliberate actions, such as shaking a rattle to make a noise. A major goal of the developmental sciences is to explain how biological and cultural processes contribute to the emergence of these new forms of organized behavior. We begin first with infant reflexes, evolution's contribution to the newborn's behavioral organization. We then explore how more complex forms of behavioral organization arise and become coordinated with the particular social world in which the child develops.

Reflexes

reflex A specific, well-integrated, automatic (involuntary) response to a specific type of stimulation.

Newborn babies come equipped with a variety of **reflexes**—specific, well-integrated, automatic (involuntary) responses to specific types of stimulation (see Table 4.2). Some reflexes are clearly adaptive throughout life. One of these is the *eyeblink reflex*, which protects the eye from overly bright lights and foreign objects that might damage it. Other reflexes are adaptive during infancy but disappear over time. For example, the *sucking reflex*, of obvious adaptive value to newborn feeding, can be elicited by a touch on the baby's lips. Needless to say, this particular reflex disappears with time.

There are also some reflexes that seem to serve no apparent function. An example is the *Moro reflex*, in which infants make a grasping motion with their arms in response to a loud noise or when suddenly experiencing a feeling of being dropped. Some developmentalists believe that these reflexes currently serve no purpose but were functional during earlier evolutionary stages, allowing infants to cling to their mothers in threatening situations, as do infants of most nonhuman primate species (Jolly, 1999). Others believe that such seemingly useless reflexes may still be functional because they promote a close relationship between mother and infant (Bowlby, 1973; Rousseau, Matton, Lecuyer, & Lahaye, 2017).

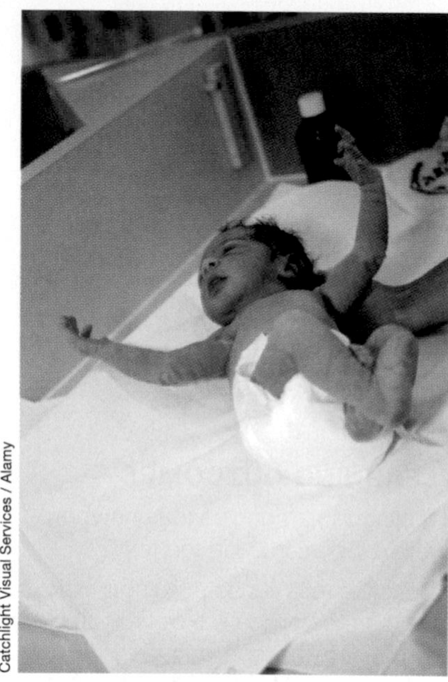

Catchlight Visual Services / Alamy

The Moro reflex occurs if a baby experiences a dropping sensation or hears a loud noise. Its presence at birth—and disappearance around 6 or 7 months of age—signals normal neurological development.

Infant reflexes are an important window into the infant's developing brain and can be used to diagnose the functioning of the central nervous system. For example, the *absence* of a neonatal reflex, such as sucking, often indicates that the infant suffers some form of brain damage. Brain damage is also indicated when a reflex *persists* beyond the age at which it should have disappeared (Konicarova & Bob, 2012). For example, the Moro reflex typically disappears in the months after birth. It is seen again only in the event of injury to the central nervous system (Zafeiriou et al., 1999).

From Reflex to Coordinated Action

action Complex, coordinated behaviors.

Virtually all developmentalists agree that reflexes are important building blocks for constructing more complex and coordinated behaviors, often referred to as **action** (Valsiner, 2007). For example, one new action that appears in early infancy is nursing. When we compare the way newborn infants feed with the nursing behavior of 6-week-old infants, a striking contrast is evident. Newborns possess several reflexes that are relevant to feeding: rooting (turning the head in the direction of a touch on the cheek), sucking, swallowing, and breathing. These component behaviors are not well integrated, however. Newborns tend to root around for the nipple in a disorganized way and may lose it as soon as they find it. They also have trouble coordinating breathing with sucking and swallowing, and they must frequently break away from sucking to come up for air.

By the time infants are 6 weeks old, a qualitative change is evident in their feeding behavior. For one thing, infants anticipate being fed when they are picked up and can prepare themselves to feed by turning toward the nipple and making sucking movements with their mouths—all without direct stimulation on their cheek or lips from the breast or bottle. Equally significant, they have worked out the coordination of all the component behaviors of feeding—sucking, swallowing, and breathing—and they can now perform them in a smooth, integrated sequence (Meyers, 2001). In short, feeding has become nursing. In fact, babies become so efficient at

TABLE 4.2 Reflexes Present at Birth

Reflex	Description	Developmental Course	Significance
Babinski	When the bottom of the baby's foot is stroked, the toes fan out and then curl	Disappears in 8 to 12 months	Presence at birth and normal course of decline are a basic index of normal neurological condition
Crawling	When the baby is placed on the stomach and pressure is applied to the soles of the feet, the arms and legs move rhythmically	Disappears after 3 to 4 months; possible reappearance at 6 to 7 months as a component of voluntary crawling	Uncertain
Eyeblink	Rapid closing of eyes	Permanent	Protection against aversive stimuli such as bright lights and foreign objects
Grasping	When a finger or some other object is pressed against the baby's palm, the baby's fingers close around it	Disappears in 3 to 4 months; replaced by voluntary grasping	Presence at birth and later disappearance is a basic sign of normal neurological development
Moro	If a baby experiences a sudden dropping sensation while being held or hears a loud noise, the baby will throw the arms outward while arching backward and then bring the arms together as if grasping something	Disappears in 6 to 7 months (although startle to loud noises is permanent)	Disputed; its presence at birth and later disappearance are a basic sign of normal neurological development
Rooting	When touched on the cheek, the baby turns head in the direction of the touch and opens mouth	Disappears between 3 and 6 months	Component of nursing
Stepping	When held upright over a flat surface, the baby makes rhythmic leg movements	Disappears in first 2 months but can be reinstated in special contexts	Disputed; it may be only a kicking motion, or it may be a component of later voluntary walking
Sucking	The baby sucks when something is put into his or her mouth	Disappears and is replaced by voluntary sucking	Fundamental component of nursing

nursing that they can get as much milk in 10 minutes as it once took them up to an hour to get. In the language of *dynamic systems theory* (see Chapter 1, p. 27), the stable and balanced behavioral system of nursing has emerged as its component parts (sucking, swallowing, breathing) interacted over time, became increasingly coordinated with each other, and ultimately unified into a complex system of action. However, as we discuss below, the emergence of nursing as an organized system of action does not happen in a vacuum but is facilitated by the active efforts of the caregiver. (See also the box "In the Field: Baby-Friendly Hospital Care" on page 145 for procedures used to promote nursing and other aspects of developing behavioral organization in premature infants who are in intensive care units.)

Whereas the connection between the sucking reflex and the emergence of nursing is readily discernible, the developmental path between other reflexes and subsequent action is less apparent and more controversial. For example, when newborn babies are held in an upright position with their feet touching a flat surface, they make rhythmic leg movements as if they were walking, a form of behavior often referred to as a "stepping reflex" (see Figure 4.16). But they stop doing so at around 2 months of age. Around 1 year of age, babies use similar motions as a component of walking, a voluntary activity that is acquired with practice.

There are competing explanations for the developmental changes in these rhythmic leg movements. According to Philip Zelazo (1983), the newborn's movements are a genuine (that is, involuntary) reflex, probably controlled by subcortical brain processes. In the first months after birth, the brain undergoes a period of reorganization as the cortex, the seat of voluntary behavior, develops, and many lower-level reflexes, including the stepping reflex, disappear. Zelazo maintains that the old stepping behavior reappears in a new form as a voluntary component of walking after this period of brain reorganization.

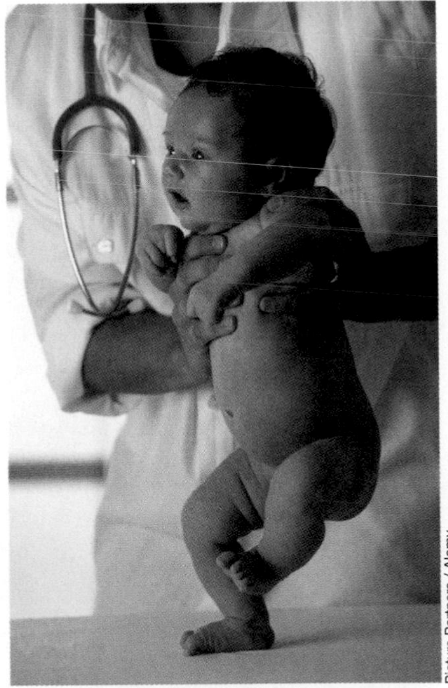
Picture Partners / Alamy

FIGURE 4.16 Babies held upright with their feet touching a flat surface move their legs in a fashion that resembles walking. Experts have debated the origins and developmental history of this form of behavior, called the stepping reflex.

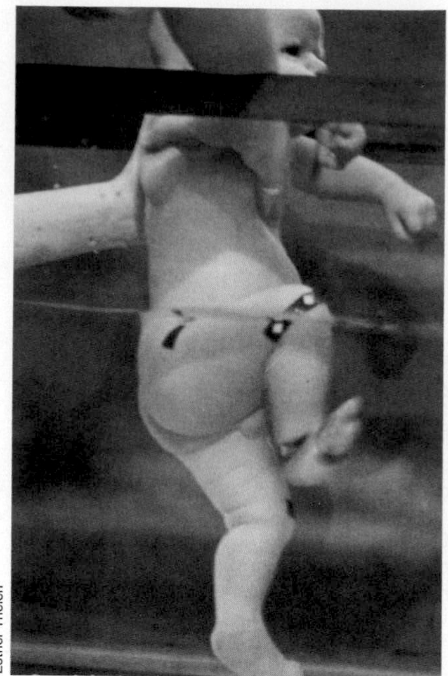

Esther Thelen

Although the stepping reflex seems to disappear around 3 months of age, Esther Thelen and her colleagues demonstrated that it would reappear if babies were given proper support. Here, a baby who no longer exhibits a stepping reflex under normal conditions makes the same stepping motions when partially submerged in water.

Esther Thelen and her colleagues rejected this explanation (Thelen, Fischer, & Ridley-Johnson, 2002). According to these researchers, early stepping disappears not because of changes in the cortex but because of changes in the baby's muscle mass and weight that make stepping difficult. In other words, for a period of time, babies' legs are just too heavy for their muscles to lift. In support of their view, Thelen and her colleagues hypothesized that if infants were partially submerged in water and supported in a standing position, stepping would reappear because the buoyancy of the water would counterbalance the infant's increased weight and relative lack of leg strength. They were correct: When infants who had stopped exhibiting stepping were held upright in water up to their waists, the stepping behavior reappeared.

Instead of invoking complex explanations about brain development in order to account for the relationship between early stepping and later walking, Thelen and her colleagues took a dynamic systems approach. In their view, infant walking is a new complex form of behavior that emerges from the interaction of a variety of less complex parts, including the infant's weight and muscle mass.

Reaching

Even from the earliest days of postnatal life, babies' arms are often moving, sometimes allowing them to bring their fingers to their mouth to initiate sucking, and sometimes bringing their hands into contact with objects in the world around them. At first, their contact with objects appears to be totally accidental. Nevertheless, research initiated by Claus von Hofsten (1982, 1984) identified an early form of movement he termed *prereaching*, which he elicited by showing very young infants a large, colorful, slow-moving object, such as a ball of yarn. As the object passed in front of them, they reached toward it. However, they were unable to grasp an object even after repeated attempts because the movements of reaching with the arm and grasping with the hand are uncoordinated in the newborn, and the babies were unable to get their fingers to close around the object.

At about 3 months of age, a time of maturational changes in the visual and motor areas of the cerebral cortex, *visually guided reaching* emerges. Now, once infants locate an object by either seeing or hearing it, they can use feedback from their own movements to adjust the trajectory of their reach and get their hands close to the object. They are also able to open their fingers in anticipation of grasping the object. Remarkably, they can do this even when a bright object is presented in a darkened room so that they cannot see their own arms, clear evidence that it is feedback from their movement relative to the object that is controlling their reaching and grasping (McCarty et al., 2001).

In an ingenious experiment, Amy Needham and her colleagues demonstrated that the process of infants' reaching and grasping can be accelerated if infants are given support (Needham, Barrett, & Peterman, 2002). The researchers put specially designed Velcro-covered mittens on the hands of a group of 3-month-old infants and placed Velcro-covered objects within their reach. The infants' successful experiences connecting their Velcro-covered mittens with objects had fascinating consequences. Compared with a control group of infants who did not have such mittens, those in the experimental group showed greater interest in objects, as well as greater skill in grasping objects when they were later tested without the special mittens. In a related study, babies who practiced reaching and grasping with the sticky mittens showed higher levels of neural processing (as measured by EEG) when they observed the experimenter reaching toward an object rather than away from an object, suggesting that their own actions have implications for understanding the actions of others (Bakker, Sommerville, & Gredebäck, 2016).

In The Field

Baby-Friendly Hospital Care

Name: HEIDELISE ALS

Education: M.S. in education and Ph.D. in human learning and education from University of Pennsylvania; additional training at the Child Development Unit at Children's Hospital Boston

Current Position: Director, Neurobehavioral Infant and Child Studies, Children's Hospital, Harvard Medical School

Career Objectives: Develop procedures to minimize premature newborns' trauma while being treated in hospital intensive care units

HEIDELISE ALS, A DEVELOPMENTAL PSYCHOLOGIST AT Harvard Medical School and Children's Hospital, has spent years trying to understand how premature babies experience the world of the traditional newborn intensive care unit (NICU), which may be their home for weeks or even months after their birth (Raeburn, 2005). Emerging from a warm, dark amniotic pool where they had bobbed in warmth, relative quiet, and constant physical and hormonal contact with their mothers, preterm babies are thrust into the high-tech environment of the NICU, where they lie on their back, with their nose, hands, chest, or feet often pinned with gauze and adhesive tape to hold medical monitors and equipment in place. It is an environment dominated by constant bright lights, the noisy hum and whir of life-support machines, the continual chatter of NICU personnel, and a daily series of by-the-clock feedings, diaper changes, and medical procedures, often painful, in which the fragile newborns are handled on average more than 200 times in a 24-hour period (Sizun & Westrup, 2004). All this, from Als's perspective, overwhelms their immature brains.

Indeed, although it is well known that premature infants are at risk for a number of neurological problems and have more difficulty maintaining alert states and behavior organization than do full-term infants (see Chapter 3, p. 115), recent research has suggested that the stress of traditional NICUs may actually contribute to babies' difficulties (Provenzi et al., 2016). For example, preterm babies often experience episodes in which the oxygen in their blood drops to dangerous levels. It now appears that routine nursing procedures trigger many of these episodes and also increase concentrations of stress hormones in the baby's system (reviewed in Sizun & Westrup, 2004). Moreover, this stress of the NICU is experienced at a critical time in the development of the brain's neuronal circuitry. More specifically, the preterm baby's brain is undergoing the radical synaptic pruning characteristic of the final weeks of pregnancy, and it is thus particularly vulnerable to lasting effects from abnormal sensory input and pain.

Fortunately, as a consequence of Als's impassioned efforts to improve the early experiences of the prematurely born, NICUs throughout the world are beginning to change the way they operate. The busy, stimulus-intense, and medically oriented NICU is being replaced by a NICU that is decidedly more baby friendly. In this new NICU, lights are dimmed and varied to suggest day–night cycles, nurses whisper, and, rather than being kept on a strict schedule, babies are watched for cues that they are hungry or need to be changed. Stethoscopes are warmed before they are placed on the baby's chest; incubators look more like cozy nests than sterile platforms (see photo); and family members are included in the baby's care.

The individualized developmental care adopted by many modern NICUs also includes procedures used to support developing behavioral organization. For example, babies are given pacifiers to suck, even though, because of their prematurity, many are fed by a tube that delivers nutrients directly into their stomachs. Interestingly, when babies are given pacifiers for sucking, they not only make an easier transition from tube to breast- or bottle-feeding than babies who are not given pacifiers, they also digest the tube-fed nutrients better, sleep better, absorb higher levels of oxygen, and have shorter hospital stays (Ahmadpour-kacho et al., 2017; Pinelli & Symington, 2001). Other procedures used to promote behavioral organization include wrapping babies tightly (swaddling) in order to reduce disorganized motor behavior, such as the frequent occurrence of the Moro (startle) reflex, which often disrupts the baby's sleep.

According to Als, "the neurological disability that many preterms are left with when they leave the NICU may in some ways be preventable" (Cassidy, 2005). It may be, then, that the new medical and nursing practices intended to decrease babies' stress may have significant, long-lasting benefits for the developing brain and neurological health of preterm babies (Symington & Pinelli, 2003).

Evan Richman/The Boston Globe via Getty Images

Heidelise Als

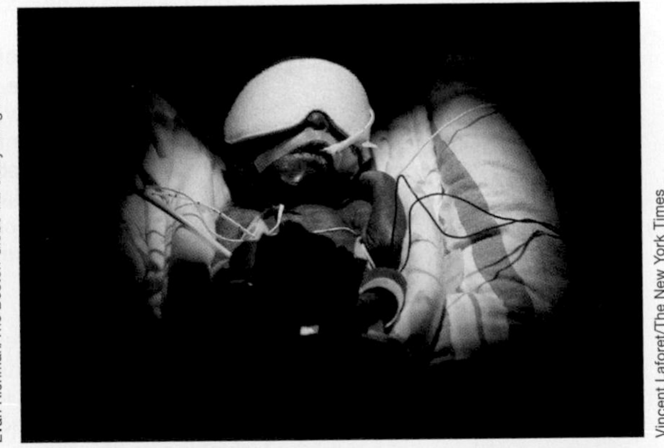
Vincent Laforet/The New York Times

Piaget's Theory of Developing Action

Jean Piaget, one of the "grand theorists" described in Chapter 1 (see p. 20), provided an impressively comprehensive explanation for the infant's transition from reflexive behavior to coordinated action. Piaget believed that children actively organize an understanding of the world through their engagement with it and that their understanding develops in distinct stages. According to Piaget, the *schema* is the most elementary form of understanding—a mental structure that provides a model for understanding the world. Piaget argued that schemas develop through *adaptation*, a twofold process involving *assimilation* and *accommodation* (see pp. 21–22).

sensorimotor stage Piaget's term for the stage of infancy during which the process of adaptation consists largely of coordinating sensory perceptions and simple motor behaviors to acquire knowledge of the world.

Piaget referred to infancy as the **sensorimotor stage** of cognitive development because during this period, the process of adaptation through which infants gain knowledge about the world consists largely of coordinating sensory perceptions and simple motor responses. Piaget saw the sensorimotor stage as consisting of six substages (Table 4.3). During the first few months of life, infants are said to progress through substages 1 and 2, *exercising reflex schemas* and *primary circular reactions*. (Substages 3–6 are covered in Chapter 5, on pp. 176–178.)

Substage 1: *Exercising reflex schemas*. Piaget believed that in the first 4 to 6 weeks, infants learn to control and coordinate the reflexes present at birth, which provide them with their initial connection to their environment. However, these initial reflexes add nothing new to development because they undergo very little accommodation (that is, they are largely unchanged). In this sense, infants seem to accomplish little more than exercising inborn reflexes.

Substage 2: *Primary circular reactions*. Accommodation first appears in this substage, which occurs from about 1 to 4 months of age. The first hints of new

TABLE 4.3 Piaget's Stages of Cognitive Development and the Sensorimotor Substages

Age (years)	Stage	Description	Characteristics of Sensorimotor Substages
Birth to 2	Sensorimotor	Infants' achievements consist largely of coordinating their sensory perceptions and simple motor behaviors. As they move through the six substages of this period, infants come to recognize the existence of a world outside themselves and begin to interact with it in deliberate ways.	Substage 1 (0–1½ months) *Exercising reflex schemas:* involuntary rooting, sucking, grasping, looking Substage 2 (1½–4 months) *Primary circular reactions:* repetition of actions that are pleasurable in themselves
2 to 6	Preoperational	Young children can represent reality to themselves through the use of symbols, including mental images, words, and gestures. Still, children often fail to distinguish their point of view from that of others, become easily captured by surface appearances, and are often confused about causal relations.	Substage 3 (4–8 months) *Secondary circular reactions:* dawning awareness of the effects of one's own actions on the environment; extended actions that produce interesting change in the environment
6 to 12	Concrete operational	As they enter middle childhood, children become capable of mental operations, internalized actions that fit into a logical system. Operational thinking allows children to mentally combine, separate, order, and transform objects and actions. Such operations are considered concrete because they are carried out in the presence of the objects and events being thought about.	Substage 4 (8–12 months) *Coordination of secondary circular reactions:* combining schemas to achieve a desired effect; earliest form of problem solving Substage 5 (12–18 months) *Tertiary circular reactions:* deliberate variation of problem-solving means; experimentation to see what the consequences will be
12 to 19	Formal operational	In adolescence, the developing person acquires the ability to think systematically about all logical relations within a problem. Adolescents display keen interest in abstract ideas and in the process of thinking itself.	Substage 6 (18–24 months) *Beginnings of symbolic representation:* images and words come to stand for familiar objects; invention of new means of problem solving through symbolic combinations

forms of behavior are that existing reflexes are extended in time (as when infants suck between feedings) or are extended to new objects (as when infants suck their thumb). Piaget acknowledged that babies might thumb-suck as early as the first day of life (we now know they may do so even before birth), but he believed that the thumb-sucking seen during substage 2 reflects a qualitatively new form of behavior. That is, in substage 1, infants suck their thumb only when they accidentally touch their mouth with their hand. During substage 2, in contrast, if a baby's thumb falls from her mouth, the baby is likely to bring the thumb back to her mouth so that she can suck it some more. In other words, infants in this substage repeat pleasurable actions for their own sake. Piaget used the term **primary circular reaction** to characterize such behavior. Behaviors of this type are considered *primary* because the objects toward which they are directed are parts of the baby's own body; they are called *circular* because they circle back to themselves (sucking leads to more sucking, which leads to more sucking, and so on).

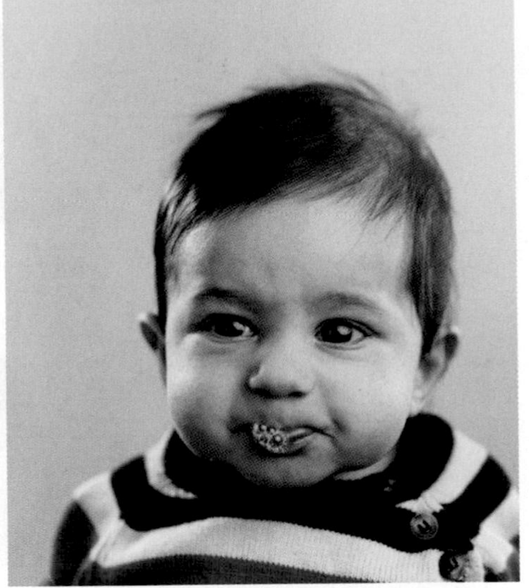
SensorSpot/Getty Images

Blowing bubbles is an early instance of a primary circular reaction in which an accidental aspect of sucking is prolonged for the sheer pleasure of continuing the sensation.

Over the course of substage 2, primary circular reactions undergo both differentiation and integration. *Differentiation* occurs as actions become increasingly fine-tuned and flexible and infants modify them in response to variations in the environment (for example, sucking on a thumb differently than on a nipple). *Integration* occurs as separate actions become coordinated into new patterns of behavior (for example, reaching becomes coordinated with grasping). Piaget believed that primary circular reactions are important because they offer the first evidence of cognitive development. "The basic law of dawning psychological activity," he wrote, "could be said to be the search for the maintenance or repetition of interesting states of consciousness" (Piaget, 1977, p. 202). By the end of substage 2, infants are ready to direct their attention to the external world.

primary circular reaction The term Piaget used to describe the infant's tendency to repeat pleasurable bodily actions for their own sake.

Learning Theories of Developing Action

Learning theorists argue that new forms of behavioral organization emerge as a consequence of **learning**, a relatively permanent change in behavior brought about when the infant makes associations between behavior and events in the environment. Several types of learning are believed to operate throughout development, including *habituation* (described previously) and *imitation* (which we will explore in Chapter 6), as well as two processes referred to as *classical conditioning* and *operant conditioning*.

learning A relatively permanent change in behavior brought about by making associations between behavior and events in the environment.

Classical Conditioning

Classical conditioning is learning in which previously existing behaviors come to be associated with and elicited by new stimuli. The existence of this very basic learning mechanism was demonstrated in the early part of the twentieth century by the Russian physiologist Ivan Pavlov (1849–1936). Pavlov (1927) showed that after several experiences of hearing a tone just before food was placed in its mouth, a dog would begin to salivate in response to the tone before it received any food. Pavlov had caused the dog to learn to expect food when it heard the tone, and its mouth watered as a result.

In the terminology of learning theories, Pavlov elicited the dog's response by pairing a **conditional stimulus (CS)**—a tone—with an **unconditional stimulus (UCS)**—food in the mouth. The food is called an unconditional stimulus because it "unconditionally" causes salivation, salivation being a reflex response to food in the mouth. Salivation, in turn, is called an **unconditional response (UCR)** because it is automatically and unconditionally elicited by food in the mouth. The tone is called a conditional stimulus because the behavior it elicits depends on (is conditional on) the way it has been paired with the unconditional stimulus. When the unconditional response (salivation in response to food in the mouth) occurs in response to the CS (the tone), it is called a **conditional response (CR)** because it

classical conditioning Learning in which previously existing behaviors come to be elicited by new stimuli.

conditional stimulus (CS) In classical conditioning, a stimulus that elicits a behavior that is dependent on the way it is paired with the unconditional stimulus (UCS).

unconditional stimulus (UCS) In classical conditioning, the stimulus, such as food in the mouth, that invariably causes the unconditional response (UCR).

unconditional response (UCR) In classical conditioning, the response, such as salivation, that is invariably elicited by the unconditional stimulus (UCS).

conditional response (CR) In classical conditioning, a response to the pairing of the conditional stimulus (CS) and the unconditional stimulus (UCS).

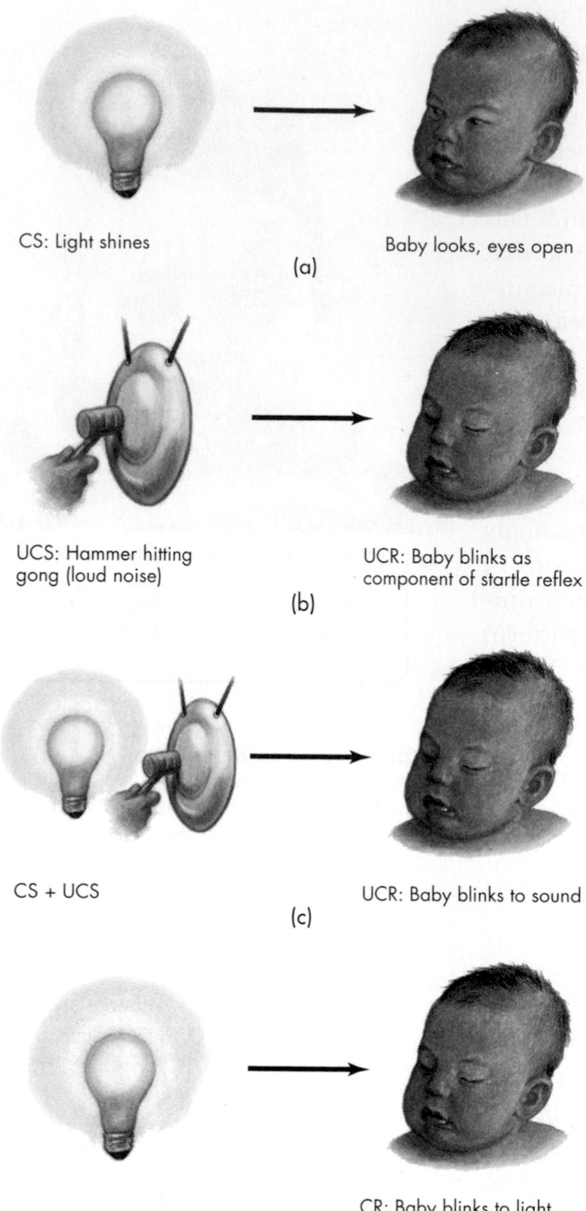

FIGURE 4.17 In the top panel, (a) the sight of a light (CS) elicits no particular response. In (b), the loud sound of a gong (UCS) causes the baby to blink (UCR). In (c), the sight of the light (CS) is paired with the sound of the gong (UCS), which evokes an eyeblink (UCR). Finally, in (d), the sight of the light (CS) is sufficient to cause the baby to blink (CR), demonstrating that learning has occurred.

operant conditioning Learning in which changes in behavior are shaped by the consequences of that behavior, thereby giving rise to new and more complete behaviors.

depends on the pairing of the CS (the tone) and the UCS (the food). The key indicator that learning has occurred is that the CS (tone) elicits the CR (salivation) before the presentation of the UCS (food) (Figure 4.17).

A number of developmentalists seized on Pavlov's demonstrations as a possible model for the way infants learn about their environment. One of Pavlov's coworkers demonstrated conditioned feeding responses in a 14-month-old infant based on the principle of classical conditioning (Krasnogorski, 1907/1967). The baby opened his mouth and made sucking motions (CRs) at the sight of a glass of milk (CS). When a bell (a new CS) was sounded on several occasions just before the glass of milk was presented, the baby began to open his mouth and suck at the sound of the bell, an indication that classical conditioning built expectations in the infant by a process of association. The crucial point of these observations is that there is no biological connection between the sound of a bell and the mouth-opening and sucking responses it elicited. Rather, the fact that the new stimuli elicited these responses shows that learning has occurred.

Operant Conditioning

Classical conditioning explains how infants begin to build up expectations about the connections between events in their environment, but it does little to explain how even the simplest new behaviors come into being. According to learning theorists, new behaviors, both simple and complex, arise from a different kind of conditioning: *operant conditioning*. The basic principle of **operant conditioning** is that behaviors are shaped by their consequences; that is, organisms will tend to repeat behaviors that lead to rewards and will tend to give up behaviors that fail to produce rewards or that lead to punishment (Skinner, 1938). A consequence (such as receiving a reward) that increases the likelihood that a behavior will be repeated is called a *reinforcement*. Operant conditioning in young infants has been experimentally demonstrated with a variety of reinforcers, such as milk, sweet substances, the opportunity to suck on a pacifier, the sound of a heartbeat or the mother's voice, and the appearance of an interesting visual display (Rovee-Collier & Giles, 2010).

An elegant procedure designed by Rovee-Collier and her colleagues demonstrates how infants will repeat behaviors in order to produce interesting visual effects (Cuevas, Learmonth, & Rovee-Collier, 2016). The researchers tied one end of a ribbon around an infant's ankle and attached the other end of the ribbon to a mobile hanging above the infant's crib (Figure 4.18). Within just a few minutes, the infant learned that kicking would animate the mobile, causing the shapes to shake and spin. The interesting visual effects of the mobile thus acted as a positive reinforcer, prompting the infant to organize her kicking behavior in order to produce additional reinforcements.

Further support for the argument that learning is an important contributor to the development of behavioral organization comes from studies that show that even very young infants are capable of remembering what they have learned from one testing session to the next, a capacity that improves markedly during the first few months of life (Learmonth, Cuevas, & Rovee-Collier, 2015).

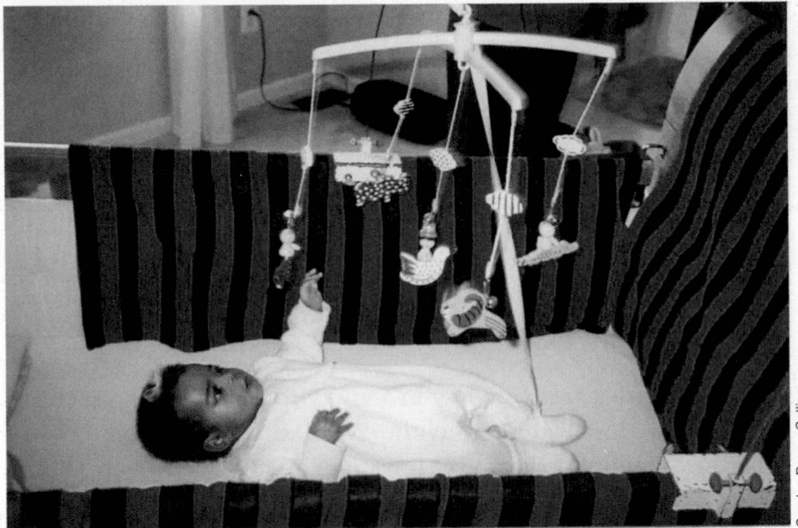

Carolyn Rovee-Collier

FIGURE 4.18 This baby has learned that her kicking produces the interesting effect of moving the objects dangling from the mobile. Such operant conditioning is an important process in the organization of infant behavior.

APPLY > CONNECT > DISCUSS

Suppose you have been hired by a local health clinic to lead a class on newborn behavioral organization for expecting parents. How would you describe "behavioral organization" to these parents? How would you explain its importance for development? What sorts of activities or interactions would you recommend to parents for promoting the development of behavioral organization in their newborn?

Temperament

LEARNING OUTCOMES

Point out the characteristics of temperament in babies.

Compare the temperament of infants in different cultures.

In our discussion of how newborns learn about and become increasingly engaged with the features of their environment, we have focused on universal capacities inherited by each individual infant as a consequence of the evolutionary history of our species. We know, however, that infants are also born with individual differences in how they respond to their environment. Some infants seem to fuss a lot, while others are usually cheerful; some wake at the slightest noise, whereas others seem able to sleep through fireworks. Individual differences such as these relate to variations in **temperament**, an individual's emotional and behavioral characteristics that appear to be consistent across situations and to have some stability over time (Bornstein et al., 2015; Calkins & Degnan, 2005).

temperament The term for the individual modes of responding to the environment that appear to be consistent across situations and stable over time. Temperament includes such characteristics as children's activity level, their intensity of reaction, the ease with which they become upset, their characteristic responses to novelty, and their sociability.

Alexander Thomas, Stella Chess, and their colleagues pioneered longitudinal studies of temperament and its role in development (Chess & Thomas, 1996; Wachs & Bates, 2001). They began their research in the late 1950s, with a group of 141 middle- and upper-class White children in the United States and later broadened their study to include 95 working-class Puerto Rican children and several groups of children suffering from diseases, neurological impairments, and developmental delays. Chess and Thomas began their study by conducting structured clinical interviews of the children's parents shortly after the children's birth. They questioned parents about such matters as how the child reacted to the first bath, to wet diapers, to the first taste of solid food. As the children grew older, these interviews were supplemented by interviews with teachers and by tests of the children themselves.

From their data, Chess and Thomas identified nine key traits of temperament: *activity level*, *rhythmicity* (the regularity or irregularity of the child's basic biological functions), *approach–withdrawal* (the child's response to novelty), *adaptability*, *threshold of responsiveness* (the minimum intensity of stimulation required to evoke a response), *intensity of reaction*, *quality of mood* (negative or positive), *distractibility*, and *attention span* or *persistence*. After scoring the children on each of these nine traits, they found that most of the children could be classified in one of three broad temperament categories:

- *Easy babies* are playful, are regular in their biological functions, and adapt readily to new circumstances.
- *Difficult babies* are irregular in their biological functions, are irritable, and often respond intensely and negatively to new situations or try to withdraw from them.
- *Slow-to-warm-up babies* are low in activity level, and their responses are typically mild. They tend to withdraw from new situations but in a calm way, and they require more time than easy babies to adapt to change.

Although the three categories of temperament described by Chess and Thomas are widely used by developmentalists, a number of researchers have tried to create a more refined set of temperament types. For example, Mary Rothbart and her colleagues created a child-behavior questionnaire that provided scores on 195 questions divided into 15 different scales. Parents were asked to decide how well each item applied to their child during the past half year. The results suggested three dimensions of temperamental variation, providing a profile of each child's temperament (see Table 4.4; Rothbart, 2007):

TABLE 4.4 Definitions of Temperament in the Children's Behavior Questionnaire

Broad Dimensions/Temperament Scales	Scale Definitions
Effortful control	
Attention control	The capacity to focus attention as well as to shift attention when desired
Inhibitory control	The capacity to plan future action and to suppress inappropriate responses
Perceptual sensitivity	Detection or perceptual awareness of slight, low-intensity stimulation in the environment
Low-intensity pleasure	Pleasure derived from activities or stimuli involving low intensity, rate, complexity, novelty, and incongruity
Negative affectivity	
Frustration	Negative affect related to interruption of ongoing tasks or goal blocking
Fear	Negative affect related to anticipation of distress
Discomfort	Negative affect related to sensory qualities of stimulation, including intensity, rate, or complexity of light, movement, sound, or texture
Sadness	Negative affect and lowered mood and energy related to exposure to suffering, disappointment, and object loss
Soothability	Rate of recovery from peak distress, excitement, or general arousal
Extraversion	
Activity	Level of gross motor activity, including rate and extent of locomotion
Low—shyness	Behavioral inhibition to novelty and challenge, especially social
High-intensity pleasure	Pleasure derived from activities involving high intensity or novelty
Smiling and laughter	Positive affect in response to changes in stimulus intensity, rate, complexity, and incongruity
Impulsivity	Speed of response initiation
Positive anticipation	Positive excitement and anticipation for expected pleasurable activities

Republished with permission of SAGE Publications, Inc. Journals. From "Definitions of Temperament in the Children's Behavior Questionnaire," in *Current Directions in Psychological Science*, by Mary K. Rothbart, 16(4), 207–212, 2007. Permission conveyed through Copyright Clearance Center, Inc.

- *Effortful control*—Control over what one attends to and reacts to
- *Negative affect*—The extent of negative emotions
- *Extraversion*—The extent to which one engages eagerly and happily with people and activities

There is widespread agreement that genetic factors provide the foundation for temperamental differences (Gaias et al., 2012; Micalizzi, Wang, & Saudino, 2017; Propper & Moore, 2006). Evidence comes from studies showing that genetically identical monozygotic twins are more similar in certain temperamental characteristics than are dizygotic twins (Planalp, Van Hulle, Lemery-Chalfant, & Goldsmith, 2017). In addition, while working with monkeys, Stephen Suomi (2000) found that an allele on a specific gene is associated with a highly reactive temperament, while a different allele is associated with a calmer temperament. A genetic basis to temperamental traits implies that one should expect to find relatively stable "biases" in the way given individuals respond to their environment and that it should thus be possible to predict the characteristic style with which they will behave at later stages of development. Indeed, studies conducted in several different societies find evidence of stability in temperamental traits such as irritability, persistence, and flexibility (Emde & Hewitt, 2001; Gartstein et al., 2015; Viddal et al., 2015).

Researchers have also found ethnic and national differences related to temperamental traits. Research on infants from a variety of countries including the United States, Japan, the People's Republic of China, the Netherlands, Israel, and Cuba find generally that U.S. infants tend to score higher in positive affect and lower in negative affect and effortful control (see Farkas & Vallotton, 2016, for a review of this research). Such differences likely reflect cultural differences in child-rearing practices, with parents from many non-U.S. countries placing greater emphasis on children's obedience and self-control.

In addition to examining the degree of innate temperamental stability, researchers have also tried to determine whether certain adjustment problems in childhood or adolescence may be related to temperament in infancy (Neal, Durbin, Gornik, & Lo, 2017). They have identified several dimensions of early temperament reflective of fearfulness, withdrawal, distress, and lack of adaptability that appear to be linked to later problems with anxiety, depression, and social withdrawal (see Calkins & Degnan, 2005, for a review of this research). Suppose, for example, that an infant tends to react negatively to new people, objects, and situations with screaming and crying. Because the infant's reactions create a state of behavioral disorganization that severs connections to the baby's environment, the baby loses opportunities to practice more adaptive coping skills such as looking away from the source of distress, sucking a pacifier, or seeking comfort from someone. And because of this failure to develop adaptive coping skills, the world continues to overwhelm the child, who may grow up generally anxious and depressed. However, caregivers and other people in the infant's world can impact how the baby emotionally responds to the environment. For example, babies are less likely to exhibit negative affect when their mothers are more sensitive and responsive to their needs and communications (Pickles et al., 2013; Thomas et al., 2017). Similarly, babies with difficult temperaments may elicit negative parenting, which reinforces the stability of their temperamental traits (Micalizzi et al., 2017).

APPLY > CONNECT > DISCUSS

How would your characterize your own temperament in light of the discussion above? In what ways have your temperamental characteristics influenced who you are?

LEARNING OUTCOMES

Describe various sleeping arrangements among babies and parents.

Identify the different states of arousal and sleep in infants.

Explain the influence of culture on infant schedules.

Point out the various purposes for infant crying.

Becoming Coordinated with the Social World

The indisputable fact that human infants are enormously dependent on others for their survival may often obscure babies' own contributions to the care they receive. Infants' survival and continued development depend not only on the actions of responsive caregivers but also on infants' ability to coordinate their actions with those of their caregivers. This ability is essential because caregivers have their own rhythms of life and work and cannot always be hovering over their infant, anticipating his or her every need. Most parents, whether they work the land or work in an office, need to sleep at night, and this need is often in direct conflict with their infant's sleep and hunger patterns. As a result, parents may attempt to modify their infant's patterns of sleeping and feeding so that they will fit into the life patterns of the household and the community. In this and other ways, infants become coordinated with their social world. (The box "Sleeping Arrangements" shows the variety of sleeping practices that are typical in different cultures.)

Sleeping

As with adults, the extent of newborns' arousal varies from deep sleep to frantic activity. The patterns of their rest and activity are quite different from those of adults, however, particularly in the first weeks after birth (Wakai & Lutter, 2016). To find out about the range and cycles of newborns' arousal patterns, developmentalists use a variety of methods, including direct observation, video recordings, and sophisticated electronic monitoring devices (Salzarulo & Ficca, 2002). In a classic study in which babies' eye movements and muscle activity were observed over the first several weeks following birth, Peter Wolff (1966) was able to distinguish seven states of arousal (Table 4.5 on page 154). Infant sleep states have since been associated with distinctive patterns of brain activity (Novelli et al., 2016).

Neonates spend most of their time asleep, although the amount of sleep they need gradually decreases. Several studies have shown that babies sleep about 16½ hours a day during the first week of life. By the end of 4 weeks, they sleep a little more than 15 hours a day, and by the end of 4 months, they sleep a little less than 14 hours a day (Thoman & Whitney, 1989).

If babies sleep most of the time, why do their parents lose so much sleep? The reason is that newborns tend to sleep in snatches that last anywhere from a few minutes to a few hours. Although sleep–wake cycles are clearly present immediately after birth, babies may be awake at any time of the day or night (Korotchikova et al., 2016). As babies grow older, their sleeping and waking periods lengthen and coincide more and more with the day–night schedule common among adults (Jenni, Deboer, & Achermann, 2006; Salzarulo & Ficca, 2002).

Although babies' adoption of the night/day sleep cycle seems natural to people who live in developed countries and urban settings, studies of infants raised in other cultures suggest that it is at least partly a function of cultural influences on the infant (Meléndez, 2005). In a widely cited example of the role of social pressure in rearranging newborns' sleep, the development of the sleep–wake behavior of infants in the United States was compared with that of Kipsigis babies in rural Kenya. In the United States, parents typically put their infants to bed at certain hours—often in a separate room—and try not to pick them up when they wake up crying at night, lest they become accustomed to someone's attending to them whenever they make a fuss. In rural Kenya, infants are almost always with their mother. During the day they sleep when they can, often while being carried on their mother's back as the mother goes about her daily round of farming, household chores, and social activities. During the night, they sleep with their mother and are permitted to nurse whenever they wake up. Among Kipsigis infants, the longest period of

Sleeping Arrangements

LULLABIES, ROCKING CHAIRS, MUSIC boxes, and cuddly stuffed toys are common features of many infants' bedtime routines. But cross-cultural research shows that the use of such objects in bedtime rituals, as well and where and with whom the baby sleeps, are steeped in cultural beliefs, values, and traditional practices.

In a study of 120 societies around the world, 64 percent of the mothers surveyed reported that their infants sleep in the same bed with them (a practice referred to as co-sleeping). Co-sleeping is widely practiced in highly urban, modern communities in countries such as Japan and Italy, as well as in rural communities in many countries including Mexico and China. For example, the prevalence of co-sleeping is 40 percent in the Netherlands, 46 percent in Australia, 72 percent in Manitoba, Canada, and nearly 50 percent in the United Kingdom (Ball, 2009). In only a few countries, such as the United States and Germany, are infants expected to sleep in their own beds in a separate room (Ward, 2015). But even within the United States, the practice of having infants sleep separately, while particularly common among college-educated, middle-class families, is far from universal across regions and groups. Data from the Centers for Disease Control and Prevention found that in 2009 and 2010, 16.5 percent of White mothers and 37.6 percent of Black mothers reported that they always or often co-slept with their infants (U.S. Department of Health and Human Services, 2013).

Sleeping practices are related to broad cultural themes regarding the organization of interpersonal relations and the moral ideals of the community (Ward, 2015). Whereas middle-class U.S. and German mothers emphasize the values of independence and self-reliance, mothers in societies where co-sleeping is the norm emphasize the need for babies to learn to be interdependent and to be able to get along with others and be sensitive to their needs. In Korea, for example, where nearly all infants sleep with their parents, that practice is considered a natural part of child-rearing and an important step in developing family bonds (Yang & Hahn, 2002).

Sleep arrangements vary considerably both within and across cultures. The co-sleeping of this mother and baby is somewhat uncommon in England, where they live.

© Peter Marlow/Magnum Photos

Some researchers have tried to determine whether one arrangement or the other is better or worse for infants. For example, compared to infants who slept apart from their parents in a separate room, those who slept in their parents' bedroom (either in their own or their parents' bed) for the first month after birth had lower stress responses to being bathed, as measured by cortisol levels (baths are considered mildly stressful for newborns) (Tollenaar et al., 2012). Likewise, a great deal of concern has been raised regarding the possible relationship between co-sleeping and sudden infant death syndrome (see the box "Sudden Infant Death Syndrome" on p. 155) because of accidental suffocation (Blair, Sidebotham, Pease, & Fleming, 2014; Carpenter et al., 2013). In contrast, on the basis of cross-cultural evidence, James McKenna (1996) reports no ill effects associated with co-sleeping and concludes that "infant–parent co-sleeping is biologically, psychologically, and socially the most appropriate context for the development of healthy infant sleep physiology." On balance, it appears that except in certain cases—when parents smoke, consume drugs or alcohol, or sleep on soft surfaces such as sofas—whether infants sleep in a bed alone or with their mother does not seem to make a great deal of difference (Blair et al., 2014; Okami, Weisner, & Olmstead, 2002). All cultural systems are relatively successful in seeing that infants get enough sleep and grow up normally.

sleep reported at 1 month is only about 3 hours; many shorter periods of sleep are sprinkled throughout the day and night. Eventually Kipsigis infants begin to sleep through the night, but not until many months later than American infants begin to do so. Even as adults, the Kipsigis are more flexible than Americans in their sleeping hours (Super & Harkness, 1972).

In the United States, the length of the longest sleep period is often used as an index of the infant's maturation. Charles Super and Sara Harkness (1972) suggest that parents' efforts to get babies to sleep for long periods of time during the early weeks of life may be pushing the limits to which young infants can adapt. They believe that the many changes that occur in a newborn's state of arousal in every 24-hour period reflect the immaturity of the infant's brain, which sets a limit on how quickly the child can conform to an adult routine. This may be

TABLE 4.5 Infant States of Arousal

State of Arousal	Characteristics
Nonrapid eye movement (NREM) sleep	Quiet rest; little motor activity; eyes closed and still; steady breathing
Rapid eye movement (REM) sleep	Increased motor activity; facial movements and smiles; some eye movements; irregular breathing
Periodic sleep	Between REM and NREM sleep—periods of deep and steady breathing alternate with periods of more rapid and shallow breathing
Drowsiness	Intermediate between NREM and REM sleep—eyes open and close, appearing glazed when open; breathing faster and more variable than in NREM sleep
Alert inactivity	Some motor activity; relaxed face; eyes open and bright; steady but more rapid breathing compared to NREM sleep
Active alert	Frequent disorganized motor activity; vocalizations and irregular breathing; skin flushed
Distress	Vigorous disorganzied motor activity; red skin; crying

Information from Wolff, 1966.

the explanation for the failure of some infants in developed countries to adopt a night/day pattern of sleeping and waking as quickly and easily as their parents would like them to. (Cultural differences in sleeping practices may also be relevant to differences in rates of infant deaths from sudden infant death syndrome; see the box "Sudden Infant Death Syndrome.")

Feeding

As you saw in the description of Afwe's awkward first efforts to feed her baby at the beginning of this chapter, a new mother's initial nursing behavior frequently may not be much more coordinated than her infant's (Page-Goertz, McCamman, & Westdahl, 2001). She must learn how to hold the baby and adjust herself so that her nipple is placed at exactly the right spot against the baby's mouth to elicit the sucking reflex but not press so tightly that the infant's breathing is disrupted.

The coordination of infant and maternal behavior during feeding is also apparent in the physical movements mothers make while they are feeding their infants by either breast or bottle. Kenneth Kaye (1982) and his colleagues found that even during the very first feeding, mothers occasionally jiggle the baby or the bottle. These jiggles come not at random intervals but during the pauses between the infant's bursts of sucking. The jiggles increase the probability of sucking and prolong the feeding session, thereby increasing the amount of milk the neonate receives. Researchers are not certain how such adaptive patterns originated. Kaye calls them "preadapted responses," implying that they may have arisen in the course of human evolution.

Like many other developments that you have encountered in this chapter, the newborn's feeding behaviors are affected by culture as well as by biology. In many parts of the world where artificial means of birth control are unavailable, breast-feeding babies is an essential birth-control strategy in that it can suppress menstruation (although not reliably in all women), increasing the intervals between pregnancies (LeVine et al., 1994; Kuti, Adeyemi, & Owolabi, 2007). The Sukuma of Tanzania, for example, try to space pregnancies by 24 to 30 months and describe someone who does not breast-feed for this length of time as a woman who "gives birth like a chicken." The Baganda of Uganda traditionally forbade sexual activity

Sudden Infant Death Syndrome

AMONG INFANTS 1 TO 6 MONTHS OF age, sudden infant death syndrome, often referred to as SIDS, is among the most common causes of death in the United States (Centers for Disease Control and Prevention, 2017). In the typical case of SIDS, an apparently healthy infant is put to bed and a few hours later is dead. The infant may be found with clenched fists, discharge from the nose or mouth, and mottled skin, but based on the infant's prior health conditions, the family and its medical history, and the surrounding circumstances, the death is inexplicable.

The first medical report about SIDS was published more than 60 years ago (Garrow & Werne, 1953); since that time there has been an increasingly intense research program to discover its causes and ways to prevent it. Early research suggested that some infants are prone to a condition referred to as sleep apnea—that is, irregular breathing due to the brain's periodic failure to activate the muscles controlling the lungs. The most effective prevention for sleep apnea in babies involves using an electronic monitoring device that sounds an alarm whenever an infant has an episode of apnea so that an adult can come and revive the baby in time.

Postmortem studies of infant brains have suggested that sleep apnea and SIDS are associated with insufficient development of a key area in the brain stem, the medulla, which is involved in the regulation of involuntary motor behaviors, including breathing and arousal from sleep (Franco et al., 2011; Lavezzi, Corna, Mingrone, & Matturri, 2010; Singh, Chowdhury, Bindu & Schaller, 2016). However, research has also shown that episodes of apnea are relatively common in early infancy and that most babies are startled awake and experience no lasting harm from such incidents. This suggests that the maturity of the medulla may not be the only factor involved in sleep apnea and SIDS.

An important turning point in the quest to eliminate SIDS came in 1994, when the American Academy of Pediatrics, in conjunction with the National Institutes of Health and other organizations, began informing parents about SIDS through a campaign called the "Back to Sleep" movement. This clever phrase identified the major strategy on which the campaign was based: placing babies on their back to sleep instead of having them sleep on their stomach, which greatly increased the chances of accidentally obstructing their breathing. Since the inauguration of this campaign, the rate of SIDS in the United States has been cut by more than half (CDC, 2017). Reductions in the incidence of SIDS have occurred in other countries where awareness of the back-to-sleep practice has been increased (Blair et al., 2006).

To the alarm of some parents, infants who spend most of their sleep time lying on their back are prone to developing "positional skull flattening" from ongoing external pressure to the same part of the head. However, the condition is not believed to harm the baby and tends to disappear during the second 6 months of infancy, as babies become capable of moving around more and their brain continues to expand, reshaping the skull (Laughlin, Luerssen, & Dias, 2011).

Despite the success of the Back to Sleep campaign, SIDS clearly remains a serious threat, so research is currently under way to discover what additional factors might, either singly or in combination, increase infants' risk. A number of prenatal and postnatal risk factors have been identified (Hauck et al., 2003; Spinelli, Collins-Praino, Van Den Heuvel, & Byard, 2017), including the following:

- Maternal malnutrition and smoking during pregnancy, which increase the risk of prematurity (Immaturity of the brain stem is almost certainly involved in apnea episodes.)
- Other teratogens
- Postnatal exposure to secondary tobacco smoke (The greater the exposure to tobacco smoke, the greater the risk of SIDS.)
- Formula-feeding of babies, which is associated with a higher SIDS rate than is breast-feeding
- Placing infants to sleep on their stomach on a soft mattress with stuffed animals or other toys in the crib

Many studies have found different rates of SIDS for different ethnicities (CDC, 2017). For example, Native Americans have a higher rate of SIDS than do European Americans, while Latinos have a lower rate. The incidence of SIDS also varies widely across countries (Murray, 2016). Current research strongly suggests that these variations result from cultural differences in eating habits, alcohol and cigarette consumption, and sleeping patterns, not from any group differences in a genetic predisposition for SIDS. Thus, preventive measures are focused on informing local populations about the factors they can change to help reduce the possibility of their babies dying from SIDS.

by a new mother because if she has another child too soon, the first child might be deprived of breast milk and therefore may be susceptible to **kwashiorkor**, an often-fatal form of protein-calorie malnutrition.

kwashiorkor A potentially fatal form of malnutrition in which the diet is extremely low in protein.

Yet another example of culture influencing infant feeding behaviors involves pediatricians' recommendations regarding when babies should be fed. Today, pediatricians in the United States often tell parents to feed their newborn baby whenever they think the baby is hungry, perhaps as often as every 2 to 3 hours. But from the early 1920s through the 1940s, pediatricians advised parents to feed their babies only every 4 hours, even if the babies showed signs of hunger long before the prescribed time had elapsed.

Although there seems to be no difference in growth rate between babies fed on demand and those fed on a strict schedule, for a very small infant, 4 hours can be a long time to go without food (Saxon, Gollapalli, Mitchell, & Stanko, 2002). A mother's sensitivity to this may depend on her experience as a mother. In a study conducted some years ago in Cambridge, England, mothers were asked to keep records of their babies' behaviors and their own caregiving activities, including when they fed their babies and the time their babies spent crying. All of the mothers were advised to feed their babies on a strict 4-hour schedule, but not all followed the advice. The less experienced mothers tended to stick to the schedule, but the more experienced mothers sometimes fed their babies as soon as 1 hour after a scheduled feeding. Not surprisingly, the reports of the less experienced mothers showed that their babies cried the most (Bernal, 1972).

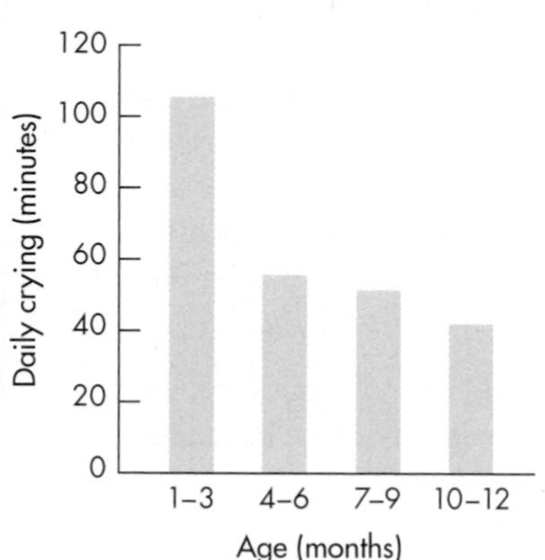

FIGURE 4.19 Crying decreases substantially between birth and 1 year of age. (Data from Bard, 2004.)

Crying

One of the most difficult problems parents face in establishing a pattern of care for their babies is how to interpret their infants' needs. Infants obviously cannot articulate their needs or feelings, but they do have one highly effective way of signaling that something is wrong: crying.

Crying is a complex behavior that involves the coordination of breathing and movements of the vocal tract. Initially it is coordinated reflexively by structures in the brain stem, but within a few months, the cerebral cortex becomes involved, enabling babies to cry voluntarily (Chittora & Patil, 2016; Sheinkopf, Righi, Marsit, & Lester, 2016). This change in the neural organization of crying is accompanied by physical changes in the vocal tract that lower the pitch of infants' cries. At this point, parents in the United States begin to report that their infants are "crying on purpose," either to get attention or because they are bored (Lester et al., 1992). Across cultures, and even in chimpanzees, there is a peak in the frequency of infant crying at 6 weeks of age, followed by a decline at approximately 12 weeks (Bard, 2004) (Figure 4.19).

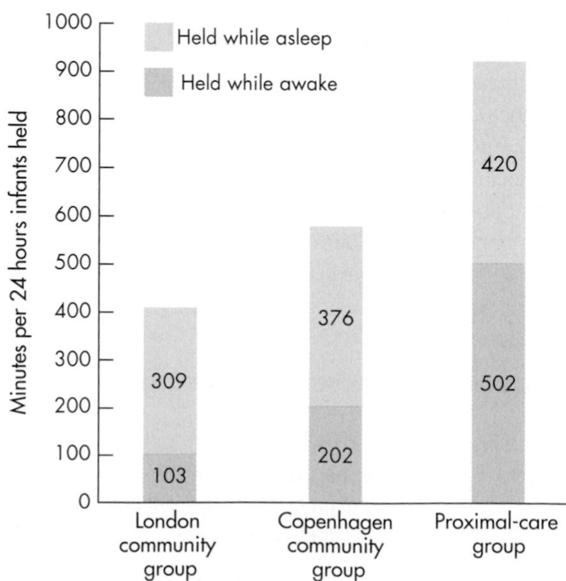

FIGURE 4.20 There are considerable differences within and across cultures in the amount of time that babies are held. In general, babies who are held more spend less time fussing and crying. (Data from St. James-Roberts et al., 2006.)

Developmentalists with an evolutionary perspective believe that human crying evolved as a signal to promote caregiving when the infant is hungry, in pain, or separated from its caregiver (Falk, 2016). Indeed, cross-cultural evidence suggests that infants cry less when their culture's caregiving practices include proximal care—that is, prolonged holding, frequent breastfeeding, rapid response to infant frets and cries, and co-sleeping with infants at night—all found, for example, in several African cultures, including the !Kung and the Aka (Bleah & Ellet, 2010; Hewlett et al., 1998; Kruger & Konner, 2010). These practices have been found to different extents in Western cultures, and the differences have similar repercussions for infant crying (St. James-Roberts et al., 2006). As shown in Figures 4.20 and 4.21, compared with mothers in London, those in Copenhagen spent significantly more time holding their infants, and in the course of a day, their babies cried and fretted significantly less.

Certainly babies' cries have a powerful effect on those who hear them. Experienced parents and childless adults alike respond to infants' cries with increases in heart rate and blood pressure, both of which are physiological signs of arousal and anxiety (Esposito et al., 2016; Out, Pieper, Bakermans-Kranenburg, & van IJzendoorn, 2010). The problem for anxious parents who hear their newborns cry is to figure out the source and seriousness of their baby's discomfort. Research shows that adults are in fact able to make certain distinctions among cries. According to Phillip Zeskind and his colleagues, the higher-pitched the cries and the shorter the pauses between them, the more urgent—and unpleasant—adults perceive them to be. Indeed, such urgent-sounding cries are more typical of infants born prematurely or exposed prenatally to drugs or alcohol (Orlandi et al., 2016; Zeskind et al., 2014).

It is widely believed that some children suffer from an unexplained medical condition called *colic*, which causes them to cry excessively. Indeed, excessive infant crying is the most common complaint heard by pediatricians from mothers with infants under 3 months of age (Forsyth, 1989). However, while there are marked individual differences in the amounts that infants cry, the cries of babies thought to suffer from colic are not distinguishable from those of others who cry frequently, although their bouts of crying tend to last longer and are more difficult to soothe (Barr et al., 2005). Thus, it would appear that it is not the specific sounds of the colicky infant's crying that trouble parents but rather the prolonged and unexplained nature of the crying.

Caregivers' efforts to get babies on a schedule for sleeping and feeding and to comfort them when they are distressed continue as the months go by. Infants' adaptations to these parenting activities are so commonplace that it is easy to overlook their significance. They are, however, the first instances of infants' coordination and active participation in the social world.

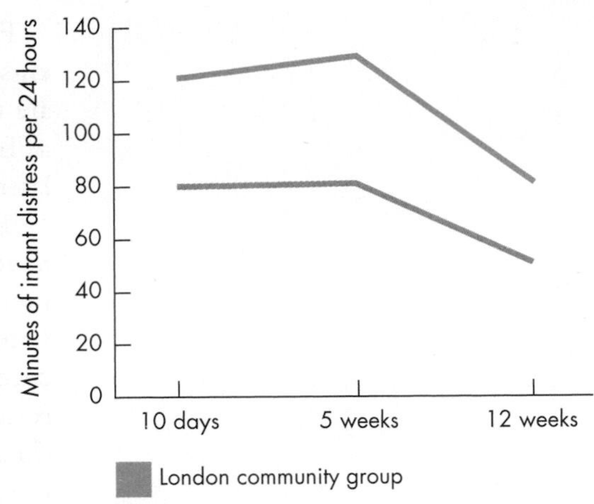

FIGURE 4.21 Although many people continue to believe that infants who are held a lot will cry more than those who are held less, research indicates just the opposite. As shown here, the amount of distress during the first 12 weeks of life of infants who are held less (the London group) is significantly higher than that of infants who are held more. (Data from the Copenhagen group.)

APPLY > CONNECT > DISCUSS

How would you respond to a new parent who takes an operant conditioning approach to newborn crying, believing that babies will cry more if their crying is "reinforced" by the parents' always responding to it?

Looking Ahead

LEARNING OUTCOMES

Summarize the developmental changes that occur in the first three months of life.

Looking back over the first 3 months of postnatal life, you can see a remarkable set of changes in the organization of infants' behaviors and how they become coordinated with social life.

Babies are born with a rudimentary ability to interact with and learn about their new environment. They have reflexes that enable them to take in oxygen and nutrients and expel waste products. They are able to perceive objects, including people, although they tend to focus on only a part of the entire stimulus. They are sensitive to the sounds of human language, and they quickly develop a preference for the sound of their mother's voice. Although they sleep most of the time, they are occasionally quite alert.

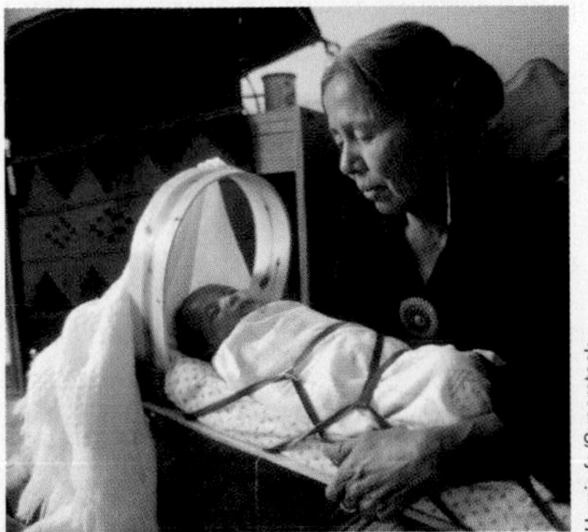
Hemis.fr /Superstock

Wallenrock/Shutterstock

Parents throughout the world employ a variety of methods to deal with infant cries and fussiness. Holding the baby close, rocking, patting, or making rhythmic sounds such as clapping, are common. Some child-care practices, including swaddling and carrying, reduce the amount and intensity of fussiness, making it easier for caregivers to soothe their infants.

From the moment of birth, infants interact with and are supported by their parents or other caregivers. Initially, the first interactions of babies and their caregivers are tentative and somewhat uncoordinated, but within a matter of days, a process of behavioral coordination has begun that will provide an essential framework for later development.

The developmental changes that characterize the first 3 months of infancy have clear origins in biology and in the physical and sociocultural environment. In the domain of biology, there is rapid maturation of the central nervous system, particularly in the connections between the brain stem and the cerebral cortex. Physically, babies become bigger and stronger; behaviorally, reflexes make way for more sophisticated actions that are increasingly coordinated and responsive to variations in the environment. This responsiveness is assisted by shifts in the infants' arousal states: Less time is spent sleeping and crying, and more time is spent in alert states, where babies can profit from and learn through active engagement with the world. All of these accomplishments converge to position the newborn at a new threshold of cognitive, social, and emotional development.

INSIGHT AND INTEGRATION

1. Explain how, in some ways, babies are born ready to encounter a vast range of experiences, but in other ways, they are born to focus on particular types of experience.
2. Provide some examples of how, despite the radical changes involved in the transition from the world of the womb to the extrauterine environment, the newborn's prenatal experiences and condition impact postnatal life.

Summary

Physical Growth

- As growth charts reveal, early physical growth is rapid, with the infant gaining about 6 pounds (2.7 kilograms) and growing more than 4 inches (10 centimeters) in just 12 weeks.
- The growing brain pushes against the bones of the skull, expanding the infant's head circumference.

Brain Development

- At birth, the brain contains most of the cells (neurons) it will ever have, but it will become four times larger by adulthood.
- Increased size results primarily from an increase in the connections among neurons and from myelination, which insulates axons and speeds the transmission of impulses.
- At birth, the cerebral cortex is less mature than the brain stem, which controls reflexes such as sucking and vital functions such as breathing. Development of the cortex occurs through both experience-expectant and experience-dependent processes.

Sensing the Environment

- Although newborns' sensory systems are all functioning, some are more developed than others. Newborns are able to perceive an object or event with more than one sensory system.
- Newborns are sensitive to the differences that distinguish the various sounds of human languages and, although they are initially able to hear and discriminate between sounds made in all the world's languages, they are soon able to perceive only those made in the language they hear around them.
- Because of immaturity of the eye's structures, newborns are very nearsighted, but visual acuity soon improves. Newborns are able to visually scan their surroundings, they can perceive patterns and discern among forms, they show a preference for faces, and they have the ability to distinguish their mother's face.
- Newborns can distinguish various tastes and smells. They prefer tastes and smells that are sweet, like breast milk, and make characteristic facial expressions in response to sour and bitter tastes and foul odors.

The Organization of Behavior

- Developing and maintaining behavioral organization is important for infants because it allows them to interact more effectively and adaptively with the world around them.
- At birth, reflexes give newborns highly organized ways of responding to the environment.

- Reflexes are building blocks for more complicated, coordinated forms of behavioral organization—for example, nursing develops from reflexes such as rooting and sucking. With maturational changes in the cerebral cortex, infants become able to coordinate reaching and grasping.
- According to Jean Piaget, infants gain knowledge largely by coordinating sensory perceptions and simple motor responses. During the first few months, they progress through the first two of the six substages of the sensorimotor stage:
    - In substage 1, infants learn to control and coordinate inborn reflexes.
- In substage 2, accommodation first appears, and infants prolong pleasant sensations arising from reflex actions.
- According to learning theorists, learning, as evidenced by a change in behavior, occurs when the infant makes associations between his or her behavior and events in the environment. Learning may take various forms:
    - In classical conditioning, previously existing behaviors come to be associated with, and elicited by, new stimuli.
- In operant conditioning, new behaviors may come about as a result of the reinforcement and punishment of behaviors.

Temperament

- Infants differ in temperament, the emotional and behavioral characteristics that show consistency across situations and some stability over time. Temperament includes such traits as activity level, quality of mood, and attention span. It is genetically based but is also subject to environmental influences.
- The same temperamental traits appear to be found in all cultures, but the strength of their expression may be influenced by cultural factors.

Becoming Coordinated with the Social World

- Infants' survival depends not only on the actions of caregivers but also on infants' ability to coordinate their own actions with those of caregivers.
- Newborns sleep approximately two-thirds of the time, but their periods of sleep are relatively brief, and they may be awake at any time. They tend to adapt gradually to adults' night/day sleep cycle, but the specifics of their sleep cycle depend in part on cultural patterns.
- The maternal–infant coordination that nursing requires has a biological underpinning. However, culture influences the age at which infants breast-feed and their feeding schedules. Newborns tend to prefer a 3-hour schedule, moving to a 4-hour schedule by 2½ months and approximating an adult schedule by 7 or 8 months.
- Infants' crying is a primitive means of communication that evokes a strong emotional response in adults and alerts them that something may be wrong. Infants tend to cry less in cultures with caregiving practices such as prolonged holding and frequent feeding. Certain distinctive patterns of early cries may indicate difficulties.

Looking Ahead

- From birth, infants have a wide range of abilities and interact with their caregivers. Developmental changes in the first 3 months, originating in biology and depending also on the environment, include rapid physical growth and maturation of the central nervous system and a shift from reflexes to complex actions. The 3-month-old is at a new threshold of cognitive, social, and emotional development.

Key Terms

growth charts, p. 124
fontanels, p. 126
neuron, p. 126
axon, p. 127
dendrite, p. 127
synapse, p. 127
neurotransmitter, p. 127
synaptogenesis, p. 127
myelin, p. 127
spinal cord, p. 128
brain stem, p. 128
cerebral cortex, p. 128
experience-expectant, p. 129
exuberant synaptogenesis, p. 130
synaptic pruning, p. 130
experience-dependent, p. 131
perceptual narrowing, p. 132
electroencephalography (EEG), p. 132
visual preference technique, p. 133
habituation, p. 133
dishabituation, p. 133
phonemes, p. 133
visual acuity, p. 134
multimodal perception, p. 140
reflex, p. 142
action, p. 142
sensorimotor stage, p. 146
primary circular reaction, p. 147
learning, p. 147
classical conditioning, p. 147
conditional stimulus (CS), p. 147
unconditional stimulus (UCS), p. 147
unconditional response (UCR), p. 147
conditional response (CR), p. 147
operant conditioning, p. 148
temperament, p. 149
kwashiorkor, p. 155

Tetra Images/Getty Images

CHAPTER

5

Physical and Cognitive Development in Infancy

It's music time in the toddler room at Tiny Tots, and 18-month-old Liam watches and laughs as his teachers stomp their feet and move their arms in rhythm to "We are the dinosaurs marching, marching." In an apparent effort to march along, Liam bends his knees a few times, bouncing in place, and waves the toy dinosaurs clutched in his hands—all of it uncoordinated and in no relation to the music. He stops to glance at some of the other children: The 2-year-olds are following along fairly well, some alternating their feet in true marching style, and chiming in, "Marching, marching," while the younger ones, to different degrees, engage—some trying to march, others waving or banging their dinosaurs together, or chewing on them; still others have fallen down or moved off to other areas of the room. The teachers stop marching and sing on, "We stop and eat our food, when we're in the mood." They pretend to gather food and put it into their mouths. Some of the 2-year-olds follow suit, while Liam continues to bend his knees, bounce in place, and wave his dinosaurs.

At 1½ years of age, Liam behaves far differently than he did as a typical 3-month-old. At that earlier age, Liam's main activities were eating, sleeping, and gazing around the room. He could hold his head up and turn it from side to side, but he could not readily reach out and grasp objects or move around on his own. He took an interest in mobiles and other objects when they were immediately in front of him, but he quickly lost interest in them when they were removed from his view, as though they no longer existed for him. His communications were restricted to cries, frowns, and smiles.

The contrast between Liam's behavior then and his behavior more than a year later gives you a hint of some of the amazing changes that occur during the period of infancy. Perhaps most obvious are the outwardly visible physical changes: Infants become markedly larger and stronger between 3 and 24 months of age. Essential maturation has also taken place in the central nervous system, particularly the cerebral cortex and other parts of the brain.

Related to these biological changes are the enormous gains that infants make in being able to move their bodies. At 3 months of age, infants are just beginning to be able to roll over, and their parents can be confident that they will remain more or less wherever they are put down. That soon changes. At about 7 to 8 months, infants begin to crawl; at about 1 year, they begin to walk; and by the time they are 2, they can run, take a few steps backward, and walk up stairs (with a helping hand). During this period, infants also become far more adept at manipulating objects. At 1 year of age, babies prod, bang, squeeze, push, and pull almost anything they can get their hands on, and they often put objects into their mouths to learn about them, as some of the 1-year-olds did with their dinosaurs; at 2 years of age, they possess enough control to feed themselves with a spoon, to toss a large ball, to open cabinets, drawers, and boxes. As infants' mobility, motor control, and curiosity about the world increase, their parents must constantly be on the watch to keep them out of harm's way.

Important changes also occur in infants' cognitive abilities. Older babies become better at focusing their attention; they learn more rapidly and remember what they have learned for longer periods of time. By the end of infancy, babies can imitate increasingly complex actions that they have observed others perform — marching or pretending to gather and eat food — and can even imitate those actions days later in play. They can follow simple directions, and they laugh when someone does something silly, such as acting like a dinosaur. They also begin to use symbols, turning a building block into a smart phone or a racing car. Of special significance is their emerging mastery of that uniquely human symbol system, language.

These changes in biological makeup, motor behavior, and cognitive capacities interact throughout infancy. We will focus on them in this chapter, and in the next, we will turn to the substantial social and emotional developments that they help make possible.

WARMING UP

1. One of the most remarkable and consequential achievements of infancy is the ability to walk. In what way does this major milestone in motor development affect how babies relate to and learn about their environments? Do you think it affects their language development, or how they understand or learn about objects and spaces?
2. Many properties of our physical world are so fundamental that they're easy to overlook: Objects continue to exist even when we can't see them; objects do not simply float around in the air but fall to the ground if not supported; if one object knocks against another, the second one moves. Do you think such knowledge of the physical world is present at birth, or does it takes time and experience to develop? Can you think of how you might answer this question by studying the behavior of infants?

LEARNING OUTCOMES

Describe physical growth during infancy.

Point out changes in the musculoskeletal system of infants.

Physical Growth

The physical differences between a 3-month-old and a 2-year-old are so striking that it's hard to believe that so much could have changed in a scant 21 months (Figure 5.1). There are changes in body size and proportions and in the muscles and bones, as well as in the brain. These changes are connected both with each other and with the development of the new behavioral capacities babies display. For example, their greater weight requires larger and stronger bones to support them and stronger muscles to enable movement. Their developing cognitive capacities make them want to explore new aspects of the world, but to explore the world, they must coordinate their constantly changing size and strength in new ways.

mother image/Getty Images

FIGURE 5.1 As is apparent in this photograph, the child's body undergoes remarkable changes over the course of infancy, enabling a host of new actions and behaviors, including climbing on Mom's back and giving her a hug.

Size and Shape

During their 1st year, most healthy babies triple in weight and grow approximately 10 inches; in the United States, the typical 1-year-old weighs 20 to 22 pounds (9 to 10 kg) and stands 28 to 30 inches (71 to 76 cm) tall. During the second year of life, children's bodies continue to grow rapidly, though at a much slower rate (Bogin, 2001); in the United States, children on average gain 5 pounds (2.2 kg) and grow 4 inches (10.6 cm), to about 27 pounds and about 34 inches (12.2 kg and 86.3 cm). (This tapering off of the growth rate, apparent in Figure 5.2, continues until adolescence, when there is a noticeable growth spurt for children growing up in many, but not all, parts of the world, as we will discuss in Chapter 14; Urlacher et al., 2016.) Also by 2 years of age, most children have all their baby teeth.

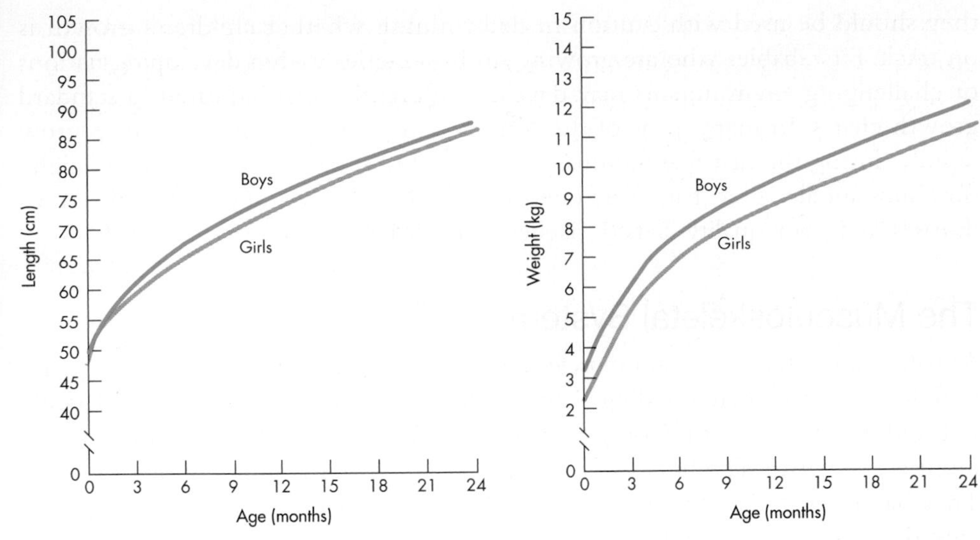

FIGURE 5.2 U.S. babies' lengths roughly double and their weights increase around 200 percent during the first 2 years of life. Note that at this stage, boys tend, on average, to be heavier and taller than girls. (Research from the Centers for Disease Control and Prevention, 2009.)

Increases in babies' height and weight are accompanied by changes in their body proportions (see Figure 5.3). At birth, the baby's head is 70 percent of its adult size and accounts for about 25 percent of the baby's total length. By 1 year of age, the head accounts for 20 percent of body length, and by adulthood, 12 percent. Infants' legs at birth are not much longer than their heads; by adulthood, the legs account for about half of a person's total height. By 12 months, the changes in body proportions have led to a lower center of gravity, making it easier for the child to balance on two legs and begin to walk (Thelen, 2002). As their bodies stretch out, most babies lose the potbellied look so characteristic of early infancy; they begin to look more like children than infants.

The norms for children's growth, such as those depicted in Figure 5.2, can be enormously helpful in determining whether a child's physical development is on track. Physical growth that differs substantially from the norms may signal illness or risk for disease. For example, significantly slower growth rates, known as *infant growth restriction*, or *stunting*, are associated with a number of serious problems, including developmental delay, infections, and poor nutrition (Eide et al., 2016; File, 2015; Shafique et al., 2016); significantly faster growth rates are associated with risk of obesity in later childhood (Druet et al., 2012; van der Willik et al., 2015). However, most standard growth norms are derived by averaging large samples of children who are developing in Western, technologically advanced countries; consequently,

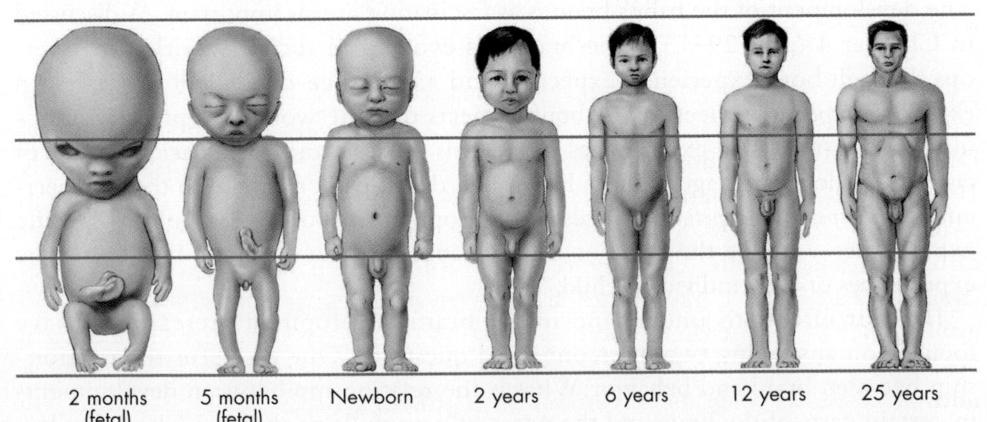

FIGURE 5.3 These drawings show the proportions of body length accounted for by the head, trunk, and legs at different stages of development. During the fetal period, the head accounts for as much as 50 percent of body length. The head decreases from 25 percent of body length at birth to 12 percent in adulthood. (Data from Fryar, Gu, & Ogden, 2012.)

they should be used with caution in determining whether children's growth is on track. First, babies who are growing up in societies within developing nations or challenging environments may develop differently than indicated in standard growth charts. In many areas of the Amazon, for example, infants tend to grow rapidly during the first few months, but their rates of growth, especially in height, slow substantially after that, likely due to some combination of genetics, infectious diseases, and poor-quality diets (Urlacher et al., 2016).

The Musculoskeletal System

As babies grow, the bones and muscles needed to support their increasing bulk and mobility undergo corresponding growth. Most of a newborn's bones are relatively soft, and they harden (ossify) only gradually, as minerals are deposited in them in the months after birth. The bones in the hand and wrist are among the first to ossify. They harden by the end of the 1st year, making it easier for a baby to grasp objects, pick them up, and play with them. At the same time, infants' muscles increase in length and thickness, a process that continues throughout childhood and into late adolescence. In infancy, increases in muscle mass are closely associated with the development of the baby's ability to crawl, stand alone, and walk.

Although boys are generally larger than girls, as Figure 5.2 clearly indicates, research supports the common wisdom that girls mature faster than boys. In fact, sex differences in growth rates are apparent even before birth: Halfway through the prenatal period, the skeletal development of female fetuses is some 3 weeks more advanced than that of male fetuses. At birth, the female skeleton is 4 to 6 weeks more mature than that of the male; by puberty, it is 2 years more advanced. (Girls are more advanced in the development of other organ systems as well. They get their permanent teeth, go through puberty, and reach their full body size earlier than boys do [Bogin, 1999].)

The physical changes of infancy described above open wholly new ways of exploring and learning about the environment. Equally significant in making these possible are the changes taking place in the brain.

APPLY > CONNECT > DISCUSS

Provide some concrete examples of how socioeconomic status may affect infants' physical growth.

LEARNING OUTCOMES

Describe brain development during infancy.

Give examples of the relationship between brain development and infant behavior.

Brain Development

The development of the baby's brain is as fascinating as it is important. As discussed in Chapter 4 (pp. 129–131), the brain has evolved in such a way that it develops through both experience-expectant and experience-dependent processes. In *experience-expectant* processes, the brain expects that the world will present particular, species-universal experiences—patterns of light and dark, various kinds of tastes and odors, language, and the like—and develops in response to those experiences. In *experience-dependent* processes, development occurs in response to specific experiences—hence the brain's amazing capacity to be changed by the unique experiences of each individual child.

In their efforts to understand infant brain development, researchers have focused on answering two interconnected questions. One concerns the relationship between brain and behavior: What is the relationship between developments in certain parts of the brain and the onset of new skills or abilities? The other key question concerns the relationship between brain and experience: To what extent does experience or the lack thereof (that is, deprivation) enhance or impede brain development and function?

Brain and Behavior

As we discussed in Chapter 4, the brain undergoes substantial development throughout infancy, although different parts grow at different times and rates (Dubois et al., 2014). The *cerebral cortex* is very immature at birth. Because the cortex is associated with such complex functions as voluntary (as opposed to reflexive) behavior, abstract thought, problem solving, and language, its development has been of special interest to researchers eager to understand brain–behavior relationships. (As detailed in the box "Now Trending in Practice: Bringing Up Babies in the Digital Age" on page 167, interest in infant brain development has fueled a multimillion-dollar industry aimed at making babies smarter.)

prefrontal cortex The part of the cortex that is located directly behind the forehead and is important to the development of voluntary behaviors.

The **prefrontal cortex** of the cortex, located behind the forehead, plays a particularly important role in the development of voluntary behavior. It begins to function in a new way sometime between 7 and 9 months of age. With this change in functioning comes an increase in infants' ability to regulate themselves (Posner, Rothbart, Sheese, & Voelker, 2014). Infants can stop themselves from grabbing the first attractive thing they see; they can cuddle their teddy bear to keep from being upset when they are put down for a nap. With the emerging ability to inhibit action, they can also better control what they attend to. In effect, they begin to be able to stop and think (Posner, Rothbart, & Voelker, 2016).

Another important development, revealed by brain-imaging techniques, involves the language-related areas of the cortex. These areas, in the frontal and temporal lobes, undergo significant myelination shortly before a characteristic spurt in toddlers' vocabulary (Pujol et al., 2006; see Chapter 7, p. 234). (Myelin, remember, is the fatty substance that covers axons, speeding the brain's communications.)

At least as important as the growth of different brain areas is that the different areas increasingly function together (Fox, Levitt, & Nelson, 2010; Posner et al., 2016). Once again, myelination plays an important role. In fact, although myelination of the brain is ongoing from the second part of pregnancy through adolescence, there is a peak rate of myelination during the first postnatal year, resulting in the formation of neural networks that allow different parts of the brain to communicate and work together (Dubois et al., 2014). For example, myelination of the neurons that link the prefrontal cortex and frontal lobes to the brain stem, where emotional responses are partially generated, creates a new potential for interaction between thinking and emotion. In general, the greater synchrony among brain areas appears vital to the emergence of functions that define late infancy, including more systematic problem solving, voluntary control of behavior, and the acquisition of language (Richmond & Nelson, 2007).

Toward the end of infancy, the length and the degree of branching of the neurons in the cerebral cortex approach adult magnitudes: Each neuron now has connections with other neurons, usually numbering in the thousands. Although brain structures mature at different rates, those that eventually will support adult behavior are present, and the pace of the brain's overall growth becomes slower and steadier until adolescence.

Brain and Experience

As we discussed in Chapter 4, everyday experience, as well as even brief periods of deprivation, can affect the brain's structures and functions. For instance, in discussing *exuberant synaptogenesis* and *synaptic pruning* (p. 130), we described how the infant's

Europics/Newscom

This young, Romanian gypsy woman was abandoned at an early age. Despite years spent in the horribly depriving conditions of an orphanage, she is doing remarkably well. She has been accepted into five universities, and her future is bright.

normal everyday experiences, such as exposure to a specific language, can affect which synapses are strengthened and which are eliminated, or pruned. We also discussed how newborns who are nearly blind due to congenital cataracts, despite corrective surgery that removes the cataracts and restores vision, may throughout their lives process auditory and visual information somewhat differently than individuals born with normal vision (p. 135; de Heering et al., 2016).

If brain development is so readily influenced by the infant's daily experience and brief periods of deprivation, how might it be affected by situations in which an infant endures more severe forms of deprivation? Profound and pervasive deprivation, referred to as **early-life adversity**, can have terrible consequences for development. Some of the most heart-wrenching and conclusive evidence comes from research on infants and children who spent time in orphanages before being adopted into families or foster care (Brett et al., 2015). The orphans, many of whom were abandoned or left without caregivers due to war or political violence, received basic physical care with little social and intellectual stimulation. Typically, they were confined to cribs for most of each day, with no social interaction and nothing to look at but bare walls. Needless to say, many of these children had significant delays in development at the time they were rescued from these horrific conditions.

early-life adversity Profound and pervasive deprivation experienced during infancy, often resulting in severe developmental delays.

In general, research finds that children who were adopted early in infancy, especially before 6 months of age, fare far better than those adopted at older ages, who were much more likely to suffer significant developmental impairments (Nelson, Zeanah, & Fox, 2007). The researchers point out that the infant brain undergoes considerable development between 6 and 24 months of age and that during such phases of rapid growth, brain structures are particularly sensitive to the infant's experiences. In Chapter 1, we described such phases as *sensitive periods*, or periods of *plasticity*, during which a particular experience (or lack of it) has a more pronounced effect on development than it would at another point in time (see p. 13). It is likely that during sensitive periods of brain development, the orphans lacked the species-universal experiences required for strengthening and fine-tuning normal experience-expectant neural connections. In addition, the infants' experience-dependent brain development may have been adversely affected by the deprived conditions of the orphanage.

But even children who seem less affected by deprivation early in development may show evidence of impairment as they age. The detrimental effects of early-life adversity that occur only later in development are referred to as **sleeper effects** (Brett et al., 2015; Zeanah et al., 2011). Sleeper effects are evident in an interesting pattern of emotional development observed in some boys who had been institutionalized as infants: As young children, the boys were less adventurous than their non-institutionalized peers; however, as adolescents, such boys engaged in excessive levels of impulsiveness and risk-taking. This pattern suggests that deprivation may have altered the development of neural connections between areas of the brain associated with impulses and the processing of emotions (the limbic system, see Chapter 11, p. 379), and those areas in the cerebral cortex responsible for higher levels of decision making and behavioral control.

sleeper effects The detrimental effects of early-life adversity that occur only later in development.

Aided by new brain-imaging technologies (see Chapter 1, p. 33), developmentalists are gaining spectacular new insights into the relationships between the developing brain and the experiences and behaviors of infants. Indeed, brain scans of a group of these orphans showed significant deficits in the functioning of certain areas in the limbic system, which is involved in emotion and motivation (Eluvathingal et al., 2006). Interestingly, work with rats and other animals indicates

Now TRENDING in PRACTICE

Bringing Up Babies in the Digital Age

One-year-old Chloe is sitting in her father's lap, video-chatting with her mother, who's out of town for a business meeting. Mom says, "Hi, Chloe! How's my girl? Are you having fun with Daddy?" With a big smile, Chloe says, "Daddy!" But she quickly begins to squirm and fret, until Dad gives her his tablet, on which bubbles are appearing as if in a foaming bath. Chloe's mood brightens immediately. She hits at the screen with her index finger, exclaiming "Pop!" as bubbles burst into brilliant colors at her touch. The interactive app occupies her attention for several minutes while mom and dad continue to chat.

The digital age has fundamentally altered the life experiences of infants and children throughout the world. Electronic devices and digital applications are used increasingly with very young children for a variety of reasons, including staying in touch with loved ones, distraction during periods of fussiness or distress, entertainment during daily routines, such as car rides and eating out, and as educational tools that promote academic skills, such as reading and counting (Radesky, Schumacher, & Zuckerman, 2015). The range and ingenuity of the products that have been created for infants and young children are staggering. Indeed, 72 percent of the top-paid apps are in the Preschool/Toddler category, and more than 80,000 apps are designated as educational (Apple, 2015; Shuler, 2012). In 2013, a nationwide survey found that 58 percent of parents in the United States reported downloading apps for their children; a survey conducted with parents in France found even higher rates of touch screen use by very young children (Cristia & Seidl, 2015). Needless to say, the app industry rakes in enormous amounts of money, with current revenues estimated to be around $40 billion (Shuler, 2012).

Early exposure to environments saturated with new technologies has raised both hope for the educational potential of interactive media and concerns about the consequences of exposure during a crucial period of rapid brain development and the formation of social and attachment relationships (Council on Communications and Media, 2016). But the scientific community has been struggling to keep up with the breakneck pace at which new devices and apps are developed, marketed, and adopted by parents of very young children, and there is no straightforward answer to the question of whether exposure to digital technologies is harmful or beneficial. Indeed, the answer depends on how and when the technologies are used.

Some research has found that screen time, typically defined as exposure to television, may disrupt the sleep of infants and young children by causing them to take longer to fall asleep, or sleep less overall (Chonchaiya, Wilaisakditipakorn, Vijakkhana, & Pruksananonda, 2017; Cespedes et al., 2014). Other research has focused on some positive consequences of interactive technologies such as distracting young children during stressful medical procedures or promoting language learning through video-chatting (McQueen, Cress, & Tothy, 2012 Roseberry, Hirsh-Pasek, & Golinkoff, 2014).

Recent studies have focused on how digital technologies affect the quality of parent–infant interactions and indicate that quality suffers compared to interactions that involve traditional toys and books. One study found that with electronic toys, parents used fewer words and responded less frequently to their infants' vocalizations and behaviors than they did with traditional toys and books (Sosa, 2016); the babies also vocalized less often. Another study compared parent–child interactions during play with a traditional sorting toy, similar to illustration "a," and a comparable, electronically enhanced toy, similar to illustration "b," with headlights that lit up, musical keys, and a puppy "driver" that would sway from side to side when the toy was moved (Zosh et al., 2015). Again, parent–child interactions were significantly affected by the nature of the toy, with the traditional sorter prompting a higher quality of parental language, overall, as well as more language specific to the types of shapes ("circle," "square") and spatial relationships ("Put it in there").

Thus, research supports critics' concerns that digital toys and apps may displace or dilute the quality of human interaction — a source of essential experiences for infant brain growth and emerging cognitive, social, and emotional development. As the prevalence of their use continues to explode, along with the industry's unfounded claims of their "educational" value, researchers continue to evaluate the risks and benefits to infant and child development (Hirsh-Pasek et al., 2015).

(a)

(b)

that the specific limbic areas affected are especially vulnerable to stress, particularly when it is experienced early in development. As the findings involving the orphans suggest, advances in developmental neuroscience hold great promise for exploring how biological and environmental processes interact in the life of the developing child.

APPLY > CONNECT > DISCUSS

Review the four central issues of developmental science that were discussed in Chapter 1 (pp. 11–12). How does current knowledge of infant brain development shed light on these issues?

LEARNING OUTCOMES

Describe the fine and gross motor skills of infants.

Indicate the steps by which infants learn to reach and grasp.

Describe the progress in locomotion that occurs during infancy.

Explain the role of practice in infant motor development.

Motor Development

One of the most dramatic developments between 3 and 24 months of age is the enormous increase in infants' ability to explore their environment by grasping and manipulating objects and by moving about. As their motor skills advance, babies gain important information about features of the world and how it is put together—for example, how objects feel to the touch and how they behave when they are poked, pulled, dropped, or banged together. Importantly, advances in motor skills give babies new opportunities to pursue people (quite literally) and to communicate to them and get feedback from them about interesting objects in the environment—from odd bits of trash ("No, don't touch—that's *dirty*") to the tail of the family dog ("Be careful, don't pull—that might *hurt*"), to a toy on a chair that was out of reach just a few months before ("What a big girl to reach that teddy bear!").

These changing motor abilities have widespread consequences for cognitive, social, and emotional development (Libertus, Joh, & Needham, 2016). For instance, infants' walking and grasping skills have been associated with the size of their vocabularies, as well as their language development at 3 years of age (He, Walle, & Campos, 2015; Wang, Lekhal, Aarø, & Schjølberg, 2014). One recent study found that 3-month-old-infants who received just 2 weeks of parent-guided training in reaching for objects engaged in higher levels of exploration and attention when they were 15-months-olds compared to infants who did not receive special training. All this suggests that the development of early motor skills may result in a cascade of developments in other areas (Libertus et al., 2016).

fine motor skills Motor skills related to the development and coordination of small muscles, such as those that move the fingers and eyes.

gross motor skills Motor skills related to the development and coordination of large muscles; important for locomotion.

locomotion The ability to move around on one's own.

Developmentalists who study motor development typically distinguish between **fine motor skills**, which involve the development and coordination of small muscles, such as those that move the fingers and eyes, and **gross motor skills**, which involve the large muscles of the body and make **locomotion** possible.

Fine Motor Skills

We pointed out in Chapter 2 that human beings are highly distinctive in their ability to make and use tools. Such tool use would be impossible without the development of fine motor skills that allow us to grasp and manipulate objects. From the perspective of parents and caregivers, increasing fine motor control and coordination mean that their baby can participate more fully in such daily activities as feeding and dressing. It also means that the baby can get into drawers, cupboards, and other spaces that may contain dangerous objects. Figure 5.4 provides a summary of the major milestones of an infant's fine motor skills.

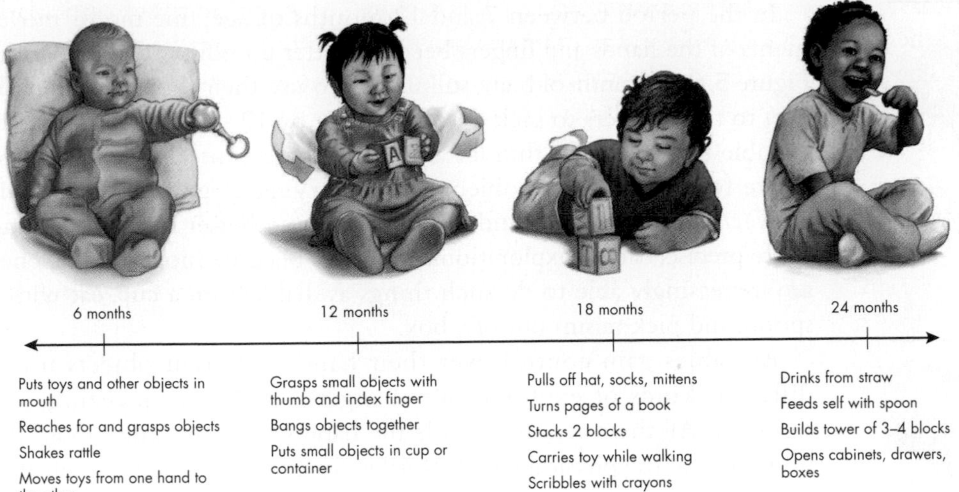

FIGURE 5.4 The development and coordination of the small muscles that control the fingers and hands are associated with a variety of important skills and follow a fairly predictable timetable.

Early Skills: Reaching and Grasping Remember from Chapter 4 (p. 144) that very young infants reach for an object moving in front of them, a reflexlike motion we referred to as *prereaching*. As we discussed, at this initial stage, the perceptions and actions involved in reaching and grasping are not yet coordinated. Infants may reach for an object but fail to close their hands around it, usually because they close their hands too soon (see Figure 5.5a). Then, around 4 to 6 months of age, babies begin to gain voluntary control over their movements, so reaching and grasping occur in the proper sequence (Berthier & Keen, 2006). At first, their reaching and grasping is hit or miss (von Hofsten, 2001). With practice, their fine motor coordination gradually improves (see Figure 5.5b), and by 2 years of age, the overall speed and smoothness of their reaching approach adult levels. During this time, caretakers need to "baby proof" their homes by putting dangerous or fragile objects out of the infant's reach. They also have to watch out for the sudden appearance of unexpected items in the grocery cart if the baby is along for the ride!

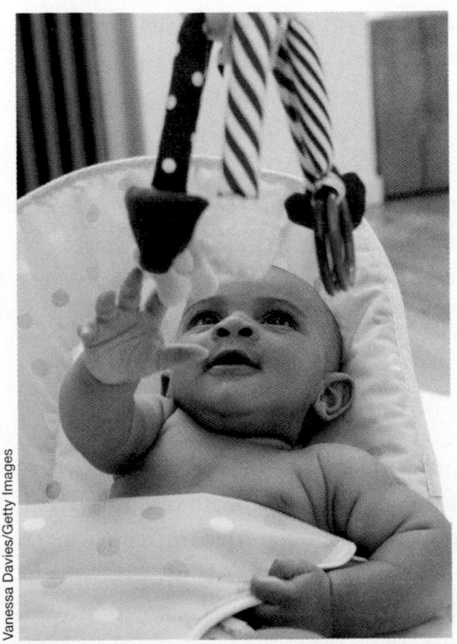
Vanessa Davies/Getty Images

(a)

Yukmin/Getty Images

(b)

FIGURE 5.5 At 3 months of age, the baby's reaching and grasping are not yet well coordinated, making it difficult to seize the object of interest (a). In contrast, by 8 months of age, motor skills are so advanced that the baby can not only grasp the object easily but also explore it intently (b).

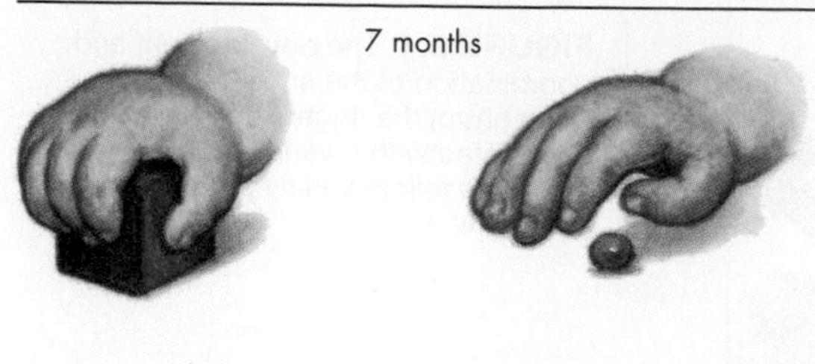

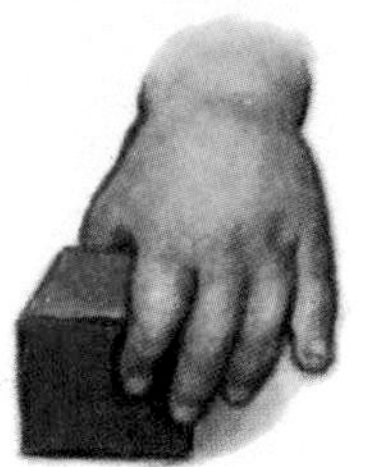

FIGURE 5.6 Babies find ways to grasp objects from an early age, but good coordination of the thumb and forefinger requires at least a year to achieve. (Research from Senna et al., 2017.)

In the period between 7 and 12 months of age, fine motor movements of the hands and fingers become better coordinated. As shown in Figure 5.6, 7-month-olds are still unable to use their thumbs in opposition to their fingers to pick up objects, but by 12 months of age, babies are able to move their thumbs and other fingers into positions appropriate to the size of the object they are trying to grasp (Senna et al., 2017). As their reaching and grasping become better coordinated and more precise, babies' explorations of objects become more refined. They are increasingly able to do such things as drink from a cup, eat with a spoon, and pick raisins out of a box.

As babies gain control over their hands, different objects invite different kinds of exploration—banging, shaking, squeezing, and throwing. All these actions provide the baby with knowledge about the properties of the physical world. Rattles, for example, lend themselves to making noises, while soft dolls lend themselves to pleasurable touching. Perceptual-motor exploration is an all-important way to find out about the environment and to gain control over it.

Later Skills: Manual Dexterity A lot of parents keep pictures of their babies' first efforts to feed themselves—pudgy faces all smeared with food. As amusing as these pictures can be, they illustrate the difficulty of mastering an act as elementary as using a spoon. Infants between 10 and 23 months of age attempt to hold a spoon in a variety of different ways as they try to learn the incredibly precise coordination that the effective use of a spoon entails. At 10 to 12 months of age, babies can do only simple things with a spoon, such as bang it on the table or repeatedly dip it into their bowl. Slightly older children can coordinate the action of dipping, opening their mouth, and bringing the spoon to it, but as often as not, the spoon is empty when it arrives. Once the baby masters the sequence of getting food on the spoon, carrying it to the mouth without spilling, and putting the food in the mouth, the sequence is adjusted until it is smooth and automatic.

Coordination of fine motor movements increases significantly during the second year of life. At age 1, infants can only roll a ball or fling it awkwardly; by the time they are age 2, they are more likely to throw it. By age 2, they can also turn the pages of a book without tearing or creasing them, snip paper with safety scissors, string beads with a needle and thread (although the bead hole usually has to be pretty big!), build a tower six blocks high with considerable ease, hold a cup of milk or a spoon of applesauce without spilling it, and dress themselves (as long as there are no buttons or shoelaces) (Bayley, 1993). Each of these accomplishments may seem minor on its own, but infants' growing ability to manipulate objects with their hands relates to one of the most sophisticated accomplishments of our species and the most effective way of transmitting and transforming culture—using and making tools.

JGI/Jamie Grill/Getty Images

Using a spoon is a lot more complicated than you might think. It will take this baby many more months of practice before the fine motor skills involved in spoon use become smooth and automatic.

Gross Motor Skills

Progress in locomotion, the ability to move around on one's own, is a central developmental change that occurs toward the end of the 1st year. As we have noted, the development of gross motor skills greatly expands infants' opportunities to learn about the world and decreases their dependence on caregivers. Although there is wide variation in the age at which the various gross motor milestones are achieved, most babies throughout the world move through the same sequence of development, which begins with reflexive creeping and ends with purposeful walking, that uniquely human form of locomotion (Figure 5.7).

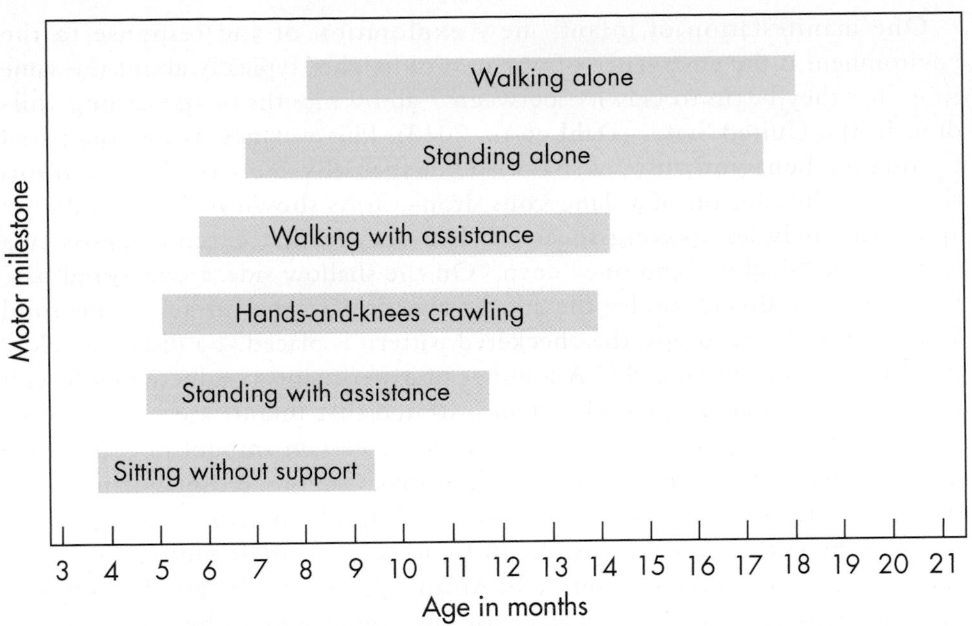

FIGURE 5.7 Despite wide variation in the ages at which specific gross motor skills are acquired, most children follow the same sequence of motor milestones, from sitting without support to independent walking.

Creeping and Crawling During the 1st month of life, when their movements appear to be controlled primarily by subcortical areas of the brain, infants may occasionally creep short distances, propelled by the rhythmic pushing movements of their toes or knees (Figure 5.8). At about 2 months of age, this reflexive pushing disappears, and it is another 5 or 6 months before babies can crawl about on their hands and knees (World Health Organization, 2006).

By the time they are 8 to 9 months of age, most infants can crawl on flat, smooth surfaces with some skill. Crawling allows babies to explore their environment in a new way and acquire new information about it, thus changing how they respond to the world.

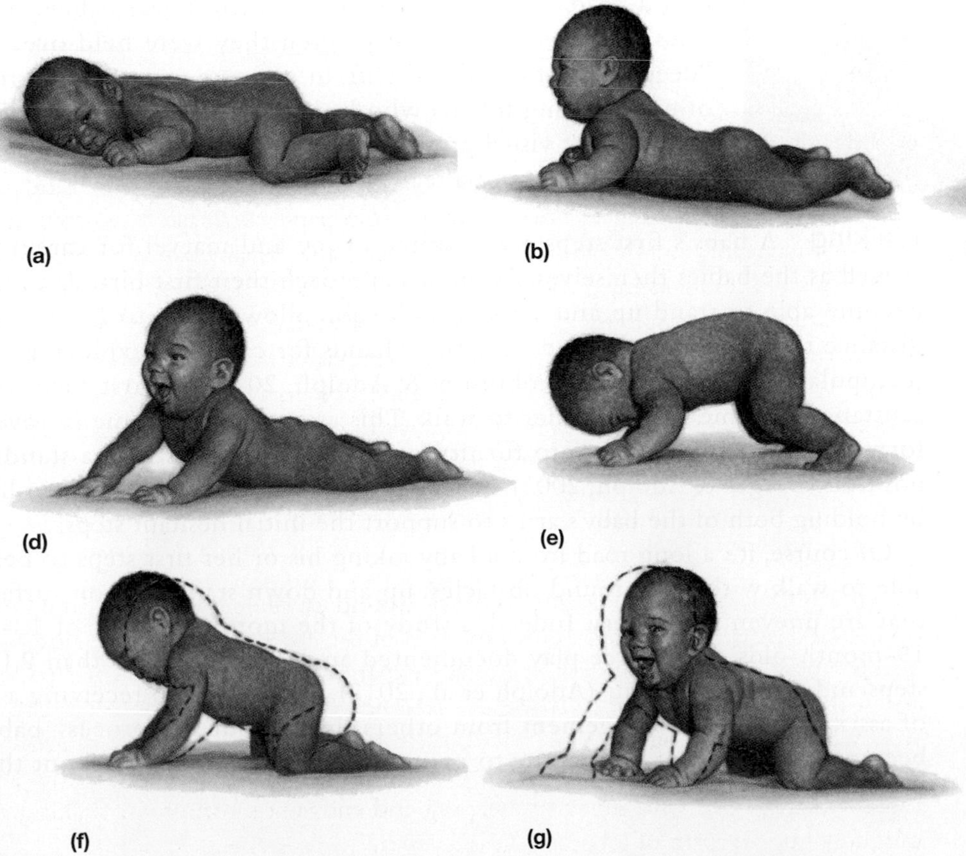

FIGURE 5.8 Phases in the development of creeping and crawling. (a) Newborns creep by making pushing movements with their knees and toes. (b) The head can be held up, but leg movements diminish. (c) Control over movement of head and shoulders increases. (d) Ability to support the upper body with the arms improves. (e) Babies have difficulty coordinating shoulders and midsection; when the midsection is raised, the head lowers. (f) Babies can keep the midsection raised but are unable to coordinate arm and leg movements, so they tend to rock back and forth (Goldfield, 2000). (g) Coordinated arm and leg movements enable the baby to crawl.

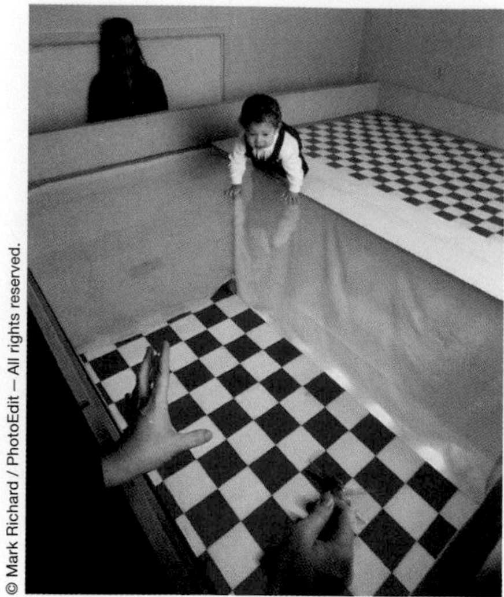
© Mark Richard / PhotoEdit – All rights reserved.

FIGURE 5.9 Despite being encouraged to do so, this little boy is hesitant about crossing the transparent surface of the visual cliff. Associated with learning to crawl, his behavior indicates a fear of heights typical of 7- to 9-month-olds.

One manifestation of infants' new exploration of and response to the environment is the emergence of wariness of heights, typically about the same time that they begin to crawl—between 7 and 9 months of age among children in the United States (Dahl et al., 2013). This wariness is demonstrated by infants' behavior on a "visual cliff," a specially constructed apparatus that gives the illusion of a dangerous drop-off. As shown in Figure 5.9, the apparatus includes a strong sheet of clear acrylic that extends across two sides—one "shallow," and one "deep." On the shallow side, a checkered pattern is placed directly under the acrylic sheeting, so the surface seems solid and safe. On the deep side, the checkered pattern is placed at a distance below the sheeting, suggesting a cliff. A number of experiments conducted by Joseph Campos and his colleagues have demonstrated that infants are not afraid to cross over to the deep side until they have had a certain amount of experience trying to crawl about on their own (Bertenthal, Campos, & Kermoian, 1994). In addition to their reluctance to cross the cliff, infants with crawling experience express their wariness of depth by looking to their mothers for cues about what to do (Striano, Stahl, & Cleveland, 2009). (As discussed below, this kind of checking in with a caregiver for cues about how to behave is known as *social referencing*.)

Appreciating that when infants crawl, they not only move across flat surfaces but also gain experience moving—and sometimes falling—over various objects, obstacles, and steps, you might assume that wariness of heights is associated with the occasionally unhappy consequences of crawling. But research does not support this interpretation. Instead, it seems that **visual proprioception**, the visual feedback that one gets from moving around, may be critical to the development of wariness. To test this idea, a team of researchers placed pre-crawling babies in self-controlled go-carts (see Figure 5.10) for 10 minutes per day over a 15-day period (Dahl et al., 2013). These babies' heart rates increased significantly when they were held over the "deep" side of the visual cliff, in contrast to a control group of pre-crawling infants who had no go-cart experience. This suggests that visual proprioception does indeed contribute to the development of a fear of heights.

visual proprioception The visual feedback that one gets from moving around, linked to the development of wariness of heights in infancy.

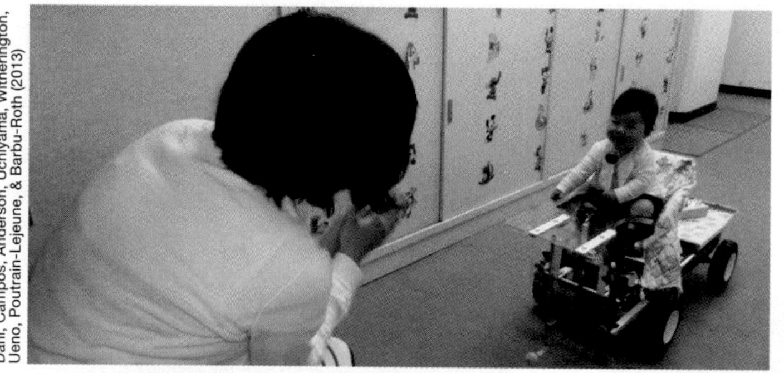
Dahl, Campos, Anderson, Uchiyama, Witherington, Ueno, Poutrain-Lejeune, & Barbu-Roth (2013)

FIGURE 5.10 When babies who do not yet crawl get experience moving around their environments in self-controlled go-carts, they develop wariness of heights. This suggests that wariness is due to visual proprioception, rather than experiences falling in the course of learning to crawl.

Walking

A baby's first steps are a source of joy and marvel for caregivers as well as the babies themselves. As infants approach their first birthday, many become able to stand up and walk, which soon allows them to cover more distance than crawling did and frees their hands for carrying, exploring, and manipulating objects (Cole, Robinson, & Adolph, 2016). At first they need assistance of some kind in order to walk. This assistance can come in several forms. Many babies grasp onto furniture to pull themselves into a standing position (Berger & Adolph, 2003). Seeing such attempts, caregivers often help by holding both of the baby's arms to support the initial hesitant steps.

Of course, it's a long road from a baby taking his or her first steps to being able to walk with ease around obstacles, up and down stairs, and on surfaces that are uneven or slippery. Indeed, a study of the motor behavior of 12- to 19-month-olds during free play documented an average of more than 2,000 steps and 17 falls per hour (Adolph et al., 2012). In addition to receiving a lot of assistance and encouragement from others throughout this process, babies become quite adept at responding to communications from others about their motor behavior. Karen Adolph's research shows an example of the ways infants use social referencing when walking down slopes that may put them at risk of falling (Adolph, Karasik, & Tamis-LeMonda, 2010). **Social referencing** refers to infants' tendency to look to their caregiver for an indication of how to feel and act in unfamiliar circumstances. Placing infants on a walkway with an adjustable slope (see Figure 5.11), Adolph and her colleagues found that even when the slope was shallow and posed little risk of falling, babies proceeded with caution (if at all) when their mother discouraged them from walking. On the other hand, they refused to walk when the slope was steep and dangerous, even when their mother encouraged walking. The researchers concluded that when social signals from the caregiver conflict with the baby's own assessment of risk, the latter generally wins the day, which is probably good news. As the researchers point out:

> In everyday situations, parents cannot be so vigilant that they can protect infants from every potential danger. With the advent of independent locomotion comes increasing autonomy. Although mothers' advice can often be useful, especially under conditions of uncertainty, infants must eventually learn to navigate the world on their own. (p. 1041)

social referencing Infants' tendency to look to their caregiver for an indication of how to feel and act in unfamiliar circumstances.

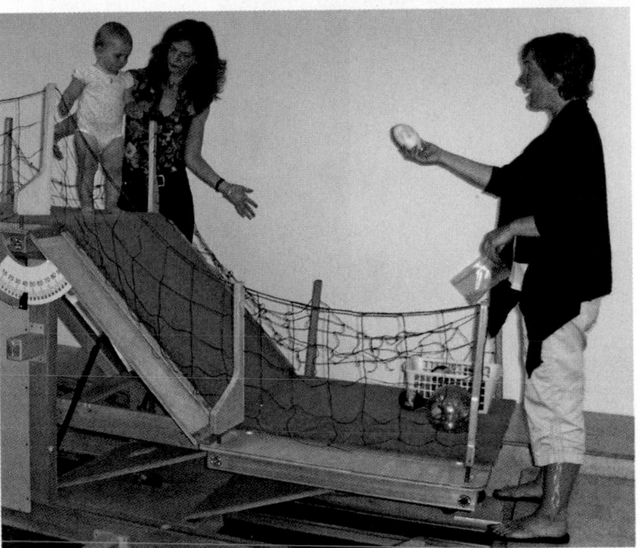

Courtesy of Karen Adolph

FIGURE 5.11 The transition from crawling to walking changes the way babies approach the task of going down a ramp. The toddler looks quite unsure, despite being lured by a toy.

No one factor can be considered the key to walking; rather, as dynamic systems theorists point out, walking becomes possible only when all the component motor skills—upright posture, leg alternation, muscle strength, weight shifting, and sense of balance—have developed sufficiently and when the child has been able to practice combining them (Thelen, Fisher, & Ridley-Johnson, 2002). These new motor skills must then be combined with an increased sensitivity to perceptual input from the environment and social information from others about where, when, and how to walk.

The Role of Practice in Motor Development

Studies of motor development were among developmentalists' earliest strategies for investigating the relative roles of nature and nurture. During the 1930s and 1940s, it was commonly believed that the attainment of such motor milestones as sitting and walking were dictated by maturation, with learning and experience playing little or no role.

One of the earliest studies to support this view was conducted by Wayne and Margaret Dennis among Hopi families in the southwestern United States (Dennis & Dennis, 1940). In traditional Hopi families, babies in the first several months after birth are tightly swaddled and strapped to a flat cradle board. They are unwrapped only once or twice a day so that they can be washed and their clothes can be changed. The wrapping allows infants very little movement of their arms and legs and no practice in such complex movements as rolling over. The Dennises compared the motor development of traditionally raised Hopi babies with that of the babies of less traditional Hopi parents who did not use cradle boards. They found that the two groups of babies did not differ in the age at which they began to walk by themselves, which is consistent with the notion that this basic motor skill does not depend on practice for its development.

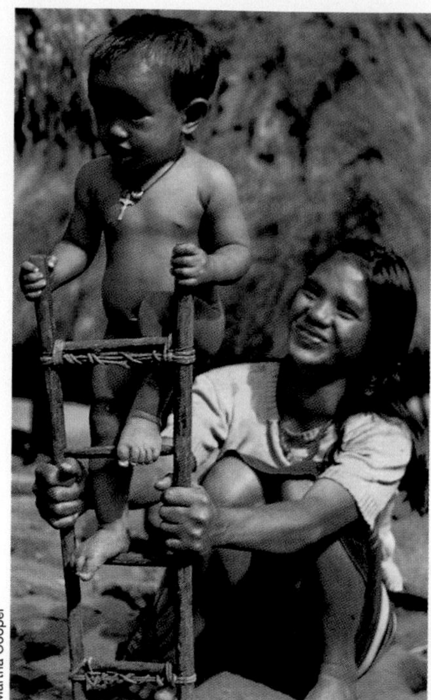
Martha Cooper

Babies who are just beginning to stand up find other people and furniture to be handy aids. This Filipino baby who lives in a house on stilts is being trained at an early age in the essential skill of climbing a ladder.

However, observations of babies from other cultural settings provide evidence that practice can affect the age at which babies reach motor milestones and may even alter the sequence of the milestones. Charles Super (1976) reported that among the Kipsigis people of rural Kenya, parents begin to teach their babies to sit up, stand, and walk not long after birth. To teach their children to sit up, for example, Kipsigis parents seat their babies in shallow holes in the ground that they have dug to support the infants' backs, or they nestle blankets around them to hold them upright. They repeat such procedures daily until the babies can sit up quite well by themselves. Training in walking begins in the 8th week after birth. The babies are held under the arms with their feet touching the ground and are gradually propelled forward. On average, Kipsigis babies reach the developmental milestones of sitting 5 weeks earlier and walking 3 weeks earlier than do babies in the United States. (Similar results have been reported among West Indian and Cameroonian children, whose mothers put them through a culturally prescribed sequence of motor exercises during the early months of infancy [Hopkins & Westen, 1988; Keller, 2003].) At the same time, Kipsigis infants are not advanced in skills they have not been taught or have not practiced. They learn to roll over or crawl no faster than children in the United States, and they lag behind children in the United States in their ability to negotiate stairs.

Further evidence about the impact that practice — or lack of it — can have on early motor development comes from the Ache, a nomadic people living in the rain forest of eastern Paraguay. Hilliard Kaplan and Heather Dove (1987) reported that Ache children under 3 years of age spend 80 to 100 percent of their time in direct physical contact with their mothers and are almost never seen more than 3 feet away from them. A major reason is that Ache hunter–gatherer groups do not create clearings in the forest when they stop to make camp. Rather, they remove just enough ground cover to make room to sit down, leaving roots, trees, and bushes more or less where they found them. For safety's sake, mothers either carry their infants or keep them within arm's reach.

As a result of these cultural patterns, Ache infants are markedly slower than U.S. infants in acquiring gross motor skills such as walking. In fact, they begin walking, on the average, at about 23 months of age, almost a full year later than children in the United States. At about the age of 5, however, when Ache children are deemed old enough to be allowed to move around on their own, they begin to spend many hours in complex play activities that increase their motor skills. Within a few years, they are skilled at climbing tall trees and at cutting vines and branches while they balance high above the ground in a manner that bespeaks normal, perhaps even exceptional, motor skills.

JGI/Jamie Grill/Getty Images

Intended to prevent sudden infant death syndrome, the practice of putting babies to sleep on their back has had the unexpected effect of delaying the onset of crawling. Pediatricians now encourage parents to provide young infants with plenty of "tummy time" in which to gain experiences important for learning to crawl.

The influence of practice, and of cultural norms on physical development, is further highlighted by the "back-to-sleep" movement in the United States to eradicate SIDS (see Chapter 4, p. 155). The widespread success of getting parents to put their infants on their back to sleep rather than on their belly has had the unexpected effect of delaying the onset of crawling in babies in the United States by as much as 2 months (Majnemer & Barr, 2005). Because time spent in the prone position (facedown) provides babies with their earliest experiences of bearing their body weight with their arms, shifting their weight to reach for a toy, and trying out coordinated movements of their arms and legs, children who spend their waking as well as sleeping hours on their back miss out on developmentally appropriate experiences. As a consequence, pediatricians in the United States urge parents to provide their young infants with "tummy time" to play so that they can practice pushing themselves up as a precursor to crawling (Pontius et al., 2001). Indeed, researchers are finding that babies with more tummy time tend to roll, crawl, and sit at earlier ages than do those who spend less time in the prone position (Kuo et al., 2008).

APPLY > CONNECT > DISCUSS

Imagine two children—one an early walker, walking well at 9 months of age, and the other a late walker, walking well at 15 months. Suppose both children live in the same neighborhood or village and have parents with similar resources and with similar child-rearing practices and beliefs. Explain how the difference in onset of walking may have significant implications for each child's development.

Cognitive Development: The Great Debate

LEARNING OUTCOMES

Point out how Piaget explains infant thinking, from sensorimotor intelligence to representational thinking.

Contrast Piaget's ideas about infant thinking with those of other developmentalists.

Distinguish the qualities of substages 3 through 6 in Piaget's sensorimotor stage of cognitive development.

Point out critiques of Piaget's theory of cognitive development during infancy.

As the physical body, and the ability to control it, continue to mature across the first 2 years after birth, so too does the mind. As we shall see in the following sections, developmentalists are engaged in a great debate about how thinking progresses during the first 2 years.

For some developmentalists, such as Piaget, the mind undergoes a radical, discontinuous shift at the end of infancy (Müller, 2009). According to Piaget's stage theory, young infants are limited to *sensorimotor intelligence*; that is, they understand the world only through their own actions and perceptions. They, therefore, cannot think about people and objects that are not immediately present to be seen, heard, or felt, and acted upon. All this changes fundamentally at 18 or so months of age, when infants become capable of *representational thinking*, forming mental pictures or images of the world. The ability to form such mental images, and to reason about them, is a significant turning point in cognitive development. Knowledge is no longer tied to the immediate here and now. Instead, infants can hold in mind past experiences, compare and contrast them with each other and with present circumstances, and use them to anticipate the future and guide their actions. Developmentalists who take this view claim that the emergence of the ability to represent the world mentally results in a mind that is truly *conceptual* rather than simply "sensorimotor."

On the other side of the debate are developmentalists who maintain that mental development is more continuous than Piaget supposed—that the ability to represent and understand the world conceptually is present very early in development, if not from birth. According to this view, conceptual understanding does not emerge out of sensorimotor knowledge, as Piaget claimed. Instead, young babies are believed to possess at least a rudimentary conceptual system. This system is thought to develop separately from, although in close association with, the sensorimotor system (Mandler, 2012; Marshall & Meltzoff, 2014). As you will see, there is much at stake in the debate about the nature and development of the human mind.

Sensorimotor Development

Piaget referred to infancy as the stage of *sensorimotor development* because of his belief that at this early age, infants acquire knowledge exclusively through motor actions that are directed at their immediate environment and guided by their sensory organs. He combined the terms *sensory* and *motor* to emphasize the intimate relationship between sensing the world and acting upon it. Each influences the other: What infants perceive depends on what they are doing, and what they do depends on what they are perceiving at the moment (Piaget, 1973). As noted above, Piaget maintained that infants are bound to this moment-to-moment, here-and-now form of understanding until the final stage of sensorimotor development, when they begin to think representationally.

As we explained in our previous discussions (Chapter 1, p. 20; Chapter 4, pp. 146–147), Piaget divided the sensorimotor period into six substages (see Table 5.1). During the first substage, the newborn learns to control and coordinate reflexes, and during the second, the newborn begins to modify and repeat behaviors, such as thumb-sucking, simply because they are pleasurable (primary circular reactions). The following sections provide an overview of the four remaining substages of sensorimotor development. As you read through the sections, notice how infants become increasingly flexible, purposeful, and inventive.

Reproducing Interesting Events (Substage 3) In contrast to the first two substages, in which infants' actions primarily involve their own body, in the third substage, 4- to 8-month-olds begin to direct their attention and their actions to the external world—to objects and outcomes. This new interest in external things gives rise to a characteristic behavior observed in infants during this substage—the repetition of actions that produce interesting changes in the environment. For example, when babies in this substage accidentally discover that a particular action, like squeezing a rubber toy, produces an interesting effect, such as squeaking, they repeat the action again and again to produce the effect. Similarly, when babies vocalize by cooing or gurgling and a caregiver responds, they repeat the sound they made. Piaget termed these new, object-oriented actions **secondary circular reactions**. They are "secondary" because they apply to something outside the infant, in contrast to primary circular reactions, which apply to the infant's own body (see Chapter 4, p. 146).

secondary circular reactions The behavior characteristic of the third substage of Piaget's sensorimotor stage, in which babies repeat actions to produce interesting changes in their environment.

The change from primary circular reactions to secondary circular reactions indicated to Piaget that infants are beginning to realize that objects are more than an extension of their own actions—that objects have their own, separate identities. In this substage, however, babies still have only a rudimentary understanding of objects and space, and their discoveries about the world seem to have an accidental quality.

The Emergence of Intentionality (Substage 4) The hallmark of the fourth sensorimotor substage, which occurs between 8 and 12 months of age, is the emergence of the ability to engage in behaviors directed toward achieving a goal. Piaget called this ability **intentionality**. He believed goal-directed behavior to be the earliest form of true problem solving.

intentionality The ability to engage in behaviors directed toward achieving a goal.

TABLE 5.1 Piaget's Sensorimotor Substages

Substage	Age (months)	Characteristics of Sensorimotor Substage
1	0–1½	*Exercising reflexive schemas:* involuntary rooting, sucking, grasping, looking
2	1½–4	*Primary circular reactions:* repetition of actions that are pleasurable in themselves
3	4–8	*Secondary circular reactions:* dawning awareness of the relationship of own actions to the environment; extended actions that produce interesting changes in the environment
4	8–12	*Coordination of secondary circular reactions:* combining schemas to achieve a desired effect; earliest form of problem solving
5	12–18	*Tertiary circular reactions:* deliberate variation of problem-solving means; experimentation to see what the consequences will be
6	18–24	*Beginning of symbolic representation:* images and words come to stand for familiar objects; invention of new means of problem solving through symbolic combinations

Piaget's son, Laurent, provided a demonstration of intentional problem solving of this kind when he was 10 months old. Piaget had given him a small tin container, which Laurent dropped and picked up repeatedly (a secondary circular reaction characteristic of behavior in substage 3). Piaget then placed a washbasin a short distance from Laurent and struck it with the tin box, producing an interesting sound. From earlier observations, Piaget knew that Laurent would repeatedly bang on the basin to make the interesting sound occur (another typical secondary circular reaction). This time Piaget wanted to see if Laurent would combine the newly acquired "dropping the tin box" schema with the previously acquired "make an interesting sound" schema. Here is his report of Laurent's behavior:

> Now, at once, Laurent takes possession of the tin, holds out his arm and drops it over the basin. I moved the latter as a check. He nevertheless succeeded, several times in succession, in making the object fall on the basin. Hence this is a fine example of the coordination of two schemas of which the first serves as a "means" whereas the second assigns an end to the action. (Piaget, 1952b, p. 255.)

In Piaget's view, then, over the course of substages 3 and 4 of sensorimotor intelligence, infants become capable of intentional action directed at objects and people around them, but these abilities come fully into play only when infants can directly perceive the objects and people in question. Piaget maintained that this is because infants lack **object permanence**—that is, the understanding that objects exist even when they are out of view. Until substage 4 of sensorimotor development, according to Piaget, infants live in a world in which objects come and go from their line of sight, each "a mere image which reenters the void as soon as it vanishes, and emerges from it for no apparent reason" (1954, p. 11). Piaget's classic test of object permanence was to put a cloth over a young infant's favorite toy as the infant watched and then observe whether the infant searched for the hidden toy. Unfailingly, infants under 8 months of age not only did not search for the vanished toy, they also showed no interest or surprise in its vanishing—as though it had never existed. Thus, Piaget believed that for young babies, out of sight is literally out of mind. In stage 4, infants begin to demonstrate some degree of object permanence (they lift the cloth off the hidden toy), but until substage 6, it is rudimentary and fragile.

object permanence The understanding that objects have substance, maintain their identity when their location is changed, and ordinarily continue to exist when out of sight.

tertiary circular reactions The fifth stage of the sensorimotor period, characterized by the deliberate variation of action sequences to solve problems and explore the world.

Exploring by Experimenting (Substage 5)

The fifth substage of the sensorimotor period, **tertiary circular reactions**, emerges between 12 and 18 months of age and is characterized by an ability to vary the actions of substage 4 systematically and flexibly. This ability makes explorations of the world more complex. Indeed, Piaget (1952b) referred to tertiary circular reactions as "experiments in order to see" because children seem to be experimenting in order to find out about the nature of objects and events (p. 272). Here is Piaget's description of this kind of behavior in Laurent, at 10 months and 11 days, lying in his crib:

> He grasps in succession a celluloid swan, a box, etc., stretches out his arm and lets them fall. He distinctly varies the positions of the fall. . . . Sometimes he stretches out his arm vertically, sometimes he holds it obliquely, in front of or behind his eyes, etc. When the object falls in a new position (for example, on his pillow), he lets it fall two or three times more on the same place, as though to study the spatial relations; then he modifies the situation. (Piaget, 1952b, p. 269.)

According to Piaget's observations, infants in substage 5 seem unable to reason systematically about actions and anticipate their probable consequences. As suggested in Laurent's behavior of trying different ways of dropping the object for the sheer purpose of seeing what might happen, infants in substage 5 live in a

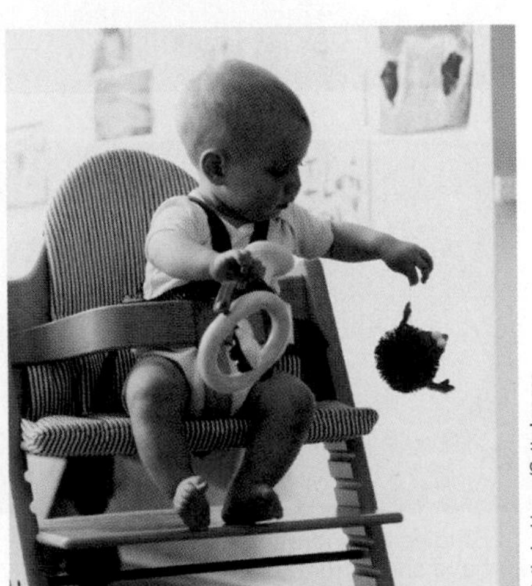

Ruth Jenkinson/Getty Images

Experimenting with objects, including dropping toys from one's high chair in order to watch them fall and bounce, is typical of Piaget's sensorimotor substage 5.

representations Internal, mental symbols of experience; according to Piaget, the ability to form mental symbols emerges during sensorimotor substage 6.

symbolic play Play in which one object stands for, or represents, another.

deferred imitation The imitation of an action observed in the past.

here-and-now, trial-and-error world. The ability to mentally plan, organize, and otherwise envision their actions and foresee their possible consequences does not begin until the arrival of *representational thinking*.

Representation (Substage 6) According to Piaget, the hallmark of substage 6, the final stage of the sensorimotor period, between 18 and 24 months of age, is that babies begin to base their actions on internal, mental symbols, or **representations**, of experience. When they can *re-present* the world to themselves—that is, when they can present it to themselves over again mentally—they can be said to be engaging in true mental actions.

www.flickr.com/photos/jeijiang/Getty Images

This little boy engages in deferred imitation, giving his bear a cookie in imitation of how he himself is given treats.

Infants' ability to represent people, objects, events, and experiences mentally has been a central focus for researchers because it has enormous ramifications in other areas of development. For example, once infants are able to represent a sequence of events, they can *solve problems* systematically rather than by trial and error. Similarly, once babies become capable of representation, they begin to engage in **symbolic play** (also known as *pretend play* or *fantasy play*), in which one object is used to stand for (represent) another, as when a child combs a baby doll's hair with a twig or gives it a drink from a small plastic block. Representation also enables **deferred imitation**, the imitation of actions observed in the past, which is of tremendous importance to children's learning and socialization. A child who observes a parent having coffee and reading the paper and then hours or days later pretends to be drinking coffee and reading is engaged in deferred imitation. Finally, of special significance is the role of representation in *language*, in which words are used to stand for (represent) people, objects, and events.

A. N. Meltzoff

Studies by Andrew Meltzoff (1988) have shown that young infants imitate live models and also imitate actions they have seen on television. This child observes a televised adult model manipulate blocks, and then immediately the child imitates the adult's actions. Meltzoff also demonstrated that infants who watch a televised model on one day are able to reproduce the model's behavior 24 hours later.

There is little disagreement about the importance Piaget attached to representation as a foundation for the development of problem solving, symbolic play, deferred imitation, and language. Nor do developmentalists disagree with Piaget's descriptions of the sequence of behavioral changes that occurs as children progress through the early stages of dealing with objects. Indeed, his observations have been widely replicated, not only in Europe and the United States but in traditional societies as well. For example, Baule infants living in rural areas of the West African country of Côte d'Ivoire have been found to proceed through the same sequence of object-related behaviors on almost exactly the same timetable as European children, despite vast differences in their cultural environments (Dasen, 1973). In fact, research conducted with infant great apes reveals the same pattern of sensorimotor development (Parker & McKinney, 1999). The sequence and timing of sensorimotor stages are so reliable that Piaget's procedures were long ago standardized for assessing the development of children who are at risk because of disease, physical impairment, or extreme environmental deprivation (Uzgiris & Hunt, 1975).

The past two decades have brought challenges both to Piaget's theory and to his methods. In general, these challenges attack the idea that infants are unable to represent objects they cannot see, arguing instead that infants are born with, or quickly develop, a conceptual system with representational powers. As we discuss below, critics argue that young infants have the competence to form representations of objects but lack various skills needed to demonstrate that ability on traditional Piagetian tests. Using a variety of ingenious methods, the critiques suggest that infants' mental lives are more complex than Piaget believed.

APPLY > CONNECT > DISCUSS

Imagine that you have been hired by a company to develop a line of toys appropriate to the ongoing sensorimotor development of infants through age 2. Prepare a presentation of some of your ideas for products, including arguments for how your products will appeal to infants at the various substages of sensorimotor development.

Conceptual Development

LEARNING OUTCOMES

Describe the development of object permanence, according to Piaget.

Explain the role of memory for infants in the A-not-B task.

Point out some alternate approaches to measuring and understanding object permanence, including the violations-of-expectations method.

Point out how infants reason about objects that involve their ability to count, understand cause–effect, and categorize.

As we have seen, Piaget maintained that before the onset of representations, infants have no knowledge that endures beyond the immediate here and now. Although they can form primitive associations as, for example, in classical and operant conditioning (see Chapter 4, pp. 147–149), it is not until the end of the sensorimotor stage of intelligence that infants gain a conceptual understanding of the characteristics of objects and events. The distinction between sensorimotor and conceptual intelligence was cleverly highlighted by Jean Mandler when she characterized the sensorimotor infant as an "absent-minded professor" who, finding herself in the kitchen unable to remember what she wanted there, searches around for a clue and, upon seeing a cup by the sink, thinks, "Aha, I came for coffee!" (2004, p. 21). From Piaget's perspective, the sensorimotor infant can be similarly cued by perceptual features of the immediate environment to "remember" past associations but cannot grasp them conceptually in the absence of such prompts.

In the sections that follow, we explore the ways that infants demonstrate capacities to understand the world in more conceptual, abstract terms. As you will see, there is strong evidence that Piaget underestimated the conceptual intelligence of infants. As yet, however, there is no unifying theory that accounts for conceptual development during the first 2 years. Should such a unifying theory take shape, the accumulating evidence indicates that it will need to account for the infant's biological preparedness to construct a typically "human" understanding of the world as well as for the consequences of the infant's experiences in specific contexts.

Understanding the Permanence of Objects

- Observation 1. A baby seated at a table is offered a soft toy (see Figure 5.12). He grasps it. While he is still engrossed in the toy, the experimenter takes it from him and places it on the table, behind a screen. The baby may begin to

Doug Goodman/Science Source

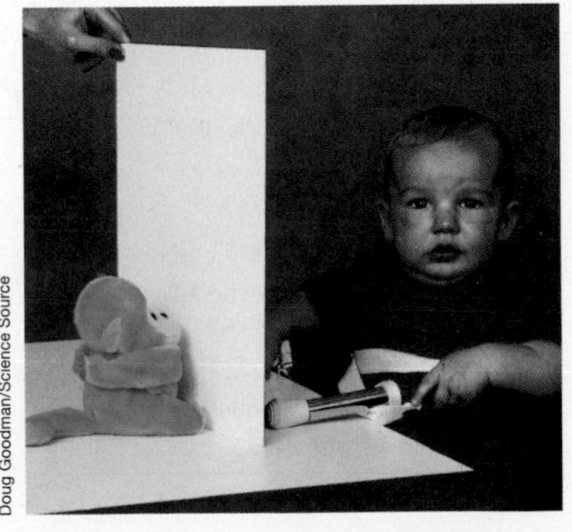
Doug Goodman/Science Source

FIGURE 5.12 Instead of searching behind the screen when his toy disappears, this infant looks dumbfounded. This kind of behavior led Piaget to conclude that objects no longer in view cease to exist for infants younger than 8 months of age.

reach for the toy, but as soon as it disappears from sight, he stops short, stares for a moment, and then looks away without attempting to move the screen (Piaget, 1954).

- Observation 2. A baby is placed in an infant seat in a bare laboratory room. Her mother, who has been playing with her, disappears for a moment. When the mother reappears, the baby sees three of her, an illusion the experimenter has created through the use of carefully arranged mirrors. The baby displays no surprise as she babbles happily to her multiple mothers (Bower, 1982).
- Observation 3. A baby watches a toy train as it chugs along a track (see Figure 5.13). When the train disappears into a tunnel, the child's eyes remain fixed on the tunnel's entrance rather than following the train's expected progress through the tunnel. When the train reappears at the other end of the tunnel, it takes the child a few seconds to catch up with it visually, and the child shows no surprise when the train that comes out of the tunnel is a different color or shape (Bower, 1982).

Infant watches train approach tunnel

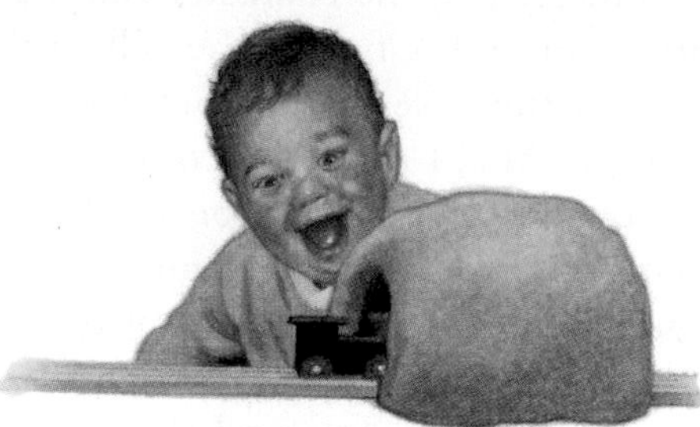

Infant watches train enter tunnel

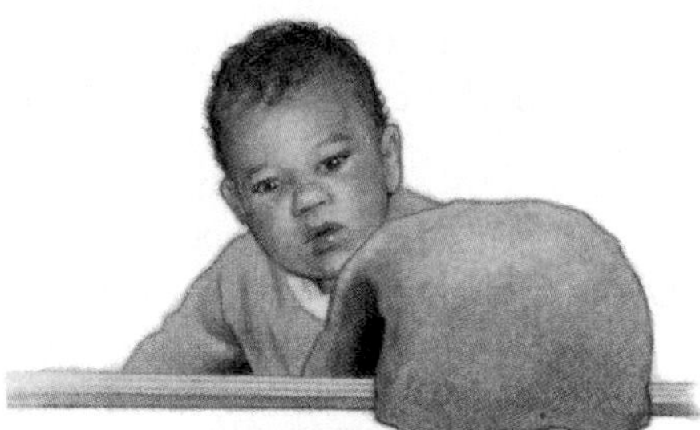

Infant's eyes remain fixed on tunnel's entrance

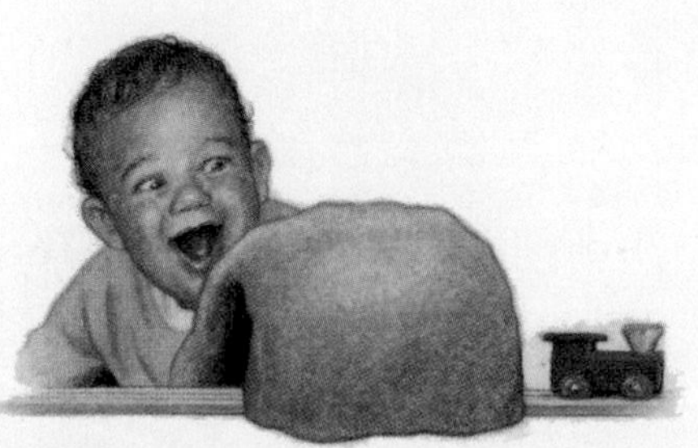

Infant notices train moving away from tunnel

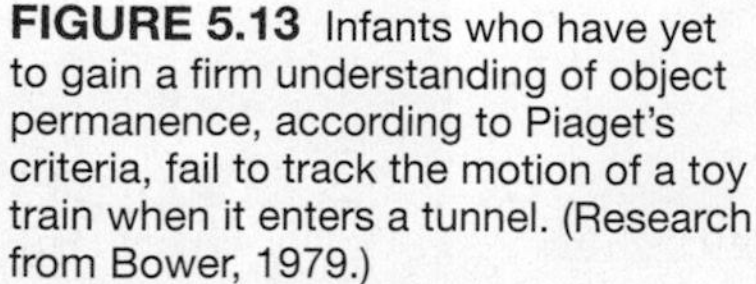

FIGURE 5.13 Infants who have yet to gain a firm understanding of object permanence, according to Piaget's criteria, fail to track the motion of a toy train when it enters a tunnel. (Research from Bower, 1979.)

Each of these observations was recorded in the context of studying *object permanence*, a full and stable grasp of which is, according to Piaget, a clear indicator that the development of mental representation and conceptual thinking is under way. As noted, Piaget contended that babies demonstrate object permanence only when they begin to search actively for an absent object, as when they uncover a toy they have just seen the experimenter hide under a cloth or behind a barrier. His research indicated that although this active searching behavior first appears at around 8 months of age, infants' mastery of object permanence is incomplete until the second half of their 2nd year. He discovered, for example, that babies between 8 and 12 months tend to make a characteristic mistake when searching for objects: If, after they have successfully searched for an object hidden in one location, A, the object is then hidden, *right before their eyes*, in a new location, B (Figure 5.14), they will still search for the object in location A, where they previously found it!

Piaget interpreted this pattern of responding—referred to as the **A-not-B error**—as evidence that the child remembers the existence of the object but cannot reason systematically about it. He believed that true representation requires the ability both to keep in mind the existence of an absent object and to reason about that absent object mentally, an achievement he did not think occurs until late in the 2nd year, during the sixth substage of the sensorimotor period.

A-not-B error A pattern of reacting in the object permanence task, in which the infant looks for the hidden object in location A, where the infant had previously found the object, instead of location B, where the infant has just observed it being hidden.

Alternative Explanations of Infants' Difficulties

Other developmentalists have disagreed with Piaget's interpretation of young infants' A-not-B error. They believe that the error is due not to a failure to represent and reason about the object but to other developmental limitations, including limitations of memory or motor skills (Cuevas & Bell, 2010; Marcovitch et al., 2016).

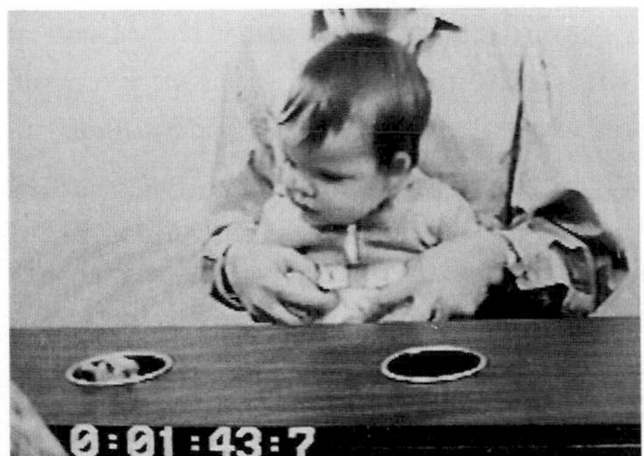

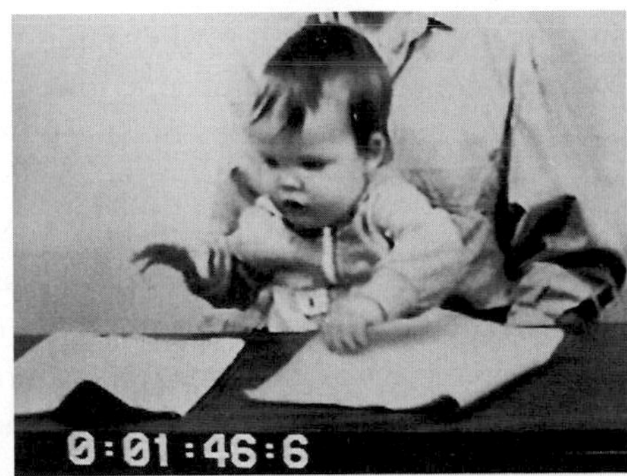

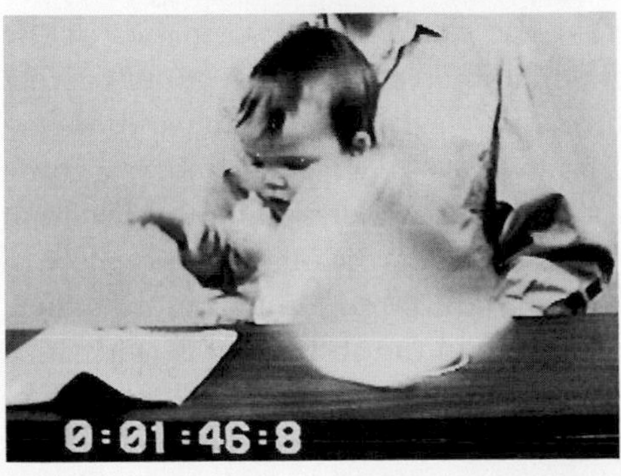

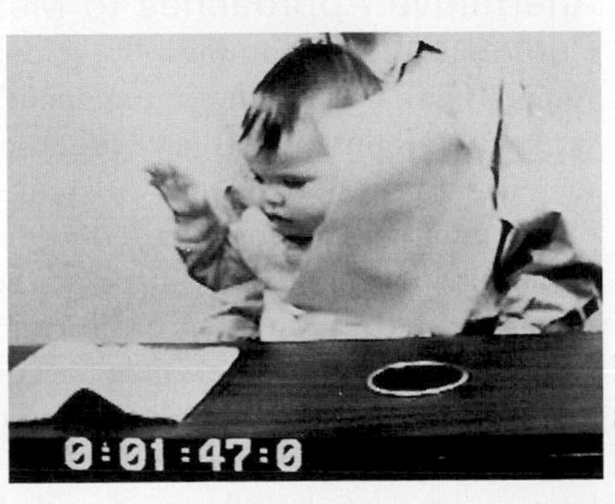

Adele Diamond

FIGURE 5.14 In this movie sequence, an object is placed in the circle on the left (position B), and then both circles (positions A and B) are covered with a cloth while the baby watches. In a previous trial, the object had been placed in the right-hand circle (position A), and the baby had correctly retrieved it. This time, while remaining oriented toward the hidden object at position B, the baby nonetheless picks up the cloth at position A, where the object was hidden before.

The Role of Memory. In an influential series of studies, Adele Diamond (1991) suggested that young infants may be capable of representation but fail Piaget's A-not-B task because they simply do not remember where the object was hidden. Diamond varied the time between the switching of an object from location A to location B and the moment when children were allowed to reach for the hidden object (Diamond, 1991, 2000). She found that, if they were allowed to reach immediately, 7½-month-old babies correctly located the object at position B, but if they were prevented from reaching for as little as 2 seconds, they exhibited the A-not-B error. By 9 months of age, infants could withstand a delay of 5 seconds before beginning to make mistakes, and by 12 months of age, they could withstand a delay of 10 seconds. These results suggest that young infants are capable of representing objects they cannot see but quickly forget their location and become confused (which may explain the behavior of the baby in Figure 5.14 on page 181). Other studies documenting a relationship between the delay of reaching and successful searching (Bremner et al., 2005; Johansson et al., 2014; Ruffman, Slade, & Redman, 2005) further suggest that the A-not-B task may impose significant demands on infants' memory system, masking their representational abilities.

The Role of Perseveration. Have you ever tried to push your ill-fitting glasses up the bridge of your nose (again), only to remember that you're wearing your contact lenses? If so, then you are familiar with *perseveration*—the persistent repetition of a particular behavior. Diamond believed that young infants may exhibit the A-not-B error not only because of their memory limitations but also because of their tendency to engage in *motor perseveration*, in which they repeat a movement rather than modify it to fit new events. She noted that some infants who make the A-not-B error in fact look at location B but reach toward location A. Research suggests that such perseveration (which could also explain the behavior of the baby in Figure 5.15) may be due to the tendency of certain motor behaviors to become habits (Clearfield et al., 2009) or may be related to immature brain development that makes it difficult for infants to inhibit responses (Diamond & Amso, 2008; Marcovitch et al., 2016).

The A-not-B error may also involve another type of perseveration that is not specifically linked to motor behavior: Babies may reach incorrectly for the object at location A because of their previous success in finding it there. This is an example of a *capture error*, a tendency of people at all ages to continue using a once-successful solution whenever possible.

Memory limitations, motor perseveration, and capture errors are all explanations for why infants may fail the A-not-B task, even though they may possess the ability to form mental representations. In other words, many developmentalists believe that infants have representational *competence* but lack the *performance* skills required to successfully demonstrate that competence on the task (Hespos & Baillargeon, 2008).

Alternative Approaches to Measuring and Understanding Object Permanence

Prompted by evidence that the performance demands of the A-not-B task obscure the young infant's representational competence about objects, several developmentalists have proposed alternative ways of measuring and understanding object permanence. Some designed new tests of Piaget's theory, arguing that if infants were not required to demonstrate their understanding by reaching for and manipulating things, it might be possible to show that infants are capable of representational thought at or near birth. Others have taken a much more radical stance, proposing that the whole idea of competence in the absence of performance is irrelevant to infants' performance on the A-not-B test. As you will see, these developmentalists do not call for new measures of object permanence as much as for a new theory about how infants behave in various testing situations.

Violation-of-Expectations Method. To challenge Piaget's theory of when representation develops, Renée Baillargeon and her colleagues devised an object permanence test that exploits the well-known tendency of infants (in fact, of everyone) to stare at events that violate their expectations (Hespos & Baillargeon, 2008; Wang, Baillargeon, & Brueckner, 2004). This test, the **violation-of-expectations method**, involves a bit of research trickery. Basically, babies are habituated to a particular event and then presented two variants of the event—one that is "possible" under normal circumstances and one that is "impossible" and comes about only through an illusion created by the researcher. The premise is that if infants are capable of mentally representing their experiences, they should develop specific expectations during the habituation phase and then look longer at events that violate those expectations—that is, at the impossible events.

violation-of-expectations method A test of mental representation in which the child is habituated to an event and then presented with possible and impossible variants of the event.

In one study, infants were habituated to two events. In one, a short carrot moved behind a screen and reappeared on the other side; in the other, a tall carrot moved behind the screen and likewise reappeared (Figure 5.15). Once the infants were habituated to these two events, they were presented with two test events in which a window had been cut out of the screen.

1. In the *possible event*, a short carrot again moved behind the screen and reappeared on the other side. The window in the screen was high enough that the small carrot was hidden from view as it passed behind the screen.
2. In the *impossible event*, a tall carrot moved behind the screen and reappeared on the other side. In this case, the tall carrot *should* have appeared in the window as it passed behind the screen—but, in violation of anyone's expectations, it did not (thanks to the experimenter's secret manipulations).

Using this method, Baillargeon demonstrated that infants as young as 2½ months of age looked longer at the impossible event than at the possible event, suggesting that they had, indeed, formed mental representations of their past experiences with the habituation events. As you will see later in this chapter, developmentalists have used similar tricks to figure out what infants do and do not understand about the physical world.

Habituation Events

Short-carrot event

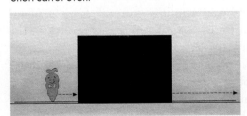

Tall-carrot event

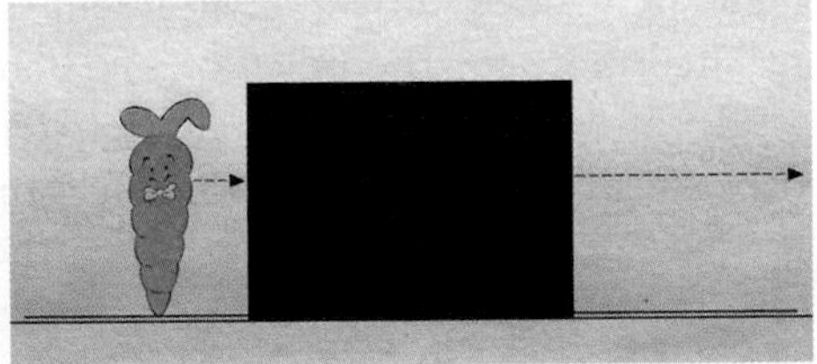

Test Events

Possible event

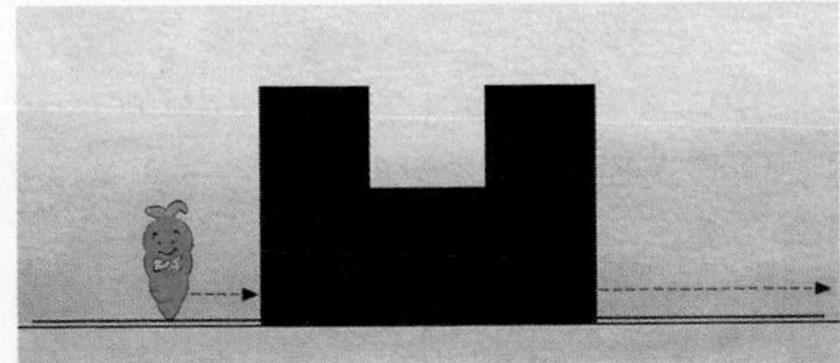

Impossible event

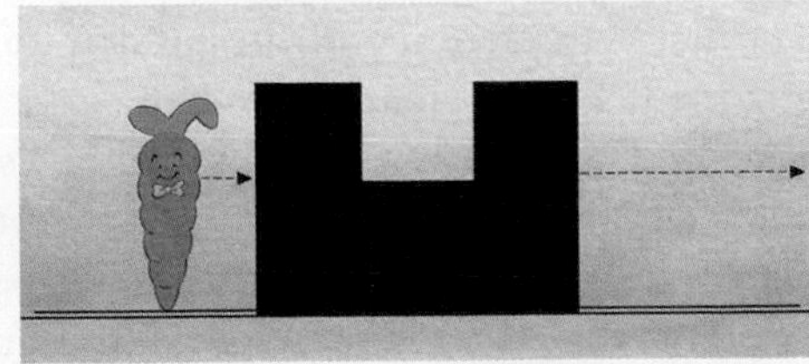

FIGURE 5.15 Using this version of the violation-of-expectations method, researchers find that infants as young as 2½ months look longer at the impossible event, suggesting that they are capable of mentally representing their past experiences.

Dynamic Systems Approach. While many developmentalists have focused on untangling infants' underlying conceptual competence from the performance demands of the tasks, Esther Thelen and her colleagues have offered an entirely different approach to thinking about the nature of knowledge and its development in infants (Thelen, Schoener, Scheier, & Smith, 2001). According to their *dynamic systems* perspective (see Chapter 1, p. 27), it is unnecessary to invoke the idea of performance limitations to explain infants' failures on the A-not-B task or to invoke the idea of mental concepts such as object permanence to account for their ultimate success. In their view, infants' behaviors on tests of object permanence—indeed, all human action in any context—are the result of the dynamics that emerge from the "immediate circumstances and the [individual's] history of perceiving and acting in similar circumstances" (p. 34). Thus, infants' experiences with specific objects, their current memory of those experiences, and their current motor skills all interact in their solving the specific problems posed by whatever task they face. From this perspective, the critical developmental process is not, as Piaget contended, a shift from sensorimotor intelligence to conceptual intelligence. Rather, it is infants' growing abilities to better coordinate all the various systems involved in both sensorimotor and conceptual intelligence (looking, reaching, perceiving, remembering, and so on) required by the task at hand (Clearfield, Diedrich, Smith, & Thelen, 2006).

The Role of Experience. Noting that infants' performance on tests of object permanence is highly sensitive to the particulars of the test itself—such as the search method (reaching or looking) and the amount of time between hiding and searching—Jeanne Shinskey and her colleagues (Shinskey & Jachens, 2014; Shinskey & Munakata, 2005, 2010) wondered if infants gradually develop stronger representations of objects through their experience with them and if stronger representations are required for some tasks than for others. In line with the dynamic systems approach, the researchers focused on the *process* through which infants build mental representations rather than on whether and at what age infants reliably demonstrate the *capacity* to represent objects mentally. Reasoning that infants' representations of objects gradually strengthen as babies gain experience perceiving and interacting with them, Shinskey and Munakata predicted that object permanence would be stronger for familiar objects than for novel objects.

To test their prediction, the researchers used an inventive method in which 7-month-olds were presented with novel and familiar objects under "visible" and "hidden" conditions (Shinskey & Munakata, 2005). In the "visible" condition, either a novel object or a familiar object was set in front of the babies. (An object was made familiar by providing an infant several opportunities to reach for it.) Infants reached more for the novel object, demonstrating a preference for novelty. In the "hidden" condition—the condition that actually tests for object permanence—the babies were presented with a novel or familiar object and then the lights were turned off, shrouding the room and the object in darkness. (The babies had been given some experience with the lights going out so that they wouldn't be surprised or scared during the test phase.) In this hidden condition, the babies tended to reverse their previous novelty preference, reaching more for the familiar object than for the novel object.

What does this shift from a novelty preference in the visible condition to a familiarity preference in the hidden condition tell us about the process of forming mental representations? As Shinskey and Munakata point out, once infants have mastered information contained in one stimulus, seeking the novelty of a new stimulus is an adaptive strategy for acquiring new information about the world—a strategy that has likely evolved in our species because of its useful role in helping us explore, learn about, and respond to changes in our environments. When the infants in their study showed a preference for the novel object in the visible condition, they were demonstrating that they had processed the familiar object sufficiently well that it had become less interesting to explore, so they were more inclined to reach for the novel object. Furthermore, the fact that the infants were more inclined to reach for the familiar object in the hidden condition suggests that their experience with the object had helped them develop a stronger representation of it than of the novel object. Evidence such as this leads some developmentalists to argue that the formation of mental representations depends heavily on experience (Shinskey & Jachens, 2014; Shinskey & Munakata, 2010; Wang & Baillargeon, 2008). Thus, it seems likely that infants' developing representations and knowledge of the world is a joint consequence of human evolutionary processes and experiences available to babies in the specific cultural contexts in which they are brought up.

Developmentalists continue to debate questions about when object permanence emerges in development and whether it is innate, learned through experience, or some combination of the two. As you will now see, these fundamental questions also inspire research on how infants understand other properties of the physical world.

Understanding Other Properties of the Physical World

There are, of course, properties of the physical world other than objects' continuing existence when out of sight. As adults, we are so thoroughly familiar with the properties of our physical world that is it easy for us to overlook their significance for our behavior and development. We walk around obstacles rather than attempt to walk through them; we expect an apple that falls from a tree to land on the ground and not fly around crazily and hit someone on the nose; we may playfully smack a friend with a pillow but would never do so with a brick; when we reach into the back of a closet, we expect to find a wall, not the land of Narnia.

What is the source of our knowledge of the physical world? Are we born with the knowledge that objects are solid and conform to physical laws, such as the law of gravity, or does that knowledge emerge from experience? By what process do we come to reason about objects, recognizing, for example, that they can be counted, that there are often cause-and-effect relationships between them, or that certain objects share some of their features with other objects and can be categorized accordingly? As they have done in their research on object permanence, developmentalists have turned to infants to explore these fundamental questions. And, as they do in their research on object permanence, developmentalists often employ the violation-of-expectations method, generally in the form of research trickery, to good advantage.

A number of such experiments found that between 3 and 9 months of age, and sometimes earlier, infants appear to have at least an initial grasp of a wide variety of physical laws concerning the behavior of objects. For instance, 5-month-old babies expect liquid and granular (sand) substances to be "pourable" when transferred from one glass to another, and they are surprised when researchers cunningly arrange for the apparently pourable substance to plop into the second glass like an ice cube; similarly, the babies expect solid substances to plop when transferred from one glass to another, they and are surprised when they pour like liquids (Hespos et al., 2016). Other research conducted by Renee Baillargeon and her colleagues has explored whether infants would expect an object that is suspended unsupported in midair would fall (Wang, Zhang, & Baillargeon, 2016). In an early study, the experimenters repeatedly presented 4½-month-old infants with the habituation event shown at the top of Figure 5.16 (p. 186), in which a hand reaches out and places one block on another before being withdrawn (Needham & Baillargeon, 1993). Then the researchers presented either an event that defies the law of gravity, in which the top

FIGURE 5.16 Evidence that very young infants have some appreciation of the laws of gravity is demonstrated by the fact that they stare longer at impossible "gravity" events, such as a block remaining suspended in air, than at possible events, such as a block being supported by a block underneath it.

block is left dangling in midair as the hand withdraws (bottom part of Figure 5.16), or a control event (not shown), in which the hand withdraws partway and continues holding the top block, which is not supported by the bottom block. Infants looked longer when the block appeared to be suspended in midair without any visible support, indicating to the researchers that the babies expected the block to fall. Similar studies have demonstrated that by 4 months of age, infants appear to believe that objects cannot move behind one screen and reappear from a separate screen without appearing in the space between screens, and they also appear to believe that if a container with an object inside is moved, the object will move with it (Figure 5.17) (Baillargeon, 2004; Spelke, Breinlinger, Macomber, & Jacobson, 1992).

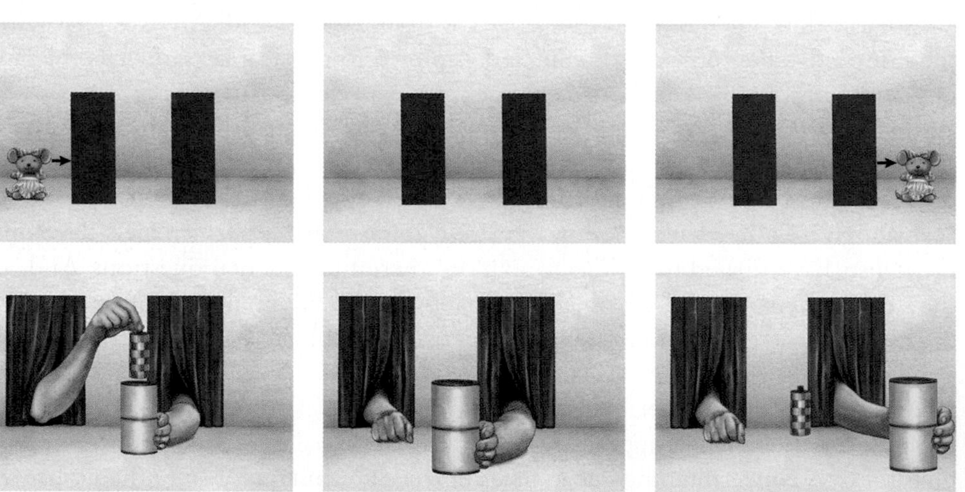

FIGURE 5.17 Studies using the violation-of-expectations method find that infants as young as 4 months look longer at events that violate certain physical laws. The first sequence shown here depicts the impossible event of an object passing behind a screen and then reappearing from behind a separate screen, without showing up in the space between the screens. The second sequence shows the impossible event of an object inside a container failing to change position when the container is moved.

Reasoning About Objects

An important part of Piaget's theory about knowledge of objects is that even after children begin to be aware of the physical properties of objects, they cannot reason about those objects; for example, they cannot count them, understand cause–effect relations between them, or categorize them according to some feature they have in common.

Counting

The question of whether young babies can count has puzzled researchers for decades. In an early study conducted by Karen Wynn (1992), 4-month-old infants were shown the events depicted in Figure 5.18. First, a mouse doll was placed on an empty stage while the baby watched. Then a screen was raised to hide

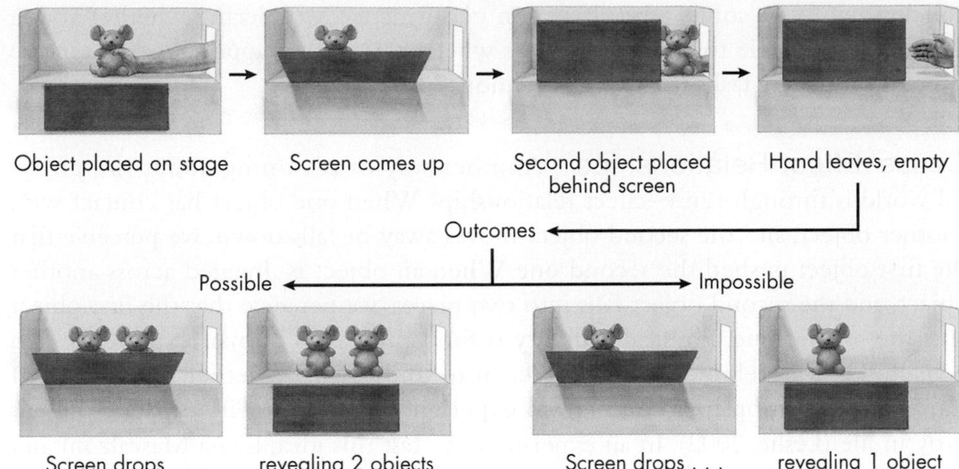

FIGURE 5.18 After 4-month-olds observe the sequence of events depicted at the top of the figure, they show surprise when the screen is removed and only one mouse remains. Apparently the babies not only remember the presence of the first mouse hidden behind the screen but mentally add the second mouse and expect to see two mice. (Research from Wynn, 1992.)

the doll from the baby's view. Next, the baby saw a hand holding a doll identical to the first one go behind the screen and then reappear without the doll. The screen was then lowered, in half the trials revealing two dolls (the possible event) and in the other half revealing only one doll (the impossible event). The infants looked longer when there was only one doll, suggesting that they had mentally calculated the number of dolls that ought to be behind the screen. Similarly, when the experiment began with two dolls on the stage and the hand removed one doll from behind the screen, the infants seemed surprised when the screen was lowered to reveal two dolls.

More recent research has confirmed that young babies recognize when the number of objects in an array increases or decreases, and there is some indication that the recognition of numerical change is associated with the activation of specific brain areas (Edwards, Wagner, Simon, & Hyde, 2016; Mou & vanMarle, 2014). In light of the fact that counting is a fundamental skill of the human species, researchers are not surprised that the brain may have evolved to include areas that are dedicated to processing number.

In addition to perceiving changes in the numbers of objects, babies seem to "match" number across sensory modalities (see the discussion of multimodal perception in Chapter 4, p. 140). For example, when 7-month-olds hear a recording of three voices speaking, they look longer at a video that shows three faces than at a video that shows only two (Jordan & Brannon, 2006). This preference for correspondence is evident at a more complex level when older babies respond to correct and incorrect counting (Slaughter, Itakura, Kutsuki, & Siegal, 2011). Eighteen-month-olds were shown a video depicting six fish. In one instance—the correct counting condition—a hand pointed to each fish while a voice counted each one, from one to six. In the other instance—the incorrect counting condition—the hand moved back and forth between only two of the six fish while the voice counted to six. The babies looked significantly longer at the correct, compared to the incorrect, counting sequence, indicating a preference for correct counting. Such experiments appear to demonstrate that infants are capable of understanding certain features of counting far ahead of Piaget's timetable regarding their ability to reason about objects.

However, as with other research suggesting precocious, possibly innate, infant abilities (such as whether infants understand the permanence of objects), research claiming to demonstrate that infants can count has not gone unchallenged. For example, Leslie Cohen and Kathryn Marks (2002) found that the infants looked longer the more objects there were and that they looked longer at a familiar display, no matter how many objects were in it. Developmentalists are still trying to reach conclusions about competence based on performance, wondering whether young babies are truly able to count objects or whether they only appear to do so in the context of specific tasks (Cordes & Brannon, 2009).

Cause–Effect Relationships Another way of reasoning about the physical world is through cause–effect relationships. When one object has contact with another object, and the second object moves away or falls down, we perceive that the first object pushed the second one. When an object is dragged across another object, and the second object falls into two pieces, we perceive that the first object cuts the second one. Physical causality is fundamental to human experience and behavior, and developmentalists are keen to understand whether knowledge of cause–effect relationships comes from experience or is an innate capacity present early in life (Leslie, 2002). In an experiment to test this idea, Elena Mascalzoni and her colleagues presented newborns with two computer displays in which one gray disc appeared to bump into a second disc, which then moved (commonly referred to as the "launching task"; Mascalzoni, Regolin, Vallortigara, & Simion, 2013). In one, the *causal* version, the second disc moved immediately, an event that adults perceive as the result of its being pushed by the first disc. In the other, the *noncausal* version, there was a delay in the movement of the second disc, suggesting that being pushed did not cause its movement. The newborns looked significantly longer at the causal version, suggesting their preference for cause–effect relationships over noncausal events.

Although research with newborns suggests that the perception of physical causality may be present at birth, other research indicates that experience can have a significant impact on infants' understanding of cause–effect relationships. An example is a clever study conducted with 4½-month-olds wearing mittens (Rakison & Krogh, 2012). Some of the babies wore regular mittens and were placed in front of several balls glued to a tray. The other babies wore mittens made of Velcro and were placed in front of a tray of loose balls that stuck easily to the mittens. Clearly, the regular-mittened babies did not experience cause–effect relationships; even if they succeeded in touching the balls by batting or swiping at them, the balls, glued to the tray, did not move. On the other hand (so to speak), babies wearing the sticky mittens experienced cause–effect relationships when their batting and swiping resulted in "catching" a ball. After some experience in wearing either regular or sticky mittens, the infants were presented with causal and noncausal displays similar to the launching task described above. As predicted, babies who had special experiences with causal relationships were more likely to show evidence of causal perception on the launching task.

Categorizing Imagine 2-year-old Sylvie playing "bedtime" with her toys. She has put her Dora doll under a cover on the table, along with Bitty Kitty and Pooh Bear. Excluded from the makeshift bed, however, are several other toys that she had just been playing with, among them Dora's truck and Pooh Bear's honey pot. Sylvie has appropriately categorized her toys into two groups: those that need sleep and those that do not.

The process of categorizing—that is, of seeing similarities in different objects and events—is an essential feature of how we make sense of the world. Without the ability to categorize, we would need to learn about each new detail of our experience from scratch. We would not be able to take knowledge gained in one situation and apply it to another similar situation, and this would make learning about the world a very slow and inefficient process. The adults of our species, however, are incredibly adept at categorization. Developmentalists are interested in when this ability emerges and how it changes over time.

Infants display an ability to form categories remarkably early in life (Cimpian, 2016). For example, if 3-month-olds are shown a series of pairs of pictures of different cats and then shown a pair consisting of a picture of a cat and a picture of a dog, the infants will look longer at the picture of the dog than they will at the picture of the new cat (Figure 5.19). This preferential looking indicates that the infants had formed a category for what they had been viewing and that a dog did not fit it (Quinn & Eimas, 1996; Quinn, Eimas, & Rosenkrantz, 1993). Brain studies have shown that when young babies form categories, the electrical activity of their brains changes in ways which suggest that basic neurological processes have evolved to support early categorizing abilities (Quinn, Westerlund, & Nelson, 2006). In addition, brain research suggests that young babies 4 to 6 months of age may categorize and process faces differently than they process other visually complex objects (de Heering, Van Belle, & Rossion, 2014).

Most research on categorization, however, has been conducted with somewhat older infants and has focused on the bases infants use to form categories. Do they rely primarily on perceptual similarities—that is, on similarities in how objects look, feel, or sound—or are they able to categorize according to more abstract, conceptual features, such as how objects function or behave? The framing of this question may remind you of the general theme that has permeated much of our discussion of infant intelligence: the extent to which an infant's knowledge is primarily perceptual and sensorimotor in nature and the extent to which it is also abstract and conceptual.

Evidence that infants form conceptual categories before the 1st year comes from an intriguing study of "generalized imitation" (Mandler, 2004; Mandler & McDonough, 1996). In this study, 9- and 11-month-old babies observed an adult model performing an action that would be appropriate either for animals as a category or for vehicles as a category—for example, giving a toy dog a drink from a cup or turning a key in a toy car door (Figure 5.20, p. 190). Then, in the imitation phase, either the dog or the car was put away, and the infants were presented with a different item that was placed next to the prop (the cup or the key). Sometimes the new item was from the same category as the previous one (a bunny was placed next to the cup or a truck was placed next to the key); sometimes it was from the other category (the bunny was placed next to the key or the truck was placed next to the cup). The researchers found that the babies would give a drink to the bunny but not to the truck, and likewise would use the key with the truck but not with the bunny. That is, while the babies were likely to imitate the action with the appropriate object, they rarely performed the action on the item from the incorrect category.

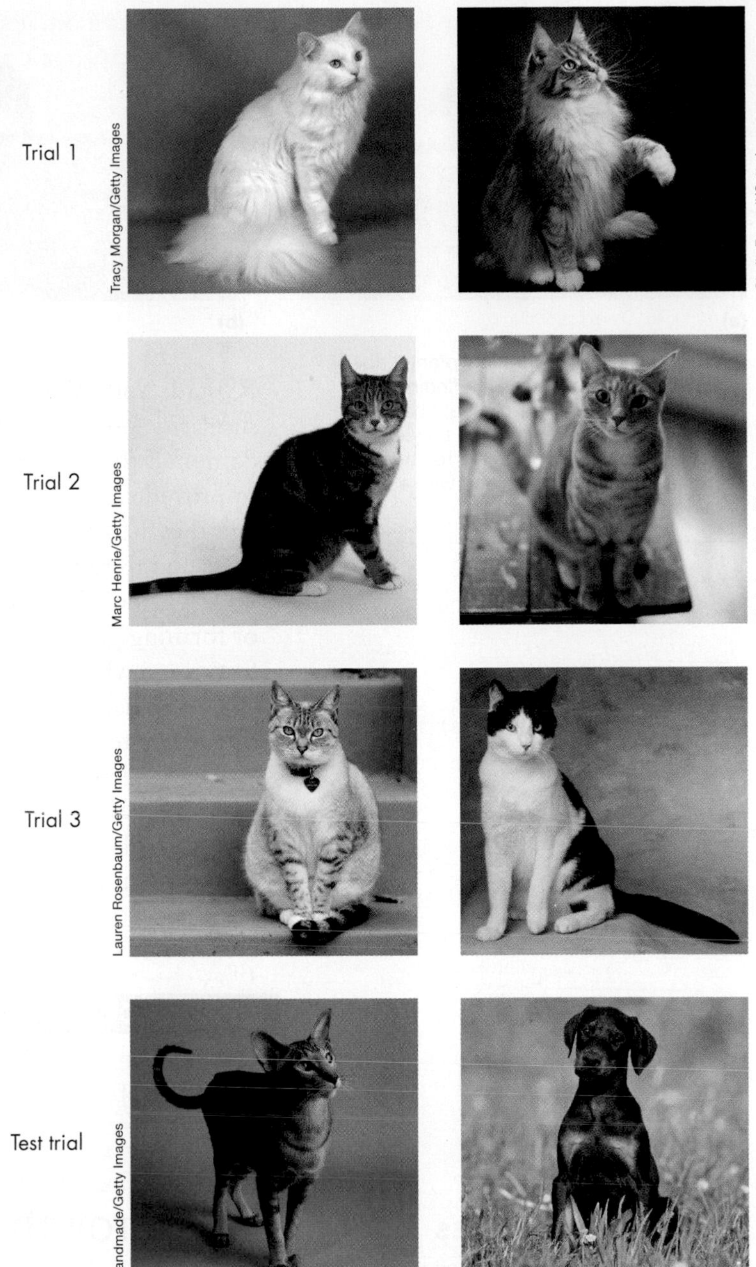

FIGURE 5.19 When 3-month-olds are shown a sequence of pictures of cats, they are surprised at the presence of a dog in the sequence, indicating that they are sensitive to the category cats.

There is still uncertainty among developmentalists about the basis for the changes in categorization observed across infancy (Booth, Schuler, & Zajicek, 2010;

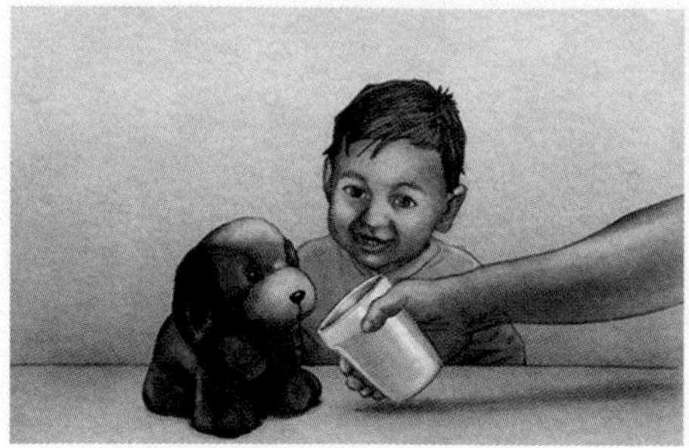
(a)

(b)

(c)

FIGURE 5.20 Illustrating infants' ability to categorize objects is the finding that when 7- to 11-month-olds (a) observe an adult give a toy dog a drink, they (b) do not imitate the action with a toy truck but (c) imitate the adult's action with a toy bunny.

Rostad, Yott, & Poulin-Dubois, 2012). Some researchers believe that perceptual similarity—whether the object has legs versus wheels, for example—remains fundamental to category formation for the entire period. Thus, older infants show improved categorization skills because their sensory systems are more developed, and they have greater experience, making them sensitive to more subtle characteristics and to relationships between characteristics (Cohen & Cashon, 2006; Quinn, 2002). Others believe that before the end of the 1st year, infants become capable of forming genuine conceptual categories—categories based on such meaningful features as what things do and how they come to be the way they are—in addition to perceptual categories (Mandler, 2004). For instance, 14-month-olds continue to categorize toy replicas of people and animals as animate objects, even though their legs have been replaced by wheels; similarly, toy wagons and boats are categorized as inanimate, even though they have been given legs (Rostad et al., 2012).

Although developmentalists are continuing to test different theories about how infants form categories, it is clear that by the end of infancy, babies are able to use them categories organize their own behavior in relation to their environments, as did Sylvie when she put some of her toys to bed but not others.

APPLY > CONNECT > DISCUSS

Design an experiment to test whether infants understand the difference between "natural" objects (trees, fish, people, etc.) and "artificial" objects (cars, watches, buildings, etc.).

LEARNING OUTCOMES

Outline the four distinct phases in the process of infant attention.

Describe increases in memory during infancy.

The Growth of Attention and Memory

Although we have not yet discussed it specifically, a baby's ability to pay attention to and remember specific aspects of the environment clearly plays an important role in many of the developments described above. Obviously, before babies can figure out whether an object with wings has feathers or a different surface, they first need to attend to the object. And it would be impossible for babies to understand cause–effect relationships if, as they were watching some effect, they could not remember the earlier event that caused it.

Developing Attention

The process of attention appears to involve four distinct phases that can be distinguished by changes in infants' heart rates (Figure 5.21) (Courage, Reynolds, & Richards, 2006):

Phase I: Stimulus-detection reflex. The stimulus-detection reflex signals the baby's initial awareness of some change in the environment. In this phase (not labeled in the figure), there is a very brief slowing and then quickening of the heart rate.

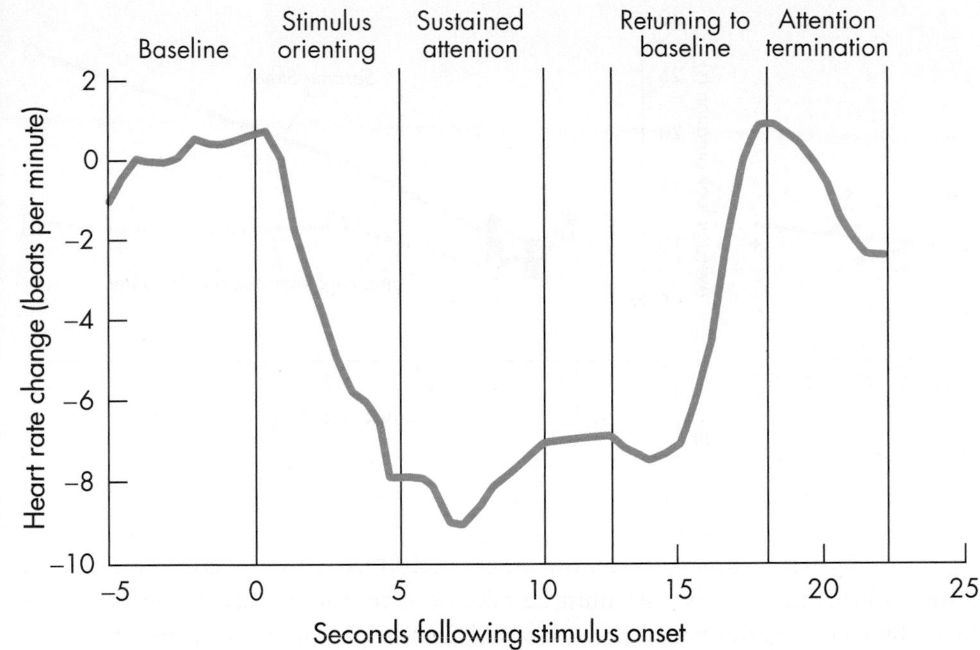

FIGURE 5.21 Attention is a process involving four phases that can be distinguished by changes in the infant's heart rate. As shown here, the heart rate drops considerably when the infant is engaged in sustained attention. (Data from Courage et al., 2006.)

Phase II: Stimulus orienting. During the second phase, the baby's attention becomes fixed on the stimulus. As you can see in the figure, the heart rate slows considerably during this period.

Phase III: Sustained attention. In the third phase, the heart rate remains slow as the baby cognitively processes the stimulus. The baby's entire body may become still, and it is relatively more difficult to distract the baby with a new stimulus (Reynolds & Richards, 2007). Sustained attention is believed to be a voluntary state; that is, the baby purposefully controls and focuses his or her attention on the stimulus (Johansson et al., 2016). At this point, the baby is truly *paying attention*.

Phase IV: Attention termination. In this phase, the baby is still looking at the object but is no longer processing its information. (It takes a moment to break contact with the stimulus.) The heart rate begins to return to prestimulus levels.

From the descriptions of these phases, you can imagine why developmentalists are particularly interested in the development of sustained attention. It is during the attention phase that babies actively learn about and remember their experiences. At 3 months of age, babies can sustain their attention only for periods of 5 to 10 seconds. Certainly, one of the most significant developments in the first 2 years is infants' increasing ability to focus their attention in a sustained way.

In addition to getting better at focusing their attention over the course of the first 2 years, babies get faster at processing information about the targets of their attention. Show 1-year-olds a picture of a bunny, and they are likely to stare with rapt attention for a long period of time. Show the same picture to 2-year-olds, and they may look at it for a few seconds and be done with it. They have processed it and recognized it, and they are ready to turn their attention elsewhere. Clearly, it is not the case that 1-year-olds have better sustained attention than 2-year-olds. Rather, 1-year-olds need more time to process the information. Indeed, research indicates that with increasing age, there is a decrease in the amount of time that babies spend looking at simple patterns or figures. It has even been found that 6-month-olds who spend relatively long periods of time looking at simple patterns tend to have lower intelligence quotients (IQs) when they are tested at the

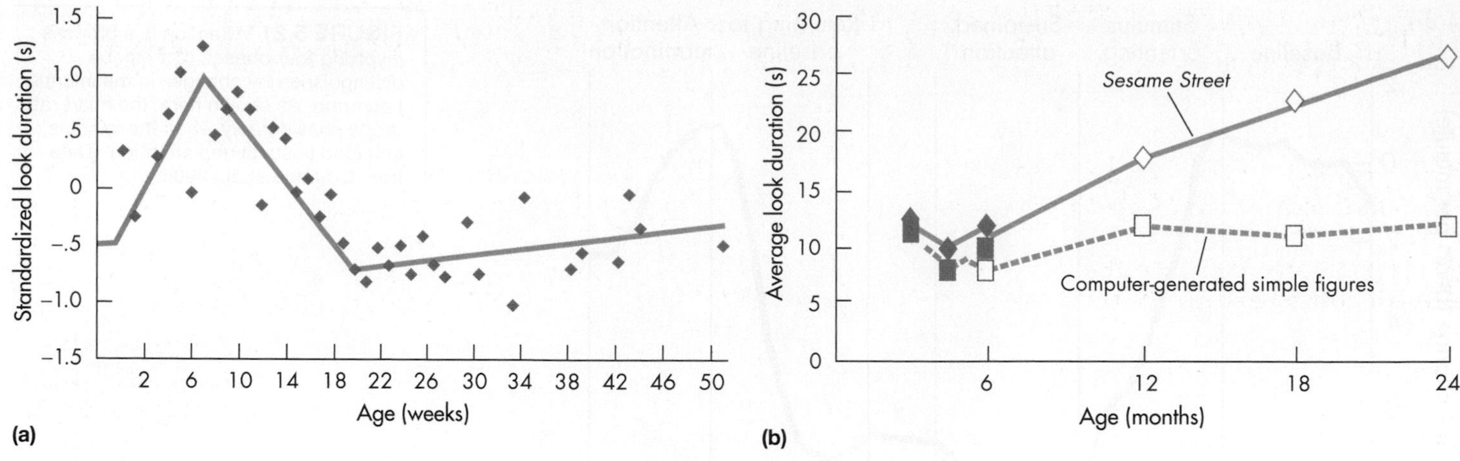

FIGURE 5.22 (a) Between 6 and 22 weeks of age, there is a significant decline in the amount of time that infants looks at simple geometric figures. (b) Between 6 and 24 months of age, however, there is a significant increase in the amount of time that infants look at complex stimuli, such as *Sesame Street* videotapes, while the amount of time they spend looking at simple figures remains stable. (Data from Rose et al., 2004.)

age of 11 (Rose, Feldman, & Jankowski, 2004, 2009; Figure 5.22a). Among other things, all this means that care must be taken not to confuse *visual attention* (how the baby processes information) with *visual fixation* (the amount of time the baby looks at an object).

While infants' attention to simple visual displays decreases after the first few months of life, attention to complex stimuli increases (Rose et al., 2009). Figure 5.22b illustrates the amount of time babies of different ages, ranging from 6 to 24 months, looked at two different videotapes. One videotape showed a computer-generated display of simple geometric patterns. The other showed a segment from *Sesame Street*. The time spent watching the computer-generated film was about the same for all babies, whereas the time spent watching the *Sesame Street* segment increased with age.

As we mentioned earlier, the development of attention, especially focused, sustained attention, is of enormous significance to the infant's emerging ability to remember past events and learn about the environment, a topic we address next.

Developing Memory

Carolyn Rovee-Collier and her colleagues explored the complexities of infants' memory development throughout the 1st year of life (Cuevas, Learmonth, & Rovee-Collier, 2016; Rovee-Collier, Mitchell, & Hsu-Yang, 2013). Using the operant-conditioning procedure described in Chapter 4 (pp. 148–149), the researchers trained babies between ages 2 and 6 months of age to kick in order to make an overhead mobile move. (One of the infants' ankles, you will recall, was connected to the mobile by a ribbon; Figure 5.23.) Following the training, the babies were returned to the lab after delays of various durations to see if they remembered how to make the mobile move. The researchers found that 2-month-olds started kicking immediately following a 24-hour delay but seemed to forget the procedure if the delay lasted 3 days. Memory for the task was better in 3-month-olds and better yet in 6-month-olds, who remembered their training 2 weeks later but not 3 weeks later. Interestingly, if infants are permitted to observe the experimenter pulling the string to shake the mobile, their apparently forgotten memories can be "reactivated" (Joh, Sweeney, & Rovee-Collier, 2002).

Infants' memories can also be strengthened by other memories. In one study, for example, 6-month-olds were trained to push a button to activate an electronic train and then returned to the lab days and weeks later to see how long they remembered the task (Rovee-Collier et al., 2013). But before learning how to operate the train, some of the babies spent time in two free-play sessions with a number of objects, including two puppets. Other babies spent time in the free-play sessions, but the two puppets were not present together—one was present in the first session; the other in the second. The two puppets were present together when the babies learned how to operate the train. Babies who had associated the two puppets together during the free-play sessions remembered how to work the train five times longer than those who saw the puppets separately. According to the researchers, these results tell a fascinating story about how young infants learn and remember. As they undergo dramatic development, young infants are especially quick to form associations between objects and events that occur in their continually and rapidly changing environments—a tendency that Rovee-Collier and her colleagues referred to as a "period of exuberant learning," which ends around 9 months of age. Exuberant learning may account for the infants' association of the two puppets and how that earlier association strengthened the memory of the association between pushing the button and the movement of the train.

Memory is considered an especially important cognitive achievement because it seems to require the generation of a mental representation for something that is not present to the senses. As we discuss in later chapters, developments in memory and attention are intertwined with the other cognitive achievements, and, over time, come under increasingly purposeful control.

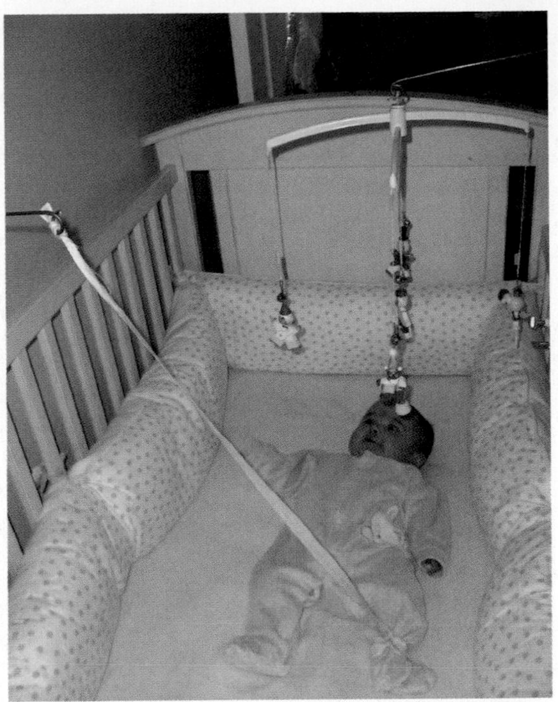

Carolyn Rovee-Collier

FIGURE 5.23 Because of the ribbon tied between her ankle and the mobile overhead, this infant will learn that kicking causes the mobile to move. Research indicates that she is likely to remember what she learned about the mobile for several days. However, she will probably be at least 6 months old before she can remember the task for 2 or more weeks.

APPLY > CONNECT > DISCUSS

In what ways might the changes in the brain discussed on p. 165 contribute to the development of attention and memory during infancy?

Looking Ahead

LEARNING OUTCOMES

Summarize how physical and cognitive development prepare infants for further development through childhood.

It is truly astonishing that babies undergo such enormous physical and cognitive changes in such a brief period of time. Equally amazing are the implications that these changes have for future development. Already, as a consequence of synaptogenesis and selective pruning, the baby's neural pathways are taking shape according to both species-universal and individual experiences. Whereas the crucial biological events during the newborn period (Chapter 4) involve changes in the connections between the sensory cortex of the brain and the brain stem, the remaining months of infancy are marked by increased myelination of the prefrontal cortex, which is associated with voluntary behavior and language, and myelination of pathways connecting different areas of the brain, which allows the brain to work in a more integrated way. Equally important are increases in height and weight, increases in the strength of muscles and bones, and a change in body proportion that shifts the baby's center of gravity—all of which are necessary to support developing motor skills.

As we noted earlier, motor development appears to orchestrate the reorganization of many other functions that have been developing in parallel during infancy. For one thing, the acquisition of new motor skills leads infants to discover many properties of objects in their immediate environment. They become capable of reaching for objects efficiently and picking them up, feeling them, tasting them, moving around them, carrying them, and using them for various purposes of their own. Their growing autonomy and ability to explore the world advances further as gross motor skills emerge, especially the uniquely human form of locomotion—walking.

These experiences would not amount to much, however, if babies were not able to represent them mentally or to remember them. The capacity to represent objects, people, events, and experiences mentally exerts a powerful influence on other areas of development that we explore in detail in later chapters, including symbolic play, imitation, and language. Indeed, as you will learn in later chapters, mental representation plays a pivotal role in how children make use of the material and symbolic tools of their culture. In the next chapter, we address the social and emotional domains of infancy and how they enter into the biocultural equation of children's development.

INSIGHT AND INTEGRATION

Advances in brain-imaging technologies have led to an explosion of research on the relationship between the growth of the brain and other physical and cognitive developments in infancy. Based on your reading of this chapter, what are some of the most interesting examples of this relationship? Does it seem to you that the growth of the brain enables physical and cognitive development, or is it the other way around, with physical and cognitive development stimulating brain development, or both?

Summary

Physical Growth

- Height and weight increase rapidly throughout infancy, especially during the 1st year. Body proportions shift, too, with the head coming to account for relatively less of the infant's length and the legs for relatively more. Soft bones gradually ossify, and muscle mass increases. Although boys tend to be larger than girls, girls tend to develop more quickly.
- Norms for children's growth can be enormously helpful in determining whether a child's physical development is on track and whether a child may be at risk for later problems. Significantly slower growth rates, known as infant growth restriction or stunting, are associated with developmental delay, infections, and poor nutrition, whereas significantly faster growth rates are associated with the risk of obesity in later childhood.

Brain Development

- Increased myelination of axons, along with other changes, such as the formation of neural networks that allow different parts of the brain to communicate and work together, leads to substantial development of the cerebral cortex, including the prefrontal and language-related areas, and to greater synchrony among the brain areas. These changes appear to be vital to the emergence in late infancy of more systematic problem solving, voluntary control of behavior, and the acquisition of language. By late infancy, most of the brain structures that will support adult behavior are present.
- As shown by studies of orphans who experienced early life adversity, prolonged deprivation in infancy leads to ongoing impairments in intellectual functioning. Because the brain undergoes considerable development between 6 and 24 months of age, lack of experiences during this sensitive period appears to affect both experience-expectant and experience-dependent brain development.

Motor Development

- Made possible by physical changes, the development of fine and gross motor skills enables infants to reduce their dependence on caregivers to get around and allows them to increasingly explore their environment.
- As the movements of their hands and fingers become better coordinated during the 1st year, infants perfect their reaching and grasping. With continuing increases in coordination of fine motor movements, by age 2 infants can do much in the way of feeding and dressing themselves and can turn book pages, cut paper, string beads, and stack blocks.
- Progress in locomotion leads to the emergence of crawling by 8 to 9 months of age, at which time wariness of heights appears. Walking begins at around 1 year and is made possible by the development of component motor skills and by practice. Studies in different cultures reveal that practice or lack of it can affect the age at which infants reach motor milestones.

Cognitive Development: The Great Debate

- For some developmentalists, including Piaget, young infants are limited to sensorimotor intelligence until about 18 months of age, when they become capable of representational thinking—thinking that is truly conceptual.

- For other developmentalists, very early in development, if not from birth, infants are capable of representing and understanding the world conceptually. A rudimentary conceptual system develops separately from, although in close association with, the sensorimotor system.
- In Piaget's stage of sensorimotor development, infants acquire knowledge exclusively through motor actions directed at their immediate environment and guided by their senses.
- Following the first two of Piaget's substages, in which infants learn to control reflexes and then to modify and repeat actions involving their bodies, infants move through four additional sensorimotor substages:
  - In substage 3, infants 4 to 8 months of age become capable of secondary circular reactions, repeating actions that involve objects, not simply those that involve their own body.
  - In substage 4, at 8 to 12 months of age, infants begin to display intentionality, engaging in goal-directed behavior.
  - In substage 5, the stage of tertiary circular reactions, infants 12 to 18 months of age deliberately vary their actions, thus experimenting in order to explore the world.
  - In substage 6, which occurs between 18 and 24 months of age, infants begin to base their actions on representations. The ability to represent mentally is crucial to problem solving, symbolic play, deferred imitation, and the use of language.
- The sequence and timing of the behaviors associated with Piaget's sensorimotor stages have been replicated with infants in a wide range of societies. However, critics of Piaget argue that young infants have representational competence that traditional Piagetian tests do not enable them to reveal.

Conceptual Development

- For Piaget, object permanence—the understanding that objects continue to exist when out of sight—emerges only gradually, beginning at about 8 months. Thus, 8- to 12-month-olds continue to search for an object in a location where they discovered it even when they have seen it hidden again in a different location. Piaget claimed that these infants still did not have true representations. Other developmentalists have argued that the infants' behavior reflects not a lack of representational competence but performance problems—specifically, memory limitations or a tendency to perseverate, repeating the same movement or the same successful strategy.
- Using the violation-of-expectations method, in which babies are habituated to an event and then presented with possible and impossible variants, researchers have obtained results suggesting that infants as young as 2½ months are capable of representations.
- According to the dynamic systems approach, cognitive development in infancy involves not a shift from sensorimotor to conceptual intelligence but the growing abilities to coordinate all the various systems involved in sensorimotor and conceptual intelligence.
- The formation of representations may depend heavily on experience. In experiments, infants' typical preference for a novel object over a familiar object is reversed when the room is darkened, perhaps because experience with an object leads to a stronger representation of it.
- Experiments using the violation-of-expectations method suggest that infants as young as 3 months of age have an initial grasp of various physical laws concerning the behavior of objects, such as the law of gravity.
- Other experiments using simplified tests suggest that, contrary to Piaget's view, young infants may be capable of understanding basic numbers and cause–effect relationships. Of particular interest is infants' abilities to categorize, evident as early as 3 months of age. Developmentalists are uncertain whether changes in categorization abilities during infancy simply reflect improved perceptual abilities or signal a change from categorization based only on perceptual features to categorization that is also conceptually based.

The Growth of Attention and Memory

- Developments in attention and memory are crucial to all the other cognitive changes of infancy.
- Infants are increasingly able to sustain their attention; in addition, they are increasingly fast at processing information about the targets of their attention. These changes are reflected in experiments showing that attention to simple visual displays decreases after the first few months but attention to complex stimuli increases.
- Memory increases rapidly during the 1st year, as shown by the increase in the length of time over which infants are able to remember procedures such as how to make a mobile move.

Looking Ahead

- Infancy is a brief period of enormous physical and cognitive changes with significant implications for development in other domains and for future development. Brain development and increases in height and weight support developing motor skills, which help make the cognitive changes possible. Among cognitive changes crucial to development is the growing capacity for mental representation and memory.

Key Terms

prefrontal cortex, p. 165
early-life adversity, p. 166
sleeper effects, p. 166
fine motor skills, p. 168
gross motor skills, p. 168
locomotion, p. 168
visual proprioception, p. 172
social referencing, p. 173
secondary circular reactions, p. 176
intentionality, p. 176
object permanence, p. 177
tertiary circular reactions, p. 177
representations, p. 178
symbolic play, p. 178
deferred imitation, p. 178
A-not-B error, p. 181
violation-of-expectations method, p. 183

Jessica Lia/Getty Images

CHAPTER

6

Social and Emotional Development in Infancy

In a creaky bus bumping along the highway from the airport to the city of Changsha, China, Jeff and Christine take in the passing scenes of marshy rice paddies and smokestacks. They want to remember this landscape so they can describe it someday to their 2-year-old daughter, Jin Yu, whom they are about to meet for the first time. They arrive at a hotel with 25 other new parents from America, all waiting to receive their children. One by one the children are handed over. And one by one they wail in protest. But not Jin Yu. And this disturbs Jeff and Christine. In preparing for this life-altering moment, the couple learned that such tears are a sign that the child has formed attachments to his or her orphanage caregivers and is therefore capable of forming new attachments to the adoptive parents. Jeff and Christine take Jin Yu to their hotel room, where she sits on the bed, silent and lethargic. They talk to her in soothing tones, stroke her, smile, and reassure her that all is well. But Jin Yu seems untouched and is unresponsive. Jeff and Christine become increasingly concerned. How long has she been like this—so socially and emotionally disconnected? Is her condition temporary or permanent? Then Jeff and Christine discover a ragged scar running across her head. They are frightened—for Jin Yu and for themselves. But she is their daughter now, and committed to this fact, they brace themselves for the unknowable. Back in the United States, doctors relieve their fears; the scar was probably a wound that became infected, but there is no evidence of permanent damage. Most reassuring, however, is Jin Yu's own rapid development. Within 6 months, she has grown 5 inches and gained 5 pounds, and she is taking an avid interest and obvious joy in her toys and playmates. If she becomes frustrated because her parents won't let her handle a cup of hot coffee or a steak knife, she makes an angry face, slams down her hand, and scolds them in Chinese. She has begun speaking in English, too. She requests, "Fries, please," and exclaims, "All done!" And she hums little melodies to herself. Jeff and Christine take great comfort in knowing that someone took time to sing to their baby. Perhaps a caregiver they would never know gave them and Jin Yu the foundation for building loving relationships in their new life together.

(Information from Gammage, 2003.)

Faced with Jin Yu's initial lack of social and emotional responsiveness, Jeff and Christine were understandably distraught. The ability to respond to others socially and emotionally is crucial to human development because it draws children into the lives of others—and into contact with their knowledge and values, goals and desires, and cultural activities and practices (Kokkinaki, Vasdekis, Koufaki, & Trevarthen, 2017; Trevarthen, 2015). Although we cannot be sure why Jin Yu was so unresponsive and "disconnected" at first, it is clear that within months of her adoption, she developed a rich emotional life that included feelings such as interest, joy, anger, and frustration. It is equally clear that she communicated these feelings effectively to others through gesture, facial expression, and language. She had become actively engaged in a social and emotional world that is, most importantly, *shared*.

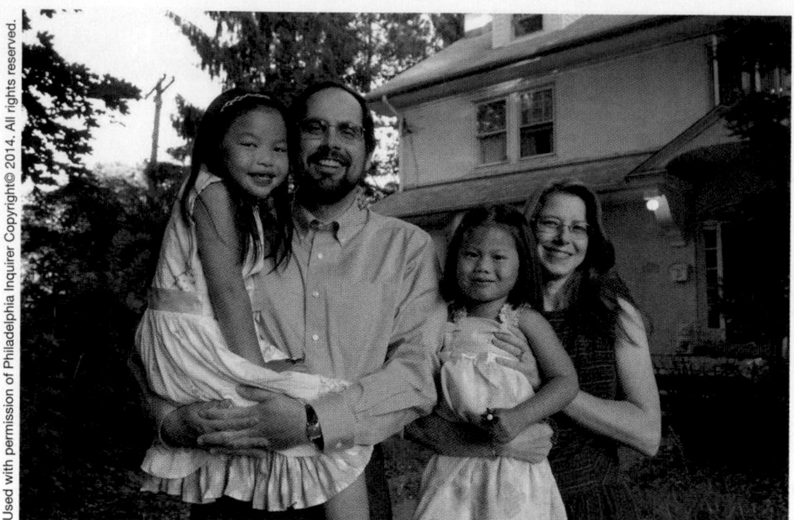
Used with permission of Philadelphia Inquirer Copyright© 2014. All rights reserved.

Jeff, holding Jin Yu, age 6, and Christine, holding their other adopted daughter, Zhao, age 4.

This chapter explores fundamental developments in the social and emotional lives of babies. We will discuss the range of infants' emotions and their origins, as well as infants' emotional attachments to caregivers and the ways in which those attachments can be affected by experience. We will also examine the changing nature of communication—how babies share their emotions, needs, and interests with others and become interactive partners in an ever-widening sphere of social life. As you will see, the fundamental social and emotional developments of the first 2 years are nurtured and shaped by interacting biological and cultural processes. Thus, some of these developments are universal and deeply rooted in the evolution of our species, and others are specific to the local contexts of children's development.

WARMING UP

1. Review this list of common emotions: joy, fear, anger, surprise, sadness, disgust, shame, guilt, and pride. Which, if any, do you think are experienced by newborns? Why? Do you think some of the listed emotions may take longer than others to develop? If so, which ones, and why? Which, if any, do you think might depend on the cultural context of the developing child? Why?
2. Our first emotional relationships are those we form in infancy with the people who take care of us. How important are these relationships? How do they affect our development? Do they impact emotional relationships formed later in life—with our siblings or romantic partners? Explain.
3. As adults, we are keenly aware of ourselves as unique persons with our own thoughts, desires, and motives. How might the seeds of self-awareness be apparent during the first 2 years? How does a baby begin to understand and express himself or herself as a singular, unique individual?

LEARNING OUTCOMES

Explain the features of emotion that develpomentalists typically consider.

Name six basic emotions expressed similarly across cultures.

Describe theories of emotional development, including their relationship to etic and emic approaches.

Give examples of how infants and their caregivers engage in primary intersubjectivity.

The Nature of Infant Emotions and Emotional Expressions

When in everyday conversation we talk about emotions, we are usually referring to the feelings aroused by an experience—feelings of happiness and excitement on unexpectedly winning a prize, of sadness on saying good-bye to a loved one whom we will not see for some time, of frustration and anger on being prevented from achieving a goal. But when we think deeply about what it is like to truly *feel* an emotion, it becomes clear that we are dealing with a process of enormous complexity. Our heart pounds; we catch our breath; our palms sweat; we shout or moan; we run away from or rush toward the source of our arousal. Recognizing the complexity of emotion, developmentalists typically define it in terms of the following features (Saarni, Campos, Camras, & Witherington, 2006):

- *A physiological aspect.* Emotions are accompanied by identifiable physiological reactions such as changes in heart rate, breathing, and hormonal functioning.
- *A communicative function.* Emotions communicate our internal feeling states to others through facial expressions, vocalizations, and other distinctive forms of behavior.
- *A cognitive aspect.* The emotions we feel depend on how we appraise what is happening to us.
- *An action aspect.* Emotions are a source of action. When something causes joy, for example, we laugh or cry or do both at once. When we are scared, we withdraw.

Technically speaking then, **emotion** can be defined as a feeling state that involves distinctive physiological responses and cognitive evaluations that motivate action (Saarni et al., 2006). But even this technically comprehensive definition of emotion fails to capture the complexity of the phenomenon fully. Emotions, for example, can emerge slowly, as when a feeling of pleasure blossoms into full-blown elation, or they can emerge rapidly, as in an explosive rage. Emotions can vary in their intensity, as indicated by the different smiles shown in Figure 6.1. Sometimes emotions mix together, as in the excitement and apprehension that many parents feel when their children go off to college. Complicating things further is the fact that people have ways of controlling the emergence and intensity of their own and others' emotions. When an older brother tries to distract his fussy baby sister with a toy, he is attempting to control her emotions; when the baby sister soothes herself by sucking on her pacifier, she is controlling her own emotions, although probably not intentionally. **Emotion regulation** is the term developmentalists use to describe how people act to modulate and control their emotions. In the sections below, we explore developmental changes in infants' emotions and how infants' emotions are expressed and regulated.

emotion A feeling state that involves distinctive physiological reactions and cognitive evaluations and that motivates action.

emotion regulation Ways of acting to modulate and control emotions.

Theories of Emotional Development

In some respects, emotions and emotional expressions seem to be universal, biologically driven, and common to all cultures. Who can mistake a broad smile and sparkling eyes for anything other than joy? Or a downturned mouth, trembling chin, and tears for anything other than sorrow? But emotions can have different meanings in different cultures. In some cultures, for instance, the expression of intense emotion, even if positive, can be viewed as a loss of control and considered socially inappropriate (Otto & Keller, 2015). As we discuss below, parents and other caregivers socialize their infants and children to express emotions in ways that conform to the specific values and expectations of their culture. A major challenge for researchers, then, is

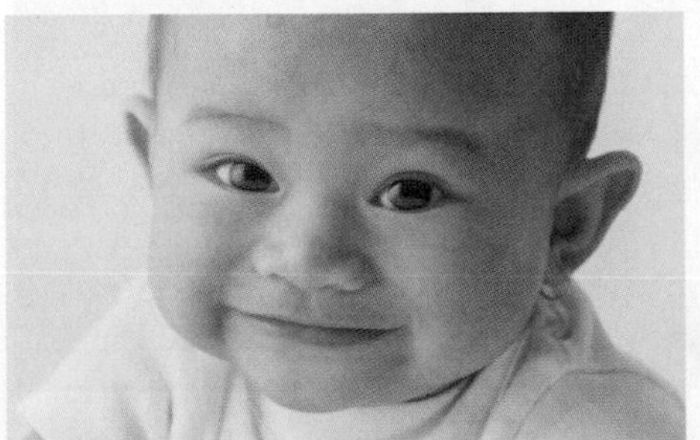

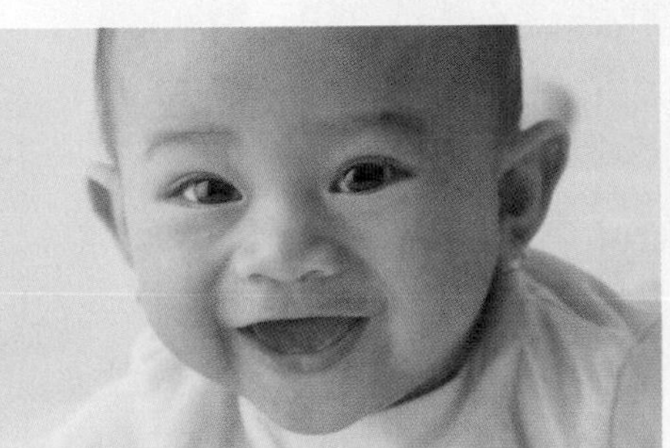

Odua Images/Shutterstock

FIGURE 6.1 Various emotional intensities are clearly apparent in the different smiles shown by this baby.

etic approach An approach that emphasizes the universal aspects of human behavior and development.

emic approach An approach that explores how behavior and development take place within specific cultural contexts.

to balance an **etic approach**, which emphasizes the universal aspects of human behavior and development, with an **emic approach**, which explores how behavior and development take place within specific cultural contexts (Lansford et al., 2016). We will now consider three different views of early emotional development that vary in the degree to which they emphasize etic or emic approaches.

basic emotions Universal emotions—such as joy, fear, anger, surprise, sadness, and disgust—that are expressed similarly in all cultures and are present at birth or in the early months.

Differential Emotions Theory

Consistent with an etic approach, most developmentalists agree that there are universal **basic emotions**—joy, fear, anger, surprise, sadness, and disgust—that are expressed in similar ways in all cultures. For example, adults from vastly different cultures, including isolated, preliterate cultures, generally agree on which facial expressions represent happiness, sadness, anger, and disgust. In addition, research finds that, across cultures, babies' smiles, expressions of distaste, and cry faces are comparable to those of adults (Camras & Shuster, 2013).

differential emotions theory The view that basic emotions are innate and emerge in their adult form either at birth or on a biologically determined timetable.

Some developmentalists believe that the basic emotions are biologically innate and present at birth in essentially adultlike form (Izard, Woodburn, & Finlon, 2010; Jessen, Altvater-Mackensen, & Grossman, 2016). Carroll Izard and his colleagues proposed **differential emotions theory** to capture the idea that infants' early emotions represent a set of distinct emotions comparable to those experienced by adults. In support of their argument, they point to the cross-cultural studies described above, which find that people from widely different cultures use similar facial expressions to signal basic emotions and to research suggesting that many infant facial expressions are similar to those of adults and can be reliably identified as such by untrained adult observers (Figure 6.2; Izard et al., 1980).

FIGURE 6.2 It's easy to see why some developmentalists believe that basic emotions are biologically innate and present from birth. Match the basic emotions (joy, fear, anger, surprise, sadness, disgust) with the images shown here.

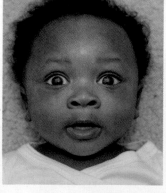

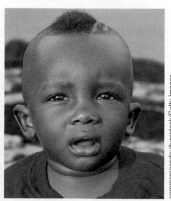

In this view, biology dictates the presence of distinct emotions at birth and the timing at which new, adultlike emotions such as guilt and shame emerge during infancy and childhood. Biology also underlies the increasing ability to regulate emotions; for example, emotion regulation is associated with brain development, including the prefrontal cortex, which, as we discussed in Chapter 5, is believed to affect a variety of voluntary behaviors (Panksepp & Smith-Pasqualini, 2005; Trevarthen, 2015).

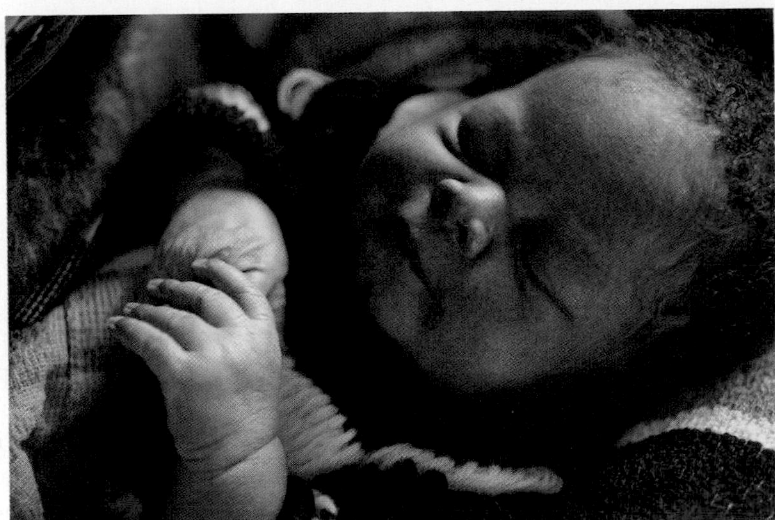
Giacomo Pirozzi / Panos

This very young Congolese infant is demonstrating an endogenous smile, which was probably a reaction to internal physiological fluctuations.

Taken together, such findings are considered strong evidence for the widely held belief that the basic emotions represent universal adaptive responses that are generated by and contribute to the biological and cultural evolution of our species (Panksepp, 2010). From a biological perspective, the basic emotions and their expression both protect children from potential sources of danger and ensure that their basic needs are met, largely by eliciting care and protection. From a cultural perspective, these emotions facilitate social connections to family and community members—connections that are vital to learning about the world and acquiring cultural knowledge and values (Liu et al., 2013; Trevarthen, 2015). Indeed, according to Vygotsky's (1978) sociocultural theory, introduced in Chapter 1 (pp. 22–23), all complex forms of reasoning and understanding develop as a consequence of the connections formed between individuals.

ontogenetic adaptation A trait or behavior that has evolved because it contributes to survival and normal development; in one view, infant emotions are ontogenetic adaptations.

Emotions as Ontogenetic Adaptations

A second view of infants' emotions, and one that blends etic and emic approaches, proposes that they are **ontogenetic adaptations**, meaning that they have evolved because they contribute to infants' survival and development (Oster, 2005; Schore, 2016). Therefore, developmentalists who take this view focus on the circumstances or situations in which babies experience and express different emotions (for example, the sorts of situations that provoke feelings of fear or joy) and on the ways infants' emotional expressions affect their interactions with their caregivers (Oster, 2005). An illustrative example is the changing nature of the infant's smile.

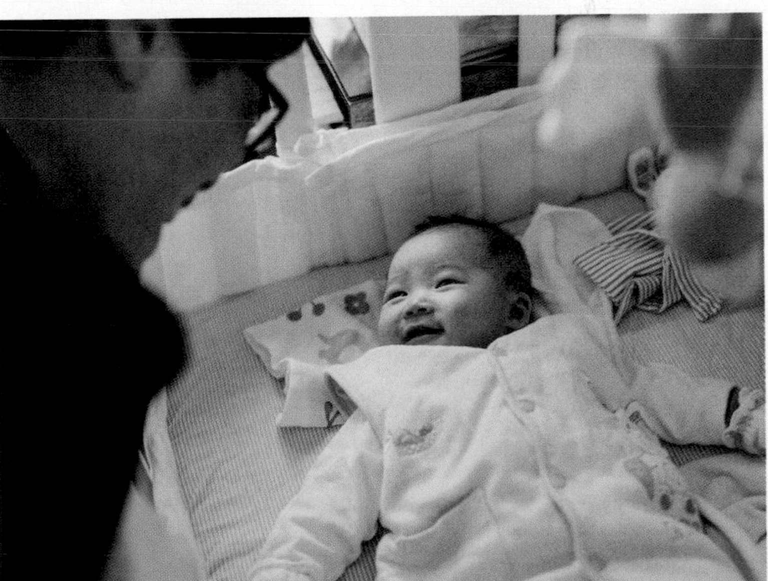
Images By Tang Ming Tung/Getty Images

Around 2 months of age, babies begin to smile in response to the smiles of others. An example of such social smiling is illustrated by this Chinese infant.

During the first weeks of life, the corners of a baby's mouth often curl up in a facial expression that looks just like a smile. Most likely to occur when the infant is asleep or very drowsy, these early smiles are called *endogenous smiles* because they seem to be associated with internal, physiological fluctuations rather than with external stimulation from the environment. However, between 1 and 2 months of age, infants begin to smile in response to mild perceptual stimulation, such as when a caregiver talks softly to them or lightly strokes their skin. Then, between 2 and 3 months of age, an infant's smile becomes truly social, both responding to and eliciting the smiles of others. At this point, parents report a new emotional quality in their relationship with their child.

According to the theory of emotions as ontogenetic adaptations, the changing nature of smiling during these early months of postnatal life demonstrates both continuities and discontinuities in infants' emotions, their origins, and the meanings they have for social interaction.

Emotions as Socialized in Cultural Contexts The third view takes the strongest stand on the significance of cultural contexts and the importance of an emic approach to understanding emotional development (Kartner et al., 2013; Keller & Kartner, 2013). Recognizing that infants are biologically prepared to express basic emotions and that parents and other caregivers are biologically primed to respond to infants' expressions, developmentalists who take an emic approach are interested in how these basic biological inclinations unfold and are shaped in the course of specific social interactions. Once again, the development of smiling provides an excellent illustration.

If you can hardly keep from smiling at the last image in Figure 6.2 on the previous page—the photo of the baby expressing intense joy—and can easily imagine trying to induce such an expression in an infant, then you are likely from a culture that prizes individuality. In such cultures, each person is unique, separate from others, with his or her own goals, preferences, and feelings. In these cultures, parents and other caregivers are likely to be highly responsive to infant social smiling and to encourage the escalation and expression of intense positive emotions (Kartner et al., 2013; Wörmann, Holodynski, Kärtner, & Keller, 2012). But if you happen to be from a culture that values interpersonal relationships more than individuality and individual expression, then it's likely you would respond very differently. In such cultures, the expression of intense emotion is discouraged beginning in infancy. For example, both the Nso of Cameroon and the Gusii of Kenya are ethnic groups that value relationships and an individual's responsibilities to others. In these types of cultural groups, it is common to socialize children to be obedient, respectful, and cooperative (Kartner et al., 2013; Keller et al., 2010; LeVine et al., 1994). Parents believe that babies should be calm and emotionally neutral; intense smiling and laughing are interpreted as signs of overexcitement and are discouraged. An early study of mother–infant interaction among the Gusii found that mothers would turn or look away when their infants expressed intense positive emotions, which typically resulted in the babies reducing the level of their emotional excitement, although they remained emotionally positive (LeVine et al., 1994). More recently, researchers found that, compared to middle-class German mothers (Germans tending to prize individuality), Nso mothers engaged in less face-to-face interactions with their infants, smiled at them less often, and were less likely to imitate the smiles of their babies (Wörmann et al., 2012). Significantly, over the course of time (between 6 and 12 postnatal weeks), Nso babies looked less often at their mothers' faces and smiled less overall compared to the German babies. All this suggests that cultural beliefs impact how mothers socialize the expression of emotion in infancy.

Infant Emotions and Social Life

We mentioned that infants' emotions play a key role in connecting infants to their social world. The coordination of movement and mood apparent in our discussion above indicates that the mother and baby are each able to recognize and share the emotional state of the other. Colwyn Trevarthen (1998; 2015) labeled this kind of well-organized, reciprocal social interaction **primary intersubjectivity**. (It is "primary" in the sense that it is direct face-to-face interaction whose focus is the interaction itself.) The importance of maintaining primary intersubjectivity is

primary intersubjectivity Organized, reciprocal interaction between an infant and a caregiver, with the interaction itself as the focus.

nowhere more apparent than in circumstances in which it breaks down, as when interactions between the baby and caregiver are disorganized and out of sync. As we discuss below, the interruption of this synchronous, or coordinated, interaction can take place for a variety of reasons. Mothers who suffer from depression, for example, often have difficulty being emotionally responsive to their babies. But before we discuss such "naturally occurring" influences on primary intersubjectivity, let us first consider what has been found in laboratory settings, when developmentalists experimentally disrupt the emotional connection between babies and their interactive partners.

Manipulating Intersubjectivity in the Laboratory Developmentalists have experimentally manipulated the synchrony of social interactions in two ways. One of these involves a procedure known as the *still-face method* (Apter et al., 2017; DiCorcia, Snidman, Sravish, & Tronick, 2016). In this procedure, after a few minutes of normal synchronous interaction with her infant, the mother is cued to pose a neutral "still face" and to stop responding to the baby (Figure 6.3). The other way of disrupting synchrony is by *delayed transmission*, a method that involves the use of TV monitors (Tremblay et al., 2005). In this method, the mother and baby interact naturally and synchronously, but they are seeing and hearing each other on the monitors. Periodically, the experimenters make transmissions from the mother's monitor run several seconds behind the baby's, so that her responses are out of sync with the infant's behavior. In both the still-face and delayed-transmission methods, babies as young as 2 months of age react to the loss of synchrony by averting their gaze and ceasing to smile. Frequently, the babies become agitated and fussy. These negative emotional responses have been found in babies interacting with mothers, fathers, and even complete strangers in several countries, including the United States, Canada, France, Taiwan, and China (Braungart-Rieker et al., 2014; Hsu & Jeng, 2008; Mesman, van IJzendoorn, & Bakermans-Kranenburg, 2009).

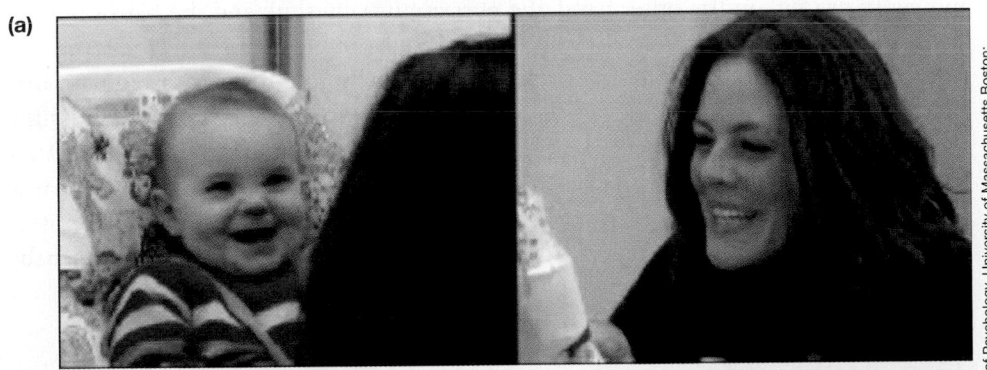

Ed Tronick, University Distinguished Professor, Department of Psychology, University of Massachusetts Boston; Research Associate and Lecturer, Department of Newborn Medicine, Brigham and Women's Hospital, Harvard Medical School, LOVETT STORIES + STRATEGIES

FIGURE 6.3 In the still-face method, after a few minutes of normal interaction (a), the mother is instructed to pose a "still face" (b) and stop responding to her baby. The baby shown here has become notably distressed, a typical reaction.

Maternal Depression: An Obstacle to Intersubjectivity Disruptions in infant–caregiver synchrony, of course, are commonplace outside the lab: Caregivers can be distracted or otherwise busy; babies can be fussy or drowsy. Usually, these disruptions are fleeting, and synchrony is quickly restored. However, there are circumstances in which infant–caregiver interactions are routinely disorganized and out of sync. For example, compared with nondepressed mothers, those who suffer from depression may be less sensitive to their infants' emotional cues. In addition to missing opportunities to share emotions, they may "transfer" their unresponsiveness to their babies (Field, Diego, Hernandez-Reif, & Fernandez, 2007). Indeed, in the still-face procedure, infants of depressed mothers act quite differently than do those of nondepressed mothers (Field, 2010; Ostlund et al., 2017). In particular, although they will avert their gaze when their depressed mothers "still face" (as do infants of nondepressed mothers), they do not fuss and protest. Helene Tremblay and her colleagues believe this reaction suggests not that the babies are undisturbed by their mothers' lack of responsiveness but that they have learned over time to disengage from stressful, unresponsive interactions with their mothers (Tremblay et al., 2005). Developmentalists speculate that many problems frequently observed in children of depressed mothers, such as anxiety and conduct disorders, are due to a history of disorganized and unresponsive emotional interactions (Pelaez, Field, Pickens, & Hart, 2008).

Emotion Regulation to Maintain Intersubjectivity Based on evidence from the still-face and delayed-transmission methods, it seems that babies have a deeply ingrained need to be emotionally connected to others. Indeed, Harriet Oster (2005) has argued that this need for connection may account for a particularly interesting and very common infant behavior: pouting. Pouting is most common when the infant is just beginning to be upset. The pout is intriguing for two reasons. First, the facial muscles involved in pouting are diametrically opposed to the facial muscles that pull the mouth into a cry face (Figure 6.4), suggesting that pouting is not simply a component of crying. Second, pouting is typically "directed" at a social partner—that is, the baby's eyes tend to remain open and focused on the other individual. In crying, on the other hand, the eyes are usually shut, and the baby's behavior becomes too disorganized for coordinated social interaction. Oster believes that pouting reflects the baby's first efforts (not necessarily intentional) to regulate distress and thereby maintain the social contact that crying would otherwise disrupt. Advocating the position that infant emotions are ontogenetic adaptations, Oster suggests that pouting has evolved as part of an emotion-regulation process because it serves to interrupt intense crying (which can deplete oxygen and lead to physical exhaustion) and also signals the caregiver to provide comfort before the baby

(a)

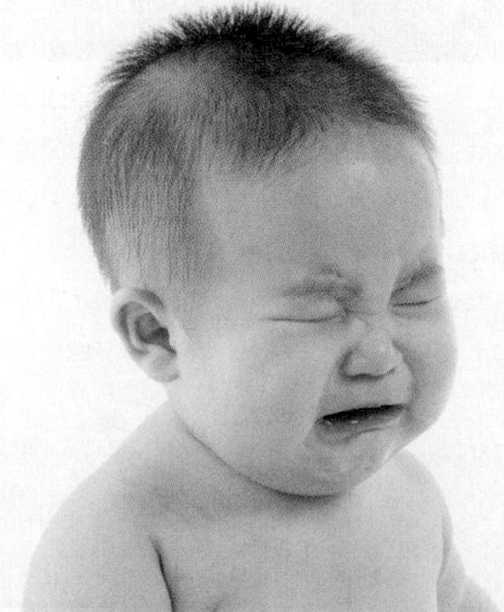
(b)

szefei/Shutterstock

FIGURE 6.4 Pouting (a) may be one of the baby's first efforts to regulate distress by signaling to another that help is needed to avoid intense crying (b).

begins to cry uncontrollably (Oster, 2005, p. 284). Her account of the evolutionary origins of emotion regulation has its roots in Darwin's observation that some of our most characteristic facial expressions are related to crying and our efforts to control it (Darwin, 1872).

Intersubjectivity and the Brain

The growing emphasis on the evolutionary origins of emotions has led to an intensive effort to discover how the brain contributes to the experience, expression, and regulation of emotions in infancy. A breakthrough in this quest occurred in a laboratory in Italy on a hot summer day in 1991. A monkey with electrodes implanted in its brain to monitor its brain activity happened to observe a graduate student enter the lab with an ice cream cone. The monkey stared at him, and then the breakthrough moment occurred: When the student raised the cone to his lips, the monkey's brain monitor began registering as if the *monkey* were eating the cone. Subsequent research by Giacomo Rizzolatti, the neuroscientist who heads the laboratory, suggested that specialized brain cells, called **mirror neurons**, fire when an animal sees or hears another perform an action, just as they would if the animal itself were carrying out the action (Rizzolatti, 2014). Since then, neuroscientists have identified a variety of *mirror neuron systems* in the human brain that are much more complex and flexible than the systems found in monkeys and that register the perceived intentions and emotions of others as if they were those of the person who is observing them in others. According to this evidence, we feel happy when those around us seem happy and sad when others seem sad because the emotional expressions of others activate our mirror neurons.

mirror neurons Specialized brain cells that fire when an individual sees or hears another perform an action, just as they would fire if the observing individual were performing the same action.

The discovery of mirror neurons has suggested a revolutionary way of understanding how infants connect emotionally with their social partners. As Rizzolatti argued,

> . . . we are exquisitely social creatures. Our survival depends on understanding the actions, intentions, and emotions of others. Mirror neurons allow us to grasp the minds of others not through conceptual reasoning but through direct stimulation. By feeling, not by thinking. (Blakeslee, 2006.)

Indeed, developmentalists have argued that mirror neurons very likely contribute to the remarkable ability of infants—even newborns within 42 minutes of birth—to imitate certain facial actions or movements of others (Simpson, Murray, Paukner, & Ferrari, 2014). Meltzoff and his colleagues consider such imitation in newborns to be innate, governed by brain processes that include mirror neurons (Meltzoff & Decety, 2003; Marshall & Meltzoff, 2014). Noting that adults across cultures play imitative games with their children, these researchers suggest that, over the period of infancy, imitation has a special role in establishing emotional connections between self and other. Young infants not only imitate the facial expressions of others, they also pay special attention when their own behaviors are imitated. If a young baby sticks out her tongue, for example, and an adult follows suit, the baby will act interested and generate more tongue protrusions. By 14 months of age, other cognitive and social processes moderate the neurological basis of imitation. At this age, infants derive a great deal of pleasure from being imitated by adults and, once the "game" is established, they modify their behaviors to make the adult follow their lead (see also Asendorpf, 2002; Nadel, 2002). Indeed, they will play such games gleefully for 20 minutes or more—a long time for a 14-month-old to do anything! Meltzoff and his colleagues argue that the joy babies derive from imitative games is a joint function of the emotional connection that comes from understanding that the adult is choosing to do "the same as me" and the sense of agency that comes from controlling the behavior of another (Meltzoff, 2007; Repacholi, Meltzoff, & Olsen, 2008). Developing a sense of agency is a key feature of an emerging sense of self, a topic we address more fully later in this chapter.

Although the concept of mirror neurons has inspired a great deal of research and theorizing about the relationship between brain and social behavior, it has also generated considerable controversy (Oostenbroek et al., 2016). Critics point out that research has yet to clearly identify specific cells as mirror neurons. Instead, the existence of mirror neurons has been inferred from brain imaging technologies that do not measure the specific activity of individual cells but, instead, measure the general activity of brain regions that include many types of neural cells. (This is why, as noted, these brain regions are referred to as "mirror neuron systems.")

All the research we have considered in this section points to the importance of well-coordinated, responsive, and synchronous social interactions in establishing emotional connections between babies and their caregivers. In the next section, we examine in depth the development of the infant's first, and what many believe to be the infant's most significant, emotional relationships—those between the baby and his or her primary caregivers. As you will see, the interactive synchrony we have been discussing is considered an essential ingredient to the formation of these first relationships.

APPLY > CONNECT > DISCUSS

Consider the nature of emotion regulation from a Vygotskian perspective (you may want to review p. 201) and discuss how maternal depression may complicate its development.

LEARNING OUTCOMES

Distinguish the differing views of attachment by Freud and Bowlby.

Summarize each of Bowlby's four phases of attachment.

Describe the purpose of the Strange Situation procedure and related research.

Distinguish among contexts in which variations for patterns of attachment arise.

The First Emotional Relationships

Our emotional relationships with others can be the source of our greatest joys, as well as our deepest despairs. They also provide a window onto the biocultural foundations of human development. Our emotions and attachments to others have tremendous significance for the evolution of the human species; but they are also substantially affected by, and adapted to, specific cultural contexts. This may remind you of the discussion we had previously regarding etic and emic approaches. Indeed, as we described about researchers exploring infant emotional development in general, those who study the infant's first emotional relationships are also challenged to integrate the universal, biologically driven aspects of relationships with the variety of ways that emotional connections with others are shaped by the cultural contexts in which they develop (Harkness, 2015).

Theories of Attachment

From mice to monkeys, to humans, mother–infant interactions are important to the survival of the baby and, by extension, the continuing evolution of the species (Esposito, Setoh, Yoshida, & Kuroda, 2015; Feldman, 2017). Taking a broad view that often encompasses mother–infant interactions across multiple species, biological accounts typically refer to the first emotional bond as *attachment*. When studied in humans, **attachment** refers to relationship characteristics emerging between children and their caregivers sometime between the ages of 7 and 9 months, when many babies begin showing distress at being separated from a primary caregiver, as well as a fear of strangers (Ainsworth, 1982). Developmentalists generally cite four signs of attachment in babies and young children:

attachment The emotional bond that children form with their caregivers at about 7 to 9 months of age.

1. They seek to be near their primary caregivers. Before the age of 7 to 8 months, few babies plan and make organized attempts to achieve contact with their caregivers; after this age, babies often follow their caregivers closely, for example.
2. They show distress if separated from their caregivers. Before attachment begins, infants show little disturbance when their caregivers walk out of the room.
3. They are happy when they are reunited with the person to whom they are attached.
4. They orient their actions to the caregiver. When they are playing, for example, they watch the caregiver or listen for the caregiver's voice.

The special relationship with their primary caregivers that babies begin to display between 7 and 9 months of age undergoes significant changes during the remainder of infancy and beyond.

Juice Images/AGE Fotostock

Even a spoonful of cereal offered by a stranger may evoke wariness in young children.

Explanations of Attachment

The fact that 7- to 9-month-old children everywhere begin to become upset when they are separated from their primary caregivers suggests that attachment is a universal feature of development (Simpson, Collins, Tran, & Haydon, 2007). This possibility has led to a lively debate about the evolutionary reasons for attachment, the causes of changes in attachment behaviors as children grow older, and the influence of the quality of attachment on children's later development.

Freud's Drive-Reduction Explanation

Early on, Sigmund Freud suggested that infants become attached to the people who satisfy their need for food. He believed that human beings, like other organisms, are motivated in large part by **biological drives**—the impulses of organisms to satisfy essential physiological needs, such as hunger or thirst, that create tension and a state of arousal in the organism. When such a need is satisfied, the drive is reduced as biological equilibrium is restored, and the organism experiences a sensation of pleasure. In this sense, pleasure-seeking is a basic principle of existence. With respect to attachment in particular, Freud asserted that "love has its origin in attachment to the satisfied need for nourishment" (1940/1964, p. 188). Thus, according to Freud, an infant becomes attached to his or her mother because she is the one most likely to nourish the child. The major problem with this explanation is that research with nonhuman primates has not substantiated Freud's notion that attachment is caused by the reduction of the hunger drive.

biological drives Impulses to attempt to satisfy essential physiological needs.

In a famous study that tested Freud's drive-reduction theory of attachment, Harry Harlow and his coworkers (Harlow, 1959) separated eight baby rhesus monkeys from their mothers a few hours after birth and placed each monkey in an individual cage with two inanimate "substitute mothers"—one made of wire and the other made of terry cloth (Figure 6.5). These substitute mothers were the monkeys' sole source of nutrition, with four babies receiving milk from the wire mothers, which had been specially equipped with milk-giving nipples, and four receiving milk from the terry cloth mothers, similarly equipped. The two types of substitute mothers were equally effective as sources of nutrition: All eight babies drank the same amount of milk and gained weight at the same rate.

Martin Rogers/The Image Bank/Getty Images

FIGURE 6.5 This baby monkey spent most of its time clinging to the terry cloth substitute mother even when its nursing bottle was attached to a wire substitute mother nearby. This preference indicates that bodily contact and the comfort it gives are important in the formation of the infant's attachment to its mother.

Nevertheless, over the 165-day period that they lived with the substitute mothers, the baby monkeys showed a distinct preference for their terry cloth mother, regularly climbing on her and clinging to her. Even those who obtained their food from a wire mother would go to it only to feed and would then go back to cling to the terry cloth mother. From the perspective of drive-reduction theory, it made no sense that the four infant monkeys who received their food from a wire mother would prefer to spend their time with a terry cloth mother that might feel good but satisfied no apparent biological drive, such as hunger or thirst. Harlow (1959) concluded, "These results attest to the importance—possibly the overwhelming importance—of bodily contact and the immediate comfort it supplies in forming the infant's attachment to its mother" (p. 70).

John Bowlby's Ethological Explanation John Bowlby's theory of attachment arose from his study of the mental health problems of British children who had been separated from their families during World War II and were cared for in institutions (Bowlby, 1969, 1973, 1980; Vicedo, 2013). Bowlby's observations of children in hospitals, nurseries, and orphanages, as well as his analyses of clinical interviews with psychologically troubled or delinquent adolescents and adults, indicated that when children are first separated from their mothers, they become frantic with fear. They cry, throw tantrums, and try to escape their surroundings. Then they go through a stage of despair and depression. If the separation continues and no new stable relationship is formed, these children seem to become indifferent to other people. Bowlby called this state of indifference **detachment**.

detachment For Bowlby, the state of indifference toward others experienced by children who have been separated from their caregivers for an extended time and have not formed new stable relationships.

In his attempt to explain the distress of young children when they are separated from their parents, Bowlby was particularly influenced by the work of ethologists, who emphasize a broad, evolutionary approach to understanding human behavior (see Chapter 1, p. 25). Ethological studies of monkeys and apes revealed that infants of these species spend their initial weeks and months of postnatal life in almost continuous direct physical contact with their biological mothers. Bowlby noted that these primate infants consistently display several apparently instinctual responses that are also essential to human attachment: clinging, sucking, crying, and separation protest. After a few weeks or months (depending on the species of primate), infants begin to venture away from their mothers to explore their immediate physical and social environments, but they scurry back to the mother at the first signs of something unusual and potentially dangerous (Suomi, 1995). These primate behaviors, Bowlby hypothesized, are the evolutionary basis for the development of attachment in human babies as well.

In contrast to their conclusions regarding Freud's drive-reduction hypothesis, Harlow and his colleagues found strong support for Bowlby's evolutionary theory in their subsequent research with monkeys placed in cages with "substitute mothers" (Harlow & Harlow, 1969). Knowing that normal human and monkey babies run to their mothers for comfort when faced with an unfamiliar and frightening situation, the researchers created such a situation for the monkeys who had received milk from the wire mothers. They introduced into these monkeys' cages a mechanical teddy bear that marched forward while loudly beating a drum. The terrified babies fled to their terry cloth mother, not to the wire one, and began rubbing their body against hers (Figure 6.6). Soon their fears were calmed, and they turned to look at the bear with curiosity. Some even left the protection of the terry cloth mother to approach the object that had so terrified them only moments before.

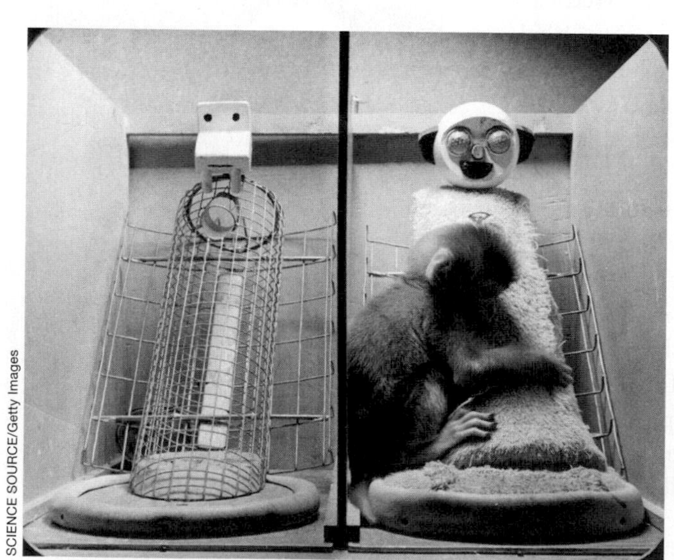
SCIENCE SOURCE/Getty Images

FIGURE 6.6 The terry cloth surrogate mother, which does not provide nourishment, acts as a secure base for the baby monkey, whereas the wire mother, which does provide nourishment, does not. This behavior contradicts drive-reduction theories of attachment.

Harlow concluded that soothing tactile sensations provide the baby with a sense of security that is more important to the formation of attachment than food. However, as Harlow's team discovered, although soothing tactile sensations appear to be necessary for healthy development, they are not sufficient. As these monkeys grew older, they showed signs of impaired development: They were either indifferent or abusive to other monkeys, and none of them could copulate normally. Noting that the substitute mother "cannot cradle the baby or communicate monkey sounds and gestures," the researchers concluded that the physical comfort provided by the cloth-covered mother in the monkey's infancy does not produce a normal adolescent or adult (Harlow & Harlow, 1962, p. 142). Applying the concept of *primary intersubjectivity* introduced earlier, it would seem that the absence of a sensitive and responsive social partner interfered with establishing the infant–mother emotional relationship considered so critical to later social and emotional development.

Phases of Attachment

Bowlby (1969) believed that attachment normally develops through four broad phases during the first 2 years of life, eventually producing a balance between infants' need for the safety provided by the caregiver and their need to explore their world (see Table 6.1). As you read through the descriptions of each phase, notice how infants take on more responsibility for maintaining the balance of the attachment system as their capacities to act and interact become more sophisticated:

1. *The preattachment phase* (birth to age 6 weeks). In the first few weeks of life, infants remain in close contact with their caregivers and do not seem to get upset when left alone with an unfamiliar caregiver.
2. *The "attachment-in-the-making" phase* (ages 6 weeks to 6 to 8 months). Infants begin to respond differently to familiar and unfamiliar people, and by the time they are 6 or 7 months old, they start to show clear preferences for their familiar caregivers as well as signs of wariness when confronted with unfamiliar objects and people.
3. *The "clear-cut attachment" phase* (between ages 6 to 8 months and 18 to 24 months). During this period, the mother becomes a **secure base** from which babies make exploratory excursions and to which they come back every so often to renew contact before returning to their explorations. This is also the time when children display full-blown **separation anxiety**, becoming visibly upset when the mother or another caregiver leaves the room.
4. *The reciprocal relationship phase* (ages 18 to 24 months and older). As the child becomes more mobile and spends increasingly greater amounts of time away from the mother, the pair enter into a more reciprocal relationship, sharing responsibility for maintaining the equilibrium of the attachment

secure base Bowlby's term for the people whose presence provides a child with the security that allows him or her to make exploratory excursions.

separation anxiety The distress that babies show when the person to whom they are attached leaves.

TABLE 6.1 Four Phases of Attachment

Attachment Phase	Age Range	Typical Attachment Behaviors
Preattachment	Birth to 6 weeks	No discrimination of different people; no distress with unfamiliar people
Attachment-in-the-making	6 weeks to 6–8 months	Discrimination of familiar and unfamiliar people; at 6 to 8 months, shows preferences for familiar people and wariness of strangers
Clear-cut attachment	6–8 months to 18–24 months	Primary caregiver (mother) becomes secure base for exploring; clear separation anxiety when separated from primary caregiver
Reciprocal relationships	18 to 24 months and older	Shared responsibility for maintaining contact; may feel secure even during separations due to growing symbolic capacities

system. When engaged in separate activities, the mother and the child will occasionally interrupt what they are doing to renew their contact. Among humans, this transitional phase lasts several years.

Once achieved, a firm attachment helps infants retain feelings of security during the increasingly frequent and lengthy periods of separation from their caregivers. It is noteworthy that this phase develops at the same time that infants' powers of mental representation are on the rise (see Chapter 5). Bowlby believed that as a consequence of infants' growing symbolic capacities, parent–child attachment begins to serve as an **internal working model**, a mental model that children construct as a result of their experiences and that they use to guide their interactions with caregivers and others (Sherman, Rice, & Cassidy, 2015). We will address the implications of the model in detail below.

internal working model A mental model that children construct as a result of their experiences with their caregivers and that they use to guide their interactions with their caregivers and others.

Patterns of Attachment

The maladaptive social behavior of Harlow's monkeys raised with inanimate substitute mothers, coupled with Bowlby's original observations of detachment in orphans, prompts a question: What kinds of interactions between primary caregivers and children provide the most effective basis for the development of healthy human social relations? (The following discussion is in terms of the mother as the attachment figure because most attachment research has focused on mother–infant pairs, a problem that we address later in the chapter.)

Mary Ainsworth initiated and inspired considerable research on how mother–child interaction affects the development of children's attachment. She designed the famous and widely used **Strange Situation** to assess different patterns of children's attachment to their mothers. The procedure, which takes place in a toy-stocked laboratory playroom, consists of eight brief episodes, including ones in which the child is with the mother, is with the mother and a stranger, is left alone with the stranger, is left entirely alone, and is reunited with the mother after a separation (see Table 6.2). The basic purpose of this procedure is to observe how infants make

Strange Situation A laboratory procedure designed to assess children's attachment on the basis of their use of their mother as a secure base for exploration, their reactions to being left alone with a stranger and then completely alone, and their response when they are reunited with their mother.

TABLE 6.2 The Strange Situation Procedure

Episode	Events	Attachment Behaviors Analyzed
1	Researcher greets parent and child, escorts them to the playroom, and leaves.	
2	Parent sits while child plays with toys; may encourage play briefly but tries to stay uninvolved.	Child's use of parent as secure base to explore toys and playroom
3	Stranger enters, sits, and talks with parent.	Child's acknowledgement of and response to unfamiliar adult
4	Parent leaves room; stranger remains; may offer comfort if child is distressed.	Child's response to separation; acceptance of comfort from unfamiliar adult
5	Parent returns, offers comfort if necessary; stranger leaves.	Child's response to reunion
6	Parent leaves; child is alone.	Child's response to separation
7	Stranger enters, offers comfort if necessary.	Child's acceptance of comfort from stranger
8	Parent returns, offers comfort if necessary; attempts to interest child in toys.	Child's response to reunion

use of the mother as a secure base from which to explore the playroom, how they respond to separation from the mother, and how they respond to a stranger. Ainsworth reasoned that different patterns of reactions would reflect different qualities of the attachment relationship.

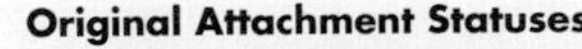

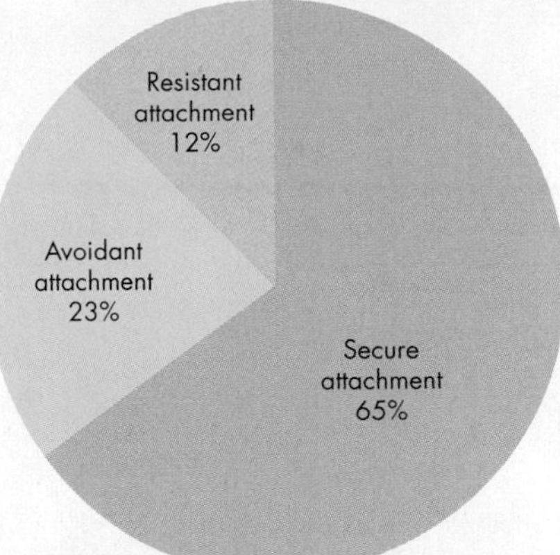

FIGURE 6.7 Early studies of middle-class children in the Strange Situation continue to serve as a yardstick for describing patterns of attachment. Initial research with samples of U.S. children identified three patterns—secure, avoidant, and resistant—with secure being the most common. Later research identified a fourth pattern—disorganized—which is associated with a number of mental health problems in later development. (Data from Ainsworth et al., 1971.)

On the basis of their findings, Ainsworth and her colleagues initially categorized infants' responses in the Strange Situation into three types that seemed to reflect the quality of the children's attachment: *secure*, *avoidant*, and *resistant* (Ainsworth, Bell, & Stayton, 1971; Ainsworth, Blehar, Waters, & Wall, 1978; see Figure 6.7). Later researchers added a fourth attachment type, *disorganized* (Main & Solomon, 1990). These types of attachment, or *attachment statuses*, and the responses they are associated with in the Strange Situation can be described as follows:

- **Secure attachment**. As long as the mother is present, securely attached children play comfortably with the toys in the playroom and react positively to the stranger. These children become visibly and vocally upset when their mother leaves. Although they may be consoled by the stranger, they clearly prefer the mother. When the mother reappears and they can climb into her arms, they quickly calm down and soon resume playing. This pattern of attachment, which reflects a healthy balance between wanting to be in close contact with the mother and wanting to explore the environment, is shown by about 65 percent of middle-class children in the United States.
- **Avoidant attachment**. During the time the mother and child are alone together in the playroom, avoidant infants are more or less indifferent to where their mother is sitting. They may or may not cry when she leaves the room. If they do become distressed, the stranger is likely to be as effective at comforting them as their mother is. When the mother returns, these children may turn or look away from her instead of going to her to reestablish contact. About 23 percent of middle-class children in the United States show this pattern of attachment.
- **Resistant attachment**. Resistant children have trouble from the start in the Strange Situation. They stay close to their mother rather than explore the playroom and appear anxious even when she is near. They become very upset when the mother leaves, but they are not comforted by her return. Instead, they simultaneously seek renewed contact with the mother and resist her efforts to comfort them. They may demand to be picked up, cry angrily with arms outstretched, but then arch away and struggle to get free once the mother starts to pick them up. These children do not readily resume playing after the mother returns. Instead, they keep a wary eye on her. This attachment pattern is shown by about 12 percent of middle-class children in the United States.
- **Disorganized attachment**. Children who fit this category seem to lack any coherent, organized method for dealing with the stress they experience. Some cry loudly while trying to climb onto the mother's lap; others may approach the mother while refusing to look at her; still others may stand at the door and scream while she is gone but move away from her silently when she returns. In some extreme cases, the children seem to be in a dazed state and refuse to move while in their mother's presence (Main & Solomon, 1990).

Over the past several decades, developmentalists have conducted a good deal of research trying to understand the causes of these four basic patterns of attachment behavior (Sherman et al., 2015). For instance, a number of studies have examined the relationship between maternal sensitivity and attachment status. Michael Lamb and his colleagues reported that parents of securely attached infants are generally more involved with their infants, more in synchrony with them, and more appropriate in their responsiveness (Lamb & Ahnert, 2006). Similar results were found in a study conducted in Colombia, Mexico, Peru, and the United States (Posada et al., 2016). The

secure attachment A pattern of attachment in which children play comfortably and react positively to a stranger as long as their mother is present. They become upset when their mother leaves and are unlikely to be consoled by a stranger, but they calm down as soon as their mother reappears.

avoidant attachment The attachment pattern in which infants are indifferent to where their mother is sitting, may or may not cry when their mother leaves, are as likely to be comforted by strangers as by their mother, and are indifferent when their mother returns to the room.

resistant attachment The attachment pattern in which infants stay close to their mother and appear anxious even when their mother is near. They become very upset when their mother leaves but are not comforted by her return. They simultaneously seek renewed contact with their mother and resist their mother's efforts to comfort them.

disorganized attachment The insecure attachment pattern in which infants seem to lack a coherent method for dealing with stress. They may behave in seemingly contradictory ways, such as screaming for their mother but moving away when she approaches. In extreme cases, they may seem dazed.

Camille Tokerud / Getty Images

This baby's attachment to his mother will be strongly affected by the role she plays in providing a secure base from which to explore the world.

mother's sensitivity to her infant's distress seems particularly important (McElwain & Booth-LaForce, 2006). This link is especially evident where such sensitivity is low. For example, maternal depression has been consistently linked to reductions in secure attachment behaviors (Brummelte & Galea, 2016; Flykt, Kanninen, Sinkkonen, & Punamäki, 2010). In addition, mothers who deny or fail to acknowledge relationship difficulties and negative emotions associated with interacting with their babies are more likely to foster the development of insecure attachments than mothers who acknowledge relationship difficulties (Bailey, Redden, Pederson, & Moran, 2016). Needless to say, babies who have been maltreated or whose mothers have mental health issues associated with decreased sensitivity—including substance abuse and addiction—are at risk for developing insecure attachments (Parolin & Simonelli, 2016; Stronach, Toth, Rogosch, & Cicchetti, 2013).

As a consequence of this large body of evidence linking maternal sensitivity to attachment development, a number of programs have been created to help mothers become more sensitive and responsive to their infants' behavior. One such program, conducted with low-income, at-risk mothers in Paris, France, included videotaping everyday interactions between mothers and infants during bath time, mealtime, play, and so forth. The mothers reviewed the videotapes with a professional trained to encourage mothers to be sensitive to the signals, intentions, and emotional states of their infants (Tereno et al., 2017). Compared with mothers in a control group, those who participated in the program showed an increase in sensitivity, and their babies were less likely to show disorganized attachment. In another program, infants who had been maltreated and their mothers participated in weekly sessions over the course of a year with a trained therapist (Stronach et al., 2013). The sessions took place in the home, and the therapist observed and commented on mother–infant interactions, encouraging a mother's sensitivity and responsiveness to her baby. At the end of the year, babies who participated in the program had higher rates of secure attachment compared to those in a different program that included only the mothers and that focused on promoting parenting skills and knowledge of children's development.

Attachment Patterns Across Development and Generations

A long-standing issue for developmentalists concerns the stability of attachment across individual development, as well as across generations (Raby, Steele, Carlson, & Sroufe, 2015). Is it the case that the security of one's attachment in infancy affects later development? In light of the strong evidence that mothers' sensitivity affects attachment security, is it possible that children inherit their parents' attachment securities? Many developmentalists agree that establishing a secure attachment relationship is crucial not only to infants' emotional well-being but also to the quality of their future relationships (Schoenmaker et al., 2015; Zeanah et al., 2009). Supporting this idea, early studies conducted by Alan Sroufe and his colleagues reported that when children who are judged to be securely attached at 12 months of age are assessed at age 3½, they are more curious, play more effectively with their age-mates, and have better relationships with their preschool teachers than do children who were insecurely attached as infants (Erikson, Sroufe, & Egeland, 1985; Frankel & Bates, 1990; Sroufe & Fleeson, 1986). In follow-up observations conducted when the children were 10 years old, and then again when they were 15, researchers found that those who had been assessed as securely attached in infancy were more skillful socially, had more friends, displayed more self-confidence, and were more open in expressing their feelings (for a summary, see Raby et al., 2015).

Researchers who see patterns of attachment as tending to remain consistent throughout development emphasize that such stability depends on one key

In The Field

Children with Reactive Attachment Disorder

Name: LARK ESHLEMAN

Education: B.A. in English and American literature, Utica College of Syracuse University; M.A. in library science, State University of New York at Geneseo; M.A. in psychology, Millersville University; Ph.D. in clinical psychology, Union Institute (also certified in school psychology and play therapy)

Current Position: Psychotherapist; developed Synergistic Trauma and Attachment Therapy, Pennsylvania

Career Objectives: Help children and families recover from the effects of early childhood trauma, including abuse, neglect, and family upheaval

LARK ESHLEMAN IS A CHILD AND ADOLESCENT psychotherapist specializing in the treatment of children who have experienced early emotional traumas such as exposure to violence, abuse, neglect, or parental separation and loss (Eshleman, 2003). Such children are at risk for reactive attachment disorder (RAD), a severe psychological disorder linked to a disruption in the development of the parent–child attachment relationship (Humphreys, Nelson, Fox, & Zeanah, 2017; Zeanah & Gleason, 2015).

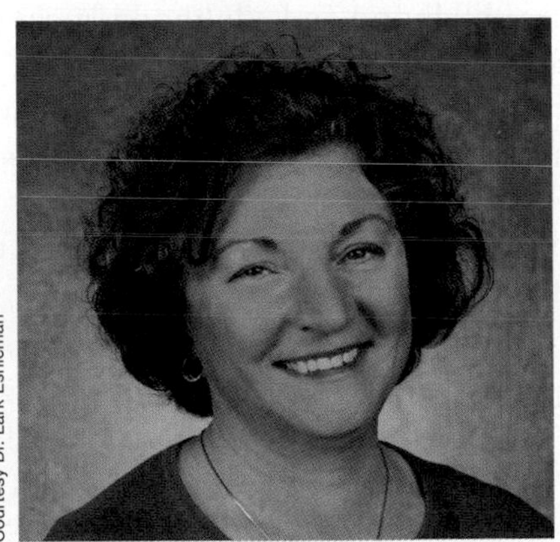

Courtesy Dr. Lark Eshleman

Lark Eshleman

According to the *Diagnostic and Statistical Manual of Mental Disorders (DSM-5)*, the main feature of RAD is extremely inappropriate social relating that takes one of two forms: (1) The child engages in indiscriminate and excessive efforts to receive comfort and affection from any adult, even strangers, or (2) the child is extremely reluctant to seek or accept comfort and affection, especially when distressed, even from familiar adults. Other symptoms used to diagnose this rare disorder include onset before 5 years of age, a history of significant neglect, and lack of a reliable, consistent primary caregiver (Humphreys et al., 2017). Barbara Braun-McDonald, another attachment therapist, explains that "if a baby cries and he's ignored, and it happens over and over again, at some level he begins to tell himself, 'I can't trust that the people who are in charge are going to meet my needs'" (in Meltz, 2004, p. H1).

Eshleman came into the international spotlight for her therapeutic interventions with orphans in Croatia and her advice to parents seeking to adopt them (Eshleman, 2003). Not surprisingly, children who have spent considerable time in orphanages, especially those of poor quality, are at special risk for developing RAD. Significantly, therapies that are specifically linked to attachment theory have been found most effective in healing children whose attachment process has been seriously disrupted by various emotional traumas. As concluded in a major review of research into various therapies for RAD,

> Services for children described as having attachment problems should be founded on the core principles suggested by attachment theory, including caregiver and environmental stability, child safety, patience, sensitivity, consistency, and nurturance. (Chaffin et al., 2006, p. 87.)

Especially important to therapeutic success, according to the review, is to focus on the parent–child relationship rather than on the individual child's pathology, and to teach positive parenting skills that promote a secure attachment relationship between parent and child.

factor—how well the individual's *internal working model* functions over time and across situations (Grossmann, Grossmann, Kindler, & Zimmermann, 2008; Waters et al., 2015). As discussed earlier Bowlby (1969) proposed that on the basis of their interactions with their primary caregiver, infants build up an internal working model of the way to behave toward other people. Enlarging on Bowlby's idea, Inge Bretherton (2005) argues that internal working models provide expectations about how others are likely to respond to the child's own behavior and emotional expressions—whether the child will be comforted or rejected, and whether others will be emotionally available to respond when the child expresses his or her feelings. These expectations influence how the child acts in new situations and with new people. The child's actions, in turn, can provoke either positive or negative reactions in others, which can confirm the child's expectations and perpetuate patterns of behavior. Changing a child's internal working model is not accomplished easily. Indeed, recent research suggests that the development of attachment may impact brain development in ways that affect behavior in adulthood (Swain et al., 2014). One study focused on low-income males whose behavior as infants in the Strange Situation was judged to be insecure and disorganized (Quevedo et al., 2017). As 20-year-old young men, these individuals were presented with gambling tasks in which they had to guess whether a number would be greater or smaller than 5, and they were told that their performance would determine how much money they would receive. Compared to a control group of securely attached males, the young men with a history of insecure attachment showed higher levels of activation in emotion-related areas of the brain (the limbic system; see Chapters 11 and 14), suggesting more intense emotional responses to the tasks.

In addition to asking about the stability of attachment across the individual's development, researchers are also interested in whether attachment patterns can be transmitted from parents to children (Waters et al., 2015; Raby et al., 2015). In general, there is little evidence that the mother's attachment pattern predicts attachment development in her children, except in the case of disorganized attachment. For example, using data collected as a part of an ongoing 37-year longitudinal study of the development of children born into poverty (Sroufe, Egeland, Carlson, & Collins, 2005), researchers found that children whose mothers had histories of disorganized attachment were significantly more likely to form disorganized attachments themselves, compared to children whose mothers had no history of attachment disorganization (Raby et al., 2015). You might wonder why disorganized attachment has such strong intergenerational effects. Researchers suggest that it is likely due to frightening or chaotic caregiving, disturbances that are especially harmful to the child's later development and known to be associated with a number of mental health problems in later childhood and adulthood, including personality disorders (Carlson, Egeland, & Sroufe, 2009).

With the exception of disorganized attachment, which tends to show fairly persistent effects across development and generations, most research finds only modest evidence of attachment stability over time. For this and other reasons that we discuss below, an increasing number of researchers have been drawn to emic approaches that explore the cultural contexts of the infant's first emotional relationships.

First Relationships and Culture

At present there is sharp disagreement among developmentalists concerning the extent to which the process of attachment is influenced by cultural variations—even whether attachment theory and the Strange Situation procedure are appropriate for understanding the development of first relationships outside middle-class families in the United States and Western Europe (Harkness, 2015; Quinn & Mageo, 2013). At one extreme are those who argue that attachment is a universal, biologically driven feature of human development and that the emotionally sensitive interactions that nourish attachment are similar across cultures (Posada et al., 2016). At the other extreme are those who claim that attachment theory and research are culturally biased and that the development of early relationships varies substantially according to the cultural beliefs and parenting practices that govern interactions between babies and their social partners (Otto & Keller, 2014). Taking a middle ground are those who suggest that there are both universal and culturally specific characteristics of attachment (Gaskins, 2013).

A common criticism of attachment theory and research is the emphasis on infants' relationships with their mothers, when in fact babies throughout the world spend considerable time with fathers and other significant caregivers. In many industrialized countries, fathers are becoming more deeply involved as parents, often for social and economic reasons associated with mothers working outside the home. Fathers' sensitivity to their children's needs is increasingly recognized as important to children's well-being, attachment, and emotional development (Davidov & Grusec, 2006; Hawkins et al., 2008; Lamb, 2010; Ryan, Martin, & Brooks-Gunn, 2006; Stoltz, Barber, & Olsen, 2005). Indeed, the infants of fathers with relatively poor parenting skills develop insecure patterns of attachment to them, as is found in the case of insensitive mothering (Brown, Schoppe-Sullivan, Mangelsdorf, & Neff, 2010). Of course, mothers and fathers are not the only people with whom infants form attachments. Babies also form attachments with nonparental caregivers, including siblings, day-care providers, teachers, and grandparents. An analysis that combined results from 40 separate studies showed that 42 percent of children were securely attached to their day-care providers. Secure attachments between children and day-care providers were more likely to develop in home-based care than in center-based care and were more prevalent among girls than among boys (Ahnert, Pinquart, & Lamb, 2006).

© Mary Kate Denny / PhotoEdit — All rights reserved.

This child is clearly distressed at the prospect of being separated from her father when he goes to work.

A second, related criticism of the traditional attachment approach is its focus on exclusive, one-to-one relationships (infant–mother, infant–father, infant–grandparent), when many babies receive care from a network of caregivers in relationships that are better described as one-to-many. It is not uncommon for families in the United States, particularly those living close to or below the poverty line, to have caregiving systems that include networks of adults, such as grandparents and other kin, to whom children become attached. (We will return to this topic in Chapter 10.) In some societies, such as that of the Aka of the Central African Republic, the involvement of multiple caregivers is extensive from birth onward. One study found that more than 50 percent of Aka infants were breast-fed not only by their mothers but by other women, that other women provided approximately 25 percent of all care to infants, and that each infant had contact with approximately 20 caregivers each day (Meehan & Hawks, 2013). Furthermore, the engagement of multiple caregivers increased dramatically over time, especially after weaning (at age 2 to 3 years), when mothers frequently left camp in order to gather food. The attachment behaviors of Aka infants were highly distinct from the patterns described in traditional attachment theory. For instance, the infants formed attachments with an average of 6 caregivers in addition to their mothers, were not particularly distressed at being separated from their mothers when they left to gather food, and did not immediately seek contact with their mothers when the women returned to camp.

The attachment behaviors of Aka infants are entirely consistent with a cultural context that includes a one-to-many network of care. Importantly, these cultural contexts often emphasize the child's relationship to a broader community rather than as a member of a nuclear family. In several such cultures, including those of Samoa, Sri Lanka, the Murik of New Guinea, and Israeli kibbutzim, children are not only cared for by a complex network of caregivers but may live in different households during the course of childhood, according to the desires of community members or their own personal choices (Barlow, 2013; Chapin, 2013; Mageo, 2013). Overall, research with other cultural groups underscores the diversity of infant care worldwide (Broesch et al., 2016). It also suggests that traditional attachment theory and research may have limited application to cultures in which exclusive relationships with a single caregiver (usually the mother) predominate (see Figure 6.8, p. 216).

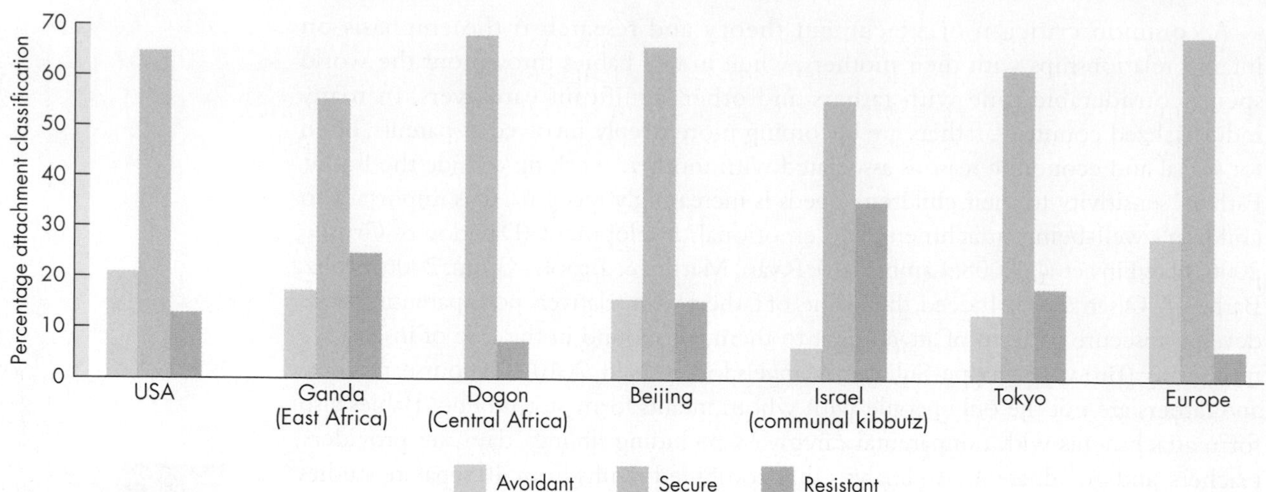

FIGURE 6.8 Secure attachments predominate in many cultures, but the percentage of different forms of insecure attachments varies (as summarized in Van IJzendoorn & Sagi-Schwartz, 2008). However, some developmentalists argue that attachment theory and the Strange Situation procedure are biased toward cultures in which exclusive relationships with a single caregiver predominate.

APPLY > CONNECT > DISCUSS

Review the descriptions of the different patterns of attachment on pages 209–210. Note that each refers to the percentages of white, middle-class children who exhibited the pattern in early research conducted by Ainsworth and her colleagues. Based on what you have learned about potential cultural bias in attachment theory and the Strange Situation, do you think there also might be bias of a socioeconomic nature? That is, do you expect children from non-middle-class backgrounds to show similar attachment patterns to their middle-class counterparts? Explain.

LEARNING OUTCOMES

Explain how secondary intersubjectivity affects the way infants and their caregivers interact.

Identify forms of communication, such as social referencing, used between infants and caregivers when infants encounter something unfamiliar.

The Changing Nature of Communication

Seated in his stroller, 12-month-old Juan is enjoying a beautiful spring day with his father. As they stroll through the park, Juan points excitedly and exclaims, "Da!" at a dog, at a bicycle, at another baby in a stroller, each time looking over his shoulder and smiling at his father, who smiles back and says, "Yes, that's a doggie [bicycle, baby]." They come across a small crowd gathered around street performers who are dressed in colorful costumes, entertaining the audience with jokes, juggling, and antics. The performers invite the children to join them—throwing or catching balls, chasing each other around, acting like various animals, and just being generally silly. Juan seems to be enjoying the spectacle—until one of the performers slinks toward him on hands and knees, like a stalking lion. First, Juan leans back into his stroller, stares warily, and looks up at his father, who is scowling at the insensitive performer. The lion-man continues his approach and begins to make growling vocalizations. Then, obviously frightened, Juan bursts into tears and raises his arms toward his father, who picks him up and gives him a reassuring hug.

As you know from our earlier discussions, by 3 months of age, infants and their caregivers are jointly experiencing pleasure in simple interactions. This early form of communication, which we referred to as *primary intersubjectivity*, is limited to direct face-to-face interactions and is supported mainly by the efforts of the caregiver (Trevarthen, 2015). Between 9 and 12 months of age, babies begin to interact with their caregivers in a new and more complex way. This new form of connection is referred to as **secondary intersubjectivity** because now the infant and the caregiver communicate with each other about the world that extends beyond themselves, such as their pleasure in seeing a passing puppy or their concern over an approaching threat.

secondary intersubjectivity A form of interaction between infant and caregiver, emerging at about 9–12 months, with communication and emotional sharing focused not just on the interaction but on the world beyond.

The emergence of secondary intersubjectivity marks a major turning point in the infant's development because it brings a new dimension to the communicative process, serving as a foundation for sharing one's thoughts, feelings, and expectations about the world.

Rick Gomez / Masterfile

The pleasure this child and mother take in their interaction using a fork is an example of the kind of emotional sharing referred to as secondary intersubjectivity.

Social Referencing

An important form of secondary intersubjectivity in infancy is *social referencing*, in which, as we explained in Chapter 5, babies look to their caregiver for an indication of how they should feel and act when they encounter some unfamiliar object or event. (Juan's looking up at his father as the street performer slunk toward him was a clear instance of social referencing.) Social referencing becomes a common means of communication as soon as babies begin to move about on their own (Campos et al., 2000; Stenberg, 2017). When approaching an unfamiliar object, for example, if they notice that their caregiver is looking at the object and appears to be concerned, they typically hesitate and become wary. If, instead, the caregiver smiles and looks pleased, they continue their approach. (Perhaps if Juan's father had not been scowling at the advancing performer, Juan would not have burst into tears.) As they grow more experienced, babies become increasingly sensitive to where their caregiver is looking and even check back to see how the caregiver responds to an object after they have made their own appraisal of it (Stenberg, 2017; Striano & Rochat, 2000). Babies also look to caregivers to help them decide whether someone acting silly is being funny or simply strange (Mireault et al., 2015).

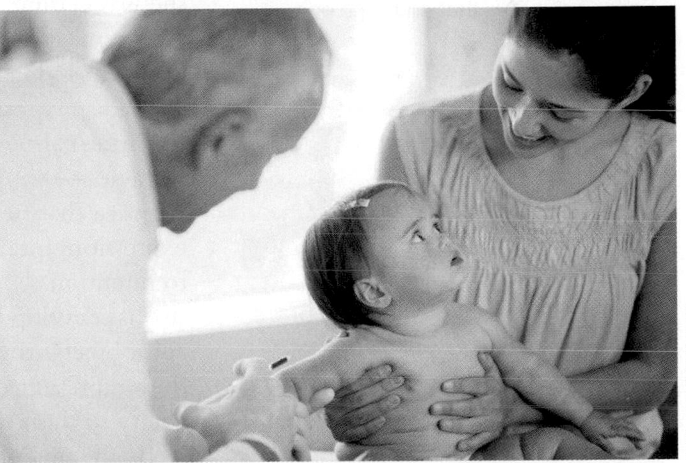

FatCamera/Getty Images

In a wonderful illustration of social referencing, this baby checks in with Mom before deciding how to react to the medical exam. Mom's reassuring smile will greatly influence how the baby interprets and emotionally responds to this unusual event.

Between approximately 9 and 12 months of age, infants' contributions to secondary intersubjectivity become more sophisticated. For example, Tricia Striano and Philippe Rochat (2000) compared the way 7- and 10-month-old infants in a laboratory playroom reacted to the appearance of a remote-controlled toy dog that barked intermittently. An experimenter in the room was instructed either to look at the infant when the dog barked or to look away. The 7-month-olds kept checking with the adult even if the adult ignored them, while the 10-month-olds immediately stopped checking with the adult unless the adult looked at them when the dog barked. Striano and Rochat believe that the 10-month-olds were beginning to engage in "selective social referencing" because the infants knew they could obtain information from the adult only if the adult was attending to them.

Following a Caregiver's Signs of Interest

Another way infants communicate with their caregivers is by following a caregiver's gaze to see what the caregiver is looking at and to look at what the caregiver is pointing at (Rohlfing, Longo, & Bertenthal, 2012). If a mother and her 5-month-old are looking at each other and the mother suddenly looks to one side, the infant will not follow the mother's gaze. And if the mother points at some object in the room, the baby is more likely to stare at the end of the mother's finger than to look in the direction in which the mother is pointing. A few months later, in similarly simple circumstances, the infant will look in the direction of the mother's gazing or pointing (Butterworth, 2001).

Like social referencing, an infant's abilities to use a caregiver's pointing and gazing strengthen and provide more reliable means of communication after their initial appearance between 7 and 9 months of age (Liebal, Behne, Carpenter, & Tomasello,

2009). A baby's ability to look in the direction of a caregiver's gaze is well established by 12 to 14 months of age, while attention to pointing begins to dominate around 2 years of age (Paulus & Fikkert, 2014). As we will discuss in Chapter 7, the ability to follow a caregiver's signs of interest has significant implications for the child's language development.

APPLY > CONNECT > DISCUSS

Social referencing emerges during infancy and persists throughout life. Give examples of events that might prompt social referencing in a 2-year-old, a 6-year-old, and a 15-year-old. What similarities are there across your three events? What differences are there? How might social referencing have important biocultural implications?

LEARNING OUTCOMES

Point out experiences that contribute to an infant's emerging sense of self.

Explain the function of self-conscious emotions in infant development.

Define behaviors that mark the end of infancy.

A Sense of Self

Strapped securely in the grocery-cart seat with a bit of a pout on her face, 10-month-old Nadia watched her mother, who had turned away from her to read the nutritional content of a cereal box. All of a sudden, Nadia let out a piercing, heart-stopping screech that could be heard throughout the store. Everyone in the cereal aisle looked at her—and Nadia looked back at them, grinning at the attention she was getting. For weeks afterward, Nadia shrieked like that whenever she wanted attention, and she acted happy and self-satisfied when she got it. It was as though she were saying, "Look at me!"

Nadia's emotional life has changed considerably since she was a newborn, when her internal feeling states seemed to trigger certain facial and other nonverbal behaviors—smiles, frowns, agitated crying, and so forth. At 10 months of age, she is aware that her emotional expressions affect those around her, and she uses her expressions intentionally to elicit predictable social responses. Clearly, Nadia's ability to intentionally draw attention her way and her delight in showing off indicate that she has developed a sense of self—that is, of being an entity separate from the people and objects around her. However, as vivid as her expressions of self-awareness are, they represent only the early phase of a long process in the development of the ability to think about oneself.

By the time they are 6 months old, infants have acquired a great deal of experience interacting with objects and other people and have developed an intuitive sense of themselves as a result (Rochat, 2009). The ability to locomote provides them with still further experience of their separateness from their caregivers. Having a more explicit sense of self as separate from others promotes new forms of social relations. Infants at that age begin to learn that they can share their own experiences and compare their own reactions with those of others, especially through their emerging use of language (Trevarthen, 1998).

Self-Recognition

Consciousness of self has been proposed to be among the major characteristics distinguishing human beings from other species. This is an interesting idea, but finding a way to demonstrate it convincingly has been problematic.

Several decades ago, Gordon Gallup (1970) argued that a form of self-consciousness is apparent in the ability to recognize one's image in a mirror. He reported an ingenious series of experiments using mirrors with chimpanzees, experiments that have since been replicated with chimpanzees and also used with children. Gallup showed adolescent wild-born chimpanzees their images in a full-length mirror. At first the chimps acted as if they were looking at another animal: They threatened, vocalized, and made conciliatory gestures to the "intruder." After a few days, however, they began to use the mirror to explore themselves; for example, they picked bits of food from their faces, which they could see only in the mirror.

To make certain of the meaning of his finding, Gallup anesthetized several chimps and painted a bright, odorless dye above one eye and on the ear on the opposite side of the head. When they woke up and looked in the mirror, the chimps immediately began to touch their faces and ears where the mirror showed the appearance of spots. Gallup concluded that they had learned to recognize themselves in the mirror.

This kind of self-recognition is by no means universal among primate species. Gallup gave a wild-born macaque monkey more than 2,400 hours of exposure to a mirror over a 5-month period, but the monkey never showed any sign of self-recognition. The problem was not simply dealing with the mirror image because the monkey quickly learned to find food that it could see only in the mirror. The monkey simply could not recognize itself.

Gallup's procedure has been used in modified form with human infants between the ages of 3 and 24 months (Bard et al., 2006; Inoue-Nakamura, 2001; Rochat & Striano, 2002). The results indicate that there are several stages in learning to recognize oneself in a mirror. When held up to a mirror in the first few months of life, infants show little interest in their own image or in anyone else's. At about 3 months of age, however, babies begin to engage in long bouts of cooing and smiling at and reaching for their images. An interesting question is whether infants at this age respond differently to their own mirror image than they do to images of other babies, which would suggest that they are able to distinguish between self and other. According to a study conducted by Tiffany Field, the answer is yes. Specifically, while the infants tended to look longer at themselves in a mirror than at images of other babies, they tended to smile and vocalize more at the images of other babies (Field, 1979). One interpretation of this intriguing finding is that the infants recognize and find their own images interesting, and they behave as if images of other babies may be potential interactive partners.

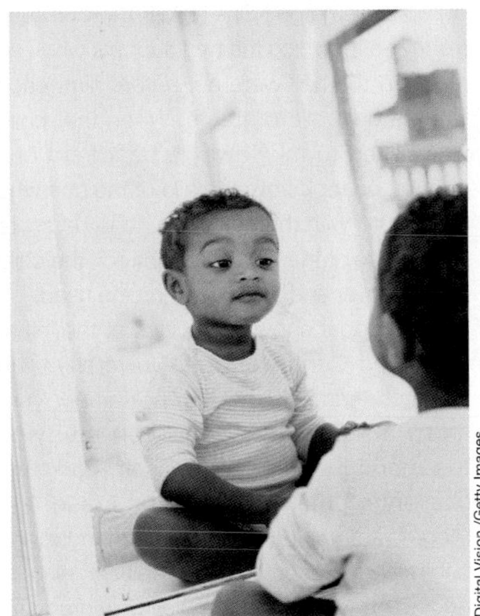
Digital Vision./Getty Images

This baby seems to take great interest in his own image in the mirror. Developmentalists use infant reactions to mirror images as a way to study the emerging understanding of self.

Some researchers have argued that infants' interest in their own mirror images may be due not to self-recognition but, rather, to their fascination with the fact that the movement of the image is exactly contingent with their own movements (Sugiura, et al., 2015). In an effort to explore this possibility, Philippe Rochat and Tricia Striano showed 4- and 9-month-olds a live video image of either themselves or an adult who mimicked their every move (Rochat & Striano, 2002). Their results indicated that even the 4-month-olds discriminated between their own images and those of the mimicking adult. While this suggests some early awareness of self/other discrimination, even 10-month-olds do not react to the sight of a red spot that has been surreptitiously applied to their nose. Not until children are 18 months old will they reach for their own nose or ask, "What's that?" when they see the red spot. Within a few months, whenever someone points to the child's mirror image and asks, "Who's that?" the child will be able to answer, unhesitatingly, "Me" (Rochat, 2015).

The Emergence of Self-Conscious Emotions

The sense of self that arises during infancy gives rise to a new class of emotions, including embarrassment, pride, shame, guilt, and envy (Reddy, 2005) (see the box "Now Trending in Research: The Moral Life of Babies," p. 220). These new emotions are referred to as **self-conscious emotions** because they depend on babies' newly acquired abilities to recognize, talk about, and think about themselves in relation to other people (Lewis, 2005; Thompson & Newton, 2010). That is, whereas basic emotions (joy, fear, anger, surprise, sadness, and disgust) bear a simple and direct relationship to the events that elicit them, self-conscious emotions involve complex combinations of cognition and emotion and cannot appear until children are able to think about and evaluate themselves in relationship to other people and the goals

self-conscious emotions Emotions such as embarrassment, pride, shame, guilt, and envy, which emerge after 8 months with infants' growing consciousness of self.

Now TRENDING in RESEARCH

The Moral Life of Babies

Imagine a show in which three puppets are playing a turn-taking game: One puppet rolls a ball to another, who rolls it back; then the first puppet rolls the ball again to a different puppet. After catching the ball, instead of rolling it back, as you might reasonably expect, the third puppet runs off with it. As an adult, you would likely consider this puppet to be behaving badly. But when do such feelings of injustice emerge? One child witnessed such a show, after which the two puppets who had received the ball were set before him, each with its own pile of treats. When that child was asked to take away a treat from one puppet, he took from the pile of the one who had run off with the ball. Then, to underscore his outrage at the puppet's behavior, the child reached over and smacked it on the head.

The puppet show took place at the Infant Cognition Center at Yale University. The research team—Kiley Hamlin, Karen Wynn, and Paul Bloom—have been studying the moral life of babies. Their work has challenged the view, held by Freud and Piaget, among others, that human beings begin life as amoral, largely selfish animals. According to this view, babies only gradually learn about right and wrong, and they only gradually develop emotions such as empathy, shame, and guilt that are associated with understanding injustice and behaving in ways that society deems are morally appropriate.

A growing body of evidence, however, suggests that humans do have a rudimentary moral sense from the very start of life (Holvoet, Scola, Arciszewski, & Picard, 2016; Thompson & Newton, 2010). A series of studies conducted by the research team at Yale bears this out. In one study, babies watched as geometric objects on a miniature stage acted out "helping" or "hindering" behaviors in various situations. (The objects were manipulated by behind-the-scenes experimenters.) For example, the babies saw a red ball trying to go up a hill. Sometimes, a yellow square got behind the ball and helpfully pushed it upwards; but other times, a green triangle got in front of the ball and pushed it back down the hill. After the babies saw each event, the experimenter presented them with the helper (yellow triangle) and the hinderer (green square) on a tray to see which object they reached for and presumably preferred. Both 6- and 10-month-old babies were overwhelming in their preference for the helper over the hinderer.

Infants' responsiveness to the "nice" and "naughty" behavior of others was assessed in another set of studies designed as puppet shows. In one, a puppet struggled to open a box. The puppet succeeded in getting the lid partly off, but then it would fall back down. In some scenes, another puppet would help out by grabbing the lid and pulling it off the box. In other scenes, another puppet would jump on the box and slam it shut. The researchers found that babies as young as 5 months of age preferred the nice puppet to the mean one. In a fascinating extension of the study, 8-month-olds saw the original helping/hindering scenes and then witnessed two other puppets either reward or punish the nice one and the mean one. The results were striking. The babies clearly preferred the puppet who rewarded the nice puppet. This finding isn't particularly surprising, however, since it had already been determined that babies like those who are helpful to others. What was especially interesting is how the babies responded when they watched the mean puppet being rewarded or punished. In this instance, they preferred the puppet who punished bad behavior over the one who rewarded it.

Issouf Sanogo/AFP/Getty Images

In addition to our own species, other highly social primate species have an apparent capacity for moral behavior, empathy, and concerns for others, as amply demonstrated by these bonobos.

Evidence of a moral sense in young babies leads some developmentalists to conclude that this capacity is deeply rooted in our species, as it is in other species that depend for survival on social relationships and community. Other developmentalists point out, however, that regardless of its biological foundation, infants are engaged in complex social and cultural systems that support the human ability to understand and act with compassion toward others and to recognize and remedy harm and injustice (Carpendale & Hammond, 2016).

(Information from Bloom, 2010.)

(a)

(b)

Reprinted by permission from Macmillan Publishers Ltd: NATURE, 450, 557–559. J. Kiley Hamlin, Karen Wynn & Paul Bloom. Social evaluation by preverbal infants. (22 November 2007) doi:10.1038/nature06288

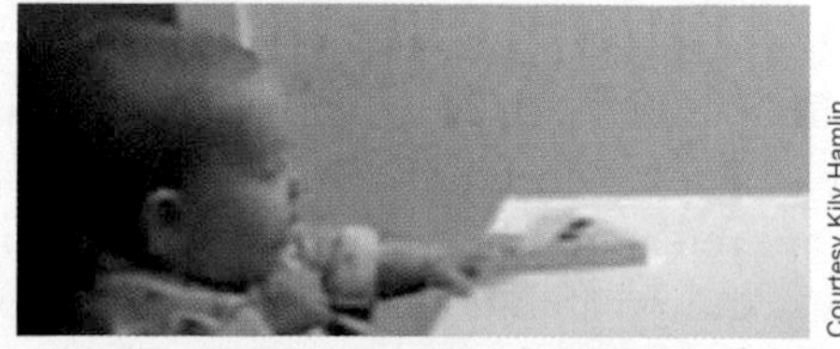

Courtesy Kily Hamlin

To explore early moral understanding, researchers presented young babies, like the baby you see in the photo to the right, with different scenarios in which geometric shapes seemed to be helping or hindering each other's efforts. This particular sequence includes a "helping" scenario, in which a triangle assists a circle in getting up a hill (a), and a "hindering" scenario, in which a square gets in the way of a circle and pushes it back down the hill (b). When presented with the geometric shapes, the vast majority of infants reached for the helpers.

they desire. To feel self-conscious emotions such as pride or embarrassment, babies must be able to consider their own behavior in relationship to how they believe other people are judging or evaluating them. Indeed, as you might expect, based on previous discussions of emotional and brain developments, self-conscious emotions appear to involve activation of the prefrontal cortex, which is associated with self-regulation and higher cognitive functions; basic emotions, in contrast, involve activation of more "primitive" areas of the brain (the limbic system; see Chapters 11 and 14) that develop earlier than the prefrontal cortex (Gilead, Katzir, Eval, & Liberman, 2016).

The baby's sense of self as a distinct person is well under way by the end of infancy. In just 2 short years, a number of developments come together to form the beginnings of a self-system: children's increasing self-awareness; their growing sensitivity to adults' standards of what is good; their new awareness of their own ability to live up to those standards; an ability to create plans of their own and judge them against adult standards; and a strong desire to see that their plans are not thwarted by adults—all of which is supported by substantial developments taking place in the brain and increasingly complex interactions with caregivers. One of the most significant consequences of the developing self is a growing sense of autonomy that Erikson (1963) says normally characterizes late infancy.

APPLY > CONNECT > DISCUSS

In what respects might the development of a sense of self contribute to the development of emotion regulation?

Developing Trust and Autonomy

LEARNING OUTCOME

Distinguish between the first two stages into which Erikon divided infancy.

Much of what we have presented in this chapter is consistent with Erik Erikson's picture of infancy. As indicated in Chapter 1 (Table 1.2, p. 18), Erikson divided infancy into two main stages. The first of these he called the stage of **basic trust versus mistrust**, in which the infant determines whether the world is a safe place to explore and discover or an unpredictable and threatening one, and whether the people in the world are reliable, loving, and kind or insensitive and hurtful. Consistent with much of the research we have reviewed, Erikson believed that warm and responsive parenting fosters infants' development of trust and that unresponsive, insensitive, or disorganized parenting fosters a mistrust of people and a wariness about exploring the world.

basic trust versus mistrust For Erikson, the first stage of infancy, during which children either come to trust others as reliable and kind and to regard the world as safe or come to mistrust others as insensitive and hurtful and to regard the world as unpredictable and threatening.

autonomy versus shame and doubt For Erikson, the second stage of infancy, during which children develop a sense of themselves as competent to accomplish tasks or as not competent.

During the 2nd year, babies enter the stage of **autonomy versus shame and doubt**, during which they develop a sense of themselves as competent or not competent to solve problems and accomplish tasks. In this important period of self-assertion, babies want to do things themselves, often resisting the assistance or control of another. Parents frequently hear the refrain "No! I do it!" (remember Jin Yu from beginning of the chapter, who scolded her parents in Chinese when they tried to keep her from handling dangerous objects). According to Erikson, when parents structure their children's environments in ways that foster success in their early, self-initiated efforts at mastery and control, babies develop confidence in their own abilities and seek challenges. On the other hand, when parents are overly controlling or fail to create contexts in which their children can demonstrate competence, a sense of doubt and shame may take hold and dampen the children's efforts to achieve.

APPLY > CONNECT > DISCUSS

Imagine that you are responsible for the infant care provided at a child-care center. Using insights from Erikson's theory, make a list of points you would cover in a training session for newly hired infant-care providers.

LEARNING OUTCOME

Assess how biological and sociocultural processes help forge social and emotional ties between infants and caregivers.

Looking Ahead

Infancy is a time during which babies and caregivers forge social and emotional ties that provide a foundation for infants' exploring and learning about the world. Consistent with a biocultural perspective, both biological and sociocultural processes contribute to the creation of these ties. On the biological side, evolution and brain development provide infants not only with certain capacities for sensitivity to the emotions of others, but also with the ability to express and share their emotions, especially through facial expressions.

On the sociocultural side, the infant's emerging emotional and social development and expressiveness are significantly shaped by the nature of early interactions. In typical Western cultures, including the United States and Europe, close, one-to-one relationships are emphasized; whereas in other cultures, caregiving networks foster the development of one-to-many relationships. In either case, adults and caregivers lay a foundation for the child that promotes engagement with others and with the community.

In the following chapter, you will learn about how emotional development in infancy both contributes to and is affected by the infant's developing ability to use and understand language. Language opens entirely new avenues for expressing one's self—one's desires, feelings, and growing independence and autonomy.

INSIGHT AND INTEGRATION

Consider the concept of agency (a condition in which exerted power achieves an end). How is agency apparent in a child's emotional development and developing attachment?

Summary

The Nature of Infant Emotions and Emotional Expressions

- Emotion can be defined as a feeling state that includes distinctive physiological responses, can be expressed to others, involves a cognitive appraisal, and can motivate action. Through emotion regulation, people modulate and control emotions.
- Certain basic emotions—joy, fear, anger, surprise, sadness, and disgust—appear to be universal and present from birth or early infancy. Several theories explain basic emotions in infancy:
  - The differential emotions theory argues that at birth or soon after, infants have distinct basic emotions similar to those of adults.
  - The etic approach focuses on the universal aspects of emotions, whereas the etic approach focuses on the cultural diversity of emotions.
  - Theorists who see infants' emotions and emotional expressions as ontogenetic adaptations believe these evolved because they contribute to babies' development and well-being by eliciting care and protection.
- Through primary intersubjectivity, which involves face-to-face interaction, infants and their caregivers share emotions that focus on the interaction itself. In the laboratory, disruption of the synchrony between infants and their interactive partners results in negative emotional responses in infants. Maternal depression may prove an obstacle to intersubjectivity since mothers may be less responsive to babies' emotional cues and infants may disengage from stressful, unresponsive interactions.
- Pouting, most common when an infant is beginning to be upset, may have evolved as a form of emotion regulation to maintain the intersubjectivity between infant and caregiver that crying would disrupt.
- Mirror neurons, which evidently fire in the same way when one is observing an action as when one is performing it, may register the intentions and emotions of others as if they were happening to the observer.

The First Emotional Relationships

- Attachment is an emotional bond between children and their caregivers, which begins to develop at around 7 to 9 months of age. According to Freud's drive-reduction explanation, attachment to the mother originates from her satisfying the infant's need for nourishment. Experiments with monkeys have failed to support Freud's explanation but do support John Bowlby's ethological explanation, according to which attachment arises from the infant's coming to feel that the mother is a source of security and a safe base from which to explore the world.
- Bowlby described attachment as developing in four phases, with infants ultimately being able to retain feelings of security

during separations and developing an internal working model for relationships.

- Using a procedure called the Strange Situation, Mary Ainsworth and other researchers found that the infant's attachment relationship could be one of secure attachment—with a healthy balance between wanting close contact with the mother and wanting to explore—or any of three types of insecure attachment—avoidant, resistant, or disorganized.
- Variations in patterns of attachment may relate to differences in several contexts:
  - Parental sensitivity correlates with secure attachment, while maternal depression and abusive or extremely insensitive caregiving appear to be linked to insecure attachment patterns.
  - Standard procedures for measuring patterns of attachment may not be valid in some cultures.
  - Establishing a secure attachment relationship may be crucial to later relationships since there appears to be continuity of attachment status from infancy to adulthood, particularly if the internal working model developed remains unchanged.

The Changing Nature of Communication

- Toward the end of the 1st year, with the emergence of secondary intersubjectivity, infants and their caregivers interact and share emotions about the world beyond themselves.
- Important forms of communication include social referencing, in which babies look to their caregiver for an indication of how to feel and act on encountering something unfamiliar, and gaze-following and pointing.

A Sense of Self

- By about age 6 months, experience interacting with objects and people, along with emerging abilities to locomote and to use language, contributes to the infant's new sense of self. Infants' ability to recognize themselves in a mirror emerges gradually and is clearly evident at around 18 months. Children's two-word utterances reflect their ability to see themselves as agents.
- The emergence of a sense of self gives rise to the self-conscious emotions—for example, embarrassment, pride, shame, guilt, and envy—which require thinking about and evaluating oneself in relationship to other people and their standards.
- The end of infancy is marked by patterns of behavior reflecting a sense of self and a new independence.

Developing Trust and Autonomy

- In the first of the two stages into which Erikson divided infancy—that is, basic trust versus mistrust—infants may come to see the world as safe for exploration and people as reliable and loving, or they may come to see the world as dangerous and people as insensitive and hurtful.
- In the second stage—autonomy versus shame or doubt—infants may acquire a sense of their ability to accomplish tasks and tackle challenges, or they may come to doubt their ability and feel shame.

Looking Ahead

- During infancy, babies and caregivers forge social and emotional ties that give infants a foundation for exploring the world. Consistent with a biocultural perspective, both biological and sociocultural processes contribute to the creation of these ties. On the side of biology, evolution provides infants with certain capacities to express and share their emotions through a variety of facial expressions and behaviors and to form early emotional relationships with social partners. The infant is also biologically endowed with a brain that seems particularly sensitive to the social and emotional behaviors of others.
- On the sociocultural side, the infant's emerging emotional and social development and expressiveness are significantly shaped by the nature of early interactions. Social interactions that are well organized and responsive to the baby's cues seem essential to healthy development and to nurturing the baby's sense of trust that the world is a safe place to explore. Furthermore, because early interactions are influenced by the values and patterns of life in the infant's culture, they serve to draw the child into the lives of others, laying the foundation for the child's engaged participation in the community.
- As babies become more mobile and able to explore their environments more actively, a new means of interaction—one that will allow babies and caregivers to communicate at a distance—becomes an urgent necessity. That new means, of course, is language. As you will learn in the next chapter, language fundamentally changes the child's relationship to the world. It enables entirely new ways of expressing and sharing thoughts, feelings, and desires. Language development also expands our insight into the intricate relationship between biology and culture.

Key Terms

emotion, p. 199
emotion regulation, p. 199
etic approach, p. 200
emic approach, p. 200
basic emotions, p. 200
differential emotions theory, p. 200
ontogenetic adaptations, p. 201
primary intersubjectivity, p. 202
mirror neurons, p. 205
attachment, p. 206
biological drives, p. 207
detachment, p. 208
secure base, p. 209
separation anxiety, p. 209
internal working model, p. 210
Strange Situation, p. 210
secure attachment, p. 211
avoidant attachment, p. 211
resistant attachment, p. 211
disorganized attachment, p. 211
secondary intersubjectivity, p. 216
self-conscious emotions, p. 219
basic trust versus mistrust, p. 221
autonomy versus shame and doubt, p. 221

PART THREE

Early Childhood

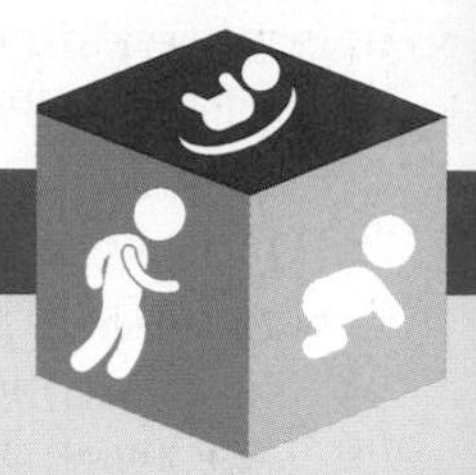

APPLICATION TO DEVELOPING LIVES PARENTING SIMULATION

Below is a list of questions you will answer in the Early Childhood simulation module. As you answer these questions, consider the impact your choice will have on the physical, cognitive, and social and emotional development of your child.

Physical Domain	Cognitive Domain	Social and Emotional Domain
• How do your child's height and weight compare to national norms? • What kinds of food will your child eat at this stage of development? • How much physical activity will you encourage for your child?	• In which stage of Piaget's stages of cognitive development is your child? • In which kind of school will you enroll your child? • Will your child demonstrate impulse control? • How will your child compare to national averages in reading, math, and language arts?	• In which kind of social environment will you place your child? • How will your child react if you and your partner split up? • How will you discipline your child during these years? • How does your stress level impact your child's emotional health?

MAJOR MILESTONES OF EARLY CHILDHOOD

	Physical Domain	Cognitive Domain	Social and Emotional Domain
What Develops . . .	• Compared to infancy, growth rates slow, while the ability to control the body increase. • Motor developments include climbing, throwing, and coloring within the lines with crayons.	• Children tend to confuse appearance and reality. • There are limitations in cause–effect reasoning. • Knowledge of physical laws such as gravity increases.	• Children develop autonomy as well as conformity to social roles and moral standards. • Ethnic identity emerges. • Ability to control thought, action, and emotion increases.
Sociocultural Contributions and Consequences . . .	• Increased access to food in developing countries may increase risk for obesity and related diseases. • Certain cultural activities impact brain development and function.	• Cultural customs and routines support developing knowledge.	• Social and cultural practices contribute to developing gender stereotypes. • Parenting practices may support developing ethnic pride. • Cultural tolerance of aggression affects children's aggression.

By the age of 2½ or 3, children are no longer infants. It is clear that they are entering early childhood—the period between ages 2½ and 6. They are losing their baby fat, their legs are growing longer and thinner, and they are moving around the world with a great deal more confidence than they did only 6 months earlier. Within a short time, they can usually ride a tricycle, control their bowels, and put on their own clothes. They can help bake cookies, gather berries, and begin to participate in cultural ceremonies and rituals—as flower girls or ring bearers at a wedding, for example. Three-year-olds can talk an adult's ears off, and they are an avid audience for an interesting story. They can be bribed with promises of a later treat, but they may try to negotiate for a treat now as well. They develop theories about everything, from where babies come from to why the moon disappears from the sky, and they constantly test their theories against the realities around them.

Dan Dalton/Getty Images

Despite their developing independence, 3-year-olds need assistance from adults and older siblings in many areas. They cannot hold a pencil properly, cross a busy road safely by themselves, or tie their shoes. They do not yet have the ability to concentrate for long on their own. As a result, they often go off on tangents in their games, drawings, and conversations. One minute a 3-year-old may be Dora the Explorer, the next minute a unicorn, and the next a little girl in a hurry to go to the toilet.

In early childhood, children still understand relatively little about the world in which they live, and they have little control over it. Thus they are prey to fears of monsters, shadows, and things that go bump in the night. They combat their awareness of being small and powerless by wishful, magical thinking that turns a little boy afraid of ghosts into a big, brave ninja who dominates the playground.

Our discussion of early childhood development spans four chapters. Chapter 7 focuses on language and its acquisition. One of our most significant cultural tools, language is the medium through which children learn about their roles in the world, about acceptable behavior, and about their culture's assumptions of how the world works. Simultaneously, language enables children to ask questions, to explain their thoughts and desires, and to make more effective demands on the people around them.

Chapter 8 examines physical and cognitive developments during early childhood. The challenge developmentalists face is to explain how children can think and behave logically at one moment and then with complete lack of logic the next. The chapter considers different explanations for the unevenness of young children's cognition.

Chapter 9 shifts attention to social development and personality formation—to children's growing sense of a distinct identity, their ability to control their actions and feelings, their ways of thinking about rules of proper behavior, and their relations with the people around them. Topics that receive particular emphasis include the acquisition of a sense of culturally acceptable gender roles and children's increasing ability to get along with one another as they learn to balance their own desires with the demands of their social group.

With these general characteristics of early childhood as background, Chapter 10 addresses the influence of various contexts on young children's development. Among these are the family, where children first learn about who they are and what adults expect of them; community settings, including day-care centers and preschools; and the media and technology, which link children's experiences in different settings and have important socializing effects.

Andy Andrews/Getty Images

CHAPTER 7

Language Acquisition

Although it has been 15 minutes since her father put her down with her "baby" and gave her a good-night kiss, the sandman has yet to arrive, and 21-month-old Emily is filling her quiet room with words:

baby no eat dinner
broccoli, soup carrots cause rice
baby eat that
baby no in night
broccoli broccoli soup carrots cabbage
no baby sleeping
then baby get sick
Emmy no eat dinner
broccoli soup cause
no baby sleeping
baby sleeping all night

One year later, Emily's bedtime monologue sounds like this:

actually it's Stephen's koala bear . . .
when Stephen wakes up I'll have to throw his koala bear in his room
'cause it's really Stephen's
as a matter of fact Stephen's
as a matter of fact it's sleeping with me now

(Information from Levy, 1989, pp. 158 and 169.)

As you can see, the first of Emily's bedtime monologues is barely interpretable. Words are missing or out of the usual order, and the monologue seems a jumble of disconnected statements with no clear meaning. The word "cause" appears in both monologues, but in the first it is next to impossible to figure out the meaning of "broccoli, soup carrots cause rice" and "broccoli soup cause." In fact, the only likely clue to what Emily might mean is the fact that many young children are not big fans of vegetables: She might be reciting her reason for not eating dinner.

By contrast, in the second monologue, Emily's words are far more grammatically organized, and they more clearly convey her meaning. The groups of words are longer and more like complete sentences now. The word "'cause" expresses a causal relationship ("'cause it's really Stephen's"), and possessive and temporal relationships are also expressed ("it's Stephen's"; "it's sleeping with me now"). It is also clear that Emily has picked up certain speech mannerisms, such as "actually" and "as a matter of fact." Although her language is not fully developed by any means, it is significantly more adultlike and easy to interpret.

The progress Emily has made in her ability to use language during the year separating the two monologues is amazing but by no means exceptional, and similar increases in language-using ability will continue for several years to come. Indeed, by her 6th birthday, Emily's mental and social life will be totally transformed by an explosive growth in the ability to comprehend and use language. Typically, developing children are estimated to learn several words a day during the preschool years, and by the time they are 6 years old, their vocabularies have grown to somewhere between 8,000 and 14,000 words (Anglin, 1993; Biemiller & Slonim, 2001). They can understand verbal instructions ("Go wash your face—and do not come back until it's clean"), chatter excitedly about the tiger they saw at the zoo, teach friends how to play a video game, or insult their siblings with a variety of colorful labels. In short, 6-year-old children are competent language users. Without this competence, they could not carry out the new cognitive tasks and social responsibilities that their society will now assign them, including acquiring the tools of their culture through formal education or other instruction.

We begin this chapter by reviewing the nature of language as a symbolic system and elaborating on the emerging foundations of linguistic communication that we discussed in earlier chapters. Next, we describe the two main keys—human biological structures and processes, and human social environments—that unlock the door to the world of language. We then trace the course of children's development in the four basic domains of language—*phonology* (sound), *semantics* (meaning), *grammar*, and *pragmatics* (the uses to which language is put). With the facts of language development in hand, we examine various theories about the processes that underlie this fundamental human capacity. Finally, we explore the unique role of language as a tool for creating and transforming reality.

1. A great number of people, including many language development experts, believe that language is uniquely human. What distinctive features permit the development of language in our species?
2. How might children's development be affected by growing up learning more than one language?

The Power and Foundations of Language

LEARNING OUTCOMES

Explain some ways in which language is considered a cultural tool.

Summarize the progress of early language development in children.

The story of Romeo and Juliet has endured for centuries. It is about a tragic love made so by the fact that one lover is a Montague and the other a Capulet, two families caught in a long and violent feud. In deep despair, Romeo challenges the idea that one's family name could stand as an obstacle to the happiness of a shared life together and asks the famous question: "What's in a name? That which we call a rose by any other name would smell as sweet." Romeo suggests that names should not matter; they are just words for things. It is the things themselves that we love or despise and that move us (as do roses) with their sweet scent and beauty. But we know better. Names, like words in general, can carry deep and complex meanings. And when names and other words are woven together into sentences and stories, like Shakespeare's *Romeo and Juliet*, they can move and inspire people for generations.

We made the point in Chapter 2 that language is a *symbolic system* of enormous scope and power (pp. 52–53). It allows communication about the past and the future; permits the expression of abstract ideas, desires, and emotions; and is one of the most significant means of preserving and passing on—and even of challenging and transforming—a culture's knowledge, values, and beliefs. We also explained that language, like other tools of culture, profoundly affects development because it organizes or *mediates* human activities, relationships, and thinking—as "Montague" and "Capulet" did for Romeo and Juliet. Alexander Luria (1981, p. 35) beautifully summarized the power human beings possess as a consequence of language:

> In the absence of words, humans would have to deal only with those things which they could perceive and manipulate directly. With the help of language, they can deal with things which they have not perceived even indirectly and with things which were part of the experience of earlier generations. Thus, the word adds another dimension to the world of humans. . . . Animals have only one world, the world of objects and situations which can be perceived by the senses. Humans have a double world.

Although many other species make a variety of communicative sounds and gestures, none has evolved a system of communication as powerful and flexible as human language (Jablonka, Ginsburg, & Dor, 2012; Lucy, 2016). Indeed, the evidence presented in previous chapters leaves little doubt that children are born predisposed to attend to language and to communicate with the people around them. At birth they show a preference for speech over other kinds of sounds and are capable of differentiating between two sounds that are distinct *phonemes* (basic sound categories) in any of the world's languages. Within a few days after birth, they can distinguish the sounds of their native language from those of a foreign language. Well before they are able to speak intelligibly, the range of sounds they recognize as distinct becomes narrowed to those that their native language treats as distinct phonemes (Kuhl et al., 2006; Luo & Baillargeon, 2005).

But to some extent, all languages are "foreign languages" to young infants. Think about what it is like for you to hear an unfamiliar language. Very probably, it seems like an uninterrupted sound stream; that is, it is difficult to tell where one word ends and another begins. Indeed, one of the first tasks of learning a language is to segment its sounds into distinct words and phrases, a process that is aided by infant-directed speech (IDS), or baby talk (Golinkoff, Can, Soderstrom, & Hirsh-Pasek, 2015). By 6 months of age, they begin to show the first signs of comprehending words for highly familiar objects, such as "Mommy" or "Daddy." These new abilities are interesting in their own right, but they also have implications for developing the ability to segment language. In particular, Roberta Golinkoff and her colleagues have found that when babies hear a familiar word—such as their own name or "Mommy" or "Daddy"—the familiar word serves as an anchor for learning the words that immediately precede or follow the familiar word (Blanchard, Heinz, & Golinkoff, 2010; Pruden, Hirsch-Pasek, Golinkoff, & Hennon, 2006). Thus, it is easier for the baby to learn the word "cup" if it is used in the sentence "Here's your cup, Amy" than if it is used in the anchorless "Here's your cup." Developmentalists use the term **perceptual scaffolding** to refer to the process through which the sound of a familiar word serves as an anchor for learning new words. At about 9 months of age, children begin to understand some common expressions, such as "Do you want your bottle?" "Wave bye-bye," and "Cookie?" when they are used in highly specific, often routine, situations.

perceptual scaffolding The way in which a familiar word serves as an anchor for learning new words that come immediately before or after it.

The ability to produce language follows several months behind the ability to understand it. Its origins can be traced back to the cooing and gurgling noises babies begin to make at 10 to 12 weeks of age (Golinkoff et al., 2015). Soon thereafter, babies with normal hearing not only initiate cooing sounds but also begin to respond to the voices of others with gurgles and coos. When their cooing is imitated, they answer with more coos, thereby engaging in a "conversation" in which turns are taken at vocalizing.

babbling A form of vocalizing, beginning at around 7 months, in which infants utter strings of syllables that combine a consonant sound and a vowel sound.

Babbling, a form of vocalizing that combines a consonant and vowel sound, such as "dadadadadadada" or "bababababa," begins at around 7 months of age (Hillairet de Boisferon, Tift, Minal, & Lewkowicz, 2017). Research indicates that babbling is controlled by the left hemisphere of the brain; thus, well before recognizable language has begun, the brain areas that will support language are already active and behaving in language-specific ways (Homae, 2014; Leroy et al., 2011; Quast et al., 2016). At first, babbling amounts to no more than vocal play, as babies discover the wealth of sounds they can make with their tongue, teeth, palate, and vocal cords. They practice making these sound combinations endlessly, much as they practice grasping objects.

Early babbling is the same the world over. No matter what language the baby's family speaks, babies produce syllables they have never heard before and will not use when they learn to speak (Kuhl, 2015). At about 8 months of age, however, babies begin to narrow their babbling to the sounds produced in the language that they hear every day (Davis, MacNeilage, Matyear, & Powell, 2000). Interestingly, when babies growing up in environments where only one language is spoken enter the babbling phase, they shift their attention from focusing on the eyes of a speaker to focusing more on the mouth (Pons, Bosch, & Lewkowicz, 2015). Then, once the babies begin talking, they no longer pay special attention to the mouth. Babies growing up in bilingual environments, in contrast, pay special attention to the mouth well before the babbling phase, and they continue to do so once they begin to speak. This suggests that as babies begin to produce language-relevant vocalizations, they zero in on the most obvious source of the speech of others—the mouth—and this is especially important for bilingual infants meeting the challenge of acquiring two languages.

Toward the end of the first year, babies begin to babble with the intonation and stress of actual utterances in the language they will eventually speak. Such vocalizations are called jargoning. At this point, babbling begins to take on distinctive intonation patterns associated with declarations, commands, and questions. Compare, for example, the sound pattern you produce as you say "I want a cookie" with the sound of "May I have a cookie?" From approximately 9 months of age, babies will begin altering the intonational patterns of their babbling when they are attempting to communicate with others (Esteve-Gibert & Prieto, 2013). Babbling also appears to play an important role in language development. The age at which it occurs in the baby predicts the onset of the baby's first words, leading researchers to speculate that babbling elicits responses from others that encourage yet more babbling, drawing the infant's attention to the ways that vocalizations can be used to communicate (McGillion et al., 2017).

By about 12 months of age, infants are able to comprehend a dozen or so common phrases, such as "Give me a hug," "Stop it!" and "Let's go bye-bye." At about this same time, the first distinguishable words make their appearance, although their use is restricted to only a few contexts or objects (Fenson et al., 1994).

It used to be thought that deaf children babbled, beginning at the same age as hearing children (Lenneberg, 1967). Research has shown, however, that, although deaf infants in their early months do vocalize, they progress to babbling only if they have some residual hearing (Koopmans-van Beinum, Clement, & van den Dikkenberg-Pot, 2001). In the case of totally deaf infants, vocalizations become rare by 1 year of age. However, if their caregivers communicate with each other in sign language, these infants "babble" with their hands—that is, just as hearing infants' babbling comes to have the sounds and sound patterns of the language they hear, so these infants make the movements that will become the elements of sign language (Takei, 2001).

At the same time that their capacity to distinguish and produce linguistic signals increases, babies become more adept at interacting with the people and objects around them. In Chapter 6, we explained how infants and their social partners establish *primary intersubjectivity*, sharing feelings as a consequence of well-coordinated and organized face-to-face social interactions (see pp. 202–203). This ability is evident in the rounds of greeting noises and smiling that caregivers and babies engage in, to their mutual delight. We noted, moreover, that between the ages of 9 and 12 months, babies and their partners become able to establish *secondary intersubjectivity*, a crucial precursor to language acquisition that allows babies and their caregivers to communicate their feelings about objects and events that are the focus of their joint attention (see pp. 216–217).

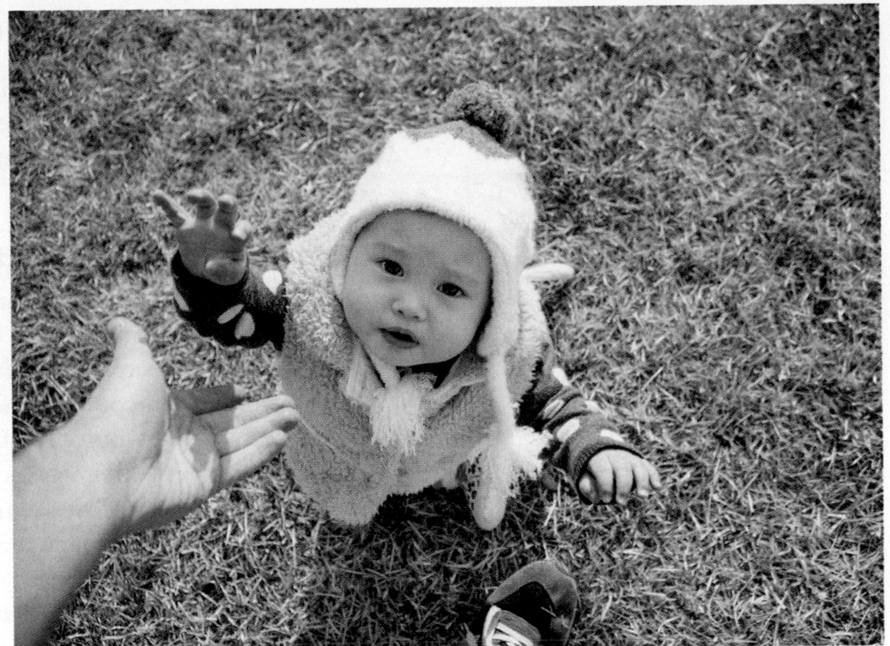

Jonathan Galione/Getty Images

There is no mistaking this baby's gesture: "Pick me up!" In just a few more months, the baby's gesturing will be accompanied by words.

Somehow, in the space of a very few years, children are launched from these early foundations and enter the world of language. (See Table 7.1 for a summary of some of the early developments.) We will now examine the special keys that unlock the door to this world.

TABLE 7.1 The Progress of Language Development

Approximate Age	Typical Behavior
Birth	Phoneme perception Discrimination of language from nonlanguage sounds Crying
3 months	Cooing
6 months	Babbling Loss of ability to discriminate between nonnative phonemes
9 months	First words
12 months	Use of words to attract adults' attention
18 months	Vocabulary spurt First two-word sentences (telegraphic speech)
24 months	Correct responses to indirect requests ("Is the door shut?")
30 months	Creation of indirect requests ("You're standing on my blocks!") Modification of speech to take listener into account Early awareness of grammatical categories

APPLY > CONNECT > DISCUSS

In the section above, what evidence suggests that innate biological processes drive language development? What evidence suggests that the child's language environment is critical?

LEARNING OUTCOMES

Distinguish biological structures from other systems that support language acquisition.

Point out how Broca's area and Wernicke's area affect language function, including during language development of infants.

Give examples of ways in which communities of language users provide models and opportunities for children's language acquisition.

Point out the effect of multilingual environments on children's language acquisition.

Keys to the World of Language

Access to the world of language is virtually guaranteed to all who hold two keys: (1) the human biological structures and systems that support language and (2) participation in a language-using community. Let us consider the biological key first.

The Biological Key to Language

Developmentalists have used two conceptually related approaches to tackle the question of how biology unlocks the door to the world of language. The first is to inquire about the capacities and limitations of nonhuman species. If humans' abilities in producing and comprehending language depart significantly from those of other species, then evolutionary forces must have produced the uniquely human biological structures and processes that make language possible. The second, related approach is to try to discover which structures and processes of the human brain support language development and what their special contributions to it are.

Is Language Uniquely Human? Research to determine whether language is uniquely human has a long and controversial history (Bohn, Call, & Tomasello, 2016; Corballis, 2015; Gillespie-Lynch, Greenfield, Lyn, & Savage-Rumbaugh, 2014). Much of the controversy has been inspired by the work of Sue Savage-Rumbaugh and Duane Rumbaugh (Rumbaugh, Savage-Rumbaugh, & Sevcik, 1994). The Rumbaughs provided chimpanzees with a "lexical keyboard"—that is, a keyboard that bore symbols that stood for words ("banana," "give," and so on)—and they used standard reinforcement learning techniques to teach the chimpanzees the meaning of these symbols. In addition, the people who worked with the chimpanzees used natural language in everyday, routine activities such as feeding.

The Rumbaughs' most successful student has been Kanzi, a bonobo ape who initially learned to use the lexical keyboard by observing his mother being trained to use it. Kanzi is able to use the keyboard to ask for things, and he can comprehend requests made of him by researchers using the lexical symbols. He has also learned to understand some spoken English words and phrases (Rumbaugh & Washburn, 2003). For example, when told to "feed your ball some tomato," Kanzi picked up a tomato and placed it in the "mouth" of a facelike soft sponge ball. He has also demonstrated some understanding of syntax: When asked to "give the shot [syringe] to Liz" and then to "give Liz a shot," he correctly handed the syringe to the girl in the first instance and touched the syringe to the girl's arm in the second.

MICHAEL NICHOLS/National Geographic Creative

Kanzi uses a specially designed keyboard composed of lexical symbols to communicate.

Kanzi's ability to produce language is not as impressive as his comprehension. Most of his "utterances" on the lexical keyboard are single words that are closely linked to his current actions, and they usually involve requests. He also uses two-word utterances in a wide variety of combinations and occasionally makes observations. For example, he produced the request "car trailer" on one occasion when he was in the car and wanted (or so his caretakers believed) to be taken to the trailer rather than to walk there. He has created such requests as "play yard Austin" when he wanted to visit a chimpanzee named Austin in the play yard. When a researcher put oil on him while he was eating a potato, he commented, "potato oil."

Using combinations of visual symbols or gestures, bonobos and chimpanzees can produce language at roughly the level of a 2-year-old child. In their productions, they form telegraphic utterances that encode the same semantic relations as do those of children (for example, a two-symbol combination relating an agent to its action—"Kanzi eat") (Greenfield & Lyn, 2007). Bonobos are also capable of comprehending English speech at roughly the level of a 2-year-old child (Savage-Rumbaugh, 1993). However, in contrast to human children, who acquire complex language with no formal teaching, nonhuman primates develop language ability only in the context of intense explicit instruction provided by their human caretakers. To explore what might account for this dramatic species difference in the ability to learn language, developmentalists have looked to species-unique features of the human brain.

A Brain for Language Scientists have long been aware that the left side of the human brain plays a dominant role in language ability, but it was not until the middle of the nineteenth century that the brain bases of language became an active area of research in medicine and psychology. In particular, it was the work of two physicians, each studying a different form of a speech disorder called *aphasia*, that led to the discovery of language areas of the brain (Luria, 1973).

In 1861, a French surgeon named Paul Broca treated a man who was unable to speak. When his patient died, Broca examined his brain and found damage on the outside surface of the left frontal lobe in an area that came to be known as *Broca's area*. Patients with damage to this area suffer from what is called *Broca's aphasia*, a condition in which speech is either absent or severely disrupted. Individuals with Broca's aphasia may speak with great effort in brief, meaningful phrases that omit small words such as "is," "and," and "the." For example, they might say "Walk dog" to mean "I will take the dog for a walk." (Those who recover from this disorder often report that they knew what they wanted to say but could not control their speech.) Generally, patients with Broca's aphasia are able to understand individual words but have difficulty understanding more complex structures.

A few years later, Carl Wernicke, a German physician, discovered that damage to an area slightly to the rear of Broca's area results in an inability to comprehend language. People with damage to this area, now called *Wernicke's area*, are often capable of producing language, but much of what they say makes little sense. Patients with what is known as *Wernicke's aphasia* thus often produce long sentences that include unnecessary words and even nonsense words. For example, they might say something like "You know that smoodle pinkered and that I want to get him round and take care of him like you want before" to mean "The dog needs to go out so I will take him for a walk" (National Institute on Deafness and Other Communication Disorders, 2012).

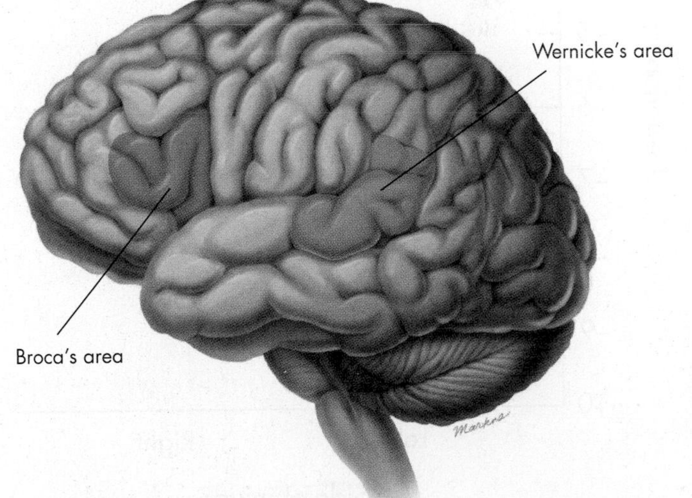

FIGURE 7.1 This view of the left hemisphere of the brain highlights two key areas for normal language processing in adults. Wernicke's area is central to processing sounds and comprehension. Damage to this area results in an inability to comprehend language. Broca's area is central to motor control and language production. Damage to this area of the brain results in the loss or severe disruption of normal speech. (Research from Chudler, 2011.)

Contemporary studies of the brain and language have shown that in adults, injuries to the left hemisphere in either Broca's or Wernicke's area are overwhelmingly more likely to cause aphasia than are injuries to the corresponding parts of the right hemisphere (Figure 7.1). This evidence appears to confirm the idea that there is indeed a part of the brain that is genetically programmed to produce and comprehend language—an idea that has gained additional support from studies using technologically sophisticated neuroimaging techniques.

Angela Friederici and her colleagues at the Max Planck Institute for Human Cognitive and Brain Sciences in Germany have been using advanced neuroimaging techniques to investigate relationships between language development and brain mechanisms

(Zaccarella, Meyer, Makuuchi, & Friederici, 2015). In one study, they tried to determine whether Broca's area plays a special role in processing complex language (Friederici et al., 2006). Their inquiry was inspired by increasing evidence suggesting that although some nonhuman species show at least a rudimentary capacity to process simple sentences (as did Kanzi when he distinguished the difference between "give the shot to Liz" and "give Liz a shot"), they are not able to process more complex sentences. When the researchers presented participants with both simple and complex speech sequences (for example, a simple sentence like "The song pleased the teacher" and a more complex sentence like "The song that the boy sang pleased the teacher"), they discovered that the complexity of the sequence determined which area of the brain became active. In particular, complex sequences activated Broca's area, which evolved fairly recently in the history of our species. Simple sequences, in contrast, activated only an evolutionarily older area of the brain that we share with other primates. In another line of research using neuroimaging, studies conducted at the University of Barcelona have shown that the characteristic spurt in toddlers' vocabulary (discussed in more detail below) occurs only after substantial myelination of language-related brain regions (Pujol et al., 2006).

Although Broca's and Wernicke's areas seem to play a significant role in humans' ability to acquire and use language, research with children strongly suggests that it is possible to develop normal, or near-normal, language abilities even if Broca's and Wernicke's areas are damaged, as long as the damage occurs early in life (Bates & Roe, 2001). Data in support of this conclusion come largely from studies of children who, just before, during, or after birth, suffered strokes that cut off the blood supply to the left or right hemisphere of the brain, resulting in damage to the cerebral cortex. These children still acquire language, although their performance may be at the lower end of the normal range. Most importantly, however, they do so even when the damage occurs in the left hemisphere, where language appears to be localized in adults! Whereas left-hemisphere damage would leave an adult considerably more language-impaired than would right-hemisphere damage, damage on either side results in little impairment for children, as Figure 7.2 shows. This is because of the plasticity of the brain in early development; in infants with left-hemisphere damage, parts of the right hemisphere become the brain center for the language.

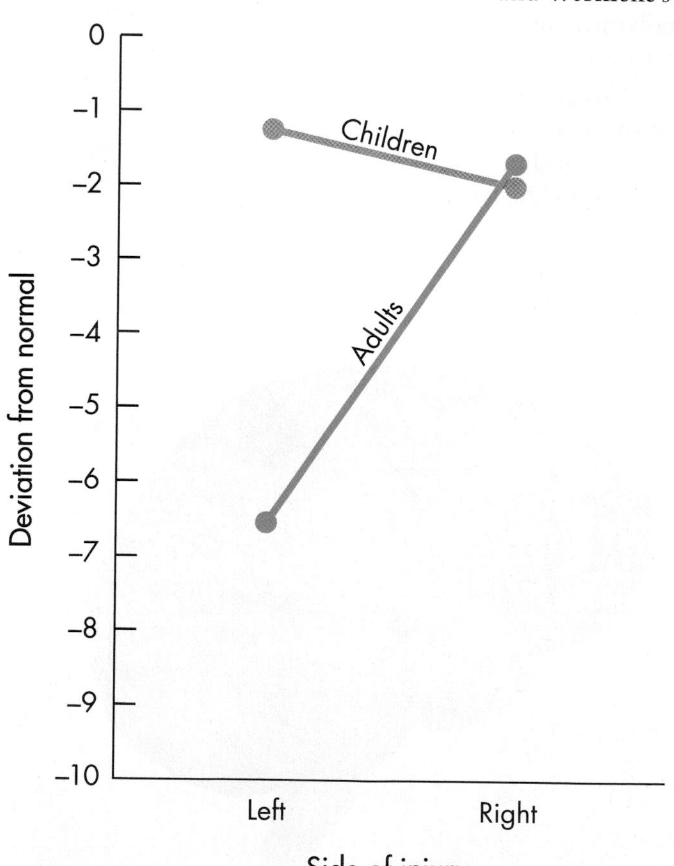

FIGURE 7.2 The figure shows the difference in the impact of brain injury to the left and right hemispheres for adults and children. When adults were presented with novel phrases, the performance of adults with left-hemisphere damage was far worse than the performance of those with right-hemisphere damage. There was no significant difference in performance between children with left-hemisphere damage and those with right-hemisphere damage. (Data from Bates & Roe, 2001.)

Some researchers interpret these and similar findings to indicate that, in the absence of any interfering factors, the infant brain is predisposed to ensure the eventual emergence of an area in the left hemisphere of the brain that is specialized to process language (Bates, 2005). Indeed, a fascinating study indicates that when 5-month-old babies babble, their mouths open more on the right side than the left; since the right side of the mouth is controlled by the left side of the brain, this suggests that the left side of the brain has already begun to specialize as a center for language processing (Holowka & Petitto, 2002). On the other hand, evidence that the newborn's brain can compensate for damage caused by strokes indicates that the brain mechanisms supporting language are not fixed at birth. Indeed, recent research indicates that the brain undergoes highly specific changes as the child's language abilities progress (Brauer, Anwander, & Friederici, 2011). The extent to which brain maturation may *cause* particular language advances remains unclear.

It is likely, however, that "learning itself plays a major role in organizing the brain for efficient language use" (Bates & Roe, 2001, p. 305).

The Environmental Key to Language

Sometime before her second birthday, a girl named Genie was permanently locked in her room by her abusive father. For more than 11 years, she spent her days chained to a potty and her nights tied up in a sleeping bag. She lived in almost total isolation, and as far as can be determined, was never spoken to after she was confined. Every time her father came to tie her in for the night or to bring her food, he growled at her like a beast and often scratched her with his fingernails. When she was finally liberated from these horrible circumstances at the age of 13, Genie was a pitiful creature. She did not make intelligible sounds, walk normally, chew solid food, or express her emotions appropriately. David Rigler, a scientist, and his wife petitioned the Department of Social Services to become Genie's foster parents and to study her extensively, along with a team of linguists and psychologists. Genie spent 4 years in the Rigler household. During that time, she was treated as much as possible like a member of the family. She was taught how to chew solid food, to behave properly at the table, to express her emotions appropriately, and to stop masturbating publicly whenever she felt the urge. However, despite the special emphasis placed on nurturing her language development, Genie's speech resembled the language used in telegrams. There is no evidence that she ever learned to ask a real question or to form a proper negative sentence (Curtiss et al., 1974).

Genie's case tells a tragic story of unimaginable deprivation and destruction. It also underscores how participation in a normal social environment is essential to the process of language acquisition (Clark, 2014). In the course of such participation, children are not only exposed to *models* of how language is used and understood, they are also provided with opportunities to communicate with others, opportunities that *motivate* them to be better communicators—that is, to use language to express and share ideas effectively (Bridges & Hoff, 2014; Tomasello, 2011). Clearly, Genie was denied both language models and communication opportunities during the years that children acquire language, and these deprivations certainly contributed to her inability to develop normal language. But Genie's horrific deprivations affected every aspect of her health and development, making it impossible to use her case to assess the specific effects that language deprivation can have on children's language development. Researchers have therefore looked to the case of deaf children whose hearing parents do not know sign language and discourage its use (Goldin-Meadow & Brentari, 2015; Goldin-Meadow, Özyürek, Sancar, & Mylander, 2009).

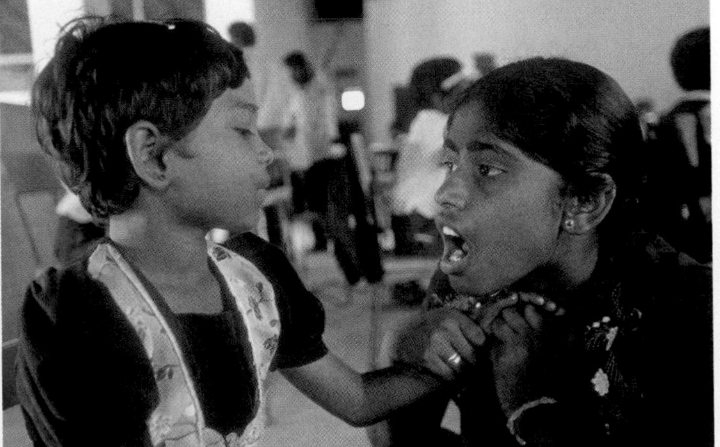

Paul Hahn/LAIF/Redux

Children with hearing impairments acquire language at a comparable rate to hearing children, especially when they receive support from the environment. Here, a deaf child learns sign language at a special school in Sri Lanka.

Language-Deprived Environments

The biological condition of deafness need not be an impediment to normal language acquisition: Deaf children born to deaf parents who communicate in sign language acquire language at least as rapidly and fully as hearing children born into hearing households (Morgan & Woll, 2002; Volterra, Iverson, & Castrataro, 2006). Thus, any delays or difficulties in deaf children's language development must result from the way the linguistic environment is organized.

When deaf children are raised with little or no exposure to a signed language, they often develop fairly sophisticated gestural systems that allow them to communicate with others (reviewed in Schick, 2006). In particular, many deaf children raised without exposure to a signed language spontaneously begin to gesture in "home sign," a kind of communication through pantomime (Goldin-Meadow, 2015; see the box "Now Trending in Research: Children Creating a Language").

Research by Susan Goldin-Meadow and her colleagues (Franklin, Giannakidou, & Goldin-Meadow, 2011) has determined that the home-sign gesturing developed by deaf children has certain characteristics of language, even when children have no one to show them the signs. Home sign begins as pointing. Children then gesture one sign at a time—at the same age that hearing children develop single-word utterances. Home-sign gestures also seem to refer to the same kinds of objects and to fulfill the same functions as the early words of hearing children or of deaf children with signing parents. Remarkably, around their second birthday, about the same time that hearing children begin to utter multiword sentences, home-signing children begin to make patterns of two, and sometimes three or more, signs. In addition, these patterns appear to involve complex sentence structures that are characteristic of all human languages and are absent from the communicative system of chimpanzees and other creatures even after long training—structures equivalent to the type of speech sequences that we described above as activating Broca's area, rather than the evolutionarily older part of the brain.

Of course, many hearing parents will learn a signed language in order to communicate with and enrich the language environments their deaf children. Naturally, as novice language learners, they are considerably less proficient compared to deaf parents who are fluent in sign language. This suggests that the quality of deaf children's language environments may vary depending on whether they are born to deaf or hearing parents. Indeed, by 2 years of age, deaf children of deaf parents—expert sign language users—have larger vocabularies and more sophisticated hand signs compared to deaf children of hearing parents who learned sign language after their deaf children were born (Lu, Jones, & Morgan, 2016).

cochlear implant A device that transforms sounds into electric pulses that directly stimulate the auditory nerve, bypassing the malfunctioning inner ear that ordinarily processes sound.

The language environments of deaf babies can also be enriched through the use of cochlear implants. A **cochlear implant** is a device that transforms sounds into electric pulses that directly stimulate the auditory nerve, bypassing the malfunctioning inner ear that ordinarily processes sound (Vavatzanidis, Murbe, Friederici, & Hahne, 2016; see Figure 7.3). Although cochlear implants provide considerably less auditory stimulation than a normally functioning ear (Zeng, Tang, & Lu, 2014), studies of children who have been using the implants for several years provide variable but encouraging results regarding the development of spoken language (Faes, Gillis, & Gillis, 2015; Kronenberger, Colson, Henning, & Pisoni, 2014; van Wieringen & Wouters, 2015). In one study, more than half of the adolescents who had used cochlear implants for at least 10 years had language skills comparable to those of their hearing counterparts (Geers & Sedey, 2011).

AP Photo/Rochester Post-Bulletin, Jerry Olson

FIGURE 7.3 This baby has a cochlear implant. The part behind the baby's ear contains microphones that pick up sounds and converts them to signals that are sent to the transmitter—the part on the baby's head. The transmitter sends the signals to an internal implant that passes the signals along to the auditory nerve in the inner ear (the cochlea), from where they are sent to the brain and perceived as sound.

Multilingual Environments

We live in an age in which vast numbers of people move from one language community to another, rear children among people whose native tongue is different than their own, or grow up in families in which more than one language is spoken. In fact, a study conducted in many European nations found that approximately

Now TRENDING in RESEARCH
Children Creating a Language

Before the 1970s, there was no national education system for deaf Nicaraguans, and there was no Nicaraguan sign language. The deaf were socially isolated and marginalized in Nicaraguan society. But in 1977, a school for 25 deaf children was built in the capital city, Managua. Two years later, the school was expanded to admit 100 children, and the following year, a vocational school was opened for deaf adolescents. These schools served more than 400 students, mostly through lip-reading instruction. Within a few years, a community of deaf people ranging in age from childhood to adulthood developed, and with it, a new language, Nicaraguan Sign Language. For a number of years, Ann Senghas and her colleagues have studied the emergence of this language within the newly formed community (Kocab, Senghas, & Snedeker, 2016; Senghas, 2011). Her findings illustrate that while the child's *capacity* for learning complex language is rooted in the evolutionary history of our species, the acquisition of a fully-fledged grammar requires social participation.

Specifically, Senghas found that when the first children to attend the school for the deaf were together on school playgrounds and buses, they began to communicate with one another using the home signs that they had invented before coming to school. Although teachers were instructing children in lip-reading and finger-spelling in Spanish, the children largely ignored these lessons outside the classroom and instead created their very own language community. As children interacted socially, the number and variety of signs they used increased dramatically, as did the complexity of their communication.

At the start of the second and third school years, new groups of children arrived at the school and, with no deliberate instruction, began combining their own individual home signs with those of their schoolmates. The new signing mix eventually became conventionalized, producing a *pidgin language*. A pidgin language is a blending of two different languages and is characterized by simplified grammar and vocabulary. (Pidgin languages most often emerge in situations of slave or immigrant labor.) Over time, the pidgin language the deaf schoolchildren used became increasingly stylized and took on more complex grammatical forms. In short, the children began to communicate with each other in a language that exhibits the same structure as any other natural language. Significantly, it was the *youngest* children who elaborated on and enriched the pidgin language they encountered and introduced new grammatical forms that were not present in the signing of the older students (Senghas, Senghas, & Pyers, 2005; Slobin, 2005).

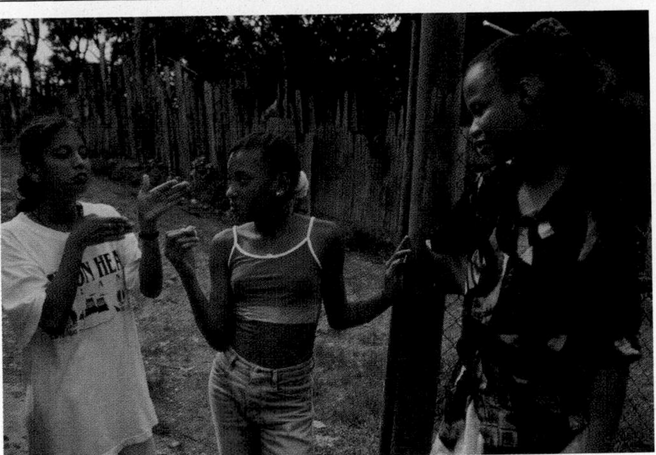

Susan Meiselas/Magnum Photos

These girls are students at the Escuelitas de Bluefields, a school for the deaf in Nicaragua, where they learn sign language as well as other literacy and academic skills.

In his review of Senghas's work, Dan Slobin has argued the point that children's creation of home signs suggests a human capacity to create the rudiments of a language system but that, for such rudimentary systems to develop further, a community of users, as in the case of the Nicaraguan school, is needed. Slobin wrote that "language is like other sorts of human technology; once it is present, it provides a 'niche'—a modified environment—creating new pressures for the refinement of that technology" (2005, p. 280). Ongoing research has found, in fact, that the grammatical complexity of Nicaraguan Sign Language continues to evolve as more and more children enter the community and learn to use it (Kocab, Pyers, & Senghas, 2015; Kocab et al., 2016).

Taken as a whole, the research on language-deprived environments suggests that even in the absence of direct experience with language, children will develop the beginnings of language during the first 2 years of life, as long they regularly have the opportunity to communicate with others. However, the language that appears under such linguistically impoverished conditions does not go beyond that of children at the two-word phase. Apparently, to fully acquire language, children must grow up in an environment that provides a language-support system.

56 percent of the respondents reported being *bilingual* or *multilingual*—that is, able to speak two or more languages (European Commission Special Eurobarometer, 2006). In the United States alone, approximately 4.5 million children in public schools are English Language Learners (ELLs) (Kena et al., 2014). This state of affairs poses interesting questions about language acquisition for parents as well as developmentalists. How does exposure to multiple languages affect a child's language acquisition? Is the child confused by clashing vocabularies and grammars? Is it better for a child to learn one language first before being exposed to another?

michaeljung/Getty Images

In today's world, the ability not only to speak but also to read and write in a foreign language is becoming an increasingly important part of every child's development.

Despite ample scientific evidence that young children can acquire two or more languages with ease (Bialystok, 2017; Petitto, 2009), many North American parents worry that early exposure to two languages might confuse children and cause them to learn language more slowly or less well than their monolingual peers. As a result of these concerns, some parents decide to withhold knowledge of one family language from their children until it is "safe" to add a second language to their repertoire (Petitto, 2009).

Despite parents' concerns, research finds very little evidence that there is anything harmful about children acquiring two languages simultaneously. A number of studies have shown that vocabulary development for children under the age of 3 is comparable for bilingual and monolingual children and that bilingual children have little trouble distinguishing between the words and grammars of the different languages they are learning (Jia, Chen, & Kim, 2008; Conboy & Thal, 2006).

Moreover, bilingual children reap surprising rewards. The constant need to switch between two active language systems—inhibiting one while using the other—may carry over to other areas of intellectual functioning (Kroll, Dussias, Bice, & Perrotti, 2015). A case in point is bilingual children's early ability to see multiple images in an ambiguous figure (Bialystok & Shapero, 2005). It is well known that children, particularly those under age 5, have difficulty identifying more than one image in ambiguous figures, such as the vase and the faces shown on this page (Diamond, 2002a, 2002b; Gopnik & Rosati, 2001). Once they see the vase, it is hard for young children to reinterpret the picture and see it in a different way—as a picture of faces. (See p. 242 regarding how preoperational children can be "captured" by a specific feature of an object.) Bilingual children, however, seem to master such tasks at earlier ages than do children learning a single language, suggesting that emersion in a multilingual environment promotes the early development of flexible attention (Bialystok, 2017). In older bilingual children, this cognitive flexibility is manifested in a number of ways, including the ability to solve problems that require dealing with various sorts of conflict or switching between different types of tasks or behaviors (Barac, Bailystok, Castro, & Sanchez, 2014).

Bilingual children are able to see both the faces and the vase in this ambiguous figure at an earlier age than can children who are learning a single language.

Ellen Bialystok and her colleagues believe that bilingual children's early mastery of tasks requiring cognitive flexibility is related to how a bilingual environment affects brain development and function (Bialystok, 2017; Grundy, Anderson, & Bialystok, 2017). When children were given tasks that involve processing sentences, brain-imaging technologies found higher levels of activation in the language centers of the brain for bilingual children and adults than for monolingual children and adults (Jasinska & Petitto, 2013). The effects were especially pronounced for individuals who were exposed to a second language during the first 3 years. These results led the researchers to a fascinating conclusion—namely, that the brain's language centers do not develop to their fullest extent in individuals who grow up speaking only one language, and further, that there may be a sensitive period during the first 3 years, after which the language centers of the brain lose the capacity to be strongly affected by exposure to more than one language. This conclusion is consistent with the notion of *experience-dependent* brain development that we introduced in Chapter 4 (pp. 129–131).

All told, research on how multilingual environments affect children's language development not only lays to rest parents' concerns about developmental delays but also indicates that there are a number of cognitive benefits to being able to communicate in more than one language.

APPLY > CONNECT > DISCUSS

In describing language as an "instinct," Stephen Pinker (1994) argued that people know how to use language for more or less the same reason that spiders know how to spin webs—because their spider brains give them both the urge to spin and the competence to succeed. In what ways might his argument be insufficient for explaining how individual children acquire language?

The Basic Domains of Language Acquisition

LEARNING OUTCOMES

Explain the relationship of phonological development to language acquisition and include examples.

Explain the relationship of semantic development to language acquisition and include examples.

Explain the relationship of grammar development to language acquisition and include examples.

Explain the relationship of pragmatic development to language acquisition and include examples.

Consider the sentence "Thomas kissed Sylvia, so she slapped his face." If someone read this sentence aloud to you, your interpretation would clearly be impaired if you heard something like "To mask issed sylvias oshes lapped his face." The first challenge in understanding a new language is segmenting the stream of sounds into separate and recognizable words. The process through which children acquire knowledge of how to segment strings of speech sounds into meaningful units of language is part of the domain of language acquisition referred to as **phonological development**.

phonological development The process of learning to segment speech into meaningful units of sound.

Beyond understanding how to segment the speech sounds of the sentence, it is necessary to understand the meaning of the words that compose the sentence. **Semantic development** refers to this process of learning the meanings of words and word combinations. We know, for example, that the word "kiss" refers to a particular type of action in which the lips are puckered and applied to some person or object. However, the fact that the action resulted in being slapped, which we understand to mean striking another with one's palm, adds another layer of meaning to the kiss: It was unwanted and resented. As this simple example illustrates, word meanings are complex and interact with each other; as you will see, the meanings of words change for children as they learn and apply them—often in error.

semantic development The process of learning meanings of words and of combinations of words.

Yet another challenge to interpreting the sentence about Thomas and Sylvia is to understand the rules about how the words are arranged in the sentence. For words to be combined into a comprehensible sentence, they must be related not only to objects and events but also to one another. That is, they must be governed by **grammar**, the rules of a particular language for sequencing words in a sentence and word parts within words. For example, the word sequence "Thomas kissed Sylvia" has a very different meaning from the sequence "Sylvia kissed Thomas." Rules of grammar also lead us to understand that the kissing and slapping are actions that happened in the past (as indicated by the "-ed" ending) and that one action (the kissing) led to the other (the slapping). Thus language acquisition includes the process of learning grammar.

grammar The rules of a given language for the sequencing of words in a sentence and the ordering of parts of words.

Finally, a full interpretation of a sentence requires that we know something about the connections between the sentence and the social or cultural context in which it occurs. **Pragmatic development**, the process of learning the social and cultural conventions that govern how language is used in particular contexts, is an especially important challenge in children's acquisition of language. Children's failure to appreciate the connections between sentences and their contexts often leads to inappropriate utterances. Indeed, young children are famous for speaking their minds without regard for context, blurting out various facts or opinions at exactly the wrong moment. One of your authors will never forget the time her 4-year-old daughter greeted the somewhat portly chairman of her psychology department with a cheery "Hi, fatso!"

pragmatic development The process of learning the conventions that govern the use of language in particular social contexts.

Phonological development, semantic development, grammar, and pragmatic development together represent the basic domains of language acquisition. We explore each of these domains in the sections below. For the sake of clarity, we will describe how children become competent in each domain separately. However, it is important to keep in mind that language is a system in which each domain is connected to all of the others, as well as to the social world of which it is an essential part (de Lemos, 2000).

Phonological Development

When children's vocalizations shift late in the 1st year from babbling to pronouncing words, children give up their indiscriminate play with sounds and begin to vocalize the particular sounds and sound sequences that make up the words in the language of their community (Kuhl, 2015). *Phonological development* refers to the process of learning to segment speech into meaningful units of sound. The process of mastering the pronunciation of the separate words of a native language takes several years (and can be complicated by, for example, malformation of structures involved in articulation; see the box, "In the Field: A Speech–Language Pathologist in Vietnam"). Children's early efforts at pronouncing words may be no more than crude stabs at the right sound pattern that frequently leave out parts of words (resulting in "ca" instead of "cat," for example). They may also include using a particular sound pattern for several different multisyllabic words that have sound similarities. For example, a child may use the sound pattern "bubba" to say "button," "bubble," "butter," and "baby." A long word, such as "motorcycle," can come out sounding like almost anything: "momo," "motokaka," or even "lomacity" (Preisser, Hodson, & Paden, 1988).

Children's command of their native sound system develops unevenly. Sometimes children find a particular sound especially difficult to master, even after they understand many words that employ that sound. At the age of 2½, for example, one of our sons, Alexander, could not pronounce /l/ sounds at the beginning of words, and whenever he referred to his friend's dog, Lucky, it came out "Yucky," much to everyone's amusement.

Alexander's transformation of "Lucky" to "Yucky" generated chuckles because when he changed the phoneme from /l/ to /y/, he changed the *meaning* of the word. As noted in Chapter 6, the close connection between phonemes and meanings becomes clear when one is attempting to learn a foreign language. Some native speakers of Spanish find it difficult to hear or produce the difference between /b/ and /v/, which in English can change meaning, because Spanish has no corresponding distinction in sound. To native English speakers, "boat" and "vote" sound quite different; to Spanish speakers, these two words sound much the same. Likewise, English speakers frequently have difficulty hearing and producing the difference between the French /u/ and /ou/, because that difference, which in French can change meaning, does not exist in English.

morpheme The smallest unit of meaning in the words of a language.

While phonemes are the basic units of sound, **morphemes** are the basic units of meaning. Words are composed of one or more morphemes. The word *horse*, for example, consists of one morpheme, which means "a member of the equine family." *Horses*, on the other hand, includes two morphemes: *horse*, meaning "a member of the equine family," plus "-s" meaning "more than one." Until the rules are pointed out, we rarely stop to think about the parts of words or the way we put together these parts. Yet every child must acquire the ability to decipher and reproduce just such intricate interweaving of sound and meaning. By the time they are 8 or 9 years old, children can use knowledge about morphemes to figure out the meanings of made-up words such as "treelet" (Anglin, 1993).

In The Field

A Speech–Language Pathologist in Vietnam

Name: CHARLOTTE DUCOTE

Education: B.A. from Louisiana State University; M.A. from Vanderbilt; Ph.D. in speech and hearing sciences from Louisiana State University

Current Position: Director of the Division of Communicative Disorders at the Ochsner Clinic; volunteer for Operation Smile

Career Objectives: Provide education and services to improve speech and language skills for children with communication disorders

GIANG, A 6-YEAR-OLD VIETNAMESE GIRL, WAS BORN IN Ho Chi Minh City (Saigon) with a cleft lip and palate, a serious birth defect caused when the structures of the mouth form abnormally during fetal development. As a consequence of the defect, Giang had difficulty eating, communicating, and even breathing. It is estimated that clefting of the lip, palate, or both occurs in 1 to 2.5 of every 1,000 births worldwide, making it one of the most common birth defects; it is the second most common birth defect in the United States (McLeod, Arana-Urioste, & Saeed, 2004; Parker et al., 2010). Fortunately for Giang and other children from impoverished areas of the world, a number of humanitarian groups have formed to provide affected children with reconstructive surgery and speech and language therapy.

Charlotte Ducote, a speech–language pathologist, has devoted considerable time to one such group—Operation Smile, a private, not-for-profit medical services organization that has helped tens of thousands of indigent children in more than 20 countries. Medical teams include plastic surgeons, anesthesiologists, pediatricians, nurses, and dentists. But realizing the important of speech therapy after surgery, Ducote cofounded a project to teach health-care providers how to screen, evaluate, and treat communication disorders.

Ducote studied Vietnamese and its phoneme system and acquainted herself with the country's customs and culture. Armed with this knowledge, she met Giang, who was brought to the clinic by her mother for speech problems that interfered with her being accepted into first grade. Giang's cleft palate and lip had been surgically corrected the previous year, and her mother was convinced that additional surgery would help her daughter speak better. Ducote's evaluation, however, showed otherwise: Rather than requiring additional surgery, Giang's speech difficulties could be drastically improved with daily speech therapy. Indeed, within minutes of treatment, Giang was able to imitate phonemes that had been particularly difficult for her in the past, moving Giang's mother to tears: "I never thought my child would be able to say that word. How did you do that? It is like magic!"

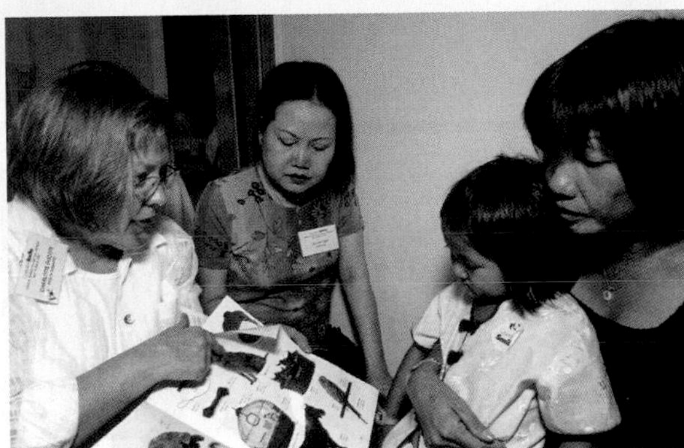

Charlotte Ducote, a speech–language pathologist with Operation Smile.

Operation Smile

Over the course of the next week, Ducote met regularly with Giang and her mother, teaching them how to form phonemes and breathe properly during speech. Ducote also encouraged Giang to open her mouth wider while talking to facilitate airflow and reduce the nasal tone of her voice. Her mother resisted this particular intervention because she worried that speaking with the mouth more open would make Giang unattractive to future suitors. She relented, however, when she witnessed the dramatic improvement in her daughter's speech.

At last report, Giang was in school and doing very well. Ducote, for her part, continues to volunteer in Vietnam and to mobilize financial and educational resources to help children with communication disorders throughout the world.

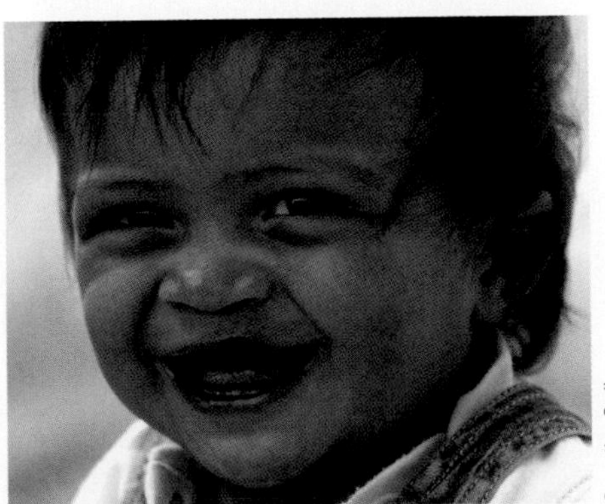

Operation Smile

One of the most common birth defects, cleft lip and palate, is caused by abnormal development of the structures of the mouth during the prenatal period. Without surgery, this baby's health and development would have been seriously affected. Fortunately, a surgical team associated with Operation Smile corrected the cleft when the baby was 5 months of age.

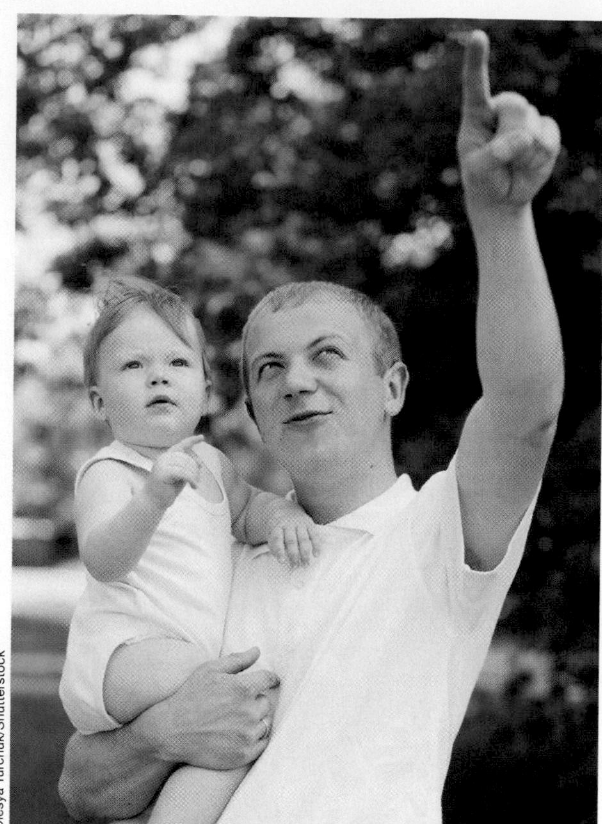
Olesya Turchuk/Shutterstock

FIGURE 7.4 For children just beginning to acquire language, the problem of learning what words refer to is particularly acute. This father may be telling his daughter to look at a squirrel—or a bird, tree, cloud, or any number of other objects in the direction of his pointing finger.

Semantic Development

Semantic development, as you may recall, refers to the process of learning the meanings of words and word combinations. As we described previously, through the example of Romeo and Juliet, words refer to something beyond themselves. Indeed, for a child acquiring language, a significant and surprisingly difficult part of the process of learning a new word involves what Sandra Waxman and her colleagues described as "mapping words to the world" and realizing the "referential power of language" (Ferguson & Waxman, 2016; Waxman & Leddon, 2011). Key to this process is the ability to identify the object to which the word refers—for example, knowing that the fluffy creature with the wet nose and wagging tail is the object referred to when the mother exclaims, "Look! It's a *puppy*!"

To get an intuitive feel for just how difficult it may be for a young child to learn the relationship between a word and its referent, examine Figure 7.4. Imagine that you are the child in the photograph, trying to figure out what Dad means when he says, "Look, there's a squirrel," when you don't yet know what a squirrel is, and the direction of his point includes a vast array of objects whose names you also don't yet know—trees, leaves, sky, clouds, sun, birds—in addition to squirrels. Even more fundamentally, babies must somehow figure out that the sounds they hear are in fact meant to refer to something in the ongoing flow of experience—to indicate an actual object, event, or feeling. According to Eve Clark (2014), the process of identifying a word's referent depends critically on the child's ability to establish joint attention with the speaker and to understand that the object or event of joint attention is what the speaker is talking about. As we will see, it takes some years before the child is fully able to appreciate the *referential intentions* of a speaker, which may account for why the child's vocabulary development is initially fairly slow but undergoes a substantial growth spurt during toddlerhood.

The Earliest Vocabulary

Much of the evidence concerning children's earliest words has come from having parents keep records of their children's vocabulary development or by making recordings of children's speech in their homes or in organized play facilities (Dromi & Zaidman-Zait, 2011). A number of studies have shown that children typically begin to produce their first comprehensible words around their 1st birthday and continue to utter single words for several months or more. Although there is a great deal of variation in the ages at which children reach particular levels of language production (Figure 7.5), infants, on average, are able to use approximately 10 words by 13 to 14 months of age, 50 words by the time they are 17 to 18 months old, and approximately 300 words by the time they reach their second birthday. More impressive still is children's *receptive vocabulary*—that is, the vocabulary they understand—which is considerably larger. For example, when they can produce 10 words, they can understand over 100 (Fenson et al., 1994).

The first words in young children's vocabularies are predominantly nouns used to label objects; this is true for children who speak languages as diverse as Spanish, Dutch, French, Hebrew, Italian, Korean, Mandarin Chinese, and American English (Bornstein et al., 2004; Hao et al., 2015). As is evident in Table 7.2, many first words refer to objects that young children can manipulate or somehow act upon, such as toys and certain foods—or objects that move on their own, such as animals and vehicles (Mandler, 2006; Tardif et al., 2008). In addition, the baby's earliest words

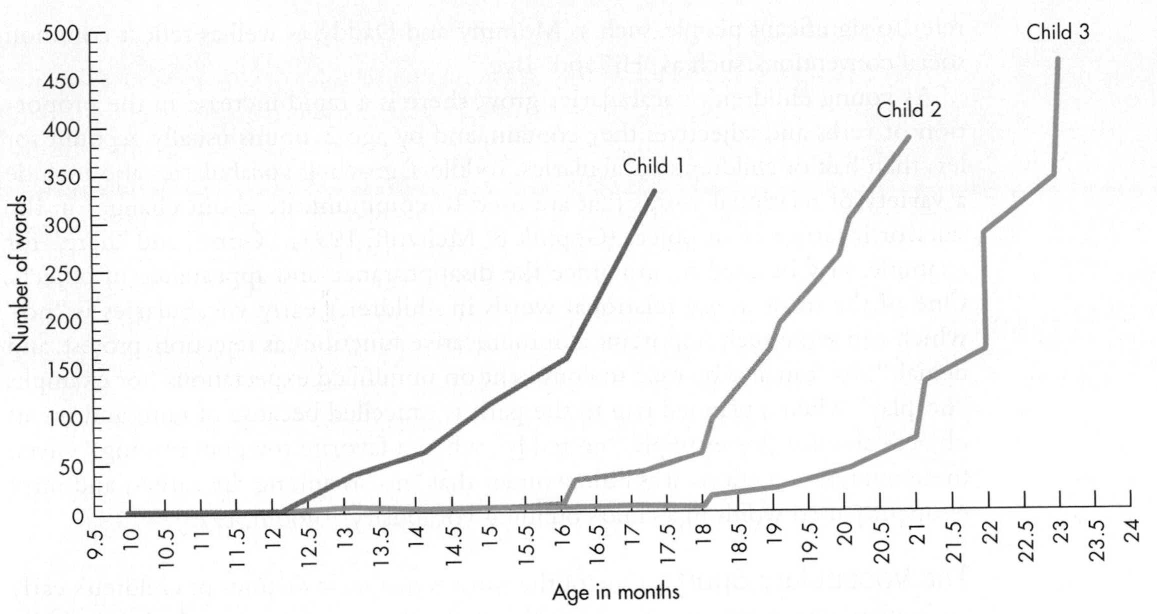

FIGURE 7.5 There are wide variations in the rates at which young children acquire new words. Each curve indicates the number of words that the designated child spoke while in the one-word phase. Note that despite the variability, each child shows the growth spurt in vocabulary that typically begins shortly before children start to produce utterances of two or more words. (Data from Dromi, 1999, p. 104.)

TABLE 7.2 Baby's First Words

United States	Hong Kong	Beijing
Daddy	**Daddy**	**Mommy**
Mommy	Ahh	**Daddy**
Baabaa	*Mommy*	*Grandma (paternal)*
Bye	*Yumyum*	*Grandpa (paternal)*
Hi	*Sister (older)*	**Hello?/Wei?**
Uhoh	**Uhoh (aiyou)**	*Hit*
Grr	*Hit*	Uncle (paternal)
Bottle	**Hello?/Wei?**	Grab/grasp
Yumyum	Milk	*Auntie (maternal)*
Dog	Naughty	**Bye**
No	*Brother (older)*	**Uhoh (aiyou)**
Woofwoof	*Grandma (maternal)*	Ya/wow
Vroom	*Grandma (paternal)*	*Sister (older)*
Kitty	**Bye**	**Woofwoof**
Ball	Bread	*Brother (older)*
Baby	*Auntie (maternal)*	Hug/hold
Duck	*Ball*	Light
Cat	*Grandpa (paternal)*	*Grandma (maternal)*
Ouch	Car	Egg
Banana	**Woofwoof**	*Vroom*

Note: Bolded words above are shared across three languages, and italicized words are shared across two languages.

Information from Tardif et al., 2008.

refer to significant people, such as Mommy and Daddy, as well as reflect common social conventions, such as "Hi" and "Bye."

As young children's vocabularies grow, there is a rapid increase in the proportion of verbs and adjectives they contain, and by age 2, nouns usually account for less than half of children's vocabularies. Toddlers' growing vocabularies also include a variety of relational words that are used to communicate about changes in the state or location of an object (Gopnik & Meltzoff, 1997). "Gone" and "here," for example, may be used to announce the disappearance and appearance of objects. One of the most useful relational words in children's early vocabularies is "no," which can serve such important communicative functions as rejection, protest, and denial. "No" can also be used to comment on unfulfilled expectations (for example, "no play" when a planned trip to the park is cancelled because of rain) and on an object's absence (for example, "no teddy" when a favorite toy goes missing). Given these multiple functions, it is little wonder that "no" is among the earliest and most frequently used words in a child's budding vocabulary (Bloom, 1973).

The Vocabulary Spurt One of the most remarkable features of children's early vocabulary development is the astonishing *growth spurt* of new words that typically occurs during toddlerhood (see Figure 7.5, p. 243). In order to reach an average-sized vocabulary by kindergarten, children must learn about nine new words each day (Samuelson & McMurray, 2017). What makes this rapid acquisition possible?

Elsa Bartlett and Susan Carey made use of the normal routine of a preschool classroom to find out what happens when a totally new word is introduced into conversation with children (Bartlett, 1977; Carey, 1978). They chose to study the acquisition of color terms. Pretesting had revealed that none of the 14 children in the classroom knew the name of the color that adults call olive, so the researchers chose olive as the experimental color but instructed the children's teacher to refer to it with the implausible name "chromium," just in case some children had partial knowledge of the real name that they had not revealed.

The researchers then arranged to have a cup and tray that had been painted "chromium" paired in the classroom with a cup and a tray of a primary color, such as red or blue. While preparing for snack time, the teacher, as instructed, created an opportunity to say to each child, "Please bring me the chromium cup; not the red one, the chromium one" or "Bring me the chromium tray; not the blue one, the chromium one." Despite the fact that the children had never heard the word "chromium" before, all of them picked the correct cup or tray, although they were likely to ask for confirmation ("You mean this one?"). Some of the children could be seen repeating to themselves the unfamiliar word.

One week after this single experience with the new word, the children were given a color-naming test with an array of color chips. Two-thirds of them showed that they had learned something about this odd term and its referents: When asked for chromium, they chose either the olive chip or a green one. Six weeks later, many of the children still showed the influence of this single experience.

As in this experiment, it appears that when children hear an unfamiliar word in a familiar, structured, and meaningful social interaction, they form a quick, "first pass" idea of the word's meaning (Clark & Wong, 2002). Developmentalists refer to this form of rapid word acquisition as **fast mapping**. Fast mapping has been observed in children as young as 15 months of age in controlled experiments (Yow et al., 2017).

fast mapping The way in which children quickly form an idea of the meaning of an unfamiliar word they hear in a familiar and highly structured social interaction.

An important question for researchers is why fast mapping occurs in toddlerhood but not before. Some research suggests that a tipping point occurs once children have achieved a vocabulary of 50 to 75 words (Bates, Thal, Finlay, & Clancy, 2002; von Koss Torkildsen et al., 2009). For example, a study conducted with

Norwegian 20-month-olds found that children with more than 75 words in their vocabulary learned new words significantly faster than did children with smaller vocabularies, perhaps because of changes in how the brain processes language. In particular, the children's brain activity was monitored as the children were presented with five repeat pairings of nonsense words and pictures of fantasy objects. In the small-vocabulary group, brain activity associated with attention persisted across all five presentations; in the large-vocabulary group, attention peaked during the third presentation and then declined. This finding suggests that children with larger vocabularies processed the word-object associations more efficiently than did the children with smaller vocabularies (von Koss Torkildsen et al., 2009). Other research, however, suggests that fast mapping is due not to brain changes but to toddlers' increased abilities to use social cues to infer a speaker's intentions. For example, Shannon Pruden and her colleagues devised an experiment in which two groups of younger babies were presented with two objects, one boring (like a kitchen cabinet latch) and one interesting (like a sparkle wand), neither of which the infants would know the name. With one group, the experimenter repeated a nonsense label like "blicket" several times while looking at the boring object; with the other group, the experimenter repeated the same label several times while looking at the interesting object. Subsequent testing in which the infants were told to look at the blicket revealed that they had applied the "blicket" label to the interesting object, regardless of which object the experimenter had been looking at while repeating the label. Thus, unlike the word learning of toddlers that takes into account the speaker's intention, word learning in younger children seems to be indifferent to the social intent of the speaker and driven instead by the children's own interest and point of view (see also Golinkoff & Hirsh-Pasek, 2006; Poulin-Dubois & Forbes, 2006). The researchers speculate that this form of word learning is necessarily slower than the fast mapping of toddlers because it probably requires repeated word-to-object pairings and may often leave infants with wrong names to unlearn. On the other hand, the pace of word learning should be considerably faster once children are able to use social information to infer a speaker's labeling intent.

Figurative Language Not long after children start to name objects, they begin to use figurative language—specifically metaphors. A **metaphor** involves using a word or a phrase to represent some other, seemingly unrelated thing. When we talk about how "time flies," complain that a grumpy person is "prickly," or tease a friend who's stealing our French fries by saying, "Quit being such a pig!" we are using metaphors. Likewise, a 2½-year-old may point at a half-peeled banana and say "Flower" or throw Styrofoam bits in the air and shout, "Snow!" Children's use of metaphor provides evidence that language production is a creative process, not simply an imitative one. To generate a metaphor, children must recognize a similarity between two unrelated things and express that similarity in a way that they have never heard before.

metaphor Use of a word in a way that draws a comparison between the thing the word usually refers to and some other, unrelated thing.

At the same time that young children appear extraordinarily creative in inventing metaphors, they can be very limited in understanding metaphors used by others. An example is the following exchange one of your authors observed at a birthday party: As one 4-year-old girl sat at the table eating cake, another child's mother, evidently a stranger to the girl, reached over and wiped chocolate frosting from the girl's cheek. "Thank you," said the little girl. "I've got your back, sister," said the mother. Obviously shaken by the mother's statement, the little girl replied, "I'm not your sister!" (We can only imagine what she made of "I've got your back.")

The ability to understand and use metaphors develops throughout childhood (Johanson & Papafragou, 2014). There is evidence that even 5-year-old children can understand certain metaphors, such as how time flies or how ideas can *escape from your head* (Özçalışkan, 2007). Nonetheless, children's understanding of metaphors takes some years to develop and is significantly related to general cognitive development. During middle childhood, for example, children still have difficulty understanding metaphors that compare people to objects. Metaphors such as "That kid is a bulldozer" are confusing to them because they lack knowledge about personality traits and thus fail to understand the similarity proposed by the metaphor. Not until adolescence are children able to understand and create metaphors of this nature (Pan & Snow, 1999).

Grammar Development

As noted earlier, a watershed of language development is reached toward the end of infancy, when children begin to produce utterances consisting of two or more words. Significantly, two-word utterances carry more than twice as much information as a single word alone because of the meaning conveyed by the relationship between the two words. With as few as two words, children can indicate possession ("Daddy chair"), nonexistence ("Gone cookie"), and a variety of other meanings. They can also create different meanings by varying the order of words ("Chase Mommy" and "Mommy chase"). This new potential for creating meaning by varying the arrangement of linguistic elements marks the birth of grammar.

Grammar and Meaning

As we indicated previously, the rules of grammar play a critical role in interpreting the meaning of sentences. Evidence that children have some grasp of grammatical rules fairly early in their language development comes from studies in which young children are asked to interpret grammatically correct sentences that contain nonsense words (Fisher, Klingler, & Song, 2006). In one experiment, 2-year-old children were shown two pictures of a duck and a bunny interacting (Gertner, Fisher, & Eisengart, 2006). One picture showed the bunny acting on the duck (Figure 7.6a); the other showed the duck acting on the bunny (Figure 7.6b). As the children viewed the pictures, they were told, "The duck is *gorping* the bunny! See?" Even though "gorping" is a nonsense word, English grammar

(a)

(b)

FIGURE 7.6 Despite the fact that "gorping" is a nonsense word, 2-year-olds—when presented with pictures similar to (a) and (b)—associate the sentence "The duck is gorping the bunny!" with image (b), demonstrating the importance of grammar in learning and understanding language.

dictates that if the duck is gorping the bunny, the duck is the active agent, and the bunny is the object being acted upon. The 2-year-olds presented with this sentence indicated their knowledge of grammar by looking significantly longer at the picture in which the duck was acting on the bunny. Developmentalists interpret results like this as evidence of an innate universal grammar that helps children interpret the language they hear (Chang, Dell, & Bock, 2006). Using grammar to learn the meaning of new words—as the children did with "gorp" in the study—is referred to as **syntactic bootstrapping** (Fisher et al., 2006; Wojcik & Saffran, 2015).

syntactic bootstrapping Use of knowledge of grammar to figure out the meaning of new words.

Young children also demonstrate their knowledge of grammar through the errors they make when they string together words. Between ages 2 and 3, English-speaking children often make statements like "My doggy runned away" or "Connor camed to play." Such errors are so common that it is easy to overlook their significance. Children cannot have been taught to say such things, nor could they have learned them by simple imitation because they virtually never hear such incorrect sentences uttered. Rather, they are revealing their knowledge of the general rule for forming the past tense with regular verbs by misapplying it to irregular verbs.

Increasing Complexity

At the same time that children begin to string together more and more words to form complete sentences, they increase the complexity and the variety of words and grammatical devices they use. These changes are illustrated by the following prodigious sentence spoken by an excited 2-year-old girl: "You can't pick up a big kitty 'cos a big kitty might bite!" (DeVilliers & DeVilliers, 1978, p. 59). This sentence is by no means typical of 2-year-olds, but it provides a good opportunity to assess how more complex utterances communicate more explicitly. The sentence communicates not only that the little girl does not want to pick up a big cat but also that no one should pick up a big cat; it also conveys her understanding that big cats sometimes bite but do not invariably do so. Such complex sentences communicate shades of meaning that help adults respond sensitively to children's experiences.

As Figure 7.7 indicates, the length of the utterances grows explosively from around 2 years of age (Eve being a bit earlier than most), along with vocabulary and grammatical ability (Devescovi et al., 2005). Note that the growth in the length of utterances (or the *mean length of utterance*) is indicated by the average number of morphemes per utterance rather than the average number of words. The phrase "That big bad boy plays ball," for example, contains six words and seven morphemes, whereas the phrase "Boys aren't playing" contains only three words but six morphemes ("boy," "s," "are," "not," "play," "ing"). Assessing linguistic complexity by counting morphemes rather than words provides an index of a child's total potential for making meaning in a particular utterance.

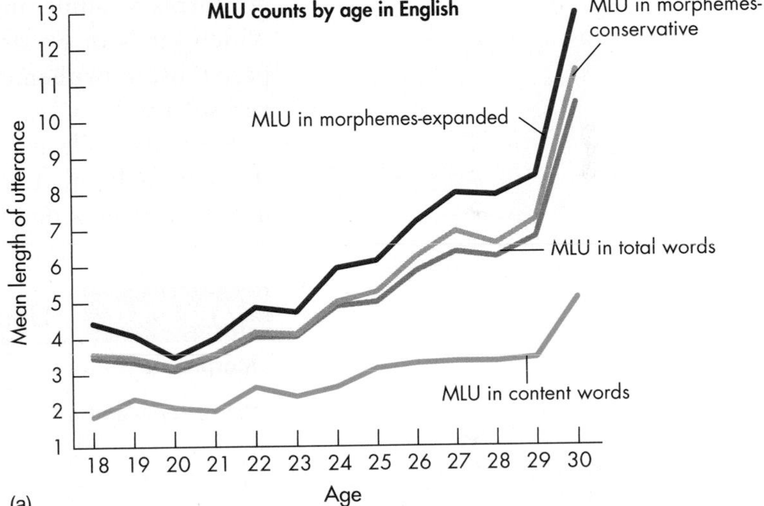

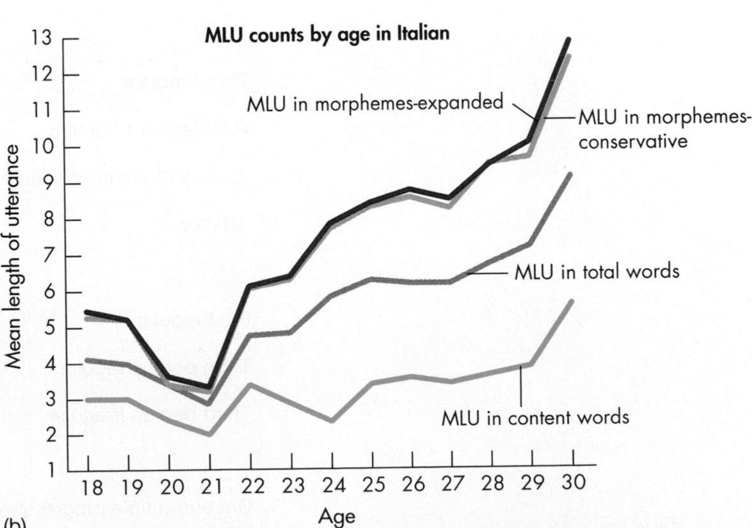

FIGURE 7.7 This graph shows the rapid increase in the mean length of utterances made by English-speaking (a) and Italian-speaking (b) children between 18 and 30 months of age. (Data from Devescovi et al., 2005.)

The complexity of the 2-year-old girl's long sentence about picking up cats is attributable in large measure just to her use of those little words and word parts that are systematically absent in two-word utterances. The article "a" ("a big kitty") indicates that it is big cats in general, not just this particular big cat, that are worrisome.

The word "'cos" connects two propositions and indicates the causal relationship between them. The contraction "can't" specifies a particular relationship of negation. These elements are special type of morphemes called **grammatical morphemes** because they create meaning by showing the relationships between other elements within the sentence.

grammatical morphemes Words and parts of words that create meaning by showing the relationships between other elements within the sentence.

Whether the rate of language acquisition is fast or slow, grammatical morphemes appear in roughly the same sequence in the speech of all children who acquire English as a first language. As Table 7.3 indicates, the grammatical morpheme likely to appear first in children's language production is *ing*, used to indicate the present progressive verb tense. This verb form allows children to describe their ongoing activity. Morphemes indicating location, number, and possession make their appearance next. Morphemes that mark complex relationships, such as the contraction *'m* in "I'm going" (which codes a relationship between the first person singular subject of the action and the present time of the action), are generally slower to emerge.

The appearance of grammatical morphemes is a strong indicator that children are implicitly beginning to distinguish nouns and verbs because their speech conforms to adult rules that specify which morphemes should be attached to which kinds of words in a sentence. Thus, for example, children do not apply past-tense morphemes to nouns ("girled"), nor do they place articles before verbs ("a walked").

Evidence collected by a number of language development researchers shows that although children begin to produce grammatical morphemes relatively late in the language acquisition process, they recognize and understand the significance

TABLE 7.3 Usual Order of Acquiring Grammatical Morphemes

Morpheme	Meaning	Example
Present progressive	Temporary duration	I walk*ing*
In	Containment	*In* basket
On	Support	*On* floor
Plural	Number	Two balls
Past irregular	Prior occurrence	It *broke*
Possessive inflection	Possession	Adam's ball
To be without contraction	Number	There it *is*
Articles	Specific/nonspecific	That *a* book That *the* dog
Past regular	Prior occurrence	Adam walk*ed*
Third person regular	Number	He walks
Third person irregular	Number	He does She has
Uncontractible progressive auxiliary	Temporary duration; number	This *is going*
Contraction of *to be*	Number; prior occurrence	That's a book
Contractible progressive auxiliary	Temporary duration	I*'m* walking

Information from Brown, 1973.

of grammatical morphemes in the language they hear at least by the time they are starting to produce their first multiword utterances (Golinkoff, Hirsch-Pasek, & Schweisguth, 1999).

Pragmatic Development

Many of us have observed a mother trying to talk to a friend while her child pulls on her pant leg, impatiently intoning, "Mommy, Mommy, Mommy." "Not now," the mother may say, or, "I'm talking; you need to wait until I'm done." Whether interrupting a conversation or using language that is inappropriate for the context (remember the little girl who greeted her mother's psychology department head with "Hi, fatso!"), young language learners are famous for saying the wrong thing at the wrong time simply because they have not yet mastered *pragmatics*, which include social and cultural conventions of language use in particular contexts (Clark, 2014). These conventions may vary markedly from one culture to another. In many cultures, children are expected to say "please" when they request something and "thank you" when they are given something. But in certain Colombian communities, such verbal formulas are frowned upon in the belief that "please" and "thank you" signal the speaker's inferiority; obedience, not formulaic politeness, is what these adults expect of their children (Reichel-Dolmatoff & Reichel-Dolmatoff, 1961).

Conversational Acts

One important aspect of pragmatics is the use of language as **conversational acts**, actions to achieve goals performed through language and gesture. According to Elizabeth Bates and her colleagues (Bates, Camaioni, & Volterra, 1975), children's earliest conversational acts fall into two categories, *protoimperatives* and *protodeclaratives*. Using **protoimperatives** is an early way of engaging another person to achieve a desired goal—for example, holding up a cup and saying "More" to get a refill on juice. Using **protodeclaratives** is a way of establishing joint attention and sustaining a dialogue. Perhaps the earliest form of a protodeclarative is the act of pointing, which may be accompanied by words, as when a baby points to a dog and says, "Doggie." Young children often use a succession of protodeclaratives for the purpose of sustaining a dialogue. A common gestural example of this is a child's bringing all of his or her toys, one after another, to show to a visitor if each presentation is acknowledged by a smile or a comment (Bates, O'Connell, & Shore, 1987).

conversational acts Actions that achieve goals through language.

protoimperatives Early conversational acts whose purpose is to get another person to do something.

protodeclaratives Early conversational acts whose purpose is to establish joint attention and sustain a dialogue.

In the process of acquiring pragmatics, children also come to understand that a single sequence of words may accomplish several alternative goals and that linguistic and other contexts can be crucial to interpretation. An amusing example of this occurs in a series of incidents in *Higglety Pigglety Pop!*, Maurice Sendak's tale of an adventurous dog who accepts a job as nanny for Baby, a child caught in the grip of the "terrible twos." At first the dog attempts to get the baby to eat, and the baby says, "No eat!" When the dog decides to eat the food himself, the baby again says, "No eat!" Finally the baby and dog find themselves confronted by a lion, and the baby says for the third time, "No eat!"

In addition to using the same words to convey different meanings, children must also gain competence in using social cues in order to understand the meaning intended by the speaker. For example, the sentence "Is the door shut?" has the grammatical form of a request for information. But it may be functioning as a request for action or as a criticism—that is, pragmatically equivalent to "Please shut the door" or "You forgot to shut the door again." Marilyn Shatz (1978) found that children as young as 2 years old responded correctly to their mother's indirect commands, such as "Is the door shut?" That is, instead of responding to the surface grammatical form and answering "Yes" or "No," Shatz's toddlers went to shut the door.

This finding is consistent with work we described earlier, linking toddlers' sensitivity to social cues to the fast mapping of vocabulary growth.

At the same time that children are recognizing that a single phrase can have multiple meanings or goals, they develop the ability to express a single meaning or goal in multiple ways. For example, a 3-year-old observed by John Dore (1979) used three different grammatical forms to achieve a single goal: "Get off the blocks!" "Why don't you stay away from my blocks?" and "You're standing on my blocks."

Viewing communications as conversational acts in which a single phrase can have more than one meaning and a single meaning can be conveyed in many ways exposes the complex relationship between the world of language and the world of objects, events, and direct experience. There is no simple and direct correspondence between the two worlds—which makes a child's apparently easy acquisition of language all the more wondrous. As they get older, children become increasingly skilled in their use and understanding of the subtleties of conversational acts—eventually knowing, for example, that despite the difference in language and tone, "I think I need some time to myself to sort things out" and "I'm dumping you" mean the same thing.

Developing Narratives As children's conversational skills develop, so too does their capacity to tell stories, or *narratives*, about their experiences. In a seminal study of developing storytelling abilities, Peterson and McCabe (2004) asked children to tell them about memorable events such as going to the doctor's office. They found that the stories of young children followed the very simple structure of **chronology**, presenting a sequence of concrete events. For example, 3½-year-old Paul describes a visit to the doctor's office to get stitches as "I get a needle. I get stitches, like first I got a needle, then I got stitches and then go home." As children's narrative abilities mature, their stories become more elaborate and more dramatic in emotional tone, as shown in the following story about a younger brother getting stung by a bee (Peterson & McCabe, 2004, p. 29):

chronology In language development, a simple story structure used by young children, in which they present a sequence of concrete events.

> Mark [brother] got a big sting when he was just first born. I, I was walking with him and, and I just and he falled and he didn't know that he falled right on a bee. And he, and his knee was on a bee and stung, he got stung on a bee. I tried to pick him up but, but he didn't want me to but I had to call my Mommy. My Daddy and everybody who I knowed who was a grown-up came. And then I, I told them and I looked down at his knee and there it was, stung.

©Elizabeth Crews/The Image Works

The conversational skills of these 4-year-olds allow them to tell each other stories about memorable events.

When children first begin to produce narratives, their stories can be hard to follow because they leave out essential information. A teacher who is approached by a tearful preschooler saying only "He broked it" does not have much to work with unless he or she asks the child to elaborate ("What was broken?" "Who broke it?"). Indeed, adults often ask young children to expand their stories in an effort to make them more organized and coherent, as the following dialogue between a mother and her 3½-year-old child demonstrates (Nelson & Shaw, 2002, p. 51):

Child: You know something?
Mother: What?
Child: Let me think . . . . What's her name again?
Mother: Who?
Child: That girl.
Mother: Who?
Child: Don't you remember her? You've seen her before.

Mother: Where is she?
Child: I don't know. I don't know her name. Somebody has a rocket. That can turn into a big rocket.
Mother: Who is this person?
Child: I don't know her.
Mother: Where'd you meet her?
Child: At our house!
Mother: Was I home for this?
Child: (shakes head)
Mother: So how would I know who this is?

Although the mother is working hard to help her child develop her story, the child has difficulty understanding that her mother's knowledge of the girl is necessarily limited by the fact that she was not home to meet her, a cognitive limitation we discuss in more detail below.

As children grow older, **cultural modeling**—that is, culturally specific ways of telling stories—influences their narrative development. Carol Lee's work with African American children has done much to advance our understanding of how children use the storytelling traditions of their culture to form stories of their own (Lee, Rosenfeld et al., 2004; Lee, 2010). For example, common features of African American narratives include the following (Lee et al., 2004, p. 47):

cultural modeling Culturally specific ways of telling stories.

- Use of dramatic language
- Use of or description of body language and gesture
- Sermonic tone (a dramatic tone of voice typically used during African American church services)
- References to culturally specific objects, events, and behaviors

To illustrate the cultural modeling of African American children's narratives, Lee and her colleagues showed pictures to 8- to 10-year-old children and asked the children to tell stories about them. One picture, "Jumping the Broom" (Figure 7.8), depicts a custom of great significance in the history of African Americans, dating back to the time of slavery, when African Americans were not legally allowed to marry. To mark their marital commitment, couples would jump over a broom in front of witnesses, a custom that is still enacted in some African American weddings. One girl who participated in Lee's study told the following story about the picture, giving names to the man and woman being married, and creating a dialogue between them. Notice how she incorporates several of the features of African American narratives described above:

> The wedding looked so pretty. There was dancing [and] Mr. Johnson said to his wife, "I love you." "I love you, too," Ms. Sara Lee said. Mr. Johnson threw up his Bible and said, "Thank you Jesus! For giving me a wonderful ceremony," and Ms. Sara said, "Amen to that." They were both happy. They jumped over the broom. (Lee et al., 2004, pp. 52–53.)

FIGURE 7.8 Developmentalist Carol Lee studies cultural modeling—that is, the ways that children draw from cultural traditions to construct meaningful stories of life and experience. To facilitate children's storytelling, Lee makes use of culturally relevant artifacts, such as Annie Lee's painting "Jumping the Broom," which depicts African American marriage traditions.

APPLY > CONNECT > DISCUSS

Consider the two exchanges on this and the next page between a mother and her son, Richard, while they were looking at a book, the first when Richard was about 1 year old and the second when he was nearly 2 years old (Bruner, 1983, cited in Clark, 2003). Analyze each in terms of the concepts presented in this section.

First exchange:
Mother: Look!
Richard: (touches pictures)
Mother: What are those?
Richard: (vocalizes a babble string and smiles)

Mother: Yes, there are rabbits.
Richard: (vocalizes, smiles, looks up at mother)
Mother: (laughs) Yes, rabbit.
Richard: (vocalizes, smiles)
Mother: Yes. (laughs)

Second exchange:
Mother: What's that?
Richard: *Mouse.*
Mother: Mouse, yes. That's a mouse.
Richard: (pointing at another picture) *More mouse.*
Mother: No, those are squirrels. They're like mice but with long tails. Sort of.
Richard: *Mouse, mouse, mouse.*
Mother: Yes, all right, they're mice.
Richard: *Mice, mice.*

LEARNING OUTCOMES

Point out some biological explanations of language acquisition.

Point out some social and cultural explanations of language acquisition.

Point out come constructivist and dynamic systems explanations of language acquisition.

Explanations of Language Acquisition

During much of the twentieth century, two widely divergent theories dominated explanations of how children acquire language. These theories correspond roughly to the polar positions on the sources of human development—nature versus nurture. Social learning theorists, for example, once attributed language acquisition largely to nurture, especially to the language environment and teaching activities provided by adults. Biological theorists, in contrast, attributed language acquisition largely to nature, assuming that as children mature, their innate language capacity enables acquisition to occur naturally, with only minimum input from the environment and without any need for special training.

In recent decades, both theoretical positions have been modified. On the nurture side, there has been a growing consensus that such mechanisms as learning by association, classical and operant conditioning, and imitation are insufficient to account for how children acquire language. Contemporary theorists who emphasize the role of the environment now focus on how social and cultural contexts are organized in ways that draw children into language-using communities. Likewise, theorists who emphasize the biological foundations of language acquisition agree that it is important to specify the ways in which the environment, however minimally, contributes to the developmental process. Thus, as we indicated at the beginning of this chapter, virtually all developmentalists agree that both biology and the environment provide important keys to the world of language. At the same time that these two dominant approaches were undergoing modification, a third approach gained attention—one that places emphasis on the distinct role of cognition in language development. We will review each of three approaches in the sections below.

Biological Explanations

For half a century, biological explanations of language acquisition have been dominated by the work of the linguist Noam Chomsky (Chomsky, 2017). According to Chomsky, the fact that children acquire language quickly and effortlessly without any direct instruction and that they produce a vast array of sentences that they have never before heard makes it impossible to claim that language could be acquired primarily through learning mechanisms. Rather, language is innate and develops through a universal process of maturation. Chomsky (1988, p. 134) phrased this idea as follows:

> Language learning is not really something that the child does; it is something that happens to the child placed in an appropriate environment, much as the child's body grows and matures in a predetermined way when provided with the appropriate nutrition and environmental stimulation.

In likening the acquisition of language to the maturation of the body, Chomsky also emphasized that language is a "mental organ." Just as the functions of a physical organ such as the liver are specific, so are the functions of the "mental organ" of language (Chomsky, 1980, p. 52). Psycholinguist Steven Pinker echoes this view in a book pointedly titled *The Language Instinct* (1994). In Pinker's words, language is a "distinct piece of the biological makeup of our brains . . . distinct from more general abilities to process information or behave intelligently" (2007). The fact that Chomsky describes language as a distinct process does not mean that he denies its connection to other psychological processes or to the environment. Indeed, he explicitly acknowledges that "children acquire a good deal of their verbal and non-verbal behavior by casual observation and imitation of adults and other children" (Chomsky, 1959, p. 49). But such factors, he argues, cannot fully account for language acquisition.

In certain formulations of this theory, Chomsky proposed that children learn language as a result of a mental mechanism he dubbed the **language acquisition device (LAD)**. Through the LAD, the child is, in essence, hardwired to recognize the abstract grammatical rules (for example, for the order of elements in sentences) of whatever language the child is regularly exposed to. According to Chomsky, at birth, the LAD is in an embryonic state, but as children mature and interact with the environment, maturation of the LAD enables them to use increasingly complex language forms. The eventual result of this process is the adult capacity to use language.

language acquisition device (LAD) Chomsky's term for an innate language-processing capacity that is programmed to recognize the universal rules that underlie any particular language that a child might hear.

Others who, like Chomsky, believe that there must be some preexisting linguistic mechanism that guides children's language acquisition argue that the feedback children get on their early utterances provides insufficient information for them to induce the rules of grammar (Dehaene-Lambertz & Spelke, 2015; Pinker, 2002). One strategy for evaluating this argument is to document how much feedback children actually receive about their use of language. The answer, based on several decades of research, is "very little" (Valian, 1999). Furthermore, even when parents do attempt to correct erroneous grammar, the effort is likely to fail, as shown in a classic exchange reported by David McNeill (1966, pp. 106–107):

Child: Nobody don't like me.
Mother: No, say "nobody likes me."
Child: Nobody don't like me.
[This interchange is repeated several times. Then:]
Mother: No, now listen carefully; say "nobody likes me."
Child: Oh! Nobody don't likes me.

Sequences like this, which are commonplace, seriously undermine the idea that specific teaching is important to language acquisition and bolster the biological view that language acquisition depends only minimally on the environment.

In summary, biological theorists contend that the essential structures that make language acquisition possible—the universals of grammar—are determined far more by the evolutionary history of our species than by the experiential history of particular children. Experience does of course determine which of the many possible human languages a child actually acquires. Children who never hear Chinese spoken will not grow up speaking Chinese, even though they are genetically capable of learning that (or any other) language. According to Chomsky's theory, however, the experience of hearing a particular language does not modify the LAD; it only triggers the innate mechanisms designed for language acquisition and implements the particular language features it encounters.

Social and Cultural Explanations

While acknowledging that innate features of the human brain play an important role in the acquisition of language, many developmentalists stress the fact that language is necessarily a social process. They argue that children acquire language in the process of using it in a particular sociocultural environment (Nelson, 2014; Schmidt, Butler, Heinz, & Tomasello, 2016; Vygotsky, 1978).

In an early and influential statement of this position, Jerome Bruner (1982) proposed that the earliest social structures for language development involve what he called **formats**—recurrent socially patterned activities in which adult and child do things together. In the United States and other cultures, for example, simple formatted activities include such games as peekaboo and the routines surrounding bathing, bedtime, and meals, which provide a structure for communication between babies and caregivers even before babies have learned any language. In this way, formats serve as "crucial vehicles in the passage from communication to language" (Bruner, 1982, p. 8). Bruner argued that, viewed as a whole, the formatted events within which children acquire language constitute a **language acquisition support system (LASS)**, which is the environmental complement to the innate, biologically constituted LAD emphasized by Chomsky.

formats Recurrent socially patterned activities in which adult and child do things together.

language acquisition support system (LASS) Bruner's term for the patterned behaviors and formatted events within which children acquire language. It is the environmental complement to the innate, biologically constituted LAD.

In a series of studies, Michael Tomasello and his colleagues (summarized in Tomasello, 2000) revealed that a key element in such language-learning support systems is the finely tuned and well-timed interaction of the participants. These researchers videotaped mothers interacting with their young children in order to identify the precise moment at which the mothers referred to objects in the immediate environment. They found that the mothers talked mostly about objects that were already a part of the child's current actions and the focus of joint attention for the child and mother, thus greatly reducing the child's problem in figuring out the referents of the mother's words. As you recall from a previous discussion, children are much more likely to learn new words for objects they find interesting (see p. 245).

Importantly, culture often influences whether and how particular objects become a focus of mother–child joint attention. This was nicely illustrated in Jeremy Anglin's comparison of two studies that explored how children learn the names for plants (Anglin, 1995). One study was conducted in a small Mayan hamlet in a highland region of central Mexico and the other in the urban area of Berkeley, California (Stross, 1973). The Mayans live on a mountain slope covered by lush and varied vegetation, including both cultivated and wild trees, bushes, grasses, and

Ariel Skelley/Getty Images

A great deal of language learning takes place in casual interactions among family members as they talk, joke, and even sing.

herbs. The Mayan community depends on this botanical environment for food and fuel, as well as for material with which to make their houses. In contrast, the residents of Berkeley, like most other urban-dwelling Americans, generally do not interact directly with the botanical world. As you might imagine, compared with that of the children in the Berkeley study, the language environment of the Mayan children contained far more words specific to the botanical world. Indeed, as early as 2½ years of age, most Mayan children knew as many as 30 different plant names and could appropriately describe a variety of ways that the different plants were used. In contrast, 2-year-olds in Berkeley had acquired just a few, very general plant words, usually labels for fruits and vegetables used in the home (for example, "banana," "spinach").

Penny Tweedie/Getty Images

This young Aboriginal Australian boy lives in a community that depends heavily on the natural environment for food, shelter, and other basic needs. Compared with his non-Aboriginal peers, his vocabulary likely includes many more terms relevant to his important relationship to nature.

Constructivist and Dynamic Systems Approaches

Other approaches to understanding language development emphasize how the child's language abilities emerge in relationship to other developing systems (D'Souza, D'Souza, & Karmiloff-Smith, 2017). Many theorists suggest that changes in the way children use language arise as a consequence of the kind of cognitive developments described by Piaget. For example, as we discussed in Chapters 5 and 6, sometime around 18 months of age, children begin to reason systematically about hidden objects; they deliberately vary their actions to achieve a goal and display increasing awareness of social standards. Correspondingly, before 18 months of age, children are restricted to words that reflect what they are experiencing at the moment—"social words" such as "Bye-bye" (when Mother is leaving for work) and "Hereyare" (when discovering a searched-for toy). After the age of 18 months, however, they can articulate knowledge of absent objects ("Gone"), describe their own activities ("Done it"), and comment on their perceived failure to meet social expectations ("Uh-oh").

Cognitive development also influences children's emerging conversational skills. Consider the following "conversation" between two preschoolers:

> Jenny: My bunny slippers . . . are brown and red and sort of yellow and white. And they have eyes and ears and these noses that wiggle sideways when they kiss.
> Chris: I have a piece of sugar in a red piece of paper. I'm gonna eat it but maybe it's for a horse.
> Jenny: We bought them. My mommy did. We couldn't find the old ones. These are like the old ones. They were not in the trunk.
> Chris: Can't eat the piece of sugar, not unless you take the paper off.
> (Stone & Church, 1957, pp. 146–147.)

Clearly, Jenny and Chris are not having a true conversation. Instead, each is voicing his or her own thoughts, without regard for the utterances of the other, a form of communication that Piaget referred to as **collective monologues**. According to Piaget, preschool-age children engage in such talk because they are egocentric and lack the cognitive ability to take into account another person's knowledge, interests, and activities. We encountered a similar example of this cognitive limitation in the dialogue between the mother and the child who were trying to figure out the name of the girl that the mother had never met (p. 251). This particular cognitive limitation, called *egocentrism*, is discussed in detail in Chapter 8 (pp. 270–271). As cognitive development progresses, collective monologues eventually give way to **true dialogue**, in which the utterance of one person takes into account the utterance of another.

collective monologues Communications in which young children each voice their own thoughts without attending to what the others are saying.

true dialogue A communication in which each person's utterances take into account the utterances of others.

In what would become a famous counterargument to Piaget's analysis, Vygotsky (1934/1986) claimed that young children's egocentric talk has an entirely different

Marko MacPherson/Masterfile

Despite their shared delight in sand, sea, and shells, it will be several years before these two toddlers develop the cognitive and language skills necessary to engage in true dialogue about their day at the beach.

inner speech According to Vygotsky, the internalization of egocentric speech that occurs during early childhood and allows individuals to mentally plan activities and solve problems.

source. Rather than being rooted in an inability to take into account another person's perspective, as Piaget posited, Vygotsky suggested that children use egocentric speech to help in their early efforts to organize their thoughts and regulate their behavior. In other words, egocentric speech is a form of "thinking out loud," a prelude to the ability to think entirely internally, as amply demonstrated in this preschool boy's verbalizations during solitary play with action figures and objects:

> Caught him! Whoops! Got him. He fell down. He's dead. Whoopsey! What's that? I caught her. Hey, you get, you get back up here. I got ya, I got her. Look what you did to the building. Stop! There you go! Show you. Argh! Pow! Boom! I got you now. I pull you. Oww, that hurt! You guys are dead. Hahaha. Boom! I'll cut that thing off. Haha. Hey what's wrong with you? Haha. You're dead! . . . What's that handcuff doing on me? Haha. You're still handcuffed on. We need the key, where's the key? Right here? Where's the key? Lock him up. We can't. Lock him up. Lock him up. I locked him. I'm the cops. Thanks. You're welcome. (Bergen, 2011, p. 237.)

Vygotsky also differed from Piaget regarding the developmental course and outcome of egocentric speech. Piaget argued that egocentric speech is simply replaced by socialized speech as the child matures cognitively. In contrast, Vygotsky believed that egocentric speech never truly disappears. Instead, it is gradually internalized as **inner speech**, the internal mental "talk" that we all engage in as we think about our experiences, plan our daily activities, and solve problems. Thus, although the *form* of egocentric speech becomes transformed with development (that is, internalized as inner speech), the *function* of egocentric speech in regulating thought and action is developmentally invariant.

Vygotsky also differed from Piaget in the way he understood social interactions as critically significant for children's development. The role of social interactions in language development is underscored in recent dynamic systems approaches, which argue that the emergence of language is highly related not only to cognitive developments but to social experiences as well (D'Souza et al., 2017; Ribot & Hoff, 2014). So, for example, and as we discussed previously, language development is affected by how parents talk to their children—how they respond to early vocalizations, what they talk about, and whether they speak more than one language. In turn, parents are known to adjust their speech according to their children's cognitive and language development (Zampini, Fasolo, & D'Odorico, 2012). According to dynamic systems approaches, then, language develops in ways that reflect its connection to a complex web of interactions with other developing factors.

Explaining Grammar Because those who adopt a cognitive approach deny that biological processes primarily drive language acquisition, a major challenge for these developmentalists is to explain how children acquire grammar, with its complex rules and structures. As we noted earlier, as children's vocabulary increases, so too does the complexity of the grammar they use. Some developmentalists propose that children's growing mastery of grammatical structures is, in fact, a by-product of the growth of their vocabulary and of their attempts to express increasingly complex thoughts (Devescovi et al., 2005; Elman et al., 1996). Evidence in support of this view comes from research demonstrating a direct link between the size of children's vocabularies and the degree of complexity of the grammatical utterances they can make (Fernald, Perfors, & Marchman, 2006). When grammatical complexity is compared directly with the number of words that children know, there is an almost perfect relationship between vocabulary size and grammatical complexity, regardless of how old the children are. Researchers argue that such data clearly demonstrate that grammar develops to deal with a growing vocabulary (Figure 7.9).

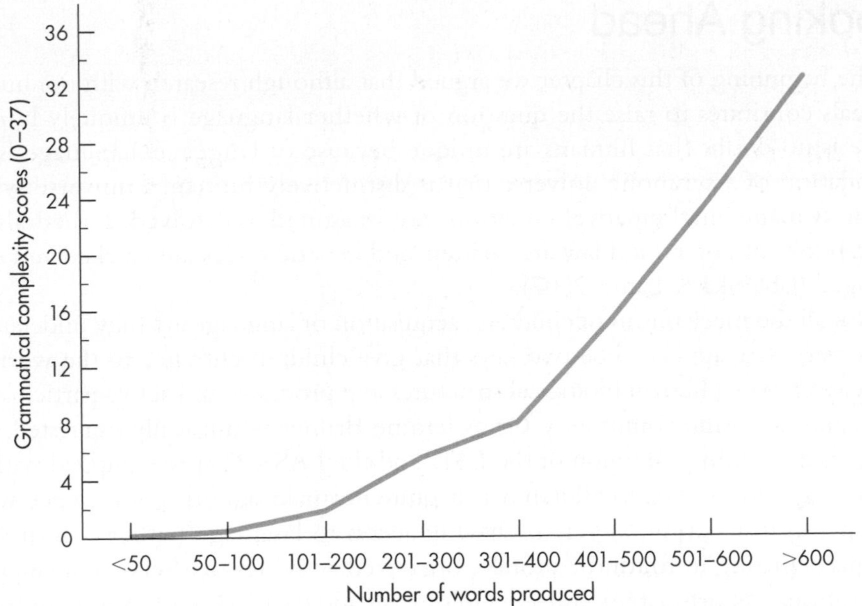

FIGURE 7.9 When the size of children's vocabulary is plotted against the degree of grammatical complexity of their utterances, there is a clear positive relationship. Elizabeth Bates and her colleagues have used these data to argue that grammar emerges from the need to use many words to convey complex messages. Note that an acceleration of grammatical complexity begins when children's vocabularies reach approximately 400 words. (Data from Bates, 1999.)

Language and Cognitive Impairments Given the extent to which cognitive development is understood to influence language development, researchers and practitioners are naturally interested in how children with various cognitive impairments acquire language (D'Souza et al., 2017). In Chapter 2 (p. 65), we briefly described Down syndrome, a genetic disorder that produces moderate to severe intellectual impairments. Children with Down syndrome are able to hold a conversation, but their vocabulary is relatively restricted, and their talk is grammatically simple. Although their language improves over the course of childhood, it reaches a plateau in adolescence, and these children remain largely incapable of producing and comprehending complex linguistic constructions (Witecy & Penke, 2017). Such results suggest that normal language development requires normal cognitive functioning.

This broad conclusion is brought into question, however, by research on children who suffer from a rare genetic disorder called *Williams syndrome*. Children afflicted with Williams syndrome are also intellectually impaired, yet their language is much less impaired than their cognitive abilities would suggest. Although initial language acquisition is often delayed, many children with Williams syndrome eventually produce sentences that are grammatical, clearly pronounced, and understandable. They are also able to tell stories that are meaningful and display considerable subtlety in their portrayal of human feelings (D'Souza et al., 2017). A much smaller proportion of children with Down syndrome reach this level of sophisticated language use, even when their level of intellectual impairment is relatively mild (Fowler, 1990).

Overall, data on children who have some form of genetic disease indicate that children are capable of developing some degree of language competence even in the face of intellectual impairment and that at least some aspects of language develop independently of general cognitive functioning.

APPLY > CONNECT > DISCUSS

Review the discussion of primary and secondary intersubjectivity presented on p. 231. In what ways are they similar to Bruner's concept of a language acquisition support system (LASS)?

LEARNING OUTCOMES

Indicate the two keys to the world of language that children use to enter the distinctly human, symbolic universe.

Looking Ahead

At the beginning of this chapter we argued that although research with nonhuman animals continues to raise the question of whether language is uniquely human, there is no doubt that humans are unique because of language. Language is the foundation of a symbolic universe that is distinctively human, a universe where music is made, mathematical equations are imagined and solved, cathedrals are built, books of poetry and law are written, and genetic codes are cracked and even changed (Jablonka & Lamb, 2007).

Not all the mechanisms of children's acquisition of language are fully understood. However, there appear to be two keys that give children entrance to the world of language: normal human biological structures and processes and active participation in a language-using community. Or, as Jerome Bruner whimsically suggested, language is born from the union of the LAD and the LASS. That is, equipped with an innate acquisition device, children may acquire normal linguistic competence without special instruction, merely by having access to language (either oral or sign) and participating in routine, culturally organized activities that serve as a language acquisition support system. Indeed, Goldin-Meadow's work with deaf children in hearing households suggests that participation in normal cultural routines can be sufficient for the rudiments of language to appear.

Although children 2½ to 3 years of age can properly be considered language-using human beings, their language development is obviously incomplete. Language continues to develop during childhood; indeed, some aspects of language develop into adulthood (Clark, 1995). Moreover, as children begin to acquire the specialized skills they will need to cope with adult life in their culture, deliberate teaching may begin to play a conspicuous role in language development. Such specialized activities as reciting nursery rhymes, acting in a play, and writing an essay are all forms of language activity that require practice and instruction. We shall return to examine some of the more specialized language developments associated with middle childhood in Chapter 11.

Review the discussion of experience-expectant and experience-dependent processes of brain development presented in Chapter 4 (pp. 129–131). In what ways might these processes be reflected in language development, especially a child's developing ability to distinguish phonemes?

Summary

The Power and Foundations of Language

- Language is a cultural tool, a symbolic system of enormous scope and power. As such, it profoundly affects development by mediating human activities, relationships, and thinking. Children are born predisposed to attend to language and to communicate. They move rapidly from cooing, babbling, and jargoning into the world of language.

Keys to the World of Language

- The two keys to language acquisition are the biological structures and systems that support language and participation in a language-using community.
- Humans differ dramatically from nonhuman primates in their ability to acquire language. Bonobos and chimpanzees can be taught to understand and (with symbols and gestures) produce

simple utterances—abilities at roughly the level of 2-year-old children.

- Studies of patients with Broca's aphasia and Wernicke's aphasia have shown the importance of the left frontal lobe in acquiring and using language. Neuroimaging studies confirm the involvement of Broca's area in the processing of complex speech. Although the left hemisphere appears to have evolved as the brain center for language, when infants suffer left-hemisphere damage, the right hemisphere can take over language functions.
- A community of language users provide children with models of, and opportunities for, language acquisition, as is clear from studies of children in language-deprived environments.
- Bilingual and multilingual environments are not known to create interference with language development; they do, however, promote specific cognitive developments, including the ability to shift and control attention.

The Basic Domains of Language Acquisition

- As part of phonological development, young children learn to segment sequences of speech into meaning units of language and to master the pronunciation and rules of their native sound system.
- Semantic development brings increasing understanding of the meaning of words and strings of words. With the help of adults, children learn to pair words to their referents.
- Infants' first words tend to be nouns, but they are soon supplemented by verbs, adjectives, and relational words. A vocabulary spurt occurs at about 2 or 3 years of age, when young children's new ability to understand speaker intent makes possible fast mapping, in which children form quick first-pass ideas of word meanings.
- With two-word utterances, the acquisition of grammar (or the rules for sequencing words) is evident. Children's utterances become increasingly long and complex, with more units of meaning, or morphemes, including grammatical morphemes.
- Pragmatic development enables children to understand and employ social and cultural conventions of language use, to use communications as conversational acts to achieve goals, and to use context to interpret communications.
- Young children increasingly understand and use figurative language such as metaphors and produce increasingly sophisticated narratives.

Explanations of Language Acquisition

- Biological explanations of language acquisition argue that children are able to acquire language on the basis of limited input because the human brain is hardwired to learn a language that follows certain universal rules.
- Social and cultural explanations emphasize the role of the sociocultural environment through, for example, formats (routine, patterned activities that adult and child do together) and interactions generally.
- Constructivist and dynamic systems approaches focus on the ways emerging language abilities relate to development in other areas. From a Piagetian perspective, for example, as egocentrism wanes, collective monologues give way to true dialogue. From a dynamic systems perspective, language development is part of a web of interacting factors, including language input from parents.

Looking Ahead

- Questions about the specifics remain, but it is clear that with the two keys to the world of language—a brain for language and participation in a language-using community—young children enter a symbolic universe that is distinctively human.

Key Terms

perceptual scaffolding, p. 229
babbling, p. 230
cochlear implant, p. 236
phonological development, p. 239
semantic development, p. 239
grammar, p. 239
pragmatic development, p. 239
morpheme, p. 240
fast mapping, p. 244
metaphor, p. 245
syntactic bootstrapping, p. 247
grammatical morphemes, p. 248
conversational acts, p. 249
protoimperatives, p. 249
protodeclaratives, p. 249
chronology, p. 250
cultural modeling, p. 251
language acquisition device (LAD), p. 253
formats, p. 254
language acquisition support system (LASS), p. 254
collective monologues, p. 255
true dialogue, p. 255
inner speech, p. 256

Daniel Grill/Getty Images

CHAPTER

8

Physical and Cognitive Development in Early Childhood

A group of 5-year-old children has been listening to their teacher read the folktale "Stone Soup," which tells the story of three hungry soldiers who trick some peasants into giving them food by pretending to make soup out of stones. The soldiers tell the peasants that they have made stone soup to share with everyone and that the soup would, of course, taste much better with some vegetables and meat. Rose, one of the children listening to the story, asks whether stones melt. The teacher, Vivian Paley, decides that the best way to answer this question is to have the children make some stone soup of their own. In the course of their experiment, she asked the children about their expectations regarding the stones—and they all agreed that the stones would melt if cooked. Ms. Paley set them to boil for an hour and then placed them on the table for inspection. Now all agreed that the stones were quite smaller—"Almost melted," said one little boy. So Ms. Paley begins another experiment. This time the class weighs the stones before and after they are boiled. After observing that the stones weighed two pounds before cooking and two pounds after, the children struggled to understand what might be going on. A few suggested that although they continued to weigh the same, the stones were nonetheless a little bit smaller. One child suggested that the stones in the story were magic.

(Information from Paley, 1981, pp. 16–18.)

This discussion among a group of kindergarten children and their teacher illustrates both the fascination developmentalists feel and the challenges they face as they study the cognitive changes that occur in the years following infancy. When the teacher prompts the children to reconcile the world of the folktale and the world of their senses, the children exhibit a pattern of thinking that is typical for their age—a mixture of sound logic and magical thinking. The children correctly believe that when things are "cooked down," they grow smaller and that small stones should be lighter than big ones. At the same time, they are willing to believe that there really are such things as magical stones that melt, and so they miss the point of "Stone Soup." Their way of thinking appears to wobble back and forth between logic and magic, insight and ignorance, the reasonable and the irrational.

A similar mixture of cognitive competence and incompetence can be found in the youngsters' ability to remember objects and events. Young children can often recall the names and descriptions of their favorite dinosaurs, details of trips to the dentist's office, or where they last left their favorite toy with an accuracy that astounds their parents (Baker-Ward et al., 2015; Fivush, Habermas, Waters, & Zaman, 2011). In fact, their memory for stories that rhyme can be better than that of adults (Király, I., Takács, S., Kaldy, Z., & Blaser, 2017). But if an adult asks them to remember a short list of words or a set of toy objects—a task that is easy for older children and adults—young children find it difficult to do so, even just a few minutes later (Tulving & Craik, 2000).

The variability of young children's intellectual performances highlights in a special way the unevenness of development, one of the key principles discussed in Chapter 3 (see p. 103 for the list of principles). At the same time, it raises important questions: Can early childhood be considered a distinct stage of development? If it can, then what explains the uneven and variable quality of thought during the years between ages 2 and 5?

As you probably expect from your reading thus far, theorists' answers to these questions depend on whether they view development as discontinuous and stagelike or continuous and gradual. Stage theorists see young children as being at a certain stage—that is, at a certain level of cognitive *competence*—which they have attained as a result of general processes of change—physical maturation and the universal experiences children have with a variety of people, objects, and other features of their environments. According to these theorists, the unevenness of thought in early childhood is of little significance or consequence: In their view, it is largely a matter of variability in *performance* resulting from such factors as the variations in children's familiarity with a particular task or the specific way in which the task is presented (see also Chapter 5, p. 179). In contrast, theorists who emphasize the continuity of development see the unevenness as consequential and as inconsistent with a stage view. These theorists tend to maintain that cognitive change and its unevenness arise either from (1) gradual increases in various general psychological mechanisms such as short-term memory capacity or (2) from changes within various isolated domains of psychological functioning, with changes in different domains occurring at different rates. In this chapter, we will examine each of these views in turn, looking at Piaget's preoperational stage, at information-processing approaches to cognitive development, and at cognitive development in specific domains.

1. Young children have charming ideas about how the world works, believing, for example, that the moon follows them around or fairies live in flowers. Where do you suppose these ideas come from?
2. It's a sad fact that young children can be victims or witnesses of crime. Do you think that young children are capable of providing reliable testimony about crimes they have experienced or witnessed? Why or why not?

LEARNING OUTCOMES

Summarize gains in early childhood gross and fine motor skills.

Explain the importance of sleep and nutritional needs in early childhood, including problems of undernutrition and obesity.

Outline how the brain develops during early childhood.

Point out unevenness of early childhood cognition in terms of variability of development.

Physical and Motor Development

Growth rates of the body and brain are considerably slower during early childhood than they were in infancy. At the same time, the ability of children to use and control their bodies grows by leaps and bounds. As you will see, these changes affect children's health and nutritional needs—needs that are not always met, for various cultural, social, and economic reasons.

The Changing Body

By the time children enter early childhood, around the age of 2½, their body proportions have changed substantially. Gone are the dimpled bottoms, pudgy thighs, and sumo-wrestler bellies so typical of the infant build. Much of the change in the body's proportions and appearance is due to the lengthening of the long bones of the arms, legs, and fingers (Duren et al., 2013; Olsen, Reginato, & Wang, 2000). This bone development occurs when new bone tissue is formed through a process of **ossification**. In general, ossification takes place at the ends of long bones, around areas of cartilage known as *growth plates* (see Figure 8.1). In addition to generating new bone tissue, ossification is associated with the hardening and strengthening of bones (Kalkwarf et al., 2007; Rauch & Schoenau, 2001). Until a bone becomes fully mature and ossified, it is vulnerable to fracture, especially the area of the growth plate, which is the last part to ossify and harden. It is estimated that 15 to 30 percent of all childhood fractures are growth-plate fractures (Sullivan & Anderson, 2000). Because they may affect future bone growth, growth-plate fractures should be treated immediately and followed over time to best prevent consequences such as crooked or uneven limbs.

ossification A process through which new bone tissue is formed at the growth plates of long bones.

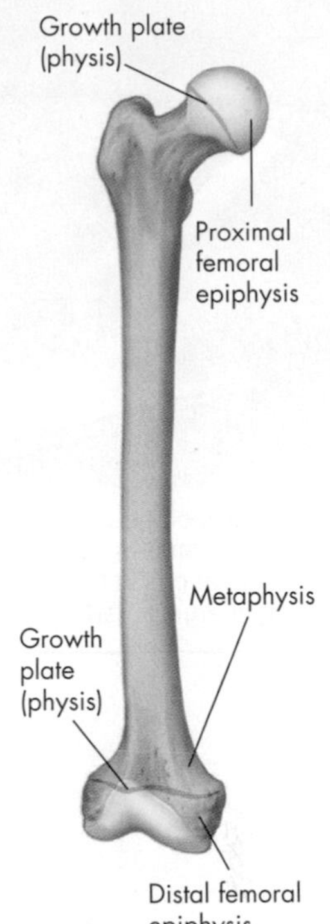

FIGURE 8.1 Growth plates (physes) are located between the widened part of the shaft of the bone (the metaphysis) and the end of the bone (the epiphysis). This diagram of a femur (thighbone) shows the location of the growth plates at both ends of the bone. (Research from Sullivan, 2000.)

Motor Development

Watching little children on a playground is a lesson in the extraordinary physical and motor developments that separate early childhood from infancy. As shown in the Table 8.1 column on gross motor skills, at 2 years of age, children can run, kick a ball, and climb the ladder of the slide, and at 3 years they can ride a tricycle. The ability to throw a ball overhand emerges at around age 4, as does skipping—that quintessentially childlike way of moving through the world. By the time they are 5, children have achieved a great deal of mastery over their bodies; they have good balance and can ride a scooter and climb nimbly on a jungle gym.

Just as impressive as these gains in motor development is the exuberance with which children practice them. Have you ever been at the grocery store or mall and noticed a young child hopping around or gyrating goofily for no apparent reason other than the sheer joy of doing so? Indeed, young children seem to take great pleasure in their newfound abilities to control their bodies, an aspect of motor development described as **motor drive**.

In addition to advances in their gross motor skills, young children's fine motor skills improve notably—to the point that 5-year-olds can fully dress themselves and

motor drive The pleasure young children take in using their new motor skills.

TABLE 8.1 Motor Milestones of Early Childhood

Age, in Years	Gross Motor Skills	Fine Motor Skills
2	Walks well Runs Goes up and down stairs alone Kicks ball	Uses spoon and fork Turns pages of a book Imitates circular stroke Builds tower of 6 cubes
3	Runs well Marches Rides tricycle Stands on one foot briefly	Feeds self well Puts on shoes and socks Unbuttons and buttons Builds tower of 10 cubes
4	Skips Standing broad jump Throws ball overhand High motor drive	Draws a person Cuts with scissors (not well) Dresses self well Washes and dries face
5	Hops and skips Good balance Skates Rides scooter	Dresses without help Prints simple letters Ties shoes

The enormous gains in gross motor development that characterize early childhood provide good reasons for South Korean parents to enroll their children in martial arts classes.

Seokyong Lee/New York Times/Redux

Steven Puetzer/Getty Images

This young boy's colorful drawing of his family demonstrates some of the remarkable advances in fine motor control that emerge in early childhood.

tie their shoes, use eating utensils effectively, pour water into a glass more or less reliably, and wield crayons with enough control to stay within the lines when they want to. Taken together, the growth and refinement of young children's gross and fine motor capacities markedly increase their abilities to explore their environments and add significantly to the variety of experiences they can have, providing ample occasions for the development of new ways to think and act.

Health

The slowed pace of physical growth during early childhood is reflected in the decreased and occasionally finicky appetites of young children (Dubois et al., 2006). Nevertheless, new levels of physical activity enabled by increased motor development and control place significant demands on the young body for appropriate amounts of both sleep and nutrition. It is fairly well known that older children and adolescents often do not get enough sleep or eat as well as they should (see Chapter 11, pp. 376–377, and Chapter 14, pp. 496–499), but research indicates that this is also often true for young children. As any parent can attest, children who do not get enough sleep or have not been eating well can be grumpy, overly emotional, and easily frustrated, and they may have trouble concentrating (Dahl & Lewin, 2002; El-Sheikh, Buckhalt, Mize, & Acebo, 2006).

Sleep Despite pediatricians' recommendations that young children get 12 to 15 hours of sleep in a 24-hour period (naps included), a study conducted by Christine Acebo and her colleagues found that children between 2 and 5 years of age typically sleep only about 8.7 hours at night and less than 9.5 hours in the course of 24 hours (Acebo et al., 2005). A study of Chinese children found similar results; in addition, it found that those who slept less were less prepared to start preschool and had lower scores on tests of emotional maturity, language development, and cognitive development (Tso et al., 2016). Furthermore, and consistent with research conducted in several other countries, including the United States and Spain, children who slept less than the recommended hours were more likely to engage in excessive use of electronic devices, including television (see Domingues-Montanari, 2017, for a review). In a Spanish study of 1,000 young children ages 2 to 6 years, viewing TV for more than 1.5 hours correlated with significantly reduced sleep duration (Marinelli et al., 2014).

Researchers continue to explore the causes and long-term effects of early sleep deprivation on later development. One significant and troubling finding is the association of shorter sleeping and obesity. This is due, at least in part, to the fact that short-sleepers consume more calories in the evenings before bed—mostly in the form of milk drinks (McDonald et al., 2015).

Nutrition In many parts of the world, breast-feeding continues well into the third and even fourth year of life (Konner, 2005; Whiting & Child, 1953). In most industrial societies, however, children usually have been fully weaned from the breast or bottle by the time they are 2 years of age. How parents meet the energy needs of young children has become a major source of concern for developmentalists, particularly in light of the obesity epidemic affecting an estimated 42 million children under the age of 5 throughout the world (Lumeng et al., 2017; Syrad, Johnson, Wardle, & Llewellyn, 2016; WHO, 2010). In the United States, a nationwide longitudinal study found that children identified as overweight between 2 and 4 years of age were five times more likely than their normal-weight peers to be overweight as adolescents, placing them at risk for a variety of health problems, including diabetes, high blood pressure, and heart disease (Nader et al., 2006). Interestingly, it appears that in addition to the amount of weight gained, the velocity of weight gain during early childhood poses significant health risks. A large study conducted in France found that young children who gained weight quickly relative to their peers were at greater risk of being overweight (Péneau et al., 2011).

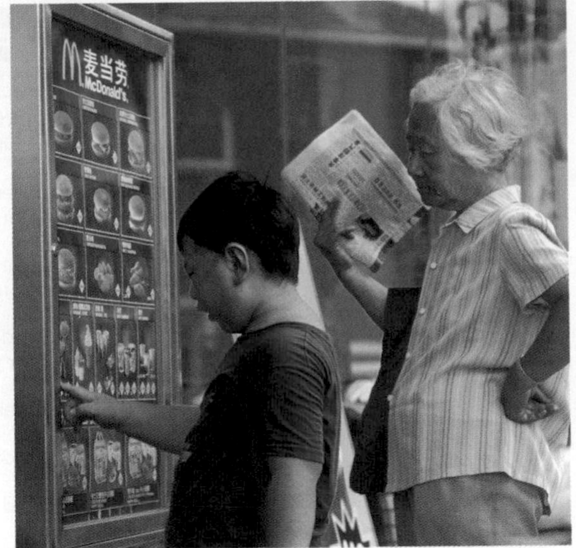

Mark Henley/Panos Pictures

Childhood obesity rates continue to rise throughout the world, including China, due in part to increased access to diets high in fats and sugars.

A similar national study of Finnish children found an interesting growth pattern associated with the emergence of heart disease in adulthood (Alastalo et al., 2009). Specifically, individuals most at risk for cardiovascular disease as adults were those who were underweight during the first 2 years of life and then underwent a period of rapid weight gain through early and later childhood. This particular pattern has worrisome implications for children in developing countries where globalization is creating major changes in access to food and in eating behavior, with an increase in calories as well as in fats and sugar in the diet. In fact, a study of children in China, India, Guatemala, Brazil, and the Philippines—all of which are experiencing the "nutrition transition" associated with globalization—found evidence for the pattern described in the Finnish study—that is, growth failure in the first few years of postnatal life followed by overweight in early and later childhood and elevated risk for diabetes and heart disease in adulthood (Stein, Thompson, & Waters, 2005).

Young children rely on parents to provide them with nutritious meals and snacks. For economic reasons, some parents may have difficulty meeting the nutritional needs of their children (Augustine, Prickett, & Kimbro, 2017). This is especially true in developing countries, where an estimated 195 million children under the age of 5 have stunted growth because their parents cannot afford to feed them adequately (UNICEF, 2009). Even in the United States, 21.3 percent of households with children (8.4 million) are considered **food-insecure** (Fiese, Gundersen, Koester, & Washington, 2011; Nord, Coleman-Jensen, Andrews, & Carlson, 2010), meaning that they do not have access to enough food to ensure good health for all family members (Figure 8.2). Table 8.2 (p. 266) lists items that are included in a national survey completed by parents in the United States to assess the food security of their children. Children who suffer food insecurity are at risk for a number of problems, including developmental delays and poor academic achievement (Cook & Frank, 2008; Jyoti, Frongillo, & Jones, 2005).

food-insecure Lacking enough food to ensure good health.

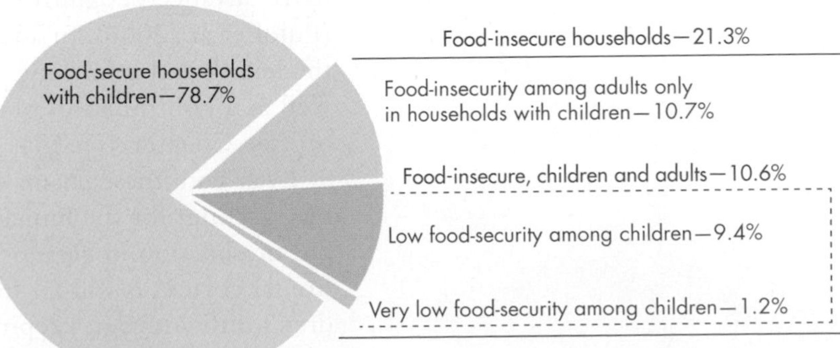

FIGURE 8.2 Food is surely at the top of the list of children's essential needs. Yet many parents around the globe have difficulty providing their children with enough food to ensure healthy growth and development. Even in the United States, one of the wealthiest countries in the world, more than 10 percent of families with children are food insecure.

Parental attitudes about food and eating can also take a toll on children's nutrition. A series of studies conducted by Thomas Joiner and his colleagues found that parents of 3-year-olds worried that their sons but not their daughters were underweight and did not eat enough, despite the fact that there was no difference in the actual average weight of boys and girls in the study (Holm-Denoma et al., 2005). This finding prompted the researchers to speculate that body-image stereotypes—specifically, that girls should be thin and boys big and strong—may be affecting the diets of very young children and possibly increasing the risk of eating disorders in the future (see Chapter 15, p. 555). And, although parents today are increasingly concerned about early-childhood obesity, researchers have made the point that these concerns must be carefully balanced with the

TABLE 8.2 Questions Used to Assess the Food Security of Children (questions refer to the past 12 months)

1. Did you often, sometimes, or never rely on only a few kinds of low-cost food to feed your children because you didn't have enough money to buy food?
2. Were you often, sometimes, or never able to feed your children a balanced meal because you couldn't afford to do so?
3. Was it often, sometimes, or never true that your children were not eating enough because you couldn't afford enough food?
4. Did you ever cut down the size of your children's meals because there wasn't enough money for food?
5. Were your children ever hungry because you couldn't afford more food?
6. Did any of your children skip a meal because there wasn't enough money for food?
7. Did any of your children not eat for a whole day because there wasn't enough money for food?

Information from Nord et al., 2010.

potential for children's undernutrition (Allen & Myers, 2006). Especially when it is severe or chronic, undernutrition can cause serious developmental problems, including for the young child's developing brain (Prado & Dewey, 2014).

Brain Development

As we discussed in Chapter 5, after infancy, the brain's development slows considerably until adolescence, when it undergoes another growth spurt. At the start of early childhood, the brain has attained about 80 percent of its adult weight; by age 5, it has grown to 90 percent of its full weight (Huttenlocher, 1994). Despite this modest growth rate, several noteworthy changes occur in the brain during early childhood (Lenroot & Giedd, 2006; Shaw et al., 2008). For example, the overall enlargement in size results from the continuing process of *myelination*, which speeds the transmission of neural impulses within and among different areas of the brain (Dean et al., 2014). During early childhood, myelination is most prominent in brain areas such as the frontal cortex that are important for more advanced cognitive functions, including planning and regulating behavior (Pujol et al., 2006). In addition to increased myelination, there is an increase in the length and branching of neurons that connect different areas of the brain, as well as a continuation of *synaptic pruning*, in which nonfunctional synapses die off (see Chapter 4, p. 130).

Even with these changes, the brain, of course, is still relatively immature, which may account for the limitations of children's problem-solving abilities. For example, myelination in parts of the brain that support memory (the hippocampus and frontal cortex) is still far from complete, which likely contributes to young children's difficulties in keeping several things in mind at once. In addition, various areas of the brain are developing and connecting at different times and at different rates, and this variability may account for the unevenness of cognitive development that is evident during this age period. When one part of the brain develops more rapidly than others, or when the neural pathways connecting a particular combination of cortical areas undergo a spurt in myelination, the psychological processes supported by the brain area or areas can be expected to undergo rapid change as well. High levels of performance are expected to occur when a given task calls on brain systems that are highly developed, and, correspondingly, low levels of performance are expected to occur when a given task calls on brain systems that are not yet mature.

A fascinating example of what happens when areas of the brain that will eventually communicate with each other are not yet connected is the *scale errors* made by toddlers. In older children and adults, the perception of the size, or scale, of an object is seamlessly integrated into the person's actions with the object. You would not, for example, try to put a really large peg into a really small hole. Children between 18 and 30 months of age, on the other hand, very well might. This is because they frequently commit **scale errors**; that is, they fail to integrate information about the size of an object into their decisions about how to use it (Ishibashi & Moriguchi, 2017). The result is serious and often amusing attempts to perform impossible actions, such as trying to sit in a dollhouse chair or get into a miniature toy car (Figure 8.3). On the basis of their research, Judy DeLoache and her colleagues argue that scale errors in young children involve a "disconnect" between children's use of visual information and their ability to plan and control their actions (DeLoache, LoBue, Vanderborght, & Chiong, 2013). The dissociation of perception and action, they speculate, may be due to the immature cortical functioning of the brain, particularly in the prefrontal cortex (see also Barsalou, 2008).

Some of the changes that occur in brain development during early childhood are influenced by the cultural context: Different culturally organized activities promote *experience-dependent* brain growth in the form of increased synaptic development and connections (see Chapter 4, pp. 129–131). For example, if a young child lives in a culture that emphasizes hunting or weaving, both of which require concentrated and sustained processing of spatial relations, it can be expected that the child's brain will undergo increased growth of cells in the area responsible for processing spatial information (the parietal cortex). By contrast, if the child's culture places a heavy emphasis on verbal expression, the language centers of the child's brain are likely to undergo additional development. The influence of culturally organized activities on brain development is intriguingly illustrated in a recent study indicating that when children take music lessons between the ages of 4 and 6, brain processes associated with attention and memory become more active when they listen to music, and their general memory capacity and IQs improve compared with those of children who do not receive music training (Fujioka, Trainor, & Ross, 2008).

scale errors Young children's inappropriate use of an object due to their failure to consider information about the object's size.

DeLoache et al., 2004

(a)

DeLoache et al., 2004

(b)

FIGURE 8.3 Two examples of scale errors. (a) This 21-month-old child has committed a scale error by attempting to slide down a miniature slide; she has fallen off in this earnest effort to carry out what is an impossible act. (b) This 24-month-old child has opened the door to the miniature car and is repeatedly trying to force his foot inside the car. (Republished with permission of Judy S. DeLoache et al. From Scale Errors Offer Evidence for a Perception-Action Dissociation Early in Life. *Science* 304, 1027 [2004]. DOI:10.1126/science.1093567. Permission conveyed through Copyright Clearance Center.)

APPLY > CONNECT > DISCUSS

Armed with the information in Table 8.1 (p. 263) and your understanding of *motor drive*, visit a playground where you can observe young children engaged in motor play. What examples of motor skills and motor drive can you identify? Focusing on one or two children, can you guess their ages, based on the motor skills they exhibit?

Preoperational Development

LEARNING OUTCOMES

Explain how early childhood thinking exemplifies Piaget's preoperational stage of cognition.

Examine centration through early childhood errors of egocentrism, confusion of appearance and reality, and precausal reasoning.

Adult: Why is it cold in winter?
Child: Because there is snow.
Adult: What is it that makes the cold?
Child: The snow.
Adult: If there were no snow would it be cold?
Child: No.
Adult: It is the snow which makes the cold, or the cold which makes the snow?
Child: The cold makes the snow.
Adult: And where does the cold come from?
Child: From the snow.

(Piaget, 1929/1979, p. 323.)

As we discussed in Chapter 5, Piaget believed that when children complete the final sensorimotor substage of infancy, they are able to think symbolically, using one thing to stand for ("re-present") another. This newfound ability to use one thing to stand for another is the foundation for developing language. It is also the bridge to the next stage of intellectual development, which Piaget called *preoperational* and considered a transitional stage between the sensorimotor intelligence of infancy and the fully *operational* intelligence of middle childhood (Piaget & Inhelder, 1969). In order to explain what Piaget meant by *preoperational thinking*, we need first to say a bit about the meaning of operational thought (which we will discuss in more detail in Chapter 11).

mental operations In Piaget's theory, the mental process of combining, separating, or transforming information in a logical manner.

According to Piaget, operational thinking involves **mental operations**—that is, mental "actions" in which children combine, separate, and transform information in a logical manner. Examples of mental operations include mathematical processes such as adding and subtracting, as well as arranging objects in particular orders (from smallest to largest, alphabetically, and so on) or putting objects into categories based on some feature they have in common. The ability to engage in such mental actions and think operationally emerges around 7 to 8 years of age, making it possible for children to arrange their stamp collections according to country of origin and estimated value, for example, or to assemble a complex new toy right out of the box. They are better able to formulate explicit problem-solving strategies because they can think through alternative actions and modify them mentally before they actually act. Piaget believed that until children are able to engage in mental operations, their thinking is subject to fluctuations of the kind Ms. Paley's class demonstrated when answering questions about "Stone Soup" and to the type of circular reasoning illustrated in the above dialogue, in which a child explains the relationship between snow and the cold of winter.

preoperational stage According to Piaget, the stage of thinking between infancy and middle childhood, in which children are unable to decenter their thinking or to think through the consequences of an action.

Piaget's belief that young children often fall into error and confusion because they are still unable to engage in true mental operations is what led him to call the period of cognitive development in early childhood the **preoperational stage**. In his view, cognitive development during early childhood involves a process of overcoming the limitations that stand in the way of operational thinking. (These limitations, discussed in the next several sections, are outlined in Table 8.3.)

Although fluctuations and errors are typical of early childhood thought, Piaget insisted that preoperational thinking is not random or unsystematic. Indeed, as you will see below, the errors children make in the preoperational stage are remarkably consistent, and this may reveal much about the nature of cognition and its development. On the other hand, as we discussed in Chapter 5, many developmentalists disagree with Piaget's conclusions and argue that his interview methods make it difficult for children to demonstrate their competence on various tasks, thereby obscuring their level of actual understanding.

Centration

centration Young children's tendency to focus on only one feature of an object to the exclusion of all other features.

Imagine that we show you two beach balls. One is red with blue stripes; the other is red with yellow stripes (see Figure 8.4). If we then ask you to point to the red ball, you would very likely want clarification: "Which red one? The one with yellow stripes or the one with blue stripes?" In contrast, a preoperational child would most likely point to one or the other of the balls with total confidence. According to Piaget, the source of such an error, and the greatest limitation to early childhood thinking, is **centration**, the tendency of young children to be "captured" by a single, usually perceptual, feature of whatever they are trying to think about and to focus on that one feature to the exclusion of all others. In the case of the beach balls, the child focuses on the perceptual feature color (blue, in this case) and

TABLE 8.3 Piaget's Stages of Cognitive Development: Preoperational

Age (years)	Stage	Description	Characteristics and Examples
Birth to 2	Sensorimotor	Infants' achievements consist largely of coordinating their sensory perceptions and simple motor behaviors. As they move through the six substages of this period, infants come to recognize the existence of a world outside themselves and begin to interact with it in deliberate ways.	Centration, the tendency to focus (center) on the most salient aspect of whatever one is trying to think about; a major manifestation of this being the tendency to consider the world entirely in terms of one's own point of view • Children engage in collective monologues, rather than dialogues, in each other's company.
2 to 6	Preoperational	Young children can represent reality to themselves through the use of symbols, including mental images, words, and gestures. Objects and events no longer have to be present to be thought about, but children often fail to distinguish their point of view from that of others; become easily captured by surface appearances; and are often confused about causal relations.	• Children have difficulty taking a listener's knowledge into account in order to communicate effectively. • Children fail to consider both the height and width of containers in order to compare their volumes. • Children confuse classes with subclasses. They cannot reliably say whether there are more wooden beads or more brown beads in a set of all wooden beads.
6 to 12	Concrete operational	As they enter middle childhood, children become capable of mental operations, internalized actions that fit into a logical system. Operational thinking allows children to mentally combine, separate, order, and transform objects and actions. Such operations are considered concrete because they are carried out in the presence of the objects and events being thought about.	Confusion of appearance and reality • Children act as if a Halloween mask actually changes the identity of the person wearing it. • Children may believe that a straight stick partially submerged in water actually does become bent. Precausal reasoning, characterized by illogical thinking and an indifference to cause-and-effect relations
12 to 19	Formal operational	In adolescence, the developing person acquires the ability to think systematically about all logical relations within a problem. Adolescents display keen interest in abstract ideals and in the process of thinking itself.	• A child may think a graveyard is a cause of death because dead people are buried there. A form of moral reasoning that sees morality as being imposed from the outside and that does not take intentions into account

consequently ignores the other feature, stripes. As you can imagine, centration results in thinking and knowledge that are highly biased and limited to the particular perceptions that happen to have captured the child's attention at a given point in time. The opposite of centration—and the key to cognitive growth beyond the preoperational stage—is **decentration**, which is the ability to mentally pull away from focusing on just one aspect of an object or problem in order to consider multiple aspects of it simultaneously. Decentration allows children's thinking and knowledge to be less subjective and reflect a broader point of view. For this reason, Piaget argued that the *consequence* of the mental distancing enabled by decentration is **objectivity**—that is, an understanding of reality as separate from one's subjective perceptions, thoughts, and actions—which Piaget regarded as the full flowering of cognitive development. Indeed, as you will see in later chapters, Piaget held that cognitive development from infancy through adolescence involves a steady march toward increasing objectivity, the hallmark of scientific reasoning.

Preoperational children, however, have just begun this journey toward objectivity. Their tendency to be captured by a single aspect or dimension of an object or event is at the root of what Piaget identified as the three most common errors in early childhood reasoning: (1) egocentrism, (2) the confusion of appearance and

FIGURE 8.4 "Captured" by the blue stripes, this child fails to recognize the ambiguity of the statement, "point to the red ball."

decentration The cognitive ability to pull away from focusing on just one feature of an object in order to consider multiple features.

objectivity The mental distancing made possible by decentration. Piaget believed the attainment of objectivity to be the major achievement of cognitive development.

reality, and (3) precausal reasoning. In the sections that follow, we will look at these three errors by first summarizing the evidence that led Piaget to his conclusions about each one and then presenting findings that challenge his interpretations.

Egocentrism If you and some friends were to walk together down a road in the dark of night, you all might notice that the moon seemed to be following you. You would all know, of course, that the moon was not *really* coordinating its movement with your own. To think otherwise, you would have to account for the fact that if each of you suddenly set off in different directions, each of you would still have the sense of being followed by the moon. The contradiction here no doubt seems obvious to you. Preoperational children, on the other hand, have no sense of such a contradiction. They will steadfastly maintain that the moon follows them around and fail to appreciate that it cannot possibly follow someone heading west at the same time it follows someone heading east.

egocentrism In Piaget's terms, the tendency to "center on oneself"—that is, to consider the world entirely in terms of one's own point of view.

In the context of Piaget's general concept of centration, **egocentrism** refers to the tendency to "center on oneself," or, in other words, to be captive to one's own point of view and unable to take another person's perspective. The child who wants to give Daddy a Care Bear or an action hero for his birthday and the child who believes that he or she is being followed around by the moon are both demonstrating egocentrism.

A famous example of egocentrism as a failure to take another person's perspective is found in young children's performance on Piaget's classic "three-mountain problem." In this procedure, young children were shown a large diorama containing models of three mountains that were distinctively different in size, shape, and landmarks (Piaget & Inhelder, 1956) (Figure 8.5). First, the children were asked to walk around the diorama and become familiar with the landscape from all sides. Once the children had done this, they were seated on one side of the diorama. Next, a doll was placed on the opposite side of the diorama so that it had a "different view" of the landscape. The children were then shown pictures of the diorama from several perspectives and were asked to identify the picture that corresponded to the doll's point of view. Even though they had seen the diorama from the doll's location, the children almost always chose the picture corresponding to their own spatial perspective, not that of the doll. Preoperational children's poor performance on Piaget's three-mountain problem has been widely replicated and long assumed to demonstrate the perspective-taking limitations of young children.

FIGURE 8.5 Preschool children shown this diorama of three mountains, each with a distinctive feature on its top, were unable to say how the scene might look from perspectives other than the one they had at the moment. (Research from Piaget & Inhelder, 1956.)

Speculating that the complexity of Piaget's task might affect children's performance, Helen Borke (1975) first replicated the classic three-mountain experiment with children between 3 and 4 years of age. She then presented the same children with an alternative form of the problem—a farm scene that included such landmarks as a small lake with a boat on it, a horse and a cow, ducks, people, trees, and a building. In this alternative version, Grover, a character from *Sesame Street*, drove around the landscape in a car, stopping from time to time to take a look at the view. The child's task was to indicate what that view looked like from Grover's perspective.

Children as young as 3 years old performed well on this perspective-taking problem, despite the fact that, as would be expected, they performed poorly on the three-mountain version of the problem. These contrasting levels of performance between the two forms of a logically identical problem led Borke to conclude that when perspective-taking tasks involve familiar, easily differentiated objects, and when care is taken to make it easy for young children to express their understanding, young children demonstrate that they are able to take spatial perspectives other than their own. In other words, young children have the *competence* to take the perspectives of others, but their *performance* may be affected by the demands of the task.

Confusing Appearance and Reality

First child: Pretend there's a monster coming, okay?
Second child: No. Let's don't pretend that.
First child: Okay. Why?
Second child: 'Cause it's too scary, that's why.
(Garvey & Berndt, 1977, p. 107.)

The tendency to confuse appearance and reality is another common error of early childhood that Piaget attributed to centration. Difficulty distinguishing between appearance and reality would explain why 2½-year-olds often become frightened when someone puts on a mask at Halloween, as if the mask had actually changed the person into a witch or a dragon.

John Flavell and his colleagues conducted early studies on children's confusion about appearance and reality by showing young children various objects that appeared to be one thing but were really another: a sponge that appeared to be a rock, a stone that appeared to be an egg, soap that appeared to be a block, and so on. After each object was presented, the children were asked, "What does that look like?" (the appearance question) and "What is it really?" (the reality question) (Flavell et al., 1986; Melot & Houde, 1998). The researchers found that 3-year-olds were likely to answer appearance–reality questions incorrectly. As expected, the children initially thought that the sponge "rock" was a rock because it was realistic enough to fool even adults. But once children discovered by touching it that the "rock" was really a sponge, they began to insist that it not only felt like a sponge but also looked like a sponge! Four-year-olds seemed to be in a transition state; they sometimes answered correctly, sometimes incorrectly. Five-year-olds had a much firmer grip on the appearance–reality distinction in these circumstances and usually answered the experimenters' questions correctly. These findings have been replicated in recent studies and in several countries, including China, Germany, and France (Huelsken, Sodian, & Pickel, 2001; Lane, Harris, Gelman, & Wellman, 2014; Melot & Houde, 1998; Woolley & McInnis, 2015). Thus, research would seem to confirm Piaget's view that centration can make it difficult for preschoolers to distinguish appearance from reality.

Rich Reid/National Geographic/Getty Images

At 2 years of age, Riley can hardly be blamed for bursting into tears when she meets the Easter Bunny for the first time. Her age-typical confusion between appearance and reality can make such encounters truly scary.

Of course, under certain circumstances, the relationship between appearance and reality can be complicated even for adults. Consider walking down a dark street late at night. Is that shape in the shadows a person—perhaps a mugger—or just a bush? Naturally, it can be hard to tell appearance from reality when things are hard to see. But how about when you can't see things at all, as in the case of microorganisms? As Jacqueline Woolley and Melissa McInnis point out, invisibility is one of the most striking examples of the discrepancy between appearance and reality—when something has no appearance, yet still exists (Woolley & McInnis, 2015). Not surprisingly, young children's understanding of the reality of invisible things is intertwined with their ability to distinguish between appearance and reality. In their study of 3- to 7-year-olds, the youngest children were more likely to say that they could actually see invisible entities, such as "air," "germs," and "songs," compared to fantasy entities such as "ghosts" and "magic spells."

Precausal Reasoning Nothing is more characteristic of 4- to 5-year-old children than their love for asking questions: "Why is the sky blue?" "What makes clouds?" "Where do babies come from?" Clearly, children are interested in the causes of things. Piaget believed, however, that because young children are not yet capable of true mental operations, they cannot engage in genuine cause-and-effect reasoning. He claimed that instead of reasoning from general premises to particular cases (deduction) or from specific cases to general principles (induction), young children think *transductively*, from one particular to another. As an example, he described how his young daughter missed her customary nap one afternoon and remarked, "I haven't had a nap, so it isn't afternoon." As a consequence of such reasoning, young children are likely to confuse cause and effect. Because he believed that transductive reasoning precedes true causal reasoning, Piaget referred to this aspect of young children's thinking as **precausal thinking** (Piaget, 1930).

precausal thinking Piaget's description of the reasoning of young children that does not follow the procedures of either deductive or inductive reasoning.

One of the most critical elements of causal relationships is the principle that *causes* must necessarily precede their *effects* (Goswami, 2008): The fly ball hits the window, and then it breaks; the child is tickled, and then he laughs. These relationships do not run in reverse, with effects preceding causes. In an exploration of how transductive reasoning interferes with this principle, a team of researchers asked whether young children understand that the cause of an action must come before, and not after, the action (Atance, Metcalf, Martin-Ordas, & Walker, 2014). For instance, children were shown a dog and asked to get some cheese to feed the dog. But when they returned, the children found a mouse instead of a dog. When asked why they had gotten the cheese, the majority of 3-, 4-, and 5-year-olds claimed it was for the purpose of feeding the mouse! Only 7-year-olds appreciated that their action was caused by a request to get cheese for a dog.

Given children's unflagging curiosity about the world around them and their persistent attempts to understand it, a team of researchers wondered what might trigger children to reason about the causes of events they observe (Legare, Gelman, & Wellman, 2010). The researchers presented preschoolers with events that included two objects—one blue, one green—and two special "light boxes." The blue object was called a "starter" and, when placed on top of one of the light boxes, activated a light, causing the box to glow. The green object was called a "do-nothing" and would not activate a light box when placed on top of it (see Figure 8.6). After observing how the objects and light boxes worked, the children were shown the two light boxes again and then watched as the blue object was placed on top of one box and the green object on top of the other. The boxes, however, did not always behave as the children had come to expect them to. In particular, the light boxes had been rigged so that, in one test trial, both were activated when the objects were placed on top of them, and, in a second test trial, neither box was activated by the objects. The researchers found that the preschoolers were much more likely to look first at the inconsistent events. That is, on Test Trial A, they tended to look first at the box being activated by the "do-nothing" green object, whereas on Test Trial B, they tended to look first at the unlit box with the "starter" blue object. When the experimenter asked, "Why did that happen?" the children were also much more likely to offer explanations for the inconsistent events than for events that were consistent with their prior knowledge. Thus, it appears that young children are most likely to look for causes and reasons when their current knowledge is challenged by new information (see also Legare, Schult, Impola, & Souza, 2016).

Introduction to task: blue object is a "starter" (turns on light box); green object is a "do-nothing" (does not turn on light box)

Test Trial A: both objects turn on light box

Test Trial B: neither object turns on light box

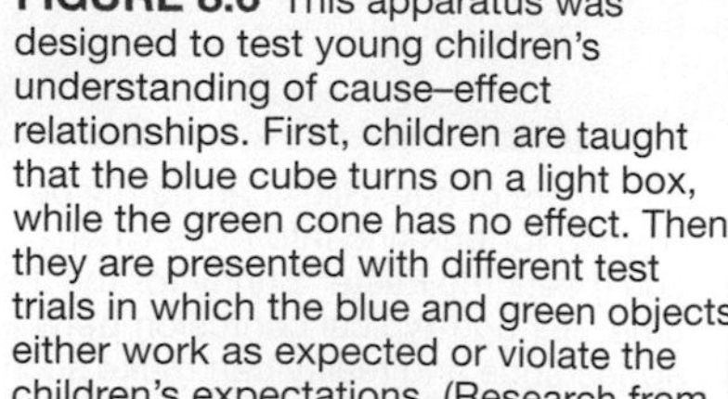

FIGURE 8.6 This apparatus was designed to test young children's understanding of cause–effect relationships. First, children are taught that the blue cube turns on a light box, while the green cone has no effect. Then, they are presented with different test trials in which the blue and green objects either work as expected or violate the children's expectations. (Research from Legare, Gelman, & Wellman 2010.)

The Problem of Uneven Levels of Performance

The examples of preoperational thinking we have provided thus far (summarized in Table 8.3 on page 269) are only a sample of the phenomena supporting the idea that there is a distinctive mode of thought associated with early childhood. But these examples are sufficient to give the flavor of the sorts of evidence collected by Piaget and others to argue that an inability to decenter one's thought pervades the preoperational stage of cognitive development, making it difficult for young children to consider multiple aspects of a situation simultaneously or to think through a problem systematically. (For an example of the real-world challenges presented by young children's cognitive limitations, see the box "Bearing Witness: Can Young Children Tell the Truth?" on p. 275.)

On the other hand, we have also discussed various studies that cast doubt on certain specifics of Piaget's tasks and on his reliance on interviews, which led him to judge young children as particularly vulnerable to errors of reasoning. Much of this new evidence indicates that cognitive development in early childhood is a good deal more uneven and less stagelike than Piaget suggested. Under some circumstances, children show evidence of cognitive abilities well before Piaget believed they emerge (Goswami, 2008; Inagaki & Hatano, 2006). Piaget himself argued that certain types of tasks may be more difficult for children to solve than others, even though the tasks require the same type of reasoning skills (as discussed in more detail in Chapter 11).

As noted earlier, some developmentalists believe that uneven levels of performance within a specific Piagetian stage are not particularly surprising. Others suggest that such unevenness poses a significant challenge to Piaget's fundamental idea that development proceeds through a sequence of qualitatively distinct, discontinuous stages (Feldman, 2004). Those in the latter camp propose two kinds of approaches that offer alternatives to Piaget's concept of a preoperational stage as characteristic of early childhood. These alternative approaches take different paths but share the twin goals of understanding the sources of unevenness in children's performance and the extent to which developmental change is general or piecemeal and stagelike or gradual (Goswami, 2008; Rose & Fischer, 2009). As you will see in the next section, information-processing approaches propose *general psychological mechanisms*, such as increases in short-term memory capacity and knowledge, to account for the process of cognitive change and the unevenness of young children's cognitive performances. A competing set of theories, which we examine later, relegates general mechanisms to a secondary role and focuses on the ways in which cognitive development builds on *domain-specific psychological processes*, such as the ability to distinguish between living things and nonliving objects.

APPLY > CONNECT > DISCUSS

When young children are asked where they live, they often confuse the name of the city with the name of the state. How is this confusion an example of preoperational thinking?

Information-Processing Approaches to Cognitive Development

LEARNING OUTCOMES

Explain the information-processing approach to cognitive development.

Summarize events or experiences during early childhood that help improve cognitive performance.

As discussed in Chapter 1, information-processing models of development depict the workings of the mind as being analogous to the workings of a digital computer (Siegler, 2005). According to such models, the neural features of the human brain are analogous to the hardware of a computer—that is, its *structural*

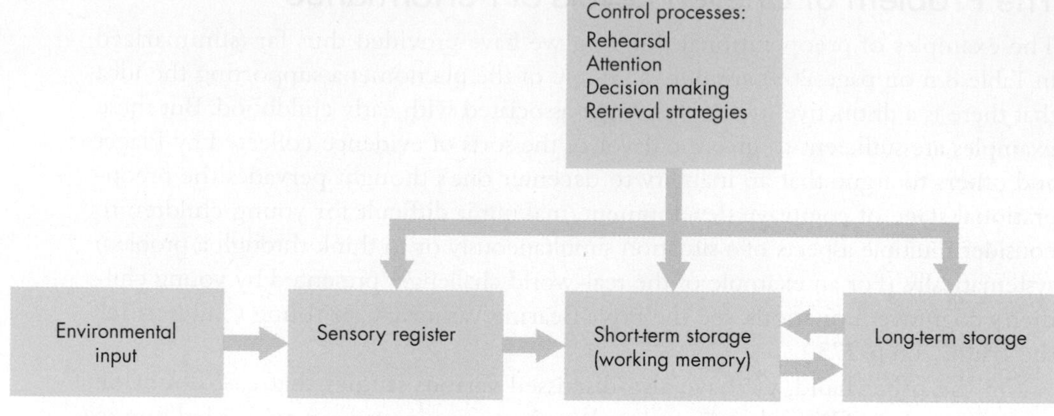

FIGURE 8.7 This figure shows the major components of an information-processing model of mental actions. (Information from Atkinson & Shiffrin, 1968.)

components—whereas the activities and practices that individuals engage in for the purpose of remembering and using information are analogous to the computer's software—that is, the programs that are written to *process* information through the system.

An overview of the essential components of this view of the mind is illustrated in Figure 8.7. The three boxes labeled "sensory register," "short-term storage," and "long-term storage" represent the basic system for attending to, interpreting, and storing information. The box at the top of the figure, labeled "control processes," represents the systems that, in effect, monitor and modify the results of the ongoing processes of the basic system.

You can follow the potential flow of information by starting at the left of the figure. The presumed starting point of any problem-solving process is the *sensory register*. Stimulation from the environment—"input," in the language of computer programming—is detected by the sensory organs and is passed on to the **sensory register**, where it is stored for a fraction of a second. If the input is not immediately attended to, it disappears. If it is attended to, it may be "read into" working memory, where it can be retained for several seconds. **Working memory** (also known as *short-term memory*) is the part of the information-processing system where active thinking takes place. Working memory combines incoming information from the sensory register with memory of past experiences, or **long-term memory**, and changes the information into new forms. If the information in working memory is not combined with information in long-term memory, it is easily forgotten.

sensory register The part of the information-processing system that stores input from the sensory organs for a fraction of a second, during which time it is either attended to and moved into working memory or lost from the system.

working memory (also known as *short-term memory*) The part of the information-processing system where active thinking takes place, and information from the sensory register may be combined with memory of past experiences.

long-term memory The part of the information-processing system that holds memories of past experiences.

Figure 8.7 also shows the way in which the flow of information between sensory register, working memory, and long-term memory is coordinated by *control processes*. These control processes determine how the information temporarily held in working memory is applied to the problem at hand. Important control processes include attention, rehearsal, and decision making. The "software" that implements the control processes determines the particular information that must be attended to, whether long-term memory must be searched more thoroughly, or whether a particular problem-solving strategy should be used. Control processes also determine whether a piece of information in short-term memory needs to be retained or can be forgotten.

You can get an overall idea of the information-processing approach by considering what occurs when a mother tries to teach her 4-year-old daughter to remember the family phone number. The mother sits with the child at the phone and shows her the sequence of numbers to tap—say, 543-1234. The child watches what her mother does and hears what her mother is saying. First, the set of numbers enters the child's sensory register as images and a sequence of sounds and is transferred to working memory. Next, meanings corresponding to those images and sounds

Bearing WITNESS Can Young Children Tell the Truth?

IT IS A SAD FACT THAT CHILDREN OF ALL ages are victims of crimes or witness crimes committed against others. Psychologists have traditionally viewed children's eyewitness testimony concerning such events as unreliable—especially in cases involving sexual abuse and other traumatic events—because young children have been considered suggestible (Stern, 1910), incapable of distinguishing fantasy from reality (Piaget, 1926), and prone to fantasizing sexual events (Freud, 1905/1953). Judges, lawyers, and prosecutors have also expressed reservations about children's reliability as witnesses (Bottoms, Goodman, Schwartz-Kenney, & Thomas, 2002; Goodman & Melinder, 2007). Legal rulings on the admissibility of children's testimony continue to reflect these long-standing doubts. In many states, for example, it is left up to the judge to determine whether a child below a certain age is competent to testify.

Due to growing concern about the prevalence of sexual and physical abuse of children in recent years, the scientific and legal communities are particularly interested in determining when and under what conditions young children can testify reliably about past events (Brown, Lewis, & Lamb, 2015; Lyon, Carrick, & Quas, 2010). Children's behavior both in actual criminal trials and in experimental psychological studies reveals a complex picture in which a child's memories and testimony about an event are affected by the child's age, the nature of the event being recalled, and a number of socioemotional factors.

A concern that has spurred considerable research is whether very young children may be unreliable witnesses because either their long-term memory is less reliable than older children's and adults' or they are particularly susceptible to misremembering events when they are coached or presented with misleading questions (Melinder et al., 2010; Warren & Peterson, 2014). Indeed, several studies have demonstrated that preschool-age children are more susceptible to false suggestions than are older children and adults (Poole & Lindsay, 2001). For example, when researchers asked young children misleading, even strange questions about what happened when they went to the doctor's office ("Did the doctor cut off your hair?" or "Did the nurse lick your knee?"), the youngest children were much more likely than the older children to say that these things happened even though they did not (Ornstein et al., 1997).

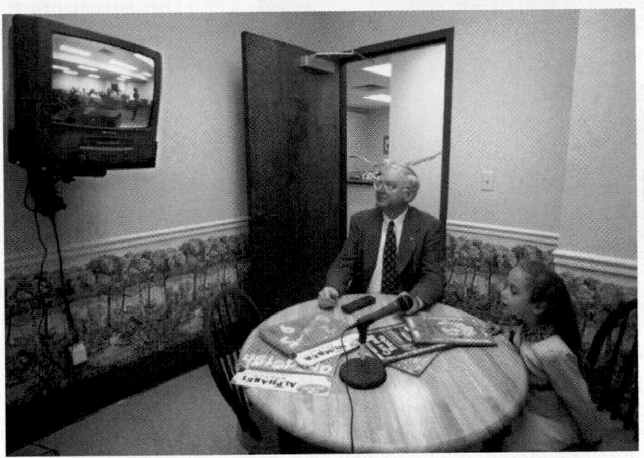
Ron Thompson/ZUMA Press/Newscom

In an effort to put young children at ease during testimony, some courts are using child witness rooms. The one shown here uses a two-way, closed-circuit television system that both displays the courtroom to the child and uses a camera to transmit the child's testimony to the court.

On the other hand, Gail Goodman and her colleagues have found that children can be remarkably resistant to misleading questions if they are interviewed soon after an event, when it is still fresh in their minds (Goodman, Jones, & McLeod, 2017; Malloy & Quas, 2009). Moreover, their memory is improved when the event in question is emotionally intense. In one study, for example, when children were asked about their experiences getting vaccinated at the doctor's office, those who were more upset and cried more recalled more information (Goodman, Hirschman, Hepps, & Rudy, 1991). In a long-term study of memory for child sexual abuse, it was found that sexual-abuse victims who had more posttraumatic stress symptoms remembered the abuse particularly well, suggesting that such trauma leads to "fear networks" that foster hypervigilance to trauma cues and reactivation of traumatic memories (Alexander et al., 2005).

Although much of the research on children's eyewitness testimony has focused on how unreliable children can be, Gail Goodman has turned her attention to finding out how to help children tell the truth about the frightening events they have witnessed or personally experienced. She has, for example, identified techniques that help children make accurate face identifications in photo lineups and that limit their suggestibility in interviews (such as the interviewer's telling children things like "I may try to trick you" and "It's OK to say 'I don't know'"). As she has pointed out, the legal system makes a number of assumptions regarding the needs and abilities of young children. It assumes, for example, that the best way to reach the truth is by confronting victims in open court, "even if the victim is a young, traumatized child. Psychological science has the potential to test many of those assumptions and, in the process, to help create a more scientifically based jurisprudence concerning children" (Goodman, 2005, p. 873).

are retrieved from long-term memory and matched with the images and sounds in working memory. The child recognizes each number and applies control processes in order to "try to remember," perhaps by using the strategy of repeating each number to herself. Remembering occurs when the information concerning the numerical sequence enters long-term memory so that it is retrievable at a later time.

AFP/Getty Images

Using a host of information-processing skills involving the sensory register, working memory, long-term memory, and retrieval processes, this boy takes a picture of a rooster contest being held in the Saudi city of Qatif.

The young child in our example may experience difficulty at any phase of this process. She may pay insufficient attention to what her mother is saying, in which case the information will not enter her sensory register. Being young, she has a small (immature) working-memory capacity and may not be able to hold all the numbers in working memory as she tries to remember them. The speed with which she can transfer information from the sensory register to working memory and to long-term memory may be relatively slow, causing her to forget some of the numbers before they can be enduringly stored in long-term memory. Finally, she may have little experience with intentional memorization and hence no repertoire of strategies for holding information in working memory for an extended period or for manipulating numbers in working memory.

Developmentalists who study children's memory find that striking changes occur across the years of early childhood. To a large extent, the dramatic increase in young children's ability to remember is due to "software" changes—that is, changes in the way information flows through the memory system as a consequence of changes in the processes by which it is encoded, stored, and retrieved (Ornstein & Light, 2010). Moreover, two factors can be key in contributing to children's increasing success: children's prior knowledge about the events or materials being remembered and adults' assisting children in remembering (Baker-Ward et al., 2015). In general, children are better at remembering when they have substantial prior knowledge on which to "hang" the new information. In the absence of prior knowledge, their memory can be greatly improved if adults talk with them about the new event or experience (Bauer, 2015). Studies of mother–child interactions (Ornstein, Haden, & Hendrick, 2004) have found that children's memories improve when mothers (and presumably other caregivers) use an **elaborative style**, which includes

elaborative style A form of talking with children about new events or experiences that enhances children's memories for those events and experiences.

- *Wh- questions* (What's happening? Who is that?)
- *Associations* that relate the new information to the child's prior knowledge
- *Follow-ins* that follow and discuss aspects of the events that the child finds interesting
- *Positive evaluations* that praise the child's verbal and nonverbal contributions to the interaction

An elaborative style is likely to facilitate children's memories because it serves to highlight the significance of events and link those events to other memories. Indeed, connections formed between new experiences and past memories may very well explain why young children are more likely than older children and adults to forget significant experiences in their lives—a phenomenon commonly known as *infantile* or *early-childhood amnesia* (Bauer & Larkina, 2015). As Patricia Bauer suggests, "metaphorically, parents serve as the training wheels on the children's memory bike" (Bauer, 2015, p. 807).

In sum, from an information-processing perspective, young children's cognitive difficulties are caused by general cognitive factors including limitations in knowledge, memory, attentional control, and the speed of processing information, as well as by limited strategies for acquiring and using information (Thompson & Siegler, 2010). Difficulties may be less in situations in which children have prior knowledge or caregivers' elaborative style encourages remembering. As children grow older, their performance improves and its unevenness diminishes because the cognitive limitations are gradually reduced through maturation of their brain ("hardware") and the development of more effective information-processing strategies ("software").

APPLY > CONNECT > DISCUSS

Suppose that two children are presented with the same set of unrelated pictures and told to remember the pictures because they will be given a memory test shortly.

Picture presented	Child 1 says	Child 2 says
Cat	cat, cat, cat	cat, cat
Shoe	shoe, shoe, shoe	cat, shoe, cat, shoe
Truck	truck, truck, truck	cat, shoe, truck
Pen	pen, pen, pen	cat, shoe, truck, pen

According to material presented in this section, why is Child 2 likely to outperform Child 1 on the memory test?

Cognitive Development in Privileged Domains

LEARNING OUTCOMES

Demonstrate privileged domains in cognition development through examples of early childhood thinking related to naïve psychology, biology, and physics.

Distinguish three different approaches that explain domain-specific cognitive development.

I talking very quiet because I don't want somebody to wake me up.

He needs more meat because he is growing long arms.

The teddy's arm fell off because you twisted it too far.

These statements are young children's explanations of different events encountered in daily life—a psychological event (an internal desire), a biological event (physical growth), and a physical event (a broken object) (Hickling & Wellman, 2001). In contrast to Piagetian and information-processing theorists, who emphasize how general intellectual processes such as centration or information storage and retrieval affect virtually all aspects of the young child's thinking, developmentalists taking another approach to cognition focus on changes in specific areas of knowledge acquisition, known as **privileged domains** (Goswami, 2008; Legare et al., 2016). These domains are "privileged" in that they involve specific kinds of reasoning that have evolutionary significance for our species. The most frequently studied privileged domains relevant to early childhood thinking are the domains psychology, biology, and physics. Although these domains obviously are rudimentary in early childhood, they nevertheless direct children to attend to and respond to highly specific and important features of the environment—in particular, the way in which objects and people and other biological organisms behave under various conditions.

privileged domains Cognitive domains that call on specialized kinds of information, require specifically designated forms of reasoning, and appear to be of evolutionary importance to the human species.

The Domain of Psychology

Just as children reason about their everyday physical world, they also reason about people—specifically about how people's actions are affected by their internal mental states. Children's early understanding of the relationship between mental states and behavior is referred to as *naïve psychology*.

In the transition from infancy to early childhood, and all during early childhood, children gain a more comprehensive idea about how other people's desires, beliefs, and knowledge are related to how they act in the world. As we explained in Chapter 6, by the end of the first year, infants possess at least an intuitive understanding that other people's actions are caused by their goals and intentions. Even at age 2, children are able to distinguish between their own desires and those of others (Wellman, 2011). If the child's own preference is for strawberry ice cream but a character in a story prefers chocolate ice cream, the child will predict that, given a choice between the two, the storybook character would choose chocolate ice cream. Children's ability to reflect on and understand the mental states of others

theory of mind Coherent theories about how people's beliefs, desires, and mental states combine to shape their actions.

false-belief task A technique used to assess children's theory of mind; children are tested on their understanding either of stories in which a character is fooled into believing something that is not true or of situations in which they themselves have been tricked into a false belief.

continues to develop throughout early childhood. As you will see, during this period, children construct coherent *theories* about how people's beliefs and desires combine to shape their actions—that is, they develop a **theory of mind**.

To determine when children develop a mature theory of mind, developmentalists use a technique called the **false-belief task**, which assesses a child's ability to recognize that others can have, and act according to, beliefs that are contrary to the facts as the child knows them (Scott & Baillargeon, 2017). In one version of this task, the child is presented with a brief story in which one of the characters comes to have a false belief. After hearing the story, the child is asked questions designed to reveal his or her understanding about what goes on in another person's mind. Here is a typical story and a follow-up question:

> **Story:** Once there was a little boy who liked candy. One day he put a chocolate bar in a drawer and went out to play for a while. While he was gone, his mother came. She took the candy out of the drawer and put it in the kitchen. When the little boy came back, he was hungry and went to get his candy.
>
> **Question:** Where do you think the little boy will look for his candy?

When 3-year-olds are asked this question, they say that the boy will look in the kitchen, where they themselves know the candy to be, and not in the drawer, where the boy left it. In short, they respond as if the boy had the same information that they do. Five-year-olds are far more likely to say that the boy will look in the drawer, presumably because they understand that he has a false belief about the current location of the candy.

A second version of the false-belief task involves tricking children themselves into a false belief. In one task of this type, children are shown a box covered with pictures of candy and are asked what they think is in the box. All, of course, answer, "Candy." Then they are shown that they are wrong—the box actually contains something else, such as a pencil. Next, the children are asked what a friend who has not yet seen inside the box would think it contains. Even though they have just gone through the process of being deceived themselves, most 3-year-olds say that the friend will think the box contains a pencil, despite the fact that it has pictures of candy on it. In contrast, 5-year-olds realize that the friend will be tricked into a false belief (Astington, 1993).

However, just as there is evidence that young children's performance on Piagetian tasks differs according to how the problem is posed for them, so there is evidence that, in some circumstances, even babies under 2 years of age can appreciate the false-belief states of others (Scott & Baillargeon, 2017). One way to induce children this young to solve false-belief tasks is to create tasks that rely on children's nonverbal, rather than verbal, behavior. For example, when an agent falsely believes that a desirable object is in a certain location, children as young as 18 months will point to show the agent the correct location of the object (Knudsen & Liszkowski, 2012). In another study, 17-month-olds watched as an agent hid two different toys in different boxes (Box A and Box B) and then left the room (Southgate, Chevallier, & Csibra, 2010). While the agent was out of the room, the experimenter switched the locations of the toys. Upon returning to the room, the agent pointed to Box A, said she wanted the toy inside, and asked the child to help her get it. But rather than retrieve the toy contained in Box A, these young children retrieved the toy from Box B, indicating their understanding that the agent had a false belief about the location of the toy they desired.

This range of evidence from different types of false-belief tasks suggests that the child's naïve psychology begins developing early in life and becomes increasingly sophisticated over time.

The Domain of Biology

Inquisitive developmentalist: How did the baby happen to be in your mommy's tummy?
Child: It just grows inside.
Developmentalist: How did it get there?
Child: It's there all the time. Mommy doesn't have to do anything. She waits until she feels it.
Developmentalist: You said the baby wasn't in there when you were there.
Child: Yeah, then he was in the other place. In . . . in America.
Developmentalist: America?
Child: Yeah, in somebody else's tummy.
Developmentalist: In somebody else's tummy?
Child: Yes, and then he went through somebody's vagina, then he went in, um, in my Mommy's tummy.
Developmentalist: In whose tummy was he before?
Child: Um, I don't know, who his, her name is. It's a her.

(Cowan, 1978, p. 86.)

Young children's ideas about conception and other biological processes are, well, different from ours, and they arise in the privileged domain referred to as *naïve biology*.

An important starting point for developing biological understandings is making the distinction between animate (living) and inanimate (nonliving) things. The distinction is more difficult than you might think because it relies on fairly abstract biological properties that are hard to observe: growth, the ability to move independently, the possession of internal parts—such as organs—and internal thoughts (Opfer & Gelman, 2001). A study conducted by Kristyn Wright and her colleagues nicely illustrates the trouble young children have in making the animate–inanimate distinction and suggests that part of the problem may be the abstractness of biological features (Wright, Poulin-DuBois, & Kelley, 2015). Adults, 4-year-olds, and 5-year-olds were set in front of a touchscreen computer that showed a series of three colored drawings. One drawing was located in the center of the screen, and two more were located beneath it, in a rectangular box. The adults and children were each asked to touch one of the two pictures in the box that was the "same kind of thing" as the centrally located picture. The pictures were of vehicles, furniture, and animals. The researchers set up the series to include three different types of picture combinations (see Figure 8.8). One type focused on basic category distinctions, such as having a German Shepard as a central figure and a Golden Retriever and a bird as comparison figures within the box; in this instance, the correct choice was the picture within the same category (dog). The second type required choosing a picture based on more abstract, "superordinate" categories, such as having an image of a bus as the central picture with a motorcycle and a chair as comparison figures; the correct choice was within the broader class vehicles. Finally, the third type of picture combination focused on the most abstract distinction, animate–inanimate, such as having a cow as a central picture and a person and truck as comparison images within the box.

FIGURE 8.8 To test his understanding of the difference between animate and inanimate objects, this boy is asked to point to the object that is "the same kind of thing" as the cow.

The researchers found, as expected, that the 4- and 5-year-olds responded much like adults on the picture combinations that assessed basic and superordinate categorization, but they made significantly more errors on the combinations that assessed the animate–inanimate distinction. Nonetheless, even the 4-year-olds responded better than chance would predict, indicating that they had an emerging if incomplete understanding of the difference between living and nonliving things.

In addition to their developing understanding that living things are different from nonliving things, young children know that living

Vivian Hoxsey

FIGURE 8.9 Children often attribute humanlike properties, including goals and intentions, to all living things. This drawing of a germ depicts an organism with humanlike arms, legs, and eyes, and spiky hair suggesting evil intent.

things grow and change their appearance, whereas inanimate objects may change in appearance due to wear or damage, but they do not grow. Moreover, as illustrated by Kayoko Inagaki and Giyoo Hatano's interviews with Japanese children, they also recognize that if neglected, living things may die. Upon seeing a sweet potato drooping, a 3-year-old boy exclaimed, "Poor thing! Are you thirsty? I give lots of water (to you). So, cheer up." When asked what would happen to a tulip if it went without water for a day, a 5-year-old girl replied, "The tulip will wither. 'Cause if the tulip doesn't drink water, it won't become very lively" (Inagaki & Hatano, 2002, p. 19).

At present, developmentalists who support the idea of a privileged domain of naïve biology are uncertain about when and how it originates. Some believe that it slowly differentiates itself from naïve psychology, as young children gain greater experience with living things. Others believe that as children come into contact with different kinds of living creatures, they draw analogies between themselves and other living creatures to reason about the biological world (Inagki & Hatano, 2004). This tendency is clearly shown in the response of a Japanese boy interviewed by Inagaki and Hatano close to his 6th birthday. Asked if it was inevitable that a baby rabbit would grow, the child replied, "We can't keep it [the rabbit] forever the same size. Because, like me, if I were a rabbit, I would be 5 years old and become bigger and bigger" (Inagaki & Hatano, 2002, p. 51). In drawing such analogies, children sometimes overlook important differences between living things, including the fact that not all living things have goals and intentions (Figure 8.9).

The Domain of Physics

In the opening to this chapter, we described how the children in Vivian Paley's class argued that stones melt when they are boiled, demonstrating an intuitive understanding of the effect that intense heat has on physical materials. Of course, for stones to melt, much greater heat would be needed than that provided by a stove. Moreover, by the time the stones would start to melt, there would not be any water left in the pot. Nevertheless, children's reasoning about melting stones indicates that they have ideas about the physical properties of objects. Indeed, Rose's question "Do stones melt?" indicates that children are interested in learning about such features of their environments. Because young children, like most adults, are not physicists but nevertheless harbor "everyday ideas" about how the physical world works—for example, about motion, the consequences of objects colliding, gravity, and changes of material state such as water turning into ice or stones melting—developmentalists refer to their reasoning as *naïve*, or *intuitive, physics* (Frick, Mohring, & Newcombe, 2014). As we discussed in Chapter 5, it appears that within months after birth, children have some grasp of at least a few very basic physical principles, including expectations that two objects cannot occupy the same location at the same time and that an object cannot pass through physical obstructions. Clearly, the foundations of a naïve physics are laid down in infancy.

Much research on the naïve physics of young children explores the developing understanding of moving objects, including the striking difficulty that young children have overcoming the so-called *gravity error* (Bascandziev, Powell, Harris, & Carey, 2016). As we all know from experience, when we drop an object, it falls straight down as a consequence of gravity. But as adults, we also know that circumstances can intervene and affect the paths of falling objects; a strong wind, for instance, can push an object off a straight-down path. More obviously, if an object—say, a ball—is dropped into a curving tube, the ball's path downward will not be straight but will follow the path of the tube. Surprisingly, children younger than about 4 years of age seem incapable of understanding this apparently obvious physical constraint on the path of the ball. So if a ball is dropped into the white "A" cup shown in Figure 8.10 and asked where the ball will go, children younger than 4 will declare that the ball will end up in the red "C" cup directly below the white "A" cup—exactly where it would go if gravity were the only force acting on the ball's trajectory. As we have found with other sorts of tasks, children's performance can be improved if the task is made easier. For example, if each tube is a distinctly different color, 3-year-olds are much better at overcoming the gravity error and understanding that the path of the ball will follow the curve of the tube (Joh & Spivey, 2012).

There is a great deal more to be learned about physical laws, as everyone who has taken an introductory physics course knows. But by the age of 5 to 6 years, children have developed a serviceable set of ideas about the physical world that appear to be shared by people all over the world.

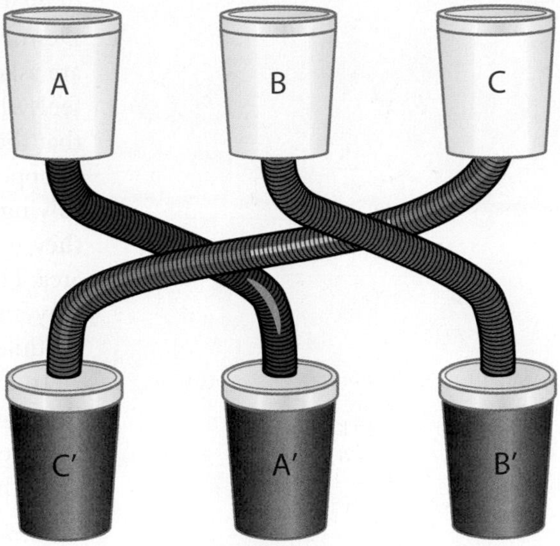

A B C
C′ A′ B′

FIGURE 8.10 This apparatus is used to test children's gravity bias. Until approximately 4 years of age, children believe that a ball dropped into a tube will fall straight down (if dropped into A, they believe it will fall into C′), even though this is physically impossible due to the shape of the tubes. (Research from Bascandziev, Powell, Harris, & Carey, 2016, p. 73.)

Explaining Domain-Specific Cognitive Development

Although it is clear that young children have an intuitive understanding of psychology, biology, and physics, there are questions about where these privileged domains come from and how they develop. There are three major approaches to explaining the source and development of privileged domains. One, *modularity theory*, views each domain of reasoning as a distinct and separate set of mental processes that has evolved to handle domain-specific information and that changes very little over the course of development. The second approach, *theory theory*, holds that children are biologically endowed with basic notions about each domain but modify their ideas as they learn more about the world. Finally, the third approach emphasizes the special role of language and culture in weaving together the contributions of biological and general cognitive factors.

Modularity Theory

Modularity theory's approach to understanding domain-specific intelligence is to conceive of it in terms of **mental modules**, innate mental faculties that are dedicated to receiving information from, and processing information about, particular types of objects in the environment, such as physical objects, people, and biological organisms (Atran, 1998; Sternberg, 2011). Each module is distinct and separate from all others; there is very little interaction among them. In addition, because they are coded in the genes, such psychological processes do not need special tutoring in order to develop. They are present "at the beginning" in the normal human genome and only need to be "triggered" by the environment.

mental modules Hypothesized innate mental faculties that receive inputs from particular classes of objects and produce corresponding information about the world.

An intriguing line of research with children with autism spectrum disorder provides strong evidence for modularity theory. **Autism spectrum disorder (ASD)** is a poorly understood, genetically induced condition that is defined primarily by an inability to relate normally to other people (American Psychiatric Association, 2013). Young children with severe ASD rarely use language to communicate; they do not engage in symbolic, pretend play; and they often engage in unusually repetitive movements such as rocking, spinning, or flapping their hands (see the box "In the Field: Supporting Siblings of Children with Autism" on p. 284).

autism spectrum disorder (ASD) A biologically based condition that includes an inability to relate normally to other people and low scores on false-belief tasks.

What makes autism spectrum disorder so interesting for modularity theorists is that children with ASD, who often exhibit high ability in some specific domains, routinely score poorly on false-belief tasks such as the one involving a story about a mother who, while her son was outside playing, moved a candy bar from the drawer, where the son had put it, to another location (Pellicano, 2010; Schroeder, Desrocher, Bebko, & Cappadocia, 2010). When children with ASD of various ages are asked where the boy will look for the candy when he returns and how he will feel when he looks there, they perform like typical 3-year-olds, failing to realize that the boy has a false belief about the candy's present location and that he will be disappointed when he acts on his belief. These same children may be very clever at solving mechanical puzzles such as putting together blocks to make a racing car, or they may have unusual abilities in music, art, math, memory, or some other specific area. The extreme difference in performance suggests that autism spectrum disorder may affect a specific module—a theory-of-mind module, perhaps—leaving other modules unaffected.

In an early study to demonstrate the domain-specific nature of ASD, Simon Baron-Cohen and his colleagues (Baron-Cohen, Leslie, & Frith, 1986) asked groups of 4-year-olds to arrange scrambled sequences of picture cards into stories. There were three types of stories, each depicted with four cards:

Mechanical sequences depicting physical interactions between people and objects—for example, a man kicks a rock, which rolls down a hill and then splashes in the water (Figure 8.11a).

Behavioral sequences depicting interactions among people—for example, a girl takes an ice cream cone from a boy and eats it, and the boy cries (Figure 8.11b).

Mentalistic sequences depicting stories that involve mental events—for example, a girl puts a toy down behind her while she picks a flower; another person sneaks up and takes the toy; the girl looks surprised when she turns around and finds the toy gone (Figure 8.11c).

The study included some children with ASD; other participants did not have ASD but had intellectual disabilities; and others were developing typically. The children with ASD outperformed the typically developing children in arranging mechanical sequences and were just as proficient as typically developing children when

FIGURE 8.11 These drawings illustrate some of the stimuli used to assess autistic children's ability to think about mental states. At the top of the figure is a *mechanical sequence* (a) showing a man kicking a rock, which rolls down a hill; the middle *behavioral sequence* (b) shows a girl taking an ice cream cone away from a boy; the bottom *mentalistic sequence* (c) shows a boy taking a girl's teddy bear when her back is turned.

arranging behavioral sequences in which the emotions of the figures in the story were obvious. But they were unable to create meaningful mentalistic sequences that reflected an understanding of thoughts or inner emotions, such as the surprise experienced by the girl whose toy disappeared (see Figure 8.11c). In addition, when asked to verbally tell the story of the mentalistic sequences, the narratives of children with ASD tended to be purely descriptive, with no reference to mental states. Of the last card in Figure 8.11c, for example, they might say something like "The girl held the flower" rather than "The girl wondered where her toy went."

Studies of naïve physics and biology have also found evidence for the domain-specific nature of ASD (Binnie & Williams, 2003; Peterson, 2005). For example, a study of Australian children conducted by Candida Peterson found that when asked questions about biological functions ("What does your heart do?" "What does your brain do?"), children with ASD performed at least as well as typically developing children. On the other hand, most of the children with ASD failed the false-belief task. Interestingly, in another study focused on the domains of physics and psychology, children with ASD performed better than did typically developing children—but they also tended to explain psychological events in terms of physical causation (Binnie & Williams, 2003). For example, when presented with a picture of a flower with a cut stem, children with ASD indicated that the wind blew the flower over, whereas normally developing children indicated that a person cut the flower. Findings like this, along with the fact that children with ASD perform very well in some privileged domains but routinely fail false-belief tasks, lead many developmentalists to argue for the existence of isolated modules and to speculate that ASD is due to a cognitive defect in a theory-of-mind module (see Figure 8.12; Baron-Cohen, Leslie, & Frith, 2007). In fact, recent research suggests that children's degree of success on false-belief and other theory-of-mind tasks may be used to predict the severity of ASD (Hoogenhout & Malcolm-Smith, 2017).

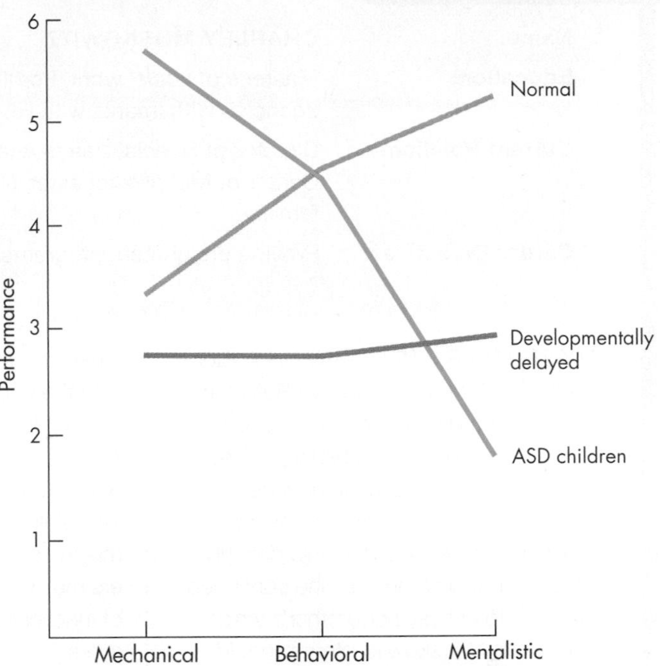

FIGURE 8.12 The graph shows the level of performance achieved by normal, developmentally delayed, and ASD children when asked to create meaningful mechanical, behavioral, and mentalistic sequences. Note that the ASD children are especially good at creating mechanical sequences but have even greater difficulty than developmentally delayed children do when asked to create mentalistic sequences.

Theory Theory

Despite the link between autism spectrum disorder and difficulty with the false-belief task, not all developmentalists agree that there is a theory-of-mind module that is present at birth and that a defect in this module explains ASD (Tager-Flusberg, 2007). Those who disagree with modularity theory point out that, when placed in intensive therapeutic programs, many autistic children show significant improvement in their social behavior and communication skills. They can learn, for example, to interact with other children and to carry out simple household routines, and some are eventually able to hold jobs (Scheuermann, 2002). Such facts naturally raise a question that modularity theory does not address: How does experience influence domain-specific development?

Developmentalists somewhat playfully refer to **theory theory** as an influential theory that addresses this question (Asakura & Inui, 2016; Mahy, Moses, & Pfeifer, 2014). According to this approach, young children, from birth or shortly thereafter, have primitive theories of how the world works. These theories direct the child's attention to domain-specific features of the environment and influence the child's actions in particular domains. Over time, the child modifies the theories in light of his or her experience (Gopnik, Wellman, Gelman, & Meltzoff, 2010).

theory theory The theory that young children have primitive theories about how the world works, which influence how children think about, and act within, specific domains.

Children's thinking within privileged domains is like scientific theorizing in at least two important respects. First, children's ideas are accompanied by causal

In The Field

Supporting Siblings of Children with Autism

Name: CHARLEY MOSKOWITZ

Education: Master's of social work, Fordham University; additional experience at various agencies with infants with HIV, pediatric hospice, and special-needs preschoolers

Current Position: Director of Special Needs Academic and Arts Center at the Jewish Community Center of Mid-Westchester, New York; private practice counseling children and families

Career Objectives: Provide enrichment programs for children with disabilities and their families

"MY BROTHER'S BEEN HAVING A BIG PROBLEM," began 6-year-old Ruthie in a quiet and anxious voice. "He's been having a hard time with beeping noises." Ruthie went on to describe how her brother would run in terror whenever he heard what most people would describe as nearly inaudible beeps. She continued anxiously to convey her brother's terror, until Charley Moskowitz interrupted. Ms. Moskowitz is a social worker who runs Sib Connection—a support group for siblings of children with disabilities. She asked Ruthie why she was so sad about her brother's reaction to beeps. In response, Ruthie explained that she doesn't want her brother to act that way, and it makes her sad when he's afraid. Ms. Moskowitz turned to the other children in the group and asked, "Can anybody help her?"

Thomas raised his hand, and explained that a lot of kids with ASD, including his own brother, will go through phases: "One month he might be afraid of beeps, and then next month he'll love beeps."

Another boy, Nick, chimed in with an interpretation based on his own personal experience. Nick told Ruthie that kids with ASD can have exceptionally keen senses. His brother, for example, "can hear things that are really low." He went on to say that there's nothing bad about this aspect of ASD, "it's just something that happens."

(Adapted from Olson, 2007)

Most of the children in Ruthie's support group have siblings with an ASD. ASDs are a group of highly heritable developmental disabilities that include autistic disorder, pervasive developmental disorder, and Asperger syndrome, all of which are characterized by significant impairments in social interaction and communication and the presence of unusual behaviors and interests—a fear of beeps, or a fascination with the whirl of electric fans, for example (American Psychiatric Association, 2013). ASD usually appears before the age of 3, and it affects the person throughout life. While some individuals with ASD may have severe intellectual deficits, others may be highly gifted in certain areas of functioning; approximately half have average or above average intellectual ability. According to a recent estimate by the Centers for Disease Control and Prevention, ASD in the United States is far more common than once supposed, affecting 1 out of every 68 children (CDC, 2014). It is five times more common in boys than in girls.

The Autism Genome Project, a massive international study involving scientists who are collecting genetic data in 19 countries, is shedding increasing light on the chromosomal changes and mutations that contribute to ASD phenotypes (Karsten et al., 2006; Ylisaukko-oja et al., 2006), including abnormalities in the number of copies of specific genes (Pinto et al., 2010). In the meantime, children like Ruthie, Thomas, and Nick struggle to make sense of their siblings' behavior. Fortunately, some of them will do so with the help of peers who have similar experiences and of people like Charley Moskowitz who are aware of the unique issues and challenges facing siblings of special-needs children. She explained to Ruthie that there are some things in the world that we can't change, including the way Ruthie's brother reacts to beeps. She then turned to Nick: "What else is she doing, Nick?" Nick responded that Ruthie was taking too much responsibility for her brother.

The sense of obligation weighs heavily on siblings of special-needs children. And as their parents age and eventually die, siblings will likely become fully responsible for the care of their special-needs family members. By participating in Sib Connection, these siblings get help understanding the disabilities of their brothers or sisters in the context of their personal lives and family relationships. Moskowitz hopes the experiences with her will give them the courage they need to develop independently from, but stay connected to, their family members, and begin preparing these siblings for the time when they will need to make important decisions concerning the welfare of their brothers or sisters.

Charley Moskowitz

Courtesy of Charley Moskowitz

Nick, who has an autistic sibling and participates in Sib Connection, designed this pin to help people better understand the behavior of autistic children.

Courtesy of Charley Moskowitz

Mark Plage, 15, right, shares a quiet moment with his 13-year-old brother, Derek, who has autism spectrum disorder.

Fred R. Conrad/New York Times/Redux

explanations. If asked why a little girl who climbs a tree and hangs from a branch soon falls to the ground, they provide a reasonable biological explanation: "She is not strong enough, so her arms get tired, and she eventually has to let go." If asked why a little boy who declares that he is going to step off a stool and float in the air actually falls to the ground, they provide explanations such as "He is too heavy to float in the air" or "Gravity brings him down." Second, their ideas generate reasonable predictions, as a theory should. They will predict that the little girl who drops from the tree will hurt herself if the branch is high off the ground and that the little boy who fails to float will be disappointed. Although 3-year-olds may sometimes confuse biological and psychological explanations, by the time they are 4 years old, American children invoke the right kinds of theory to fit what needs to be explained (Wellman, Hickling, & Schult, 1997).

An important source of information for children's developing theories is their interactions and conversations with their parents (Hughes et al., 2005). For example, a study of Mexican American parents and their children attending an agricultural science exhibition found that the context prompted children to ask questions that fall within the domain of biology and that parents offered domain-appropriate causal explanations. For instance, when one child asked, "Why can't I water the plants too much?" his mother answered, "Because they are going to drown; they don't need that much water." Another parent used an analogy to provide a basis for the child's theory development. When asked "Why do insects eat each other?" the mother answered, "Because insects are food for other animals just like other animals are food for us" (Tenenbaum, Callanan, Alba-Speyer, & Sandoval, 2002, p. 237). Sometimes parents spontaneously offered up explanations of puzzling phenomena, providing a rich source of information that confirmed or denied children's initial theories. This study highlights the important role that parents play in the process of children's theory-testing; teachers, peers, and personal experience also contribute to children's construction of their knowledge base.

The Special Role of Language and Culture

The third approach to explaining domain-specific development focuses primarily on how language and culture influence the emergence and growth of various domains. Considerations of language and culture are important for thinking about the nature of privileged domains because cultures vary dramatically in their use of domain-specific language. As an example, take the domain of psychology. Language, as Janet Astington and Eva Filippova point out, helps a young child figure out what other people might think, want, or feel (Astington & Filippova, 2005). Ample evidence from cultures around the world suggests that there is enormous variety in the extent and ways that mental states and actions are conceived (Lillard, 2006; Vinden, 2002). In terms of sheer number, English is at one extreme of the continuum, possessing more than 5,000 words for emotions alone. By contrast, the Chewong people of Malaysia are reported to have only five terms to cover the entire range of mental processes, translated as "want," "want very much," "know," "forget," and "miss or remember" (Howell, 1984).

At present, it is unclear whether the lack of mental terms in a culture's language slows down, or even eliminates altogether, the development of the kind of naïve psychology found in cultures where such language is prevalent. In some cases, there appears to be no lag in performance, for example, on standard false-belief tasks (Avis & Harris, 1991). In other cases, there does seem to be a significant delay, and in still other cases, it appears that the sort of theory of mind assumed to be universal by privileged-domain theorists does not appear at all (De Gracia, Peterson, & de Rosna, 2016; Vinden, 2002). In cultures where talk about minds and mental processes is prevalent, positive correlations have been found between the pace at which children demonstrate competence on standardized tests for theory of mind and the amount of conversation parents devote to mental processes in the course of their daily interactions with their children (Morgan et al., 2014; Nelson et al., 2003). A study of how hearing parents talk to their deaf children and hearing children found that parents of deaf children were less likely than parents of hearing children to use mental state language such as "think," "know," "happy," "sad," "want," and "like." These differences in language input may account for findings from numerous studies that deaf children born to hearing parents show delays in performance on false-belief and other theory of mind tests (Meristo et al., 2012; Schick, de Villiers, de Villiers, & Hoffmeister, 2007).

The influence of language and cultural variation on privileged domains is not restricted to the domain of naïve psychology. Among the Tainae of Papua New Guinea, for example, Penelope Vinden (1999) found that it is common for people to believe that certain individuals can literally change themselves into a pig or another animal and that such changelings can, and occasionally do, physically assault young children. Such beliefs defy the distinction we ordinarily make between human beings, other animals, and inanimate natural objects, calling into question the extent to which naïve biology and naïve psychology are distinct domains.

Indeed, some developmentalists have challenged the very idea that knowledge can be compartmentalized into distinct domains on the grounds that it represents a specifically Western perspective, which is at odds with the belief systems of many non-Western cultures. It has been found, for example, that certain African societies have a more integrated view of knowledge. According to Bame Nsamenang, who studies African beliefs about knowledge, the knowledge, skills, and values children learn are not "compartmentalized into this or that activity, knowledge, or skill domain, but are massed together as integral to social interaction, cultural life, economic activity, and daily routines" (Nsamenang, 2006, p. 296).

APPLY > CONNECT > DISCUSS

Of *modularity theory* and *theory theory*, which is more consistent with Piaget's understanding of development? Why?

LEARNING OUTCOMES

Explain how cultural scripts and generalized representations contribute to the cognitive development of young children.

Name three ways in which cultural scripts may influence unevenness in children's development.

Cognitive Development and Culture

As we discussed in Chapter 1, Vygotsky's sociocultural theory has had a significant impact on understanding how development in general and cognitive development in particular are influenced by the cultural contexts in which children live. As we have noted on numerous occasions, children's active participation in cultural activities, especially their interactions and communications with others, seems to be essential to their developing knowledge of the world (Nelson, 2003; Rogoff, 2003). One aspect of these cultural activities that has received much attention is *cultural scripts*, which are said to account for both the acquisition and unevenness of knowledge during early childhood.

Cultural Scripts

scripts Event schemas that specify who participates in an event, what social roles they play, what objects they are to use during the event, and the sequence of actions that make up the event.

Katherine Nelson (2009, 2015) suggested that as a result of their participation in routine, culturally organized events, children acquire *generalized event representations*, or **scripts**. These scripts, which are also referred to as *cultural scripts*, specify who participates in an event, what social roles they play, what objects they are to use during the event, and the sequence of actions that make up the event. Scripts exist both as external, material tools of culture—observable patterns of behavior expressed in the words and the customary practices of daily life—and as internal representations of those tools (see Chapter 2, pp. 52–53). Scripts are, in both their internal and external aspects, *resources* for cognitive development that affect the child's thinking and reasoning skills.

Tim Rock/Lonely Planet-Getty Images/ Getty Images

As she participates in basket-weaving lessons over time, this young Palauan girl will develop a generalized script of what it means to "have a lesson," including the guidance of a teacher, the use of particular materials, and the sequence of activities performed.

Initially, cultural scripts are a good deal more external than internal. Anyone who has made the attempt to bathe a 2-month-old knows that "taking a bath" is something the adult does to the baby. The adult fills a sink or an appropriate basin with warm water; lays out a towel, a clean diaper, and clothing; and then slips the infant into the water, holding on firmly to keep the infant's head above water. The infant's contribution consists of squirming around. Gradually, however, as they become stronger and more familiar with the script of bath taking (and their caregivers perfect their role as bath-givers), babies acquire more competence in parts of the activity and assume a greater role in the process.

By the age of 2 years, most children have "taken" many baths. Each time, roughly the same sequence is followed, the same kinds of objects are used, the same cast of characters participates, and the same kinds of talk accompany the necessary actions. Water is poured into a tub, clothes are taken off, the child gets into the water, soap is applied and rinsed off, and the child gets out of the water, dries off, and gets dressed. There may be variations—a visiting friend may take a bath with the child or the child may be allowed to play with water toys after washing—but the basic sequence has a clear pattern to it.

During early childhood, adults still play the important role of "bath-giver" in the scripted routine called "taking a bath." Adults initiate children's baths, scrub their ears, wash their hair, or help them dry off. Not until adulthood will the child be responsible for the entire event, including scouring the tub and worrying about clean towels, hot water, and the money to pay for them.

Nelson points out that, as in the "taking a bath" script, children grow up inside other people's cultural scripts. As a consequence, human beings rarely, if ever, experience the natural environment "raw." Rather, they experience the world, including such simple activities as taking a bath and eating a meal, in a way that has been prepared (cooked up!) according to the scripts prescribed by their culture.

Nelson and her colleagues have studied the growth of scripted knowledge by interviewing children and recording the conversations of children playing together. When Nelson asked children to tell her about "going to a restaurant," for example, she obtained reports like the following:

> **Boy aged 3 years, 1 month:** Well, you eat and then go somewhere.
> **Girl aged 4 years, 10 months:** Okay. Now, first we go to restaurants at nighttime and we, um, we, and we go and wait for a while, and then the waiter comes and gives us the little stuff with the dinners on it, and then we wait for a little bit, a half an hour or a few minutes or something, and, um, then our pizza comes or anything, and um, then when we're finished eating the salad that we order, we get to eat our pizza when it's done, because we get the salad before the pizza's ready. So then when we're finished with all the pizza and all our salad, we just leave.
> (Nelson, 1981, p. 103.)

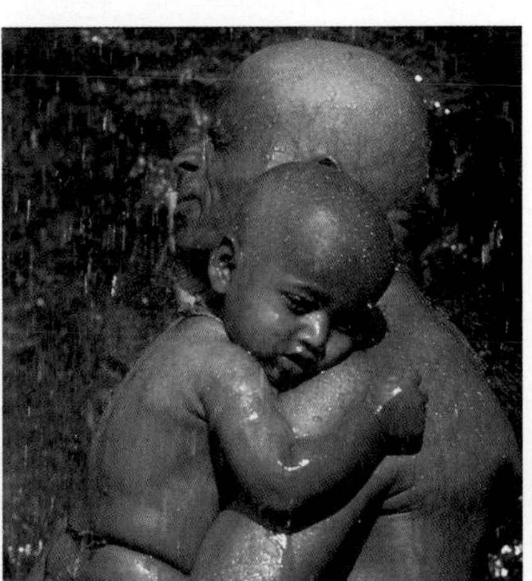
Micah Hanson/Alamy

Even a script such as "taking a bath" can vary considerably from one culture to another. This image shows a pilgrim and a child bathing in a sacred waterfall near a temple in India.

Even these simple reports demonstrate that scripts represent generalized knowledge. For one thing, the children are describing general content: They are

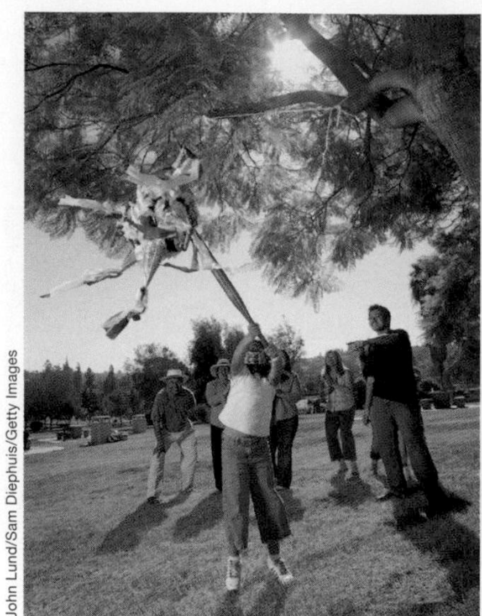
John Lund/Sam Diephuis/Getty Images

This particular cultural script for celebrating a birthday, common in Mexico, involves taking turns batting at a swinging piñata until it breaks, spilling its candies and toys on the ground for the children to collect.

clearly referring to more than a single, unique meal. The 3-year-old uses the generalized form "you eat" rather than a specific reference to a particular time when he ate. The little girl's introduction ("First we go to restaurants at nighttime") indicates that she, too, is speaking of restaurant visits in general.

Besides containing general content, children's cultural scripts are organized into a general structure, similar to that of adult scripts. Even very young children know that the events involved in "eating at a restaurant" do not take place haphazardly but, rather, occur sequentially: "First we do this, then we do that." Children evidently abstract the content of a script and its structure from many events and then use that knowledge to organize their behavior.

Cultural scripts are guides to action. They are mental representations that individuals use to figure out what is likely to happen next in familiar circumstances. Until children have acquired a large repertoire of scripted knowledge from which they can generalize in unfamiliar circumstances, they must pay attention to the details of each new activity. As a consequence, they may be less likely to distinguish between the essential and the superficial features of a novel context. The little girl interviewed by Nelson, for example, seemed to think that eating pizza is a basic part of the "going to a restaurant" script, whereas paying for the meal was entirely absent. However, because the little girl has grasped a small part of the restaurant script, and going to restaurants is a routine activity in her family, she will be free to attend to new aspects of the setting the next time she encounters it. Over time, she will gain a deeper understanding of the events she participates in and the contexts of which they are a part.

Cultural scripts also allow people within a given social group to coordinate their actions with each other because, in a very important sense, scripts are *shared*. That is, they are a source of common meanings, expectations, and ways of understanding how and why people behave as they do in particular contexts. For this reason, Nelson argued that "the acquisition of scripts is central to the acquisition of culture" (Nelson, 1981, pp. 109–110). Knowing the script, especially its variants and nuances, is an important marker of maturity and adaptation. For example, when children go to a "sit-down" restaurant in the United States, they learn that first a host or hostess seats you, and later you tell a server what you want to eat. However, a different script applies to fast-food establishments, where you first go to the counter and place your order and then seat yourself. If someone were to take the sit-down script to a fast-food establishment, or she would go hungry. Likewise, someone who took the fast-food script to a sit-down restaurant would be viewed as very peculiar.

Cultural Context and the Unevenness of Development

Once children leave the confines of their cribs and their caregivers' arms, they begin to experience a great variety of contexts that compel them to acquire a variety of new scripts, as well as refine those with which they are already familiar. Thus, it is natural that cognitive development during early childhood should appear to be so uneven. In familiar contexts, where they know the expected sequence of actions and can properly interpret the requirements of the situation, young children are most likely to behave in a logical way and adhere to adult standards of thought. But when the contexts are unfamiliar, they may apply inappropriate scripts and resort to magical or illogical thinking.

Overall, cultures influence the unevenness of children's development in several basic ways (Rogoff, 2003; Super & Harkness, 2002):

1. *By making specific activities available:* One cannot learn about something without observing or hearing about it. A 4-year-old growing up among the !Kung of the Kalahari Desert is unlikely to learn how to use a TV remote, and children growing up in Seattle are unlikely to learn how to find water-bearing roots.
2. *By determining the frequency of basic activities:* Dancing is an activity found in all societies but with varying degrees of emphasis. Due to the importance placed on traditional dancing in Balinese culture, many Balinese children become skilled dancers by the age of 4 (McPhee, 1970), whereas Norwegian children are likely to become better skiers and skaters than dancers.
3. *By relating different activities to each other:* If pottery-making is a valued cultural activity, children are likely to not only become skilled pottery makers but also to learn a variety of related skills, such as digging clay from a quarry, firing clay, glazing clay, painting designs, and selling the products. Molding clay as part of a nursery school curriculum will be associated with a distinctively different pattern of experiences, skills, and knowledge.
4. *By regulating the child's role in the activity:* Children enter most activities as novices who bear little responsibility for the outcome. As their roles and responsibilities change, so do the specialized abilities they develop.

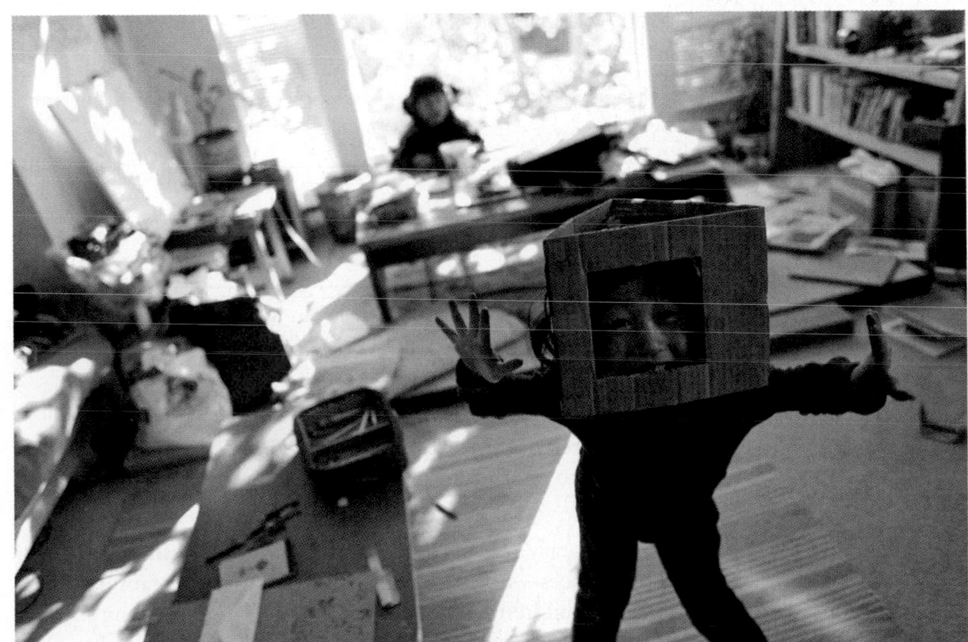

Toshi Kawano/Getty Images

Whether she is pretending to be a monster, a character peering out from a television set, or both, this young Japanese girl has created an imaginary "play space" within a highly supportive cultural context that provides her with play materials, a play room, a vast variety of TV monster characters, and cultural expectations that pretend play is appropriate behavior for young children. According to Kurt Fischer, the specific cognitive processes used in such play, and supported by the culture, should result in stagelike changes in her development.

APPLY > CONNECT > DISCUSS

In arguing against the notion that knowledge can be compartmentalized into separate domains, Bame Nsamenang asserts that, according to African beliefs, knowledge is integrated into social life and daily routines. To what extent is this consistent with Katherine Nelson's theory of cultural scripts?

LEARNING OUTCOMES

Assess the importance of reconciling alternative approaches as a way to understanding events and experiences that contribute to development during early childhood.

Looking Ahead

At this point, you should be convinced that the exceedingly uneven and complex picture that emerges from studies of childhood thought in the first few years following infancy cannot be explained by any single approach. Indeed, there have been a number of attempts to formulate more inclusive theories that are capable of accounting for both general and domain-specific changes in young children's competence and performance and for the fact that cognitive development sometimes appears to occur in discontinuous leaps and at other times as a process of gradual change. For example, Kurt Fischer has proposed that whether change appears continuous and gradual or abrupt and stagelike depends crucially on the relationship between the specific cognitive process being investigated and the context in which it occurs (Fischer & Yan, 2002). Fischer has demonstrated that under conditions of optimal support from the context, increases in the level of children's performance go through a series of stagelike changes. But when support is low (and a child has many distracting problems to deal with simultaneously), change is continuous. Thus, the culturally organized context of children's developing competence and performance is an element that must always be taken into account.

Recall the scenario at the beginning of the chapter—the story about the young children making stone soup. Using at least two different theories presented in the chapter, explain the children's understanding about whether stones melt when cooked.

Summary

Physical and Motor Development

- Early childhood is marked by impressive gains in both gross and fine motor skills.
- Young children's sleep needs often are not adequately met. Nutrition is also a common problem, and undernourishment and obesity are both causes for concern.
- Brain development, which is slower than in infancy, includes myelination of the frontal cortex, as well as increases in the length and branching of neurons connecting different areas of the brain. Variability in the development of different areas may contribute to the unevenness of early childhood cognition.

Preoperational Development

- According to Piaget, children in the preoperational stage are in the process of overcoming limitations that stand in the way of their attaining mental operations—that is, the ability to perform logical transformations of information. He considered the greatest such limitation to be centration, in which the child focuses on one aspect of an object or problem to the exclusion of others. Centration explains three common early childhood errors:
- Egocentrism, the tendency to be captive to one's own perspective and unable to take that of another.
- The tendency to confuse appearance and reality.
- Precausal reasoning, or the tendency to reason from one particular to another rather than engaging in cause-and-effect reasoning.
- Contemporary research suggests that under certain circumstances—for example, with tasks involving familiar objects—children do not commit these errors, showing evidence of cognitive abilities well before Piaget thought possible and hence more unevenness of cognitive development.

Information-Processing Approaches to Cognitive Development

- Information-processing approaches explore the workings of the mind through analogy to the digital computer, with the brain's neural features being likened to a computer's hardware and the practices that people engage in to process information likened to its software.
- Input from the environment goes to the sensory register and may be read into short-term (working) memory, where it

may combine with information from long-term memory. The flow of information among these components is coordinated by control processes, which include attention, rehearsal, and decision making.

- As children grow older, their cognitive performance improves as a result of both the maturation of their brains and their development of more effective information-processing strategies. Prior knowledge and caregivers' elaborative style in interactions with children can help children encode and store memories.

Cognitive Development in Privileged Domains

- Another approach to early childhood cognitive development focuses on changes within privileged domains, specific areas of knowledge that may have evolutionary significance.
- Within naïve psychology, young children develop a theory of mind, as is reflected by their improving performance on false-belief tasks.
- Naïve biology includes an understanding of differences between living things and inanimate objects.
- Naïve physics traces to infancy and, in early childhood, extends to an understanding of laws such as gravity and inertia and of properties of objects.
- Several approaches seek to explain domain-specific cognitive development.
- Modularity theory holds that distinct and separate mental modules—mental processes present from birth—are dedicated to the different privileged domains. Autistic children's having difficulties in the psychological domain while being normal or even exceptional in some others is seen as support for this approach.
- Theory theory holds that from birth or shortly thereafter, children have primitive theories about how the world works—theories that direct their attention to domain-specific features of the environment and that they modify over time in light of their experience.
- A third approach focuses on the influence of language and other aspects of culture on the emergence and development of domains. The idea of domains of knowledge may be a Western construct.

Cognitive Development and Culture

- As children participate in routine events of their culture, they acquire increasingly accurate scripts, or generalized representations, of these events.
- Cultures influence cognitive development by determining the frequency of basic activities, the specific activities that are available, and children's roles in activities.

Looking Ahead

- Studies of cognition in early childhood yield a picture not of a homogeneous stage but of complexity and unevenness. More inclusive theories are probably needed in order to account for processes that are both domain specific and general and for developmental changes that are both continuous and discontinuous (stagelike).

Key Terms

ossification, p. 263
motor drive, p. 263
food-insecure, p. 265
scale errors, p. 267
mental operations, p. 268
preoperational stage, p. 268
centration, p. 268
decentration, p. 269
objectivity, p. 269
egocentrism, p. 270
precausal thinking, p. 272
sensory register, p. 274
working memory (also known as *short-term memory*), p. 274
long-term memory, p. 274
elaborative style, p. 276
privileged domains, p. 277
theory of mind, p. 278
false-belief task, p 278
mental modules, p. 281
autism spectrum disorder (ASD), p. 281
theory theory, p. 283
scripts, p. 286

Bartosz Hadyniak/Getty Images

CHAPTER

9

Social and Emotional Development in Early Childhood

Didi, a 2-year-old Chinese boy, is talking with his mother and older sister about an event in which he cried and made a scene at his sister's music lesson, causing his mother to lose face:
Mother to Didi: That day when you went to music lesson with Mama and older sister. Was that fun?
Didi: It was fun.
Mother: What didn't the teacher give you?
Didi: Didn't give me a sticker.
Mother: Didn't give you a sticker. . . . Then what did you do?
Didi: Then I cried.
Sister: Cried loudly! "Waah! Waah! Waah!"
Mother: Oh, then you cried? Yeah, you constantly went, "Waah! Why didn't you give me a sticker?" (Mother says in a whining tone, rubbing her eyes with her fists.) "Why didn't you give me a sticker? Why didn't you?"
Didi looks up from a picture book he's holding, looks at his mother and smiles, and looks back at the book.
Sister: Yes, you said, "Why didn't you give me a sticker?"
Mother to Didi, with a sigh: "A sticker. Ai, you made Mama lose face. I wanted to dig my head into the ground! Right?
Didi points to the picture book.
Sister: Mommy wanted to faint! She almost began to faint!

(Information from Miller, Fung, & Mintz, 2010.)

As they do for children everywhere, Didi's lessons in proper behavior and emotional expression begin early. And as they are for children everywhere, his lessons are steeped in cultural values and expectations. Chinese culture expects personal desire to be carefully controlled. Indeed, individual goals and needs are considered secondary to those of the group, and children's behaviors are believed to reflect strongly on the family. Didi's outburst about not getting a sticker was consequently not only contrary to his culture's values about containing one's emotions but also an embarrassment to his mother—a fact not lost on his older sister. In chastising Didi for his behavior, his mother and sister are giving him a lesson in the importance of regulating his feelings, as well as in being a member of Chinese society. This chapter explores how children learn to act appropriately and how they develop a sense of themselves in relation to the societies in which they live.

socialization The process by which children acquire the standards, values, and knowledge of their society.

personality formation The process through which children develop their own unique patterns of feeling, thinking, and behaving in a wide variety of circumstances.

During early childhood, children's social and emotional lives develop along two closely connected paths. One is the path of **socialization**, which leads children toward the standards, values, and knowledge of their society. The second path is **personality formation**, in which children develop their own unique patterns of feeling, thinking, and behaving in a wide variety of circumstances.

Children begin their trek down the paths of socialization and personality formation as soon as they are born and with plenty of help from the significant people in their lives. It is not just idle talk when a father says of his newborn daughter, "She could be a concert pianist with these long fingers," and her mother adds, "Or a basketball player." The beliefs that give rise to such statements lead parents to shape their child's experience in a variety of ways—some obvious, others quite subtle. Socialization is apparent in the ways parents communicate to children about how they should and should not behave ("Ai, you made Mama lose face"). Socialization is also apparent in the ways parents—and their social and economic circumstances—influence the neighborhoods children live in, the day-care centers or preschools they attend, and a variety of other contexts in which they become conversant with their culture's funds of knowledge and rules of behavior.

But children do not automatically or passively absorb adults' lessons. They interpret and select from the many socializing messages they receive according to their budding and unique personalities. The early origins of personality formation are present in infancy. As we saw in Chapter 4 (p. 149), neonates display individual differences in characteristic levels of activity, responses to frustration, and readiness to engage in novel experiences. We referred to these patterns of responsivity and associated emotional states as *temperament* and noted that it tends to be moderately stable over time: Children who draw back from novel experiences in infancy, for example, are more likely to behave shyly when they first enter a nursery school. Personality formation expands as children's initial temperamental styles of interacting with people and objects in their environments are integrated with their developing cognitive understanding, emotional responses, and habits (McAdams, 2015; Odden, 2009).

Courtesy Sheila Cole

In addition to fulfilling a traditional role in a wedding ceremony, these little flower girls are learning about many important aspects of the social roles and behaviors expected of them when they grow up.

Thus, the paths of socialization and personality formation are closely connected. In traveling these paths, children, along with the significant others in their lives, play an active role in *co-constructing* the course of development (Hutto, 2008; Valsiner, 2007). That is, as we learned in Chapter 2, the behaviors, activities, and choices both of children and of the people with whom they interact, shape and modify the environments in which children develop. In this chapter, we will examine the social and emotional development of young children as they gain experience interacting with a variety of people, develop a more explicit sense of themselves and their abilities, and come to understand the ways in which they can (and cannot) use the rules and tools that society attempts to press upon them. These changes in social and emotional development do not, of course, occur independently of the biological and cognitive changes discussed in Chapter 8. Socialization, personality formation, biological maturation, and cognitive development occur simultaneously.

WARMING UP

1. In thinking about your own personality development, what aspects of your socialization have contributed to the person you are today? How have you developed in ways that are unexpected based on your socialization experiences?
2. Do you think it is part of human nature to be violent and aggressive? Do you think there could ever be "peace on earth" for all human beings? Why or why not?

Identity Development

LEARNING OUTCOMES

Explain identification as part of the socialization process that children experience.

Distinguish the five different approaches to gender identity.

Provide examples of ethnic identity and the role it plays in the lives of young children.

Explain how a sense of self, or personal identity, plays out in the lives of young children, including the influence that their caregivers have on children.

Erik Erikson (1950) claimed that the path of identity takes a sharp and fateful turn in early childhood. As discussed in Chapter 6 (p. 221), in the stage of *autonomy versus shame and doubt* (associated with the "terrible twos"), children acquire and confidently declare their sense of free will and their ability to control their environment: "*I* do it!" "No! I don't want that one; I want *that* one!" During early childhood, in contrast, children face the challenge of **initiative versus guilt**—that is, the challenge of continuing to declare their autonomy and existence as individuals but in ways that begin to conform to the social roles and moral standards of society. According to Erikson, we see evidence of this in children's initiative and eagerness to join both peers and adults in constructing, planning, and making things. From building "forts" in which to play to baking cookies or repairing broken toys, children of this age take special delight in cooperating with others for the purpose of accomplishing specific goals and tasks. In Erikson's words, "the child is at no time more ready to learn quickly and avidly, to become bigger in the sense of sharing obligation and performance" (1950, p. 258). Such enthusiasm during early childhood underscores identity development as a process by which children come to express and believe in their own value as social participants—as individuals who can contribute to the plans and goals of a group.

initiative versus guilt According to Erikson's theory, the stage in early childhood during which children face the challenge of continuing to declare their autonomy and existence as individuals but in ways that begin to conform to the social roles and moral standards of society.

identification A psychological process in which children try to look, act, feel, and be like significant people in their social environment.

One factor that is essential to socialization is **identification**, a psychological process in which children try to look, act, feel, and be like significant people in their social environment. The development of identification can be studied with respect to almost any social category—a family, a religious group, a neighborhood clique, or a nationality. We could ask, for example, how a boy goes about identifying with his father, his Hindu religion, his soccer team, or his country, India. The overwhelming majority of studies on identification in early childhood, however, focus on the acquisition of sex-role identity and ethnic identity. As the social categories and role expectations regarding gender and ethnicity become increasingly visible in our rapidly globalizing world, developmentalists are eager to understand the processes of identification through which children come to understand themselves as members of various social categories and adopt behaviors consistent with various social roles. In this section we look at sex-role and ethnic identity in turn and then at the sense of self of which they are part. As you will see, there is much disagreement about the processes through which identification in these areas is achieved.

Gender Identity

If an infant wearing nothing but a diaper and a bright-eyed smile were placed in your arms, you would probably have a hard time determining whether the baby was a boy or a girl. But you likely wouldn't have that problem with a 3-year-old! In the short span of 3 years, children come to behave in ways that give clear signals about whether they are boys or girls (Golombok et al., 2012). These signals begin as early as age 2, when both girls and boys tend to produce more same-gender-typed words ("boy," "girl," "truck," "dress") than other-gender-typed words (Stennes, Burch, Sen, & Bauer, 2005). By the time children enter preschool, most boys and girls differ in both what they play and how they play. Most have distinctly different toy preferences, and most boys are more active and rough-and-tumble, whereas most girls tend to be more verbal and nurturing. Even their selection of playmates becomes gender-typed, and they are more likely to have more positive attitudes toward their own gender (Cvencek, Greenwald, & Meltzoff, 2016; Kurtz-Costes, DeFreitas, Halle, & Kinlaw, 2011). In a study of 95 children ages 1 to 3 years, researchers found distinct gender-typed patterns in *affiliative behaviors*—that is, behaviors involving seeking and establishing friendly contact with peers. By age 2, girls affiliated with other girls rather than with boys, and by age 3, boys affiliated with other boys rather than with girls (Blicharski, Bon, & Strayer, 2011). The phenomenon of same-gender preference in young children has been observed throughout the world and is known as **gender segregation** (Gasparini et al., 2015).

gender segregation The term for the preference of girls to play with other girls, and of boys to play with other boys.

Because one's gender is so central to a person's adult experience, the question of how children acquire **gender identity**—that is, a personal sense of themselves as boys or girls—is of great interest to developmental psychologists. In the sections that follow, we will explore five major views of gender identity development: the psychodynamic, social learning, constructivist, gender schema, and cultural views (see Table 9.1 for a summary). As you will see in Figure 9.1, all views attempt to explain gender identity in terms of an evolving relationship between the developing individual's *biological sex* (typically male or female) and the *gender roles* of their culture. **Gender roles** are sets of beliefs about how boys/men and girls/women should behave. (We discuss the relationship between gender roles and identity and sexual orientation in Chapter 13.)

gender identity A personal sense of self as a boy or girl

gender role A set of beliefs about how boys/men and girls/women should behave.

The Psychodynamic View By far the best-known account of gender identity formation is that of Sigmund Freud (1921/1949, 1933/1964). Although many of Freud's specific hypotheses about development have not been substantiated, his theories remain influential. Certainly, many parents can tell stories of "Freudian moments" when their own young children began to test the boundaries between

TABLE 9.1 Paths to Sex-Role Identity

View	Process
Psychodynamic	**Differentiation and identification:** Boys differentiate from their mothers and identify with their fathers through resolution of the Oedipus complex. Girls' resolution of the Electra complex results in identification with their mother, with the attempt to differentiate from her being short-circuited.
Social learning	**Modeling and differential reinforcement:** Boys and girls observe and imitate sex-typed behaviors of males and females, respectively, because they are rewarded for doing so.
Constructivist	**Conceptual development:** Children develop sex-role constancy (an understanding that their sex remains the same no matter what), and sex-role identity then begins to guide their thoughts and actions.
Gender schema	**Gender schemas *and* observation and imitation:** As in cognitive-developmental theory, children form concepts—gender schemes, which they use to process gender-relevant information. As in social learning theory, observation and imitation play roles.
Cultural	**Mediation:** The acquisition of gender roles occurs as children's activities are organized (mediated) by cultural conceptions and stereotypes of gender.

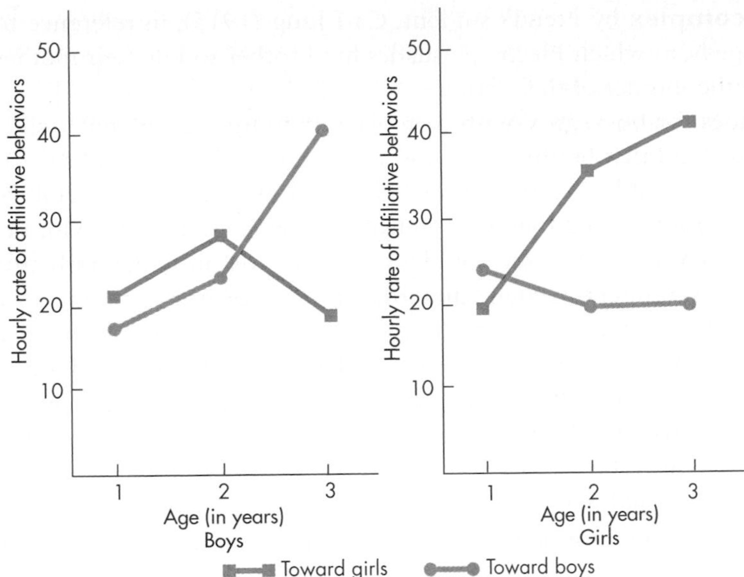

FIGURE 9.1 Gender segregation in children's play is clearly established by 3 years of age, with boys tending to affiliate with other boys, and girls tending to affiliate with other girls.

their personal desires and culturally accepted behavior, as reflected in the following conversation:

> "When I grow up," says [4-year-old] Jimmy at the dinner table, "I'm gonna marry Mama."
> "Jimmy's nuts," says the sensible voice of 8-year-old Jane. "You can't mary Mama and anyway, what would happen to Daddy?"
> "He'll be old," says [Jimmy], through a mouthful of string beans. "And he'll be dead."
>
> Then, awed by the enormity of his words, [Jimmy] adds hastily, "But he might not be dead, and maybe I'll marry Marcia instead."
>
> (Fraiberg, 1959, pp. 202–203.)

phallic stage In Freudian theory, the period beginning around the age of 3 or 4 years when children start to regard their own genitals as a major source of pleasure.

Oedipus complex In Freudian theory, the desire young boys have to get rid of their father and take his place in their mother's affections.

By Freud's account, when Jimmy says that he wants to "marry Mama," he is playing out the universal predicament of boys around the age of 3 or 4, who have moved beyond the oral and anal stages to the **phallic stage** of development, at which children have become capable of deriving pleasure from their genitals. Jimmy's feelings toward his mother and father cause him a lot of mental anguish. He is old enough to know that feelings like wanting your father to die are bad, and he is young enough to believe that his parents, who are powerful figures in his life, are always aware of what he is thinking. So he lives in fear of being punished and feels guilty about his bad thoughts.

Freud called this predicament the **Oedipus complex**, referring to the ancient Greek tragedy in which Oedipus, king of Thebes, unknowingly kills his father and marries his mother. To resolve these feelings, little boys, as they leave infancy and enter childhood, must mentally reorder their emotional attachments by *differentiating*, or distancing, themselves from their mothers and becoming closer to their fathers, identifying with them and taking on their characteristics, beliefs, and values. This process is driven by complex social emotions such as guilt and envy.

Chris Whitehead/Getty Images

Many young boys are fascinated by their father's typical activities, just as many young girls are fascinated by the typical activities of their mother. Less often, however, are children fascinated with the gender-related activities of the other-sex parent. Why this is the case would be explained differently by each of the major theoretical perspectives.

According to Freud, girls go through a very different process of sex-role identity development. The key event in the development of a girl's sex-role identity is her discovery that she does not have a penis: The girl is "mortified by the comparison with boys' far superior equipment" (Freud, 1933/1964, p. 126). She blames her mother for this "deficiency" and transfers her love to her father. Then she competes with her mother for her father's affection. This process was dubbed the

Electra complex In Freudian theory, the process by which young girls blame their mother for their "castrated" condition, transfer their love to their father, and compete with their mother for their father's affection.

Electra complex by Freud's student, Carl Jung (1915), in reference to another Greek tragedy, in which Electra persuades her brother to kill their mother in order to avenge the murder of their father.

As it does for boys, girls' wish to replace the same-sex parent results in guilt. The girl is afraid that her mother knows what she is thinking and that she will be punished by loss of her mother's love. She overcomes her fear and guilt by repressing her feelings for her father and intensifying her identification with her mother. Freud believed that this pattern of identity formation, in which girls affiliate with their mothers, renders women "underdeveloped" versions of men because their attempts to differentiate themselves from their mothers are short-circuited.

Not surprisingly, Freud's argument has been strongly attacked, on numerous grounds. For example, critics reject Freud's belief that females are somehow underdeveloped compared with males. Indeed, if any priority were to be given to one sex, it would more plausibly be given to the female. As we saw in Chapter 3 (pp. 84–86), the sex organs of all human embryos initially follow a female path of development, becoming male only if modified through the action of male hormones. Moreover, modern research indicates that there is more to children's achievement of gender identities than identifying with the same-sex parent around the age of 4 or 5 because aspects of identity formation can be discerned well before this age (Ruble & Martin, 1998). Freud's ideas, however criticized, continue to influence both popular and scholarly thinking about the acquisition of sex roles. The challenge facing those who dispute his theories is to provide a better account of the processes at work.

Anders Ryman/Alamy

Dressed in a traditional costume, this little Swedish girl learns to clap and dance at a midsummer festival by observing and imitating the behavior of adults.

The Social Learning View

Freudian theories of identification assume that young children are caught in hidden conflicts between their fears and their desires. Identification with the same-sex parent is their way of resolving those conflicts. The social learning view differs from this in two fundamental ways. First, social learning theories emphasize entirely different developmental processes. Second, they assume that parents are not the only ones responsible for the child's gender-role and identity development (Eagly & Koenig, 2006).

Social learning theory proposes that identification arises through two related processes. The first is **modeling**, in which children observe and imitate others; the second is **differential reinforcement**, in which children are rewarded for engaging in specific types of behavior. In the particular case of acquiring gender roles and gender identity, social learning theorists believe that children model the behavior of individuals of the same sex as themselves and receive differential reinforcement for engaging in gender-appropriate behavior (Ewing & Taylor, 2009).

modeling In acquiring gender roles and identities, the process by which children observe and imitate individuals of the same sex as themselves.

differential reinforcement In acquiring gender roles and identities, the process by which girls and boys are rewarded for engaging in ways that are considered gender appropriate in their culture.

Social learning theory also proposes that it is simplistic to think that children acquire gender-role identity primarily by imitating their same-sex parents. Instead, in coming to understand their gender role, children rely also on peers, siblings, and other adults in their lives, as well as on the gender stereotypes communicated in their cultures through television and other media (Kornienko, Santos, Martin, & Granger, 2016; Martin & Kazyak, 2009) (Figure 9.2).

Siblings, for example, are known to be important resources in the child's construction of gender roles. In a major longitudinal study, John Rust and his colleagues (Rust, Golombok, Hines, & Johnston, 2000) examined the gender development of more than 5,000 preschoolers. In some cases the preschooler had an older sister, in some cases an older brother, and in some cases no siblings. They found that boys with older brothers and girls with older sisters showed the greatest amount of gender-typed behavior—that is, behavior traditionally considered characteristic of one's gender. In contrast, boys with older sisters and girls with older brothers were the least sex typed. Those without siblings were somewhere in the middle. Clearly, older siblings exert significant influence on the gender-role development of their little brothers and sisters.

The Constructivist View Many developmentalists believe that a child's cognitive development must be taken into account when explaining gender-role and identity development. Developmentalists taking this view argue that children actively, cognitively construct gender roles in the course of interacting with their physical and social environments (Coyle & Liben, 2016; Weisgram, 2016). One approach that attempts this is *gender schema theory*.

Gender schema theory emphasizes that the environment affects the child's understanding of gender indirectly, through a *schema*, or cognitive structure. Once formed, this schema guides the way the child selects and remembers information from the environment and leads the child to act in ways that are considered gender appropriate in the child's culture (Martin & Ruble, 2010). A **gender schema**, then, can be considered a mental model containing information about boys/men and girls/women that is used to process gender-relevant information, such as which types of toys, clothing, activities, and interests are appropriate for which gender (Liben & Bigler, 2002).

Children form gender schemas not only for objects ("boy things" and "girl things") and people but also for familiar events and routines, such as how Daddy barbecues or how Mommy shops for groceries. Accordingly, at the same time that they are discovering how to classify people and objects in terms of gender, gender information is becoming a part of the scripts that boys and girls draw upon and apply—so that their barbecuing script features a man, for example, and their grocery shopping script features a woman.

Figure 9.3 provides an illustration of how gender schemas work (Martin & Ruble, 2010). A little girl who can say that she is a girl and that her brother is a boy is presented with four objects with which to play. Two of the objects are gender neutral—an orange and an artichoke—and two are stereotypically male or female—a truck and a doll. When the girl is presented with the doll, she must first decide if it is specifically relevant to her. She will think "Dolls are for girls" and "I am a girl" and thus conclude that dolls are relevant to her. As a result of this decision, the girl will interact with the doll—playing with it, exploring it, and learning about it. (The green arrows in the diagram depict this sequence.) In contrast, when the little girl is presented with a truck, she will think "Trucks are for boys" and "I am a girl" and thus conclude that the truck is not relevant to her. As a result, she will avoid the truck and not be interested in knowing anything else about it. (The orange arrows in the diagram depict this sequence.) Asked about these toys later on, she will remember more about the doll than about the truck.

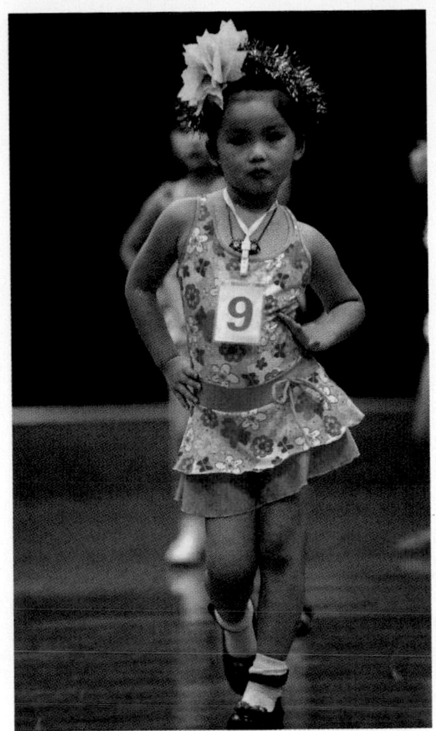
AFP/Getty Images

FIGURE 9.2 These girls are participating in a modeling contest—the first of its kind in their province in south China. Like many young girls from Western countries, they are learning that physical appearance in girls is valued and rewarded in their community.

gender schema A mental model containing information about boys and girls that is used to process gender-relevant information.

FIGURE 9.3 An example of an information-processing sequence associated with gender-schema formation. In this case, the child is a girl who has been offered four objects with which to play. (Information from Martin & Halverson, 1981.)

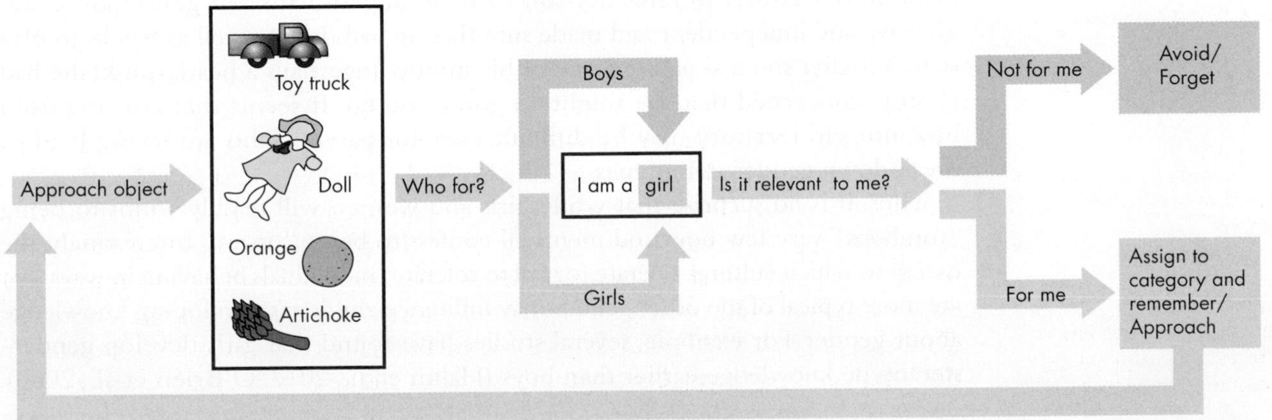

Gallo Images - Emielke van Wyk/Getty Images

Trucks and little boys just seem to go together. Understanding the source of gender-specific toy preferences is an important focus of developmental research.

Naturally, children's ability to associate particular objects, such as toy trucks and dolls, with one gender or the other depends on the presence and use of such objects in the child's environment. Indeed, our understanding of gender-role development would be incomplete without exploring the impact of culture—the gender-specific objects, expectations, values, and beliefs that *mediate* children's activities and experiences from very early in life.

The Cultural View The acquisition of gender roles provides an excellent illustration of how the tools of culture (in this case, gender roles) organize children's activities and the way children relate to their environment. Evidence that such mediation may have significant consequences for children's gender identity development comes from studies of children's responses to various contexts in which the amount of emphasis on gender varies (Hilliard & Liben, 2010). For example, preschool teachers may differ widely in their emphasis on gender in classroom activities (Lynch, 2015; Markström & Simonsson, 2011; Chapman, 2016). One preschool teacher may greet her class with an enthusiastic "Good morning, boys and girls!" During circle time, she may say, "All the boys with blue socks stand up! Now, all the girls wearing sweaters stand up!" Later, when it is time to go outside, she may say, "Okay, let's line up boy-girl-boy-girl." And lunch may provide an opportunity to reinforce arithmetic: "How many boys are at the table? How many girls?" In her classroom, gender categories organize activities, and gender-typed language is used frequently. Another teacher may make an effort to establish the classroom as a gender-neutral environment. A number of studies find that teachers harbor a variety of assumptions regarding the gender-role behavior of the young children in their classrooms, and toys are often gender coded (dolls and trucks). Children who spend time in preschool classrooms that emphasize gender have higher levels of gender stereotyping and gender-typical play than do children in classrooms that are more gender neutral (Hilliard & Liben, 2010; Lynch, 2015).

Children's behavior is mediated not only by the *content* of gender categories (what sorts of behaviors count as specifically "boy/man" or "girl/woman") but also by the rigidness of the categories and the consequences of crossing category boundaries (Ruble & Martin, 2002). In many Western cultures, the stereotype of boys and men is defined more clearly—and more rigidly—than the stereotype of girls and women. In the United States, for example, this difference is reflected in the relative permissiveness toward girls' engaging in typically male-identified behaviors and much greater intolerance toward boys' engaging in typically female-identified behavior. One young mother told us of a time when her 2-year-old son snuggled up to her on the sofa while she was painting her fingernails, extended his hand, and said, "Me, too, Mommy." This mother took great pride in her efforts to raise her son to be as affectionate and gentle as he was assertive and independent and made sure that he had dolls as well as trucks to play with. Yet after she had painted one of his stubby fingernails a pearly pink, she had to stop, concerned that she might be going too far. It seems that crossing from boy into girl territory may be difficult even for parents who are trying hard to break down gender stereotypes.

Thus, it is no surprise that while girls and women will readily admit to being "tomboys," very few boys and men will confess to being "sissies." Interestingly, the extent to which cultures tolerate (or fail to tolerate) individuals behaving in ways that are more typical of the other gender may influence children's developing knowledge about gender. For example, several studies have found that girls develop gender-stereotype knowledge earlier than boys (Halim et al., 2017; O'Brien et al., 2000), perhaps because girls are allowed to experiment with behaviors typical of both gender roles, whereas boys are confined to behaviors that are consistent with what society defines as the "male domain."

Ethnic Identity

Ethnic identity refers to a personal sense of belonging to an ethnic group—a group defined according to a cultural heritage, including cultural values, traditions, and language—and the feelings and attitudes one holds regarding one's sense of belonging to that group (Phinney & Ong, 2007; Schwartz et al., 2014). In a society populated by many ethnic groups, children's developing sense of their own ethnic identity* has a host of social, psychological, and economic implications (Phinney & Baldelomar, 2011). These implications range from whether there are ethnic grocery stores in particular communities and whether ethnically relevant after-school clubs and activities are available for students to whether ethnic-minority youths are at elevated risk for suicide (see Chapter 15, pp. 544–550). As a consequence, researchers have studied how children identify their own ethnic group and how they form stable attitudes toward their own and other groups (Cross & Cross, 2008; Schwartz et al., 2014). Studies have explored the different kinds of feelings and attitudes that children might associate with their ethnic identity and the possible effects such feelings and attitudes might have on children's self-esteem.

ethnic identity A sense of belonging to an ethnic group and the feelings and attitudes that accompany the sense of group membership.

Photograph by Gordon Parks, Copyright the Gordon Parks Foundation

Kenneth and Mamie Clark conducted groundbreaking research in the 1930s and 1940s and found that African American children of that era tended to make more positive attributions to light-colored rather than dark-colored dolls.

Perhaps the most famous research on the development of ethnic identity was carried out by Kenneth and Mamie Clark (1939, 1950), who asked African American and European American children to indicate their preferences between pairs of dolls. The children, who were 3 years old and older, were presented with pairs of dolls representing the two ethnic groups and were asked to choose "which boy would you would like to play with" or "which girl you don't like." The Clarks reported that most of the youngest children could distinguish between the categories of dolls and, more importantly, that African American children of all ages seemed to prefer the white dolls, a phenomenon that has come to be called "the white bias" (Justice, Lindsey, & Morrow, 1999). On the basis of this research, many psychologists concluded that African American children define themselves entirely in terms of the majority group, thereby denying the importance of their own families and communities in shaping their identities (Jackson, McCullough, & Gurin, 1997).

Studies conducted since the 1950s have confirmed the Clarks' findings (Jordan & Hernandez-Reif, 2009; Justice et al., 1999) and have extended them to children of other minority groups, including Native Americans (Annis & Corenblum, 1987) and Bantu children in South Africa (Gregor & McPherson, 1966). However, these studies have also cast doubt on the notion that minority-group children acquire a negative ethnic self-concept (Spencer, 2006). Margaret Spencer (1988), for example, showed that while many of the 4- to 6-year-old African American children she interviewed said that they would prefer to play with a white doll, 80 percent of

*The difference between ethnic identity and racial identity is complicated. Typically, ethnic identity refers to how individuals understand themselves in relation to cultural beliefs, values, and practices, whereas racial identity refers to how individuals understand themselves in light of oppressive and racialized societies (Cokley, 2007). Although distinct in many ways, there is considerable overlap between these terms, prompting many researchers to use *race* and *ethnicity* interchangeably, as we have done here.

these children displayed positive self-esteem. Several other studies confirm that the "white bias" is not connected to the way that children think about and evaluate themselves (Justice et al., 1999). Ann Beuf (1977) reported incident after incident in which Native American children who chose white dolls made evident their understanding of the economic and social circumstances that make their lives difficult in contrast to the lives of White people. In one study, 5-year-old Dom was given several dolls representing Caucasians and Native Americans (whose skins were depicted as brown) to put into a toy classroom:

> Dom: (holding up a white doll) The children's all here and now the teacher's coming in.
> Interviewer: Is that the teacher?
> Dom: Yeah.
> Interviewer: (holding up a brown doll) Can she be the teacher?
> Dom: No way! Her's just an aide.
> (Beuf, 1977, p. 80.)

In Beuf's view, the children's choices are less a reflection of their sense of personal self-worth than of their desire for the power and wealth of the White people with whom they had come in contact. Her views are echoed by James Jackson (2006), whose review of existing data provided little support for the idea that minority-group children's recognition that they are members of a less powerful group translates into a negative personal sense of themselves. Similarly, a study conducted with Black and multiracial children in South Africa—a country marked by profound racial status differences—found that the children's pro-White bias correlated highly with their positive attitudes toward people with wealth (Newheiser et al., 2014).

Decades of research on ethnic-identity development make clear that understanding oneself as a member of a particular ethnic group emerges in the first years of life. An important question is how ethnic identity is affected by children's social experiences. To address this question, developmentalists have explored how parents communicate with their children about issues of ethnicity (Dunbar et al., 2017; Rodriguez, Umaña-Taylor, Smith & Johnson, 2009). **Ethnic socialization** refers to the ethnicity-related messages communicated to children. Developmental researchers most commonly study two general forms of ethnic socialization: *cultural socialization*, which emphasizes ethnic heritage and pride, and *preparation for bias*, which emphasizes awareness of racial bias and ways to cope with it, including through spirituality, academic achievement, and managing negative emotions (Dunbar et al., 2017; Lesane-Brown, 2006).

ethnic socialization Ethnic-based messages communicated to children.

Rolf Bruderer/Getty Images

Despite an early awareness that White Americans are more likely than Black Americans to have wealth and power, African American children generally display positive self-esteem. The traditional dress of his young girl and her grandmother express their sense of ethnic pride.

A number of studies have found that parents of ethnic-minority youths in the United States (including African American, Puerto Rican, Dominican, Mexican American, and Hmong) routinely incorporate a variety of ethnic socialization messages when interacting with their young children (Hughes et al., 2006; Knight et al., 2011; Moua, & Lamborn, 2010). These messages most often focus on cultural socialization, although, as children approach adolescence, preparation for bias messages becomes more salient (see Chapter 15).

Differences in the form of ethnic socialization bear importantly on children's cognitive abilities and behavioral adjustment. Children whose parents promote ethnic pride and provide a home rich in culture tend to have stronger cognitive abilities and problem-solving skills and fewer behavior problems compared to children whose parents provide lower levels of ethnic socialization (Dunbar et al., 2017). This research indicates that the process of forming an ethnic identity is well under way in early childhood.

Personal Identity

> I'm 3 years old and I live in a big house with my mother and father and my brother, Jason, and my sister, Lisa. I have blue eyes and a kitty that is orange and a television in my own room. I know all my ABC's, listen: A, B, C, D, E, F, G, H, L, K, O, M, P, Q, X, Z. I can run real fast. I like pizza and I have a nice teacher at preschool. I can count up to 100, want to hear me? I love my dog Skipper. I can climb to the top of the jungle gym, I'm not scared! I'm never scared! I'm always happy. I have brown hair and I go to preschool. I am really strong. I can lift this chair, watch me! (Harter, 1999, p. 37.)

The preceding monologue is a composite of the kinds of statements 3- to 4-year-olds typically make when describing themselves, revealing their sense of personal identity. Traditionally, developmentalists define **personal identity** as consisting of two parts, the *I-self* and the *me-self*. The I-self is the person's subjective sense of being a particular individual who exists over time and who acts and experiences the world in a particular way. The me-self, in contrast, is the person's sense of his or her objective characteristics, such as physical appearance, abilities, and other personal features that can be objectively known ("I live in a big house. I have blue eyes and a kitty.") The "I" and the "me" are two sides of the same coin; they shape each other continuously over the course of development (see also Chapter 15).

personal identity A person's sense of his or her self as persisting over time (*I-self*), as well as a sense of personal characteristics such as appearance and abilities that can be objectively known (*me-self*).

For reasons of cognitive immaturity, young children's descriptions of themselves focus mainly on the objective self and typically list highly specific, loosely connected behaviors, abilities, and preferences that are usually seen in an unrealistically positive way. These self-descriptions are rarely combined into generalized traits such as "being shy" or "being smart." That is, young children's self-descriptions are not well integrated into a *personality structure*. Instead, they tend to be fluid and shifting, as well as disjointed. As we discussed in Chapter 8, reasoning that proceeds from particular to particular (transductive reasoning) is characteristic of preoperational thought. The integration of the "self" into a mature identity is a gradual process that continues in step with cognitive development throughout childhood and adolescence (see Chapter 15, p. 542).

Cognitive limitations also contribute to young children's tendency to see themselves in the most favorable light. Their self-evaluations tend to be unrealistically positive because they have difficulty distinguishing between what they want to do and what they actually are able to do. For example, a child will say "I know all my ABCs" and "I can swim the whole way across the pool" when he or she can do neither of these things. One reason young children describe themselves in such glowing and unrealistic terms is that they are not yet capable of distinguishing between a "real" self and an "ideal" self—a cognitive ability that doesn't emerge until middle childhood (Chapter 13, pp. 442–445).

The continuing process of developing personal identity is greatly influenced in early childhood by children's increasingly sophisticated use of language. We discussed in Chapter 7 (pp. 254–255) that language is acquired in routine, scripted activities during which young children interact with their caregivers. The same routine activities in family settings are crucial contexts for further development of the self. Not only do caregivers tell children that they are boys or girls, good or bad, Black or White, Japanese or Irish, but they also help them acquire an enduring sense of themselves by helping them to create a personal narrative about themselves. This personal narrative is referred to as **autobiographical memory**.

autobiographical memory A personal narrative that helps children acquire an enduring sense of themselves.

Adults typically contribute to children's development of autobiographical memory by helping children recall and interpret events in which they have participated (Fivush, 2011; Merrill & Fivush, 2016). Initially, adults carry the burden of helping the child remember. Gradually, with increasing age and growing facility with language, the child assumes a more active role, as one of our daughters, Jenny, did when she was about 2 years old. "Tell me what Jenny did," she would say every night at bedtime, and her parents would oblige her by recounting the events of the day in a schematic way that highlighted events that were particularly interesting or worrisome to her. These conversations would go like this: "Do you remember this morning, when we went to pick up Michael, and Mandy [the dog] came running out?" and Jenny would say, "Doggie go wuff, wuff, wuff." "And what did Mandy do?" her parents would prompt. "Wagged her tail," Jenny would respond. "And what else did Mandy do?" they would ask, and she would laugh remembering, "She kissed me!" Although her parents continued to guide the narrative, as Jenny grew older, she increasingly corrected them and added details of her own until she stopped asking them to tell her what happened and started telling them the events of her day (or refusing to tell, as she often did).

Like all other parents in such interactions, Jenny's parents were not simply mirrors reflecting their child's experiences. As participants in creating the stories of children's experience, parents strongly influence their children's autobiographical memories and are themselves influenced by the larger culture as well as by their own personal histories, values, and interests. What is more, as illustrated in Jenny's case, parents are not necessarily objective in their contributions to the stories. Some parents may tend to embellish and exaggerate to heighten the stories and make them more exciting, or to play down children's incompetence or fears and exaggerate their capabilities and bravery. Other parents might stay closer to the objective facts in recounting the events in their children's lives. Yet others might tend to structure the stories of prior events so that they teach moral lessons. There are great variations among parents in what events they remember and include in these narratives as well as in how they structure the narratives (Nelson, 2003). Despite this variation, by the time most children are 4 years old, they have internalized the narrative structures appropriate to their culture and can recount their personal experiences by themselves, a significant step in developing personal identity.

APPLY > CONNECT > DISCUSS

Visit a major toy store and look for evidence of social categories of gender and ethnicity. What sorts of toys are marketed for boys, girls, or children of specific ethnic backgrounds? How might these toys mediate children's behavior?

Visit the children's section of a public library and look for similar evidence of social categories in books appropriate for 3- to 5-year-olds. (You might enlist the help of the librarian.) What similarities and differences do you note between books and toys?

LEARNING OUTCOME

Distinguish young children's moral development and behavior according to the psychodynamic view, the constructivist view, and the social domain theory.

A New Moral World

Eddie: Sometimes I hate myself.
Teacher: When?
Eddie: When I'm naughty.
Teacher: What do you do that's naughty?
Eddie: You know, naughty words. Like "shit." That one.
Teacher: That makes you hate yourself?
Eddie: Yeah, when my dad washes my mouth with soap.
Teacher: What if he doesn't hear you?
Eddie: Then I get away with it. Then I don't hate myself.
(Paley, 1981, p. 54.)

Children's early ideas of what is good and what is bad come from the ways in which the significant people in their lives respond to their behavior. In the conversation above, it is clear that for Eddie, as for young children generally, "[b]ad and good depended on the adult response. . . . An angry parent denoted a naughty child" (Paley, 1981, p. 55). As discussed in Chapter 6, the seeds of this moral development are apparent at the end of infancy when children acquire sensitivity to adult standards and become frustrated or disappointed when they fail to meet them.

To get a sense of the vast territory between these early beginnings and fully mature moral reasoning, take a moment to think about your own moral standards—what you consider right, just, and fair. It is very likely that you believe these standards are not based on the dictates of authority. That is, although you may share your parents' or community's moral values, it is unlikely that you embrace your moral standards because you were told to do so or because you worry about what will happen if you get caught violating a moral standard. Instead, you probably have a deeply *personal* sense of right and wrong. Developmentalists are intent on discovering how such personally felt moral standards are acquired. In the sections below, we examine three perspectives that have dominated research on children's moral development: psychodynamic theory, constructivist theory, and social domain theory.

The Psychodynamic View

According to psychodynamic theory, we acquire a personal sense of what is right and wrong because we have *internalized* the moral standards of our parents, especially those of our same-sex parent. Indeed, our previous discussion of Freud's views on sexual identity development contains the kernel of his thinking about the development of moral reasoning.

According to Freud, the internalization of moral standards that occurs as a consequence of identifying with a same-sex parent is responsible for the creation of the last of the three mental structures that, he said, develop in early childhood (previewed in Chapter 1). The first, the **id**, which is present at birth, functions unconsciously and operates on the basis of the *pleasure principle*; that is, it strives for the immediate satisfaction of bodily drives and does so impulsively (Freud, 1933/1964). Over the first few years of life, the id comes gradually to be held in check by the emergence of the second mental structure, the **ego**. The ego serves as the intermediary between the demands of the id and the demands of the social world, enabling children to control and regulate their behavior. The ego is said to operate on the basis of the *reality principle*—that is, it is concerned with how bodily drives can be satisfied while taking reality into account. Sometime later, around age 5, children internalize adult standards, rules, and admonitions, resulting in the formation of the **superego**. In Freud's words, the superego "continues to carry on the functions which have hitherto been performed by the [parents]: it observes the ego, gives it orders, judges it and threatens it with punishments, exactly like the parents whose place it has [partially] taken" (1940/1964, p. 205). The emergence of the superego, and all its associated emotions of shame and guilt, is fundamental to children's abilities to regulate their behaviors according to their personal sense of right and wrong.

id In Freudian theory, the mental structure present at birth that is the main source of psychological energy. It is unconscious and pleasure-seeking and demands that bodily drives be satisfied.

ego In Freudian theory, the mental structure that develops out of the id as the infant is forced by reality to cope with the social world. The ego mediates between the id and the social world, allowing children to control and regulate behavior.

superego In Freudian terms, the conscience. It represents the authority of the child's parents and sits in stern judgment of the ego's efforts to hold the id in check. It becomes a major force in the personality in middle childhood.

The Constructivist View

Consider two scenes. In one, a young child named Luke is warned by his mother to stay away from the freshly baked cookies cooling on the kitchen counter. When she leaves the room, Luke snitches a cookie and, in his clumsy haste, knocks over a cup that falls to the floor and breaks. Now consider the second scene, in which young Zack is helping his mother set the dining room table for dinner. With hands full of napkins and silverware, he pushes open the door leading from the kitchen to the dining room. When the door swings open, it hits a tray on which are stacked a dozen cups, all of which fall to the floor and break. Who, in your judgment, is the naughtier child—Luke, who broke one cup while snitching a cookie, or Zack, who broke a dozen while helping his mother set the table?

When Piaget presented similar contrasts to children of different ages, he found that young, preoperational children considered Zack the naughtier of the two because he broke more cups. Older children, in contrast, chose Luke because he was deliberately violating his mother's order, whereas Zack was trying to do good and simply had an unfortunate accident.

As you might predict from previous discussions of preoperational thinking, when young children reason about moral issues, they tend to focus on objective consequences—how much damage is done (in the case of Luke and Zack) or whether the person gets caught and in trouble (as when Eddie's father washed his mouth out with soap). Jean Piaget (1932/1965) called this pattern of thinking **heteronomous morality**—that is, morality defined in terms of externally imposed controls and objective consequences. According to Piaget, as children enter middle childhood and begin to interact increasingly with their peers outside situations directly controlled by adults, heteronomous morality gives way to *autonomous morality*, in which one's moral judgments are freely and personally chosen. (This idea and its extension by Lawrence Kohlberg and other contemporary researchers will be discussed further in Chapter 14.)

heteronomous morality Piaget's term for young children's tendency to define morality in terms of objective consequences and externally imposed controls.

As you can see, the cognitive-developmental and psychodynamic views both focus on how children move past their reliance on external authority and objective consequences to define right and wrong. But whereas the psychodynamic view emphasizes processes such as identification, internalization, and the development of the superego, the cognitive-developmental view links changes in moral reasoning to broader cognitive developments that are supported by the expansion of children's social lives.

The Social Domain View

The social domain view of moral development stands apart from the other two views we have considered because it emphasizes that there are different *types* of "right" and "wrong" (Killen, Elenbaas, & Rutland, 2016; Killen & Smetana, 2007). For example, jaywalking is a very different type of transgression than pushing someone off a bridge. According to **social domain theory**, rules that dictate right and wrong fall into three domains, which are at different levels of generality: Some rules are *moral rules*, others are *social conventions*, and yet others are rules within the *personal sphere* (Lagattuta, Nucci, & Bosacki, 2010; Turiel, 2008a) (Table 9.2).

social domain theory The theory that the moral domain, the social conventional domain, and the personal domain have distinct rules that vary in how broadly the rules apply and in what happens when they are broken.

Moral rules are the most general; they are based on principles of justice and the welfare of others. Thus, moral rules specify, for example, that others be treated fairly, in a way that preserves their rights and avoids causing them harm. Often believed to derive from a divine source (for example, to be God's law), and found in all societies, moral rules are obligations that are not to be transgressed.

At the next level of generality are social conventions—rules that are important for coordinating social behavior in a given society, such as rules about how men or women should act, or what constitutes appropriate dress at a house of worship or on the beach, or who has authority over whom. Social conventions are important aspects of the cultural scripts that young children are acquiring. Social conventions vary tremendously, not only among societies but also among subcultural groups within a society. This variation can contribute to difficulties children may have in knowing whether a rule they have broken is a moral rule or a social

TABLE 9.2 Social Domain Theory Approach to Rules and Infractions

Rule Type	Sample Infractions
Moral rules—rules related to	
Physical harm	Hitting, pushing
Psychological harm	Hurting feelings, ridiculing
Fairness and rights	Refusing to take turns
Social conventions—rules related to	
School behavior	Chewing gum in class, talking back to the teacher
Forms of address	Calling a physician "Mr." when he is working
Attire and appearance	Wearing pajamas to school
Sex roles	Boy wearing barrette to keep hair out of eyes while playing football
Personal sphere—rules related to	
Personal habits	Making loud noises while eating
Hygiene	Not brushing teeth
Social events	Not sending a thank-you card for a gift

convention. For example, some families may treat cursing as violating a social convention ("That's not a nice word; you definitely shouldn't say it in front of your grandmother"), but when Eddie says "shit" and gets his mouth washed out with soap, he might well believe that he has broken a moral rule!

At the most specific level are rules that govern the personal sphere, in which children can make decisions on the basis of their personal preferences. They are allowed to choose whether to call or send a note to thank an uncle for a birthday gift. It is in the personal sphere that children are able to develop what is unique about the way they deal with the world (Johnson, Tasimi, & Wynn, 2017; Lagattuta, Nucci, & Bosacki, 2010).

Several studies have found that children as young as 3 or 4 years old from a variety of cultures can distinguish among moral, social, and personal rules (Yau & Smetana, 2003). For example, they respond quite differently to moral rule violations, such as hurting another child or taking another's favorite toy, than they do to violations of a social convention, such as wearing inappropriate clothes to school (Turiel, 2006).

As already suggested, the borders between the three levels of rules are not easy to learn and keep straight. Parents, for example, may treat their young children's wearing a bathing suit at the beach as a matter of social convention. Their young children, however, may treat wearing a bathing suit as a matter of personal choice, so they take it off to play naked in the water. It takes children many years to acquire their culture's normative separations, and even then, deciding which rules should be applied in which situations often requires a good deal of thought and flexibility (Ball, Smetana, & Sturge-Apple, 2017; Nucci, 2004).

APPLY > CONNECT > DISCUSS

Erikson believed that identity development and moral development are closely related. Using material presented in this chapter, pull together evidence for his argument.

LEARNING OUTCOMES

Explain how self-regulation acts as a cornerstone in a child's development.

Point out different types of play that contribute to children's social and emotional development.

Explain the role of emotions, including the ability to interpret emotional stages in others, in helping children develop socioemotional competence.

Point out how cultures influence a child's emotional development and emotion regulation.

Developing Self-Regulation

In the process of learning about basic social roles and rules and developing their sense of self, children are also learning to act in accordance with the expectations of their caregivers, even when they do not want to and are not being directly monitored. Learning to control one's thoughts, emotions, and behaviors, an ability referred to as **self-regulation**, spans various developmental stages and involves all the developmental domains (Kochanska, Philibert, & Barry, 2009; Montroy et al., 2016). As we have noted in previous chapters, the capacity for self-regulation begins to emerge early in development, as infants first acquire the ability to regulate their sleep/wake cycles, their crying, and later, to a certain degree, their behavior. As they get older, children's regulatory capacities expand and deepen, allowing them, for example, to increasingly control their attentional state and tune out distractions in order to complete a task, to put aside hurt feelings in order to patch up a friendship, and to keep secrets.

Infants and young children require a great deal of assistance with regulation. They are soothed by caregivers when they cry, their interpersonal relationships are often orchestrated by others ("Tell him you're sorry and make up"), and their emotional expressions are monitored and managed ("No hitting! Use words!"). Even the large and simple figures contained in young children's coloring books reflect the culture's response to children's need for assistance in regulating their attention and behavior (in this case, their fine motor behavior).

Dynamic Graphics/Getty Images

Culture helps these girls' immature motor skills by making extra big shovels for filling buckets with sand.

Because the ability to regulate one's own thoughts, emotions, behaviors, and attentional states is such an important part of what it means to function independently, many developmentalists consider self-regulation to be a cornerstone of children's development (Carlson, 2005; Connor et al., 2016).

Regulating Thought and Action

Intentionally focusing one's attention, or remembering to do something, or mapping out a plan to solve a problem involves the regulation of cognitive processes. Consider a preschooler who is stringing beads (after Shonkoff & Phillips, 2000, p. 116). Accomplishing this task requires that she regulate her thoughts in order to:

- Generate and maintain a mental representation that directs her behavior: "I need to hold up the string and put the end through the hole in the bead."
- Monitor her own progress: "I got one on; now I'll try another."
- Modify her problem-solving strategies: "This bead won't go on; I need one with a bigger hole."

self-regulation The ability to control one's thoughts, emotions, and behaviors.

effortful control The inhibition of impulsive or dominant actions.

The simple act of stringing beads calls on a host of skills that require the child to select certain actions (holding the bead to the string), eliminate impulsive actions that do not fit the goal (throwing the bead), and inhibit dominant actions as the task requires (stop trying the bead with the too-small hole). The inhibition of impulsive or dominant actions, also called **effortful control**, can be particularly difficult for young children, as anyone who has observed a game of "Red Light, Green Light" or "Simon Says" knows. Once a behavior has been initiated, especially in a highly exciting situation, it can be difficult to stop.

Effortful control is considered an aspect of children's temperament (Rothbart & Bates, 2006). Researchers typically measure effortful control in one of two ways. One way is to survey parents or teachers about children's abilities to follow instructions and inhibit inappropriate behaviors when told to do so: "Can wait before entering

dmbaker/Getty Images

Lawrence Manning/Getty Images

The ability to share requires that children control their own desires and regulate their behaviors in order to comply with social norms and the expectations of friends.

into new activities if s/he is asked to," "Can quit working on a project if asked," "When drawing or coloring in a book s/he shows strong concentration" (Palermo, Mikulski, & Conejo, 2017). Another way is to give children behavioral tests that require effortful control; for example, setting a desirable toy in front of them and telling them not to touch it or having them put large blocks in a large bucket and small blocks in a small bucket and then reversing their behavior and put large blocks in a small bucket and small blocks in a large bucket (Di Norcia et al., 2015).

A large number of studies conducted with children growing up in a variety of countries—including Italy, Turkey, China, and the United States—find that effortful control is associated with academic performance and social adjustment and that girls tend to exhibit higher levels than boys. Children with higher levels of effortful control do better in school, exhibit fewer problem behaviors with peers and teachers, and engage in lower levels of aggression (Chen et al., 2015; Gestsdottir et al., 2014; Zhang & Rao, 2017). But researchers are beginning to think that these findings depend on different types of effortful control. Consider, for example, the two types of behavioral measures of control mentioned above—being told not to touch a desirable toy and reverse sorting blocks into buckets. The first task is considered a "hot task" because it requires regulating emotion and motivation, whereas the second is considered a "cool task" because it requires regulating behavior to solve a problem relatively lacking in emotional salience (Allan & Lonigan, 2014). A study conducted with Italian preschool-aged children found that those who performed well on hot tasks were rated by their teachers as good at working in groups and cooperating with other children; those who performed poorly on the hot tasks were reported to be more aggressive than their peers (Di Norcia et al., 2015).

A child's developing effortful control is affected by the nature of his or her culture's values. For instance, Confucian values strongly influence Chinese culture, placing considerable emphasis on self-control, obedience, modesty, and respect for authority; Chinese children who are self-restrained are considered mature and well behaved (Rao, Sun, & Zhang, 2014; Zhang & Rao, 2017). Not surprisingly, Chinese children typically show higher levels of effortful control than peers growing up in cultures that place less value on these behaviors (Chung et al., 2016).

The development of effortful control is also strongly influenced by children's socioeconomic circumstances. Children living in or near poverty tend to exhibit lower levels than their more economically advantaged peers (Chung et al., 2016; Lengua et al., 2015). However, preschool programs that include training on effortful control—including physical training in martial arts and yoga—appear successful in improving the self-regulation skills of low-income children (Diamond, 2012; Diamond & Lee, 2011).

The research cited above makes clear that the development of children's effortful control and self-regulation is better fostered in some contexts than others—in cultures that value self-restraint and programs that emphasize types of activities that encourage children to monitor and regulate their behavior. Yet children also create their own contexts for developing effortful control—in play.

Self-Regulation and Play

Play occupies a conspicuous role not only in young children's physical development but also in their cognitive and social development. According to Vygotsky and those who have followed in his footsteps, the development of self-regulation is a crucial function of play (Goncu & Gaskins, 2011; Kroll, 2017; Nicolopoulou et al., 2015).

Chris Stowers/Panos Pictures

Play provides an important opportunity for acquiring self-control. These young children are regulating their behavior so that it is coordinated with that of their playmates.

Key to Vygotsky's theory about how play leads to self-regulation are his ideas regarding children's ability to separate the objects they play with from their thoughts about those objects. Remember that early in development, children have difficulty separating their thoughts and actions from the objects and situations they think about and act upon. For example, before they are 2 years old, children pretend to talk on a cell phone only if the toy really looks and acts like a cell phone, complete with buttons to tap and a shape that allows it to be held up to the mouth and ear. Not until age 2 can children let one object substitute for another; at 2 years old, for instance, they might play "phone" with a rectangular block that has the general shape of a real cell phone. The ability to detach the *idea* of the phone from the *object itself* increases through the next year, and by the age of 3, the attributes of the play symbol can be entirely independent of the object that it represents. So, for example, children can play "phone" using a ball or a stuffed animal or any other object. Their ability to separate thought—which carries the *idea* or *meaning* of the object—from the object that is thought about indicates that they are regulating their thoughts and actions. They are making themselves imagine that an object that is not a cell phone is a cell phone and are acting on it accordingly. Vygotsky believed that children's self-regulation is most required in, and hence most developed through, this type of imaginary play.

sociodramatic play Make-believe play in which two or more participants enact a variety of related social roles.

A particularly important and complex type of imaginary play is **sociodramatic play**—make-believe play in which two or more participants enact a variety of related social roles (Berk & Meyers, 2013). Sociodramatic play requires a shared understanding of what the play situation involves, which often must be negotiated as part of the play. As an example, consider the following scene involving several children in preschool. The girls in the group have just agreed upon the roles they will play: mother, sister, baby, and maid.

Karen: I'm hungry. Wa-a-ah!
Charlotte: Lie down, baby.
Karen: I'm a baby that sits up.
Charlotte: First you lie down and sister covers you and then I make your cereal and then you sit up.
Karen: Okay.
Karen: (to Teddy, who has been observing) You can be the father.
Charlotte: Are you the father?
Teddy: Yes.

Charlotte: Put on a red tie.
Janie: (in the "maid's" falsetto voice) I'll get it for you, honey. Now don't that baby look pretty? This is your daddy, baby.
(Adapted from Paley, 1984, p. 1.)

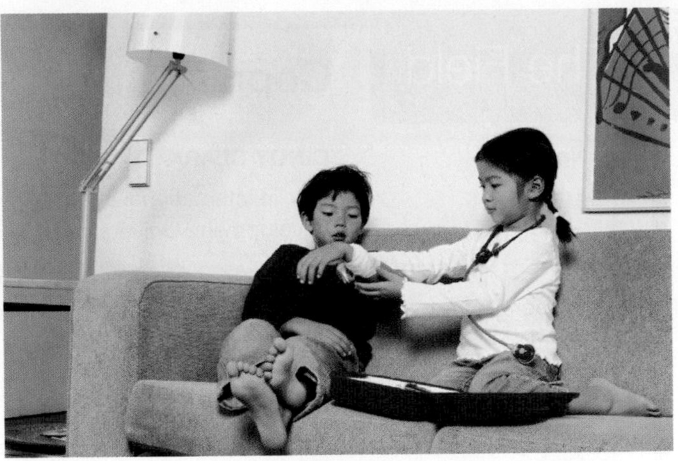
Edith Held/age fotostock

The sociodramatic play of these two children involves enacting the roles of doctors or nurses. According to Vygotsky, such play is fundamental to the emergence of self-regulation.

This transcript illustrates several features of young children's sociodramatic play. The children are enacting social roles and using scripts that they have encountered numerous times in their daily lives, on television, or in stories. Babies make stereotypic baby noises, maids get things for people, and fathers wear ties. At the same time that they are playing their roles in the pretend world, the children are also outside of it, giving stage directions to one another and commenting on the action. The "baby" who sits up has to be talked into lying down, and the boy is told what role he can play. The children here are clearly acting against immediate impulse and regulating their thoughts and behaviors according to the imaginary situation as it evolves in the course of interacting with their playmates.

Recently, developmentalists have sought empirical evidence for the link between sociodramatic play and the more general ability of children to regulate their actions. An example is a study conducted by Cynthia Elias and Laura Berk (2002), in which they observed 51 children ages 3 and 4 in their preschool classrooms. Elias and Berk recorded and assessed the children's involvement in sociodramatic play, and they assessed their level of self-regulation by observing how well the children participated in cleanup and how attentive they were when they gathered in a circle to listen to the teacher. They used a short-term longitudinal design, assessing both play and self-regulation in the fall and assessing self-regulation again several months later.

Their findings support Vygotsky's main idea regarding the role of play in facilitating self-regulation (see also the box "In the Field: Coping with Chronic Illness Through Play," p. 312). In particular, children who engaged in a lot of sociodramatic play in the fall showed high levels of self-regulation several months later, even though there was no correlation between the two variables at the time of the first assessment. Interestingly, the correlation was especially strong for the most impulsive

"I would share, but I'm not there developmentally."

Barbara Smaller/The New Yorker Collection/Cartoonbank.com.

As an important aspect of children's play, sharing requires that children act against their own impulses and coordinate their thoughts and behaviors with those of their friends.

In The Field

Coping with Chronic Illness Through Play

Name: CINDY CLARK

Education: B.A. in international relations, University of Pennsylvania; M.A. and Ph.D. in human development, University of Chicago

Current Position: Visiting associate professor, Rutgers University

Career Objectives: Use research to learn about and reduce the stress and anxiety of children with chronic illnesses

> *The sight of a child unable to breathe carries unspeakable anxiety. Life begins with the first breath and ends when breathing does. Children's connection to life is only as reliable as inhaling and exhaling. Against this fact of life, asthma stalks, specterlike.*
> (Cindy Clark, 2003, p. 89.)

A parent's letter to Mr. Rogers:

> *Our 5½-year-old daughter has an inoperable brain tumor. Our only hope to remove the tumor is radiation. On the first day of her radiation treatment, she screamed and cried when she found out that she would have to be in the room all by herself. . . . We kept saying that it would only take a minute. . . . Finally, she asked me, "What is a minute?" . . . I looked at my watch and started singing, "It's a beautiful day in this neighborhood, a beautiful day for a neighbor," and before I could finish the song I said "Oops, the minute's up. I can't even finish Mr. Rogers' song." Then Michelle said, "Is that a minute? I can do that." And she did. She laid perfectly still for the entire treatment; but there was a catch to it. I have to sing your song every time over the intercom.*

From an interview with a child living with chronic asthma:

> *If I had a magic wand, all asthma medicine would taste good, not like the yucky stuff. And my inhaler and breathing machine would work as fast as I can snap my fingers, so I could start breathing and go play. My breathing machine takes 10,000 years. That's how slow it seems to me. Sometimes, I play games with myself when I do my breathing machine. I pretend I have a friend who is a dragon, and the dragon breathes smoke. You know the steam coming from the machine? That's dragon smoke. Another game is, I have a toy airplane.*
> *I fly my airplane through the steam. I pretend to fly away, to a place away from this. That's really fun to pretend, getting up and away.*

Children afflicted with serious illness and disease face a number of challenges. The disease itself can be painful and physically exhausting—and terribly frightening. It can also be socially isolating, as when children need to stay home or in hospitals, away from their friends and schoolmates.

Beyond the physical, psychological, and social costs of the disease itself, chronically ill children pay a heavy toll as a consequence of the medical procedures required to heal them (Nabors et al., 2013; Nabors & Liddle, 2017). As expressed in the stories above, the procedures can be scary and may seem to make time stand still. Medical procedures can also unnerve the very people on whom sick children count for support, friendship, and comfort. That is, peers often inadvertently shun children with chronic illness, as do some family members, who may be squeamish in the face of the diabetic child's insulin shots and blood tests, the hair loss that typically accompanies chemotherapy, or the disfigurement of surgery.

Bill and Cindy Dell Clark

Cindy Clark

How do children cope with chronic illness? According to Cindy Clark's

children, indicating that they benefited more from opportunities to engage in sociodramatic play than did their less impulsive peers. On the basis both of their findings and on what is known about the social and academic difficulties that go along with poor self-regulation skills (a matter we will address below), Elias and Berk argued that sociodramatic play deserves a significant place in preschool curricula and may provide an important form of early intervention for highly impulsive children.

intensive study (2003), they cope surprisingly well, particularly when they are allowed to play. In her interviews with children living with chronic severe asthma or diabetes, Clark found that play has an important role in altering the meanings of medical procedures and devices and symbolically recasting what it means to be ill. Play provides children with a sense of control and empowerment over conditions and circumstances that are otherwise forced upon them by doctors, parents, and the medical regimens that keep them alive.

Thus, Clark found that parents and children often develop games and playful routines that transform unpleasant medical experiences into something fun—or at least endurable. The examples above of singing Mr. Rogers's song or imagining smoke-breathing dragons are cases in point. Parents of children with asthma described a variety of playful ways of counting off the breaths their children needed to take on their inhalers (also known as puffers)—they counted in French, in pig Latin, in the voice of the Count from *Sesame Street*. Some parents got their children inhalers that look like toys (see the figure). Sometimes, children themselves transformed the medical devices into toys. Certain types of inhalers make a whistling sound to signal to patients that they are inhaling too quickly, so, as you might imagine, a lot of asthmatic children get the giggles by using their inhalers (improperly) as musical instruments. One mother recounted how her daughter played with a breathing mask used with the nebulizer (a machine that delivers asthma medication automatically as a breathable aerosol, often to children too young to manipulate the more complicated puffer). The mother had intentionally acquired a second mask, thinking that using it in the context of play might facilitate her daughter's coping with asthma. Sure enough, the girl "played asthma" with her friends, placing the mask on their faces, instructing them to sit quietly, and promising that mommy would read stories to pass the time.

Bill and Cindy Dell Clark

Puffa Pals introduce a playful dimension to asthma inhalers, making them more attractive to the young children who must use them to manage the symptoms of their disease.

Clark also found playful approaches adopted with chronic illness in other contexts. At an "illness camp" for children with diabetes, syringes and paint were used to create art; at an asthma camp, some of the children put on a "Three Little Pigs" skit in which the big, bad wolf was unable to blow the house down because he had life-threatening asthma. He was taken to the hospital, received a lung transplant, and, to the delight of the audience, was thereafter able to blow down just about anything.

In her child-centered approach to understanding chronic illness, Clark attempts to reveal how children attach meaning to their illness and to the medical procedures and devices that they endure and use on a daily basis. What she found is a child's world in which fear, pain, embarrassment, and confusion are ordered and controlled through song, jokes, art, pranks, and funny stories. From a Vygotskian perspective, the blending of fantasy play and medical treatment creates a zone of proximal development through which the child gains a sense of control over the uncontrollable and frightening. Children spontaneously generate much of the play. However, some adults encourage it—especially parents who are sensitive to how children can regulate their thoughts and feelings in the context of play.

The medical community is increasingly recognizing the therapeutic value of play. At one hospital, the pediatric blood-testing machine is named "Herbie"; his most distinctive characteristic is his inclination to "suck your blood." One of Herbie's child "victims" claimed that his encounter with blood-sucking Herbie was the best part of his hospital stay and that Herbie made the procedure seem like it did not hurt quite so much. Other hospitals have systematically incorporated play into children's treatment regimens. Many now employ *child life specialists*, whose primary duties involve familiarizing children with the treatment they will be undergoing and facilitating their coping and adjustment to it through the use of play and games.

Currently, developmentalists such as Clark are seeking new ways of using the functions of play to help children deal with debilitating diseases and medical procedures. Clark is now engaged in a study that incorporates inhalers that are shaped like toys, as in the photo above. And you can bet that if they whistle, it is not when they are being used improperly.

Although sociodramatic play provides an important context for the development of self-regulation, it is but one of many contexts through which children come to master themselves. Children encounter a vast array of social norms, parenting practices, school curricula, and work demands, which vary according to the child's culture, gender, and age. All provide possible contexts in support of the child's journey toward independence in thought and action.

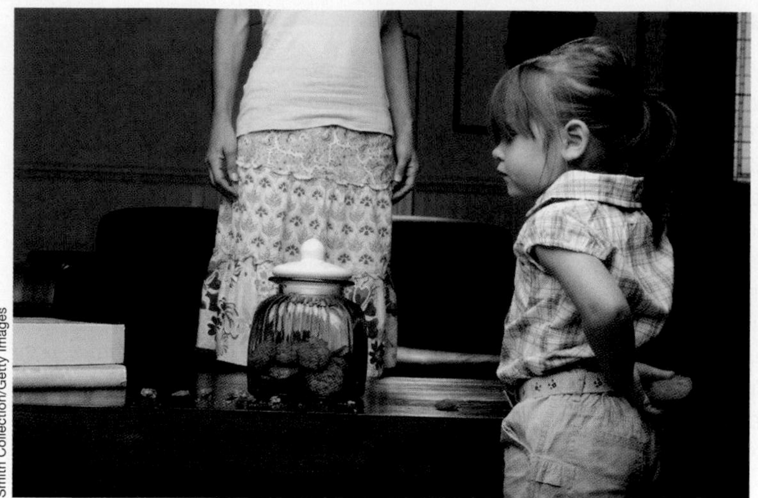

Smith Collection/Getty Images

Caught in the act of making a big mess, this girl has unmistakable signs of guilt on her face. Self-conscious emotions, including guilt, first emerge during early childhood.

Regulating Emotions

To be competent members of society, children must learn how to control their emotions as well as their thoughts and actions. As we noted in Chapter 6 (pp. 219–221), the development of self-conscious emotions—pride, shame, guilt, envy, and embarrassment—is one of the key changes associated with the transition from infancy to early childhood. In combination with anger, joy, and the other basic emotions, self-conscious emotions enable children to participate in new and more complex social relationships (Mascolo, Fischer, & Li, 2003). Children must now begin to understand how their emotional states and expressions affect others and learn to manage their emotions and, when necessary, to mask their true feelings.

Controlling Feelings Most of us know what it feels like to carry a chip on one's shoulder, to stew over a negative experience, or to react explosively to a frustrating situation. Such feelings present special challenges to children's developing self-regulation abilities. However, between 2 and 6 years of age, children develop a number of strategies to help them keep their emotions under control (Saarni, 2007; Thompson & Newton, 2010). For example, they avoid or reduce emotionally charged aversive information by closing their eyes, turning away, and putting their hands over their ears. They also regulate negative emotions by distracting themselves with pleasurable activities. Further, they use their budding language and cognitive skills to reinterpret events to create a more acceptable version of what is occurring ("I didn't want to play with her anyway; she's mean"), to reassure themselves ("Mommy said she'll be right back"), and to encourage themselves ("I'm a big girl; big girls can do it").

The emerging ability to control emotions helps a preschool-age child deal with the disappointments, frustrations, and injured feelings that are so common at this stage. In addition, emotional regulation can be helpful in the increasingly important realm of social behavior. For example, when children observe a playmate fall down and get hurt, they will likely feel anxious themselves. Children who can moderate their personal distress are more likely to show sympathy toward the playmate and offer help than are children who cannot manage their own emotional reactions (Eisenberg, 2010). Indeed, in order to sustain play with each other, children must create and maintain a delicate balance of emotional expression and regulation (Halberstadt, Denham, & Dunsmore, 2001). As you will see, the skills associated with this balance are significantly related to children's altruistic, or *prosocial*, behaviors.

Culture and Emotions Young children must learn not only to control their feelings but also to express their feelings in a socially appropriate way. Young infants display no such ability. They communicate their emotions directly, regardless of the circumstances. A 1-year-old who starts to fidget and fuss during a wedding because she's hungry and tired is not going to settle down until she's been fed and had a nap. It takes several years for children to learn to control their emotional expressions. Likewise, it takes time before children are able to appreciate that the emotional expressions of others may not correspond to their true feelings—that they may hide or even fake their emotions in order to be polite or achieve particular social goals (acting brave to avoid teasing, for instance). The ability to control one's emotional experiences and to understand that others do so as well requires the cognitive capacity to distinguish between emotional *expressions* and emotional *experiences* (Agostino, Im-Bolter, Stefanatos, & Dennis, 2017). This cognitive capacity is closely related to the development of a *theory of mind*—that is, the understanding that people have internal beliefs, desires, and emotions that may not be expressed in their behavior (Hudson & Jacques, 2014; see Chapter 8, pp. 278).

In many cultures, for example, it is considered socially inappropriate to express disappointment when someone gives you a present you don't like. You are expected to thank the giver and say something nice, masking your true feelings. A social or cultural group's informal conventions regarding whether, how, and under what circumstances emotions should be expressed are known as **display rules**. Several researchers have studied the ability of children to use display rules and to understand their use by others. In some studies, children were asked to interpret stories about a child who expects an exciting present and gets something undesirable instead. In other studies, the children themselves were led to expect a desirable object but received a disappointing one (as when, for example, they were led to expect a toy car as a prize for playing a game but got a picture book instead).

display rules A social or cultural group's informal conventions regarding whether, how, and under what circumstances emotions should be expressed.

Several general results come from this type of research in different cultures (see summary in Saarni, Campos, Camras, & Witherington, 2006). First, during early childhood, children around the world appear to gain the ability to recognize when someone is masking his or her feelings. Second, girls tend to be better than boys at recognizing and displaying masked emotions. Third, there are wide cultural variations in the age at which children learn about masking emotion or use display rules. For example, one study found that Iranian children were more likely than Dutch children to report using display rules, a finding consistent with the different cultural values of the two countries (Novin, Banerjee, Dadkhah, & Rieffe, 2009). In particular, Iranian culture stresses the importance of social hierarchy and group harmony, whereas Dutch culture values individual autonomy and the acknowledgement of personal needs and desires. With these radically different cultural value systems, it is not surprising that Iranian children are socialized to monitor and control their emotions in ways that are deemed socially appropriate, while Dutch children are given greater latitude in directly expressing their thoughts and feelings.

In addition to affecting the development of emotion regulation, cultural beliefs and values impact the emergence of different types of emotions. Western cultures, common in Europe, Canada, and the United States, place great emphasis on individualism and hence on personal achievement. Children are socialized to express themselves and take pleasure in their own accomplishments. Accordingly, parents act to bolster their children's pride, and also their self-esteem, when they succeed ("Good girl! You did it all by yourself!"). Because failure is associated with children's incompetence and feelings of self-reproach ("I'm not smart enough to do this"), parents may act to protect their children from feelings of shame and failure by emphasizing the difficulty of the task in relation to the competence of the child ("That puzzle is too hard for you; let's do this one instead"). In contrast, many Asian cultures elevate the needs and well-being of the group over individual desires and success. For instance, the Chinese embrace the philosophy of Confucianism, which emphasizes harmony with others as a principal goal. When a child succeeds at a task, the culturally appropriate response is not self-celebration but modesty and praise for others. Accordingly, parents might respond to their child's achievement with a caution like, "You did all right, but now you need more practice. Play down your success." When a child fails, the failure is viewed as a discredit to the family and to the child's larger social group. Chinese parents thus often utilize a variety of "shaming techniques" to promote good behavior and effortful performance. Mascolo and his colleagues report that if a child does

Klaus Tiedge/Getty Images

Consistent with the philosophy of Confucianism, Chinese parents commonly play down their children's successes and use "shaming techniques" when their children perform poorly.

socioemotional competence The ability to behave appropriately in social situations that evoke strong emotions.

poorly in school, a parent might say things like "Shame on you!" "You didn't study hard enough!" "Everyone will laugh at you!" Because of such use of shame as a strategy of control, Mascolo and his colleagues argue, shame emerges for Chinese children at an earlier point in development than it does for American children (Mascolo et al., 2003). As shown in Figure 9.4, children's emotional responses to their accomplishments follow radically different pathways as a consequence of their cultural traditions.

Children's increasing abilities to control their own emotional expression and read the emotions of others are considered forms of **socioemotional competence**, the ability to behave appropriately in social situations that evoke strong emotions. Carolyn Saarni (2007) proposed that socioemotional competence involves a variety of skills, most of which are acquired in early childhood. The skills include an awareness of one's own emotional state and the emotional states of others, as well as the realization that outward expressions of emotion do not necessarily reflect inner emotional states. It should come as no surprise that preschool children who display the characteristics of socioemotional competence are better liked by both their peers and their teachers (Eisenberg, Losoya, & Spinrad, 2003; Saarni, 2011).

United States
Individualism

Emphasized goal
PERSONAL ACHIEVEMENT

If child succeeds... If child fails...
child is seen as showing...

Competence (high ability) — associated with feelings of... — Pride — expressed through... — Self-esteem Self-celebration ...or... Bragging

Incompetence (low ability) — associated with feelings of... — Shame and guilt — expressed through... — Self-reproach

CHINA
Confucianism

Emphasized goal
MEETING SOCIAL OBLIGATIONS

If child succeeds... If child fails...
child is seen as showing...

Good effort — associated with feelings of... — Feelings of bringing honor to group — expressed through... — Modesty Praise for others

Poor effort — associated with feelings of... — Shame and guilt — expressed through... — Self-reproach

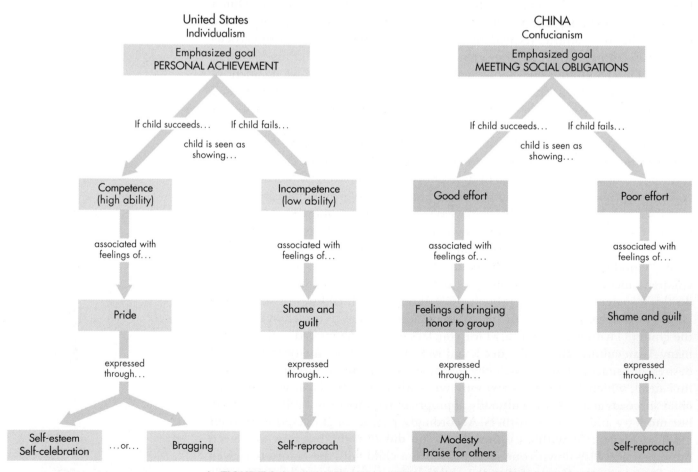

FIGURE 9.4 While children in the United States are socialized to strive for, and take pride in, personal achievements, children in China are encouraged to strive to meet social obligations and to feel honor in doing so. This figure shows the emotional outcomes for children who are successful or unsuccessful in meeting their culture's expectations.

APPLY > CONNECT > DISCUSS

We argued in Chapter 6 that one of the earliest purposes of emotion regulation is to maintain intersubjectivity. Review pages 202–205 in Chapter 6 and discuss the similarities and differences between infancy and early childhood in the purposes and consequences of emotion regulation.

Understanding Aggression

LEARNING OUTCOMES

Explain the purposes and forms of aggression.

Point out gender differences in children's aggression.

Distinguish among biological, social and cultural, and emotional and cognitive contributions to the causes and/or control of aggression in children.

In order to be accepted as members of their social group, young children must learn not only to subordinate their personal desires to the good of the group when the situation demands it but also to regulate their anger when their goals are thwarted. Such anger can lead to aggression, and learning to control aggression is one of the most basic tasks of young children's social development. Indeed, researchers have argued that early childhood holds the key to understanding both the origins of aggressive behavior and the ways to control such behavior (Provençal, Booij, & Tremblay, 2015).

The Development of Aggression

Although it seems odd to imagine babies engaging in aggressive behavior, the capacity to use force against another—by pulling at toys, pushing, hitting, or biting—is present in infancy. Some developmentalists believe that these early forceful behaviors, often shown when babies are angry or frustrated, are early manifestations of aggression that evolve over the course of a few short years into intentional aggression (Hay, 2017). Children's aggressive behavior can take a variety of forms (Ettekal & Ladd, 2017). Some of the most common forms exhibited by children include *physical aggression*, such as hitting, kicking, and pushing; *verbal aggression*, such as name-calling and teasing; and **relational aggression**, which involves harming someone's friendships by, for example, gossiping about them or excluding them from group activities or play. As with other types of behaviors, the form of aggression may change at different points in the child's development. For example, as children develop cognitive and language skills, they become capable of teasing. Teasing is a subtle form of aggression that requires the ability to understand something about the mental states and desires of another—how destroying a favorite toy or calling someone a name may be hurtful. Likewise, as children grow, both adults and peers become less tolerant of physical aggression, and children learn that it is socially unacceptable. Until the age of about 18 months, teasing and physical aggression occur with equal frequency. But as children approach their 2nd birthday, teasing increases enormously, and they are much more likely to tease their siblings than to hurt them physically.

relational aggression Aggression intended to harm someone's friendships or exclude an individual from the group.

Many studies of childhood aggression from around the world have reported that boys are more aggressive than girls in a wide variety of circumstances (Lansford et al., 2012). Boys are more likely than girls to hit, push, hurl insults, and threaten to beat up other children; they are also up to five times more likely that girls to engage in highly aggressive behavior (Dodge, Coie, & Lynham, 2006; Lussier, Corrado, & Tzoumakis, 2012; Zsolnai, Lesznyák, & Kasik, 2012). When asked to pretend about conflict situations that might happen to them in preschool (for instance, a peer's knocking over a block tower or refusing to share a toy), boys are more likely than girls to offer aggressive rather than positive solutions (Walker, Irving, & Berthelsen, 2002). This difference seems to emerge during the 2nd and 3rd years of life, with girls engaging is less aggression and boys engaging in more (Blicharski, Bon, & Strayer, 2011; Underwood, 2002). Consistent with our earlier discussion of *gender*

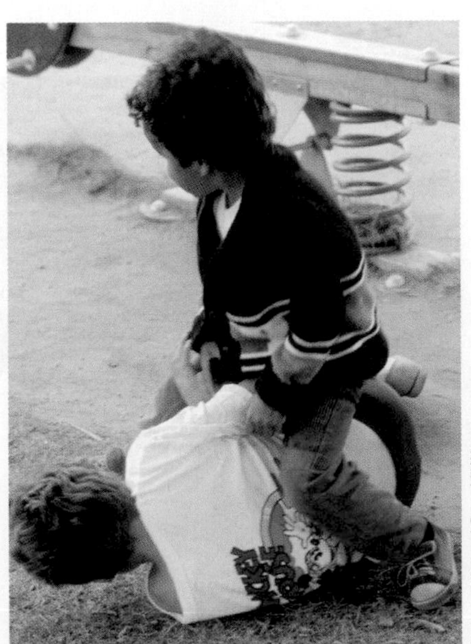

Sally and Richard Greenhill/Alamy

Playground fights, especially among boys, are common scenes in preschools.

segregation, while boys' aggression toward girls declines between the ages of 1 and 3, boys' aggression toward other boys increases dramatically (Blicharski et al., 2011).

What Causes and Controls Aggression?

Patterns of aggressive behavior often emerge during early childhood as personality becomes more defined. There is substantial evidence that 3-year-old children who behave defiantly and disobediently with adults, act aggressively toward their peers, and are impulsive and hyperactive are likely to still have these problems during middle childhood and adolescence (Campbell, Spieker, Burchinal, & Poe, 2006; Hay, 2017). A number of longitudinal studies have found that, for boys in particular, the earlier the age at which children begin to exhibit such problem behaviors, the greater the likelihood that they will continue to behave in those ways later in life (Baillargeon et al., 2007). But what initiates these behaviors in young children? And how can such aggression be controlled? In studying aggression—both problematic patterns of aggressive behaviors and aggression more generally—developmentalists have tended to focus on one of three sets of factors: biological, social and cultural, or emotional and cognitive factors.

Biological Contributions

Those who emphasize the role of biology in the development of aggression base their arguments on evolutionary factors (Bjorklund, 2015; Ellis & Bjorklund, 2005). Noting that no group in the animal kingdom is free of aggression, many students of animal behavior have proposed that aggression is an important and adaptive force in animal evolution. According to Darwin (1859/1958), individuals compete with each other for the resources necessary for survival and reproduction. Consequently, evolution favors individuals with more aggressive phenotypes. In many species, including our own, phenotypic characteristics such as territoriality, which ensures that a mating pair will have access to food, are believed to contribute to survival (Wilson, 1975). According to this interpretation, aggression is natural and necessary and appears automatically in the development of the young of many animal species.

While aggression is widespread among animal species, so are mechanisms that limit it. The aggressive behavior in litters of puppies, for example, changes in accordance with a maturational timetable (James, 1951). At about 3 weeks, puppies begin to engage in rough-and-tumble play, mouthing and nipping one another. A week later, the play becomes rougher; the puppies growl and snarl when they bite, and the victims may yelp in pain. Once injurious attacks become really serious, however, a hierarchical social structure emerges, with some animals dominant and others subordinate. After such a dominance hierarchy is formed, the dominant puppy needs only to threaten in order to get its way; it has no need to attack. At this point, the frequency of fighting diminishes (Cairns, 1979). Throughout the animal kingdom one finds such hierarchies, which regulate interactions among members of the same species (Figure 9.5).

Michael Weber/Getty Images

FIGURE 9.5 Many species of animals have innate behaviors for signaling defeat to allow the establishment of a social dominance hierarchy without bloodshed. One such behavior is reflected in the submissive crouching posture of the wolf on the left.

The developmental history of aggression and its control among puppies is similar in some interesting ways to the development of aggression in human children. F. F. Strayer (1991) and his colleagues observed a close connection between aggression and the formation of dominance hierarchies among 3- and 4-year-olds in a nursery school. They identified a specific pattern of hostile interactions among children: When one child would behave aggressively, the other child would almost always submit by crying, running away, flinching, or seeking help from an adult. Dominance encounters like these led to an orderly pattern of social relationships within the group. Once children knew their position in such a hierarchy, they challenged only those whom it was safe for them to challenge and left others alone, thereby reducing the amount of aggression within the group. As you will see in Chapter 13 (p. 453), the formation of dominance hierarchies may explain the increase in bullying that is associated with children's transitions into the new social environment of middle school.

Social and Cultural Contributions A second explanation for the causes of aggression, and for different levels of aggression, is that people learn to behave aggressively because aggressive behavior is sanctioned or socially adaptive in their families, peer groups, or cultures. According to this perspective, children learn aggression in the course of social interactions—because they observe aggressive behaviors in others and imitate or are rewarded for it, or because the particular context permits the expression of aggression. For example, when the marital relationship of parents is marked by aggression, children are more likely to behave aggressively themselves (Nomaguchi, Johnson, Minter, & Aldrich, 2017). Likewise, parents of aggressive children have been found to reward their children's aggressive behaviors by paying more attention to them, laughing, or otherwise signaling approval (Dishion, Veronneau, & Myers, 2010). In addition to parent influences, researchers find that some contexts are more likely than others to inspire aggressive behavior. Young children in group-based child care, for instance, are more likely to engage in aggressive behaviors than those in home-based care, presumably because a larger social group increases the likelihood of conflicts with peers and teachers' rules and expectations (Pingualt et al., 2015).

Social and cultural expectations and beliefs may also contribute to young children's aggressive behavior. We mentioned earlier that overall aggression tends to decrease as children age, in part because it is deemed unacceptable by peers and adults alike. The social acceptability of aggression may also impact gender differences commonly observed between boys and girls. Evidence of this comes from a study showing that parents' stereotypic gender-role attitudes have pronounced effects on the aggressive behavior of young sons and daughters (Endendijk et al., 2017). The study, conducted in the Netherlands with families with 3-year-old children, found that fathers with strong traditional gender stereotypes (associating women with family and men with careers) were more likely to be physically controlling of their sons when the boys misbehaved, and their sons engaged in higher levels of aggressive behavior at the age of 4 compared to sons of fathers who did not maintain strong gender-role stereotypes. Interestingly, fathers with strong *counter*-stereotypes (associating women with careers and men with family) tended to be more physically controlling with their daughters when they misbehaved compared to fathers with less strong counter-stereotypes, and their daughters behaved more aggressively at age 4 compared to daughters of dads with less strong counter-stereotypes.

Cross-cultural studies have yielded evidence both that children model the aggressive behavior of adults and that societies differ markedly in the levels of interpersonal violence they consider normal (Lansford et al., 2015; see also the box "The Spanking Controversy," p. 320). For example, Douglas Fry (1988) compared the levels of aggression of young children in two Zapotec Indian towns in central Mexico. On the basis of anthropological reports, Fry chose one town that was notable for the degree to which violence was controlled and a second town that was notable for the fact that people often fought at public gatherings, husbands beat their wives, and adults punished children by beating them with sticks.

Fry and his wife established residences in both towns so that they could get to know the people and develop enough rapport to be able to make their observations unobtrusively. They then collected several hours of observations of 12 children in each town as they played in their houses and around the neighborhood. When the researchers compared the aggressive acts of the children in the two towns, they found that those in the town with a reputation for violent behavior performed twice as many violent acts as did the children in the other town.

Emotional and Cognitive Contributions Another way to explore the development of aggression is to focus more particularly on how children feel and think about social situations that might provoke aggressive responses. Children's emotional reactions to events and their ability to regulate their emotional reactions depend to a great extent on how they interpret social contexts and on their ability to understand the emotions and intentions of others. It is known, for example, that

The Spanking Controversy

"THIS IS GONNA HURT ME MORE than it hurts you."

—Prelude to a whuppin'

Two-year-old Mairin is starting to get the upper hand in her house—but not the kind of upper hand she had in mind. She throws her food across the kitchen, pitches tantrums when anyone touches "her" television, and recently got up and marched out the door when asked to sit still at the dinner table. So how is her mother responding? With a firm swat on the backside. "I know some people think it's awful," says her mother, "But how many of them have a 2-year-old?" (as reported by Costello, 2000).

Despite evidence that spanking can be harmful to children, a national survey in 2014 indicated that 76 percent of U.S. men, and 65 percent of women, agreed that a child sometimes needs a "good hard spanking" (Child Trends Data Bank, 2015). In addition, although there has been a notable decrease in the rate of parental use of corporal punishment on children 12 years and older over the past few decades, the rate of decrease for younger children, especially toddlers, has been relatively minor. Further, in the face of international efforts to discourage spanking, several states have recently passed laws explicitly granting parents the right to spank their children. The right to spank, moreover, extends well beyond the home front. As of 2010, 20 states permitted the practice in public schools.

In addition to being one of the more common forms of discipline in the United States, spanking is also one of the most controversial. Most parents do not like to hit their children and resort to spanking only after other tactics, such as reasoning and time-outs, fail to produce the desired results. However, the argument made by those who oppose spanking is that it can damage children psychologically and emotionally. In fact, the practice has been outlawed in many European countries, where public opinion takes a much dimmer view of its effectiveness.

In the United States, most mothers do the spanking, largely because they spend more time with their children than fathers do (Dietz, 2000). The acceptability and frequency of spanking also varies by ethnicity, family income, and geographic region. Spanking is most commonly practiced in African American families (Straus, 2009). Researchers have speculated that African American parents may use spanking as a means of tightening their control over their children because they worry that highly active behavior in their children, particularly in boys, may draw negative attention from others who harbor racial stereotypes regarding aggression in African American youths. Spanking is also more common among low-income families and is most acceptable in southern regions of the United States (Straus, 2009).

Universal Images Group/Getty Images

Spanking is outlawed in many countries because it is thought to contribute to the development of aggression in children.

Is spanking an effective form of discipline? This question is at the heart of developmental research on the effects of spanking, as well as of the advice given to parents by pediatricians and other child-care experts. In general, developmentalists discourage the practice. A host of studies conducted across a number of countries link physical discipline to increased aggression, lower-quality relationships, low self-esteem, and poorer mental health in children and adolescents (Choe, Olson, & Sameroff, 2013; Baumrind, Larzelere, & Owens, 2010; Gershoff & Grogan-Kaylor, 2016). For example, a large study of nearly 2,500 children found that 3-year-olds who are spanked frequently are at increased risk for high levels of aggressiveness as 5-year-olds (Taylor, Manganello, Lee, & Rice, 2010). A study of nearly 1,000 children in eight different countries—China, Colombia, Italy, Jordan, Kenya, Philippines, Thailand, and the United States—found significant relationships between the frequency of corporal punishment and negative child outcomes (Lansford, Cappa, Putnick, Bornstein, Deater-Deckard, & Bradley, 2017). In addition, abusive parents are known to spank their children more than nonabusive parents, prompting speculation that relying on spanking may increase parents' risk for using more severe forms of punishment (Afifi Mota, Sareen, & MacMillan, 2017). Overall, research and most professional opinion suggest that parents should seek alternatives to spanking.

children inclined toward aggressive outbursts have poor emotion regulation skills and score at lower levels on theory-of-mind tasks (Yeh, Lin, Liu, & Fang, 2017).

According to one view, aggression has its origins in the negative affect that arises in frustrating or otherwise unpleasant (aversive) situations (Berkowitz, 2003). These general negative feelings might come about when a child fails to achieve a goal, encounters a parent's disapproval, or is rejected by a peer. The negative feelings initiate a fight-or-flight process, an impulsive reaction to be aggressive or to withdraw. The impulse to fight is associated with aggression-related thoughts, memories, physiological reactions, and motor responses; the flight impulse has corresponding escape-related associations. In this way, the initial general negative feelings become the more specific emotions of rudimentary, or basic, anger (in the case of the fight impulse) or fear (in the case of the flight impulse). These rudimentary emotions can be significantly modified by cognitive processes, including the child's anticipation of consequences or thoughts about what he or she understands to be acceptable behavior. As a result, the child experiences more differentiated feelings—feelings different from and more complex than the rudimentary anger or fear—and the response of the child whose initial impulse was aggressive may or may not be aggression.

Suppose, for example, that a preschooler is playing with a toy, and a playmate takes it away. According to the model shown in Figure 9.6, children in such a situation will experience negative feelings, and, depending on their temperament and past social experiences, may be inclined to act aggressively. However, if they have internalized the "no hitting" rule of the classroom and know that violating the rule carries the consequence of a time-out, they may, as a result of their thought processes, refrain from using physical confrontation to get the toy back and enlist the help of the teacher instead.

Developmentalists are building a strong case for the role of thought processes in children's aggressive behavior. A major influence on young children's aggressive tendencies is their understanding of their own and others' emotions, goals, and behaviors and of how these are all linked together. The general argument is that children who have a more advanced understanding of emotions, including what causes them and how they are expressed, are less likely to behave aggressively (Arsenio, 2006; Halberstadt et al., 2001; Lemerise & Arsenio, 2000).

Susanne Denham and her colleagues (Denham et al., 2002) tested this argument in a longitudinal study that followed 127 children between preschool and kindergarten. To assess children's emotional knowledge, the researchers used puppets that had several attachable faces, depicting different emotions. The procedure involved asking children questions about a puppet's emotions in a variety of circumstances—its basic emotions ("What does she look like when she's sad?"), its emotions in particular situations ("What does she look like when she's had a nightmare?"), and its emotions in social situations that require masking emotions ("What does she look like if she's getting teased, but if she shows she's upset, she'll get teased even more?"). The children responded by choosing and attaching a face to the puppet. Children's anger and aggressive behaviors were assessed through both naturalistic observation of their play and through teacher reports. In general, the researchers found that both boys and girls who, as preschoolers, had less advanced knowledge of emotions and their expression were, as kindergarteners, more likely to behave aggressively toward their peers.

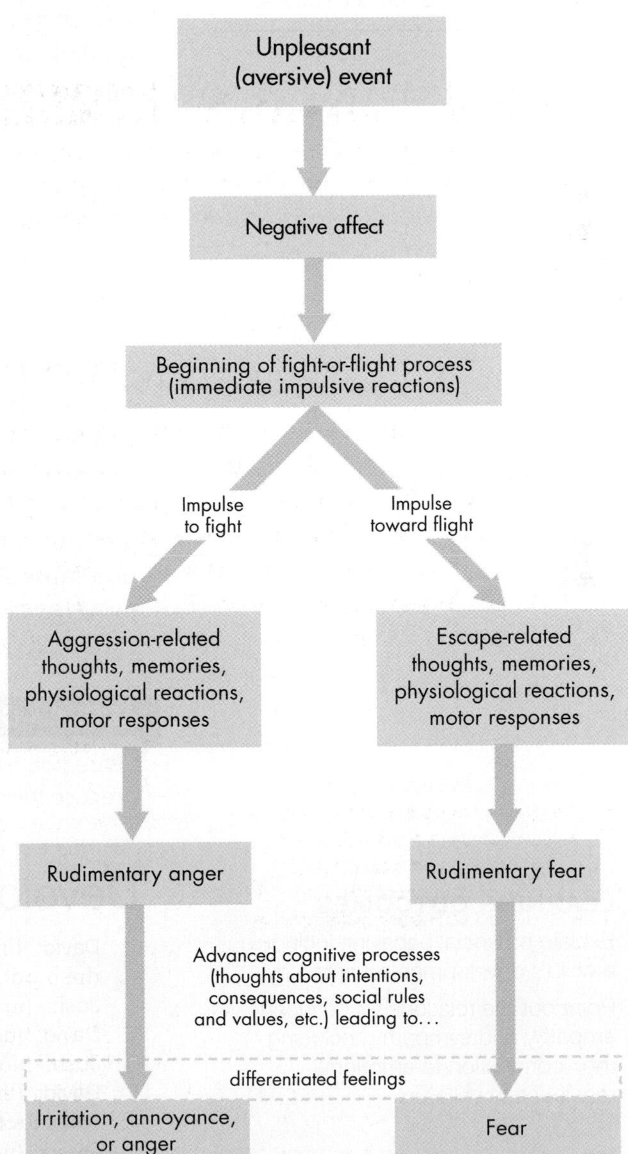

FIGURE 9.6 According to Len Berkowitz, aggression has its source in the negative feelings aroused by an unpleasant event, but these feelings can be significantly modified by cognitive processes.

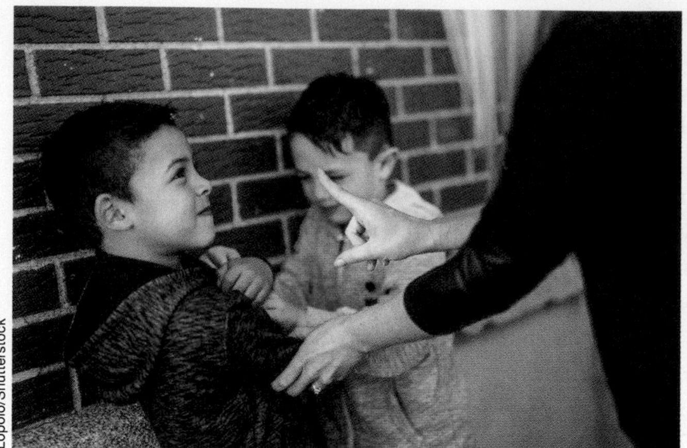
Lopolo/Shutterstock

Children rely on adults to help them regulate the expression of emotions.

Another study of preschoolers looked at how beliefs about aggression—specifically, the belief that aggression is an enduring trait rather than a changeable behavior—might contribute to children's use of aggression (Giles, Legare, & Samson, 2008). Jessica Giles and her colleagues argued that children who take an *essentialist* view of aggression—that is, believe that individuals who are aggressive in one situation will very likely be aggressive in the future—may be more likely to jump to conclusions about the hostile intention of a peer who behaves aggressively and, therefore, may be more likely to endorse the use of aggressive solutions.

To test preschoolers' essentialist beliefs about aggression, Giles and Heyman (2003) presented a group of 100 children with brief scenarios such as "Imagine there is a new girl in your class. She steals things from people, calls people mean names, and trips kids at recess. Do you think this new girl will always act this way?" Some children tended to believe that aggressiveness would endure over time, whereas others rejected this idea.

The children's endorsement of aggressive solutions was tested by presenting scenarios such as "Renee scribbled all over Belinda's art project. So Belinda hit Renee. What else could Belinda have done to solve the problem?" Some children said things such as "Well, she could kick her instead"; others, however, provided more socially appropriate solutions, such as "She could tell the teacher." Consistent with their hypothesis, Giles and Heyman found that children who believed in aggressiveness as an enduring trait were more likely to endorse aggressive solutions.

Using testing methods such as those described above, developmentalists are amassing significant evidence that aggression must be understood in light of children's thoughts and beliefs about their own and others' emotional lives. This general idea suggests the possibility of controlling aggression by using reason. Though it is sometimes difficult to hold a rational discussion with a 4-year-old who has just grabbed a toy away from a playmate, discussions that emphasize how aggression hurts another person and how conflicts can be resolved by sharing and taking turns have been found to reduce aggression even at this early age (Conners-Burrow, Patrick, Kyzer, & McKelvey, 2017).

APPLY > CONNECT > DISCUSS

Based on evidence presented in this section, design an activity for preschoolers that might reduce their aggressive behavior.

LEARNING OUTCOMES

Explain prosocial behavior, including a child's development of empathy.

Point out the relationship between empathy and sympathy, including their connection to emotional regulation in children.

Developing Prosocial Behaviors

David: I'm a missile robot who can shoot missiles out of my fingers I can shoot them out of everywhere—even out of my legs. I'm a missile robot.
Josh: (in a teasing tone) No, you're a fart robot.
David: (defensively) No, I'm a missile robot.
Josh: No, you're a fart robot.
David: (hurt, almost in tears) No, Josh!
Josh: (recognizing that David is upset) And I'm a poo-poo robot.
David: (in good spirits again) I'm a pee-pee robot.
(From Rubin, 1980, p. 55.)

As suggested in the dialogue above between two 4-year-olds, young children can be remarkably sensitive to the emotional needs of their playmates. Josh not only recognized his friend's distress at being teased but was able to remedy the situation by making similar deprecating remarks about himself. Such diplomacy becomes relatively common during early childhood as children acquire a number of sophisticated prosocial skills.

Prosocial behavior is defined as voluntary action intended to benefit others (Eisenberg, VanSchyndel, & Spinrad, 2016). Sharing, helping, caregiving, and showing compassion are all examples of prosocial behaviors. Two psychological states—*empathy* and *sympathy*—correspond to prosocial behavior in the way that anger corresponds to aggression.

prosocial behavior Behavior such as sharing, helping, caregiving, and showing compassion.

Empathy

Empathy, the sharing of another person's emotions and feelings, is widely believed to provide the essential foundations for prosocial behavior (Taylor et al., 2013). According to Martin Hoffman (2002), a child can feel empathy for another person at any age. As children develop, however, their ability to empathize broadens, and they become better able to interpret and respond appropriately to the distress of others.

empathy Sharing another person's emotions and feelings.

Hoffman has proposed that empathy develops in four stages that are significantly linked to stages in the child's self-development. The first stage occurs during the 1st year of life. As we noted earlier, babies as young as 2 days old become stressed and cry at the sound of another infant's cries. Hoffman calls this phenomenon *global empathy*. This early form of empathic crying is reflexive, since babies obviously can have no understanding of the feelings of others. Yet they respond as if they were having those feelings themselves.

During the 2nd year of life, as children develop a sense of themselves as distinct individuals, their responses to others' distress change, and *egocentric empathy* emerges. When confronted by someone who is distressed, babies are now capable of understanding that it is the other person who is upset. This realization allows children to turn their attention from concern for their own comfort to comforting others. Since they have difficulty keeping other people's points of view in mind, however, some of their attempts to help may be inappropriate and *egocentric* (see Chapter 7, p. 270), such as giving a security blanket to an adult who looks upset.

The third stage of empathy occurs in early childhood, when role-taking skills increase. Being able to distinguish one's own emotional needs from those of another allows the child to respond in a way that is less egocentric and more sensitive to the other. In addition, the growing command of language vastly increases the contexts in which children can behave empathically. Language allows children to empathize with people who are expressing their feelings verbally, without visible emotions, as well as with people who are not present. Information gained indirectly through stories, pictures, or television permits children to empathize with people whom they have never met. (The fourth stage of empathy emerges in middle childhood, when the child understands that emotional responses may be tied to an individual's unique history of past experiences.)

Note that Hoffman's theory of empathy is linked to Piaget's theory of cognitive development. Each new stage of empathy corresponds to a new stage of cognitive ability in which decreasing egocentrism and increasing *decentration* (see Chapter 7, p. 269) allow children to understand themselves better in relation to others.

Perhaps because it is linked so closely to what children understand, Hoffman's explanation of the development of empathy tends to leave out children's own personal feelings. It is tacitly assumed that the more children understand, the more intensely they adopt the feelings of the person in distress. The catch, as Judy Dunn (1988) has pointed out, is that children may understand perfectly well why another child is in distress and feel glad as a result.

RuslanDashinsky/Getty Images

The increasing capacity to separate his own emotional state from that of others contributes to this preschooler's effectiveness in responding empathetically to his distressed friend.

Sympathy

Other researchers have been more attentive to the emotional component of empathy, particularly with regard to its role in prosocial behaviors. One of the best examples is found in the work of Nancy Eisenberg and her colleagues (Eisenberg, Hofer, & Vaughan, 2007). Like Hoffman, Eisenberg sees empathy as an emotional reaction that stems from, and is similar to, what is experienced by another. However, she proposes that empathy can turn into either sympathy or personal distress. **Sympathy** involves feelings of sorrow or concern for another person. A child who is being sympathetic is not feeling the same emotion as the other person. Instead, he or she feels "other-oriented concern." In contrast, **personal distress** is a self-focused emotional reaction in the face of another's distress.

sympathy Feelings of sorrow or concern for another.

personal distress A self-focused emotional reaction to another person's distress.

Eisenberg argues that it is important to distinguish between sympathy and personal distress because they have entirely different consequences for prosocial behavior. For example, when shown films that depict characters who are distressed, children who exhibit concern or sadness are more likely to engage in prosocial behaviors than are children who exhibit personal distress (Eisenberg, Spinrad, & Sadovsky, 2006).

Personal distress, according to Eisenberg, stems from empathic overarousal in response to the negative emotions of another (Eisenberg, Spinrad, & Knafo-Noam, 2015). When another person's distress generates too much negative emotion in the child, the result is a focus on the self rather than the other-directed focus that underlies sympathy. Not surprisingly, personal distress is associated with poor social skills.

A deciding factor in whether the child's initial empathic response becomes personal distress or sympathy is the child's capacity to regulate his or her emotions. The relationship between emotional regulation and sympathy is illustrated in a series of studies involving 6- to 8-year-olds. The studies focused on three variables: (1) general emotional intensity—the children's personal tendencies to respond to another's distress with strong feelings; (2) emotional regulation—the ability to modulate their negative feelings; and (3) sympathy—the expression of concern for the other. The first study found that children who were rated low in regulation were also low in sympathy, regardless of their general emotional intensity (Eisenberg et al., 1996). However, for children who could regulate their emotions, greater emotional intensity was associated with greater levels of sympathy.

The second study went one step further and examined how the ability to focus one's attention—another form of self-regulation—might enter the picture (Eisenberg et al., 1998). The researchers argued that children who are more capable of focusing their attention may take in more information about other people and their circumstances, leading to increased perspective-taking and, by extension, greater sympathy. They found that children who were low in emotional intensity and attention-focusing were also low in sympathy. However, children who were low in emotional intensity but high in attention-focusing were relatively high in sympathy.

All of this suggests that sympathy results from an optimal level of emotional arousal but that an optimal level can be achieved by different routes. Children who are inclined to extreme emotional reactions need to be able to regulate their emotions in order to be sympathetic. For children who are not as emotional, the ability to focus attention on others may enhance their understanding of others' needs.

APPLY > CONNECT > DISCUSS

From a Vygotskian perspective, what might account for whether children react to someone's distress with their own personal distress or with sympathy?

Looking Ahead

LEARNING OUTCOME
Summarize the development of mental states that children understand about themselves and others as a way of responding to their social relationships and cultures.

The kindergartners in Vivian Paley's classroom are discussing the story of Tico, a wingless bird who is cared for by his black-winged friends. In the story, the wishingbird visits Tico one night and grants him a wish. Tico wishes for golden wings. When his friends see his golden wings in the morning, they are angry. They abandon him because he wants to be better than they are. Tico is upset by his friends' rejection and wants to gain readmission to the group. He discovers that he can exchange his golden feathers for black ones by performing good deeds. When at last he has replaced all the golden feathers with black ones, he is granted readmission by the flock, whose members comment, "Now you are just like us" (Leoni, 1964).

> Teacher: I don't think it's fair that Tico has to give up his golden wings.
> Lisa: It is fair. See, he was nicer when he didn't have any wings. They didn't like him when he had gold.
> Wally: He thinks he's better if he has golden wings.
> Eddie: He is better.
> Jill: But he's not supposed to be better. The wishingbird was wrong to give him those wings.
> Deana: She has to give him his wish. He's the one who shouldn't have asked for golden wings.
> Wally: He could put black wings on top of the golden wings and try to trick them.
> Deana: They'd sneak up and see the gold. He should just give every bird one golden feather and keep one for himself.
> Teacher: Why can't he decide for himself what kind of wings he wants?
> Wally: He has to decide to have black wings.
> (Paley, 1981, pp. 25–26.)

This conversation shows that the children understand that by wishing for golden wings, Tico has wished himself a vision of perfection. Each child has done the same thing countless times: "I'm the beautiful princess"; "I'm Superman; I'll save the world." For the blissful, magical moments when the world of play holds sway, perfection is attainable, even by a lowly bird or a preschool child. Wally and his friends also appreciate the dilemmas of perfection. In their eyes, Tico not only thinks he is better but is better—yet he is not supposed to be. Try as they may to conceive of a way for Tico to retain his prized possessions, the children realize that conformity is unavoidable. Wally's summary is difficult to improve upon: Tico has to choose to conform.

Kevin Dodge/Getty Images

This little girl's ability to understand her younger brother's mental state helps her draw him into the storybook, providing an opportunity for sharing a happy emotional experience.

The children's discussion of Tico and his community of birds reveals more than an appreciation of the pressure of group norms as experienced by children everywhere. It also shows the children's awareness that individuals have a responsibility for regulating social relations. They understand that it is the wishingbird's job to grant wishes and therefore not the wishingbird's fault that Tico wished to be better than the others. Tico should have been able to control himself and make a reasonable wish.

This story returns us to the theme with which this chapter began—that socialization and personality development are two aspects of a single process. When children engage in acts of sharing and comforting, they reveal their ability to know another person's mental state. At the same time, they are displaying their own ways of thinking and feeling—in other words, their personalities.

Before we turn in Part IV to the wide range of new roles and rules that children encounter in middle childhood and the corresponding changes that take place in their sense of themselves, we need to round out the discussion of early childhood by investigating the range of contexts that make up the world of young children and structure their everyday experiences. As you will see in Chapter 10, the many different social influences and cultural prescriptions that children encounter in these contexts play a key role in the processes through which their personality and sense of personal and social identity develop.

INSIGHT AND INTEGRATION

1. How might self-regulation be related to the development of gender-role and ethnic identity?
2. Using the concept of *co-construction* discussed at the beginning of the chapter and defined in Chapter 2 (p. 71), explain how children contribute to their own moral development.
3. How can society promote the development of less aggression and more prosocial behavior in children?

Summary

- Children's social and emotional lives develop along two paths—the path of socialization, through which they acquire the standards, values, and knowledge of their society, and the path of personality formation, through which they develop their own unique patterns of feeling, thinking, and behaving in a wide variety of situations.

Identity Development

- Crucial to socialization is identification, a psychological process in which children try to look, act, feel, and be like significant people in their social environment. Identification includes acquisition of sex-role and ethnic identities.
- Gender-role identity development has been explained in various ways:
  - In Freud's psychodynamic view, during the phallic stage, boys experience the Oedipus complex and girls experience the Electra complex, both of which are resolved by the child's identifying with the same-sex parent, at around the age of 4 or 5.
  - According to the social learning view, identification occurs through modeling, in which children observe and imitate people of their gender, and through differential reinforcement, in which they are rewarded for gender-appropriate behavior.
  - In the constructivist view, cognitive development contributes to the child's construction of gender. Gender schema theory emphasizes that children form mental models containing information about males and females that are used to process gender-relevant information, such as which types of toys, clothing, activities, and interests are "male" or "female."
  - In the cultural view, gender categories are tools of culture, mediating children's behavior by organizing their activities and the ways they relate to the environment as "boys" or "girls."
- Ethnic identity is the sense of belonging to an ethnic group and having the feelings and attitudes associated with being a member of that group. Young children show awareness of the status of their own ethnic group and those of others. Parents can communicate different sorts of ethnicity-related messages.
- Young children's personal identity, or sense of self, tends to be fluid and, as reflected in self-descriptions, focused on disconnected concrete attributes, which the children often see in an unrealistically positive light. Caregivers contribute to children's developing sense of self by helping them create an autobiographical memory, or personal narrative.

A New Moral World

- According to Freud's psychodynamic view, children's internalization of adult standards and rules results, at about age 5, in the formation of the superego, a third personality structure (along with the already existing id and ego). The superego functions within the child to regulate the child's behavior.
- The constructivist view held by Piaget maintains that, as part of broader cognitive developments, children's moral reasoning moves from a focus on external authority and objective

consequences to, in middle childhood, a sense of morality as personally chosen.

- According to social domain theory, young children can distinguish among three categories of rules—moral rules, social conventions, and personal sphere rules. The boundaries between these categories vary across and within cultures.

Developing Self-Regulation

- The ability to control one's thoughts, behaviors, and emotions, referred to as self-regulation, is considered a cornerstone of children's development. Children must regulate myriad thoughts and actions to solve problems or achieve social goals.
- According to Vygotsky, play is important in the development of self-regulation, in part because it requires control of thoughts and actions. Sociodramatic play is particularly important in that children must negotiate a shared understanding of the evolving situation and control their thoughts and actions to enact their roles.
- To function socially, young children must learn to interpret the emotional states of others, manage their own emotions, and mask their feelings when necessary—all part of socioemotional competence, the ability to behave appropriately in social situations that evoke strong emotions.
- Cultures can influence the development of children's emotions and of their regulation of emotions.

Understanding Aggression

- The ability to regulate anger and control aggression is a basic task of young children's social development.
- Aggression can take different forms, including physical, verbal, and relational, which is intended to harm someone's friendships.
- Boys' and girls' expressions of aggression differ after age 2, with boys engaging in more physical aggression and girls engaging in less.
- Developmentalists studying causes and control of aggression have focused on:
    - *Biological contributions:* Aggression is evident across animal species, a natural consequence of competition for resources. In groups of human children, as in other species, the development of dominance hierarchies can control aggression.
    - *Social and cultural contributions:* Children learn aggression in the course of social interactions—because they observe aggression in others and imitate or are rewarded for aggressive behavior or because the context permits the expression of aggression.
    - *Emotional and cognitive contributions:* Negative feelings in frustrating situations may or may not lead to violence, depending on factors including the child's cognitions and ability to regulate emotion. Children who have a better understanding of emotions and their expression are less likely to behave aggressively.

Developing Prosocial Behaviors

- Prosocial behavior, or voluntary action intended to benefit others, may have as its foundation empathy, the sharing of another person's emotions and feelings. Development of empathy in early childhood may correspond to decreasing egocentrism.
- According to some developmentalists, empathic feelings may, depending on emotional regulation, become sympathy (feelings of sorrow or concern for another) or personal distress, with sympathy being more likely to lead to prosocial behavior.

Looking Ahead

- Young children are increasingly able to understand others' mental states and to be aware that individuals have a responsibility for regulating social relations. They also increasingly display their own ways of thinking and feeling.

Key Terms

socialization, p. 294
personality formation, p. 294
initiative versus guilt, p. 295
identification, p. 295
gender segregation, p. 296
gender identity, p. 296
gender role, p. 296
phallic stage, p. 297
Oedipus complex, p. 297
Electra complex, p. 298
modeling, p. 298
differential reinforcement, p. 298
gender schema, p. 299
ethnic identity, p. 301
ethnic socialization, p. 302
personal identity, p. 303
autobiographical memory, p. 303
id, p. 305
ego, p. 305
superego, p. 305
heteronomous morality, p. 306
social domain theory, p. 306
self-regulation, p. 308
effortful control, p. 308
sociodramatic play, p. 310
display rules, p. 315
socioemotional competence, p. 316
relational aggression, p. 317
prosocial behavior, p. 323
empathy, p. 323
sympathy, p. 324
personal distress, p. 324

Contexts of Development

CHAPTER 10

Africa is the continent of drums. Formed from the wood of special trees and animal skins, drums are slapped or beaten with sticks to celebrate birth, mourn the dead, and coronate kings. When beaten with special skill and grace, the drums of the Republic of Burundi resemble rolling thunderclaps; they are to be heard "not with your ear, but your heartbeat." For 13-year-old Thierry, beating the drums with his friends, all orphans of Burundi's genocidal war, is a source of pride and honor. Thierry and his friends are among 823,000 war orphans, 20,000 of whom lead desperate lives on the streets. Although such a dire existence places children at considerable risk for a number of physical, emotional, and intellectual problems, the lives of Thierry and his friends have taken a decided turn for the better. They have been recruited to a special program sponsored by UNICEF, which provides war orphans, including former child soldiers, with homes, education, and life skills, while also promoting Burundi's cultural traditions, such as beating the sacred drums. The newfound hope of young Thierry and his friends was apparent when they met with an international peace delegation and explained how young people must avoid the mistakes of their elders and work together in beating the drums and rebuilding their country. Education, Thierry emphasized, is essential to Burundi's children, as well as to its future as a nation.

(Information from Ajia, 2007.)

It is hard to imagine what it might be like growing up on the street in Burundi, where "family" may be nothing more than a few other child associates with whom you steal food; where "education" involves learning how to avoid being captured by soldiers who would force you to fight in a war you do not understand; where "neighborhood" is a territory scarred by burned and abandoned buildings; and where "government"—including the policies and programs meant to provide a safety net in times of strife—has been brought to its knees by years of civil war. Developmental scientists and practitioners recognize the importance of these contexts for children's health and well-being. International organizations such as UNICEF help children like Thierry by repairing the damaged contexts of their lives and development or by creating new ones.

Families, neighborhoods, schools, governments, the media—these and other settings constitute the contexts of children's development. As we shift our attention to these contexts, it is helpful to remember Urie Bronfenbrenner's idea that children's development occurs within nested, interacting ecosystems (see Figure 1.5, p. 28). The innermost system is the *microsystem*, which includes the various settings children experience directly in their daily lives, such as the home, the church, the neighborhood, and the child-care center. The *mesosystem* comprises connections among these microsystem settings, such as parents' involvement with their children's school. Elements of the *exosystem*, such as caregivers' workplaces,

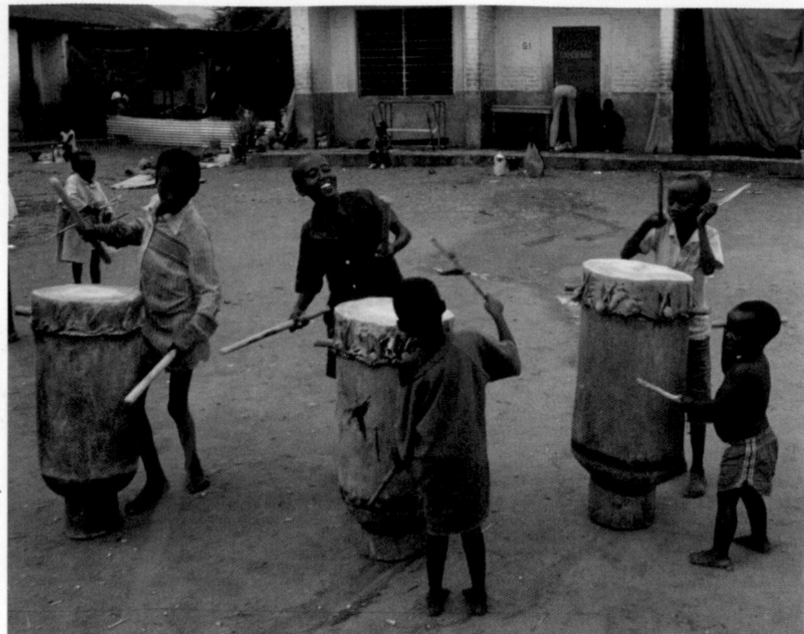

Danita Delimont / Alamy

These Burundi children, displaced by genocidal violence, engage in the traditional practice of beating drums.

government agencies, and mass media, may influence children either directly, as television does, or indirectly, through their impact on parents and other family members. The *macrosystem* includes cultural values and beliefs that infuse the entire ecology, affecting everything from the content of television, to educational programs and health-care policies, to beliefs parents have about how to raise their children. Finally, the outermost *chronosystem* includes life-altering personal transitions (divorce, deaths of family members or friends), major environmental events (crop failures, floods, earthquakes), and significant sociohistorical circumstances (new technologies and medicines, war and peace) that occur over the life span of the individual.

Our discussion of the major contexts of children's development begins with the more immediate and personal contexts of *family* and *child care*. We then move to consider the broader contexts of *neighborhoods and communities* before discussing what may be the broadest context that directly influences children—the *media*. As you read this chapter, you will come to appreciate how each context can provide children with resources for positive growth and development or present significant challenges and risks to their health and well-being.

WARMING UP

1. Think back on how you were raised by your primary caregivers—parents, grandparents, or whoever provided you with the most care. Consider how close your relationships with them were, whether they were more or less strict with you, and how much freedom they gave you in your activities and behaviors. What do you think accounted for these features of caregiving? How do you think these caregiving features affected your development? Save your answers, as we will return to them at the end of the chapter.
2. Because of technological advances and access to the Internet, increasing numbers of children worldwide are exposed to television and interactive media such as video games. What are some of the pros and cons of increased Internet use by children? Do you think exposure to television and interactive media affects children differently than adults? Why?

LEARNING OUTCOMES

Distinguish cultural and social factors associated with nuclear and extended family structures.

Identify three main goals for parenting in families around the world.

Compare the four different patterns of parenting that are based on research initiated by Diana Baumrind.

Indicate some influences on parenting and children's development of the following status of families: immigrant parents, single parents, sexual-minority parents, socioeconomic status, and adolescent parents.

Explain child abuse in terms of cultural influences and/or parents' childhood experiences.

The Family Context

According to an ancient Latin proverb, "the hand that rocks the cradle rules the world." Although many hands shape each child's development—teachers, coaches, and playmates and other peers—the hand of the family is the first influence on the child and remains one of the most significant. Through their traditions, routines, stories, and cultural artifacts, families communicate their perceptions and values about the world to their children. These communications shape their children's behavior and relationships to the world (Pratt & Fiese, 2004).

According to Bronfenbrenner's theory, families are a part of the developing child's *microsystem*—that is, one of the various settings that the child inhabits on a daily basis (Chapter 1, p. 28). The microsystem, as we explained, is the innermost part of the child's entire ecological system; it extends outward from the face-to-face settings of home, school, and peer groups, to the values, customs, hazards, and resources of the larger culture that shape what happens in all the systems nested within. An important feature of all systems in Bronfenbrenner's model, including the family, is that they are *dynamic*. In general, *dynamic systems*, also described in Chapter 1 (p. 27), are complex networks that develop over time from the changing interactions of less complex parts. Families are dynamic systems in the sense of involving a complex network of relationship styles and communication patterns that emerge and change according to the interaction and development of family members. Over the course of time, families face transitions and challenges that their members cope with and adjust to in a variety of ways. Family interactions change as members experience birth, adoption, marriage, divorce, children going off to and returning home from work or school, or relatives moving in or out. And family members themselves change over time as they develop and adjust to the challenges, complexities, and circumstances of their lives.

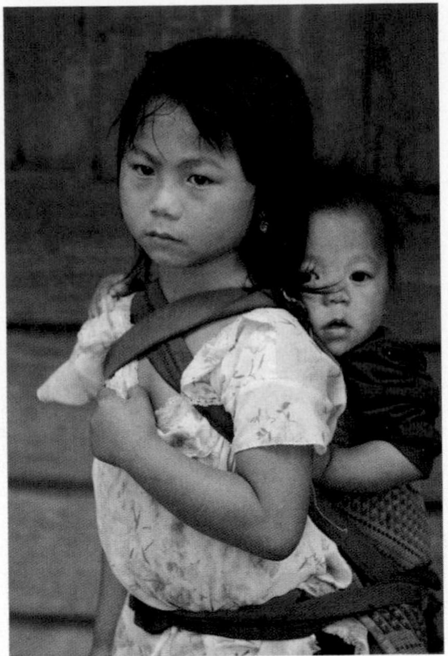

Digitalpress/age fotostock

In many cultures, children care for younger children. This responsibility requires both nurturance and control.

A classic study by Beatrice and John Whiting (1975) illustrates how differences in family life influence children's development. The Whitings organized teams of anthropologists to observe child-rearing in six communities from vastly different cultures. A comparison of two of the groups, the Gusii of Nyansongo, Kenya, and Americans in a small New England town, demonstrates how cultural belief systems, practices, and economics are expressed in the microsystem of family.

At the time of the Whitings' work, the 1950s, the Gusii were agriculturalists living in the fertile highlands of western Kenya. The basic family unit was large, commonly including three generations headed by a grandfather. Polygyny was the traditional marriage form, with several wives living in a compound that included a separate house for the husband. Women, who did most of the farm work, often left their infants and toddlers in the care of older siblings and elderly family members. Beginning at the age of 3 or 4, Gusii children were expected to start helping their mothers with simple domestic tasks. By the age of 7, their economic contributions to the family were indispensable.

The small New England town, referred to as "Orchard Town" by the researchers, represented the opposite extreme in family organization and social complexity. Most of the men of Orchard Town were wage earners who lived with their wives and children in single-family dwellings. The children of Orchard Town divided their time between playing at home (they were rarely asked to do chores) and attending school.

The Whitings' observations of children's behavior patterns in these two cultures documented notable overall differences. The Gusii children, for example, were more likely to offer help and support and to make responsible suggestions to others. At the same time, they were more likely to aggressively reprimand other children. Both of these tendencies were consistent with their child-tending duties: They needed to be nurturing and responsible, but they also needed to exert high levels of control both for safety's sake and to communicate the cultural value of respecting one's elders.

Orchard Town children, in contrast, were more often observed seeking, rather than giving, help and attention, and were more often observed engaging in sociable horseplay, touching others, and joining groups in an amiable way. According to the Whitings, children of industrialized societies, such as those in Orchard Town, are less nurturing and responsible because they do not contribute economically to the family and because they spend most days in school competing with other children rather than helping them. On the other hand, the higher level of intimacy shown by the Orchard Town children is likely a reflection of the close bonds that develop between individuals living in small families. Gusii, in contrast, socialize attachments to the broader group, consistent with a family living pattern that includes many members from several generations.

The Biocultural Origins of Family

Cultural comparisons like the one conducted by the Whitings show that families can differ in many ways that affect children's lives and development. Take a moment to think about your own family. Were you raised by one parent, or two, or even three, or perhaps by a grandparent? Do you have brothers and sisters? Half-siblings or step-siblings? Did other people or relatives live with you while you were growing up? An important feature that defines your family is the members it includes and their relationships to you and each other. Developmentalists use the term **family structure** to refer to how a family is organized socially. There are two major forms of family structure—**nuclear families**, which consist of parents (including single parents) and their children, and **extended families**, which consist of parents (again including single parents) and their children as well as other kin, who may include grandparents, cousins, aunts, uncles, and others. Why are some families nuclear, while others are extended? And what difference does family organization make in the lives and development of children? As you will see below, answers to these questions hinge on the cultural and evolutionary processes that influence how families are socially organized.

family structure The social organization of a family. Most commonly, the structure is nuclear or extended.

nuclear families Families consisting of parents (including single parents) and their children.

extended families Families in which not only parents and their children but other kin—grandparents, cousins, nieces and nephews, or more distant family relations—share a household.

Family and Culture

A major source for understanding the origins and significance of family is the historical work of Philippe Ariès (1962). According to Ariès, the nuclear family is a highly private structure unique to modern societies. Especially in the late eighteenth and early nineteenth centuries, large migrations from rural areas into newly industrialized cities contributed to a shift from extended-family farm life to nuclear-family patterns. In the relative isolation of nuclear families, close, intimate relationships between parents and children took on greater importance than the less personal relationships that are central to the extended-family pattern and bind children to their ancestral line. The greater isolation of nuclear families had other repercussions for children's lives. For example, Ariès contrasts the private nuclear family with the more sociable families of premodern times, in which "people lived on top of one another, masters and servants, children and adults, in houses open at all hours." Children reared in these conditions were exposed to an enormous diversity of roles, relationships, and patterns of interacting—experiences quite different from those of children growing up in nuclear families.

Despite the predominance of the nuclear-family structure in the United States, the proportion of extended families has been steadily increasing in recent decades for families of all ethnicities, and it rose dramatically during the recent Great Recession. According to a recent national study, approximately 19 percent of the entire population—a total of 60.6 million people—lives in a household with two or more adult generations or a household that includes grandparents and grandchildren (Cohn & Passel, 2017; see Figure 10.1). This arrangement

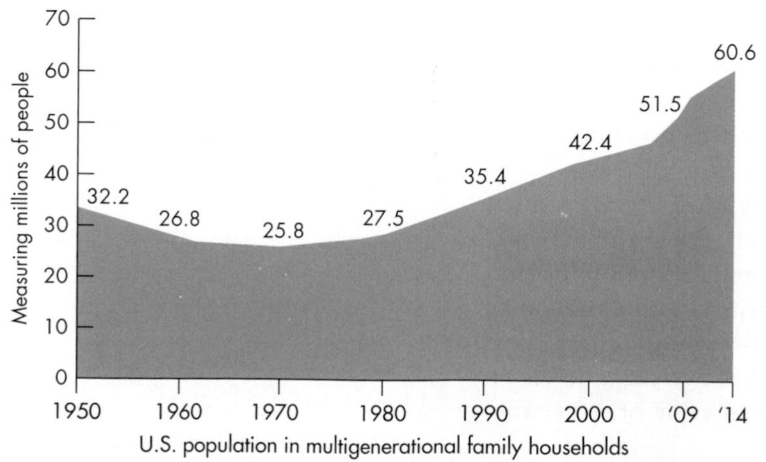

FIGURE 10.1 The number of people in the United States who live in extended families has grown dramatically over the past three decades. Today, approximately 60.6 million people in the United States live in multigenerational family homes. (Data from Cohn & Passel, 2017.)

is more common when families are experiencing economic stress, when the mother is young and single, or when cultural traditions and values are consistent with extended-family living arrangements, as they are among those of Asian or Hispanic descent and African Americans (Goodman & Rao, 2007; Taylor et al., 2010; see Figure 10.2).

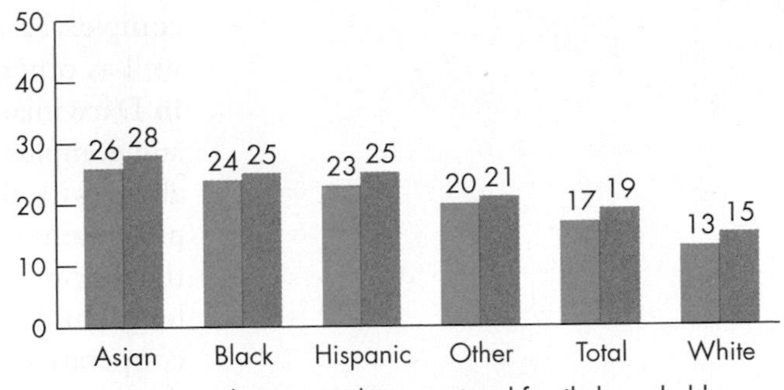

FIGURE 10.2 In the United States, Asians, Blacks, and Hispanics are much more likely than Whites to live in extended families. (Data from Cohn & Passel, 2017.)

Many scholars see living as an extended family as a natural strategy for dealing with the combined handicaps of low income and low social standing (Goodman & Silverstein, 2006). Young, economically disadvantaged minority children are particularly likely to benefit from the problem-solving and stress-reducing resources provided by the extended family (Smith, 2002). Moreover, recent studies of children in sub-Saharan African countries who have been orphaned due to the HIV/AIDS epidemic or famine, or those in Middle Eastern countries who have been forced to migrate due to political violence, find that they are more likely to do well when they live in extended family situations (Kazeem & Jensen, 2017; Pieloch, McCullough, & Marks, 2016).

allocaregiving Child care and protection provided by group members other than the parents, usually other relatives.

cooperative breeding In humans and certain other species, a system involving networks of support in which individuals other than parents contribute resources toward rearing the young.

Family and Evolution

Extended kin make a difference in the lives of children because they provide essential *resources*, including food, income, child care, and help in maintaining the household, as well as less tangible assistance in the form of emotional support and counseling and, in some cultures, opportunities for the mother to improve the family's economic situation by furthering her education (Jarrett, 2000). Such significant contributions to child and family well-being have been recognized by anthropologists and evolutionary theorists who study **allocaregiving**—that is, child care and protection provided by group members other than the parents (Hrdy, 2016; Kruger & Konner, 2010). Allocaregivers may include a child's siblings, uncles, aunts, and grandmothers, as well as non-kin such as foster children who live within the group. Several studies of highly diverse cultures have found that the presence of allocaregivers increases the likelihood that mothers will have more children (Hrdy, 2016). Some of these studies have shown the advantages of having a grandmother living with the family; others have pointed to the importance of having a big sister. For example, in villages in Micronesia, the Caribbean, and Gambia, West Africa, it has been found that women whose firstborn child is a daughter tend to have more births, and more *surviving* children, than do women whose firstborn is a son.

Evidence that allocaregiving increases mothers' reproductive success has also been documented in nonhuman species. In addition to humans, many species of birds, as well as wild dogs, lions, and elephants, form networks of support in which nonparental individuals contribute resources toward rearing the young—that is, networks of allocaregivers—a practice referred to as **cooperative breeding** (Kramer, 2014; Shen et al., 2017). Cooperative breeding is rather rare in the animal kingdom; an estimated 8 to 17 percent of bird species and only 3 percent of mammalian species breed cooperatively. However, when it occurs, cooperative breeding results not only in more numerous births and larger, healthier offspring but also in prolonged periods of childhood dependency, since offspring can take longer to mature without becoming too burdensome to their mothers, who are busy producing new offspring (Hrdy, 2009; McDonald et al., 2008).

Huber H.-B./laif/Redux

From bandaging toes and braiding hair to providing educational resources that allow his daughter to read a letter, the parenting practices of this father will profoundly affect the development of his offspring.

With respect to our own species, evidence regarding the effects of cooperative breeding has ignited a fascinating controversy about why human offspring take so long to mature. According to the traditional view, an extended childhood evolved in our species because it provides the time necessary for the maturation of large, complex brains and the development of cognitive, symbolic, and linguistic skills, as well as other tools of culture that are important to children's survival and success. In Darwinian terms, *natural selection* assures that individuals with *phenotypically* large and complex brains, and the spectacular cognitive, social, and linguistic skills that go along with them, are more likely to reproduce than are individuals with less complex brains (presumably due to shorter childhoods; see Chapter 2, pp. 57–58). From this perspective, delayed maturation is a by-product of brain evolution; we have long childhoods because we grow big brains. Evolutionary theorists who study cooperative breeding, however, have turned this perspective on its head, arguing that we grow big brains because we have long childhoods, and we have long childhoods because we have families. More specifically, the lengthy childhood enabled by the resources of extended family networks opened the door that allowed brain evolution to occur.

Parenting Practices

Regardless of who raised you, or how, there can be little doubt that the caregiving you received growing up has had a powerful impact on who you are today. As you will see in the next section, virtually all people who raise children share a common set of goals. Efforts to reach these goals, however, vary considerably depending on the family's ecological context, cultural values, and beliefs about how children should behave.

Parenting Goals

On the basis of his study of child-rearing practices in diverse cultures, the anthropologist Robert LeVine (1988) has proposed that three major goals are shared by parents the world over:

1. *The survival goal:* To ensure that their children survive, by providing for their health and safety
2. *The economic goal:* To ensure that their children acquire the skills and other resources needed to be economically productive adults
3. *The cultural goal:* To ensure that their children acquire the basic cultural values of the group

LeVine found that the way parents raise their children reflects the extent to which local ecology threatens any of these goals. For example, child-care practices in places with high infant-mortality rates look fairly uniform throughout the world. In places as different as Africa, South America, and Indonesia, when there is a general threat to children's physical survival, parents tend to keep their infants on their bodies at all times, respond quickly to infants' cries, and nurse their babies often. Under such threat conditions, parents show little concern for the emotional and behavioral development of their infants and young children, rarely attempting, for instance, to elicit smiles from their babies or engage them in vocal play. In contrast, in places where children's physical survival is more or less guaranteed, parents are more likely to focus on ensuring their children's future economic success. In industrialized societies, for example, where education is crucial to earning a living wage, many child-care practices are oriented toward enhancing cognitive development and supporting "school readiness" and children's achievement in the classroom. Indeed, as discussed in Chapter 5, this trend in the United States has led to the development of a highly profitable industry devoted to toys and games that supposedly foster intellectual development in infants and young children.

Thus, LeVine's research contributes to understanding both the universality of parental goals and the diversity of parenting practices observed throughout the world. For example, it gives insight into the "no-nonsense parenting" or "tough love" practiced by many African American and Mexican American parents (LeCuyer & Swanson, 2017; Steele, Nesbitt-Daly, Daniel, & Forehand, 2005; White et al., 2016). A mixture of high parental control, including physical restraint and punishment, and warm affection characterize **no-nonsense parenting**. Developmentalists who study no-nonsense parenting in African American and Mexican American families find that it is used more frequently by mothers who live in urban areas than by those in rural areas, as well as by mothers who are better educated. A study of Mexican American families found that children in high-adversity neighborhoods (high levels of poverty and unemployment), compared to peers living in low-adversity neighborhoods, showed fewer behavior problems over time if their fathers engaged in no-nonsense parenting (White et al., 2016). These patterns are consistent with LeVine's conclusions, which would suggest that no-nonsense parenting, with its mix of control and warmth, is a protective response to the threats—social as well as physical—that urban life poses for children, especially in inner cities. Similarly, better-educated mothers may have higher aspirations for their children and consequently exert high levels of control over their behavior to see that they do what is needed to succeed.

no-nonsense parenting Parenting characterized by a mix of high parental control—including punishment—and warmth, and associated especially with African American single mothers.

authoritative parenting pattern Parenting style identified by Baumrind in which parents set standards and limits for children but also encourage discussion and independence and express warmth.

authoritarian parenting pattern Parenting style identified by Baumrind in which parents enforce obedience and conformity to traditional standards (including by use of punishment) and lack verbal give-and-take or expressions of warmth with children.

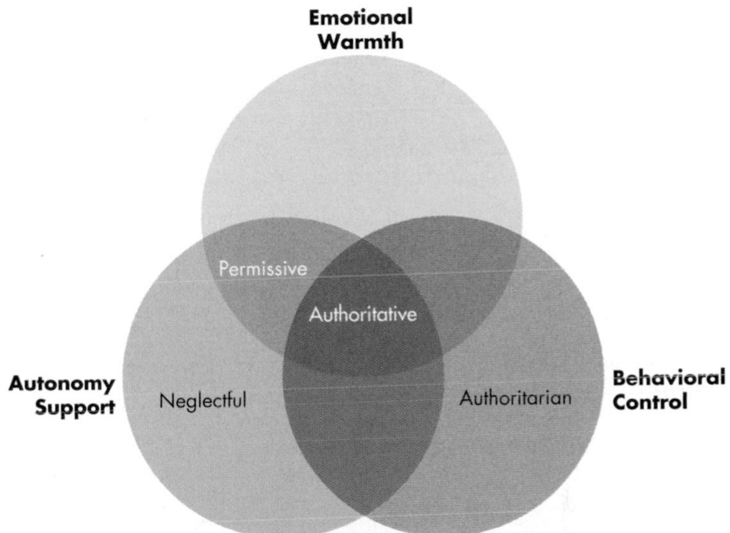

FIGURE 10.3 Parenting styles vary in the extent of warmth, control, and support.

Parenting Styles

Although parenting practices vary widely, they can be analyzed in terms of three key dimensions: emotional warmth, behavioral control, and autonomy support (Kerr, Stattin, & Ozdemir, 2012; Pinquart, 2017). *Emotional warmth* is associated with parents' expressions of caring and acceptance. *Behavioral control* refers to parents' efforts to monitor and control their children's behavior. Finally, *autonomy support* concerns the extent to which parents support and respect their children's feelings and perspectives (see Figure 10.3).

In the early 1970s, Diana Baumrind (1971, 1980) launched what would become one of the best-known research programs on the developmental consequences of *parenting styles*. On the basis of interviews and observations of predominantly White, middle-class preschoolers and their parents, Baumrind and her colleagues found that parenting behaviors in 77 percent of their families fit one of three patterns—*authoritative*, *authoritarian*, and *permissive*. Baumrind also found that each parenting pattern tended to be associated with a different pattern of children's behavior in preschool (see Table 10.1, p. 336):

- *Authoritative parenting pattern:* Parents who follow an **authoritative parenting pattern** set high standards for their children's behavior and expect them to respect established limits, but they also recognize that their children have needs and rights. They tend to be warm and also responsive, and they attempt to control their children by reasoning with them rather than by using physical punishment. In general, their children tend to be more self-reliant and self-controlled and willing to explore compared to children raised by permissive or authoritarian parents.
- *Authoritarian parenting pattern:* Parents who follow an **authoritarian parenting pattern** try to shape, control, and evaluate the behavior and attitudes of their children according to a set traditional standard. Comparatively lacking in the expression of warmth and responsiveness,

Ed Bock / Getty Images

This mother disciplines her son by attempting to explain why his behavior was inappropriate.

TABLE 10.1 Baumrind's Parenting Styles

Parenting Style	Description
Authoritative	• Demanding but reciprocal relationship • Favor reasoning over physical punishment • Encourage independence
Authoritarian	• Demanding and controlling • Favor punitive methods over reasoning • Stress obedience over independence
Permissive	• Undemanding and little control exercised • Allow children to learn through experience as a result of indulgence • Neither independence nor obedience stressed • Emotionally warm
Neglectful	• Undemanding and little control exercised • Allow children to learn through neglect • Emotionally distant

they stress obedience to authority and tend to favor punitive measures over reasoning to curb their children's behavior. With this parenting pattern, children tend to lack social competence, often withdrawing from social contact, and may lack intellectual curiosity.

permissive parenting pattern Parenting style identified by Baumrind in which parents express warmth but do not exercise control over their children's behavior.

neglectful parenting pattern Parenting style identified by Baumrind in which parents do not exercise control over children's behavior and are emotionally distant.

- *Permissive parenting pattern:* Parents who exhibit a **permissive parenting pattern** exercise less explicit control over their children's behavior than do authoritarian and authoritative parents, often because they believe children must learn how to behave through their own experience. Although these parents tend to be emotionally warm, they do not demand the same levels of achievement or standards of behavior from their children.
- *Neglectful parenting pattern:* Those who engage in a **neglectful parenting pattern**, similar to those with a permissive parenting pattern, make few demands on their child's behavior and provide little supervision. However, unlike permissive parenting, neglectful parenting is characterized by emotional distance, with little effort by these parents to acknowledge their children's emotions and perspectives.

Baumrind's pioneering work inspired hundreds of studies on how parenting practices affect children's development. In more recent research, however, developmentalists have attempted to view patterns of parenting from a broader, more dynamic perspective. Some developmentalists have examined how children's behavior and temperament may elicit different styles of parenting (Collins, 2005; Maccoby, 2007). Children with attention-deficit/hyperactivity disorder (ADHD) or autism spectrum disorder, for instance, who may display relatively low levels of executive control, are more likely to elicit authoritarian or permissive parenting styles compared to their counterparts with higher levels of executive control (Hutchison, Feder, Abar, & Winsler, 2016). Similarly, parents may change their style over time in response to developmental changes in their child's behavior. For example, as their children move out of the "terrible twos" and are better able to understand and comply with their parents' verbal directives, some parents may become less controlling and physically coercive.

A broader, more dynamic approach to parenting styles is also apparent in research focused on the cultural contexts of parenting practices. A team of researchers headed by Heidi Keller compared parenting styles in two countries with very different cultural beliefs and values—Germany and India (Keller et al., 2010). German culture cherishes independence, personal freedom, and autonomy; India embraces the interdependence of family and social connections and relationships. The researchers studied mother–child interactions when the babies were 3 months old and then again when they were 19 months old. The researchers found significant cultural differences in the mothers' parenting goals, as well as in how they talked to and played with their babies. To a greater extent than German mothers, Indian mothers emphasized the importance of learning self-control and talked more often to their babies about other people's feelings and needs and the social consequences of their actions. German mothers, in contrast, tended to emphasize the importance of developing self-confidence and talked more about their babies' own internal states and personal needs. These differences were apparent when the babies were both 3 and 19 months of age. Cultural differences in parenting styles have been identified in other cultures as well, including in China (Huang, Cheah, Lamb, & Zhou, 2017; Wu et al., 2002).

The Role of Siblings

Our friend Laureen is the oldest of three siblings. Reflecting on her experiences growing up with two younger brothers, she remembers a lot of fighting (but does not remember what was being fought about), babysitting (when she would rather have gone out with her friends), and sticking up for her brothers when they got into trouble with peers or parents (which was often). In her words, "It was fine for *me* to push them around, but everyone else had better keep their hands off my little brothers!" Laureen also vividly remembers when her brothers overtook her in physical size and strength. "After that, my power as the 'big sister' was entirely psychological." Despite the fact that all three of them are now in their 50s and fairly good friends, Laureen still considers herself the big sister. Her relationships with her brothers, which have existed longer than any other relationships in her life, still bear the mark of their early experiences.

Studies indicate that, across cultures, siblings are influential in one another's development (Pike & Oliver, 2017; Whiteman, McHale, & Crouter, 2007). The socializing role of siblings is obvious in agricultural societies, like the Gusii, discussed earlier in the chapter, in which much of the child care is performed by older siblings. But even in industrialized societies, siblings spend tremendous amounts of time in each other's company; according to one estimate, by middle childhood, children in the United States spend more time with their siblings than with their parents (McHale, Whiteman, Kim, & Crouter, 2007). The behavior of older siblings can have a strong and lasting impact on the behavior of younger siblings, for good and ill. Older siblings using drugs and alcohol increases the likelihood that their younger brothers and sisters will also engage in illicit drug and alcohol use (Litt, Stock, & Gibbons,

Of all the relationships an individual may ever have, those with siblings may be the longest lasting. Developmentalists are just beginning to understand the complexity of these relationships and how they are affected by the ages and gender mix of the sibling pair.

Hugh Sitton/Getty Images

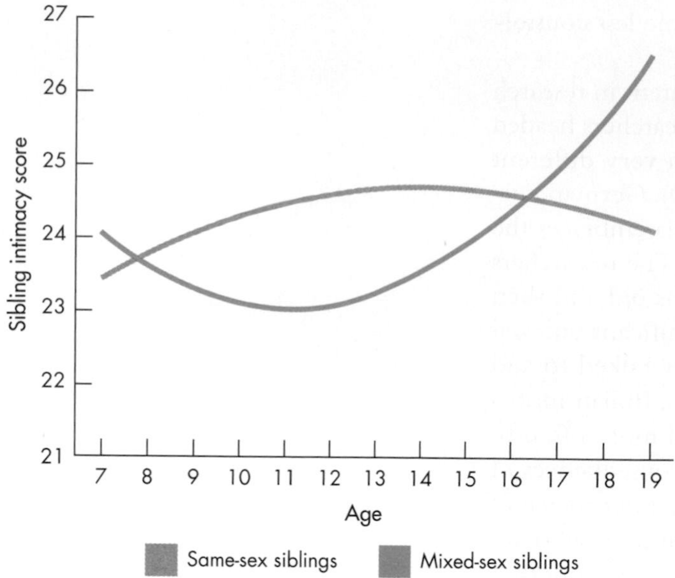

FIGURE 10.4 Intimacy between siblings varies depending on the age and gender mix of the sibling pair. Intimacy of same-sex sibling pairs is fairly constant over time, whereas the intimacy of mixed-sex pairs declines during middle childhood and increases throughout adolescence and early adulthood. (Data from Kim, McHale, Osgood, & Crouter, 2006, p. 1753.)

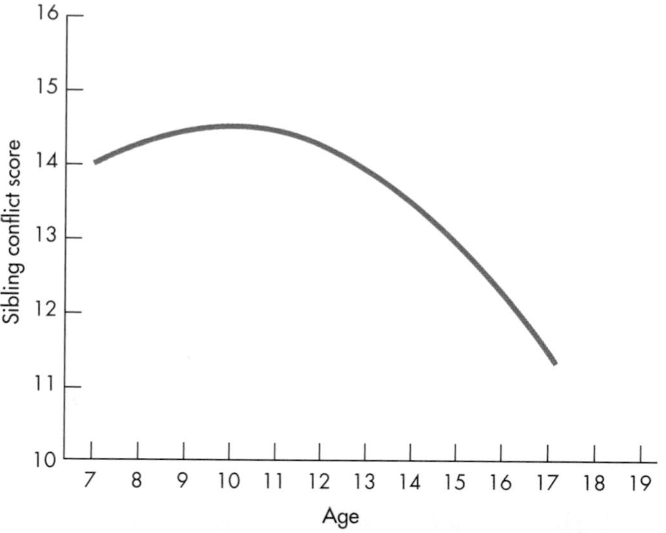

FIGURE 10.5 Conflicts between siblings peak during middle childhood and decline throughout adolescence. (Data from Kim et al., 2006, p. 1753.)

2015; Samek, McGue, Keyes, & Iacono, 2015). Older siblings can also protect their younger brothers and sisters from such risks and can even lessen the influence of their younger siblings' drug-using peers (Pomery, Gibbons, Gerrard, Cleveland, Brody, & Wills, 2005). According to some social learning theories (Chapter 1, pp. 25–26), siblings may provide each other with models of how to act (Chapter 1, p. 25). It is important to keep in mind, however, that biological siblings also share genetic materials and grow up in highly similar environments, and these factors are also known to influence the development of these types of behaviors.

As suggested by Laureen, sibling relationships are often ambivalent, sometimes loving and supportive, sometimes hostile and competitive. Indeed, siblings provide children with opportunities to learn about sharing and trust, as well as about conflict and negotiation. The degree of intimacy and conflict in sibling relationships depends on a variety of factors, including the sex and age of the children. In a longitudinal study of U.S. siblings between 9 and 20 years of age, there appeared to be higher levels of intimacy between sisters than between brothers or between brothers and sisters (Kim, Han, & McCubbin, 2007). In addition, whereas the intimacy of same-sex sibling pairs remained fairly stable over time, that of mixed-sex pairs declined during middle childhood, perhaps as a consequence of *gender segregation* (see Chapter 9, p. 296), and then increased in mid-adolescence, when siblings may turn to each other for advice and support on matters of peer and dating relationships (Figure 10.4).

Sibling intimacy and conflict have been associated with children's mental health and adjustment. In general, warmth and intimacy in sibling relationships tend to be associated with emotional understanding and sharing in later childhood. In contrast, negative sibling relationships are associated with later adjustment problems. Sibling conflict is common across the years of childhood, peaking during middle childhood and declining thereafter (Figure 10.5). A large longitudinal study of more than 2,000 sibling pairs documented the pronounced influence of sibling relationships on children's development (Pike & Oliver, 2017). In particular, when mothers reported that their 4-year-old children got along well with older siblings, the younger of the two, at age 7, was more likely to develop higher levels of prosocial behavior and consideration for others, compared to younger siblings with poorer-quality relationships. Likewise, when the 4-year-olds had poor-quality relationships with their older siblings, they were more likely to develop conduct problems at age 7. Another case in point is a study that examined the relationship between adjustment to war-related trauma and sibling relationships in a group of Palestinian schoolchildren in the Gaza Strip (Peltonen, Qouta, El Sarraj, & Punamäki, 2010). Palestinian boys and girls aged 10 to 14 years were asked to report their exposure to war-related trauma (such as the shelling of their home, being wounded, or losing a family member) and were assessed for depression and psychological distress. Relationships with their siblings were also analyzed, including their degree of intimacy, conflict, and rivalry. Specifically, the children used a 5-point scale to indicate how well specific sentences applied to their own sibling relationships. Some of the sentences that the children were asked to rate on a scale ranging from 1 ("not at all") to 5 ("very well") were:

- "We usually laugh and joke together."
- "I usually tell him/her about my secrets."
- "He/she annoys and teases me."
- "I feel jealous of him/her when he/she takes all of my mother's attention."

The researchers found that children who witnessed or were themselves the target of military violence had higher levels of sibling rivalry than children exposed to lower levels of trauma. As the researchers point out, increased sibling rivalry under life-threatening conditions makes sense from an evolutionary perspective, as siblings may be competing for limited parental attention and resources. On the other hand, the researchers also found that higher levels of sibling intimacy appeared to provide some protection against depression and psychological distress in children exposed to the traumatizing conditions of war (see also p. 363 for a discussion of "protective factors").

Family Diversity

Changes in values, politics, economies, and transportation technologies have altered the face of "family" in many parts of the world, bringing to it a wide diversity of ethnic backgrounds, cultural heritages, and lifestyles. As immigrant populations swell across the globe, family ethnicity has become a special focus of developmentalists' attention. Likewise, research on families with single parents or sexual-minority parents has increased in recent years due to ever-growing numbers of single parents and of gay couples raising children.

Immigrant Families

Life can change, often dramatically, when a family emigrates to a new country and culture. The mother quoted below prided herself on doing everything for her children before the family moved from their native Korea. In the United States, altered circumstances required that the children of this family work in the family store on non-school days. As the mother noted:

> I had to completely change my parenting style. . . . I can do very little for my kids. . . . My daughter cooks for us, . . . and she is taking care of her little brother. While she was in Korea, she was like a princess . . . but now she is different.
>
> (Kim, Conway-Turner, Sherif-Trask, & Wolfolk, 2006, p. 51.)

In 2015, 244 million people (3.3 percent of the world population) lived outside their country of birth (United Nations Population Fund, 2015). Many had fled life-threatening violence and famine. Europe, in particular, has experienced massive movements of migrants seeking refuge from armed conflicts, mass killings, and pervasive sexual and gender-based violence (United Nations Population Fund, 2016).

Ethnic diversity has been present in the United States throughout its history as a result of the colonization of Native Americans, the importation of slaves from Africa, and a continuous stream of immigrants, mostly from Europe. Moreover, in the past few decades, the United States has had an enormous influx of families from other parts of the globe. As shown in Figure 10.6, the vast majority of U.S.

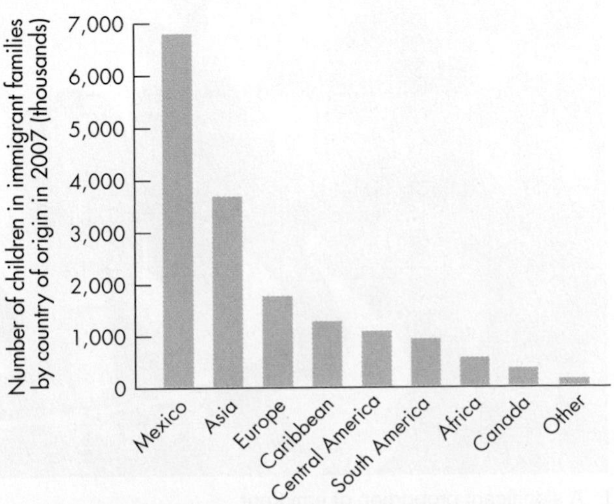

FIGURE 10.6 In the United States, about two-fifths of all children in immigrant families were born in Mexico or had a parent who was born in Mexico. (Data from Mather, 2009.)

immigrants now come from Mexico, followed by Asia and Europe. Between 1995 and 2014, the population of first- and second-generation immigrant children grew by 51 percent to 18.7 million. Currently, one-quarter of all children in the United States are living in immigrant families, with 40 percent having at least one parent who was born in Mexico (Child Trends, 2014). Similar changes in the influx of immigrants have also occurred in Canada, Australia, and Germany and other European countries (United Nations Department of Economic and Social Affairs Population Division, 2017).

Just as parenting styles vary across cultures, so do the values that parents seek to instill in their children. Many recent immigrants to the United States come from cultures that place great value on education as a means of achieving a successful life. Indeed, immigrant parents tend to emphasize the importance of education more than do native-born Americans. In his ethnographic case study of a Hispanic immigrant family, Gerardo Lopez (2001) reported that the parents would often take their children with them as they worked in the fields in order to underscore important "life lessons" about how hard they worked and how poorly they were compensated. The most important lesson, however, was that education is the key to a better life.

What accounts for this difference in the valuing of education? Many developmentalists have pointed to the "ideologies of opportunity" and "cultures of optimism" that motivate families to migrate in the first place (Suárez-Orozco, Suárez-Orozco, & Todorova, 2008). In short, parents believe that life in the new country will provide increased opportunities for their children. However, as with the family of the Korean mother quoted earlier, many immigrant families experience a significant drop in economic and social status when they arrive in the United States (Kim et al., 2007). Sadly, and perhaps counterintuitively, research indicates that, among immigrant Asian and Latino children alike, length of residence in the United States is associated with declines in health, school achievement, and aspirations (Portes & Rumbaut, 2001; Suárez-Orozco, Bang, & Onaga, 2010). Carola Suárez-Orozco and her colleagues (2008) suggest that the "Americanization" of foreign-born children often includes exposure to persistent forms of racism and to peer influence that together undermine their initial sense of optimism and regard for education.

familism A sense of family obligation, common in Hispanic families.

© Kayte Deioma/PhotoEdit – All rights reserved.

A significant proportion of emigrant families to the United States come from Asia. This Cambodian family has made their new home in Long Beach, California.

Immigrant families in the United States also often differ from native-born families in the extent of their devotion and loyalty to family, particularly parents. For example, a sense of family obligation, or **familism** is common in Hispanic families (Landale, Oropesa, & Noah, 2014; Yahirun, Perreira, & Fuligni, 2015). Familism has several important dimensions (Yahirun et al., 2015):

1. *Structural dimension:* Hispanic families often are extended rather than nuclear, and marriage and childbearing tend to occur earlier than in native-born families.
2. *Behavioral dimension:* Activities that fulfill family obligations, including those that provide economic and social support, are highly valued.
3. *Attitudinal dimension:* Values and attitudes that emphasize family loyalty and solidarity are common.

Hispanic parents socialize their children from an early age to value spending time with family, assisting in household chores, and showing respect to elders (Umana-Taylor, et al., 2014). Indeed, Hispanic youths report a greater sense of responsibility toward parents and extended family members compared to non-Hispanic youths, especially when parent–child relationships are strong (Baer & Schmitz, 2007; Tsai, Telzer, Gonzales, & Fuligni, 2015).

Single-Parent Families It is estimated that half of all children born in the United States today will spend at least some portion of their childhood in a single-parent home. Studies of children from single-parent families report a number of behavioral, social, and academic problems (Vespa, Lewis, & Kreider, 2013). One explanation for this pattern is that the quality of the home environment may be lower in single-parent homes (Son & Peterson, 2017). Single parents typically assume the role of sole breadwinner, caregiver, and household manager, and they often have higher levels of depressive symptoms and stress (Price, Price, & McKenry, 2010).

Other researchers argue that the presence of only one parent is not itself a problem; rather, other factors that often correlate strongly with single-parenthood are to blame. For example, with only one wage earner, single-parent families have fewer material resources and have greater financial stress than do two-parent families. In addition, children in single-parent families are likely to have experienced substantial family instability in the form of divorce or remarriage. (You will learn more about the effects of divorce in Chapter 13.) According to this view, whether there is one parent or two in the household is not the issue; exposure to poverty and family instability are the critical factors (Landale, Oropesa, & Noah, 2014).

In an effort to untangle these competing explanations, Gunilla Weitoft and her colleagues (2003) launched a nationwide study comparing health outcomes for children in single-parent and two-parent families in Sweden. They identified almost 1 million children who were living with the same single parent or the same two opposite-sex adults in both 1991 and 1999. Using national records of child deaths, social welfare benefits, and hospital discharges, they found that, compared with their peers in two-parent homes, children in the single-parent homes fared less well on a variety of physical and mental health indicators. Although the researchers found that socioeconomic status was the most important factor in accounting for a number of differences between the two groups, children in single-parent families, regardless of SES, remained at greater risk for psychiatric disorders, suicide, injury, and addiction.

The results of such large-scale studies can provide important information about populations of individuals in general, as Weitoft and her colleagues suggest. However, they reveal little about family dynamics, family communication patterns, child-rearing practices, the reasons for single-parenthood, kin relationships outside the immediate family, and other factors that may influence the well-being of children in single-parent families.

Another problem with conclusions about children in single-parent families is that most of the relevant research has been conducted primarily with Caucasian families, raising the question of whether the results apply as well to ethnic-minority families. As early researchers to address this question, John Kesner and Patrick McKenry (2001) studied 68 preschool children and their parents living in a large city in the southeastern United States. Most of the families were African American (66 percent) or Hispanic (10 percent). Sixty-six percent of the children lived with both parents, and 34 percent lived with their mothers, who had never been married. There were no differences between the single- and two-parent families in terms of ethnicity or socioeconomic level.

Kesner and McKenry examined the children's social skills and styles of conflict management and found no differences between children from single-parent families and those from two-parent families. In discussing their results, the researchers noted that compared with European Americans, African Americans are more supportive of single-parent families and attach less stigma to them. In addition, the extended-family pattern characteristic of the Hispanic and African American cultural traditions (as discussed earlier) may mean that children have a network of kin that provides additional support. Finally, Kesner and McKenry pointed out that because the single mothers in their study had never been married, their families were not exposed to the sudden emotional and financial changes typically experienced by divorced families. These mothers may also have had stronger commitments to their nonconventional family structure than mothers who may have been divorced against their choice.

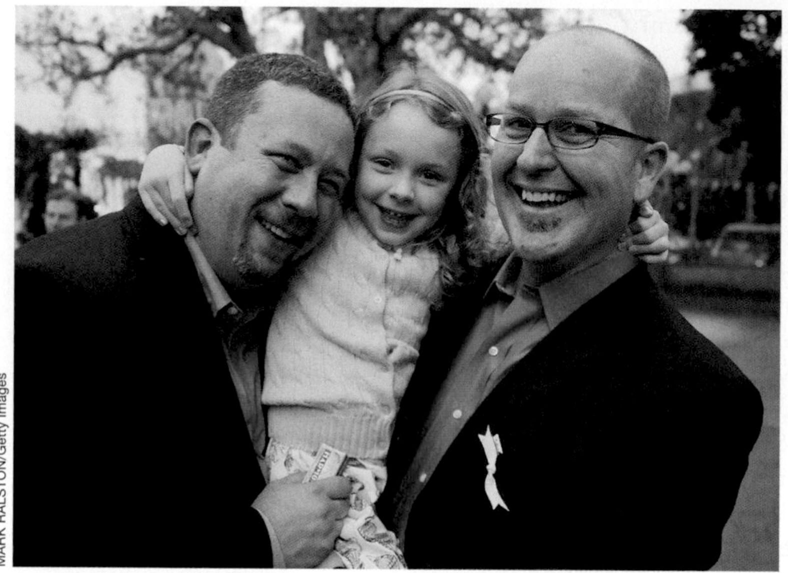

MARK RALSTON/Getty Images

The families of gay couples are diverse in size, ethnicity, religion, and socioeconomic status.

Sexual Minority Parents Another significant change in the nature of families is the increasing number of sexual-minority parents (Patterson & Riskind, 2010). Estimates of both the number of same-sex parents and the number of children they are raising vary considerably. According to a widely cited study, there were 116,000 same-sex couples raising approximately 250,000 children in the United States in 2010, and same-sex couples were four times more likely than mixed-sex couples to adopt children (Gates, 2013).

Like other families, families with sexual-minority parents are diverse in size and structure, ethnicity, religion, and socioeconomic class. A number of studies have sought to determine whether children raised by sexual-minority parents are different from children raised by heterosexual parents. Reviews of this research paint a generally positive picture of development and adjustment for children of sexual-minority parents (Biblarz & Savci, 2010; Fedewa, Black, & Ahn, 2015). For example, on measures of psychological well-being, peer relationships (number and quality of friendships), and behavioral adjustment, a number of studies find no differences between children raised by heterosexual parents and those raised by sexual-minority parents (Bos, van Balen, & van den Boom, 2007; MacCallum & Golombok, 2004; Wainright & Patterson, 2008). On the other hand, children of same-sex parents are often teased about their parents' sexual orientation, as documented by research in several countries, including the United States, the Netherlands, and Belgium (Bos & van Balen, 2008; Farr et al., 2016; Vanfraussen, Ponjaert-Kristoffersen, & Brewaeys, 2002). Interestingly, a rare cross-national study found that peer teasing about parents' sexual orientation is more likely to take place in the United States than in the Netherlands (Bos, Gartrell et al., 2008). Not surprisingly, children of sexual-minority parents seem to be more tolerant of same-sex experimentation and may be somewhat more likely to develop a sexual-minority identity than are children growing up with heterosexual parents (Biblarz & Savci, 2010; Bos, Sandfort, de Bruyn & Hakvoort, 2008).

Distressed Families

Because the family is the first and perhaps the most important developmental context, *distressed families*—that is, families facing significant social, economic, and/or psychological challenges—are of special concern to those interested in children's well-being. According to developmentalists who study distressed families, the most significant family factors that impede children's development are poverty, parenthood in adolescence, abuse, and divorce. We will look at the first three of these factors below (and at divorce in Chapter 13).

Families in Poverty One of the most consistent findings in research on families is the relationship between economic hardship and children's well-being. As discussed in Chapter 6, socioeconomic status includes education level and occupation as well as income. It therefore serves as a predictor of the amount of hardship experienced by families, especially those in poverty.

Poverty touches all aspects of family life: the quality of housing and health care, access to education and recreational facilities, and even safety when walking along the street (Leventhal & Brooks-Gunn, 2011; Shonkoff, Garner et al., 2012). Interest in the influence of poverty on children's development has increased in recent years, due in part to the increasing numbers of poor children in the United States. According to the National Center for Children in Poverty (NCCP), approximately 21 percent of all children in the United States live in poverty, part of the approximately 43 percent who live in low-income families (Jiang, Granja, & Koball, 2017; see Figure 10.7). As we discussed in Chapter 8, nearly 11 percent of children in the United States are considered *food insecure*, meaning that they do not have access to enough food to ensure their good health; and 1.2 percent are considered to have "very low food security," meaning that they have so little food that they are often hungry. In addition, it is estimated that 2.5 million children in the United States—1 in every 30 children—become homeless at some point each year (National Center for Family Homelessness, 2014).

Contrary to popular belief, only half of all poor children and families in the United States are chronically and persistently poor. In a nationwide study, Duncan and his colleagues found that family income fluctuates significantly across the family's life cycle and tends to increase as children age (Duncan & Raudenbush, 1999). However, they also found that being poor during early childhood presents a greater challenge to children's well-being, particularly to their academic achievement, than does being poor during later stages of development. Considering that a family's SES is the most powerful predictor of intellectual skills when children enter school and that early school success forecasts lifelong achievement and adjustment, the effects of poverty are particularly serious (Stipek, 2001).

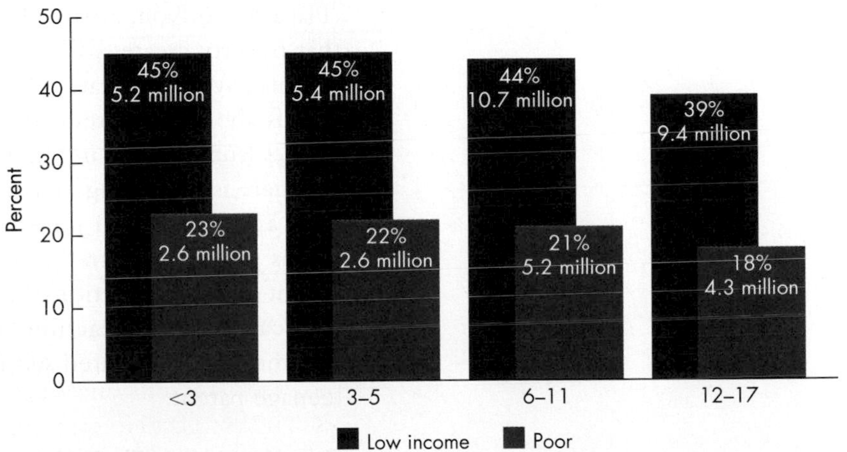

FIGURE 10.7 This figure shows the percentages of children in the United States living in low-income (Red) or poor (Blue) families (Jiang et al., 2017). The National Center for Children in Poverty defines "poor" families as those with incomes below the federal poverty level ($22,050 for a family of 4 in 2010). It defines "low income" families as those with incomes at or below twice the federal poverty level. Defining low-income families is important because research indicates that families cannot meet their basic needs of food, clothing, shelter, transportation, and medical care unless their income is at least 200 percent higher than the federal poverty level. (Data from Engelhardt & Skinner, 2013.)

Poverty-stricken children are at an elevated risk for mental health problems, but this risk can be significantly reduced if their family's income rises above the poverty level. Jane Costello and her colleagues (2003) demonstrated this in an 8-year study of Native American children growing up on a reservation. Some of the children lived in poverty; others did not. Halfway through the study, a casino opened on the reservation, lifting many of the poor families out of poverty. Overall, children in these families subsequently showed a significant decrease in mental health disorders, whereas the children whose families remained in poverty showed no improvement in their mental health. A similar effect was found in a study of very poor rural Mexican families who participated in a program that gave them access to cash resources (Fernald & Gunnar, 2009). Preschool-age children whose families were assigned to participate in the program had lower levels of the stress hormone cortisol than did children whose families were not assigned to participate.

In addition to mental health problems, poverty is also associated with physical health problems and problems in intellectual development. For example, environmentally induced illnesses such as tuberculosis and asthma are observed at higher rates in poor children than in nonpoor children (Shonkoff, Boyce, & McEwen, 2009). Lead poisoning, which is associated with learning disabilities and impaired intellectual functioning, is also a significant threat to impoverished children, who tend to live in rundown housing where they may be exposed to contaminated chips and dust from deteriorating lead-based paint. Water supplies can also be contaminated with lead, as happened beginning in 2014 in Flint, Michigan, an economically struggling industrial town. Dr. Mona Hanna-Attisha, a pediatrician in Flint, became concerned when increasing numbers of parents brought their children in with rashes and hair loss. Analyses showed substantially elevated lead levels in the children's blood (Gupta, Tinker, & Hume, 2016).

Poverty may also affect parents' approach to child-rearing. In particular, studies have found that in families experiencing economic hardship, parents are likely to be harsher and more controlling, in some cases to discourage children's curiosity and restrict their movements because of the dangerous circumstances of their daily lives (Placa & Corlyon, 2016). However, this pattern may also arise because of the stress that poverty creates for parents. Compared with higher-SES parents, low-income parents have higher rates of depression, negative feelings of self-worth, and negative beliefs about the extent to which they have control over their own life circumstances (summarized in Shonkoff & Phillips, 2000).

There is increasing evidence that children can be protected from a number of risks associated with poverty if their families are involved in intervention programs focused on strengthening parents' social support and increasing positive parent–child interactions (Morris et al., 2017). Nonetheless, it is clear that poverty can have far-reaching and long-lasting effects on children's development. Another risk associated with poverty arises in adolescence—that of becoming a teenage parent.

Families with Teen Mothers Many women who are raising children are still teenagers. In contrast to older mothers, teen mothers are less knowledgeable about child development, are less confident in their ability to parent their children, and have less positive attitudes about parenting (Bornstein & Putnick, 2007). As Figure 10.8 indicates, the proportion of adolescents giving birth in the United States has been declining steadily since 2007 and is now among the lowest ever recorded (Centers for Disease Control and Prevention, 2017).

Despite the relatively recent decline, the teen birthrate in the United States is still among the highest in the developed world (Sedgh et al., 2015). This situation is of grave concern because research has shown that children of unmarried teenage mothers suffer significant deficits in several developmental areas. In general, they tend to be more aggressive, less self-controlled, and less intellectually advanced than the children of older, married mothers (Jaffe et al., 2001; Khatun et al., 2017).

A number of factors may contribute to the negative developmental effects of being raised by a young unmarried mother. First, young mothers often are less prepared to bring up children and have little interest in doing so. One consequence is that they tend to vocalize less with their babies than older mothers do. As we

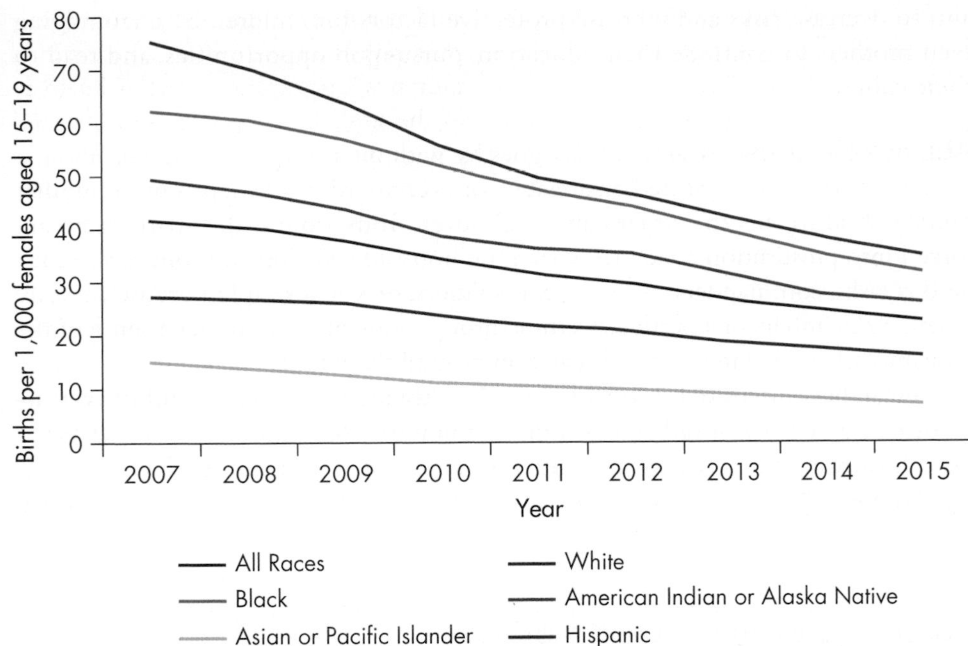

FIGURE 10.8 The proportion of adolescents giving birth in the United States dropped dramatically between 1991 and 2015, particularly among Hispanic and Black teens. Overall, this downward trend has continued for younger and older adolescents across all groups. (Data from Martin, Hamilton, & Osterman, 2015.)

discussed in Chapter 6, mother–infant communication is an important source of intellectual stimulation. Second, young mothers, especially those without husbands, are likely to have very limited financial resources; one-half of all children living in poverty are in single-parent families (Jiang et al., 2017). As a consequence, they are likely to be poorly educated, to live in disadvantaged neighborhoods, to lack quality health care, and to be socially isolated. In addition, typical of teenagers in general, teen mothers are less intellectually mature than adults, which may affect their parenting. Indeed, teen mothers who score lower on tests of executive function are less sensitive in interactions with their babies compared to those who scored at higher levels (Chico et al., 2014).

It is important to recognize that not all children born to teenage mothers have negative developmental outcomes. Tom Luster and his colleague (Luster & Haddow, 2005) compared "more successful" and "less successful" children of adolescent mothers. Children who were most successful, as measured by a standardized test of intellectual and language functioning, were likely to live in environments that were more intellectually stimulating and less stressful than those of their less successful peers. In addition, the mothers of the most successful children had received more years of education, were more likely to be employed, had fewer children, resided in more desirable neighborhoods, and lived with a male partner. Likewise, a study of adolescent mothers' participation in welfare-reform programs indicates that highly involved mothers—those who take advantage of center-based child care, educational opportunities, and job-training programs—have children with more developed cognitive abilities than do children whose mothers are less involved (Yoshikawa, Rosman, & Hsueh, 2001). Social programs for teen mothers, such as the one described in the box "In the Field: Louisiana Swamp Nurse" (p. 348),

Despite the stresses of teen parenting, this young mother takes time to play with her toddler in the park.

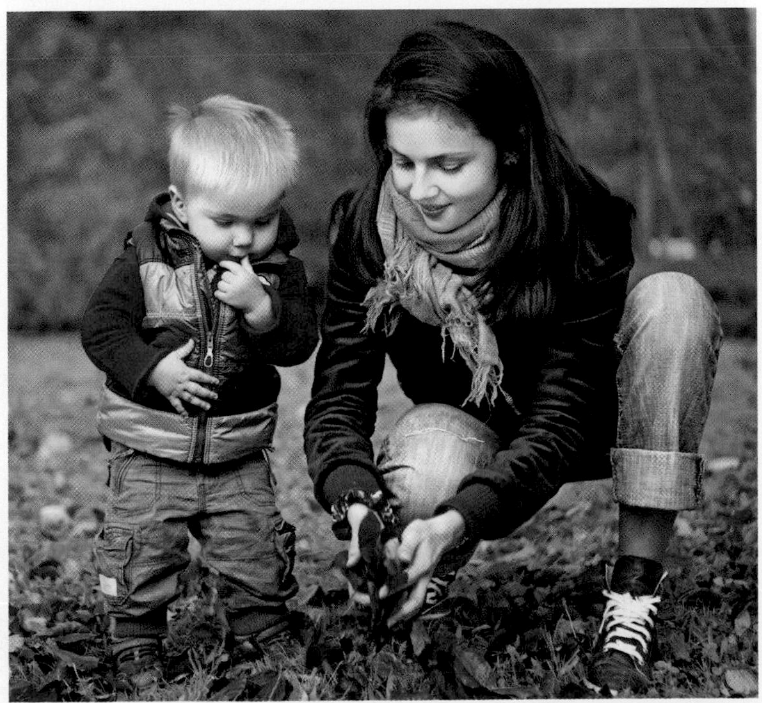

Lorado / Getty Images

aim to decrease risks and increase protective factors for children by encouraging teen mothers to continue their education, pursue job opportunities, and read to their babies.

Abusive Families Scarcely a day goes by without a story in the media about a child who has been neglected, maltreated, or even murdered by a parent or another relative. Add to this the stories about children from around the world who are forced into prostitution, made to work long hours at grueling and sometimes dangerous tasks, commandeered to serve as soldiers, or killed simply because they are female or members of a particular ethnic group, and you begin to get a sense of the enormity of child abuse and maltreatment around the world.

Researchers interested in tracking the worldwide incidence of child maltreatment face a number of difficulties. One of the most common difficulties relates to how "maltreatment" is defined in different cultures. As you can see in Table 10.2, with the exception of extreme physical and sexual abuse, there is wide regional

TABLE 10.2 What Constitutes Abuse? Views from Around the Globe

	Agreement by Region (%)			
Type of Abuse	**Africa**	**Americas**	**Asia**	**Europe**
Sexual abuse (e.g., incest, sexual touching, pornography)	100.0%	100.0%	100.0%	100.0%
Physical abuse (e.g., beating, burning)	90.9	100.0	100.0	100.0
Failure to provide adequate food, clothing, or shelter (neglect)	72.7	100.0	91.7	92.0
Abandonment by parent or caretaker	81.8	100.0	83.3	92.0
Emotional abuse (e.g., repeatedly belittling or insulting a child)	63.6	100.0	62.5	88.0
Failure to secure medical care for child based on religious beliefs	72.7	80.0	60.9	84.0
Psychological neglect (e.g., failure to provide emotional support/attention)	63.6	80.0	54.2	79.2
Parental substance abuse	63.6	70.0	45.8	88.0
Domestic violence	63.6	60.0	41.7	76.0
Parental mental illness	36.4	40.0	37.5	64.0
Physical discipline (e.g., spanking)	45.5	60.0	37.5	60.0
Nonorganic failure to thrive (FTT)	36.4	50.0	37.5	56.0
Child prostitution	100.0	100.0	100.0	96.0
Children living on the street	100.0	100.0	83.3	92.0
Physical beating of a child by any adult	72.7	90.0	83.3	96.0
Forcing a child to beg	63.6	90.0	87.5	84.0
Female/child infanticide	72.7	70.0	82.6	88.0
Child labor	63.6	80.0	70.8	68.0
Abuse by another child	63.6	80.0	62.5	76.0
Children serving as soldiers	60.0	66.7	59.1	50.0
Female circumcision	60.0	60.0	45.0	60.9

This table reflects results from a 2006 mail survey of key informants identified by the International Society for the Prevention of Child Abuse as knowledgeable about child maltreatment issues within their respective countries. The number of informants from each region ranged from 10 (Americas) to 25 (Europe).

variation in the sorts of behaviors that are recognized as abusive (ISPCAN, 2006). Definitional problems arise because what is deemed appropriate and inappropriate treatment of children, including the frequency and severity of physical punishment, varies dramatically from one family and community to the next (Holden, 2002). As noted in Chapter 9, nearly three out of four parents in the United States approve of spanking, a practice that is viewed as unacceptable in countries such as Sweden (see the box "The Spanking Controversy," Chapter 9, p. 320). Clearly, the borders between culturally acceptable physical punishment and physical punishment that is defined as maltreatment depend very much on parents' beliefs about children and the modes of interaction sanctioned in the children's families and communities.

Why do parents abuse their own children? Answers to this question paint a complicated picture. First, there is considerable evidence that parents are more likely to abuse their children if they were themselves victims of child abuse (Bartlett, Kotake, Fauth, & Easterbrooks, 2017). Another major contributor to abuse is stress on the family, including chronic poverty, recent job loss, marital discord, and social isolation (Gordon et al., 2003). The likelihood of abuse is also higher when the mother is very young, is poorly educated, abuses drugs or alcohol, or receives little financial support from the father (U.S. Department of Health and Human Services, 2017).

Any child may be neglected or abused, but some characteristics seem to put certain children at increased risk (U.S. Department of Health & Human Services, 2017). For example, in the United States, infants under the age of 1 are at considerably higher risk compared to other age groups, girls are slightly more likely than boys to be abused, and African American children, followed by American Indian and Alaska Native children, are more likely to experience abuse compared to those from other ethnic backgrounds.

Many scholars who have studied the physical abuse of children in the United States see it as a social disease that accompanies the acceptance of violence by families, local communities, and society at large. Research shows, for instance, that in countries that frown upon physical punishment of children, such as Sweden and Japan, there are very low rates of physical abuse of children (Lansford et al., 2015).

Although adults who have been maltreated as children are more likely to be depressed, abuse drugs and alcohol, have sexual problems, and engage in criminal behavior, nearly one-fourth of maltreated children show no long-term problems (McGloin & Widom, 2001). Factors that seem to buffer children from long-term consequences of abuse include having a warm relationship with at least one adult, having a fairly stable family residence (not moving around a lot), having positive experiences in school, and participating in extracurricular activities (Zielinski & Bradshaw, 2006). The multiple cultural, family, parent, and child factors that operate together in cases of child maltreatment suggest that broad-based, systematic intervention campaigns would offer the best hope for reducing the problem in the long run (Hughes, Graham-Bermann, & Gruber, 2001).

Family Affluence As surprising as it may seem, another family factor that may place children at risk for behavioral and emotional problems is wealth (Racz, McMahon, & Luthar, 2011). Suniya Luthar and Bronwyn Becker (2002) studied middle school students living in one of the most affluent suburban communities in the United States. Their results showed high levels of depression, particularly among girls, as well as high levels of substance abuse. Another study found that children from affluent families were more likely than less affluent peers to be bullies (Shetgiri, Lin, & Flores, 2012). What might cause this pattern of distress among affluent young people? According to the findings, many children of wealth feel themselves to be under a great deal of pressure to achieve—in school,

In the Field

Louisiana Swamp Nurse

Name: **LUWANA MARTS**
Education: B.S. in nursing
Current Position: Nurse visitor for the Nurse–Family Partnership of Louisiana

LUWANA MARTS IS A NURSE WHO WORKS with teen mothers living in a swampy, isolated region southwest of New Orleans. In Louisiana, nearly one in three children are poor, nearly half are born to single mothers, and the proportion of people unable to read or write is among the highest in the nation. Myths about children and their development abound: It is better to feed babies formula than breast milk; babies held by menstruating women will suffer from constipation; brain damage may occur if the baby's hair is cut before the first birthday. In this context, a beautiful young woman named Alexis became pregnant with her first child and became part of Luwana's caseload.

Until her 8th month of pregnancy, Alexis lived with her parents, but their constant fighting became more than she could bear, so she moved out. She made other changes as well. At Luwana's urging, Alexis gave up drinking and smoking, and she began to get regular medical checkups. When her son, Daigan, was born, Luwana visited regularly to educate Alexis about her son's development and how to be a good parent.

At one visit, Alexis told Luwana that she was beginning to recognize that her baby cries a certain way when he is hungry. Luwana praised her for making the distinction: "You're listening. . . . soon now he'll be making other sounds, and when he does you'll want to make that noise right back. He'll babble, and then you'll talk to him, and that's how you'll develop his language."

Explaining that the amount of Daigan's crying would likely increase around 5 to 8 weeks of age, as it does for most infants, Luwana asked Alexis what she would do if the crying ever became frustrating or upsetting. Alexis knew that she should never shake her baby, as this can result in brain damage. With some prompting from Luwana, she also said that she would call someone to help.

On another occasion, Luwana took up the subject of infant attachment, which she skillfully tailored to Alexis's limited education on such matters. She explained "the love link" that babies need to feel in order to have a foundation for trust. To establish the love link, she said that Alexis should satisfy Daigan's needs, provide comfort when he is distressed, and respond to his communications. Luwana explained, "because that's how Daigan is going to learn how to love."

Luwana is part of a growing legion of visiting nurse practitioners whose work is dedicated to helping families raise healthy children. They bring their skills, knowledge, and resources to where they are most needed in the first few years of children's lives: the home. Visiting nurse practitioners focus on improving mothers' prenatal care, educating parents about how to provide sensitive and competent child care, and helping parents plan future pregnancies, complete their education, and find work (Zielinski, Eckenrode, & Olds, 2009). In addition to making intervention programs more accessible to families who are unable or unlikely to attend programs offered elsewhere in the community, home visits provide rich detail about the often-changing characteristics and needs of specific families. Consequently, nurse practitioners are able to individualize their interventions, as well as provide critical feedback regarding program effectiveness.

© Alec Soth/Magnum Photos

Luwana Marts, visiting nurse, with two of her clients.

Research on the effectiveness of visiting nurse programs is mixed (Pinquart & Teubert, 2010). In general, the programs are somewhat effective in promoting positive parenting practices, reducing parents' stress, increasing children's social and cognitive development, and reducing risk for child abuse and children's later criminal behavior, although their effectiveness tends to decline over time in what is commonly described as a "fade-out" effect (Olds, 2006; Pinquart & Teubert, 2010). These modest results apply, of course, only to families that persist in the programs. Sadly, Alexis and Daigan did not. But despite the odds, visiting nurse practitioners such as Luwana continue delivering intervention programs to families in need.

(Information from Katherine Boo, 2006.)

in sports, socially, and financially. They also tend to be isolated from adults and feel emotionally distant from their mothers. Luthar and Becker's study supports recent concerns voiced in the popular press that wealthy families have become overly invested in performance and achievement issues and that their children are suffering as a consequence. Their children's time is overscheduled, especially with activities driven by the need to succeed. Such free time as children do have is often spent in the company of peers who endorse the use of drugs and alcohol as a means of "letting off steam." The study stands as a cautionary note against the assumption that children of means lack for nothing.

It is clear that families have pronounced effects on children's development. In addition to exerting influence through the ways they are structured (nuclear or extended) and the styles of care and interaction they provide, families influence children by linking them to other developmentally important contexts, including nonparental child-care settings.

home child care Child care provided in the child's own home, primarily by a grandmother or other family member, while the parents are at work.

family child care Child care provided in the home of a relative or someone else.

child-care center An organized child-care facility supervised by licensed professionals.

APPLY > CONNECT > DISCUSS

Using Bronfenbrenner's model (Chapter 1, pp. 27–29), analyze the ecology of Alexis and her baby as described in the box about the Louisiana swamp nurse. Describe features of the microsystems, exosystems, mesosystems, and macrosystems. If you lack specific information about the features of a system, try to speculate on the basis of features in the other systems.

Nonparental Child Care

LEARNING OUTCOMES

Distinguish home child care, family child care, and child-care centers as forms of nonparental child care.

Give examples of what constitutes high-quality child care.

Explain some impacts of child care on children's social and emotional development.

Nonparental child care is a fact of life for nearly all children in the United States. In 2012, approximately 60 percent of children between birth and 5 years of age with employed mothers spent some time in nonparental child care (Redford, Desrochers, & Hoyer, 2017). These numbers alone suggest the importance of nonparental child care as a context for young children's development. In this section, we focus on the varieties and general developmental consequences of nonparental care. (In Chapter 12, we will take up the more particular case of academically focused care, such as preschools.)

Varieties of Child Care

One of the most popular child-care arrangements for children younger than 5 years is **home child care**—care provided for children in their own homes, primarily by their grandmothers or other relatives, while their parents are at work. (Nearly half of all children in nonparental care are cared for by other family relatives.) Children cared for at home experience the least change from normal routine: They eat food provided by their parents and take naps in their own beds. They also come in contact with relatively few children their own age.

Child care provided in someone else's home, that of either a relative or nonrelative, is called **family child care**. Family child care often exposes children not only to caretakers from outside the family circle but also to new settings and to children of other families. The children in a family child-care setting may range widely in age, forming a more diverse social group than is likely to exist in the children's own home. The routine of activities in family child care, however, is usually very similar to the routine at home.

Child-care centers—organized child-care facilities supervised by licensed professionals—provide care for 24 percent of children receiving nonparental care and have attracted the most public attention (Rathburn & Zhang, 2016). The programs available vary in style and philosophy. Some offer an academic curriculum,

High-quality child-care centers offer children a variety of educational and social experiences.

E+/Getty Images

Arthur Tilley/Getty Images

Preschool provides an important context for developing "children's culture." Hand-clapping games and ball-tossing, shown here, are examples of the many games and rituals that children learn from each other.

emphasize discipline, and have a school-like atmosphere. Others emphasize social development and allow children to exercise more initiative in their activities. Programs vary widely in quality as well. An important task many parents face is selecting the high-quality child-care facility or preschool that they feel best meets their children's needs. (See Table 10.3 for information that may help parents formulate questions about the quality of a child-care program they may be considering.) Because licensed child-care centers often receive public financing, they have been more accessible than other nonparental care settings to researchers, who have studied both their characteristics and the way these characteristics affect children's development.

Developmental Effects of Child Care

The effects of child care during the first 2 years of life depend primarily on the quality of the care provided and not on the mere fact of parent–child separation during the day. Nevertheless, concerns about the later effects of early child care continue to be raised, primarily regarding children's intellectual development, social development, and emotional well-being.

TABLE 10.3 Characteristics of High Quality Child-Care Centers

Characteristics of the Program

- Licensed by a government office
- Accredited by the National Association for the Education of Young Children or the National Association of Family Child Care
- Provides medical benefits, leave, and professional-development opportunities (conferences and workshops) for caregivers
- Staff-to-child ratio conforms to regulated standards
- Encourages parental involvement through volunteering in classroom, joining parent-teaching association

Characteristics of the Environment

- Safe and sanitary
- Attractive, comfortable lighting, acceptable noise level
- Appropriate accommodations for children with special needs
- Toys, books, and other materials well organized so children can choose what interests them

Characteristics of the Caregivers

- Caregivers certified by relevant professional society, and hold appropriate educational degree credential for infant/toddler caregivers
- Caregivers responsive, showing the following characteristics:
  - Play with the children, and introduce new ideas and games
  - Support children in their social contacts with other children and adults
  - Respect the child's individual development, recognizing strengths and limitations
  - Respect the child's native culture or ethnicity

Information from Zero to Three, 2010.

Physical and Intellectual Effects When children enter care outside the home, they enter a whole new world. There are new routines and expectations, new toys and children to play with, new adults who will provide care and comfort, and, as any parent will tell you—new germs. In fact, children under 3 years of age in care arrangements with more than six other children are at increased risk for upper respiratory infections, gastrointestinal illnesses, and ear infections (de Hoog et al., 2014). Although cold and flu bugs make regular rounds in child-care facilities, and often follow children home to their families, there is no evidence that increased illness takes a toll on children's overall development or school readiness; indeed, effects on the child's immune system may be protective against future illnesses (Hullegie et al., 2016).

Stress is another physical consequence of time spent in child care. A number of studies have found that children's time in child care is associated with higher levels of salivary cortisol, a hormone commonly used to measure stress (Geoffroy, Cote, Parent, & Séguin, 2006; Wagner et al., 2016). In turn, higher level of cortisol have been associated with poorer executive functioning in children in daycare, prompting concern about whether school readiness may be affected by daycare experience (Wagner et al., 2016). Importantly, some research suggests that the levels of cortisol may be influenced by the quality of care, with low-quality day-care conditions resulting in more elevated levels (Geoffroy et al., 2006).

Despite the evidence that children in child care may have higher levels of stress, research conducted in Europe as well as the United States indicates that intellectual development of children in high-quality child-care centers is at least as good as that of children raised at home by their parents (Campbell et al., 2001; Jaffee, Van Hulle, & Rodgers, 2011). For children of low SES, being in a high-quality child-care program can lessen or prevent the decline in intellectual performance that is sometimes seen in their counterparts who remain at home after the age of 2 and whose parents are poorly educated (Dearing, McCartney, & Taylor, 2009). The caregivers' level of training, as well as appropriate child-to-staff ratios are of special importance to the quality of child-care centers (Auger et al., 2014).

Impact on Social and Emotional Development Children who attend child-care centers tend to be more self-sufficient and more independent of parents and teachers, more verbally expressive, more knowledgeable about the social world, and more comfortable in new situations than are children who do not attend child-care centers. They are also more enthusiastic about sharing toys and participating in fantasy play. This development of greater social competence is not simply a matter of the children's learning how to get along by interacting with a variety of playmates. Caregivers play a crucial role as well. Children's social play and peer interactions become more complex and skilled when they are monitored and facilitated by warm, responsive caregivers (NICHD, 2003).

By attending Head Start, a federally funded preschool program, these preschoolers from low-income families acquire learning skills and attitudes designed to help them succeed in school in the years ahead.

© Octavio Jones/Tampa Bay Times/ZUMAPRESS.com

Not all the social and emotional effects of child care are positive, however. A longitudinal study followed 1,544 Canadian children from 5 months of age through their years of elementary school (Pingault et al., 2015). Children who received nonparental care, mostly in the form of center care, were more oppositional and more aggressive when they entered school at 6 years of age than those who did not receive nonparental care. However, the differences disappeared as children who received exclusive parental care caught up to those who had spent time in nonparental care settings, likely due to the fact that interacting with larger groups of peers provided more opportunities for the expression of oppositional and aggressive behaviors.

Other developmentalists have reasoned that the quality, not the quantity, of child-center care exerts the biggest influence on children's adjustment. For example, a controlled study of children from low-income families (who would be expected to be at special risk for behavioral problems) found that those who received high-quality child care benefited in many ways and had fewer aggressive behavior problems than did similar children who received lesser-quality care (Love et al., 2003).

Next we turn to research that goes well beyond the typical focus on parental versus nonparental child care. In particular, this research calls attention to the ways in which other features of the ecology—the neighborhood and the community and its culture—contribute to how children experience and adapt to different contexts of care.

APPLY > CONNECT > DISCUSS

Imagine that you are preparing to have or adopt your first baby, and you are trying to figure out when to return to work. To help you decide, outline the arguments for and against enrolling your baby in a child-care center. Based on the evidence of your arguments, what do you decide to do?

LEARNING OUTCOMES

Identify ways in which neighborhoods and communities provide social capital for families and children.

Point out how economic disadvantages, physical disorder, and social disorganization affect the well-being of families and children.

Neighborhoods and Communities

As children mature, their spheres of action expand beyond the microsystem settings of home and child care to include other developmentally important microsystem settings within the neighborhood and community. From the ecological perspective that we have been emphasizing throughout this chapter, these microsystem settings not only influence each other but also can be affected by other systems—for example, by local politics and the mass media (elements of the exosystem), as well as by the dominant beliefs and values of the culture (elements of the macrosystem).

Neighborhoods and communities differ substantially in the resources they provide to children and families, including whom they interact with, the activities they engage in, the health services available to them, and even the food they eat. Researchers use the term **social capital** to refer to such resources, which also include a community's social structures, its expectations for behavior, and the levels of trust and cooperation of its members (Wu, 2017). These features of social capital are associated with children's quality of life and mental health outcomes (Frissen et al., 2015).

social capital The resources that communities provide children and families, including not only schools, health services, and so on, but also social structures, expectations for behavior, and levels of trust and cooperation among community members.

Community and Culture

Like families and other child-care settings, communities play an important role in transmitting the values and beliefs of culture. An excellent illustration of this is provided by Donna Marie San Antonio's (2004) study of children from two neighboring but vastly different communities in the rural northeastern United States. One community, Hillside, is a working-class community with one of the lowest levels of education and median family income in the state. The other, Lakeview, is more affluent, a white-collar community built around a thriving tourist industry. Beyond social class differences, San Antonio found that the two communities have profoundly divergent perspectives on what constitutes a good life and how to secure it for one's children. For example, the people of Hillside cherish tradition, community, and family ties, with social status being determined "more by social and civic connections than by material wealth" (p. 87). In contrast, the people of Lakeview embrace the values of independence, family privacy, achievement, and upward mobility. San Antonio's study revealed that these two very different sets of beliefs and values are reflected in children's language and social interaction. Her observations of the children's behavior as she rode with them on school buses make the point:

> [On Lakeview buses], most students spaced out in separate seats. Students were polite, but I was not drawn into conversations as I was on the Hillside–Two Rivers buses. The words spoken between students [on the Lakeview buses] seemed fragmented; they were not conversations I could follow. Conversations between friends sitting together were whispered privately. In some instances, the communication seemed intended for power and position rather than for peer connection. On the Hillside bus, I heard students talk to each other in whole sentences—they included others, they said hello and good-bye to each other; on the Lakeview buses, I had an entirely different experience. (p. 170)

San Antonio's observations demonstrate how the values and beliefs of communities are expressed in children's behaviors and interactions. As we emphasized in Chapter 2, culture affects children's development so profoundly precisely because it is rooted in the everyday activities of families and peers.

Distressed Communities

Jasmine's elementary school is just two short blocks from her home. Nevertheless, her mother walks her back and forth each day because she worries about Jasmine's safety. The street and sidewalk between the steps of their small row house and the school is strewn with litter and garbage; a street intersection they have to cross is a hang-out for mean-looking older kids who harass passersby for spare change. A few weeks ago, a boy was shot and killed in front of the school—an innocent victim caught in the crossfire of a drug-related shootout. How will Jasmine be affected by growing up in such a neighborhood?

The past several years have seen an explosion in research on the impact that distressed neighborhoods and communities have on children's development (Habibi, Sarkissian, Gomez, & Ilari, 2015). This work has focused on economic disadvantage and physical and social disorder.

Economic Disadvantage

You know from our previous discussion that children growing up in poverty-stricken families often suffer a variety of health, intellectual, social, and emotional problems. As you also know, most poverty-stricken families live in economically disadvantaged neighborhoods, which themselves contribute risk factors, including lack of decent housing and health care services, lack of grocery stores with fresh fruits and vegetables, and lack of recreational facilities. Plagued by excessive noise, crowding, and street traffic, economically disadvantaged neighborhoods generally have few parks or natural settings where children can play.

Research on communities indicates that neighborhood economic disadvantage profoundly affects children's development and well-being, over and above the effects of the income levels of their families. For example, a number of studies show that low-SES children living in substandard housing are at greater risk for emotional and academic problems, get sick and injured more often, and

The ways that families cope with economic misfortune can dramatically affect their children's risk for developmental problems. If the children living here are cared for as well as their beautiful garden suggests, they may escape many of the usual consequences of poverty.

Gideon Mendel/Getty Images

Busà Photography/Getty Images

Tony Savino/The Image Works

These two neighborhoods, both in New York, demonstrate the stark differences between clean and organized physical environments and those that are disordered and deteriorating.

miss more school compared with low-SES children living in better housing (Evans, 2006). Not surprisingly, children show significant improvements in school when their families move from substandard to better-quality housing.

Physical and Social Disorder In addition to their poor economic conditions, distressed neighborhoods and communities are often ugly, congested, and confusing. One problem associated with such conditions is referred to as **neighborhood physical disorder**, which includes both *physical deterioration*, such as abandoned buildings and cars, garbage on the streets, broken windows, and graffiti on buildings, and *chaotic activity*, such as crowding, heavy street traffic, and high noise levels. Overall, children growing up in physically disordered environments are at risk for a variety of developmental problems. Compared with their peers in nondisordered environments, they are more likely to do poorly in school, be easily frustrated, have less motivation to master difficult tasks, and suffer health problems such as being overweight (Slater et al., 2010; Zuberi & Teixeira, 2017).

neighborhood physical disorder A problem in distressed communities that includes both physical deterioration (garbage on the streets, rundown buildings, etc.) and chaotic activity (crowding, high noise levels, etc.).

Another problem associated with the conditions of distressed neighborhoods is **social disorganization** (Riina, Martin, & Brooks-Gunn, 2014), which includes weak *social cohesion* (the sense of trust and connection between people), poor *neighborhood climate* (the level of fear related to crime and violence), and *perceived racism*. Social disorganization is associated with poor parent–child relationships, reduced parental warmth, and higher levels of parent–child conflict.

social disorganization A problem in distressed communities that includes weak social cohesion (lack of trust and connection among community members), poor neighborhood climate (fear related to crime and violence), and perceived racism.

Although most studies of physical and social disorganization have been conducted in North America, the effects of chaotic environments on children's development and well-being can be found everywhere. Recently, researchers have turned their attention to a particularly troubling source of community disorganization that affects children in many parts of the world: the disruptive and destructive consequences of war (see the box "Now Trending in Practice: Children and War").

APPLY > CONNECT > DISCUSS

A newly elected mayor campaigned on promises to tackle the problems affecting a distressed community in his city. He has put you in charge of a task force and wants you to develop a plan for reducing social disorganization. Generate a list of possible community programs that you think might help reduce social disorganization and explain why and how they would improve the lives of children in the community.

Now TRENDING in PRACTICE

Children and War

POLITICAL VIOLENCE HAS BEEN IDENTIFIED as a major risk that threatens the lives and well-being of children around the globe (Daiute, 2016; Wainryb, 2010). A United Nations General Security Council (2011) report catalogs a list of horrifying traumas and rights violations suffered by children and their families. Children are recruited as soldiers and forced to commit murder and other atrocities (including suicide bombings); they are exposed to disease and malnutrition when they are forced to flee their homes or while living in refugee camps; their access to education and health care is severely curtailed due to relocation, or because their schools and hospitals have been destroyed; children are injured, permanently disabled, or killed in conflict, often intentionally, sometimes by stumbling on unexploded land mines; they are raped and otherwise exploited sexually; they witness the murder of family members and neighbors; and they are orphaned.

In light of these horrors, it is not surprising that children exposed to war often show symptoms of traumatic stress, including irritability, sleep difficulties, separation anxiety, depression, and nightmares (Cummings et al., 2017; Klasen et al., 2010; Moussa et al., 2015). However, studies on the long-term effects of war on children present a complex picture. While some children suffer greatly, becoming depressed and developing psychosocial problems, many others appear to be relatively resilient and cope reasonably well in everyday life (Betancourt et al., 2010; Veronese et al., 2017). In trying to identify the factors that may contribute to children's successful coping with the traumas of war, developmentalists have focused on two particular factors—quality of parenting and the cultural traditions in which the child develops.

The importance of parenting in helping children cope with the devastations of war has been suggested by parenting-intervention programs especially designed for wartime conditions. Because of the significant stress warfare places on families, parenting may deteriorate, with parents often becoming less emotionally supportive in their interactions with their children (Murphy, Rodrigues, Costigan, & Annan, 2017). Intervention programs focused on supporting good parenting skills in the face of wartime conditions have been shown to benefit children's adjustment and overall well-being. In one study, mothers and children who were refugees from the Bosnian War in the 1990s were randomly assigned either to a control group or to an experimental group that was counseled on the importance of emotionally responsive communication with their children and of providing an emotionally warm and supportive environment (Dybdahl, 2001). (The war experiences faced by the parents and children who participated in the study are shown in the table.) Compared with the control group, mothers in the experimental group showed fewer trauma symptoms and greater life satisfaction. On the basis of the mothers' reports, the children of mothers in the experimental group appeared less anxious and sad and had fewer nightmares compared with the children whose mothers were in the control group. In addition, they gained more weight, showed higher levels of improvement on tests of cognitive reasoning, and perceived their mothers as more emotionally supportive.

War Experiences of Children and Families Participating in Parenting Program

Type of Event	*n*	%
Had to flee from my home	76	100
Thought I would die	70	92
Experienced war activities	68	90
Been shot at	64	84
Separated from close family	57	75
Family members missing	50	66
Family members wounded	49	65
Serious food deprivation	48	63
Saw dead bodies of victims	46	61
Family members killed	44	58
Witnessed home destroyed	23	30
Forced to do things against own will	22	29
Witnessed torture	17	22
Wounded	16	21
Abused, tortured	9	12
Been in concentration camp	6	8

Data were collected during the war in Bosnia and Herzegovina (1992–1995); $n = 76$.
Republished with permission of John Wiley & Sons, Inc. From "Children and mothers in war: An outcome study of the psychosocial intervention program," in *Child Development*, by Dybdahl, R., 72, 1214–1230, 2001. Permission conveyed through Copyright Clearance Center, Inc.

PA Images/Alamy

Children who experience the horrors of war firsthand often show psychological symptoms that are similar to those associated with posttraumatic stress disorder (PTSD).

Christophe Calais/Getty Images

One of the most disturbing ways that children become victims of war is by being recruited into armies and other militant groups as armed combatants.

Cultural traditions can also help children cope with the trauma of war. An example of this is provided in studies of child soldiers (Honwana, 2000; Summerfield, 1999). In many African nations torn by war over the years—including Zimbabwe, Mozambique, Angola, and Ethiopia—children have been recruited to fight. Part of the process of their recovering from the emotional effects of war involves participating in ritualized cleansing ceremonies. In contrast to Western traditions that view dealing with trauma as a personal matter, African traditions view it as a process that involves the entire community. Thus, when child soldiers return home from fighting, they must undergo ceremonies that symbolically purge them of the contaminating ancestral spirits of their victims, which would otherwise spread from the soldiers to the entire social body (Honwana, 2000). The children are forbidden to speak of their war experiences, since this would "open a door" for the harmful spirits to infect the community. Instead, the former child soldiers proclaim a complete break from the past, often burning anything associated with their role as warriors, and through reintegration rituals, they are welcomed back into their community of origin.

LEARNING OUTCOMES

Explain the relationship between literature and children's emotional development.

Point out concerns about the effects of television content on children.

Give examples of interactive media and their effects on children's cognitive skills as well as their thinking and behavior.

media Forms of mass communication, including newspapers, magazines, books, comic books, radio, television, films, video games, and the Internet.

Media Contexts

The term **media** refers to forms of mass communication, such as newspapers, books, magazines, comic books, radio, television, film, video games, and the Internet. Needless to say, children in technologically advanced societies are immersed in modern communications media to a staggering degree. As you can see from Figure 10.9, children spend considerable amounts of time using media, especially between the ages of 11 and 14, when media use occupies an astonishing 8½ hours on a typical day (Rideout, Foehr, & Roberts, 2010). What children see on TV, read in books, and learn from video games influences their behavior in other contexts. Research from Germany, Israel, South Korea, and the United States indicates that children across cultures take themes and characters from media and fold them into their play and make-believe worlds (Gotz, Lemish, Aidman, & Moon, 2005). Concerns about how children are affected by media are apparent in movie ratings and television V-chips and in the way parents worry about their children's vulnerability to everything from nightmares induced by fairy tales to Internet sexual predators.

Research on how the various media affect children's development focuses on two general issues. The first concerns whether the *physical form* of the medium affects development. For example, could the vivid images on television confuse young children regarding differences between reality and make-believe? Does excessive Internet use contribute to social isolation from one's peers and interfere with developing social skills? The second issue concerns whether the *content* of the medium affects development. Does Mr. Rogers really teach children that "you are special; you are the only one like you"? Does a steady diet of violent television teach children that aggression is an appropriate way to solve problems?

It is clear from the nature of these questions that considerable controversy surrounds the subject of media effects on children. Below we outline the controversies as they have surfaced in research on the effects of print media, television, and interactive media.

Print Media

Children's exposure to print media—books, comics, magazines, and newspapers—is relatively small and fairly stable throughout childhood compared with their exposure to the other media forms. Although children with more books in the home,

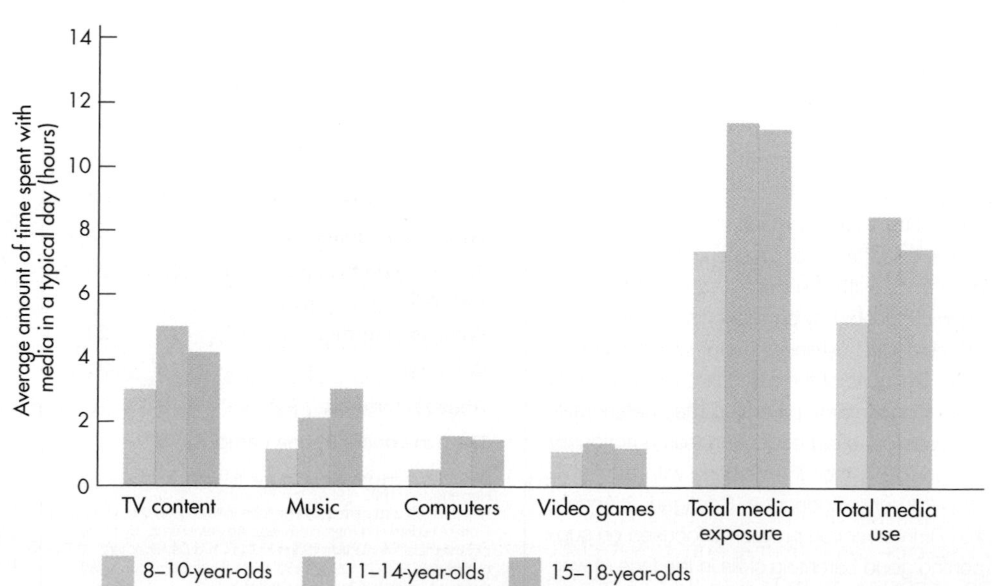

FIGURE 10.9 As shown here, media exposure between the ages of 8 and 18 varies according to the type of media, with television being the most common. It also varies according to the age of the child, with 11- to 14-year-old children being the most frequent users overall. (Data from Rideout, Foehr, & Roberts, 2010.)

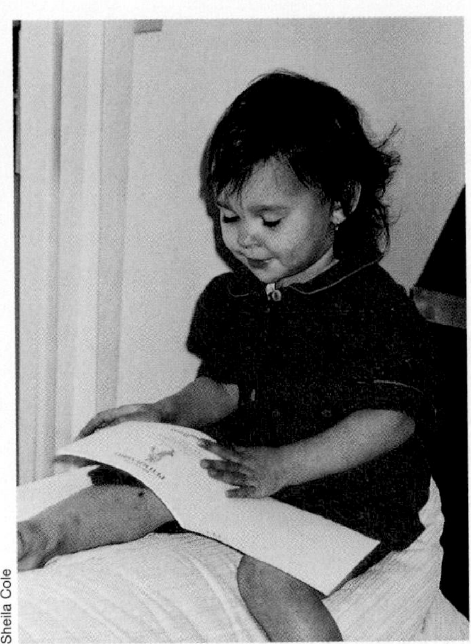
Sheila Cole

Learning to read involves understanding how to hold a book and turn pages and what to look for on the page.

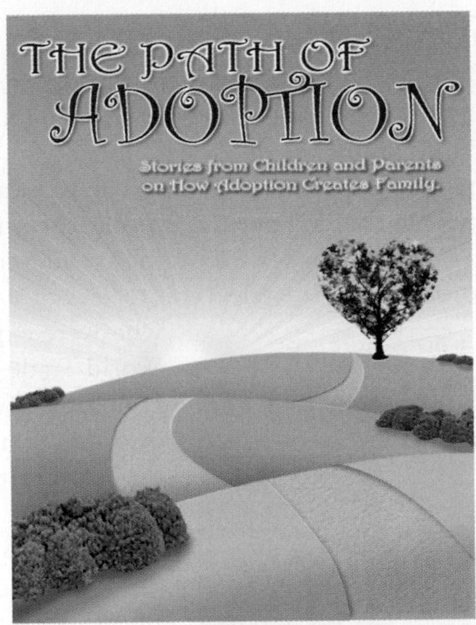

One common purpose of children's books is to help parents discuss significant family events and experiences, such as adoption.

who also read more frequently, tend to use other forms of media less frequently, and because young children typically prefer electronic over print media, we can reasonably conclude that many children read, or are read to, just about every day (Duursma, Meijer, & deBot, 2017; Natsiopoulou & Bletsou, 2011). Certainly, this is consistent with the fact that children's literature is a growing multimillion-dollar industry. In general, developmentalists have approached children's literature from two directions. One direction, which we examine in Chapter 12, considers children's literature as a means of fostering intellectual development and "school readiness"—in particular, the development of language, reading, and writing skills. The other direction, which we examine here, explores why certain types of literature—adventures, mysteries, fantasies, and fairy tales, in particular—appeal to children and what functions they may serve in children's emotional development (Riquelme & Montero, 2013).

One of the most famous analyses of the role of fairy tales in children's emotional development is that of the psychoanalyst Bruno Bettelheim (1977). Noting that many fairy tales include symbolic representations of universal childhood anxieties, such as abandonment and aggression, Bettleheim argued that children need fairy tales in order to find solutions to their own inner conflicts and fears. Consider, for example, Maurice Sendak's wonderful tale *Where the Wild Things Are*. If you read this book, you may remember that naughty Max is sent to his room, where he imagines sailing to an enchanted land and becoming king of the wild things. From a psychoanalytic perspective, the story traces Max's feelings of anger and aggression as they are projected into the forms of imaginary "wild things." When Max masters his emotions—that is, tames and becomes king of the wild things—he returns to the reality of his room, his mother, and his dinner, which is, comfortingly, "still hot."

In addition to serving as a tool of emotional control and development, children's literature has been used as a therapeutic device to help children cope with and communicate about a variety of emotionally troubling events, such as divorce, illness, death, and even the birth of a sibling (Arruda-Colli, Weaver, & Wiener, 2017).

Whether intended to delight, instruct, or comfort, children's literature reflects a centuries-old cultural belief that children's thoughts and emotions can be affected by exposure to specific types of print media.

Television

In 2001, television screens throughout the world, but especially in the United States, were full of images showing airplanes slicing into the Twin Towers on 9/11, plumes of smoke, and the towers collapsing into clouds of dust. TVs showed people leaping from 80 floors up to escape the inferno and of the streets filled with people running in panic, or sitting, confused or hurt, on sidewalk curbs. There was a flurry of concern about how children might be harmed by viewing—over and over again—the television replays of 9/11. In fact, research suggests that children who were exposed to extensive television replays of the World Trade Center attack were more likely to show symptoms of separation anxiety and posttraumatic stress disorder than were children who had less television exposure to the event (Gershoff & Aber, 2004; Hoven et al., 2004).

Bill Clark/Getty Images

The Muppet Julia is a newcomer to the cast of *Sesame Street*. With red hair and bright green eyes, she's a bit shy and loves to paint and pick flowers. She also has autism spectrum disorder.

Television is powerful. It communicates information, sways opinions, and moves viewers emotionally. And, clearly, young children are exposed more to television than to any other medium. Between birth and 6 years of age, children watch nearly 1 hour of television each day, while between ages 8 and 10, the amount of viewing time jumps to just under 4 hours per day. Extensive research has focused on television as a potentially positive or destructive influence on children's development.

Television Form

> The Count von Count: (with a bad Transylvanian accent) I am the Count, and I *love* to count. Today I will count my bats. I see *one* bat. Now I see *two* bats. Now there is another. That makes how many bats?
>
> Tens of thousands of children watching the Count on TV respond as one: *Three bats!!!!*
>
> The Count: Yes! There are *three bats.*

Before asking how television viewing affects children's thoughts, feelings, and behavior, it is necessary to understand how children make sense of television sounds, images, and plots. For example, a special concern about television viewing is that young children easily confuse TV make-believe and reality. Consistent with our earlier discussion of preoperational thinking (see Chapter 8, p. 268), research suggests that young children have difficulty understanding the reality status of what they see on TV—whether what they see can "really" happen or is make-believe (Li, Boguszewski, & Lillard, 2015; Mares & Sivakumar, 2014). Even 4- and 5-year-olds may display such difficulty, believing that Sesame Street is a real place or that television characters can see and hear the people who are watching them. This no doubt contributes to the enthusiasm with which young children enter into conversations with TV characters such as the Count and to how special they may really feel when Daniel Tiger looks them right in the eye and invites them in to his home to meet his loving family.

In addition to problems distinguishing between appearance and reality, young children often fail to comprehend what they watch, especially if understanding requires linking together fast-paced scenes (Juston, Bickham, Lee, & Wright, 2007). Consequently, they may fail to appreciate the overarching meaning of a

TV story, not recognizing, for example, that the point of a typical police drama is that even if a character's bad behavior results in short-term gains, it does not pay off in the long run. Problems understanding the relationship between one scene and another may also contribute to the difficulty children have distinguishing between television programs and advertisements. Indeed, not until they are 7 or 8 years of age do children both distinguish between TV programs and advertisements and appreciate the persuasive intent of the latter (Calvert, 2008; Gunter, Oates, & Blades, 2005). Concerns that children who do not understand the persuasive intent of advertising may be highly susceptible to it have led some countries, including Sweden, to ban television advertising to children under the age of 12 (Bjurström, 1994).

vario images, Inh. Susanne Baumgarten e.K. / Alamy

Television remains the most popular form of media among children.

Television Content Television exposes children to a great range of content. The Count teaches counting; Mr. Rogers counsels on the importance of caring for others; cartoon characters meet violent ends (sometimes more than once); popular dramas, as well as the evening news, depict sexuality, violence, and aggression but also empathy and tenderness. For decades, developmentalists have been deeply interested in how television content affects children's behavior, attitudes, and development—both positively and negatively.

Violence. The aggressive and violent content of children's television in the United States has received considerable attention from researchers, as well as from society at large. Nearly 70 percent of children's television shows contain acts of physical aggression, averaging 14 violent acts per hour, compared with fewer than 4 in programming not aimed at children (Wilson et al., 2002). Researchers estimate that by age 18, children have witnessed 200,000 acts of television violence and 16,000 television murders. To be sure, a large portion of these images are in the form of cartoons, in which the likes of Road Runner and Wile E. Coyote commit mayhem on each other, only to recover miraculously to fight another day. But there is a great deal of graphic and realistic violence as well.

Research conducted in numerous countries indicates that the amount of exposure to violent television predicts later problems, including both acting aggressively with peers and being victimized by bullies (Coker et al., 2015; Pagani, Levesque-Seck, & Fitzpatrick, 2016). But studies also find considerable verbal and relational aggression in popular children's programs (Martin & Wilson, 2012). Often, the perpetrators of these forms of aggression are attractive, likable characters—ones who children may be more inclined to identify with and imitate.

As we have pointed out on many occasions, children are not passive recipients of what goes on around them but actively select and interpret particular messages and information from their environments, including their television sets. This was demonstrated by Jamie Ostrov and his colleagues, who conducted a longitudinal study of 78 preschoolers whose parents reported on their children's three favorite TV and video shows and assessed how violent and how educational the shows were (Ostrov, Gentile, & Crick, 2006). For this group of children, who were from families of relatively high SES, educational shows (mostly from PBS) were significantly preferred over violent shows. Interestingly, teachers and observers rated the children who watched the most television as engaging in more prosocial behaviors than children who watched less. Furthermore, although no gender differences were found in the type of programs watched by boys and girls, results suggested that boys and girls were learning different behaviors from the shows. In particular, for boys, greater exposure to violent shows predicted higher levels of future physical, verbal, and relational aggression. In girls, however, higher levels of exposure to violent shows were associated only with future verbal aggression. On the basis of this gender difference, the researchers speculated that boys and girls might be keying in on different forms of aggression depicted on TV. Additional support for this idea comes from the provocative finding that high levels of exposure to educational shows predict future relational aggression in girls but not in boys. These results suggest that even educational programs may be exposing children to relational aggression and, further, that gender socialization processes may be influencing how the content of television affects children's behavior (see Chapter 9, pp. 317–318, to review gender socialization in young children).

Social Stereotypes. Another area of special concern to researchers and society is the social stereotypes in children's television programming, especially the stereotypes pertaining to gender and to ethnic minorities.

Regarding gender stereotyping, throughout the history of television in North America, the people who dominate the television screen have tended to be strong, powerful, and resourceful European American men, with women playing more passive and less visible roles. Although this is changing to some extent, gender stereotypes remain, even in children's programming. For example, a study of the gender content of such favorites as *Drake and Josh*, *Hannah Montana*, *iCarly*, and *Wizards of Waverly Place* indicates that boy characters commonly target girls' appearance and sexuality, with statements such as "Hey, baby!" and "You're hot!" and girl characters often dress provocatively and act coy to impress boys (Kirsch & Murnen, 2015). Gender stereotypes also abound in music videos, and studies indicate that adolescents who watch a lot of music videos tend to hold more traditional attitudes toward gender roles than do peers who are less frequent viewers (van Oosten, Peter, & Valkenburg, 2015).

In light of the changing demographics of American society, developmentalists have become increasingly interested in TV ethnic stereotypes and their impact on the multicultural awareness of children. Research examining the presence and characteristics of ethnic-minority television characters finds ample evidence of negative stereotyping. Ethnic minorities tend to be underrepresented on network television programs, and when they do appear on the screen, they are more often depicted as behaving immorally than are White characters (Monk-Turner et al., 2010). The misrepresentation of ethnic minorities on television is of concern because it may both create or maintain negative attitudes toward minority groups and influence young minority children's attitudes about their own group and place in society.

Interactive Media

Although television continues to claim the lion's share of children's leisure time, interactive media, in which the actions of the user—clicking the mouse, turning the joystick, tapping the keyboard—are closing in quickly. The new media are appealing to children because of both their form and their content, and as you will see, many of the issues and controversies surrounding children's television viewing loom equally large in the case of children's use of interactive media.

The Form of Interactive Media From your own experience, you probably have a good sense of how exciting and mentally challenging playing interactive video games can be. The amazing special effects of computer games provide children with highly sophisticated cartoonlike scenes that they can interact with, controlling the characters' actions and engaging in active problem solving at the same time. In general, computer games call upon a number of cognitive skills, including divided attention, spatial imagery, and representation (Subrahmanyam & Renukarya, 2015).

Purepix / Alamy

The ability to use technology is considered key to success in an increasingly wired world, so many government and nongovernment organizations have special projects intended to increase children's access to technology. These boys are using a laptop in their rural village in India.

In addition to stimulating cognitive and intellectual processes, interactive media can stimulate emotional responses beyond excitement in children.

One concern about new media technologies—games, as well as e-mail, text messaging, blogging, and so forth—is how they affect relationships with peers. It has been suggested, for example, that spending time on a machine necessarily cuts into time that otherwise would be spent interacting with friends. However, research does not entirely support this concern. Indeed, studies indicate that Internet communication is positively related to both the number and quality of adolescent friendships, perhaps because it encourages a form of behavior long associated with intimacy: self-disclosure (Valkenburg & Peter, 2007). In addition, social media use may be especially helpful for children who have trouble with social relationships, such as those with autism spectrum disorder (van Schalkwyk, Ortiz-Lopez, Volkmar, & Silverman, 2016).

Another concern is about the ways that new interactive media affect family relationships. An early study found that new computer games brought families together for shared play and interaction (Mitchell, 1985). However, now that games and computers are common, and children are often more knowledgeable than their parents about how to operate them, such sharing may be less frequent (Subrahmanyam & Šmahel, 2011). Indeed, most parents are fairly ignorant about the interactive games that appeal to their children, perhaps because many games, including "Bloody Days," "Sniper Assassin 2," and "Beat Me Up," are available free on computers, tablets, and cell phones, and children play them away from the watchful eyes of parents. Despite all the public controversy over violent video games, one national survey found that only 17 percent of parents check their children's video game ratings (Rideout, Roberts, & Foehr, 2005), and only 30 percent set rules about the type of video games their children are allowed to play (Rideout, Foehr, & Roberts, 2010).

Children's literature is recognized by parents and developmentalists alike as a tool for children's developing emotional control.

"I can't protect you from everything, but I can read you stories that make you believe I can protect you from everything."

Peter C. Vey The New Yorker Collection/The Cartoon Bank

The Content of Interactive Media As with television, developmentalists and parents alike worry about how children may be affected by the aggressive content of many video games (Bushman, Gollwitzer, & Cruz, 2015). For the most part, research finds strong support for the conclusion that violent video game play is associated with increased aggression and antisocial behavior. One study of more than 5,000 fifth-graders and their parents in the United States found that children with higher levels of violent video game play were more likely that those who played less to engage in problem behaviors (Coker et al., 2015).

As video games become increasingly graphic, explicit, and realistic, they may have stronger and broader effects on children's behavior (Comstock & Scharrer, 2007). For example, in addition to their association with aggression and antisocial behavior, violent video games would appear to affect children's perceptions of real-world crime. For instance, a study of more than 300 Flemish third- through sixth-graders found that children who played a lot of violent video games tended to overestimate the amount of violent crime occurring in the real world (Van Mierlo & Van den Bulck, 2004). This finding contributes to the concern that repeated exposure to video game violence may desensitize children to actual violence, making it seem normal and acceptable and reducing children's capacity to respond empathically to the emotional distress of others (Funk, Baldacci, Pasold, & Baumgardner, 2004). Although this concern about the effects of repeated exposure arises with other violent media as well, it is heightened in the case of interactive media because children are actively and constantly making violent choices and being rewarded (receiving more points, getting to the next level) for making these choices.

All told, research on the effects of media on children's development paints a consistent, if complex, picture. Children are immersed in media, and the media can have pronounced effects on how and what children think and feel. At the same time, however, children are active agents in the process; their individual differences and preferences shape how they are affected.

APPLY > CONNECT > DISCUSS

Some argue that exposure to violent and aggressive interactive games causes children to be more aggressive. Others believe that such games are a symptom, not a cause, of the fact that our species and/or society is inherently aggressive and that children's exposure to these games is unlikely to make much difference. What is your own position on this classic chicken-or-egg debate? What evidence supports your position?

LEARNING OUTCOMES

Identify risk factors as well as protective factors that help determine the resilience of children.

Appraise various institutions—from the United Nations to individual governments—in their efforts to advance children's development.

Looking Ahead

Questions about the impact of different contexts on children's development are motivated by a desire to protect children from harm and to promote their health and well-being. In recent years, a new area of research called **prevention science** has emerged to examine the biological and social processes that lead to maladjustment, as well as those that are associated with healthy development (Bradshaw, 2015; Shonkoff & Fisher, 2013).

prevention science An area of research that examines the biological and social processes that lead to maladjustment as well as those that are associated with healthy development.

risk factors Personal characteristics or environmental circumstances that increase the probability of negative outcomes for children. Risk is a statistic that applies to groups, not individuals.

Developmentalists working within this field are particularly interested in identifying **risk factors**—personal characteristics or environmental circumstances that increase the probability of negative outcomes for children. Risk is a statistic that applies to groups, not individuals. One can say, for example, that children who have parents who are depressed are more likely than the general population to become depressed themselves, but one cannot say that a particular child whose father or mother is depressed is necessarily at risk for becoming depressed. Most risk factors are not the direct cause of the developmental problems or disorders with which they are associated but, instead, interact in complex ways with other risk factors in contributing to a problem (Shonkoff & Fischer, 2013). For example, having a poorly educated mother is a risk factor for school failure—but not a cause of it. Rather, if a child with a poorly educated mother is failing in school, despite being of normal intelligence, the failure can be seen as a large puzzle in which one piece is the mother's lack of education and of familiarity with the demands of school (for example, the need for the child to spend time at home studying), with other pieces, possibly including a peer group that does not value academic achievement, a school with limited resources due to its location in an economically distressed community, and other risk factors such as poor nutrition and exposure to environmental pollutants.

Many studies have demonstrated that most serious developmental problems are associated with a combination of biological, social, and environmental risk factors interacting over a considerable period of time (Cicchetti, 2016; Kochanska, Kim, & Boldt, 2015; Nigg, 2016). Thus, an increase in the number of risk factors increases the likelihood of problems; see Figure 10.10 for a related example involving academic achievement. However, all of these studies have also demonstrated marked individual differences in outcomes among children who live in highly stressful circumstances. Many children who grow up in the face of adversity—who are raised by alcoholic parents, attend substandard schools, have siblings who belong to gangs, experience dislocation due to war or homelessness due to poverty—are able to rise above their circumstances and lead healthy, productive lives. That is, they seem to have **resilience**—the ability to recover quickly from the adverse effects of early experience or to persevere in the face of stress with no apparent negative psychological consequences. Such cases have led developmentalists to search for the sources of children's resilience, referred to as **protective factors** (Ernestus & Prelow, 2015; Lin & Seo, 2017).

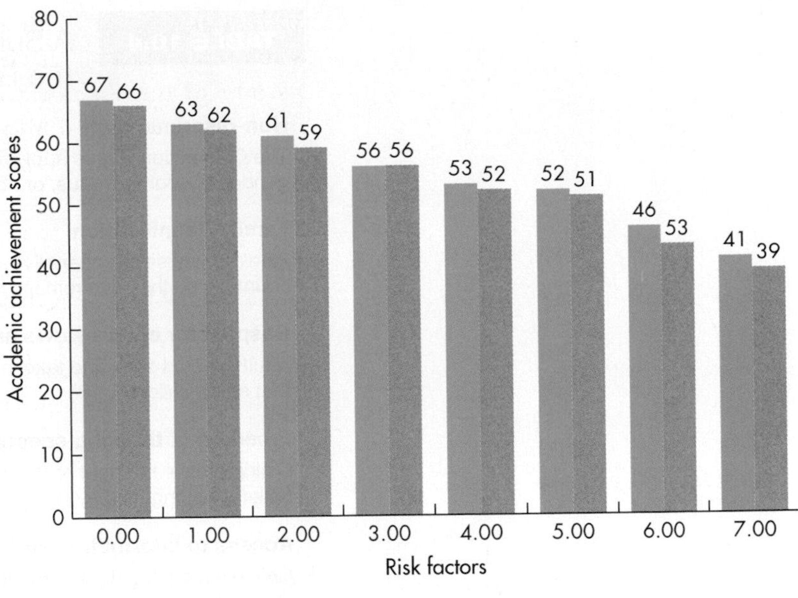

FIGURE 10.10 The consequences of risk are cumulative, such that children's academic achievement scores decline in proportion to the number of risk factors children experience. (Data from Ragnarsdottir, L., Kristjansson, A., Thorisdottir, I., Allegrante, J., Valdimarsdottir, H., Gestsdottir, S., & Sigfusdottir, I. [2017]. Cumulative risk over the early life course and its relation to academic achievement in childhood and early adolescence. *Preventive Medicine*, 96, 36-41. P. 39.)

resilience The ability to recover quickly from the adverse effects of early experience or persevere in the face of stress with no apparent special negative psychological consequences.

protective factors Environmental and personal factors that are the source of children's resilience in the face of hardship.

At this point, you are well aware of how children's development can be impaired by risks present in family, community, and media contexts. When children are harmed by social chaos, poverty, abuse, hunger, or disease, responsible adults look for ways to reduce their suffering. This is, in fact, the goal of prevention science. A question that reaches deeply to address this goal is: What fundamental needs must be met to assure that children will develop into healthy, well-adjusted adults? In an effort to answer this question, the General Assembly of the United Nations in 1959 produced a document called the "United Nations Declaration of the Rights of the Child" (see Table 10.4, p. 364). This document reflected governments' recognition of the importance of coming together for the sake of protecting and nurturing the world's children (Colon, Colon, & Colon, 2001). The declaration was followed, in 1989, by the "United Nations Convention on the Rights of the Child," a binding resolution to provide children with specific protections. As of this writing, it has been ratified by all countries except the United States.

In addition to international organizations such as the United Nations, individual governments have worked to develop programs to optimize children's development. **Public policies** are governmental laws and programs designed to promote the welfare of children and families. In the United States, public policies range from nutritional and education programs such as Women, Infants, and Children (WIC) and Head Start to policies regarding children's television programming and advertising and laws that govern the age at which children can be employed, married, vote, admitted to military service, or required to attend school.

public policies Governmental laws and programs designed to promote the welfare of children and families.

TABLE 10.4 A Summary of the United Nations Convention on the Rights of the Child

Non-discrimination
The Convention Rights apply to all children, whatever their race, religion, culture, language, gender, economic status, or abilities.

Family Reunification
Families whose members live in different countries should be allowed to move between those countries so they can remain in contact, or be reunited as a family.

Respect for child's views and opinions
Adults should seek and take into account children's opinions and ideas when making decisions that affect children.

Freedom of thought, speech, and religion
Children have the right to think and believe what they want, and to express their thoughts and beliefs, as long as they do not interfere with the rights and freedoms of others.

Access to Information and Mass Media
Children have the right to get information that is important to their health and well-being. Governments and mass media should provide such information in ways that children understand, including in languages that minority and indigenous children can understand.

Protection from all Forms of Violence and Abuse
Children have the right to be protected from being physically or mentally hurt or mistreated. They should be protected from violence, sexual exploitation, cruel punishment, and participation in war and armed conflicts.

Juvenile Justice
Children accused of breaking the law have the right to legal help and fair treatment. Governments should have a justice system that respects children's rights, and sets a minimum age below which children are not held criminally responsible for their behavior.

Health and Health Services
Children have the right to health care, safe drinking water, nutritious food, and a clean and safe environment. More wealthy countries need to help less wealthy countries achieve this.

Education
Children have the right to free, primary education. Wealthy countries should help less wealthy countries achieve this. Education should respect the dignity of all students, and should encourage students to respect others, understand human rights, and protect the environment. It should also promote learning about other cultures, and how to live peaceably.

Special Protections
Children who have disabilities, or cannot be looked after by their own family, or are refugees who have been forced to leave their home and live in another country, have the right to special care, protection, and help by people who respect their ethnic group, religion, culture and language.

Information from http://www.unhcr.org/en-us/protection/children/50f941fe9/united-nations-convention-rights-child-crc.html.

Cliff Volpe / Getty Images

These young Uzbek children are helping each other wash in preparation for a meal. Violent ethnic clashes that took place in Kyrgyzstan in 2010 left many families, including this one, living outdoors in the ruins of what once were their homes.

This chapter has by no means surveyed all the contexts that influence the lives and development of children. Many children also spend considerable time in peer-group contexts and the special contexts created by religious or ethnic traditions and backgrounds. Indeed, children's ecologies include a great variety of interacting systems that can be mutually supportive or mutually damaging or that can present a mixture of risk and protective factors. Each child finds, and responds to, a myriad of meanings across a vast array of contexts according to his or her unique characteristics and past experiences, underscoring the incredible diversity of developmental pathways and outcomes.

APPLY > CONNECT > DISCUSS

Visit the Web site of the United Nations Children's Fund (UNICEF) at www.unicef.org. What are the priorities of the organization (see "What We Do")? Explore the most recent *State of the World's Children* report.

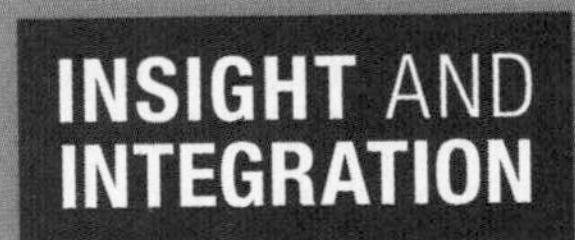

1. Review the answer you provided at the beginning of the chapter regarding how you were parented. How do you answer the question now, in light of what you learned in this chapter?
2. In this chapter, you learned about a number of contexts through which children are exposed to violence. Review each of Bronfenbrenner's interacting ecosystems (microsystem, mesosytem, exosystem, macrosystem, chronosystem) and identify how exposure to violence may occur.

Summary

- The contexts of children's development can be thought of as nested, interacting ecosystems. Each context can provide resources for positive growth or present significant challenges to health and well-being.

The Family Context

- Families are the first influence on development and one of the most important. The culture affects the way parents treat and socialize their children.
- The two major forms of family structure are nuclear families (parents and their children) and extended families (parents and their children and other kin), each with different implications for children's socialization. Although industrialization brought a shift to the nuclear family, the extended family prevailed for most of human history and remains important as a support for dealing with low income. From an evolutionary perspective, caregiving by extended kin may have made possible humans' extended childhood and large brain.
- Parents the world over have three goals: first, ensuring their children's survival; second, ensuring that their children will be economically productive adults; and third, ensuring that their children will share the group's values. Parenting practices reflect this hierarchy of goals.
- Research initiated by Diana Baumrind found four patterns of parenting:
  - Authoritative parents exert some control, explain the reasoning behind standards and punishments, and express warmth. The authoritative parenting pattern style is associated with more self-reliant and self-controlled child behavior.
  - Authoritarian parents focus on obedience and control, use physical punishment, and tend not to express warmth.
  - Permissive parents express warmth but fail to set standards or exert control.
  - Neglectful parents set few standards and exert little control, and are emotionally distant.
- Siblings play important roles in one another's social and cognitive development, and their relationships are influenced by culture and by factors such as age and gender and the family's emotional climate.
- In many of the world's countries, families are becoming increasingly diverse, through immigration and through changes in family composition.
- Approximately 25 percent of children in the United States have immigrant parents. Parenting styles and values vary across cultures, with education, for example, being more

highly valued by new U.S. immigrant parents than by those who have been established in the United States for a generation or more.

- About half of all children born in the United States today will spend at least some of their childhood in a single-parent home. Children from single-parent families have more behavioral, social, and academic problems. Various explanations have been offered, and it appears that cultural contexts may mitigate problems.
- Research on the increasing number of children in sexual-minority households paints a generally positive picture of these children's development.
- Various family factors may impede children's development. The most significant of these factors are poverty, having an adolescent parent, and abuse.
  - Poverty, affecting more than one in five children in the United States, touches all aspects of life—housing, health care, education, and even safety. Poverty in early childhood is associated with mental and physical health problems and problems in intellectual development.
  - Although declining, the teen birthrate in the United States remains among the highest in the industrialized world. Children of unmarried teenage mothers tend to be more aggressive, less self-controlled, and less intellectually advanced than other children.
  - Definitions of abuse vary widely across cultures. Causes of abuse by parents are not clear, but a parent's childhood experience of abuse, stresses on the family, certain maternal and child characteristics, and cultural acceptance of violence may increase its likelihood.

Nonparental Child Care

- By age 4, approximately 60 percent of children in the United States spend time in regular nonparental care, which takes three forms: home child care (in the children's own home), family child care (in someone else's home), and care in child-care centers (organized facilities supervised by licensed professionals).
- The effects of early child care depend largely on the quality of the care. Children in child-care centers may be subject to higher levels of stress than are children who receive care in their own homes. Nevertheless, if they are in high-quality child-care centers, their intellectual development is at least as good as that of their peers being cared for in the home. Social and emotional effects appear to be both positive (e.g., more self-sufficiency and verbal expressiveness) and negative (e.g., more aggressive behavior). Children from low-income families may especially benefit from high-quality care.

Neighborhoods and Communities

- Neighborhoods and communities differ substantially in the resources they provide children and families, with consequences for children's quality of life and mental health outcomes. Communities may also differ in the values and beliefs transmitted to children.
- Children are often adversely affected by living in distressed communities—communities characterized by economic disadvantage, physical disorder, and social disorganization.

Media Contexts

- Children in technologically advanced societies are extensively exposed to a wide range of media. Research has investigated how the form and content of different media affect development.
- Children's literature may help children with emotional control and development.
- Young children are exposed more to television than to any other medium. A concern about TV viewing is that young children have trouble distinguishing between appearance and reality. Other causes for concern are TV violence, which is especially common in children's shows, and stereotyping, evident in the somewhat limited roles of female and ethnic-minority characters.
- Increasingly important, interactive media such as video games help children develop cognitive skills. Like television, interactive media raise various concerns, including regarding the effects on relationships with peers and with family and the effects that playing games with violent content may have on children's thinking and behavior.

Looking Ahead

- Prevention science seeks to protect children from harm and promote their well-being by identifying risk factors—personal and environmental characteristics that increase the probability of negative outcomes—as well as protective factors—factors that may be sources of children's resilience.
- International organizations such as the United Nations and individual governments, through public policies, work to optimize children's development.

Key Terms

family structure, p. 332
nuclear families, p. 332
extended families, p. 332
allocaregiving, p. 333
cooperative breeding, p. 333
no-nonsense parenting, p. 335
authoritative parenting pattern, p. 335
authoritarian parenting pattern, p. 335
permissive parenting pattern, p. 336
neglectful parenting, p. 336
familism, p. 340
home child care, p. 349
family child care, p. 349
child-care centers, p. 349
social capital, p. 352
neighborhood physical disorder, p. 354
social disorganization, p. 354
media, p. 356
prevention science, p. 362
risk factors, p. 362
resilience, p. 363
protective factors, p. 363
public policies, p. 363

PART FOUR

Middle Childhood

APPLICATION TO DEVELOPING LIVES PARENTING SIMULATION

Below is a list of questions you will answer in the Middle Childhood simulation module. As you answer these questions, consider the impact your choice will have on the physical, cognitive, and social and emotional development of your child.

	Physical Domain	Cognitive Domain	Social and Emotional Domain
	• How will you adjust your child's diet and activity level during middle childhood? • Will you follow the recommended immunization schedule? • Will you regulate your child's TV time or video game time?	• In which stage of Piaget's stages of cognitive development is your child? • How will your child score on an intelligence test? • Will you have your child tutored if needed? • Will you help your child with his or her homework?	• Will you eat meals as a family around the table or follow a different routine? • What kind of elementary school will you choose for your child? • In which stage of moral development is your child? • Will your son or daughter be a popular child?

MAJOR MILESTONES OF MIDDLE CHILDHOOD

	Physical Domain	Cognitive Domain	Social and Emotional Domain
What Develops ...	• Increased muscle mass results in greater strength. • Brain growth and connections continue between cortex and limbic systems.	• Emergence of mental operations allows sorting, classification, and experimenting with variables. • Memory strategies develop. • Knowledge of cognition and memory increases, including one's own limitations in both.	• Stage of industry versus inferiority is linked to greater expectations for mature behavior. • Playing games with rules emerges. • Moral behavior is regulated by social relationships rather than fear of authority. • Gender-typed behaviors increase. • Social comparison becomes key in defining self in relation to peers.
Sociocultural Contributions and Consequences . . .	• Access to healthy food influences changes in height and weight. • Cultures provide different opportunities for boys and girls to engage in sports and physical activities.	• School experience is associated with the development of specific intellectual skills and memory abilities. • Different cultures may support the development of different cognitive strategies.	• What constitutes moral behavior varies across cultures. • Bullying increases during middle childhood. • Culture impacts parenting strategies and extent of parental monitoring.

Anthropological descriptions of a wide variety of cultures indicate that as children reach the ages of 5 to 7 years, they are no longer restricted to the home or to settings where they are carefully watched by adults. Instead, they become responsible for behaving themselves and are given responsibilities in a variety of new contexts, including contexts where they are alone or interacting with peers. The new activities they engage in vary from one society to the next. Among some of the Mayan people in the highlands of Guatemala, for example, boys go out to gather wood, a solitary activity that takes them well beyond the range of watchful adults, while girls spend more time doing domestic work in the company of their mothers and the older women of the village (Rogoff, 2003). In the United States, by contrast, boys and girls alike spend long hours in school receiving formal education; both in and out of school, their interactions with peers increase.

All these shifts are important to children. Thus, solitary activities, such as gathering wood or chasing birds away from a growing rice crop, and peer interactions, such as playing games, exchanging secrets, or simply hanging out, can be as significant for development as time spent in the classroom. Being in charge of the family cornfield or a younger sibling or engaging in informal interaction with peers provides children with important opportunities to learn what it means to take responsibility, to explore social relationships, and to develop moral understanding and personal identity.

Angelo Cavalli/AGE Fotostock

The fact that cultures everywhere give children greater autonomy and responsibility as they enter middle childhood both reflects and supports the significant expansion of children's physical and cognitive capacities. For example, as you shall see, evidence from experiments, naturalistic observations, and clinical interviews makes it clear that during middle childhood, children are increasingly able to think more deeply and logically, to follow through on a task once it is undertaken, and to keep track of several aspects of a situation at one time.

Our discussion of middle childhood is divided into three chapters. Chapter 11 focuses on the changes in children's physical and cognitive capacities between the ages of 6 and 12 that support the new freedoms and responsibilities adults place upon them. Chapter 12 examines the influence of schooling on development, with particular attention to the organization of school activities and to the intellectual capacities that schooling both demands and fosters. Chapter 13 focuses on emotional development and on the significance of the new social relationships that emerge during middle childhood, particularly among peers. The influence of physical, cognitive, and social factors, as they are woven together in different cultural contexts, creates the particular tapestry of middle childhood as it is encountered around the world.

Floresco productions/Getty Images

CHAPTER

11

Physical and Cognitive Development in Middle Childhood

A girl from the Kukatja community, a hunter-gatherer society in the desert of Western Australia, provides the following, translated description of life in her camp:

Mothers and fathers gone out hunting and leave us kids in camp. When we got hungry we go hunting for little lizard, get him and cook it and eat him up. Me little bit big now, I go hunting myself, tracking goanna [a type of lizard] and kill him. . . . Soon as mother leave him, little ones go hunting, kill animals, blue tongue, mountain devil [both lizards], take them home before mother and father come back, cook and eat it. Mothers, they bring him goannas and blue tongue and father one still long way. Mother come back and feed all them kids. . . . After lunch mother and father go hunting for supper, all the little kids walk and kill little lizard, take him home, cook and eat him. . . .

Morning again, father one he go hunting. All little kids go hunting self. . . . Mother go out separate from father and come back with big mob of animals. Me big enough to hunt around self. . . . Morningtime, father one bin for hunting long way way. He bin get and kill an emu, bring and cook him. Everyone happy, they bin say he good hunter. Mother and father sometime bin come back late from hunting. They bin go long way.

(Kapanankga, 1995; cited in Bird & Bird, 2005, p. 129.)

Despite being a "little bit big now," and able to track, kill, and cook goanna, the Kukatja girl quoted above remains dependent on her mother and father to provide adequate nutrition and care throughout the years of middle childhood. As we have discussed in earlier chapters, our species is unique in its prolonged period of childhood dependency; once weaned, children in all societies rely on their elders for care and protection for well over a decade (Bird & Bird, 2005; Hartman & Belsky, 2016).

On the other hand, research conducted in many societies shows that adults begin to have new expectations when their children approach 6 years of age. Among the Ngoni of Malawi, in central Africa, for example, adults believe that the loss of milk teeth and the emergence of permanent teeth (starting around the age of 6) signal that children should begin to act more independently. They are supposed to stop playing childish games and start learning skills that will be essential when they grow up. They are also expected to understand their place and are held accountable for being discourteous. The boys leave the protection and control of women and move into dormitories, where they must adapt to a system of male dominance and male life. Margaret Read (1983) describes the difficulties that this transition to a new stage of life causes for Ngoni boys:

> There was no doubt that this abrupt transition, like the sudden weaning [several years earlier], was a shock for many boys between six-and-a-half and seven-and-a-half. From having been impudent, well fed, self-confident, and spoiled youngsters among the women many of them quickly became skinny, scruffy, subdued, and had a hunted expression. (p. 49)

Observations of life among the Ifaluk of Micronesia provide a similar picture. The Ifaluk believe that at the age of 6 years, children gain "social intelligence," which includes the ability to acquire important cultural knowledge and skills, as well as the ability to work, to adhere to social norms, and to demonstrate compassion for others—all valued adult behaviors (Lutz, 1987). In Western Europe and the United States, this same transition has long been considered the beginning of the "age of reason" (White, 1996).

Adults' expectations that their children will begin to behave more maturely at around the age of 6 or 7 arise from a combination of cultural traditions, ecological circumstances and demands (for example, whether children must learn to cross busy streets or fast-moving streams), and their observations of how well their children now cope with new demands (Morelli, 2017). At the age of 6, children are strong and agile enough to catch a runaway goat or to carry their little sisters on their hips. They become more proficient at hunting and gathering food and know not to let a baby crawl near an open fire (Bock, 2005; Bird & Bird, 2005). They can wait for the school bus without wandering off. They can, sometimes under duress, sit still for several hours at a time while adults attempt to instruct them, and they are beginning to be able to carry out their chores in an acceptable manner. In short, they can perform tasks independently, formulate goals, and resist the temptation to abandon them.

In this chapter, we focus on the physical and cognitive changes of middle childhood that lead to these advances and might justify adults' new demands and expectations of children. The physical changes of middle childhood—continued growth, improved motor skills, and increased brain maturation and activity—are readily measurable. Changes in children's cognitive functioning, however, are more difficult to measure and, as you might expect, have been addressed by different theoretical approaches.

Margie Politzer/Getty Images

The transition to middle childhood is often marked by new responsibilities, privileges, and rituals. These young Nicaraguan children are walking to church for their first Communion.

WARMING UP

1. What were your special interests between 6 and 12 years of age? Were you into sports, collecting something special, reading certain types of books, or playing certain types of video games? Do you think your interests may have been influenced by your gender or culture?
2. What do you think it means to be "intelligent"? How is intelligence related to performance in school? To life in general? What are the differences between intelligence and school performance?

Physical and Motor Development

LEARNING OUTCOMES

Describe changes in size and strength during middle childhood.

Identify genetic and environmental factors that affect height and weight during middle childhood.

Distinguish the motor abilities of boys and girls during middle childhood.

Summarize some brain developments that underlie children's cognitive skills during middle childhood.

An obvious reason that children can do more on their own is that they are bigger, are stronger, and have more endurance than they had when they were younger. Size and strength increase significantly during middle childhood, although more slowly than in earlier years. Motor development shows marked improvement as children perfect the skills needed for running, throwing, catching, and turning somersaults.

Patterns of Growth

Children in the United States are on average about 39 inches tall and about 36 pounds at age 4; by the time they are 6 years old, they are about 45 inches tall and weigh about 45 pounds. At the start of adolescence, 6 or 7 years later, their average height will have increased to almost 5 feet, and their weight to approximately 90 pounds (Cameron, 2002). During middle childhood, increases in muscle mass contribute to increased strength in both boys and girls. In addition, beginning at approximately age 7 for girls and age 8 for boys, there is a gradual increase in fat tissue that contributes to the changing appearance of the body. Like all other aspects of development, children's growth during middle childhood continues to depend on the interaction of environmental and genetic factors.

Height

Now fully grown, Amita just barely reaches the 5′3″ mark on the measuring stick. There would be nothing remarkable about her small stature except for the fact that she comes from a very tall family. Growing up with jokes that question her mother's relationship with the milkman, Amita is good-natured about defying what we know regarding how genetic factors influence one's height: Tall parents tend to have tall children. Monozygotic twins reared together are very similar in their patterns of growth, and those reared apart still tend to resemble each other more than do dizygotic twins. Yet environmental conditions also play a significant role, as attested to by the existence of many cases in which one monozygotic twin is significantly smaller than the other because of the effects of illness (Amita attributes her short stature to several severe infections suffered during infancy) or a poor environment, as when, in the case of twins reared apart, one twin is raised in a healthy environment and the other is raised in impoverished conditions.

The environmental contribution to size can also be seen in the variations in the height and rate of growth typical of populations that undergo changes in living conditions. From the late 1970s to the early 1990s, Mayan families from Guatemala migrated to the United States in record numbers due to a violent civil war

(Jonas, 2013). Barry Bogin and his colleagues measured the heights of more than 400 5- to 12-year-old Mayan American children in 1999 and 2000 (Bogin et al., 2002). These data were compared with data for a sample of more than 1,000 Mayan children living in Guatemala at the time. The Mayan American children were about 4½ inches taller, on average, than their Mayan peers living in Guatemala. These results illustrate how the heights of human populations can be sensitive indicators of the quality of the environment for growth.

One of the key environmental factors that moderates genetic growth potential is nutrition. Poor children, who have less access to nutritious food and good health care than do children in well-off families, are usually smaller than their well-off peers. This difference is especially evident if the lack of access is extreme. For example, in a study of the physical development of North Korean children whose families fled to South Korea because of North Korea's chronic food shortages, the children's malnourishment was so severe that, by the time they reached their 14th birthdays, the boys were approximately 6 inches shorter and the girls 3 inches shorter than their South Korean counterparts (Pak, 2010).

As indicated, health also plays a role in a child's growth. Growth slows during illnesses, even mild ones. When children are adequately nourished, this slowdown is usually followed by a period of rapid "catch-up growth," which quickly restores them to their genetically normative path of growth (Huynh et al., 2015). When nutritional intake is inadequate, however, the children never do catch up, and their growth is stunted (deRegnier, Long, Georgieff, & Nelson, 2007).

Weight Body weight, like height, is influenced by genetic factors. A study of 540 Danish adoptees found a strong correlation between the adoptees' weight as adults and the weight of their biological parents, especially their mothers (Stunkard et al., 1986). Yet environmental factors—including the quantity and quality of food available—play a significant role in determining weight (Whitaker et al., 1997). For example, the number of calories consumed in an average day can have long-term effects for a child's growth. The consumption of as few as 50 extra calories a day can lead to an excess weight gain of 5 pounds over the course of a year (Kolata, 1986). Given that the average 12-ounce can of soda contains 150 calories and that soda has replaced bread as a major source of calories in the diets of American children and adults, it is not surprising that scores of studies have implicated the consumption of soft drinks as a major contributor to childhood obesity (Morgan, 2013).

Because of the growing problem of obesity among American children, increasing attention has been focused on the factors that contribute to it (Harrison, Bost, McBride, & Donovan, 2011). (See the box "Let's Move! A National Campaign to Battle Childhood Obesity," pp. 376–377.) While obesity is commonly measured by weight, many researchers have argued that it can be diagnosed earlier and more accurately by measuring *body mass index* (*BMI*), the ratio of weight to height (American Academy of Pediatrics, 2003). A recent nationwide survey of U.S. children aged 2–19 years revealed that 17.2 percent were obese and another 16.2 percent were overweight (Frayar, Carroll, & Ogden, 2016).

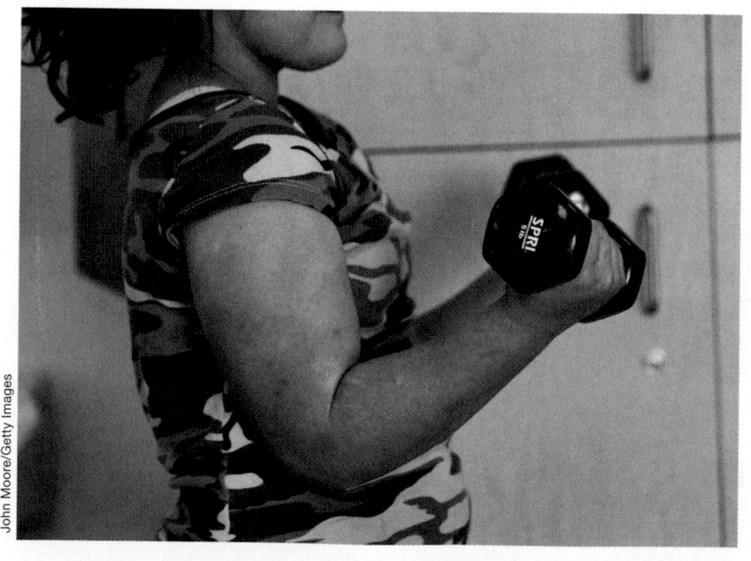

Rising rates of obesity among children throughout the world have spurred efforts to prevent it, including the exercise program in which this girl is participating.

John Moore/Getty Images

A vast variety of biological and environmental factors are known to contribute to childhood overweight and obesity. In an effort to organize these factors into a "big picture," Kristen Harrison and her colleagues proposed the Six-Cs developmental ecological model (Harrison et al., 2011; Dev et al., 2013). As indicated in the following list, the six Cs range from the microscopic level of genes to the most general level of culture.

- *Cell:* Biological and genetic characteristics, such as the inheritance of genes that contribute to fat storage
- *Child:* Behaviors, attitudes, and knowledge relevant to weight gain, including eating patterns, exercise, and the ability to control behavior (self-regulation)
- *Clan:* Family characteristics, such as parents' encouragement to exercise and eat healthy foods, family media use, and whether the child was fed breast or artificial milk during infancy
- *Community:* Factors in the local community, including school meal programs and vending-machine options, availability of grocery stores, and access to recreational activities
- *Country:* State and national characteristics such as government funding for nutrition programs, healthy-eating media campaigns, and state or federal dietary guidelines
- *Culture:* Cultural and social beliefs and practices, including gender-role expectations concerning eating and activity, cultural standards for beauty, and norms regarding portion sizes served in restaurants

Given that the risk of childhood obesity resides at multiple levels, Harrison and her colleagues are not surprised that most intervention efforts to reduce overweight and obesity have been unsuccessful; they say that such efforts are narrowly focused at a single level. For example, one approach may target the *child level* by engaging children in physical activity programs, whereas another may target the *community level* by introducing healthier lunch menus at schools. Ecological models such as the Six-Cs underscore the importance of comprehensive interventions that tackle childhood overweight and obesity at multiple levels simultaneously.

Motor Development

Walking along the beach one day, we saw a girl about 7 years old and her little brother, who was about 4 years old, following their father and their older brother, who was 10 or 11 years old. The father and older brother were tossing a ball back and forth as they walked. The girl was hopping along the sand on one foot, and her younger brother scrambled to keep up with her. Suddenly the little girl threw her arms up in the air, leaned over, threw her feet up, and did a cartwheel. She then did another cartwheel. Her younger brother stopped to watch her. Then he tried one. He fell in a heap in the sand, and she continued doing one perfect cartwheel after another.

In such everyday scenes, you can see the increases in motor development that occur over the course of middle childhood (see Figure 11.1, p. 376). Children become stronger and more agile, and their balance improves. They run faster; they throw balls farther and with greater efficiency and are more likely to catch them. They also jump farther and higher than they did when they were younger, and they

In The Field

Let's Move! A National Campaign to Battle Childhood Obesity

Name: MICHELLE OBAMA
Education: B.A. in sociology, Princeton University; J.D., Harvard University
Profession: Lawyer
Objectives: Used resources of position as First Lady of the United States to promote initiatives to reduce childhood overweight and obesity

WHILE FIRST LADY OF THE UNITED STATES, MICHELLE OBAMA TOOK ON A MISSION TO ELIMINATE childhood obesity in a generation. To this end, she launched a nationwide campaign called "Let's Move!" which targets four areas regarded as being key to children's healthy nutrition and weight: parental knowledge about nutrition and exercise, the quality of food in schools, accessibility and affordability of healthy food in communities, and physical education.

Since 1980, the incidence of childhood obesity has tripled among school-age children (Frayar, Carrol, & Ogden, 2016). The consequences of becoming obese during childhood and adolescence are severe. Obese children are often rejected by their peers, leading many of them to become withdrawn and lose self-esteem. Obese children are also more vulnerable to a variety of serious health problems, such as asthma, heart disease, diabetes, respiratory disease, and orthopedic disorders (Davies & Fitzgerald, 2008). In recent years, there has been an alarming increase among obese minority children in the incidence of type 2 diabetes, a serious condition that can lead to kidney disease, eye disorders, and nervous system problems, as well as heart disease and stroke.

There appear to be three important periods during which there is an increased risk for developing obesity that persists into adulthood. The first is the prenatal period, during which maternal overnutrition or maternal undernutrition (see Chapter 4, pp. 92–94), as well as smoking during pregnancy, raise the risk that the child will become overweight (Tabacchi, Giammanco, La Guardia, & Giammanco, 2007). The second important period is related to what is known as the *adiposity rebound period*, during which children's body fat begins to increase again after a period of decreasing. Normally, the adiposity rebound period occurs at around age 6. Longitudinal studies have found that children whose body fat increases before the age of 5½ are significantly more likely than other children to become and remain obese (Centers for Disease Control and Prevention, 2009; McCarthy et al., 2007). The third important period for the development of persistent obesity is adolescence, when there are changes in the quantity and location of body fat. This period is especially critical for girls. In boys, the quantity of body fat normally decreases by about 40 percent, whereas in girls, the quantity of body fat increases by about 40 percent, putting girls at elevated risk for becoming and staying obese.

Tim Boyle/Getty Images

Although many school cafeterias are now offering a greater variety of fruits and vegetables, children often bypass the salads and reach for the fries. It is also common for children to supplement their lunches with unhealthy foods that they bring from home, such as potato chips and sports drinks.

Obviously, children's risk of obesity is influenced substantially by the family, including its mealtime habits, food preferences, and leisure activities—how

(a)

(b)

(c)

FIGURE 11.1 The physical changes of childhood make possible a range of new activities. The ability to kick a ball, for example, improves dramatically. (a) A young child learning to kick will simply push the leg forward, while (b) an older child will step forward, cock the leg, and take a limited swing at the ball. (c) By the end of middle childhood, the child is able to take a full swing at the ball while simultaneously moving arms and trunk to provide support and balance. (Research from Haywood & Getchell, 2005.)

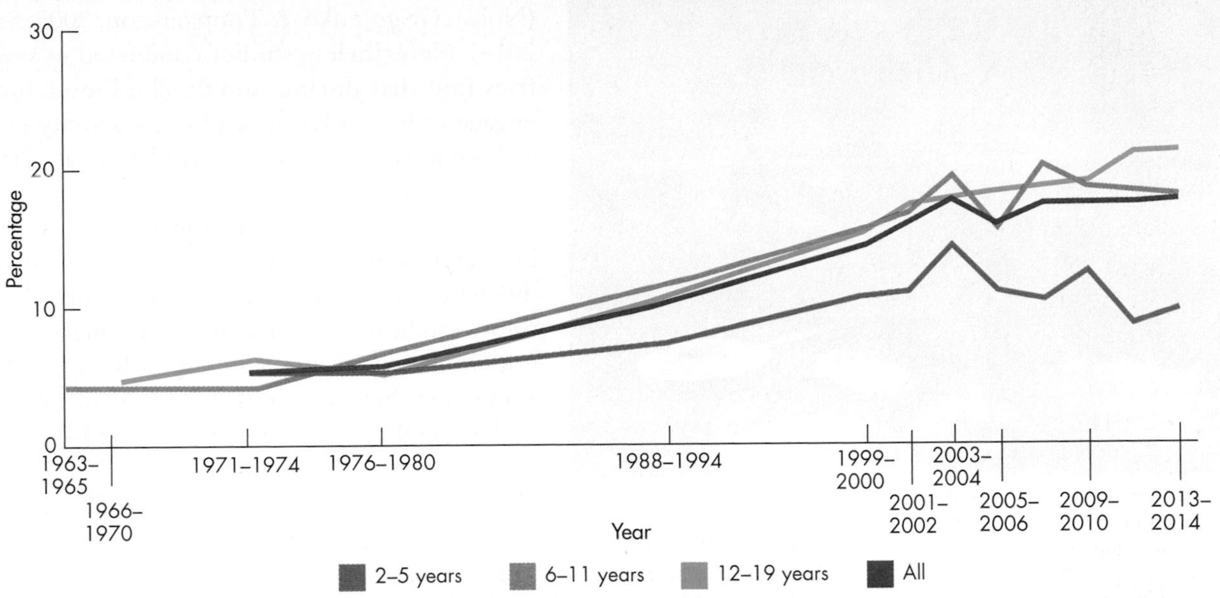

Since the late 1970s, there have been dramatic increases in the percentages of children and adolescents in the United States who are overweight and obese. (Data from Fryar, Carroll, & Ogden, 2016.)

much time is spent watching television and using other electronic devices or going for walks, for example (Domingues, Montanari, 2017; Larson, Neumark-Sztainer, Hannan, & Story, 2007). It is also influenced by parents' knowledge of nutrition and access to healthy food in the community. Michelle Obama's Let's Move! campaign helps families make informed choices at the supermarket by working with governmental agencies to improve nutrition labeling on food packages.

Social institutions, including schools, bear significant responsibility for children's eating behavior. For example, sugary drinks and snacks high in fat, sugar, and salt once were regular fare in school cafeterias and vending machines, and they remain readily available in many states (Hennessy et al., 2014; Prentice & Jebb, 2003). Increasingly, however, many new school programs have tackled the obesity epidemic by including a greater variety of fresh fruits and vegetables, reducing the amount of soda and candy sold in vending machines, and educating children about the importance of a healthy diet. Nutritionists and other health care professionals agree that to combat childhood obesity effectively, public attitudes must continue to shift responsibility from children and families to include the schools and other social institutions that provide children with meals and snacks when they are away from home. Let's Move! includes government support for schools to provide more nutritious meals. Noting that many schools are reducing or eliminating recess, physical education, and gym classes, Obama is also encouraging renewed attention to the importance of physical activity for children's health.

Let's Move! is a broadly focused effort that encourages the cooperation of local, state, and federal governments, along with schools, businesses, and nonprofit agencies. As Obama explained, "We all know the numbers. I mean, one in three kids are overweight or obese, and we're spending $150 billion a year treating obesity-related illnesses. So we know this is a problem and there's a lot at stake."

---

learn to skate, ride bikes, dance, swim, and climb trees as well as acquire a host of other physical skills during this period.

Gender Differences As a general rule, motor development follows different patterns for boys and girls (Gidley Larson et al., 2007). During middle childhood, there are no gender differences in strength, although girls typically are faster and better coordinated than boys, perhaps because of differences in patterns of brain development. Girls are better at maintaining a steady rhythm when tapping their fingers and putting pegs in a board, and they are also better than boys at

In an example of how culture supports the development of fine motor skills, Armine makes a Chinese drum as a part of a school program celebrating the Chinese New Year.

balancing—including standing and hopping on one foot (Nolan, Grigorenko, & Thorstensson, 2005; Smith et al., 2014). Nevertheless, studies conducted in several countries find that during middle childhood, boys tend to engage in higher levels of physical activity compared to girls (Baptista et al., 2012; Klinker et al., 2014; Seabra et al., 2013).

Cultural conceptions of the activities appropriate to boys and to girls also play a large role in shaping these differences in physical activity. For example, being able to throw, catch, and hit a baseball is a valued set of skills for boys in many cultures. Correspondingly, parents usually encourage their sons, much more than their daughters, to develop these skills by buying them balls and bats, taking them to ball games, talking about baseball with them, playing catch with them, and enrolling them in Little League. And in all cultures, it is also much truer for boys than for girls that those who are considered to be good athletes are more popular with their peers than those who show no athletic ability. While the participation of girls in such sports as baseball, soccer, and tennis has increased significantly in a number of countries in recent decades, girls are still less likely than boys to participate in sports—but significantly more likely to engage in sports when their parents and friends encourage it (Seabra et al., 2013). It is clear, however, that both boys and girls appear to profit from being active in sports. As shown in Figure 11.2, compared with peers who do not participate in sports, children who are highly involved in sports have (1) more positive friends who encourage behaviors such as doing well in school, (2) fewer negative friends who encourage behaviors such as disobeying parents, (3) higher self-esteem, (4) a greater sense of belonging at school, and (5) lower levels of depression (Simpkins et al., 2006). As discussed later in this chapter, regular aerobic exercise may even increase the mathematics achievement and cognitive functioning of overweight children.

FIGURE 11.2 Youths who are highly involved in sports report more positive friends, fewer negative friends, higher self-esteem, lower levels of depression, and a greater sense of belonging at school compared with youths who do not participate in sports. (Data from Simpkins et al., 2006, p. 298.)

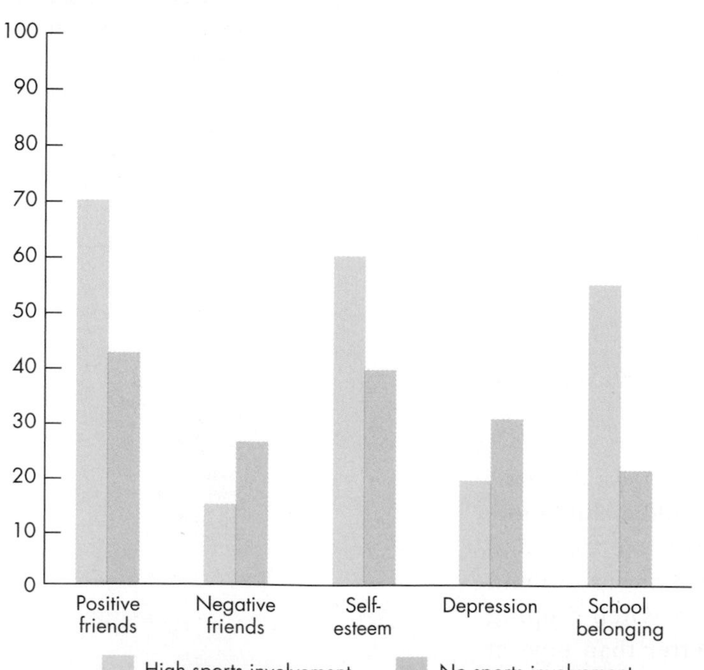

The Role of Practice As suggested above, and as we have discussed in previous chapters, the practice of motor skills is essential to furthering motor development. A striking demonstration is provided in a laboratory study of how children bicycle across traffic-filled intersections (Plumert et al., 2011). As you will see, crossing the street involves considerably more than just looking both ways.

The study used a bicycling simulator—a very high-tech stationary bike surrounded by enormous screens that projected a complex virtual town environment (see Figure 11.3). The participants—10-year-olds, 12-year-olds, and adults—"rode" the bicycle through the virtual town along a two-lane residential roadway with stop signs at 12 intersections. The high-tech bicycle generated data about each participant's pedal speed and steering, while video cameras recorded other behavior, such as head turns. After a short warm-up session in which a participant became acquainted with how the bike works, he or she was given the following instructions:

> Your job is to cross every intersection without getting hit by a car. So, when you get to an intersection, you will see a stream of cars coming from your left-hand side. Some of the spaces

Hank Virtual Environments Laboratory at the University of Iowa

Hank Virtual Environments Laboratory at the University of Iowa

FIGURE 11.3 To study the role of practice in the development of motor skills, researchers designed a high-tech bicycling simulator. Participants in the study rode a stationary bike surrounded by giant screens that made it seem as if they were riding through a town, complete with stop signs and intersections.

between the cars will be too small to get across without getting hit, and some will be big enough for you to get across without getting hit. You can wait as long as you need to before going across.

The researchers found that over the course of riding through 12 intersections, both children and adults chose to cross the street through increasingly smaller gaps between cars. This finding suggests that participants of all ages learned from their experiences in the virtual environment. In addition, there were interesting age differences in the timing of participants' riding through the intersections. At the first several intersections, the 10-year-olds had very little time to spare between clearing the intersection and the passing of the oncoming car. But by the end of their ride, they had increased their time-to-spare by an average of 25 percent. In contrast, the time-to-spare changed very little throughout the ride for 12-year-olds and adults. It seems that the 10-year-olds had much more room for improvement than did the older participants. Indeed, at later intersections, they crossed at higher rates of speed and also cut in closer behind the lead car. Their increased speed was likely due to the effects of practice on their ability to control the bike. Not only did they pedal faster, they became better able to look left for traffic without veering around like drunken sailors.

Brain Development

Middle childhood—particularly the early years, between ages 6 and 8—is a period of continued growth of the brain and of the development of specific kinds of brain functioning that is believed to underlie changes in cognitive skills. Until fairly recently, researchers believed that most changes in the brain take place well before middle childhood. However, new technologies such as magnetic resonance imaging (MRI) provide evidence that the brain remains a work in progress through childhood, adolescence, and into young adulthood.

Although the brain, which has attained 90 percent of its adult weight by the age of 5, grows very little in size during middle childhood, recent longitudinal MRI studies point to complex changes in its organization and functioning (Durston & Casey, 2006; Gogtay et al., 2004). Two areas of the brain—the cerebral cortex (introduced in Chapter 4, p. 128) and the limbic system (discussed below)—have received a good deal of scientific attention because of the significant roles they may play in children's behavior (see Figure 11.4).

FIGURE 11.4 In evolutionary terms, the cortex is a fairly recent development for our species and is associated with executive function—that is, the ability to control thoughts, feelings, and behaviors. The limbic system, which includes the amygdala, hippocampus, basal ganglia, and hypothalamus, evolved earlier than the cortex in our species and is associated with the expression and interpretation of emotions.

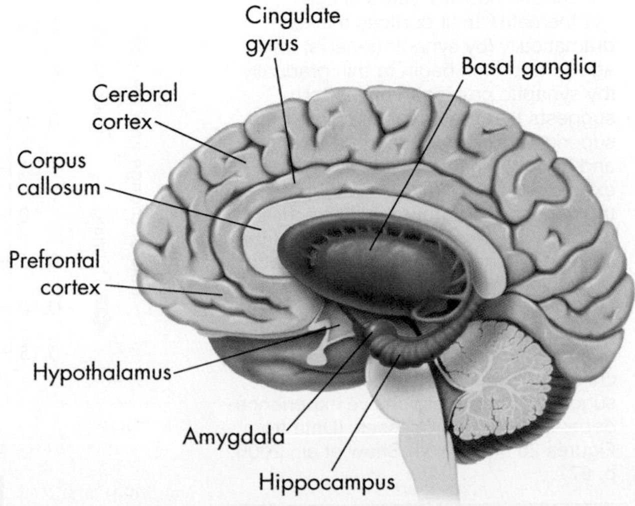

Cerebral Cortex Changes

The cerebral cortex continues to develop throughout the years of childhood and into early adulthood (Luciana, 2010). Neuroscientists have paid particular attention to changes in the frontal lobes of the cortex, which have emerged fairly recently in the brain evolution of our species and are associated with a number of advanced behaviors and processes, including memory, decision making, reasoning, impulse control, and the ability to multitask. As we discussed in Chapter 5 (p. 165) the *prefrontal cortex* resides directly behind your forehead and is thought to contribute to a host of abilities that involve controlling and regulating one's thoughts, feelings, and behaviors.

As we discussed in Chapter 4 (p. 127), changes in the volume of the brain involve changes in *gray matter*—that is, the size and number of dendrites and axons that transmit neural information—as well as changes in *white matter*, the myelin that forms the insulating sheath around certain axons, speeding the transmission of neural information. An example of how cortical brain volume may impact children's behavior comes from a study linking differences in brain development to individual differences in children's intelligence (Shaw et al., 2006). On the basis of standardized tests of intelligence (which we discuss in detail later in this chapter), more than 300 children and adolescents were classified as being of superior intelligence, high intelligence, or average intelligence. Neuroimaging techniques were used to measure the thickness of each child's cortex. Interestingly, the researchers found that intelligence test scores correlated not with cortical thickness per se but with a certain *developmental pattern* of cortical thickening and thinning over the course of childhood. Specifically, as shown in Figure 11.5, children with superior intelligence tended to have thinner cortices at age 7 but then showed a marked increase in

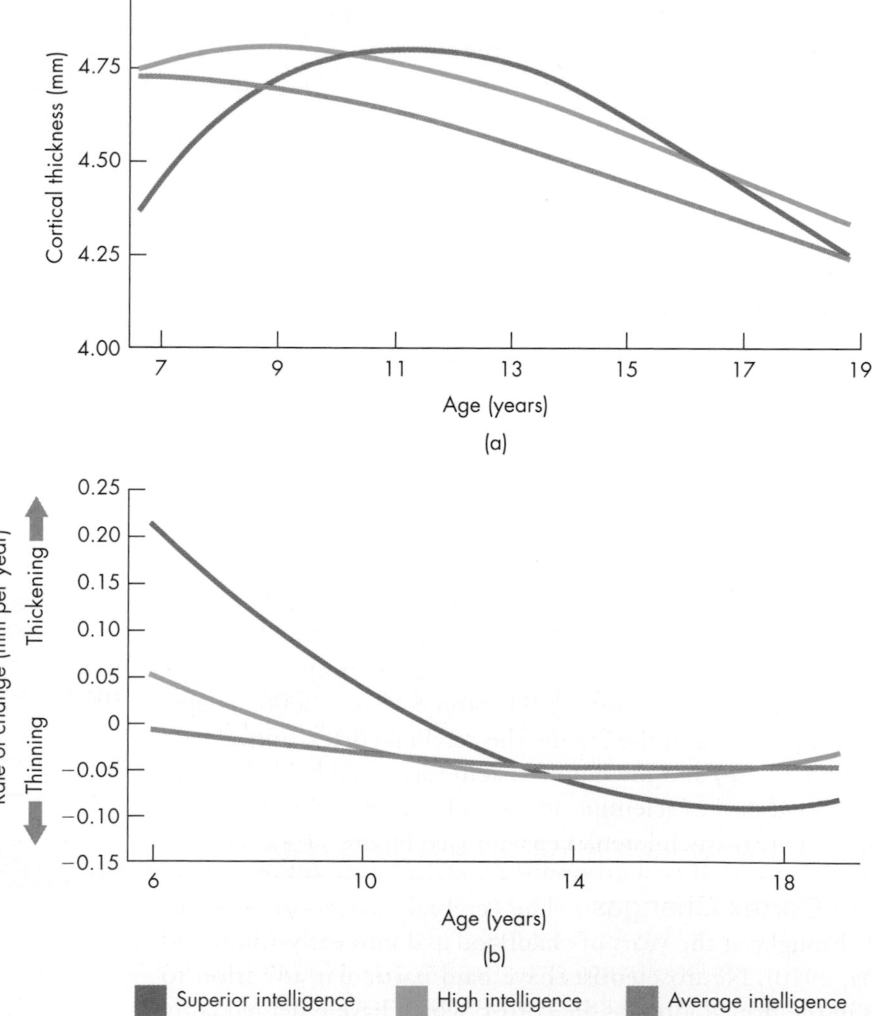

FIGURE 11.5 (a) Compared with children of high or average intelligence, children with superior intelligence have thinner cortices at 7 years of age, but thereafter their cortices thicken dramatically (by synaptogenesis) until age 11 and then begin to thin gradually (by synaptic pruning). This pattern suggests that the brains of children of superior intelligence are more flexible and better able to respond to children's experiences. (The data shown are for the right superior frontal gyrus; similar patterns are found for other parts of the cortex.) (b) The rate of change in cortical thickening (indicated by positive values) and thinning (indicated by negative values) is much more dynamic in children of superior intelligence than it is in children of high or average intelligence, suggesting more responsive experience-dependent brain processes. (Data from Figures 2a and 3 from Shaw et al., 2006, p. 677.)

cortical thickening that peaked around 11 years of age and then rapidly declined. In contrast, children with average intelligence showed a fairly steady decline in cortical thickening from age 7, while children with high intelligence demonstrated an intermediate pattern, but one more closely approximating that of the average intelligence group. Maximum cortical thickness occurred at 5.6 years for the average intelligence group, 8.5 years for the high intelligence group, and 11.2 years for the superior intelligence group.

What do we make of the waxing and waning of cortical thickness in these different groups of children? As the researchers point out, an increase in cortical thickness may be due to a proliferation of brain cells and synapses and/or an increase in myelin. Cortical thinning, in contrast, takes place as a consequence of "pruning" unused synapses. The researchers speculate that cortices of the "brainy" children, which thicken and then thin at a rapid rate through middle childhood and adolescence, are more flexible and dynamic compared with those of other children—that the pattern of cortical development provides a larger window in which neural circuitry can be laid down in response to learning experiences, a process of brain development we previously described as *experience-dependent* (see Chapter 4, p. 129). Thus, these children are smarter not because of the sheer amount of brain matter but because of the dynamic properties of cortical development.

Limbic System Changes

Notwithstanding the significance of the developing cerebral cortex, important developments occur in other, evolutionarily older parts of the brain as well (Casey et al., 2010; Whittle et al., 2008). Positioned deep beneath the cortex and above the brain stem are several brain structures, including the *amygdala*, the *hippocampus*, the *basal ganglia*, and the *hypothalamus* (review Figure 11.4, p. 379), that are often referred to collectively as the **limbic system**. Because these brain structures are associated more with emotion than with reasoning, the limbic system is often described as the "emotion brain" (in contrast to the cerebral cortex, which some have dubbed the "reasoning brain"). Neuroscientists, however, warn against distinguishing too sharply between two brains, one associated with emotions and the other with reasoning, primarily because of evidence suggesting that the two systems share in, or cooperate on, certain functions. For example, some limbic structures are involved in processing complex memories, and certain areas of the cortex are essential to understanding and interpreting emotional events and experiences (LeDoux, 2012).

limbic system A group of brain structures, including the amygdala, hippocampus, basal ganglia, and hypothalamus. Because these brain structures are associated more with emotion than with reasoning, the limbic system is often described as the "emotion brain" (in contrast to the cerebral cortex, which some have dubbed the "reasoning brain").

One of the most significant features of brain development during middle childhood concerns the communication that takes place between the cortical and limbic areas of the brain as neural networks are established (Posner, Rothbart, Sheese, & Voelker, 2014). A special brain structure—the *cingulate gyrus*—plays an important role in this communication process. Although formally a part of the limbic system, you can see in Figure 11.4 that it lies in close proximity to the cortex.

Despite these various research findings, we must be cautious about inferring direct causal links between particular changes in the brain and specific changes in behavior. The evidence we have cited is correlational: As children grow older, we observe changes in their brains and changes in their behavior, but the direction of causation remains uncertain. As explained in Chapter 4, the development and strengthening of neural pathways in the brain both affects and is affected by the individual's experience.

APPLY > CONNECT > DISCUSS

Discuss some of the ways that physical activity affects the physical and psychological development of girls and boys during middle childhood. In your discussion, consider how the effects are similar for boys and girls, how they may differ, and the extent to which culture may contribute to any gender differences you identify.

LEARNING OUTCOMES

Outline Piaget's stage of concrete-operational development.

Provide examples for Piaget's principles of conservation, centration, classification, planning, and metacognition.

Point out some limitations to thinking during the stage of concrete operations.

Concrete-Operational Development

The apparatus shown in Figure 11.6 is one that Piaget presented to children of different ages to assess their level of cognitive development. The apparatus involves a toy wagon, suspended by a cable, that can be moved up and down a slope by manipulating three variables: the number of counterweights at the end of the cable, the weight of the load being carried by the wagon, and the angle of the track on which the wagon moves (Inhelder & Piaget, 1958, pp. 182–198). When a 6-year-old was asked how the wagon could be made to move, he pushed it down the track with his hand.

> **Experimenter:** Can you do anything else?
> **Child:** You drive in the train.
> **Experimenter tried a suggestion:** And with the weights?
> **Child adds a counterweight to the cable:** I put something on.
> **Experimenter:** Why does it go up?
> **Child:** I don't know. Because it's heavy.
> **Experimenter:** And to make it go down?
> **Child:** I don't know. You could push it.

A 10-year-old responded quite differently.

> **Child:** To make it go up, you have to put a heavier weight here [at the end of the cable].
> **Experimenter:** What else could you do?
> **Child:** Unload the wagon.
> **Experimenter tried a suggestion:** Can you do something with the rail?
> **Child:** Maybe you could lower it; it's easier for the wagon to go forward because the track isn't as high.

In accounting for the vastly different ways in which these two children responded to the problem, Piaget points out that the 6-year-old is unable to identify the relevant variables (wagon load, counterweight, slope of incline); indeed, he is unable to separate the variables from his own actions of pushing, pulling, and "putting something on." The older child, in contrast, appreciates that the wagon's movement will depend on changes to the load, counterweight, and incline, independent of the child's own actions on the apparatus.

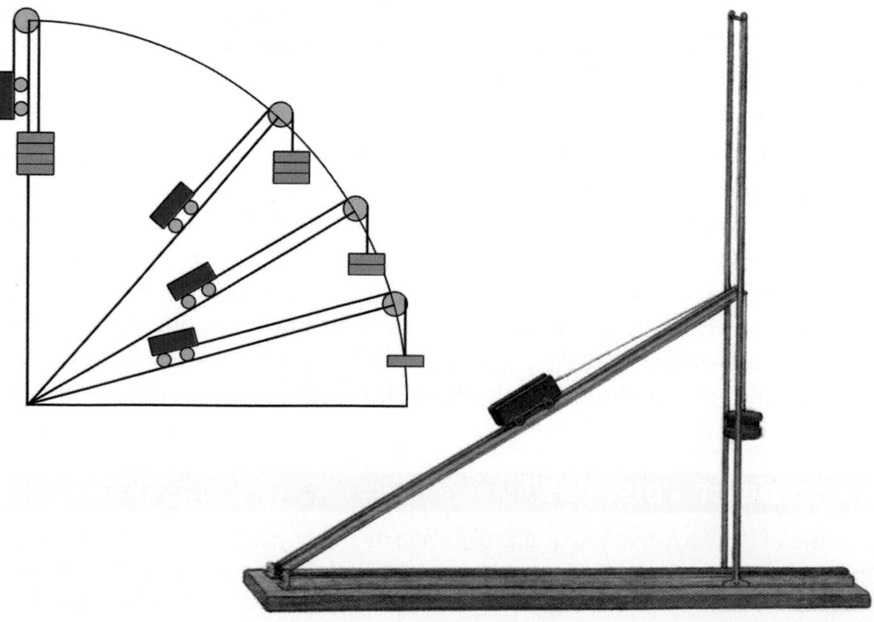

FIGURE 11.6 In this classic Piagetian task, a toy wagon, suspended by a cable, is hauled up the inclined plane by the counterweights at the other end of the cable. The counterweights can be varied, and the angle of the plane is adjustable; weights placed in the wagon provide the third variable. (Research from Inhelder & Piaget, 1958, p. 183.)

their attention on a single aspect of the new beaker—its height. Even when the experimenter points out that no liquid was added or subtracted—and even after the experimenter pours the liquid back into the original beaker to demonstrate that the amount has not changed—3- and 4-year-olds generally stick to their claim that there was more liquid in the taller, narrower beaker.

Piaget found that around the age of 5 or 6 years, children's understanding of conservation goes through a transitional stage. At this point, children seem to realize that it is necessary to consider both the height and the circumference of the beakers, but they have difficulty keeping the dimensions of both beakers in mind simultaneously and coordinating the differences between them in order to make a valid comparison.

According to Piaget, children fully master the principle of conservation around the age of 8, when they understand not only that the new beaker is both taller and narrower but also that a change in one dimension of the beaker (increasing height) is offset by a change in the other (decreasing circumference). Children who have mastered conservation recognize the logical necessity that the amount of liquid remains the same despite the change in appearance. When asked the reasons for their judgment, they offer arguments such as the following, showing that they understand the logical relationships involved:

Laura Dwight

FIGURE 11.8 The procedure that Piaget used to test for the conservation of volume follows three simple steps. First, present the child with two beakers of equal size containing equal amounts of liquid. Second, present a taller, narrower beaker and pour the contents of one of the other beakers into it. Third, ask the child, "Which beaker has more liquid, or do they contain the same amount?" Like most other children under age 6, this girl appears to lack an understanding of conservation of volume.

- "They were equal to start with and nothing was added, so they're the same." This mental operation is called **identity**; the child realizes that a change limited to outward appearance does not change the actual amounts involved.
- "The liquid is higher, but the glass is thinner." This mental operation is called **compensation**; changes in one aspect of a problem are mentally compared with, and compensated for, by changes in another.
- "If you pour it back, you'll see that it's the same." This mental operation is called *negation*, or **reversibility**; the child realizes that one operation can be negated, or reversed, by the effects of another.

Whether they are asked to reason about number or volume, children's ability to conserve leads to the logical conclusion that a change in visual *appearance* does not change the logical *reality* of amount.

identity A mental operation in which a child realizes that a change limited to outward appearance does not change the substances involved.

compensation A mental operation in which a child realizes that changes in one aspect of a problem are compared with and compensated for by changes in another aspect.

reversibility A mental operation in which a child realizes that one operation can be negated, or reversed, by the effects of another.

Classification

Another significant change associated with concrete operations is the ability to understand the hierarchical structure of categories—in particular, the logical *relation of inclusion* that holds between a superordinate class and its subclasses (for example, the subclass of cats being included in the superordinate class of mammals; see Figure 5.19 in Chapter 5, p. 189).

When 4- to 6-year-old children are shown a set of wooden beads that includes some brown beads and a smaller number of white beads and are asked, "Are there more brown beads or more beads?" they are likely to say there are more brown beads than beads. According to Piaget, they answer this way because they cannot attend to the subclass (brown beads) and the superordinate class (beads) at the same time. Instead, they compare one subclass (brown beads) with another subclass (white beads). In middle childhood, understanding of subordinate–superordinate relations become more stable, and children realize that brown beads are a subset of the overall set of beads and answer correctly.

Serious young trading card collectors will have fairly elaborate classification systems that organize their cards according to multiple criteria.

Christina Kennedy / Alamy

A more difficult classification ability that emerges during middle childhood is the capacity to categorize objects according to multiple criteria. This kind of logical classification can be seen when children begin to collect stamps, baseball cards, or Pokémon cards, many of which are traded in order to fill certain categories. Stamp collections, for example, can be organized according to multiple criteria. Stamps come from different countries. They are issued in different denominations and in different years. There are stamps depicting insects, animals, sports heroes, rock stars, and space exploration. Children who organize their stamps according to type of animal and country of origin (so that, for example, within their collection of stamps from France, all the birds are together, all the rabbits are together, and so on) are creating a multiple classification for their collections. The result is a marked increase in the number of relations among objects and events that children can think about and increased flexibility in the particular relations they choose to use in particular circumstances.

Planning

The abilities of decentering, considering multiple variables, and thinking flexibly in new situations are all cognitive prerequisites to efficient and effective planning. Preschoolers can be heard saying to one another things like, "When you come over, we'll play house and have a party," but they have no plans to achieve their goal aside from informing their parents that they want to play with the other child. During middle childhood, children begin to plan in the sense that they form cognitive representations of the actions needed to achieve a specific goal. To make a plan, they have to keep in mind what is presently happening, what they want to happen in the future, and what they need to do in order to get from the present to the future. They must also have enough self-control to keep their attention on achieving the goal (a topic we address in more detail later in the chapter).

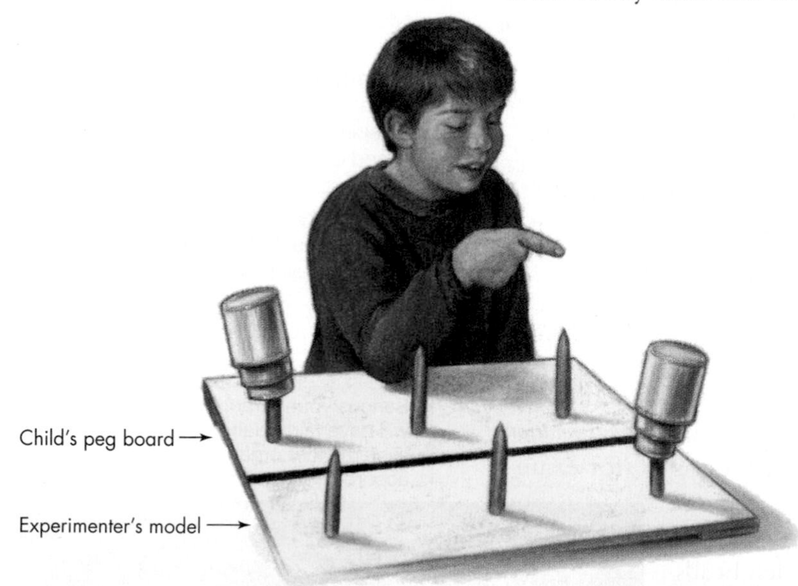

FIGURE 11.9 To solve the Tower of Hanoi problem, this child must, using the three pegs in front of him, reorder the cans one at a time to re-create the experimenter's model stack of cans. The task requires careful planning because it is against the rules to place a small can on top of a large can when moving the cans from peg to peg. (Research from Klahr, 1989.)

Planning is important in reasoning tasks (Friedman et al., 2014). Games that require children to solve logical problems, like Minecraft or Robot Factory, become popular in middle childhood. To play these games skillfully, children have to analyze both the goals and the means of attaining them. A good example of such a game is the Tower of Hanoi, the goal of which is to move a set of size-graded objects from one location to another in accordance with two rules: (1) Only one object can be moved at a time; and (2) a larger object must go on top of a smaller one.

In an experimental form of this game shown in Figure 11.9, the child is presented with a peg board with three pegs, on one of which there are three cans of different sizes—the smallest on the bottom, the largest on the top. The task is to move the cans individually from one peg to another so that they end up on the third peg at the other end of the board in their original order, as illustrated by the experimenter's model. The solution to this problem requires a minimum of seven moves.

A variety of research shows that between the ages of 6 and 7 years, children become better at playing the game (Best & Miller, 2010; Senn, Espy, & Kaufmann, 2004). This trend is not surprising because, according to the evidence, older children are increasingly able to keep in mind both their current circumstances and the circumstances they want to create. Three-year-olds could not keep the rules in mind at all. Six-year-olds began to form subgoals that would take them part of the way to a solution, but they could not think the problem all the way through, and they still found it difficult to assemble their subgoals into an overall plan. When, however, children are given opportunities to reflect on their planning, either by watching videotapes of themselves working on the task or by being instructed in efficient problem strategies, their performance improves (Fireman & Kose, 2002).

As you might imagine, the planning skills described above are important not just to solving mazes and playing games. They are also essential to children's routine activities, including, for example, their ability to safely cross busy streets (Barton & Morrongiello, 2011). And, of course, planning skills are associated with a lot of skills required to perform well in school. In fact, performance on the Tower of Hanoi problem during first grade predicts reading and mathematics achievement during third grade (Friedman et al., 2014).

Elisabeth Andanson/Getty Images

In middle childhood, children enjoy the intellectual challenges of board games that call on newly acquired cognitive skills.

Metacognition

The fact that children's problem solving can be enhanced by calling their attention to effective strategies and ways to use them suggests that *knowledge* about how to think things through may facilitate problem-solving performance. Indeed, **metacognition**, the ability to think about and regulate one's own thoughts, allows one to assess how difficult a problem is likely to be and to be flexible in choosing strategies to solve it (Flavell, 2007; O'Leary & Sloutsky, 2016). The development of metacognition has received considerable attention from researchers, who generally find large mismatches between young children's estimates of what they think they know about a problem and what they actually know. Preschoolers and kindergartners are especially prone to overestimating their knowledge. As metacognition develops over the course of middle childhood, children become more accurate in recognizing the limits of their knowledge and problem-solving skills.

metacognition The ability to think about one's own thought processes.

An example of metacognitive development is provided by Candice Mills and Frank Keil, who asked kindergartners, second-graders, and fourth-graders to estimate their understanding of mechanical devices such as toasters, gum-ball machines, and staplers (Mills & Keil, 2004). First, the children were trained to use a five-point scale to show how much they thought they knew about how the device worked. The low end of the scale was one star, indicating very little understanding; the high end was five stars, indicating a lot of understanding. Next, the children were asked to estimate their knowledge of how, for instance, a toaster works by pointing to the appropriate number of stars on the scale. Then they were asked to provide an explanation for how toasters toast, after which they once again used the scale to estimate their knowledge. (Explanations of younger children tended to focus on pressing a lever, heat, and toast popping out, while those of older children typically referred to electricity coming through the cord.) The idea behind this was that the children might sense the holes in their explanations and downgrade their original estimates of their knowledge. Finally, to really drive home the children's lack of knowledge, the researchers explained the workings of toasters as reported by an expert "who knows five stars about how a toaster works," after which children had one last opportunity to rate their knowledge on the star scale.

FIGURE 11.10 Age differences in children's ratings of their own toaster knowledge. (Data from Mills & Keil, 2004, p. 11.)

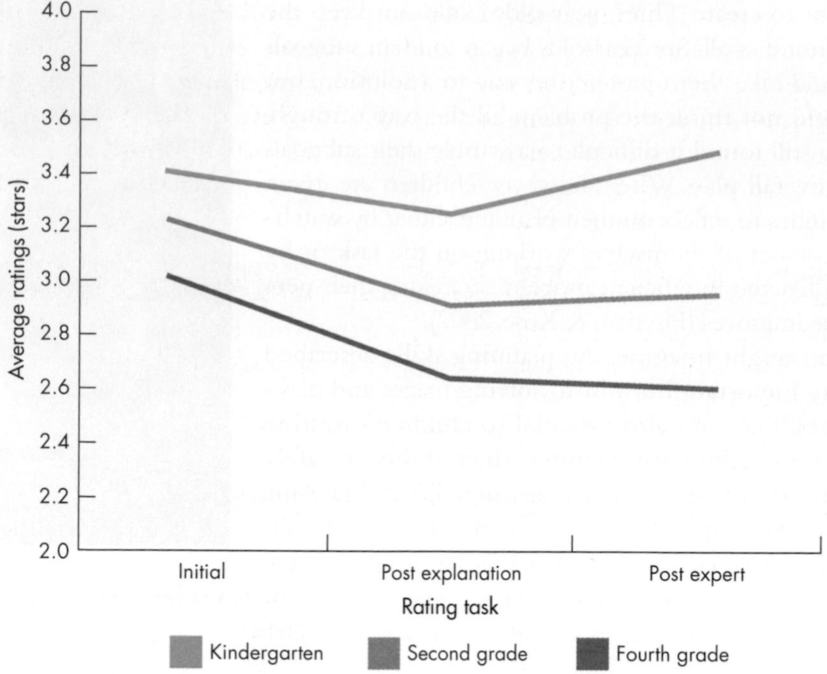

As shown in Figure 11.10, the researchers found clear overall age differences in children's ratings of their toaster knowledge: Fourth-graders were significantly more conservative than kindergartners, and second-graders fell in between. Only the second- and fourth-graders significantly downgraded their estimates after they were asked to explain how the device works or were told of the "five-star" expert's explanation. Indeed, at the end of the study, several of them remarked that they were surprised at how little they knew about toasters. Kindergartners' ratings, as you can see in the figure, actually *increased* after hearing the expert's account. Why? Apparently, they believe that the expert's explanation simply reminded them of what they already knew but forgot to mention. This is a classic example of egocentrism—in this case, the youngsters' obvious difficulty separating their own perspective and knowledge from that of the expert.

The growth of metacognitive skills provides children with important cognitive resources. As metacognitive skills increase, children are better able to keep track of how successfully they are accomplishing their goals, and this allows them to modify their strategies in order to be more successful.

Limitations of Concrete Operations

With the emergence of concrete operations, children take a significant step toward objectivity and the ability to think logically and apply their knowledge flexibly to new problems and situations. However, as we indicated previously, children's intellectual functioning and problem solving are at their best when they involve concrete objects and events that children have experienced directly. As soon as children are asked to reason about abstract phenomena, their problem solving falters.

The difficulty children encounter when reasoning about abstract situations with which they have no direct experience is apparent in a study undertaken by Jason Low and Steve Hollis (Low & Hollis, 2003). These researchers asked groups of 6-, 9-, and 12-year-olds and college students in New Zealand to draw a portrait of themselves as they would look if they had three eyes instead of two and then to explain why they had placed the third eye where they had. Given good reasons for believing that no one in the sample had ever encountered a three-eyed person, the self-portrait task constituted a true challenge to abstract thinking.

All three groups of children tended to place the third eye close to the other two. In their concrete experience, this is, after all, where eyes belong. In addition to drawing similar portraits, children's reasons for their particular eye placements were fairly uniform—and concrete—emphasizing that a third eye on the forehead would help them see better or see farther. In contrast, the self-portraits of college students were much more imaginative and diverse, permitting not only better eyesight but an entirely different, 360-degree view.

APPLY > CONNECT > DISCUSS

Explain how Piaget's fundamental concepts of *decentration* and *objectivity* are apparent in the ability of children who are at the concrete-operational stage to solve conservation and classification tasks.

Information-Processing Approaches

LEARNING OUTCOMES

Point out ways in which information-processing theory accounts for changes in cognition during middle childhood.

Give examples of memory strategies that involve rehearsal, organizational strategies, and elaboration.

Describe improvements in cognition due to metamemory during middle childhood.

Describe changes of attention and executive functioning that occur during middle childhood.

Point out some cultural variations during childhood in memory and attention.

In contrast to Piaget's focus on decentration as a source of increasing objectivity in reasoning, information-processing theorists account for cognitive changes during middle childhood by pointing to processes such as increased memory capacity and attention, more rapid and efficient mental operations, and the acquisition of a variety of mental strategies. According to these theorists, children's increased memory and attention abilities play a central role in allowing them to hold two or more aspects of a problem in mind while they are thinking. For example, a young soccer player racing for the goal can pay attention to, and keep in mind, the positions of teammates, the goalie's well-known difficulty blocking low shots, and an appropriate fake-out move to use on a charging defender. Younger players may have a difficult time simply remembering they are in a soccer game and may run after the ball only when it passes in front of them or when they are encouraged to do so by coaches or parents.

The Role of Memory

Three factors, taken together, appear to bring about the memory changes characteristic of middle childhood (Schneider, 2011):

1. Increases in the speed and capacity of working memory
2. Increases in knowledge about the things one is trying to remember
3. The acquisition of more effective strategies for remembering

Increased Speed and Capacity of Working Memory

Working memory has received a great deal of attention as a source of improved intellectual functioning during middle childhood because it is considered the "active" memory system that holds and manipulates information needed to reason about complex tasks and problems (Simmering & Wood, 2017). Developmentalists have been particularly interested in the *capacity* of children's working memory to "hold" larger amounts of information with age, as well as in the increases of its *speed* in manipulating (or processing) information.

A common behavioral method of measuring the changing capacity of working memory is to assess children's **memory span**, the number of randomly presented items of information children can repeat immediately after the items are presented (Barrouillet et al., 2009). Most 4- and 5-year-olds can recall four digits presented one after another; most 9- and 10-year-olds can remember about six; most adults can remember about seven (Schneider, Knopf, & Sodian, 2009). Although it seems clear that the older child's memory capacity is larger than that of the younger child, developmentalists are keenly aware that other factors also come

memory span The number of randomly presented items of information that can be repeated immediately after they are presented.

into play. For example, in order to store several randomly presented numbers into working memory, individuals must somehow represent each number to themselves, perhaps by silently repeating them. It takes young children longer than older children simply to repeat a number such as 10 or 2, making their memory for the numbers already presented more likely to decay and be lost. Because, by comparison, older children name individual numbers quite quickly, reducing the time interval between storing numbers, they have a greater likelihood of retaining the numbers in memory (Gaillard, Barrouillet, Jarrold, & Camos, 2011).

Cross-cultural research enriches these conclusions. When Chuansheng Chen and Harold Stevenson (1988) compared the memory spans of U.S. and Chinese children 4 to 6 years of age, they found that the Chinese children were able to recall more digits at each of the ages tested. At first, this finding might seem to suggest that the working memory of Chinese children was larger than that of the American children. However, as Chen and Stevenson pointed out, the Chinese words for the digits are shorter than their English equivalents. Thus the task was easier for the Chinese children for the same reason that it was easier for the older North American children: There was a shorter interval between repeated items. This hypothesis was supported by a study in which Stevenson and his colleagues used lists of objects whose names were equal in length in English and Chinese. When these words were presented for remembering, Chinese and American children were found to have equal memory capacities (Stevenson et al., 1985).

Not surprisingly, developmentalists have looked increasingly at brain development as a source of the change in working memory observed during middle childhood (Jog et al., 2016). Neuroimaging studies indicate that the speed at which children's brains can respond to complex stimuli increases throughout childhood (Vogan et al., 2016), and as you know from our discussion thus far, increased speed of processing may help prevent information from being lost. In addition to processing speed, increases in the connections between brain regions and greater efficiency in information processing have also been directly linked to memory performance in children aged 7 to 16 years (Jog et al., 2016; Scherf, Sweeney, & Luna, 2006).

Expanded Knowledge Base

The second factor that contributes to improved memory during childhood is the greater knowledge that older children are likely to have about any given topic simply because they have accumulated more experience (Ornstein & Haden, 2009). This experience provides older children with a richer knowledge base, or store of information, with which to relate, and remember, new information.

A classic demonstration of how a rich knowledge base contributes to children's ability to remember was provided by Michelene Chi (1978), who studied the ability of 10-year-old chess experts and college-student chess novices to remember the arrangement of chess pieces that might occur in a game. She found that the 10-year-olds' memory for the positioning of chess pieces was better by far than that of the college students. However, when the two groups were compared on their ability to recall a random series of numbers, the college students' performances were far superior. More recent studies comparing child experts and novices indicate that experts are also better at seeking out and incorporating new information, distinguishing relevant from irrelevant information, and monitoring their behavior and strategies to improve performance on tasks relevant to their expertise, such as video game play (Geurten, Lejeune, & Meulemans, 2016; VanDeventer & White, 2002).

Improved Memory Strategies

A third source of improved memory ability is children's increased use of **memory strategies**—that is, their deliberate use of actions to enhance remembering (Geurten, Catale, & Meulemans, 2016). A large

memory strategies Specific actions used deliberately to enhance remembering.

number of studies have shown that children's spontaneous use of strategies for remembering undergoes a marked increase between early and middle childhood (Ornstein & Haden, 2009). Three memory strategies that have been intensively studied are rehearsal, organization, and elaboration.

Rehearsal is the process of repeating to oneself the material that one is trying to memorize, such as a word list, a song, or a phone number (Lehmann, 2015). In a classic study of the development of rehearsal strategies in children, John Flavell and his colleagues (Keeney, Cannizzo, & Flavell, 1967) presented 5- and 10-year-olds with seven pictures of objects to remember. The children were asked to wear a "space helmet" with a visor that was pulled down over their eyes during the 15-second interval between the presentation of the pictures and the test for recall. The visor prevented the children from seeing the pictures and allowed the experimenter to watch their lips to see if they repeated to themselves what they had seen. Few of the 5-year-olds were observed to rehearse, but almost all the 10-year-olds did. Within each age group, children who had rehearsed the pictures recalled more of them than did children who had not.

rehearsal The process of repeating to oneself the material that one is trying to remember.

Marked changes are also found in **organizational strategies**—that is, strategies involving mentally grouping the materials to be remembered in meaningful clusters of closely associated items so that remembering only one part of a cluster brings to mind the rest. The use of organizational strategies is often studied by means of a procedure called *free recall.* In a free-recall task, children are shown a large number of objects, or read a list of words one at a time, and then asked to remember them. This kind of memory is called *free* recall because the children are free to recall the items in any order they choose.

organizational strategies Memory strategies in which materials to be remembered are mentally grouped into meaningful categories.

Research has demonstrated that 7- and 8-year-olds are more likely than younger children to group the items they have to remember into easy-to-remember categories (Schlagmüller & Schneider, 2002). The kinds of groupings that children impose on lists of things to be remembered also change with age. Younger children often use sound features such as rhyme ("cat," "sat") or situational associations ("cereal," "bowl") to group words they are trying to remember. Indeed, preschoolers are better than adults at remembering rhyming text (Király, Takács, Kaldy, & Blaser, 2017). In middle childhood, children are more likely to link words according to categories such as animals ("cat," "dog," "horse"), foods ("cereal," "milk," "bananas"), or geometric figures ("triangle," "square," "circle"). These changes in strategy enhance the ability to store and retrieve information deliberately and systematically.

Children who do not spontaneously use rehearsal and organizing strategies can be taught to do so (Pressley & Hilden, 2006; Shing, Werkle-Bergner, Li, & Lindenberger, 2008). In the "space helmet" experiment by Flavell and his colleagues, for example, those who had not rehearsed were later taught to do so and subsequently did as well on the memory task as those who had rehearsed on their own. The effectiveness of such training indicates that there is no unbridgeable gap between the memory performance of 4- to 5-year-olds and that of 7- to 8-year-olds or between children who use strategies spontaneously and those who do not. Over the course of middle childhood, children become increasingly better at using various strategies to help themselves remember.

A third strategy, **elaboration**, is a process in which children identify or make up connections between two or more things they have to remember. In a typical study of elaboration strategies, children are presented with pairs of words and are asked to remember the second one when they hear the first. For example, they might be asked to remember the word "street" after hearing the word "tomato." An elaboration strategy for this word pair might be to think of a tomato squashed in the middle of a street. The spontaneous use of elaboration strategies emerges during

elaboration A memory strategy that involves making connections between two or more things to be remembered.

middle childhood, and children's skill in using them continues to increase with age (Bjorklund, Dukes, & Brown, 2009).

Thinking About Memory

metamemory The ability to think about one's memory processes.

Not only do most 7- and 8-year-olds know and remember more about the world in general than do 3- to 5-year-olds but they also are likely to know more about memory itself—knowledge referred to as **metamemory**, which is a particular form of *metacognition*. Even 5-year-olds have some understanding of how memory works. In a study that stimulated a great deal of the subsequent research on memory development, 5-year-olds said they knew that it was easier to remember a short list of words than a long one, easier to relearn something you once knew than to learn it from scratch, and easier to remember something that happened yesterday than something that happened last month (Kreutzer, Leonard, & Flavell, 1975).

Nevertheless, most 8-year-olds have a better understanding of the limitations of their own memories than do most 5-year-olds. When shown a set of 10 pictures and asked if they could remember them all (something not many children at these ages can do), the majority of the 5-year-olds—but only a few of the 8-year-olds—claimed that they could. The 5-year-olds also failed to correctly evaluate how much effort they would require in order to remember the pictures. Told that they could take all the time they needed to commit the set of pictures to memory, the 5-year-olds announced that they were ready right away, and, of course, succeeded in remembering only a few of the items. The 8-year-olds, by contrast, knew enough to study the materials and to test themselves on their ability to remember (Flavell, Friedrichs, & Hoyt, 1970). However, another study found that even though young children are inclined to be overly confident of their memory abilities, they might adjust their self-assessments downward in the face of evidence that they remembered less than they expected (Bertrand, Moulin, & Souchay, 2017).

Not surprisingly, later research seemed to find a connection between children's metamemory and their use of memory strategies (Pressley & Hilden, 2006).

JHPhoto / Alamy

During middle childhood, activities may challenge children's memory strategies as well as their developing control of attention—such as finding the figure of Waldo in popular books and games known as "Where's Waldo?"

In one study, children 8 to 12 years of age, adolescents 13 to 17 years of age, and adults 18 to 25 years of age were asked about the effectiveness of different types of memory strategies for remembering pairs of common words (Daugherty & Ofen, 2015). Some strategies, such as saying the word pair once, were relatively "shallow" and known to produce only modest increases in memory. Other strategies, such as creating a sentence or imagining a scene that featured both words, were "deep" and known to produce larger memory gains. The study found that children were more likely to use and prefer "shallow" over "deep" strategies, whereas adolescents and adults used and preferred the deeper, more effective strategies.

Increased Control of Attention

With his distinctive red-and-white striped shirt, goofy hat, and nerdy glasses, Waldo is a popular figure in children's books. Attractive to children during the middle childhood years, "Where's Waldo?" and similar seek-and-find puzzles, as seen on p. 392, call upon developing abilities to regulate attention, stay focused on relevant aspects of a task, and ignore irrelevant distractions.

A classic study by Elaine Vurpillot (1968) illustrates the kinds of changes observed by later researchers. She recorded the eye movements of children ages 3 to 10 while the children examined pairs of line drawings of houses such as those shown in Figure 11.11. In some trials, children were shown identical houses; in others, the houses differed in one or more fairly subtle ways. The children were asked to say whether or not the houses were identical.

FIGURE 11.11 Vurpillot used stimuli like these to assess the development of visual search strategies. It is not until middle childhood that children systematically compare the two houses of each pair in order to discover the subtle differences between them. (Research from Vurpillot, 1968.)

Vurpillot found that all the children responded correctly when the houses were identical but that the younger children were more likely to make mistakes when the houses differed, especially if the houses differed in only one way. Her recordings of eye movements pinpointed the difficulty. Rather than systematically paying attention to each of the houses to see how they differed, the younger children scanned the houses in a haphazard order. By contrast, the older children paid attention to each of the houses, scanning, and sometimes rescanning, row by row or column by column. It seems from this experiment that older children have a greater ability to select and execute an effective attentional strategy.

During early and middle childhood, better regulation of attention is also seen in children's increasing ability to ignore distractions and gain voluntary control over what they choose to pay attention to in order to obtain information more efficiently (Connor et al., 2016; Huang-Pollack, Carr, & Nigg, 2002). This type of voluntary control over attention helps children in school when, for example, they need to ignore distractions while reading. Interestingly, research suggests a reciprocal relationship between the ability to control attention and reading performance: More control enables better reading comprehension, and better reading comprehension stimulates yet higher abilities of regulation (Connor et al., 2016).

Executive Function

You have probably noticed that a key component of cognitive development in middle childhood is the increasing ability to *control* and *monitor* one's own thinking and behavior in order to make plans, solve

executive function Higher-level cognitive processes, such as aspects of cognition associated with supervising and controlling lower-level cognitive processes.

problems, and pursue goals. Developmentalists use the term **executive function** to describe higher-level cognitive processes, such as planning and problem solving, that involve supervising and controlling lower-level cognitive processes, such as attention and memory (Fuhs & Day, 2011; Zelazo & Müller, 2011; Müller et al., 2012). For example, when children attempt to solve a problem—such as a math problem—they need to utilize their executive function to keep their attention focused and avoid distractions, consider whether problem-solving strategies they've used in the past can be used in this instance, and monitor whether the strategy they are employing seems to be working or should be changed for a different strategy. As you can see, executive function is highly similar to the *self-regulation* we discussed in Chapter 9 (pp. 308–310). Indeed, developmentalists are divided on whether and where to draw the boundaries between the two (Blair, Zelazo, & Greenberg, 2005). Nevertheless, there is broad agreement that the skills involved in executive function and self-regulation are essential to academic success and are related to developing areas of the brain, especially the frontal cortex, associated with higher cognitive processes.

Given the importance of executive function to children's academic performance, developmentalists have been eager to discover whether it can be improved. An interesting study conducted by Catherine Davis and her colleagues suggested that executive function may be affected by children's health and that improving health through exercise may benefit executive function as well as academic achievement, especially in children who are overweight (Davis et al., 2011). Their experiment included approximately 170 overweight children 7 to 11 years of age who were randomly assigned to one of three groups: *low-exercise* (20 minutes per day of aerobic exercise for approximately 3 months), *high-exercise* (same exercise for 40 minutes per day), and a *no-exercise* control group. As shown in Figure 11.12, aerobic exercise significantly improved the children's math achievement and executive function (as measured by a test of planning ability). In addition, the researchers found a significant "dose effect," meaning that children in the high-exercise group performed significantly better than those in the low-exercise group. An especially intriguing result concerned changes in the children's brain activity over the course of the 13-week program. Specifically, neuroimaging data (fMRI) showed significant increases in prefrontal cortex activity for children in the exercise groups. These results have important implications for educational policies, suggesting that physical activity programs may pay off not only in terms of children's health but also in terms of their academic success in elementary school.

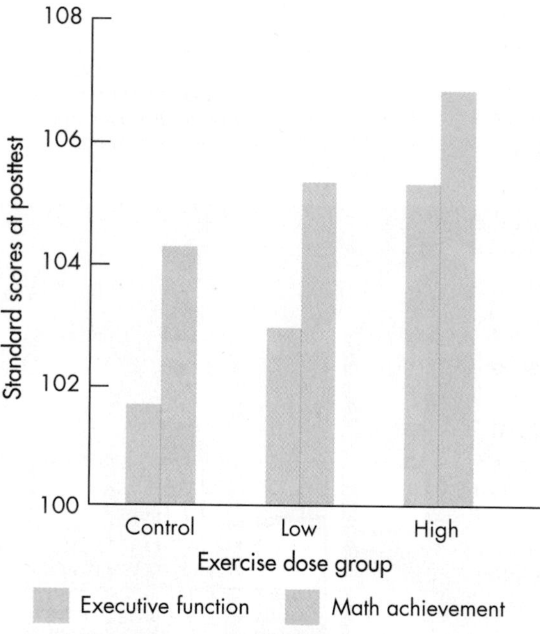

FIGURE 11.12 A study conducted with overweight children found that aerobic exercise significantly improved children's math achievement and executive function. (Data from Davis et al., 2011.)

APPLY > CONNECT > DISCUSS

Many people believe that a really good memory involves the ability to store a lot of information for considerable periods of time. However, good memory is not just about the *quantity* of information stored over time; it also involves how the information is organized. In what specific ways does it seem that children's memories may be organized differently in middle childhood than in early childhood?

LEARNING OUTCOMES

Explain how cross-cultural studies address the universality of concrete operations during middle childhood.

Give examples of cultural variations that influence children's performance when using concrete operations that involve memory, attention, or planning.

The Role of Social and Cultural Contexts

Thus far we have treated cognitive changes between early and middle childhood as if they were entirely determined by development of the brain and the specific internal mental processes brought to bear on the task at hand. But as Usha Goswami cautions, "the functioning of even these relatively specific developmental mechanisms . . . turns out to be influenced by the social . . . and cultural context in which learning takes place" (Goswami, 2002, p. 227). Cross-cultural research on developmental changes in cognitive ability underlines this point.

Is the Acquisition of Conservation Universal?

It was Piaget's (1966/1974) belief that the development of conservation is a universal achievement of human beings, regardless of the cultural circumstances in which they live. The only cultural variation he expected in the acquisition of conservation was that children in some cultures might acquire this form of reasoning earlier than children in others because their culture provided them with more extensive relevant experiences.

However, cross-cultural research on the acquisition of conservation has provoked a great deal of controversy regarding its presumed universality and age of onset (Mishra, 2014). Using Piaget's conservation tasks, several researchers found that children in traditional, non-industrialized societies who have not attended school lag a year or more behind the norms established by Piaget—and, in some cases, appear not to acquire this form of reasoning at all, even as adults. Reviewing the evidence available in the early 1970s, Pierre Dasen (1972) wrote, "It can no longer be assumed that adults of all societies reach the concrete operational stage" (p. 31).

This conclusion was quickly challenged because of its wide-reaching implication that traditional, nonliterate adults think like the preschool children of industrialized countries. For example, Gustav Jahoda (1980), a leading cross-cultural psychologist, rejected outright the possibility that in some cultures people never achieve the ability to think operationally. Jahoda pointed out that it is difficult to see how a society could survive if its members were indifferent to causal relations, incapable of thinking through the implications of their actions, or unable to adopt other people's points of view. He concluded that "no society could function at the preoperational stage, and to suggest that a majority of any people are at that level is nonsense almost by definition" (Jahoda, 1980, p. 116).

To resolve this issue, developmentalists who questioned nonschooled children's apparent failure to understand conservation designed new tests or otherwise modified research procedures. They sought to demonstrate that Piaget's research methods somehow misrepresented such children's mental capacities, either because the test situation was too unfamiliar to the children or because the experimenters, working in an unfamiliar culture and language, did not make their intentions clear. (Similarly, as noted in Chapter 8, researchers in early childhood cognition designed new tasks because they felt Piaget's tasks underestimated the thought processes of preschool-age children.) Ashley Maynard and Patricia Greenfield (2003) addressed this problem in a study comparing task performance of children growing up in a city in the United States (Los Angeles) with that of *Zinacantan* Mayan children growing up in a rural community in the highlands of Chiapas, Mexico.

Through their extensive field work in the Mexican community, Maynard and Greenfield noted that young girls are introduced to the cultural practice of backstrap-loom weaving when they are as young as 3 years of age. Weaving,

The kinds of work that children are assigned afford different kinds of learning opportunities. Young street vendors who have no formal education often acquire a variety of arithmetic skills that, in some respects, may surpass those of children of the same age who attend school.

Ton Koene/AGE Fotostock

FIGURE 11.13 Backstrap loom weaving is an important cultural practice learned through apprenticeship. Simple toy looms are used in early lessons. After the girls gain basic skills and develop physically, they graduate to adult looms.

considered an alternative to schooling, is a complex technical skill acquired by virtually all the girls in the community through apprenticeship (see Chapter 12, pp. 411–412). The girls begin weaving on relatively simple toy looms and later graduate to adult looms (see Figure 11.13). In analyzing the cognitive skills involved in using the looms, the researchers found that the adult loom, but not the toy loom, requires concrete operational reasoning. Significantly, Mayan girls usually begin using adult looms between the ages of 8 and 10 years. Because most girls in the study had never been to school, this finding contradicts the assertion that schooling is essential to the acquisition of concrete operations.

To further explore the results of their field observations and analysis of loom skill-level differences, Maynard and Greenfield presented 160 boys and girls from the Zinacantec community and from Los Angeles with two types of concrete operational tasks. One was a traditional Piagetian task (referred to as the knots problem because it involves twisted/knotted strings of beads that study participants are required to mentally untwist/unknot); the other was based on traditional weaving practices (see Figure 11.14). Although the children in Los Angeles performed significantly better on the Piagetian task, the Zinacantec Mayan children, especially girls, performed significantly better on the weaving task.

While some developmentalists, including Maynard and Greenfield, focus on how standard Piagetian tasks may underestimate the cognitive abilities of unschooled children, others suggest that the tasks may pose special difficulties even for schooled children, if their native language is different from that used to administer the tasks. Raphael Nyiti (1982), for example, compared the conservation performances of 10- and 11-year-old children of two cultural groups, both living on Cape Breton, Nova Scotia. Some of the children were of English-speaking European backgrounds, and some were of the Micmac tribe. The Micmac children all spoke Micmac at home, but they had spoken English in school since first grade. The children of European backgrounds were all interviewed in English by an English

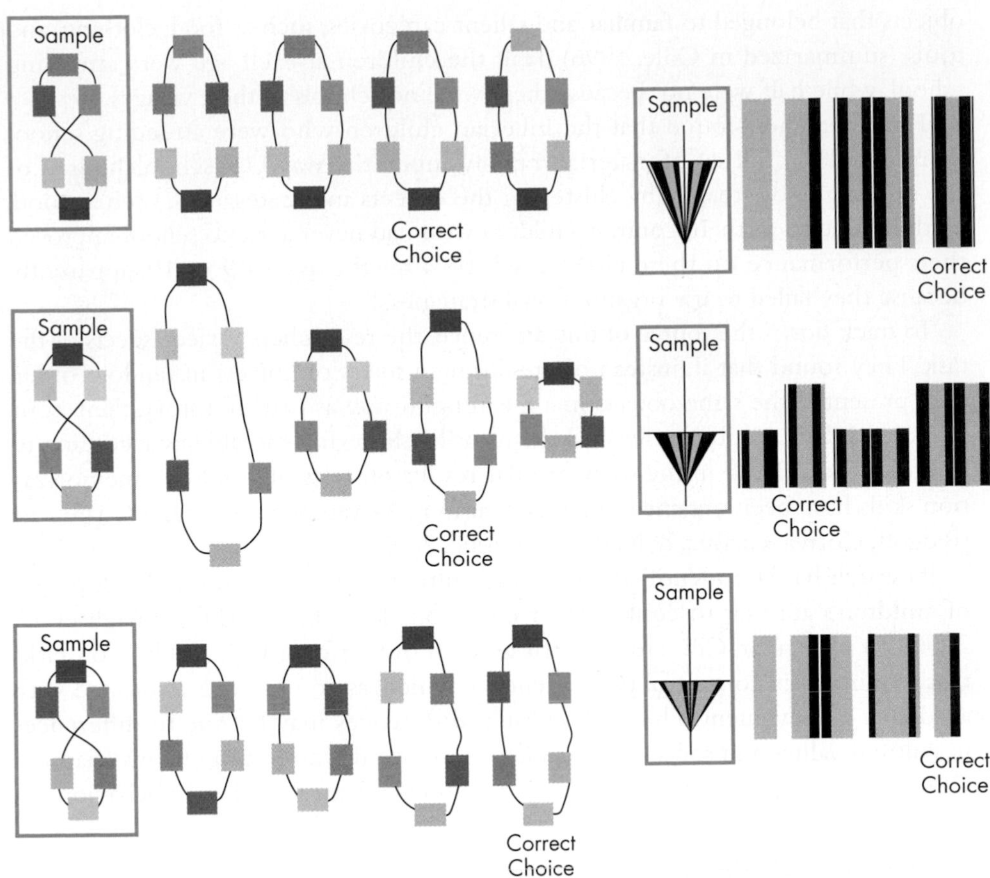

FIGURE 11.14 The knots problem is a traditional Piagetian task that measures cognitive development. (Research from Maynard & Greenfield, 2003.)

speaker of European background. The Micmac children were interviewed once in English and once in Micmac.

Nyiti found that when the Micmac children were interviewed on the conservation tasks in their native language, there was no difference between their performance and that of the other group. But when the Micmac children were interviewed in English, only half as many seemed to understand the concept of conservation. Nyiti (1976) obtained similar results in a study of children in his native Tanzania, as did other researchers in the West African country of Sierra Leone (Kamara & Easley, 1977).

Taken as a whole, these studies, along with others, demonstrate that when Piaget's clinical procedures are applied appropriately, using materials with which people have extensive experience, conservation (and by extension, concrete operations) is a universal cognitive achievement of middle childhood, just as Piaget assumed it to be (Segall, Dasen, Berry, & Poortinga, 1999). However, the evidence also shows that there are quite dramatic cultural variations in children's familiarity with the contents and procedures used in standard Piagetian tests of conservation and that these variations clearly influence children's performances on the tests. Modern researchers are less concerned with finding cultural differences and similarities in cognitive development than understanding how and why particular cognitive abilities are adaptive within the specific contexts of children's lives (Maynard, 2008).

Cultural Variations in Memory and Attention

Cross-cultural research has revealed striking variations in the development of memory and attention. In the case of memory, a study conducted in rural Liberia involved presenting groups of children of different ages with a set of 20 common objects that belonged to familiar and salient categories, such as food, clothing, and tools (summarized in Cole, 1996). Half the children at each age were attending school, while half were not because there were no schools in their villages.

The researchers found that the Liberian children who were attending school memorized the full set of materials rapidly, much the way U.S. schoolchildren of the same age do—that is, by clustering the objects into categories, such as food, clothing, and so forth. In contrast, children who had never gone to school improved their performance on these tasks very little after the age of 9 or 10, apparently because they failed to use organizational strategies.

To track down the source of this difference, the researchers varied aspects of the task. They found that if, instead of presenting a series of objects in random order, they presented the same objects in a meaningful way as part of a story, their non-schooled Liberian subjects recalled them easily, clustering the objects according to the roles they played in the story. Similar results on tests of children's memorization skills have been obtained in research among Mayan people of rural Guatemala (Rogoff, Correa-Chávez, & Navichoc-Cotuc, 2005).

Research has also identified fascinating cultural differences in the development of children's abilities to control their attention (Lan et al., 2011; Sabbagh et al., 2006). In particular, Chinese children tend to outperform U.S. children on tasks that require them to control their attention, which, as you know, is associated with academic achievement. The stark cultural differences may be due to differences in cultural values and socialization practices. As we discussed in previous chapters, Chinese culture places great value on controlling and regulating one's behavior.

Cultural Variations in Planning

A cross-cultural study by Shari Ellis and Bonnie Schneiders (reported in Ellis & Siegler, 1997) shows how differences in cultural values can shape the way and extent to which children plan ahead. Using a schematic drawing of a maze representing a rural scene, Ellis and Schneiders studied the way that Navajo and European American children planned their routes to and from different parts of the maze. The researchers were interested in contrasting these two groups because the two cultures place different values on doing things speedily. The Navajo emphasize doing things thoughtfully rather than quickly (John, 1972). By contrast, speed of mental performance is often treated as an index of intelligence among Americans of European background (Sternberg, 1990). This cultural difference in values was expressed in the children's behavior as they planned their routes through the maze. The Navajo children spent almost 10 times as long planning their movements as the European-American children did—and, as a result, they made significantly fewer errors.

APPLY > CONNECT > DISCUSS

In what ways does Michael Cole's study of Liberian children suggest that culture contributes both to children's knowledge bases and to the type of memory strategies that children favor?

LEARNING OUTCOMES

Point out how different cultures emphasize either cognitive or social competence when defining intelligence.

Explain intelligence quotient (IQ) in relationship to intelligence tests.

Distinguish among the concepts fluid intelligence, crystallized intelligence, and spatial intelligence.

Identify the three questions that dominate research by developmentalists in intelligence.

Individual Differences in Cognitive Development

If you were a hungry 10-year-old Australian Aborigine, and your parents were out hunting and gathering, how would you know where to go to find the edible goanna lizard? With all the various scratches and scuffs in the sand, how would you recognize the special tracks that would lead you to your prey? How would you catch and carry your lizards? How would you prepare them for cooking? Acquiring your afternoon snack would obviously require a good deal of knowledge and planning, characteristics of intelligent behavior. And if you nearly always returned to camp with a goanna sack brimming with lizards, while your peers rarely did, you might even be considered the most intelligent child in the village.

But all those intelligent behaviors associated with successful goanna hunting wouldn't protect you from having an empty stomach. They would, for example, get you nowhere at the corner store where you and your friends might stop for a snack on the way home from school. In this instance, your superior intelligence might be manifested by your having brought enough money with you, being able to count your change, and knowing that a granola bar and an apple are better choices than a bag of chips and a soda.

The fact that intelligence is so securely anchored to the cultural contexts in which it is used has led many developmentalists to argue that intelligence has no clear meaning outside its cultural context (Sternberg & Grigorenko, 2008). Indeed, although all languages have terms that describe individual differences in people's ability to solve various kinds of problems, the precise meanings of these terms vary among cultures, and it has proved difficult—some say impossible—to define intelligence so that individual differences in intelligence can be measured as precisely as weight or height or the number of lizards in a goanna sack. Some cultures, including the Chewa of eastern Zambia, define intelligence largely in social terms, emphasizing cooperation and obedience (Serpell, 2000). Other cultures, including those of Europe and North America, define intelligence in mainly cognitive terms. Still others, including many Asian and African cultures, believe that intelligence includes both social and cognitive features. A case in point is the conception of intelligence of rural Kenyans, which has been studied by Elena Grigorenko and her colleagues (Grigorenko et al., 2001). These researchers report that among the Luo of rural Kenya, there are four words that people apply to different kinds of problem-solving abilities. One of these words appears to correspond to the notion of cognitive competence at the heart of European and North American conceptions of intelligence. The others refer to social qualities such as diligence or obedience, or personal qualities with social implications, such as a willingness to take initiative.

While cultural notions of intelligence vary, almost all children growing up today in industrialized countries can expect to take an intelligence test intended to assess their cognitive competence. Such tests are used to decide the kind of education they will receive and the kind of work they seem best suited for, which will, in turn, influence the lives they will lead as adults. It is thus important to understand the concept of intelligence that underlies these tests, as well as intelligence testing itself as a factor in children's development.

Measuring Intelligence

Interest in measuring intelligence became widespread at the beginning of the twentieth century, when mass education was becoming the norm in industrialized countries. Though most children seemed to profit from the instruction they were given, some had considerable difficulty learning. In France, the minister of public instruction named a commission to determine how to distinguish between what he termed "defective" children, who needed special educational treatment, and children who were failing to learn in school for other reasons. The commission asked Alfred Binet, a professor of psychology at the Sorbonne, and Théodore Simon, a physician, to create a means of identifying those children who needed special educational treatment. Binet and Simon set out to construct a test for diagnosing mental subnormality that would have all the precision and validity of a medical examination. They especially wanted to avoid incorrectly diagnosing children as "mentally subnormal" (Binet & Simon, 1916).

After considerable research on various test items presented to children of various ages, Binet and Simon concluded that they had succeeded in constructing a scale of intelligence. They called the basic index of intelligence for this scale *mental age* (*MA*). A child who performed as well on the test as an average 7-year-old was said to have an MA of 7, a child who did as well as an average 9-year-old was said to have an MA of 9, and so on. The MA provided a convenient way to characterize mental subnormality. A "dull" 7-year-old child was one who performed like a normal child 1 or more years younger.

Shortly after Binet and Simon introduced their scale, psychologist William Stern recognized a serious limitation in using MA as an index of intelligence. To get a sense of this limitation, consider two children, an 18-year-old with an MA of 16 and a 5-year-old with an MA of 3. Although both children are 2 years "behind" the average, there would be reason to be much more concerned about the 5-year-old's intellectual development than about the 18-year-old's. To address the fact that 2 years of development in the life of a very young child is not equivalent to 2 years of development in the life of an older child, Stern (1912) introduced a new way of calculating intelligence. He used the simple strategy of dividing children's mental age by their chronological age (CA) to obtain a measure of their intelligence—the **intelligence quotient (IQ)**:

intelligence quotient (IQ) The ratio of mental age to chronological age, calculated as IQ = (MA/CA)100.

$$IQ = (MA/CA) \times 100$$

Calculation of IQ in this fashion ensures that when children are performing precisely as expected for their age, the resulting score will be 100; thus 100 is an "average IQ" by definition (Figure 11.15). Applied to the two children described above, the calculation generates an IQ score of 89 for the 18-year-old and 60 for the 5-year old.

Intelligence tests have undergone substantial refinement since the seminal work of Binet, Simon, and Stern. One of the most common tests used today is the Wechsler Intelligence Scale for Children (WISC), which assesses general intellectual ability, as well as abilities in five distinct cognitive areas: verbal comprehension, fluid reasoning working memory, processing speed, and visual-spatial reasoning. These refinements provide a much more nuanced view of the child's intellectual functioning.

FIGURE 11.15 This figure illustrates an idealized bell-shaped curve of the distribution of IQ scores. A bell-shaped curve is a distribution of scores on a graph in which the most frequent value, the mode, is in the center, and the less frequent values are distributed symmetrically on either side. By definition, the modal IQ score is 100.

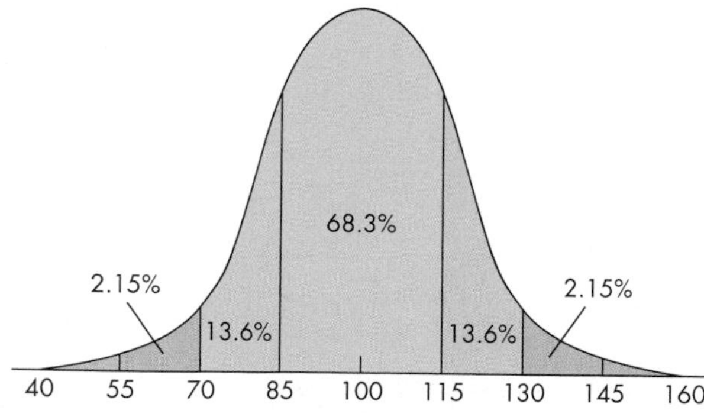

Persistent Questions About Intelligence

The adoption and refinement of IQ testing methods by later generations of developmentalists represent only part of the contribution that Binet and Simon made to the study of intelligence. Equally important have been the questions they brought to the fore, three of which have dominated research on intelligence ever since. The first question focuses on the nature of intelligence itself: Is it a general characteristic of a person's entire mental life, or is it a bundle of relatively specific abilities? Second is the question of how biological and environmental factors contribute to variations among individuals and groups in test performance. The third question is about the nature of IQ tests and their relationship to culture: To what extent might tests be biased in their assessment of intelligence?

The Nature of Intelligence: General or Specific?

Although Binet and Simon (1916) were skeptical about the possibility of defining intelligence, they attempted to specify the quality of mind they were trying to test for:

> It seems to us that in intelligence there is a fundamental faculty, the alteration or lack of which is of the utmost importance for practical life. This faculty is judgment, otherwise called good sense, practical sense, initiative, the faculty of adapting oneself to circumstances. To judge well, to comprehend well, to reason well, these are the essential activities of intelligence. (p. 43)

By referring to intelligence as "a fundamental faculty," Binet and Simon signaled their belief that intelligence can be considered holistically. Many others have followed this approach, noting, for example, that an individual's performance tends to be similar across types of intelligence-test items, a tendency consistent with the existence of a general intelligence (Mackintosh, 2011).

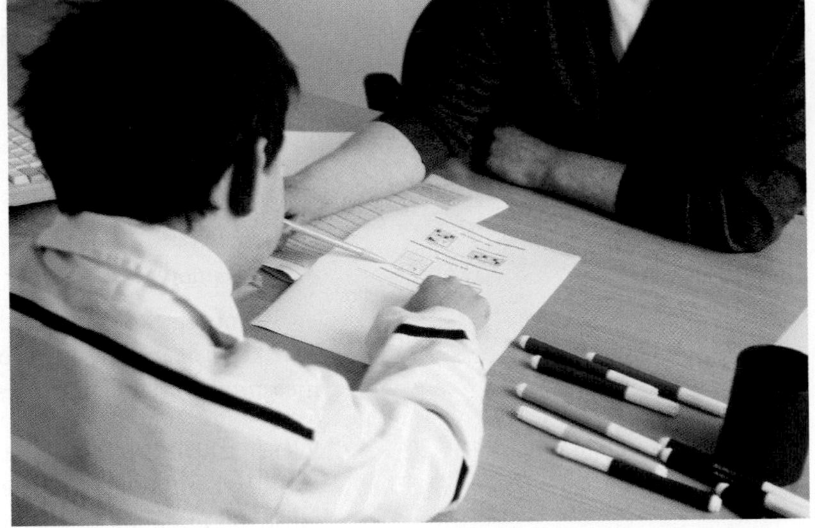

BSIP/UIG Via Getty Images

Despite persistent questions about the nature of intelligence and how to measure it, IQ tests are a routine part of many children's lives.

However, many psychologists reject the idea of general intelligence, arguing instead that intelligence is composed of several distinct and separate abilities (Ekinci, 2014; Lynch & Warner, 2012). Two approaches that depict intelligence in terms of distinctive capacities have been particularly influential. Howard Gardner (1983, 2006) has proposed a theory of *multiple intelligences*, each of which coincides with a different cognitive module and follows its own developmental path (Table 11.2). For example, musical intelligence often appears at an early age; logical mathematical intelligence seems to peak in late adolescence and early adulthood; and the kind of spatial intelligence on which artists rely may reach its peak much later. Gardner argues that the expression of each kind of intelligence depends upon a combination of three factors: (1) innate biological brain structures, (2) the extent to which the particular kind of intelligence is emphasized in a given culture, and (3) the extent to which a child is provided deliberate instruction in activities associated with the particular kind of intelligence.

These talented young dancers display their creative intelligence in a dance competition at a ceremonial powwow in New Mexico.

Chuck Place / Alamy

TABLE 11.2 Gardner's Multiple Intelligences

Kind of Intelligence	Characteristics
Linguistic	Special sensitivity to language, which allows one to choose precisely the right word or turn of phrase and to grasp new meanings easily
Musical	Sensitivity to pitch and tone, which allows one to detect and produce musical structure
Logical-mathematical	Ability to engage in abstract reasoning and manipulate symbols
Spatial	Ability to perceive relations among objects, to transform mentally what one sees, and to re-create visual images from memory
Bodily-kinesthetic	Ability to represent ideas in movement; characteristic of great dancers and mimes
Personal	Ability to gain access to one's own feelings and to understand the motivations of others
Social	Ability to understand the motives, feelings, and behaviors of other people

Information from Gardner, 1983.

The second approach that views intelligence as consisting of distinct capacities is Robert Sternberg's (1985) "triarchic" theory of intelligence, which proposes that there are three kinds of intelligence:

1. *Analytic:* The abilities we use to analyze, judge, evaluate, compare, and contrast
2. *Creative:* The abilities we use to create, invent, discover, and imagine or suppose
3. *Practical:* The abilities we use to apply knowledge by putting it into practice

Sternberg (2007) reports that an individual's performance level can vary from one kind of intelligence to another and argues that only analytic intelligence is measured by standard IQ tests.

What Explains Population Differences?

Along with their disagreements about what intelligence means and whether it is specific or general, developmentalists disagree about the significance of differences across individuals and across groups in performance on tests. The debate dates back to the beginning of World War I, when Robert Yerkes proposed that all military recruits be given an intelligence test to determine their fitness to serve in military capacities. In addition to determining individual recruits' fitness, the testing was perceived as generating data about the U.S. population as a whole (Yerkes, 1921). Approximately 1.75 million men were given IQ tests—written tests for those who could read and write English and a picture-completion test for those who could not (Figure 11.16). Never before had IQ tests been administered to such large groups of people at one time or to people for whom the language of the tests was not their native language.

FIGURE 11.16 In the picture-completion test used by Robert Yerkes and his colleagues to test recruits during World War I, each picture is incomplete in some way; the task was to identify what was missing. (From Yerkes, 1921.)

Robert Yerkes, 1921

Yerkes's research began a controversy that continues to the present time. Two results appeared to be particularly provocative. First, the average mental age of native-born Anglo Americans was assessed to be 13 years. Since, by the standards of the time, a mental age of 8 to 12 years was considered subnormal for an adult, it appeared that a substantial part of the Anglo population consisted of "morons." Second, there was a substantial difference between the scores obtained by recruits of European American and of African American origin. Overall, the average for recruits of European origin was a mental age of 13.7 years, whereas African Americans averaged slightly more than 10 years.

Several of the pioneer testers of intelligence interpreted such differences as resulting from innate, immutable differences in natural intelligence ("nature"). According to this *innatist hypothesis of intelligence*, some people are born generally smarter than others, and no amount of training or variation in the environment can alter this fact. The generally lower test scores of members of ethnic-minority groups and the poor (who often, but not always, are the same people) were widely interpreted to mean that such groups were innately and irrevocably inferior (Herrnstein & Murray, 1994).

During the 1930s and 1940s the general-intelligence, innatist position was countered by an *environmental hypothesis of intelligence*, which asserted that intelligence is both specific—that is, includes distinct and separate abilities—and heavily dependent on experience. It was demonstrated, for example, that after people had moved from rural areas to the city, their intelligence test scores rose (Klineberg, 1935) and that when orphans were removed from very restricted early environments, their intelligence test scores improved markedly.

One of the most striking new lines of evidence for the environmental hypothesis of intelligence is the fact that worldwide there has been a steady increase in IQ test performance since testing began roughly 100 years ago, a trend called the **Flynn effect**, named after the scientist who discovered it (Flynn, 1984, 2007). Although the amount of improvement differs somewhat according to the kind of test that is used and the particular country in which it is administered, the general result for the 20 countries where intelligence testing has been widely carried out for many decades indicates that IQ scores have been going up. One team of researchers reviewed and analyzed more than 200 studies of the IQs of nearly 4 million participants over the course of 105 years (Pietschnig & Voracek, 2015). Their **meta-analysis**—a statistical analysis of results collected from multiple scientific studies—documented the Flynn effect for three broad categories of intellectual performance (Figure 11.17):

Flynn effect The steady increase over the past 100 years in IQ test performance, an increase believed to support the environmental hypothesis of intelligence.

meta-analysis A statistical analysis of results collected from multiple scientific studies.

- **Fluid intelligence** is derived from tests involving tasks that require reasoning but not prior knowledge, such as figuring out the next number in a series that begins 1, 3, 5, 7.
- **Crystallized intelligence** is derived from tests involving knowledge-based questions, such as "What is the capital of France?"
- **Spatial intelligence** is derived from tests of the ability to mentally rotate objects in order to solve problems, such as deciding whether a cube, if rotated in a certain direction, will look the same as a stimulus cube.

fluid intelligence The intelligence quotient derived from tests involving tasks that require reasoning but not prior knowledge.

crystallized intelligence The intelligence quotient derived from tests involving knowledge-based questions.

spatial intelligence The intelligence quotient derived from tests of the ability to mentally rotate objects in order to solve problems.

There is no clear consensus about what environmental factors are causing IQ scores to go up, but it is certain that the change must involve the environment, since rapid change in the genetic constitution of people all over the world has not taken place, but large changes in the environment have (Dickens & Flynn, 2006; Pietschnig & Voracek, 2015). As Flynn points out, it is almost impossible to determine precisely how the environment contributes to the development of intelligence because all the possible causal factors are closely connected with each other, and they all lead to changes that are in the same direction. The list of the possible causal factors includes improved nutrition and decreased family size, which may impact fluid IQ; increasing years of and greater access to education, which may impact crystallized IQ; and the spread of technology and interactive video games, which may impact spatial IQ.

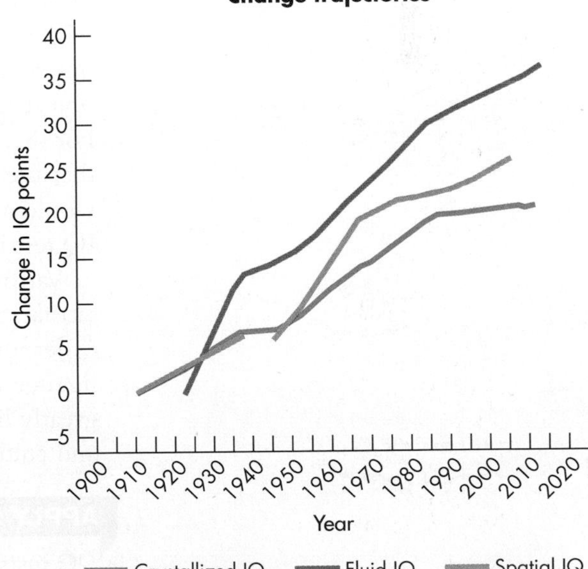

FIGURE 11.17 Increases in IQ across generations, a phenomenon dubbed the "Flynn effect," have been reported in research in many countries. (Data from Pietschnig & Voracek, 2015.)

Are IQ Tests Culturally Biased?

At the present time, no responsible scholar believes that the variation in intelligence test scores from person to person can be attributed entirely to either environmental or genetic factors. As we pointed out in Chapter 2, the attempt to tease apart the specific gene–environment interactions that shape human beings is especially difficult in relation to traits like intelligence that are *polygenic*—that is, that are shaped by several or many genes acting in combination in a given set of environmental conditions. Thus, even when it has been possible to estimate the genetic contribution to a trait, little can be said about precisely which genes are interacting with the environment in what way. Efforts to separate the various influences of nature and nurture on the phenotype are further complicated

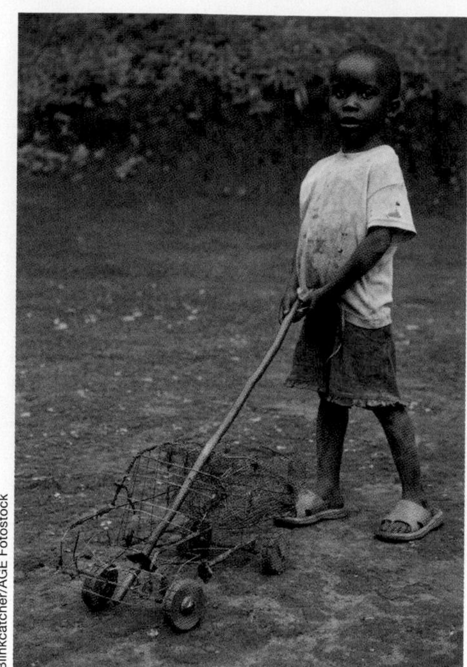

Blinkcatcher/AGE Fotostock

Although children from traditional agricultural societies sometimes perform poorly on psychological tests, their cognitive abilities are often manifested in other ways. This Ugandan boy has constructed his toy car out of bits of wire and some wooden wheels.

by the fact that parents contribute both to their children's genetic constitution and to the environment in which their children grow up. And then there is the final knot in untangling gene–environment interaction: Children actively shape their own environments in response to both genetic and environmental influences.

Attempts to understand how genetic and environmental factors combine to create the phenotypic behavior called "intelligence" face another, even greater difficulty. As we noted earlier, psychologists disagree profoundly about what, precisely, they are measuring when they administer an intelligence test. All they can say with any confidence is that these tests predict later school performance to a moderate degree.

At first glance, IQ tests may appear to be standard measures logically similar to a yardstick. But this appearance is an illusion. Precisely because intelligence tests derive their validity from their correlation with academic achievement, they are rooted in the schooled society in which they are developed and bound to the graphic systems of representation that are central to all schooling. But these modes of representation are generally absent in nonliterate societies. To be administered to a !Kung child, every existing intelligence test would thus require some modification—and not just translation from English to !Kung. If, for example, one of the test questions asks how many fingers are on two hands, the testers might assume that the test could be adapted to !Kung with only minimal modification—but that assumption would be wrong. The number system used by the !Kung is not the same as that used by Westerners, and it plays a different role in their lives. There is not much to count in a hunting-and-gathering society; in !Kung society, the relative importance of knowing the number of fingers on a hand is less important than knowing how to tie knots with those fingers. Indeed, research suggests that performance on tests of intelligence and cognitive abilities depends on the extent to which particular cultures value, and consequently provide opportunities to practice, different intellectual and cognitive skills (Bakos, Denburg, Fonseca, & Parente, 2010). Furthermore, the developing brain is substantially affected by cultural experiences in ways that affect children's behavior, likely contributing to their test performance (Miller & Kinsbourne, 2012).

When it comes to the tests that require interpretation of pictures or some form of written answer, even more serious difficulties arise. The !Kung have no tradition of either drawing or writing, and research with nonliterate peoples in several parts of the world and with young children in the United States shows that people without such experience do not automatically interpret two-dimensional pictures of objects as they would the objects themselves (Pick, 1997; Serpell & Haynes, 2004). For them, interpreting the pictures requires additional mental work. As a result, tests that use pictures or require copying figures graphically would be inappropriate, as would any tests that depend on the ability to read. We thus cannot assume that an IQ test is like a yardstick, yielding equivalent measures in all cultural environments.

Various attempts have been made to create "culture-free" tests, but no generally satisfactory approach has been found: All tests of intelligence draw on a background of learning that is culture specific (Serpell & Haynes, 2004). The fact that intelligence cannot be tested independently of the culture that gives rise to the test greatly limits the conclusions that can be drawn from IQ testing in different social and cultural groups.

APPLY > CONNECT > DISCUSS

IQ tests were first developed in order to identify children who needed special education. Today, the use of IQ tests in making decisions to place children on different "academic ability tracks" is hotly debated. Using concepts and research evidence presented in this section, describe the pros and cons of IQ testing and ability tracking in schools.

Looking Ahead

LEARNING OUTCOMES

Assess how changes in cognitive ability affect a child's relationship with the adults in his or her life.

The changes in children's biological and cognitive abilities between early and middle childhood point to specific features of children's physical abilities and thought processes that are becoming more systematic and can be applied across a broader variety of settings. Particularly important is the extent to which children are gaining increasing understanding of, and control over, their new powers of thought and action. Considered as a whole, rather than as isolated achievements, these changes help explain why adults begin to grant their children more independence during this developmental period.

Although the cognitive skills and capacities of children everywhere change dramatically over the course of middle childhood, our discussions of cross-cultural work suggest that the specific contexts of children's daily lives support intellectual development in what can be radically different ways. To properly address the issue of how culturally organized environments exert their effects on cognitive development, we need to reach beyond the relatively narrow range of tasks that has been featured in psychologists' studies and investigate the changes that children display in a variety of social contexts, especially in classrooms and peer groups, where many children in middle childhood begin to spend much of their time. Many developmentalists believe that experiences in both of these contexts are crucial to the cognitive changes associated with middle childhood. We will examine these contexts in the next two chapters.

1. How do the neurological changes of middle childhood relate to cognitive development?
2. Executive function is a critical aspect of cognitive development during middle childhood. Consider how culture might support this development.

Summary

- The beginning of middle childhood is recognized in cultures around the world, particularly in adults' new expectations of their 6- and 7-year-olds. These expectations relate to children's increased physical capacities and cognitive abilities.

Physical and Motor Development

- Size and strength increase significantly during middle childhood although more slowly than in earlier years. Muscle mass and fat tissue both increase.
- Although height and weight are both influenced by genetic factors, environmental factors, such as nutrition and health, also play an important role. For example, in the United States, changes in diet in recent decades have contributed to an increase in childhood obesity.
- Strength, agility, and balance all improve in middle childhood, with girls tending to be more advanced than boys.
- Brain developments include changes to the cortex and limbic system. The cortex, especially the prefrontal cortex, is associated with higher forms of reasoning and decision making. The limbic system is associated with the experience and interpretation of emotions. In addition:
    - The thickness of the cortex changes, increasing with the growth of neurons (synaptogenesis) and decreasing with consolidation of neural pathways (pruning).

The developmental pattern of cortical thickening and thinning may vary between children.

- The cingulate gyrus plays an important role in communications between the cortex and the limbic system.

Concrete-Operational Development

- According to Piaget, as a result of increasing decentration, at about age 7 or 8, children become capable of mental operations—of logically combining, separating, and transforming information. With the advent of this stage of concrete operations, children can think in a more organized, flexible way, and the world becomes more predictable to them.
- Concrete-operational thinking is reflected in new abilities related to:
  - Conservation, Piaget's term for the understanding that some properties of an object or a substance remain the same even when its appearance is altered in some way
  - Classification, with children now able to understand the relation between a superordinate class and its subclasses and to categorize objects according to multiple criteria
  - Planning, which requires forming mental representations of actions needed to achieve a goal
  - Metacognition, with children better able to think about and regulate their thoughts
- The limitations of concrete operations are apparent in the difficulty children encounter when reasoning about abstract, unfamiliar situations.

Information-Processing Approaches

- According to information-processing theorists, the cognitive changes in middle childhood are made possible by changes such as:
  - Improvements in memory arising from increased processing speed and capacity of working memory; increases in knowledge; and greater use of more effective strategies for remembering, such as rehearsal, organizational strategies, and elaboration
  - Improvements in metamemory, or knowledge about memory, including about memory limitations and strategies
  - Increases in children's ability to regulate their attention, which enables them to stay focused and ignore distractions
- Developmentalists have suggested that the mechanisms for cognitive change suggested in Piaget's stage theory and those suggested by information-processing theorists may in fact work together.

The Role of Social and Cultural Contexts

- Cross-cultural studies suggest the universality of concrete operations in middle childhood as well as significant cultural variations that influence performance.
- Across cultures, memory strategies differ significantly depending on whether children have had schooling. Cross-cultural differences in planning relate to cultural differences in values.

Individual Differences in Cognitive Development

- Definitions of intelligence differ among cultures and may focus on social, rather than cognitive, competence.
- Intelligence tests, as they have been developed since their introduction by Binet and Simon, attempt to measure cognitive competence by producing an IQ score based on a child's performance compared with that of children of the same age.
- Research on intelligence has been dominated by three questions:
  1. Is intelligence a general characteristic, or are there specific kinds of intelligence? Two approaches taking the second position are Gardner's theory of multiple intelligences and Sternberg's triarchic theory of intelligence.
  2. Are differences among individuals and among groups in performance on IQ tests the result of genetic or environmental factors? Evidence for an environmental role comes from the Flynn effect, the increase across generations in performance on IQ tests in areas of fluid, crystallized, and spatial reasoning intelligence.
  3. To what extent might IQ tests be culturally biased? All tests draw on learning that is culture specific, limiting the conclusions that can be drawn.

Looking Ahead

- The cognitive changes of middle childhood are associated with children's increasing control over their thoughts and actions. This is consistent with the greater independence that children of this age are granted by adults.

Key Terms

limbic system, p. 381
concrete operations, p. 383
conservation of number, p. 384
conservation of volume, p. 384
identity, p. 385
compensation, p. 385
reversibility, p. 385
metacognition, p. 387
memory span, p. 389
memory strategies, p. 390
rehearsal, p. 391
organizational strategies, p. 391
elaboration, p. 391
metamemory, p. 392
executive function, p. 394
intelligence quotient (IQ), p. 400
Flynn effect, p. 403
meta-analysis, p. 403
fluid intelligence, p. 403
crystallized intelligence, p. 403
spatial intelligence, p. 403

uart Fox/Getty Images

CHAPTER 12

School as a Context for Development

Ben Charma is the headmaster at a primary school in the heart of rural Zambia. More than one half of the 1,700 children who attend the school have been orphaned by AIDS. The son of a copper miner, Mr. Charma worked hard at school and avoided the mining life that ruined his father's health. He knows what lies in store for children when educational chances are limited by poverty. It is the end of the school year, and exam results show that the graduating students have done well. Yet, this is the most heartbreaking time of all for the teachers that have worked so hard to achieve a good pass rate for their pupils. They know that for many of their students—particularly girls—this will be their very last day at school, even though they are just 11 or 12 years old. Their families don't have enough money for school clothing, shoes, books, stationery, and fees needed to go on to secondary school. And so it is that parents come to beg. They understand that without an education, their daughters will be forced to marry young and face lives of backbreaking labor. They know, as well, that their daughters' babies will also be born into families too poor to give them more than life.

Many millions of girls in sub-Saharan Africa are unable to go to school, with devastating consequences for rural communities. When mothers do not learn about basic hygiene and how to prevent diseases such as AIDS, children die younger, diseases spread throughout the community, and earnings are lower. When girls go to school, the benefits multiply across whole communities. When women farmers have the same access to education as their brothers and husbands, crop yields rise by 22 percent. In Africa, if mothers receive just 5 years of education, their children are 40 percent more likely to live to their fifth birthday. Fortunately, the world has begun to heed the urgent message that educating girls is the key to eradicating poverty, and literacy rates are on the rise. Former United Nations Secretary-General Kofi Annan once said: "Without achieving gender equity for girls in education, the world has no chance of achieving many of the ambitious health, social and development targets it has set for itself."

(Information from Cotton, 2006.)

In contrast to the students in Mr. Charma's school, it is unlikely that at the tender age of 11 or 12, you worried that your education might be about to end or thought about school in terms of its consequences for your future. But as Ann Cotton argues in her heartfelt plea to increase educational access for Africa's children, especially girls, going to school not only improves the life circumstances of individuals, it also contributes substantially to the health and economic well-being of local communities and to human society as a whole. Indeed, in the case of Africa, where children spend less time in school than do children anywhere else on earth (see Figure 12.1, p. 410), increasing access to education may provide countries with a powerful defense against the devastation of poverty and diseases that are killing so many of their citizens.

FIGURE 12.1 Compared with most other countries in the world, many African countries face significantly greater challenges in providing education to children, especially girls. (Data from UNESCO, 2015.)

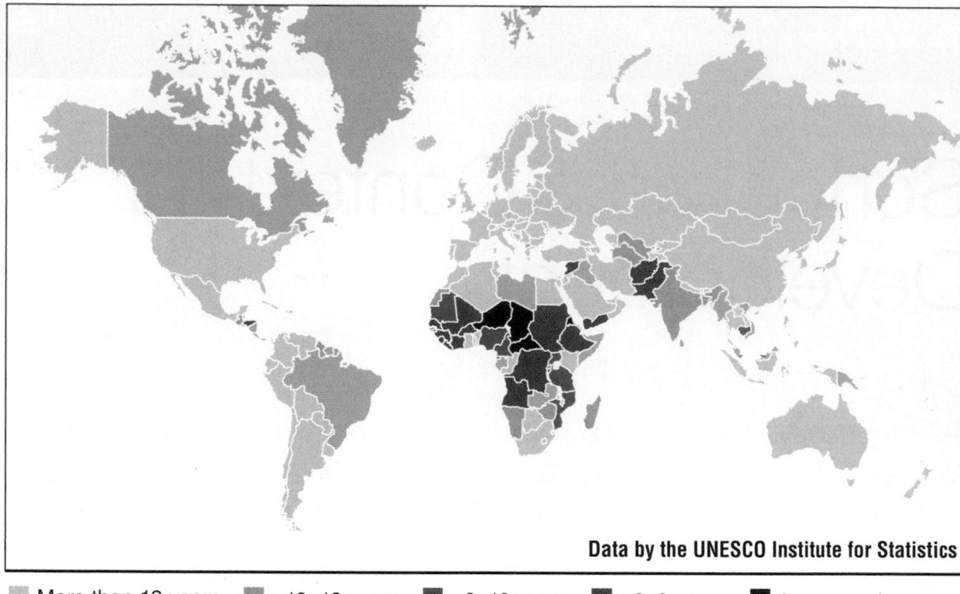

Although access to education is not nearly as restricted in the United States and other wealthier nations as it is in Africa, disparities in who has access to quality education can be quite pronounced for a number of reasons. It is well known, for example, that educational quality in the United States suffers substantially in schools located in economically impoverished neighborhoods, where large numbers of ethnic-minority children grow up. Yet conditions in such neighborhoods make educational quality all the more important. For example, living in poor neighborhoods makes it more likely not only that children will be exposed to environmental toxins that have been shown to harm cognitive development but also that they will be exposed to violence, which increases the likelihood of psychiatric disorders. To make matters more complicated, financing for schools in poor neighborhoods is often inadequate, and such schools are disproportionately assigned inexperienced teachers because experienced teachers, who often have more choice in where they teach, are reluctant to work in them.

This chapter is devoted to exploring the extraordinary impact of school as a context for children's development. We begin by discussing the unique features of school that set it apart from other contexts of learning and consider the particular contributions that school makes to intellectual development. We then examine *school readiness*, arising from the academic building blocks that children bring with them into the classroom, including those provided by family, community, and culture. Next, we examine the different ways of "doing school"—that is, the various forms of classroom instruction and their implications for learning. Finally, we confront contemporary challenges to school access and school success in our rapidly globalizing world.

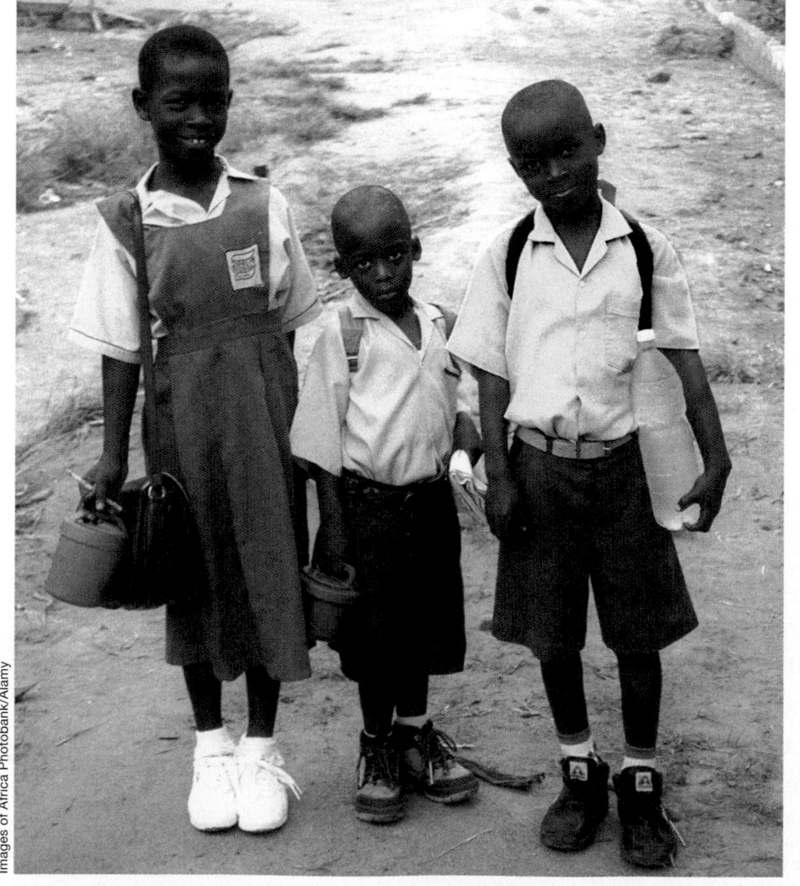

These Ghanaian children are ready for school. Children in many other African countries tend to leave school at earlier ages compared with those in Ghana, placing entire communities at greater risk for AIDS and poverty.

Images of Africa Photobank/Alamy

WARMING UP

1. Think back on your years in school. Which aspects of school contributed in positive ways to your learning? What would you have changed to make your school experience more effective?
2. Students have different attitudes and motivations about school and the importance of doing well. Think about two people you know—one highly motivated, the other less so. What do you think accounts for the differences?

The Contexts of Learning

LEARNING OUTCOMES

Summarize the transmission of knowledge and skills to children from the culture of past hunter-gatherer societies through to the emergence of schooling.

Distinguish by various dimensions schooling from traditional apprenticeship training.

In Chapter 2, we introduced the idea that children acquire the material and symbolic tools of culture through three fundamental social processes: *social enhancement* (making use of resources present in the immediate environment), *imitation* (observing and copying the behaviors of others), and, the process we examine here, *explicit instruction* (deliberate teaching of knowledge and skills). The most structured type of explicit instruction is **formal education**, through which adults instruct the young in the specialized knowledge and skills of their culture.

formal education The most structured type of explicit education, through which adults instruct the young in the specialized knowledge and skills of their culture.

It is not known if education existed among the hunter-gatherer peoples who roamed the earth hundreds of thousands of years ago, but explicit instruction is not a conspicuous part of socialization in contemporary hunter-gatherer societies (Hewlett & Roulette, 2016; Lancy & Grove, 2010). Among the Aka and Bofi "Pygmy" societies of the Central African Republic and the Republic of Congo, for instance, most teaching takes place through observation and imitation, as well as direct instruction provided by other—often older—children (Hewlett, Fouts, Boyette, & Hewlett, 2011).

When societies achieve a certain degree of complexity and specialization in the roles people play, the tools they use, and the ways they secure food and housing, preparation for some occupations is likely to occur through **apprenticeship**, a form intermediate between learning through participation in family and community life and the explicit instruction of formal education. A young apprentice learns a craft or a skill by spending an extended period of time working for an adult master (Collins, 2006; Downey, Dalidowicz, & Mason, 2015). The settings in which apprentices learn are not organized solely for the purpose of teaching. Rather, instruction and productive labor are combined; from the beginning, apprentices contribute to the work process.

apprenticeship A form of education in which a young person learns a craft or skill by spending an extended period of time working for an adult master.

DCPhoto/Alamy

Apprenticeship arrangements in which children learn by observing adults and working alongside them are still an important form of education, despite the spread of formal schools. This young boy is learning to tune a guitar from his grandfather, in their family workshop where they make instruments.

Researchers have found that novice apprentices receive relatively little explicit instruction but, instead, are given ample opportunity to observe skilled workers and to practice specific tasks (Rogoff, 2003). In many societies, the apprentice's relationship with the master is part of a larger web of family relationships. Often the apprentice lives with the master and does farm or household chores to help pay for his or her upkeep. In this way, the tasks of education and community building are woven together (Rogoff et al., 2007).

Formal education differs from traditional apprenticeship training (and from informal instruction in the family) in four main ways (Lave & Wenger, 1991; Singleton, 1998):

1. *Motivation.* Apprentices get to practice their craft from the beginning and see the fruits of their labor. Students in schools must work for years to perfect their skills before they can put their knowledge to use in adult work. In the meantime, the tasks they are engaged in may seem pointless to them.
2. *Social relations.* Unlike masters of apprentices, schoolteachers are rarely kin or family acquaintances, and they may not even live in the community.
3. *Social organization.* Apprentices are most likely to learn in a work setting among people of diverse ages and skill levels, so they have more than one person to turn to for assistance. At school, children typically learn in the company of other children who are about their age and one adult, who instructs them, and they are often expected to work individually. (In fact, asking for assistance from their peers may be considered cheating.)
4. *Medium of instruction.* Apprenticeship instruction is usually conducted orally in the context of production. Oral instruction is important in formal schooling as well, but, as we will see later, it is speech of a special kind, closely associated with the use of written symbols as a means of acquiring skills and knowledge.

Not only does schooling differ from other learning contexts in these ways, but also the types of problems posed to children in school differ considerably from those they encounter in other learning contexts (Table 12.1). Consider, for example, a problem in which a child needs to figure out the distance between two locations. In a school context, the child might be asked to use a scientific instrument, such as a ruler, to precisely measure abstract units (centimeters, inches) between two points. The goal of this problem solving is to learn or demonstrate mastery over a mathematical system of measurement that can be applied to measure distances in any situation. In an everyday context, in contrast, the child might be faced with a problem of finding and cutting tree saplings of sufficient length to bridge a small stream so that people can cross into crop fields without getting their feet wet. In this instance, problem solving is undertaken in the service of a highly specific goal that is important to the local community. In all likelihood, the child works with others to find saplings that are tall enough and strong enough to accomplish the task at hand. The measuring "tools" are specific to the particular, concrete problem and

TABLE 12.1 School Problems Versus Everyday Problems

School Problems	Everyday Problems
• Tend to draw on analytic intelligence	• Tend to draw on practical intelligence
• Abstract in nature and goals	• Concrete in nature and goals
• Formulated for the learner by other people	• Must be recognized or formulated by learners themselves
• Generally have little or no intrinsic interest to the learner	• Are intrinsically important to the learner
• Are clearly defined	• Generally are poorly defined
• Usually have a single correct answer that can be reached by a single, generalizable method	• Usually have several acceptable solutions that can be reached by a variety of routes
• Include all the information needed to deal with them	• Require people to seek new information
• Are detached from ordinary experience	• Are embedded in ordinary experience

may be as variable as the sense that the saplings should be "taller than my house" or "young trees of at least 4 winters." The outcomes of such measuring will also be variable, lacking the precision of scientifically calibrated measurement instruments.

Thus, it appears that school problem solving supports the development and use of abstract reasoning, whereas everyday problem solving supports reasoning based on particular concrete experience (Cole, 2005). Indeed, Alexander Luria, a Russian developmentalist who studied the cognitive effects of literacy, found evidence of this when he presented illiterate peasants with school-type problems that required the application of abstract reasoning, as in the following (adapted from Luria, 1976, pp. 108–109):

> Luria: In the North, where there is snow, all bears are white. Novaya Zemlya is in the Far North, and it always has snow. What color are the bears there?
> Peasant: I don't know. I've never been to Novaya Zemlya.
> Luria: But on the basis of my words [repeats the problem].
> Peasant: I've only seen black bears.
> Luria: But if you just think about my words [repeats the problem again].
> Peasant [becoming annoyed]: Look. . . . If a king or a czar had been to Novaya Zemlya and saw a bear and told about it, then maybe he could be believed. But I have never been there, and I have not seen the bears there, so I can't say. That's my last word!

Clearly, different contexts pose different types of intellectual challenges and support the development of different forms of reasoning. Formal education, according to Luria's research, encourages the development of abstract, hypothetical reasoning crucial to success in technologically advanced societies.

APPLY > CONNECT > DISCUSS

Using concepts presented in this section, explain some ways that going to school might contribute to the health and economic well-being of local communities and human society as a whole.

School Readiness

LEARNING OUTCOMES

Explain the building blocks that help children learn to read, write, and do math.

Describe the role of graphemes and phonemes as children learn to decode text.

Describe the number-related abilities that allow children to learn math.

Point out some family contexts that prepare children for school and academic success.

Extrapolate how situations in which preschool is available or not available in various countries affects the ability of children to be ready for school.

Four-year-olds Dawn and Heshan are coloring pictures when Dawn invites, "Let's play lieberry." "Okay," says Heshan, agreeably. Gesturing to a collection of books stacked on a toy shelf, Dawn suggests, "You can get some books over there." Heshan chooses several books while Dawn prepares a "check-out" by clearing toys from a space on the table and assembling some crayons and paper. "I'll take these," Heshan announces. Dawn takes the books he offers, looks at each one, gives them back, and warns, "They're due in 1 week." Heshan retreats to a corner of the room and begins "reading" a book about animal babies. Meanwhile, Dawn is scratching marks on small pieces of paper. After some minutes, she approaches Heshan and hands him a piece of paper. "You owe 5 dollars," she says. "What?" asks Heshan, clearly puzzled. Dawn explains, "You're overdue 1 week. If you don't pay 5 dollars that will be 5 weeks and you have to pay 100 dollars." "Oh," says Heshan, uncertainly. "Here," says Dawn, handing him another piece of paper. "This can be 5 dollars."

It is clear from our previous discussions of development during infancy and early childhood that by the time they start school, children already possess a number of building blocks relevant to literacy and math instruction. **Emergent literacy** and **emergent numeracy** include knowledge, skills, and attitudes that are precursors to learning to read, write, and do math. In the example above, it is clear that Dawn and Heshan have had experiences relevant to developing literacy and numeracy. They know about books and libraries and enjoy them well enough to include them in their play. Dawn pretends to write; Heshan pretends to read. And Dawn expresses the rudiments of mathematical knowledge. She not

emergent literacy Knowledge, skills, and attitudes that provide the building blocks for learning to read and write.

emergent numeracy Knowledge, skills, and attitudes that provide the building blocks for learning how to do math.

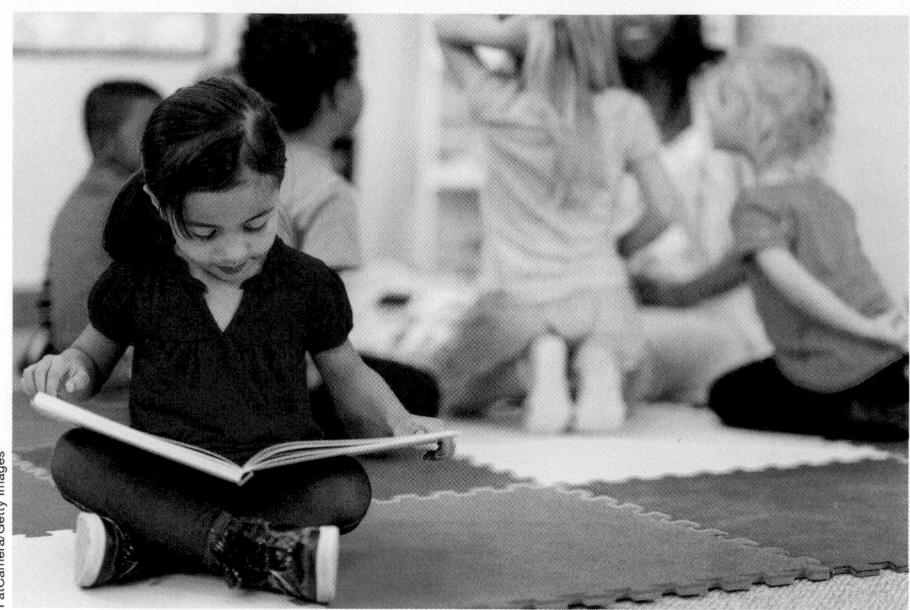

FatCamera/Getty Images

During play time, this preschooler chose to look at a book. Early childhood teachers often mix books and toys together on shelves for the purpose of increasing children's exposure to books and promoting emergent literacy skills.

only uses number words—"one," "five," "one hundred"—but also demonstrates an understanding of which words reflect larger amounts (and higher library fines). When Dawn and Heshan start school, their emergent literacy and numeracy skills will provide an important foundation for academic success. In the following sections, we will examine several emergent literacy and numeracy skills associated with school readiness, as well as a number of factors known to contribute to the development of these skills, including experiences provided by families and preschools.

Precursors to Reading and Writing

The first step children must take in learning to read and write is to realize that there is a correspondence between the marks on the printed page and the spoken language. Once they understand that each cluster of graphic signs represents a word, they still have to figure out how each graphic sign is related to a linguistic sound. One of the most basic reading skills is **decoding** text—that is, translating units of print, or *graphemes*, to units of sound, or *phonemes* (Nunes, Bryant, & Barros, 2012). Obviously, before this process of translation can occur, children must be able to distinguish between letters, as well as detect and manipulate phonemes. As we discussed in Chapter 4 (see p. 133), the capacity to discriminate between phonemes occurs very early in life. However, this infant capacity is quite different from the ability to detect and manipulate the phonemes that make up words. So, for example, your own capacity to detect and manipulate phonemes makes it easy for you to fill in the blanks below, each of which represents a phoneme:

decoding The process of translating units of print into units of sound.

Fuzzy Wu_y wa_ a bear.
Fuzzy Wu_y had no h_ _.
Fuzzy Wu_y wa_ n't fuzzy, wa_ he?

Research suggests that the *phonological awareness* you used to fill in the blanks of the "Fuzzy Wuzzy" ditty—your ability to detect and manipulate the phonemes in words—does not occur without deliberate instruction: Nonliterate adults in various parts of the world do not seem able to identify the phonemic units that make up individual words (Scholes, 1998).

A wealth of research conducted by Terizinha Nunes and Peter Bryant in different countries demonstrated that children who find it difficult to break words into their constituent syllables and phonemes in a purely oral task have difficulty linking sounds and letters (Nunes & Bryant, 2009). This research has spawned special educational programs that provide children with enriched experiences in oral language analysis before they are taught to read or when they experience difficulty in reading (Henry, 2017). The lessons include practice in rhyming, breaking words into syllables, and special language games such as Pig Latin, in which the first phoneme of each word is moved to the end of the word and then followed by an "ay" (as in "igpay atinlay"). Such special instruction has been found to increase the literacy skills of poor readers substantially (Blachman et al., 2004).

Precursors to Learning Mathematics

Like learning to read and write, learning mathematics involves a process of translation. In the case of mathematics, however, children must learn to translate their culture's number words and symbols (e.g., Arabic numerals) into an understanding of specific quantities (Bryant & Nunes, 2011; Izard, Streri, & Spelke, 2014). Although very young babies (as well as a wide variety of nonhuman species) demonstrate the ability to discriminate between different amounts—distinguishing, for example, between a set containing 6 objects and a set containing 12 objects—the vastly more complex process of mapping symbols to quantities does not begin in earnest until 2 to 3 years of age (Beran & Beran, 2004; Gilmore & Spelke, 2008; Gordon, 2004).

As we all know, early counting efforts are prone to error, as when a child says "three, five" when asked to count two crayons, and "three, five, six" when asked to count three crayons. However, errors like this actually reveal several competencies that are central to mathematics learning. First, when asked to count, the child responded with number words, not color words, demonstrating awareness of the special language of mathematics. Furthermore, the child used each count word only once, suggesting an understanding that different number words correspond to different quantities. Finally, the word order the child used—"three, five" and "three, five, six"—indicates awareness that the sequence of words matters in counting (Sarnecka & Gelman, 2004).

With increasing age, children become more proficient at mapping number words onto specific quantities. Interestingly, research indicates that this developmental process unfolds differently depending on the language spoken in the child's environment (LeCorre et al., 2016; Marusic et al., 2016). Consider, for instance, the singular/plural distinction in English: A singular noun is used to refer to a single thing (apple, balloon, cartwheel), whereas a plural noun refers to more than one of a thing (apples, balloons, cartwheels). Other languages, in contrast, have different ways of indicating such quantities. Najdi Arabic and some Slovenian dialects have three forms—singular, dual (referring to two things), and plural (referring to more than two things). Still other languages, such as Japanese, rarely mark the numbers of things at all. Children growing up in these different language environments follow different developmental pathways in understanding number words. Arabic and Slovenian children, growing up with languages that have ways of marking two of a thing using a dual form, learn the meaning of "two" at earlier ages than English-speaking children but are not faster at learning other number words (Almoammer et al., 2013). Similarly, Japanese children, growing up with a language that rarely marks number through grammar, are slower to acquire the meanings of number words compared to English and Russian-speaking children (Russian, like English, has a singular/plural distinction) (Sarnecka et al., 2007).

As children gain mathematical experience during elementary school, they become able to envision quantities in terms of a mental number line. That is, they can imagine an abstract number line composed of discrete units and identify the placement of a particular number on the line (Figure 12.2). As we found with children's abilities to identify and manipulate the phonemic units of words, the ability to identify and manipulate numeric units seems to emerge

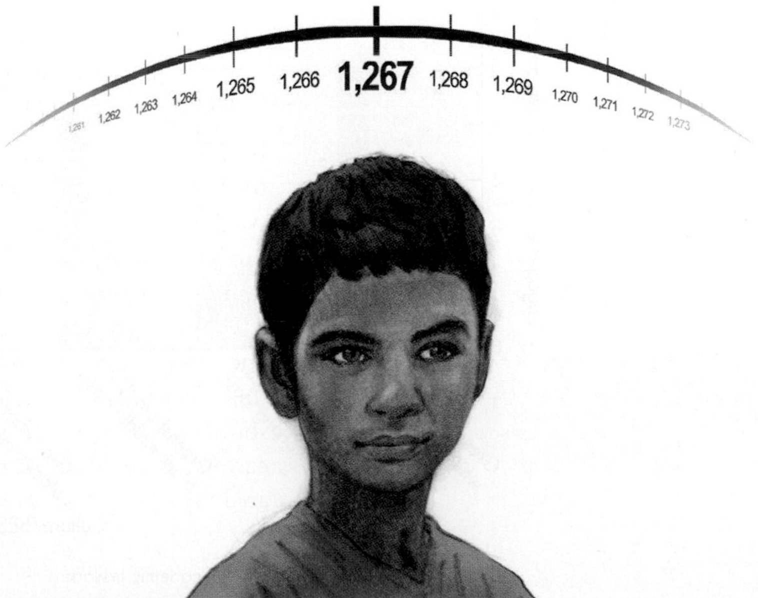

FIGURE 12.2 The ability to locate a specific number on an abstract number line emerges during middle childhood.

only in the context of deliberate instruction (Siegler & Opfer, 2003). Later in the chapter, we will examine other ways in which formal education fosters the development of abstract thinking.

The Role of Family

The family's important role in supporting the child's emergent literacy and numeracy skills has long been recognized by teachers and researchers alike. In many cultures, parents provide their children with special toys, games, and activities designed to promote learning mathematics, reading, and writing (Ginsburg, 2008; Tudge et al., 2006). When Jonathan Tudge and his colleagues conducted an ethnographic study of 3-year-olds growing up in the United States, Kenya, and Brazil, they found important differences in children's school-readiness activities, depending on the children's culture and socioeconomic status (Tudge et al., 2006). For example, as shown in Figure 12.3, in all cultures, children from middle-class families were more likely than their working-class counterparts to engage with their parents in academically oriented play and academically oriented lessons such as counting, spelling, and learning shapes and colors—findings that have been replicated in more recent research conducted in the United States (Bennett, Lutz, & Jayaram, 2012). Significantly, in Kenya, but not in the other cultures, children from working-class families were more likely than their middle-class counterparts to be engaged with their parents in "world lessons," such as learning how things work, why things happen, and how to be safe. Interestingly, Kenyan working-class children also spent considerably more time engaged in work-related activities, such as cleaning, shopping, and repairing, than did children in any of the other cultural/socioeconomic groups. As the researchers suggest, it is likely that the concentration on "world lessons" and work-related activities helps move Kenyan working-class children "on a trajectory more to do with the world of work than the world of school" (Tudge et al., 2006, p. 1463). In contrast, Kenyan middle-class children spent more time than any other

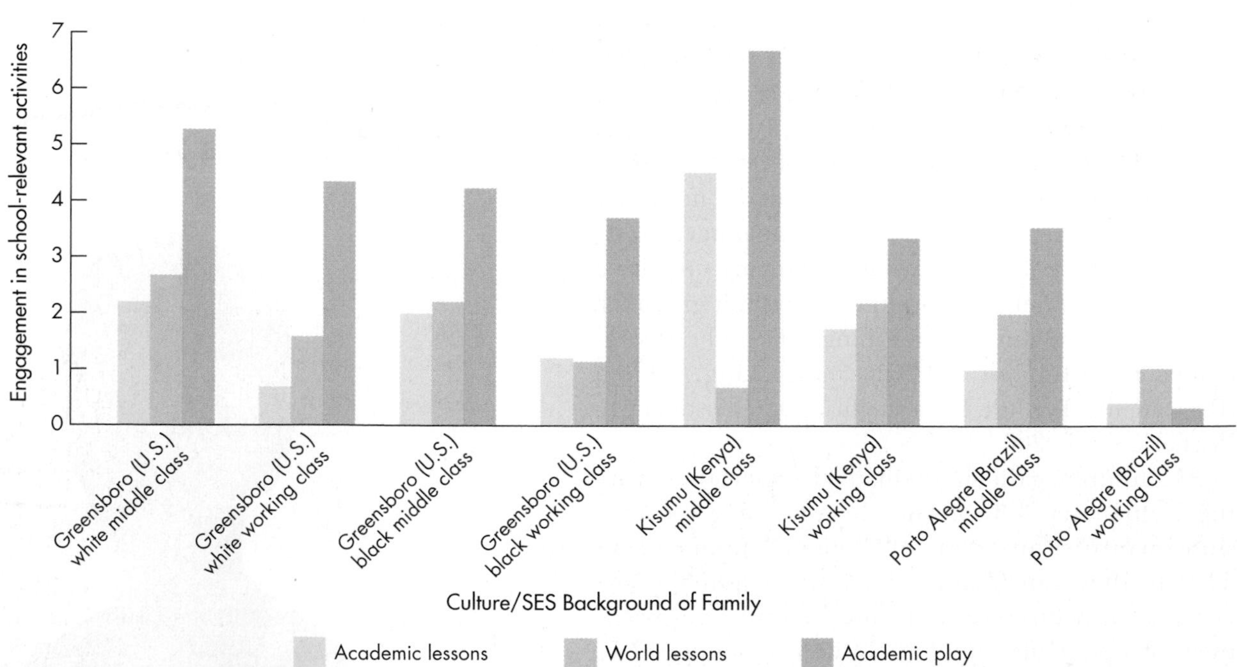

FIGURE 12.3 Ethnographic studies find that families prepare their children for school in a number of ways, emphasizing academic lessons, world lessons, and/or academic play. The extent to which a family may stress one or more of these ways depends on the specific culture and socioeconomic status of the family. (Data from Tudge et al., 2006.)

group engaged in academically oriented play and academic lessons with parents. In Kenyan society, children must pass school-readiness tests to be admitted to the more prestigious schools. In preparation for these tests, most middle-class families enroll their children in preschools that provide substantial school-relevant content.

Taken together, results from Tudge's exhaustive analysis of children's everyday activities underscore the importance of family in creating contexts for children to engage in activities relevant to school readiness. There is, in fact, a wealth of research indicating that such activities have a significant bearing on children's intellectual development and academic success (Inoa, 2017). Strong relationships have been found, for example, between being read to at 14 months of age and language comprehension, vocabulary size, and cognitive functioning at 2 years (Raikes et al., 2006). In addition, it seems that such early reading experience and emergent literacy skills enhance one another. Thus, when young children are read to on a daily basis, their vocabularies increase, and as their vocabularies increase, so, too, do their daily reading experiences. Helen Raikes, who discovered this relationship in a study involving more than 2,500 children and families, described it as a "snowball" effect, in which reading and vocabulary lead to more opportunities to use and learn language.

GoGo Images Corporation/Alamy

It is well documented that children who are read to on a daily basis will develop larger vocabularies and, in turn, have even more reading experiences compared to children who are read to less often.

Preschools

Preschools came into being early in the twentieth century, initiated by concerns of educators and physicians that the complexities of urban life were overwhelming children and stunting their development. The preschool was conceived as a protective environment designed with children's developmental levels and needs in mind.

In the 1960s, a variety of scientific and social factors combined to create great interest in the potential of preschools to increase the educational chances of the poor. On the scientific side was a growing belief that environmental influence during the first few years of life is crucial to all later abilities, especially intellectual ones. This belief coincided with growing political concern that social barriers between the rich and the poor and between Whites and Blacks were creating a dangerous situation in the United States. In 1963 Michael Harrington warned that the United States was creating "an enormous concentration of young people who, if they do not receive immediate help, may well be the source of a kind of hereditary poverty new to American society" (Harrington, 1963, p. 188). Commentators on the lives of poor young children issue the same warning today.

This combination of social, political, and scientific factors led the U.S. Congress to declare a "war on poverty" in 1964. One of the key programs in this "war" was Project Head Start. Its purpose was to intervene in the cycle of poverty at a crucial time in children's lives by providing them with important learning experiences that they might otherwise miss. Federal support enabled Head Start programs to offer these experiences at no charge to low-income families.

This strategy of social reform through early childhood education rested on three crucial assumptions:

1. The environmental conditions of poverty-level homes are insufficient to prepare children to succeed in school.
2. Schooling is the social mechanism that permits children to succeed in U.S. society.
3. Poor children could succeed in school, and thereby overcome their poverty, if they were given extra assistance during the preschool years.

Originally conceived as a summer program, Head Start soon began to operate year-round, serving approximately 200,000 preschool children at a time. Many decades later, Head Start programs have expanded to provide services for more than 750,000 children. Since its inception in 1965, more than 30 million children have enrolled in the program (Head Start, 2015).

In recent decades, a large number of studies have evaluated preschool programs for poor children, including Head Start and a variety of similar efforts (Friedman-Krauss, Connors, & Morris, 2017; Zigler & Styfco, 2010). Some of the studies have been able to do follow-up evaluations of children as they have reached their early 20s and to include broader developmental indicators, such as crime rates and earned income, in the assessment. These broad evaluations have revealed a variety of positive findings, although success has not been uniform. On the positive side, children who attend regular Head Start or special model programs show meaningful gains in intellectual performance and socioemotional development (Shager et al., 2013). Children who attend Head Start are also less likely to be assigned to remedial special-education classes when they attend school. As is the case with child-care programs, however, the success of Head Start programs depends on the quality of the classroom experience; and, unfortunately, while most classrooms have been rated as adequate in quality, fewer than half are considered to be of high quality (National Center for Education Statistics, 2013).

Nonetheless, the success of well-run programs is now broadly accepted (Friedman-Krauss et al., 2017). In one of the best and most heavily studied cases, the Perry Preschool Program in Ypsilanti, Michigan, it has been possible to follow up the progress of experimental and control children for more than 35 years. The children in the experimental group had higher achievement scores than those in the control group at ages 9 and 14. They were more likely to graduate from high school, more likely to be employed at age 19, less likely to have run afoul of the law by age 28, and less likely to have gone on welfare. A recent cost–benefit analysis of the Perry Preschool Program showed that the money invested was more than recovered in savings on other social services and interventions (Heckman et al., 2010).

With the recognition of the importance of school readiness to academic success and of education in general to the health and well-being of children, their communities, and society as a whole, enrollment in preschools throughout the world has expanded significantly over the past several decades, and in 2015, nearly one-half of the world's children were enrolled in preschools (UNESCO Institute for Statistics, 2017). Nevertheless, consistent with our earlier discussion about children's access to education, significant cross-national disparities exist in preschool enrollments (Figure 12.4). Sadly, the children most likely to benefit from preschool education—for example, those at highest risk for poor health due to malnourishment and contracting preventable diseases—are the least likely to be enrolled in a preschool program (UNESCO, 2015).

paylessimages/Getty Images

Preschool programs can boost children's readiness for primary school, especially when children are from immigrant families.

In addition to cross-national differences in preschool enrollments, there are differences within countries. In countries as diverse as the United States and Nepal, for example, children of ethnic-minority immigrant families are less likely than ethnic-majority peers to participate in preschool (Crosnoe et al., 2016; Jaganath et al., 2015). And, consistent with our previous discussions about gender differences in access to formal education, in some countries, girls are less likely than boys to attend preschool. In rural Nepal, for example, girls and ethnic minorities are underrepresented in preschool enrollments—statistics that are especially unfortunate in light of the well-documented advantages of preschool participation, especially for children from ethnic-minority or low-income families (Jaganath et al., 2015).

Taken as a whole, research presents a strong case for the role of preschool programs in boosting a variety of school-readiness indicators for children of immigrant families. This would seem to suggest that the larger the number of immigrant

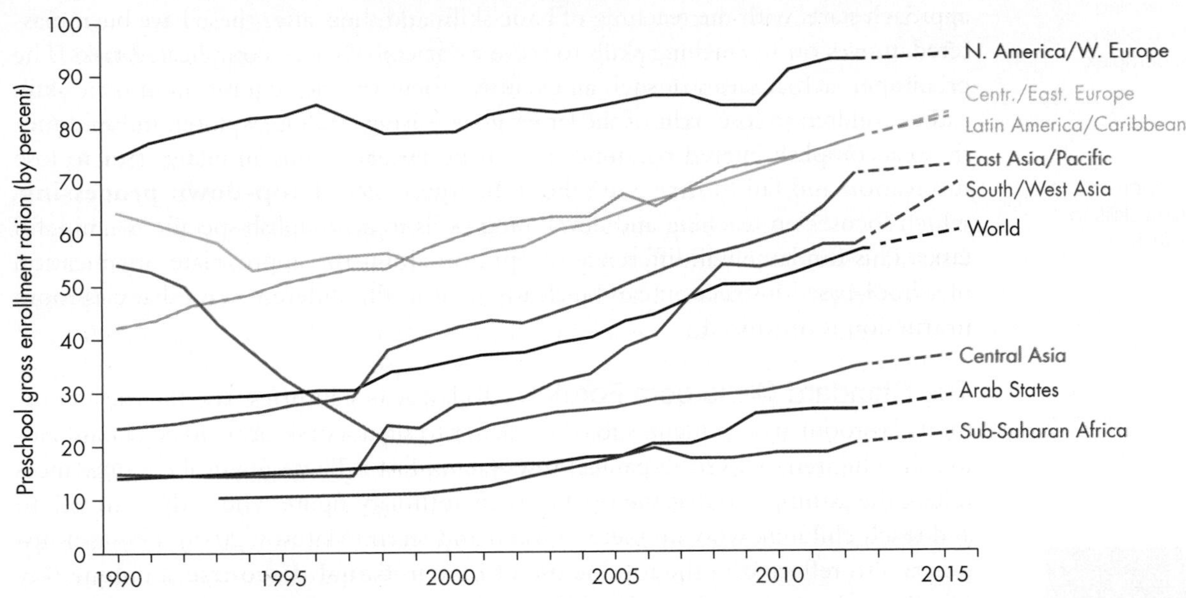

FIGURE 12.4 There are vast differences in preschool enrollments throughout the world. Children who are most at risk for malnourishment and disease are least likely to be enrolled in preschool. (Data from UNESCO, 2015.)

children enrolled in preschool, the better. But accomplishing this goal requires understanding the barriers that may exist to preschool participation and knowing how to remove them.

APPLY > CONNECT > DISCUSS

Both phonemic awareness and the ability to identify and manipulate numeric units appear to emerge only in the context of formal education. What do these two developments have in common, and how might formal schooling stimulate their development?

In the Classroom

LEARNING OUTCOMES

- Compare a bottom-up and a top-down approach to educating children.
- Give examples of how teachers use instructional discourse.
- Distinguish among the instructional formats for reciprocal teaching, realistic mathematics in education, and playworld practice.
- Describe how specific learning disabilities such as dyslexia pose a barrier to a child's school success.
- Distinguish between the incremental model of intelligence and the entity model of intelligence.

At this point in your education, you are no doubt aware of the vastly different ways in which students experience school. Students come to have different feelings about school and, accordingly, put more or less energy into doing well. Students also experience different types of instruction according to the educational philosophy of the particular schools they attend or the teachers they have. In your own extensive experience, you have surely encountered some teachers who rely on workbooks and tests and others who emphasize hands-on projects and papers. In this section, we explore various factors that shape students' school experiences, including the social organization of classroom instruction and personal and cultural barriers to school success.

Social Organization of the Classroom and Instructional Design

From the earliest schools of the ancient Middle East to neighborhood schools throughout the modern world, there has been controversy about how to design instruction more effectively. Opinion seems to oscillate between two extreme

bottom-up processing An approach to education that starts with teaching basic skills and, once they have been mastered, moves on to more complex tasks.

top-down processing An approach to education that focuses on using skills to accomplish specific, meaningful tasks.

approaches. One approach begins with the assumption that instruction should proceed from the simple to the complex. Known as **bottom-up processing**, this approach starts with the teaching of basic skills and then, after these have been mastered, moves on to teaching skills to solve a variety of more complicated tasks. The other approach argues that such an exclusive focus on the acquisition of basic skills causes children to lose sight of the larger goal—using reading, writing, and arithmetic to accomplish interesting, important purposes—and, thus, in many cases, to lose motivation and fail to thrive in school. It urges, instead, **top-down processing**, which focuses on teaching and developing skills to accomplish specific meaningful tasks. This fundamental difference of opinion about the appropriate organization of school-based instruction can be clearly seen in the different ways that classroom instruction is organized.

instructional discourse A distinctive way of talking and thinking that is typical in school but rarely encountered in everyday interactions in the community or home.

The Standard Classroom Format

Today, as in centuries past, the most common classroom arrangement is for the teacher to sit at a desk or stand at a board facing the children, who sit in parallel rows facing front. These physical circumstances reflect the assumption that the teacher is an authority figure who is there to talk to and teach children, who are there to listen and learn (Matusov, 2015). This assumption is also reflected in the routine use of **instructional discourse**, a unique way of talking that is typical in school but rarely encountered in everyday interactions in the community or home. A common pattern for instructional discourse is the "known-answer question." When the teacher asks a student, "What does this word say?" the teacher already knows the answer (a fact the student fully understands) and is actually seeking information about the student's progress in learning to read. Learning to respond easily to known-answer questions, in addition to learning the academic content of the curriculum, is an important early lesson of schooling.

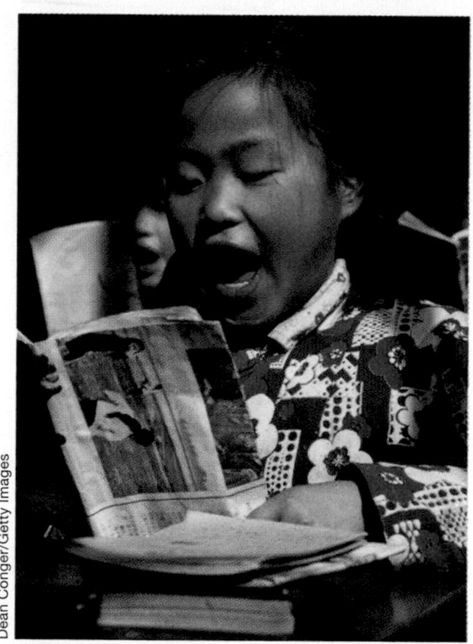

Dean Conger/Getty Images

Reading in unison is common in classrooms throughout the world.

Alternative Forms of Classroom Instruction

Although the standard classroom format is widespread in classrooms around the world, many developmentalists argue that it is not the best way of organizing instruction. Among other shortcomings, children taught in this manner are placed in the role of passive recipients of predigested information and therefore gain very little practice in formulating and solving problems for themselves (Matusov, Smith, Soslau, Marianovic-Shane, & Von Duyke, 2016). In contrast, the instructional alternatives we will consider next make children active participants in the educational process—a strategy that is closely aligned with the developmental theories of Piaget and Vygotsky.

reciprocal teaching A method of teaching reading in which teachers and children take turns reading text in a manner that integrates decoding and comprehension skills.

Reciprocal Teaching. One alternative to the recitation script is **reciprocal teaching**, which was designed as a way to integrate bottom-up and top-down processing, through small-group discussion at the time of reading. It was designed initially for children who are able to read in the sense that they can decode simple texts but who have difficulty making sense of what they read (Brown, Palincsar, & Armbruster, 1994).

In the reciprocal-teaching procedure, a teacher and a small group of students read silently through a text one segment at a time and take turns leading discussions about what each segment means (Palincsar et al., 2007; Tarchi & Pinto, 2016). The discussion leader (teacher or child) begins by asking a question about the main idea of the segment and then answers the question by summarizing the content in his or her own words. If members of the group disagree with the summary, the group rereads the segment and discusses its contents to clarify what it says. Finally, the leader asks for predictions about what will come next in the text.

Note that each of the key elements in reciprocal teaching—asking questions about content, summarizing it, clarifying it, and predicting narrative progression—presupposes that the purpose of the activity is comprehension—that is, figuring out what the text means. And because these strategies involve talking about (and arguing over) textual meaning, children are able to see and hear the teacher and other children model metacognitive behaviors that aid comprehension. For example, as a way of making sense of what is being read, the teacher might point to relevant information in a prior paragraph that needs to be considered or might relate an idea in the text to some common experience that all the children have had. Reciprocal teaching is an application of Vygotsky's notion of the "zone of proximal development" (Chapter 1, p. 23) that allows children to participate in the act of reading for meaning even before they have acquired the full set of abilities that independent reading requires. A number of studies have found that reciprocal teaching can produce rapid and durable increases in children's reading skills, including those of children with learning disabilities (Koch, & Spörer, 2017; Lee & Tsai, 2017).

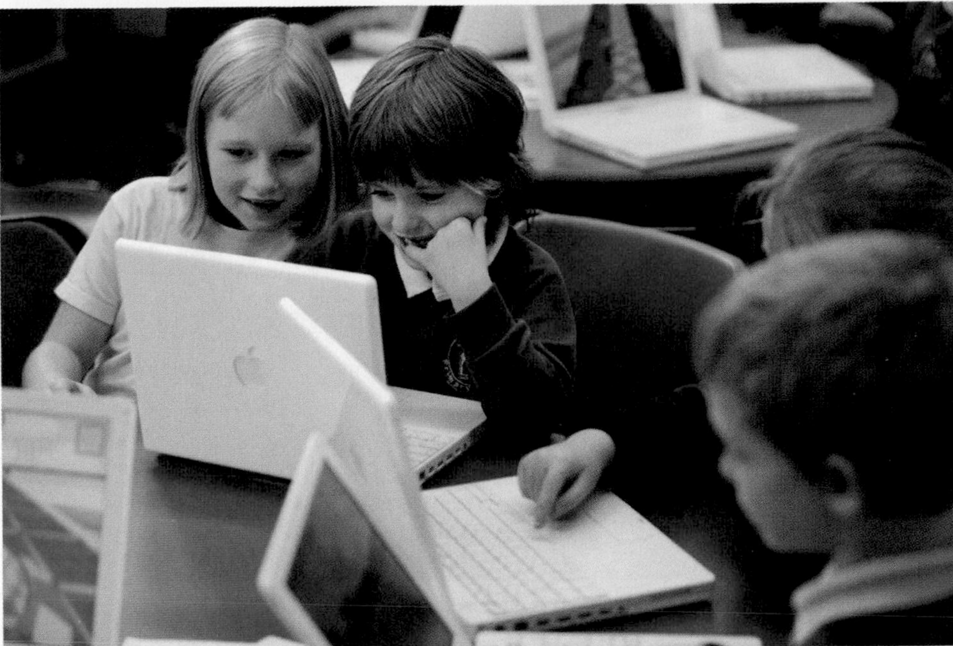
Andrew Fox/Getty Images

Instructional methods that encourage students to work together and participate actively in the learning process, as shown here in a classroom in the United Kingdom, often result in higher levels of learning and language skills than those achieved through more traditional instructional approaches.

In one study, Cathy Block and her colleagues studied the effectiveness of various instructional approaches to reading with nearly 700 elementary school students in 30 different classrooms. Over the course of an academic year, some students received standard reading instruction, while others received alternative instructional approaches. The researchers found that alternative approaches that included student-guided, teacher-led group discussion of the texts were significantly more effective than the standard approach (Block et al., 2009). Similar results were found in a study conducted in 40 schools in the Netherlands (Droop, van Elsacker, Voeten, & Verhoeven, 2016).

Realistic Mathematics Education. Recognizing the limitations of recitation scripts and the bottom-up approach, the National Council of Teachers of Mathematics adopted a set of standards for improving mathematics education that shifts the focus of mathematics instruction from training in basic skills, procedures, and memorization toward conceptual understanding and linkages between mathematics and real-world problems (Koestler, Felton-Koestler, Bieda, & Otten, 2013). An example of a mathematics program designed to implement these goals is **realistic mathematics education**, which includes the following features (Hirza, Kusumah, Darhim, & Zulkardi, 2014; Shanty, 2016; Zakaria & Syamaun, 2017):

realistic mathematics education An approach to mathematics education that focuses on developing the student's understanding of how math can be used to solve real-world problems

1. *Using meaningful activities.* For example, a first-grade teacher might introduce counting up to 20 by creating a make-believe situation in which a bus conductor has to keep track of how many people are on a double-decker bus that has 10 seats on each deck. As we have learned from the experimental research on children's problem solving discussed in previous chapters, such stories help provide a meaningful context for carrying out cognitive operations.

SARAH Network of Rehabilitation Hospitals

Research supports the idea that learning is effective when teachers link lessons to real-world issues and problems, as suggested here by the teacher's use of a newspaper in working with her student.

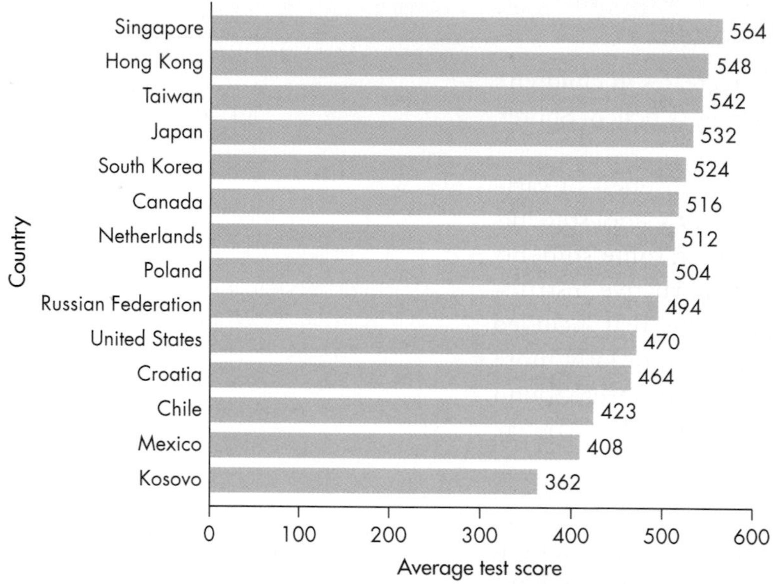

FIGURE 12.5 Average mathematics scores in 2015 of 15-year-olds in countries in different parts of the world. (Data from DeSilver, 2017.)

2. *Supporting basic mathematical skills.* In the case of the double-decker bus, for example, the teacher wants children to learn how to group numbers for calculation and to realize that there are 8 people on the bus if there are 4 on top and 4 on the bottom or 6 on the top and 2 on the bottom or 2 on the top and 6 on the bottom, and so on. Each configuration is a different way of representing a total of 8.
3. *Employing models in educational activity.* Cobb describes a number of studies that use an "arithmetic rack," with two rows containing 10 beads each. For the conductor-on-the-bus context, the arithmetic rack provides a rather precise spatial model, with each of its rows corresponding to a deck of the bus. But the beads on the rack can also be used to represent the number of cookies put in or taken out of a cookie jar and a variety of other story contexts involving similar mathematical concepts.

Over time, children gradually master the conceptual structures that the stories and models initially support, and they can carry out the needed calculations without such aids.

As in the case of reciprocal teaching, a social organization of the classroom that supports the mixing of bottom-up knowledge with top-down conceptual and utilization knowledge is key. Teachers work to establish a classroom culture in which children are expected to justify their reasoning when they answer a question and to try to understand the reasoning behind other children's answers, appreciating that there may be different ways of solving problems. In addition, children are expected to be helpful to the group, to solicit help from others, and to share what they have learned. This type of mathematics instruction is observed more commonly in some countries than others and may account in part for cross-national differences in mathematics achievement scores (see Figure 12.5).

Playworld Practice. In contrast to the recent educational trend in the United States to emphasize content that will help students pass mandatory statewide tests, several European countries are moving in the direction of integrating play and art into classroom activities (Nilsson & Ferholt, 2014). Devised on the basis of developmental theory pointing to the importance of play in children's understanding and representation of the world (see Chapter 9, p. 311), **playworld practice** involves discussing, enacting, and making art about themes based on children's literature (Ferholt & Lecusay, 2010). Although playworld practice has been featured in Swedish and Finnish classrooms for some years (Hakkarainen, 2004; Sandberg & Samuelsson, 2003), only recently have efforts been made to experimentally compare playworld practice with other instructional formats. In one such effort, Sonja Baumer and her colleagues studied two classrooms

playworld practice A type of classroom activity that is based on theories regarding the importance of play in intellectual development and involves students enacting and discussing various themes in children's literature.

of 5- to 7-year-olds who were learning about the C. S. Lewis fantasy novel *The Lion, the Witch, and the Wardrobe* (Baumer, Ferholt, & Lecusay, 2005). One classroom used the playworld-practice approach; the other used standard instruction. In the playworld-practice classroom, the children, teacher, and researchers enacted scenes from the story; drew pictures of the scenes; and played with costumes and props used in the enactments. In the standard-instruction classroom, in contrast, the teacher read from the book, guided the students in a discussion of the story, and had the children draw pictures or write stories about the novel. Results from the study indicated that compared with standard instruction, the playworld-practice format generated significantly larger increases in children's language skills, especially their abilities to tell and understand stories. (For another example of an alternative educational method, see the box "Now Trending in Practice: Educating Naturally in Forest Schools.")

Now TRENDING in PRACTICE | Educating Naturally in Forest Schools

After the children drop their backpacks at the base of the oak tree, they gather in a circle with their teacher and two aides, sing a "good morning" song that includes each child's name, and rehearse the days of the week in a funny dance. "What's next?" asks the teacher. "The bridge!" "The creek!" And they take off like a shot, with the adults trailing behind. Their destination is the project they have been working on for several days: building a wooden bridge to cross a small creek running through the forest, which also serves as their classroom.

Popular for decades in many European countries, Forest Schools—in which children spend significant time in natural environments, regardless of weather—are increasingly common in the United States, Canada, China, and other places around the world. A good deal of instruction takes place in Forest Schools. Teachers and aids enhance children's experiences by explaining the biology of the woodland plants and animals, the geology of rocks and minerals, and the physics and engineering associated with activities like building bridges across creeks. But it is the children's interests and motivations that initiate the lessons. Tamira finds a pretty rock, and the teacher points out the lines of granite running through it; Devon points to scattered bird feathers on the trail, inspiring a discussion of foxes and food chains; and as Sakim inspects a rotting log, the teacher shows how it supports the growth of mushrooms and millions of insects. (The children decide that it is poor bridge-building material.)

Advocates argue that the nature-based learning of Forest Schools provides a number of advantages over traditional classrooms. Although the subject of Forest Schools is relatively new territory for developmental researchers, some studies are beginning to find evidence for health benefits associated with increased physical activity, more complex language use, and higher levels of creativity (Kiewra & Veselack, 2016; Richardson & Murray, 2017; Ridgers, Knowles, & Sayers, 2012). According to one summary of 61 studies conducted with children under the age of 12, children's experiences with nature (in Forest Schools as well as in gardening projects and in play in natural environments) have the following benefits (Gill, 2014):

- Improvements in mental health and emotion regulation, including for children with learning disabilities
- Improved scientific learning
- Healthier eating habits
- Greater physical activity and improved motor fitness
- Greater environmental knowledge

The worldwide proliferation of Forest Schools is itself strong evidence of the value of learning in natural environments—at least in the eyes of educators and parents. Based on their enthusiastic engagement, children like Tamira, Devon, and Sakim agree.

Lumi Images/Alamy

Forest schools provide children with hands-on opportunities to learn about the world by manipulating natural objects.

Overall, the evidence indicates that when properly organized, instructional methods that induce students to be active contributors to classroom discourse can be quite effective. But such methods are more complex to organize than the recitation script and are still used in only a minority of classrooms.

Barriers to School Success

There is, of course, more to children's school experience than the ways classroom instruction is organized and designed. Many students experience difficulty in school, regardless of instructional organization and design, often because they have learning disabilities or because they lack motivation to learn.

specific learning disabilities (SLD) A term used to refer to the academic difficulties of children who fare poorly in school despite having normal intelligence.

Specific Learning Disabilities

Specific learning disabilities (SLD) is a term used to refer to the academic difficulties of children who fare poorly in school despite having normal IQ test scores. The U.S. government defines specific learning disabilities as

> a disorder in one or more of the basic psychological processes involved in understanding or in using language, spoken or written, that may manifest itself in an imperfect ability to listen, think, speak, read, write, spell, or to do mathematical calculations, including conditions such as perceptual disabilities, brain injury, minimal brain dysfunction, dyslexia, and developmental aphasia. . . . The term does not include learning problems that are primarily the result of visual, hearing, or motor disabilities, of mental retardation, of emotional disturbance, or of environmental, cultural, or economic disadvantage. (34 Code of Federal Regulations §300.7[c][10])

Diagnosing SLD can be complicated, and experts do not agree on a single best process (Schroeder, Drefs, & Cormier, 2017; Zirkel, 2017). These are the three most commonly used methods of identifying and diagnosing SLD (Cottrell & Barrett, 2017):

1. *Severe discrepancy* (*SD*) refers to substantial differences between a student's performance on a measure of intellectual functioning, such as an IQ test, and their academic achievement, as measured, for example, by their grades in school.
2. *Response to intervention* (*RTI*) is a method that identifies students with SLD based on their lack of responsiveness to interventions designed to increase performance in problem areas, such as reading, writing, or mathematics.
3. *Patterns of strengths and weaknesses* (*PSW*) refers to discrepant performance on different subscales of tests of intellectual or cognitive functioning, as when a student scores well in the area of spatial reasoning but very poorly in reading comprehension.

Despite considerable criticism, SD continues to be the most commonly used method for diagnosing SLD. Critics of SD consider it to reflect an underlying assumption that SLD are general, rather than specific, learning deficits, and SD consequently provides little guidance in terms of targeted interventions. In contrast, both RTI and PSW are gaining increasing interest among educators as ways of identifying specific areas of concern. For example, a child with a low verbal-ability score and a high quantitative-ability score, or one who responds poorly to interventions focused on increasing verbal ability, would be expected to have difficulty in learning to read but not in learning arithmetic. This pattern of performance, called *dyslexia*, is the most common form of specific learning disability. Other children display a pattern of performance called *dyscalculia*, in which their verbal IQ is high and their quantitative IQ is low: Correspondingly, they do not have difficulty learning to read but have difficulty learning arithmetic. Yet another specific learning disability is *dysgraphia*, which involves special difficulties in learning to write, including poor handwriting, problems with spelling, and difficulty putting thoughts on paper. In the remainder of our discussion of special learning disabilities, we focus on dyslexia, which is not only the most common such disability but also the one about which the most is known.

The primary question regarding children with dyslexia is: Why do they have difficulty reading? As we saw earlier, phonological awareness—the ability to detect and manipulate the phonemes in words—is crucial to learning to decode text—that is, to relate graphemes (symbols of the writing system) to phonemes. More directly, phonological awareness is a crucial part of *phonological processing*—of understanding and applying the rules relating phonemes and graphemes. Like problems with phoneme awareness, delays in the development of phonological processing skills may indicate that a child has dyslexia (Helland et al., 2008).

The leading test of phonological processing skills employs *pseudowords*, pronounceable combinations of letters that are not real words—for example, "shum," "laip," and "cigbet"—but can be read by following the rules for converting graphemes into phonemes. Because they are not real words, they cannot be recognized and therefore permit an accurate assessment of phonological processing.

To demonstrate the link between deficient phonological processing and dyslexia, Linda Siegel compared normal and dyslexic readers in their ability to read pseudowords (Siegel, 2008, 2017). By 9 years of age, the normal readers were quite proficient in reading the pseudowords, but 14-year-old dyslexic readers were no better at reading pseudowords than were normal 7-year-old readers. Even when dyslexic readers and normal readers were matched for reading level on a standardized test (the dyslexic readers being considerably older than the normal readers), the dyslexic readers performed more poorly on the pseudowords task.

Current theories about the causes of dyslexia assume that the difficulties arise because of biological anomalies (Neef et al., 2017; Papagiannopoulou & Lagopoulos, 2017). Recent brain-imagining studies have, in fact, indicated that the brains of children with dyslexia have decreased information processing capacity and speed, which affects attention and working memory (Papagiannopoulou & Lagopoulos, 2017; Xia, Hancock, & Hoeft, 2017). Furthermore, children with dyslexia may have genetic anomalies that impair their ability to process auditory information, making it difficult for them to discriminate phonemes (Neef et al., 2017).

Motivation to Learn

As we noted earlier, a distinctive aspect of formal education is that children are expected to pay attention and try to master material that may be difficult to learn and that may hold little interest for them. They must also learn to cope with the fact that they will not always be successful in their schoolwork. In such circumstances, a significant proportion of children lose their **academic motivation**—the ability to try hard and persist at school tasks in the face of difficulties. On the other hand, many children seem to thrive on the challenges presented by formal education.

academic motivation The ability to try hard and persist at school tasks in the face of difficulties.

What accounts for these differences? Researchers who study this question distinguish between two ways in which children approach school tasks (Jozsa, Wang, Barrett, & Morgan, 2014; Martin, Sokol, & Elfers, 2008): **mastery orientation**, in which children are motivated to learn, to try hard, and to improve; and **performance orientation**, in which children are motivated by their level of performance, ability, and incentives for trying.

mastery orientation A way that children approach school tasks in which they are motivated to learn, to try hard, and to improve their performance.

performance orientation A way of approaching school tasks in which students are motivated by their level of performance, ability, and incentives for trying.

Mastery and performance orientations have consistently been associated with two different outcomes in terms of children's academic success. Children who adopt a mastery orientation are more likely to succeed in the long run, to use more advanced learning strategies, and to relate what they are trying to accomplish at

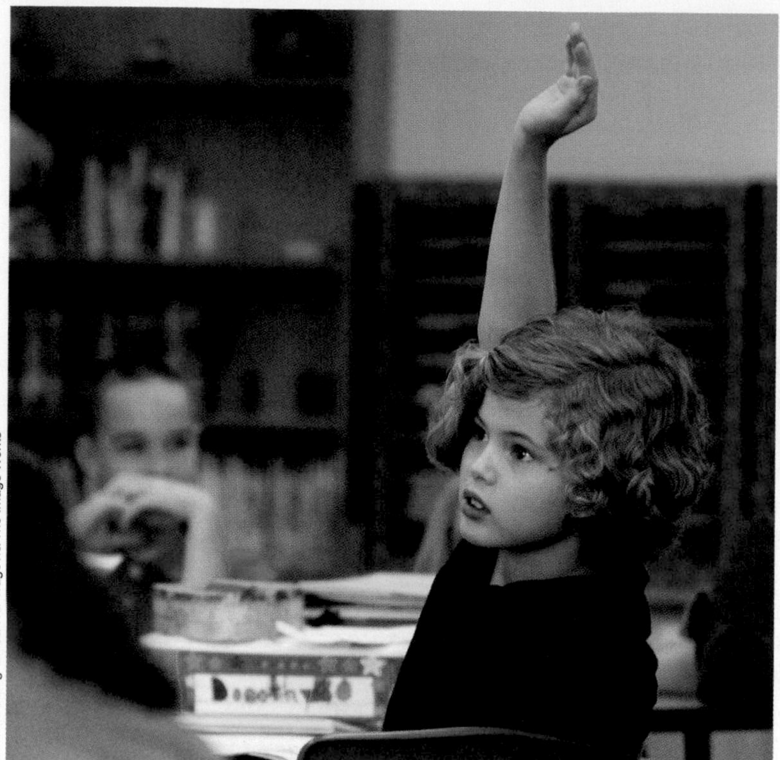
St. Petersburg Times/Will Vragovic/The Image Works

This student seems to be the personification of academic motivation: If she happens to give an incorrect answer this time, she will not give up and is likely to work harder to get it right the next time.

the moment to relevant prior knowledge. Even if these children have just done poorly or failed at a task, they remain optimistic and tell themselves, "I can do it if I try harder next time." As a result of this kind of thinking, they tend to persist in the face of difficulties and to seek out new intellectual challenges. Over time, this kind of motivational pattern allows these children to improve their academic performance. By contrast, children who adopt a performance orientation are more likely, when failing at a task, to tell themselves, "I can't do this." They may give up trying altogether and, when they encounter similar tasks in the future, tend to avoid them.

It might be thought that more-able students would typically display the mastery-oriented pattern and that less-able students would be the ones to adopt a performance orientation, quickly giving up in the face of difficulty and avoiding challenges. However, the evidence concerning motivational orientation and school achievement is mixed. Carol Dweck and her colleagues reported that these two patterns are not related to children's IQ scores or their academic achievement: Many able students give up in the face of difficulty, and many weaker students show a mastery orientation (Dweck & Master, 2009). But a number of studies conducted with typically developing children, as well as children with Down syndrome, indicate that mastery motivation does promote cognitive development and academic achievement (Gilmore & Cuskelly, 2017; Jennings & Dietz, 2003).

In an extensive series of studies looking at factors that might lead to the two different motivational patterns, Carol Dweck and Allison Master related the patterns to two different conceptions of ability, conceptions that children develop as they progress through school (Dweck & Master, 2009). According to Dweck and Master, children as young as 2½ years old are sensitive to success or failure in their problem-solving attempts and are vulnerable to becoming discouraged and unmotivated when they fail. But it is not until the onset of formal schooling, when, through grading practices, children's academic abilities are directly compared with those of their peers, that the notion of ability becomes a distinctive category that children use to evaluate themselves and their relationship to academic challenges. Children's conceptions of ability continue to change during the elementary school years, and children are increasingly less likely to engage in wishful thinking about problems they can solve and increasingly more likely to see ability as a fixed characteristic of people.

entity model of intelligence The belief that intelligence is a quality of which each person has a certain fixed amount.

incremental model of intelligence The belief that intelligence is something that can grow over time as one learns.

Around the age of 12, when children make the transition from elementary to middle school, North American children begin to articulate theories about what it means to "be intelligent." Some children adopt an **entity model of intelligence**; that is, they see intelligence as quantitatively fixed in each individual. Other children, by contrast, adopt an **incremental model of intelligence**; they see intelligence as something that can grow as one learns and has new experiences. These theories about intelligence include ideas about how effort is related to outcome. Children who adopt the entity model see academic success as depending primarily on fixed ability and thus remaining relatively unaffected by effort; children who adopt the incremental model see academic success, along with ability, as depending on the effort expended. Dweck found that children who adopt an entity model of intelligence are likely to develop a performance orientation to problems. When they fail, they believe that it is because they lack ability and that nothing they can do will change this. Because they view intelligence as a fixed entity, they try to avoid situations that put them at risk for failure and feel hopeless when they are confronted with challenging tasks. Children who adopt an incremental model of intelligence, on the other hand, tend to develop a mastery orientation to challenging situations. They believe that if they apply themselves and try hard enough, they will succeed and become more intelligent; and when they fail at a particular task, their response is to try harder the next time. As children encounter the more challenging environment of middle school, notable achievement gaps arise between students who have one or the other of the basic motivational patterns.

Findings such as these have led developmentalists to emphasize the importance of assisting students to develop mastery motivation and to educate teachers on the differences between incremental and entity models of intelligence (Smith & Skrbis, 2017; Stump, Husman, & Corby, 2014).

School Engagement

In addition to mastery motivation, students' engagement in the classroom environment may affect academic performance (Ladd & Dinella, 2009). **School engagement** refers to the thoughts, behaviors, and emotions that children have about school and learning. It makes sense that a child who likes school, cooperates willingly in classroom activities, and devotes effort to learning will perform better than a child who dislikes school, resists involvement, and invests little intellectual effort.

school engagement The thoughts, behaviors, and emotions that children have about school and learning.

Gary Ladd and Lisa Dinella explored the relationship between school engagement and academic achievement in nearly 400 children as they progressed from first grade to eighth grade (Ladd & Dinella, 2009). They focused on two dimensions of engagement. The first dimension was *school liking/avoidance*, as measured by teacher and parent reports about factors such as whether the child "likes being in school," "complains about school," and "enjoys most classroom activities." The second dimension was *cooperative/resistant classroom participation*, as measured by teacher reports about factors such as whether the child "responds promptly to teacher requests," "breaks classroom rules," and "acts defiant." Ladd and Dinella discovered that school engagement was moderately stable over time; that is, most children maintained their degree of engagement—whether high or low—from first grade through eighth grade. In addition, the researchers found that children with higher levels of engagement made greater academic progress than did those with lower levels; also, that children who were increasingly resistant and avoidant of school and classroom activities were at greater risk for academic problems.

APPLY > CONNECT > DISCUSS

Write a letter to the best or worst teacher you have ever had. Using concepts presented in this section, explain how the format of the classroom and method of instruction affected your motivation.

The Cognitive Consequences of Schooling

LEARNING OUTCOME

Discuss the school-cutoff strategy, school–nonschool comparisons, and second-generation studies as research strategies for assessing schooled and nonschooled children.

Because formal schooling is widely available throughout the world, it is difficult to do research that directly compares groups of schooled and nonschooled children for the purpose of assessing the cognitive consequences of formal education. Given this limitation, three research strategies have generally been found useful:

1. The *school-cutoff strategy* compares 6-year-olds who have experienced formal schooling with 6-year-olds who have not yet experienced it.

2. *School–nonschool comparisons* take advantage of circumstances in which schooling has been introduced unevenly into a society, providing formal education for some children but not for others.
3. *Second-generation studies* focus on differences between children whose mothers have attended school and children whose mothers have not, looking for effects that the mothers' schooling might have on their children.

The School-Cutoff Strategy

Nearly all countries have cutoff dates for when children are allowed to begin school. For example, children may be eligible to start kindergarten as long as they have reached their fifth birthday by September first (Bedard & Dhuey, 2006). This means that in any given grade, the oldest students are about 20 percent older than the youngest. The **school-cutoff strategy** raises questions about children's relative maturity and preparedness for school and also allows researchers to assess the impact of early schooling while holding the factor of age virtually constant: They simply compare the intellectual performances of children who turn 5 in July or August with that of children who turn 5 in September (after the first) or October, testing both groups at the beginning and at the end of the school year.

school-cutoff strategy A means of assessing the impact of early education by comparing the intellectual performance of children who are almost the same age but begin schooling a year apart because of school rules that set a specific cutoff birthday date for starting school.

Researchers have used the school-cutoff strategy to explore children's development in a number of countries and have found substantial and long-lasting effects with the age at which children begin their formal schooling (Bedard & Dhuey, 2006; Matsubayashi & Ueda, 2015; Ponzo & Scoppa, 2014). One large, cross-national study involving children from a wide range of countries in Europe, Canada, and the United States found that children who started at younger ages were more likely than their older counterparts to score lower on tests of achievement at both fourth and eighth grade and to be held back a year or repeat a grade during primary school, particularly in the United States (Bedard & Dhuey, 2006). Children who started school at relatively young ages in Canada and the United States were even less likely to attend college. Thus, it seems that the disadvantages of relative immaturity in the early school years do not dissipate over time but accumulate across a child's years in school.

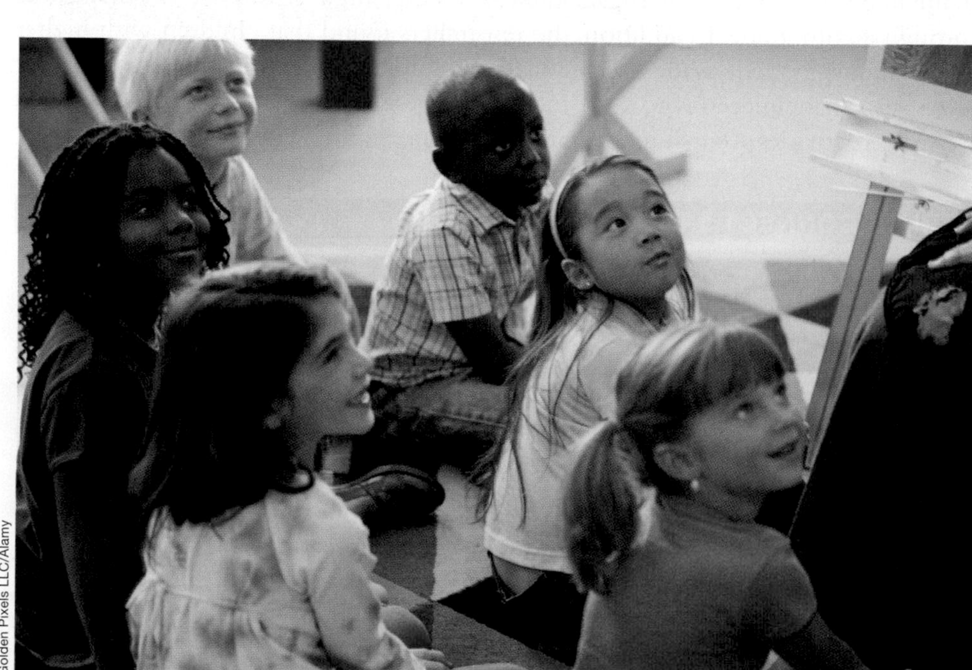

Golden Pixels LLC/Alamy

Because of the school-cutoff strategy, some children in this first-grade class may be just a month or so older than some children in the kindergarten class next door. Research shows that over the course of the school year, memory development of the first-graders will significantly surpass that of similar-aged kindergarteners, illustrating the importance of schooling to intellectual development.

Comparing Schooled and Nonschooled Children

Although the school-cutoff strategy provides an excellent way to assess the cognitive consequences of schooling over time, another approach is to study children who have no experience at all with formal education. As we mentioned previously, access to education varies widely around the globe, especially for girls. But it is also the case that some children do not attend school due to family circumstances, such as needing to work or care for younger siblings. Research on children with little or no formal schooling has focused on three major areas of cognitive development: logical thinking, memory, and metacognitive skills.

Logical Thinking

A large number of cross-cultural studies have been conducted to determine if participation in formal schooling enhances performance on Piagetian conservation tasks and other tasks created to reveal concrete-operational thinking (Keller, 2011; Maynard, 2008). In terms of results, the studies have split more or less evenly between those that found enhanced performance among schooled children and those that did not. Consistent with the evidence presented in Chapter 11 (pp. 397–398), when schoolchildren do better than their unschooled peers on the standard Piagetian tests, their greater success appears to have less to do with more rapid achievement of concrete-operational thinking than with their greater familiarity with the circumstances of test-taking. Such familiarity includes experience with the forms in which test questions are asked, greater ease in speaking to unknown adults, and fluency in the language in which the test is given when the testing is not conducted in the child's native language. When these factors are taken into account, the overall pattern of results indicates that the development of concrete-operational thinking increases with age and is relatively unaffected by schooling.

Memory

As we discussed in Chapter 11 (pp. 397–398), unlike North American children, children in some other cultures do not show an increase in free-recall memory performance as they grow older, and the difference is related to the fact that the children did not attend school. Indeed, research comparing schooled and nonschooled children in other societies, like the research on first-graders and kindergartners presented here, has shown that schooling is the crucial experience underlying differences in performance on free-recall tasks. The performance of children in other cultures who attended school is more similar to that of their North American counterparts in the same grade than it is to that of their age-mates in the same village who have not been to school (Rogoff, 2003).

A classic study by Daniel Wagner (1974) suggested the kind of memory-enhancing information-processing skills that children acquire as a consequence of schooling. Wagner conducted his study among Mayans in Yucatán, Mexico, who had completed different amounts of schooling. He asked 248 people ranging in age from 6 years to adulthood to recall the positions of picture cards laid out in a line. (To ensure that the items pictured on the cards would be familiar to all the participants, the pictures were taken from a local version of bingo called *Lotería*, which uses pictures instead of numbers.) On each trial, each of seven cards was displayed for 2 seconds and then turned facedown. After all seven cards had been presented, a duplicate of one of the cards was shown faceup, and the participant was asked to point to the facedown card that it matched.

For participants who attended school, performance improved markedly with age, as in similar research in the United States. In contrast, among those who did not attend school, older children and adults remembered no better than young children did, leading Wagner to conclude that it was schooling that made the difference. Additional analyses of the data revealed that increasingly efficient use of the memory strategy rehearsal (discussed in Chapter 11, p. 391) by those who attended school was largely responsible for the improvement in their performance.

Evidence such as this does not mean that memory simply fails to develop among children who have not attended school. The difference between schooled and nonschooled children's performance in cross-cultural memory experiments is most noticeable when the items to be remembered are not related to one another according to any everyday script. When the items are part of a meaningful setting, such as the animals found in a barnyard or the furniture placed in a toy house, the effects of schooling on memory performance disappear (Rogoff & Waddell, 1982). Similarly, as observed in Chapter 11, although schooled children were better than unschooled children in a free-recall task because they used a clustering strategy for the items to be remembered, the difference between the two groups' successful recall disappeared when the items to be remembered were presented in a story context. It appears that schooling helps children to develop specialized strategies for remembering and thereby enhances their ability to commit arbitrary material to memory for purposes of later testing. There is no evidence to support the conclusion that schooling increases memory *capacity* per se.

Metacognitive Skills Schooling appears to influence children's metacognitive skills, which, as we discussed in Chapter 11, involve the ability to reflect on and talk about one's own thought processes (Rogoff, 2003). When children have been asked to explain how they arrived at the answer to a logical problem or what they did to make themselves remember something, those who have not attended school are likely to say something like "I did what my sense told me" or to offer no explanation at all. Schoolchildren, on the other hand, are likely to talk about the mental activities and logic that led to their responses. The same pattern applies to *metalinguistic skills*—that is, the ability to think logically about language—understanding, for example, that language has rules of grammar, that words can be dissected into phonemes, and so on. A study conducted with Mexican children aged 6 to 13 found that metalinguistic skills were substantially lower for illiterate compared to literate children than for literate children (Matute et al., 2012). One test of metalinguistic skills asked children to count the number of words in a spoken sentence. In contrast to their literate peers, illiterate children were much less accurate. In general, metalinguistic skills improve when children begin reading and writing, likely because these activities provide opportunities to reflect on the properties of language and how it is used.

Assessing the Second-Generation Impact of Schooling

The evidence from both school-cutoff and cross-cultural research supports the conclusion that the cognitive consequences of schooling are quite specific to the particular skill being tested. The clearest evidence for a general cognitive impact of schooling comes from studies of the child-rearing practices of mothers who have, or have not, gone to school and the subsequent school achievement of their children.

Considerable evidence collected in many countries finds that mothers' literacy skills have profound consequences for children's health and development. Children born to mothers who can read and write have a lower level of infant mortality, better health during childhood, and greater academic achievement (Ataguba, Ojo, & Ichoku, 2016; Smith-Greenaway, 2013). These researchers propose a set of habits, preferences, and skills that mothers acquire in school that might help account for these differences. Beyond rudimentary literacy and numeracy skills, this set includes the mothers':

1. Ability to understand written texts concerning, and engage in discussion about, health and educational issues involving children

2. Use of teaching and learning models based on the scripted activities and authority structure of schooling, which they then employ in the home, talking more to their children and using less directive child-rearing methods
3. Ability and willingness to acquire and accept information from governmental agencies and the mass media regarding their children's health and development

LeVine and his colleagues hypothesized that girls who have been to school retain these habits of mind into adulthood and apply them in the course of raising their own children (LeVine, LeVine, & Schnell, 2001). The work of these researchers was supported by direct observations of the teaching styles of Mayan mothers who have, or have not, been to school. Pablo Chavajay and Barbara Rogoff found that mothers with 12 years of schooling used school-like teaching styles when asked to teach their young children to complete a puzzle, whereas mothers with 2 years or less of schooling participated with their children in completing the puzzle but did not explicitly teach them (Chavajay & Rogoff, 2002). There is nothing wrong with the unschooled mothers' teaching style, but it does not prepare their children well for school, which relies heavily on instructional discourse as the primary mode of instruction.

When we consider how school affects health-related behaviors, including mothers' use of modern social welfare institutions and ways of interacting with their children, it is clear that schooling can have profound consequences for society.

Overall, extensive research on the cognitive consequences of schooling has produced a mixed picture. The idea that schooling is directly responsible for broad changes in the way the mind works is, at best, only minimally supported. When schooling has been found to improve cognitive performance, the effect appears to work in one of three ways: (1) by increasing children's knowledge base, including ways of using language; (2) by teaching specific information-processing strategies that are relevant primarily to school itself; and (3) by changing children's overall life situations and attitudes, which they later pass on to their children in the form of new child-rearing practices that promote school achievement. As we emphasized at the beginning of the chapter, it may be that the most important consequences of schooling for the majority of the world's people are not simply cognitive. Schooling is a gateway to health and nutrition, to economic power, and to social status.

APPLY > CONNECT > DISCUSS

Your local government has earmarked a special pool of money to support services for the rising population of immigrant families in your community. Concerned about the school readiness of immigrant children, officials plan to apply most of the money to a vast preschool expansion project. You believe this focus would be too narrow and want to convince the officials to divert funds to support adult education for immigrant parents. Map out the evidence that you will use to persuade the officials to your point of view.

Contemporary Challenges in a Globalizing World

LEARNING OUTCOME

Explain the challenges of increasing access to quality education, serving diverse populations of students, and sensitively integrating home cultural values into classroom practices.

As we pointed out earlier, access to quality education continues to be a major challenge for educators and policy makers. There are vast disparities among countries in the proportions of children who are able to go to school. Within many countries, there are also vast disparities among children in the amount and quality of the schooling they receive. As we discussed previously, a child's gender, ethnicity,

Gideon Mendel/Getty Images

Children of immigrant families are the fastest-growing group of children in the United States.

and socioeconomic status all can profoundly affect both the amount and the quality of schooling.

In addition to the challenge of access, schools are challenged by the increasing cultural and linguistic diversity of the students they serve. Throughout the world, large numbers of families are moving away from their native lands and cultures, seeking new lives in places where the language, cultural practices, and values and beliefs are radically different from their own. Indeed, as we discussed in Chapter 10, children of immigrant families are the fastest-growing group of children in the United States, accounting for approximately 25 percent of all U.S. children (Child Trends, 2014).

Although some areas in the United States, especially border states, attract a preponderance of Spanish-speaking immigrants, an increasing number of school districts are seeing an enormous rise in the cultural and linguistic diversity of their immigrant students. Given that studies routinely find that children of immigrant families are overrepresented among students who experience academic difficulties and school failure (Motti-Stefanidi, Masten, & Asendorpf, 2015; Suárez-Orozco et al., 2010), schools face a particularly difficult challenge in identifying and responding to the unique academic needs of immigrant students who vary so widely in native language and heritage culture. Indeed, as we will see, many immigrant children and their families must adjust not only to a new culture and language but also to the unique culture and language of school.

The Culture of School

A number of scholars have proposed that every culture can be described in terms of its own particular worldview, a dominant way of thinking about and relating to the world that arises from a people's common historical experience. This dominant pattern of interpreting events is called a **cultural style** (Gratier, Greenfield, & Isaac, 2009; Greenfield, Keller, Fuligni, & Maynard, 2003). An important dimension of cultural style is independence–interdependence. An *independent*, or *individualistic*, cultural style emphasizes the individual and the individual's personal choices and goals; an *interdependent*, or *collectivist*, style emphasizes the group and group harmony, downplaying individual achievement.

cultural style A dominant way of thinking about and relating to the world that arises from a people's common historical experience.

Cultural style is not just a matter of abstract values and beliefs; it is embodied in daily life and patterns of social interaction and how parents socialize their children to express cultural values and beliefs (Mosco & Atzaba-Poria, 2016). But in addition to affecting family life, cultural style is also embodied in school. In the United States, for example, an individualistic cultural style is apparent in the emphasis placed on academic achievement and obligations to school and studies. This emphasis is readily apparent when students are publically rewarded for writing the best essay or getting the highest score on a test. A critical issue for developmentalists and educators is the extent to which the cultural style of a child's background may conflict with the culture of school.

Patricia Greenfield and her colleagues have addressed the potentially problematic relationship between children's traditional cultural practices and the

Christian Kober/Robert Harding Picture Library Ltd

Developmentalists point out that schools have different cultural styles that influence classroom practices and the assumptions and attitudes of teachers and students. Because of the increasing number of students from immigrant families, some U.S. schools are training their teachers to be sensitive to the possibility of "culture clashes" between the cultural style of the school and the children's culture of origin.

practices they encounter in school. In particular, they have proposed that, given the competitive nature of the American education system, the cultural practices of standard American classrooms favor children who come from homes that promote the prevailing American cultural style of independence, with the goal of socializing children to become autonomous individuals who enter into social relations by personal choice (an individualistic orientation). They also propose that the standard culture of American schools is correspondingly disadvantageous to children from homes that promote a cultural style of interdependence—that is, children whose parents have been socializing them to place a strong value on social networks and downplaying personal achievement (Vasquez-Salgado, Greenfield, & Burgos-Cienfuegos, 2015).

Research indicates that first-generation immigrant Hispanic children can be disadvantaged by conflicting cultural styles between home and school. In one study, first-generation college students who had emigrated from Mexico to southern California were presented with a common home–school conflict, such as being asked by their mothers to attend a family reunion on Sunday but needing to study for an important exam (Vasquez-Salgado et al., 2015). Although most students indicated that they would remain at school to study, all described similar conflicts in their own lives and the stress associated with having to decide between family and school obligations.

Other researchers emphasize the point that many children who come from families with an interdependent orientation thrive in the standard American classroom. The success of these children appears to be due in large measure to the positive role the parents play in their schooling. For example, Nathan Caplan and his colleagues studied the children of refugees who fled to the United States from Vietnam, Cambodia, and Laos during the 1970s and 1980s. These children, whose home cultures were characterized by an interdependent cultural style, became conspicuously successful in educational pursuits (Caplan, Choy, & Whitmore, 1991). Although they had lost from 1 to 3 years of formal education in refugee camps, and most were unable to speak English when they entered school in the United States, 8 out of 10 students surveyed had a B average or better within 3 to 6 years. Almost half received A's in mathematics. These achievements are all the more noteworthy because they were

Pablo Chavajay, Organizational patterns in problem solving among Mayan fathers. *Developmental Psychology* 44.3 (May 2008) 882–888, page 885. APA. Reprinted with permission.

Researchers have found that Mayan parents who have at least 12 years of schooling typically use school-like teaching styles when helping their children complete a puzzle. These styles may reinforce their children's classroom learning.

attained in schools in low-income, inner-city areas traditionally associated with limited resources and poorly motivated, often disruptive students.

In trying to account for the spectacular success of these children, Caplan and his colleagues found parents' involvement to be crucial. Almost half of the parents surveyed said that they read to their children, many in their native language. That the parents didn't know English well evidently mattered less to the children's school performance than did the children's positive emotional associations of being read to and the connection to their culture.

Aspects of culture other than an interdependent cultural style can prove to be poorly supported by, and disadvantageous in the context of, the standard American classroom culture. According to Wade Boykin, African American children inherit a rich tradition of using expressive movement as a part of their everyday communicative behavior—a tradition they are required to suppress in classrooms that emphasize sitting quietly while learning. Hypothesizing that this suppression of an important cultural asset has a negative impact on their learning, Boykin conducted experiments with African American children in which they listened to stories under different conditions and were then asked questions about the stories. The story conditions varied in terms of the activity levels of the stories' characters, whether the storytelling was accompanied by music with a lively beat, and whether children were instructed to sit quietly or were told they could clap and dance while they listened to the story. As shown in Figure 12.6, the children performed significantly better on the questions when the story involved high levels of character activity and music and they were encouraged to clap and dance, supporting Boykin's idea about the importance of this cultural factor for the children's learning (Boykin & Cunningham, 2001).

Taken together, these different studies strongly implicate home cultural values and modes of behavior as important factors in children's school success. But they also indicate that there is no "one right way" to incorporate such differences into classroom practices.

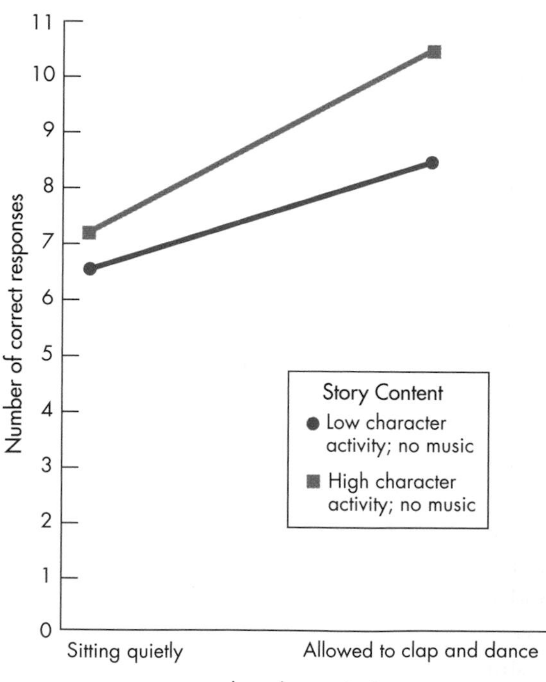

FIGURE 12.6 As indicated by the number of correct responses on a memory task, students were much better at remembering a story when it had a high level of character activity and when the children were allowed to clap and dance while they heard the story. (Data from Boykin & Cunningham, 2001.)

The Language of School

Even when people speak the same language, they do not necessarily use language in the same way. Indeed, some developmentalists and educators use the term *Englishes* to capture the rich diversity of English dialects that children in the United States bring from their homes and communities into the classroom (Flores & Rosa, 2015; Martinez, Morales, & Aldana, 2017). As we have noted, language is used in schools in rather distinctive ways, and children's experience of oral and written language in the home will differ to some extent not only from language practices at school but also from those of other homes within the community.

In order to gain insight into how language used in the home may differ from language practices associated with school and school success, Shirley Heath (1983) conducted a groundbreaking ethnographic study of three populations of children and their families over a period of years. The populations she studied, all from the same geographical locale, included the families of a group of European American schoolteachers, a group of European American textile workers, and a group of African Americans engaged in farming and textile jobs.

Conducting observations both in homes and in classrooms, Heath found that the families of European American teachers experienced the least mismatch with the school. About half of the conversations she recorded in the teachers' homes included the "instructional discourse" that is a prominent feature of classrooms. In addition, these parents involved their children in labeling objects, naming letters, and reading. When reading with their children, they went well beyond the text itself to make clear the relationships between what was in the book and experiences the child might have had or might have in the future. In a sense, the teachers were being teachers at home as well as at school. Perhaps as a result, their children tended to do well in school.

The pattern in the homes of European American textile workers differed from the pattern in schools and in the teachers' homes in that the parents limited their storybook conversations to the text itself. They asked their children questions about the characters and events in stories they read to them but did not encourage their children to imaginatively link the stories to the world around them. Overall, the children from these working-class European American families tended not to do well in school. More precisely, in what may have been a reflection of the language-use pattern in their homes, they tended to perform well in the early grades of school, where a focus on the literal meaning of a text fits most tasks, but they did less well in the higher grades, where it becomes necessary to draw inferences from complex texts.

Unlike the two groups of European American parents, the African American parents rarely used the known-answer questions of instructional discourse ("What color is your jacket?"). Rather, they most often asked children questions that encouraged them to think about similarities across situations related to the children's own experience ("Do you think you can get along with your cousin on this visit?"). Such questions often served as the pretext for discussing some interesting event and helped children think about shifting roles and responsibilities in different situations. Heath also documented many inventive uses of language in teasing and storytelling. But the children's language experience generally did not expose them to the kinds of language patterns they would be expected to use in school. Again, perhaps in part because of the mismatch, these African American working-class children tended not to perform well in school. Similar findings were reported for Latino children (Vasquez, 2002).

These differences in academic success among the children from the three groups are understandable in terms of the relative fit between school and home language use and culture. At the same time, it is the goal of teachers to be successful with all children. So the question becomes one of how to design educational interventions to make it possible for everyone to learn effectively.

Culturally Responsive Classroom Strategies

In recognition of the importance of children's home language and culture to their success in the classroom, schools have begun to make a place for them in academic curricula and to host special events to explore and celebrate the cultural heritages of

Roberto E. Rosales/Albuquerque Journal/ZUMAPRESS.com/Alamy

Illustrating culturally responsive education, a professional artist works with school children to create a mural, "El Ritmo de la Agua" ("The Rhythm of the Water"), to represent the region's agricultural and Hispanic heritages.

the young people they serve. Common programs for English language learners (ELLs), including bilingual education programs and heritage language classes, are intended to help immigrant students make the transition to an all-English curriculum. The overarching goal is to foster assimilation while valuing cultural diversity (Padilla, 2006).

An early and influential example of the culturally responsive approach to education occurred in a classroom of students from the Odawa Indian tribe in Canada, taught by an expert Odawa teacher (Erickson & Mohatt, 1982). On the surface, the teacher appeared to adhere to a recitation-script approach, talking for most of the lessons, asking many known-answer questions, and limiting the students' role to answering her questions. But she did so in a special way consistent with the language use and cultural patterns employed in Odawa homes. When she was giving instruction, she organized students into small groups instead of rows, approximating the way the children interacted in groups at home. She generally addressed the children as a group and did not single out individual children. Instead of saying "good" when students answered her questions correctly, she signaled her acceptance of their answers by moving on to the next question. She praised but did not reprimand students in public, in accordance with Odawa norms against public criticism. This culture-sensitive way of implementing classroom lessons worked well to improve children's academic performance.

Another example of the importance of culture-sensitive instruction was provided by an experiment conducted by Carol Lee, who drew on African American high school students' familiarity with, and appreciation of, the linguistic form called *signifying* (Lee, 2010). Within the African American community, to signify means to speak in a manner that uses innuendo and words with double meanings, to play with the sounds and meanings of words, and to be quick-witted and funny, all at the same time. According to Lee, African American adolescents use signifying for a wide variety of speech functions, including:

- To challenge someone in a verbal duel but remain friendly
- To persuade someone by driving home a message in a distinctive way
- To criticize someone in a way that is difficult to pin down

Lee began by presenting students examples of signifying dialogues of the sort they were familiar with and getting the students to analyze and explain how each example of signifying worked to achieve a specific goal. Then she had them read stories and novels by African American writers that included signifying and asked them to apply the rules, which they knew intuitively, to the interpretation of complex inferential questions from the literary texts.

When Lee compared the performance of students who engaged in this kind of culturally responsive instruction with that of students who took the regular literature course, she found that they demonstrated a significantly higher level of literary understanding and active engagement with the problem of literary interpretation.

On the basis of available research, these examples could be multiplied to encompass a wide variety of ethnic and social-class groups—wide enough to make a convincing case that it is possible to organize effective contexts for education by taking into account local variations in culture and social class (Lee, 2017; Martinez et al., 2017; Tharp, 2005). At the same time, it needs to be recognized that there is no single "right way" to connect classroom instruction to home culture. Research on this topic makes it clear that a wide variety of specific classroom strategies can successfully engage students from the vast variety of backgrounds characteristic of American society.

APPLY > CONNECT > DISCUSS

In her research with African American children, Carol Lee found that, compared with traditional instruction, culturally responsive instruction results both in a higher level of literary understanding (of how to analyze and interpret texts) and in increased engagement. Review the curriculum she developed around the concept of "signifying" and explain how it led to both of these results.

Looking Ahead

LEARNING OUTCOME

Point out how peer-group experiences outside school help prepare students for adult life.

As important as schooling is to middle childhood, it is not the only context beyond the family that influences children. Especially important is the time spent in new kinds of activities with friends and one's peer group. On weekday afternoons and evenings, on weekends and holidays, children of elementary-school age are likely to be found among other children their own age, engaged in activities of their own choosing. Some of these settings have an adult or two present, but in many cases, adults are not on the scene.

Participation in these peer groups provides a kind of preparation for adult life that is quite different from that organized by adults in classrooms or at home. At the same time, peer-group experiences influence life at home and in school. Consequently, a full understanding of the nature of middle childhood requires investigation of peer contexts as well, so we turn to this important topic in Chapter 13.

SUMMARY

- The children of the world have vastly unequal access to education, yet school can have an extraordinary impact as a context for children's development.

The Contexts of Learning

- Education refers to explicit instruction of children in order to transmit a culture's knowledge and skills.
- Early hunter-gatherer societies most likely transmitted cultural knowledge and skills through social enhancement and imitation as children participated in everyday activities rather than through explicit instruction. Increasing specialization led to the emergence of apprenticeship—an intermediate form involving some explicit instruction but relying mainly on participation—and to the emergence of education, or schooling.
- Schooling differs from traditional apprenticeship training in dimensions including motivation, social relations, social organization, and mediums of instruction. Its problems are abstract, in contrast to those of everyday life.

School Readiness

- Children often start school with knowledge, skills, and attitudes that serve as building blocks for learning to read and write and to do math.
- A basic reading skill is decoding text—translating graphemes (units of print) to phonemes (units of sound). This, in turn, requires the ability to detect and manipulate the phonemes in words, an ability that comes only with instruction.
- To learn math, children must be able to relate number words and symbols to quantities. Children learn to envision the placement of numbers on an abstract number line and to manipulate numeric units.
- Families play a key role in promoting school readiness by creating contexts for children to engage in relevant activities. School readiness promotes academic success.
- Preschools also promote school readiness. Although worldwide preschool enrollment has continued to grow at an encouraging rate in recent decades, there are significant disparities in enrollment across and within countries, with lower enrollments among many groups of children who might most benefit from preschool, including immigrant children in the United States.

In the Classroom

- Educators have debated the merits of a bottom-up approach, which initially focuses on basic skills, versus a top-down approach, which focuses on the big picture of which the basic skills are part.
- The standard classroom format features a teacher at the head of the class, instructing students through the use of a special instructional discourse, typified by the teacher's asking known-answer questions.
- Alternative forms of classroom instruction seek to counter the passivity of students in the standard format and make them active participants in their education. Examples include:
  - Reciprocal teaching, in which a teacher and a small group of students read segments of text and take turns leading discussions of their meaning.
  - Realistic mathematics education, which encourages development of conceptual understanding as well as basic skills through the use of models and meaningful problem-oriented activities.
  - Playworld practice, which involves enacting, making art about, and playing with themes based on children's literature.
- For many children, specific learning disabilities (SLD) pose a barrier to school success. These children have normal IQs but fare poorly in at least some academic areas. The most common specific learning disability is dyslexia, a reading problem that typically involves difficulties detecting phonemes and understanding the rules that relate graphemes and phonemes.
- While some students thrive on the challenges of schooling, others lose their academic motivation. Researchers exploring the reasons have found two patterns:
  - Children who adopt an incremental model of intelligence see intelligence as something that can grow as one learns. They tend to have a mastery motivation that motivates them to learn and improve.
  - Children who adopt an entity model of intelligence see intelligence as fixed. They tend to develop a performance orientation that motivates them to perform well but also to give up when they experience failure.

The Cognitive Consequences of Schooling

- The cognitive consequences of schooling have been assessed through three research strategies for comparing schooled and nonschooled children:
  - The school-cutoff strategy, which compares 6-year-olds in first grade with those in kindergarten, finds that schooling makes a difference mainly to a range of relatively specific cognitive abilities.
  - School–nonschool comparisons show few clear differences other than increased use of specialized memory strategies and increased metacognitive skills.
  - Second-generation studies, comparing schooled and unschooled mothers, suggest that habits and skills acquired in school may influence child-rearing practices in such a way as to lead to better health and educational outcomes for children. Thus, school's greatest impact may be other than cognitive.

Contemporary Challenges in a Globalizing World

- A major challenge is to increase access to quality education, reducing disparities across and within countries, including disparities related to gender, ethnicity, and socioeconomic status.
- Another major challenge in many countries is to serve student populations that are increasingly diverse in terms of language and culture.
- Home cultural values are important to children's school success. A good match between home and school language also favors success. Although the culture of U.S. schools reflects the dominant cultural style, classroom practices can be sensitive to other cultural styles, thereby benefiting a wider range of children.

Looking Ahead

- In addition to school, peer groups become another important context of development during middle childhood.

Key Terms

formal education, p. 411
apprenticeship, p. 411
emergent literacy, p. 413
emergent numeracy, p. 413
decoding, p. 414
bottom-up processing, p. 420
top-down processing, p. 420
instructional discourse, p. 420
reciprocal teaching, p. 420
realistic mathematics education, p. 421
playworld practice, p. 422
specific learning disabilities (SLD), p. 424
academic motivation, p. 425
mastery orientation, p. 425
performance orientation, p. 425
entity model of intelligence, p. 426
incremental model of intelligence, p. 426
school engagement, p. 427
school-cutoff strategy, p. 428
cultural style, p. 432

SM Rafiq Photography/Getty Images

CHAPTER

13

Social and Emotional Development in Middle Childhood

Cassie and Becca had been best friends since first grade. When the girls were in fifth grade, Kelly moved into town. At first, the three of them were quite close. But something happened a few weeks ago. According to 10-year-old Cassie:

> *Becca kind of forgot me. They started to get really close and they just forgot me. And then they started ganging up on me and stuff. Like, after lunch we have a place where we meet and stuff. We get in a circle and just talk. And they'd put their shoulders together and they wouldn't let me, you know, in the circle. They would never talk to me, and they would never listen to what I had to say. I don't think I've ever done anything to them. I've always been nice to them. I feel like I don't want to go to school, because I don't know what they'll do every day. I talk to my mom but it kind of makes her mad because she says I should ignore them. But I can't. And I can't concentrate. They're like—they look at me and stuff like that. They stare at me. I can hear them saying stuff and whispering and they look right at me.*

(Information from Simmons, 2002.)

Very few of us pass through middle childhood without experiencing the sting of peer rejection. As children between the ages of 6 and 12 spend more time in the company of age-mates, and correspondingly less time with parents, peers begin to assume a more prominent place in their lives and exert more influence on their behavior and development. Indeed, one of the most significant changes of middle childhood is the emergence of peer influence as a considerable power in shaping behavior. Sometimes the rule of "might makes right" prevails, as when an especially strong child dominates group activity. At other times, the complexity of social relationships, including popularity, sets the tone, as Cassie came to experience.

The emergence of new forms of *social control*—that is, ways of organizing behavior in relation to group life and society—is also apparent in the changing nature of children's relationships with their parents. Parents can no longer successfully demand blind obedience from their children, nor can they easily just pick them up and remove them from danger or from situations in which they are behaving badly. Parents can still monitor their children's whereabouts, but they must rely on their children's greater understanding of the consequences of their actions and on their desire to conform to the standards that have been set for them about behaving in ways that are safe, socially appropriate, and morally acceptable. As a result, parents' socialization techniques become more indirect, and they rely increasingly on discussion and explanation to influence their children's behavior.

As their relationships with others change, so, too, do children's sense of themselves. As long as they spend their time primarily among family members, their social roles and sense of self are more or less predefined and determined. They are little brothers or older sisters, with all the expectations and privileges that go along with those roles. When children spend more time among their peers, however, the sense of self they acquired in their families no longer suffices, and they must form new identities appropriate to the new contexts they inhabit. The child who seems fearless at home and who dominates younger siblings may find that he or she needs to be more restrained on the playground with peers.

This chapter focuses on how new forms of social control are manifested in children's changing sense of self, moral development, peer interactions and friendships, and relationships with parents.

WARMING UP

1. Think about Cassie's experience of being excluded by Becca and Kelly. What might have led to that situation? Why would Becca and Kelly treat her that way? Should Cassie's mom intervene? If so, how? How might Cassie's rejection by her friends affect her in the future?
2. In the middle childhood years, children begin to spend increasing amounts of time using digital technologies and social networking. What are the pros and cons for children's social relationships?

LEARNING OUTCOMES

Describe changes in the sense of self that occur during middle childhood.

Explain how self-esteem affects the middle childhood crisis that Erikson called *industry versus inferiority*.

A New Sense of Self

> On our quests to create ourselves we brown girls play dress up. What is most fascinating about this ritual of imitation is what we choose to mimic—what we reach for in our mothers' closets. We move right on past the unglamorous garb of our mothers' day-to-day realities—the worn housedresses or beat-up slippers—and reach instead for the intimates. Slip our sassy little selves into their dressiest of dresses and sexiest of lingerie like being grown is like Christmas or Kwanzaa and can't come fast enough. Then we practice the deadly art of attitude—rollin' eyes, necks, and hips in mesmerizing synchronization, takin' out imaginary violators with razor-sharp tongues. (Morgan, 1999, pp. 29–30.)

Joan Morgan's reflection on playing dress-up surely resonates with anyone who remembers clomping around in their mother's high heels, with the hems of fancy dresses trailing behind. Dress-up is a common play activity toward the end of early childhood and in the first years of middle childhood. Morgan's point that it tends to reflect glamour, success, and even power is especially interesting in light of Erik Erikson's theory that the main challenge of middle childhood is to establish a sense of *competence.* As we explained in Chapter 1 (see p. 19), Erikson believed that development throughout life involves seeking answers to the question "Who am I?" At each *psychosocial stage*, the individual faces a particular challenge in his or her quest for identity. In middle childhood, when children are expected to develop more mature forms of behavior—pitching in around the house or solving more complicated problems at school—the main challenge is **industry versus inferiority**. Children who emerge from middle childhood with a sense of industry believe that

industry versus inferiority According to Erikson's theory, the stage during which children judge themselves to be industrious and successful at meeting the new challenges posed by adults at home and school, or inferior and incapable of meeting such challenges.

they are competent and effective at activities valued by adults and peers. Those who emerge with a sense of inferiority feel inadequate, believing themselves incapable of mastering the tasks expected of them.

In addition to general feelings of competence, the transition from early to middle childhood is accompanied by equally striking developments in how children think about themselves, the emergence of a new level of sensitivity to their personal standing among their peers, and their resulting efforts to maintain their self-esteem.

Changing Conceptions of the Self

A sizable body of evidence suggests that as children move from early childhood to middle childhood and then to adolescence, their sense of self undergoes marked changes that are significantly intertwined with cognitive and social developments (Côté, Bouffard, & Vezeau, 2014; Harter, 2015). One avenue of research concerns changes over time in the *structure* of the self—that is, how the self becomes increasingly complex, encompassing multiple features. The simplest distinction is between the *I-self*, and the *me-self*. As we discussed in Chapter 9 (p. 303), the *I-self* is a person's subjective sense of being a self-aware, unique individual who experiences the world in a particular way, whereas the *me-self* is the person's sense of his or her objective characteristics, such as physical appearance, abilities, and other personal features that are easily observed. The cognitive development of younger children is such that self-descriptions focus mainly on the concrete, objective self and include highly specific, loosely connected behavior, abilities, and preferences: "I live in a big house. I have brown eyes. I like to ride my pony." Rarely are children's self-descriptions combined into generalized, more abstract traits such as "being shy," or "being smart" (Côté, 2009; Harter, 2012). In middle childhood, however, self-descriptions become more abstract and increasingly oriented toward the possibilities of the self in the future.

The development of individual self-concepts based on limited, concrete characteristics to more abstract and stable conceptions is fueled by **social comparison**, the process of defining oneself in relationship to one's peers (Nesi & Prinstein, 2015; Sheskin, Bloom, & Wynn, 2014). There is no mystery about why social comparison begins to play a significant role in children's sense of themselves during middle childhood. The increased time they spend with their peers in both face-to-face and digital environments, and their greater ability to understand others' points of view, lead children to engage in a new kind of questioning about themselves. They must determine their answers to questions such as "Am I good at sports?" "Am I a good friend?" "Do the other kids like me?" Such questions have no absolute answer because there are no absolute criteria for success. Rather, success is measured in relationship to the performance of others in the social group. The many comparisons children make in a wide variety of settings provide them with a new overall sense of themselves.

social comparison The process of defining oneself in relationship to one's peers.

With greater maturity, the use of social comparison becomes increasingly complex and subtle. When deliberate and pervasive social comparison becomes important at around 8 years of age, children are initially inclined to make overt social comparisons in interactions with their peers, saying such things as, "I'm finishing the math problems a lot faster than you are"

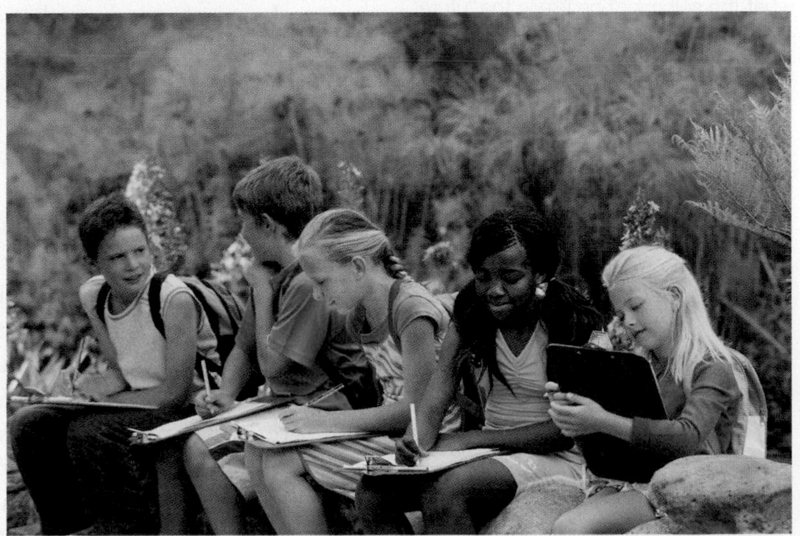

moodboard/Getty Images

Social comparison often takes the form of asking how one's friends are doing on a school assignment.

or "I bet I beat your score in the video game." But they soon discover that this kind of comparison is perceived as bragging and is likely to evoke negative reactions. As a consequence, they begin to develop more subtle ways of making social comparisons, asking questions such as, "What problem are you on?" or "What was your highest score?"

The targets of social comparison also change across middle childhood, extending well beyond one's immediate peers. An example is the way that children begin to compare themselves with the vast array of characters portrayed in the media (Eyal & Te'eni-Harari, 2013; Gleason, Theran, & Newberg, 2017). By 12 years of age, television characters are common targets of social comparison (Comstock & Scharrer, 2010). Indeed, as we discuss in Chapter 15, social comparison with media characters is related to the body image of adolescents, as when teens compare their bodies to those of ultra-thin super models—comparisons that may impact mental and physical health (Eyal & Te'eni-Harari, 2013; Santarossa & Woodruff, 2017).

Finally, the opportunities for social comparison expand considerably as children gain increasing access to social media through various electronic devices. Posted text and images provide fertile ground for social comparison with friends, acquaintances, and media characters (Reinecke, 2017).

differentiated self A sense of self as including many fluctuating attributes.

The many comparisons children make in a wide variety of settings contribute to a **differentiated self** —a sense of themselves as including a number of attributes that fluctuate in significance according to particular circumstances, roles, and relationships (Cohen, Spiegler, Young, Hankin, & Abela, 2014). In middle childhood, children may describe themselves as rowdy with friends, obnoxious with parents, and polite with grandparents. They may consider themselves to be smart at languages and dumb at biology. The appearance of such multiple selves in children's self-descriptions makes it necessary for them to deal with the fact that they are, in certain respects, different people in different contexts. Interestingly, in middle childhood, children seem unconcerned about the proliferation of selves, even when the different selves they present are inconsistent. For example, when a researcher confronted a boy who claimed to be both rude and caring, the boy replied, "Well, you are caring with your friends and rude to people who don't treat you nicely. There's no problem" (Harter, 2015 p. 79).

possible selves Possibilities about what the self might be like in the future.

The differentiated self is also apparent in children's ability to construct **possible selves**—that is, hypothetical possibilities about what the self might be like in the future (Hardy et al., 2014; Oyserman, Bybee, & Terry, 2006). Such possible selves may include *ideal*, or *hoped-for*, selves (what one wishes to become) or *feared selves* (what one is afraid of becoming). Such possible selves are evidence that the child is beginning to understand that the current, actual self is but one of many possible hypothetical selves.

Some developmentalists have argued that because the construction of multiple selves and self-possibilities intersects with changing social expectations to engage in different, more mature behavior, in middle childhood the self is inherently unstable (Harter, 2012). In the context of this instability, children may be especially motivated to explore the self and experiment with different self-possibilities. Increasing access to digital media during middle childhood presents a myriad of new ways to explore self-possibilities. One fascinating study used a questionnaire to examine how and why 600 9- to 18-year-olds in the Netherlands might use chat or instant messaging to present themselves as somehow different than they really are—for example, older, more "macho," or more attractive (Valkenburg, Schouten, & Peter, 2005). They found that young adolescents (9- to 13-year-olds) were significantly more likely than older adolescents (14- to 18-year-olds) to engage in such self-experimentation. When asked for their reasons for pretending to be someone else on the Internet, adolescents reported three general motives:

- *Social compensation*: To feel less shy; to talk more easily about certain topics
- *Social facilitation*: To make new friends; to get a date; to get to know people more easily
- *Self-exploration*: To explore how others react to me; to try out how it feels to be someone else

The researchers found that, in addition to engaging in more self-experimentation overall, young adolescents were especially more likely than older adolescents to engage in experimentation for purposes of social facilitation—that is, to make new friends or get to know people more easily. This underscores an important point regarding the relationship between self-development and social relationships: Young adolescents may experiment with possible selves in the context of pursuing possible social relationships.

It is interesting to speculate about how recent technological advances may impact exploration and development of self. From personal Web pages and blogs to popular social networking sites—these new electronic forums are radically public and interactive, accessible to literally billions of people, any of whom may comment on the documents' contents. These personal digital expressions can be entirely rewritten to present an entirely different self—or selves—to the world.

Self-Esteem

Having and being a self is much more than an intellectual experience of comparing oneself to others or imagining future self possibilities. Indeed, one of the most powerful forms of evidence that selves exist at all is that they make trouble for us: We can lack confidence in ourselves, feel sorry for ourselves, or even despise ourselves. Selves, in other words, are important targets of evaluation that can profoundly affect how we act, learn, and experience our lives. **Self-esteem**, our evaluations of our own worth, is of considerable interest to developmentalists and clinicians precisely because of its pervasive influence on individual development and mental health.

self-esteem One's evaluation of one's own worth.

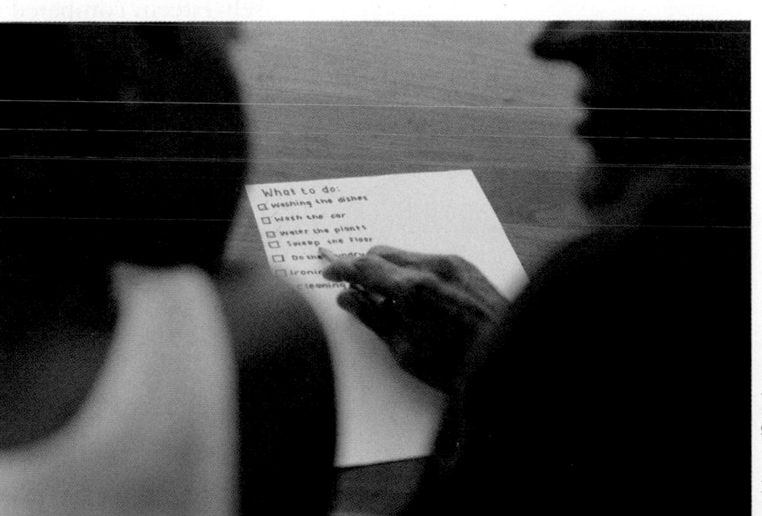

Peopleimages/Getty Images

The positive feedback this girl receives for completing a list of tasks for the day will likely have an important impact on her developing self-esteem.

Susan Harter, a developmental researcher and clinician, has been intrigued for decades by the question of children's development of self-esteem—that is, their evaluations of their own worth (1999). Consistent with the differentiation of self-conceptions described above, research on the development of self-esteem indicates that self-evaluations during middle childhood become similarly differentiated. During this period, children make distinctive evaluations of their competence and worth in several different areas, such as schoolwork, friendships, and sports. Self-esteem is also affected by the fact that children can now compare and evaluate their current, actual self against an ideal, hoped-for self.

Foundations of Self-Esteem Developmentalists and clinicians agree that self-esteem is an important index of mental health. High self-esteem during childhood and adolescence has been linked to satisfaction and happiness in later life, while low self-esteem has been linked to depression, anxiety, and maladjustment in school, work, and social relationships (Harter, 2012;

Steiger, Allemand, Robins, & Fend, 2014; Sowislo, & Orth, 2013). Researchers, educators, counselors, and other developmentalists have therefore been eager to understand the foundations of self-esteem and how it can be nurtured.

Not surprisingly, self-esteem has been linked to patterns of child rearing and the quality of parent–child relationships (Khaleque, 2017; von Soest, Wichstrom, & Kvalem, 2016). In an early, extensive study of 10- to 12-year-old boys, Stanley Coopersmith (1967) found that parents of boys with high self-esteem (as determined by their answers to a questionnaire and their teachers' ratings) employed a style of parenting characterized by a mixture of firm control, promotion of high standards of behavior, encouragement of independence, and willingness to reason with their children. Coopersmith's data suggest that three parental characteristics combine to produce high self-esteem in middle childhood:

1. *Parents' acceptance of their children.* The mothers of sons with high self-esteem had closer, more affectionate relationships with their children than did mothers of children with low self-esteem. The children tended to interpret their mothers' interest as an indication of their personal importance.
2. *Parents' setting of clearly defined limits.* Parents who set and enforced strict limits on their children's activities gave their children a sense that norms are real and significant and made in the children's best interest.
3. *Parents' respect for individuality.* Within the limits set by the parents' sense of standards and social norms, the children with high self-esteem were allowed a great deal of individual self-expression. Parents showed respect for these children by reasoning with them and considering their points of view.

More recently, developmentalists have explored the relationship between parent–child relationships and developing self-esteem from middle childhood to late adolescence, and in numerous countries (Harris et al., 2015; Khaleque, 2017). A meta-analysis of more than 13,000 children in 16 countries found that children who perceived their parents as hostile or aggressive were significantly more likely to have poor self-esteem compared to peers who had no such perceptions of parents (Khaleque, 2017). Overall, this research supports the notion that parenting practices and the quality of parent–child relationships exert a positive impact on the development of self-esteem. According to a number of studies, children with lower self-esteem are more likely to define their self-worth in the context of their peer relationships and are more likely to associate with deviant peers, a topic to which we will return in Chapter 15.

APPLY > CONNECT > DISCUSS

In what ways do changing conceptions of self appear related to the cognitive developments characteristic of middle childhood (see Chapter 11)?

How might self-esteem be related to the development of self-regulation discussed in Chapter 9 (see pp. 308–316)?

LEARNING OUTCOMES

Contrast moral development during middle childhood according to stages described by Piaget and levels and stages described by Kohlberg.

Explain what the social domain theory suggests about the moral development of children.

Point out the relationship between moral development and children's developing theory of mind.

Moral Development

During middle childhood, the child's new ability to internalize society's rules and standards leads to significant changes in moral development, just as it does in social development generally. Remember from Chapter 9 that as children develop, their reasoning and behaviors become less dependent on external rewards and punishments and more dependent on an internal, personal sense of right and wrong. According to Freud's *psychodynamic theory* (see Chapter 9, p. 305), this transition occurs with the development of the superego. The *superego*, remember, is the part of the personality that monitors and evaluates whether the individual's actions are morally appropriate. It is the individual's conscience—the *internalization* first of the same-sex parent's standards and moral codes and then of society's. Once the superego has formed, the child is able to draw upon his or her own internal notions of right and wrong in making moral judgments rather than be driven by hope of reward or fear of reprisal.

Interest in the shift from external to internal control is also apparent in the *constructivist* view of moral development held by Piaget and those who follow in his footsteps (see Chapter 9, pp. 305–306). Much of their work has focused on exploring children's reasoning about what is morally right or wrong and the relationship between moral reasoning and moral behavior.

Constructivist View of Moral Development

In Chapter 9, we explained that for Piaget, moral development involves a shift from *heteronomous morality*—in which right and wrong are defined according to objective consequences of behavior—to **autonomous morality**, in which right and wrong are defined according to the person's internal motives and intentions (see p. 306). Piaget argued that the shift in moral reasoning takes place in the context of peer activities—playing games, in particular.

autonomous morality The second and final stage of Piaget's theory of moral development, in which right and wrong are defined according to internal motives and intentions rather than objective consequences.

Around the age of 7 or 8, children begin to engage in a new form of play—games based on rules. By observing changes in how children play the game of marbles, Piaget found that young children (6 to 8 years of age) have a "mystical respect" for the rules of the game. They believe that rules are "eternal and unchangeable" because they have been handed down by authority figures such as parents, grandparents, or even God (Piaget, 1965/1995, pp. 206–207; see the box "Children's Ideas About God, pp. 450–451"). This way of thinking about rules corresponds, of course, to heteronomous morality. In contrast, and consistent with the onset of autonomous morality, older children (10 to 12 years of age) recognize that the rules are not mystical and unchangeable but are rational; and since they have been agreed upon by the players, they can be modified with the players' consent.

Piaget (1932/1965) believed that games are models of society—that is, that rule-based games have certain fundamental characteristics of social institutions. First, rule-based games remain basically the same as they are passed from one generation to the next. Thus, like social institutions, rule-based games provide an existing structure of rules about how to behave in specific social circumstances. Second, rule-based games can exist only if people agree to participate in them. There would be no religions, for example, if there were no practicing believers; there would be

AFP/Getty Images

These Yemeni boys are playing street soccer. Throughout the world, children in middle childhood begin to play games based on rules, activities that Piaget considered fundamental to developing moral reasoning.

Jim West / Alamy

These members of the Michigan Grosse Point girls' ice hockey team know that breaking the rules is cheating. According to Piaget, participating in rule-governed games such as hockey contributes to children's moral development.

no game of marbles if children stopped playing it. In order to participate in social institutions, people must subordinate their immediate desires and behavior to a socially agreed-upon system, be it the beliefs and rituals of a religion or the rules of marbles. Piaget (1932/1965) linked this ability to play within a framework of rules to children's acquisition of respect for rules and a new level of moral understanding.

In Piaget's (1932/1965) view, it is through game-playing—that is, through the give-and-take of negotiating plans, settling disagreements, making and enforcing rules, and keeping and breaking promises—that children come to understand that social rules make cooperation with others possible. As a consequence of this understanding, peer groups can be self-governing and their members capable of autonomous moral thinking.

Whereas Piaget argued for the existence of two stages of moral reasoning, heteronomous and autonomous, Kohlberg proposed a sequence of six stages extending from childhood into adolescence and adulthood (Table 13.1). These six stages are grouped into three levels of moral reasoning: *preconventional*, *conventional*, and *postconventional* (Colby & Kohlberg, 1987; Kohlberg, 1969, 1976, 1984).

TABLE 13.1 Kohlberg: Six Moral Stages

Level/Stage	Doing Right	Doing Right: Reasons	Social Perspective
Preconventional Level I			
Stage 1—Heteronomous morality	• Conform to rules. • Obey for the sake of obedience. • Avoid causing physical harm to objects or people.	• Avoid punishment. • Follow the power of higher authority.	Egocentric: doesn't distinguish the concerns and interest of others from the individual; actions evaluated according to external, physical consequences rather than internal, psychological motivations
Stage 2—Instrumental morality	• Follow rules when in your best interest to do so. • Act to serve your own interests and needs and allow others to do the same. • Be fair, seen as an equal exchange.	• Allow yourself and others to achieve interests and fulfill desires.	Concrete individualistic: aware that each individual has personal interests that may conflict with those of others; what is "right" is relative
Conventional Level II			
Stage 3—Good-child morality	• Live up to expectations of those who are close to you. • Have good intentions and concern for others. • Show trust, loyalty, respect, and gratitude—all fundamental to mutual relationships.	• Be a good person according to your own and others' standards. • Care for others. • Believe in the Golden Rule. • Desire to maintain rules that enforce good behavior.	Perspective of the individual in relation to others: awareness of shared feelings, agreements, and expectations; ability to relate points of view through the Golden Rule
Stage 4—Law-and-order morality	• Uphold the law.	• Keep the community viable.	Perspective of the individual in relation to the social group
Postconventional, or Principled, Level III			
Stage 5—Social-contract reasoning	• Be aware of the variety of values and opinions that may be held by individuals.	• Have a sense of obligation to obey the law due to a social contract that requires you to act for the welfare of the group.	Perspective of the individual as a rational agent aware of the values and rights of others
Stage 6—Universal ethical principles	• Have self-chosen ethical principles.	• Believe in universal moral principles.	Perspective of a moral point of view that interprets the meanings and significance of social and individual actions

Information from Kohlberg, 1976.

The stages are characterized by ideas about what is right and the reasons for doing right, all of which evolve over time as egocentrism declines and is replaced by social perspective-taking. (In Chapter 14, we will discuss moral development in adolescence and evaluate Kohlberg's view as a whole.)

Kohlberg's method for studying moral reasoning was to ask children about stories in which people faced dilemmas involving the value of human life and property, people's obligations to each other, and the meaning of laws and rules. His most famous story is the "Heinz dilemma." In this story, a woman was near death from cancer. One drug might save her, but the druggist who had discovered it was charging $2,000, 10 times what the drug cost him to make. The sick woman's husband, Heinz, borrowed money from friends but could only come up with about $1,000. He pleaded with the druggist to sell it cheaper, or let him pay later, but the druggist refused. In desperation, Heinz broke into the pharmacy and stole the drug for his dying wife. After hearing the story, children are asked, "Should Heinz have done that? Why or why not?"

In Kohlberg's theory of moral development, individuals who are at the *preconventional level* see right and wrong in terms of external consequences to the individual for following or not following the rules. This level comprises stages 1 and 2.

Stage 1, *heteronomous morality*, coincides with the beginning of middle childhood, when children still exhibit egocentric thinking: In making judgments about right and wrong, they do not recognize the interests of others as distinct from their own. What is right or wrong for them must be right or wrong for others. Moreover, their judgments about the rightness and wrongness of an action are based on its objective outcome, which in this case is how powerful authorities would respond to the action. In stage 1, children might assert that Heinz must not steal the medicine because he will be put in jail.

Stage 2, *instrumental morality*, ordinarily is reached at around the age of 7 or 8, with a decline in egocentrism: Children can now recognize that different people have different perspectives and interests and that these may conflict with their own. Consequently, morality is seen as serving one's immediate interests and needs and letting others do the same. Similarly, fairness is understood in the context of an exchange system, of giving as much as you receive. Children at this stage might respond to the Heinz dilemma by saying that Heinz should steal the drug because someday he might have cancer and would want someone to steal it for him.

Stage 2 is the key transition associated with school-age children's ability to get along without adult supervision. Children no longer depend on a strong external source to define right and wrong; instead, reciprocal relationships between group members regulate their behavior. Sometimes the resulting behaviors are desirable ("I'll help you with your model if you help me with mine"); other times, they are less so ("I won't tell Mom you got detention today if you don't tell her I failed my math quiz"). In either case, this form of thinking allows children to regulate their actions with each other.

At the *conventional level* of moral reasoning, children's focus shifts from external consequences to society's standards and rules. The first phase of this shift occurs in stage 3, *good-child morality*, which children begin to reach around the age of 10 or 11. Children at this stage have come to see shared feelings and agreements, especially with people close to them, as more important than individual self-interest. One child quoted by Kohlberg (1984) said, "If I was Heinz, I would have stolen the drug for my wife. You can't put a price on love, no amount of gifts make love" (p. 629). Stage 3 is often equated with the golden rule (treat others as you wish to be treated), a moral rule of reciprocity found in scriptures in all major religions.

Clearly, the development of moral reasoning is closely associated with the child's increasing ability to consider the feelings and perspectives of others. In Chapter 8 (p. 278), we explained that around 4 to 5 years of age, children develop a *theory of mind*—that is, the ability to think about other people's mental states. Indeed, when judges and juries deliberate a criminal case, they devote a lot of time to understanding the mental

Children's Ideas About God

CAREN, AGE 9:

> Once upon a time in Heaven. . . . God woke up from his nap. It was his birthday. But nobody knew it was his birthday but one angel. . . . And this angel rounds up all these other angels, and when he gets out of the shower, they have a surprise party for him. (Heller, 1986, cited in Barrett, 2001.)

An adult:

> God is infinite, pervasive, and man finite and limited to a locality. Man cannot comprehend God as he can other things. God is without limits, without dimensions. (Ullah, 1984, cited in Barrett, 2001.)

The quotes above would seem to support the conclusion shared by many developmentalists that children's understanding of God moves from primitive, anthropomorphic conceptions—God has birthdays, naps, and showers—to abstract concepts that refer to God's infinite knowledge and power and existence beyond the realm of physical and natural laws.

This was certainly the view held by both Freud and Piaget, who believed that, early on, children's conceptions of God are similar to their conceptions of parents. Freud, for example, argued that the idea of God is a projection of our need for a protective parent figure. Piaget, as you would expect, adopted an approach that links children's changing conceptions of God to their changing cognitive systems. In particular, children initially attribute godlike properties to both God and their parents. Once they realize that their parents are fallible—vulnerable to errors in judgment and knowledge—they differentiate the divine from the merely human, granting ultimate supremacy to God alone. Not until adolescence and the advent of abstract reasoning do children begin to understand God in terms of "infinite knowledge" and being "without limits."

Children's developing conceptions of God have been studied using a variety of methods. Children have been asked to describe God, or to draw pictures of God or the house that God lives in. In general, the studies suggest that major cognitive shifts occur across childhood. For example, Dimitris Pnevmatikos (2002) asked first- through fifth-grade Catholic and Greek Orthodox children living in Luxembourg to draw the house where God lives. He found a tendency for first- and second-graders to draw real houses or churches on Earth, sometimes next door to their own homes. Many third-graders, however, located the buildings in clouds, suggesting a more heavenly neighborhood. With increasing age, material buildings became less frequent in the drawings, which began to include symbolic elements, including heaven's gates, angels, and planets. Not until fourth grade did a very few children, perhaps on the threshold of adolescent abstract reasoning, begin to depict God as coexisting with qualities such as goodness, love, peace, and so on rather than as residing in tangible structures.

On the other hand, some developmentalists have argued that the differences between younger and older children's views of God, or even between children's and adults', are not as robust or dramatic as once believed and depend greatly on the demands of the task used to elicit those views. Some studies have found evidence that under certain circumstances, adults are prone to anthropomorphize God, much as children do. In one such study, adults of several faith traditions in the United States and India were told a story in which a boy was swimming in a swift and rocky

state of the accused: Did he or she intend to commit the crime? Was it premeditated? What was the motive? Research conducted with children in a number of countries indicates that the way that children judge someone's moral behavior may depend on their ability to understand the person's mental state (Ball, Smetana, & Sturge-Apple, 2017; Cowell et al., 2017; Fu, Xiao, Killen, & Lee, 2014; Sokol & Chandler, 2004).

Social Domain Theory

Freud, Piaget, and Kohlberg all shared the view that young children rely on external consequences and authority in order to determine right and wrong. However, as we indicated in Chapter 9 (see p. 307), research within the social domain perspective has suggested that a relatively strong sense of fairness and others' welfare, as well as an ability to question the legitimacy of authority, may emerge at earlier ages than developmentalists once thought (Turiel, 2010). In this research, children often are presented with stories that create a conflict between authority on the one hand and fairness or others' welfare on the other. For example, children might be told of a situation in which two children are fighting on the school playground. A peer tells the two to stop fighting; however, a teacher says that it is okay for the fight to continue. Researchers find that children as young as 5 or 6 years of age will insist that

(a)

(b)

(c)

(a, b) Young children's drawings of the house where God lives often depict real houses, whereas (c) older children's drawings link God's house to abstract ideas such as "happiness," "love," and "peace."

river. His leg became caught between two rocks, and he began to struggle and pray. Although God (or Vishnu, Shiva, Brahman, or Krishna, depending on the adult's faith) was answering another prayer in another part of the world when the boy started praying, before long God responded by pushing one of the rocks so the boy could get his leg out. The boy then struggled to the riverbank and fell over, exhausted (Barrett, 2001).

When asked to interpret the story, most adults reported that God had been busy answering another prayer and attended to the drowning boy as soon as business allowed. Attributing to God such qualities as limited attention suggests that adults, like children, are quite capable of anthropomorphizing God. The discrepancy between the findings that in some situations adults will anthropomorphize God but in others will describe God as infinite and without limits suggests that adults' conceptions of God are complex and depend at least in part on the context of reasoning.

Yet another challenge to the idea of a dramatic shift in conceptions of God comes from evidence that young children, like adults, are capable of distinguishing between merely human knowledge and abilities and the infinite knowledge and power associated with God. In a version of the "false-belief task" (see Chapter 8, p. 278), 3- to 6-year-old children saw a closed cracker box that, when opened, revealed rocks. The children were asked what their mother, in another room, would think was in the closed box if she were to come in and see it on the table. Consistent with much of the theories-of-mind research, the youngest children replied "rocks," not appreciating that their mother could have a different point of view, whereas the 5- and 6-year-olds replied "crackers." However, when asked what God would think was in the box, children of all ages were equally likely to say "rocks." Similar results have been found for both U.S. and Mayan children (Barrett, Richert, & Driesenga, 2001; Knight, Sousa, Barrett, & Atran, 2004). Thus, the 5- and 6-year-olds seemed to understand that a "God's-eye view" is much different, and less limited, than their mother's.

Evidence that children's and adults' understanding of God may not be as different as once supposed suggests that anthropomorphic and abstract conceptions of God are not mutually exclusive but interact and remain relevant to the ways in which individuals try to make sense of the divine.

the peer's position to stop the fight is more legitimate than the teacher's position to allow it to continue (Laupa, Turiel, & Cowan, 1995).

The priority that children give to the morality of a particular act over the status of the authority figure has been found even in cultures, such as in Korea and China, that are assumed to attach great weight to authority (Helwig et al., 2011). This suggests that instead of deferring to rules and authority, children rely on concepts of harm and welfare in judging moral behavior. This fact led Elliot Turiel (2010) to conclude that reasoning about moral issues is quite different from reasoning about authority and social conventions.

Considerable evidence supports the claim that children distinguish between the moral domain and the social conventional domain when they judge how people should and should not behave (Killen, Elenbaas, & Rutland, 2016; Nucci, Creane, & Powers, 2015). Consequently, researchers have begun to look at the development of children's reasoning in the two separate domains. They have found that, while the bases for reasoning are different in the two domains, in both cases the pattern of reasoning develops from more concrete to more abstract.

Despite sometimes getting into fights, even young children know that fighting is generally wrong. This suggests that they are able to use concepts of harm and welfare in judging moral behavior.

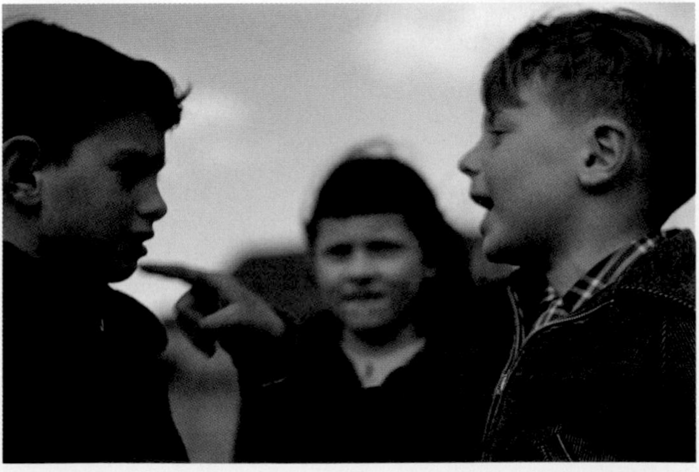
Steven Gottlieb/Getty Images

In the moral domain, research indicates that young children's judgments are based on concepts of harm or welfare, whereas the judgments of older children and adolescents make use of the more abstract concepts of justice and rights. Children of all ages, however, are unlikely to judge moral transgressions, such as hitting or stealing, according to rules, the dictates of authority, or common practices. Hitting, for example, is wrong even if there is no rule against it, even if the school principal says it is okay, and even if hitting is a common behavior in a particular context.

In contrast to judgments in the moral domain, reasoning about social conventions takes into account rules, authority, and custom. However, whereas young children's reasoning about social conventions tends to emphasize social rules, that of older children tends to emphasize more abstract concepts such as social roles and the social order. For example, a young child might argue that it is wrong to call a teacher by her first name because there is a rule against it, but an older child might express concern that the students would begin to treat the teacher as a peer rather than as someone in authority (Turiel, 1983). Over the course of middle childhood, children become increasingly concerned with social group roles and effective group functioning (Killen et al., 2016). As you will discover later in this chapter, age-related changes in reasoning in the social conventional domain influence children's interpretations of peer rejection and social exclusion.

A current controversy among the developmental psychologists who study moral reasoning concerns cultural variations in distinguishing between the moral and social conventional domains. Using culturally appropriate versions of Turiel's stories, researchers have replicated his basic findings in a wide variety of societies (Fu et al., 2014). Other researchers, using slightly different methods to elicit judgments, have concluded that certain issues North Americans tend to see as matters of social convention may in some other cultures tend to be considered moral issues (Shweder et al., 2006). We will discuss the question of cross-cultural variation in this area again in Chapter 14 because most of the relevant data have been collected from adolescents and adults.

APPLY > CONNECT > DISCUSS

Academic integrity is a "hot button" issue on many high school and college campuses. Review your school's definition of academic integrity.

To what extent does your school emphasize academic integrity as a moral issue rather than a social conventional issue?

Do you think middle-school children are more or less likely to view cheating as a moral or social conventional issue? Why?

Drawing on the theoretical insights of Piaget and Kohlberg, describe how middle schools might encourage the development of academic integrity in their students.

LEARNING OUTCOMES

Describe social structures that emerge during middle childhood, along with the influence on these structures by dominant children.

Distinguish among children who are classified as popular, rejected, neglected, and controversial, as well as those affected by bullying.

Explain the role of cooperative experiences and competition in the development of children.

Provide examples of gender differences through gender relationships that often occur during middle childhood.

Explain the role of friendship in the lives of children during the middle childhood years.

Peer Relationships

Once children begin to spend significant amounts of time among their peers, they must learn to create a satisfying place for themselves within the social group. Their greater appreciation of social rules and their increased ability to consider other people's points of view are essential resources for this developmental task. But no matter how sensitive or sophisticated children may be about social relationships, there is no guarantee that other children will accept these children. In creating a life for themselves among peers, all children must learn to deal with issues of social status, come to terms with the possibility that they may not be liked, and deal with the peer conflicts that inevitably arise.

Peer Relationships and Social Status

Whenever a group of children exists over a period of time, a social structure emerges. **Social structures** are complex organizations of relationships among individuals. Developmentalists describe children's social structures in a couple of ways: One focuses on degree of *dominance* (who does and does not hold power over group members); the other focuses on degree of *popularity* (who is liked or disliked).

social structures Complex organizations of relationships between individuals.

Dominance

As is true for many other species, dominance hierarchies contribute to the functioning of human social groups, including those of children (see Chapter 9, pp. 318–319). Dominance hierarchies are usually established through a repeated pattern of fighting or arguing and then making up (Roseth et al., 2011). Over time, individuals who are skilled at managing the conflict–reconciliation pattern establish dominance within the group. **Dominant children** are those who control "resources"—toys, play spaces, the determination of group activities, and so forth.

dominant children In reference to social hierarchies, those children who control "resources" such as toys, play spaces, and decisions about group activities.

Although dominance hierarchies are evident even in preschool social groups (Grueneisen & Tomasello, 2017), there are critical moments in development when children work hard to negotiate their positions with each other. One such moment is the transition between elementary and middle school, when new social groupings are being formed. In a longitudinal study that followed more than 100 students from fifth through seventh grades, Andrew Pellegrini and Jeffrey Long (2002) found that, while bullying is used by elementary and middle school children to influence the dominance hierarchy, its incidence peaks during the sixth grade, the first year of middle school, when children are working to establish dominance in new social groups, and then diminishes significantly during seventh grade, once the dominance patterns have been fully formed.

Popularity

Beyond their relative position in a dominance hierarchy, children acquire social status based on how well they are liked by their peers. The importance of being popular with peers increases substantially during middle childhood (LaFontana & Cillessen, 2010). In this period, children become keenly aware of their social structures and may attempt to influence their social standing among peers by seeking or avoiding relationships with particular individuals. So, for example, children of low social status will try to increase their status by befriending higher-status peers, while high-status individuals will attempt to distance themselves from their less-popular classmates (Dijkstra, Cillessen, & Borch, 2013). Who are the popular children? Who are the outcast or excluded children? What effect does having a particular peer status have on a child's development? Researchers who study the relative social status of group members usually begin in one of two ways. Using a *nomination procedure*, they may ask children to name their friends or to name children whom they would like to sit near, play with, or work with. Using a *rating procedure*, they may ask children to rank every child in the group according to a specific criterion, such as popularity within the group or desirability as a friend or as a teammate in sports. Data obtained through these techniques can then be used to construct *sociograms*, graphic representations of each child's relationship to all others in the group (Figure 13.1).

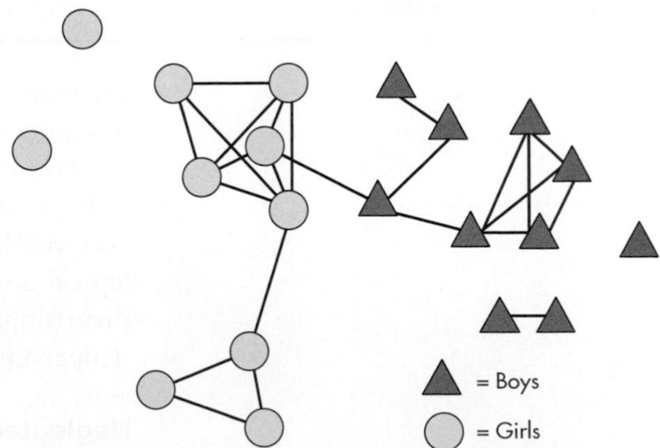

FIGURE 13.1 This sociogram shows the relationships among a group of fifth-grade boys and girls. Notice that the one boy who has a friendship with a girl has a friendship with two other boys but is not part of the larger group of boys, whereas the girl in this friendship is part of a group of girls. Two girls and one boy are social isolates. (Data from Gronlund, 1959.)

As you can imagine, an enormous amount of research has focused on children's social status and its implications for development. What follows is a summary of that work, grouped according to the four main *popularity statuses* that have been identified (Asher & Coie, 1990; Ladd, 1999; Rubin, Bukowski, & Parker, 2006).

Popular Children. *Popular children* are those who receive the highest numbers of positive nominations, or the highest rankings, from their peers. In general, popular children tend to be rated as more physically attractive than children with other statuses, more skilled at social relationships, and, consistent with our discussion of social dominance, more aggressive (Kornbluh & Neal, 2016; Rubin et al., 2006). There are, however, important cultural differences in what constitutes "popular." For instance, a study comparing Chinese and U.S. fifth-graders' perceptions of what makes a peer popular found that Chinese children emphasized the importance of prosocial behaviors and academic competence and had unfavorable perceptions of aggression (Li, Xie, & Shi, 2012). The U.S. children, in contrast, emphasized the positive impact of social connections and appearance, as well as aggression and interactions with the opposite gender.

Rejected Children. *Rejected children* are those who receive few positive nominations or receive low rankings from their peers. They are actively disliked. Studies conducted in the United States, the Netherlands, and Korea found that some children are rejected because they are shy and withdrawn (Parke et al., 1997; Shin, 2007). These children are often aware of their social failure, an awareness that makes them lonelier and more distressed about their social relationships. Other children may be rejected because of their appearance—particularly in the case of severe obesity (Harrist et al., 2016). Children who are not accepted or who are actively rejected by their peers are also at greater risk for being the victims of bullying, a topic we address in the following pages (Elledge, Elledge, Newgent, & Cavell, 2016). Interestingly, one of the most common reasons for rejection is aggressive behavior; children quite naturally do not like to be around others who behave unpleasantly or hurt them (Dodge et al., 2003). Aggressive rejected children overestimate their social skills and competence and underestimate how much their peers dislike them (Bellmore & Cillessen, 2006; McQuade et al., 2016). They are also more likely to misinterpret various innocuous behaviors by peers (joking remarks, accidental bumping) as deliberate and hostile and to retaliate.

Toby Maudsley/Getty Images

Peer rejection is not only emotionally painful but is also associated with a number of difficulties that can extend well into the future, including delinquency, substance abuse, and psychological disturbances.

Rejected children experience difficulties that extend beyond the classroom into everyday life. They show higher levels of delinquency, substance abuse, and psychological disturbances compared with children who are accepted by their peers. Not surprisingly, they are almost twice as likely to be arrested as juvenile delinquents (Kupersmidt, Coie, & Howell, 2004).

Neglected Children. *Neglected children* are those who receive few nominations of any kind (McQuade et al., 2016). These children seem to be ignored by their peers rather than disliked. Neglected children, like rejected children, are less sociable than their peers, but they are neither aggressive nor overly shy and appear less concerned about their social status. Whereas severely obese children are at risk for peer rejection, children who are overweight are at risk for being neglected by their peers (Harrist et al., 2016). Neglected children also perform better academically than rejected children, are more compliant in school, and are better liked by their teachers (Wentzel & Asher, 1995).

Controversial Children. As the label suggests, *controversial children* are those who receive both positive and negative nominations. Controversial children tend to behave even more aggressively than rejected children. However, they compensate for their aggression by joking about it or by using other social and cognitive skills to keep their social partners from becoming angry enough to break off the relationship (Newcomb, Bukowski, & Pattee, 1993). Children who engage in high levels of relational aggression often generate a mixture of liking and disliking in their peers (Cillessen & Mayeux, 2004; Rose, Swenson, & Carlson, 2004). Like neglected children, controversial children tend not to be particularly distressed by their relative lack of social success. The reason may be that such children are usually liked by at least one other child—and this may be sufficient to prevent loneliness. As we discuss below, chronically friendless children are at risk for a variety of psychosocial problems (Ladd & Troop-Gordon, 2003).

Bullies and Their Victims

When 12-year-old Rebecca Sedwick leapt to her death, apparently in response to being bullied physically and on Facebook (some of the postings said, "Drink bleach and die"; "kill yourself because you're ugly"), she brought national attention to the terrible consequences that can come from aggressive peer relationships. There is, in fact, mounting evidence that associates bullying with a variety of poor psychological and academic outcomes throughout childhood and adolescence and into adulthood (Cornell & Bradshaw, 2015; Copeland et al., 2013; Geoffroy et al., 2016; Salmivalli, Sainio, & Hodges, 2013). Bullies engage in unprovoked aggression intended to harm, intimidate, and/or dominate. Their attacks can be physical—pushing and hitting, for example—or verbal, as in teasing and name-calling. Children's access to communication technologies—cell phones and the Internet, in particular—creates a whole new world in which bullies can intimidate through text messages and social media such as Facebook, ASKfm, Instagram, Twitter, and so on, anytime, anywhere (Tokunaga, 2010).

Because bullying is instrumental—that is, a means of controlling other people and getting one's way—developmentalists consider it a form of **proactive aggression** (Pellegrini et al., 2010). Proactive aggression is distinguished from **reactive aggression**, which is usually impulsive and displayed in response to a perceived threat or provocation. Research on aggression in middle childhood finds that proactive aggression may even be valued in some peer groups and a basis for friendship and group formation, especially among middle school boys (Sentse et al., 2013). In the same vein, some researchers argue that bullies often have quite well-developed social skills (Peters, Cillessen, & Scholte, 2010) and are sometimes considered to be most popular by their 11- to 12-year-old classmates (Rodkin, Farmer, Pearl, & Van Acker, 2000).

proactive aggression A form of aggression, common to bullying, used as a means of controlling other people and getting one's way.

reactive aggression A form of aggression that is usually impulsive and displayed in response to a perceived threat or provocation.

The U.S. Department of Justice conducted a nationwide survey of schoolchildren in grades 6 through 12 (Musu-Gillette et al., 2017) and found that boys are somewhat more inclined than girls to report bullying; bullying is reported more often by children from rural communities than by those from urban or suburban communities; and reports of bullying are highest among sixth-graders and then drop off dramatically between seventh and eighth grades. This last finding is consistent with the results of longitudinal studies showing that bullying reaches a peak during the transition between the elementary and middle school years, perhaps due to children's need to establish dominance in their new peer groups (Pellegrini & Long, 2002).

peer victimization The experiences of children who are chronically harassed, teased, and bullied by peers.

Bullies often target the same children in their attacks. In middle childhood, victims of chronic bullying are known by other children as the kids most often teased, bullied, and "picked on." Developmentalists use the term **peer victimization** to describe the experiences of children who are chronically harassed, teased, and bullied at school, as was certainly the case for Rebecca Sedwick. Studies indicate that boys are more often victimized than girls, probably because they tend to hang out with other boys, and across a number of countries, boys are more likely to bully (Casper & Card, 2017; see Figure 13.2). And while bullies engage in proactive aggression, their victims are most likely to engage in reactive aggression—that is, retaliate against their aggressors (Lamarche, Brendgen, Boivin, Vitaro, Dionne, & Perusse, 2007; Ettekal & Ladd, 2017).

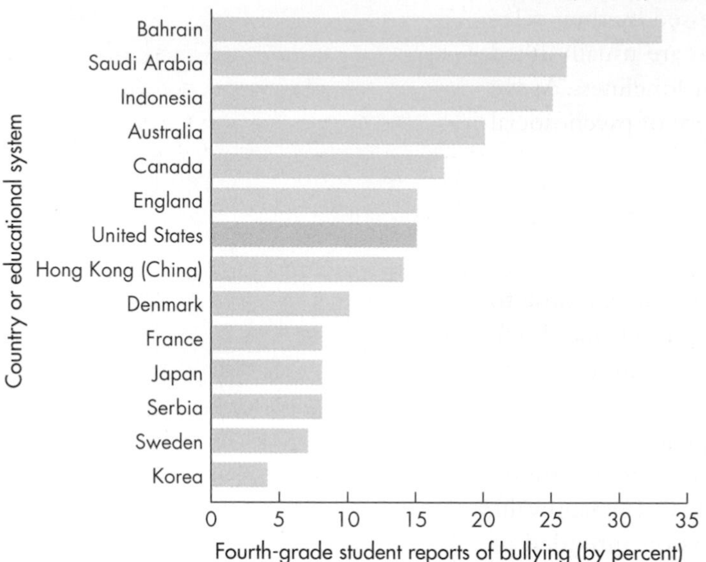

FIGURE 13.2 All too common for children in many countries, bullying is associated with a number of social and psychological problems, especially when it is experienced repeatedly over time. This figure presents experiences of bullying that occurred at least once a month in 2015, as reported by fourth-graders. (Data from Musu-Gillette et al., 2017.)

Victimized children experience a variety of social difficulties in addition to the mistreatment they receive directly from their peers. In general, they lose their tempers easily and are prone to depression, have difficulty in school, and act in an immature and dependent way (Schwartz, Lansford, Dodge, Pettit, & Bates, 2015; Prinstein, Cheah, & Guver, 2005; Sweeting, Young, West, & Der, 2006). It isn't clear, however, whether bullying causes these social difficulties or merely exacerbates preexisting problems that may make children easier targets of peer aggression. For example, a longitudinal study of fourth- through sixth-graders found that children who exhibited more symptoms of depression in fourth grade were more likely than their less-depressed counterparts to be victims of peer aggression in fifth grade and then more likely to be disliked by peers in sixth grade (Kochel, Ladd, & Rudolph, 2012). Peer victimization decreases from the middle school years through adolescence in part because bullying decreases but also because children learn to ignore, avoid, and/or retaliate against their aggressors (Pellegrini & Long, 2003).

The longitudinal research on bullies and victims has important implications for the timing and content of prevention and intervention efforts. It would seem that the early elementary school years are a ripe time to introduce prevention measures that help children recognize and respond to bullying behaviors. However, intervention efforts may be most effective if applied during that part of early adolescence when children experience the major social transition from primary to secondary schools (Goodman, Stormshak, & Dishion, 2001; Pellegrini et al., 2010). With the understanding that a major function of bullying is to establish status and relationships in the peer group, some researchers have suggested that schools devise ways to help children foster more varied and closer peer relationships as they move from the socially more intimate context of elementary school to the larger, hard-to-navigate social scene of secondary school (see the box "Now Trending in Practice: Katy Butler Takes on Hollywood").

Competition and Cooperation Among Peers

Spending significant time with one's peers creates conditions for both competition and cooperation, facets of social life that bear importantly on children's relationships with others. As you will see, the extent to which children are competitive or cooperative in their interactions and the effects of such interactions on peer relationships depend on both the contexts and cultures in which they occur.

Now TRENDING in PRACTICE | Katy Butler Takes on Hollywood

For Katy Butler, seventh and eighth grades were horrible. When she was 12, she came out as a lesbian to her best friend, who betrayed Katy's trust, spreading news about her sexual orientation throughout the school. Katy was devastated by the betrayal of someone she'd been close to for so many years. She also was profoundly affected by the bullying she experienced by her peers when they learned of her sexual orientation.

Katy attended a fairly large school, with more than 200 students in her grade. When homosexuality came up, which wasn't often, it was discussed in negative, disparaging terms. As word of Katy's sexual orientation spread, students began talking behind her back and would even approach her directly in hallways and classrooms to tell her that being gay was "gross" and "wrong," and call her names such a "fag" and a "dyke." Katy often heard the expression, "That's so gay," used in casual conversation, which deeply offended her. The bullying Katy experienced wasn't only verbal. On several occasions, students physically pushed her into walls. One time, her hand was slammed into her locker, breaking her finger.

Katy decided to work with anti-bullying legislators on a better anti-bullying bill. She joined a lot of anti-bullying listservs and one day received an e-mail about a new movie focused on bullying. When she first watched it, she cried. The eye-opening and controversial documentary *Bully* provides a stark and honest account of five students who are mercilessly bullied at school. Two of the victims, both boys, killed themselves as a consequence of the relentless bullying. Katy easily identified with the students and felt that the movie had great value as an educational tool in schools. Victims would see that they are not alone in being bullied, and bullies might see and understand the profound social and emotional consequences of their behavior—more so than when they are simply lectured to by adults.

When *Bully* (directed by Lee Hirsch) was first released in 2011, the Motion Picture Association of America (MPAA) rated it as R, meaning that it couldn't be viewed by anyone younger than 17 years of age unless accompanied by a parent or an adult guardian. Katy realized that with the R rating the film was unlikely to reach those most likely to be bullies or victims: middle schoolers. So she took action. She went on Change.org, a Web site that allows individuals to start their own petitions in the interest of human rights and social justice. Katy set up a petition demanding that the MPAA change the rating to PG-13. A PG-13 rating doesn't prohibit children from viewing a film; it simply cautions parents that the film may include material that may be inappropriate for children younger than 13 years of age. The petition garnered approximately 500,000 signatures. More importantly, it convinced the MPAA to adjust the rating from R to PG-13 (though the film had to be stripped of all expletives). Now the film is being used in middle schools across the country just as Katy had hoped: to educate kids about the devastating effects of bullying.

Katy's extraordinary experiences as a victim of bullying and an advocate for bully prevention and LGBTQ (lesbian, gay, bisexual, transgender, queer) rights, shaped her goal of becoming a political activist. Her experiences and advocacy also led to her meeting and being mentored by the television talk-show host Ellen DeGeneres—which Katy described as "Awesome!"

(a)

Damian Dovarganes/AP Images

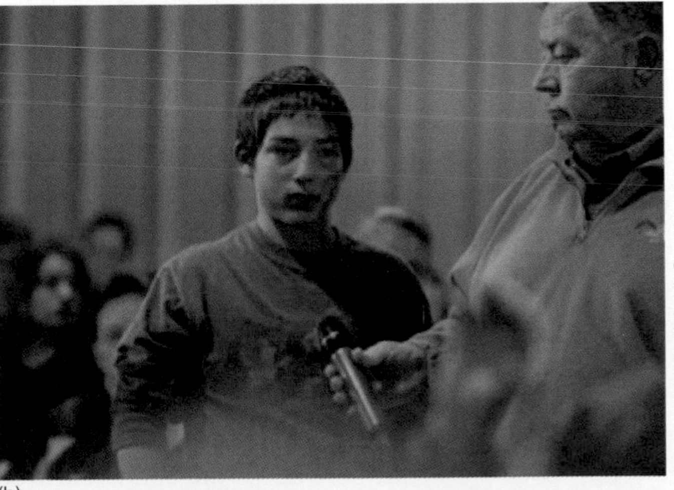
(b)

Scene from *Bully*, The Weinstein Company

"Katy Butler (a) led a crusade to change the rating of the movie *Bully* (b) so that it could be used for antibullying education in middle school."

The Role of Context A classic series of studies by Muzafer Sherif and Carolyn Sherif (1956) provides the best evidence to date about the role of context in fostering cooperation and competition in children's social groups. In the most famous of these studies, 11-year-old boys, who were from similar backgrounds but were all strangers to one another, were divided into two groups and brought to two separate summer camps in Robbers Cave State Park in Oklahoma. To ensure that the boys at each encampment formed a cohesive group, the adults arranged for them to encounter problems they could solve only by cooperating. They provided the ingredients for each day's dinner, for example, but left it to the boys themselves to prepare and apportion the food. By the end of the week, friendships had formed, and leaders had emerged within each group. Each group had adopted a name: the *Rattlers* and the *Eagles.*

When it was clear that both groups had formed a stable pattern of interactions, the adults let each group know about the other. The two groups soon expressed a keen desire to compete against each other, and the adults arranged for a tournament between the two, with prizes for the winners. On the first day of competition, the Eagles lost a tug-of-war with the Rattlers. Stung by their defeat, they burned the Rattlers' flag. In retaliation, the Rattlers seized the Eagles' flag. Scuffling and name-calling ensued. After 5 days in which hostility escalated, the experimenters took steps to reverse it by introducing a series of problems requiring cooperation between the groups. For example, they arranged for the food delivery truck to get stuck in mud (imagine kids at summer camp without food!). When efforts to push the truck failed, the boys came up with the idea of using their tug-of-war rope to pull out the truck, resulting in what Sherif and Sherif (1956) described as "jubilation over the common success" (p. 323). After the two groups had banded together to solve several other problems requiring cooperation, the boys' opinions of each other changed significantly. Mutual respect largely replaced hostility, and several of the boys formed intergroup friendships.

As developmentalists interested in peer-group relationships, Sherif and Sherif intentionally manipulated the contexts of children's interactions in ways that encouraged competitive or cooperative behavior. But as a moment's reflection will no doubt reveal, such context manipulations by adults are far from unusual in children's lives. Take your own educational experiences as an example. If you attended school in a Western culture, it is likely that you were part of educational practices that foster interpersonal comparisons and competition in which children who show themselves better than their peers are publicly praised and rewarded: Their papers and tests are showcased on classroom bulletin boards; they make honor roll; and their parents display bumper stickers proclaiming their academic excellence.

In the face of growing criticism of competition in U.S. classrooms, some educators have made efforts to manipulate the contexts of children's schooling through *cooperative learning programs.* These programs, which focus on students' working together on projects, sharing information, studying together for tests, and developing respect for each other's particular strengths, are meant to foster children's appreciation for their peers' successes as well as their own (Choi, Johnson, & Johnson, 2011). Research suggests that cooperative experiences in school promote prosocial behaviors and decrease bullying and aggression.

Sherif and Sherif's classic experiment and the research on cooperative learning environments carry an important lesson. Cooperation and competition are not fixed characteristics of individuals or of groups but are heavily influenced by the context in which they occur. The research also carries an important but controversial message—that competition is detrimental to peer group relationships, whereas cooperation nurtures relationships and children's sense of belonging. This message has been called into question, however, by research documenting cultural differences in the extent to which competition is valued and rewarded (Schneider et al., 2006).

The Role of Culture Most studies of cultural differences in children's tendencies to behave competitively or cooperatively with peers involve bringing children together to play games that have been specifically designed to distinguish between children's use of competitive and cooperative game strategies. In one such example, two children play a board game in which they move tokens toward a goal. In some instances, the player who reaches the goal first gets a toy as a prize. In other instances, one player is given a toy before the game begins, and the children are told that if the child who was given the toy loses the game, the experimenter will take the toy away, and neither child will have a prize. Playing such games, children can, for example, play competitively, trying to maximize their own "wins" at the other child's expense, and even choose to compete when the only consequence for winning is to see the other player lose a toy. Alternatively, children can play cooperatively, allowing their opponents to win when there are no consequences for their own losses.

Using such experimentally designed games, researchers find that North American children tend to adopt competitive strategies, whereas children from Asia, Latin America, and other cultures that emphasize interdependence and the well-being of the group over individual success tend to adopt cooperative strategies (Domino, 1992; Kagan & Madsen, 1971; Shapira & Madsen, 1969).

At present there is no overarching explanation for which cultural factors in particular foster cooperation over competition. One leading possibility is that societies that value interdependence over independence also foster collaboration over competition (Kagitçibasi, 2013). However, a study of more than 1,000 preadolescent seventh-graders in Canada, Costa Rica, Cuba, and Spain suggests a more complicated picture. In this study, Barry Schneider and his colleagues (Schneider et al., 2006) reasoned that a cultural emphasis on interdependence or independence would tend to be reflected at the individual level in children's *basic social goals* and that these goals would influence the extent to which children were inclined to be competitive in peer interactions. The researchers divided goals into three types, and to assess how strong each type was for the children, they had them fill out a questionnaire indicating the extent to which they agreed or disagreed with particular statements, such as:

1. *Ego-oriented goals*—"I feel really successful when I can do better than my friends."
2. *Task-oriented goals*—"I feel really successful when I keep practicing hard."
3. *Cooperation goals*—"I feel really successful when my friends and I help each other do our best."

The researchers also distinguished between two forms of competition, which they assessed through a second questionnaire.

1. *Hypercompetitiveness* (the desire to win at any cost as a means of maintaining feelings of self-worth, often with manifestations of aggressiveness)—"[Friend's name] and I often compare our school marks to see who did better, and he [she] gets upset if I do better in our tests or assignments."
2. *Nonhostile social comparison* (friendly competition with little emotional investment in who wins)—"[Friend's name] and I often play sports or games against each other; we see who's better, but we don't really care who wins."

Hero Images/Getty Images

Schools are important sources of cooperative and competitive experiences with peers.

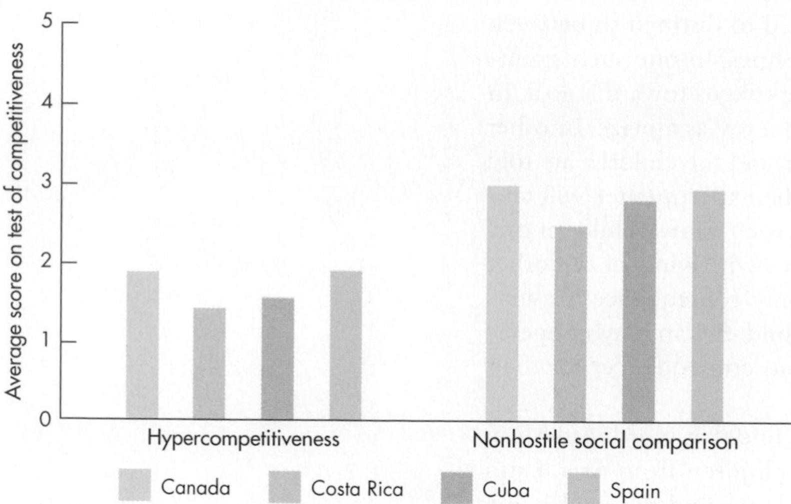

FIGURE 13.3 Hypercompetitiveness—that is, the desire to win at any cost—is significantly more common in the friendships of Canadian and Spanish children than in the friendships of Costa Rican and Cuban children. In contrast, nonhostile social comparison—that is, friendly competition—is not significantly different across the four cultures. (Data from Schneider et al., 2006.)

As shown in Figure 13.3, there was much more hypercompetitiveness in the friendships of Spanish and Canadian children than there was in the friendships of the Costa Rican and Cuban children. The researchers also found significant gender differences, with boys of all the cultures scoring significantly higher than girls in hypercompetitiveness. On the other hand, there were no significant cultural differences in nonhostile social comparison. As expected, competitive behavior correlated strongly with children's social goals. Across all four cultures, children with high ego orientation also tended to be more hypercompetitive and less cooperative. Importantly, the researchers found significant cultural differences in the effects of hypercompetition on children's relationships. In particular, whereas friendly competition seemed to enhance the closeness of Latin American boys, hypercompetition correlated with friendship termination. In the case of Canadian boys, a moderate amount of hypercompetition was associated with closer relationships, but higher levels threatened friendship bonds.

In short, this research suggests that certain kinds of competition among children are common across cultures and are not detrimental to peer relationships. It also suggests that even hypercompetitiveness may not necessarily be detrimental, depending in part on the culture in which it occurs.

Relationships Between Boys and Girls

During middle childhood, children of all cultures spend a great deal of time in sexually segregated groups (Fouts, Hallam, & Purandare, 2013; Pellegrini & Long, 2003). Studies in several countries have found that preferences for same-sex friends dominate children's social interactions both at home and in school, and they strengthen across the years of middle childhood, perhaps because of gender differences in activity preferences (Munroe & Romney, 2006; Neal, Neal, & Cappella, 2014; Poulin & Pedersen, 2007). In particular, the *male-style play* preferred by boys includes high levels of physical activity, such as horseplay and play fighting, whereas the *female-style play* preferred by girls includes more cooperative and prosocial forms of play, such as clapping and jump-rope games.

As children increasingly play with same-sex peers, they amplify each other's gender-typed behavior, further socializing gender-typed activity preferences. Eleanore Maccoby, a pioneer in the field of the development of gender differences, pointed out, however, that these two styles of play can be moderated depending on the extent of gender differentiation in the culture (Maccoby, 1998). That is, gender-typed play styles may be more subtle in children growing up in cultures that make few distinctions between males and females in terms of work, activities, and status but more evident in children in cultures that draw strict lines around male and female behavior. In many Western-style schools, for example, boys and girls are not seated or grouped together by gender, providing more opportunities for cross-gender interaction in the context of the classroom. These same children, however, are likely to be segregated on sports teams. Other cultures, in contrast, draw strict lines around boys and girls, perhaps sending only boys to school or sending boys and girls to separate schools. Regardless of how it might be moderated, gender segregation in middle childhood is so common, and its consequences for socialization are so large, that Maccoby famously proposed the existence of "two cultures of childhood"—one for boys, the other for girls (Maccoby, 1998, p. 32; see the box "In the Field: Gender Politics on the Playground, p. 462").

Jeongmee Yoon

Advertising and popular culture feed the pervasive notion that "pink is for girls; blue is for boys." But children's gender-based color preferences often change with age. Despite her years-long attachment to pink, 8-year-old Maia's preferences have expanded to include purple.

The role of culture in gender segregation and socialization has become increasingly visible in questions about the rights and needs of **gender-variant (transgender) children**—that is, children whose gender identity and/or preferences regarding clothing, activities, and/or playmates do not match what is culturally normative for the gender assigned at birth (Gray, Sweeney, Randazzo, & Levitt, 2016; Pfeffer, 2012; Rahilly, 2015). In the United States, for instance, questions of whether public schools should provide gender-neutral bathrooms or whether transgender individuals should serve in the military have recently risen to national prominence and sparked nationwide protests both for and against. Although research on the causes of gender variance is relatively new and inconclusive, much discussion centers on the constraints of what has been dubbed the **gender binary**—the cultural belief system that there are two "opposite" categories of gender (boys and girls). Developmentalists, educators, and parents seeking to provide safe and nurturing environments for gender-variant children suggest that the gender binary is an overly simplistic belief system that fails to capture the diversity of gender identity development, and it consequently creates profound difficulties for children whose emerging gender identities are misaligned with cultural norms (Dierckx, Motmans, Mortelmans, & T'sjoen, 2016; Pullen Sansfacon, Robichaud, & Dumas-Michaud, 2015; Steensma & Cohen-Kettenis, 2015). It is interesting to note in this context that the gender binary is not universal across cultures. In Samoa, for instance, individuals may identify as *fa'afafine*, a gender that is neither boy nor girl (Bartlett & Vasey, 2006). Increasingly, especially among young people, the cultural belief in the gender binary is eroding and being replaced with a view that gender identity is more of a continuum than a collection of opposing categories, as we discuss in more detail in Chapter 15.

gender-variant (transgender) children Children whose gender identity and/or preferences regarding clothing, activities, and/or playmates do not match what is culturally normative for the gender assigned at birth.

gender binary The cultural belief system that there are two "opposite" categories of gender (boys and girls).

LYNN JOHNSON/National Geographic Creative

Dancing with friends and family members, these best friends identify as fa'afafine, a gender other than boy or girl.

Friendship: A Special Type of Relationship

Harry Stack Sullivan (1953), an American psychiatrist, proposed that the formation of close, one-on-one relationships, which he called *chumships*, is key to the development of social skills and competencies during middle childhood. In Sullivan's words:

> If you will look very closely at one of your children when he finally finds a chum . . . you will discover something very different in the relationship—namely, that your child begins to develop a new sensitivity to what matters to another person. And this is not in the sense of "what should I do to get what I want," but instead "what should I do to contribute to the happiness or to support the prestige and feeling of

In The Field

Gender Politics on the Playground

Name: MARJORIE GOODWIN

Education: B.A. in Spanish (junior year in Spain), Lake Erie College; Ph.D. in anthropology, University of Pennsylvania

Current Position: Professor of anthropology, University of California, Los Angeles

Career Objectives: Study the culture and development of girls in the contexts of their relationships with each other and their position in society

MARJORIE GOODWIN, WHO DOES RESEARCH ON language, gender, and children's social organization, is taking notes during lunchtime at an elementary school in southern California. The children are gulping down their food in order to rush off to play. They understand that whichever group is first to occupy a particular area—the soccer field, the jungle gym, the basketball courts—is the group allowed to use the space. But the competition for space isn't overwhelming; this is no free-for-all. Although girls might argue over who gets the hopscotch area first, and boys might quarrel over the basketball court, there are traditions about which groups gain access to different play areas. Research on children's play (Thorne, 1993)—and probably your own personal memories of your elementary school days—indicate that boys and girls occupy different territories on elementary school playgrounds. Boys control large spaces intended for team sports. They occupy the grassy soccer fields, baseball diamonds, and basketball courts. In contrast, the space controlled by girls is only a small portion of that controlled by boys and tends to be cemented and closer to the school building.

Courtesy Margorie Goodwin

Marjorie Goodwin

But as Goodwin is about to discover, today is different. A group of fifth-grade girls who like to play soccer is beginning to challenge the idea that the playing fields are an exclusively male space (Goodwin, 2002). Today these girls have rushed through lunch in order to beat the boys to the soccer field. Once they have secured the space, they begin to organize their teams. Soon, however, two boys arrive, demanding their right to the field.

Amy: We have it today.

Paulo: We play soccer every day, okay?

Mark: It's more boys than girls.

Amy: So? Your point?

Mark: This is our field.

Amy: It's not your field. Did you pay for it? No. Your name is not written on this land.

Kathy: Mine is. K-A-T-H-Y. [as she writes her name]

The boys move away but return moments later with the male playground aide, who confronts the girls:

Male aide: Girls. Go somewhere else! The boys are coming to play and you took over their field. I think I'm gonna go and tell the vice principal. . . . When the boys are coming out here to play soccer, okay? You have no right to kick them off the field. Listen, I've seen it happen more than once. . . . You can go over there and play soccer [pointing to the jungle gym area]. You girls can go anywhere to do what you're doing.

> worth-whileness of my chum." So far as I have been ever able to discover, nothing remotely like this appears before the age of, say, 8½, and sometimes it appears decidedly later. (pp. 245–246)

Sullivan believed that children's tendency to pick out one or a few other children with whom they feel this kind of special affinity is the childhood precursor of the need for interpersonal intimacy that will be called love when it is encountered again in adolescence. He further claimed that the failure to form such friendships in childhood creates a social deficit that is difficult to remedy later.

Laura: Why can't they go anywhere?

Male aide: They can't go on the blacktop and play soccer. Somebody's gonna fall and hurt their knee.

Kathy: Well neither can we!

In her analysis of the dispute presented above, Goodwin argued that in negotiating access to the territory, the girls resisted and challenged not only the arguments of the boys ("Your name is not written on this land") and those of the male aide ("Why can't they go anywhere?") but also the very social structure of the playground. Historically the field had indeed belonged to boys. In all probability, this had been the case for generations of children attending the school.

True to his word, the aide summoned the vice principal, who, after hearing from all parties, formulated the problem in terms of exclusion, asking, "At school do we exclude anyone?" The girls responded with a long list of exclusionary practices typical of the boys' behavior: "They hog the ball," "Boys are always team captains," "They always pick boys first and then girls last." Apparently taking the girls' complaints to heart, the following year the school administrators instituted a rotating system for using the fields that allowed boys and girls equal access. Yet, despite the changes, Goodwin found that "boys continued to favor passing the ball to other boys; when they did pass to girls they did it with such force that girls often stopped playing. In addition, during the sixth grade, girls had to contend with boys grabbing their breasts in the midst of the game." The playground aides responsible for supervising the children's activities often looked on the boys' rejection of the girls on the playing field as part of a natural order. One even suggested that it prepared girls for their "appropriate" and "eventual" adult sex roles as sports spectators rather than participants.

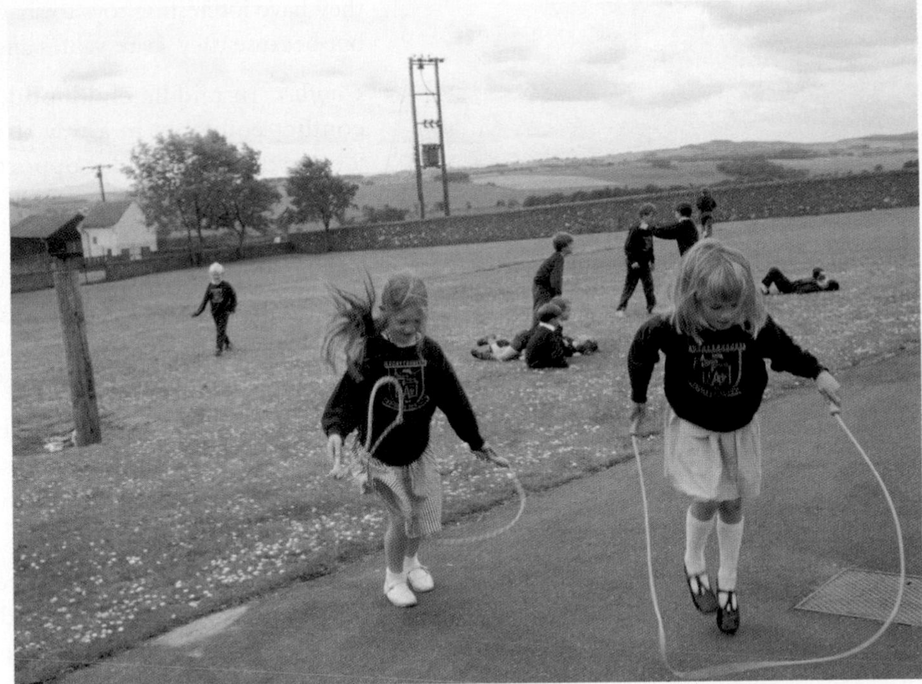

Photofusion Picture Library / Alamy

At many schools, including this one in the United Kingdom, girls tend to play on small, paved places close to the school building, whereas boys tend to occupy large fields.

Traditions by definition resist change. However, Goodwin's research indicates that some girls on some playgrounds are staging microrevolutions, challenging the status quo, and working to define a new moral order on their own terms. In addition to providing insight into transformation in cross-gender relationships, Goodwin's research also challenges the idea, proposed by some, that girls, compared with boys, are less concerned about matters of justice and fairness and instead tend to be more cooperative and focused on preserving harmony and cohesion (Goodwin, 2011). Goodwin argues that a narrow view of girls and women as nurturing and noncompetitive prevents us all—developmental scientists included—from seeing and studying girls and women as wielders of power and instruments of change (Goodwin, 2015). A broader view, Goodwin contends, permits the understanding that "we can not only obtain a better picture of children's worlds but also attempt to implement equity policies which promote children's fundamental democratic right to be spared oppression and humiliation in school" (Goodwin, 2006).

Sullivan's general view of the importance of friendships is widely shared by developmentalists who find that children with best friends score higher on measures of self-esteem and positive feelings of self-worth, whereas children with fewer or no friends tend to be timid, lacking in emotion regulation, and at risk for later psychological problems and bullying (Blair et al., 2015; Rubin et al., 2006; Burgess et al., 2006). Expanding on Sullivan's early work, researchers have identified several developmental functions of friendships (Adams, Santo, & Bukowski, 2011; Ciarrochi et al., 2017):

- *Companionship and play*. Children of all ages recognize that friends do fun things together. However, only in middle childhood does the developing person appreciate that friends enjoy each other's company not only because they have interesting toys to share or live conveniently nearby to one another but because they share values and interests.

- *Conflict.* In middle childhood, friends become concerned with resolving conflict equitably, in a way that will repair and preserve the relationship. Thus, conflict provides opportunities to develop conflict resolution and communication skills, as well as an understanding of other points of view.
- *Help and support.* From loaning clothes or athletic equipment to defending against gossip or rumors, friends provide each other with many forms of help and support. Friends are also counted on to stick up for each other in the face of social threats or peer aggression.
- *Security and trust.* Security and trust are widely regarded as central features of friendships. Despite quarrels and conflicts, friends trust that their relationship is strong enough to transcend current difficulties and will endure over time.
- *Closeness and intimacy.* Compared to friendships of young children, those of middle childhood are marked by closeness and intimacy. Friends share feelings of acceptance, validation, and attachment. Self-disclosure and the sharing of secrets become defining features of close friends, especially among girls (Berndt, 2007).

Given the importance of friendships for children's feelings of well-being and social success, developmentalists are naturally interested in understanding the processes through which children form and maintain close relationships with their peers.

Friendship Stability Having close friends is critically important to children's development and well-being. Research indicates, however, that only about one-half of all close friendships are stable over the course of a school year (Bowker, 2004). What characteristics distinguish friendships that endure over time and those that fall apart? And is the ability to keep friends any more or less important than the ability to make friends?

It makes sense that the reasons for one's initial choice of friends would have a bearing on whether the relationship is likely to endure. Indeed, a key characteristic of a lasting relationship is the degree to which two new friends are similar to each other at the start of their friendship. Developmentalists find that similarity promotes equality in the relationship, positive reinforcement, and cooperative interactions—all factors associated with friendship stability (Poulin & Chan, 2010). Thus, friend-keeping is enhanced when children share similar behavioral characteristics, even when those characteristics are maladaptive. For example, the stability of shy, with-drawn children's friendships is as high as that of non-shy peers *if* their friends are also shy and withdrawn (Rubin, Wojslawowicz, Rose-Krasnor et al., 2006).

The role of behavioral similarity in friendship stability is further illuminated in a short-term longitudinal study conducted by Wendy Ellis and Lynne Zarbat-any (2007) that involved more than 600 children in fifth through eighth grades. Over the course of the first 3 months of a school year, the researchers collected information on the children's friendships, as well as on their behavioral char-acteristics, such as engaging in overt aggression (harming through physical or verbal actions such as hitting or threatening), engaging in relational aggression (harming by disrupting social relationships or self-esteem), and being bullied by peers. They found that behavioral similarity tended to predict friendship stability and that some of the most unstable relationships were those in which the children were behaviorally mismatched. For example, children's relationships were more stable when both friends scored either high or low on a measure of relational aggression than when they were mismatched on this measure. The same was true when the characteristic was being bullied. New friendships between girls who had not been bullied by peers and those who had been bullied tended to falter quickly. The researchers speculated that girls face negative social consequences for hanging out with unpopular (bullied) peers and may abandon these new friends at the first sign that their relationship with them may be diminishing their own social status. In contrast, when both girls were victims of bullying, the friendship was relatively stable, probably because the girls could provide each other with much-needed comfort and support, with little risk of further drop in social status.

Importantly, the one exception Ellis and Zarbatany found to the pattern involved children who were high in measures of overt aggression. That is, when an aggressive child became friends with another aggressive child, the relationship was no more likely to endure than when the aggressive child became friends with a nonaggressive child. Although aggressive children had no trouble making new friends, they were at a distinct disadvantage in holding on to the friendships for any length of time.

A Constructivist Approach In addition to becoming skilled at making and keeping friends, during middle childhood, children develop a more sophisticated understanding of their friendships and the unique needs, motives, and goals of their friends. According to Robert Selman and his colleagues, this more complex understanding, which is a crucial ingredient for successful relationships, arises as a consequence of the higher levels of *perspective-taking* and declining *egocentrism* associated with the transition from preoperational to concrete-operational thinking (see Chapter 11, pp. 383–384). Based on extensive studies of children with and without friendship problems, Robert Selman and his colleagues (Selman, Levitt, & Schultz, 1997) proposed that friendship involves three general spheres of influence that are affected by the development of perspective-taking: friendship understanding, friendship skills, and friendship valuing.

Friendship understanding refers to the child's developing knowledge of the nature of friendship. Selman describes children as young philosophers who have theories about how to make friends, sustain relationships, and manage conflicts. For example, an immature friendship philosophy, typical of preschoolers, is "a friend is someone who gives me toys." Somewhat more mature, and typical of the early elementary school years, is the idea that "a friend is someone who always does what you want." With increasing interpersonal understanding and decreasing egocentrism, children will eventually come to define friendships with reference to balancing, and even cherishing, different perspectives as a means of ensuring both personal autonomy and intimacy in relationships. (We discuss this aspect further in Chapter 15.)

The second influence on friendships, *friendship skills*, refers to the specific action strategies that children use in developing their relationships. Like friendship understanding, friendship skills become increasingly sophisticated over time. The action strategies used by preschoolers are often impulsive and focused on getting immediate needs met. In a conflict over a toy, for example, there may be grabbing and crying. In just a few years, however, children develop a capacity to take turns. Later, they manage conflicts by using complex strategies such as compromise, with each side agreeing to give up something in order to achieve a goal.

The final influence, *friendship valuing*, is the child's ability to make a personal commitment to a relationship and be emotionally invested and motivated to maintain it. As Selman and his colleagues observed, "to know friendship and practice friendship one must be involved in the process of being a good friend—one must take the risk of investing oneself in meaningful friendship experiences" (Selman, Levitt, & Schultz, 1997, p. 44). To see the development of friendship valuing, consider a girl who breaks a play date with a close friend because a new acquaintance invited her to go to the circus. If the girl is in the early years of middle childhood, she may defend her decision in a way that is dismissive of the relationship, saying something like "Well, I love the circus." An older child would be more likely to consider her action in light of the relationship and the needs of her friend, reasoning "Alex's feelings may be hurt if I go to the circus with Janine, so I'll invite her for a sleepover this weekend." Selman argues that friendship valuing depends on children's increasing capacity to take responsibility for their own contributions to the friendship and to see the personal consequences of their actions for the relationship.

Overall, middle childhood is a time during which children acquire a variety of resources for managing their relationships. This is particularly apparent when friends argue and fight. Whereas younger children rely on coercion to resolve their conflicts, as children progress through middle childhood, they become aware of several alternatives. In a major review of research on children's conflict resolutions, Danielle Popp and her colleagues (2008) found that, in middle childhood, children are more aware of the importance of **social repair mechanisms**, strategies that allow friends to remain friends even when serious differences temporarily drive them apart. Examples of social repair mechanisms include negotiation, disengaging before a disagreement escalates into a fight, staying nearby after a fight to smooth things over, and minimizing the importance of a conflict once it is over. Each of these strategies increases the likelihood that when the conflict is over, the children will still be friends. Social repair mechanisms take on importance in middle childhood because of children's changed social circumstances. When no caregiver is present, children must settle conflicts on their own.

social repair mechanisms Strategies that allow friends to remain friends even when serious differences temporarily drive them apart.

APPLY > CONNECT > DISCUSS

Refer to the story of Cassie and Becca, at the beginning of the chapter. Using concepts presented in this section, explain what might have motivated Becca and Kelly's behavior toward Cassie.

The Influence of Parents

LEARNING OUTCOMES

Describe parent–child relationships and changes in those relationships that may happen during middle childhood.

Point out some impacts of divorce on children and their development.

In addition to monumental shifts in the nature and influence of peer relationships and friendships, middle childhood is a time of significant change in the relationship between children and their parents. As you will see, the new patterns of interaction that emerge in the family are felt also in other social arenas, including children's peer relationships.

Changing Interactions

As children grow older, the nature of parent–child interactions changes in a number of ways. For one thing, there is a marked decline in the amount of time that children and parents spend in each other's company, and there is an increase in the time children spend with their peers. This reflects a process of **social reorientation** that begins in middle childhood, when children expand their focus and engagement from the family to the peer group. Social reorientation takes place in the context of significant changes in the ways that children and family members interact and communicate. As the child progresses through middle childhood, parents increasingly share control over their children's lives with the children themselves (Lancaster et al., 2015; Martinez, Pérez, & Cumsille, 2014). This sharing of responsibility between parents and children, called **coregulation**, is built on parent–child cooperation. It requires that parents work out methods of monitoring, guiding, and supporting their children when adults are not present; using the time parents are with their children to reinforce their children's understandings of right and wrong, safe and unsafe, and when children need to go to adults for help. For coregulation to succeed, children must be willing to inform their parents of their whereabouts and activities and talk about their problems (Stattin, Kerr, & Tilton-Weaver, 2015).

social reorientation A process that begins in middle childhood, when children expand their focus and engagement from the family to the peer group.

coregulation A form of indirect social control in which parents and children cooperate to reinforce the children's understandings of right and wrong and what is safe and unsafe when they are not under direct adult control.

Some other changes that take place in parent–child interactions are due to cognitive developments. Beginning in middle childhood, children undergo a process of **de-idealization** with respect to their parents—that is, they come to understand that their parents are not all-knowing or perfect but, rather, have faults; parents can make mistakes, miscommunicate, misunderstand, overreact, or underreact. Many children begin to take issue with the way their parents dress, their manner of speaking, or their behavior. A friend of ours reported that her 10-year-old once complained that she walked "like a nerd." When children reach middle childhood, many parents—once revered and idolized—become not only mere humans but annoying sources of embarrassment. It is during this time that children begin to question the legitimacy of their parents' authority and desire higher levels of autonomy in what they do, where they go, and with whom.

de-idealization Children's understanding that their parents are not all-knowing or perfect but, rather, have faults and can make mistakes.

Parents, for their part, continue to consider their authority more legitimate than do their children. They also want to grant autonomy at later ages than their children desire. Parents worry about how involved they should become in their child's schoolwork, what they should do if a child has academic problems, and how they should deal with behavior problems at school. Parents also wonder how much they should monitor their children's social life and whether they should require their children to do chores around the house and, if so, what standards of performance to expect from them. In less developed countries, where a family's survival often depends on putting children to work as early as possible, parents may be more likely to worry instead about their children's ability to take care of younger siblings in the absence of adult supervision and to help with important economic tasks such as caring for livestock, hoeing weeds, or selling goods at the market (Weisner, 2014).

TAO Images Limited / Alamy

These girls are being taught to weave tapestry in China's Nawei Village. In this cultural context, it is likely that their parents' expectations and standards for behavior center on the quality of their work.

Cultural differences in parents' standards of performance and the ways that parents monitor and control their children's behaviors, reflect different *parental ethnotheories.*

parental ethnotheories Parents' values, beliefs, and goals about the development and care of children that reflect the traditions of their cultural communities.

Parental ethnotheories are parents' values, beliefs, and goals about the development and care of children that reflect the traditions of their cultural communities (Harkness & Super, 1996; Martinez et al., 2014). Different cultural traditions motivate parents to adopt particular parenting practices and prioritize particular goals in raising their children.

Parental ethnotheories are an example of how the macrosystem of the culture affects the microsystem of the family. As we would expect from Bronfenbrenner's theory (Chapter 1, p. 28), parental ethnotheories are not set in stone but respond to changes in other components of the ecological system. A case in point is how Chilean parental ethnotheories have transformed as a consequence of dramatic social and political changes associated with globalization (Martinez et al., 2014). For many generations, Chile was an authoritarian state characterized by limited personal freedoms. In such a context, promoting the development of children's autonomy made little sense. But Chile experienced radical social and political transitions in the 1970s and 1980s, and a democratic government was instituted in 1990. Parents who grew up in the context of democracy, which values the importance of individuals rights and responsibilities, were considerably less likely than their own parents to use controlling, authoritarian practices with their children (Martinez et al., 2014). Modern-day Chilean parents emphasize agency and autonomy as critical aspects of development that require careful give and take of freedom and control, geared to the developing competencies of their children (Martinez et al., 2014).

Peter Cavanagh / Alamy

Although parent–child relationships change dramatically during the middle childhood years, parents continue to play an important and influential role in their children's lives and development.

Parents and Peers

While family life and peer relationships sometimes appear to be two separate social worlds, they are linked in several important ways. As we explained in our discussion of parents' roles in *niche construction* (see Chapter 2, pp. 70–71), parents have considerable power in determining the contexts in which their children spend their time. They choose, for example, the neighborhood in which they live and where their children go to school (and, hence, who their children have as potential playmates and schoolmates). They also provide or deny their children opportunities to interact with other children in specific activities during nonschool hours, although this form of managing their children's social contacts with peers begins to decline during middle childhood (Schneider, 2000). The influence of parents on children's peer relationships is also apparent in the way parents monitor where their children are, whom they are with, and what they are doing. In general, when parents know about and monitor their children's activities and whereabouts, their children are less likely to engage in rule-breaking, delinquent behavior, and other forms of antisocial behavior (Ahmad, Smetana & Klimstra, 2015; Hadley et al., 2015; Marceau et al., 2015).

In addition to these very direct ways of organizing their children's social lives, parents affect peer relationships indirectly by providing working models of the ways people should interact with each other. There is ample evidence that interactional patterns established between parents and children influence peer relationships. Aggressive behavior is a good case in point. As noted in Chapter 9, parents may unwittingly encourage their children to behave aggressively when they themselves engage in coercive, power-assertive modes of discipline and socialization. Such *coercive family interaction patterns* have been linked to aggressive behavior in peer relationships, gang involvement, and sexual coercion in middle childhood and adolescence (Dishion & Snyder, 2016; Van Ryzin & Dishion, 2013).

Developmentalists have proposed a *developmental cascade model* to explain the relationship between coercive family interaction patterns and later peer relationships (Eiden et al., 2016; Waller et al., 2016). In general, coercive or callous, unemotional parenting practices result in low levels of behavioral control and social competence and higher levels of aggression in early and middle childhood. These behaviors, in turn, result in peer rejection, further limiting children's opportunities for positive peer socialization. Consequently, children are more likely to seek relationships with other rejected, aggressive peers, who reinforce aggressive, antisocial behaviors.

In light of overwhelming evidence for the developmental cascade model, developmentalists have been eager to establish interventions that disrupt the process (Shaw et al., 2016). Whether or not this developmental cascade actually takes place depends critically on the stability of the environmental conditions and the extent to which they permit or disrupt parent–child interaction patterns. One very common example of such instability is the case of divorce.

Divorce

Although divorce rates in the United States have be declining over the past two decades, they remain among the highest in the world. Divorce impact tens of thousands of children annually (Anderson, 2016; U.S. Census Bureau, 2011). In contrast, divorce rates are rising in many other countries, including in Asian, Eastern European, and other areas undergoing major social and economic transitions associated with globalization (Antonov & Medkov, 2007; Bourreau-Dubois & Doriat-Duban, 2016).

A range of problems has been associated with divorce. Children whose parents have divorced are twice as likely as children whose parents are still together to have problems in school, to act out, to be depressed and unhappy, to have lower self-esteem, and to be less socially responsible and competent (Amato, 2010). As adults, they are also more likely to have unstable romantic relationships, and their marriages are more likely to end in divorce or separation (Amato & Patterson, 2017).

Divorce leads to several changes in children's life experiences that might be expected to contribute to these negative outcomes. First, divorce often brings changes in children's economic status, often plunging families into poverty, especially for households headed by divorced women (Ananat & Michaels, 2008). Moreover, in the United States, nearly 25 percent of the custodial parents (more than 80 percent of whom are mothers) who are due child support receive no money at all from their former spouses, and roughly 30 percent receive only a portion of what is owed to them (Grail, 2009). As a consequence, about 25 percent of all custodial parents in 2007 found themselves living below the poverty threshold—twice the rate of the overall population. The changes in economic status often mean that after their parents' divorce, children have to move away from their friends and neighbors to poorer neighborhoods with different schools and lower-quality child care. These changes are difficult for children to deal with.

Second, parents raising children alone are trying to accomplish by themselves what is usually a demanding job for two adults. Both fathers and mothers who have sole custody of their children complain that they are overburdened by the necessity of juggling child care and household and financial responsibilities by themselves (Amato & Patterson, 2017). Divorce forces many parents to enter the workforce at the same time that they and their children are adapting to a new family configuration. In the United States, approximately 80 percent of custodial parents are in the labor force; most of them work full time (Grail, 2009). Because of the many demands on their parents' time, children of divorce not only receive less guidance and assistance but also tend to lose out on important kinds of social and intellectual stimulation (Hetherington, Collins, & Laursen, 1999).

In studying the consequences of divorce, some developmentalists employ a *crisis model* that views divorce as a time-limited disturbance to which parents and children gradually adjust. Recently, however, developmentalists have created a *chronic strain model*, which recognizes that ongoing hardships, including financial insecurity and continuing conflict between parents, may affect children's lives and adjustment for many years to come. Paul Amato (2006) has attempted to capture the insights of both models—representing both the short-term trauma associated with divorce and its long-term effects—with the *divorce-stress-adjustment perspective.* This more inclusive model views marital dissolution not as a discrete event but as a complex process that varies depending on the specific stressors and protective factors influencing the short- and long-term adjustment of the family as a whole and of its individual members.

Although it makes intuitive sense that the losses associated with the breakup of a family are the cause of the various behavioral and social problems exhibited by children of divorce, a number of studies that collected data about children before their parents divorced have cast doubt on this idea.

UpperCut Images/SuperStock

One effect of high rates of divorce is high rates of remarriage, resulting in "blended families." This photograph includes children from their parents' previous marriages who were blended into a new family.

An alternative to the divorce-stress-adjustment perspective, in which child problems begin with the divorce itself, is the *selection perspective.* According to this model, most of the negative effects of family disruption may be accounted for by problems that predate the divorce (Kim, 2011; Sun & Li, 2008). Several large longitudinal studies indicate that long-standing dysfunctional family patterns and inherent characteristics of parents, such as antisocial personality traits, create unhealthy environments for children, thereby contributing to their adjustment problems (Hetherington, 2006; Sun & Li, 2008).

There is, of course, a range of individual differences in how children adjust to divorce. In his comprehensive review of research in the area, Amato identified factors that have been found to affect adjustment (Amato, 2010; Amato & Hohmann-Marriott, 2007). Factors that facilitate adjustment include active coping skills such as seeking social support; support from peers; and access to therapeutic interventions, including school-based support programs. Factors that impede adjustment include avoidant coping mechanisms, a tendency toward self-blame, and feelings of lack of control.

Amato, among others, realizes that research on the consequences of divorce fuels a contentious debate. Some see divorce as a source of a variety of social ills and child problems. Others, however, see it as a benign force that allows parents to seek happiness in new relationships and provides an escape for children otherwise trapped in dysfunctional families. On the strength of several decades of research, Amato concludes that "divorce benefits some individuals, leads others to experience temporary decrements in well-being that improve over time, and forces others on a downward cycle from which they might never fully recover" (Amato, 2000, p. 1285). Given the high divorce rates in the United States and the rising ones in other countries, continued research on the consequences of divorce remains a high priority.

APPLY > CONNECT > DISCUSS

This section has presented evidence that coercive parenting practices are associated with the development of aggressive behavior and peer rejection in children. Review the previous section on peer relationships and suggest how parents might interact with children in ways that promote their ability to form successful friendships.

Looking Ahead

LEARNING OUTCOMES

Summarize the new responsibilities and expectations that occur for children at around ages 6 and 7.

Sigmund Freud described the years of middle childhood as a period of *latency*, during which the sexual instincts that drive development lay dormant and the child experiences relative stability. Freud's idea that not much happens during middle childhood no doubt accounts for the lack of attention he devoted to the period. As documented in this and the previous two chapters, however, a host of significant changes occur between the ages of 6 and 12. Surveys of the world's cultures make it clear that adults everywhere assign 6- and 7-year-olds to a new social category, characterized by new responsibilities and by expectations for higher levels of independence, autonomy, and self-control.

Another universal characteristic of middle childhood is the rise of the peer group as a major context for development. For the first time, children must define their status within a group of relative equals without the intervention of adults. In many cultures, interactions with peers become coordinated, with games governed by rules serving as substitutes for adult control. The experience of negotiating these interactions and comparing themselves with peers contributes to children's mastery of the social conventions and moral rules that regulate their communities. Peer interactions also contribute to changing conceptions of self, providing crucial contexts within which children arrive at a new, more complex, and global sense of themselves. The significance of peer interactions is especially revealing in the damage they cause when characterized by rejection and bullying.

The new cognitive capacities that develop at this time are less obvious than changes in the social domain but are no less important. As we discussed in Chapters 11 and 12, thought processes in middle childhood become more logical, deliberate, and consistent. Children become more capable of thinking through actions and their consequences; they are able to engage in concentrated acts of deliberate learning in the absence of tangible rewards; they keep in mind the points of view of other people in a wider variety of contexts; and they learn to moderate their emotional reactions in order to facilitate smooth relationships with their parents and their peers. As we have emphasized several times, these cognitive changes must be considered as both cause and effect of the social changes discussed in this chapter.

Least visible are the biological changes that underpin children's apparent new mental capacities and modes of social interaction. The fact that children are bigger, stronger, and better coordinated is obvious enough. But only recently has modern anatomical and neurophysiological research provided evidence of such subtle changes as the proliferation of brain circuitry, changing relationships between different kinds of brain-wave activity, and the greatly expanded influence of the brain's frontal lobes. Without such biological changes, the cognitive and social changes we have reviewed would not be possible. By the same token, when children are severely deprived of experience, such biological changes are disrupted.

The existence of a universal pattern of changes associated with middle childhood in no way contradicts the fact that there are significant cultural variations in the particular ways that 6- to 12-year-old children's lives are organized. The beliefs and values of a culture shape and are transmitted through parenting practices, parental ethnotheories, and school curricula. Both interpersonal (family and peers) and institutional (schools) practices contribute to the *niche construction* of middle childhood and position children for their next developmental step: adolescence.

1. Consider the progression of moral development during the middle childhood years (from the preconventional through the conventional levels). How does this progression relate to children's social relationships and friendships?
2. Explain how identity development and social status might be connected. What is the role of culture in this connection?

SUMMARY

A New Sense of Self

- In middle childhood, there is a shift from self-concepts based on limited, concrete characteristics to more abstract, stable conceptions arrived at through social comparison.
- For Erikson, the crisis of middle childhood is that of industry versus inferiority. Positive self-esteem is associated with a sense of self as industrious.
- According to Harter, in middle childhood, self-evaluations become more differentiated, more integrated into an overall sense of self-worth, and more in keeping with judgments made by others. Children measure themselves against an "ideal self."
- High self-esteem may be linked to an authoritative parenting style. However, cross-cultural research suggests a more complicated picture of both self-esteem and the role of parenting practices.

Moral Development

- According to Piaget, in middle childhood there is a shift to autonomous morality, in which judgments of right and wrong are based on people's intentions rather than on the objective consequences of their behavior. Experience with rule-based games makes possible this shift and the emergence of self-governing peer groups.
- Kohlberg proposed six stages of moral reasoning, with children in middle childhood moving from the stage of heteronomous morality, based on authority and objective consequences, to the stage of instrumental morality, based on one's own and others' self-interests, and then to good-child morality, characterized by concern about others and their expectations and needs.
- Social domain theory suggests that even young children distinguish between moral and social conventional domains, basing moral judgments on concepts of harm and welfare, a basis that shifts, over time, to more abstract concepts of justice and rights.
- The shift in moral reasoning from objective consequences to internal motives may be made possible by children's developing theories of mind, especially with respect to their increasing ability to interpret other people's behaviors in light of their mental states.

Peer Relationships

- Whenever a peer group forms, a social structure emerges. These structures are often described in one of two ways:
  - In terms of dominance hierarchies, which are often influenced by bullying.
  - In terms of relative popularity, with children often falling into one of four popularity statuses—popular, rejected, neglected, or controversial.
- Bullies engage in proactive aggression, intending to control and dominate others; victims often experience social and psychological problems; bullying peaks between the elementary and middle school years.
- Contexts may promote cooperation or competition in children's interactions. The extent, nature, and effects of competition may be influenced by culture.
- In middle childhood, gender differences in play style increase gender segregation, although the boundaries between boys and girls are far from impermeable.
- Friendship becomes important in middle childhood, and close friendships may contribute to self-esteem, providing models and contexts for developing social skills.
- Children tend to choose friends who are similar to themselves and with whom they interact well.
- Friendship stability is promoted by similarity, including in behavioral characteristics. Overly aggressive children have difficulty maintaining friendships.
- The changes in friendship of middle childhood may be possible because declining egocentrism and increased perspective-taking lead to increases in children's understanding of friendship, friendship skills, and commitment to friendships.

The Influence of Parents

- Associated with the social reorientation that takes place during middle childhood, parents and children spend less time together, and parents increasingly share control over their children's lives with the children themselves—a process called *coregulation*.

- Parental ethnotheories, that is, parents' beliefs and goals about how children should be raised, reflect cultural traditions and impact how parents interact with their children.
- Children whose parents divorce are more likely than other children to have problems in a range of areas. According to the divorce-stress-adjustment perspective, these problems stem from both the short-term trauma of divorce and its long-term effects. The selection perspective attributes problems not to divorce but to long-standing family patterns and to parents' characteristics that children have inherited.

Looking Ahead

- Around the world, despite considerable cultural variations, the ages of 6 and 7 mark the beginning of new responsibilities and expectations. Closely associated with these changes are the rise of the peer group as a context for development and new cognitive capacities.

Key Terms

industry versus inferiority, p. 442
social comparison, p. 443
differentiated self, p. 444
possible selves, p. 444
self-esteem, p. 445
autonomous morality, p. 447
social structures, p. 453
dominant children, p. 453
proactive aggression, p. 455
reactive aggression, p. 455
peer victimization, p. 456
gender-variant (transgender) children, p. 461
gender binary, p. 461
social repair mechanisms, p. 466
social reorientation, p. 467
coregulation, p. 467
de-idealization, p. 467
parental ethnotheories, p. 468

PART **FIVE**

Adolescence

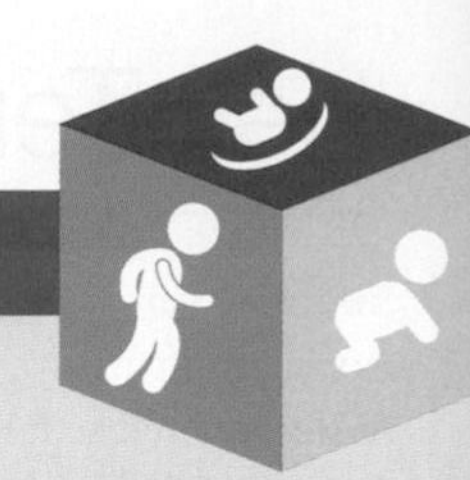

APPLICATION TO DEVELOPING LIVES PARENTING SIMULATION

Below is a list of questions you will answer in the Adolescence simulation module. As you answer these questions, consider the impact your choice will have on the physical, cognitive, and social and emotional development of your child.

	Physical Domain	Cognitive Domain	Social and Emotional Domain
	• Will your child experiment with smoking, drinking, or drugs during adolescence? • How will you respond if you learn that your child is experimenting with drugs? • How will you encourage your child to spend his or her free time after school (sports, part-time job)?	• In which stage of Piaget's cognitive stages of development is your child? • What life path do you see your teenager pursuing after high school (i.e., college, military, work program)?	• How will you respond if your child is struggling to fit in with his or her peers? • How often do you think you and your teenager will have conflicts? • How social will your child be during his or her teen years? • How much privacy will you grant your teenager? • How will you respond when your teenager starts dating?

MAJOR MILESTONES

	Physical Domain	Cognitive Domain	Social and Emotional D
What Develops . . .	• Rapid increase in height and weight, changing the requirements for food and sleep • For boys, increase in muscle tissue, decrease in body fat • For girls, increase in both muscle tissue and body fat • Influx of hormones, which stimulates growth and functioning of reproductive organs • Significant changes in brain regions associated with impulse control, decision making, and the ability to multitask	• Emergence of new forms of mental operations associated with scientific reasoning abilities • Increased ability to think hypothetically • Increase in working memory, which enables higher-level problem-solving strategies • Increased decision-making skills • Increased ability to use reasoning in making moral judgments	• Compared with emotions in chi decreased daily experience of positive emotions and increase experience of negative emotion • Increased ability to regulate em • New basis for friendships, ide balancing intimacy and autono needs • Peer-group opportunities for ex identity possibilities • Increased gender-typed behavi • Increased parent–child conflict i but not all domains • Emergence of a more coherent, s sense of identity • Emergence of sexual orientation a ethnic identities
Sociocultural Contributions and Consequences . . .	• Access to nutritious food and health care, lowering the age of pubertal onset for general populations • Diets excessively high in fat that result in overweight and obesity, further lowering the age of pubertal onset, as in low-income minority populations in the United States • Physical changes marking sexual maturity (breast development, facial hair, etc.), affecting how peers, parents, and others interact with the child • Cultural stereotypes regarding ideal body types possibly impacting girls' experience of normal weight gain and contributing to the development of eating disorders • Some cultures marking pubertal onset with special rites and ceremonies	• Highly variable emergence of various forms of reasoning and problem-solving skills across cultures • Social and emotional aspects of a context possibly affecting decision making substantially • Cultures varying in the extent to which they support the emergence of different moral standards and values • Both parent and peer relationships and interaction styles possibly affecting moral development	• Parental warmth and behavior aff the adolescent's developing emo regulation ability • Cultural expectations affecting g differences in the regulation and expression of emotion • Cultural variations existing in su developing autonomy • Cultural differences existing in s of developing sexual orientation ethnic-minority identities

Most of us look back on our adolescence and see it as a special time in our lives—a time that we still associate with intense friendships, dramatic and often embarrassing bodily changes, parents who were as maddening as they were supportive, experimentation with everything from sports and drama to drugs and alcohol, a feeling of freedom derived from such simple things as driving around in a car with friends. For some, adolescence was especially wonderful; for others, it was downright awful. But however we remember it, it is unlikely that any of us feel neutral about those few years that included such momentous events as the onset of reproductive maturity and that first sexually charged kiss.

Jack Hollingsworth/Getty Images

Puberty begins around the end of the first decade of life, with a cascade of biochemical events that alters the body's size, shape, and functioning. The most revolutionary of these alterations is the emergence of the ability to produce offspring—new human beings to carry forward the genetic and cultural heritages of the species. This biological fact has profound interpersonal implications. As their reproductive organs reach maturity, boys and girls begin to engage in new forms of social behavior because of emerging sexual attractions.

Although reproductive maturity is the biological signal of adulthood, most societies attempt to delay many social changes associated with adulthood, including marriage and parenting. In the United States and other developed countries, a gap of 7 to 9 years typically separates the biological changes of sexual maturity from the social roles that confer adult status. This lengthy period is necessary because it takes young people many years to acquire the knowledge and skills they will need to achieve independence and to contribute to their society. Nonetheless, some societies have only a brief delay between the beginnings of sexual maturity and adulthood (Whiting, Burbank, & Ratner, 1986). These are usually societies in which biological maturity occurs late by Western standards and in which the level of technology is relatively low. In such societies, by the time biological reproduction becomes possible, at about the age of 14 or 15, young people already know how to perform the basic tasks of their culture, such as farming, weaving cloth, preparing food, and caring for children.

In Chapter 14 we examine the advent of biological maturity, including both hormonal processes associated with reproduction and changes in the architecture of the brain that may contribute to adolescent behavior. We also explore the changes in intellectual functioning and moral reasoning that underpin the adolescent's ability to be an effective member of society. Chapter 15 concentrates on aspects of emotional and social life, including new abilities to regulate the intense emotions of adolescence, changing relationships with parents and peers, sexual relationships, and a changing sense of personal identity. We also examine the implications of adolescents' social and emotional development for their health and well-being and take a look at recent theories and methods intended to promote positive youth development by establishing ties between adolescents and their communities and cultural institutions. Throughout, we will address the many ways that adolescence is a unique and essential time for establishing advanced ways of thinking and reasoning, forming healthy social and emotional relationships and identities, and acquiring the tools, practices, and traditions of culture.

Alistair Berg/Getty Images

CHAPTER

14

Physical and Cognitive Development in Adolescence

My Dear Girls,

I write to answer your questions about the path you follow from childhood to womanhood. There is often confusion about hygiene of the menstrual period. If the girl is well and strong this period should cause her no trouble. It happens, however, that many young girls are neither well nor strong. Their habits of life are not always regular, or wise, and they may be living under conditions which are not normal. If this is the case, it may happen that they feel unusually nervous or irritable or depressed; they may complain of feeling discomfort in the pelvic region, or suffer a discomfort which amounts even to intense pain, accompanied by nausea and vomiting. The discomfort may be relieved by lying down for a while well covered and warmed, to induce perspiration. It frequently happens that resting carefully at this period for some months in succession will entirely cure the trouble.

If the individual is entirely normal and experiences no pain at this period moderate exercise is not in the least objectionable; however, extreme exercise, such as dancing or late parties attended with excitement should be omitted at the time of the menstrual period. One should also be careful not to get wet or be chilled. Ordinary local bathing should be continued, for cleanliness is even more necessary at this time. The feet and other parts of the body may be bathed as usual and even a full sponge bath may be taken, but sea bathing, or even tub bathing, should be omitted until the flow has ceased.

It occasionally happens that annoying pimples appear on the face or between the shoulder blades. This has been puzzling and disagreeable to many young people. More rest and quiet during the first two days of the menstrual period will aid very much in preventing this annoying appearance. Many have questioned the effect of school upon the menstrual period. The problem of the girl is not that she is unfit for intellectual labor but that she often adds music, dancing, social life and many home demands to the requirement of school. She therefore becomes overanxious, overtense, and overworried. The first indication of her failure in strength and health is likely to appear at the menstrual period.

As you face the sacred responsibilities of wifehood and motherhood I hope these words give courage and cause to rejoice in your increasing beauty and womanliness.

Yours sincerely,

Dr. Mary Hood

(Source: Hood, 1914.)

The letter above contains excerpts from a book written by a physician, Mary G. Hood, to all young girls facing the "sacred responsibilities of wifehood and motherhood." We don't need to tell you that it was written many years ago; this is clear from Dr. Hood's old-fashioned prose, which sounds flowery and stuffy to our modern ears, as well as from her outdated advice. Hood attributes the discomforts of menstruation to "habits of life" and promotes remedies such as sweating and prolonged resting. To maintain the good health essential to normal menstruation, she urges young girls to avoid stress, anxiety, and excessive excitement, such as dancing and parties. With the exception of sponge baths, she warns against getting wet or being submersed in water while menstrual blood flows. Although her letter may seem old-fashioned (it was written in 1914), Dr. Hood was in many respects ahead of her time. She was one of the first physicians to talk about female biological development openly, candidly, and directly to young girls. She was also among the first to discuss the relationships between girls' biological events, their knowledge and behavior about those events, and the way they experience their own biological development. As you will see in this chapter, 100 years later, the nature and course of these complex relationships continue to drive questions and discussion about puberty and health.

As discussed in previous chapters, the challenges facing individuals at any given period in development and the challenges facing those who want to study and understand development are deeply rooted in the views of society at a particular moment in history. So we begin our discussion of the physical and cognitive changes of adolescence by tracing the roots of current conceptions of adolescence. As you will see, many beliefs about adolescence have endured for thousands of years, whereas others relate to the issues and concerns of the modern world. These beliefs reflect the relationship between adolescents and society and influence the efforts of researchers and practitioners who want to understand adolescent development and devise strategies for promoting healthy developmental outcomes.

WARMING UP

If you were to write a letter to today's young people as a way to prepare them for the onset of puberty and adolescence, what would you say? What challenges would you address? What positive aspects of growing up would you tell them about?

LEARNING OUTCOMES

Give some examples of how societies through history have described adolescence.

Explain the connection between industrialization and the increased attention society pays to adolescence.

What consequences do adolescents and emerging adults face due to prolonged education and delayed marriage and/or childbearing?

Adolescents and Society

The relationship between adolescents and society is no less complex than adolescent development itself. One source of this complexity is the fact that adolescents inhabit a gray, transitional area in between childhood and maturity. In some ways, adolescents are pressed to be responsible, knowledgeable, independent, and adultlike; in other ways, they are encouraged to remain childlike and immature. For example, in some societies, adolescents may be urged to take on certain adult responsibilities but discouraged from mature sexual behavior. Societies guide their children through adolescence in various ways, depending on such factors as cultural beliefs and values and economic structures. However, virtually all societies recognize adolescence as an important transition that requires special attention.

Historical Views

The idea of a transitional period between childhood and adulthood is an ancient one, and many contemporary views of the problems and turmoil of adolescents are strikingly similar to views expressed millennia ago. Literature from the Middle Ages onward is filled with images of young people as passionate, sensual, and impulsive (Kiell, 1959; Violato & Wiley, 1990). In Chaucer's *Canterbury Tales*, for example, young squires are portrayed as seekers of high adventure, willing to take risks in love as well as in battle; Shakespeare's *Romeo and Juliet* depicts what is probably the most famous literary example of a teenage romance and suicide. The Greek philosopher Plato also wrote of the passions and perils of youth when he proposed what may well have been the first formal argument for a minimum drinking age:

> Boys shall not taste wine at all until they are eighteen years of age . . . fire must not be poured upon fire, whether in the body or in the soul, until they begin to go to work—this is a precaution which has to be taken against the excitableness of youth; afterwards they may taste wine in moderation up to the age of thirty, but while a man is young he should abstain altogether from intoxication and from excess of wine. (*Laws, Book 2.*)

Romeo et Juliette/CCI (RDA)/Bridgeman Images

The story of Romeo and Juliet remains current in depicting the trials and tribulations of transitioning to adulthood.

Plato's student Aristotle also wrote about youthful passions and impulses and the unfortunate consequences they could lead to. However, he also viewed the period of adolescence as an especially fertile one for the development of new powers of thought and suggested that individuals are not able to profit from "the education of reason" until they reach puberty.

The notion that adolescence is a period of both peril and promise—of emotional conflict and instability as well as higher intellectual functioning—persisted into modern times. We will now consider how this notion came to prominence in contemporary societies.

Adolescents in Modern Society

In the late eighteenth and early nineteenth centuries, widespread interest in adolescence was sparked by two trends stemming from industrialization. One trend was increased urbanization and its related problems; the other was increased education.

Because industrialization generated wage-paying job opportunities, a great many young people flocked to the cities. Once in the cities, as child welfare advocates (among others) noted, many of these youths were not only joining the workforce, they were also getting into trouble (Addams, 1910; Kett, 1977). Adolescent drinking, sexual promiscuity, and card playing were identified as major social problems (Mintz, 2004). By the mid-nineteenth century, delinquent gangs were common throughout the major cities of Europe and North America, and they were the focus of considerable public concern. Jacob Riis, a journalist and photographer of the period who documented the living conditions of impoverished children and youths, described an encounter he had with a group of young "rascals" in Manhattan, New York. Worried about his safety, he appealed to the vanity of the teens and asked them to show "cigarette-poses" for his camera. He shot the famous photo shown here, certain that his photo taking is all that saved him from getting beaten up (Savage, 2007).

The Museum of the City of New York / Art Resource, NY

Worried that he was going to be beaten up, a photographer from the late 1800s appealed to the vanity of these "rascals," asking them to pose with their cigarettes for his camera.

In response to the rising social problems created by adolescents, efforts were made to provide teenagers with organized services and structured activities that would occupy them during their leisure hours. Jane Addams, a founder of the famous Hull House of Chicago, which provided a wide range of services for the working class, initiated several programs designed specifically to deal with problems of youth—programs that were among the first of their type in United States. The Juvenile Protective Association, for example, was designed to prevent juvenile delinquency and was associated with the campaign that led to the establishment of the nation's first juvenile court (Smuts & Smuts, 2006). Addams also spearheaded the creation of the Juvenile Psychopathic Institute for the purpose of determining the degree to which juvenile delinquency is influenced by mental disorders.

Although increased industrialization is thought to have led to an increase in youth problems, it also created demands for more educated workers. Children were staying in school longer to prepare for the ever-increasing number of jobs that were available in the new industrial age. The massive expansion of education that took place during this period meant that high school attendance soared by over 700 percent between 1890 and 1918, and a new high school opened on average every day between 1900 and 1930 (Mintz, 2004). As education for adolescents became more extensive, educators were faced with the need to develop new ways of teaching that were appropriate to adolescents' advanced mental capacities. Likewise, as the adoption of adult roles and responsibilities was extended to the age of 18 or so, a host of new issues arose related to dating, work, and leisure activities. These issues affected family and peer relationships, as well as the young person's identity development.

In contemporary technologically advanced societies, prolonged education and delayed marriage and childbearing have expanded even further the years of transition from childhood to maturity. In the modern world, young people who are adults chronologically often continue to rely on their parents for support, engage in an extended period of identity exploration, and feel unprepared for the roles and responsibilities typically associated with adulthood. Does this description capture how you see yourself? If so, are you experiencing a prolonged adolescence or an entirely new stage of development? If you resist describing yourself as an "adolescent," you are not alone. Partly on the basis of how college students and slightly older young adults feel about themselves, some developmentalists have argued for the existence of a new stage of development. This stage has been named **emerging adulthood**, which is meant to capture the unique developmental challenges facing many individuals between the ages of 18 and 25 in technologically advanced societies (Arnett, 2016; Swanson, 2016). Although the term is relatively recent, the idea behind it—that changing social conditions have set the stage for the emergence of a distinctive new period in the life cycle—was suggested decades ago (Keniston, 1963; Parsons, 1963).

emerging adulthood The name of what some developmentalists propose is a new stage of development facing many individuals between the ages of 18 and 25 in technologically advanced societies.

Kenneth Keniston, in particular, proposed that the term *youth* be used to describe individuals in their late teens and early 20s who are coming of age in rapidly changing societies (1963). He argued that societies undergoing fast-paced technological change also experience a high degree of social, political, and cultural change as they adapt to these new technologies. Such societies tend to value innovation over tradition. As a consequence, the connections that once bound generations together are weakened: The knowledge and values of the parent generation feel less relevant to their children's interests and concerns. According to Keniston, under such conditions, youth turn to each other, rather than to their elders, to sort out fundamental identity issues. They create their own "youth culture," separate and distinct from the culture of the prior generation. The cultural discontinuity between generations contributes to a number of attitudes and behaviors that Keniston observed in youth, including their sense of powerlessness to make a personal difference in their societies and their lack of interest and involvement in politics. Regardless of the specific label used to describe the period, it is widely agreed that the economic and social conditions of modern life have prolonged the transition to adulthood for many adolescents (Côté & Bynner, 2008), complicating development in a variety of areas, including family relationships, sexuality and romantic relationships, and the transition from school to work.

Clearly, the development and life experiences of young people are closely anchored to changes taking place in their societies. For just this reason, the scientific study of adolescence has undergone important changes over the course of time. In the next section of this chapter, we explore theories and research that focus on the biological development of adolescence. We begin with the contributions of three early theorists—G. Stanley Hall, Sigmund Freud, and Margaret Mead—and then turn our attention to the evolutionary and ethological approaches they helped to inspire.

APPLY > CONNECT > DISCUSS

Provide some personal examples of how social and cultural pressures to be both child-like and adultlike affected your adolescence. To what extent might these examples be associated with contemporary social and cultural issues facing adolescents and their families?

The Emergence of a Scientific Approach

LEARNING OUTCOMES

Differentiate the views of adolescence by Stanley H. Hall, Sigmund Freud, and Margret Mead.

In Chapter 1, we explained that early theories of children's development were heavily influenced by Darwin's theory of evolution. In the case of adolescence, this influence is readily apparent in the attention that developmentalists paid to the relationship between adolescent behavior and the survival of the species.

G. Stanley Hall

G. Stanley Hall, the first president of the American Psychological Association and a major figure in the shaping of developmental psychology, was instrumental in promoting the idea that understanding the unique qualities of adolescence is essential to understanding the proper education and counseling of adolescents, as well as to understanding the evolution of the species (Cairns, 1998; Hall, 1904). Two key features of his theory continue to influence modern thinking and research (Arnett & Cravens, 2006; White, 1991).

The more influential feature of Hall's theory is the notion that adolescence is a time of heightened emotionality and oppositions: stratospheric highs and deep depressions, boundless self-confidence and nagging insecurity, astounding generosity and equally astounding selfishness. In Hall's view, adolescence is a time of "storm and stress," attributable to "raging hormones" associated with the biological processes of puberty. Contemporary research indicates that the relationship between adolescent hormonal levels and emotions is considerably more complex than Hall suggested, involving significant changes to the brain, as we discuss later in the chapter. Nonetheless, there is evidence that early adolescence can be a time of emotional ups and downs and an increase in mental health problems, as we will discuss in detail in Chapter 15.

The second key feature of Hall's theory that remains influential is the idea that the stage of adolescence is the consequence of evolutionary processes. Consistent with most other theorists of his time, Hall believed that the developing child passes through stages that correspond to the evolutionary steps of the species, beginning with the primitive, animal-like stage of infancy and progressing toward the civilized, mature stage of modern adults. According to Hall, middle childhood corresponds to an ancient period of human evolution when reason, morality, feelings of love toward others, and religion were underdeveloped. He believed that it is only when they reach adolescence that young people go beyond the biologically predetermined past to create new ways of thinking and feeling. As a consequence, Hall believed, adolescence is more flexible and creative than any other period of development. For this reason, Hall asserted (as many others have) that adolescents are literally the future of our species.

Sigmund Freud

As we discussed in Chapter 1 (p. 17) that Freud's psychodynamic theory reflects a largely biological position with respect to the sources of development. Freud viewed adolescence as a distinctive stage because it is the time during which human beings become capable of fulfilling the biological imperative to reproduce, and sexual intercourse becomes a major motive of behavior. Accordingly, he considered adolescence to be the beginning of the *genital stage*, the final stage in his theory of psychosexual development.

Like Hall, Freud emphasized both storm and stress and evolutionary processes as major features of the stage. In Freud's theory, the emotional storminess associated with adolescence is the culmination of a psychological struggle among the three components of personality—the id, the ego, and the superego (see Chapter 9, p. 305). As Freud saw it, the upsurge in sexual excitation that accompanies puberty reawakens primitive instincts, increases the power of the id, and upsets the psychological balance achieved during middle childhood. This imbalance produces psychological conflict and erratic behavior. The main developmental task of adolescence is therefore to reestablish the balance of psychological forces by reintegrating them in a new and more mature way that is compatible with the individual's new sexual capacities.

Margaret Mead

While Hall and Freud focused on the biological aspects of adolescent development, the anthropologist Margaret Mead (1909–1978) emphasized the role of culture in adolescent development and experience. At age 23, Mead went to the Samoan Islands in the South Pacific, seeking to answer two simple yet brilliant questions: (1) "Are the disturbances which vex our adolescents due to the nature of adolescence itself or to the civilization?" and (2) "Under different conditions does adolescence present a different picture?" As revealed in her classic book *Coming of Age in Samoa* (1928), the answer to both questions is a resounding yes! Based on observations and interviews with young women between the ages of 9 and 20, Mead concluded that Samoan youth experience little of the storm and stress that Hall and Freud considered biologically rooted and universal. In a significant departure from biologically oriented developmentalists, Mead suggested that the experience of adolescence—the extent to which it is marked by emotional upheaval and psychological distress—depends crucially on the nature of the society in which adolescents develop. According to Mead, societies vary in how they organize key transitions to maturity, including the transitions from play to work, from dependence to independence, from being asexual to being sexually active, and from lacking responsibilities to being fully responsible. In **continuous societies**, such as Samoa, the transitions to maturity are slow and steady, resulting in little emotional storm and stress: The young are introduced *gradually* to work and other adult responsibilities; they are not shielded from sex, childbirth, or death; and they have little if any exposure to cultural beliefs and practices that differ from their own. In **discontinuous societies**, such as the United States and many other developed societies, transitions to maturity are abrupt, resulting in considerable anxiety and distress; the young are intentionally excluded from the world of adults until a certain age, at which point they are expected to rapidly assume adult behaviors and responsibilities, and they are exposed to widely divergent values and beliefs.

continuous societies Societies in which transitions to maturity, including work and other adult responsibilities, are slow and steady, resulting in little emotional storm and stress.

discontinuous societies Societies in which transitions to maturity are abrupt, resulting in considerable anxiety and distress.

The theoretical perspectives of Hall, Freud, and Mead have had a lasting impact on developmental science, particularly on the study of the biological and social foundations of adolescence. Although there is currently some dispute regarding the extent to which adolescence is necessarily a period of stress and conflict (Lerner et al., 2011), it is widely accepted that adolescents are especially prone to argue with their parents, engage in risky and rebellious behaviors, experience mood fluctuations, and generally think and act in creative, imaginative ways.

APPLY > CONNECT > DISCUSS

From a biocultural perspective, why might it be advantageous to develop advanced social, economic, and cognitive skills and abilities prior to, rather than after, reaching sexual maturity?

Puberty

LEARNING OUTCOMES

Summarize the biological developments that occur in males and in females during puberty.

Identify both male and female primary sexual characteristics and secondary sexual characteristics that develop during puberty.

Point out adolescent brain developments—including the function of the hypothalamic-pituitary-gonadal (HPG) axis—and their role in behavior.

Give examples of the timing of puberty for males and for females based on individual variations, involving on-time maturation as well as early or late maturation.

List health concerns and particular demands on health for adolescents.

As the period during which a person becomes capable of sexual reproduction, **puberty** is of enormous biological, social, and psychological significance. For individual boys and girls, it is a memorable time of growth—of arms and legs, hips and shoulders, breasts and penis—and all that hair! But change in the body's outward appearance is just the start of a long list of transformations and new beginnings associated with the onset of puberty. The body doesn't just *look* different, it *acts* differently as well: It sweats, menstruates or ejaculates, and becomes capable of higher levels of strength and endurance. Taken together, the changes in the body's outward appearance and in bodily functions have important consequences for family dynamics, peer relationships, cultural expectations for "age-appropriate" behavior, and, most importantly, for self-understanding. Puberty inspires a wide array of social and psychological reactions. Indeed, depending on characteristics such as the individual's gender, culture, and family situation, the onset of puberty can generate any combination of dread, fear, joy, and celebration.

The Growth Spurt

Plenty of parents have had the expensive experience of seeing their children's clothes outgrown well before they were outworn. Indeed, one of the first visible signs of puberty is the onset of the *growth spurt*, during which boys and girls grow more quickly than at any other time since they were babies (Rosenfeld, 2015). The **growth spurt** is the rapid change in height and weight that marks the onset of puberty and the processes that culminate in the capacity to sexually reproduce. Over the 2 to 3 years that the growth spurt lasts, up to 45 percent of skeletal growth takes place, and up to 37 percent of total bone mass may be accumulated (Ballabriga, 2000; Whiting et al., 2004). A boy may grow as much as 9 inches taller, and a girl as much as 6 to 7 inches taller. Although adolescents continue to grow throughout puberty, they reach 98 percent of their adult height by the end of their growth spurt (Sinclair & Dangerfield, 1998).

puberty The series of biological developments that transforms individuals from a state of physical immaturity into one in which they are biologically mature and capable of sexual production.

growth spurt A rapid change in height and weight that signals the onset of puberty.

I BRING YOU SOCIAL ANXIETY! AND HAIR!
Nobody likes The Puberty Fairy.

SMBC-Comics

Puberty brings a wealth of changes to the mind and body.

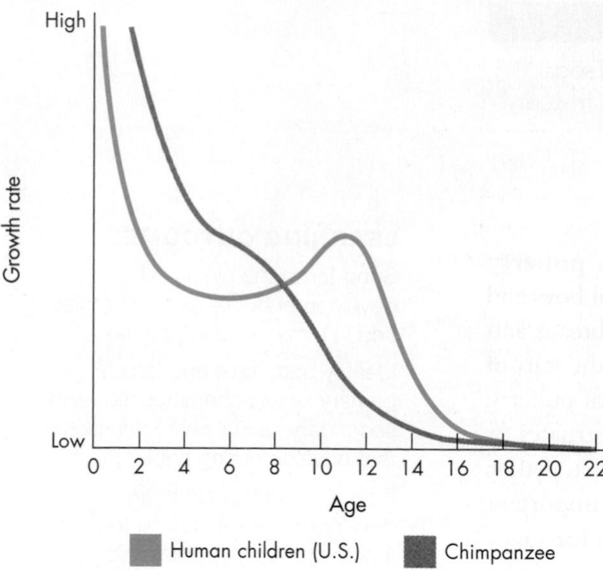

FIGURE 14.1 Compared with other primate species, the human species is markedly delayed in reaching physical maturity and experiences a spurt of growth during adolescence.

Interestingly, it seems that human beings are the only primate species to experience a spurt of growth after early childhood (Locke & Bogin, 2006; Rosenfeld, 2015). Figure 14.1 shows the speed of growth from birth to maturity for females in the United States and for captive female chimpanzees (Walker, Hill, Burger, & Hurtado, 2006). As you can see, for girls, the *takeoff velocity*, when growth first begins its radical surge, begins at around 7½ years of age. (For boys, takeoff velocity is closer to 10½ years of age.) In contrast, the speed of growth of the female chimpanzees continues to decline in a relatively straight line over the course of time.

Figure 14.1 illustrates another interesting species difference that has captured the attention of developmentalists: the slow rate of growth of humans relative to that of other primate species (Charnov, 2004). As you can see in the figure, although the speed of growth decreases substantially in both species, it remains dramatically slower in humans than in chimpanzees until the adolescent growth spurt. Thus, in our species, the onset of puberty and the capacity to reproduce is radically delayed compared with its onset in our evolutionarily closest relatives.

Given that evolution operates to maximize species survival through reproduction, it would seem to follow that the sooner human beings start producing offspring, the better. So why the delay in reaching reproductive maturity? Evolutionary theorists have argued that delayed maturation in humans actually contributes to our reproductive success. (See the box "Early Maturation and Reproductive Success: The Case of the Pumé Foragers" for an example of the relationship between maturation and reproductive success.) Energy that would be spent on rapid physical development is instead diverted to disease prevention (McDade, 2003) and to other functions that give humans time to develop the complex brain associated with capacities such as language, sophisticated problem solving, and an extraordinary ability to make and use the tools of culture. Moreover, from a biocultural perspective, the phenotype of delayed maturation confers significant reproductive advantages to our species "by allowing the adolescent to learn and practice adult economic, social, and sexual behavior before reproducing" (Bogin, 1999, p. 216).

The rate of growth during adolescence varies for different parts of the body, prompting James Tanner (1978) to quip, "A boy stops growing out of his trousers (at least in length) a year before he stops growing out of his jackets" (p. 69). As a result of asynchronous growth patterns, many adolescents develop a gangly appearance and become awkward in their movements.

Changes in physical size are accompanied by changes in overall shape. Girls develop breasts, and their hips expand. Boys undergo a marked increase in muscle development and shoulder width and a decrease in body fat, giving them a more muscular and angular appearance than that of girls, who continue to have a higher ratio of fat to muscle and hence continue to have a rounder, softer look (Smith & Mittendorfer, 2016).

Most boys not only *appear* to be stronger than girls at the end of puberty, they *are* stronger. Before puberty, boys and girls of similar size differ little in strength. But by the end of puberty, boys can exert more force per ounce of muscle than girls of the same size. Boys can also exercise for longer periods. They develop relatively larger hearts and lungs, which give them higher blood pressure when their heart muscles contract, a lower resting heart rate, and a greater capacity for carrying oxygen in the blood (oxygen in the blood neutralizes the chemicals that lead to fatigue during physical exercise; Weisfeld & Janisse, 2005). In general, the aerobic power associated with the cardiovascular and muscular systems peaks earlier for females but is of greater magnitude in males (Geithner et al., 2004).

The physiological differences between males and females may help to explain why males have traditionally been the warriors, hunters, and heavy laborers throughout human history. They also help to explain why most superior male athletes can

Early Maturation and Reproductive Success: The Case of the Pumé Foragers

THE OLD SAYING THAT "THE EXCEPTION proves the rule" has very recently become relevant to understanding the adolescent growth spurt and its role in species evolution. In particular, two anthropologists, Karen Kramer and Russell Greaves, discovered a dramatic exception to the familiar pattern found in developed nations in which physical growth slows considerably during middle childhood and then enters the growth spurt characteristic of pubertal onset, with peak height and weight velocities staggered by a year or two (Kramer & Greaves, 2011). The pattern doesn't hold for the Pumé, an isolated people living in the forest of southwestern Venezuela. In contrast to the typical pattern, Kramer and Greaves found that Pumé girls continue to grow at a fairly even pace throughout middle childhood and adolescence, with no evidence of entering a growth spurt, and they achieve peak height and weight velocities at considerably earlier ages than their Western counterparts do. Their skeletal growth is particularly strong and steady, with peak height velocity beginning several years ahead of both peak weight velocity and the age of the first menstrual period. On average, by the time of her first period, a Pumé girl will have achieved 93 percent of her adult stature and 70 percent of her adult weight.

What might account for these unique patterns of growth among the Pumé? Kramer and Greaves suggest that they are a consequence of evolutionary processes that operate to prepare girls for early childbearing under conditions of nutritional stress and short life expectancy. Pumé children grow up, mature, and begin to have children of their own under conditions of severe nutritional stress. (They eat reasonably well during the dry season but struggle not to starve during the wet season.) One of the most startling indicators of the Pumé's harsh developmental circumstances is their life expectancy—a scant 30 years, with almost half of all Pumé children dying before reaching puberty (Coale & Demeny, 1983). On average, Pumé girls begin bearing children when they are 15½ years old. Such early childbearing is common when life expectancy is short (Migliano, Vinicius, & Lahr, 2007). But while we might simply expect an earlier growth spurt, such an energy-expensive developmental pattern would be extremely risky for the Pumé; girls who entered the growth spurt during the nutrition-poor rainy season would likely suffer delayed maturation, limiting their reproductive success. On the other hand, if the physical body, especially the important pelvic structures of the skeletal system, is underdeveloped, early childbirth can have dire, life-threatening consequences for both mother and baby. Consequently, girls who are genetically disposed not to an adolescent growth spurt but to strong and steady skeletal growth throughout middle childhood and adolescence, well in advance of the first period, are physically better prepared for early childbearing under conditions of vastly fluctuating food availability. (Unlike weight, height is considerably less sensitive to nutritional fluctuations.) In general, at the time her first baby is born, a Pumé girl will have achieved 97 percent of her adult height and 84 percent of her adult weight. From a biocultural perspective, girls who develop according to these patterns can be expected to have more surviving offspring who, in turn, will pass on to subsequent generations the propensity for early maturation and reproductive success.

The unique patterns of Pumé reproductive maturation stand as an example of the remarkable ability of the human species to adapt to vastly different and swiftly changing environments. They also illustrate the essential role of developmental variation to the overall success of our species (see Chapter 2).

Russell D. Greaves

Growing up under especially harsh developmental conditions, including severe nutritional stress, Pumé girls typically begin having children around 15½ years of age. Their physical growth is unique: Rather than undergo a growth spurt during adolescence, the bodies of Pumé girls grow steadily throughout middle childhood and adolescence.

outperform superior female athletes. In some important respects, however, females exhibit greater physical prowess than males do. On average, they are healthier, live longer, and are better able to tolerate long-term stress (Weisfeld & Janisse, 2005).

Sexual Development

The sexual development of many species, including our own, involves two distinctive components. The first component is the maturation of **primary sex characteristics**, also known as the reproductive organs or gonads, which consist of the egg-producing ovaries in the case of females and the sperm-producing testes in the case of males. The second component of sexual development is the emergence

primary sex characteristics The organs directly involved in reproduction.

secondary sex characteristics The anatomical and physiological signs that outwardly distinguish males from females.

of **secondary sex characteristics**—outward traits, such as breasts and facial hair, that distinguish males from females in a species but are not part of the reproductive system. Let's take a closer look at these two critical components of sexual maturation.

Primary Sex Characteristics

During puberty, the sexual organs grow and become functional. Essential to reproduction, they provide not only the raw material (eggs/ova and sperm) for constructing new life but also produce hormones—primarily *estrogen* and *testosterone*—that play a fundamental role in the individual's development. While estrogen is generally associated with females and testosterone with males, both are present in the two sexes, and both are present before the onset of puberty, although in different amounts.

semenarche The first ejaculation. Ejaculation often occurs spontaneously during sleep, in which case it is called a nocturnal emission.

During puberty, testosterone in boys increases to 18 times its level in middle childhood, stimulating the testes to manufacture sperm cells and the prostate to produce semen, the fluid that carries the sperm cells (Bogin, 1999). A boy's first ejaculation, also known as **semenarche**, typically occurs spontaneously during sleep, in which case it is often called a nocturnal emission. For the first year or so after semenarche, the boy's sperm will be less numerous and less fertile than they will be in his later adolescent years and in early adulthood (Katchadourian, 1977).

menarche The first menstrual period.

In the case of girls, estrogen undergoes an eightfold increase during puberty (Malina & Bouchard, 1991). In conjunction with progesterone, another important hormone, estrogen stimulates the ovaries to release ova into the fallopian tubes. When conception does not take place, menstruation occurs. A girl's first menstrual period, also known as **menarche**, usually occurs relatively late in puberty, about 18 months after her growth spurt has reached its peak velocity, or upper limit. Similar to the boy's period of relative infertility, the girl's early menstrual periods tend to be irregular and often occur without ovulation—the release of a mature egg. Regular ovulation typically begins about 12 to 18 months after menarche (Bogin, 1999). During all of this, the uterus is growing, and the vaginal lining thickens. Importantly, the pelvic inlet, the bony opening of the birth canal, does not reach adult size until most girls are about 18 years of age, which makes childbirth more difficult and potentially more dangerous for young adolescents (Bogin, 1999).

Secondary Sex Characteristics

Unlike primary sex characteristics, which are directly involved in reproduction and largely hidden from view, secondary sex characteristics play an important role in communicating an individual's status as a reproductively mature male or female (Figure 14.2). Their communicative function lies in the fact that others easily observe them. Some of nature's most dramatic secondary sex characteristics belong to males: the great shaggy mane of the lion or the elegant if entirely impractical plumage of the peacock. Regardless of species, ethologists maintain that secondary sex characteristics are essential to reproductive success because they signal biological readiness for reproduction and trigger sexually relevant responses in others—flirting, for example, in our own species.

Radius Images/Corbis

This photograph underscores the dramatic secondary sex characteristics that emerge as a consequence of reaching reproductive maturity. The shaggy mane of the lion communicates that males are biologically prepared for reproduction.

The development of secondary sex characteristics in boys and girls follows a fairly predictable sequence. The first signs that boys are entering puberty include growth of the testes, a thickening and reddening of the scrotal sac containing the testes, and the appearance of pubic hair. These changes usually occur about 3 years before a boy

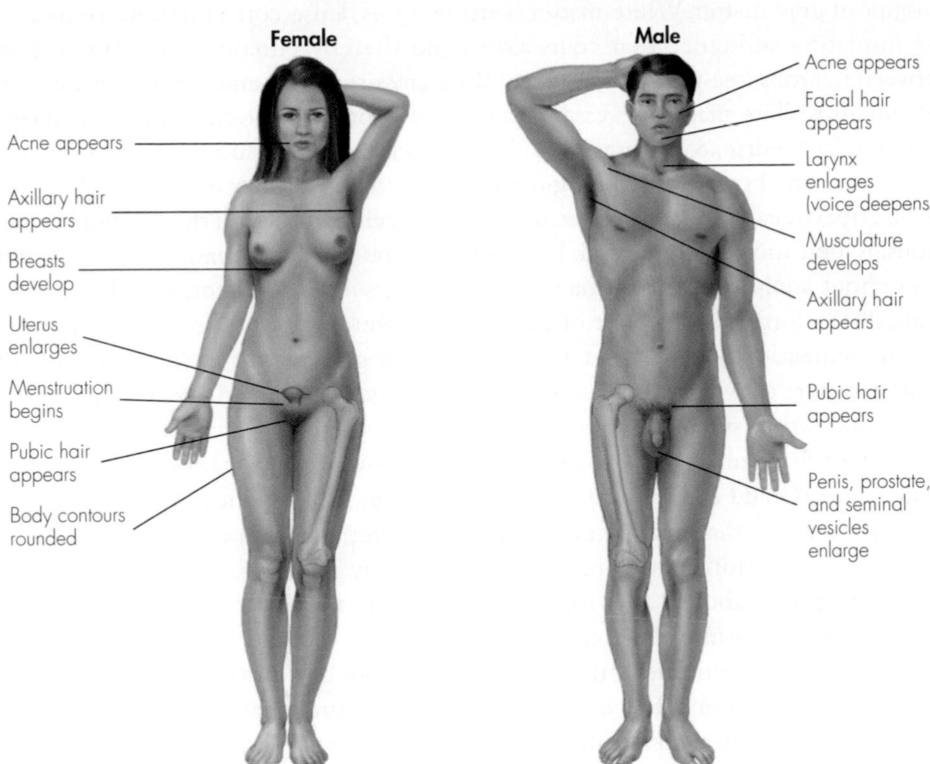

FIGURE 14.2 The hormonal changes that accompany puberty cause a wide variety of physical changes both in males and in females. (Information from Netter, 1965.)

reaches the peak of his growth spurt. When the growth spurt begins, the boy's penis begins what will be a 2-year period of growth. Halfway into this period, the ejaculation of semen becomes possible. Another noticeable change concerns the deepening of the boy's voice. In late puberty, testosterone stimulates the growth of the larynx and vocal cords, which results in the deeper voice characteristic of mature males. Until this process is complete, a boy's voice may crack and squeak, to the embarrassment of the boy and the amusement of his family and friends.

In the case of girls, the onset of sexual maturity is usually marked by the appearance of a small rise around the nipples called the breast bud. Pubic hair appears a little later, just before the girl enters her growth spurt. The breasts continue to grow throughout puberty as a function of both the development of mammary glands (the source of milk) and the increase of adipose (fatty) tissue, which gives them their adult shape.

Clearly, the sexual development of the human body is a dramatic and complex process. Less obvious, but just as important, are the radical changes that take place in the adolescent brain.

Brain Development

New technologies for imaging the brain have revealed a host of changes to both the cerebral cortex, sometimes referred to as the "reasoning brain," and the limbic system, sometimes referred to as the "emotion brain" (see Chapter 11, p. 381). As we discuss below, these changes are associated with important developments in adolescents' behavior.

Synaptic Changes The cerebral cortex continues to develop into early adulthood (Luciana, 2010). Neuroscientists have paid particular attention to changes in the frontal lobes of the cortex, which have emerged fairly recently in the brain evolution of our species and are associated with a number of advanced behaviors and processes, including memory, decision making, reasoning, impulse control, and the ability to multitask—abilities that are collectively referred to as *executive function* (see p. 394).

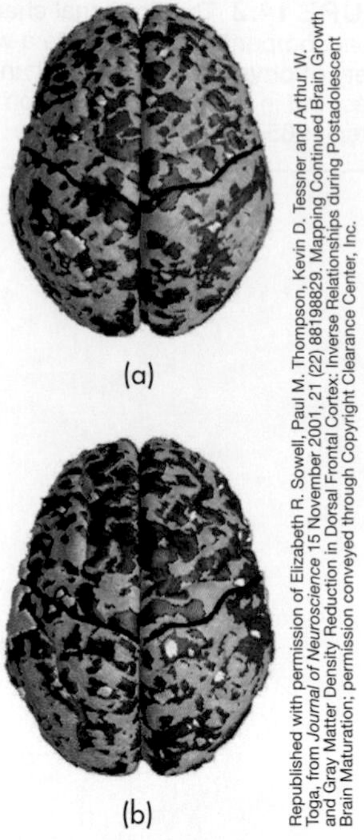

Republished with permission of Elizabeth R. Sowell, Paul M. Thompson, Kevin D. Tessner and Arthur W. Toga, from *Journal of Neuroscience* 15 November 2001, 21 (22) 88198829. Mapping Continued Brain Growth and Gray Matter Density Reduction in Dorsal Frontal Cortex: Inverse Relationships during Postadolescent Brain Maturation; permission conveyed through Copyright Clearance Center, Inc.

FIGURE 14.3 These images are composites derived from brain scans of normally developing (a) children and adolescents and (b) adolescents and adults. The red areas indicate where there is both an increase in the size of the brain and a decrease in gray matter. As you can see, there are substantially more areas of red in the adolescent and adult image, most of which are concentrated in the frontal area of the brain, which is associated with complex cognitive processes. The fact that areas of the brain are growing even though their gray matter is decreasing suggests that the growth is most likely due to an increase in white matter.

Results from MRI studies show that changes in the prefrontal cortex are of two kinds (Figure 14.3). One concerns the amount of white matter; the other, the amount of gray matter. White matter is made up of dense concentrations of myelin, the insulating substance that coats axons and thereby enhances communication between neurons (see p. 127 for review). Both cross-sectional and longitudinal studies indicate that white matter increases fairly steadily from childhood to early adulthood (Koolschijn, Cédric, & Crone, 2013; Menzies et al., 2015), suggesting that during adolescence, the brain is continuing on its course toward greater efficiency.

The story regarding gray matter, the neuronal cell bodies with their dendrites and axons, is a bit more complicated. In contrast to the steady increase of white matter throughout adolescence, gray matter first increases and then decreases (Koolschijn et al., 2013). Since the amount of gray matter is believed to reflect the number of neural connections, or synapses, these changes in gray matter during adolescence suggest a spurt of synapse production, or synaptogenesis, in early puberty followed by a reduction in synapses, or synaptic pruning, in late adolescence. Neuroscientists believe that pubertal hormones may trigger the overproduction of synapses in adolescence (Giedd & Gordon, 2010; Herting et al., 2014). They base their speculation on the fact that peak amounts of gray matter occur in early puberty, when hormone production is at its highest, and that gray matter reaches a peak rate of growth in females about 1 year earlier than it does in males, consistent with the pattern of pubertal hormonal activity.

In addition to hormones, other factors are known to contribute to brain development in adolescence. For example, one study found that the hippocampus, a brain structure central to memory (see Figure 11.4, p. 379), is smaller in adolescents growing up in economically impoverished families compared to those living in relative affluence (Noble et al., 2012). Another study found significant differences in synaptic white matter between children and adolescents from lower-SES families compared to those from higher-income families (Ursache & Noble, 2016). The specific ways that poverty affects the developing brain are not yet clear, but poverty is known to increase levels of stress, and research has demonstrated that stress hormones—especially when experienced chronically—generate a number of negative effects on children's and adolescents' brain development (de Araújo et al., 2017).

This spurt of synaptogenesis, followed by a period of synaptic pruning, parallels the pattern of brain development during infancy (see Chapter 4, p. 130). As you may recall from our earlier discussion, it is believed that the surge of synapse formation prepares the brain to learn and respond to a great variety of experiences that might be encountered by the developing individual. If the individual does not have experiences that stimulate the functioning of particular synapses, those synapses atrophy and die off, which decreases the amount of gray matter in the brain, leading to more efficient neural functioning (Bramen et al., 2011).

Although the details of these synaptic changes are far from clear, developmentalists believe that they represent evidence of the brain's capacity to adapt to, and be shaped by, the individual's experiences (Herting et al., 2014; Lenroot & Giedd, 2011). From the child hunter–gatherer's lessons in distinguishing edible from poisonous plants to the Buddhist youth's spiritual awakening, such neural flexibility and responsiveness is highly adaptive when you consider the vast landscape of experiences made possible by different cultures, families, neighborhoods, peer groups, and so forth. It is important to understand, however, that the brain responds to negative experiences as well as to opportunities for learning and positive adaptation. For example, some researchers have argued that the radical surge in gray matter during early adolescence makes the brain not only highly responsive to learning opportunities but also especially vulnerable to the effects and addictive properties of drugs, alcohol, and tobacco (Heikkinen et al., 2017).

Brain and Behavior Although the limbic system also undergoes significant synaptic changes during adolescence, one of the most fascinating changes occurs in the spiking of **dopamine**, the limbic system's primary neurotransmitter (Galvan & Rahdar, 2013). Dopamine stimulates the **reward system**—that is, areas of the limbic system associated with motivating people to seek out resources, such as food, water, shelter, and sex, that are critical to individual and species survival (Casey, Jones, & Hare, 2008; Goddings et al., 2014; Shulman et al., 2016). The dopamine spike results in the "hyperactivation" of the reward system, which developmentalists have linked to adolescents' motivations to seek out new experiences and take risks.

dopamine The limbic system's primary neurotransmitter, which activates the reward system.

reward system Areas of the limbic system associated with motivations to seek resources critical to individual and species survival, such as food, shelter, and sex.

Developmentalists have long argued that risky behavior may be related to an enhanced motivation for greater independence and new experiences, which emerges not only in our own adolescence but during the adolescence of many other mammalian species as well. Neuroscientists have suggested that this behavioral transition toward novelty-seeking and adventurousness is associated with the hyperactivation of the reward system and is likely necessary for procreation, as well as for the learning of tasks and skills essential to mature functioning. However, the drive for novelty also increases exposure to potential danger. And because the cortex—the neurological seat of impulse control, decision making, and reasoning—remains immature through early adulthood, the developing organism is particularly vulnerable to negative outcomes. In the case of the human child, such outcomes include substance abuse, unprotected sex, inflicting harm on others, injuries, and death (Somerville, Jones, & Casey, 2010).

Research conducted with both human and nonhuman species suggests that adolescent risk-taking declines in late adolescence and early adulthood as the cortex matures and executive function improves, increasing the individual's ability to control the way he or she thinks, feels, and acts in particular situations (Peters et al., 2017; Van Leijenhorst et al., 2010). As you will learn in Chapter 15, many nonneurological factors are also known to influence adolescent risk-taking, including the tolerance of such behavior by the individual's culture and family and the involvement of peers in such behavior. Recent research on brain development and adolescent behavior adds an important piece to the puzzle of why adolescents are especially attracted to novelty and risk.

"Young man, go to your room and stay there until your cerebral cortex matures."

Barbara Smaller The New Yorker Collection/The Cartoon Bank

Some developmentalists, as well as parents, speculate that immaturities in the adolescent cerebral cortex contribute to risky behavior and poor decision making.

An important question for developmental neuroscientists concerns the role of pubertal hormones in facilitating brain development during adolescence. The brain is a major target of pubertal hormones (Herting et al., 2014; Lenroot & Giedd, 2010). Indeed, pubertal hormones have important *organizing effects* on the brain, meaning that they trigger structural brain changes. As we have noted, evidence suggests that pubertal hormones may affect synaptogenesis. Hormones also appear to affect synaptic pruning and myelination. In the early phase of puberty, increases in cerebral white matter seem to be triggered by elevated levels of *luteinizing hormone*, the precursor of the sex hormones, which we describe below (Peper et al., 2008). A bit later, when sex hormones begin to surge, gray matter decreases in the frontal and parietal brain areas. The complex relationship between neurological changes and various pubertal hormones underscores the dynamic nature of brain development and the importance of hormones to the developing individual, a topic that we will now address in more detail.

The Neuro-Hormonal System

It has been known for decades that puberty involves the activation of the so-called **hypothalamic-pituitary-gonadal (HPG) axis**, a circuit that extends from the brain to the sex organs (testes or ovaries) and back again and that is

hypothalamic-pituitary-gonadal (HPG) axis A circuit that extends from the brain to the sex organs (testes or ovaries) and back again; activated in adolescence, the HPG regulates the hormones that affect the body's growth and functions.

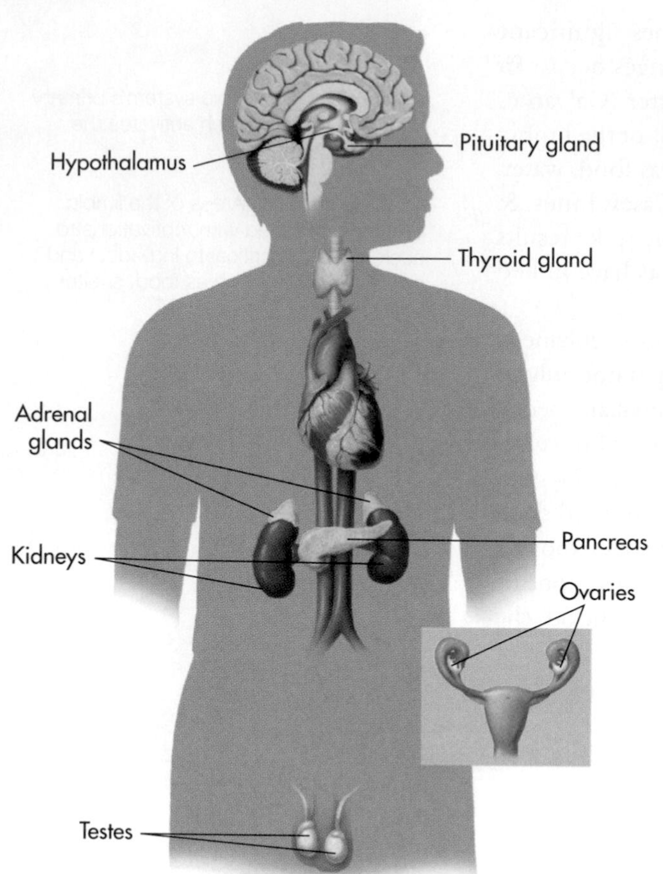

FIGURE 14.4 The hypothalamic-pituitary-gonadal (HPG) axis is a complex, interactive system involving the brain (hypothalamus and pituitary) and the sex glands.

responsible for regulating the hormones that affect the body's growth and functions. The anatomical components of this circuit are shown in Figure 14.4. At the top of the circuit is the **hypothalamus**, a brain structure about the size of an almond, located just above the brain stem. The hypothalamus is a jack-of-all-trades that performs a number of important tasks, including the regulation of hunger, thirst, and sexual desire. One of the most important functions of the hypothalamus is to connect the nervous system to the **endocrine system**, a network of hormone-secreting glands associated with changes in the individual's mood, metabolism, and growth. The glands associated specifically with puberty include the *pituitary gland*, the *thyroid gland*, the *adrenal glands*, and the *sex glands* (*gonads*).

The anatomical components (the hypothalamus and glands) of the HPG axis form a highly complex system of hormonal communication associated with the onset of puberty. Specifically, puberty begins when the hypothalamus increases its production of *gonadotropin-releasing hormone* (*GnRH*), stimulating the pituitary gland to release hormones called *gonadotropins.* The gonadotropins travel to the sex glands, where they trigger the production of estrogens and androgens, which are the two classes of **sex hormones**. Most of the changes observed during puberty are due to *estradiol*, which is an estrogen, and *testosterone*, which is an androgen. Completing the circuit, the sex hormones travel through the bloodstream and communicate with special hormone-perceiving receptors located throughout the body, including in the skeletal system, where they contribute to bone strength and growth, and the brain, where they contribute to sex differences in the brain's neural pathways.

An important question for developmentalists is What condition or set of conditions activates the HPG circuit, triggering the onset of puberty? Until very recently, it was thought that the developing person's energy store, or amount of body fat, was critical. The gradual increase in body fat that occurs over the course of childhood results in higher levels of **leptin**, a hormone that plays a key role in appetite and metabolism. Researchers believed that the cascade of hormones associated with pubertal onset is triggered when the levels of leptin reach a certain threshold in the hypothalamus. This belief is consistent with research demonstrating that puberty is delayed when adolescents are excessively thin as a consequence of illness, excessive exercise, eating disorders, or poverty. It is also consistent with the fact that, worldwide, adolescents from well-off communities begin puberty at earlier ages than do their counterparts living in underprivileged communities. (We will discuss these differences in more detail below.)

Despite support for the notion that leptin triggers the activation of the HPG axis, a fascinating new discovery shows the story to be a bit more complicated. In what may well be the most significant breakthrough in pubertal science in the past three decades, researchers have discovered **kisspeptin**, a small protein produced by specialized cells in the hypothalamus of several mammalian species, including our own (Marraudino et al., 2017; Navarro & Tena-Sempere, 2011). Kisspeptin production is influenced by leptin, as well as by circulating levels of estrogens and androgens, and plays a principal role in activating the HPG axis. Thus, puberty seems to be triggered not by any single factor but by a system of interacting neural and hormonal processes (see Figure 14.5).

hypothalamus A brain structure, located just above the brain stem, that performs a number of important tasks, including the regulation of hunger, thirst, and sexual desire, and connects the nervous system to the endocrine system.

endocrine system A network of hormone-secreting glands associated with changes in the individual's mood, metabolism, and growth. The glands associated specifically with puberty include the pituitary gland, the thyroid gland, the adrenal glands, and the sex glands (gonads).

sex hormones Estrogens and androgens that circulate in the bloodstream and activate hormone-perceiving receptors located throughout the body.

leptin A hormone that plays a key role in appetite and metabolism.

kisspeptin A small protein that is produced by specialized cells in the hypothalamus and plays a key role in the activation of the HPG axis.

The biological processes governing the onset of puberty are complex indeed. No less dramatic are their effects on the growing body. They are responsible for the maturation and functioning of the sex organs and the visible bodily changes that announce to the world that the individual is now capable of reproduction. Our exploration of puberty now turns to consider the *timing* of these changes and the implications of timing for the individual's physical health, social relationships, and personal feelings.

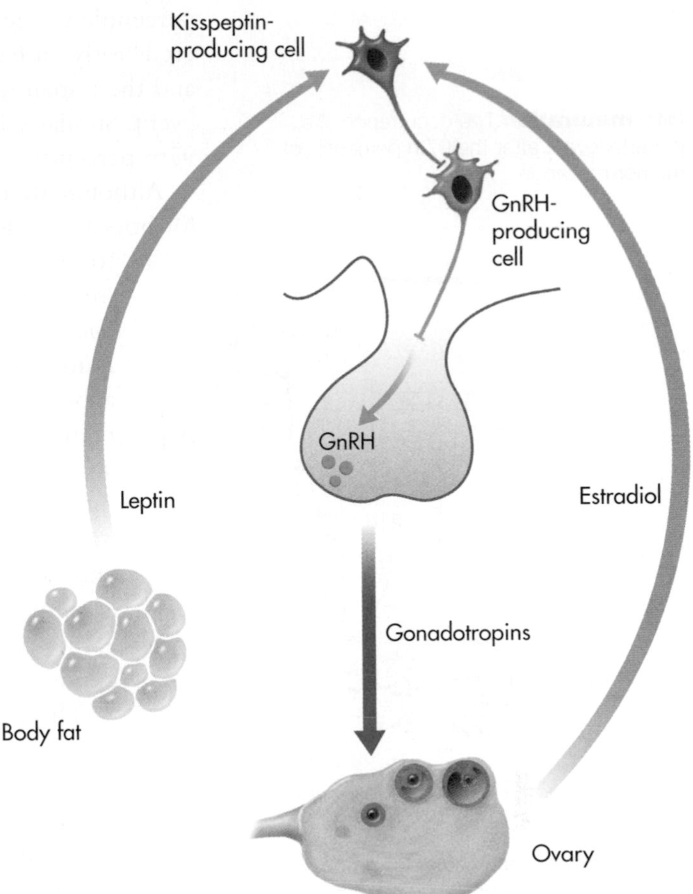

FIGURE 14.5 Scientists have discovered recently that the hypothalamus produces a small protein, kisspeptin, that has a major role in the activation of the HPG axis. As shown here, in females, kisspeptin production is influenced by the level of leptin circulating in the body (leptin levels are associated with body fat), as well as the level of estradiol, a hormone produced by the ovaries. Kisspeptin stimulates the release of gonadotropin-releasing hormone (GnRH) from the hypothalamus, which stimulates the release of gonadotropins from the pituitary gland. In turn, the gonadotropins travel to the ovaries, stimulating them to produce sex hormones, primarily estrogens. (Research from Roa et al., 2010, p. 92.)

The Timing of Puberty

Five-year-old Tracey is taken to the doctor by her mother, who is concerned because Tracey's breasts have started to develop. Sixteen-year-old Jamal is worried because he has no pubic or facial hair, has never experienced a nocturnal emission, and still looks like a child. At 18 years of age, Michelle makes an appointment with a gynecologist because she has not yet begun to menstruate, although she has developed breasts and other secondary sex characteristics. Each of these cases raises the question of what constitutes the "normal" timing of various pubertal events—an anxiety-provoking question for adolescents as well as their parents. As you have probably observed, some children enter puberty earlier and some later than most of their peers. In addition to individual variations in the timing of puberty, there are significant variations across generations, ethnic groups, and nations. If you are African American, you probably reached puberty before most of your Asian American peers; if you were born and raised in South Korea, the chances are high that you reached puberty well in advance of your North Korean counterparts. The answer to the question of what constitutes the "normal" timing of pubertal events depends on many different factors: the nature of the event in question (menstruation, breast development, facial hair growth, etc.), the status of other pubertal events (whether several events are early or late or on time), and other biological and environmental characteristics of the individual (genetic makeup, ethnicity, and the location and historical era in which they grew up). The sources of such variations are associated with a number of physical, social, and psychological conditions, some of which are entirely normal, others of which signal an underlying pathology. In this section, we will focus on individual and group variations in pubertal timing related to health and disease.

Individual Variation

It is not uncommon for adolescents to wonder (and worry) whether the changes occurring in their body and bodily functions are all as they should be. Many of their concerns focus on the timing of pubertal events. Should certain of their body parts be bigger or not so big at this or that stage? Is their menstruation or first ejaculation early or late compared with that of their peers? Can pubertal events somehow be hurried along or delayed? As suggested above, whether an individual's pubertal development is early, on time, or late can only be determined in comparison with the development of a group of similar individuals. For example, in order to determine whether the initial appearance of facial hair on a particular Japanese boy is occurring at the "normal" time, one would have to know when most other Japanese boys begin to show facial hair. As a general rule, **early maturation** occurs when a pubertal event (or set of events) emerges before the 3rd

early maturation The occurrence of a pubertal event (or set of events) before the 3rd percentile of the normal range.

percentile of the normal range. The growth of a boy's facial hair would be considered "early" if fewer than 3 percent of boys of the same age have grown facial hair, and the remaining 97 percent have not yet begun to enter this particular pubertal event. Similarly, **late maturation** occurs when a pubertal event emerges after the 97th percentile of the normal range (Brämswig & Dübbers, 2009).

late maturation The occurrence of a pubertal event after the 97th percentile of the normal range.

Although there can be very real and lasting social and psychological consequences for boys and girls who are significantly off time in pubertal development compared to their peers, early or late maturation usually poses no long-term health risks (see Table 14.1). Two of the most common "normal variants" of puberty are *constitutional delay of growth* and *constitutional acceleration of growth* (Brämswig & Dübbers, 2009). As the term *constitutional* suggests, both types of variants appear to be heavily influenced by genetic factors, affecting multiple family members across generations (Wohlfahrt-Veje et al., 2016). In *constitutional delay*, children are healthy but enter puberty and the pubertal growth spurt significantly later than normal. These children tend to be shorter and thinner than their peers (Wit, 2015). In *constitutional acceleration*, healthy children enter puberty (as indexed by breast development or testicular enlargement) at significantly earlier ages than normal. The HPG axis may be activated earlier than usual; however, if activation occurs too early, the condition is considered pathological rather than constitutional.

Barbara Smaller The New Yorker Collection/The Cartoon Bank

"I think I'll be more relaxed once my secondary sex characteristics kick in."

Although late maturation may produce anxiety, it usually poses no long-term health problems.

The hereditary basis of *constitutional delay* and *constitutional acceleration* is consistent with research indicating that the age of pubertal onset of one's parents is one of the strongest predictors of age of pubertal onset in a child (Belsky et al., 2007). Evidence that pubertal onset is closer for genetically identical twins than non-identical (fraternal) twins provides further support for the role of heredity in sexual maturation (Mustanski et al., 2004).

In addition to genetic contributions, ethnicity has been identified as a source of normal variation in pubertal onset. For example, African American girls mature earlier than Mexican American girls, who mature earlier than White girls; similarly, African American boys mature earlier than Hispanic boys, who mature earlier than White boys (Chumlea et al., 2003; Herman-Giddens et al., 2012). Various physical and emotional stressors such as family dysfunction and exposure to violence and war can also contribute to variation in pubertal onset (Belsky, et al., 2015; Koziel & Jankowska, 2002; see the box "Now Trending in Research: Family Stress and Pubertal Timing"). Recent research, much of it conducted with nonhuman species, indicates

TABLE 14.1 Normal Variants of Puberty

Condition	Contributing Factors and Indicators
Constitutional delay	Influenced by genetic factors; children are healthy, enter puberty and the growth spurt significantly later than normal; they tend to be shorter and thinner than peers.
Constitutional acceleration	Influenced by genetic factors; children are healthy; breast development or testicular enlargement begins at significantly earlier ages than normal.
Premature thelarche	Girls without other signs of puberty develop breast tissue mature earlier than normal; may occur as early as the second year of life and has been observed even in newborns.
Premature pubarche	In the absence of other signs of puberty, pubic, facial, and/or armpit hair emerge before age 8 in girls or age 9 in boys.
Pubertal gynecosmastia	A common condition of the development of breast tissue in boys; it affects between 50 percent and 90 percent of all boys between 12 and 14 years of age, especially those who are overweight. It is usually confined to a small area under the nipple and usually disappears on its own in 6 to18 months.

Information from Brämswig & Dübbers, 2009; Narula & Carlson, 2007.

Now TRENDING in RESEARCH

Family Stress and Pubertal Timing

Decades of developmental research have shown that development in general and puberty in particular will be delayed in children who grow up under conditions of chronic stress. When a growing child's physical needs are unmet due to poor nutrition, inadequate medical care, or exposure to environmental toxins, the child's body will be deprived of the resources required for normal maturation. Emotional stress also deprives a child of resources crucial to development. Developmentalists were therefore surprised to discover that girls who experience stress in the family tend to enter puberty at *earlier* ages compared with girls who do not experience such stress. There is now considerable evidence that family disruption in the form of parental divorce or separation, absent fathers, and insensitive mothering is associated with early pubertal onset in girls. Boys, in contrast, do not seem to be similarly affected by family stress. (See Belsky et al., 2007, for a review.)

Naturally, researchers are eager to find out what might account for this unexpected link between family stress and early pubertal onset in girls. Three possible explanations have been identified (Tither & Ellis, 2008):

1. *Conditional adaptation.* According to this account, humans have evolved to respond to specific conditions that may threaten a child's ability to successfully adapt to and function in the world. One such condition is "paternal investment"—that is, the father's contribution of resources, time, and effort to the child's developmental success. Another condition is "sensitive mothering," or the mother's general responsiveness to the child's needs. When either of these conditions is inadequate, pubertal development associated with sexual behavior and motivations to leave the family accelerates, promoting the likelihood of a girl's early reproductive success.
2. *Family-wide environmental conditions.* In contrast to the notion of conditional adaptation, in which family stress causes early puberty, it is possible that some other family condition underlies both family stress *and* accelerated pubertal development. Poverty, for example, is associated with both father absence and obesity (Votruba-Drzal et al., 2016), both of which are associated with early puberty in girls (Braithwaite et al., 2009 Ellis & Essex, 2007).
3. *Gene–environment correlation.* Some developmentalists have speculated that family stress doesn't actually *cause* early puberty; the two simply go hand-in-hand in a *correlational relationship*. As you know, the mother's age of pubertal onset is a strong predictor of the daughter's age of onset, suggesting a genetic component. In addition, early puberty is linked with early childbirth, which, in turn, is strongly associated with later divorce and father absence (Amato & Patterson, 2017; Amato et al., 2015).

In an effort to tease apart these three competing explanations, the researchers studied the ages of pubertal onset in sisters who were several years apart in age. Some sisters grew up together with their biological mothers and fathers; others grew up together in families that experienced divorce or father absence before the younger sister reached puberty. This clever design assured that family-wide environmental conditions (#2 above) and gene-environment correlations (#3 above) would be comparable for each sister pair. The distinguishing feature between the younger and older sisters in the disrupted families would consequently be limited to the amount of time that each was exposed to family stress. Specifically, the researchers expected that the younger sisters, who experienced stress for a longer period in their childhood, would enter puberty at an earlier age than did their older sisters. In contrast, no differences in pubertal onset were expected for the sister pairs developing in families that did not experience divorce or father absence. In fact, the results of the study confirmed these expectations (see the figure below). Interestingly, the degree of difference in pubertal onset between sisters developing in disrupted families was magnified substantially when the father was reported to have serious behavioral or mental health issues, such as substance abuse, a record of criminal offenses, or a history of violence. Under such conditions, the younger sister entered puberty at a radically earlier age than did her older sibling.

Tither and Ellis interpret their findings as supporting an evolutionary account (#1 above) of the relationship between family stress and girls' pubertal timing. Their research also contributes to an ever-growing body of evidence underscoring the importance of fathers to their children's development, health, and well-being.

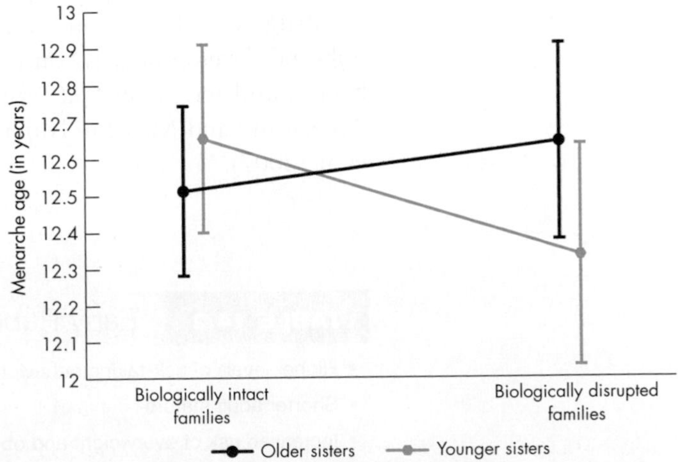

Pubertal onset is not significantly different for sisters living with both biological parents, but younger sisters enter puberty at significantly earlier ages if they experience parental divorce or father absence, presumably due to increased levels of stress.

that exposure to certain environmental chemicals, such as DDT, lead, and phthalates (common in plastic bottles), may disrupt the endocrine system and alter the normal onset and course of sexual maturation (reviewed in Toppari & Juul, 2010).

While the variants of puberty described above can be anxiety provoking for children and parents, they are not generally associated with increased risk for disease and are not considered pathological. **Precocious puberty**, on the other hand, is a serious condition that involves the activation of the HPG axis before the age of 8 in girls and 9 in boys. As shown in Table 14.2, precocious puberty is associated with predispositions to a number of diseases, including cancer, diabetes, and overweight (Lazar et al., 2015; Lee, Yoon, & Hwang, 2016). It has an estimated prevalence rate of between 1:5,000 and 1:10,000 and is 5 to 10 times more common in girls than in boys (Carel & Léger, 2008). Interestingly, higher rates of precocious puberty are found in foreign adopted and migrant children in the United States, perhaps due to a rapid increase in fat mass resulting from a switch in diet and eating patterns (Parent et al., 2003).

precocious puberty A serious condition that involves the activation of the HPG axis before the age of 8 in girls and 9 in boys.

Individual Variation and Gender

Regardless of the factors underpinning the early sexual maturation of one child or the late pubertal onset of another, the timing of puberty can be a psychological burden or an asset, depending on whether the child's maturing is early or late relative to that of peers and whether the child is male or female. If you were an early-maturing girl, or knew one, you may remember being acutely aware of some of the consequences of being "off time" in relation to your peers. Early-maturing girls can be magnets of unwanted sexual attention from older boys; they may have trouble sharing the trials and tribulations of puberty with their less mature girlfriends; and their parents, teachers, and even peers may expect more mature behavior from them, despite the likelihood that their intellectual and emotional abilities are relatively less developed than their bodies would suggest. If you can think of other social or psychological consequences of girls' early sexual maturation, it is likely that they, too, are negative rather than positive. Indeed, the past two decades have produced a wealth of studies documenting the difficulties experienced by girls who mature early. Although most girls weather the storms of early maturation without lasting problems, many develop depressive disorders, eating disorders, anxiety, and poor self-esteem—all associated with their early pubertal onset (Graber, Nichols, & Brooks-Gunn, 2010; Stojković, 2013; Sun et al., 2016). Early-maturing girls are also at risk for having problems in school, engaging in delinquent behaviors, abusing drugs and alcohol, and having sex at earlier ages compared with girls whose pubertal development is "on time" or late. In the United States, such effects have been found across multiple ethnic groups, including European Americans, African Americans, and Mexican Americans (Ge, Brody, Conger, & Simons, 2006; Lynne et al., 2007).

TABLE 14.2 Early Puberty: Associated Risks

- Higher levels of risk-taking behavior in adolescence
- Shorter adult stature
- Increased risk of overweight and obesity due to elevated BMI
- Increased risk of disease, including adult-onset diabetes, heart disease, and premenopausal breast cancer
- Increased mortality

Information from Ahmed, Ong, & Dunger, 2009.

Early maturation is quite a different story for boys. Compared with their on-time and late-maturing counterparts, early-maturing boys tend to be more popular with peers and, in stark contrast to girls, generally pleased with their changing bodies (Stojković, 2013). As we discussed earlier, the growth spurt in muscle mass and the physiological changes to the respiratory and circulatory systems result in a more athletic body capable of higher levels of athletic performance. Given that athletic ability in boys and men is highly prized in many cultures, it is little wonder that boys are eager to develop physically and usually adjust well if development occurs relatively early. However, despite these apparent benefits, researchers point out that early-maturing boys share some risk factors with their female counterparts, including delinquency, substance abuse, and academic problems.

Researchers have pointed to several possible reasons early-maturing youths are at risk for engaging in such problem behaviors. One explanation, which we address more fully in Chapter 15, relates to changes in friends and peer-group affiliations. In particular, when youths become sexually mature at relatively early ages, they may begin to form friendships with older peers or become involved with deviant peer groups, exposing themselves to contexts that promote risk-taking or rebelliousness (Rudolph, 2008; Wiesner, Silbereisen, & Weichold, 2008). A second, related explanation is that although their bodies are mature, and they may be experiencing hormone-related impulses and desires, their powers of reason may be relatively unsophisticated and childlike. Indeed, pubertal development and cognitive development seem to be largely unrelated (Giedd et al., 2006). Early sexual maturation is also associated with lower self-control and less emotional stability, as measured by psychological tests. The degree of adult supervision is yet another possible explanation for the relationship between early maturation and problem behavior. Compared with on-time and late maturers, early-maturing boys and girls are subject to less monitoring by parents and teachers (Silbereisen & Kracke, 1997).

Altogether, research on individual variation in pubertal timing suggests that understanding why one child might enter puberty earlier or later than another or respond to the timing of his or her own puberty with anxiety and depression or with satisfaction and well-being requires understanding how pubertal development intersects with the personal history and the current context of the child in question.

Population Variation Developmentalists are interested not only in variations in pubertal timing that take place at the level of the individual; they are also interested in such variations as they occur in whole populations. Studies devoted to examining population differences in pubertal onset have been conducted in hundreds of countries and over the course of several centuries; their numbers may very well run into the thousands. What accounts for this extensive and enduring interest? The answer lies in the fact that the average age of sexual maturation is strongly associated with the health of the general population. In particular, sexual maturation, as well as other physical developments, can be significantly delayed in populations that suffer widespread malnutrition and exposure to disease as a consequence of poor medical care. Consider Figure 14.6, from a classic study conducted in 1978. The figure shows the average age of menarche for girls growing up at the time in urban and rural environments in several different countries. (Most studies of population variation rely on menarche to gauge pubertal onset because, unlike ejaculation, it is not tied to sexual behavior yet is readily observable and reasonably memorable [Herman-Giddens, 2007].) The differences are dramatic, and they are more so in some countries than in others. Cross-national differences raise several important questions: Why does menarche occur earlier in some countries than in others? Why are the rural/urban differences relatively small

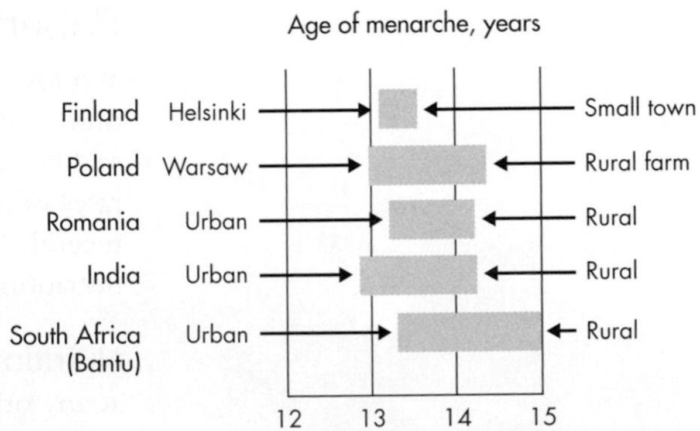

FIGURE 14.6 Complex interactions between genetic and environmental factors result in large regional differences in the average age of pubertal onset. In general, puberty begins earlier in urban areas than in rural areas. (Data from Tanner, 1978.)

in some countries (Finland, for example) but quite large in others (such as India and South Africa)? Identifying the factors that affect the onset of puberty would help developmentalists understand these national differences and might help policy makers identify areas of the world in need of greater levels of health care.

secular trend A pattern in which the average age of puberty in developed countries declines across decades.

In addition to cross-national differences, the age at which puberty is reached has also undergone striking historical changes. The **secular trend** refers to a pattern of decline in the average age of puberty that has occurred across all social, ethnic, and economic populations in developed countries and, to a lesser extent, in developing countries. For a time, the secular trend in both developed and developing countries was taken as evidence of good health. In developed countries, for example, the average age of menarche dropped from about 16 years in the mid-1800s to about 13 years in the 1960s (Parent et al., 2003), presumably due to increased access to food, prenatal and child care, immunizations, and medicines and technologies that combat infectious diseases. Likewise, the downward trend in pubertal onset in developing countries is likely due to better nutrition and quality health care (Jaruratanasirikul & Sriplung, 2015; Pawloski, Ruchiwit, & Pakapong, 2008; Ying-Xiu & Shu-Rong, 2008).

Since the 1960s, the secular trend has continued in developed countries, although at a slower rate than that observed between the mid-1800s and mid-1900s. This was demonstrated in a study of a nationally representative sample of girls in the United States who were surveyed 10 years apart in the late 1980s and 1990s. The study found that the average age of pubertal onset had declined from 12.09 to 12.06 for Black girls, from 12.24 to 12.09 for Mexican American girls, and from 12.57 to 12.52 years for (non-Hispanic) White girls (1999–2002 NHANES data, analyzed in Anderson, Bandini, & Must, 2005). Although these differences may seem slight, researchers argue that they are nonetheless highly meaningful. In particular, there is grave concern that the factors underpinning the trend have changed from positive ones, such as improved nutrition and access to health care, to ones that are decidedly unhealthy, including "overnutrition" associated with overweight and obesity, declining physical activity, and chemical pollution in the environment (Herman-Giddens, 2006; Song et al., 2016; Surana et al., 2017). Given the number of health and psychological problems associated with early sexual maturation (discussed above), it is clearly essential to continue monitoring pubertal onset around the globe and to explore connections to genetic and environmental factors.

Puberty and Health

Worldwide, adolescence is a period of relatively good health. Compared with children and older people, adolescents experience fewer infections, chronic diseases, and life-threatening illnesses (WHO, 2017). Nevertheless, the astronomical growth rates of adolescence place new demands on the body, and developmentalists have recently begun to focus attention on the unique needs of adolescents for adequate nutrition, sleep, and physical activity.

Nutrition

The body's total nutrient needs are greater during adolescence than at any other time in life. These needs are especially great during the growth spurt; in fact, it has been estimated that at the peak of the growth spurt, the body needs twice the nutrients that it needs at other points during adolescence. Optimal nutrition during adolescence is essential not only for achieving full growth potential but also for preventing a number of diseases in later life, including heart disease, cancer, and osteoporosis (Wideman et al., 2016). Unfortunately, the average diet of adolescents, at least in the United States, is low in essential vitamins and minerals and high in fats and sugars.

The importance of a healthy diet to adolescent development cannot be overemphasized. Vitamins and minerals are known to influence essential physiological processes, including facilitating healthy sexual maturation and protecting against chromosomal damage.

What accounts for adolescents' tendency toward poor diets and bad dietary choices? In many parts of the world, of course, adolescents simply do not have access to healthy food. This is obviously true in economically poor, developing nations, but it is also true in many communities in wealthy countries. In the United States, for example, people in poor, urban neighborhoods have far fewer grocery stores and fewer means of transportation to them than do those in more affluent neighborhoods (Gittelsohn et al., 2010; Suarez et al., 2015).

Christian Science Monitor/Getty Images

Concerns about the nutrition of cafeteria lunches have prompted many schools to expand the healthy choices offered to students.

Limited access to food is just one of a variety of social, psychological, and cultural factors that contribute to nutritional problems in adolescence. Unfortunately, while poor, urban communities lack adequate grocery stores, they have a plethora of fast-food outlets—nearly twice the number found in wealthier neighborhoods—that are notorious for their "super-sized," high-caloric menus. This combination of factors may help account for the higher levels of obesity among African Americans and other ethnic-minority populations in the United States (Block, Scribner, & DeSalvo, 2004). Compounding the problem is the fact that foods high in calories and low in nutritional value are often less expensive than more nutritious foods and therefore may be purchased often by families with limited resources (Drewnowski & Darmon, 2005). Interestingly, adolescents of food-insecure families (see Chapter 8, p. 265) are more likely than their food-secure counterparts to report that eating healthy foods is inconvenient and that healthy food doesn't taste very good. As reported by one team of researchers, adolescents from food-insecure families develop eating patterns that are different from those of food-secure families. In particular, they are more likely to eat fast food, less likely to eat meals with their families, and eat breakfast less often. They are also more likely to be obese (Widome et al., 2009).

Sleep In addition to not getting enough nutrients, many adolescents do not sleep enough. Adolescents are night owls, tending to stay up later at night than they did as children and, when their schedule permits, to sleep later in the morning (Laberge et al., 2001). This shift in the sleep–wake pattern, called the **delayed circadian phase**, is not particularly problematic in cultural contexts that do not require adolescents to rise early for school. However, for adolescents enrolled in school, late bedtimes combined with early rising create morning classrooms full of bleary-eyed teens who are less prepared to learn than they would be if they had had a good night's rest (not to mention a nutritious breakfast!). There is also concern that adolescents are inclined to use chemical stimulants to cope with sleep deprivation. The most commonly used stimulants are nicotine and, especially, caffeine, including the increasingly popular and caffeine-concentrated energy drinks (Bryant Ludden & Wolfson, 2010; Calamaro, Mason, & Ratcliffe, 2009).

delayed circadian phase A shift in the sleep–wake pattern in which adolescents tend to stay up later at night than they did as children and then sleep later in the morning.

Concerns about the effects of sleep deprivation on academic performance are not new. Over a century ago, G. Stanley Hall argued that adolescents should not be allowed to go to school at all without 9 hours of sleep (1904). His recommendation is not far from that of contemporary developmentalists, who believe that 8 hours of sleep is optimal for most adolescents (Carskadon, Acebo, & Jenni, 2004). However, during the school week, the average bedtime for high school students in the United States is later than 11 P.M., and the average high school senior rises (or tries to,

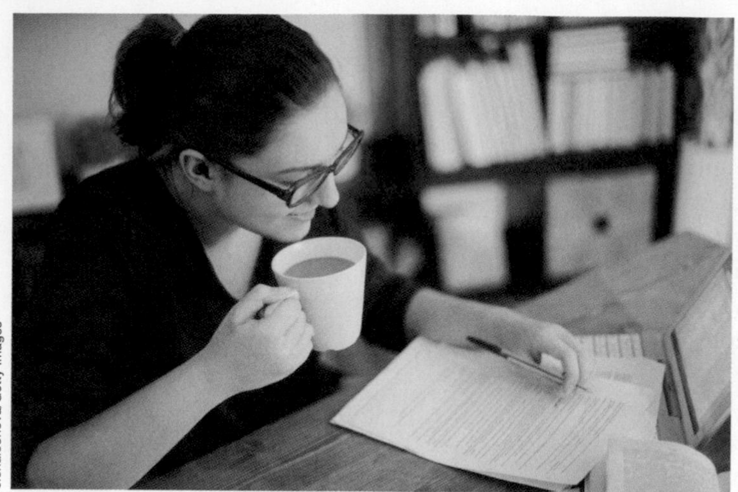
elenaleonova/Getty Images

This student is doing her homework under the influence of caffeine, a practice that may interfere with a good night's sleep.

at least) before 6:15 A.M., resulting in *chronic sleep deprivation* for a large portion of students (Dahl & Hariri, 2005). The reason to be concerned over adolescents' sleep patterns was highlighted by a recent analysis of scores of studies that concluded that sleepiness, sleep quality, and sleep duration all affect school performance (Lewin et al., 2017).

Sleep researchers recognize that the delayed circadian phase results from an interaction of biological and environmental influences. It is known to occur earlier in girls than boys and has been linked to hormones that affect the brain's biological clock, suggesting that pubertal status may play a role (Hagenauer, Perryman, Lee, & Carskadon, 2009). However, the later bedtime of teenagers has also been linked to decreased parental control, increased schoolwork, and other social pressures, including the 24/7 lifestyle enabled and even encouraged by electronic social networking media (Calamaro et al., 2009; Keyes, et al., 2015). For example, researchers at the National Taiwan University studied sleep patterns in nearly 1,600 Taiwanese students between fourth and eighth grades (Gau & Soong, 2003). In Taiwan, only a limited number of students are admitted to senior high school (beginning in tenth grade), and academic competition and parental pressure to achieve in school are both extremely intense. The researchers found that the increased academic demands of the higher grade levels were more strongly associated with the sleep–wake shift than pubertal status.

Yet another factor complicating the delayed circadian phase of adolescence is school start times, which tend to get progressively earlier as children move from elementary to middle to high school (Carskadon, 2011). Despite the overwhelming evidence that *later* start times would be better suited to the changing biorhythms of adolescence, efforts to delay the first bell of high school have met with intense resistance because of the myriad ways it would complicate family life and after-school activities (Wahlstrom, 2002).

Although the delayed circadian phase has enormous significance for adolescents, as well as for their families, schools, and communities, it is not the only change in sleep patterns observed during this particular developmental period. There is also a significant and fascinating decline in the amount of time adolescents spend in nonrapid eye movement (NREM) sleep. NREM sleep is identified by large, slow "delta" waves and is associated with deep, quiet sleep. The size of the delta waves increases sharply during the first years of life, declines through early childhood, and then drops off dramatically during adolescence, apparently due to developmental changes in the brain (Feinberg & Campbell, 2010; Feinberg et al., 1978). In particular, as in infancy, as the number of neural connections increases during the adolescent spurt of synaptogenesis, so too does the amplitude of delta waves. Likewise, when synaptic density declines sharply in adolescence as a consequence of synaptic pruning, delta-wave amplitude diminishes accordingly. In short, adolescents' difficulties in getting a good night's sleep may be a consequence of a number of biological, social, and cultural factors.

Physical Activity As you have been advised for years, in addition to eating and sleeping well, it is important to get plenty of exercise. Indeed, adolescents who engage in higher levels of physical activity experience greater well-being than less physically active adolescents. Studies indicate that high levels of athletic activity are generally associated with less depression, less drug use, better relationships with parents, and higher academic performance for adolescent girls and boys alike (Korczak, Madigan, & Colasanto,

2017; Lebron et al., 2017; Suchert, Hanewinkel, & Isensee, 2016). On the basis of intensive interviews with adolescent girls and boys on issues of sexuality and pubertal development, Karin Martin concluded that girls who are involved in sports feel confidence in themselves and their bodies and show a good deal of admiration and respect for each other (Martin, 1996).

Despite the importance of physical activity to body, mind, and social relationships, many adolescents get woefully little of it, spending, as discussed in Chapter 10, far too much time engaged in sedentary activities such as watching TV, playing computer games, and electronic surfing and social networking. We have already noted that excessive sedentary behavior increases the risk for obesity in children, and this risk becomes more prevalent during puberty (Bradley, McMurray, Harrell, & Deng, 2000). Activity level may also affect adolescents' emotional state. A large-scale study of British 11- and 12-year-olds documented a significant relationship between low levels of emotional well-being and high levels of sedentary behavior (Brodersen, Steptoe, Williamson, & Wardle, 2005).

Obvious to all are some of puberty's most dramatic changes; less visible transformations, including brain functions, are nonetheless highly influential in adolescent development. Taken together, the changes of puberty both support new ways of thinking and provide the developing adolescent with significant new issues to think about, as you will see in the next section.

© Steve Skjold/PhotoEdit, Inc.

Girls who are involved in team sports may feel more confidence in themselves and show higher levels of admiration and respect for each other.

APPLY > CONNECT > DISCUSS

What might be done to protect girls from the negative consequences of early maturation? Consider various contexts of prevention, including families, schools, and culture.

Cognitive Development

LEARNING OUTCOMES

Describe Piaget's formal operational stage of cognitive development and provide examples of scientific thinking that use hypothetical-deductive reasoning.

Describe post-formal-operational thinking and provide examples of epistemic developments that reflect objectivist, subjectivist, and evaluativist theories of knowledge.

Explain the relationship between information-processing approaches and adolescent thinking.

Explain the relationship between sociocultural approaches and adolescent thinking.

How adolescents interpret and react to their changing bodies, as well as to their changing social life and relationships, is influenced by their developing intellectual abilities—that is, the ways in which they reason about themselves and their development and about the world around them. Indeed, some of the most fascinating developments of the adolescent period are those that concern the workings of the mind. When G. Stanley Hall argued that adolescents are the future of our species, he was thinking in particular of their newly acquired capacities for reasoning, planning, deciding, and imagining—intellectual ingredients that are essential to our species' proudest accomplishments, as well as to the individual's success in the world. As in earlier chapters, we look at various approaches to cognition—at Piaget's theory and then at information-processing and sociocultural approaches.

Piaget's Theory of Formal Operations

It was Piaget's contention that changes in the way adolescents think about themselves, their personal relationships, and the nature of their society have a common source: the emergence of **formal operations** (Table 14.3, p. 500). An "operation" in Piaget's terminology is a mental action that fits into a logical system. Examples of *concrete operations*, typically achieved in middle childhood, include the mathematical operations of adding and subtracting as well as other logical operations, such as placing items in a serial order—say, from shortest to tallest. The concrete-operational child is able to apply operations to the real world. What distinguishes the formal-operational adolescent is the ability to apply operations to operations—that

formal operations In Piaget's terms, mental operations in which all possible combinations are considered in solving a problem. Consequently, each partial link is grouped in relationship to the whole; in other words, reasoning moves continually as a function of a structured whole.

TABLE 14.3 Piaget's Stages of Cognitive Development: Formal Operational

Age (years)	Stage	Description	Characteristics and Examples
Birth to 2	Sensorimotor	Infants' achievements consist largely of coordinating their sensory perceptions and simple motor behaviors. As they move through the six substages of this period, infants come to recognize the existence of a world outside themselves and begin to interact with it in deliberate ways.	
2 to 6	Preoperational	Young children can represent reality to themselves through the use of symbols, including mental images, words, and gestures. Objects and events no longer have to be present to be thought about, but children often fail to distinguish their point of view from that of others, become easily captured by surface appearances, and are often confused about causal relationships.	
6 to 12	Concrete operational	As they enter middle childhood, children become capable of mental operations, internalized actions that fit into a logical system. Operational thinking allows children to mentally combine, separate, order, and transform objects and actions. Such operations are considered concrete because they are carried out in the presence of the objects and events being thought about.	
12 to 19	Formal operational	In adolescence, the developing person acquires the ability to think systematically about all logical relations within a problem. Adolescents display keen interest in abstract ideas and in the process of thinking itself.	Formal-operational reasoning, in which each partial link in a chain of reasoning is related to the problem as a whole • Capacity to solve scientific problems by systematically testing all possible combinations • In forming a personal identity, taking into account how young people judge others, how others judge them, how they judge the judgment process of others, and how all this corresponds to social categories available in the culture Application of formal-operational thinking to a wide variety of life's problems for young people • In thinking about politics and law in terms of abstract principles and seeing the beneficial, rather than just the punitive, side of laws • Being interested in universal ethical principles and critical of adults' hypocrisies

is, to systematically relate sets of relationships to each other. For this reason, formal operations are also called *second-order operations.* David Moshman provides the following illustration:

> Consider the following proportion:
>
> $$10/5 = 4/2$$
>
> To comprehend the logic of this proportion, it must be understood that the relation of 10 to 5 is equal to the relation of 4 to 2 (that is, that in both cases, the first number is twice as great as the second). The focus is on a relation (of equality, in this case) between two relations. A proportion, in other words, is a relation between two relations, a second-order relation. (Moshman, 1999, p. 13.)

Nicholas K. Geranios/AP Images

New powers of reasoning and imagination emerging in adolescence no doubt contributed to Kira Powell's science project, which gained international attention. Her project involved lacing farmland in drought-stricken areas with a moisture-retaining material used in disposable diapers.

Formal-operational thinking is the kind of thinking needed by anyone who has to solve problems systematically. To give two examples from the adult world of work, the ability to use formal-operational thinking is needed by the owner of a gasoline station who, to make a profit, has to take into account the wholesale price of gasoline, the kinds of customers who pass by the station, the types of services the station needs to offer, the hours it needs to stay open, and the cost of labor, supplies, rent, and utilities; or by a lawyer who must consider a wide variety of alternative strategies, legal precedents, and possible consequences in deciding how best to present a case and counter the arguments of the attorney on the opposing side.

Scientific and Hypothetical Reasoning Inhelder and Piaget's studies of formal-operational thinking focused on very basic versions of the kinds of problems encountered in scientific laboratories. Typically, these problems require participants to hold one variable of a complex system constant while systematically searching mentally through all the other variables. To illustrate, suppose you remembered the first two digits of your combination lock (2, 5) but could not remember the last two. Thus, you need to solve the problem: 2–5–*x*–*y*, where *x* and *y* are variables that can vary from 0 to 9. Solving the problem without formal operations, you might plug in values randomly, or insert your brother's age, the number of times you have been late for class, and so on. This strategy is obviously flawed. For one thing, it would be very difficult for you to keep track of all your previous entries and separate the "tried" from the "to be tried." A formal-operational strategy, on the other hand, would systematically test every possible pair of digits—0–0, 0–1, 0–2 . . . 1–0, 1–1, 1–2 . . . all the way through to 9–0, 9–1 . . . 9–9, if necessary.

A central feature of scientific thinking is **hypothetical-deductive reasoning**, which involves the ability to judge an argument entirely on the basis of its logical form, regardless of whether the argument is true. Consider, for example, the following arguments (information from Moshman, 2011):

hypothetical-deductive reasoning Reasoning that involves the ability to judge an argument entirely on the basis of its logical form, regardless of whether the argument is true.

Argument 1
First premise: Elephants are bigger than mice.
Second premise: Dogs are bigger than mice.
Conclusion: Therefore, elephants are bigger than dogs.

Argument 2
First premise: Mice are bigger than dogs.
Second premise: Dogs are bigger than elephants.
Conclusion: Therefore, mice are bigger than elephants.

Because all the statements in the first argument are true, the concrete-operational child will judge it to be more logical than the second argument, for which all of the statements are false. The formal-operational individual, on the other hand, will understand that the second argument is logical—that is, the conclusion follows from the premises—whereas the first argument is not. Correctly solving this task demonstrates the ability of formal thinkers to distinguish between truth and logic, an ability of vital importance in thinking beyond actual experience to consider and evaluate the possible.

In general, research finds a steady increase in logical reasoning between the 4th and 12th grades (roughly, between 10 and 18 years of age; Markovits, 2014). In fact, formal-deductive reasoning is very rare before 6th grade (11 to 12 years of age).

Variability in Formal-Operational Thinking

Cross-cultural evidence that people failed to reach formal operations without extensive schooling led Piaget to conclude that the stage of formal operations is not universal but, instead, depends on certain types of experience. In fact, even extensive schooling does not guarantee the attainment of formal operations. For example, studies find that as few as 30 to 40 percent of well-educated Americans in their late teens and early 20s are able to solve the combination-of-liquids and other formal-operational problems (Moshman, 2013). In addition, formal operations show a high degree of variability within individuals; that is, many individuals who are capable of formal-operational thought do not employ formal-operational strategies in all situations (Markovits & Barrouillet, 2002). Thus, a car mechanic who uses formal-operational thought to troubleshoot an engine problem may use concrete-operational thinking in most other domains of life. Indeed, there is mounting evidence that most decisions in everyday contexts, whether by adolescents or adults, do not employ the strategies of formal-operational thinking (Keating, 2004; Klaczynski & Cottrell, 2004; Kokis et al., 2002).

Post-Formal-Operational Thinking In addition to questioning the pervasiveness of formal-operational thinking in everyday contexts, researchers have asked whether there might be additional cognitive developments through late adolescence and into early, emerging adulthood. One of the most interesting and productive areas of research to address this question has examined changes in how individuals reason about the nature of knowledge, known also as **epistemic development** (Magolda, 2008; Perry, 1970; Weinstock, 2015). How do you know that something is true, that it can be believed? What makes one argument persuasive and another sound like so much poppycock? The following examples of epistemic reasoning, which were taken from college students who were interviewed about their experiences in school, reflect three types of epistemic reasoning that represent very different views of the nature of knowledge (Perry, 1970):

epistemic development Refers to changes in how individuals reason about the nature of knowledge.

1. I feel rather insecure thinking about these philosophical things all the time and not coming up with any definite answers. Definite answers are, well, they're sort of my foundation point. In physics you get definite answers to a point. Beyond that point you know there *are* definite answers, but you can't reach them (yet).
2. The instructor kept trying to force her ideas about the poem on us. . . . I mean, what makes her ideas any better than mine, anyway?
3. So here were all these theorists and theories and stuff—and hell, I said, "These are *games*, just *games* and everybody makes up their own rules! So it's gotta be bullshit." But then I realized "What else have we got?" and now every time I get into a thing I set out to learn all its rules, 'cause that's the only way I can tell whether *I'm* talking bullshit.

The first example reflects an **objectivist theory of knowledge**—that is, a belief that knowledge involves an accumulation of objective facts and "definite answers." In contrast, the second example reflects a **subjectivist theory of knowledge**, according to which there is no absolute truth because truth can change depending on one's perspective. Finally, the third example expresses an **evaluativist theory of knowledge**, in which it is recognized that although truth can change, it is nevertheless subject to particular standards of evaluation—the "rules of the game" (Hallett, Chandler, & Krettenauer, 2002; Weinstock, 2015).

objectivist theory of knowledge A belief that knowledge involves an accumulation of objective facts and "definite answers."

subjectivist theory of knowledge A belief that there is no absolute truth because truth can change depending on one's perspective.

evaluativist theory of knowledge A belief that although truth can change, it is nevertheless subject to particular standards of evaluation—the "rules of the game."

Most studies of epistemic reasoning in late adolescence and early adulthood find that these three types of reasoning form a developmental hierarchy: An objectivist theory of knowledge emerges first, followed by a subjectivist theory, and then by an evaluativist theory. However, recent studies have found that cultural factors may influence epistemic development, with some cultures emphasizing one theory of knowledge over another (Hofer, 2008; Weinstock, 2015). Cultures that value tradition, for example, may believe that knowledge resides in, and is transmitted by, authority figures (worldly or spiritual), thereby tending to support the objectivist theory of knowledge. Other cultures, in contrast, may believe that knowledge must be evaluated in terms of scientific standards, thereby supporting the evaluativist theory of knowledge.

In light of the high degree of variability of formal-operational thinking both between and within cultures, as well as evidence that additional cognitive developments occur in late adolescence and early adulthood, modern researchers have argued that the study of advanced intellectual development should shift from focusing on a general stage of formal operations to looking at specific forms of reasoning associated with particular types of tasks and cultural practices.

Information-Processing Approaches

Whereas in the Piagetian view the advances in adolescents' cognition result from global, qualitative change, information-processing theorists believe that adolescents' expanded cognitive abilities are better explained as resulting from the continuing development of various cognitive structures and processes and the ability to control them. So, for example, information-processing approaches emphasize how adolescents' ability to think systematically arises from the increased capacity of their working memory and from their ability to apply more powerful problem-solving strategies with increasing reliability (Markovits & Lortie-Forgues, 2011). In problem solving, increased memory capacity makes it possible to coordinate several different factors at once, keep intermediate results in mind, and come up with a solution that is comprehensive and consistent.

Information-processing approaches also examine increasing abilities to control one's thoughts. As we first introduced in Chapter 11 (p. 394), *executive function* refers to cognitive skills that control and regulate one's cognitive processes in order to achieve particular goals—for example, inhibiting or resisting an impulsive or desirable behavior, such as going out to a party with friends, in order to go to the library to study for an important exam. Although executive functions are apparent in middle childhood, they expand considerably during the years of adolescence and are associated with the maturation of the brain (Treit, Chen, Rasmussen, & Beaulieu, 2014; Vara et al., 2014). High levels of executive function in adolescence have been linked to academic achievement, whereas low levels have been linked to a number of problem behaviors, including eating disorders and risk-taking (Kittel, Schmidt, & Hilbert, 2017; Schiebener et al., 2015).

Not surprisingly, developmentalists have been eager to identify factors that support or impede the development of executive function. An interesting example is **multitasking**, which involves attending and responding to multiple sources of information simultaneously, such as following a text stream on a phone while also watching a video. Needless to say, in this age when many adolescents are using multiple digital devices simultaneously, questions have emerged about the benefits of multitasking to the development of executive function. Does multitasking contribute to the development of executive function by providing practice in switching attention from one task to another? Perhaps counterintuitively—certainly counter to what many adolescents will claim when their parents urge them to put away the phone in order to better focus on their online homework—it does not. Instead, multitasking appears to interfere with attention, causing heightened distractibility and decreased performance on tasks (Courage et al., 2015; Moisala et al., 2016). So put that phone away while you're studying—and driving!

multitasking Cognitive processes involving attending and responding to multiple sources of information simultaneously.

Whereas multitasking appears to interfere with executive function, another common adolescent behavior may provide benefits: action video game play (Courage et al., 2015). A number of studies suggest that action video game play has positive effects on attention, cognition, and motor control (Bavelier & Green, 2016; Cardoso-Leite, et al., 2016). For instance, gamers, in contrast to non-gamers, are more able to control their attention and visually track moving objects. In light of evidence that gaming increases adolescents' cognitive strategies and skills, developmentalists and educators have questioned whether these skills may impact academic achievement. At this point, there is no clear consensus (Blumberg, Altschuler, Almonte, & Mileaf, 2013). Although gaming and schoolwork are similar in some respects—both involve solving difficult and benefit from practice—it remains unclear whether the strategies and skills developed through video game play are relevant to solving the sorts of problems that teens are likely to encounter in school. Some developmentalists, however, argue that gaming could be used to foster higher levels of student engagement in and learning of course material (Morris et al., 2013).

GoGo Images/AGE Fotostock

Sociocultural approaches focus on how social interactions, relationships, and cultural norms contribute to intellectual development and learning. It is likely that these boys, thoroughly engrossed in their books, receive a lot of support from family, teachers, and peers for excelling at school.

Sociocultural Approaches

Like information-processing theorists, developmentalists who examine adolescent thinking from a sociocultural perspective focus mainly on specific forms of thinking used in particular problem-solving situations. In addition, however, sociocultural theorists emphasize how the means of solving problems are influenced and guided by the social interactions of the participants (Rogoff, 2003; Subrahmanyam & Greenfield, 2008).

From a sociocultural perspective, games provide an ideal setting for exploring the development of complex reasoning skills in adolescence. As we discussed in Chapter 13 (pp. 447–448), games typically include material and symbolic tools of culture, provide a means of transmitting cultural values and norms, and often involve quite sophisticated forms of reasoning. In addition, many games are highly social, requiring players to coordinate goals and strategies with each other. Using a Vygotskian sociocultural approach, Na'ilah Nasir has explored reasoning in the context of a game of strategy popular in many African American communities—dominoes (Nasir, 2005).

In the version of the game used in Nasir's study, pairs of individuals play in teams against one another. Each player selects 7 dominoes from the total set of 28 tiles placed facedown. The faces of the dominoes are divided into halves, each of which is embossed with 0 to 6 dots, or pips. Whoever draws the double-6 tile (the one with 6 pips in each half) places it faceup on the board, and the game begins. If the next player has a domino with 6 pips at one end, the player lays the 6 end against one side of the first domino. The game then proceeds with the players taking turns similarly "matching" their pips with those that have been laid down. If a match can't be made, the player must "pass." If, after a domino is played, the sum of all the end dominoes is a multiple of five, then the player receives those points; if the sum is not a multiple of five, no points are scored. Playing the game well involves scoring points by making the right sorts of matches (resulting in multiples of five), assisting one's partner to make matches, and blocking matches of opponents, thereby preventing them from scoring. (Successful blocking requires keeping track of the opponent's passes, which provide clues to the possible matches available.)

As you can see, dominoes can be a complexly strategic game involving the ability to calculate various point values associated with different possible moves, remembering earlier moves by partners and opponents, thinking hypothetically about possible future moves, and making inferences about how to help or hinder those possibilities through one's own game play. Nasir's analysis documents fascinating transformations in domino play from childhood to adolescence. As we would expect from Piagetian research, adolescents were much more adept at generating and evaluating the point value of possible moves—for themselves as well as for their partner and opponents—than were younger children, who were primarily concerned with the matching of ends. Likewise, adolescents were also much more skilled than younger children in using information about previous moves and passes to anticipate and make inferences about future possible moves of opponents and partners. However, the Vygotskian approach adopted by Nasir emphasized how individuals sought and received help from other players in ways that scaffolded their developing knowledge of the game and their mastery of various scoring, blocking, and partner-assisting strategies. Consider the following examples, the first involving elementary school students and the second involving high school students:

> David isn't sure which domino to play, so he holds one out towards his partner, Tyrell, saying, "Man, put that down there, dog." Tyrell says, "It goes right there!" and plays the domino for David.
>
> Deondre begins the game by playing a double 6. Aaron, on the opposing team, follows with the 6–4 (Figure 14.7). Realizing that this move opens the possibility that Deondre's team can score 20 points by playing the 4-4 (known as the "hit rock"), Aaron's teammate, James, immediately criticizes this play by saying "What you doin' over there, man?" Deondre's teammate, Latrisha, chimes in, affirming James's criticism, "He lucky I ain't got the hit rock. I sho' would tax your butt." (Nasir, 2005, pp. 13, 20.)

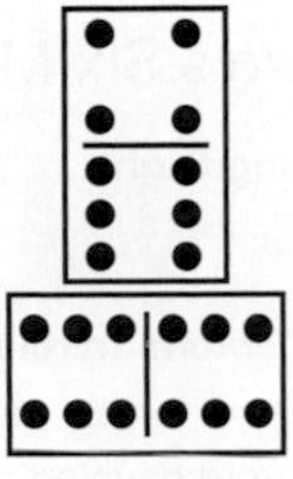

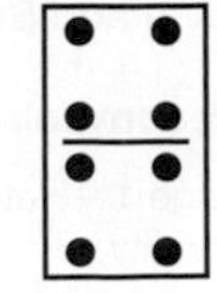

FIGURE 14.7 Popular in many African American communities, the game of dominoes calls on complex formal-operational reasoning skills.

From a Vygotskian perspective in which intellectual development is emphasized not as a solitary process but as one that emerges in the course of social participation, these types of social interactions are critical to the learning process. Whether responding to a peer's uncertainty (like David's) or mistake (like Aaron's), adolescents are often able to engage each other in new forms of thinking and acting. Just as social participation contributes to intellectual development, intellectual development, as we will see below, contributes to the adolescent's social participation by affecting moral reasoning and behavior.

APPLY > CONNECT > DISCUSS

Consider the various forms of reasoning described in this section: formal operations, post-formal operations, and decision making. To what extent are they relevant to reasoning in everyday contexts, including gaming? Do you think it's possible to design games that would promote these types of reasoning? What would they look like?

Moral Development

LEARNING OUTCOMES

- Apply Kohlberg's levels and stages of moral reasoning to moral development in adolescents.
- Explain Gilligan's theory of moral reasoning as it relates to moral development during adolescence.
- Point out some contributions of parents and peers in the moral development of adolescents.
- Identify some cultural variations in moral development for adolescents around the world.

Regardless of their theoretical orientation, developmentalists agree that adolescence is a time during which issues of moral behavior take on special importance for young people, typified by such questions as What is right? What is wrong? What principles should I base my behavior on and use to judge the behavior of others? Evidence suggests that the processes used to think about such questions, like those used to think about science problems, undergo important changes between the ages of 12 and 19 years (Moshman, 2011; Nucci, 2016).

Kohlberg's Theory of Moral Reasoning

As we noted in Chapter 13 (pp. 447–450), the study of moral development has been greatly influenced by Lawrence Kohlberg, who proposed that moral reasoning may progress across three broad levels, each consisting of two stages (Table 14.4 on page 506 summarizes these levels and stages). As they develop from one stage to the next, children make more-complex analyses both of moral obligations among individuals and of moral obligations between individuals and their social groups.

Recall that, according to Kohlberg, at the start of middle childhood, moral reasoning is at the *preconventional level* (stages 1 and 2), with children judging the

TABLE 14.4 Kohlberg's Six Moral Stages

Level and Stage	Doing Right	Doing Right: Reasons	Social Perspective
Preconventional Level I			
Stage 1—Heteronomous morality	• Conform to rules. • Obey for the sake of obedience. • Avoid causing physical harm to objects or people.	• Avoid punishment. • Follow the power of higher authority.	Egocentric point of view
Stage 2—Instrumental morality	• Follow rules when in your best interest to do so. • Act to serve your own interests and needs and allow others to do the same. • Be fair, seen as an equal exchange.	• Allow yourself and others to achieve interests and fulfill desires.	Concrete individualistic perspective: right is relative, an equal exchange
Conventional Level II			
Stage 3—Good-child morality	• Live up to expectations of those who are close to you. • Have good intentions and concern for others. • Show trust, loyalty, respect, and gratitude—all fundamental to mutual relationships.	• Be a good person according to your own and others' standards. • Care for others. • Believe in the Golden Rule. • Desire to maintain rules that enforce good behavior.	Perspective of the individual: sharing feelings, agreements, and expectations with others
Stage 4—Law-and-order morality	• Uphold the law.	• Keep the community viable.	Perspective of an individual in relationship to the social group: takes the point of view of the system that defines roles and rules
Postconventional, or Principled, Level III			
Stage 5—Social-contract reasoning	• Be aware that people hold a variety of values and opinions, most of which are relative to the group that holds them. • Understand rules as a social contract, upheld in order to be impartial. • Let universal values and rights, such as life and freedom, take precedence over the majority opinion.	• Have a sense of obligation to the law because of a social contract to make and abide by laws for the welfare of all and for the protection of all people's rights. • Implement a freely chosen commitment to a contract, which results in feelings of obligation to others and your relationships with them. • Believe that laws and duties should be based on reasons of overall utility, "the greatest good for the greatest number."	Prior-to-society perspective: perspective of a rational individual aware of values and rights prior to social attachments and contracts
Stage 6—Universal ethical principles	• Choose to follow universal principles of justice: human rights, equality, and respect for the dignity of each individual. • Evaluate laws or social agreements according to how well they exemplify such principles. • Let principles take priority over laws.	• Believe in the validity of universal moral principles. • Act with a sense of personal commitment to those principles.	Perspective of a moral point of view from which social arrangements derive: understanding that rational individuals recognize the moral nature of actions, and that all individuals must be treated with equality, respect, and dignity

Information from Kohlberg, 1976.

rightness or wrongness of actions purely in light of their own wants and fears. Toward the end of middle childhood, children attain the first stage of the *conventional level*, stage 3, in which they begin to make moral judgments in terms of their relationships with others, taking into account shared feelings, expectations, agreements, and standards of right and wrong, especially those shared with people whom they are close to (see Chapter 13, p. 451). Kohlberg called stage 3 reasoning "good-child morality" because he believed that for individuals in this stage, being moral means living up to the expectations of one's family and other significant people in one's life.

In adolescence, moral reasoning at stage 4, the second stage of the conventional level, begins to appear, although stage 3 remains the dominant mode of moral reasoning until people reach their mid-20s (Figure 14.8; Colby, Kohlberg, Gibbs, & Lieberman, 1983). Reasoning at stage 4 is like that at stage 3 except that its focus—the social perspective from which judgments are made—shifts from relationships between individuals to relationships between the individual and the larger society. People who reason at stage 4 believe that society has legitimate authority over individuals, and they feel an obligation to accept its laws, customs, and standards of decent behavior. Moral behavior from this point of view is behavior that upholds the law, maintains the social order, and contributes to the group. For this reason, stage 4 reasoning is also called "law-and-order morality" (Brown & Herrnstein, 1975, p. 289).

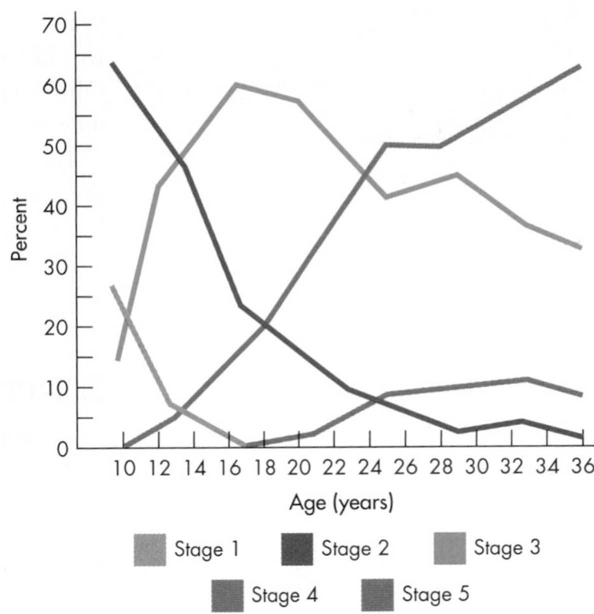

FIGURE 14.8 Mean percentage of U.S. citizens at each of Kohlberg's stages of moral reasoning at different ages. (Data from Colby et al., 1983.)

Kohlberg believed that moral thinking at stages 3 and 4 depends on a partial ability to engage in formal-operational reasoning; specifically, it requires the ability to consider simultaneously the various existing factors relevant to moral choices (Kohlberg, 1984). People who are reasoning at stages 3 and 4, however, are still reasoning concretely insofar as they do not yet simultaneously consider all possible relevant factors or form abstract hypotheses about what is moral.

With the transition from stage 4 to stage 5 comes another basic shift in the level of moral judgment. Reasoning at the *postconventional* (or *principled*) level requires people to go beyond existing social conventions to consider more abstract principles of right and wrong. Reasoning at stage 5, called *social contract reasoning*, is based on the idea of a society as bound by a social contract designed and agreed upon by the group to serve the needs of its members. People still accept and value the social system, but instead of insisting on maintaining society as it is, they are open to democratic processes of change and continual exploration of possibilities for improving the existing social order. Recognizing that laws are sometimes in conflict with moral principles, they become creators as well as maintainers of laws. Kohlberg found that stage 5 moral reasoning never appears before early adulthood and then only rarely.

To reach stage 6 in Kohlberg's system, the stage of *universal ethical principles*, the individual must make moral judgments in accordance with ethical principles that he or she believes transcend the rules of individual societies—principles of the equality of human rights and respect for the dignity of human beings as individuals. From this perspective, laws are valid only insofar as they rest on these principles. Kohlberg and his colleagues failed to observe stage 6 reasoning in their research on moral dilemmas, and Kohlberg eventually concluded that this stage is more usefully thought of as a philosophical ideal than as a psychological reality. Nonetheless, there are examples of people who have put their lives at risk because of moral beliefs guided by stage 6 reasoning. Such was the case during World War II, when many European gentiles attempted to

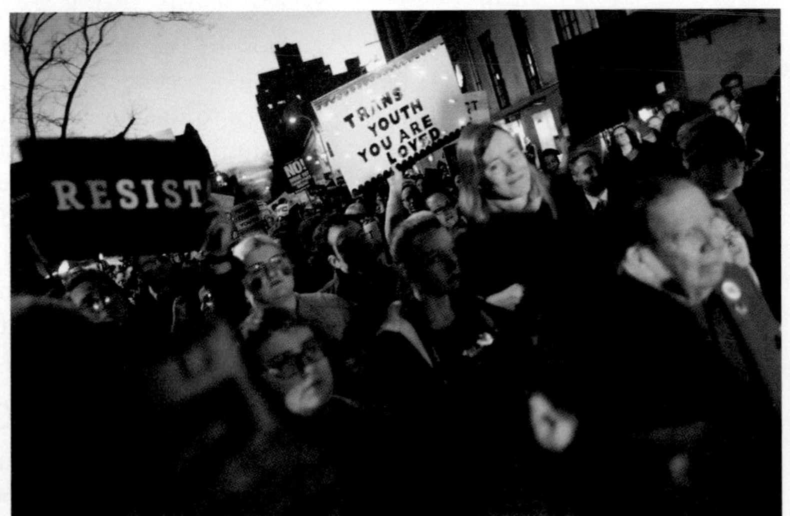

Spencer Platt/Getty Images

These protestors at the Stonewall Inn in New York City—a historical LGBTQ site—are protesting against the possible withdrawal of transgender protections.

protect Jews from the Nazi efforts to exterminate them, even though being caught would have resulted in their own execution. According to Samuel Oliner and Pearl Oliner (1988), most of these individuals were motivated by ethical principles that they believed apply to all of humanity, the hallmark of stage 6 moral reasoning.

By and large, research confirms that children and adolescents progress through the sequence of moral reasoning proposed by Kohlberg (Rest, Narvaez, Bebeau, & Thoma, 1999). However, Kohlberg's approach is not without its difficulties (Moshman, 2011; Turiel, 2002). Three important critiques address specific limitations associated with Kohlberg's theory.

Gilligan's Theory of Moral Reasoning

Since her car accident, Tara had been in a persistent vegetative state, kept alive by sophisticated medical machinery. Her case became headline news in Canada when doctors refused the request of Tara's family to disconnect her life-support system and allow Tara to die. Emotionally charged arguments emerged on both sides of the issue as the case went to court. Some insisted that acceding to the family's request would violate Tara's right to life; others insisted that failing to do so would violate her right to die with dignity. At one point in the hotly debated and highly publicized drama, the press interviewed Tara's older sister, Kim. "Everyone is talking about rights—the right to life; the right to die. It's become a big legal thing," said Kim. "But this isn't about rights at all. It's about my sister, and about our family, and how we take care of each other. I wish people could see that, and feel some compassion for what we're going through."

morality of justice A morality that emphasizes issues of rightness, fairness, and equality.

morality of care A morality that stresses relationships, compassion, and social obligations.

One of the most strident criticisms of Kohlberg's theory is that its conception of the nature of morality is too narrow. Taking a different approach to moral reasoning, Carol Gilligan (1982) asserted that Kohlberg's theory reflects a **morality of justice**—that is, a morality that emphasizes issues of rightness, fairness, and equality. As Kim illustrated in her comments to the press, the debate regarding her sister's right to life or right to die with dignity reflects a morality of justice orientation. However, from Gilligan's perspective on moral development, Kohlberg's emphasis on justice neglects a key dimension of moral reasoning and action that Gilligan termed the **morality of care**. This second dimension focuses on relationships, compassion, and social obligations—just the sort of issues that Kim said were being overlooked in the case of her sister.

Gilligan's work inspired a great deal of debate not because of her conception of a morality of care but because of her claim, based on largely anecdotal evidence, that there is a gender difference in moral orientation, with girls and women being oriented to the morality of care and boys and men being oriented toward the morality of justice (Moshman, 2011). More systematic research, including a meta-analysis of 180 studies, has found few gender differences in moral reasoning (Jaffe & Hyde, 2000; Weisz & Black, 2003). Despite the lack of evidence for strong gender differences, Gilligan's conception of a morality of care provides a broader, more inclusive view of moral reasoning than Kohlberg's original formulation and has helped orient researchers to the broader contexts of moral development and judgment (Held, 2014).

Parent and Peer Contributions to Moral Development

Kohlberg maintained that parents have a minimal role in the moral development of their children and that peer interactions are essential to promoting moral growth (Walker, Hennig, & Krettenauer, 2000). This is due, he argued, to the differences in power inherent in the two types of relationships. Because children are under the unilateral authority of their parents, they are not inclined to try to understand their parents' point of view when it differs from their own or to negotiate and compromise on issues of disagreement.

Recently, however, developmentalists have challenged Kohlberg's idea that parents have little impact in the moral realm (Augustine & Stifter, 2015; Carlo et al., 2011). Research finds that authoritative, democratic, responsive parenting is generally associated with higher levels of moral maturity in children. For instance, adolescents whose parents express disappointment—as opposed to love, withdrawal, or power assertion in response to their children's misbehavior—are more likely to describe themselves in terms of moral dimensions ("I am a kind person" or "I am a fair person") rather than in non-moral terms ("I am smart" or "I am athletic"; Patrick & Gibbs, 2012).

Research also finds that peers can impact teens' moral reasoning. In one study, young adolescent best friends were videotaped as they discussed social dilemmas, such as whether to tell on a friend who had done something wrong or dangerous (McDonald, Malti, Killen, & Rubin, 2014). Best friends who reported that they were able to constructively resolve their own conflicts also engaged in more moral reasoning in discussing the social dilemmas. The upshot of this research is that both parent and peer relationships were highly influential in moral development and reasoning, but each type of relationship contributes in distinctive ways.

Cultural Variations in Moral Reasoning

Like studies showing cross-cultural variability in formal-operational reasoning, studies using Kohlbergian dilemmas (such as the Heinz dilemma) reveal significant differences between cultural groups in moral reasoning (Sachdeva, Singh, & Medin, 2011; Turiel, 2008b). Although there are some exceptions (Shweder, Mahapatpa, & Miller, 1987), most studies show that people who live in relatively small, technologically unsophisticated communities have primarily face-to-face interactions with others and have not received extensive schooling that exposes them to ways of life other than their own rarely reason beyond stage 3 on Kohlberg's scale (Figure 14.9). Furthermore, social relationships in these communities may be strongly hierarchical in nature throughout life, providing little opportunity for the sort of equality of power that Kohlberg argued is essential to moral development (Eberhardt, 2014).

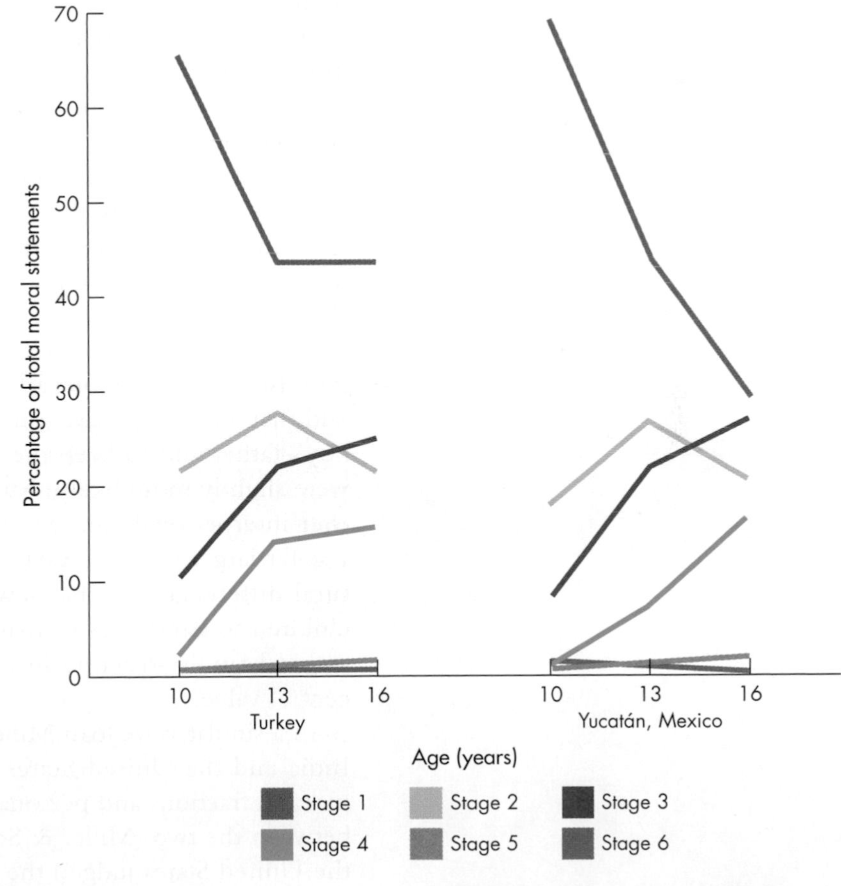

FIGURE 14.9 This figure reflects trends in the moral judgments of boys in small, isolated villages in two nations. Note the continuing high incidence of stage 1 responses even by 16-year-olds. (Data from Kohlberg, 1969.)

Kohlberg suggested that cultural differences in social stimulation produce differences in moral reasoning. However, several developmentalists have argued that Kohlberg's stage sequence, particularly in the higher stages, contains built-in value judgments that reflect the moral views of Western culture and democracy. Are we really to believe, such critics ask, that people who grow up in a traditional village in a developing country and reason at stage 2 of Kohlberg's sequence are less moral than the residents of a city in a more developed country (Shweder, Minow, & Markus, 2002)?

Kohlberg (1984) denied that cultural differences in performance on his dilemmas lead to the conclusion that some societies are more moral than others. He echoed the classical position of modern anthropology that cultures should be thought of as unique configurations of beliefs and institutions that help the social group adapt to both local conditions and universal aspects of life (Eberhardt, 2014). In this view, a culture in which stage 3 is the height of moral reasoning would be considered "morally equivalent" to a culture in which some people reason at stage 5 or 6, even though the specific reasoning practices could be scored as less "developed" according to Kohlberg's criteria.

Nevertheless, other approaches to moral reasoning have produced results that depart markedly from those obtained using Kohlberg's methods. Cross-cultural studies have reported that by adulthood, a shift from conventional to postconventional moral reasoning is quite widespread if not universal (Gielen & Markoulis, 2001). For example, using their *social domain theory*, which emphasizes the need to separate moral issues from issues involving social convention and personal choice (see Chapter 13, pp. 451–452), Elliot Turiel and his colleagues also provide evidence that the pattern of development for moral reasoning, defined in terms of justice and rights, is universal across cultures. The areas in which cultural differences *do* appear tend to be those related to social conventions and personal choice, the importance of obedience to authority, and the nature of interpersonal relationships (Turiel, 2002; Wainryb, 1995).

An extensive study by Cecilia Wainryb provides an excellent example of how moral reasoning is culturally universal while reasoning in other social domains is culturally specific. Wainryb compared judgments about social conflicts given by a large sample of Israeli 9- to 17-year-olds. Half the participants were Jews from a secular, Westernized part of the Israeli population. The other half were from Druze Arabic villages, where the cultural norms emphasize hierarchical family structures, fixed social roles, and severe punishment for violating traditional duties and customs. The study pitted questions about justice and personal choice against questions about authority and interpersonal considerations.

Wainryb found no cultural or age differences in response to questions involving justice. For example, an overwhelming percentage of participants at all ages said that a boy who saw someone lose money should return it, even though the boy's father said to keep the money—a conflict with authority. Jewish children were slightly more likely than Druze children to choose personal considerations over interpersonal considerations, but the variability within each cultural group was far larger than the variation between them. The only really significant cultural difference was that Jewish children were much more likely than Druze children to assert personal rights over authority—a result in line with the hierarchical family structure in Druze culture, in which obedience to authority is a central value.

In a similar vein, Joan Miller and her colleagues found that while people from India and the United States may differ in where they draw the line between moral infractions and personal conventions, members of both groups distinguish between the two (Miller & Schaberg, 2003). For example, people from India and the United States judged the violation of dress codes in terms of social conventions, not moral issues; and members of both societies judged theft to be a moral issue, not a matter of social convention. These studies suggest that by dividing up questions of morality into separate domains, it is possible to obtain a subtler picture of cultural influences on moral reasoning in which there are both universal and culture-specific elements.

The Relationship Between Moral Reasoning and Moral Action

At some points in your life, you have probably acted in ways that violated your moral principles; you may have lied to your parents, cheated on an exam, betrayed a friend's confidence, or stolen someone's property. In adolescence (as in childhood; see Chapter 13, pp. 446–451), the links between moral reasoning and moral action are not particularly close, prompting developmentalists to examine factors that contribute to the variability in moral behavior—that is, why young people sometimes make moral choices in accordance with their moral principles and sometimes do not (Nucci, 2016).

In some cases, societal standards and expectations contribute to variability in moral behavior. For example, studies of cheating among U.S. school students generally find that it is widespread and is heavily influenced by school norms and the attitudes of teachers and friends (Galloway, 2012; Lucifora & Tonello, 2015). High school students seem to be less guilt-stricken than college students and more apt to blame others—schools, teachers, and society—for their dishonesty (Anderman & Murdock, 2007). As a participant in Donald McCabe's study explained, one reason that cheating is common is because there is no threat of being caught:

> I don't know if it's just our school, but like everybody cheats. . . . And the teachers don't care. . . . The students keep on doing it because they don't get in trouble. (McCabe, 1999, p. 683.)

snapphoto/Getty Images

According to a 2009 national survey, over one-third of adolescents admitted to having used their cell phone to cheat on tests and about one-quarter of those surveyed didn't think there was anything wrong in such behavior.

However, even in the absence of an obvious deterrent, some students expressed ambivalence about their behavior, suggesting that although initial cheating may result in feelings of guilt, repeated cheating becomes easier over time. However, cheating takes its toll in ways that can be easily discerned by students. One student claimed that he was at a point where "I don't know nothing. . . . If I don't cheat, I just fail" (McCabe, 1999, p. 682).

A factor that helps adolescents to act morally is their increasing ability to understand the plight of others and to reason prosocially (Carpendale, Hammond, & Lewis, 2010; Peter, Tasker, & Horn, 2016). One study found, for example, that teens were significantly less likely to engage in sexual and gender-based harassment when they believed that such behaviors caused harm to the victims; in contrast, knowing that harassment violated school policies had no impact on the likelihood of teens engaging in harassment (Peter et al., 2016). And as we will discuss in Chapter 15, moral behavior is also tied to identity issues and the degree to which individuals are motivated to lead exemplary moral lives.

Yet another way to examine the relationship between moral reasoning and behavior is to approach it from the perspective of social domain theory. In the same way that this theory has proved useful in accounting for cross-cultural variability in moral reasoning, it provides insight into the relationship between adolescents' moral reasoning and their moral actions. In particular, the behaviors that researchers (and parents, as we discuss in Chapter 15) define as "moral" may not be defined as such by adolescents. An example comes from a study of the relationship between moral reasoning and risky behavior. Tara Kuther and Ann Higgins-D'Alessandro (2000) found that, compared with adolescents who report lower levels of drugs and alcohol use, those who report higher levels are more likely to see their risky behaviors as personal decisions rather than as moral or conventional decisions. The researchers suggested that directors of drug and alcohol intervention programs take heed of this tendency and encourage youth to explore their views of the personal-choice, social convention, and moral realms and examine their behavior in light of each realm.

APPLY > CONNECT > DISCUSS

Suppose you want to facilitate moral development in juvenile delinquents participating in a counseling program. How would you go about this from a Kohlbergian perspective? How would you do this from the perspective of social domain theory? In each case, consider whether your intervention programs would be most effective if carried out with teens individually or in family or peer groups.

LEARNING OUTCOMES

Appraise influences that affect the development of people during adolescence.

Looking Ahead

Bodily changes that signal sexual maturity; wholly new ways of thinking, deciding, and processing information; a new sense of what constitutes morally appropriate behavior—all of these are significant changes that are part of the transitions of adolescence. But however private and personal these changes may be, the expectations, technologies, and institutions of an adolescent's culture provide maps for the journey toward maturity. In the following chapter, we explore the social and emotional developments that interweave with the physical and cognitive changes we have been examining.

Based on your reading of this chapter, what are some of adolescents' most critical needs for healthy development and well-being—from parents and society?

SUMMARY

- Adolescence is characterized by remarkable changes in physical and intellectual development, presenting challenges whose specifics depend on the particular society.

Adolescents and Society

- Virtually all societies recognize adolescence as an important transition requiring special attention. In philosophy and literature through the ages, adolescence has been seen as a period of unique peril and promise.
- Industrialization led to increased attention to adolescence because it led to urban youth problems and to a need for a more educated workforce.
- Prolonged education and delayed marriage and childbearing are common in many contemporary societies. Consequences for young people include increasing reliance on parents for support, an extended period of identity exploration, and feelings of being unprepared for the roles and responsibilities of adulthood.

The Emergence of a Scientific Approach

- G. Stanley Hall saw adolescence as a time of "storm and stress" and as evolutionarily corresponding to a period beyond the biologically predetermined past, with adolescents thus representing the future of the species.
- Sigmund Freud saw adolescence as the beginning of the genital stage of psychosexual development and its main task as reestablishing the balance among the id, ego, and superego that was upset by the upsurge of sexual excitation at puberty.
- Margaret Mead viewed the experience of adolescence as embedded in cultural contexts, with discontinuous societies provoking higher levels of stress compared to continuous societies.
- Modern biological approaches focus on evolutionary implications of such aspects as delayed maturation followed by the growth spurt at puberty, an evolutionarily advantageous pattern that is unique to humans.

Puberty

- Puberty refers to the biological developments that lead to physical maturity and the capacity for reproduction.
- The growth spurt is one of the first signs of puberty.
- In girls, the development of primary sex characteristics, or reproductive organs, includes the maturation of the ovaries, which leads to ovulation, typically beginning after menarche, the first menstrual period. In boys, it includes the maturation of the testes, which leads to sperm production and to semenarche, the first ejaculation. Development of secondary sex characteristics, beginning with breast buds in girls and pubic hair in both sexes, provides evidence that puberty is under way.

- Significant brain developments in adolescence include changes to the cortex and limbic system. The cortex, especially the prefrontal cortex, which is associated with higher forms of reasoning and decision making, undergoes a period of rapid synaptic growth and pruning. The limbic system, associated with the experience and interpretation of emotions, undergoes a period of myelination and synaptic pruning, and the associated reward system becomes hyperactivated.
- The timing of puberty, earlier for girls than for boys, varies widely as a result of complex interactions between genetic and environmental factors. Caloric intake may be among the crucial environmental factors, as a certain level of body fat may be required for the onset of puberty; thus, nutritional improvements may have led to the secular trend of decline over the decades in the average age of puberty. However, "overnutrition"—that is, diets excessively high in calories, has been identified as a source of recent trends toward earlier pubertal onset in many developed and developing countries. Changing circadian phase affects the adolescent's sleep–wake cycle and conflicts with the typical schedule of most schools.
- Although adolescence is generally a time of good health, its astronomical growth rates place new demands on the body, creating special needs for nutrition, sleep, and physical activity—needs that all too often are not fully met.
- Puberty has profound social and psychological consequences, which are influenced by cultural beliefs and values. For cultural reasons, puberty may tend to be more psychologically difficult for girls than for boys, especially if its timing is early rather than on time or late.

Cognitive Development

- According to Piaget, adolescence is marked by the emergence of a capacity for formal-operational thinking, for relating sets of relationships to each other. Formal-operational thinkers can reason by systematically manipulating variables and can use hypothetical-deductive reasoning, judging an argument based on logical form alone.
- Multitasking interferes with attention processes and reduces performance on academically relevant tasks.
- Epistemic development, involving how individuals reason about the nature of truth and knowledge, takes different forms during adolescence: the objectivist theory of knowledge, the subjectivist theory of knowledge, and the evaluativist theory of knowledge.
- Information-processing approaches attribute adolescents' more systematic thinking to increased capacity in working memory and to the use of more powerful problem-solving strategies.
- Sociocultural approaches demonstrate the role of social interactions in scaffolding the development of adolescent thinking.

Moral Development

- According to Lawrence Kohlberg, moral reasoning at stage 4 ("law-and-order morality") appears during adolescence, although reasoning at stage 3 ("good-child morality") remains more typical. Kohlberg believed that postconventional reasoning (based on principles) is relatively rare.
- Carol Gilligan argued that Kohlberg had emphasized a morality of justice at the expense of a morality of care.
- Although Kohlberg's approach showed significant differences between cultures in members' moral reasoning, cross-cultural studies taking other approaches suggest that differences between cultures are few and that the shift to postconventional reasoning is widespread. Social domain theory, one such approach, shows the importance of separating issues of morality from issues of social convention and personal choice.
- Parents and peers make important but distinct contributions to adolescents' moral development.
- Adolescents' actions do not always accord with their morals, perhaps reflecting inconsistent societal standards, as well as whether adolescents perceive particular behaviors as being in the domain of morality, social convention, or personal choice. Perspective-taking and prosocial reasoning encourage moral behavior.

Looking Ahead

- Critical changes of adolescence include sexual maturity, new ways of thinking, and new ways of understanding moral development.
- Social expectations, use of technologies, and participation in cultural institutions provide roadmaps for the developing adolescent.

Key Terms

emerging adulthood, p. 480
continuous societies, p. 482
discontinuous societies, p. 482
puberty, p. 483
growth spurt, p. 483
primary sex characteristics, p. 485
secondary sex characteristics, p. 486
semenarche, p. 486
menarche, p. 486
dopamine, p. 489
reward system, p. 489
hypothalamic-pituitary-gonadal (HPG) axis, p. 489
hypothalamus, p. 490
endocrine system, p. 490
sex hormones, p. 490
leptin, p. 490
kisspeptin, p. 490
early maturation, p. 491
late maturation, p. 492
precocious puberty, p. 494
secular trend, p. 496
delayed circadian phase, p. 497
formal operations, p. 499
hypothetical-deductive reasoning, p. 501
epistemic development, p. 502
objectivist theory of knowledge, p. 502
subjectivist theory of knowledge, p. 502
evaluativist theory of knowledge, p. 502
multitasking, p. 503
morality of justice, p. 508
morality of care, p. 508

wundervisuals/Getty Images

CHAPTER

15

Social and Emotional Development in Adolescence

When 16-year-old Kimberly and her boyfriend had been together for four months, they decided together that they wanted to start having sex. "We both, just really find each other to be, like, interesting people, and, just as we progress in our relationship, it's, like, you want to touch this interesting person, and you want to see what they're like." Although Kimberly believes that her parents are aware of her sexual activity, she hides that part of her life from her parents. "I'm not completely open," she says. "Before I wanted to share everything with my parents, but I realized that doesn't really work. For them, it's just easier not to know. So, now I just do my own thing and . . . (just) let them see what makes them happy. . . . They're doing a very good job of being oblivious. . . ."

Similar to Kimberly, when 16-year-old Natalie reflects on her thoughts and feelings about having sex for the first time, she says, "I think you need to be VERY sure about him, that you know for sure that you love him; that he accepts you as you are; that you have a great time together. I was just really happy with him so. . . . It hurt, but I don't regret it in any case. It was pretty fun." According to sociologist Amy Schalet who interviewed Natalie and other teen girls about having sex for the first time, one reason Natalie's first intercourse was "pretty fun" is that Natalie had been taking birth control pills, and had no reason to fear pregnancy. Indeed, several months before she had sex with her boyfriend, she read an article about the pill in a magazine for teenage girls, and, in sharp contrast to Kimberly, showed it to her mother, saying, "I want that too." Her mother responded positively: "Sure! Go to the doctor tomorrow. Let's go together." When Natalie informed her parents that she and her boyfriend had had sex, they "weren't shocked." In fact, Natalie says that her mother "thought it was really great. She didn't mind because she knows how serious we are." Her father, for his part, simply said, "Sixteen is a beautiful age." Natalie is confident that her parents will soon allow her boyfriend to spend the night with her in her room.

(Information from Schalet, 2011.)

If Kimberly's story sounds familiar, and Natalie's sounds unusual—perhaps even shocking—then it is likely that you are from the United States, where Kimberly grew up, and not from Natalie's country, the Netherlands. In the Netherlands, parent–teen communication about contraception and romantic relationships and feelings is the norm, and parents readily acknowledge their adolescents' emerging sexuality and sexual desires. In her study comparing girls in the Netherlands to those in the United States, Schalet found that even U.S. girls from "liberal" families were highly resistant to communicating directly with parents about their sexual lives and feelings. Regarding the possibility of her

wundervisuals/Getty Images

David R. Frazier/The Image Works

Whether they grow up in California in the United States or Tierra del Fuego in Argentina, adolescents increasingly turn to each other to share ideas, feelings, and experiences.

boyfriend ever sleeping over in her bedroom, one such girl, Caroline, said, "My parents would *kill* me. No, my parents would not go for that at all." Although her mother knows that Caroline has sex and supports her contraceptive use, and really likes Caroline's boyfriend, Caroline must keep the door open when he is in her room: "They don't want to know that I'm doing it. It's kind of like, 'Oh my God, my little girl is having sex'" (Schalet, 2011, pp. 315–316).

Natalie and Caroline underscore the vast differences in the contexts in which adolescents' sexual behaviors develop and how their feelings and desires are expressed—the focus of this chapter. You will see that adolescence is, indeed, "a beautiful age" of exploring and developing as a sexual being. But it can also be a perilous one during which teens are exposed to an array of factors that place them at risk for serious physical and health problems.

In this chapter, we examine the new feelings, relationships, and ways of interacting with family and friends that are typical of adolescence and that mark a new beginning in adolescents' sense of themselves and their place in the world. Adolescence is a time of seeking answers to fundamental questions of identity: Who am I? Who will I become? What do I want? How do I fit in?

We begin our examination by exploring adolescents' emotional development, focusing on the different types of feelings that adolescents experience and how they come to express and control them. We then shift our attention to adolescents' changing relationships—with friends, romantic partners, sexual partners, and family. Our third topic is identity development and its relationship to adolescents' social lives and cultures. Finally, we consider adolescents' health and well-being, including health problems and diseases that typically emerge in adolescence, as well as approaches to positive youth development.

WARMING **UP**

1. Think back to the teens that you knew in high school. Think about someone who seemed very well adjusted and another who did poorly or struggled. What do you suppose accounted for the differences between these two people?
2. What do you think adolescents need to feel good about themselves? To what extent does society contribute to meeting these needs? What changes can society make to better meet adolescents' needs?

Emotional Development in Adolescence

LEARNING OUTCOMES

Assess the idea of adolescence as an emotional, roller-coaster experience against the research findings of developmentalists.

Summarize biological events associated with adolescents' emotion regulation, experience of intense emotions, and sensation-seeking.

Explain the place of social and cultural contexts for adolescents' expression of emotion.

Adolescence is widely regarded as a period fraught with emotional highs and lows and with behavior that is often driven by impulse rather than rational thought. We described in Chapter 14 that adolescents' reputation for emotional intensity, instability, and flaming passion was well established as early as Plato's day and noted Plato's warning that adolescents should not consume wine: "Fire must not be poured upon fire." Two thousand years later, Freud described the adolescent as a "boiling cauldron of desire." Needless to say, these images of adolescence are as vivid today as they ever have been.

In this section, we take the age-old notion of adolescence as an emotional roller-coaster ride punctuated with impulse-driven behavior and hold it up to the light of scientific analysis. Is it true that adolescents experience especially intense emotions and dramatic mood swings? If so, why, and how is emotional stability eventually achieved as adolescents mature? Is it true that adolescents' behavior is exceptionally impulsive? If it is, how can behavioral impulsivity be reconciled with the significant advances that occur in adolescents' cognitive development and reasoning? In addressing these questions, we will continue the approach we used in examining emotional development during infancy and childhood, distinguishing between how emotions are experienced and how they are controlled and regulated (see Chapters 6, 9, and 13).

The Experience of Emotions

Many believe that peaks and valleys of emotional experience are a defining feature of adolescence. However, as you know from our discussions regarding infants and children, the study of emotional experiences poses significant challenges for researchers. Consequently, it is difficult to document whether, and to what extent, adolescence is the emotional roller coaster that so many believe it to be.

The effective study of emotional development in adolescence requires research tools that provide access to adolescents' emotional lives. One such tool is the **experience sampling method (ESM)**, in which research participants receive text messages containing Web links to a survey. Depending on the particular study, the survey may ask teens to describe recent positive and negative experiences, who they are with, their physical location, and how they feel. Although the ESM is time-intensive and disruptive for participants (typically, the research participants receive text messages to fill out at least five surveys per day for a week or more), it has been praised for its *ecological validity* (see Chapter 1, p. 35) (Uink, Modecki, & Barber, 2017). It has also generated a wealth of information about the types and intensities of adolescents' emotions, the situations in which they occur, and the extent to which they are related to gender, age, pubertal status, and psychological problems (Uink et al., 2017; van Roekel et al., 2015).

experience sampling method (ESM) A tool used by developmentalists in which study participants, when signaled by text message at random intervals, fill out brief reports on their feelings. ESM has been used to study adolescents' emotional lives.

In general, ESM studies find strong evidence for the idea that emotional states change in type and intensity throughout the adolescent years. Reed Larson and his colleagues conducted a comprehensive, longitudinal study using ESM data collected from 220 participants over a period spanning early to late adolescence (Larson, Moneta, Richards, & Wilson, 2002). When the participants were signaled to complete the surveys, they rated their emotional states (happy–unhappy, cheerful–irritable, friendly–angry) on a 7-point scale. Twice a year, they also filled out questionnaires about whether they had experienced major life events, including stressful events, during the past 6 months. The researchers found that more than 70 percent of the time, the participants reported experiencing positive emotions. However, they also found some interesting changes in the participants' emotional

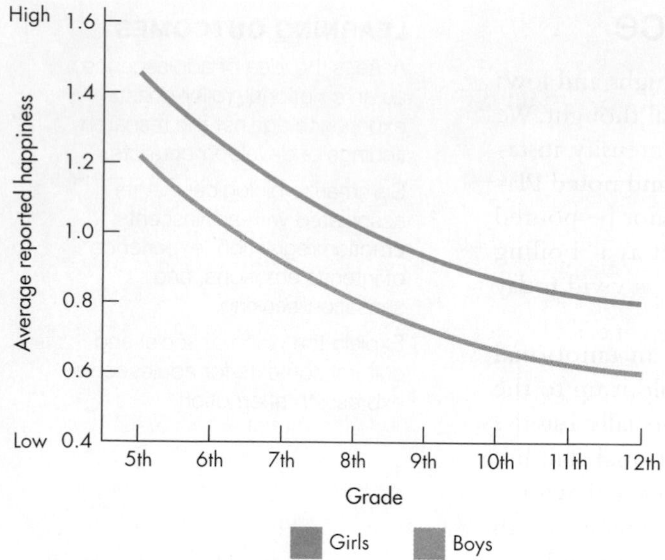

FIGURE 15.1 In general, girls report higher levels of happiness than do boys, although happiness declines for both girls and boys over the course of adolescence, as found in several countries. (Data from Larson et al., 2002; Gonzalez-Carrasco et al., 2017.)

life between early and late adolescence, several of which have been documented in teens growing up in other countries as well (Gonzalez-Carrasco et al., 2017):

- On average, daily emotions became less positive between early adolescence and middle adolescence (10th grade) and remained relatively low through late adolescence; in other words, average happiness decreased during adolescence (Figure 15.1).
- The decline in average happiness was due in part to a decrease in intense positive emotions but due mostly to an increase in negative emotions.
- Throughout adolescence, girls tended to have more positive emotions on average than boys did, as shown in Figure 15.1.
- Stressful life events were associated with equal amounts of negative emotion throughout adolescence, suggesting that there was no time during which adolescents were particularly emotionally sensitive or reactive to major life events.
- Over the course of adolescence, emotions became less intense, and emotional ups and downs became less frequent.

In general, research suggests that an emotional roller coaster may be a poor metaphor for adolescent emotional life. There does not seem to be a particular time when adolescents are hypersensitive to stressful events, and the intensity and fluctuations of emotion seem to decrease over time.

Regulating Emotions

One of the primary explanations for why emotions become less intense and more stable over the course of adolescence is that teenagers become better able to control and regulate them, as well as the behaviors they might inspire (Steinberg, 2005). When his mom complains yet again that Josh's tongue-piercing looks gross and makes him sound like he has a speech impediment, Josh may retreat to fume in his room rather than lash out in fury, "It's my @#$#% tongue, and I'll do what I want to it!" Or when Marisha's friends are heading out to party, she may stay home to study chemistry, not because she is passionate about the subject (she hates it, actually) but because she wants to do well on tomorrow's exam.

Both Josh and Marisha are acting against impulse and inhibiting certain behaviors that would very likely lead to unsatisfying consequences. In addition, Marisha is persisting on a task (studying chemistry) despite a total lack of desire to do so, and in the face of a much more attractive alternative (partying). *Impulse control*, *inhibition*, and *persistence* are among the main features of emotion regulation, and they underlie the abilities to "down regulate" negative emotions (as Josh did when he cooled his fury) and "up regulate" positive ones (as Marisha did when she mustered enthusiasm for studying). Adolescents who have difficulty regulating their emotions, especially negative emotions, are more likely to experience depression, anger, and a variety of social and behavior problems (Compas et al., 2017; Hughes, Gullone, & Watson, 2011).

As you may recall from earlier chapters, regulating emotions involves a complex interplay of biological and sociocultural processes. In adolescence, these processes interact in a unique way that has recently garnered considerable interest from developmentalists (see the box "Now Trending in Research: Neuroscience Meets Buddhist Philosophy in Mindfulness Education").

Now TRENDING in RESEARCH

Neuroscience Meets Buddhist Philosophy in Mindfulness Education

Thirteen-year-old Andrew describes a newly found ability to think about and then put aside his thoughts, in order to "see things how it is." He is able to consider his reactions to events, rather than reacting impulsively.

Eighteen-year-old Matt indicates that he is now better able to focus on relevant thoughts and filter out distractions. When his attention strays, he refocuses with special breathing exercises. He describes being "more in tune with reality," and being "brought out of" his own mind into "what's actually happening."

Eighteen-year-old Catherine notes that she's better able to be "in the moment," and identify and cope with her ADHD: "You're like, 'oh crap, being extremely ADHD right now, need to try and leave that alone,' and you can try and leave it alone."

Fifteen-year-old Tony explains that he is now able to embrace experiences more fully, appreciating them in ways he wasn't able to in the past.
(Information from Haydicky, Wiener, & Shecter, 2017.)

The lessons these students learned—about focusing their thoughts, being more in tune with reality, and embracing experiences more fully—came through their participation in a mindfulness education program designed for children diagnosed with ADHD (Haydicky et al., 2017). Mindfulness is rooted in the Buddhist practice of meditation, and increasing interest in mindfulness education aims to strengthen adolescents' emotion regulation, stress management skills, and awareness of and respect for self and others (Roeser & Zelazo, 2012).

Mindfulness includes two primary components. One component is the *self-regulation of attention*, which promotes awareness of one's thoughts, feelings, and physical experiences as they occur from one moment to the next. The second component is the *nonjudgmental awareness of experience*. When one's thoughts and feelings are experienced nonjudgmentally, instead of either avoiding or becoming overly preoccupied with them, the individual becomes more open, curious, and accepting of them (Metz et al., 2013). Mindfulness education is not intended to change, control, or analyze what one thinks or feels but to promote an awareness of one's mental and emotional states and an understanding that those states are temporary. Examples of mindful practices currently used in various educational and treatment settings include intensive meditation, small-group discussion focused on deep listening and authentic communication, yoga and other forms of mindful movement, and guided discussion regarding issues of gender, diversity, and social justice.

Developmentalists believe that mindfulness may be particularly beneficial during the period of adolescence when individuals are undergoing substantial and often stressful changes at home, in school, and with friends. Mindfulness education provides adolescents with tools to cope with and tolerate distressing thoughts and uncomfortable feelings that otherwise might provoke anxiety, self-blame, low self-esteem, and stress—all of which have been associated with mental health and adjustment problems, including poor school achievement, substance abuse, and depression. Several studies conducted with high school students have found that mindfulness education may indeed increase adolescents' emotion regulation skills, reduce stress, and promote feelings of well-being (Kuyken et al., 2013). One such study found that, compared to a control group, high school students who participated in a mindfulness education program showed significant increases in their self-reported abilities to regulate emotions, as well as declines in perceived stress and psychosomatic problems, such as headaches, poor concentration, and fatigue (Metz et al., 2013). There is mounting evidence that emotion regulation, especially the ability to regulate emotions during stressful experiences, is a critical feature of psychological health, academic success, and positive adjustment (Eisenberg, Spinrad, & Eggum, 2010). In contrast, emotion regulation difficulties have been associated with a variety of problems including anxiety, depression, self-injury, and substance abuse (Kaufman et al., 2017).

In addition to providing coping skills for dealing with the normal emotional ups and downs of adolescence, mindfulness education may also contribute to brain development by altering neural activity at a time when the brain is undergoing substantial development, particularly in areas associated with emotional regulation and attention (Lutz, Slagter, Dunne, & Davidson, 2008). Neuroscientists have discovered that mindfulness education with adults can affect the brain in ways that are associated with emotion regulation, attention, and well-being. They speculate that the practice and repetition of mindful practices during adolescence may enhance neural pathways that support the development of complex emotion regulation skills (Metz et al., 2013; Wetherill & Tapert, 2013).

Currently, mindfulness is being explored as a therapeutic treatment for teenagers dealing with a variety of physical and mental problems, including substance abuse, depression, cancer, chronic illnesses, sleep disturbances, and attention problems (Bei et al., 2013; Britton, 2010; Raes et al., 2014 Tan & Martin, 2015). Overall, the research suggests that mindful practices are beneficial to adolescent health and development. However, developmentalists point out that it is still in its infancy and recommend caution in interpreting these early, if encouraging, findings (Greenberg & Harris, 2012).

Andrew Errington/Photographer's Choice/Getty Images

The mindfulness associated with meditation may strengthen adolescents' self-regulation and stress-management skills.

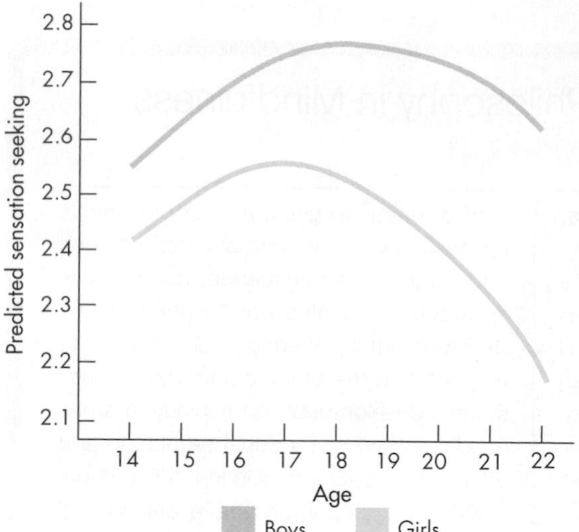

FIGURE 15.2 Adolescent males are much more likely than their female counterparts to engage in sensation-seeking behaviors. However, individuals of both genders appear particularly vulnerable to sensation-seeking within a window of time during which pubertal hormones are on the rise and maturation of the frontal lobes is incomplete. (Data from Romer & Hennessy, 2007.)

sensation-seeking The desire to participate in highly arousing activities; it is especially common in early and mid-adolescence.

Biological Processes As discussed in Chapter 14, adolescence includes several significant biological events that are associated with the experience and regulation of emotions. There is, for instance, an influx of pubertal hormones during early adolescence. There are also several significant changes to the brain. In particular, synaptic changes affect the cortex (the "thinking brain"), and the limbic system (the "emotion brain"). In addition, the reward system (a component of the limbic system) becomes "hyper-activated." Several studies suggest that pubertal hormones are associated with emotional intensity and may account for adolescents' **sensation-seeking**, or desire to participate in highly arousing activities (Icenogle et al., 2017; Figure 15.2). In Chapter 14, we noted that novelty-seeking (sensation-seeking) seems to be a common feature in adolescents in many mammalian species, and this fact has led some developmentalists to argue that it may play an instrumental role in encouraging youth to leave their families to join with peers for the purpose of exploring new territory and selecting mates (Spear, 2007, 2009). The infusion of hormones occurs at a time when the brain is undergoing considerable development, especially in regions of the frontal lobes associated with higher mental processes such as decision making, judgment, and impulse control (see p. 487). Some developmentalists, including Laurence Steinberg, have speculated that in early adolescence, there is a gap between intense emotions triggered by pubertal hormones and the brain's ability to regulate those emotions (Figure 15.3). As a consequence, until the maturation of the frontal lobes is complete, an adolescent is especially vulnerable to risk-taking, recklessness, and emotional problems (Crone, Duijvenvoorde, & Peper, 2016).

Social Processes While biological processes may very well influence the maturity of adolescents' emotional responses, most developmentalists agree that the ways adolescents regulate their emotions depend importantly on the social and cultural contexts in which the adolescents develop. In particular, they depend on family interaction patterns and on social expectations regarding the expression of emotion.

Families play a critical role in how adolescents learn to manage their feelings. In a longitudinal study that followed children from 9 to 13 years of age, Nancy Eisenberg and her colleagues explored the relationships between the emotional quality of parent–child interactions, adolescents' abilities to regulate their emotions, and adolescents' behavioral problems such as aggression (Eisenberg et al., 2005). The longitudinal design allowed the researchers to discover an interesting pattern: Parents' emotional warmth and expression of positive emotions during their children's mid-elementary school years (when the children were about 9 years old) predicted higher levels of children's emotion regulation 2 years later (early adolescence), which in turn predicted fewer behavioral problems 2 years after that (middle adolescence).

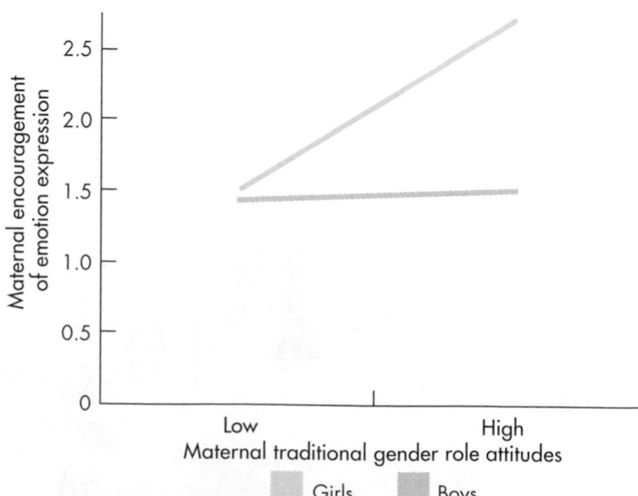

FIGURE 15.3 Mothers who tend to endorse traditional gender roles are significantly more likely to encourage the expression of emotions in daughters than in sons. (Data from Cox, Mezulis, & Hyde, 2010.)

In addition to examining the role of family, developmentalists have explored how adolescents' gender affects their regulation of emotion. It is widely believed that males and females are socialized to manage their emotional expressions in vastly different ways. In particular, girls and women are considered to be "more emotional" than boys and men—that is, they are believed to experience emotions more intensely and to communicate them more willingly, presumably due to social conventions and cultural expectations that represent females as emotionally nurturing and expressive and males as independent and self-reliant.

Evidence that gender differences in the expression of depressed emotions may be related to gender-role socialization comes from an observational home study in which adolescents and their mothers were videotaped as the adolescents took a math test that the researchers had designed and put on a computer (Cox, Mezulis, & Hyde, 2010). The adolescents first went through sets of practice problems, which had been designed to be within their abilities. Then came the test, which had been designed to ensure failure. After the test had been completed and the computer had revealed the test-taker's low score, the adolescents and their mothers discussed the test and the adolescents' disappointing performance. The researchers found that mothers of boys were less likely than mothers of girls to encourage their children's expression of negative emotion. This was particularly true for mothers who scored high on a test of how much they adhered to traditional gender roles, as measured by items such as "I would not allow my son to play with dolls" and "Men who cry have weak character" (p. 846; see Figure 15.3).

Kaz Chiba/Getty Images

The extent to which boys and girls differ in the expression of emotions depends importantly on their culture's conceptions of what is appropriate behavior for males and females. In some Asian cultures, it is considered impolite for girls to laugh without covering their mouths. The same convention does not apply to boys.

Altogether, research provides ample evidence that the experience and regulation of emotions undergo substantial change over the course of adolescence and are influenced by both biological and sociocultural factors. These changes have important implications for adolescents' relationships with peers, family, and sexual partners, topics that we address below.

APPLY > CONNECT > DISCUSS

In general, girls are considered "more emotional" than boys. Evaluate this belief in light of research on gender differences in emotional experience and emotion regulation.

Relationships with Peers

LEARNING OUTCOMES

- Explain the role of social reorientation in adolescents' experience with friends and peers.
- Describe the important qualities of friendships for adolescent boys and for adolescent girls.
- Explain how digital media influences intimacy and interactions among adolescents.
- Describe adolescent peer relationships related to cliques and crowds, as well as antisocial behavior.
- Outline romantic relationships according to the findings of Dexter Dunphy.

As we discussed in Chapter 13, one of the most significant changes associated with middle childhood and adolescence is *social reorientation*—that is, an expansion of the child's social focus from family to the broader contexts of friends and peers. Even for children who get along well with their parents, their social activities and relationships with peers undergo several major changes. First, the sheer amount of time spent with peers increases dramatically. Second, compared with younger children, adolescents are more mobile and better able to avoid the watchful eyes of parents and other authorities, so their peer activities are more likely to go unsupervised. As you will see, not only does the amount of time spent with peers change but so, too, does the nature of peer interactions and relationships. Peer groups increase in size and diversity during adolescence, and friendships and other close relationships increase in intensity. When exploring the nature of these changes and the implications they have for other areas of adolescent growth and adjustment, developmentalists tend to distinguish between adolescents' *close relationships* with friends and romantic partners and their *peer networks*—that is, their connections to groups of teens that may include casual acquaintances as well as good friends. As we discuss below, each type of relationship has different functions and fulfills different needs in adolescents' social and emotional development.

Friendships

In general, a **friendship** refers to a close relationship between two individuals. As you saw in previous chapters, the friendships of young children are often based on such shifting and transitory factors as playing with the same toys or being on the

friendship A close relationship between two individuals. Friendships in adolescence are characterized by reciprocity, commitment, and equality.

same sports team. Several large-scale studies conducted in the United States and other developed countries document the changing basis of friendships as children enter adolescence (Berndt, 2007; De Goede, Branje, & Meeus, 2009; Schneider, Woodburn, del Pilar Soteras del Toro, & Udvari, 2005). In contrast to the apparently superficial characteristics that bind younger children together, the characteristics that adolescents see as fundamental to their friendships are reciprocity, commitment, and equality (Hartup, 1998; Larsen, 1996). *Reciprocity*, the give-and-take of close relationships, includes emotional sharing as well as the sharing of interests and activities; *commitment* refers to the loyalty and trust between friends; and *equality* refers to the equal distribution of power among them.

Developmental Functions of Friendships The dyadic friendships of adolescence serve two significant developmental functions: intimacy and autonomy—the yin and yang of social life (Selman, Levitt, & Schultz, 1997). If you were asked which of the two is more salient in friendship, you would likely say **intimacy**, which, as defined by Selman and colleagues, is "the gratifying connection between two individuals through some combination of shared feelings, thoughts, and activities" (p. 32). However, as Selman and his colleagues have demonstrated in numerous studies of normally developing and psychosocially troubled children and adolescents, in healthy relationships, intimacy is balanced with **autonomy**—the ability to govern the self and assert one's own needs. Indeed, unhealthy friendships can place a child at significant risk, depending on whether the scales tip more toward intimacy or autonomy. Selman and his colleagues point out, for example, that the inability to assert one's needs without jeopardizing friendship intimacy contributes to a child's willingness to bow to peer pressure. On the other hand, an excess of autonomy can also be problematic—for example, bullying one's peers into risky behaviors.

intimacy A sense of close connection between two individuals, resulting from shared feelings, thoughts, and activities.

autonomy The ability to assert one's own needs in a relationship.

Evidence from various studies indicates that close, well-balanced friendships have a positive influence on adolescents' social and personality development (Eccles, Brown, & Templeton, 2008; Allen, Chango, & Szwedo, 2014). Adolescents who perceive their friends as supportive report fewer school-related and psychological problems, greater confidence in social acceptance by their peers, and less loneliness. Difficulty in making friends during adolescence is usually part of a broader syndrome of poor social adjustment often first apparent in early childhood (Pedersen, Vitaro, Barker, & Borge, 2007).

Friendships and Gender While friends are important to both boys and girls during adolescence, there are differences in the quality of boys' and girls' friendships. In particular, research finds that girls' friendships are more intense and intimate (Radmacher & Azmitia, 2006; Rose et al., 2012; Rose & Asher, 2017). Several explanations have been offered. According to one, male adolescent friendships are less intimate because, compared with teenage girls, teenage boys are less trusting of their friends, perhaps worried that intimacy is not "tough" or masculine (Kirby & Kirby, 2017). Consequently, boys may be less likely than girls to share the emotional details of their lives with their friends (Berndt & Murphy, 2002; Rubin, Bukowski, & Laursen, 2009). Indeed, a study of Indian and English adolescents indicated that boys in both cultures tend to share more superficial aspects of emotionally charged experiences with friends, whereas girls are more likely to share their feelings (Singh-Manoux, 2000). Consider, for example, 13-year-old Michael's description of how boys discuss sex and sexual arousal "more openly" than girls:

> I think guys can speak about it [sex] more openly with each other from what I've seen from the girls in my school. . . . We talk about girls and wet dreams. . . . With guys you can just say, "Oh, I saw this really good-looking chick on TV and I cracked a boner." (Martino & Pallotta-Chiarolli, 2003, p. 65.)

Although Michael describes boys as more open with each other regarding these highly sensitive subjects, his language suggests that humor may be used to diffuse the emotional intensity of shared events. Indeed, Michael goes on to suggest that his friends keep some of their most deeply significant emotional experiences to themselves:

> [But] I've got a friend of mine whose mom died a few years ago and he never brought it up in school and even now he rarely talks about it. I've got another friend of mine whose dad is in the hospital with a disease and he never talks about that. (Martino & Pallotta-Chiarolli, 2003, p. 65.)

Yet another explanation proposed for why the friendships of boys are less intimate than those of girls is that **homophobia**—a fear of homosexuality—prevents adolescent males from demonstrating or admitting to strong feelings of intimacy toward their male friends. Homophobia, often expressed in the form of name-calling, is remarkably common in schools, with some studies finding that students hear words like "fag," "dyke," and "homo" nearly every day (Kosciw & Diaz, 2008). Research finds that homophobic name-calling is significantly more common in adolescent boys compared to girls, is more common in some peer groups compared to others (evidence of peer socialization effects), and is strongly associated with traditional attitudes toward masculinity—for example, agreeing with the statement "It's important for a boy to act like nothing is wrong, even when something is bothering him" (Birkett & Espelage, 2015).

homophobia A fear of homosexuality. Homophobia may diminish intimacy among adolescent males.

The possibility that adolescent boys may be fearful of the perceived link between intimacy and homosexuality is also apparent in the use of phrases like "no homo" when discussing closeness in their friendships (Way, 2013). In an interview focused on friendships among male high school students of multiple ethnicities, common phrases included, "we're close, no homo. We talk, no homo" (Way, 2013, p. 205). The use of the phrase "no homo" is especially interesting in light of the teens' reported desire for intimacy with other boys and their feelings of sadness and loss at the fact that their closest friends had become distant over time. When asked to describe how his friendships had changed during high school, one junior responded that he had no best friend anymore: "I feel pretty lonely and sometimes depressed... because I don't have no one to out with, no one to speak on the phone, no one to tell my secrets, or to help me solve my problems" (Way, 2013, p. 205). According to the researcher, the junior's sense of the fading connection with his close friends was echoed broadly by the other boys who participated in the study.

Another threat to adolescents' friendship intimacy—one that may affect both boys and girls—is digital media.

Digital Media: A Threat to Intimacy?

The vast world of cyberspace—text messaging, Facebook, Instagram, Twitter, Tumblr, Snapchat, and other electronic social media—has created an entirely new context for peer interactions. Developmentalists as well as parents have wondered whether teens' extensive use of social media impacts peer relationships and social skills. Although some are concerned that digital media may replace face-to-face interactions with friends and peers and may contribute to social isolation, research suggests a more complicated picture (Alloway, Horton, Alloway, & Dawson, 2013; Valkenburg & Peter, 2013). Studies conducted with teenagers in several countries indicate that adolescents typically use social media to communicate with existing friends rather than to replace face-to-face interactions and that social media use is associated with greater intimacy with friends and peers. For instance, a survey conducted with Dutch youth found that those who used the Internet primarily to communicate with friends reported higher levels of closeness with peers compared to those who used social media less frequently (Valkenburg & Peter, 2008). And research conducted with high school students in the United Kingdom found that teens who frequently used Facebook reported higher levels of social connection than those who used a less socially engaging form of electronic media, such as YouTube (Alloway et al., 2013). Similarly, a longitudinal study of Canadian high school students found that online communication with existing friends and romantic partners was associated with an improvement of relationships over the course of a year. On the other hand, teens' satisfaction with romantic and sexual partners was greater when the relationship was initiated offline than online (Blunt-Vinti et al., 2016).

With evidence suggesting that active involvement in social media—posting comments on friends' sites, writing on their walls, "liking" photos, and so on—may actually increase feelings of social connection and intimacy, a natural question is whether social media may benefit teens who are shy or uncomfortable in face-to-face social contexts. Indeed, one study found that although teens who reported being anxious in social settings were less likely than their more socially comfortable counterparts to use the Internet, when these socially anxious adolescents did make use of electronic media, they felt that it expanded their opportunities to communicate with peers in ways that were less anxiety provoking than face-to-face interaction (Valkenburg & Peter, 2008).

clique A group of several young people that remains small enough to enable its members to be in regular interaction with one another and to serve as the primary peer group.

Adolescent Peer Group Life and Culture

Spend time on a playground or on an overnight camping trip with Boy Scouts or Girl Scouts, and you'll see plenty of evidence of children's culture: jump-rope and handclapping games, ghost stories, rude jokes, pranks, and other childish, occasionally naughty behavior. They learn their special behavior from each other—not from adults—and pass these cultural practices on to other children. But as children move into middle adolescence, peer culture becomes considerably more diverse. This diversity begins with the development of two kinds of peer groups that gain prominence in adolescence: *cliques* and *crowds*. Adolescent cliques and crowds are significant social groups in societies that group children by age, usually for the purpose of education. In such societies, adolescents spend a lot of time with each other and consequently learn to establish and maintain relationships with groups of peers. Cliques and crowds differ in size as well as in the developmental functions they serve (Figure 15.4).

Late Adolescence
Stage 5: Beginning of crowd disintegration. Loosely associated groups of couples.
Stage 4: The fully developed crowd. Heterosexual cliques in close association.
Stage 3: The crowd in structural transition. Unisexual cliques with upper status members forming a heterosexual clique.
Stage 2: The beginning of the crowd. Unisexual cliques in group-to-group interaction.
Stage 1: Pre-crowd stage. Isolated unisexual cliques.
Early Adolescence
Boys
Girls
Boys and girls

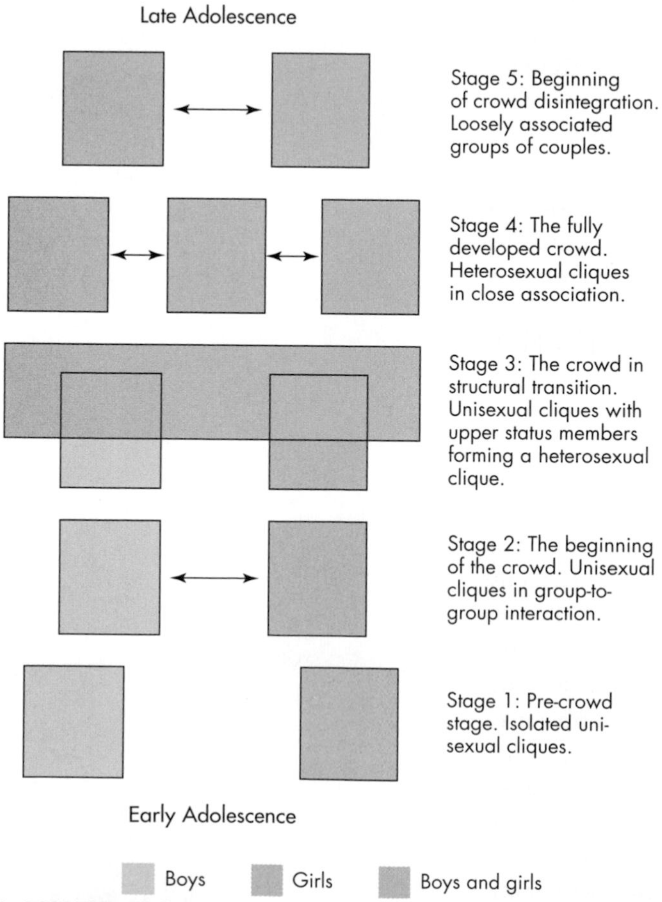

FIGURE 15.4 Stages of adolescents' social relationships from early to late adolescence, according to Dexter Dunphy.

In general, **cliques** are small and intimate and have the function of serving adolescents' emotional and security needs (Pattiselanno et al., 2015). A clique typically includes five to seven members who are relatively good friends. Dexter Dunphy (1963), one of the first researchers to study cliques and crowds, noted that cliques are about the size of a family and serve a similar emotional function as an "alternative center of security" (p. 233). Furthermore, cliques have an internal structure that usually includes a leader who tends to be more mature and more socially connected than the other members of the group. In early adolescence, clique members are usually of the same gender, but by middle adolescence, mixed-gender cliques are common. Most adolescents belong to several different cliques, and their association with them may depend on the particular setting. For example, an adolescent may be a member of one clique in science class, another during sports practice, and still another in the neighborhood on the weekends.

A **crowd** is a larger group of friends and acquaintances that emerges when cliques interact, as they might at a big party or another get-together. In contrast to the emotional functions of cliques, crowds appear to provide opportunities to meet new people, explore one's social identity (Barber, Eccles, & Stone, 2001), and develop new relationships, especially romantic relationships.

crowd A large, reputation-based and mixed-gender social network observed when cliques interact.

The importance of crowds to adolescents' exploration of identity comes especially from the fact that crowds typically have public identities of their own—that is, reputations for engaging in certain types of behaviors and having particular values, norms, and goals (Brown & Klute, 2003; Brown, Hippensteele, & Lawrence, 2014). Crowd reputations are apparent in stereotyped labels such as "jocks," "goths," "skater/punks," "stoners/druggies," "normal," "smart kids/nerds," and "outcasts" (Cross & Fletcher, 2011; Daddis, 2010). As names such as "jocks," "smart kids/nerds," and "skaters/druggies" indicate, crowds vary in the extent to which their norms and values conform to those of the adult community. Other labels, such as "normal" and "outcast," indicate how the crowd's norms and values adhere to those of the adolescent community.

Mondadori Portfolio/Getty Images

This crowd of Disclosure fans probably includes a number of cliques—smaller groups of good friends who came to the concert together and will depart together. According to Dunphy, the crowd serves the important function of providing opportunities for adolescents to meet new people and develop new relationships.

Being identified as a member of a particular crowd may have a significant impact on an adolescent's social status, depending on the local peer culture. For example, as a rule, "brains" occupy a status somewhere between the elite groups and groups that are unpopular. However, in some peer cultures, poor academic achievement is associated with high levels of popularity—as is the case where aggressive, low-achieving individuals are highly popular (Estell, Farmer, Cairns, & Cairns, 2002; Rodkin et al., 2000)—and "brains" are disparaged. Similarly, in some working-class African American communities, being labeled as a "brain" can lead to being ostracized, causing many academically able young people try to mask their abilities (Ogbu, 1997; Webb, 2016). In general, crowds and the way they are categorized help adolescents learn about the alternative social identities that are available to them and strongly influence whom they are likely to meet and spend time with (Brown, Palincsar, & Armbruster, 1994).

Peer Pressure, Conformity, and Deviance

An aspect of adolescent social relationships that has been extensively examined is peer pressure and conformity (Brown, Bakken, Ameringer, & Mahon, 2008). Conformity, also known as **homophily**, refers to the degree to which friends are similar to each other in their behavior, their taste in clothes and music, and their goals and aspirations for the future (Kandel, 1978; McCormick, Cappella, Hughes, & Gallagher, 2015). Although adolescents in the United States are more mobile than younger children, attend larger schools, and have more opportunities to meet peers of other social classes and ethnic backgrounds, their close friends tend to be even more similar to them than their close friends in elementary school were—a trend that continues throughout adolescence (Berndt & Keefe, 1995). High school friends are particularly likely to be similar in their values, their views of school, their academic achievement, and their dating and

homophily The degree to which friends are similar to each other.

other leisure-time activities (Berndt & Murphy, 2002; Patrick, Anderman, & Ryan, 2002). They also tend to feel the same way about drug use, drinking, and delinquency (Solomon & Knafo, 2007; Tani, Chavez, & Deffenbacher, 2001; Urberg, Degirmencioglu, & Tolson, 1998).

In a year-long seminal study of homophily in adolescent friendships, Denise Kandel (1978) focused on the areas of drug use, educational goals, and delinquency. Her findings suggested that two developmental processes are involved in the establishment of homophily: selection and socialization. Through *selection*, adolescents target others as potential friends, seeking out teenagers who seem similar to them in important traits and behaviors, especially those that are relevant to the adolescent's social reputation. Hockey players are more likely to hang out with other hockey players, delinquents with other delinquents, good students with other good students, and so on. Once selection has occurred, socialization comes into play. Through *socialization*, socially significant behaviors are modeled and reinforced in the course of ongoing interactions. Socialization accounts for the tendency of individuals to become increasingly more alike—to show higher levels of behavioral agreement—as their relationships develop over time. For example, studies have found that children who are at risk for antisocial behavior and who become friendly with delinquent peers are likely to become delinquent themselves (Mann et al., 2016).

Photodisc/Getty Images

Adolescent gangs have been studied since the early 1900s. Modern developmentalists have focused on understanding the risk factors associated with gang involvement, as well as the social processes involved in deviant behavior.

Recognizing the role of socialization in adolescent delinquency, developmentalists have worried for decades that it may be unhealthy for adolescents to spend excessive time with their peers, removed from the observation and control of adults. Frederic Thrasher (1927) argued as much in his classic study of more than 1,300 Chicago gangs in existence during the early years of the 1900s. The problem, he argued, was not due to the nature of the boys who joined the gangs, many of which began as neighborhood play groups. Gangs became problematic only when they functioned without supervision and opportunities to participate in socially acceptable activity. In a similar vein, Urie Bronfenbrenner (1970) made the point that "if children have contact only with their own age-mates, there is no possibility for learning culturally established patterns of cooperation and mutual concern" (p. 121).

It is an open question whether adolescents, left entirely to their own devices, would create a "Lord of the Flies" society, in which cooperation and concern for others would be overshadowed by self-interested, deviant behavior. There is, however, plenty of evidence to support the notion that deviancy can be socialized in the context of peer relationships (Blanton & Burkley, 2008; Fujimoto & Valente, 2012). The concept of *deviancy training* accounts for the homophily of antisocial behavior among adolescent peers (Dishion & Tipsord, 2011; Forgatch et al., 2016). **Deviancy training** occurs when friends respond to talk about rule-breaking and other deviant forms of behavior by laughing or reacting in other positive ways. This process was documented in a series of longitudinal studies in which boys were videotaped as they engaged in discussions with friends. The researchers coded the discussion sessions for "deviant talk" and whether it was reinforced. They found that deviancy training in discussions at age 13 or 14 predicted increased violent behavior, as well as the initiation of tobacco, alcohol, and marijuana use, by age 15 or 16 (Dishion, McCord, & Poulin, 1999).

deviancy training Positive reactions to discussions of rule-breaking.

Peer processes similar to deviancy training have been blamed for the surprising finding that group counseling and therapy for delinquent adolescents may, in some circumstances, do more harm than good (Dishion, Poulin, & Burraston, 2001). This was demonstrated in a study conducted with delinquent and nondelinquent teenage boys in Belgium (Mathys, Hyde, Shaw, & Born, 2013). For this study, the researchers put the participants into one of three types of groups. One group was made up of only delinquent boys; another was composed entirely of nondelinquents; the third was a mix of delinquent and nondelinquent boys. The adolescents in the mixed groups engaged in significantly less antisocial talk than did those in the delinquent-only groups. In addition, teens in both mixed and nondelinquent-only groups reinforced each other in discussions of socially appropriate activity. Although more research is needed to understand the conditions under which delinquent teens socialize nondelinquent teens toward increased deviancy and nondelinquent teens socialize delinquent teens toward socially appropriate activity, it is clear that deviancy training flourishes when delinquent youth are together. It also underscores the importance of designing and using developmentally appropriate therapies. Therapeutic strategies that are effective with adults may backfire when used with adolescents.

Romantic Relationships

In many cultures, a key function of the peer group is to provide an avenue to romantic relationships (Connolly & McIsaac, 2009; Furman & Simon, 2008). It has been noted, in fact, that romantic relationships are central to adolescents' sense of belonging and group status.

Dexter Dunphy argued that the process of developing romantic relationships takes place through a series of stages, as shown in Figure 15.4 (p. 524): The same-sex cliques of early adolescence give way to the mixed-sex crowds of mid-adolescence, which gradually disintegrate as members become involved in romantic relationships. Contemporary work generally supports the stages that Dunphy proposed and also marks mid-adolescence as a major turning point during which nearly 50 percent of adolescents report involvement in relatively intense romantic relationships (Kuttler & La Greca, 2004).

Although these studies provide convincing evidence of a stage-like process, there are important cultural and historical variations in adolescent romantic relationships (Berndt & Savin-Williams, 1993; Brown et al., 1994). On the basis of the data he collected in the late 1950s, Dunphy reported that the crowd disintegrated into couples who were going steady or were engaged to get married. Fifty years later, this pattern may continue in some parts of the world, but it does not appear to be generally characteristic of contemporary industrialized societies. Instead, marriage is often postponed until several years after the initiation of sexual activity. In addition, adolescents typically do not stop hanging out with their friends once they become involved in romantic relationships (De Goede et al., 2012). Thus, romantic relationships take place alongside other peer relationships, creating a context in which adolescents must maneuver between relationships with their friends and their romantic partners. Developmentalists have found that adolescents often feel neglected when their friends start dating, particularly in the early phases of new romantic relationships (Roth & Parker, 2001; Shulman & Seiffge-Krenke, 2001).

Juice Images/Alamy Stock Photo

Romantic relationships become increasingly important during the adolescent years. In addition to providing opportunities for exploring intimacy and identity, romantic relationships are important to adolescents' sense of belonging and group status.

Romantic relationships may evolve differently within different cultural subgroups. In the United States, for example, Black adolescents are less likely than

White adolescents to have romantic experiences, although when they do, they are more likely to be involved in steady relationships. Black adolescents who have steady relationships are also more likely to cohabit in early adulthood than are White youth (Meier & Allen, 2009). It also appears that male gangs in economically depressed neighborhoods actively discourage involvement in significant relationships and often ridicule members who have them (Anderson, 1990). And given that most, presumably heterosexual, adolescent peer groups generally disapprove of homosexual relationships, as we will discuss below, it is likely that peer influences are quite different in the formation of gay and lesbian relationships.

In addition, cultures vary widely in the extent to which they support and provide opportunities for the development of romantic relationships (Dhariwal, Connolly, Paciello, & Caprara, 2009). In many Middle Eastern cultures, particularly those influenced by Islamic religious traditions, dating is either carefully monitored by adults or actively discouraged (Mahdi, 2003). In Iraq, for example, even casual contact between adolescent boys and girls can have dire social consequences, as 16-year-old Samira reports:

> Yes, of course I would like to be able to speak with boys and get to know how they think about girls, but this is getting more and more difficult. I have heard some cases where a boy tried to drag a girl to speak with him by claiming that he was in love with her. But the truth is that he just wanted to show his friends that he had "a sexual affair" with her. This is a very dangerous thing to say about a girl in Iraq. Such incidents would mean that the girl has desecrated her family's honor—something for which she might be severely punished by her father or her brother. It would also mean that her chances of getting a husband become very slim. (Al-Ali & Hussein, 2003, p. 48.)

APPLY > CONNECT > DISCUSS

How does Dunphy's distinction between cliques and crowds fit your own adolescent experience of peer groups? Reflect on the social structure of your high school and try to map out the different crowd types and the different cliques within them. How do the concepts of homophily, selection, and socialization apply?

LEARNING OUTCOMES

Explain how researchers approach sexual behavior when they work with adolescents.

Differentiate among influences as adolescents establish their sexual values, attitudes, and behaviors.

Explain the role of the sexual debut, including cultural variations, in the lives of adolescents.

Sexual Behavior

Our understanding of adolescent sexual behavior has expanded considerably in recent years. However, our knowledge has been seriously hampered by several problems, not the least of which is how to define "sex" (Tolman & McClelland, 2011). When researchers ask teens about such issues as whether they are having sex, their age of first intercourse, how many sexual partners they have had, and so forth, the researchers nearly always mean "penile–vaginal intercourse" (PVI; Savin-Williams & Joyner, 2014). Teens and young adults, however, may have very different definitions in mind—definitions that may, for instance, include oral or anal intercourse or stroking or fondling another person's genitals (Horowitz & Spicer, 2013).

Wary of such definitional issues, researchers often try to use very clear and explicit language to ensure that teens are interpreting the research questions as intended. So, for example, adolescents participating in a study of sexual behavior may have vaginal intercourse defined as "when a man inserts his penis into a woman's vagina" and oral sex as when a partner puts "his/her mouth on your sex organs or you put your mouth on his/her sex organs" (Reese, Haydon, Herring, & Halpern, 2013).

Giving clear and explicit definitions of various sexual behaviors provides greater confidence that teens are interpreting sexual terms as researchers intend. However, such explicit language can be a thorny issue because it is, well, *explicit*. School officials and parents are often reluctant to give consent for adolescents, especially young adolescents, to participate in research that asks such pointed questions about sexual behavior.

Despite such complications, researchers find that adolescent sexual behavior, and its impact, meaning, and significance, varies considerably from one teen to the next. Variations include the *type* of sexual behavior engaged in (masturbation, oral, anal, penile–vaginal, etc.), the adolescent's age at first sexual activity with a partner, the age of their partner, and the sex of their partner (same sex or opposite sex). There is also considerable variation in whether contraceptives are used and how the adolescent feels about the experience afterward. These variations are influenced by a number of factors, such as the adolescent's gender, sexual orientation, family values and parenting, ethnic background, cultural beliefs, and education about sexual matters.

Learning About Sex

Adolescents learn about sexuality from a variety of sources—parents, peers, media, and special educational and counseling programs that have been devised by schools and public health agencies (see the box "In the Field: Sex and . . . Pizza?, p. 530"). And, of course, they learn from their own sexual experiences. Like contexts of learning in general, the contexts of learning about sex can range from casual and subtle to rigorous and formal. Developmentalists are interested in adolescents' sources of sexual information because of the potential consequences of those sources for teens' sexual attitudes, behavior, and health. Some sources of information promote informed decision making, effective communication skills, and self-reflection around sex and sexuality; other sources provide inaccurate or biased information and may contribute to unhealthy attitudes and practices. Altogether, sources of sexual information contribute to the development of **sexual scripts**—cognitive frames of knowledge used by individuals to guide and interpret sexual behavior, including who does what, when, and with whom (Drury, Bukowski, Velasquez, & Stella-Lopez, 2013).

sexual scripts Cognitive frames of knowledge used by individuals to guide and interpret sexual behavior, including who does what, when, and with whom.

family sexual culture Family practices that socialize and reinforce sexual values, attitudes, and behaviors of family members.

Families play an important role in the development of sexual scripts. **Family sexual culture** refers to family practices that socialize and reinforce sexual values, attitudes, and behaviors of family members. Some examples include conventions regarding touching and nudity, words for genitals, parents' dating behaviors, parental control or monitoring of children's sexual exposure (for instance, controlling access to sexually explicit media or limiting opportunities for being home "alone" after school), and ways of talking about sex, sexuality, and reproduction (Fortenberry, 2013).

Most research on family sexual culture has focused on parent–teen communication about sexuality and parental monitoring of their children's sexual exposure. In a recent study, 70 percent of male adolescents and 78 percent of female adolescents reported talking with a parent about sexual health topics such as birth control and sexually transmitted infections (STIs) (Lindberg, Maddow-Zimet, & Boonstra, 2016). The same study found, however, that the information provided to teens by their parents was often inaccurate or incomplete. Nonetheless, when teens have conversations with parents about sexual issues, and when their parents monitor or control their sexual exposure, they are less likely to engage in risky sexual behaviors, experience pregnancy, and contract sexually transmitted infections, and they are more likely to be older when they begin having sex with a partner (Steiner, Liddon, & Dittus, 2017; Han, Miller, & Waldfogel, 2010). It is important to note, however, that this research was conducted with heterosexual adolescents, and results may not apply to teens with other sexual orientations. In one study of homosexual adolescent males, higher levels of parental monitoring and communication were generally not protective against risky sexual behaviors, as typically found for heterosexual males (Thoma & Huebner, 2014). In fact, homosexual males who reported that their parents knew little to nothing about their sexual orientation were at greater sexual risk when they perceived high levels of parental monitoring or communication.

Adolescents, of course, also seek out information about sex on their own. Digital media provide easy and confidential access to sexual topics and material, and

In The Field

Sex and . . . Pizza?

Name: AL VERNACCHIO

Education: BA, Theology, St. Joseph's University; MSEd, Human Sexuality, University of Pennsylvania

Current Position: High school teacher and author

Career Objectives: To educate children about sexual behavior and relationships

Courtesy Al Vernacchio

Al Vernacchio

Al Vernacchio teaches human sexuality to high school students at a private suburban school outside Philadelphia. He begins a lesson by urging students to reflect on sexual metaphors, including the baseball metaphor of running the bases and scoring a home run. One girl mentions grass. Vernacchio confirms that when there's grass on the field, you play ball, which, he notes, is a rather unusual application of the metaphor these days, in light of the popularity of shaving pubic hair. But a boy offers that grass was mowed, creating a landing strip. His joke inspires giggles and laughter from his classmates.

Vernacchio presses his students to consider the deeper meaning of describing sex in terms of sports metaphors. It implies that sex is a game; with the boy playing offense, and the girl playing defense; that the game is played until it is over—you can't just stop because you're happy on second base.

In the United States, sex education typically emphasizes abstinence in one form or another. Most "abstinence only" programs, present abstinence as the only reasonable choice because contraceptives are unreliable and premarital sex results in physical and emotional harm. In other programs that are "comprehensive" (also known as "disaster prevention" programs), abstinence is emphasized as the best choice, but pregnancy and disease protection methods are taught for those who choose to be sexually active. But Vernacchio's program is decidedly different, taking on topics such as female ejaculation and sexual anatomy, complete with medical videos and photos. His rationale is to educate students about what genitals—especially female genitals—look like. Other subjects that rarely if ever come up in most U.S. sex education courses but are routinely addressed in Vernacchio's classes include hooking up, oral sex, pornography, and sexual pleasure.

---

the fact that these media may make possible easy and unsupervised access to online sexual information and sexually explicit material has raised concerns. Teens' exposure to pornography, for instance, has been the focus of considerable attention. Many concerned parents install "family friendly" filters that limit their children's access to television channels and Internet sites that might display sexually explicit images and content. Despite these efforts, research in a number of different countries indicates that a vast number of teens have been exposed to online pornography ("cyberporn"), either intentionally or accidentally (Flood, 2007; Wolak, Mitchell, & Finkelhor, 2007). One online survey completed by nearly 500 college students in Spain found that 63 percent of men and 30 percent of women reported that they had been exposed to pornography before they were 18 years old (Gonzalez-Ortega & Orgaz-Baz, 2013). The vast majority of male college students (84.3 percent) indicated that they viewed cyberporn because they wanted sexual excitement, whereas only 20 percent of female students indicated that sexual excitement motivated their viewing. And male students were significantly more likely than their female counterparts to report that curiosity about sexual behavior or wanting information about sex inspired their viewing.

The gender differences found in the study of Spanish college students are consistent with gender differences found in many other countries. In general, compared to females, males report significantly higher rates of exposure to cyberporn, are more likely to consider viewing pornography as "normal" behavior, and are more likely to report that they have viewed cyberporn for purposes of sexual arousal and

Importantly, Vernacchio's teaching style avoids lecturing students and filling the lessons with scary statistics on what can go wrong as a consequence of having sex: pregnancy, sexually transmitted infections, rape, discrimination based on sexual orientation—all standard fare of traditional sex education programs. Instead, he creates a classroom climate that encourages questioning and open discussion about topics that the students themselves consider important and relevant to their lives and relationships. According to Michele Fine, a developmentalist who has studied sexual identity and development of girls, all teens crave such a "safe space" in which to ponder the complexities of sex, romance, and relationships—including desire, betrayal, and coercion.

At a major sex-education conference, Paul Joannides, author of a highly successful manual for older teens and adults called "The Guide to Getting It On," made the point that today's middle-school and high-school students use pornography as a model of sexual behavior, and likely find it much more relevant than traditional sex education to their interests and concerns. He went on to argue that when sex education is focused exclusively on all the things that can go wrong, educators are turning a blind eye to the issues that most teens grapple with as they move into the world of sex and romance—whether they're sexually attractive; whether their own experiences will be as exciting as those they see in porn; whether their sexual feelings are unique or common.

Threaded throughout Vernacchio's course is an emphasis on exploring one's attitudes and beliefs about sex and sexuality and communicating about sex with one's partner. One class focused on the pros and cons of different types of relationships, from friendship to old-school dating to hookups. On the benefits of hookups, students pointed to sexual pleasure and the value of not having expectations of commitment and prolonged attachments.

Vernacchio conceded the point that sometimes a "hookup is all you want." But he then asked them about the downside of hooking up. In response, the students said that it may be difficult to keep one's affections in check and that it may be "confusing." Vernacchio suggested that two people may even have different ideas about what it means to hook up, which is why communication is so important.

To underscore his point, he suggested that eating pizza may be a better metaphor than baseball for having sex. First of all, when you share a pizza with someone, you usually talk with the person about what to order—what size, which type of crust, and what sorts of toppings. Vernacchio pointed out that there's nothing wrong with any of vast varieties of pizzas that can be made. Instead, when your pizza arrives made to your specifications, you open the box and it looks and smells wonderful, and makes your mouth water in anticipation.

Like eating pizza, sexual activity can be a whole-body experience, stimulating multiple senses at once, not just the person's genitals. And eating pizza and having sex can also have the same goal of being full or satisfied. The definition of "full" or "satisfied" may vary from one person to the next, and even for the same person at different times. The important point, for Veracchio, is that, "(n)obody's like, 'You failed, you didn't eat the whole pizza.' So what if the goal wasn't to finish the bases? What if it just was, "Wow, I feel like I had enough. That was really good.'"

(Information from Abraham, 2011.)

to learn about sex (Beaver & Paul, 2011; Carroll et al., 2008; Sevcikova et al., 2014). In light of these motives, it's not surprising that rates of males' exposure increase substantially with the onset of puberty (Beyens, Vandenbosch, & Eggermont, 2015).

Parents are not the only ones concerned about how online pornographic material may affect teens' developing sexual knowledge, behavior, and attitudes. A study conducted in Sweden found that professionals who work with adolescents share a number of worries, including the possibility that teens are exposed to conflicting information about sex, that they may use pornography as a source of information and sexual stimulation, and that pornography may contribute to the development of unhealthy expectations and anxieties regarding looks (including the appearance and size of genitalia), sexual behaviors and practices (including pressure to engage in certain types of sex), and stereotypic gender norms in which males are dominant and females are more passive (Mattebo et al., 2016).

Analyses of contemporary pornography provide ample reasons for the specific worries expressed by the Swedish professionals (Bloom & Hagedorn, 2015). In contrast to erotic media of decades past, contemporary pornography increasingly depicts "unaffectionate sex" devoid of expressions of emotional warmth or love, with themes of men using women for their own satisfaction and without regard for women's sexual desires or gratification (Peter & Valkenburg, 2010). Sexual violence is also increasingly common, portraying men's violence against women, often followed by sex (Foubert, Brosi, & Bannon, 2011). It's little wonder that adults are concerned about what teens might be learning from this type of pornographic material.

Research on the effects of adolescents' exposure to pornography paints a complex and largely inconclusive picture. A large and growing body of *correlational* research finds that exposure to cyberporn is associated with a number of troubling behaviors, including dating violence (Rothman & Adhia, 2016) and, in girls, a history of family, sexual, or dating violence (Romito & Beltramini, 2015). On the other hand, studies have found no correlations between exposure to pornography during adolescence and risky sexual practices (Luder et al., 2011) or relationship intimacy in early adulthood (Štulhofer, Buško, & Schmidt, 2012). As always, it's important to keep in mind that correlational research should not be used to draw conclusions about the *causes* of behavior.

The Sexual Debut

sexual debut Having sexual intercourse for the first time.

For teens around the globe, having sexual intercourse for the first time—the **sexual debut**—is a milestone event brimming with issues and questions never encountered before. For example, many teens will wonder about their relationships with their partners and ask themselves: Do I love him or her? Will this change our relationship? Having sex also involves questions about whether and how (and how much) to talk about it with parents and friends: Will they think more or less of me? Will it affect my reputation? Many teens also question their own emotional readiness for the experience: Will I like it? How will I feel afterward—about my partner, about myself? And, more practically, having sex often (but not often enough) involves advanced planning regarding protections against unwanted pregnancy and STIs: Should I ask her about whether she's on birth control? How can I buy condoms where I can be sure I won't run into someone I know—like my Mom?

As you can see in Figure 15.5, the average age at which adolescents first engage in sexual intercourse varies considerably around the world. There are also some interesting cultural differences between boys' and girls' sexual debuts. For example, in the United States and most Western European cultures, boys tend to first have sexual intercourse at slightly earlier ages than girls do. However, the situation is reversed in many other countries, sometimes radically so (Centers for Disease Control and Prevention, 2004). In Ethiopia, the median age of first intercourse is 15½ years for girls and 18½ years for boys; in Nepal, it is 16½ for girls and 18½ for boys. Cross-cultural

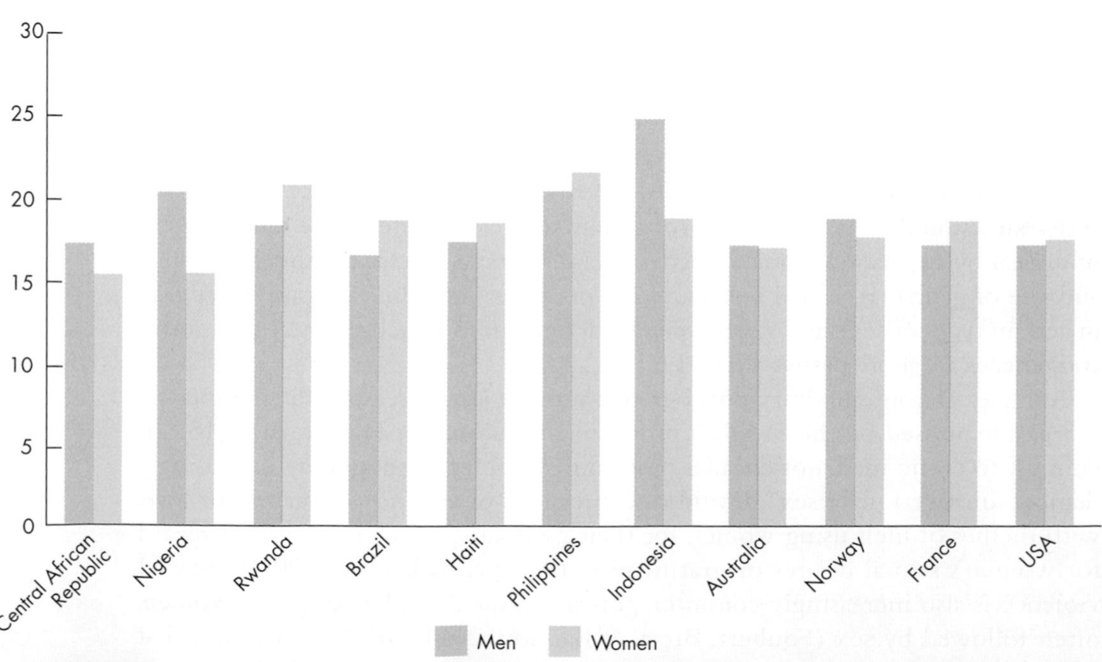

FIGURE 15.5 Median age at first intercourse (age by which half of the population becomes sexually active). (Data from Wellings et al., 2006.)

variations in the adolescent sexual debut are likely due to a variety of biological and cultural factors, including the age of pubertal onset, social norms, age of marriage, and cultural practices regarding sexuality.

In today's world of widescale immigration of children and families, the issue of ethnic differences in sexual development takes on special significance. Many adolescents around the world have relocated to entirely new cultures and are immersed in communities, schools, and peer groups with vastly different norms and expectations for sexual behavior and development. Developmentalists are working to understand how immigrant youth navigate between the sexual norms of their native cultures and those of their new homes. One study compared the sexual attitudes and experiences of native French adolescents with those who had immigrated to France from Maghreb, an area of North Africa strongly influenced by the conservative values of Islam (Yahyaoui et al., 2013). Compared to the native French adolescents, the sexual attitudes and experiences of the immigrant teens were significantly more conservative and influenced by cultural taboos regarding nonmarital sexual relations. Immigrant girls, in particular, influenced by their cultural values and beliefs, feared being publically shamed and stigmatized for not adhering to tradition.

As you can see in Table 15.1, which is based on the largest study of sexual behavior conducted to date in the United States (Herbenick, Reece, Schick, & Sanders, 2010), the proportion of U.S. adolescents and young adults who have had various sexual

TABLE 15.1 Percentage of Different Age Groups Indicating Ever Having Had Specific Sexual Experiences

	Age Group			
Specific Sexual Experience	**14–15**	**16–17**	**18–19**	**20–24**
Males				
Masturbated alone	67.5	78.9	88.1	91.8
Masturbated with other	6.7	20.3	49.3	54.5
Oral received from female	13.0	34.4	59.4	73.5
Oral received from male	1.6	3.2	8.8	9.3
Oral given to female	8.3	20.2	60.9	70.9
Oral given to male	1.6	2.8	10.1	9.3
Penile-vaginal intercourse	9.9	30.3	62.5	70.3
Penis inserted into other's anus	3.7	6.0	9.7	23.7
Other's penis inserted in own anus	1.0	0.9	4.3	10.8
Females				
Masturbated alone	43.3	52.4	66.0	76.8
Masturbated with other	9.0	19.7	38.6	46.9
Oral received from female	3.8	6.6	8.0	16.8
Oral received from male	10.1	25.8	62.0	79.7
Oral given to female	5.4	8.0	8.2	14.0
Oral given to male	12.8	29.1	61.2	77.6
Penile-vaginal intercourse	12.4	31.6	64.0	85.6
Other's penis inserted in own anus	4.3	6.6	20.0	39.9

Information from Herbenick et al., 2010.

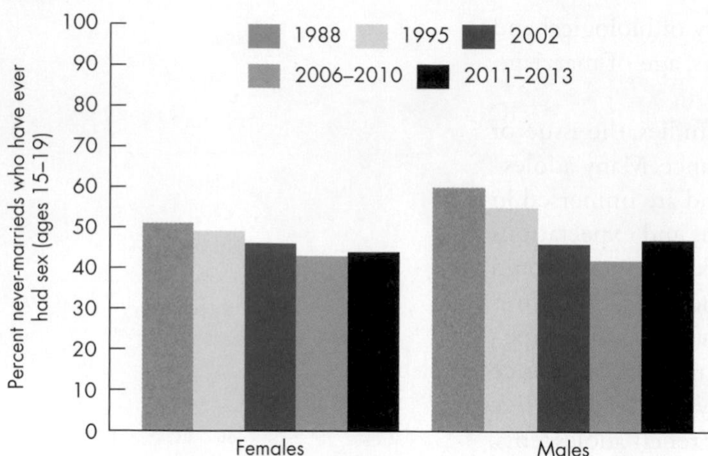

FIGURE 15.6 Percentage of 15- to 17-year-olds who have never been married or had sexual intercourse. (Data from CDC, 2015; Abma, Martinez, & Copen, 2010.)

experiences increases gradually between 14 and 24 years of age, including never-married teens who have never engaged in sexual intercourse (Figure 15.6). The table also shows interesting gender differences over time. In particular, the proportion of males reporting ever having had vaginal intercourse increases from 10 to 70 percent between the ages of 14 and 24, whereas it increases for girls from 12 to 85 percent.

How do adolescents feel about their first experience of sexual intercourse? In the United States, research on this question has found that boys tend to report more positive feelings about first intercourse than do girls (Figure 15.7). For example, in a nationwide study, more than 10,000 young adults between 18 and 24 years of age were asked how much they had wanted to have sex at the time they had their first sexual experience (Abma, Martinez, & Copen, 2010). Very few young men said that they really had not wanted to have intercourse at the time; in contrast, young women were much more likely to report either that they had not wanted to have sex at the time or that they had had mixed feelings about it. Many girls are less positive about their initial experience of intercourse—for a good reason: They were coerced into having sex (see the box "Now Trending in Practice: Exposing and Ending Child Marriage"). About 60 percent of the girls who had sex before they were 15 years old say that they did so involuntarily (Guttmacher Institute, 2006). Cultural attitudes, such as those expressed by Natalie and Caroline at the beginning of this chapter, likely also play a role in adolescents' feelings about their early sexual experiences.

One reason developmentalists are so interested in the sexual debut—especially the age of first sexual experiences—is that there are certain health risks associated with becoming sexually active at early ages. Given what you have learned in previous chapters about cognitive and emotional development during middle childhood, you can understand why young adolescents are not thought to be sufficiently mature to engage in safe and consensual sexual interactions. In general, young adolescents are less knowledgeable about sex and sexual risks, are more impulsive and sensitive to social pressures to have sex, and are less assertive and confident with sexual partners (Boislard, van de Bongardt, & Blais, 2016; De Graaf, Vanwesenbeeck, & Meijer, 2015). All of these developmental immaturities place sexually active

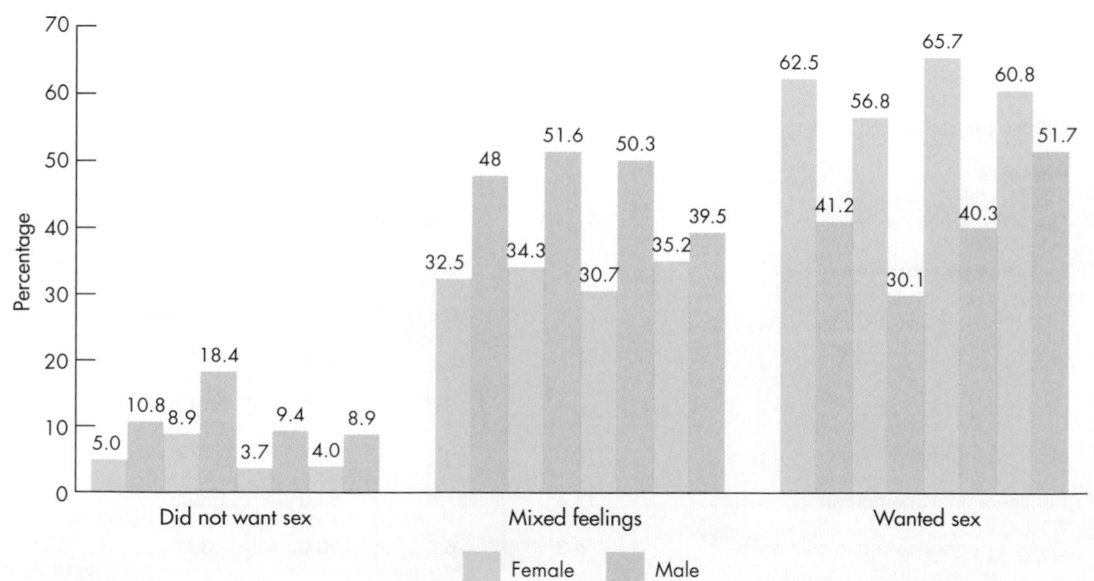

FIGURE 15.7 Percentage of males and females who reported intercourse before age 20 and whether they wanted intercourse, did not want intercourse, or had mixed feelings, according to age of first intercourse. More females than males either did not want intercourse or had mixed feelings, whereas more males than females reported that they wanted intercourse. (Data from Martinez et al., 2011.)

Now TRENDING in PRACTICE

Exposing and Ending Child Marriage

Born in Niger, Africa, 24-year-old Halima Laoual Bachir used the UNICEF Twitter account to tell the world about the plight of many of her friends who were taken out of school and forced to marry at very young ages—many before they reached their 13th birthdays. She was joined by other young women, several of whom were themselves child brides. Born in Chad, 31-year-old Mariam Agrei Musa described how she was forced to marry at the age of 16. She soon became pregnant and fled to Cameroon with her daughter, where she finished high school and started college. When she returned to Chad to look for work, her husband's family took her child from her. Twenty-four-year-old "Jennifer," whose name has been changed to protect her identity, told of how she was abducted from her home in Uganda when she was just 13 years old. Along with other abducted girls from her community, she was forced to walk to a town, and from there she and the other girls were transported to the country of Sudan and "given" to different military commanders who became their "husbands." She managed to escape after many years and return home with her daughter.

Halima, Mariam, and Jennifer have all pledged themselves to eliminating child marriage. Their activism includes working with human rights groups such as UNICEF, starting agencies to deliver programs and services to vulnerable girls and young women, and telling their stories to national and international policy makers, urging for reform to make the practice of child marriage illegal.

FADEL SENNA/Getty Images

Lakshmi Sundaram, the global coordinator of Girls Not Brides.

According to a recent UNICEF report, more than 700 million women alive today were married as children, and of these, more than one-third were married before the age of 15 (UNICEF, 2014). Data released in 2016 indicate that the prevalence of child marriage has slightly declined over the past three decades. However, it remains widespread in many regions of the world, especially in South Asia and many African countries (see the bar graph below). In the least-developed countries of the world, nearly half of all girls are married before the age of 18.

That the poorest countries of the world have the highest rates of child marriage is consistent with the understanding that poverty plays a central role in perpetuating the practice (Nour, 2009; Okonofua, 2013). Parents want their daughters to be financially secure, but food, clothing, and education are expensive, and many families give their daughters up for marriage in exchange for a "bride price" (sums of money or goods). Because the bride price can be quite high, requiring years of working and saving money, the men who marry girls are often considerably older than their brides. In addition, because of the fear of HIV/AIDS infection, men will often seek younger, virginal brides believing them to be uninfected.

Child marriage is associated with a host of negative consequences (Mace, 2016; McFarlane, Nava, Gilroy, & Maddoux, 2016). Girls typically end their schooling when they are married, and they face increased risk of sexually transmitted infections, diseases such as malaria and cervical cancer, and increased risk of death due to complications of pregnancy (UNICEF, 2014; Okonofua, 2013). When marriage is forced, as it often is for the youngest girls, there is significant risk for domestic abuse, neglect, and abandonment. Although the prevalence in the United States of forced marriage and child marriage is unknown, a 7-year longitudinal study of 300 mothers who sought shelter or legal services as a consequence of intimate partner violence (physical abuse, sexual abuse, or both) found that 17 percent reported that someone had tried to force them into marriage. Of these, 45 percent were younger than 18 years of age (McFarlane et al., 2016).

Child marriage is widely considered a violation of human rights affecting girls around the globe. As described by Susan Bissell, UNICEF's Chief of Child Protection, "child marriage robs girls of their childhoods and can scar their lives forever" (UNICEF, 2014). But the stories and work of inspiring young activists like Halima, Mariam, and Jennifer are making a difference. "These incredible young activists are beacons of hope," says Bissell. "We need all parts of society to follow their example and take urgent action to protect those at risk."

Child marriage is highly prevalent in South Asia and sub-Saharan Africa

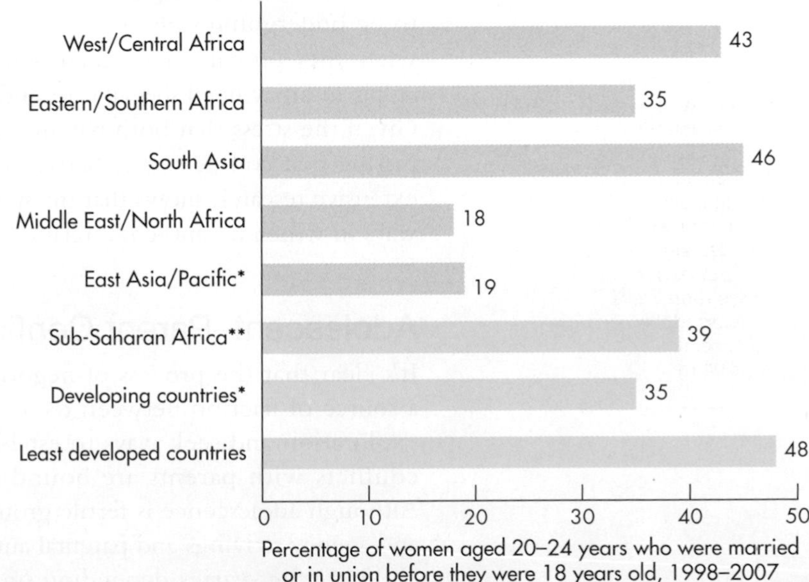

* Excludes China. ** Sub-Saharan Africa comprises the regions of Eastern/Southern Africa and West/Central Africa.
(Data from http://www.unicef.org/rightsite/sowc/pdfs/statistics/SOWC_Spec_Ed_CRC_TABLE9.CHILDPROTECTION_EN_111309.pdf.)

young adolescents at risk for not using condoms, being coerced into sex, contracting sexually transmitted infections, and becoming pregnant.

Clearly, initiating sex at early ages is associated with a host of negative outcomes, which may account for why it has received so much attention by researchers. Recently, however, developmentalists have turned their attention to adolescents who initiate sex at significantly older ages than their peers—"postponers." Most studies of adolescents who remain virgins into their late teens find that they have chosen to be sexually abstinent for religious reasons or because of their moral principles (Buhi, Goodson, Neilands, & Blunt, 2011; Okigbo et al., 2015; Young et al., 2015). But certain problems have been associated with postponing virginity into early adulthood. For instance, adult virgins are more likely to be overweight and less likely to have ever had a romantic relationship (Adamczyk, 2009; Haydon et al., 2014). So it seems that adolescents whose sexual debut is significantly "off time" compared to their peers—either very early or very late—may face additional challenges in their development. This serves to underscore the importance of experiencing significant developmental milestones *in sync* with one's peers, as we discussed in the case of pubertal development in Chapter 14.

APPLY > CONNECT > DISCUSS

Watch a few television shows that are popular among adolescents and young adults that feature teens or young adults as central characters (e.g., *Teen Wolf, Broad City, Undeclared*). How do they depict sexual relationships and communication about sex? How do they depict the social and physical (e.g., pregnancy, STIs) consequences of sex?

LEARNING OUTCOMES

Describe the role of adolescent–parent relationships or conflicts, including cultural variations, as teens engage in identity exploration.

Relationships with Parents

The increasing time that adolescents spend with their peers and romantic partners and the increasing importance adolescents place on those relationships inevitably change the relationships between adolescents and their parents. In fact, the amount of time that adolescents in the United States spend with their families drops by approximately 50 percent between fifth and ninth grades (Larson & Richards, 1991). At the most general level, adolescents become more distant from their parents and more likely to turn to peers than to parents for support and advice on questions about how to conduct themselves in a wide range of contexts (see Figure 15.8; Meeus, 2003; Steinberg & Silk, 2002). Furthermore, parents of adolescents are likely to be undergoing significant life changes of their own. They are reaching an age when they probably have increased responsibilities at work; their own parents are aging and may need special care; and their physical powers are beginning to decline. Given the stress that both parents and their adolescent children feel, it is not surprising that conflicts arise between them (Steinberg & Duncan, 2002). However, extensive research shows that the specifics of such conflicts, and, more generally, the ways in which parent–child relationships change, depend on a host of factors.

Adolescent–Parent Conflicts

It's clear that the process of negotiating between control and autonomy can be a source of friction between teens and parents. As adolescents engage in identity exploration and seek ways to establish their autonomy and express their agency, conflicts with parents are bound to arise (Branje, Laursen, & Collins, 2013). Although adolescence is fertile ground for struggle between adolescent autonomy and agency strivings and parental authority and control, you will learn that parent–child conflict varies depending on family characteristics and culture (Jensen & Dost-Gozkan, 2015).

On the basis of a review of a large number of studies, Brett Laursen and his colleagues found that both the frequency and the intensity of conflict between parents and adolescents change over the course of adolescence, peaking early in adolescence and then decreasing (Branje et al., 2013; Hadiwijaya et al., 2017). When conflicts do arise, they can evoke strong feelings. Very often, however, adolescent–parent conflict is inspired by seemingly trivial matters such as household responsibilities and privileges, dating and curfews, involvement in athletics, financial independence, and perceived privacy invasions (Hawk, Keijsers, Hale, & Meeus, 2009). Arguments over "big issues," such as religion and politics, are much less common (Smetana, 2008).

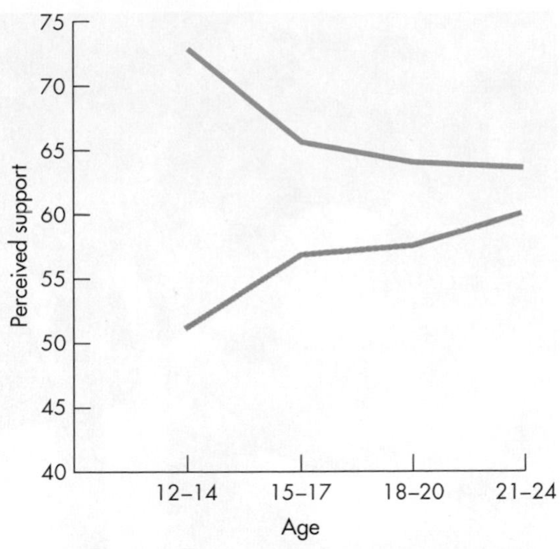

FIGURE 15.8 Although teens generally perceive their parents as highly supportive through their adolescence and early adulthood, their perception of support declines gradually across these years. In contrast, teens' perceptions of the support they receive from peers increases gradually across these years but remains lower than perceptions of parent support. (Data from Meeus, 2003.)

Many parent–adolescent conflicts emerge as a result of parents and adolescents differing in their understanding of what constitutes the domain of "personal space" (Milnitsky-Sapiro, Turiel, & Nucci, 2006; Turiel, 2010). As we explained in the discussion of social domain theory in Chapters 9 and 13, people distinguish among three domains—the moral, the social conventional, and the personal—but may differ in how they distinguish among them. Conflicts between parents and adolescents often relate to differences in where they draw boundaries between the social conventional and personal domains. A parent who insists, for example, that an adolescent dress in a socially appropriate way and an adolescent who insists that dress is a matter of personal choice are disputing the boundaries of the social conventional and the personal (Milnitsky-Sapiro et al., 2006; Smetana, 2006).

Research on parent–adolescent relationships in different ethnic groups shows broad cultural differences in where the boundaries between domains are drawn (Smetana, 2008; Smetana & Gettman, 2006). Judith Smetana has found, for example, that compared with middle-class European American families, middle-class African American families have relatively restricted definitions of what constitutes the adolescent's personal jurisdiction. Even so, negotiating the boundary of authority is still a significant source of parent–adolescent conflict for African American families. It seems that conflicts over "little things" represent deeper disagreements about the major issues of growing up—the power to decide for oneself and to take responsibility for oneself.

Conflicts between many adolescents and parents reflect struggles associated with developing independence and autonomy.

"Can't you keep your parenting to yourselves?"

Barbara Smaller The New Yorker Collection/The Cartoon Bank

© Mark Richard/PhotoEdit – All rights reserved.

This mother is helping her son prepare for his Bar Mitzvah, a Jewish ritual celebrating coming of age. Although she may continue to play an important role in her son's adolescence, her sphere of influence may shrink as he spends more time away from home with his peers.

Smetana argues that African American families' parenting practices can be better described in terms of social domain theory than by such global terms as authoritarian or parent centered. According to social domain theory, parents' expectations for obedience will vary from one domain of action to the next. This also suggests that parent–adolescent conflict need not characterize the entire relationship; rather, it is confined to certain areas where the authority to have one's way in the face of contentious issues is in dispute. Few adolescents take issue with parents' authority in the domain of moral action but will challenge it when it is applied to how they dress or color their hair.

Attachment and Adjustment

As we discussed in Chapter 6, the security of emotional bonds developed during infancy is carried forward into the interpersonal relationships of adolescence (Ainsworth & Bowlby, 1991; Kobak, Rosenthal, Zajac, & Madsen, 2007). Some infants form *secure attachments* to caregivers: They feel accepted and worthy of their caregiver's affection and trust that their caregiver will be available to provide warmth and support. One significant consequence of these feelings of trust and availability is the developing individual's ability to use the caregiver as a secure base from which to explore the world (Ainsworth & Bowlby, 1991). In contrast, other infants form *insecure attachments*: They often feel anxious and apprehensive, anticipate rejection, and feel that their caregivers are not reliable sources of comfort and safety. These infants may avoid unfamiliar people and places, and they may be less inclined than securely attached infants to explore their environments.

Adolescents' attachments to parents also have significant implications for adjustment and well-being. Those who are securely attached have higher levels of *self-efficacy*, which refers to beliefs about one's own abilities to effectively meet standards and achieve goals (Chapter 1, p. 26). This sort of confidence in oneself may contribute to the fact that securely attached adolescents are more likely than less secure counterparts to seek help when they encounter academic trouble in school (Holt, 2014). Adolescents with secure attachments to parents are also more likely to be involved in sports, which is itself associated with behavioral and mental well-being (Sukys, Lisinskiene, & Tilindiene, 2015). On the flip side, less secure attachments are associated with depression and anxiety, as well as drinking problems (Agerup et al., 2015; Breinholst, Esbjorn, & Reinholdt-Dunne, 2015; McKay, 2015). These problems can persist for years, even into adulthood. One study found that insecure attachments at age 15 were associated with depression at age 20 (Agerup et al., 2015); another found that insecure and unstable attachments throughout the adolescent years were associated with higher levels of depression in adulthood (Cook, Heinze, Miller, & Zimmerman, 2016).

Attachment theorists maintain that the child's attachment history with the primary caregivers forms an *internal working model*—a mental model that children construct as a result of their experiences and that they use to guide their interactions with caregivers and, later, with peers and romantic partners (Chapter 6, p. 210). In essence, the internal working model provides a psychological framework for the adolescent to seek out nonfamilial relationships that have similar qualities to those experienced within the context of the family (Dykas & Cassidy, 2011). In this respect, the internal working model provides *attachment continuity* over time (from infancy through adolescence and beyond) and across people (from primary caregivers to friends and romantic partners). Research with adolescents generally supports the notion of attachment continuity from family to peer relationships (Pascuzzo, Cyr, & Moss, 2013). In college students, secure attachments to parents predict secure attachment to peers, which in turn is associated with higher levels of connection to college and academic success (Wilson & Gore, 2013). However, attachment continuity varies as a function of the developing individual's ethnicity. Studies of European American adolescents, for example, have found that reported intimacy with best friends is strongly linked to feelings of being accepted by both mothers and fathers. But research conducted with U.S. ethnic-minority teens—including Latino, Black, and Asian American—found that father support or acceptance is unrelated to friendship intimacy (Updegraff et al., 2012; Way & Pahl, 2001). These ethnic variations likely reflect cultural differences in the caregiving roles of mothers and fathers in family life and the degree to which mothers and fathers participate in their children's daily lives and activities.

While the research cited above provides general support for the notion of an internal working model, other evidence challenges the idea of attachment continuity between family and peer relationships. In particular, some adolescents appear to use peer relationships as a way of *compensating* for poor family relationships. This was demonstrated in a four-year longitudinal study of more than 200 ethnically diverse high school students attending an urban school serving a low-income community (Way & Greene, 2006). The researchers found two patterns of change in the adolescents' attachments to parents and peers. One pattern reflected attachment continuity, with teens reporting improvement over time in their relationships with both parents and peers. The other pattern reflected compensation, with teens who reported the worst family relationships showing the sharpest increase in the quality of close-friend relationships. These findings illustrate the remarkable capacities of adolescents to create emotionally healthy environments.

APPLY > CONNECT > DISCUSS

Your 16-year-old daughter announces that she intends to leave home and school in order to join a spiritual community that encourages its members to "find themselves" by working toward the common good. As an informed and sensitive parent, you recognize this as an expression of developing autonomy but, for obvious reasons, believe it would be a terrible mistake for her to pursue such a plan at this point in her life. Keeping in mind the evidence presented in this section on effective parenting, write your daughter a letter about what you think of her plan.

Self and Identity Development

"Who are you?" said the Caterpillar.

Alice replied, rather shyly, "I—I hardly know, sir . . . at least I know who I was when I got up this morning, but I think I must have been changed several times since then."

(Lewis Carroll, *Alice's Adventures in Wonderland*.)

Despite having fallen down a rabbit hole into a fantasy world, Alice's confusion about who she is underscores one of the most challenging tasks and significant accomplishments of adolescence—the formation of a coherent and stable identity. **Identity development** is the process through which individuals achieve a sense of who they are, what moral and political beliefs they embrace, the sort of occupation they wish to pursue, and their relationship to their communities and culture. In this section, we will explore various paths of identity development and their relationship to adolescents' families, friends, and culture.

identity development The process through which individuals achieve a sense of who they are and of their moral and political beliefs, their career preferences, and their relationship to their culture and community.

LEARNING OUTCOMES

Describe how developing a sense of self as a self-determining, active agent relates to identity development.

Explain how the sexual self is a component of adolescents' identity.

Explain qualities that help adolescents achieve a mature identity, including the formation of ethnic identity and experiences of racial/ethnic socialization.

Describe how adolescents develop an understanding of their sexual identity, including their sexual orientation.

Self-Determination and Agency

Key to the development of self and identity in adolescence is the developing sense of being a *self-determining, active agent*. Agency is a person's sense of being able to influence, control, and be responsible for his or her actions and experiences. Agency emerges early in development. Consider the 2-year-old's classic demand: "I do it!" Over the course of childhood, and particularly during adolescence, opportunities for agency and self-determined behavior expand considerably. Compared to children, adolescents experience less parental control and later curfews, and they are allowed increasing independence in using public transportation or transporting themselves on bikes or in cars. As adolescents become physically and sexually mature and increasingly motivated to pursue exciting and novel experiences, they have many more opportunities than do children to determine their own actions.

As a sense of being in control, able to make choices, and consequently accountable for one's actions, agency is importantly linked to adolescents' strivings to be more autonomous and independent (Hitlin & Endler, 2007; Kocayörük, Altıntas, & İçbay, 2015). Parents make important contributions to their teens' developing agency. In a study of nearly 500 Turkish high school students 14 to 18 years of age, researchers used a number of surveys to assess adolescents' feelings of choice in their behaviors, their general awareness of self and emotional well-being, and their perceptions of their parents as warm, involved, and supportive of their autonomy strivings (Kocayörük et al., 2015). As expected, teens who reported high levels of parental support scored significantly higher on measures of well-being and agency compared to teens who perceived their parents as less supportive. The researchers speculated that when parents encourage and support the autonomy strivings of their teens, they provide them with opportunities to exercise increasing levels of agency and take increasing responsibility over greater parts of their lives.

resilience The ability to adapt and be successful despite being in circumstances of high risk and adversity.

In adolescence, agency has been associated with **resilience**—that is, the ability to adapt and be successful despite being in circumstances of high risk and adversity. One study found that at-risk African American females between 16 and 21 years of age were less likely to be depressed when they felt in control of their lives and futures (Sales, Merrill, & Fivush, 2013). Another study found that adolescents who had engaged in high levels of delinquent behavior were less likely to continue down

Ekaterina Korneva/Alamy

These eastern European teens are hanging out at an event in Belarus. Their strivings to be autonomous and independent reflect their developing agency.

a path of delinquency if they had a strong sense of agency and self-determination (McLean, Wood, & Breen, 2013). It may be that a strong sense of agency contributes to resiliency because teens feel more responsible for their actions. A strong sense of agency is also relevant to the developing adolescent's sexual behavior and experience.

sexual self Cognitions and feelings about who one is as a sexual being.

The Sexual Self

The **sexual self**—that is, cognitions and feelings about who one is as a sexual being—emerges over time, and influences how sexuality and sexual behaviors develop across the adolescent years (Fortenberry, 2013; Hensel, Fortenberry, O'Sullivan, & Orr, 2011). Developmentalists have explored several aspects of the sexual self. The first, *sexual agency*, or *sexual self-efficacy*, refers to the individual's sense of being in control of their sexual experiences. Sexual agency involves the ability to assert one's sexual preferences and desires, including the desire to not have sex, to make choices about using contraceptives and condoms, and to take responsibility for one's sexual activities and behavior. Sexual agency, then, is more than being able to say "no"; it means being an active agent regarding one's sexuality and sexual experiences. In general, sexual agency has been associated with sexual health (Van Campen & Romero, 2012). A study of Latino 13- to 16-year-olds found that higher levels of sexual agency were related to stronger beliefs in Latino cultural values, including *simpatía* (the importance of harmony in interpersonal relationships) and *respecto* (respect toward parents and authority); sexual agency was also associated with having fewer sexual partners and greater condom use (Ma et al., 2014).

A second aspect of the sexual self, *sexual openness*, refers to the individual's willingness to experience sexual desire and sense of agency in expressing sexuality and exploring and enjoying sexual experiences. Although it generally increases between middle and late adolescence, sexual openness varies from one individual to the next (Hensel et al., 2011). Compared to peers with lower levels of sexual openness, adolescents and young adults who report higher levels of sexual openness begin having sex with a partner at later ages, are more likely to use condoms and less likely to experience pregnancy, and report higher levels of general well-being (Horne & Zimmer-Gembeck, 2006; Rostosky, Galiher, Welsh & Kawaguchi, 2000; Zimmer-Gembeck & French, 2016).

Another aspect of the sexual self is *sexual self-esteem*—that is, how individuals feel about their sexual thoughts, desires, and behaviors, as well as feelings they have about their bodies in sexual contexts (for instance, whether they feel comfortable and attractive when they are with a partner in a sexual context) (Deutsch, Hoffman, & Wolcox, 2013). Teens and young adults who are at ease with the sexual nature of their bodies and genitals have more satisfying sexual experiences, more positive views, and greater confidence regarding sexual activities, and they are less likely to engage in risky sexual behaviors compared to those with lower sexual self-esteem (Impett & Tolman, 2006; Schick, Calabrese, Rima, & Zucker, 2010). Interestingly, sexual self-esteem may have implications for responding to sexual harassment. This was suggested in a study of 13- to 14-year-olds attending 25 schools in the Netherlands (de Lijster, Felten, Kocken, & Docken, 2016). The students participated in a program that included several lessons on how to avoid, resist, and respond to sexual harassment, as well as an educational play performed by peers who enacted short scenes involving sexual harassment. At the conclusion of the program, adolescents who participated in the program had higher levels of sexual self-esteem compared to peers who did not participate. They also had stronger social norms against sexual harassment.

Finally, the sexual self includes *sexual anxiety*—that is, negative emotions such as guilt and shame surrounding issues of sex and sexuality. Sexual anxiety may be related to social and family values that aim to control or restrain adolescents' sexual feelings and expression. Adolescents who experience higher levels of sexual anxiety are more likely than their less anxious peers to believe in the importance of sexual abstinence until marriage and less likely to feel "ready" for sexual intercourse (O'Sullivan et al., 2006). Developmentally, sexual anxiety tends to decrease over the course of adolescence, likely due to having more sexual experiences (Hensel et al., 2011).

Research on the sexual self is relatively new, but it is consistent with studies finding that sexual health and behavior are strongly related to similar factors, such as self-esteem and independence. For example, college women with higher levels of self-esteem and independence are more likely to consistently use contraceptives compared to peers with lower levels of self-esteem and independence (Morrison et al., 2016). Despite being a new focus of research, there is mounting evidence that the sexual self has considerable influence over adolescents' sexual behaviors and experiences.

Achieving a Mature Identity

The possibility that adolescents may be troubled by the feeling of multiple selves makes the search for one's "true self" one of the dominant developmental themes of adolescence (Meeus & de Wied, 2007). As we discussed in Chapter 1, Erik Erikson believed that the quest for identity is a lifelong task, through which individuals achieve a coherent understanding of themselves in relation to their societies. Although the identity quest lasts a lifetime, its challenges come to a climax during adolescence, when young people must deal with biological pressures to become sexually active and social pressures to adopt culturally valued roles and beliefs. According to Erikson (1968a), in order to successfully navigate these multiple pressures (regarding, for example, occupational goals, intimate relationships, social and political values, and religious beliefs), the adolescent has to integrate a stable sense of self across various roles and responsibilities, creating a unified sense of identity. Adolescents who fail this developmental task lack a vision of what their role is or might be. For Erikson, then, the crisis of adolescence is one of *identity versus role confusion*.

The popularity of Erikson's ideas created a demand for an assessment method that could both depict an identity in the process of being formed and provide quantitative

EyesWideOpen/Getty Images

In many cultures, adolescent identity development is complicated by the multiple identity possibilities that exist within the peer group and the larger culture.

measures of the different states of identity formation (Kroger, Martinussen, & Marcia, 2010; Marcia, 2002). In an early and influential effort at such an assessment method, James Marcia (1966) focused on two factors identified by Erikson as being essential to achieving a mature identity: exploration and commitment. **Exploration** refers to the process through which adolescents actively examine their possible future roles and paths in life, think about the choices their parents have made, and begin to search for alternatives that they find personally satisfying. **Commitment** refers to individuals' personal involvement in, and allegiance to, the goals, values, beliefs, and future occupation that they have adopted for themselves.

exploration According to Marcia, the process through which adolescents actively examine their possible future roles and paths.

commitment According to Marcia, individuals' sense of allegiance to the goals, values, beliefs, and occupation they have chosen.

On the basis of interviews with male college students about their choice of occupation and beliefs about politics and religion, Marcia (1966, 2002) identified four patterns of coping with the task of identity formation that arise from four possible patterns of exploration and commitment (Figure 15.9):

1. *Identity achievement.* Adolescents who display this pattern have gone through a period of decision making about their choice of occupation, their political commitment, their religious beliefs, and so on and are now actively pursuing their own goals. When asked about their political commitment, for example, they might respond with such answers as "I've thought it over, and I've decided to support the ________ party. Their program is the most sensible one for the country to be following." When asked about their occupational aspirations, they might say, "It took me quite a while to figure it out, but now I really know what I want to try for a career."
2. *Foreclosure.* Young people who display this pattern are also committed to occupational and ideological positions, but they show no signs of having gone through a period of exploration. Instead, they have just adopted the values, beliefs, and aspirations of their parents. They respond to questions about their political beliefs with such answers as "I really never gave politics much thought. Our family always votes for the ________ party, so that's how I vote." In the area of occupational choice, a typical answer might be "My parents decided a long time ago what I should take in school or go into for a career, and I'm following through on their plans."
3. *Moratorium.* This pattern is displayed by adolescents actively engaged in a process of exploration. They might answer questions about their political beliefs by saying "I'm not sure about my political beliefs, but I'm trying to figure out what I can truly believe in." Likewise, in responding to questions about their future occupation, they might say, "I'm still trying to decide how capable I am as a person and what jobs or school programs will be right for me."
4. *Identity diffusion.* Adolescents who manifest this pattern have neither explored nor committed to identity possibilities. They are likely to take a cynical attitude toward the issues confronting them, so they may answer questions about political commitment by declaring, "I stopped thinking about politics ages ago. There are no parties worth supporting." Regarding occupational choices, a typical response might be "I'm really not interested in finding the right job; any job will do. I'll just do whatever is available."

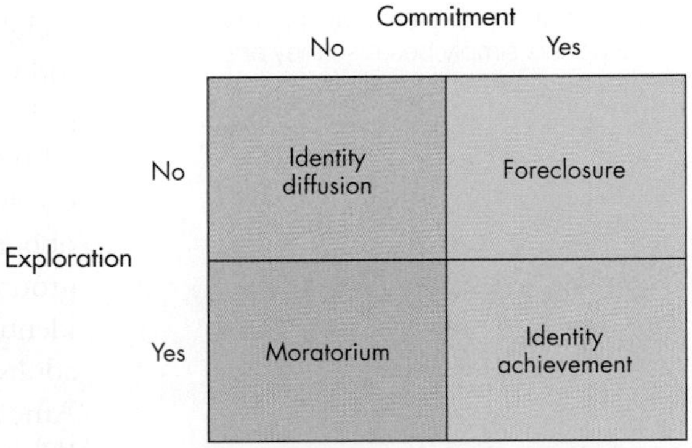

		Commitment: No	Commitment: Yes
Exploration	No	Identity diffusion	Foreclosure
	Yes	Moratorium	Identity achievement

FIGURE 15.9 When the combinations of Erikson's two factors in identity formation—exploration and commitment—are considered together, the result is the four patterns of adolescent identity formation proposed by Marcia.

Other researchers have extended Marcia's methods to incorporate additional domains of experience, including family life, friendships, dating, and sex roles (Grotevant, 1998; Luyckx et al., 2005). In general, the research has shown that identity achievement increases with age, whereas diffusion and moratorium decrease (see Figure 15.10, p. 544; Meeus, 2003). The increase in identity achievement and the decrease in diffusion are both steady trends over the period from the years before high school to the late college years (Kroger et al., 2010; Moshman, 2011).

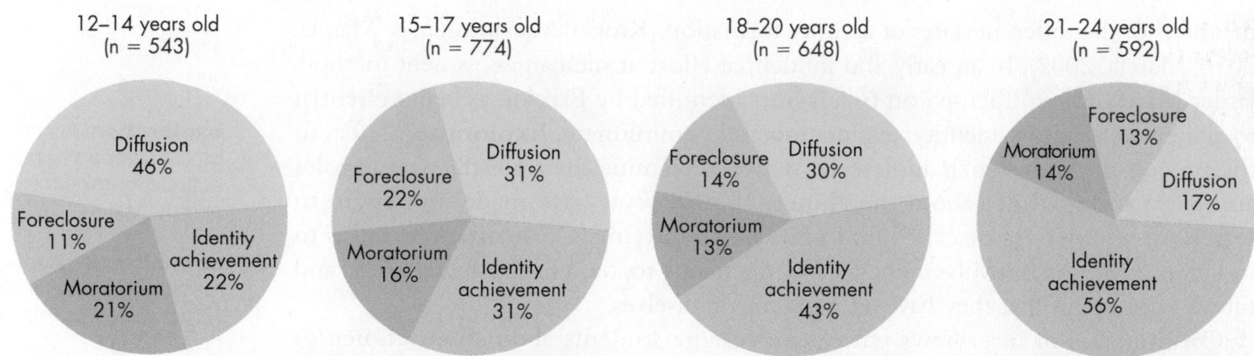

FIGURE 15.10 The proportion of identity statuses change across the adolescent years such that most individuals in the United States have an achieved identity by the time they reach their early 20s. (Data from Meeus, 2003.)

Because identity achievement is considered so important to normal adolescent development, researchers have given special effort to identifying factors that facilitate or complicate identity formation for adolescents growing up in different contexts and cultures.

Forming an Ethnic Identity

ethnic identity A sense of oneself as a member of a particular ethnic group.

bicultural stress Stress experienced by many ethnic-minority and immigrant adolescents as they negotiate two cultures simultaneously.

White privilege Social and economic benefits that are automatically granted to individuals simply because they are members of the White majority.

Ethnic identity refers to an enduring sense of oneself as a member of a particular ethnic group, including the feelings and attitudes one holds regarding one's membership in that group (Umana-Taylor et al., 2014). The process of identity formation can be complicated for ethnic-minority and immigrant children (Kiang, Witkow, & Thompson, 2016; Phinney, 2010). Developmentalists use the term **bicultural stress** to describe the stress experienced by many ethnic-minority and immigrant adolescents as they negotiate two cultures simultaneously (Roche & Kupermінc, 2012; Pina-Watson, Bornhecker, & Salinas, 2015). There are many sources of bicultural stress. Ethnic-minority and immigrant teens may experience conflicts between the values, beliefs, and customs of their family's ethnic culture and those of their peer's majority culture. In addition, many young people from minority or immigrant groups experience biocultural stress in the form of prejudice, discrimination, pressure to speak certain languages, and barriers to educational and economic opportunities.

Some scholars of ethnic and racial identity have argued that for ethnic-majority individuals in Western cultures, a lack of reflection on one's ethnicity is associated with *White privilege.* **White privilege** is famously defined by Peggy McIntosh as "an invisible weightless knapsack" of social and economic benefits that are automatically granted to individuals simply because they are members of the White majority (McIntosh, 1988, p. 10). Similar forms of ethnic privilege have been found in other cultures in which ethnic majority and minority populations have unequal access to social resources and economic opportunities (Walton, 2013). Cultural diversity and globalization increase opportunities for developing close relationships with individuals from other ethnic backgrounds and may very well change the unreflective nature of White privilege and ethnic identity for young people of ethnic majority groups. A case in point is research on young adults in interracial dating relationships (Asian American women and White European American men), which found evidence that young men became more aware of their White privilege and young women more reflective and appreciative of their ethnic heritages as a consequence of their interracial relationship (AhnAllen & Suyemoto, 2011).

Stages of Ethnic-Identity Formation As we discussed in Chapter 9 (pp. 301–302), ethnic-identity development is well under way by middle childhood, when ethnic-minority children know particular characteristics of their ethnic group and have

Paul W. Liebhardt/Getty Images

Multicultural influences are pervasive in many parts of the world, creating a special challenge for adolescents who may feel the tug of both traditional and modern beliefs, values, and expectations of behavior.

developed basic attitudes about their ethnicity. During middle childhood and adolescence, children in ethnic-minority groups move through three additional stages of ethnic-identity formation (Cross, 2003; Ong, Fuller-Rowell, & Phinney, 2010). Although researchers apply different labels to these stages, they agree on the basic content of each stage and the general kinds of experiences associated with movement from one stage to the next. In this discussion, we have adopted the labels suggested by Jean Phinney (2008) because she explicitly links the stages to the processes of exploration and commitment discussed above.

Stage 1: Unexamined Ethnic Identity. In stage 1, children tend to accept and show a preference for the cultural values of the majority culture in which they find themselves. In some cases, this stage appears to correspond to Marcia's category of foreclosure because the person refuses to consider the relevant issues and adopts the views of others unquestioningly. One Mexican American boy told Phinney, "I don't go looking for my culture. I just go by what my parents say and do, and what they tell me to do, the way they are" (Phinney, 2008, p. 68). In other cases, the failure to examine questions of ethnic identity is more similar to identify diffusion. For example, an African American girl remarked, "Why do I need to learn about who was the first Black woman to do this or that? I'm just not too interested" (p. 68).

Stage 2: Ethnic Identity Search. Movement beyond stage 1 is often initiated by a shocking experience in which the young person is rejected or humiliated because of his or her ethnic background. The specifics of such encounters are quite varied (Cross, 2003; Fuller-Rowell, Ong, & Phinney, 2013). A minority student who does extremely well on tests may be accused of cheating simply because the teacher assumes that members of the student's ethnic group are incapable of such work; or a boy and girl who have been friends for years may be forbidden to socialize with each other romantically because they have different skin colors, ethnic backgrounds,

Michael J. Doolittle/The Image Works

Responding to an increasingly multiethnic population, schools and communities provide opportunities to celebrate the cultural heritage of young people. This girl is demonstrating Korean drumming at her school's "International Day."

or religious affiliations. However, a shocking encounter is not necessary for young people to begin pondering their ethnic identity: For some, this move into stage 2 is precipitated simply by a growing awareness that the values of the dominant group may not be beneficial to ethnic minorities.

In stage 2, young people show an intense concern for the personal implications of their ethnicity and often engage in an active search for information about their group. They are likely to become involved in social and political movements in which ethnicity is a core issue. They may also experience intense anger at the majority group and glorify their own ethnic heritage.

Signithia Fordham and John Ogbu (1986) describe cases in which African American adolescents go through a process of *oppositional identity formation*, rejecting the patterns of dress, speech, mannerisms, and attitudes associated with European American society and adopting an identity that opposes them. These researchers believe that the process of oppositional identity formation provides one of the major explanations for the school failure of African American children. For many of these young people, who feel automatically shut out of the economic opportunities of the majority culture, successful identity formation requires that they look upon the academic activities of school as irrelevant to their lives. Evidence suggests that similar identity processes are at work in the development of adolescents of many minority groups in the United States (Phinney, 2008; Bisin et al., 2011; Sharkey, 2012).

Stage 3: Ethnic-Identity Achievement. Individuals who achieve a mature ethnic identity have resolved the conflicts characteristic of stage 2 and now have a secure self-confidence in their ethnicity and a positive self-concept (Cross, 2003). Researchers have found that mature ethnic identity may be a protective factor against particular risks (LaFromboise, Hoyt, Oliver, & Whitbeck, 2006). An example comes from a study of 434 seventh-grade students living in a large southwestern city who self-identified as American Indian: Students who had a greater sense of ethnic pride also had stronger antidrug norms (Kulis, Napoli, & Marsiglia, 2002).

Becoming Bicultural

In explaining how one's ethnicity becomes a lens through which teens view themselves in relation to society, the discussion above highlights the two processes—exploration and commitment—that Erikson considered key to successful identity formation. The discussion also illustrates how ethnicity becomes a salient feature of one's identity to the extent that it contrasts with other ethnicities—such as that of a majority culture. Missing from the discussion, however, is the way that adolescents form a coherent identity as members of more than one cultural background—that is, how they form a **bicultural identity** that includes identifications with one's ethnic heritage as well as with the majority culture (Schwartz, Unger & Baezconde-Garbanati et al., 2015).

bicultural identity Identifications with one's ethnic heritage as well as with the majority culture.

John Berry and his colleagues have been studying bicultural identity development for a number of years (Berry, 1984, 2015). Whereas the ethnic-identity approach described previously focuses on the single dimension of identification with one's ethnic heritage (sometimes referred to as *enculturation*), Berry suggests that there are two dimensions: one relating to the individual's preferences for maintaining their heritage culture and identity and the second relating to preferences for having contact with others outside their own group and participating in the larger society (sometimes referred to as *acculturation*). When these two dimensions are considered simultaneously, four possible ways of bicultural identity formation can be distinguished (see Table 15.2; examples in Phinney & Devich-Navarro, 1997):

1. *Marginalization* describes adolescents who feel little connection with either the heritage culture of their family or the majority culture. As reported by

one Native American teenager who didn't feel connected to any culture, "When I'm with my Indian friends I feel White, and when I'm with my White friends I feel Indian."

TABLE 15.2 Ethnic Identity Statuses

		Heritage Culture Identification	
		Low	High
Majority Culture Identification	Low	*Marginalization*	*Separation*
	High	*Assimilation*	*Integration*

2. *Separation* refers to adolescents who identify strongly with their heritage culture but have little interest in or attachment to the majority culture. For example, "I am just Black."
3. *Assimilation* describes adolescents who identify strongly with the majority culture but feel disconnected from their ethnic background. An example is teens who feel like Americans rather than Asian Americans, Mexican Americans, and so on.
4. *Integration* refers to individuals who identify strongly with both heritage and majority cultures—for example, "Being both Mexican and American means having the best of both worlds" (see Figure 15.11). Considerable research indicates that an integrated identity is positively correlated with self-esteem, self-mastery, and general well-being and negatively correlated with mental health problems including depression, anxiety, and feelings of hopelessness (Yoon et al., 2013).

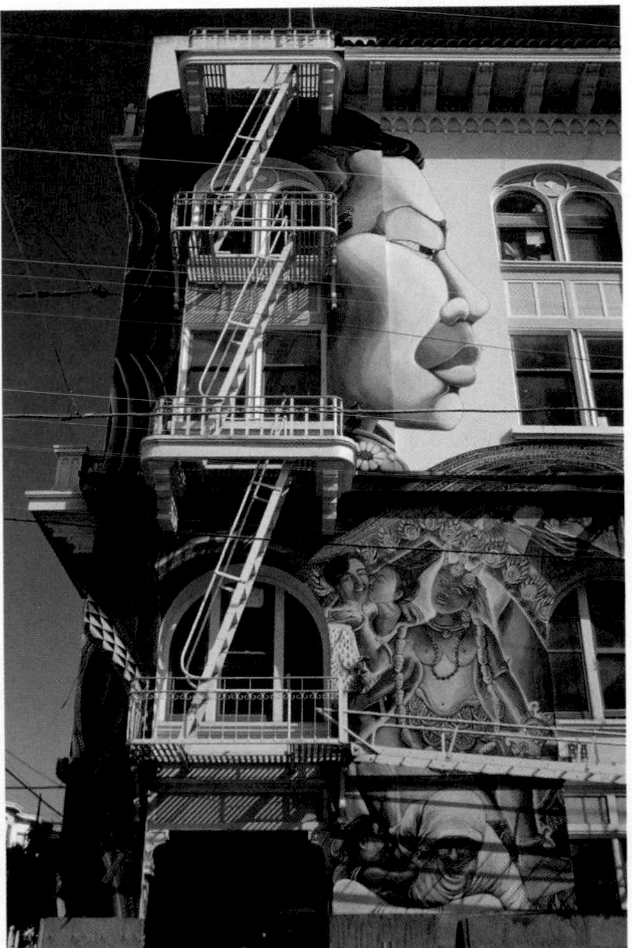
TravelStock44/LOOK/Robert Harding

FIGURE 15.11 Popular among U.S. adolescents of Hispanic descent, lowrider art often includes symbols of Latin American and Mexican cultures, encouraging teens' bicultural expression.

The extent to which an adolescent is likely to follow any of the four pathways described above depends on a number of factors, not the least of which is the teen's specific ethnic background (Berry, 2013). In the case of ethnic-minority or immigrant teens living in the United States, for example, Mexican American and Asian American adolescents are likely to develop toward *integration* (Marks, Patton, & Coll, 2011). In contrast, *separation* is the more common pathway of African American teens, and *marginalization* is more common among Native Americans (Markstrom, 2011; Yoon et al., 2013). Interestingly, although *integration* is strongly associated with well-being for many ethnic-minority groups, *separation* is associated with well-being in African American teens. To help understand this apparent discrepancy, we can compare the experiences of Asian American teens, who tend toward *integration*, and their African American counterparts, who tend toward separation (Yoon et al., 2012). Both groups are persistent targets of discrimination, although for different reasons. The discrimination experiences of Asian Americans are associated with their English language skills and cultural distance from mainstream U.S. culture (Yoo, Steger, & Lee, 2010). This type of discrimination, coupled with the traditional Asian value of conforming to social norms and not "rocking the boat," may encourage Asian minority adolescents toward identification with the majority culture. African Americans, on the other hand, have a history of oppression in the United States, so identification with their ethnic group may help teens develop a strong sense of self-esteem as members of their ethnic communities and may help them cope with discrimination (Yoon et al., 2011).

Ethnic and Racial Socialization Many teenagers associate "the talk" with an embarrassing and one-sided "conversation" in which a parent explains the risks and responsibilities of sexual behavior. But for African American teens, especially boys, "the talk" involves a serious discussion with parents about how their ethnicity may single them out as suspicious, potentially dangerous individuals and make them targets for law enforcement officers. In many African American families, "the talk" may be stimulated by particular events that take place in the community or are widely publicized in the media, such as the recent series of fatal shootings of unarmed Black boys, including Trayvon Martin and Michael Brown, and the Black Lives Matter movement that was inspired by such killings.

racial/ethnic socialization Parents' efforts to help their children understand their race/ethnicity and cope effectively with discrimination.

"The talk" is but one example of how parents and families act to influence their children's developing ethnic identity and racial awareness. **Racial/ethnic socialization**—that is, parents' efforts to help their children understand their race/ethnicity and cope effectively with discrimination—is widely practiced by ethnic-minority parents (Peck et al., 2014). Typically, racial/ethnic socialization includes two general features that are consistently associated with adolescent development (Paasch-Anderson & Lamborn, 2014). One feature socializes knowledge and pride about one's ethnic heritage, including one's native language, traditional religious beliefs, and ethnic family routines. The other socializes awareness of and preparation for racial discrimination and bias. Significantly, adolescents and young adults are very much aware of their parents' racial/ethnic socialization efforts. Here are some examples from African American adolescents who responded to questions about how their mothers tried to instill ethnic and racial understanding and prepare them for experiences with racism (Paasch-Anderson & Lamborn, 2014, pp. 173–174):

- "Attended a Black elementary school where African American culture was emphasized."
- "Home is full of African art and masks; African music played."
- "While cooking traditional African American food, such as greens and cornbread, mother explains their significance and how she was taught to cook."
- "Mother makes connections between child's achievements and those of slaves famous for their high levels of performance and activism, such as Harriet Tubman and others who participated in the Underground Railroad."
- "Mother cautions that Black males are often targets of racism."
- "Mother instructs importance of avoiding conflict situations."

Racial/ethnic socialization is strongly associated with positive developmental outcomes for adolescents. In a study of immigrant Armenian, Vietnamese, and Mexican families, Jean Phinney and her colleagues found that ethnic-identity formation is strongest when the native language is maintained in the home and when adolescents spend significant amounts of time with peers who share their ethnic heritage (Phinney & Ong, 2002). Positive ethnic-identity formation also seems to be fostered when parents deliberately uphold cultural traditions in the home and instruct their children in them (Fuligni et al., 2009; Hughes et al., 2006). There are, however, ethnic differences in the extent to which parents engage in racial/ethnic socialization practices. A recent longitudinal study of White, African

American, Latino, and Asian American adolescents and their parents found that African American parents engaged in the highest amount of socialization, in terms of both promoting knowledge and pride of their ethnic heritage and preparing their children for discrimination and bias (Else-Quest & Morse, 2015). Furthermore, and consistent with the expectation that racial/ethnic socialization fosters ethnic identity development, African American adolescents reported higher levels of ethnic identity exploration and commitment compared to adolescents in the other ethnic groups.

The strong impact of racial/ethnic socialization on ethnic identity is yet another example of how the adolescent's development results from the dynamic interaction of multiple systems—from the microsystem of the family through the chronosystem of historically and socially significant events, such as the killing of Trayvon Martin in 2012.

Ethnicity and Peer Culture In addition to family influences, ethnic-identity development is also influenced by peer culture. This is nowhere more apparent than in the case of hip-hop culture. From its beginnings in gangsta rap, through its expansion into B-boying, MC'ing, DJ'ing, graffiti, and styles of dress and speech, hip-hop has expressed the damage and injustice of growing up poor—especially Black and poor—in the inner cities of the United States (Chang, 2005; Dyson, 1995; Richardson & Scott, 2002). Researchers of hip-hop argue that it constitutes a genuine culture that influences the formation of identity among adolescents, particularly those of African and Latino descent. A striking example is Murray Forman's (2002) ethnographic study of Somali immigrant adolescents, which documents how these minority youth expand the frontiers of their own identity through the medium of hip-hop.

Since the early 1990s, Somalis have immigrated to the United States in unprecedented numbers to escape the political violence and oppression of their homeland. Uprooted from their traditional ways of life and transplanted to an entirely foreign environment, Somali adolescents face a clash of cultures. Moreover, upon their arrival in North America, "being Black" becomes a salient identity issue; cultural codes of race are simply not relevant in Somalia, where virtually the entire population is Black. According to Forman, an important means of coping with this cultural transition is to try to find a sense of self and belonging in peer groups. Hip-hop, Forman argues, provides an important vehicle by which Somali adolescents can understand the racial basis of their new social status because it generates an awareness of Blackness and the situation of Black urban youth: "There is a sense of comfort—even a sense of security—in the students' identification with hip hop" (2002, p. 110). Since Forman's groundbreaking work, hip-hop has taken on a global, multicultural dynamic in many parts of the world, having been infused with the language and the musical and dance traditions of multiple ethnicities. This makes it especially appealing to multicultural and immigrant youth seeking to express the diversity of their identities (Moran, 2016; Langnes & Fasting, 2016).

As you can see, in many ways the development of ethnic identity follows a similar course to the development of identity in general. Developmentalists point out, however, that ethnic-identity development is unique in some

Music and dance play important roles in adolescent identity development and peer culture. Originated by African American teenagers in the 1970s, breakdancing swept the North American continent and crossed the oceans, affecting youth culture throughout the world.

Nick Onken/Getty Images

very important respects (Phinney, 2010; Côté, 2009). Unlike general identity development, which is believed to involve a certain degree of choice (of occupations, spiritual beliefs, political positions, and so on), one cannot choose one's ethnic heritage. In addition, as underscored by Forman's research, one's ethnic heritage can take on different degrees of salience, depending on its relation to other groups in the community. The unique issues of choice (or lack thereof) and salience also apply to the process of forming a sexual identity.

Forming a Sexual Identity

sexual identity An individual's understanding of himself or herself as heterosexual, homosexual, or bisexual.

sexual-minority (LGBTQ) youth Adolescents who develop an identity as gay, lesbian, bisexual, transgendered, or queer.

If identity can be defined as an answer to the question "Who am I?" then sexual identity development can be defined as answering the question "Who am I as a sexual being?" More specifically, **sexual identity** refers to the name and meaning that individuals assign to themselves based on important sexual aspects of their lives, including sexual attractions, fantasies, desires, and behaviors (Savin-Williams, 2017). However, as you might imagine, it simply does not happen that young heterosexual people discover and declare to the world (or themselves), "I'm straight!" (Striepe & Tolman, 2003). Instead, developing a sexual identity can be particularly pressing and complicated for **sexual-minority (LGBTQ) youth**—that is, adolescents who develop an identity as lesbian, gay, bisexual, transgendered, or queer (Hu, Xu, & Tornello, 2016). Large national samples of adolescents indicate that by age 19, over 8 percent of males and females have had same-sex attractions or relationships (Chandra, Mosher, Copen, & Sionean, 2011; Russell & Joyner, 2001). Interestingly, whereas most females who report same-sex attractions also identify themselves as lesbian or bisexual, fewer than 2 percent of males identify themselves as gay or bisexual (Chandra et al., 2011; Garofalo et al., 1999). For both males and females, there tends to be a gap between acknowledging same-sex attractions, which usually occurs around 8 to 9 years of age, and identifying oneself as gay or bisexual, which varies between 14 and 21 years of age (Savin-Williams & Diamond, 2000). Clearly, adolescence is a critical time for developing one's sexual orientation.

Early research on the development of sexual orientation suggested that adolescents seem to go through a series of stages in the process of defining themselves as gay or bisexual (Ferrer-Wreder et al., 2002; Troiden, 1993). Richard Troiden developed the following stage model of forming a sexual-minority identity.

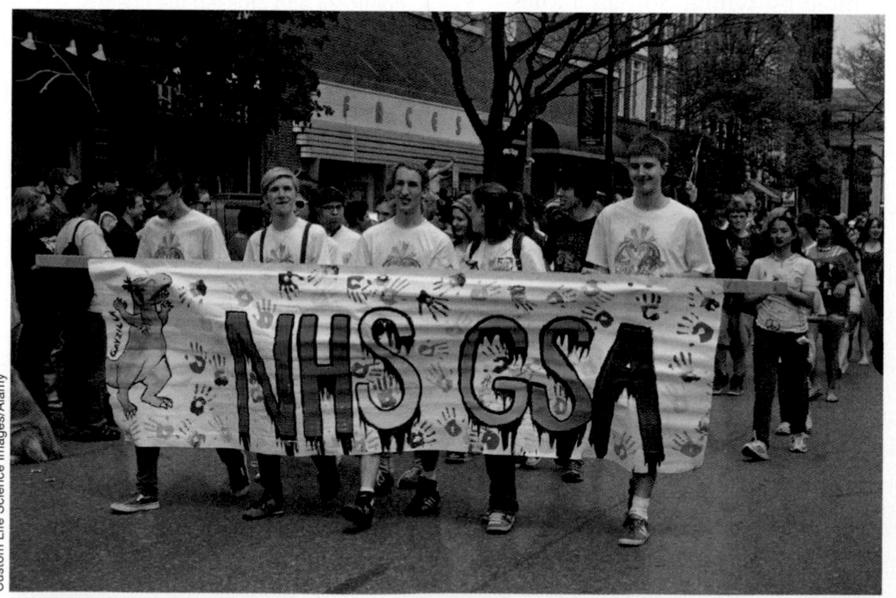

Custom Life Science Images/Alamy

More than 6,000 high school students participated in the annual Gay Straight Youth Pride Celebration that took place in Massachusetts.

Stage 1: Sensitization; Feeling Different. During early adolescence, many sexual-minority youth begin to experience a feeling of being "different." This is consistent with research finding that by 8 years of age, two-thirds of youth who later identified as gay were viewed by others as unusual in their gender behavior (D'Augelli et al., 2008).

Stage 2: Self-Recognition; Identity Confusion. With puberty, young adolescents may realize that they are attracted to members of the same sex and begin to label such feelings as "gay," "lesbian," "bisexual," "pansexual," or "omnisexual." This recognition can be the source of considerable inner turmoil and identity confusion. By middle or late adolescence, sexual-minority youth begin to believe that they are probably LGBTQ because they are uninterested in the heterosexual activities of their peers. Many sexual-minority adults recall adolescence as a time when they were loners and social outcasts.

Stage 3: Identity Assumption. Some young people who have had same-sex sexual experiences and who recognize that they prefer sexual relations with members of their own sex do not openly acknowledge their preference. Many others, however, move from private acknowledgment of their LGBTQ orientation to disclosing it publicly, at least to other sexual-minority individuals. Young people who have achieved this level of LGBTQ identity deal with it in a variety of ways. Some try to avoid same-sex contacts and attempt to pass as heterosexual because they are afraid of being stigmatized. Others begin to align themselves with the LGBTQ community.

Stage 4: Commitment; Identity Integration. This final stage of sexual-minority orientation is reached by those who come to terms with their sexual orientation. They have experienced a fusion of their sexuality and emotional commitments, express satisfaction with their sexual orientation, and have "come out"—that is, publicly disclosed their orientation.

Troiden notes that commitment to an LGBTQ identity may vary from weak to strong, depending on such factors as the individual's success in forging satisfying personal relationships, being accepted by family members, and functioning well at work or in a career. Indeed, the social stigma, oppression, and threats to physical safety facing sexual-minority youth, along with fear of being rejected by parents, can make coming out a major challenge (Baiocco et al., 2016 Samarova, Shilo, & Diamond, 2014). Retrospective accounts of gay men indicate that "living a lie," "alienation and isolation," and "telling others" were significant issues in their adolescent experiences (Flowers & Buston, 2002). This is not surprising given that well over half of all sexual-minority youth report experiencing levels of distress from face-to-face or online harassment that affect school performance and relationships with family and peers (Mitchell, Ybarra, & Korchmaros, 2014; see the box "Now Trending in Practice: Katy Butler Takes on Hollywood," in Chapter 13, p. 457).

Whereas much of the traditional work on sexual-orientation development has viewed it as a stagelike process leading to a relatively stable "identity integration," more recent work has focused on **sexual-orientation mobility**—that is, how sexual attractions, behaviors, and identities may shift over time (Ott et al., 2011; Savin-Williams & Ream, 2007). In a study conducted with young adults (21 to 26 years old), sexual-orientation mobility was higher for those who initially reported same-sex attractions compared to those who reported opposite-sex attractions, especially for young women (Dickson, Paul, & Herbison, 2003). Another study of 14- to 21-year-old LGB youth found that about half reported a change in their sexual orientation over the course of 6 to12 months (Rosario, Schrimshaw, Hunter, & Braun, 2006). Several longitudinal studies conducted in the United States and New Zealand indicate that sexual-orientation mobility of LGBTQ youth is relatively high across the early years of adolescence and becomes more stable during late adolescence and early adulthood (Dickson, van Roode, Cameron, & Paul, 2013; Hu, Xu, & Tornello, 2016; Ott et al., 2011; Savin-Williams & Ream, 2007). In general, teens who initially identify as bisexual have greater sexual-orientation mobility compared to those who initially report that they are attracted exclusively to the same or opposite sex (Dickson et al., 2013). Overall, this research underscores the dynamic nature of sexual-orientation development

sexual-orientation mobility The shifting of sexual attractions, behaviors, and identities over time.

across the adolescent years and adolescence as an important period in achieving a stable sexual identity.

One of the most critical and complicated issues for sexual-minority youth is disclosing their sexual orientation to family members and friends. Indeed, parents' reactions to their teens' disclosure is a source of considerable concern to teens and may impact their mental health and well-being (Baiocco et al., 2015; D'Augelli, 2003; Samarova, Shilo, & Diamond, 2014). A study of 117 young adults who were approximately 20 years of age and self-identified as gay or bisexual found that the average age of disclosure was similar across the subgroups, at approximately 16 years of age (Maguen, Floyed, Bakeman, & Armistead, 2002). However, the subgroups were significantly different in the average age both of awareness of same-sex attractions and of acting on these attractions. For example, lesbians were more likely than gay men to report sexual contacts with both males and females; moreover, they were more likely than gay men to have had their first sexual contact with a person of the other sex. The distinctive pattern that characterizes lesbians is consistent with arguments that sexual-minority women may be more likely than men to be attracted to both sexes and that girls may be under more social pressure to date boys (Chandra et al., 2011; Ellis, Kitzinger, & Wilkinson, 2002; Savin-Williams & Diamond, 2004).

It has been pointed out that in most respects, the needs and concerns of youth with same-sex attractions are simply those of all youth: "Regardless of sexual orientation, youths need the love and respect of their parents, must negotiate their ongoing relationships as they move toward adulthood, are concerned with peer status, desire love and sex, and wonder about their future" (Savin-Williams, 2001, p. 6). However, as a consequence of social stigma and harassment, sexual-minority youth are at special risk for a variety of mental health problems, including depression and suicide (Shearer et al., 2016). In order to help mental health practitioners and researchers working with sexual minority teens, the Society of Adolescent Health and Medicine developed a set of guidelines (see Table 15.3).

TABLE 15.3 Society of Adolescent Health and Medicine's Guidelines for Working with Sexual Minority Teens

- All adolescent health-care providers should receive training in how to provide nonjudgmental care for lesbian, gay, bisexual, transgendered, or queer (LGBTQ) youth, oriented toward understanding that the majority of LGBTQ youth are healthy and well-adjusted. Attempts to change the sexual orientation, often referred to as "reparative therapy," are coercive and inconsistent with modern standards of care.
- Training should foster understanding of adolescent sexuality development and health, as well as mental health issues associated with the coming-out process or victimization.
- Because sexual orientation may evolve over time, caution should be exercised in attaching labels to an adolescent's sexual orientation. Instead, youth should be asked how they self-identify, and professionals should use these self-identifications as a guide.
- Family connections and support are important in protecting LGBTQ teens from depression, drug use, and high-risk sexual behavior. When teens disclose their sexual orientation or gender identity to their families, professionals should be prepared to help families accept their LGBTQ children.
- Victimization and bullying of LGBTQ youth put youth at risk for depression and suicide. Professionals should be comfortable discussing these common issues with their LGBTQ clients and should screen for mental health issues. Professionals also should actively engage with schools and other community agencies to prevent and stop victimization.
- Sexual-minority adolescents should be fully and legally protected from victimization under both local and federal laws.

Information from Society for Adolescent Health and Medicine, 2013.

Clearly, developing a coherent identity is a complex process. For some adolescents, this process is further complicated by social and emotional problems, as we discuss next.

APPLY > CONNECT > DISCUSS

How does the distinction between an independent and an interdependent sense of self apply to your own sense of self?

Adolescent Health and Well-Being

LEARNING OUTCOMES

Differentiate between internalizing problems and externalizing problems that affect the health and well-being of adolescents.

Point out findings about the relationship between adolescents and the experience of depression, eating disorders, and delinquency.

Examine the qualities that promote positive youth development in adolescents.

As you have learned, the changes associated with adolescence have profound social and psychological consequences—not only for young people themselves but for their families, friends, and communities as well. Cultural beliefs, family values, and peer-group norms all contain changing, and sometimes conflicting, expectations about how adolescents should behave in their new, sexually mature bodies. And, of course, the adolescent body itself is undergoing enormous transformations in both external appearance and internal hormonal functioning and neural organization. Remarkably, most adolescents weather these stormy changes without lasting difficulties. For some, however, the challenges of adolescence pose significant problems for health and well-being, by either aggravating preexisting problems or creating conditions for the emergence of new problems which may or may not persist into adulthood.

Emotional Health

One of the most extensively studied topics of adolescence is the increase of social and emotional problems during this period (Steinberg, 2008). In general, developmentalists distinguish between two categories of emotional problems: internalizing problems and externalizing problems. **Internalizing problems**, which are more common in girls, include disturbances in emotion or mood such as depression, worry, guilt, and anxiety. **Externalizing problems**, which are more common in boys, include social and behavioral problems such as aggression and delinquency—ranging from the violation of age-appropriate social norms, such as skipping school and running away, to law-breaking behaviors such as drug use and vandalism (Farrington, 2004; Graber, 2004).

internalizing problems Disturbances in emotion or mood such as depression, worry, guilt, and anxiety; more common in girls than in boys.

externalizing problems Social and behavioral problems such as aggression and delinquency; more common in boys than in girls.

Developmentalists seeking to understand and help adolescents with social and emotional problems have focused on three broad questions: Why do these problems seem to erupt during adolescence? What are the differences between adolescents who develop these problems and those who do not? Why is it that when problems do arise, girls tend to have internalizing problems and boys externalizing problems?

Depression and Anxiety On the basis of decades of research conducted throughout the world, it is now widely accepted that there is a surge during adolescence in feelings of depression, sadness, and anxiety, and that it mostly affects girls (Costello, Swendsen, Rose, & Dierker, 2008; Twenge & Nolen-Hoeksema, 2002). Several studies have examined adolescents' **emotional tone**, or their sense of well-being versus depression and anxiety. In general, findings show that for adolescents in the United States and many other countries, positive emotional tone increases throughout adolescence for boys but plateaus after early adolescence for girls (Sweeting & West, 2003). Gender differences in emotional distress are reflected in research finding that by the age of 15, girls were about twice as likely as boys to experience serious depression (Keenan et al., 2010). Similar trends have been found in Mexican adolescents (Borges et al., 2008).

emotional tone One's sense of well-being versus depression and anxiety.

depression An emotional state involving some combination of sadness, apathy, hopelessness, poor self-esteem, and trouble finding pleasure in activities that one used to enjoy. Depression is one of the most common psychological problems of adolescence, especially for girls.

Characterized by some combination of sadness, apathy, hopelessness, poor self-esteem, and trouble finding pleasure in activities that one used to enjoy, **depression** is one of the most common psychological problems of adolescence. The incidence of depression in adolescence depends on the number and severity of the symptoms. Virtually all adolescents (and adults, for that matter) experience episodes of sadness, or *depressed mood*; approximately 25 percent of teens report regular bouts of feeling sad (Avenevoli & Steinberg, 2001). In contrast, approximately 16 percent of adolescent girls and 8 percent of boys meet the criteria for the more serious *depressive disorder*. (Table 15.4 lists the criteria, set out by the American Psychiatric Association's *Diagnostic and Statistical Manual of Mental Disorders, Fifth Edition* [*DSM*-5], 2013.)

A great deal of research has been devoted to identifying the causes of depression and to finding ways to prevent and treat it. Although a number of studies have found that both genetic and environmental factors play important roles, some of the most consistent and intriguing findings relate to the risk factors of puberty and gender (Conley, Rudolph, & Bryant, 2012; Price & Marzani-Nissen, 2012). As you probably have heard, there is a striking gender difference in rates of depression: Women are twice as likely as men to be diagnosed with the disorder. What you may not know is that there is no gender difference in depression rates during childhood and that the gender difference emerging later in development seems largely due to surging rates for girls at the time of puberty (the rates for boys remain fairly stable throughout adolescence and adulthood; Rudolph et al., 2000; Twenge & Nolen-Hoeksema, 2002). Developmentalists are eager to discover why girls in general, and girls at the point of puberty in particular, are so vulnerable to depression.

In an effort to explain the relationship between puberty, gender, and depression, developmentalists have pointed to the interaction of biological and sociocultural processes. As you read earlier, for example, girls are more likely than boys to be stressed by the events of puberty, with many reacting to their sexually maturing bodies with negativity and self-consciousness, possibly because their body image conflicts with a cultural ideal of feminine thinness. In addition, girls' maturing bodies tend to be viewed as sexual objects to a greater extent than are boys' bodies, making girls feel more self-conscious (Brooks-Gunn & Warren, 1989; Martin, 1996; Thorne, 1993). It may be that the sexualization of the female body also accounts for the different reactions that parents have to their sons' and daughters' development. In contrast to boys, who report that their parents grant them greater freedom as they become sexually mature, many girls report that their parents become more restrictive (Martin, 1996). The perception of higher levels of parental control may contribute to feelings of anxiety and depression to the extent that girls resent and attempt to resist parents' efforts to restrict their behavior.

TABLE 15.4 DSM-5 Criteria for Diagnosing Major Depressive Disorder*

- Feeling depressed for most of the day
- Taking less interest and pleasure in activities
- Significant changes in weight or appetite
- Sleeping too little or too much
- Physical movements that are unusually agitated or slow
- Feeling tired or without energy nearly every day
- Feelings of extreme guilt or worthlessness
- Difficulties concentrating, reasoning, or making decisions
- Frequent thoughts of death or suicide

*A diagnosis requires that at least five of these symptoms are present over a 2-week period and reflect change from previous functioning.

Treatment options for adolescents suffering from depression and anxiety range from drug therapies to individual and family therapy. Research indicates that one of the most effective treatments is **cognitive-behavioral therapy (CBT)**, which is based on the theory that negative thoughts and/or poor coping behaviors may cause the adolescent to feel depressed and anxious (Kennard et al., 2009). CBT involves helping the adolescent to develop adaptive communication and problem-solving skills, monitor and regulate changing emotions, and schedule time for relaxing and enjoyable activities.

cognitive-behavioral therapy (CBT) A treatment for depression and anxiety that is based on the theory that these problems are related to negative thoughts and/or poor coping behaviors. CBT is designed to help the adolescent develop adaptive communication and problem-solving skills, monitor and regulate changing emotions, and schedule time for relaxing and enjoyable activities.

Eating Disorders

One pubertal change that carries significant consequences for emotional tone is the increase in weight. As we have noted, for boys, this increase comes largely from a gain in muscle mass, whereas for girls, the increase is largely the result of the addition of body fat, estimated to be, on average, a little more than 24 pounds over the course of adolescence (Bogin, 1999). These changes are perfectly normal but can carry very different psychological consequences for boys and girls, depending on cultural values and beliefs. For boys in many cultures, bulking up is valued—as an athletic advantage and as a step toward becoming "buff" and sexy. For girls, in contrast, the increase in fat can deviate from cultural ideals and thus may be a source of significant psychological distress (Polivy & Herman, 2004). In the United States, for example, a thin, prepubertal body shape is the current ideal for women, an ideal reflected in everything from television, movie, and magazine images to dolls given to young girls (Dittmar, Halliwell, & Ive, 2006). In general, girls exposed to media that directly or indirectly promotes thinness as the physical ideal are at risk for developing a negative body image that can persist over time (Groesz, Levine, & Murnen, 2002; Hausenblaus, Janelle, Gardner, & Focht, 2004).

It is now widely acknowledged that many adolescent girls who are dissatisfied with their bodies go on fad diets that may cut out entire classes of food such as fats or carbohydrates, or take drugs to suppress their appetite, or induce vomiting and take laxatives to avoid gaining weight. All of these practices endanger their health and, in extreme forms, can lead to eating disorders such as **anorexia nervosa**, or intentional self-starving, and **bulimia nervosa**, or cycles of binge eating followed by self-induced vomiting (Keel, Gravener, Joiner, & Haedt, 2010; Keel & Klump, 2003). A third disorder, often called **unspecified feeding or eating disorder**, is diagnosed when the criteria for anorexia or bulimia nervosa are not quite met; it is the most common diagnosis for adolescents with eating disorders (Golden, Katzman, & Kreipe, 2003).

anorexia nervosa An eating disorder that involves intentional self-starving.

bulimia nervosa An eating disorder that involves cycles of binge eating followed by self-induced vomiting.

unspecified feeding or eating disorder An eating disorder that is diagnosed when the criteria for anorexia or bulimia nervosa are not quite met; it is the most common diagnosis for adolescents with eating disorders.

Table 15.5 (p. 556) shows the criteria most commonly used to diagnose anorexia nervosa and bulimia. When these criteria are applied, very few adolescents are diagnosed with eating disorders: Fewer than 1 percent of adolescents are diagnosed with anorexia, while approximately 3 percent are diagnosed with bulimia nervosa. However, this particular classification system is not entirely applicable to children and adolescents, the age groups during which eating disorders typically emerge (Miller & Golden, 2010). For example, wide variation in the adolescent growth spurt, the absence of menstrual periods in early puberty, and the unpredictability of menstrual periods immediately following menarche limit the application of the diagnostic criteria presented in the table. In addition, the developmental immaturity of children and adolescents may hinder their ability to express abstract concepts such as self-awareness, motivation to lose weight, or feelings of anxiety or depression (Golden et al., 2003).

Furthermore, clinicians have long recognized the importance of identifying and treating children with "subthreshold" conditions (which include some, but not all, of the standard criteria), as well as children exhibiting other "disordered" behaviors

TABLE 15.5 Criteria for Diagnosing Anorexia and Bulimia Nervosa

Condition	DSM-5 Criteria
Anorexia nervosa	1. Restricting caloric intake, resulting in a significantly low body weight in relation to the individual's age, sex, developmental status, and physical health
	2. Intense fear of weight gain or becoming overweight, or frequent behavior that interferes with weight gain, despite being significantly underweight
	3. Disturbed image and evaluation of one's body, body weight or shape, or persistent lack of acknowledging the seriousness of the current low body weight
	Specific types of anorexia nervosa
	Restricting type: In the past three months, weight loss due primarily to restricting food intake and/or excessive exercise, and not from self-induced vomiting, or the misuse of laxatives, diuretics, or enemas
	Binge-eating/purging type: In the past three months, frequent binge eating or self-induced vomiting, or misuse of laxatives, diuretics, or enemas
Bulimia nervosa	1. Eating a substantially larger than normal amount of food within a specific time period (2 hours or so), and feeling a lack of control over how much one is eating
	2. To prevent weight gain from overeating, compensating through harmful behaviors such as self-induced vomiting, misuse of laxatives or diuretics, fasting, or excessive exercise
	3. Both binge eating and harmful compensatory behaviors occurring at least once a week for 3 months, on average
	4. Feelings about one's self influenced to an excessive degree by one's body shape and weight
	5. The disturbed behavior not only during episodes of anorexia nervosa

associated with eating that are not included in the standard description of anorexia nervosa and bulimia nervosa. Examples include *functional dysphagia*, in which food avoidance is associated with a fear of choking or vomiting, and *pervasive food refusal*, which involves refusal not only to eat but also to drink, walk, talk, or care for oneself (Nicholls, Chater, & Lask, 2000). Using a broader set of criteria for defining disordered eating behaviors, a recent 8-year longitudinal study conducted in a large U.S. city found that 12 percent of adolescent girls developed eating disorders (Stice, Marti, Shaw, & Jaconis, 2009).

The road to recovery from eating disorders can be long and difficult, with frequent relapses. This is especially true with anorexia nervosa. More than 20 percent of individuals diagnosed with anorexia nervosa continue to have an eating disorder many years later. In addition, these individuals frequently suffer from other psychiatric problems, including depression, anxiety, and substance abuse. Sadly, according to some reports, as many as 15 percent die either from complications related to their eating disorder or from committing suicide (see Miller & Golden, 2010, for review). Although there is less longitudinal research on individuals with bulimia nervosa and unspecified feeding or eating disorder, their recovery seems more promising, with 60 to 75 percent achieving good outcomes or full recovery (Keel et al., 2010; Herzog et al., 1999).

Delinquency and Other Externalizing Problems

Like internalizing problems, externalizing problems seem to peak in adolescence. For both boys and girls, delinquent behaviors such as skipping school, stealing or destroying property, getting into fights, and taking illegal drugs rise sharply between early and mid-adolescence, after which they decline (Dodge & Pettit, 2003; Storvoll & Wichstrom, 2002; Steinberg, 2008). However, the gender differences, which, as noted, are reversed from those of internalizing problems, are much greater than those of internalizing problems (Lahey et al., 2000). In fact, it has been estimated that boys account for 70 percent of all juvenile *person offenses*, such as assault, robbery, homicide, and other crimes involving force or threat of force against persons (Puzzanchera & Adams, 2011).

The incidence of delinquent behaviors during adolescence poses an important question: Is the increase due to the fact that a larger proportion of teens are involved, perhaps minimally, in behaviors such as skipping school, drinking alcohol, smoking pot, getting into fights, and so forth, or is it the case that a small number of teens become increasingly active in such behavior? Studies indicate that the increase reflects both factors: an increase in the number of teens involved and an increase in the involvement of specific individuals (Maccoby, 2004). For example, in a nationwide longitudinal study of Norwegian adolescents, more than 75 percent of all 15- to 16-year-old boys and girls reported some involvement in delinquent behaviors (with the percentage being somewhat higher for boys than for girls), but only 25 percent of boys and 15 percent of girls reported high levels of involvement (Storvoll & Wichstrom, 2002). This is consistent with other research indicating that over 50 percent of all juvenile violent behaviors are perpetrated by only 6 percent of all adolescents, most of whom are also involved in other externalizing behaviors such as theft and the frequent use of drugs and alcohol (Dodge & Pettit, 2003; Moffitt, Caspi, Rutter, & Silva, 2002).

Naturally, developmentalists are especially concerned about this small minority of adolescents who show high levels of delinquency, as well as about those who exhibit other serious forms of chronic externalizing problems. Adolescents in these groups account for the majority of referrals to outpatient adolescent mental health clinics and the largest proportion of placements in special education classes (reviewed in Dodge & Pettit, 2003).

To shed light on these groups, a team of researchers studied approximately 1,000 individuals growing up in New Zealand, following them from birth to adulthood (Moffitt, 2007; Moffitt et al., 2002). The researchers identified two highly distinctive developmental patterns of externalizing problems. In one, called *adolescent onset*, externalizing problems emerged in adolescence and had a fairly brief time course, declining significantly in young adulthood. In the other, called *childhood onset*, or *life-course persistent*, high levels of aggression emerged in preschool and persisted throughout childhood and adolescence and into adulthood. Although boys outnumbered girls in both groups, the boy/girl ratio was much smaller (1.5 to 1) in the adolescent-onset group than in the childhood-onset group, in which boys outnumbered girls by a ratio of 10 to 1. Note that these results are similar to those of the Norwegian study described previously, in which gender differences were much greater for reports of high involvement in externalizing behaviors than for overall reports of involvement.

The developmental histories of adolescents who exhibit childhood-onset problems are strikingly different from those of their adolescent-onset peers (Patterson, DeBaryshe, & Ramsey, 1989; Dodge et al., 2009). As shown in Figure 15.12 (p. 558), boys who go on to develop life-course-persistent problems such as substance use and addiction typically have difficult temperaments and receive inconsistent parenting during early childhood. (The developmental histories of life-course-persistent girls have not yet been well studied.) In essence, by virtue of their difficult temperaments, these young boys are hard to handle, and their parents lack the skills necessary to cope effectively with their behaviors. Instead, they tend to respond either by ignoring the boys' inappropriate and often aggressive behaviors, which fails to teach the boys social skills, including self-control, or by using excessive punishment, which, as described in Chapter 9, creates a family system in which parents and children are caught in a dynamic of escalating negative interactions. Both approaches increase the chances that, when such boys begin school, they are

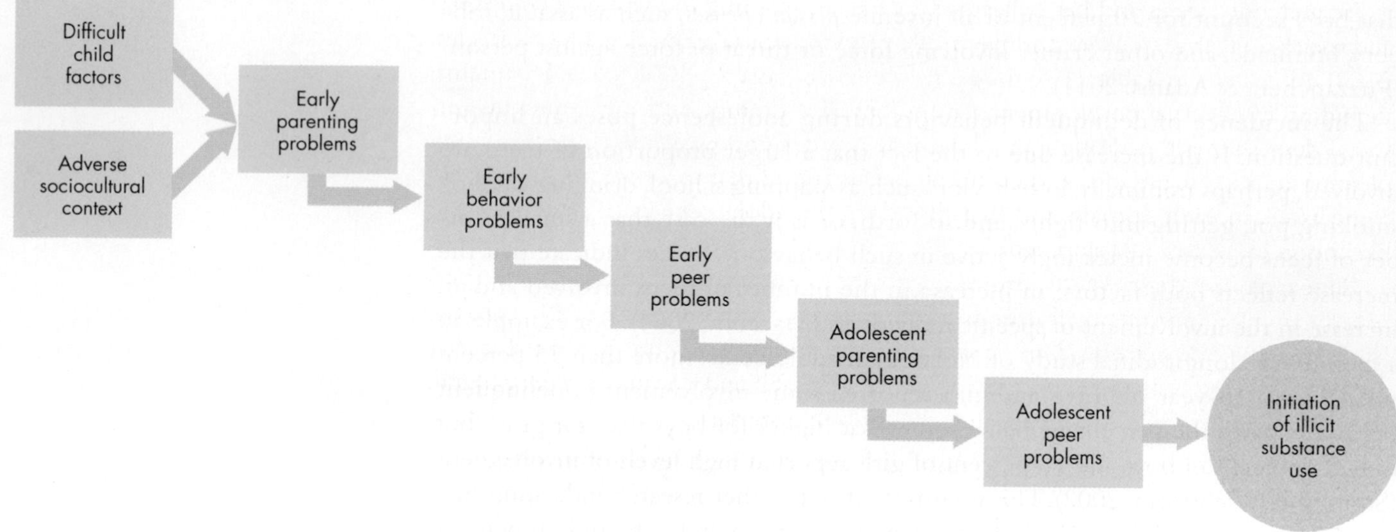

FIGURE 15.12 Research suggests that adolescent substance use may be rooted in a long history of interacting peer, family, and child temperament factors. (Data from Dodge et al., 2009.)

both aggressive and undersocialized. As a consequence, by middle childhood, they are often rejected by peers and performing poorly in school. By late childhood and adolescence, they typically form alliances with other deviant peers, who further reinforce their externalizing behaviors.

As noted above, there has been little research into how and why some girls develop externalizing problems. On the other hand, there has been a great deal of speculation as to why such problems are less common in girls than in boys. In general, most developmentalists maintain that the gender differences are largely due to an interaction of biological and sociocultural processes. As discussed in Chapter 9 (pp. 317–318), boys and girls may have different biological predispositions to behave aggressively (Maccoby, 2004). Coupled with this are the considerable differences in the socialization of boys and girls by parents as well as by peers (Zahn-Waxler & Polanichka, 2004). In particular, norm-violating behaviors are less tolerated in girls and more often ignored in boys. Moreover, the *communal orientation* of girls discussed earlier would seem to further diminish their involvement in externalizing behaviors.

All told, evidence indicates that adolescence is a vulnerable period for the onset of social and emotional problems and that these problems are significantly affected by sociocultural norms and expectations.

Positive Youth Development

Given that adolescents are generally healthier than any other age group, it is somewhat ironic that the lion's share of research on adolescent health and well-being has focused on illness and disease. Recently, however, many developmentalists have begun to balance the scales by defining a general approach to adolescence—**positive youth development (PYD)**—that emphasizes the strengths and positive qualities of youth that contribute to their psychological health as well as the welfare of their communities (Lerner, Phelps, Forman, & Bowers, 2009). As described by Jacqueline Lerner and her colleagues, the PYD perspective has its origins in the concept of the plasticity of development. As we have discussed earlier, *plasticity* refers to the degree to which development is open to change and intervention as a consequence of specific experiences. Extending the notion of plasticity to adolescent development, the PYD approach examines individual strengths such as future-mindedness, optimism, honesty, and insight, as well as the role of youth programs, communities, and societies in both promoting such strengths and profiting from them.

positive youth development (PYD) A general approach to adolescence that emphasizes the strengths and positive qualities of youth that contribute to their psychological health as well as to the welfare of their communities.

Jacquelynne Eccles and her colleagues have been working to identify the personal and social assets that facilitate positive youth development (Zaff, Malanchuk, & Eccles, 2008). As shown in Table 15.6, they have identified assets within several domains, including intellectual development, psychological and emotional development, and social development. Although an adolescent can develop positively in the absence of some or even many of the assets listed, Eccles argues that it is best to have at least some assets in each domain and that the more the adolescent has, the greater the likelihood of positive development.

Research on what, exactly, promotes positive youth development has focused mostly on the influence of after-school programs such as 4-H, Big Brothers/Big Sisters, and Boy Scouts/Girl Scouts, which share in the common goal of learning and working with others for the betterment of self and community. In general, programs are most effective when they meet three criteria:

1. Allow for the development of positive adult–youth relationships that last at least 1 year
2. Provide activities that promote skill building
3. Provide opportunities to use skills

Another important factor in the success of such programs is leadership. In general, research finds that the most successful adult program leaders are those who seek the input of the youth, follow the lead of youth, and push the youth toward higher levels of achievement (Larson, 2007; Larson & Tran, 2014).

TABLE 15.6 Assets Supporting Positive Youth Development

Cognitive development
Reasoning and critical thinking skills
Skills at making good decisions
Significant knowledge of multiple cultures
Strong achievement in school
Emotional and psychological development
Good mental health and positive self-esteem
Good emotion regulation and coping skills
Strong mastery and achievement motivation
Sense of personal agency and autonomy
Socially and culturally informed values
Social development
Perception of good relationships, connection, and trust with parents and peers
Sense of belonging to school, church, youth development programs, and other institutions
Commitment to civic engagement
Characteristics of the developmental context
Appropriately structured environment, including age-appropriate monitoring, clear and consistent rules and expectations
Emotional support, warmth, and responsiveness
Strong expectations and norms for prosocial and ethical behaviors, moral reasoning, and expectations for service to others
Opportunities to participate in activities that support agency, and to develop mastery in valued activities

Information from Eccles, Brown, & Templeton, 2008.

In a study of how participation in an urban art project may contribute to positive development, Reed Larson and his colleagues traced a fascinating developmental pattern. Specifically, when youth were engaged in an internship that involved real-life challenges to plan and create murals for their communities, they progressed from an egocentric focus on their own ideas to developing strategies and skills for teamwork that were applied to accomplish their artful goals (Larson, 2007). Needless to say, this structured civic engagement not only bolstered the positive development of the youth but also benefited the community in which they lived. The mutuality of positive youth and community development is at the heart of the PYD perspective: Youth thrive when they are meaningfully engaged in community affairs, and communities thrive when their youth are healthy, happy, and committed to the well-being of those around them.

APPLY > CONNECT > DISCUSS

Your school board is once again seeking your assistance, this time to revamp its sex education program, which is considered outdated and out of touch with issues facing today's youth. The goal is to develop programs aimed at seventh-graders (12-year-olds) and tenth-graders (15-year-olds). Outline a general plan for each program. What topics should each program include? What "issues facing today's youth" should be addressed? Should boys and girls participate in the program together or separately? Explain how the program would take into account differences between 12- and 15-year-olds.

LEARNING OUTCOMES

Summarize the developmental transformations and conflicts that occur during adolescence.

Describe how adolescent development lays a foundation for the next stages in a person's life span.

Looking Ahead

Evidence presented in this chapter, as well as in Chapter 14, indicates that the biocultural transition of adolescence universally involves dramatic transformation across the physical, cognitive, social, and emotional domains and is often accompanied by conflict, anxiety, and uncertainty.

Compared with all other primate species, humans are radically delayed in reaching reproductive maturity. Many have argued that the delay is to allow the brain to develop areas associated with advanced processes—language, reasoning, decision making—required to make and use the sophisticated tools of human culture. Even so, at the onset of puberty, the frontal lobes are not sufficiently mature for the effective regulation of the surge of emotional intensity associated with the release of hormones, and poorly regulated emotions make the adolescent vulnerable to risk-taking, recklessness, and emotional problems.

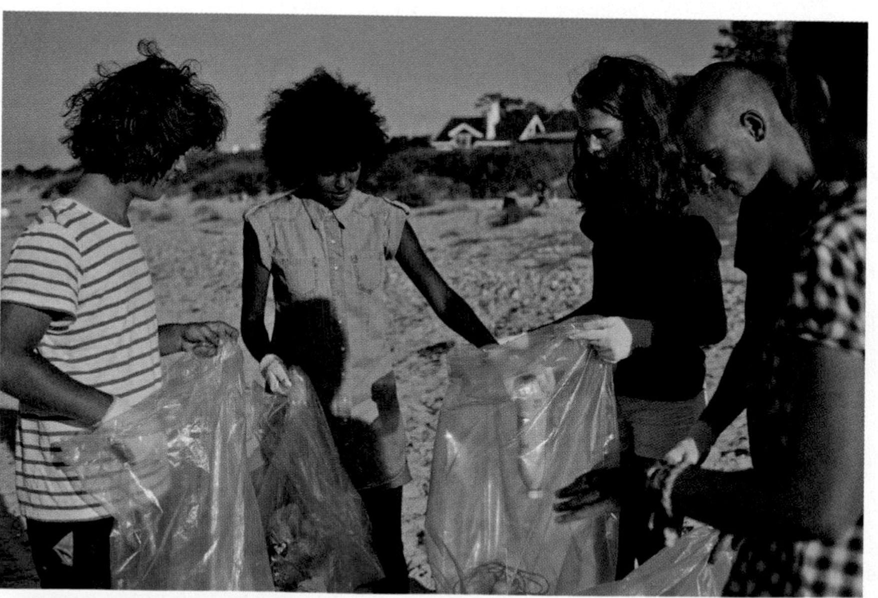

Klaus Vedfelt/Getty Images

Working together to clean up a beach in their community, these teens are not only improving the environment, but also developing a sense of their relationship to society.

While the onset and course of adolescence are heavily influenced by such biological factors, the many contexts of development—from the physical environment to cultural values and practices—also play significant roles in adolescent development. Thus, culture has played a role in the timing of the onset of puberty, as evidenced by the secular trend—the increasingly early pubertal onset associated with changes in the contexts of development across recent generations. In the past, the secular trend was attributed to increased access to nutritious food and health care. The continuing downward trend of the past few decades, however, has been associated with the rising tide of obesity and poor health, particularly among low-income minority populations in the United States, providing an unfortunate illustration of how phenotypic development is constrained by both biological and cultural processes.

Similarly, research provides strong evidence that the adolescent experience—how individuals navigate the passage to adulthood—is to a large extent structured by families, communities, and institutions and dependent on cultural beliefs, values, and practices. For example, many of the questions that concern adolescents—Who am I? Who will I become? Who will be my mate? What is right and just?—may be less significant in cultures where identity, career, and social role possibilities are mapped out in advance according to long-standing cultural traditions and where traditional beliefs and values are rarely open to question.

And then there is the issue of whether the cumulative cultural evolution of technologically advanced societies has created a context for the emergence of yet another way station between childhood and adulthood, a new stage of "emerging adulthood," in which the developing individual comes to terms with a kaleidoscopic array of possibilities—for identity, relationships, education, and ways of understanding the nature of truth and knowledge. But regardless of whether emerging adulthood proves to be a specific stage in the life course, we can be sure that the transition to adulthood reflects a special relationship between developing individuals and the cultures they will transform and carry into the future.

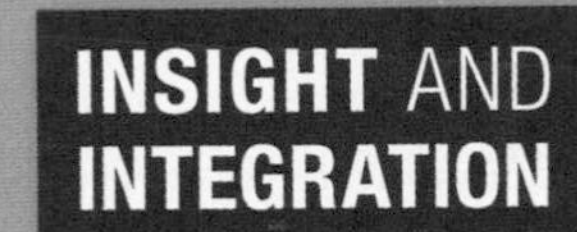

1. In what ways do adolescents engage in *niche construction*, as described in Chapter 2 (p. 70)?
2. It's often proclaimed that adolescents and young adults are the future of human culture and society. Support this claim, based on ideas presented in this chapter.
3. Review the discussion of *mediation*, described in Chapter 2 (p. 53). Explain how adolescents' use of technology mediates their development.

SUMMARY

Emotional Development in Adolescence

- Contrary to perceptions of adolescence being an emotional roller coaster, research indicates that over adolescence, ups and downs become less frequent and emotions become less intense, although average happiness decreases.
- Decreased emotional intensity is in large part explained by increased emotional regulation. In early adolescence, the cortex is not fully mature, and the reward system component of the limbic system becomes hyperactivated, leaving adolescents vulnerable to risk-taking; later maturation of the brain facilitates emotional regulation. Emotional regulation also appears to be promoted by parental warmth and to be shaped by social expectations related to gender.

Relationships with Peers

- During adolescence, time spent with peers increases dramatically, peer groups become larger, and peer relationships become more important and intense.
- Adolescents seek friendships marked by reciprocity, commitment, and equality. Close friendships serve the functions of intimacy and autonomy and thus promote social and personality development. Girls' friendships are more intense and intimate than boys' friendships, with expressions of intimacy between boys curtailed perhaps by lack of trust, stereotypes about masculinity, or homophobia; gender differences in relationship goals may also explain friendship differences.
- Adolescents' extensive use of social media does not appear to affect the intimacy of peer relationships, especially if the relationships have been initially established in face-to-face contexts. Online communications with existing friends and romantic partners improves relationships over time. The use of social media can be especially helpful for teens who struggle with social anxiety.
- In addition to friendships, adolescent peer relations take the form of cliques—small, intimate peer groups that serve emotional and security needs—and crowds—larger groups that provide opportunities to meet people, to develop romantic relationships and, because different crowds have different reputations, to explore social identity.

- Adolescent peer relationships tend to be characterized by high levels of homophily, or similarity in behaviors, tastes, views, and goals. A study by Denise Kandel showed homophily as resulting from two successive processes: selection, in which adolescents target as potential friends peers with whom they share similarities, and socialization, in which friends mutually model and reinforce significant behavior. Thus, deviancy can be socialized in the context of peer relationships, in a process that has been labeled deviancy training.
- According to classic research by Dexter Dunphy, romantic relationships develop in a stagelike process in which same-sex cliques of early adolescence give way to mixed-sex crowds, which gradually give way to romantic relationships. Significant cultural variations exist, however, and in contemporary industrialized societies, marriage is postponed and romantic relationships take place alongside other peer relationships.

Sexual Behavior

- Research on adolescent sexual behavior is hampered by multiple meanings of "sex," which can vary from one teen to the next.
- Adolescents learn about sexuality from various sources—parents, peers, media, and educational programs—and there is great variability in what is taught and how it is taught.
- Family sexual culture contributes to how adolescents and parents communicate about sex and sexuality. When parents and teens talk about sexual issues, and parents monitor teens' sexual exposure, teens are less likely to engage in risky sexual behaviors.
- Exposure to cyberporn is common during adolescence. Adolescents may use pornography to learn about sexual behavior. Some studies find that exposure is related to family and dating violence; other studies find no relationship to risky sexual practices.
- The sexual debut (age at first intercourse) varies considerably across countries and over time. Boys tend to report more positive feelings about first intercourse than do girls. Early sexual intercourse, especially when it is coercive, is related to a number of problem behaviors. Significant late sexual intercourse is associated with challenges in establishing romantic relationships.

Relationships with Parents

- In intensity and frequency, parent–child conflict reaches a peak in early adolescence and then decreases. Conflicts tend to focus on such matters as responsibilities and curfews—seemingly trivial but related to major issues of growing up. They often reflect differences between parents' and adolescents' understanding of what belongs to the personal, as opposed to the social conventional, domain.
- Parent–child attachment relationships have implications for adolescents' adjustment, with secure attachments associated with self-confidence and academic achievement, and insecure attachments associated with depression. Peer relationships may sometimes compensate for poor relationships with parents.
- Parents of adolescents generally continue to be an important influence in their children's lives and to be called on for advice, particularly if parents provide a safe environment for communication and have an authoritative parenting style. Over adolescence, parents and their teenagers typically negotiate a new form of interdependence.

Self and Identity Development

- A key challenge of adolescence is forming a coherent, stable identity through the process of identity development.
- A key component of identity is the sense of being a self-determining, active agent. Agency is promoted by parents who support their teens' autonomy strivings. High levels of agency are associated with resilience, the ability to adapt and be successful even in circumstances of high risk and adversity.
- The sexual self includes sexual agency, sexual openness, sexual self-esteem, and sexual anxiety. A positive sexual self is associated with more satisfying sexual experiences and lower probability of engaging in risky sexual practices.
- For Erik Erikson, the quest for identity, although lifelong, is particularly the task of adolescence. Focusing on exploration and commitment, the factors Erikson considered essential to achieving a mature identity, James Marcia identified four patterns young people fall into: identity achievement, with commitment following exploration; foreclosure, or commitment without exploration; moratorium, or active exploration with commitment not yet reached; and identity diffusion, with neither commitment nor exploration. Over the course of adolescence, there is an increase in achievement and a decrease in diffusion.
- Families can effectively promote identity development if they offer support and encourage exploration.
- The development of an ethnic identity can be more complicated for ethnic-minority youth and may result in bicultural stress, especially if their ethnic group's culture differs significantly from the majority culture or if the group faces prejudice. White privilege refers to social and economic benefits automatically granted to individuals. Jean Phinney has identified a process that leads from unexamined ethnic identity through an identity search to ethnic-identity achievement. Bicultural identity involves positive identifications with one's ethnic heritage, as well as the majority culture. Racial/ethnic socialization occurs with parents' efforts to understand their race/ethnicity and cope with discrimination. Peer culture, as well as hip-hop, provide contexts for teens to express and explore their biculturalism.
- The development of sexual identity—individuals' understanding of themselves as heterosexual or LGBTQ (lesbian, gay, transsexual, or queer)—can be especially pressing and complicated for sexual-minority youth. According to Richard Troiden's stage model, sexual-minority youth move from sensitization and feeling different, generally in early adolescence, through self-recognition and identity confusion and then identity assumption, before finally reaching, in many cases, commitment and identity integration. However, sexual identity development is often marked by sexual-orientation mobility—a shifting of identities over time.

Adolescent Health and Well-Being

- For some individuals, the challenges of adolescence pose significant problems for health and well-being by either aggravating preexisting problems or creating conditions for the emergence of new problems which may or may not persist into adulthood.
- Some emotional problems that may emerge during adolescence include internalizing problems, such as depression and anxiety, which are more common among girls, and externalizing problems, such as aggression and delinquency, which are more common among boys.
- Gender differences in the emergence of emotional problems are likely due to the biological and cultural factors that contribute to girls' concerns about how they are evaluated by others and boys' propensities to engage in aggressive behaviors.
- Depression is one of the most common psychological problems of adolescence. Risk factors associated with depression include biological inheritance (risk is elevated when a biological parent has a history of depression), as well as characteristics of the environment (poor peer relationships, family conflict) and cultural values and stereotypes (the sexualization of the female body).
- Cognitive-behavioral therapy (CBT) is one of the most effective treatments for depression. Based on the idea that negative thoughts and/or poor coping behaviors may cause a person to feel depressed and anxious, this approach involves helping the adolescent monitor and regulate his or her emotions and to develop adaptive communication and problem-solving skills.
- A girl's negative body image can result in the development of an eating disorder, such as anorexia nervosa (intentional self-starving), bulimia nervosa (cycles of binge eating followed by self-induced vomiting), or unspecified feeding or eating disorder when the criteria for diagnosing anorexia or bulimia are not quite met. Recovery from eating disorders is difficult, and relapses are common; however, most individuals achieve good outcomes over time.
- Delinquency and other externalizing problems are distinguished according to whether they emerge during adolescence ("adolescent onset") or emerge from problem behavior evident earlier in childhood ("childhood onset"). Adolescent-onset problems typically decline in young adulthood, whereas childhood-onset problems may persist into adulthood.
- Positive youth development (PYD) is a relatively new approach to adolescence that emphasizes the strengths and positive qualities of youth that contribute to their psychological health as well as to the welfare of their communities.

Looking Ahead

- Although humans are radically delayed in reaching puberty compared with other primate species, the frontal lobes of the human brain remain immature at the onset of puberty, perhaps contributing to adolescents' vulnerability to risk-taking and emotional problems.
- Culture, in addition to biology, plays a significant role in the onset and course of adolescent development. Increased access to health care and nutrition has resulted in the decline of pubertal onset in many countries. In many contemporary societies, overnutrition has further reduced the average age of pubertal onset.
- In societies in which education continues to be prolonged, and marriage and family are delayed, adolescents confront an increasing array of possibilities for identity, occupation, and relationships, prompting some developmentalists to posit a new stage for late adolescents—emerging adulthood.

Key Terms

GLOSSARY

A-not-B error A pattern of reacting in the object permanence task, in which the infant looks for the hidden object in location A, where the infant had previously found the object, instead of location B, where the infant has just observed it being hidden. (p. 181)

academic motivation The ability to try hard and persist at school tasks in the face of difficulties. (p. 425)

action Complex, coordinated behaviors. (p. 142)

adoption study A study that focuses on children who have been reared apart from their biological parents. (p. 69)

age of viability The age at which the fetus is able to survive outside the uterus. (p. 86)

allele The specific form of a gene that influences a particular trait. (p. 61)

allocaregiving Child care and protection provided by group members other than the parents, usually other relatives. (p. 333)

amniocentesis A prenatal test that involves inserting a needle into the uterus and withdrawing amniotic fluid containing fetal cells that can be analyzed for genetic disorders. (p. 62)

amnion A thin, tough, transparent membrane that holds the amniotic fluid and surrounds the embryo. (p. 83)

anorexia nervosa An eating disorder that involves intentional self-starving. (p. 555)

Apgar scale A quick, simple test used to diagnose the physical state of a newborn infant. (p. 112)

apprenticeship A form of education in which a young person learns a craft or skill by spending an extended period of time working for an adult master. (p. 411)

attachment The emotional bond that children form with their caregivers at about 7 to 9 months of age. (p. 206)

authoritarian parenting pattern Parenting style identified by Baumrind in which parents enforce obedience and conformity to traditional standards (including by use of punishment) and lack verbal give-and-take or expressions of warmth with children. (p. 335)

authoritative parenting pattern Parenting style identified by Baumrind in which parents set standards and limits for children but also encourage discussion and independence and express warmth. (p. 335)

autism spectrum disorder (ASD) A biologically based condition that includes an inability to relate normally to other people and low scores on false-belief tasks. (p. 281)

autobiographical memory A personal narrative that helps children acquire an enduring sense of themselves. (p. 303)

autonomous morality The second and final stage of Piaget's theory of moral development, in which right and wrong are defined according to internal motives and intentions rather than objective consequences. (p. 447)

autonomy The ability to assert one's own needs in a relationship. (p. 522)

autonomy versus shame and doubt For Erikson, the second stage of infancy, during which children develop a sense of themselves as competent to accomplish tasks or as not competent. (p. 221)

avoidant attachment The attachment pattern in which infants are indifferent to where their mother is sitting, may or may not cry when their mother leaves, are as likely to be comforted by strangers as by their mother, and are indifferent when their mother returns to the room. (p. 211)

axon The main protruding branch of a neuron; it carries messages to other cells in the form of electrical impulses. (p. 127)

babbling A form of vocalizing, beginning at around 7 months, in which infants utter strings of syllables that combine a consonant sound and a vowel sound. (p. 230)

Baldwin effect The role of cultural factors in determining which phenotypes are adaptive. (p. 72)

basic emotions Universal emotions—such as joy, fear, anger, surprise, sadness, and disgust—that are expressed similarly in all cultures and are present at birth or in the early months. (p. 200)

basic trust versus mistrust For Erikson, the first stage of infancy, during which children either come to trust others as reliable and kind and to regard the world as safe or come to mistrust others as insensitive and hurtful and to regard the world as unpredictable and threatening. (p. 221)

behaviorism Theories that focus on development as a result of learning and on changes in behavior as a result of forming associations between behavior and its consequences. (p. 19)

bicultural identity Identifications with one's ethnic heritage as well as with the majority culture. (p. 546)

bicultural stress Stress experienced by many ethnic-minority and immigrant adolescents as they negotiate two cultures simultaneously. (p. 544)

bioecological model A model that sees children in the context of five interrelated systems: microsystem, mesosystem, exosystem, macrosystem, and chronosystem. (p. 27)

biological drives Impulses to attempt to satisfy essential physiological needs. (p. 207)

bottom-up processing An approach to education that starts with teaching basic skills and, once they have been mastered, moves on to more complex tasks. (p. 420)

brain stem The base of the brain, which controls such elementary reactions as blinking and sucking, as well as such vital functions as breathing and sleeping. (p. 128)

Brazelton Neonatal Assessment Scale A scale used to assess a newborn's neurological condition. (p. 112)

bulimia nervosa An eating disorder that involves cycles of binge eating followed by self-induced vomiting. (p. 555)

canalized Refers to a trait that follows a strictly defined path, regardless of most environmental and genetic variations. (p. 68)

carriers Individuals who are heterozygous for a trait with a dominant and recessive allele and thus express only the characteristics associated with the dominant allele but may pass the recessive allele, including one for a recessive disorder, on to their offspring. (p. 61)

causation When the occurrence of one event depends upon the occurrence of a prior event. (p. 36)

centration Young children's tendency to focus on only one feature of an object to the exclusion of all other features. (p. 268)

cephalocaudal pattern The pattern of development that proceeds from the head down. (p. 84)

cerebral cortex The brain's outermost layer. The networks of neurons in the cerebral cortex integrate information from several sensory sources with memories of past experiences, processing them in a way that results in human forms of thought and action. (p. 128)

child-care center An organized child-care facility supervised by licensed professionals. (p. 349)

chorion A membrane that surrounds the amnion and becomes the fetal component of the placenta. (p. 83)

chorionic villus sampling (CVS) A prenatal test that samples tissue from the placenta to analyze for genetic disorders. (p. 64)

chromosome A threadlike structure made up of genes. In humans, there are 46 chromosomes in every cell except sperm and ova. (p. 58)

chronology In language development, a simple story structure used by young children, in which they present a sequence of concrete events. (p. 250)

classical conditioning Learning in which previously existing behaviors come to be elicited by new stimuli. (p. 147)

cleavage A series of mitotic cell divisions that transform a zygote into a blastocyst. (p. 82)

clinical interview A research method in which questions are tailored to the individual, with each question depending on the answer to the preceding one. (p. 35)

clique A group of several young people that remains small enough to enable its members to be in regular interaction with one another and to serve as the primary peer group. (p. 524)

co-construction The shaping of environments through interactions between children and their caregivers, siblings, neighbors, and friends. (p. 71)

cochlear implant A device that transforms sounds into electric pulses that directly stimulate the auditory nerve, bypassing the malfunctioning inner ear that ordinarily processes sound. (p. 236)

codominance An outcome in which a trait that is determined by two alleles is different from the trait produced by either of the contributing alleles alone. (p. 61)

coevolution The combined process that emerges from the interaction of biological evolution and cultural evolution. (p. 72)

cognitive-behavioral therapy (CBT) A treatment for depression and anxiety that is based on the theory that these problems are related to negative thoughts and/or poor coping behaviors. CBT is designed to help the adolescent develop adaptive communication and problem-solving skills, monitor and regulate changing emotions, and schedule time for relaxing and enjoyable activities. (p. 555)

cohort A group of persons born about the same time who are therefore likely to share certain experiences. (p. 39)

cohort sequential design A research design in which the longitudinal method is replicated with several cohorts. (p. 40)

collective monologues Communications in which young children each voice their own thoughts without attending to what the others are saying. (p. 255)

commitment According to Marcia, individuals' sense of allegiance to the goals, values, beliefs, and occupation they have chosen. (p. 543)

compensation A mental operation in which a child realizes that changes in one aspect of a problem are compared with and compensated for by changes in another aspect. (p. 385)

concrete operations Piaget's term for coordinated mental actions that allow children to mentally combine, separate, order, and transform concrete objects and events that the children experience directly. (p. 383)

conditional response (CR) In classical conditioning, a response to the pairing of the conditional stimulus (CS) and the unconditional stimulus (UCS). (p. 147)

conditional stimulus (CS) In classical conditioning, a stimulus that elicits a behavior that is dependent on the way it is paired with the unconditional stimulus (UCS). (p. 147)

conservation of number Recognition of the one-to-one correspondence between sets of objects of equal number. (p. 384)

conservation of volume The understanding that the amount of a liquid remains unchanged when poured from one container into another that has different dimensions. (p. 384)

constructivist theory Piaget's theory, in which cognitive development results from children's active construction of reality, based on their experiences with the world. (p. 20)

continuity/discontinuity A fundamental issue concerning the process of development that addresses the extent to which development tends to be *continuous*, consisting of the gradual accumulation of small changes, and the extent to which it is *discontinuous*, involving a series of abrupt, radical transformations. (p. 13)

continuous societies Societies in which transitions to maturity, including work and other adult responsibilities, are slow and steady, resulting in little emotional storm and stress. (p. 482)

control group The group in an experiment that is treated as much as possible like the experimental group except that it does not participate in the experimental manipulation. (p. 34)

conversational acts Actions that achieve goals through language. (p. 249)

cooperative breeding In humans and certain other species, a system involving networks of support in which individuals other than parents contribute resources toward rearing the young. (p. 333)

coregulation A form of indirect social control in which parents and children cooperate to reinforce the children's understandings of right and wrong and what is safe and unsafe when they are not under direct adult control. (p. 467)

correlation coefficient The degree of association between factors, symbolized as r and ranging between -1.0 and $+1.0$. (p. 36)

correlation The condition that exists between two factors when changes in one factor are associated with changes in the other. (p. 36)

cross-sectional design A research design in which individuals of various ages are studied at the same time. (p. 39)

crowd A large, reputation-based and mixed-gender social network observed when cliques interact. (p. 525)

crystallized intelligence The intelligence quotient derived from tests involving knowledge-based questions. (p. 403)

cultural modeling Culturally specific ways of telling stories. (p. 251)

cultural style A dominant way of thinking about and relating to the world that arises from a people's common historical experience. (p. 432)

culture Material and symbolic tools that accumulate through time, are passed on through social processes, and provide resources for the developing child. (p. 51)

cumulative cultural evolution The dynamic ongoing process of cultural change that is a consequence of variation that individuals have produced in the cultural tools they use. (p. 55)

de-idealization Children's understanding that their parents are not all-knowing or perfect but, rather, have faults and can make mistakes. (p. 467)

decentration The cognitive ability to pull away from focusing on just one feature of an object in order to consider multiple features. (p. 269)

decoding The process of translating units of print into units of sound. (p. 414)

deferred imitation The imitation of an action observed in the past. (p. 178)

delayed circadian phase A shift in the sleep–wake pattern in which adolescents tend to stay up later at night than they did as children and then sleep later in the morning. (p. 497)

dendrites The protruding parts of a neuron that receive messages from the axons of other cells. (p. 127)

depression An emotional state involving some combination of sadness, apathy, hopelessness, poor self-esteem, and trouble finding pleasure in activities that one used to enjoy. Depression is one of the most common psychological problems of adolescence, especially for girls. (p. 554)

detachment For Bowlby, the state of indifference toward others experienced by children who have been separated from their caregivers for an extended time and have not formed new stable relationships. (p. 208)

developmental science The field of study that focuses on the range of children's physical, intellectual, social, and emotional developments. (p. 3)

developmental stage A qualitatively distinctive, coherent pattern of behavior that emerges during the course of development. (p. 13)

deviancy training Positive reactions to discussions of rule-breaking. (p. 526)

differential emotions theory The view that basic emotions are innate and emerge in their adult form either at birth or on a biologically determined timetable. (p. 200)

differential reinforcement In acquiring gender roles and identities, the process by which girls and boys are rewarded for engaging in ways that are considered gender appropriate in their culture. (p. 298)

differentiated self A sense of self as including many fluctuating attributes. (p. 444)

discontinuous societies Societies in which transitions to maturity are abrupt, resulting in considerable anxiety and distress. (p. 482)

dishabituation The term used to describe the process in which an infant's interest is renewed after a change in the stimulus. (p. 133)

disorganized attachment The insecure attachment pattern in which infants seem to lack a coherent method for dealing with stress. They may behave in seemingly contradictory ways, such as screaming for their mother but moving away when she approaches. In extreme cases, they may seem dazed. (p. 211)

display rules A social or cultural group's informal conventions regarding whether, how, and under what circumstances emotions should be expressed. (p. 315)

dizygotic (DZ) twins Twins who come from two zygotes. (p. 60)

DNA (deoxyribonucleic acid) A long, double-stranded molecule that makes up chromosomes. (p. 58)

dominant allele The allele that is expressed when an individual possesses two different alleles for the same trait. (p. 61)

dominant children In reference to social hierarchies, those children who control "resources" such as toys, play spaces, and decisions about group activities. (p. 453)

dopamine The limbic system's primary neurotransmitter, which activates the reward system. (p. 489)

dynamic systems theory A theory that addresses how new, complex systems of behavior develop from the interaction of less complex parts. (p. 27)

early maturation The occurrence of a pubertal event (or set of events) before the 3rd percentile of the normal range. (p. 491)

early-life adversity Profound and pervasive deprivation experienced during infancy, often resulting in severe developmental delays. (p. 166)

ecological inheritance Environmental modifications, as a result of niche construction, that affect the development of offspring and descendants. (p. 71)

ecological systems theory A theory focusing on the organization and interactions of the multiple environmental contexts within which children develop. (p. 27)

ecological validity The extent to which behavior studied in one environment (such as a psychological test) is characteristic of behavior exhibited by the same person in a range of other environments. (p. 35)

ectoderm Cells of the inner cell mass of the embryo that develop into the outer surface of the skin, the nails, part of the teeth, the lens of the eye, the inner ear, and the central nervous system. (p. 83)

effortful control The inhibition of impulsive or dominant actions. (p. 308)

ego In Freudian theory, the mental structure that develops out of the id as the infant is forced by reality to cope with the social world. The ego mediates between the id and the social world, allowing children to control and regulate behavior. (p. 305)

egocentrism In Piaget's terms, the tendency to "center on oneself"—that is, to consider the world entirely in terms of one's own point of view. (p. 270)

elaboration A memory strategy that involves making connections between two or more things to be remembered. (p. 391)

elaborative style A form of talking with children about new events or experiences that enhances children's memories for those events and experiences. (p. 276)

Electra complex In Freudian theory, the process by which young girls blame their mother for their "castrated" condition, transfer their love to their father, and compete with their mother for their father's affection. (p. 298)

electroencephalography (EEG) A common physiological method used to evaluate infant sensory capacities, which involves attaching sensors to the baby's head and measuring changes in brain waves in response to the presentation of different stimuli. (p. 132)

embryonic period The period that extends from the time the organism becomes attached to the uterus until the end of the 8th week of pregnancy, when all the major organs have taken primitive shape. (p. 81)

emergent literacy Knowledge, skills, and attitudes that provide the building blocks for learning to read and write. (p. 413)

emergent numeracy Knowledge, skills, and attitudes that provide the building blocks for learning how to do math. (p. 413)

emerging adulthood The name of what some developmentalists propose is a new stage of development facing many individuals between the ages of 18 and 25 in technologically advanced societies. (p. 480)

emic approach An approach that explores how behavior and development take place within specific cultural contexts. (p. 200)

emotion A feeling state that involves distinctive physiological reactions and cognitive evaluations and that motivates action. (p. 199)

emotion regulation Ways of acting to modulate and control emotions. (p. 199)

emotional tone One's sense of well-being versus depression and anxiety. (p. 553)

empathy Sharing another person's emotions and feelings. (p. 323)

endocrine system A network of hormone-secreting glands associated with changes in the individual's mood, metabolism, and growth. The glands associated specifically with puberty include the pituitary gland, the thyroid gland, the adrenal glands, and the sex glands (gonads). (p. 490)

endoderm Cells of the inner cell mass of the embryo that develop into the digestive system and the lungs. (p. 83)

entity model of intelligence The belief that intelligence is a quality of which each person has a certain fixed amount. (p. 426)

epigenesis The process by which a new phenotypic form emerges through the interactions of the preceding form and its current environment. (p. 84)

epistemic development Refers to changes in how individuals reason about the nature of knowledge. (p. 502)

equilibration The main source of development, consisting of a process of achieving a balance between the child's present understanding and the child's new experiences. (p. 22)

ethnic identity A sense of belonging to an ethnic group and the feelings and attitudes that accompany the sense of group membership. (p. 301)

ethnic identity A sense of oneself as a member of a particular ethnic group. (p. 544)

ethnic socialization Ethnic-based messages communicated to children. (p. 302)

ethnography The study of the cultural organization of behavior. (p. 34)

ethology An interdisciplinary science that studies the biological and evolutionary foundations of behavior. (p. 25)

etic approach An approach that emphasizes the universal aspects of human behavior and development. (p. 200)

evaluativist theory of knowledge A belief that although truth can change, it is nevertheless subject to particular standards of evaluation—the "rules of the game." (p. 502)

evolutionary theories Theories that explain human behavior in terms of how it contributes to the survival of the species and that look at how our evolutionary past influences individual development. (p. 24)

executive function Higher-level cognitive processes, such as aspects of cognition associated with supervising and controlling lower-level cognitive processes. (p. 394)

experience sampling method (ESM) A tool used by developmentalists in which study participants, when signaled by text message at random intervals, fill out brief reports on their feelings. ESM has been used to study adolescents' emotional lives. (p. 517)

experience-dependent Development of neural connections that is initiated in response to experience. (p. 131)

experience-expectant Processes of brain development that seem to *anticipate* experiences that are universal in all normally developing members of our species. (p. 129)

experiment In psychology, research in which a change is introduced into a person's experience and the effect of that change is measured. (p. 34)

experimental group The group in an experiment whose experience is changed as part of the experiment. (p. 34)

explicit instruction The social process in which children are purposefully taught to use the resources of their culture. (p. 53)

exploration According to Marcia, the process through which adolescents actively examine their possible future roles and paths. (p. 543)

extended families Families in which not only parents and their children but other kin—grandparents, cousins, nieces and nephews, or more distant family relations—share a household. (p. 332)

externalizing problems Social and behavioral problems such as aggression and delinquency; more common in boys than in girls. (p. 553)

exuberant synaptogenesis A rapid growth in synaptic density that prepares the brain for a vast range of possible experiences. (p. 130)

false-belief task A technique used to assess children's theory of mind; children are tested on their understanding either of stories in which a character is fooled into believing something that is not true or of situations in which they themselves have been tricked into a false belief. (p. 278)

familism A sense of family obligation, common in Hispanic families. (p. 340)

family child care Child care provided in the home of a relative or someone else. (p. 349)

family sexual culture Family practices that socialize and reinforce sexual values, attitudes, and behaviors of family members. (p. 529)

family structure The social organization of a family. Most commonly, the structure is nuclear or extended. (p. 332)

family study A study that compares members of the same family to determine how similar they are on a given trait. (p. 69)

fast mapping The way in which children quickly form an idea of the meaning of an unfamiliar word they hear in a familiar and highly structured social interaction. (p. 244)

fetal alcohol spectrum disorder (FASD) A range of problems, such as abnormal appearance and low intelligence, found in babies whose mothers consumed alcohol while pregnant. (p. 97)

fetal alcohol syndrome (FAS) A syndrome found in babies whose mothers were heavy consumers of alcohol while pregnant. Symptoms include an abnormally small head and underdeveloped brain, eye abnormalities, congenital heart disease, joint anomalies, and malformations of the face. (p. 97)

fetal period The period that begins in the 9th week after conception, with the first signs of the hardening of the bones, and continues until birth. (p. 81)

fine motor skills Motor skills related to the development and coordination of small muscles, such as those that move the fingers and eyes. (p. 168)

fluid intelligence The intelligence quotient derived from tests involving tasks that require reasoning but not prior knowledge. (p. 403)

Flynn effect The steady increase over the past 100 years in IQ test performance, an increase believed to support the environmental hypothesis of intelligence. (p. 403)

fontanels "Soft spots," or spaces, that separate the bones of the skull prenatally and in early infancy. (p. 126)

food-insecure Lacking enough food to ensure good health. (p. 265)

formal education The most structured type of explicit education, through which adults instruct the young in the specialized knowledge and skills of their culture. (p. 411)

formal operations In Piaget's terms, mental operations in which all possible combinations are considered in solving a problem. Consequently, each partial link is grouped in relationship to the whole; in other words, reasoning moves continually as a function of a structured whole. (p. 499)

formats Recurrent socially patterned activities in which adult and child do things together. (p. 254)

friendship A close relationship between two individuals. Friendships in adolescence are characterized by reciprocity, commitment, and equality. (p. 521)

gender binary The cultural belief system that there are two "opposite" categories of gender (boys and girls). (p. 461)

gender identity A personal sense of self as a boy or girl. (p. 296)

gender role A set of beliefs about how boys/men and girls/women should behave. (p. 296)

gender schema A mental model containing information about boys and girls that is used to process gender-relevant information. (p. 299)

gender segregation The term for the preference of girls to play with other girls, and of boys to play with other boys. (p. 296)

gender-variant (transgender) children Children whose gender identity and/or preferences regarding clothing, activities, and/or playmates do not match what is culturally normative for the gender assigned at birth. (p. 461)

gene pool The total variety of genetic information possessed by a sexually reproducing population. (p. 62)

genes The segments on a DNA molecule that act as hereditary blueprints for the organism's development. (p. 57)

genotype The genetic endowment of an individual. (p. 57)

germ cells The sperm and ova, which are specialized for sexual reproduction and have half the number of chromosomes normal for a species. (p. 59)

germinal period The period that begins at conception and lasts until the developing organism becomes attached to the wall of the uterus about 8 to 10 days later. (p. 81)

gestational age The amount of time between conception and birth. The normal gestational age is between 37 and 43 weeks. (p. 94)

grammar The rules of a given language for the sequencing of words in a sentence and the ordering of parts of words. (p. 239)

grammatical morphemes Words and parts of words that create meaning by showing the relationships between other elements within the sentence. (p. 248)

gross motor skills Motor skills related to the development and coordination of large muscles; important for locomotion. (p. 168)

growth charts Charts that show average values of height, weight, and other measures of growth, based on large samples of normally developing infants; the charts are used to evaluate an infant's development. (p. 124)

growth spurt A rapid change in height and weight that signals the onset of puberty. (p. 483)

habituation The process in which attention to novelty decreases with repeated exposure. (p. 133)

heredity The biological transmission of characteristics from one generation to the next. (p. 57)

heritability A measure of the degree to which a variation in a particular trait among individuals in a specific population is related to genetic differences among those individuals. (p. 68)

heterochrony Variability in the rates of development of different parts of an organism. (p. 82)

heterogeneity Variability in the levels of development of different parts of an organism at a given time. (p. 82)

heteronomous morality Piaget's term for young children's tendency to define morality in terms of objective consequences and externally imposed controls. (p. 306)

heterozygous Having inherited two genes of different allelic forms for a trait. (p. 61)

home child care Child care provided in the child's own home, primarily by a grandmother or other family member, while the parents are at work. (p. 349)

homophily The degree to which friends are similar to each other. (p. 525)

homophobia A fear of homosexuality. Homophobia may diminish intimacy among adolescent males. (p. 523)

homozygous Having inherited two genes of the same allelic form for a trait. (p. 61)

hypothalamic-pituitary-gonadal (HPG) axis A circuit that extends from the brain to the sex organs (testes or ovaries) and back again; activated in adolescence, the HPG regulates the hormones that affect the body's growth and functions. (p. 489)

hypothalamus A brain structure, located just above the brain stem, that performs a number of important tasks, including the regulation of hunger, thirst, and sexual desire, and connects the nervous system to the endocrine system. (p. 490)

hypothesis A statement about expected research results that is precise enough to be shown to be true or false. (p. 29)

hypothetical-deductive reasoning Reasoning that involves the ability to judge an argument entirely on the basis of its logical form, regardless of whether the argument is true. (p. 501)

id In Freudian theory, the mental structure present at birth that is the main source of psychological energy. It is unconscious and pleasure-seeking and demands that bodily drives be satisfied. (p. 305)

identification A psychological process in which children try to look, act, feel, and be like significant people in their social environment. (p. 295)

identity A mental operation in which a child realizes that a change limited to outward appearance does not change the substances involved. (p. 385)

identity development The process through which individuals achieve a sense of who they are and of their moral and political beliefs, their career preferences, and their relationship to their culture and community. (p. 539)

imitation The social process through which children learn to use their culture's resources by observing and copying the behaviors of others. (p. 53)

implantation The process by which a developing organism becomes attached to the uterus. (p. 82)

incremental model of intelligence The belief that intelligence is something that can grow over time as one learns. (p. 426)

industry versus inferiority According to Erikson's theory, the stage during which children judge themselves to be industrious and successful at meeting the new challenges posed by adults at home and school, or inferior and incapable of meeting such challenges. (p. 442)

information-processing theories Theories that look at cognitive development in terms of how children come to perceive, remember, organize, and manipulate information in increasingly efficient ways. (p. 26)

initiative versus guilt According to Erikson's theory, the stage in early childhood during which children face the challenge of continuing to declare their autonomy and existence as individuals but in ways that begin to conform to the social roles and moral standards of society. (p. 295)

inner speech According to Vygotsky, the internalization of egocentric speech that occurs during early childhood and allows individuals to mentally plan activities and solve problems. (p. 256)

institutional review boards (IRBs) Groups responsible for evaluating and overseeing the ethical soundness of research practices at an institution. (p. 42)

instructional discourse A distinctive way of talking and thinking that is typical in school but rarely encountered in everyday interactions in the community or home. (p. 420)

intelligence quotient (IQ) The ratio of mental age to chronological age, calculated as IQ = (MA/CA)100. (p. 400)

intentionality The ability to engage in behaviors directed toward achieving a goal. (p. 176)

internal working model A mental model that children construct as a result of their experiences with their caregivers and that they use to guide their interactions with their caregivers and others. (p. 210)

internalizing problems Disturbances in emotion or mood such as depression, worry, guilt, and anxiety; more common in girls than in boys. (p. 553)

intimacy A sense of close connection between two individuals, resulting from shared feelings, thoughts, and activities. (p. 522)

kinship studies Studies that use naturally occurring conditions provided by kinship relations to estimate genetic and environmental contributions to a phenotypic trait. (p. 69)

kisspeptin A small protein that is produced by specialized cells in the hypothalamus and plays a key role in the activation of the HPG axis. (p. 490)

kwashiorkor A potentially fatal form of malnutrition in which the diet is extremely low in protein. (p. 155)

language acquisition device (LAD) Chomsky's term for an innate language-processing capacity that is programmed to recognize the universal rules that underlie any particular language that a child might hear. (p. 253)

language acquisition support system (LASS) Bruner's term for the patterned behaviors and formatted events within which children acquire language. It is the environmental complement to the innate, biologically constituted LAD. (p. 254)

large for gestational age Babies whose weight at birth is above the 90th percentile of babies of the same sex who are the same gestational age. (p. 94)

late maturation The occurrence of a pubertal event after the 97th percentile of the normal range. (p. 492)

law of effect Thorndike's notion that behaviors that produce a satisfying effect in a given situation are likely to be repeated in the same or similar situations, whereas behaviors that produce an uncomfortable effect are less likely to be repeated. (p. 19)

learning A relatively permanent change in behavior brought about by making associations between behavior and events in the environment. (p. 147)

leptin A hormone that plays a key role in appetite and metabolism. (p. 490)

limbic system A group of brain structures, including the amygdala, hippocampus, basal ganglia, and hypothalamus. Because these brain structures are associated more with emotion than with reasoning, the limbic system is often described as the "emotion brain" (in contrast to the cerebral cortex, which some have dubbed the "reasoning brain"). (p. 381)

locomotion The ability to move around on one's own. (p. 168)

long-term memory The part of the information-processing system that holds memories of past experiences. (p. 274)

longitudinal design A research design in which data are gathered about the same group of people as they grow older over an extended period of time. (p. 37)

low birth weight The term used to describe babies weighing 5 pounds, 8 ounces (2,500 grams) or less at birth, whether or not they are premature. (p. 114)

mastery orientation A way that children approach school tasks in which they are motivated to learn, to try hard, and to improve their performance. (p. 425)

material tools Cultural tools, including physical objects and observable patterns of behavior such as family routines and social practices. (p. 52)

media Forms of mass communication, including newspapers, magazines, books, comic books, radio, television, films, video games, and the Internet. (p. 356)

mediation The process through which tools organize people's activities and ways of relating to their environments. (p. 53)

meiosis The process that produces sperm and ova, each of which contains only half of the parent cell's original complement of 46 chromosomes. (p. 59)

memory span The number of randomly presented items of information that can be repeated immediately after they are presented. (p. 389)

memory strategies Specific actions used deliberately to enhance remembering. (p. 390)

menarche The first menstrual period. (p. 486)

mental modules Hypothesized innate mental faculties that receive inputs from particular classes of objects and produce corresponding information about the world. (p. 281)

mental operations In Piaget's theory, the mental process of combining, separating, or transforming information in a logical manner. (p. 268)

mesoderm Cells of the inner cell mass of the embryo that give rise to the muscles, the bones, the circulatory system, and the inner layers of the skin. (p. 83)

meta-analysis A statistical analysis of results collected from multiple scientific studies. (p. 403)

metacognition The ability to think about one's own thought processes. (p. 387)

metamemory The ability to think about one's memory processes. (p. 392)

metaphor Use of a word in a way that draws a comparison between the thing the word usually refers to and some other, unrelated thing. (p. 245)

microbiome The millions of microorganisms that live on and in our bodies, some of which are pathogenic but many of which are essential to the healthy functioning of critical systems. (p. 111)

microgenetic design A research method in which individuals' development is studied intensively over a relatively short period of time. (p. 41)

mirror neurons Specialized brain cells that fire when an individual sees or hears another perform an action, just as they would fire if the observing individual were performing the same action. (p. 205)

mitosis The process of cell duplication and division that generates all of an individual's cells except sperm and ova. (p. 59)

modeling In acquiring gender roles and identities, the process by which children observe and imitate individuals of the same sex as themselves. (p. 298)

monozygotic (MZ) twins Twins who come from one zygote and therefore have identical genotypes. (p. 60)

morality of care A morality that stresses relationships, compassion, and social obligations. (p. 508)

morality of justice A morality that emphasizes issues of rightness, fairness, and equality. (p. 508)

morpheme The smallest unit of meaning in the words of a language. (p. 240)

motor drive The pleasure young children take in using their new motor skills. (p. 263)

multimodal perception The ability to perceive an object or event by more than one sensory system simultaneously. (p. 140)

multitasking Cognitive processes involving attending and responding to multiple sources of information simultaneously. (p. 503)

mutation An alteration in the molecular structure of an individual's DNA. (p. 62)

myelin An insulating material that forms a sheath around certain axons and speeds the transmission of nerve impulses from one neuron to the next. (p. 127)

natural selection The process through which species survive and evolve, in which individuals with phenotypes that are more adaptive to the environmental conditions survive and reproduce with greater success than do individuals with phenotypes that are less adaptive. (p. 57)

naturalistic observation Observation of the actual behavior of people in the course of their everyday lives. (p. 32)

neglectful parenting pattern Parenting style identified by Baumrind in which parents do not exercise control over children's behavior and are emotionally distant. (p. 336)

neighborhood physical disorder A problem in distressed communities that includes both physical deterioration (garbage on the streets, rundown buildings, etc.) and chaotic activity (crowding, high noise levels, etc.). (p. 354)

neural tube An embryonic structure that later develops into the brain and spinal cord. (p. 92)

neuron A nerve cell. (p. 126)

neurotransmitter A chemical secreted by a neuron sending a message that carries the impulse across the synaptic gap to the receiving cell. (p. 127)

niche construction The active shaping and modification of individuals' environments by the individuals' own behaviors, activities, and choices. (p. 70)

no-nonsense parenting Parenting characterized by a mix of high parental control—including punishment—and warmth, and associated especially with African American single mothers. (p. 335)

noninvasive prenatal diagnosis (NIPD) A prenatal test that samples blood from the mother and extracts fetal blood cells to analyze for genetic disorders. (p. 64)

nuclear families Families consisting of parents (including single parents) and their children. (p. 332)

object permanence The understanding that objects have substance, maintain their identity when their location is changed, and ordinarily continue to exist when out of sight. (p. 177)

objectivist theory of knowledge A belief that knowledge involves an accumulation of objective facts and "definite answers." (p. 502)

objectivity The mental distancing made possible by decentration. Piaget believed the attainment of objectivity to be the major achievement of cognitive development. (p. 269)

objectivity The requirement that scientific knowledge not be distorted by the investigator's preconceptions. (p. 31)

Oedipus complex In Freudian theory, the desire young boys have to get rid of their father and take his place in their mother's affections. (p. 297)

ontogenetic adaptation A trait or behavior that has evolved because it contributes to survival and normal development; in one view, infant emotions are ontogenetic adaptations. (p. 201)

operant conditioning Learning in which changes in behavior are shaped by the consequences of that behavior, thereby giving rise to new and more complete behaviors. (p. 148)

organizational strategies Memory strategies in which materials to be remembered are mentally grouped into meaningful categories. (p. 391)

ossification A process through which new bone tissue is formed at the growth plates of long bones. (p. 263)

parental ethnotheories Parents' values, beliefs, and goals about the development and care of children that reflect the traditions of their cultural communities. (p. 468)

peer victimization The experiences of children who are chronically harassed, teased, and bullied by peers. (p. 456)

perceptual narrowing A process in which infants lose their apparently innate abilities to detect certain sensory features because those features do not occur very often in their environments. (p. 132)

perceptual scaffolding The way in which a familiar word serves as an anchor for learning new words that come immediately before or after it. (p. 229)

performance orientation A way of approaching school tasks in which students are motivated by their level of performance, ability, and incentives for trying. (p. 425)

permissive parenting pattern Parenting style identified by Baumrind in which parents express warmth but do not exercise control over their children's behavior. (p. 336)

personal distress A self-focused emotional reaction to another person's distress. (p. 324)

personal identity A person's sense of his or her self as persisting over time (*I-self*), as well as a sense of personal characteristics such as appearance and abilities that can be objectively known (*me-self*). (p. 303)

personality formation The process through which children develop their own unique patterns of feeling, thinking, and behaving in a wide variety of circumstances. (p. 294)

phallic stage In Freudian theory, the period beginning around the age of 3 or 4 years when children start to regard their own genitals as a major source of pleasure. (p. 297)

phenotype An organism's observable characteristics that result from the interaction of the genotype with the environment. (p. 57)

phenotypic plasticity The degree to which the phenotype is open to influence by the environment rather than determined by the genotype. (p. 67)

phonemes The smallest sound categories in human speech that distinguish meanings. Phonemes vary from language to language. (p. 133)

phonological development The process of learning to segment speech into meaningful units of sound. (p. 239)

placenta An organ made up of tissue from both the mother and the fetus that serves as a barrier and filter between their bloodstreams. (p. 83)

plasticity The degree to which, and the conditions under which, development is open to change and intervention. (p. 13)

playworld practice A type of classroom activity that is based on theories regarding the importance of play in intellectual development and involves students enacting and discussing various themes in children's literature. (p. 422)

polygenic inheritance Refers to the contribution of a variety of genes—sometimes very many—to a particular trait. (p. 61)

positive youth development (PYD) A general approach to adolescence that emphasizes the strengths and positive qualities of youth that contribute to their psychological health as well as to the welfare of their communities. (p. 558)

possible selves Possibilities about what the self might be like in the future. (p. 444)

pragmatic development The process of learning the conventions that govern the use of language in particular social contexts. (p. 239)

precausal thinking Piaget's description of the reasoning of young children that does not follow the procedures of either deductive or inductive reasoning. (p. 272)

precocious puberty A serious condition that involves the activation of the HPG axis before the age of 8 in girls and 9 in boys. (p. 494)

preconception tests Analysis of parents' DNA using blood or saliva samples to determine the risk of genetic disorders in offspring. (p. 62)

preformationism The belief that adultlike capacities, desires, interests, and emotions are present in early childhood. (p. 8)

prefrontal cortex The part of the cortex that is located directly behind the forehead and is important to the development of voluntary behaviors. (p. 165)

prenatal tests Tests such as amniocentesis and chorionic villus sampling (CVS) that are used to analyze the DNA of an embryo or a fetus to determine genetic disorders. (p. 62)

preoperational stage According to Piaget, the stage of thinking between infancy and middle childhood, in which children are unable to decenter their thinking or to think through the consequences of an action. (p. 268)

preterm The term for babies born before the 37th week of pregnancy. (p. 113)

prevention science An area of research that examines the biological and social processes that lead to maladjustment as well as those that are associated with healthy development. (p. 362)

primary circular reaction The term Piaget used to describe the infant's tendency to repeat pleasurable bodily actions for their own sake. (p. 147)

primary intersubjectivity Organized, reciprocal interaction between an infant and a caregiver, with the interaction itself as the focus. (p. 202)

primary sex characteristics The organs directly involved in reproduction. (p. 485)

privileged domains Cognitive domains that call on specialized kinds of information, require specifically designated forms of reasoning, and appear to be of evolutionary importance to the human species. (p. 277)

proactive aggression A form of aggression, common to bullying, used as a means of controlling other people and getting one's way. (p. 455)

prosocial behavior Behavior such as sharing, helping, caregiving, and showing compassion. (p. 323)

protective factors Environmental and personal factors that are the source of children's resilience in the face of hardship. (p. 363)

protodeclaratives Early conversational acts whose purpose is to establish joint attention and sustain a dialogue. (p. 249)

protoimperatives Early conversational acts whose purpose is to get another person to do something. (p. 249)

proximodistal pattern The pattern of development that proceeds from the middle of the organism out to the periphery. (p. 84)

psychodynamic theories Theories, such as those of Freud and Erikson, that explore the influence on development and developmental stages of universal biological drives and the life experiences of individuals. (p. 17)

puberty The series of biological developments that transforms individuals from a state of physical immaturity into one in which they are biologically mature and capable of sexual production. (p. 483)

public policies Governmental laws and programs designed to promote the welfare of children and families. (p. 363)

racial/ethnic socialization Parents' efforts to help their children understand their race/ethnicity and cope effectively with discrimination. (p. 548)

reactive aggression A form of aggression that is usually impulsive and displayed in response to a perceived threat or provocation. (p. 455)

realistic mathematics education An approach to mathematics education that focuses on developing the student's understanding of how math can be used to solve real-world problems. (p. 421)

recessive allele The allele that is not expressed when an individual possesses two different alleles for the same trait. (p. 61)

reciprocal teaching A method of teaching reading in which teachers and children take turns reading text in a manner that integrates decoding and comprehension skills. (p. 420)

reflex A specific, well-integrated, automatic (involuntary) response to a specific type of stimulation. (p. 142)

rehearsal The process of repeating to oneself the material that one is trying to remember. (p. 391)

relational aggression Aggression intended to harm someone's friendships or exclude an individual from the group. (p. 317)

reliability The scientific requirement that when the same behavior is measured on two or more occasions by the same or different observers, the measurements must be consistent with each other. (p. 31)

replicability The scientific requirement that other researchers be able to use the same procedures as an initial investigator did and obtain the same results. (p. 32)

representations Internal, mental symbols of experience; according to Piaget, the ability to form mental symbols emerges during sensorimotor substage 6. (p. 178)

research design The overall plan that describes how a study is put together; it is developed before conducting research. (p. 37)

resilience The ability to adapt and be successful despite being in circumstances of high risk and adversity. (p. 540)

resilience The ability to recover quickly from the adverse effects of early experience or persevere in the face of stress with no apparent special negative psychological consequences. (p. 363)

resistant attachment The attachment pattern in which infants stay close to their mother and appear anxious even when their mother is near. They become very upset when their mother leaves but are not comforted by her return. They simultaneously seek renewed contact with their mother and resist their mothers' efforts to comfort them. (p. 211)

reversibility A mental operation in which a child realizes that one operation can be negated, or reversed, by the effects of another. (p. 385)

reward system Areas of the limbic system associated with motivations to seek resources critical to individual and species survival, such as food, shelter, and sex. (p. 489)

risk factors Personal characteristics or environmental circumstances that increase the probability of negative outcomes for children. Risk is a statistic that applies to groups, not individuals. (p. 362)

scale errors Young children's inappropriate use of an object due to their failure to consider information about the object's size. (p. 267)

school engagement The thoughts, behaviors, and emotions that children have about school and learning. (p. 427)

school-cutoff strategy A means of assessing the impact of early education by comparing the intellectual performance of children who are almost the same age but begin schooling a year apart because of school rules that set a specific cutoff birthday date for starting school. (p. 428)

scripts Event schemas that specify who participates in an event, what social roles they play, what objects they are to use during the event, and the sequence of actions that make up the event. (p. 286)

secondary circular reactions The behavior characteristic of the third substage of Piaget's sensorimotor stage, in which babies repeat actions to produce interesting changes in their environment. (p. 176)

secondary intersubjectivity A form of interaction between infant and caregiver, emerging at about 9–12 months, with communication and emotional sharing focused not just on the interaction but on the world beyond. (p. 216)

secondary sex characteristics The anatomical and physiological signs that outwardly distinguish males from females. (p. 486)

secular trend A pattern in which the average age of puberty in developed countries declines across decades. (p. 496)

secure attachment A pattern of attachment in which children play comfortably and react positively to a stranger as long as their mother is present. They become upset when their mother leaves and are unlikely to be consoled by a stranger, but they calm down as soon as their mother reappears. (p. 211)

secure base Bowlby's term for the people whose presence provides a child with the security that allows him or her to make exploratory excursions. (p. 209)

self-conscious emotions Emotions such as embarrassment, pride, shame, guilt, and envy, which emerge after 8 months with infants' growing consciousness of self. (p. 219)

self-esteem One's evaluation of one's own worth. (p. 445)

self-regulation The ability to control one's thoughts, emotions, and behaviors. (p. 308)

semantic development The process of learning meanings of words and of combinations of words. (p. 239)

semenarche The first ejaculation. Ejaculation often occurs spontaneously during sleep, in which case it is called a nocturnal emission. (p. 486)

sensation-seeking The desire to participate in highly arousing activities; it is especially common in early and mid-adolescence. (p. 520)

sensitive period A time in an organism's development when a particular experience has an especially profound effect. (p. 13)

sensorimotor stage Piaget's term for the stage of infancy during which the process of adaptation consists largely of coordinating sensory perceptions and simple motor behaviors to acquire knowledge of the world. (p. 146)

sensory register The part of the information-processing system that stores input from the sensory organs for a fraction of a second, during which time it is either attended to and moved into working memory or lost from the system. (p. 274)

separation anxiety The distress that babies show when the person to whom they are attached leaves. (p. 209)

sex hormones Estrogens and androgens that circulate in the bloodstream and activate hormone-perceiving receptors located throughout the body. (p. 490)

sexual debut Having sexual intercourse for the first time. (p. 532)

sexual identity An individual's understanding of himself or herself as heterosexual, homosexual, or bisexual. (p. 550)

sexual scripts Cognitive frames of knowledge used by individuals to guide and interpret sexual behavior, including who does what, when, and with whom. (p. 529)

sexual self Cognitions and feelings about who one is as a sexual being. (p. 541)

sexual-minority (LGBTQ) youth Adolescents who develop an identity as gay, lesbian, bisexual, transgendered, or queer. (p. 550)

sexual-orientation mobility The shifting of sexual attractions, behaviors, and identities over time. (p. 551)

sleeper effects The detrimental effects of early-life adversity that occur only later in development. (p. 166)

small for gestational age Newborns whose birth weight falls in the lowest 10 percent for their gestational age because they have not grown at the normal rate. (p. 114)

social capital The resources that communities provide children and families, including not only schools, health services, and so on, but also social structures, expectations for behavior, and levels of trust and cooperation among community members. (p. 352)

social comparison The process of defining oneself in relationship to one's peers. (p. 443)

social disorganization A problem in distressed communities that includes weak social cohesion (lack of trust and connection among community members), poor neighborhood climate (fear related to crime and violence), and perceived racism. (p. 354)

social domain theory The theory that the moral domain, the social conventional domain, and the personal domain have distinct rules that vary in how broadly the rules apply and in what happens when they are broken. (p. 306)

social enhancement The most basic social process of learning to use cultural resources, in which resources are used simply because others' activities have made them available in the immediate environment. (p. 53)

social learning theories Theories that emphasize the behavior–consequences associations that children learn by observing and interacting with others in social situations. (p. 25)

social referencing Infants' tendency to look to their caregiver for an indication of how to feel and act in unfamiliar circumstances. (p. 173)

social reorientation A process that begins in middle childhood, when children expand their focus and engagement from the family to the peer group. (p. 467)

social repair mechanisms Strategies that allow friends to remain friends even when serious differences temporarily drive them apart. (p. 466)

social structures Complex organizations of relationships between individuals. (p. 453)

socialization The process by which children acquire the standards, values, and knowledge of their society. (p. 294)

sociocultural theory The theory associated with Vygotsky that emphasizes the influence of culture on development. (p. 22)

sociodramatic play Make-believe play in which two or more participants enact a variety of related social roles. (p. 310)

socioemotional competence The ability to behave appropriately in social situations that evoke strong emotions. (p. 316)

somatic cells All the cells in the body except for the germ cells (the ova and sperm). (p. 59)

spatial intelligence The intelligence quotient derived from tests of the ability to mentally rotate objects in order to solve problems. (p. 403)

specific learning disabilities (SLD) A term used to refer to the academic difficulties of children who fare poorly in school despite having normal intelligence. (p. 424)

spinal cord The part of the central nervous system that extends from below the waist to the base of the brain. (p. 128)

Strange Situation A laboratory procedure designed to assess children's attachment on the basis of their use of their mother as a secure base for exploration, their reactions to being left alone with a stranger and then completely alone, and their response when they are reunited with their mother. (p. 210)

subjectivist theory of knowledge A belief that there is no absolute truth because truth can change depending on one's perspective. (p. 502)

superego In Freudian terms, the conscience. It represents the authority of the child's parents and sits in stern judgment of the ego's efforts to hold the id in check. It becomes a major force in the personality in middle childhood. (p. 305)

symbolic play Play in which one object stands for, or represents, another. (p. 178)

symbolic tools Cultural tools, such as abstract knowledge, beliefs, and values. (p. 52)

sympathy Feelings of sorrow or concern for another. (p. 324)

synapse The tiny gap between the axon of one neuron and the dendrite of another. (p. 127)

synaptic pruning The process of selective dying-off of nonfunctional synapses. (p. 130)

synaptogenesis The process of synapse formation. (p. 127)

syntactic bootstrapping Use of knowledge of grammar to figure out the meaning of new words. (p. 247)

systems theories Theories that envision development in terms of complex wholes made up of parts and that explore how these wholes and their parts are organized and interact and change over time. (p. 27)

temperament The term for the individual modes of responding to the environment that appear to be consistent across situations and stable over time. Temperament includes such characteristics as children's activity level, their intensity of reaction, the ease with which they become upset, their characteristic responses to novelty, and their sociability. (p. 149)

teratogens Environmental agents that can cause deviations from normal development and can lead to abnormalities or death. (p. 95)

tertiary circular reactions The fifth stage of the sensorimotor period, characterized by the deliberate variation of action sequences to solve problems and explore the world. (p. 177)

theory A broad framework or set of principles that can be used to guide the collection and interpretation of a set of facts. (p. 16)

theory of mind Coherent theories about how people's beliefs, desires, and mental states combine to shape their actions. (p. 278)

theory theory The theory that young children have primitive theories about how the world works, which influence how children think about, and act within, specific domains. (p. 283)

top-down processing An approach to education that focuses on using skills to accomplish specific, meaningful tasks. (p. 420)

totipotent stem cells Cells that have the potential to grow into a complete embryo and, ultimately, to become a normal, healthy infant. (p. 82)

true dialogue A communication in which each person's utterances take into account the utterances of others. (p. 255)

twin study A study in which groups of monozygotic (identical) and dizygotic (fraternal) twins of the same sex are compared to each other and to other family members for similarity on a given trait. (p. 69)

umbilical cord A flexible helical structure containing blood vessels that connects the developing organism to the placenta. (p. 83)

unconditional response (UCR) In classical conditioning, the response, such as salivation, that is invariably elicited by the unconditional stimulus (UCS). (p. 147)

unconditional stimulus (UCS) In classical conditioning, the stimulus, such as food in the mouth, that invariably causes the unconditional response (UCR). (p. 147)

unspecified feeding or eating disorder An eating disorder that is diagnosed when the criteria for anorexia or bulimia nervosa are not quite met; it is the most common diagnosis for adolescents with eating disorders. (p. 555)

validity The scientific requirement that the data being collected must actually reflect the phenomenon being studied. (p. 32)

violation-of-expectations method A test of mental representation in which the child is habituated to an event and then presented with possible and impossible variants of the event. (p. 183)

visual acuity Sharpness of vision. (p. 134)

visual preference technique A common behavioral method used to evaluate infant sensory capacities, which involves presenting two different stimuli at once to determine if the baby displays a preference by looking at one longer than the other. (p. 133)

visual proprioception The visual feedback that one gets from moving around, linked to the development of wariness of heights in infancy. (p. 172)

White privilege Social and economic benefits that are automatically granted to individuals simply because they are members of the White majority. (p. 544)

working memory (also known as *short-term memory*) The part of the information-processing system where active thinking takes place, and information from the sensory register may be combined with memory of past experiences. (p. 274)

X chromosome One of the two chromosomes that determine sex; in females, both members of the 23rd pair of chromosomes are X, and in males, one member of the 23rd pair is X. (p. 60)

Y chromosome One of the two chromosomes that determine sex; in males, one member of the 23rd pair of chromosomes is Y. (p. 60)

zone of proximal development (ZPD) For Vygotsky, the gap between what children can accomplish independently and what they can accomplish when interacting with others who are more competent. (p. 23)

zygote The single cell formed at conception from the union of the sperm and the ovum. (p. 59)

REFERENCES

Abma, J. C., Martinez, G. M., & Copen, C. E. (2010). Sexual activity, contraceptive use, and childbearing, National Survey of Family Growth 2006–2008. *National Center for Health Statistics. Vital Health Statistics, 23*(30).

Abraham, L. (2011). Teaching good sex. *New York Times Magazine,* November 16.

Abrams, R., Gerhardt, K., & Antonelli, P. J. (1998). Fetal hearing. *Developmental Psychobiology, 33,* 1–3.

Acebo, C., Sadeh, A., Seifer, R., Tzischinsky, O., Hafer, A., & Carskadon, M. A. (2005). Sleep/wake patterns derived from activity monitoring and maternal report for healthy 1- to 5-year-old children. *Sleep, 28,* 1568–1577.

Acharya, O., Zotor, F. B., Chaudhary, P., Deepak, K., Amuna, P., & Ellahi, B. (2016). Maternal nutritional status, food intake and pregnancy weight gain in Nepal. *Journal of Health Management, 18*(1), 1–12.

Adamczyk, A. (2009). Socialization and selection in the link between friends' religiosity and the transition to sexual intercourse. *Sociology of Religion, 70*(1), 5–27.

Adams, R., Santo, J., & Bukowski, W. (2011). The presence of a best friend buffers the effects of negative experiences. *Developmental Psychology, 47*(6), 1786–1791.

Addams, J. (1910). *The spirit of youth and the city streets.* New York: Macmillan.

Adolph, K. E., Cole, W. G., Komati, M., Garciaguirre, J. S., Badaly, D., Lingeman, J. M., et al. (2012). How do you learn to walk? Thousands of steps and dozens of falls per day. *Psychological Science, 23*(11), 1387–1394.

Adolph, K. E., Karasik, L. B., & Tamis-LeMonda, C. S. (2010). Using social information to guide action: Infants' locomotion over slippery slopes. *Neural Networks, 23,* 1033–1042.

Afifi, T. O., Mota, N., Sareen, J., & MacMillan, H. L. (2017). The relationships between harsh physical punishment and child maltreatment in childhood and intimate partner violence in adulthood. *BMC Public Health, 17,* 493.

Agerup, T., Lydersen, S., Wallander, J., & Sund, A. M. (2015). Associations between parental attachment and course of depression between adolescence and young adulthood. *Child Psychiatry & Human Development, 46*(4), 632–642.

Agostino, A., Im-Bolter, N., Stefanatos, A. K., & Dennis, M. (2017). Understanding ironic criticism and empathic praise: The role of emotive communication. *British Journal of Developmental Psychology, 35*(2), 186–201.

Ahmad, L., Smetana, J., & Klimstra, T. A. (2015). Maternal monitoring, adolescent disclosure, and adolescent adjustment among Palestinian refugee youth in Jordan. *Journal of Research on Adolescence, 25*(3), 403–411.

Ahmadpour-kacho, M., Pasha, Y. Z., Hahdinejad, Z., & Khafri, S. (2017). The effect of non-nutritive sucking on transcutaneous oxygen saturation in neonates under the nasal continuous positive airway pressure (CPAP). *International Journal of Pediatrics, 5*(3), 4511–4519.

Ahmed, M. L., Ong, K. K., & Dunger, D. B. (2009). Childhood obesity and the timing of puberty. *Trends in Endocrinology & Metabolism, 20*(5), 237–242.

AhnAllen, J. M., & Suyemoto, K. L. (2011). Influence of interracial dating on racial and/or ethnic identities of Asian American women and white European American men. *Asian American Journal of Psychology, 2*(1), 61–75.

Ahnert, L., Pinquart, M., & Lamb, M. E. (2006). Security of children's relationships with nonparental care providers: A meta-analysis. *Child Development, 77*(3), 664–679.

Ainsworth, M. D. S. (1982). Attachment: Retrospect and prospect. In C. M. Parkes & J. Stevenson-Hinde (Eds.), *The place of attachment in human behavior.* New York: Basic Books.

Ainsworth, M. D. S., Bell, S. M., & Stayton, D. J. (1971). Individual differences in strange-situation behavior of one-year-olds. In H. R. Schaffer (Ed.), *The origins of human social relations.* New York: Academic Press.

Ainsworth, M. D. S., Blehar, M. C., Waters, E., & Wall, S. (1978). *Patterns of attachment: A psychological study of the strange situation.* Mahwah, NJ: Lawrence Erlbaum Associates.

Ainsworth, M. D. S., & Bowlby, J. (1991). An ethological approach to personality development. *American Psychologist, 46*(4), 333–341.

Ajia, O. (2007). *Drumming up pride among post-war Burundi's street children.* Retrieved from http://www.unicef.org/infobycountry/burundi_39331.html

Akileswaran, C. P., & Hutchison, M. S. (2016). Making room at the table for obstetrics, midwifery, and a culture of normalcy within maternity care. *Obstetrics & Gynecology, 128*(1), 176–180.

Al-Ali, N., & Hussein, Y. (2003). Iraq. In A. Mahdi (Ed.), *Teen life in the Middle East.* Westport, CT: Greenwood Press.

Alastalo, H., Raikkonen, K., Pesonen, A.-K., Osmond, C., Barker, D. J. P., Kajantie, E., et al. (2009). Cardiovascular health of Finnish war evacuees 60 years later. *Annals of Medicine, 41*(1), 66–72.

Alexander, K., Quas, J., Goodman, G., Ghetti, S., Edelstein, R., Redlich, A. D., et al. (2005). Traumatic impact predicts long-term memory of documented child sexual abuse. *Psychological Science, 16,* 33–40.

Allan, N. P., & Lonigan, C. J. (2014). Exploring dimensionality of effortful control using hot and cool tasks in a sample of preschool children. *Journal of Experimental Child Psychology, 122,* 33–47.

Allen, J. P., Chango, J., & Szwedo, D. (2014). The adolescent relational dialectic and the peer roots of adult social functioning. *Child Development, 85*(1), 192–204.

Allen, R. E., & Myers, A. L. (2006). Nutrition in toddlers. *American Family Physician, 74,* 1527–1532.

Alloway, T. P., Horton, J., Alloway, R. G., & Dawson, C. (2013). Social networking sites and cognitive abilities: Do they make you smarter? *Computers & Education, 63,* 10–16.

Almoammer, A., Sullivan, J., Donlan, C., Marušič, F., Žaucer, R., O'Donnell, T., & Barner, D. (2013). Grammatical morphology as a source of early number word meanings. *Proceedings of the National Academy of Sciences of the United States of America, 110*(46), 18448–18453.

Alqahtani, M. M. J. (2016). Neurobehavioral outcomes of school-age children born preterm: A preliminary study in the Arabic community. *Journal of Pediatric and Neonatal Individualized Medicine, 5*(2), e050211–e050211.

Altamura, M. M., Della Rovere, F., Fattorini, L., D'Angeli, S., & Falasca, G. (2016). Recent advances on genetic and physiological bases of in vitro somatic embryo formation. *Methods in Molecular Biology, 1359,* 47.

Altvater-Mackensen, N., & Grossmann, T. (2016). The role of left inferior frontal cortex during audiovisual speech perception in infants. *Neuroimage, 133,* 14–20.

Amato, P. (2000). The consequences of divorce for adults and children. *Journal of Marriage and the Family, 62,* 1269–1287.

Amato, P. R. (2006). Marital discord, divorce, and children's well-being: Results from a 20-year longitudinal study of two generations. In A. Clarke-Stewart & J. Dunn (Eds.), *Families count: Effects on child and adolescent development. The Jacobs Foundation series on adolescence* (pp. 179–202). New York: Cambridge University Press.

Amato, P. R. (2010). Research on divorce: Continuing trends and new developments. *Journal of Marriage and Family, 72,* 650–666.

Amato, P. R., Booth, A., McHale, S., & Van Hook, J. (2015). *Families in an era of increasing inequality: Diverging destinies.* Cham, Switzerland: Springer International Publishing.

Amato, P. R., & Hohmann-Marriott, B. (2007). A comparison of high- and low-distress marriages that end in divorce. *Journal of Marriage and Family, 69,* 621–638.

Amato, P. R., & Patterson, S. E. (2017). The intergenerational transmission of union instability in early adulthood. *Journal of Marriage and Family, 79*(3), 723–738.

American Academy of Pediatrics. (2003). Policy statement. *Pediatrics, 112,* 424–430.

American College of Obstetricians and Gynecologists. (2009). Induction of labor. *Obstetrics & Gynecology. ACOG Practice Bulletin No. 107,* 114–386.

American Pregnancy Association. (2017). *Genetic counseling.* Retrieved from http://americanpregnancy.org/getting-pregnant/genetic-counseling/

American Psychiatric Association. (2013). *Diagnostic and statistical manual of mental disorders* (5th ed.). Arlington, VA: American Psychiatric Association.

Ananat, E. O., & Michaels, G. (2008). Effect of marital breakup on the income distribution of women with children. *Journal of Human Resources, 43*(3), 611–629.

Anderman, E. M., & Murdock, T. B. (2007). In E. M. Anderman & T. B. Murdock (Eds.), *Psychology of academic cheating* (pp. 1–5). San Diego, CA: Elsevier Academic Press.

Anderson, E. (1990). *Streetwise: Race, class, and change in an urban community.* Chicago, IL: University of Chicago Press.

Anderson, L. (2016). Divorce rate in the U.S.: Geographic variation, 2015. *Family Profiles,* FP-16-21. National Center for Family & Marriage Research. Retrieved from www.bgsu.edu/ncfmr/resources/data/family-profiles/anderson-divorce-rate-us-geo-2015-fp-16-21.html

Anderson, S. E., Bandini, L. G., & Must, A. (2005). Child temperament does not predict adolescent body composition in girls. *International Journal of Obesity, 29,* 47–53.

Andreas, N., Kampmann, B., & Le-Doare, K. (2015). Human breast milk: A review on its composition and bioactivity. *Early Human Development, 91*(11), 629–635.

Anglin, J. M. (1993). Vocabulary development: A morphological analysis. *Monographs of the Society for Research in Child Development, 58*(10), 1–166.

Anglin, J. M. (1995). Classifying the world through language: Functional relevance, cultural significance, and category name learning. *International Journal of Intercultural Relations, 19,* 161–181.

Annis, R. C., & Corenblum, B. (1987). Effect of test language and experimenter race on Canadian Indian children's racial and self-identity. *Journal of Social Psychology, 126,* 761–773.

Antonov, A. I., & Medkov, V. M. (2007). Demographic processes in the countries of Eastern Europe, the CIS, and the Baltic: Trends in the 1990s and what we should expect in the next decade. In A. S. Loveless & T. B. Holman (Eds.), *The family in the new millennium: World voices supporting the "natural" clan: Vol. 1. The place of family in human society* (pp. 296–315). Westport, CT: Praeger Publishers/Greenwood Publishing Group.

Antonov, A. N. (1947). Children born during the siege of Leningrad in 1942. *Journal of Pediatrics, 30,* 250.

Apgar, V. (1953). A proposal for a new method of evaluation of the newborn infant. *Current Researches in Anesthesia and Analgesics, 32,* 260–267.

Apple. (2015). *iPad in education.* Retrieved from http://www.apple.com/education/ipad/apps-books-and-more/

Apple, R. (2006). *Perfect motherhood: Science and childrearing in America.* New Brunswick, NJ: Rutgers University Press.

Apter, G., Devouche, E., Garez, V., Valente, M., Genet, M.-C., Gratier, M., et al. (2017). The still-face: A greater challenge for infants of mothers with borderline personality disorder. *Journal of Personality Disorders, 31*(2), 156.

Arey, L. (1974). *Developmental anatomy* (7th ed.). Philadelphia, PA: Saunders Publishers.

Ariès, P. (1962). *Centuries of childhood.* Translated from the French by Robert Baldick. London: Cape.

Ariès, P. (1965). *Centuries of childhood: A social history of family life.* Oxford, England: Vintage Books.

Arnett, J. J. (2016). *The Oxford handbook of emerging adulthood.* New York: Oxford University Press.

Arnett, J. J., & Cravens, H. (2006). G. Stanley Hall's adolescence: A centennial reappraisal: Introduction. *History of Psychology, 9,* 165–171.

Arruda-Colli, M. N. F., Weaver, M. S., & Wiener, L. (2017). Communication about dying, death, and bereavement: A systematic review of children's literature. *Journal of Palliative Medicine, 20*(5), 548–559.

Arsenio, W. F. (2006). Happy victimization: Emotion dysregulation in the context of instrumental, proactive aggression. In W. F. Arsenio (Ed.), *Emotion regulation in couples and families: Pathways to dysfunction and health* (pp. 101–121). Washington, DC: American Psychological Association.

Asakura, N., & Inui, T. (2016). A Bayesian framework for false belief reasoning in children: A rational integration of theory–theory and simulation theory. *Frontiers in Psychology, 7.*

Asendorph, J. (2002). Self-awareness, other-awareness, and secondary representation. In A. Meltzoff & W. Prinz (Eds.), *The imitative mind: Development, evolution, and brain bases.* Cambridge, England: Cambridge University Press.

Asher, S. R., & Coie, J. D. (Eds.). (1990). *Peer rejection in childhood.* New York: Cambridge University Press.

Astington, J. W. (1993). *The child's discovery of the mind.* Cambridge, MA: Harvard University Press.

Astington, J. W., & Filippova, E. (2005). Language as the route into other minds. In B. F. Malle & S. D. Hodges (Eds.), *Other minds: How humans bridge the divide between self and others* (pp. 209–222). New York: Guilford Press.

Ataguba, J., Ojo, K., & Ichoku, H. (2016). Explaining socio-economic inequalities in immunization coverage in Nigeria. *Health Policy and Planning, 31*(9), 1212–1224.

Atance, C. M., Metcalf, J. L., Martin-Ordas, G., & Walker, C. L. (2014). Young children's causal explanations are biased by post-action associative information. *Developmental Psychology, 50*(12), 2675.

Atkinson, J. (1998). The "where and what" or "who and how" of visual development. In F. Simion & G. Butterworth (Eds.), *The development of sensory, motor and cognitive capacities in early infancy: From perception to cognition.* Hove, England: Psychology Press/Lawrence Erlbaum Associates.

Atkinson, R. C., & Shiffrin, R. M. (1968). Human memory: A proposed system and its control processes. In K. W. Spence & J. T. Spence (Eds.), *The psychology of learning and motivation: Advances in research and theory: Vol. 2.* Orlando, FL: Academic Press.

Atran, S. (1998). Folk biology and the anthropology of science: Cognitive universals and cultural particulars. *Behavioral & Brain Sciences, 21,* 547–609.

Auger, A., Farkas, G., Burchinal, M., Duncan, G., & Vandell, D. (2014). Preschool center care quality effects on academic achievement: An instrumental variables analysis. *Developmental Psychology, 50*(12), 2559–2571.

Augustine, J. M., Prickett, K. C., & Kimbro, R. T. (2017). Health-related parenting among U.S. families and young children's physical health. *Journal of Marriage and Family, 79*(3), 816–832.

Augustine, M. E., & Stifter, C. A. (2015). Temperament, parenting, and moral development: Specificity of behavior and context. *Social Development, 24*(2), 285–303.

Auyeung, B., Baron-Cohen, S., Ashwin, E., & Knickmeyer, R. (2009). Fetal testosterone predicts sexually differentiated childhood behavior in girls and in boys. *Psychological Science, 20,* 144–148.

Avenevoli, S., & Steinberg, L. (2001). The continuity of depression across the adolescent transition. *Advances in Child Development and Behavior, 28,* 139–173.

Avis, J., & Harris, P. L. (1991). Belief-desire reasoning among Baka children: Evidence for a universal conception of mind. *Child Development, 62,* 460–467.

Azad M. B., Konya T., Maughan H., Guttman D. S., Field C. J., Chari R. S., et al. (2013). Gut microbiota of healthy Canadian infants: Profiles by mode of delivery and infant diet at 4 months. *Canadian Medical Association Journal, 185,* 385–394.

Badiee, Z., Asghari, M., & Mohammadizadeh, M. (2013). The calming effect of maternal breast milk odor on premature infants. *Pediatrics & Neonatology, 54*(5), 322–325.

Baer, J. C., & Schmitz, M. F. (2007). Ethnic differences in trajectories of family cohesion for Mexican American and non-Hispanic white adolescents. *Journal of Youth and Adolescence, 36*(4), 583–592.

Bahrick, L. E., Lickliter, R., & Castellanos, I. (2013). The development of face perception in infancy: Intersensory interference and unimodal visual facilitation. *Developmental Psychology, 49*(10), 1919–1930.

Baibazarova, E., de Beek, C., Cohen-Kettenis, P., Buitelaarc, J., Shelton, K., & van Goozen, S. (2013). Influence of prenatal maternal stress, maternal plasma cortisol and cortisol in the amniotic fluid on birth outcomes and child temperament at 3 months. *Psychoneuroendocrinology, 38*(6), 907–915.

Bailey, H., Redden, E., Pederson, D., & Moran, G. (2016). Parental disavowal of relationship difficulties fosters the development of insecure attachment. *Canadian Journal of Behavioural Science, 48*(1), 49–59.

Bailey, R. L., West, J., Keith P, & Black, R. E. (2015). The epidemiology of global micronutrient deficiencies. *Annals of Nutrition & Metabolism, 66*(Suppl. 2), 22–33.

Baillargeon, R. (2004). Infants' physical world. *Current Directions in Psychological Science, 13,* 89–94.

Baillargeon, R., Zoccolillo, M., Keenan, K., Côté, S., Pérusse, D., Wu, H., et al. (2007). Gender differences in physical aggression: A prospective population-based survey of children before and after 2 years of age. *Developmental Psychology, 43,* 13–26.

Baiocco, R., Fontanesi, L., Santamaria, F., Ioverno, S., Baumgartner, E., & Laghi, F. (2016). Coming out during adolescence: Perceived parents' reactions and internalized sexual stigma. *Journal of Health Psychology, 21*(8), 1809–1813.

Baiocco, R., Fontanesi, L., Santamaria, F., Ioverno, S., Marasco, B., Baumgartner, E., et al. (2015). Negative parental responses to coming out and family functioning in a sample of lesbian and gay young adults. *Journal of Child and Family Studies, 24*(5), 1490–1500.

Baker-Ward, L., Quinonez, R., Milano, M., Lee, S., Langley, H., Brumley, B., & Ornstein, P. A. (2015). Predicting children's recall of a dental procedure: Contributions of stress, preparation, and dental history. *Applied Cognitive Psychology, 29*(5), 775–781.

Bakker, M., Sommerville, J. A., & Gredebäck, G. (2016). Enhanced neural processing of goal-directed actions after active training in 4-month-old infants. *Journal of Cognitive Neuroscience, 28*(3), 472–482.

Bakos, D. S., Denburg, N., Fonseca, R. P., & Parente, M. A. (2010). A cultural study on decision making: Performance differences on the Iowa gambling task between selected groups of Brazilians and Americans. *Psychology & Neuroscience, 3*(1), 101–107.

Balas, B. (2012). Bayesian face recognition and perceptual narrowing in face-space. *Developmental Science, 15*(4), 579–588.

Ball, C. L., Smetana, J. G., & Sturge-Apple, M. L. (2017). Following my head and my heart: Integrating preschoolers' empathy, theory of mind, and moral judgments. *Child Development, 88*(2), 597.

Ball, H. (2009). Bed-sharing and co-sleeping: Research overview. *NCT New Digest, 48,* 22–27.

Ballabriga, A. (2000, March). Morphological and physiological changes during growth: An update. *European Journal of Clinical Nutrition, 54*(Suppl. 1), S1–S6.

Bandura, A. (2012). On the functional properties of perceived self-efficacy revisited. *Journal of Management, 38*(1), 9–44.

Baptista, F., Santos, D. A., Silva, A. M., et al. (2012). Prevalence of the Portuguese population attaining sufficient physical activity. *Medicine and Science in Sports and Exercise, 44,* 466–473.

Barac, R., Bialystok, E., Castro, D. C., & Sanchez, M. (2014). The cognitive development of young dual language learners: A critical review. *Early Childhood Research Quarterly, 29,* 699–714.

Barber, B., Eccles, J., & Stone, M. (2001). Whatever happened to the jock, the brain, and the princess? Young adult pathways linked to adolescent activity involvement and social identity. *Journal of Adolescent Research, 16,* 429–455.

Bard, K. (2004). What is the evolutionary basis for colic? *Behavioral and Brain Sciences, 27,* 459.

Bard, K. A., Todd, B., Bernier, C., Love, J., & Leavens, D. (2006). Self-awareness in human and chimpanzee infants: What is measured and what is meant by the mark and mirror test? *Infancy, 9,* 191–219.

Barlow, K. (2013). Attachment and culture in Murik society: Learning autonomy and interdependence through kinship, food, and gender. In N. Quinn & J. M. Mageo (Eds.), *Attachment reconsidered: Cultural perspectives on a Western theory*. New York: Palgrave Macmillan.

Baron-Cohen, S., Leslie, A. M., & Frith, U. (1986). Mechanical, behavioural, and intentional understanding of picture stories in autistic children. *British Journal of Developmental Psychology, 4,* 113–125.

Baron-Cohen, S., Leslie, A. M., & Frith, U. (2007). Does the autistic child have a 'theory of mind'? In B. Gertler & L. Shapiro (Eds.), *Arguing about the mind* (pp. 310–318). New York: Routledge/Taylor & Francis Group.

Barr, R., Paterson, J., MacMartin, L., Lehtonen, L., & Young, S. (2005). Prolonged and unsoothable crying bouts in infants with and without colic. *Journal of Developmental and Behavioral Pediatrics, 26*(1), 14–23.

Barrett, J. (2001). Do children experience God as adults do? In J. Andressen (Ed.), *Religion in mind: Cognitive perspectives on religious belief, ritual, and experience.* Cambridge, England: Cambridge University Press.

Barrett, J. L., Richert, R. A., & Driesenga, A. (2001). God's beliefs versus mother's: The development of nonhuman agent concepts. *Child Development, 72,* 50–65.

Barrouillet, P., Gavens, N., Vergauwe, E., Gaillard, V., & Camos, V. (2009). Working memory span development: A time-based resource sharing model account. *Developmental Psychology, 45,* 477–490.

Barsalou, L. W. (2008, April). Cognitive and neural contributions to understanding the conceptual system. *Current Directions in Psychological Science, 17*(2), 91–95.

Bartlett, E. (1977). The acquisition of the meaning of color terms. In P. T. Smith & R. N. Campbell (Eds.), *Proceedings of the Sterling Conference on the psychology of language.* New York: Plenum Press

Bartlett, J., Kotake, C., Fauth, R., & Easterbrooks, M. (2017). Intergenerational transmission of child abuse and neglect: Do maltreatment type, perpetrator, and substantiation status matter? *Child Abuse & Neglect, 63,* 84–94.

Bartlett, N. H., & Vasey, P. L. (2006). A retrospective study of childhood gender-atypical behavior in Samoan fa'afafine. *Archives of Sexual Behavior, 35*(6), 659.

Barton, B. K., & Morrongiello, B. A. (2011). Examining the impact of traffic environment and executive functioning on children's pedestrian behaviors. *Developmental Psychology, 47,* 182–191.

Bascandziev, I., Powell, L. J., Harris, P. L., & Carey, S. (2016). A role for executive functions in explanatory understanding of the physical world. *Cognitive Development, 39,* 71–85.

Basow, S. A. (2006). Gender role and gender identity development. In J. Worell & C. D. Goodheart (Eds.), *Handbook of girls' and women's psychological health: Gender and well-being across the lifespan. Oxford series in clinical psychology* (pp. 242–251). New York: Oxford University Press.

Bassuk, E. L., DeCandia, C. J., Beach, C. A., & Berman, F. (2014). *Reference: America's youngest outcasts: A report card on child homelessness.* Waltham, MA: The National Center on Family Homelessness at American Institutes for Research.

Bates, E. (1999). On the nature and nurture of language. In E. Bizzi, P. Calissano, & V. Volterra (Eds.), *Frontiere della biologia* [Frontiers of biology]. Rome: Giovanni Trecanni.

Bates, E. (2005). Plasticity, localization, and language development. In S. T. Parker, J. Langer, & C. Milbrath (Eds.), *Biology and knowledge revisited: From neurogenesis to psychogenesis. The Jean Piaget symposium series* (pp. 205–253). Mahwah, NJ: Lawrence Erlbaum Associates.

Bates, E., Camaioni, L., & Volterra, V. (1975). The acquisition of performatives prior to speech. *Merrill Palmer Quarterly, 21,* 205–226.

Bates, E., O'Connell, B., & Shore, C. (1987). Language and communication. In J. D. Osofsky (Ed.), *Handbook of infant development* (2nd ed.). New York: Wiley.

Bates, E., & Roe, K. (2001). Language development in children with unilateral brain injury. In C. A. Nelson & M. Luciana (Eds.), *Handbook of developmental cognitive neuroscience.* Cambridge, MA: The MIT Press.

Bates, E., Thal, D., Finlay, B., & Clancy, B. (2002). Language development and its neural correlates. In I. Rapin & S. Segalowitz (Eds.), *Handbook of neuropsychology* (pp. 109–176). Amsterdam: Elsevier.

Bauer, P. J. (2015). Conversations and memory processes: A commentary. *Applied Cognitive Psychology, 29*(6), 805–807.

Bauer, P. J., & Larkina, M. (2015). Predicting remembering and forgetting of autobiographical memories in children and adults: A 4-year prospective study. *Memory, 24*(10), 1345–1368.

Baumer, S., Ferholt, B., & Lecusay, R. (2005). Promoting narrative competence through adult–child joint pretense: Lessons from the Scandinavian educational practices of playworld. *Cognitive Development, 20,* 576–590.

Baumrind, D. (1971). Current patterns of parental authority. *Developmental Psychology Monographs, 4*(1, Part 2).

Baumrind, D. (1980). New directions in socialization research. *American Psychologist, 35,* 639–652.

Baumrind, D., Larzelere, R. E., & Owens, E. B. (2010). Effects of preschool parents' power assertive patterns and practices on adolescent development. *Science and Practice, 10,* 157–201.

Bavelier, D., & Green, C. (2016). The brain-boosting power of video games. *Scientific American, 315,* 26–31.

Bayley, N. (1993). *The Bayley scales of infant development.* San Antonio, TX: Psychological Corporation.

Beaver, W., & Paul, S. (2011). Internet pornography: Variables related to use among traditional-aged college students. *Sociological Viewpoints, 27*(1), 25–38.

Bedard, K., & Dhuey, E. (2006). The persistence of early childhood maturity: International evidence of long-run age effects. *The Quarterly Journal of Economics, 121*(4), 1437–1472.

Bei, B., Byrne, M. L., Ivens, C., Waloszek, J., Woods, M. J., Dudgeon, P., et al. (2013). Pilot study of a mindfulness-based, multi-component, in-school group sleep intervention in adolescent girls. *Early Intervention in Psychiatry,* 7(2), 213–220.

Bellmore, A. D., & Cillessen, A. H. N. (2006). Reciprocal influences of victimization, perceived social preference, and self-concept in adolescence. *Self and Identity, 5*(3), 209–229.

Belsky, J., Ruttle, P. L., Boyce, W. T., Armstrong, J. M., & Essex, M. J. (2015). Early adversity, elevated stress physiology, accelerated sexual maturation, and poor health in females. *Developmental Psychology, 51*(6), 816–822.

Belsky, J., Steinberg, L. D., Houts, R. M., Friedman, S. L., DeHart, G., Cauffman, E., et al. (2007). Family rearing antecedents of pubertal timing. *Child Development, 78,* 1302–1321.

Bengtson, V. L. (2005). *Sourcebook of family theory and research.* Thousand Oaks, CA: Sage Publications.

Bengtson, V. L., Silverstein, M., Putney, N. M., & Harris, S. C. (2015). Does religiousness increase with age? Age changes and generational differences over 35 years. *Journal for the Scientific Study of Religion, 54*(2), 363–379.

Bennett, P. R., Lutz, A. C., & Jayaram, L. (2012). Beyond the schoolyard: The role of parenting logics, financial resources, and social institutions in the social class gap in structured activity participation. *Sociology of Education, 85*(2), 131–157.

Beran, M., & Beran, M. (2004). Chimpanzees remember the results of one-by-one addition of food items to sets over extended time periods. *Psychological Science, 15,* 94–99.

Bergen, D. (2011). Communicative actions and language narratives in preschoolers' play with "talking" and "non-talking" rescue heroes. In D. Sluss & O. Jarrett (Eds.), *Investigating play in the 21st century* (pp. 229–249). New York: University Press of America.

Berger, S. E., & Adolph, K. E. (2003). Infants use handrails as tools in a locomotor task. *Developmental Psychology, 39*(3), 594–605.

Bergman, K., Glover, V., Sarkar, P., Abbott, D. H., & O'Connor, T. G. (2010). In utero cortisol and testosterone exposure and fear reactivity in infancy. *Hormones and Behavior, 57,* 306–312.

Berk, L. E., & Meyers, A. B. (2013). The role of make-believe play in the development of executive function: Status of research and future directions. *American Journal of Play, 6*(1), 98.

Berkowitz, L. (2003). Affect, aggression and antisocial behavior. In R. Davidson, K. Scherer, & H. Goldsmith (Eds.), *Handbook of affective sciences.* Oxford, England: Oxford University Press.

Berland, J. (1982). *No five fingers are alike.* Cambridge, MA: Harvard University Press.

Bernal, J. F. (1972). Crying during the first few days and maternal responses. *Developmental Medicine and Child Neurology, 14,* 362–372.

Berndt, T. J. (2007). Children's friendships: Shifts over a half-century in perspectives on their development and their effects. In G. Ladd (Ed.), *Appraising the human development sciences: Essays in honor of Merrill-Palmer Quarterly (Landscapes of childhood series).* Detroit, MI: Wayne State University Press.

Berndt, T. J., & Keefe, K. (1995). Friend's influence on adolescent's adjustment in school. *Child Development, 66,* 1312–1329.

Berndt, T. J., & Murphy, L. M. (2002). Influences of friends and friendships: Myths, truths, and research recommendations. In R. V. Kail (Ed.), *Advances in child development and behavior: Vol. 30* (pp. 275–310). San Diego, CA: Academic Press.

Berndt, T. J., & Savin-Williams, R. C. (1993). Peer relations and friendships. In P. H. Tolan & B. J. Cohler (Eds.), *Handbook of clinical research and practice with adolescents.* New York: Wiley.

Berry, J. W. (1984). Cultural relations in plural societies: Alternatives to segregation and their sociopsychological implications. In N. Miller & M. Brewer (Eds.). *Groups in contact.* San Diego, CA: Academic Press

Berry, J. W. (2013). *Intercultural psychology.* New York: Oxford University Press.

Berry, J. W. (2015). Acculturation. In J. E. Grusec & P. D. Hastings (Eds.), *Handbook of socialization: Theory and research* (2nd ed.). New York: Guilford Press.

Bertenthal, B. I., Campos, J. J., & Kermoian, R. (1994). An epigenetic perspective on the development of self-produced locomotion and its consequences. *Current Directions in Psychological Science, 3*(5), 140–145.

Berthier, N. E., & Keen, R. (2006). Development of reaching in infancy. *Experimental Brain Research, 169*(4), 507–518.

Bertrand, J. M., Moulin, C. J. A., & Souchay, C. (2017). Short-term memory predictions across the lifespan: Monitoring span before and after conducting a task. *Memory, 25*(5), 607–612.

Best, J. R., & Miller, P. H. (2010). A developmental perspective on executive function. *Child Development, 81*(6), 1641–1660.

Betancourt, T. S., Brennan, R. T., Rubin-Smith, J., Fitzmaurice, G. M., & Gilman, S. E. (2010). Sierra Leone's former child soldiers: A longitudinal study of risk, protective factors and mental health. *Journal of the American Academy of Child & Adolescent Psychiatry, 49,* 606–615.

Bettelheim, B. (1977). *The uses of enchantment: The meaning and importance of fairytales.* New York: Vintage Books.

Beuf, A. H. (1977). *Red children in white America.* Philadelphia, PA: University of Pennsylvania Press.

Beyens, I., Vandenbosch, L., & Eggermont, S. (2015). Early adolescent boys' exposure to internet pornography: Relationships to pubertal timing, sensation seeking, and academic performance. *The Journal of Early Adolescence, 35*(8), 1045–1068.

Bialystok, E. (2017). The bilingual adaptation: How minds accommodate experience. *Psychological Bulletin, 143*(3), 233–262.

Bialystok, E., & Shapero, D. (2005). Ambiguous benefits: The effect of bilingualism on reversing ambiguous figures. *Developmental Science, 8,* 595–604.

Biancotti, J. C., Narwani, K., Buehler, N., Mandefro, B., Golan-Lev, T., Yanuka, O., et al. (2010). Human embryonic stem cells as models for aneuploid chromosomal syndromes. *Stem Cells, 28,* 1530–1540.

Biblarz, T. J., & Savci, E. (2010). Lesbian, gay, bisexual, and transgender families. *Journal of Marriage and Family, 72,* 480–497.

Biemiller, A., & Slonim, N. (2001). Estimating root word vocabulary growth in normative and advantaged populations: Evidence for a common sequence of vocabulary acquisition. *Journal of Educational Psychology, 93*(3), 498–520.

Bilder, D. A., Noel, J. K., Baker, E. R., Irish, W., Chen, Y., Merilainen, M. J., et al. (2016). Systematic review and meta-analysis of neuropsychiatric symptoms and executive functioning in adults with phenylketonuria. *Developmental Neuropsychology, 41*(4), 245–260.

Billimoria, Z. C., & Kamat, D. (2014). A pediatrician's guide to caring for the complex neonatal intensive care unit graduate. *Pediatric Annals, 43*(9), 369.

Binet, A., & Simon, T. (1916). *The development of intelligence in children.* Vineland, NJ: Publications of the Training School at Vineland (reprinted by Williams Publishing Co., Nashville, TN, 1980).

Binnie, L., & Williams, J. (2003). Intuitive psychology and physics among children with autism and typically developing children. *Autism, 7,* 173–193.

Birch, L. (2015). Early influences on the development of children's eating behavior. *Frontiers in Integrative Neuroscience, 9.*

Bird, D., & Bird, R. (2005). Martu children's hunting strategies in the Western desert, Australia. In B. Hewlett & M. Lamb (Eds.), *Hunter-gatherer childhoods: Evolutionary, developmental & cultural perspectives.* New Brunswick: Transaction Publishers.

Birkett, M., & Espelage, D. L. (2015). Homophobic name-calling, peer-groups, and masculinity: The socialization of homophobic behavior in adolescents. *Social Development, 24*(1), 184–205.

Bisin, A., Patacchini, E., Verdier, T., Zenou, Y., Stockholms universitet, Samhällsvetenskapliga fakulteten, & Nationalekonomiska institutionen. (2011). Formation and persistence of oppositional identities. *European Economic Review, 55*(8), 1046–1071.

Bjorklund, D., Dukes, C., & Brown, R. (2009). The development of memory strategies. In M. Courage & N. Cowan (Eds.), *The development of memory in infancy and childhood*. Hove, UK: Psychology Press.

Bjorklund, D., & Ellis, B. (2014). Children, childhood, and development in evolutionary perspective. *Developmental Review, 34*(3), 225–264.

Bjorklund, D. F. (2015). Developing adaptations. *Developmental Review, 38,* 13–35.

Bjorklund, D. F., & Pellegrini, A. D. (2002). *The origins of human nature: Evolutionary developmental psychology.* Washington, DC: American Psychological Association.

Bjorn, G. J., Gustafsson, P. A., Sydsjö, G., & Berterö, C. (2013). Family therapy sessions with refugee families; A qualitative study. *Conflict and Health, 7,* 7.

Bjurström, E. (1994). *Children and television advertising.* Vallingby, Sweden: Konsumentverket.

Blachman, B. A., Schatschneider, C., Fletcher, J. M., Francis, D. J., Clonan, S. M., Shaywitz, B A., & Shaywitz, S. E. (2004). Effects of intensive reading remediation for second and third graders and a 1-year follow-up. *Journal of Educational Psychology, 96,* 444–461.

Blair, B. L., Perry, N. B., O'Brien, M., Calkins, S. D., Keane, S. P., & Shanahan, L. (2015). Identifying developmental cascades among differentiated dimensions of social competence and emotion regulation. *Developmental Psychology, 51*(8), 1062.

Blair, C., Zelazo, P. D., & Greenberg, M. T. (2005). The measurement of executive function in early childhood. *Developmental Neuropsychology, 28*(2), 561–571.

Blair, M. M., Glynn, L. M., Sandman, C. A., & Davis, E. P. (2011). Prenatal maternal anxiety and early childhood temperament. *Stress, 14,* 644–651.

Blair, P., Sidebotham, P., Berry, P., Evans, M., & Fleming, P. (2006). Major epidemiological changes in sudden infant death syndrome: A 20-year population-based study in the UK. *Lancet, 367,* 314–319.

Blair, P. S., Sidebotham, P., Pease, A., & Fleming, P. J. (2014). Bed-sharing in the absence of hazardous circumstances: Is there a risk of sudden infant death syndrome? An analysis from two case-control studies conducted in the UK. *PLOS ONE, 9*(9), e107799.

Blakeslee, S. (2006, January 6). Cells that read minds. *New York Times.*

Blanchard, D., Heinz, J., & Golinkoff, R. (2010). Modeling the contribution of phonotactic cues to the problem of word segmentation. *Journal of Child Language, 37*(3), 487–511.

Blanton, H., & Burkley, M. (2008). Deviance regulation theory: Applications to adolescent social influence. In M. J. Prinstein & K. A. Dodge (Eds.), *Understanding peer influence in children and adolescents. Duke series in child development and public policy* (pp. 94–121). New York: Guilford Press.

Bleah, D. A., & Ellett, M. L. (2010). Infant crying among recent African immigrants. *Health Care for Women International, 31*(7), 652–663.

Bleidorn, W., Kandler, C., & Caspi, A. (2014). The behavioural genetics of personality development in adulthood—Classic, contemporary, and future trends. *European Journal of Personality, 28*(3), 244–255.

Blicharski, T., Bon, M., & Strayer, F. (2011). *Origins of gender differences during the preschool years.* Paper presented as a part of the symposium, The sociogenesis of gender during early childhood (T. Blicharski, organizer), at the Annual Meeting of the Jean Piaget Society, Berkeley, CA.

Block, C. C., Parris, S. R., Reed, K. L., Whiteley, C. S., & Cleveland, M. D. (2009). Instructional approaches that significantly increase reading comprehension. *Journal of Educational Psychology, 101,* 262–281.

Block, J., Scribner, R., & DeSalvo, K. (2004). Fast food, race/ethnicity, and income: A geographic analysis. *American Journal of Preventive Medicine, 27,* 211–217.

Bloom, L. (1973). *One word at a time: The use of single word utterances before syntax.* The Hague: Mouton.

Bloom, P. (2010, May 9). The moral life of babies. *New York Times Magazine.*

Bloom, Z. D., & Hagedorn, W. B. (2015). Male adolescents and contemporary pornography: Implications for marriage and family counselors. *The Family Journal, 23*(1), 82–89.

Blumberg, F., Altschuler, E., Almonte, D., & Mileaf, M. (2013). The impact of recreational video game play on children's and adolescents' cognition. *New Directions for Child and Adolescent Development, 139,* 41–50.

Blunt-Vinti, H. D., Wheldon, C., McFarlane, M., Brogan, N., & Walsh-Buhi, E. R. (2016). Assessing relationship and sexual satisfaction in adolescent relationships formed online and offline. *The Journal of Adolescent Health: Official Publication of the Society for Adolescent Medicine, 58*(1), 11–16.

Bock, J. (2005). Farming, foraging, and children's play in the Okavango Delta, Botswana. In A. D. Pellegrini & P. K. Smith (Eds.), *The nature of play: Great apes and humans* (pp. 254–281). New York: Guilford Press.

Bogin, B. (1999). *Patterns of human growth* (2nd ed.). New York: Cambridge University Press.

Bogin, B. (2001). *The growth of humanity.* New York: Wiley-Liss.

Bogin, B., Smith, P., Orden, A. B., Varela Silva, M. I., & Loucky, J. (2002). Rapid change in height and body proportions of Maya American children. *American Journal of Human Biology, 14,* 753–761.

Bohn, M., Call, J., & Tomasello, M. (2016). Comprehension of iconic gestures by chimpanzees and human children. *Journal of Experimental Child Psychology, 142,* 1–17.

Boislard, M., van de Bongardt, D., & Blais, M. (2016). Sexuality (and lack thereof) in adolescence and early adulthood: A review of the literature. *Behavioral Sciences (Basel, Switzerland), 6*(1), 8.

Boo, K. (2006, February 6). A reporter at large: Swamp nurse. *The New Yorker,* p. 54.

Booth, A. E., Schuler, K., & Zajicek, R. (2010). Specifying the role of function in infant categorization. *Infant Behavior and Development, 33,* 672–684.

Borges, G., Medina-Mora, M. E., Benjet, C., Ruíz, J. Z., & Breslau, J. (2008). Descriptive epidemiology of depression in Latin America and Hispanics in the United States. In S. A. Aguilar-Gaxiola & T. P. Gullotta (Eds.), *Depression in Latinos: Assessment, treatment, and prevention* (pp. 53–71). New York: Springer.

Borke, H. (1975). Piaget's mountains revisited: Changes in the egocentric landscape. *Developmental Psychology, 11,* 240–443.

Bornstein, M. H., Cote, L. R., Maital, S., Painter, K., Park, S.-Y., Pascual, L., et al. (2004). Cross-linguistic analysis of vocabulary in young children: Spanish, Dutch, French, Hebrew, Italian, Korean, and American English. *Child Development, 75,* 1115–1139.

Bornstein, M. H., & Putnick, D. L. (2007). Chronological age, cognitions, and practices in European American mothers: A multivariate study of parenting. *Developmental Psychology, 43,* 850–864.

Bornstein, M. H., Putnick, D. L., Gartstein, M. A., Hahn, C., Auestad, N., & O'Connor, D. L. (2015). Infant temperament: Stability by age, gender, birth order, term status, and socioeconomic status. *Child Development, 86*(3), 844–863.

Bos, H. M. W., Gartrell, N. K., van Balen, F., H, P., & Sandfort, T. G. (2008). Children in planned lesbian families: A cross-cultural comparison between the United States and the Netherlands. *American Journal of Orthopsychiatry, 78,* 211–219.

Bos, H. M. W., Sandfort, T. G. M., de Bruyn, E. H., & Hakvoot, E. M. (2008). Same-sex attraction, social relationships, psychosocial functioning, and school performance in early adolescence. *Developmental Psychology, 44,* 59–68.

Bos, H. M. W., & van Balen, F. (2008). Children in planned lesbian families. Stigmatisation, psychological adjustment and protective factors. *Culture, Health and Sexuality, 10,* 221–236.

Bos, H. M. W., van Balen, F., & van den Boom, D. C. (2007). Child adjustment and parenting in planned lesbian-parent families. *American Journal of Orthopsychiatry, 77,* 38–48.

Boss, P., & Ishii, C. (2015). Trauma and ambiguous loss: The lingering presence of the physically absent. In K. Cherry (Ed.), *Traumatic stress and long-term recovery* (pp. 271–289). Cham, Switzerland: Springer International.

Bottoms, B. L., Goodman, G. S., Schwartz-Kenney, B. M., & Thomas, S. N. (2002). Understanding children's use of secrecy in the context of eyewitness reports. *Law & Human Behavior, 26*(3), 285–314.

Bourreau-Dubois, C., & Doriat-Duban, M. (2016). Covering the costs of divorce: The role of the family, the state and the market. *Population, 71*(3), 457.

Bower, T. G. R. (1979). *Human development.* San Francisco: W. H. Freeman.

Bower, T. G. R. (1982). *Development in human infancy.* New York: W. H. Freeman.

Bowker, A. (2004). Predicting friendship stability during early adolescence. *Journal of Early Adolescence, 24,* 85–112.

Bowlby, J. (1969). *Attachment and loss: Vol. 1. Attachment.* New York: Basic Books.

Bowlby, J. (1973). *Attachment and loss: Vol. 2. Separation.* New York: Basic Books.

Bowlby, J. (1980). *Attachment and loss: Vol. 3. Loss, sadness, and depression.* New York: Basic Books.

Boyd, R., Richerson, P. J., & Henrich, J. (2011). The cultural niche: Why social learning is essential for human adaptation. *Proceedings of the National Academy of Sciences, 108*(Suppl. 2), 10918–10925.

Boyer, L. A., Lee, T. I., Cole, M. F., Johnstone, S. E., Levine, S. S., Zucker, J. P., et al. (2005). Core transcriptional regulatory circuitry in human embryonic stem cells. *Cell, 122*(6), 947–956.

Boykin, A. W., & Cunningham, R. T. (2001). The effects of movement expressiveness in story content and learning context on the analogical reasoning performance of African American children. *Journal of Negro Education, 70,* 72–83.

Braddick, O., & Atkinson, J. (2011). Development of human visual function. *Vision Research, 51*(13), 1588–1609.

Bradley, C., McMurray, R., Harrell, J., & Deng, S. (2000). Changes in common activities of 3rd through 10th graders: The CHIC study. *Medicine and Science in Sports and Exercise, 32,* 2071–2078.

Bradley, K. A. L., Colcombe, S., Henderson, S. E., Alonso, C. M., Milham, M. P., & Gabbay, V. (2016). Neural correlates of self-perceptions in adolescents with major depressive disorder. *Developmental Cognitive Neuroscience, 19,* 87–97.

Bradshaw, C. (2015). Translating research to practice in bullying prevention. *American Psychologist, 70*(4), 322–332.

Braithwaite, D., Moore, D. H., Lustig, R. H., Epel, E. S., Ong, K. K., Rehkopf, D. H., et al. (2009). Socioeconomic status in relation to early menarche among black and white girls. *Cancer Causes & Control, 20*(5), 713–720.

Brakke, K. (2015). Story and history in fetal behavior research. *Monographs of the Society for Research in Child Development, 80*(3), 114–123.

Bramen, J. E., Hranilovich, J. A., Dahl, R. E., Forbes, E. E., Chen, J., Toga, A. W., et al. (2011). Puberty influences medial temporal lobe and cortical gray matter maturation differently in boys than girls matched for sexual maturity. *Cerebral Cortex, 21,* 636–646.

Brämswig, J., & Dübbers, A. (2009). Störungen der pubertätsentwicklung. [Disorders of pubertal development.] *Deutsches Ärzteblatt International, 106,* 295–304.

Branje, S. J. T., Laursen, B., & Collins, W. A. (2013). Parent–child communication during adolescence. In A. L. Vangelisti (Ed.), *The Routledge handbook of family communication* (2nd ed., pp. 271–286). New York: Routledge.

Brauer, J., Anwander, A., & Friederici, A. D. (2011). Neuroanatomical prerequisites for language functions in the maturing brain. *Cerebral Cortex, 21,* 459–466.

Braungart-Rieker, J. M., Zentall, S., Lickenbrock, D. M., Ekas, N. V., Oshio, T., & Planalp, E. (2014). Attachment in the making: Mother and father sensitivity and infants' responses during the still-face paradigm. *Journal of Experimental Child Psychology, 125,* 63–84.

Brazelton, T. B. (1984). *Neonatal behavioral assessment scale* (2nd ed.). London: Spastics International Medical Publications.

Breinholst, S., Esbjorn, B., & Reinholdt-Dunne, M. (2015). Effects of attachment and rearing behavior on anxiety in normal developing youth: A mediational study. *Personality and Individual Differences, 81,* 155–161.

Bremner, J., Johnson, S., Slater, A., Mason, U., Foster, K., & Cheshire, A. (2005). Conditions for young infants' perception of object trajectories. *Child Development, 76,* 1029–1043.

Bremner, J. G., Slater, A. M., Mason, U. C., Spring, J., & Johnson, S. P. (2016). Limits of object persistence: Young infants perceive continuity of vertical and horizontal trajectories, but not 45-degree oblique trajectories. *Infancy, 22*(3), 303–322.

Bretherton, I. (2005). In pursuit of the internal working model construct and its relevance to attachment relationships. In K. E. Grossmann, K. Grossmann, & E. Waters (Eds.), *Attachment from infancy to adulthood: The major longitudinal studies* (pp. 13–47). New York: Guilford Press.

Brett, Z. H., Humphreys, K. L., Fleming, A. S., Kraemer, G. W., & Drury, S. S. (2015). Using cross-species comparisons and a neurobiological framework to understand early social deprivation effects on behavioral development. *Development and Psychopathology, 27*(2), 347–367.

Bridges, K., & Hoff, E. (2014). Older sibling influences on the language environment and language development of toddlers in bilingual homes. *Applied Psycholinguistics, 35*(2), 225–241.

Britton, J. (2010). Cognitive inflexibility and frontal-cortical activation in pediatric obsessive-compulsive disorder. *Journal of the American Academy of Child and Adolescent Psychiatry, 49*(9), 944–953.

Brodersen, N. H., Steptoe, A., Williamson, S., & Wardle, J. (2005). Sociodemographic, developmental, environmental, and psychological correlates of physical activity and sedentary behavior at age 11 to 12. *Annals of behavioral medicine a publication of the Society of Behavioral Medicine, 29*(1), 2–11.

Broesch, T., Rochat, P., Olah, K., Broesch, J., & Henrich, J. (2016). Similarities and differences in maternal responsiveness in three societies: Evidence from Fiji, Kenya, and the United States. *Child Development, 87*(3), 700–711.

Bronfenbrenner, U. (1970). *Two worlds of childhood: U.S. and U.S.S.R.* New York: Russell Sage Foundation.

Bronfenbrenner, U. (2005). *Making human beings human: Bioecological perspectives on human development.* Thousand Oaks, CA: Sage Publications.

Bronson, G. W. (1991). Infant differences in rate of visual encoding. *Child Development, 62,* 44–54.

Bronson, G. W. (1994). Infants' transitions toward adult-like scanning. *Child Development, 65,* 1243–1261.

Bronson, G. W. (1997). The growth of visual capacity: Evidence from infant scanning patterns. *Advances in Infancy Research, 11,* 109–141.

Brooke, J. (1991, June 15). Cubato journal: Signs of life in Brazil's industrial valley of death. *New York Times,* Pt. 1, p. 2.

Brooks-Gunn, J., & Warren, M. (1989). Biological and social contributions to negative affect in young adolescent girls. *Child Development, 60,* 40–55.

Brown, A. L., Palincsar, A. S., & Armbruster, B. B. (1994). Instructing comprehension-fostering activities in interactive learning situations. In R. B. Ruddell & N. J. Unrau (Eds.), *Theoretical models and processes of reading* (pp. 757–787). Newark, DE: International Reading Association.

Brown, B. B., Bakken, J. P., Ameringer, S. W., & Mahon, S. D. (2008). A comprehensive conceptualization of the peer influence process in adolescence. In M. J. Prinstein & K. A. Dodge (Eds.), *Understanding peer influence in children and adolescents. Duke series in child development and public policy* (pp. 17–44). New York: Guilford Press.

Brown, B. B., Hippensteele, I. M., & Lawrence, S. M. (2014). Commentary: Developmental perspectives on adolescents and gangs. *Journal of Research on Adolescence, 24*(2), 284–292.

Brown, B. B., & Klute, C. (2003). Friendships, cliques, and crowds. In G. R. Adams & M. D. Berzonsky (Eds.), *Blackwell handbook of adolescence* (pp. 330–348). Malden, MA: Blackwell Publishing.

Brown, D. A., Lewis, C. N., & Lamb, M. E. (2015). Preserving the past: An early interview improves delayed event memory in children with intellectual disabilities. *Child Development, 86*(4), 1031–1047.

Brown, G., Schoppe-Sullivan, S., Mangelsdorf, S., & Neff, C. (2010). Observed and reported supportive coparenting as predictors of infant-mother and infant-father attachment security. *Early Child Development and Care, 180,* 121–137.

Brown, R. (1973). *A first language: The early stages.* Cambridge, MA: Harvard University Press.

Brown, R., & Herrnstein, R. J. (1975). *Psychology.* Boston: Little, Brown.

Brummelte, S., & Galea, L. A. M. (2016). Postpartum depression: Etiology, treatment and consequences for maternal care. *Hormones and Behavior, 77,* 153–166.

Bruner, J. S. (1982). Formats of language acquisition. *American Journal of Semiotics, 1,* 1–16.

Brüske, I., Pei, Z., Thiering, E., Flexeder, C., Berdel, D., von Berg, A., et al. (2015). Caesarean section has no impact on lung function at the age of 15 years. *Pediatric Pulmonology, 50*(12), 1262–1269.

Bryant, P., & Nunes, T. (2011). Children's understanding of mathematics. In U. Goswami (Ed.), *The Wiley-Blackwell handbook of childhood cognitive development* (2nd ed., pp. 549–573). New York: Wiley-Blackwell.

Bryant Ludden, A., & Wolfson, A. R. (2010). Understanding adolescent caffeine use: Connecting use patterns with expectancies, reasons, and sleep. *Health Education & Behavior, 37,* 330–342.

Buhi, E. R., Goodson, P., Neilands, T. B., & Blunt, H. (2011). Adolescent sexual abstinence: A test of an integrative theoretical framework. *Health Education & Behavior, 38*(1), 63–79.

Bureau of Labor Statistics. (2015). Genetic counselors. *Occupational Outlook Handbook.* Retrieved from https://www.bls.gov/ooh/healthcare/genetic-counselors.htm

Burgess, K. B., Wojslawowicz, J. C., Rubin, K. H., Rose-Krasnor, L., & Booth-LaForce, C. (2006). Social information processing and coping strategies of Shy/Withdrawn and aggressive children: Does friendship matter? *Child Development, 77*(2), 371–383.

Bushman, B., Gollwitzer, M., & Cruz, C. (2015). There is broad consensus: Media researchers agree that violent media increase aggression in children, and pediatricians and parents concur. *Psychology of Popular Media Culture, 4*(3), 200–214.

Bushnell, I. W. R. (2001). Mother's face recognition in newborn infants: Learning and memory. *Infant and Child Development, 10,* 67–74.

Buss, C., Davis, E., Muftuler, L., Head, K., & Sandman, C. (2010). High pregnancy anxiety during mid-gestation is associated with decreased gray matter density in 6–9-year-old children. *Psychoeuroendocrinology, 35,* 141–153.

Butterworth, G. (2001). Joint visual attention in infancy. In G. Bremner & A. Fogel (Eds.), *Blackwell handbook of infant development. Handbooks of developmental psychology* (pp. 213–240). Malden, MA: Blackwell Publishers.

Byers-Heinlein, K., & Fennell, C. T. (2014). Perceptual narrowing in the context of increased variation: Insights from bilingual infants. *Developmental Psychobiology, 56*(2), 274–291.

Cain, M. A., Bornick, P., & Whiteman, V. (2013). The maternal, fetal, and neonatal effects of cocaine exposure in pregnancy. *Clinical Obstetrics Gynecology, 56*(1): 124–132.

Cairns, R. B. (1979). *Social development: The origins of interchanges.* New York: W. H. Freeman.

Cairns, R. B. (1998). The making of developmental psychology. In W. Damon & R. M. Lerner (Eds.), *Handbook of child psychology: Vol. 1. Theoretical models of human development* (5th ed.). New York: Wiley.

Calamaro, C. J., Mason, T. B., & Ratcliffe, S. (2009). Adolescents living the 24/7 lifestyle: Effects of caffeine and technology on sleep duration and daytime functioning. *Pediatrics,* e1005–e1010.

Caldwell, C. A., Atkinson, M., & Renner, E. (2016). Experimental approaches to studying cumulative cultural evolution. *Current Directions in Psychological Science, 25*(3), 191–195.

Calkins, S., & Degnan, K. (2005). Temperament in early development. In R. T. Ammerman (Ed.), *Comprehensive handbook of personality and psychopathology: Vol. 3. Child psychopathology.* Hoboken, NJ: John Wiley & Sons.

Calvert, S. L. (2008). Children as consumers: Advertising and marketing. *The Future of Children, 18*(1), 205–234.

Cameron, N. (Ed.). (2002). *Human growth and development.* New York: Academic Press.

Camp, K. M., Parisi, M. A., Acosta, P. B., Berry, G. T., Bilder, D. A., Blau, N., et al. (2014). Phenylketonuria scientific review conference: State of the science and future research needs. *Molecular Genetics and Metabolism, 112*(2), 87–122.

Campbell, F., Pungello, E., Miller-Johnson, S., Burchinal, M., & Ramey, C. (2001). The development of cognitive and academic abilities: Growth curves from an early childhood educational experiment. *Developmental Psychology, 37,* 231–242.

Campbell, S., Spieker, S., Burchinal, M., & Poe, M. (2006). Trajectories of aggression from toddlerhood to age 9 predict academic and social functioning through age 12. *Journal of Child Psychology and Psychiatry, 47*(8), 791–800.

Campos, J. J., Anderson, D. I., Barbu-Roth, M. A., Hubbard, E. M., & Hertenstein, M. J. (2000). Travel broadens the mind. *Infancy, 1,* 149–219.

Camras, L. A., & Shuster, M. M. (2013). Current emotion research in developmental psychology. *Emotion Review, 5*(3), 321–329.

Caplan, N., Choy, M. H., & Whitmore, J. K. (1991). *Children of the boat people: A study of educational success.* Ann Arbor, MI: University of Michigan Press.

Capron, A. (2016). Henry Knowles Beecher, Jay Katz, and the transformation of research with human beings. *Perspectives in Biology and Medicine, 59*(1), 55–77.

Cardoso-Leite, P., Kludt, R., Vignola, G., Ma, W. J., Green, C. S., & Bavelier, D. (2016). Technology consumption and cognitive control: Contrasting action video game experience with media multitasking. *Attention, Perception, & Psychophysics, 78*(1), 218–241.

Carel, J.-C., & Léger, J. (2008). Precocious puberty. *The New England Journal of Medicine, 358,* 2366–2377.

Carey, S. (1978). The child as word learner. In M. Halle, J. Bresnan, & G. A. Miller (Eds.), *Linguistic theory and psychological reality.* Cambridge, MA: The MIT Press.

Carlo, G., Mestre, M. V., Samper, P., Tur, A., & Armenta, B. E. (2011). The longitudinal relations among dimensions of parenting styles, sympathy, prosocial moral reasoning, and prosocial behaviors. *International Journal of Behavioral Development, 35,* 116–124.

Carlson, E. A., Egeland, B., & Sroufe, L. A. (2009). A prospective investigation of the development of borderline personality symptoms. *Development and Psychopathology, 21,* 1311–1334.

Carlson, S., Davis, A., & Leach, J. (2005). Less is more: Executive function and symbolic representation in preschool children. *Psychological Science, 16,* 609–616.

Carlson, S. M. (2005). Developmentally sensitive measures of executive function in preschool children. *Developmental Neuropsychology, 28,* 595–616.

Carpendale, J., & Hammond, S. (2016). The development of moral sense and moral thinking. *Current Opinion in Pediatrics, 28*(6), 743–747.

Carpendale, J. I. M., Hammond, S. I., & Lewis, C. (2010). The social origin and moral nature of human thinking. *Behavioral and Brain Sciences, 33,* 334.

Carpenter, R., McGarvey, C., Mitchell, E. A., Tappin, D. M., Vennemann, M. M., Smuk, M., & Carpenter, J. R. (2013). Bed sharing when parents do not smoke: Is there a risk of SIDS? An individual level analysis of five major case-control studies. *BMJ Open, 3*(5), e002299.

Carr, V., & Luken, E. (2014). Playscapes: A pedagogical paradigm for play and learning. *International Journal of Play, 3*(1), 69–83.

Carroll, J. S., Padilla-Walker, L. M., Nelson, L. J., Olson, C. D., McNamara Barry, C., & Madsen, S. D. (2008). Generation XXX: Pornography acceptance and use among emerging adults. *Journal of Adolescent Research, 23*(1), 6–30.

Carskadon, M. A. (2011). Sleep in adolescents: The perfect storm. *Pediatric Clinics of North America, 58,* 637–647.

Carskadon, M. A., Acebo, C., & Jenni, O. G. (2004). Regulation of adolescent sleep: Implications for behavior. *Annals of the New York Academy of Sciences, 1021,* 276–291.

Carter, R. C., Wainwright, H., Molteno, C. D., Georgieff, M. K., Dodge, N. C., Warton, F., et al. (2016). Alcohol, methamphetamine, and marijuana exposure have distinct effects on the human placenta. *Alcoholism: Clinical and Experimental Research, 40*(4), 753–764.

Casey, B. J., Jones, R. M., & Hare, T. A. (2008). The adolescent brain. *Annals of the New York Academy of Sciences, 1124*(1), 111–126.

Casey, B. J., Jones, R. M., Levita, L., Libby, V., Pattwell, S. S., Ruberry, E. J., et al. (2010). The storm and stress of adolescence: Insights from human imaging and mouse genetics. *Developmental Psychobiology, 52,* 225–235.

Casper, D. M., & Card, N. A. (2017). Overt and relational victimization: A meta-analytic review of their overlap and associations with social-psychological adjustment. *Child Development, 88*(2), 466.

Caspers, K. M., Romitti, P. A., Lin, S., Olney, R. S., Holmes, L. B., Werler, M. M., & National Birth Defects Prevention Study. (2013). Maternal periconceptional exposure to cigarette smoking and congenital limb deficiencies. *Paediatric and Perinatal Epidemiology, 27*(6), 509–520.

Cassidy, T. (2005, December 4). Special care of early babies; New studies of neonatal brain development are changing the way hospitals manage premature births. *The Boston Globe,* p. 34.

Center for Behavioral Health Statistics and Quality. (2015). *Results from the 2015 National Survey on Drug Use and Health: Detailed tables.* Retrieved from http://www.samhsa.gov/data/sites/default/files/NSDUH-DetTabs-2015/NSDUH-DetTabs-2015/NSDUH-DetTabs-2015.htm

Centers for Disease Control and Prevention. (2004). *National vital statistics report* (Vol. 52, No. 3, September 18, 2003). Washington, DC: Department of Health and Human Services.

Centers for Disease Control and Prevention. (2006). *Births: Final data for 2004.* National Vital Statistics Report, 55.

Centers for Disease Control and Prevention. (2007). *Autism spectrum disorders overview.* Retrieved from http://www.cdc.gov/ncbddd/autism/overview.htm

Centers for Disease Control and Prevention. (2009). *Childhood overweight and obesity.* Retrieved from http://www.cdc.gov/obesity/childhood/index.html

Centers for Disease Control and Prevention. (2010). *Sexually transmitted disease surveillance 2009.* Atlanta: U.S. Department of Health and Human Services, Centers for Disease Control and Prevention.

Centers for Disease Control and Prevention. (2014). *Prevalence of autism spectrum disorder among children aged 8 years: Autism and developmental disabilities monitoring networks, 11 sites, United States, 2010.* Retrieved from https://www.cdc.gov/mmwr/preview/mmwrhtml/ss6302a1.htm?s_cid=ss6302a1_w

Centers for Disease Control and Prevention. (2015). *Sexual activity, contraceptive use, and childbearing of children aged 15–19 in the United States.* Retrieved from https://www.cdc.gov/nchs/data/databriefs/db209.pdf

Centers for Disease Control and Prevention. (2017). *Preterm birth.* Retrieved from https://www.cdc.gov/reproductivehealth/maternalinfanthealth/pretermbirth.htm

Centers for Disease Control and Prevention. (2017). *Sudden unexpected infant death and sudden infant death syndrome.* Retrieved from https://www.cdc.gov/sids/data.htm

Centers for Disease Control and Prevention. (2017). *Teen pregnancy in the United States.* Retrieved from https://www.cdc.gov/teenpregnancy/about/index.htm

Cespedes, E. M., Gillman, M. W., Kleinman, K., Rifas-Shiman, S. L., Redline, S., & Taveras, E. M. (2014). Television viewing, bedroom television, and sleep duration from infancy to mid-childhood. *Pediatrics, 133*(5), e1163–e1171.

Chaffin, M., Hanson, R., Saunders, B., Nichols, T., Barnett, D., Zeanah, C., et al. (2006). Report of the APSAC task force on attachment therapy, reactive attachment disorder, and attachment problems. *Child Maltreatment, 11,* 76–89.

Chandra, A., Mosher, W., Copen, C., & Sionean, C. (2011). *Sexual behavior, sexual attraction, and sexual identity in the United States: Data from the 2006–2008 National Survey of Family Growth.* National Health Statistics Report Number 36. Retrieved from www.cdc.gov/nchs/data/nhsr/nhsr036.pdf

Chang, F., Dell, G., & Bock, K. (2006). Becoming syntactic. *Psychological Review, 113,* 234–272.

Chang, J. (2005). *Can't stop won't stop: A history of the hip-hop generation.* New York: Picador.

Chang, S., Skakkebaek, A., & Gravholt, C. (2015). Klinefelter syndrome and medical treatment: Hypogonadism and beyond. *Hormones, 14*(4), 531–548.

Chapin, B. (2013). Attachment in rural Sri Lanka: The shape of caregiver sensitivity, communication, and autonomy. In N. Quinn & J. M. Mageo (Eds.), *Attachment reconsidered: Cultural perspectives on a Western theory.* New York: Palgrave Macmillan.

Chapman, R. (2016). A case study of gendered play in preschools: How early childhood educators' perceptions of gender influence children's play. *Early Child Development and Care, 186*(8), 1271–1284.

Charnov, E. (2004). The optimal balance between growth rate and survival in mammals. *Evolution and Ecological Research, 6,* 307–313.

Charpak, N., Ruiz-Pelaez, J. G., Figueroa de Calume, Z., & Charpak, Y. (2001). A randomized, controlled trial of kangaroo mother care: Results of follow-up at 1 year of corrected age. *Pediatrics, 108*(5), 1072–1079.

Chaudhury, K., & Mukherjee, K. (2016). Sensitivity and specificity of a prenatal screening method using the combination of maternal age and fetal nuchal translucency thickness for fetal aneuploidy: A clinical study in eastern India. *International Journal of Reproduction, 5*(1), 148–153.

Chavajay, P., & Rogoff, B. (2002). Schooling and traditional collaborative social organization of problem solving by Mayan mothers and children. *Developmental Psychology, 38,* 55–66.

Chen, C., & Stevenson, H. W. (1988). Cross-linguistic differences in digit span of preschool children. *Journal of Experimental Child Psychology, 46,* 150–158.

Chen, Q., Brikell, I., Lichtenstein, P., Serlachius, E., Kuja-Halkola, R., Sandin, S., et al. (2016). Familial aggregation of attention-deficit/hyperactivity disorder. *Journal of Child Psychology and Psychiatry, 58*(3), 219–334.

Chen, S. H., Main, A., Zhou, Q., Bunge, S. A., Lau, N., & Chu, K. (2015). Effortful control and early academic achievement of Chinese American children in immigrant families. *Early Childhood Research Quarterly, 30,* 45–56.

Cheng, L., Wang, S., Jia, N., Xie, M., & Liao, X. (2014). Environmental stimulation influences the cognition of developing mice by inducing changes in oxidative and apoptosis status. *Brain & Development, 36*(1), 51–56.

Chess, S., & Thomas, A. (1996). *Temperament: Theory and practice.* New York: Brunner-Mazel.

Chi, M. T. H. (1978). Knowledge structures and memory development. In R. S. Siegler (Ed.), *Children's thinking: What develops?* Mahwah, NJ: Lawrence Erlbaum Associates.

Chico, E., Gonzalez, A., Ali, N., Steiner, M., & Fleming, A. S. (2014). Executive function and mothering: Challenges faced by teenage mothers. *Developmental Psychobiology, 56*(5), 1027–1035.

Child Trends. (2014). *America's Hispanic children: Gaining ground, looking forward.* Retrieved from https://www.childtrends.org/hispanic-institute/americas-hispanic-children-presentation/

Child Trends. (2014). *Databank indicators of child and youth well-being: Immigrant children.* https://www.childtrends.org/wp-content/uploads/2013/07/110_Immigrant_Children.pdf

Child Trends. (2015). *Attitudes toward spanking.* Retrieved from https://www.childtrends.org/indicators/attitudes-toward-spanking/

Chittora, A., & Patil, H. A. (2016). Newborn infant's cry analysis. *International Journal of Speech Technology, 19*(4), 919–928.

Cho, E., Kim, S., Kwon, M. S., Cho, H., Kim, E. H., Jun, E. M., & Lee, S. (2016). The effects of kangaroo care in the neonatal intensive care unit on the physiological functions of preterm infants, maternal–infant attachment, and maternal stress. *Journal of Pediatric Nursing, 31*(4), 430–438.

Choe, D. E., Olson, S. L., & Sameroff, A. J. (2013). Effects of early maternal distress and parenting on the development of children's self-regulation and externalizing behavior. *Development and Psychopathology, 25*(2), 437.

Choi, J., Johnson, D. W., & Johnson, R. (2011). Relationships among cooperative learning experiences, social interdependence, children's aggression, victimization, and prosocial behaviors. *Journal of Applied Social Psychology, 41*(4), 976–1003.

Chomsky, N. (1959). Review of verbal behavior by B. F. Skinner. *Language, 35,* 26–58.

Chomsky, N. (1980). Initial states and steady states. In M. Piatelli-Palmerini (Ed.), *Language and learning: The debate between Jean Piaget and Noam Chomsky.* Cambridge, MA: Harvard University Press.

Chomsky, N. (1988). *Language and problems of knowledge.* Cambridge, MA: The MIT Press.

Chomsky, N. (2017). Language architecture and its import for evolution. *Neuroscience & Biobehavioral Reviews,* doi: 10.1016/j.neubiorev.2017.01.053

Chonchaiya, W., Wilaisakditipakorn, T., Vijakkhana, N., & Pruksananonda, C. (2017). Background media exposure prolongs nighttime sleep latency in Thai infants. *Pediatric Research, 81*(2), 322–328.

Christian, P., Mullany, L. C., Hurley, K. M., Katz, J., & Black, R. E. (2015). Nutrition and maternal, neonatal, and child health. *Seminars in Perinatology, 39*(5), 361–372.

Christianson, A., Howson, C., & Modell, B. (2006). *March of Dimes global report on birth defects.* Retrieved from http://www.marchofdimes.org/materials/global-report-on-birth-defects-the-hidden-toll-of-dying-and-disabled-children-full-report.pdf

Chudler, E. H. (2011). *Neuroscience for kids: The brain and language.* Retrieved from http://faculty.washington.edu/chudler/lang.html

Chumlea, W. C., Dwyer, J., Bergen, C., Burkart, J., Paranandi, L., Frydrych, A., et al. (2003). Nutritional status assessed from anthropometric measures in the HEMO study. *Journal of Renal Nutrition, 13,* 31–38.

Chung, K. K. H., Liu, H., McBride, C., Wong, A. M. Y., & Lo, J. C. M. (2016). How socioeconomic status, executive functioning and verbal interactions contribute to early academic achievement in Chinese children. *Educational Psychology, 37,* 1–19.

Ciarrochi, J., Parker, P. D., Sahdra, B. K., Kashdan, T. B., Kiuru, N., & Conigrave, J. (2017). When empathy matters: The role of sex and empathy in close friendships. *Journal of Personality, 85*(4), 494–504.

Cicchetti, D. (2016). Socioemotional, personality, and biological development: Illustrations from a multilevel developmental psychopathology perspective on child maltreatment. *Annual Review of Psychology, 67,* 187–211.

Cillessen, A., & Mayeux, L. (2004). From censure to reinforcement: Developmental changes in the association between aggression and social status. *Child Development, 75,* 147–163.

Cimpian, A. (2016). The privileged status of category representations in early development. *Child Development Perspectives, 10*(2), 99–104.

Clark, C. (2003). *In sickness and in play: Children coping with chronic illness.* New Brunswick, NJ: Rutgers University Press.

Clark, E. V. (1995). Later lexical development and word formation. In P. Fletcher & B. MacWhinney (Eds.), *The handbook of child language* (pp. 393–412). Oxford, England: Blackwell Publishing.

Clark, E. V. (2014). Pragmatics in acquisition. *Journal of Child Language, 41*(Suppl. 1), 105.

Clark, E. V., & Wong, A. D.-W. (2002). Pragmatic directions about language use: Words and word meanings. *Language in Society, 31,* 181–212.

Clark, K. B., & Clark, M. P. (1939). The development of consciousness of self and the emergence of racial identity in Negro pre-school schoolchildren. *Journal of Social Psychology, 10,* 591–599.

Clark, K. B., & Clark, M. P. (1950). Emotional factors in racial identification and preference in Negro children. *Journal of Negro Education, 19,* 341–350.

Clarke, A. M., & Clarke, A. D. B. (2000). *Early experience and the life path.* London: Jessica Kingsley.

Clarke-Stewart, A., & Koch, J. B. (1983). *Children: Development through adolescence.* New York: Wiley.

Clearfield, M. W., Diedrich, F. J., Smith, L. B., & Thelen, E. (2006). Young infants reach correctly in A-not-B tasks: On the development of stability and perseveration. *Infant Behavior & Development, 29,* 435–444.

Clearfield, M. W., Dineva, E., Smith, L. B., Diedrich, F. J., & Thelen, E. (2009). Cue salience and infant perseverative reaching: Tests of the dynamic field theory. *Developmental Science, 12,* 26–40.

Coale, A., & Demeny, P. (1983). *Regional model life tables and stable populations.* New York: Academic Press.

Coghlan, D., & Jacobs, C. (2005). Kurt Lewin on reeducation: Foundations for action research. *Journal of Applied Behavioral Science, 41,* 444–457.

Cohen, J. R., Spiegler, K. M., Young, J. F., Hankin, B. L., & Abela, J. R. Z. (2014). Self-structures, negative events, and adolescent depression: Clarifying the role of self-complexity in a prospective, multiwave study. *The Journal of Early Adolescence, 34*(6), 736–759.

Cohen, L. B., & Cashon, C. H. (2006). Infant cognition. In D. Kuhn, R. S. Siegler, W. Damon, & R. M. Lerner (Eds.), *Handbook of child psychology: Vol. 2. Cognition, perception, and language* (6th ed., pp. 214–251). Hoboken, NJ: Wiley.

Cohen, L. B., & Marks, K. S. (2002). How infants process addition and subtraction events. *Developmental Science, 5*(2), 186–201.

Cohn, D., & Passel, J. (2017). *A record 60.6 million Americans live in multi-generational households.* Retrieved from http://www.pewresearch.org/fact-tank/2016/08/11/a-record-60-6-million-americans-live-in-multigenerational-households/

Coker, T., Elliott, M., Schwebel, D., Windle, M., Toomey, S., Tortolero, S., et al. (2015). Media violence exposure and physical aggression in fifth-grade children. *Academic Pediatrics, 15*(1), 82–88.

Cokley, K. (2007). Critical issues in the measurement of ethnic and racial identity: A referendum on the state of the field. *Journal of Counseling Psychology, 54*(3), 224–234.

Colby, A., & Kohlberg, L. (1987). *The measurement of moral judgment.* New York: Cambridge University Press.

Colby, A., Kohlberg, L., Gibbs, J., & Lieberman, M. (1983). A longitudinal study of moral development. *Monographs of the Society for Research in Child Development, 48* (1–2, Serial No. 200).

Cole, M. (1996). *Cultural psychology: A once and future discipline.* Cambridge, MA: The Belknap Press of Harvard University Press.

Cole, M. (2005). Cross-cultural and historical perspectives on the developmental consequences of education. *Human Development, 48,* 195–216.

Cole, W. G., Robinson, S. R., & Adolph, K. E. (2016). Bouts of steps: The organization of infant exploration. *Developmental Psychobiology, 58*(3), 341–354.

Coleman, T., Chamberlain, C., Davey, M., Cooper, S. E., & Leonardi-Bee, J. (2015). Pharmacological interventions for promoting smoking cessation during pregnancy. *The Cochrane Database of Systematic Reviews, 12,* CD010078.

Coles, C. D., Goldstein, F. C., Lynch, M. E., Chen, X., Kable, J. A., Johnson, K. C., et al. (2011). Memory and brain volume in adults prenatally exposed to alcohol. *Brain and Cognition, 75,* 67–77.

Coller, R. J., & Kuo, A. A. (2014). Youth development through mentorship: A Los Angeles school-based mentorship program among Latino children. *Journal of Community Health, 39*(2), 316–321.

Collins, A. (2006). Cognitive apprenticeship. In A. Collins (Ed.), *The Cambridge handbook of the learning sciences* (pp. 47–60). New York: Cambridge University Press.

Collins, W. A. (2005). Commentary: Parsing parenting: Refining models of parental influence during adolescence. *Monographs of the Society for Research in Child Development, 70*(4), 138–145.

Colon, A., Colon, A., & Colon, P. (2001). *A history of children.* Westport, CT: Greenwood Press.

Compas, B. E., Jaser, S. S., Bettis, A. H., Watson, K. H., Gruhn, M. A., Williams, E., & Thigpen, J. C. (2017). Coping, emotion regulation, and psychopathology in childhood and adolescence: A meta-analysis and narrative review. *Psychological Bulletin, 143*(9), 939–991.

Comstock, G., & Scharrer, E. (2007). *Media and the American child.* New York: Elsevier.

Comstock, G. A., & Scharrer, E. (2010). *Media and the American child* (rev. ed.). Burlington, MA: Elsevier.

Conboy, B. T., & Thal, D. J. (2006). Ties between the lexicon and grammar: Cross-sectional and longitudinal studies of bilingual toddlers. *Child Development, 77,* 712–735.

Conley, C. S., Rudolph, K. D., & Bryant, F. B. (2012). Explaining the longitudinal association between puberty and depression: Sex differences in the mediating effects of peer stress. *Development and Psychopathology, 24*(2), 691.

Conner, S. N., Bedell, V., Lipsey, K., Macones, G. A., Cahill, A. G., & Tuuli, M. G. (2016). Maternal marijuana use and adverse neonatal outcomes: A systematic review and meta-analysis. *Obstetrics and Gynecology, 128*(4), 713–723.

Conners-Burrow, N. A., Patrick, T., Kyzer, A., & McKelvey, L. (2017). A preliminary evaluation of REACH: Training early childhood teachers to support children's social and emotional development. *Early Childhood Education Journal, 45*(2), 187.

Connolly, J., & McIsaac, C. (2009). Adolescents' explanations for romantic dissolutions: A developmental perspective. *Journal of Adolescence, 32*(5), 1209–1223.

Connor, C. M., Day, S. L., Phillips, B., Sparapani, N., Ingebrand, S. W., McLean, L., et al. (2016). Reciprocal effects of self-regulation, semantic knowledge, and reading comprehension in early elementary school. *Child Development, 87*(6), 1813–1824.

Connor, J. M., & Ferguson-Smith, M. A. (1993). *Essential medical genetics* (3rd ed.). Oxford, England: Blackwell Publishing.

Cook, J. T., & Frank, D. A. (2008). Food security, poverty, and human development in the United States. *Annals of the New York Academy of Sciences, 1136,* 193–209.

Cook, S. H., Heinze, J. E., Miller, A. L., & Zimmerman, M. A. (2016). Transitions in friendship attachment during adolescence are associated with developmental trajectories of depression through adulthood. *The Journal of Adolescent Health, 58*(3), 260.

Coopersmith, S. (1967). *The antecedents of self-esteem.* New York: W. H. Freeman.

Copeland, W. E., Wolke, D., Angold, A., & Costello, E. J. (2013). Adult psychiatric outcomes of bullying and being bullied by peers in childhood and adolescence. *JAMA Psychiatry, 70*(4), 419–426.

Corballis, M. C. (2015). What's left in language? Beyond the classical model. *Annals of the New York Academy of Sciences, 1359*(1), 14–29.

Cordes, S., & Brannon, E. M. (2009). Crossing the divide: Infants discriminate small from large numerosities. *Developmental Psychology, 45,* 1583–1594.

Cornell, D., & Bradshaw, C. (2015). From a culture of bullying to a climate of support: The evolution of bullying prevention and research. *School Psychology Review, 44*(4), 499–503.

Costello, D. (2000, June 9). Spanking makes a comeback. *Wall Street Journal.*

Costello, D. M., Swendsen, J., Rose, J. S., & Dierker, L. C. (2008, April). Risk and protective factors associated with trajectories of depressed mood from adolescence to early adulthood. *Journal of Consulting and Clinical Psychology, 76,* 173–183.

Costello, E. J., Compton, S. N., Keeler, G., & Angold, A. (2003, October). Relationships between poverty and psychopathology: A natural experiment. *Journal of the American Medical Association, 290,* 2023–2029.

Côté, J., & Bynner, J. M. (2008). Changes in the transition to adulthood in the UK and Canada: The role of structure and agency in emerging adulthood. *Journal of Youth Studies, 11,* 251–268.

Côté, J. E. (2009). Identity formation and self-development in adolescence. In R. M. Lerner & L. Steinberg (Eds.), *Handbook of adolescent psychology: Vol 1. Individual bases of adolescent development* (3rd ed.). Hoboken, NJ: John Wiley & Sons.

Côté, S., Bouffard, T., & Vezeau, C. (2014). The mediating effect of self-evaluation bias of competence on the relationship between parental emotional support and children's academic functioning. *British Journal of Educational Psychology, 84*(3), 415–434.

Cotton, A. (2006). *Camfed founder receives Women of the Year award.* Retrieved from http://uk.camfed.org/news/2006/03/08/marking-international-womens-day/#more-71

Cottrell, J. M., & Barrett, C. A. (2017). Examining school psychologists' perspectives about specific learning disabilities: Implications for practice. *Psychology in the Schools, 54*(3), 294–308.

Council on Communications and Media. (2016). Media and young minds. *Pediatrics, 138*(5), e20162591–e20162596.

Courage, M. L., Bakhtiar, A., Fitzpatrick, C., Kenny, S., & Brandeau, K. (2015). Growing up multitasking: The costs and benefits for cognitive development. *Developmental Review, 35,* 5–41.

Courage, M. L., Reynolds, G. D., & Richards, J. E. (2006). Infants' attention to patterned stimuli: Developmental change from 3 to 12 months of age. *Child Development, 77*(3), 680–695.

Cousins, S. D. (2014). The semiotic coevolution of mind and culture. *Culture & Psychology, 20*(2), 160–191.

Cowan, P. A. (1978). *Piaget: With feeling: Cognitive, social, and emotional dimensions.* New York: Holt, Rinehart and Winston.

Cowell, J. M., Lee, K., Malcolm-Smith, S., Selcuk, B., Zhou, X., & Decety, J. (2017). The development of generosity and moral cognition across five cultures. *Developmental Science, 20*(4).

Cox, B. D. (in press). *The evolution of psychology: A history of psychological science.* New York: Routledge.

Cox, S. J., Mezulis, A. H., & Hyde, J. S. (2010). The influence of child gender role and maternal feedback to child stress on the emergence of the gender difference in depressive rumination in adolescence. *Developmental Psychology, 46,* 842–852.

Coyle, E., & Liben, L. S. (2016). Affecting girls' activity and job interests through play: The moderating roles of personal gender salience and game characteristics. *Child Development, 87,* 414–428.

Cristia, A., & Seidl, A. (2015). Parental reports on touch screen use in early childhood. *PLOS ONE, 10*(6), e0128338.

Crone, E. A., Duijvenvoorde, A. C. K., & Peper, J. S. (2016). Annual research review: Neural contributions to risk-taking in adolescence—Developmental changes and individual differences. *Journal of Child Psychology and Psychiatry, 57*(3), 353–368.

Crosnoe, R., Purtell, K. M., Davis-Kean, P., Ansari, A., & Benner, A. D. (2016). The selection of children from low-income families into preschool. *Developmental Psychology, 52*(4), 599–612.

Cross, J. R., & Fletcher, K. L. (2011). Associations of parental and peer characteristics with adolescents' social dominance orientation. *Journal of Youth and Adolescence, 40*(6), 694–706.

Cross, W. E. (2003). Tracing the historical origins of youth delinquency and violence: Myths and realities about black culture. *Journal of Social Issues, 59*(1), 67–82.

Cross, W. E., & Cross, T. B. (2008). Theory, research, and models. In S. M. Quintana & C. McKown (Eds.), *Handbook of race, racism, and the developing child* (pp. 154–181). Hoboken, NJ: John Wiley & Sons.

Cuevas, K., & Bell, M. A. (2010). Developmental progression of looking and reaching performance on the A-not-B task. *Developmental Psychology, 46*(5), 1363–1371.

Cuevas, K., Learmonth, A. E., & Rovee-Collier, C. (2016). A dissociation between recognition and reactivation: The renewal effect at 3 months of age. *Developmental Psychobiology, 58*(2), 159–175.

Cummings, E., Merrilees, C., Taylor, L., Goeke-Morey, M., & Shirlow, P. (2017). Emotional insecurity about the community: A dynamic, within-person mediator of child adjustment in contexts of political violence. *Development and Psychopathology, 29*(1), 27–36.

Cunningham, S., Elo, I., Herbst, K., & Hosegood, V. (2010). Prenatal development in rural South Africa: Relationship between birth weight and access to fathers and grandparents. *Population Studies, 64,* 229–246.

Curtis, H. (1979). *Biology.* New York: Worth.

Curtiss, S., Fromkin, V., Krashen, S., Rigler, D., & Rigler, M. (1974). The Linguistic Development of Genie. *Language, 50,* 528–554.

Cvencek, D., Greenwald, A. G., & Meltzoff, A. N. (2016). Implicit measures for preschool children confirm self-esteem's role in maintaining a balanced identity. *Journal of Experimental Social Psychology, 62,* 50–57.

Daddis, C. (2010). Adolescent peer crowds and patterns of belief in the boundaries of personal authority. *Journal of Adolescence, 33*(5), 699–708.

Dahl, A., Campos, J. J., Anderson, D. I., Uchiyama, I., Witherington, D. C., Ueno, M., et al. (2013). The epigenesis of wariness of heights. *Psychological Science, 24*(7), 1361–1367.

Dahl, R. E., & Hariri, A. R. (2005). Lessons from G. Stanley Hall: Connecting new research in biological sciences to the study of adolescent development. *Journal of Research on Adolescence, 15,* 367–382.

Dahl, R. E., & Lewin, D. (2002). Pathways to adolescent health: Sleep regulation and behavior. *Journal of Adolescent Health, 31,* 175–184.

Daiute, C. (2016). Collective practices of human development in political violence and its long shadow. *Human Development, 59*(2–3), 53–63.

Dalgaard, N. T., & Montgomery, E. (2015). Disclosure and silencing: A systematic review of the literature on patterns of trauma communication in refugee families. *Transcultural Psychiatry, 52*(5), 579.

Darwin, C. (1859/1958). *The origin of species.* New York: Penguin.

Darwin, C. (1872). *The expression of emotion in man and animals.* London: John Murray.

Dasen, P. R. (1972). Cross-cultural Piagetian research: A summary. *Journal of Cross-Cultural Psychology, 3,* 29–39.

Dasen, P. R. (1973). Preliminary study of sensori-motor development in Baoule children. *Early Child Development & Care, 2,* 345–354.

D'augelli, A. R., Grossman, A. H., & Starks, M. T. (2008). Gender atypicality and sexual orientation development among lesbian, gay, and bisexual youth: Prevalence, sex differences, and parental responses. *Journal of Gay & Lesbian Mental Health, 12*(1–2), 121.

D'Augelli, A. R. (2003). Coming out in community psychology: Personal narrative and disciplinary change. *American Journal of Community Psychology, 31*(3), 343–354.

Daugherty, A. M., & Ofen, N. (2015). That's a good one! Belief in efficacy of mnemonic strategies contributes to age-related increase in associative memory. *Journal of Experimental Child Psychology, 136,* 17.

Davidov, M., & Grusec, J. E. (2006). Untangling the links of parental responsiveness to distress and warmth to child outcomes. *Child Development, 77,* 44–58.

Davies, H. D., & Fitzgerald, H. E. (Eds.). (2008). *Obesity in childhood and adolescence: Vol. 1. Medical, biological, and social issues. Praeger perspectives: Child psychology and mental health.* Westport, CT: Praeger Publishers/ Greenwood Publishing Group.

Davis, B. L., MacNeilage, P. F., Matyear, C. L., & Powell, J. K. (2000). Prosodic correlates of stress in babbling: An acoustical study. *Child Development, 71,* 1258–1275.

Davis, C., Yanasak, N., Allison, J., Tomporowski, P., et al. (2011). Exercise improves executive function and achievement and alters brain activation in overweight children: A randomized, controlled trial. *Health Psychology, 30,* 91–98.

de Araújo, C. F. O. A., Bahia, C. P., de Aguiar, G. P. S., Herculano, A. M., Coelho, N. L. G., de Sousa, M. B. C., et al. (2017). Effect of chronic stress during adolescence in prefrontal cortex structure and function. *Behavioural Brain Research, 326,* 44–51.

De Goede, I. H. A., Branje, S. J. T., & Meeus, W. H. J. (2009). Developmental changes and gender differences in adolescents' perceptions of friendships. *Journal of Adolescence, 32,* 1105–1123.

De Goede, I. H. A, Branje, S., van Duin, J., VanderValk, I. E., & Meeus, W. (2012). Romantic relationship commitment and its linkages with commitment to parents and friends during adolescence. *Social Development, 21*(3), 425–442.

De Graaf, H., Vanwesenbeeck, I., & Meijer, S. (2015). Educational differences in adolescents' sexual health: A pervasive phenomenon in a national Dutch sample. *The Journal of Sex Research, 52*(7), 747–757.

De Gracia, M. R. L., Peterson, C. C., & de Rosnay, M. (2016). A cultural conundrum: Delayed false-belief understanding in Filipino children. *Journal of Cross-Cultural Psychology, 47*(7), 929–940.

de Heering, A., Dormal, G., Pelland, M., Lewis, T., Maurer, D., & Collignon, O. (2016). A brief period of postnatal visual deprivation alters the balance between auditory and visual attention. *Current Biology, 26*(22), 3101–3105.

de Heering, A., Van Belle, G., & Rossion, B. (2014). Categorization of faces versus objects in the infants right occipito-temporal cortex by means of fast periodic visual stimulation. *Journal of Vision, 14*(10), 695.

de Hoog, M., Venekamp, R., van der Ent, C., Schilder, A., Sanders, E., Damoiseaux, R., et al. (2014). Impact of early daycare on healthcare resource use related to upper respiratory tract infections during childhood: Prospective Whistler cohort study. *BMC Medicine, 12*(1), 107.

de Lijster, G. P., Felten, H., Kok, G., & Kocken, P. L. (2016). Effects of an interactive school-based program for preventing adolescent sexual harassment: A cluster-randomized controlled evaluation study. *Journal of Youth and Adolescence, 45*(5), 874.

de Lemos, C. (2000). Questioning the notion of development: The case of language acquisition. *Culture & Psychology, 6*(2), 169–182.

De Villiers, J. G., & De Villiers, P. A. (1978). *Language acquisition.* Cambridge, MA: Harvard University Press.

de Vrijer, B., Harthoorn-Lasthuizen, E. J., & Oosterbaan, H. P. (1999). The incidence of irregular antibodies in pregnancy: A prospective study in the region of the 's-Hertogenbosch. *Nederlands Tijdschrift voor Geneeskunde, 143,* 2523–2527.

Dean, D. C., O'Muircheartaigh, J., Dirks, H., Waskiewicz, N., Lehman, K., Walker, L., et al. (2014). Modeling healthy male white matter and myelin development: 3 through 60 months of age. *Neuroimage, 84,* 742–752.

Dearing, E., McCartney, K., & Taylor, B. A. (2009). Does higher quality early child care promote low-income children's math and reading achievement in middle childhood? *Child Development, 80*(5), 1329–1349.

Dehaene-Lambertz, G., & Spelke, E. S. (2015). The infancy of the human brain. *Neuron, 88*(1), 93–109.

DeJager, J. (2016). Baldwin's remarkable effect. *Biological Theory, 11*(4), 207–219.

Delaney, C. (2000). Making babies in a Turkish village. In J. S. DeLoache & A. Gottlieb (Eds.), *A world of babies: Imagined childcare guides for seven societies.* Cambridge, England: Cambridge University Press.

DeLoache, J. S., LoBue, V., Vanderborght, M., & Chiong, C. (2013). On the validity and robustness of the scale error phenomenon in early childhood. *Infant Behavior & Development, 36*(1), 63–70.

Deng, Q., Lu, C., Li, Y., Sundell, J., & Norbäck, D. (2016). Exposure to outdoor air pollution during trimesters of pregnancy and childhood asthma, allergic rhinitis, and eczema. *Environmental Research, 150,* 119–127.

Denham, S., Caverly, S., Schmidt, M., Blair, K., DeMulder, E., Caal, S., Hamada, H., & Mason, T. (2002). Preschool understanding of emotions: Contributions to classroom anger and aggression. *Journal of Child Psychology and Psychiatry, 43,* 901–916.

Dennis, W., & Dennis, M. (1940). The effect of cradling practices upon the onset of walking in Hopi children. *Journal of Genetic Psychology, 56,* 77–86.

deRegnier, R.-A., Long, J. D., Georgieff, M. K., & Nelson, C. A. (2007). Using event-related potentials to study perinatal nutrition and brain development in infants of diabetic mothers. *Developmental Neuropsychology, 31*(3), 379–396.

Desai, R. J., Huybrechts, K. F., Hernandez-Diaz, S., Mogun, H., Patorno, E., Kaltenbach, K., et al. (2015). Exposure to prescription opioid analgesics in utero and risk of neonatal abstinence syndrome: Population based cohort study. *BMJ, 350*(1), h2102–h2102.

DeSilver, D. (2017). *U.S. students' academic achievement still lags that of their peers in many other countries.* Pew Research Center FactTank. Retrieved from http://www.pewresearch.org/fact-tank/2017/02/15/u-s-students-internationally-math-science/

Deutsch, A. R., Hoffman, L., & Wilcox, B. L. (2014). Sexual self-concept: Testing a hypothetical model for men and women. *Journal of Sex Research, 51*(8), 932–945.

Dev, D. A., McBride, B. A., Fiese, B. H., Jones, B. L., & Cho, H. (2013). Risk factors for overweight/obesity in preschool children: An ecological approach. *Childhood Obesity, 9*(5), 399–408.

Devescovi, A., Caselli, M. C., Marchione, D., Pasqualetti, P., Reilly, J., & Bates, E. (2005). A cross-linguistic study of the relationship between grammar and lexical development. *Journal of Child Language, 32*(4), 759–786.

Dhariwal, A., Connolly, J., Paciello, M., Caprara, G. V. (2009). Adolescent peer relationships and emerging adult romantic styles: A longitudinal study of youth in an Italian community. *Journal of Adolescent Research, 24,* 579–600.

Di Norcia, A., Pecora, G., Bombi, A., Baumgartner, E., & Laghi, F. (2015). Hot and cool inhibitory control in Italian toddlers: Associations with social competence and behavioral problems. *Journal of Child and Family Studies, 24*(4), 909–914.

Diamond, A. (1991). Neuropsychological insights into the meaning of object concept development. In R. Gelman (Ed.), *The epigenesis of mind: Essays on biology and cognition* (pp. 67–110). Mahwah, NJ: Lawrence Erlbaum Associates.

Diamond, A. (2000). Close interrelation of motor development and cognitive development and of the cerebellum and prefrontal cortex. *Child Development, 71,* 44–56.

Diamond, A. (2002a). A model system for studying the role of dopamine in prefrontal cortex during early development in humans. In M. H. Johnson & Y. Munakata (Eds.), *Brain development and cognition: A reader* (pp. 441–493). Malden, MA: Blackwell Publishing.

Diamond, A. (2002b). Normal development of prefrontal cortex from birth to young adulthood: Cognitive functions, anatomy, and biochemistry. In D. Stuss & R. Knight (Eds.), *Principles of frontal lobe functioning* (pp. 466–503). New York: Oxford University Press.

Diamond, A. (2012). Activities and programs that improve children's executive functions. *Current Directions in Psychological Science, 21*(5), 335–341.

Diamond, A., & Amso, D. (2008). Contributions of neuroscience to our understanding of cognitive development. *Current Directions in Psychological Science, 17,* 26–40.

Diamond, A., & Lee, K. (2011). Interventions shown to aid executive function development in children 4 to 12 years old. *Science, 333,* 959–964.

Dickens, W. T., & Flynn, J. R. (2006, October). Black Americans reduce the racial IQ gap: Evidence from standardization samples. *Psychological Science, 17*(10), 913–920.

Dickson, N., Paul, C., & Herbison, P. (2003). Same-sex attraction in a birth cohort: Prevalence and persistence into early adulthood. *Social Science & Medicine, 56*(8), 1607.

Dickson, N., van Roode, T., Cameron, C., & Paul, C. (2013). Stability and change in same-sex attraction, experience, and identity by sex and age in a New Zealand birth cohort. *Archives of Sexual Behavior, 42*(5), 753–763.

DiCorcia, J. A., Snidman, N., Sravish, A. V., & Tronick, E. (2016). Evaluating the nature of the still-face effect in the double face-to-face still-face paradigm using different comparison groups. *Infancy, 21*(3), 332–352.

Dierckx, M., Motmans, J., Mortelmans, D., & T'sjoen, G. (2016). Families in transition: A literature review. *International Review of Psychiatry, 28*(1), 36–43.

Dietz, T. (2000). Disciplining children: Characteristics associated with the use of corporal punishment. *Child Abuse and Neglect, 24,* 1529–1542.

Dijkstra, J. K., Cillessen, A. H. N., & Borch, C. (2013). Popularity and adolescent friendship networks: Selection and influence dynamics. *Developmental Psychology, 49*(7), 1242–1252.

Dishion, T. J., McCord, J., & Poulin, F. (1999). When interventions harm. *American Psychologist, 54,* 755–764.

Dishion, T. J., Poulin, F., & Burraston, B. (2001). Peer group dynamics associated with iatrogenic effects in group interventions with high-risk young adolescents. *New Directions for Child and Adolescent Development, 91,* 79.

Dishion, T. J., & Snyder, J. J. (2016). *The Oxford handbook of coercive relationship dynamics.* New York: Oxford University Press.

Dishion, T. J., & Tipsord, J. M. (2011). Peer contagion in child and adolescent social and emotional development. *Annual Review of Psychology, 62*(1), 189–214.

Dishion, T. J., Véronneau, M.-H., & Myers, M. W. (2010). Cascading peer dynamics underlying the progression from problem behavior to violence in early to late adolescence. *Development and Psychopathology, 22,* 603–619.

Dittmar, H., Halliwell, E., & Ive, S. (2006). Does Barbie make girls want to be thin? The effect of experimental exposure to images of dolls on the body image of 5- to 8-year-old girls. *Developmental Psychology, 42,* 283–292.

Dodge, K. A., Coie, J., & Lynam, D. (2006). Aggression and antisocial behavior in youth. In N. Eisenberg, W. Damon, & R. M. Lerner (Eds.), *Handbook of child psychology: Vol. 3. Social, emotional, and personality development* (6th ed., pp. 719–788). Hoboken, NJ: John Wiley & Sons.

Dodge, K. A., Lansford, J. E., Burks, V. S., Bates, J. E., Pettit, G. S., Fontaine, R., & Price, J. M. (2003). Peer rejection and social information-processing factors in the development of aggressive behavior problems in children. *Child Development, 74,* 374–393.

Dodge, K. A., Malone, P. S., Lansford, J. E., Miller, S., & Pettit, G. S. (2009). A dynamic cascade model of the development of substance-use onset: I. Introduction. *Monographs of the Society for Research in Child Development, 74,* 1–31.

Dodge, K. A., & Pettit, G. S. (2003, March). A biopsychosocial model of the development of chronic conduct problems in adolescence. *Developmental Psychology. Special Issue: Violent Children, 39,* 349–371.

Domingues-Montanari, S. (2017). Clinical and psychological effects of excessive screen time on children. *Journal of Paediatrics and Child Health, 53*(4), 333–338.

Domino, G. (1992). Cooperation and competition in Chinese and American children. *Journal of Cross-Cultural Psychology, 23,* 456–467.

Dore, J. (1979). Conversational acts and the acquisition of language. In E. Ochs & B. B. Schieffelin (Eds.), *Developmental Pragmatics.* New York: Academic Press.

Downey, G., Dalidowicz, M., & Mason, P. H. (2015). Apprenticeship as method: Embodied learning in ethnographic practice. *Qualitative Research, 15*(2), 183–200.

Draganova, R., Eswaran, H., Murphy, P., Lowery, C., & Preissl, H. (2007). Serial magnetoencephalographic study of fetal and newborn auditory discriminative evoked responses. *Early Human Development, 83,* 199–207.

Drewnowski, A., & Darmon, N. (2005). Food choices and diet costs: An economic analysis. *The Journal of nutrition, 135,* 900–904.

Dromi, E. (1999). Early lexical development. In M. Barrett (Ed.), *The development of language* (pp. 99–131). Philadelphia, PA: Psychology Press/Taylor & Francis.

Dromi, E., & Zaidman-Zait, A. (2011). Interrelations between communicative behaviors at the outset of speech: Parents as observers. *Journal of child language, 38,* 101–120.

Droop, M., van Elsäcker, W., Voeten, M. J. M., & Verhoeven, L. (2016). Long-term effects of strategic reading instruction in the intermediate elementary grades. *Journal of Research on Educational Effectiveness, 9*(1), 77–102.

Druet, C., Stettler, N., Sharp, S., Simmons, R. K., Cooper, C., Davey Smith, G., et al. (2012). Prediction of childhood obesity by infancy weight gain: An individual-level meta-analysis. *Paediatric and Perinatal Epidemiology, 26*(1), 19–26.

Drury, K., Bukowski, W. M., Velásquez, A. M., & Stella-Lopez, L. (2013). Victimization and gender identity in single-sex and mixed-sex schools: Examining contextual variations in pressure to conform to gender norms. *Sex Roles, 69*(7), 442–454.

D'Souza, D., D'Souza, H., & Karmiloff-Smith, A. (2017). Precursors to language development in typically and atypically developing infants and toddlers: The importance of embracing complexity. *Journal of Child Language, 44*(3), 591.

Dubois, J., Dehaene-Lambertz, G., Kulikova, S., Poupon, C., Hüppi, P. S., & Hertz-Pannier, L. (2014). The early development of brain white matter: A review of imaging studies in fetuses, newborns and infants. *Neuroscience, 276,* 48–71.

Dubois, L., Farmer, A., Girard, M., & Peterson, K. (2006). Preschool children's eating behaviors are related to dietary adequacy and body weight. *European Journal of Clinical Nutrition,* 61, 846–855.

Dunbar, A. S., Leerkes, E. M., Coard, S. I., Supple, A. J., & Calkins, S. (2017). An integrative conceptual model of parental racial/ethnic and emotion socialization and links to children's social-emotional development among African American families. *Child Development Perspectives, 11*(1), 16–22.

Duncan, G., & Raudenbush, W. (1999). Assessing the effects of context in studies of children and youth development. *Educational Psychology, 34,* 29–41.

Dunlop, A. L., Salihu, H. M., Freymann, G. R., Smith, C. K., & Brann, A. W. (2011). Very low birth weight births in Georgia, 1994–2005: Trends and racial disparities. *Maternal and Child Health Journal, 15*(7), 890–898.

Dunn, J. (1988). *The beginnings of social understanding.* Cambridge, MA: Harvard University Press.

Dunphy, D. C. (1963). The social structure of urban adolescent peer groups. *Sociometry, 26,* 230–246.

DuPaul, G. J., Morgan, P. L., Farkas, G., Hillemeier, M. M., & Maczuga, S. (2016). Academic and social functioning associated with attention-deficit/hyperactivity disorder: Latent class analyses of trajectories from kindergarten to fifth grade. *Journal of Abnormal Child Psychology, 44*(7), 1425–1438.

Duren, D. L., Seselj, M., Froehle, A. W., Nahhas, R. W., & Sherwood, R. J. (2013). Skeletal growth and the changing genetic landscape during childhood and adulthood. *American Journal of Physical Anthropology, 150*(1), 48–57.

Durston, S., & Casey, B. J. (2006). What have we learned about cognitive development from neuroimaging? *Neuropsychologia. Special Issue: Advances in developmental cognitive neuroscience, 44*(11), 2149–2157.

Duursma, E., Meijer, A., & de Bot, K. (2017). The impact of home literacy and family factors on screen media use among Dutch preteens. *Journal of Child and Family Studies, 26*(2), 612–622.

Dweck, C. S., & Master, A. (2009). Self-theories and motivation: Students' beliefs about intelligence. In K. R. Wenzel & A. Wigfield (Eds.), *Handbook of motivation at school* (pp. 123–140). New York: Routledge/Taylor & Francis.

Dybdahl, R. (2001). Children and mothers in war: An outcome study of a psychosocial intervention program. *Child Development, 72,* 1214–1230.

Dykas, M. J., & Cassidy, J. (2011). Attachment and the processing of social information across the life span: Theory and evidence. *Psychological Bulletin, 137,* 19.

Dyson, M. (1995). *Between god and gangsta rap.* New York: Oxford University Press.

Eagly, A. H., & Koenig, A. M. (2006). Social role theory of sex differences and similarities: Implication for prosocial behavior. In K. Dindia & D. J. Canary (Eds.), *Sex differences and similarities in communication* (2nd ed., pp. 161–177). Mahwah, NJ: Lawrence Erlbaum Associates.

Eberhardt, N. (2014). Piaget and Durkheim: Competing paradigms in the anthropology of morality. *Anthropological Theory, 14*(3), 301–316.

Eccles, J., Brown, B. V., & Templeton, J. (2008). A developmental framework for selecting indicators of well-being during the adolescent and young adult years. In B. V. Brown (Ed.), *Key indicators of child and youth well-being: Completing the picture* (pp. 197–236). Mahwah, NJ: Lawrence Erlbaum Associates.

Edvardsen, J., Torgersen, S., Roysamb, E., Lygren, S., Skre, I., Onstad, S., et al. (2008). Heritability of bipolar spectrum disorders. Unity or heterogeneity? *Journal of Affective Disorders, 106,* 229–240.

Edwards, L. A., Wagner, J. B., Simon, C. E., & Hyde, D. C. (2016). Functional brain organization for number processing in pre-verbal infants. *Developmental Science, 19*(5), 757–769.

Eide, K., Fadnes, L., Engebretsen, I., Onarheim, K., Wamani, H., Tumwine, J., et al. (2016). Impact of a peer-counseling intervention on breastfeeding practices in different socioeconomic strata: Results from the equity analysis of the PROMISE-EBF trial in Uganda. *Global Health Action, 9*(1), 30578.

Eiden, R., Lessard, J., Colder, C., Livingston, J., Casey, M., & Leonard, K. (2016). Developmental cascade model for adolescent substance use from infancy to late adolescence. *Developmental Psychology, 52*(10), 1619–1633.

Eimas, P. D. (1985). The perception of speech in early infancy. *Scientific American, 252*(1), 66–72.

Einspieler, C., Marschik, P. B., & Prechtl, H. F. R. (2008). Human motor behavior: Prenatal origin and early postnatal development. *Zeitschrift fur Psychologie, 216,* 147–153.

Eisenberg, N. (2010). Empathy-related responding: Links with self-regulation, moral judgment, and moral behavior. In N. Eisenberg (Ed.), *Prosocial motives, emotions, and behavior: The better angels of our nature* (pp. 129–148). Washington, DC: American Psychological Association.

Eisenberg, N., Fabes, R. A., Murphy, B., Karbon, M., Smith, M., & Maszk, P. (1996). The relations of children's dispositional empathy–related responding to their emotionality, regulation, and social functioning. *Developmental Psychology, 32,* 195–209.

Eisenberg, N., Fabes, R. A., Shepard, S., Murphy, B., Jones, J., & Guthrie, I. (1998). Contemporaneous and longitudinal prediction of children's sympathy from dispositional regulation and emotionality. *Developmental Psychology, 34,* 910–924.

Eisenberg, N., Hofer, C., & Vaughan, J. (2007). Effortful control and its socioemotional consequences. In J. J. Gross (Ed.), *Handbook of emotion regulation* (pp. 287–306). New York: Guilford Press.

Eisenberg, N., Losoya, S., & Spinrad, T. L. (2003). Affect and prosocial responding. In R. Davidson, K. Scherer, & H. Goldsmith (Eds.), *Handbook of affective sciences.* Oxford, England: Oxford University Press.

Eisenberg, N., Spinrad, T. L., & Eggum, N. D. (2010). Emotion-related self-regulation and its relation to children's maladjustment. *Annual Review of Clinical Psychology, 6*(1), 495–525.

Eisenberg, N., Spinrad, T. L., & Knafo-Noam, A. (2015). Prosocial development. In M. E. Lamb & R. M. Lerner (Eds.), *Handbook of child psychology and developmental science: Vol. 3. Social, emotional and personality development* (7th ed., pp. 610–656). New York: Wiley.

Eisenberg, N., Spinrad, T. L., & Sadovsky, A. (2006). Empathy related responding in children. In M. Killen & J. G. Smetana (Eds.), *Handbook of moral development* (pp. 517–549). Mahwah, NJ: Lawrence Erlbaum Associates.

Eisenberg, N., VanSchyndel, S. K., & Spinrad, T. L. (2016). Prosocial motivation: Inferences from an opaque body of work. *Child Development, 87*(6), 1668–1678.

Ekinci, B. (2014). The relationships among Sternberg's triarchic abilities, Gardner's multiple intelligences, and academic achievement. *Social Behavior and Personality, 42*(4), 625–633.

Elder, G. H. J. (1998). The life course and human development. In W. Damon & R. M. Lerner (Eds.), *Handbook of child psychology: Vol. 1. Theoretical models of human development* (5th ed., pp. 939–992). New York: Wiley.

Elias, C., & Berk, L. (2002). Self-regulation in young children: Is there a role for sociodramatic play? *Early Childhood Research Quarterly, 17,* 216–238.

Elledge, L. C., Elledge, A. R., Newgent, R. A., & Cavell, T. A. (2016). Social risk and peer victimization in elementary school children: The protective role of teacher–student relationships. *Journal of Abnormal Child Psychology, 44*(4), 691.

Ellis, B., & Bjorklund, D. (Eds.). (2005). *Origins of the social mind: Evolutionary psychology and child development.* New York: Guilford Press.

Ellis, B. J., & Essex, M. J. (2007). Family environments, adrenarche, and sexual maturation: A longitudinal test of a life history model. *Child Development, 78*(6), 1799–1817.

Ellis, S., & Siegler, R. S. (1997). Planning as a strategy choice, or why don't children plan when they should? In S. L. Friedman & E. K. Scholnick (Eds.), *The developmental psychology of planning: Why, how, and when do we plan?* (pp. 183–208). Mahwah, NJ: Lawrence Erlbaum Associates.

Ellis, S. J., Kitzinger, C., & Wilkinson, S. (2002). Attitudes towards lesbians and gay men and support for lesbian and gay human rights among psychology students. *Journal of Homosexuality, 44,* 121–138.

Ellis, W. E., & Zarbatany, L. (2007). Explaining friendship formation and friendship stability. The role of children's and friends' aggression and victimization. *Merrill-Palmer Quarterly, 53*(1), 79–104.

Elman, J. L., Bates, E. A., Johnson, M. J., Karmilof-Smith, A., Parsi, D., & Plunkett, K. (1996). *Rethinking innateness: A connectionist perspective on development.* Cambridge, MA: The MIT Press.

Else-Quest, N., & Morse, E. (2015). Ethnic variations in parental ethnic socialization and adolescent ethnic identity: A longitudinal study. *Cultural Diversity & Ethnic Minority Psychology, 21*(1), 54–64.

El-Sheikh, M., Buckhalt, J., Mize, J., & Acebo, C. (2006). Marital conflict and disruption of children's sleep. *Child Development, 77,* 31–43.

Eluvathingal, T. J., Chugani, H. T., Behen, M. E., Juhasz, C., Muzik, O., Maqbool, M., et al. (2006). Abnormal brain connectivity in children after early severe socioemotional deprivation: A diffusion tensor imaging study. *Pediatrics, 117*(6), 2093–2100.

Emde, R. N., & Hewitt, J. K. (Eds.). (2001). *Infancy to early childhood: Genetic and environmental influences on developmental change.* New York: Oxford University Press.

Endendijk, J. J., Groeneveld, M. G., Pol, L. D., Berkel, S. R., Hallers-Haalboom, E. T., Bakermans-Kranenburg, M. J., & Mesman, J. (2017). Gender differences in child aggression: Relations with gender-differentiated parenting and parents' gender-role stereotypes. *Child Development, 88*(1), 299–316.

Enfield, N. J., & Levinson, S. C. (2006). *Roots of human sociality: Culture, cognition and interaction* (Wenner-Gren International Symposium Series). Oxford, England: Berg Publishers. New York: Oxford University Press.

Engelhardt, L. E., Mann, F. D., Briley, D. A., Church, J. A., Harden, K. P., & Tucker-Drob, E. M. (2016). Strong genetic overlap between executive functions and intelligence. *Journal of Experimental Psychology. General, 145*(9), 1141–1159.

Engelhardt, W., & Skinner, C. (2013). *Knowing what works: State and cities build smarter social policy with new and improved poverty measure.* Retrieved from http://www.nccp.org/publications/pub_1081.html

Erickson, F., & Mohatt, G. (1982). Cultural organization of participation structures in two classrooms of Indian students. In G. Spindler (Ed.), *Doing the ethnography of schooling: Educational anthropology in action* (pp. 132–175). Prospect Heights, IL: Waveland Press.

Erikson, E. H. (1950). *Childhood and society.* New York: W. W. Norton.

Erikson, E. H. (1963). *Childhood and society* (2nd ed.). New York: W. W. Norton.

Erikson, E. H. (1963). *The challenge of youth.* New York: Doubleday.

Erikson, E. H. (1968). *Identity: Youth and crisis.* New York: W. W. Norton.

Erikson, E. H. (1968). Life cycle. In D. L. Sills (Ed.), *International encyclopedia of the social sciences: Vol. 9.* New York: Crowell, Collier.

Erikson, M. F., Sroufe, L. A., & Egeland, B. (1985). The relationship between the quality of attachment and behavior problems in preschool in a high-risk sample. *Monographs of the Society for Research in Child Development, 50,* 1–2, No. 209.

Ernestus, S. M., & Prelow, H. M. (2015). Patterns of risk and resilience in African American and Latino youth. *Journal of Community Psychology, 43*(8), 954–972.

Eshleman, L. (2003). *Becoming a family: Promoting healthy attachments with your adopted child.* Dallas, TX: Taylor Publishing Company.

Esposito, G., Setoh, P., Yoshida, S., & Kuroda, K. O. (2015). The calming effect of maternal carrying in different mammalian species. *Frontiers in Psychology, 6,* 445.

Esposito, G., Truzzi, A., Setoh, P., Putnick, D. L., Shinohara, K., & Bornstein, M. H. (2016). Genetic predispositions and parental bonding interact to shape adults' physiological responses to social distress. *Behavioural Brain Research, 325*(Pt. B), 156–162.

Estell, D. B., Farmer, T. W., Cairns, R. B., & Cairns, B. D. (2002). Social relations and academic achievement in inner-city early elementary classrooms. *International Journal of Behavioral Development, 26,* 518–528.

Esteve-Gibert, N., & Prieto, P. (2013). Prosody signals the emergence of intentional communication in the first year of life: Evidence from Catalan-babbling infants. *Journal of Child Language, 40*(5), 919–944.

Estren, M. J. (2012). The neoteny barrier: Seeking respect for the non-cute. *Journal of Animal Ethics, 2*(1), 6–11.

Ettekal, I., & Ladd, G. (2017). Developmental continuity and change in physical, verbal, and relational aggression and peer victimization from childhood to adolescence. *Developmental Psychology, 53*(9), 1709–1721.

European Commission Special Eurobarometer. (2006). *Europeans and their languages.* Retrieved from http://ec.europa.eu/public_opinion/archives/ebs/ebs_243_en.pdf

Evans, G. W. (2006.) Child development and the physical environment. *Annual Review of Psychology, 57,* 423–451.

Ewing, A. R., & Taylor, A. R. (2009). The role of child gender and ethnicity in teacher–child relationship quality and children's behavioural adjustment in preschool. *Early Childhood Research Quarterly, 24*(1), 92–105.

Eyal, K., & Te'eni-Harari, T. (2013). Explaining the relationship between media exposure and early adolescents' body image perceptions: The role of favorite characters. *Journal of Media Psychology: Theories, Methods, and Applications, 25*(3), 129–141.

Fadiman, A. (2012). *The spirit catches you and you fall down: A Hmong child, her American doctors, and the collision of two cultures.* New York: Farrar, Straus, and Giroux.

Faes, J., Gillis, J., & Gillis, S. (2015). Syntagmatic and paradigmatic development of cochlear implanted children in comparison with normally hearing peers up to age 7. *International Journal of Pediatric Otorhinolaryngology, 79,* 1533–1540.

Falk, D. (2016). Evolution of brain and culture: The neurological and cognitive journey from Australopithecus to Albert Einstein. *Journal of Anthropological Sciences, 94,* 99–111.

Fantz, R. L. (1961). The origins of form perception. *Scientific American, 204*(5), 66–72.

Fantz, R. L. (1963). Pattern vision in newborn infants. *Science, 140,* 296–297.

Farkas, C., & Vallotton, C. (2016). Differences in infant temperament between Chile and the US. *Infant Behavior & Development, 44,* 208–218.

Farr, R. H., Crain, E. E., Oakley, M. K., Cashen, K. K., & Garber, K. J. (2016). Microaggressions, feelings of difference, and resilience among adopted children with sexual minority parents. *Journal of Youth and Adolescence, 45*(1), 85–104.

Farrington, D. (2004). Conduct disorder, aggression, and delinquency. In R. M. Lerner & L. Steinberg (Eds.), *Handbook of adolescent psychology* (2nd ed.). Hoboken, NJ: John Wiley & Sons.

Fedewa, A. L., Black, W. W., & Ahn, S. (2015). Children and adolescents with same-gender parents: A meta-analytic approach in assessing outcomes. *Journal of GLBT Family Studies, 11*(1), 1–34.

Feinberg, I., & Campbell, I. G. (2010). Sleep EEG changes during adolescence: An index of a fundamental brain reorganization. *Brain and Cognition, 72,* 56–65.

Feinberg, I., March, J. D., Fein, G., Floyd, T. C., Walker, J. M., & Price, L. (1978). Period and amplitude analysis of 0.5-3 c/sec activity in NREM sleep of young adults. *Electroencephalography and Clinical Neurophysiology, 44*(2), 202–213.

Feldman, D. H. (2004). Piaget's stages: The unfinished symphony of cognitive development. *New Ideas in Psychology, 22,* 175–231.

Feldman, R. (2017). The neurobiology of human attachments. *Trends in Cognitive Sciences, 21*(2), 80–99.

Feng, X., Harkness, S., Super, C. M., & Jia, R. (2014). Shyness and adaptation to school in a Chinese community. *Infant and Child Development, 23*(6), 662–671.

Fenson, L., Dale, P. S., Reznick, J. S., Bates, E., Thal, O. J., & Pettnick, S. J. (1994). Variability in early communicative development. *Monographs for Research in Child Development, 59*(5, Serial No. 242).

Ferguson, B., & Waxman, S. (2017). Linking language and categorization in infancy. *Journal of Child Language, 44*(3), 1–26.

Ferholt, B., & Lecusay, R. (2010). Adult and child development in the zone of proximal development: Socratic dialogue in a playworld. *Mind, Culture, and Activity, 17,* 59–83.

Fernald, A., Perfors, A., & Marchman, V. (2006). Picking up speed in understanding: Speech processing efficiency and vocabulary growth across the 2nd year. *Developmental Psychology, 42*(1), 98–116.

Fernald, L. C., Gunnar, M. R. (2009). Poverty-alleviation program participation and salivary cortisol in very low-income children. *Social Science and Medicine, 68,* 2180–2189.

Fernandez, M., Blass, E., Hernandez-Reif, M., Field, T., & Miguel, S. (2003). Sucrose attenuates a negative electroencephaliographic response to aversive stimulus for newborns. *Journal of Developmental and Behavioral Pediatrics, 24,* 261–266.

Ferrer-Wreder, L., Lorente, C. C., Kurtines, W., Briones, E., Bussell, J., Berman, S., & Arrufat, O. (2002). Promoting identity development in marginalized youth. *Journal of Adolescent Research, 17,* 168–187.

Field, T. (2010). Postpartum depression effects on early interactions, parenting, and safety practices: A review. *Infant Behavior & Development, 33,* 1–6.

Field, T. M. (1979). Differential behavioral and cardiac responses of 3-month-old infants to a mirror and peer. *Infant Behavior & Development, 2*(2), 179–184.

Field, T. M., Diego, M., Hernandez-Reif, M., & Fernandez, M. (2007). Depressed mothers' newborns show less discrimination of other newborns' cry sounds. *Infant Behavior & Development, 30,* 431–435.

Fiese, B., Gundersen, C., Koester, B., & Washington, L. (2011). Household food insecurity: Serious concerns for child development. *SRCD Social Policy Report, 25* (3), 1–19.

Figueras, F., & Gardosi, J. (2011). Intrauterine growth restriction: New concepts in antenatal surveillance, diagnosis, and management. *American Journal of Obstetrics and Gynecology, 204*(4), 288–300.

File, C. (2015). Gut in focus symposium Nobel Forum, Karolinska Institutet, February 2nd, 2015. *Microbial Ecology in Health and Disease, 26,* 1–45.

Fireman, G., & Kose, G. (2002, December). The effect of self-observation on children's problem solving. *Journal of Genetic Psychology, 163,* 410–423.

Fischer, K. W., & Yan, Z. (2002). The development of dynamic skill theory. In R. Lickliter & D. Lewkowicz (Eds.), *Conceptions of development: Lessons from the laboratory.* Hove, England: Psychology Press.

Fishbein, H. D. (1976). *Evolution, development and children's learning.* Pacific Palisades, CA: Goodyear.

Fisher, C., Klingler, S., & Song, H. (2006). What does syntax say about space? 2-year-olds use sentence structure to learn new prepositions. *Cognition, 101*(1), b19–b29.

Fivush, R. (2011). The development of autobiographical memory. *Annual Review of Psychology, 62*(1), 559–582.

Fivush, R., Habermas, T., Waters, T. E. A., & Zaman, W. (2011). The making of autobiographical memory: Intersections of culture, narratives and identity. *International Journal of Psychology, 46*(5), 321–345.

Flavell, J. H. (2007). Theory-of-mind development: Retrospect and prospect. In G. W. Ladd (Ed.), *Appraising the human developmental sciences. Landscapes of childhood series* (pp. 38–55). Detroit, MI: Wayne State University Press.

Flavell, J. H., Friedrichs, A. G., & Hoyt, J. D. (1970). Developmental changes in memorization processes. *Cognitive Psychology, 1,* 324–340.

Flavell, J. H., Green, F. L., & Flavell, E. R. (1986). Development of knowledge about the appearance-reality distinction. *Monographs of the Society for Research in Child Development, 51*(1, Serial No. 212).

Flood, M. (2007). Exposure to pornography among youth in Australia. *Journal of Sociology, 43*(1), 45–60.

Flores, N., & Rosa, J. (2015). Undoing appropriateness: Raciolinguistic ideologies and language diversity in education. *Harvard Educational Review, 85,* 149–171.

Flowers, P., & Buston, K. (2002). "I was terrified of being different": Exploring gay men's accounts of growing up in a heterosexist society. *Journal of Adolescence, 24,* 51–65.

Flykt, M., Kanninen, K., Sinkkonen, J., & Punamäki, R.-L. (2010). Maternal depression and dyadic interaction: The role of maternal attachment style. *Infant and Child Development, 19,* 530–550.

Flynn, E., & Siegler, R. (2007). Measuring change: Current trends and future directions in microgenetic research. *Infant and Child Development, 16,* 1135–1149.

Flynn, J. R. (1984). The mean IQ of Americans: Massive gains 1932 to 1978. *Psychological Bulletin, 95,* 29–51.

Flynn, J. R. (2007). *What is intelligence? Beyond the Flynn effect.* New York: Cambridge University Press.

Fordham, S., & Ogbu, J. U. (1986). Black students' school success: Coping with the "burden of 'acting white.'" *Urban Review, 18*(3), 176–206.

Forgatch, M. S., Snyder, J. J., Patterson, G. R., Pauldine, M. R., Chaw, Y., Elish, K., et al. (2016). Resurrecting the chimera: Progressions in parenting and peer processes. *Development and Psychopathology, 28*(3), 689–706.

Forman, M. (2002). Keeping it real: African youth identities and hip hop. In R. Young (Ed.), *Critical Studies, 19, Music, popular culture, identities.* New York: Rodopi.

Forsman, A. (2015). Rethinking phenotypic plasticity and its consequences for individuals, populations and species. *Heredity, 115*(4), 276–284.

Forsyth, B. W. C. (1989). Colic and the effect of changing formulas: A double-blind, multiple crossover study. *Journal of Pediatrics, 115,* 521–552.

Fortenberry, J. D. (2013). Puberty and adolescent sexuality. *Hormones and Behavior, 64*(2), 280–287.

Fortenberry, J. D. (2014). Sexual learning, sexual experience, and healthy adolescent sex. *New Directions for Child and Adolescent Development, 144,* 71–86.

Foubert, J. D., Brosi, M. W., & Bannon, R. S. (2011). Pornography viewing among fraternity men: Effects on bystander intervention, rape myth acceptance and behavioral intent to commit sexual assault. *Sexual Addiction & Compulsivity, 18*(4), 212–231.

Fouts, H. N., Hallam, R. A., & Purandare, S. (2013). Gender segregation in early-childhood social play among the Bofi foragers and Bofi farmers in central Africa. *American Journal of Play, 5*(3), 333.

Fowler, A. (1990). Language abilities in children with Down syndrome: Evidence for a specific syntactic delay. In D. Cicchetti & M. Beeghly (Eds.), *Children with Down syndrome: A developmental perspective* (pp. 302–328). Cambridge, UK: Cambridge University Press.

Fox, S. E., Levitt, P., & Nelson, C. A. (2010). How the timing and quality of early experiences influence the development of brain architecture. *Child Development, 81,* 28–40.

Fraiberg, S. H. (1959). *The magic years: Understanding and handling the problems of early childhood.* New York: Scribner.

Franco, P., Montemitro, E., Scaillet, S., Groswasser, J., Kato, I., Lin, J., & Villa, M. P. (2011). Fewer spontaneous arousals in infants with apparent life-threatening event. *Sleep, 34*(6), 733–743.

Frankel, K., & Bates, J. (1990). Mother-toddler problem solving: Antecedents in attachment, home behavior, and temperament. *Child Development, 61,* 810–819.

Franklin, A., Giannakidou, A., & Goldin-Meadow, S. (2011). Negation, questions, and structure building in a homesign system. *Cognition, 118*(3), 398–416.

Franz, M., & Matthews, L. J. (2010). Social enhancement can create adaptive, arbitrary and maladaptive cultural traditions. *Proceedings: Biological Sciences, 277*(1698), 3363–3372.

Freed, K. (1983, March 14). Cubatao—A paradise lost to pollution. Los Angeles *Times,* pp. 1, 12, 13.

Freigang, C., Richter, N., Rübsamen, R., & Ludwig, A. A. (2015). Age-related changes in sound localisation ability. *Cell and Tissue Research, 361*(1), 371–386.

Freud, S. (1905/1953). Three essays on the theory of sexuality. In J. Strachey (Ed.), *The standard edition of the complete psychological works of Sigmund Freud: Vol. 7.* London: Hogarth Press.

Freud, S. (1920/1955). Beyond the pleasure principle. In J. Strachey (Ed.), *The standard edition of the complete psychological works of Sigmund Freud: Vol. 18.* London: Hogarth Press.

Freud, S. (1921/1949). Group psychology—The analysis of the ego. In J. Strachey (Ed.), *The standard edition of the complete psychological works of Sigmund Freud: Vol. 18.* London: Hogarth Press.

Freud, S. (1933/1964). *New introductory lectures in psychoanalysis.* New York: W. W. Norton.

Freud, S. (1940/1964). An outline of psychoanalysis. In J. Strachey (Ed.), *The standard edition of the complete psychological works of Sigmund Freud: Vol. 32.* London: Hogarth Press.

Frick, A., Mohring, W., & Newcombe, N. (2014). Development of mental transformation abilities. *Trends in Cognitive Sciences, 18*(10), 536–542.

Friederici, A. D., Bahlmann, J., Heim, S., Schubotz, R. I., & Anwander, A. (2006). The brain differentiates human and non-human grammars: Functional localization and structural connectivity. *Proceedings of the National Academy of Sciences, 103,* 2458–2463.

Friedman, S. L., Scholnick, E. K., Bender, R. H., Vandergrift, N., Spieker, S., Hirsh Pasek, K., et al. (2014). Planning in middle childhood: Early predictors and later outcomes. *Child Development, 85*(4), 1446–1460.

Friedman-Krauss, A. H., Connors, M. C., & Morris, P. A. (2017). Unpacking the treatment contrast in the head start impact study: To what extent does assignment to treatment affect quality of care? *Journal of Research on Educational Effectiveness, 10*(1), 68–95.

Frissen, A., Lieverse, R., Drukker, M., van Winkel, R., Delespaul, P., & GROUP Investigators. (2015). Childhood trauma and childhood urbanicity in relation to psychotic disorder. *Social Psychiatry and Psychiatric Epidemiology, 50*(10), 1481–1488.

Frith, U. (1989). *Autism.* Oxford, England: Oxford University Press.

Fry, D. P. (1988). Intercommunity differences in aggression among Zapotec children. *Child Development, 59,* 1008–1018.

Fryar, C., Carrol, M., & Ogden, C. (2016). *Prevalence of overweight and obesity among children and adolescents aged 2–19 years: United States, 1963–1965 through 2013–2014.* Retrieved from www.cdc.gov/nchs/data/hestat/obesity_child_13_14/obesity_child_13_14.pdf

Fryar, C. D., Gu, Q., & Ogden, C. L. (2012). Anthropometric reference data for children and adults: United States, 2007–2010. *Vital Health Statistics, 11*(252), 1–40.

Fu, G., Xiao, W. S., Killen, M., & Lee, K. (2014). Moral judgment and its relation to second-order theory of mind. *Developmental Psychology, 50*(8), 2085–2092.

Fuhs, M. W., & Day, J. D. (2011). Verbal ability and executive functioning development in preschoolers at Head Start. *Developmental Psychology, 47,* 404–416.

Fujimoto, K., & Valente, T. W. (2012). Social network influences on adolescent substance use: Disentangling structural equivalence from cohesion. *Social Science & Medicine, 74*(12), 1952–1960.

Fujioka, T., Trainor, L. J., & Ross, B. (2008). Simultaneous pitches are encoded separately in auditory cortex: An MMNm study. *Neuroreport: For Rapid Communication of Neuroscience Research, 19,* 361–366.

Fuligni, A. J., Telzer, E. H., Bower, J., Irwin, M. R., Kiang, L., & Cole, S. W. (2009). Daily family assistance and inflammation among adolescents from Latin American and European backgrounds. *Brain Behavior and Immunity, 23*(6), 803–809.

Fullard, W., & Reiling, A. M. (1976). An investigation of Lorenz's babyness. *Child Development, 47,* 1191–1193.

Fuller-Rowell, T. E., Ong, A. D., & Phinney, J. S. (2013). National identity and perceived discrimination predict changes in ethnic identity commitment: Evidence from a longitudinal study of Latino college students. *Applied Psychology, 62*(3), 406–426.

Funk, J. B., Baldacci, H. B., Pasold, T., & Baumgardner, J. (2004). Violence exposure in real-life, video games, television, movies, and the internet: Is there desensitization? *Journal of Adolescence, 27,* 23–39.

Furman, W., & Simon, V. A. (2008). Homophily in adolescent romantic relationships. In M. J. Prinstein & K. A. Dodge (Eds.), *Understanding peer influence in children and adolescents. Duke series in child development and public policy* (pp. 203–224). New York: Guilford Press.

Futagi, Y., Ozaki, N., Matsubara, T., Futagi, M., Suzuki, Y., & Kitajima, H. (2016). Eye–mouth associated movement in the human newborn and very young infant. *Pediatric Neurology, 58,* 75–82.

Gabbe, S., Niebyl, J., Simpson, J., Landon, M., Galan, H., & Jauniaux, E. (2016). *Obstetrics: Normal and problem pregnancies* (7th ed.). Philadelphia, PA: Elsevier.

Gaias, L. M., Räikkönen, K., Komsi, N., Gartstein, M. A., Fisher, P. A., & Putnam, S. P. (2012). Cross-cultural temperamental differences in infants, children, and adults in the United States of America and Finland. *Scandinavian Journal of Psychology, 53,* 119–128.

Gaillard, V., Barrouillet, P., Jarrold, C., & Camos, V. (2011). Developmental differences in working memory: Where do they come from? *Journal of Experimental Child Psychology, 110*(3), 469–479.

Galloway, M. K. (2012). Cheating in advantaged high schools: Prevalence, justifications, and possibilities for change. *Ethics & Behavior, 22*(5), 378–399.

Gallup, G. G. J. (1970). Chimpanzees: Self-recognition. *Science, 167,* 86–87.

Galván, A., & Rahdar, A. (2013). The neurobiological effects of stress on adolescent decision making. *Neuroscience, 249,* 223–231.

Gammage, J. (2003, June 14). Bringing Jin Yu home. *The Philadelphia Inquirer.*

Gardella, B., Iacobone, A. D., Bogliolo, S., Musacchi, V., Orcesi, S., Tzialla, C., & Spinillo, A. (2015). Obstetric risk factors and time trends of neurodevelopmental outcome at 2 years in very-low-birthweight infants: A single institution study. *Developmental Medicine & Child Neurology, 57*(11), 1035–1041.

Gardner, H. (1983). *Frames of mind: The theory of multiple intelligences.* New York: Basic Books.

Gardner, H. (2006, September–October). On failing to grasp the core of MI theory: A response to Visser et al. *Intelligence, 34*(5), 503–505.

Garofalo, R., Wolf, R., Wissow, L., Woods, E., & Goodman, E. (1999). Sexual orientation and risk of suicide attempts among a representative sample of youth. *Archives of Pediatrics and Adolescent Medicine, 153,* 487–493.

Garrow, I., & Werne, J. (1953). Sudden apparently unexplained death during infancy: III. Pathological findings in infants dying immediately after violence, contrasted with those after sudden apparently unexplained death. *American Journal of Pathology, 29,* 833–851.

Gartstein, M., Putnick, D., Kwak, K., Hahn, C., & Bornstein, M. (2015). Stability of temperament in South Korean infants from 6 to 12 to 18 months: Moderation by age, gender, and birth order. *Infant Behavior & Development, 40,* 103–107.

Garvey, C., & Berndt, R. (1977). Organization of pretend play. *Catalog of Selected Documents in Psychology, 7,* 107.

Gaskins, S. (2013). The puzzle of attachment: Unscrambling maturational and cultural contributions to the development of early emotional bonds. In N. Quinn & J. M. Mageo (Eds.), *Attachment reconsidered: Cultural perspectives on a Western theory.* New York: Palgrave Macmillan.

Gasparini, C., Sette, S., Baumgartner, E., Martin, C. L., & Fabes, R. A. (2015). Gender-biased attitudes and attributions among young Italian children: Relation to peer dyadic interaction. *Sex Roles, 73*(9), 427–441.

Gates, G. (2013). *LGBT parenting in the United States.* Retrieved from http://williamsinstitute.law.ucla.edu/wp-content/uploads/LGBT-Parenting.pdf

Gau, S., & Soong, W. (2003). The transition of sleep–wake patterns in early adolescence. *Sleep, 26,* 449–454.

Ge, X., Brody, G. H., Conger, R. D., & Simons, R. L. (2006). Pubertal maturation and African American children's internalizing and externalizing symptoms. *Journal of Youth and Adolescence, 35,* 531–540.

Geers, A. E., & Sedey, A. L. (2011). Language and verbal reasoning skills in adolescents with 10 or more years of cochlear implant experience. *Ear and Hearing, 32,* 39S–48S.

Geithner, C. A., Thomis, M. A., Vanden Eynde, B., Maes, H. H., Loos, R. J., Peeters, M., et al. (2004, September). Growth in peak aerobic power during adolescence. *Medicine & Science in Sports & Exercise, 36*(9), 1616–1624.

Gelis, J. (1991). *History of childbirth.* Cambridge, England: Polity Press.

Geoffroy, M., Boivin, M., Arseneault, L., Turecki, G., Vitaro, F., Brendgen, M., et al. (2016). Associations between peer victimization and suicidal ideation and suicide attempt during adolescence: Results from a prospective population-based birth cohort. *Journal of the American Academy of Child and Adolescent Psychiatry, 55*(2), 99–105.

Geoffroy, M., Cote, S., Parent, S., & Seguin, J. (2006). Daycare attendance, stress, and mental health. *Canadian Journal of Psychiatry, 51*(9), 607–615.

Gershoff, E. T., & Aber, J. L. (2004, July). Editors' introduction: Assessing the impact of September 11th, 2001, on children, youth, and parents: Methodological challenges to research on terrorism and other nonnormative events. *Applied Developmental Science, 8*(3), 106–110.

Gershoff, E. T., & Grogan-Kaylor, A. (2016). Race as a moderator of associations between spanking and child outcomes: Race as a moderator of spanking. *Family Relations, 65*(3), 490–501.

Gertner, Y., Fisher, C., & Eisengart, J. (2006). Learning words and rules: Abstract knowledge of word order in early sentence comprehension. *Psychological Science, 17,* 684–691.

Gestsdottir, S., Von Suchodoletz, A., Wanless, S. B., Hubert, B., Guimard, P., Birgisdottir, F., et al. (2014). Early behavioral self-regulation, academic achievement, and gender: Longitudinal findings from France, Germany, and Iceland. *Applied Developmental Science, 18*(2), 90–109.

Geurten, M., Catale, C., & Meulemans, T. (2016). Involvement of executive functions in children's metamemory. *Applied Cognitive Psychology, 30*(1), 70–80.

Geurten, M., Lejeune, C., & Meulemans, T. (2016). Time's up! Involvement of metamemory knowledge, executive functions, and time monitoring in children's prospective memory performance. *Child Neuropsychology, 22*(4), 443.

Gidley Larson, J. C., Mostofsky, S. H., Goldberg, M. C., Cutting, L. E., Denckla, M. B., & Mahone, E. M. (2007). Effects of gender and age on motor exam in typically developing children. *Developmental Neuropsychology, 32*(1), 543–562.

Giedd, J. N., Clasen, L. S., Lenroot, R., Greenstein, D., Wallace, G. L., Ordaz, S., et al. (2006). Puberty-related influences on brain development. *Molecular and Cellular Endocrinology, 254–255*(3), 154–162.

Giedd, J. N., & Gordon, D. (2010). The teen brain: Primed to learn, primed to take risks. *The Dana Foundation's Cerebrum, 72,* 46–55.

Giedd, J. N., & Rapoport, J. L. (2010, Sep 9). Structural MRI of pediatric brain development: What have we learned and where are we going. *Neuron, 67,* 728–734.

Gielen, U. P., & Markoulis, D. C. (2001). Preference for principled moral reasoning: A developmental and cross-cultural perspective. In L. L. Adler & U. P. Gielen (Eds.), *Cross-cultural topics in psychology* (2nd ed., pp. 81–101). Westport, CT: Praeger.

Gilead, M., Katzir, M., Eyal, T., & Liberman, N. (2016). Neural correlates of processing "self-conscious" vs. "basic" emotions. *Neuropsychologia, 81,* 207–218.

Giles, J., & Heyman, G. (2003). Preschoolers' beliefs about the stability of antisocial behavior: Implications for navigating social challenges. *Social Development, 12,* 182–197.

Giles, J. W., Legare, C., & Samson, J. E. (2008). Psychological essentialism and cultural variation: Children's beliefs about aggression in the United States and South Africa. *Infant and Child Development, 17*(2), 137–150.

Gill, T. (2014). The benefits of children's engagement with nature: A systematic literature review. *Children, Youth and Environments, 24*(2), 10–34.

Gillespie-Lynch, K., Greenfield, P. M., Lyn, H., & Savage-Rumbaugh, S. (2014). Gestural and symbolic development among apes and humans: Support for a multimodal theory of language evolution. *Frontiers in Psychology, 5,* 1228.

Gilligan, C. (1982). *In a different voice: Psychological theory and women's development.* Cambridge, MA: Harvard University Press.

Gilmore, C. K., & Spelke, E. S. (2008, June). Children's understanding of the relationship between addition and subtraction. *Cognition, 107,* 932–945.

Gilmore, L., & Cuskelly, M. (2017). Associations of child and adolescent mastery motivation and self-regulation with adult outcomes: A longitudinal study of individuals with Down syndrome. *American Journal on Intellectual and Developmental Disabilities, 122*(3), 235.

Gingras, J. L., Mitchell, E. A., & Grattan, K. E. (2005). Fetal homologue of infant crying. *Archives of Disease in Childhood, 90*(5), F415–F418.

Ginsburg, H. (1977). *Children's arithmetic.* New York: Van Nostrand.

Ginsburg, H. P. (2008). Challenging preschool education: Meeting the intellectual needs of all children. In B. Z. Presseisen (Ed.), *Teaching for intelligence* (2nd ed., pp. 212–229). Thousand Oaks, CA: Corwin Press.

Gittelsohn, J., Song, H.-J., Suratkar, S., Kumar, M. B., Henry, E. G., Sharma, S., et al. (2010). An urban food store intervention positively affects food-related psychosocial variables and food behaviors. *Health Education & Behavior, 37,* 390–402.

Gleason, T., Theran, S., & Newberg, E. (2017). Parasocial interactions and relationships in early adolescence. *Frontiers in Psychology, 8,* 255.

Gluck, M. E., Venti, C. A., Lindsay, R. S., Knowler, W. C., Salbe, A. D., & Krakoff, J. (2009). Maternal influence, not diabetic intrauterine environment, predicts children's energy intake. *Obesity, 17,* 772–777.

Goddings, A., Mills, K. L., Clasen, L. S., Giedd, J. N., Viner, R. M., & Blakemore, S. (2014). The influence of puberty on subcortical brain development. *Neuroimage, 88,* 242–251.

Gogtay, N., Giedd, J., Lusk, L., Hayashi, K. I., Sreenstein, D., & Vaituzis, A. (2004). Dynamic mapping of human cortical development during childhood through early adulthood. *Proceedings of the National Academy of Sciences of the United States of America, 101,* 8174–8179.

Golden, N. H., Katzman, D. K., & Kreipe, R. E. (2003). Eating disorders in adolescents: A position paper of the Society for Adolescent Medicine. *Journal of Adolescent Health, 33,* 496–503.

Goldfield, E. C. (2000). Development of infant action systems and exploratory activity: A tribute to Edward S. Reed. *Ecological Psychology, 12*(4), 303–318.

Goldin-Meadow, S. (2015). The impact of time on predicate forms in the manual modality: Signers, homesigners, and silent gesturers. *Topics in Cognitive Science,* 7(1), 169–184.

Goldin-Meadow, S., & Brentari, D. (2015). Gesture, sign and language: The coming of age of sign language and gesture studies. *Behavioral and Brain Sciences, 40,* e46.

Goldin-Meadow, S., Özyürek, A., Sancar, B., & Mylander, C. (2009). Making language around the globe: A crosslinguistic study of homesign in the United States, China, and Turkey. In S. Goldin-Meadow, A. Özyürek, B. Sancar, & C. Mylander (Eds.), *Crosslinguistic approaches to the psychology of language: Research in the tradition of Dan Isaac Slobin* (pp. 27–39). New York: Psychology Press.

Goldsmith, H. H., & Campos, J. J. (1982). Toward a theory of infant temperament. In R. N. Emde & R. Harmon (Eds.), *The development of attachment and affiliative systems.* New York: Plenum Press.

Golinkoff, R. M., Can, D. D., Soderstrom, M., & Hirsh-Pasek, K. (2015). (Baby)Talk to me: The social context of infant-directed speech and its effects on early language acquisition. *Current Directions in Psychological Science, 24*(5), 339–344.

Golinkoff, R., & Hirsh-Pasek, K. (2006). Baby wordsmith: From associationist to social sophisticate. *Current Directions in Psychological Science, 15,* 30–33.

Golinkoff, R. M., Hirsh-Pasek, K., & Schweisguth, M. A. (1999). A reappraisal of young children's knowledge of grammatical morphemes. In J. Weissenborn & B. Hoehle (Eds.), *Approaches to bootstrapping: Phonological, syntactic, and neurophysiological aspects of early language acquisition.* Amsterdam and Philadelphia, PA: John Benjamins.

Golombok, S., Rust, J., Zervoulis, K., Golding, J., & Hines, M. (2012). Continuity in sex-typed behavior from preschool to adolescence: A longitudinal population study of boys and girls aged 3–13 years. *Archives of Sexual Behavior, 41*(3), 591–597.

Goncu, A., & Gaskins, S. (2011). Comparing and extending Piaget's and Vygotsky's understandings of play: Symbolic play as individual, sociocultural, and educational interpretation. In A. Pellegrini (Ed.), *The Oxford Handbook of the Development of Play.* New York: Oxford University Press.

González-Carrasco, M., Casas, F., Malo, S., Viñas, F., & Dinisman, T. (2017). Changes with age in subjective well-being through the adolescent years: Differences by gender. *Journal of Happiness Studies, 18*(1), 63–88.

González-Ortega, E., & Orgaz-Baz, B. (2013). Minors' exposure to online pornography: Prevalence, motivations, contents and effects. *Anales De Psicología, 29*(2), 319–327.

Goodman, C., & Silverstein, M. (2006). Grandmothers raising grandchildren: Ethnic and racial differences in well-being among custodial and coparenting families. *Journal of Family Issues, 27,* 1605–1626.

Goodman, G. S. (2005). Wailing babies in her wake. *American Psychologist, 60*(8), 872–881.

Goodman, G. S., Hirschman, J. E., Hepps, D., & Rudy, L. (1991, January). Children's memory for stressful events. *Merrill-Palmer Quarterly, 37*(1), 109–157.

Goodman, G. S., & Melinder, A. (2007). Child witness research and forensic interviews of young children: A review. *Legal and Criminological Psychology, 12*(1), 1–19.

Goodman, G. S., Jones, O., & McLeod, C. (2017). Is there consensus about children's memory and suggestibility? *Journal of Interpersonal Violence, 32*(6), 926.

Goodman, M. R., & Rao, S. P. (2007). Grandparents raising grandchildren in a US–Mexico border community. *Qualitative Health Research, 17*(8), 1117–1136.

Goodman, M. R., Stormshak, E., & Dishion, T. (2001). The significance of peer victimization at two points in development. *Applied Developmental Psychology, 22,* 507–526.

Goodwin, M. H. (2002). Exclusion in girls' peer groups: Ethnographic analysis of language practices on the playground. *Human Development, 45*(6), 392–415.

Goodwin, M. H. (2006). *The hidden life of girls: Games of stance, status, and exclusion.* Oxford, England: Blackwell Publishing.

Goodwin, M. H. (2011). Engendering children's play: Person reference in children's conflictual interaction. In S. A. Speer & E. Stokoe (Eds.), *Conversation and gender* (pp. 250–271). New York: Cambridge University Press.

Goodwin, M. H. (2015). A care-full look at language, gender and embodied intimacy. In A. Jule (Ed.), *Shifting visions: Gender and discourses* (pp. 27–48). Cambridge Scholars Pub.

Gopnik, A. (2012). Scientific thinking in young children: Theoretical advances, empirical research, and policy implications. *Science, 337*(6102), 1623–1627.

Gopnik, A., & Meltzoff, A. N. (1997). *Words, thoughts, and theories.* Cambridge, MA: The MIT Press.

Gopnik, A., & Rosati, A. (2001). Duck or rabbit? Reversing ambiguous figures and understanding ambiguous representations, *Developmental Science, 4,* 175–183.

Gopnik, A., Wellman, H. M., Gelman, S. A., & Meltzoff, A. N. (2010). A computational foundation for cognitive development: Comment on Griffths et al. and McLelland et al. *Trends in Cognitive Sciences, 14,* 342–343.

Gordon, P. (2004, October 15). Numerical cognition without words: Evidence from Amazonia. *Science, 306,* 496–499.

Gordon, R. A., Savage, C., Lahey, B. B., Goodman, S. H., Jensen, P. S., Rubio-Stipic, M., et al. (2003). Family and neighborhood income: Additive and multiplicative associations with youths' well-being. *Social Science Research, 32,* 191–219.

Goswami, U. (Ed.). (2002). *Blackwell handbook of childhood cognitive development.* Oxford, England: Blackwell Publishing.

Goswami, U. (2008). *Cognitive development: The learning brain.* Hove, England: Psychology Press.

Gottlieb, A. (2000). Luring your child into this life: A Beng path for infant care. In J. S. DeLoache & A. Gottlieb (Eds.), *A world of babies: Imagined childcare guides for seven societies* (55–88). Cambridge, England: Cambridge University Press.

Gottlieb, A. (2005). *The afterlife is where we come from: The culture of infancy in West Africa.* Chicago, IL: University of Chicago Press.

Gotz, M., Lemish, D., Aidman, A., & Moon, H. (2005). *Media and the make-believe worlds of children.* Mahwah, NJ: Lawrence Erlbaum Associates.

Gould, S. J. (1980). *The panda's thumb: More reflections in natural history.* New York: Norton.

Graber, J. A. (2004). Internalizing problems during adolescence. In R. M. Lerner & L. Steinberg (Eds.), *Handbook of adolescent psychology* (2nd ed.). Hoboken, NJ: John Wiley & Sons.

Graber, J. A., Nichols, T. R., & Brooks-Gunn, J. (2010). Putting pubertal timing in developmental context: Implications for prevention. *Developmental Psychobiology, 52,* 254–262.

Grail, T. S. (2009). http://www.census.gov/prod/2009pubs/p60-237.pdf, Washington, DC: U.S. Department of Commerce, Census Bureau.

Gratier, M., Greenfield, P. M., & Isaac, A. (2009). Tacit communicative style and cultural attunement in classroom interaction. *Mind, Culture, and Activity, 16,* 296–316.

Gray, S. A. O., Sweeney, K. K., Randazzo, R., & Levitt, H. M. (2016). "Am I doing the right thing?" Pathways to parenting a gender variant child. *Family Process, 55*(1), 123–138.

Greenberg, M. T., & Harris, A. R. (2012). Nurturing mindfulness in children and youth: Current state of research. *Child Development Perspectives, 6*(2), 161–166.

Greenfield, P. M., Brazelton, T. B., & Childs, C. P. (1989). From birth to maturity in Zinacantan: Ontogenesis in cultural context. In V. Bricker & G. Gossen (Eds.), *Ethnographic encounters in southern Mesoamerica: Celebratory essays in honor of Evon Z. Vogt.* Albany: Institute of Mesoamerican Studies, State University of New York.

Greenfield, P. M., Keller, H., Fuligni, A., & Maynard, A. (2003). Cultural pathways through universal development. *Annual Review of Psychology, 54,* 461–490.

Greenfield, P. M., & Lyn, H. (2007). Symbol combination in Pan: Language, action, and culture. In D. A. Washburn (Ed.), *Primate perspectives on behavior and cognition* (pp. 255–267). Washington, DC: American Psychological Association.

Greenfield, P. M., Suzuki, L., & Rothstein-Fisch, C. (2006). Cultural pathways through human development. In K. Renninger, I. Sigel, W. Damon, & R. Lerner (Eds.), *Handbook of child psychology: Vol. 4. Child psychology in practice* (6th ed.). Hoboken, NJ: Wiley.

Gregor, J. A., & McPherson, D. A. (1966). Racial preference and ego identity among White and Bantu children in the Republic of South Africa. *Genetic Psychology Monographs, 73,* 218–253.

Griffey, J. A. F., & Little, A. C. (2014). Infant's visual preferences for facial traits associated with adult attractiveness judgements: Data from eye-tracking. *Infant Behavior & Development, 37*(3), 268–275.

Grigorenko, E. L., Geissler, P., Wenzel, P. R., Okatcha, F., Nokes, C., Kenny, D. A., et al. (2001). The organization of Luo conceptions of intelligence: A study of implicit theories in a Kenyan village. *International Journal of Behavioral Development, 25,* 367–378.

Groeschel, S., Vollmer, B., King, M. D., & Connelly, A. (2010). Developmental changes in cerebral grey and white matter volume from infancy to adulthood. *International Journal of Developmental Neuroscience, 28,* 481–489.

Groesz, L. M., Levine, M. P., & Murnen, S. K. (2002). The effect of experimental presentation of thin media images on body satisfaction: A meta-analytic review. *International Journal of Eating Disorders, 31,* 1–16.

Gronlund, N. E. (1959). *Sociometry in the classroom.* New York: Harper Brothers.

Grossmann, K., Grossmann, K. E., Kindler, H., & Zimmermann, P. (2008). A wider view of attachment and exploration: The influence of mothers and fathers on the development of psychological security from infancy to young adulthood. In K. Grossmann, K. E. Grossmann, H. Kindler, & P. Zimmermann (Eds.), *Handbook of attachment: Theory, research, and clinical applications* (2nd ed., pp. 857–879). New York: Guilford Press.

Grotevant, H. D. (1998). Adolescent development in family contexts. In W. Damon & N. Eisenberg (Eds.), *Handbook of child psychology: Vol. 3. Social, emotional, and personality development* (5th ed., pp. 1097–1150). New York: Wiley.

Grueneisen, S., & Tomasello, M. (2017). Children coordinate in a recurrent social dilemma by taking turns and along dominance asymmetries. *Developmental Psychology, 53*(2), 265–273.

Grundy, J. G., Anderson, J. A. E., & Bialystok, E. (2017). Neural correlates of cognitive processing in monolinguals and bilinguals. *Annals of the New York Academy of Sciences, 1396*(1), 183–201.

Gunter, B., Oates, C., & Blades, M. (2005). *Advertising to children on TV: Content, impact and regulation.* Mahwah, NJ: Lawrence Erlbaum Associates.

Gupta, S., Tinker, B., & Hume, T. (2016). *"Our mouths were ajar": Doctor's fight to expose Flint's water crisis.* Retrieved from http://www.cnn.com/2016/01/21/health/flint-water-mona-hanna-attish/index.html

Guralnick, M. J. (2005). Early intervention for children with intellectual disabilities: Current knowledge and future prospects. *Journal of Applied Research in Intellectual Disabilities, 18*(4), 313–324.

Guttmacher Institute. (2006). *Abortion in women's lives.* Retrieved April 25, 2007. Retrieved from http://www.guttmacher.org/pubs/2006/05/04/AiWL.pdf

Habibi, A., Sarkissian, A. D., Gomez, M., & Ilari, B. (2015). Developmental brain research with participants from underprivileged communities: Strategies for recruitment, participation, and retention. *Mind, Brain, and Education, 9*(3), 179–186.

Hadiwijaya, H., Klimstra, T., Vermunt, J., Branje, S., & Meeus, W. (2017). On the development of harmony, turbulence, and independence in parent–adolescent relationships: A five-wave longitudinal study. *Journal of Youth and Adolescence, 46*(8), 1772–1788.

Hadley, W., Barker, D. H., Brown, L. K., Almy, B., Donenberg, G., DiClemente, R. J., et al. (2015). The moderating role of parental psychopathology on response to a family-based HIV prevention intervention among youth in psychiatric treatment. *Journal of Family Studies, 21*(2), 178–194.

Hagenauer, M., Perryman, J., Lee, T., & Carskadon, M. (2009). Adolescent changes in homeostatic and circadian regulation of sleep. *Developmental Neuroscience, 31,* 276–284.

Haith, M. M. (1980). *Rules that babies look by: The organization of newborn visual activity.* Mahwah, NJ: Lawrence Erlbaum Associates.

Hakkarainen, P. (2004). Narrative learning in the fifth dimension. *Outlines: Critical Social Studies, 6,* 5–20.

Halberstadt, A., Denham, S., & Dunsmore, J. (2001). Affective social competence. *Social Development, 10,* 79–119.

Halim, M. L. D., Ruble, D. N., Tamis-LeMonda, C. S., Shrout, P. E., & Amodio, D. M. (2017). Gender attitudes in early childhood: Behavioral consequences and cognitive antecedents. *Child Development, 88*(3), 882–899.

Hall, G. S. (1904). *Adolescence.* New York: Appleton.

Hallett, D., Chandler, M. J., & Krettenauer, T. (2002). Disentangling the course of epistemic development: Parsing knowledge by epistemic content. *New Ideas in Psychology. Special Issue: Folk epistemology, 20,* 285–307.

Han, W., Miller, D. P., & Waldfogel, J. (2010). Parental work schedules and adolescent risky behaviors. *Developmental Psychology, 46*(5), 1245–1267.

Hanawalt, B., & Kobialka, M. (Eds.). (2000). *Medieval practices of space.* Minneapolis, MN: University of Minnesota Press.

Hao, M., Liu, Y., Shu, H., Xing, A., Jiang, Y., & Li, P. (2015). Developmental changes in the early child lexicon in Mandarin Chinese. *Journal of Child Language, 42*(3), 505–537.

Hardelid, P., Cortina-Borja, M., Munro, A., Jones, H., Cleary, M., Champion, M. P., et al. (2008). The birth prevalence of PKU in populations of European, South Asian and Sub-Saharan African ancestry living in southeast England. *Annals of Human Genetics, 72*(1), 65–71.

Hardy, S., Walker, L., Olsen, J., Woodbury, R., & Hickman, J. (2014). Moral identity as moral ideal self: Links to adolescent outcomes. *Developmental Psychology, 50*(1), 45–57.

Harkness, S. (2015). The strange situation of attachment research: A review of three books. *Reviews in Anthropology, 44*(3), 178–197.

Harkness, S., & Super, C. M. (1996). *Parents' cultural belief systems: Their origins, expressions, and consequences.* New York: Guilford Press.

Harlow, H. F. (1959). Love in infant monkeys. *Scientific American, 200*(6), 68–74.

Harlow, H. F., & Harlow, M. K. (1962). Social deprivation in monkeys. *Scientific American, 207*(5), 136–146.

Harlow, H. F., & Harlow, M. K. (1969). Effects of various mother-infant relationships on rhesus monkey behaviors. In B. M. Foss (Ed.), *Determinants of infant behavior: Vol. 4* (4th ed.). London: Methuen.

Harrington, M. (1963). *The other America: Poverty in the United States.* New York: Touchstone.

Harris, B. S., Bishop, K. C., Kemeny, H. R., Walker, J. S., Rhee, E., & Kuller, J. A. (2017). Risk factors for birth defects. *Obstetrical & Gynecological Survey, 72*(2), 123–135.

Harris, M. A., Gruenenfelder-Steiger, A. E., Ferrer, E., Donnellan, M. B., Allemand, M., Fend, H., et al. (2015). Do parents foster self-esteem? Testing the prospective impact of parent closeness on adolescent self-esteem. *Child Development, 86*(4), 995–1013.

Harrison, D., Beggs, S., & Stevens, B. (2012). Sucrose for procedural pain management in infants. *Pediatrics, 130*(5), 918–925.

Harrison, K., Bost, K., McBride, B., & Donovan, S. (2011). Toward a developmental conceptualization of contributors to overweight and obesity in childhood: The six-Cs model. *Child Development Perspectives, 5,* 50–58.

Harrist, A. W., Swindle, T. M., Hubbs-Tait, L., Topham, G. L., Shriver, L. H., & Page, M. C. (2016). The social and emotional lives of overweight, obese, and severely obese children. *Child Development, 87*(5), 1564–1580.

Hart, C., Young, C., Nelson, D., Jin, S., Bazarskaya, N., Nelson, L., et al. (1999). Peer contact patterns, parenting practices, and preschoolers' social competence in China, Russia, and the United States. In P. Slee & K. Rigby (Eds.), *Children's peer relationships* (pp. 3–30). London: Routledge.

Harter, S. (1999). *The construction of the self: A developmental perspective.* New York: Guilford Press.

Harter, S. (2015). *The construction of the self: Developmental and sociocultural foundations* (2nd ed.). New York: Guilford Press.

Hartley, C. A., & Lee, F. S. (2015). Sensitive periods in affective development: Nonlinear maturation of fear learning. *Neuropsychopharmacology: Official Publication of the American College of Neuropsychopharmacology, 40*(1), 50–60.

Hartman, S., & Belsky, J. (2016). An evolutionary perspective on family studies: Differential susceptibility to environmental influences. *Family Process, 55*(4), 700–712.

Hartup, W. W. (1998). The company they keep: Friendships and their developmental significance. In A. Campbell & S. Muncer (Eds.), *The social child* (pp. 143–163). Hove, UK: Psychology Press/Erlbaum.

Hauck, F. R., Herman, S. M., Donovan, M., Iysau, S., Moore, C. M., Donoghue, E., et al. (2003). Sleep environment and the risk of sudden infant death syndrome in an urban population: The Chicago Infant Mortality Study. *Pediatrics, 111,* 1207–1214.

Hausenblas, H. A., Janelle, C. M., Gardner, R. E., & Focht, B. C. (2004). Viewing physique slides: Affective responses of women at high and low drive for thinness. *Journal of Social and Clinical Psychology, 23,* 45–60.

Hawk, S., Keijsers, L., Hale, W. W., & Meeus, W. H. J. (2009). Mind your own business! Longitudinal relations between perceived privacy invasion and adolescent-parent conflict. *Journal of Family Psychology, 23,* 511–520.

Hawkins, A. J., Lovejoy, K. R., Holmes, E. K., Blanchard, V. L., & Fawcett, E. (2008). Increasing fathers' involvement in child care with a couple-focused intervention.

Hay, D. F. (2017). The early development of human aggression. *Child Development Perspectives, 11*(2), 102–106.

Haydicky, J., Wiener, J., & Shecter, C. (2017). Mechanisms of action in concurrent parent–child mindfulness training: A qualitative exploration. *Mindfulness, 8*(4), 1018–1035.

Haydon, A. A., Cheng, M. M., Herring, A. H., McRee, A., & Halpern, C. T. (2014). Prevalence and predictors of sexual inexperience in adulthood. *Archives of Sexual Behavior, 43*(2), 221–230.

Haywood, K. M., & Getchell, N. (2005). *Life span motor development* (4th ed.). Champaign, IL: Human Kinetics.

He, M., Walle, E. A., & Campos, J. J. (2015). A cross-national investigation of the relationship between infant walking and language development. *Infancy, 20*(3), 283–305.

Head Start. (2015). *Head Start timeline.* Retrieved from https://eclkc.ohs.acf.hhs.gov/about/ohs/history/timeline

Heath, S. B. (1983). *Ways with words: Language, life, and work in communities and classrooms.* Cambridge, England: Cambridge University Press.

Heckman, J. J., Moon, S. H., Pinto, R., Savelyev, P., & Yavitz, A. (2010). New cost-benefit and rate of return analysis for the Perry Preschool Program: A summary. In J. J. Heckman, S. H. Moon, P. S. Rodrigo Pinto, & A. Yavitz (Eds.), *Childhood programs and practices in the first decade of life: A human capital integration* (pp. 366–380). New York: Cambridge University Press.

Heifetz, S. A. (1996). The umbilical cord: Obstetrically important lesions. *Clinical Obstetric Gynecology, 39,* 571–587.

Heikkinen, N., Niskanen, E., Könönen, M., Tolmunen, T., Kekkonen, V., Kivimäki, P., et al. (2017). Alcohol consumption during adolescence is associated with reduced grey matter volumes. *Addiction, 112*(4), 604–613.

Held, V. (2014). The ethics of care as normative guidance: Comment on Gilligan. *Journal of Social Philosophy, 45*(1), 107–115.

Helland, T., Asbjornsen, A. E., Hushovd, E., & Hugdahl, K. (2008). Dichotic listening and school performance in dyslexia. *Dyslexia: An International Journal of Research and Practice, 14,* 42–53.

Helwig, C. C., Yang, S., Tan, D., Liu, C., & Shao, T. (2011). Urban and rural Chinese adolescents' judgments and reasoning about personal and group jurisdiction. *Child Development, 82,* 701–716.

Hendrickson, J. E., & Delaney, M. (2016). Hemolytic disease of the fetus and newborn: Modern practice and future investigations. *Transfusion Medicine Reviews, 30*(4), 159–164.

Hennessy, E., Oh, A., Agurs-Collins, T., Chriqui, J. F., Mâsse, L. C., Moser, R. P., & Perna, F. (2014). State-level school competitive food and beverage laws are associated with children's weight status. *Journal of School Health, 84*(9), 609–616.

Henrich, J. (2004). Demography and cultural evolution: Why adaptive cultural processes produced maladaptive losses in Tasmania. *American Antiquity, 69,* 197–218.

Henrich, J., & Henrich, N. (2006). Culture, evolution and the puzzle of human cooperation. *Cognitive Systems Research. Special Issue: Cognition, Joint Action and Collective Intentionality, 7*(2–3), 220–245.

Henry, M. K. (2017). Morphemes matter: A framework for instruction. *Perspectives on Language and Literacy, 43*(2), 23.

Hensel, D. J., Fortenberry, J. D., O'Sullivan, L. F., & Orr, D. P. (2011). The developmental association of sexual self-concept with sexual behavior among adolescent women. *Journal of Adolescence, 34*(4), 675–684.

Hepper, P. (2015). Behavior during the prenatal period: Adaptive for development and survival. *Child Development Perspectives, 9*(1), 38–43.

Hepper, P. G., Wells, D. L., Dornan, J. C., & Lynch, C. (2013). Long-term flavor recognition in humans with prenatal garlic experience. *Developmental Psychobiology, 55*(5), 568–574.

Herbenick, D., Reece, M., Schick, V., & Sanders, S. (2010). Sexual behavior in the United States: Results from a national probability sample of men and women ages 14–94. *Journal of Sexual Medicine, 7,* 255–265.

Herlihy, A., & McLachlan, R. (2015). Screening for Klinefelter syndrome. *Current Opinion in Endocrinology Diabetes and Obesity, 22*(3), 224–229.

Herman-Giddens, M. E. (2006). Recent data on pubertal milestones in United States children: The secular trend toward earlier development. *International Journal of Andrology, 29*(1), 241–246.

Herman-Giddens, M. E. (2007). The decline in the age of menarche in the United States: Should we be concerned? *Journal of Adolescent Health, 40,* 201–203.

Herman-Giddens, M. E., Steffes, J., Harris, D., Slora, E., Hussey, M., Dowshen, S. A., et al. (2012). Secondary sexual characteristics in boys: Data from the pediatric research in office settings network. *Pediatrics, 130*(5), e1058–e1068.

Hernandez, L. M., Rudie, J. D., Green, S. A., Bookheimer, S., & Dapretto, M. (2015). Neural signatures of autism spectrum disorders: Insights into brain network dynamics. *Neuropsychopharmacology, 40*(1), 171–189.

Herrnstein, R. J., & Murray, C. (1994). *The bell curve: Intelligence and class structure in American life.* New York: Free Press.

Herting, M. M., Gautam, P., Spielberg, J. M., Kan, E., Dahl, R. E., & Sowell, E. R. (2014). The role of testosterone and estradiol in brain volume changes across adolescence: A longitudinal structural MRI study. *Human Brain Mapping, 35*(11), 5633–5645.

Herzog, D. B., Dorer, D. J., Keel, P. K., Selwyn, S. E., Ekeblad, E. R., Flores, A. T., et al. (1999). Recovery and relapse in anorexia and bulimia nervosa: A 7.5-year follow-up study. *Journal of the American Academy of Child & Adolescent Psychiatry, 38,* 829–837.

Hespos, S. J., & Baillargeon, R. C. (2008). Young infants' actions reveal their developing knowledge of support variables: Converging evidence for violation-of-expectation findings. *Cognition, 107,* 304–316.

Hespos, S. J., Ferry, A. L., Anderson, E. M., Hollenbeck, E. N., & Rips, L. J. (2016). Five-month-old infants have general knowledge of how nonsolid substances behave and interact. *Psychological Science, 27*(2), 244–256.

Hetherington, E. M. (2006). The influence of conflict, marital problem solving and parenting on children's adjustment in nondivorced, divorced and remarried families. In A. Clarke-Stewart & J. Dunn (Eds.), *Families count: Effects on child and adolescent development. The Jacobs Foundation series on adolescence* (pp. 203–237). New York: Cambridge University Press.

Hetherington, E. M., Collins, W. A., & Laursen, E. (1999). Social capital and the development of youth from nondivorced, divorced and remarried families. In W. A. Collins (Ed.), *Relationships as developmental contexts* (pp. 177–209). Mahwah, NJ: Lawrence Erlbaum Associates.

Hewlett, B., & Roulette, C. (2016). Teaching in hunter-gatherer infancy. *Royal Society Open Science, 3*(1), 150403.

Hewlett, B. S., Fouts, H. N., Boyette, A. H., & Hewlett, B. L. (2011). Social learning among Congo Basin hunter-gatherers. *Philosophical Transactions: Biological Sciences, 366*(1567), 1168–1178.

Hewlett, B. S., Lamb, M. E., Shannon, D., Leyendecker, B., & Schölmerich, A. (1998). "Culture and early infancy among central African foragers and farmers": Correction to Hewlett et al. (1998). *Developmental Psychology, 34,* 891.

Heyer, D. B., & Meredith, R. M. (2017). Environmental toxicology: Sensitive periods of development and neurodevelopmental disorders. *Neurotoxicology, 58,* 23–41.

Heyer, E., Brazier, L., Ségurel, L., Hegay, T., Austerlitz, F., Quintana-Murci, L., et al. (2011). Lactase persistence in Central Asia: Phenotype, genotype, and evolution. *Human Biology, 83*(3), 379–392.

Heyn, H., Moran, S., Hernando-Herraez, I., Sayols, S., Gomez, A., Sandoval, J., et al. (2013). DNA methylation contributes to natural human variation. *Genome Research, 23*(9), 1363.

Heywood, C. (2001). *A history of childhood: Children and childhood from medieval to modern times.* Malden, MA: Polity Press.

Hickling, A. K., & Wellman, H. M. (2001). The emergence of children's causal explanations and theories: Evidence from everyday conversation. *Developmental Psychology, 37*(5), 668–683.

Hillairet de Boisferon, A., Tift, A. H., Minar, N. J., & Lewkowicz, D. J. (2017). Selective attention to a talker's mouth in infancy: Role of audiovisual temporal synchrony and linguistic experience. *Developmental Science, 20*(3).

Hilliard, L. J., & Liben, L. S. (2010). Differing levels of gender salience in preschool classrooms: Effects on children's gender attitudes and intergroup bias. *Child Development, 81,* 1787–1798.

Hindman, H. D. (2002). *Child labor: An American history.* Armonk, NY: Sharpe.

Hindmarsh, P. C., Geary, M. P., Rodeck, C. H., Kingdom, J. C., & Cole, T. J. (2008). Factors predicting ante- and postnatal growth. *Pediatric Research, 63*(1), 99–102.

Hirsh-Pasek, K., Zosh, J. M., Golinkoff, R. M., Gray, J. H., Robb, M. B., & Kaufman, J. (2015). Putting education in "educational" apps: Lessons from the science of learning. *Psychological Science in the Public Interest, 16*(1), 3–34.

Hirza, B., Kusumah, Y. S., Darhim, D., & Zulkardi, Z. (2014). Improving intuition skills with realistic mathematics education. *Journal on Mathematics Education, 5*(1), 27–34.

Hitlin, S., & Elder, G. H. (2007). Time, self, and the curiously abstract concept of agency. *Sociological Theory, 25*(2), 170–191.

Hofer, B. (2008). Personal epistemology and culture. In M. Khine (Ed.), *Knowing, knowledge and beliefs: Epistemological studies across diverse culture* (pp. 3–22). New York: Springer Science 1 Business Media.

Hoff-Ginsberg, E., & Tardiff, T. (1995). Socioeconomic status and parenting. In M. H. Bornstein (Ed.), *Handbook of parenting: Biology and ecology of parenting: Vol. 2* (pp. 161–188). Mahwah, NJ: Lawrence Erlbaum Associates.

Hoffman, M. L. (2002). How automatic and representational is empathy, and why. *Behavioral and Brain Sciences, 25*(1), 38–39.

Holcroft, C. J., Blakemore, K. J., Allen, M. A., & Graham, E. M. (2003). Prematurity and neonatal infection are most predictive of neurologic morbidity in very low birthweight infants. *Obstetrics & Gynecology, 101,* 1249–1254.

Holden, G. W. (2002). Perspectives on the effects of corporal punishment: Comment on Gershoff (2002). *Psychological Bulletin, 128,* 590–595.

Holm-Denoma, J. M., Lewinsohn, P. M., Gau, J. M., Joiner, T. E., Jr., Striegel-Moore, R., & Otamendi, A. (2005, November). Parents' reports of the body shape and feeding habits of 36-month-old children: An investigation of gender differences. *International Journal of Eating Disorders, 38*(3), 228–235.

Holowka, S., & Petitto, L. A. (2002). Left hemisphere cerebral specialization for babies while babbling. *Science, 297*(5586).

Holsti, L., Grunau, R. V. E., & Whitfield, M. F. (2002). Developmental coordination disorder in extremely low birth weight children at nine years. *Journal of Developmental and Behavioral Pediatrics, 23,* 9–15.

Holt, L. (2014). Attitudes about help-seeking mediate the relation between parent attachment and academic adjustment in first-year college students. *Journal of College Student Development, 55*(4), 418–423.

Holvoet, C., Scola, C., Arciszewski, T., & Picard, D. (2016). Infants' preference for prosocial behaviors: A literature review. *Infant Behavior & Development, 45,* 125–139.

Homae, F. (2014). A brain of two halves: Insights into interhemispheric organization provided by near-infrared spectroscopy. *Neuroimage, 85*(Pt. 1), 354–362.

Honwana, A. (2000). Children of war: Understanding war and war cleansing in Mozambique and Angola. Retrieved April 25, 2006, from http://cas.uchicago.edu/workshops/African/papers/honwana.htm

Hood, M. (1914). *For girls and the mothers of girls: A book for the home and the school concerning the beginnings of life.* Indianapolis: The Bobbs-Merrill Company Publishers.

Hoogenhout, M., & Malcolm-Smith, S. (2017). Theory of mind predicts severity level in autism. *Autism, 21*(2), 242–252.

Hopkins, B., & Westen, T. (1988). Maternal handling and motor development: An intracultural study. *Genetic Psychology Monographs, 14,* 377–420.

Hopkins, D., Steer, C., Northstone, K., & Emmett, P. (2015). Effects on childhood body habitus of feeding large volumes of cow or formula milk compared with breastfeeding in the latter part of infancy. *American Journal of Clinical Nutrition, 102*(5), 1096–1103.

Horne, S., & Zimmer-Gembeck, M. J. (2006). The female sexual subjectivity inventory: Development and validation of a multidimensional inventory for late adolescents and emerging adults. *Psychology of Women Quarterly, 30*(2), 125–138.

Horowitz, A. D., & Spicer, L. (2013). "Having sex" as a graded and hierarchical construct: A comparison of sexual definitions among heterosexual and lesbian emerging adults in the U.K. *Journal of Sex Research, 50*(2), 139.

Hoshower, L. M., Buikstra, J. E., Goldstein, P. S., & Webster, A. D. (1995). Artificial cranial deformation at the Omo M10 site: A Tiwanaku complex from the Moquegua Valley, Peru. *Latin American Antiquity, 6,* 145–164.

Hoven, C. W., Duarte, C. S., Wu, P., Erickson, E. A., Musa, G. J., & Mandell, D. J. (2004, October). Exposure to trauma and separation anxiety in children after the WTC attack. *Applied Developmental Science, 8*(4), 172–183.

Howell, S. (1984). Equality and hierarchy in Chewong classification. *Journal of the Anthropological Society of Oxford, 15*(1), 30–44.

Hoyt, A. T., Canfield, M. A., Romitti, P. A., Botto, L. D., Anderka, M. T., Krikov, S. V., et al. (2016). Associations between maternal periconceptional exposure to secondhand tobacco smoke and major birth defects. *American Journal of Obstetrics and Gynecology, 215*(5), 613–613.e11.

Hrdy, S. (2009). *Mothers and others: The evolutionary origins of mutual understanding.* Cambridge, MA: Harvard University Press.

Hrdy, S. (2016). Variable postpartum responsiveness among humans and other primates with "cooperative breeding": A comparative and evolutionary perspective. *Hormones and Behavior, 77,* 272–283.

Hsu, H., & Jeng, S. (2008). Two-month-olds' attention and affective response to maternal still face: A comparison between term and preterm infants in Taiwan. *Infant Behavior & Development, 31*(2), 194–206.

Hu, Y., Xu, Y., & Tornello, S. L. (2016). Stability of self-reported same-sex and both-sex attraction from adolescence to young adulthood. *Archives of Sexual Behavior, 45*(3), 651–659.

Huang, C., Cheah, C. S. L., Lamb, M. E., & Zhou, N. (2017). Associations between parenting styles and perceived child effortful control within Chinese families in the United States, the United Kingdom, and Taiwan. *Journal of Cross-Cultural Psychology, 48*(6), 795–812.

Huang-Pollack, C. L., Carr, T. H., & Nigg, J. T. (2002). Development of selective attention: Perceptual load influences early versus late attentional selection in children and adults. *Developmental Psychology, 38,* 363–375.

Hubel, D., & Wiesel, T. (2004). *Brain and visual perception: The story of a 25-year collaboration.* New York: Oxford University Press.

Hudson, A., & Jacques, S. (2014). Put on a happy face! Inhibitory control and socioemotional knowledge predict emotion regulation in 5- to 7-year-olds. *Journal of Experimental Child Psychology, 123,* 36–52.

Huelsken, C., Sodian, B., & Pickel, G. (2001). Distinguishing between appearance and reality in a dressing-up game—a problem of dual coding or preserving identity? *Zeitschrift für Entwicklungspsychologie und Paedagogische Psychologie, 33*(3), 129–137.

Hughes, C., Jafee, S., Happe, F., Taylor, A., Caspi, A., & Moffitt, T. (2005). Origins of individuals differences in theory of mind: From nature to nurture. *Child Development, 76*(2), 356–370.

Hughes, D., Rodriguez, J., Smith, E., Johnson, D. J., Stevenson, H. C., & Spicer, P. (2006, September). Parents' ethnic-racial socialization practices: A review of research and directions for future study. *Developmental Psychology, 42,* 747–770.

Hughes, E. K., Gullone, E., & Watson, S. D. (2011). Emotional functioning in children and adolescents with elevated depressive symptoms. *Journal of Psychopathology and Behavioral Assessment, 33,* 335–345.

Hughes, H., Graham-Bermann, S., & Gruber, G. (2001). Resilience in children exposed to domestic violence. In S. Graham-Bermann & J. Edleson (Eds.), *Domestic violence in the lives of children: The future of research, intervention and social policy.* Washington, DC: American Psychological Association.

Hullegie, S., Bruijning-Verhagen, P., Uiterwaal, C. S., van der Ent, C. K., Smit, H. A., & de Hoog, M. L. (2016). First-year daycare and incidence of acute gastroenteritis. *Pediatrics, 137*(5), 1.

Humphreys, K. L., Nelson, C. A., Fox, N. A., & Zeanah, C. H. (2017). Signs of reactive attachment disorder and disinhibited social engagement disorder at age 12 years: Effects of institutional care history and high-quality foster care. *Development and Psychopathology, 29*(2), 675.

Hurd, Y. L., Wang, X., Anderson, V., Beck, O., Minkoff, H., & Dow-Edwards, D. (2005). Marijuana impairs growth in mid-gestation fetuses. *Neurotoxicology and Teratology, 27,* 221–229.

Hurt, H., Betancourt, L. M., Malmud, E. K., Shera, D. M., Giannetta, J. M., Brodsky, N. L., et al. (2009). Children with and without gestational cocaine exposure: A neurocognitive systems analysis. *Neurotoxicology and Teratology, 31,* 334–341.

Hutchison, L., Feder, M., Abar, B., & Winsler, A. (2016). Relations between parenting stress, parenting style, and child executive functioning for children with ADHD or autism. *Journal of Child and Family Studies, 25*(12), 3644–3656.

Huttenlocher, P. R. (1994). Synaptogenesis in human cerebral cortex. In G. Dawson & K. W. Fischer (Eds.), *Human behavior and the developing brain.* New York: Guilford Press.

Hutto, D. D. (2008, April). *Folk psychological narratives: The sociocultural basis of understanding reasons.* Cambridge, MA: The MIT Press.

Huynh, D. T. T., Estorninos, E., Capeding, R. Z., Oliver, J. S., Low, Y. L., & Rosales, F. J. (2015). Longitudinal growth and health outcomes in nutritionally at-risk children who received long-term nutritional intervention. *Journal of Human Nutrition and Dietetics, 28*(6), 623–635.

Icenogle, G., Steinberg, L., Olino, T. M., Shulman, E. P., Chein, J., Alampay, L. P., et al. (2017). Puberty predicts approach but not avoidance on the Iowa gambling task in a multinational sample. *Child Development, 88*(5), 1598–1614.

Impett, E. A., & Tolman, D. L. (2006). Late adolescent girls' sexual experiences and sexual satisfaction. *Journal of Adolescent Research, 21*(6), 628–646.

Inagaki, K., & Hatano, G. (2002). *Young children's naive thinking about the biological world.* New York: Psychology Press.

Inagaki, K., & Hatano, G. (2004). Vitalistic causality in young children's naive biology. *Trends in Cognitive Sciences, 8*(8), 356–362.

Inagaki, K., & Hatano, G. (2006). Young children's conception of the biological world. *Current Directions in Psychological Science, 15,* 177–181.

Inhelder, B., & Piaget, J. (1958). *The growth of logical thinking from childhood to adolescence.* New York: Basic Books.

Inoa, R. (2017). Parental involvement among middle-income Latino parents living in a middle-class community. *Hispanic Journal of Behavioral Sciences, 39*(3), 316–335.

Inomata, S., Yoshida, T., Koura, U., Tamura, K., Hatasaki, K., Imamura, H., et al. (2015). Effect of preterm birth on growth and cardiovascular disease risk at school age. *Pediatrics International, 57*(6), 1126–1130.

Inoue-Nakamura, N. (2001). Mirror self-recognition in primates: An ontogenetic and a phylogenetic approach. In T. Matsuzawa (Ed.), *Primate origins of human cognition and behavior* (pp. 297–312). New York: Springer-Verlag.

Ishibashi, M., & Moriguchi, Y. (2017). Understanding why children commit scale errors: Scale error and its relation to action planning and inhibitory control, and the concept of size. *Frontiers in Psychology, 8.*

ISPCAN. (2006). *World perspectives on child abuse* (7th ed.). Chicago, IL: National Society for the Prevention of Child Abuse and Neglect.

Itard, J. M. G. (1801/1982). *The wild boy of Aveyron.* New York: Appleton-Century-Crofts.

Ivey, P. (2000). Cooperative reproduction in Ituri Forest hunter-gatherers: Who cares for Efe infants? *Current Anthropology, 41,* 856–866.

Izard, C. E., Huebner, R. R., Risser, D., McGinnes, G. C., & Dougherty, L. M. (1980). The young infant's ability to produce discrete emotion expressions. *Developmental Psychology, 16,* 132–140.

Izard, C. E., Woodburn, E. M., & Finlon, K. J. (2010). Extending emotion science to the study of discrete emotions in infants. *Emotion Review, 2,* 134–136.

Izard, V., Streri, A., & Spelke, E. (2014). Toward exact number: Young children use one-to-one correspondence to measure set identity but not numerical equality. *Cognitive Psychology, 72,* 27–53.

Jablonka, E., Ginsburg, S., & Dor, D. (2012). The co-evolution of language and emotions. *Philosophical Transactions: Biological Sciences, 367*(1599), 2152–2159.

Jablonka, E., & Lamb, M. (2005). *Evolution in four dimensions.* Cambridge, MA: The MIT Press.

Jablonka, E., & Lamb, M. J. (2007). Precis of evolution in four dimensions. *Behavioral and Brain Sciences, 30,* 353–365.

Jablonka, E., & Lamb, M. J. (2015). The inheritance of acquired epigenetic variations. *International Journal of Epidemiology, 44*(4), 1094.

Jackson, J. P., Jr. (2006). The historical context of the African American social scientist. *Monographs of the Society for Research in Child Development, 71*(1), 218–223.

Jackson, J. S., McCullough, W. R., & Gurin, G. (1997). Family, socialization environment, and identity development in Black Americans. In H. P. McAdoo (Ed.), *Black families* (3rd ed., pp. 251–266). Thousand Oaks, CA: Sage.

Jackson, M. I. (2015). Early childhood WIC participation, cognitive development and academic achievement. *Social Science & Medicine, 126,* 145–153.

Jaffe, J., Beebe, B., Feldstein, S., Crown, C. L., & Jasnow, M. D. (2001). *Monographs of the Society for Research in Child Development, 66*(2), vii–131.

Jaffee, S., & Hyde, J. S. (2000). Gender differences in moral orientation: A meta-analysis. *Psychological Bulletin, 126*(5), 703–726.

Jaffee, S. R., Van Hulle, C., & Rodgers, J. L. (2011). Effects of nonmaternal care in the first 3 years on children's academic skills and behavioral functioning in childhood and early adolescence: A sibling comparison study. *Child Development, 82*(4), 1076–1091.

Jaganath, D., Khatry, S. K., Murray-Kolb, L. E., LeClerq, S. C., & Christian, P. (2015). The role of pre-primary classes on school-age cognition in rural Nepal. *Journal of Pediatrics, 166*(3), 717–722.

Jahoda, G. (1980). Theoretical and systematic approaches in cross-cultural psychology. In H. C. Triandis & W. W. Lambert (Eds.), *Handbook of crosscultural psychology: Vol. 1.* Boston: Allyn & Bacon.

James, D. (2010). Fetal learning: A critical review. *Infant and Child Development, 19,* 45–54.

James, D., Pillai, M., & Smoleniec, J. (1995). Neurobehavioral development in the human fetus. In J. P. Lecanuet & W. P. Fifer (Eds.), *Fetal development: A psychobiological perspective* (pp. 101–128). Mahwah, NJ: Lawrence Erlbaum Associates.

James, W. T. (1890). *The principles of psychology.* New York: Holt, Rinehart and Winston.

James, W. T. (1951). Social organization among dogs of different temperaments: Terriers and beagles reared together. *Journal of Comparative and Physiological Psychology, 44,* 71–77.

Janssen, P. (2009). Outcomes of planned home birth with registered midwife versus planned hospital birth with midwife or physician. *Canadian Medical Association Journal, 181*(6), 377.

Jarrett, R. (2000). Voices from below: The use of ethnographic research for informing public policy. In J. Mercier, S. Garasky, & M. Shelly (Eds.), *Redefining family policy: Implications for the 21st century.* Ames, IA: Iowa State University Press.

Jaruratanasirikul, S., & Sriplung, H. (2015). Secular trends of growth and pubertal maturation of school children in southern Thailand. *Annals of Human Biology, 42*(5), 447–454.

Jasinska, K. K., & Petitto, L. A. (2013). How age of bilingual exposure can change the neural systems for language in the developing brain: A functional near infrared spectroscopy investigation of syntactic processing in monolingual and bilingual children. *Developmental Cognitive Neuroscience, 6,* 87–101.

Jayaraman, S., Fausey, C. M., & Smith, L. B. (2015). The faces in infant-perspective scenes change over the first year of life. *PLOS ONE, 10*(5), e0123780.

Jenkins, H. (Ed.). (1998). *The children's culture reader.* New York: New York University Press.

Jenni, O., Deboer, T., & Achermann, P (2006). Development of the 24-h rest-activity pattern in human infants. *Infant Behavior & Development, 29,* 143–152.

Jennings, K. D., & Dietz, L. J. (2003). Mastery motivation and goal persistence in young children. In M. H. Bornstein, L. Davidson, C. L. Keyes, K. A. Moore, & the Center for Child Well Being (Eds.), *Well-being: Positive development across the life course. Crosscurrents in contemporary psychology* (pp. 295–309). Mahwah, NJ, Lawrence Erlbaum Associates.

Jensen, L. A. and Dost-Gözkan, A. (2015), Adolescent–parent relations in Asian Indian and Salvadoran immigrant families: A cultural–developmental analysis of autonomy, authority, conflict, and cohesion. *Journal of Research on Adolescence, 25,* 340–351.

Jessen, S., Altvater-Mackensen, N., & Grossmann, T. (2016). Pupillary responses reveal infants' discrimination of facial emotions independent of conscious perception. *Cognition, 150,* 163–169.

Jia, G., Chen, J., & Kim, H. (2008). Bilingual vocabulary development among infants and toddlers with Chinese or Korean as home languages. Unpublished manuscript.

Jiang, Y., Granja, M., & Koball, H. (2017). *Basic facts about low-income children: Children under 18 years, 2015.* Retrieved from http://www.nccp.org/publications/pub_1170.html

Jin, J., Shahbazi, S., Lloyd, J., Fels, S., de Ribaupierre, S., & Eagleson, R. (2014). Hybrid simulation of brain–skull growth. *Simulation, 90*(1), 3–10.

Jog, M. A., Yan, L., Kilroy, E., Krasileva, K., Jann, K., LeClair, H., et al. (2016). Developmental trajectories of cerebral blood flow and oxidative metabolism at baseline and during working memory tasks. *Neuroimage, 134,* 587–596.

Joh, A., & Spivey, L. (2012). Colorful success: Preschoolers' use of perceptual color cues to solve a spatial reasoning problem. *Journal of Experimental Child Psychology, 113*(4), 523–534.

Joh, A., Sweeney, B., & Rovee-Collier, C. (2002). Minimum duration of reactivation at 3 months of age. *Developmental Psychobiology, 40*(1), 23–32.

Johanson, M., & Papafragou, A. (2014). What does children's spatial language reveal about spatial concepts? Evidence from the use of containment expressions. *Cognitive Science, 38*(5), 881–910.

Johansson, M., Forssman, L., Bohlin, G., Humanistisk-samhällsvetenskapliga vetenskapsområdet, Samhällsvetenskapliga fakulteten, Uppsala universitet, & Institutionen för psykologi. (2014). Individual differences in 10-month-olds' performance on the A-not-B task. *Scandinavian Journal of Psychology, 55*(2), 130–135.

Johansson, M., Marciszko, C., Brocki, K., Bohlin, G., Humanistisk-samhällsvetenskapliga vetenskapsområdet, Samhällsvetenskapliga fakulteten, et al. (2016). Individual differences in early executive functions: A longitudinal study from 12 to 36 months. *Infant and Child Development, 25*(6), 533–549.

John, V. P. (1972). Styles of learning—styles of teaching: Reflections on the education of Navajo children. In C. Cazden, V. P. John, & D. Hymes (Eds.), *Functions of language in the classroom* (pp. 331–343). New York: Teachers College Press.

Johnson, M. K., Tasimi, A., & Wynn, K. (2017). Children's decision making: When self-interest and moral considerations conflict. *Journal of Experimental Child Psychology, 161,* 195.

Johnson, S. P., Amso, D., Frank, M., & Shuwairi, S. (2008). Perceptual development in infancy as the foundation of event perception. In S. P. Johnson, D. Amso, M. Frank, & S. Shuwairi (Eds.), *Understanding events: From perception to action* (pp. 65–95). Oxford University Press.

Johnson, S., & Wolke, D. (2013). Behavioural outcomes and psychopathology during adolescence. *Early Human Development, 89*(4), 199–207.

Jolly, A. (1999). *Lucy's legacy: Sex and intelligence in human evolution.* Cambridge, MA: Harvard University Press.

Jonas, S. (2013). *Guatemalan migration in times of civil war and post-war challenges.* Migration Policy Institute, Washington, DC. Retrieved from http://www.migrationpolicy.org/article/guatemalan-migration-times-civil-war-and-post-war-challenges

Jones, H. E. (2006). Drug addiction during pregnancy: Advances in maternal treatment and understanding child outcomes. *Current Directions in Psychological Science, 15*(3), 126–130.

Jones, H. E., Kaltenbach, K., Heil, S. H., Stine, S. M., Coyle, M. G., Arria, A. M., et al. (2010). Neonatal abstinence syndrome after methadone or buprenorphine exposure. *New England Journal of Medicine, 363*(24), 2320–2331.

Jordan, B. (1993). *Birth in four cultures: A cross-cultural investigation of childbirth in* Yucatan, Holland, Sweden, and the United States. Prospect Heights, IL: Waveland Press.

Jordan, K., & Brannon, E. (2006). The multisensory representation of number in infancy. *Proceedings of the National Academy of Sciences, 103,* 3486–3489.

Jordan, P., & Hernandez-Reif, M. (2009). Reexamination of young children's racial attitudes and skin tone preferences. *Journal of Black Psychology, 35*(3), 388–403.

Jordan-Young, R. (2010). *Brain storm.* Cambridge, MA: Harvard University Press.

Joseph, K. S., Liston, R. M., Dodds, L., Dahlgren, L., & Allen, A. C. (2007). Socioeconomic status and perinatal outcomes in a setting with universal access to essential health care services. *Canadian Medical Association Journal, 177,* 583–590.

Jozsa, K., Wang, J., Barrett, K. C., & Morgan, G. A. (2014). Age and cultural differences in self-perceptions of mastery motivation and competence in American, Chinese, and Hungarian school age children. *Child Development Research, 2014,* 1–16.

Julian, M. M. (2013). Age at adoption from institutional care as a window into the lasting effects of early experiences. *Clinical Child and Family Psychology Review, 16*(2), 101–145.

Jung, C. (1915). *The theory of psychoanalysis.* New York: Nervous and Mental Disease Publishing Company.

Justice, E., Lindsey, L., & Morrow, S. (1999). The relation of self-perceptions to achievement among African American preschoolers. *Journal of Black Psychology, 25,* 48–60.

Juston, A., Bickham, D., Lee, J., & Wright, J. (2007). From attention to comprehension: How children watch and learn from television. In N. Pecora, J. Murray, & E. Wartella (Eds.), Children and television: Fifty years of research. Mahwah, NJ: Lawrence Erlbaum Associates.

Jyoti, D. F., Frongillo, E. A., & Jones, S. J. (2005). Food insecurity affects school children's academic performance, weight gain, and social skills. *Journal of Nutrition, 135,* 2831–2839.

Kagan, J. (2001). Biological constraint, cultural variety, and psychological structures. In A. Harrington (Ed.), *Unity of knowledge: The convergence of natural and human science* (pp. 177–190). New York: New York Academy of Sciences.

Kagan, S., & Madsen, M. C. (1971). Cooperation and competition of Mexican, Mexican-American, and Anglo-American children of two ages under four instructional sets. *Developmental Psychology, 5,* 32–39.

Kagitçibasi, C. (2013). Adolescent autonomy-relatedness and the family in cultural context: What is optimal? *Journal of Research on Adolescence, 23*(2), 223–235.

Kalkwarf, H. J., Zemel, B. S., Gilsanz, V., Lappe, J. M., Horlick, M., Oberfield, S., et al. (2007). The Bone Mineral Density in Childhood Study: Bone mineral content and density according to age, sex, and race. *Journal of Clinical Endocrinology & Metabolism, 92,* 2087–2099.

Kamara, A. I., & Easley, J. A. (1977). Is the rate of cognitive development uniform across cultures? A methodological critique with new evidence from Themne children. In P. R. Dasen (Ed.), *Piagetian psychology: Cross-cultural contributions.* New York: Gardner.

Kandel, D. (1978). Homophily, selection, and socialization in adolescent friendships. *American Journal of Sociology, 84,* 427–436.

Kaplan, H., & Dove, H. (1987). Infant development among the Ache of Eastern Paraguay. *Developmental Psychology, 23,* 190–198.

Karsten, S. L., Sang, T.-K., Gehman, L. T., Chatterjee, S., Liu J., Lawless, G. M., et al. (2006). A genomic screen for modifiers of tauopathy identifies puromycin-sensitive aminopeptidase as an inhibitor of tau-induced neurodegeneration. *Neuron, 51,* 549–560.

Kartner, J., Holodynski, M., & Wörmann, V. (2013). Parental ethnotheories, social practice and the culture-specific development of social smiling in infants. *Mind, Culture, and Activity, 20*(1), 79–95.

Katchadourian, H. A. (1977). *The biology of adolescence.* San Francisco, CA: W. H. Freeman.

Kaufman, E. A., Puzia, M. E., Mead, H. K., Crowell, S. E., McEachern, A., & Beauchaine, T. P. (2017). Children's emotion regulation difficulties mediate the association between maternal borderline and antisocial symptoms and youth behavior problems over 1 year. *Journal of Personality Disorders, 31*(2), 170.

Kaur, N., Singh, Z., & Kaur, G. (2017). Growth in head circumference from birth to 3 years in Jat Sikh and Bania males. *Human Biology Review, 6*(1), 96–104.

Kaye, K. (1982). *The mental and social life of babies.* Chicago, IL: University of Chicago Press.

Kazeem, A., & Jensen, L. (2017). Orphan status, school attendance, and their relationship to household head in Nigeria. *Demographic Research, 36.*

Keating, D. (2004). Cognitive and brain development. In R. M. Lerner & L. Steinberg (Eds.), *Handbook of adolescent psychology* (2nd ed.). Hoboken, NJ: John Wiley & Sons.

Keel, P. K., Gravener, J. A., Joiner, T. E., Jr., & Haedt, A. A. (2010). Twenty-year follow-up of bulimia nervosa and related eating disorders not otherwise specified. *International Journal of Eating Disorders, 43,* 492–497.

Keel, P. K., & Klump, K. L. (2003). Are eating disorders culture-bound syndromes? Implications for conceptualizing their etiology. *Psychological Bulletin, 129,* 747–769.

Keenan, K., Hipwell, A., Chung, T., Stepp, S., Stouthamer-Loeber, M., Loeber, R., et al. (2010). The Pittsburgh girls study: Overview and initial findings. *Journal of Clinical Child and Adolescent Psychology, 39,* 506–521.

Keeney, T. J., Cannizzo, S. D., & Flavell, J. H. (1967). Spontaneous and induced verbal rehearsal in a recall task. *Child Development, 38,* 935–966.

Keller, H. (2003). Socialization for competence: Cultural models of infancy. *Human Development, 46*(5), 228–311.

Keller, H. (2011). Culture and cognition: Developmental perspectives. *Journal of Cognitive Education and Psychology, 10,* 3–8.

Keller, H., Borke, J., Chaudhary, N., Lamm, B., & Kleis, A. (2010). Continuity in parenting strategies: A cross-cultural comparison. *Journal of Cross-Cultural Psychology, 41,* 391–409.

Keller, H., & Kärtner, J. (2013). Development—The cultural solution of universal developmental tasks. In M. Gelfand, C.-Y. Chiu, & Y.-Y. Hong (Eds.), *Advances in culture and psychology: Vol. 3.* New York: Oxford University Press.

Kellman, P. J., & Banks, M. S. (1998). Infant visual perception. In R. Siegler & D. Kuhn (Eds.), *Handbook of child psychology: Vol. 2* (5th ed., pp. 103–146). New York: Wiley.

Kelly, D. J., Liu, S., Lee, K., Quinn, P. C., & Pascalis, O. (2009). Development of the other-race effect during infancy: Evidence toward universality? *Journal of Experimental Child Psychology, 104,* 105–114.

Kena, G., Aud, S., Johnson, F., Wang, X., Zhang, J., Rathbun, A., et al. (2014). *The condition of education 2014* (NCES 2014-083). Washington, DC: U.S. Department of Education, National Center for Education Statistics.

Keniston, K. (1963). Social change and youth in America. In E. Erikson (Ed.), *Youth: Change and challenge.* New York: Basic Books.

Kennard, B. D., Clarke, G. N., Weersing, V. R., Asarnow, J. R., Shamseddeen, W., Porta, G., et al. (2009). Effective components of TORDIA cognitive–behavioral therapy for adolescent depression: Preliminary findings. *Journal of Consulting and Clinical Psychology, 77,* 1033–1041.

Kennard, J. A., Brown, K. L., & Woodruff-Pak, D. S. (2013). Aging in the cerebellum and hippocampus and associated behaviors over the adult life span of CB6F1 mice. *Neuroscience, 247,* 335.

Kerr, M., Stattin, H., Ozdemir, M., Örebro universitet, & Institutionen för juridik, psykologi och socialt arbete. (2012). Perceived parenting style and adolescent adjustment: Revisiting directions of effects and the role of parental knowledge. *Developmental Psychology, 48*(6), 1540–1553.

Kesmodel, U. (2001). Binge drinking in pregnancy: Frequency and methodology. *American Journal of Epidemiology, 154*(8), 777–782.

Kesner, J., & McKenry, P. (2001). Single parenthood and social competence in children of color. *Families in Society, 82,* 136–144.

Kett, J. F. (1977). *Rites of passage: Adolescence in America 1790 to the present.* New York: Basic Books.

Keunen, K., Counsell, S. J., & Benders, M. J. N. L. (2017). The emergence of functional architecture during early brain development. *Neuroimage,* doi: 10.1016/j.neuroimage.2017.01.047

Keyes, K., Maslowsky, J., Hamilton, A., & Schulenberg, J. (2015). The great sleep recession: Changes in sleep duration among US adolescents, 1991–2012. *Pediatrics, 135*(3), 460–468.

Khaleque, A. (2017). Perceived parental hostility and aggression, and children's psychological maladjustment, and negative personality dispositions: A meta-analysis. *Journal of Child and Family Studies, 26*(4), 977–988.

Khatun, M., Al Mamun, A., Scott, J., William, G., Clavarino, A., & Najman, J. (2017). Do children born to teenage parents have lower adult intelligence? A prospective birth cohort study. *PLOS ONE, 12*(3), e0167395.

Kiang, L., Witkow, M. R., & Thompson, T. L. (2016). Model minority stereotyping, perceived discrimination, and adjustment among adolescents from Asian American backgrounds. *Journal of Youth and Adolescence, 45*(7), 1366–1379.

Kiell, N. (1959). *The adolescent through fiction: A psychological approach.* New York: International Universities Press.

Kiewra, C., & Veselack, E. (2016). Playing with nature: Supporting preschoolers' creativity in natural outdoor classrooms. *International Journal of Early Childhood Environmental Education, 4*(1), 70–95.

Killen, M., Elenbaas, L., & Rutland, A. (2016). Balancing the fair treatment of others while preserving group identity and autonomy. *Human Development, 58*(4–5), 253–272.

Killen, M., & Smetana, J. (2007, September). The biology of morality: Human development and moral neuroscience. *Human Development, 50*(5), 241–243.

Kim, E., Han, G., & McCubbin, M. A. (2007). Korean American maternal acceptance-rejection, acculturation, and children's social competence. *Family & Community Health, 30*(Suppl. 2), S33–S45.

Kim, H. S. (2011). Consequences of parental divorce for child development. *American Sociological Review, 76*(3), 487–511.

Kim, J.-Y., McHale, S. M., Osgood, D. W., & Crouter, A. C. (2006). Longitudinal course and family correlates of sibling relationships from childhood through adolescence. *Child Development, 77,* 1746–1761.

Kim, S., Conway-Turner, K., Sherif-Trask, B., & Wolfolk, T. (2006). Reconstructing mothering among Korean immigrant working class women in the United States. *Journal of Comparative Family Studies, 37,* 43–65.

Király, I., Takács, S., Kaldy, Z., & Blaser, E. (2017). Preschoolers have better long-term memory for rhyming text than adults. *Developmental Science, 20*(3), e12398.

Kirby, J. N., & Kirby, P. G. (2017). An evolutionary model to conceptualise masculinity and compassion in male teenagers: A unifying framework. *Clinical Psychologist, 21*(2), 74–89.

Kirsch, A. C., & Murnen, S. K. (2015). "Hot" girls and "cool dudes": Examining the prevalence of the heterosexual script in American children's television media. *Psychology of Popular Media Culture, 4*(1), 18–30.

Kisilevsky, B. S., & Hains, S. M. (2010). Exploring the relationship between fetal heart rate and cognition. *Infant and Child Development, 19,* 60–75.

Kisilevsky, B. S., & Low, J. A. (1998). Human fetal behavior: 100 years of study. *Developmental Review, 18,* 1–29.

Kittel, R., Schmidt, R., & Hilbert, A. (2017). Executive functions in adolescents with binge-eating disorder and obesity. *International Journal of Eating Disorders, 50*(8), 933–941.

Klaczynski, P. A., & Cottrell, J. M. (2004). A dual-process approach to cognitive development: The case of children's understanding of sunk cost decisions. *Thinking & Reasoning, 10,* 147–174.

Klahr, D. (1989). Information-processing approaches. In R. Vasta (Ed.), *Annals of child development: Vol. 6. Six theories of child development: Revised formulations and current issues.* Greenwich, CT: JAI Press.

Klasen, F., Oettingen, G., Daniels, J., Post, M., & Hoyer, C. (2010). Posttraumatic resilience in former Ugandan child soldiers. *Child Development, 81,* 1096–1113.

Kline, M., & Boyd, R. (2010). Population size predicts technological complexity in Oceania. *Proceedings of the Royal Society (B), 277,* 2559–2564.

Klineberg, O. (1935). *Race differences.* New York: Harper & Row.

Klinker, C. D., Schipperijn, J., Christian, H., Kerr, J., Ersbøll, A. K., & Troelsen, J. (2014). Using accelerometers and global positioning system devices to assess gender and age differences in children's school, transport, leisure and home-based physical activity. *International Journal of Behavioral Nutrition and Physical Activity, 11*(1), 8.

Knight, G. P., Berkel, C., Umaña-Taylor, A. J., Gonzales, N. A., Ettekal, I., Jaconis, M., & Boyd, B. M. (2011). The familial socialization of culturally related values in Mexican American families. *Journal of Marriage and Family, 73*(5), 913–925.

Knight, N., Sousa, P., Barrett, J., & Atran, S. (2004). Children's attributions of beliefs to humans and god: Cross-cultural evidence. *Cognitive Science, 28*(1), 117–126.

Knudsen, B., & Liszkowski, U. (2012). 18-month-olds predict specific action mistakes through attribution of false belief, not ignorance, and intervene accordingly. *Infancy, 17*(6), 672–691.

Kobak, R., Rosenthal, N. L., Zajac, K., & Madsen, S. D. (2007). Adolescent attachment hierarchies and the search for an adult pair-bond. *New Directions for Child and Adolescent Development, 2007*(117), 57–72.

Kocab, A., Pyers, J., & Senghas, A. (2015). Referential shift in Nicaraguan sign language: A transition from lexical to spatial devices. *Frontiers in Psychology, 5.*

Kocab, A., Senghas, A., & Snedeker, J. (2016). The emergence of temporal language in Nicaraguan sign language. *Cognition, 156,* 147–163.

Kocayörük, E., Altıntas, E., & İçbay, M. A. (2015). The perceived parental support, autonomous-self and well-being of adolescents: A cluster-analysis approach. *Journal of Child and Family Studies, 24*(6), 1819–1828.

Koch, H., & Spörer, N. (2017). Students improve in reading comprehension by learning how to teach reading strategies. An evidence-based approach for teacher education. *Psychology Learning & Teaching, 16*(2), 197–211.

Kochanska, G., Kim, S., & Boldt, L. (2015). (Positive) power to the child: The role of children's willing stance toward parents in developmental cascades from toddler age to early preadolescence. *Development and Psychopathology, 27*(4), 987–1005.

Kochanska, G., Philibert, R. A., & Barry, R. A. (2009). Interplay of genes and early mother–child relationship in the development of self-regulation from toddler to preschool age. *Journal of Child Psychology and Psychiatry, 50,* 1331–1338.

Kochel, K. P., Ladd, G. W., & Rudolph, K. D. (2012). Longitudinal associations among youth depressive symptoms, peer victimization, and low peer acceptance: An interpersonal process perspective. *Child Development, 83*(2), 637–650.

Koestler, C., Felton-Koestler, M. D., Bieda, K., & Otten, S. (2013). *Connecting the NCTM process standards and the CCSSM practices.* Reston, VA: National Council of Teachers of Mathematics.

Kohlberg, L. (1969). Stage and sequence: The cognitive-developmental approach to socialization. In D. A. Goslin (Ed.), *Handbook of socialization theory and research.* Chicago, IL: Rand McNally.

Kohlberg, L. (1976). Moral stages and moralization: The cognitive-developmental approach. In J. Lickona (Ed.), *Moral development behavior: Theory, research and social issues.* New York: Holt, Rinehart and Winston.

Kohlberg, L. (1984). *The psychology of moral development: The nature and validity of moral stages: Vol. 2.* New York: Harper & Row.

Kokis, J., Macpherson, R., Toplak, M., West, R., & Stanovich, K. (2002). Heuristic and analytic processing: Age trends and associations with cognitive ability and cognitive styles. *Journal of Experimental Child Psychology, 83,* 26–52.

Kokkinaki, T. S., Vasdekis, V. G. S., Koufaki, Z. E., & Trevarthen, C. B. (2017). Coordination of emotions in mother–infant dialogues. *Infant and Child Development, 26*(2).

Kolata, G. (1986). Obese children: A growing problem. *Science, 232,* 20–21.

Konicarova, J., & Bob, P. (2012). Retained primitive reflexes and ADHD in children. *Activitas Nervosa Superior, 54*(3–4), 135–138.

Konner, M. (2005). Hunter-gatherer infancy and childhood: The !Kung and others. In B. S. Hewlett & M. E. Lamb (Eds.), *Hunter-gatherer childhoods.* New Brunswick, NJ: Aldine Transaction.

Koolschijn, P., Cédric M. P., & Crone, E. A. (2013). Sex differences and structural brain maturation from childhood to early adulthood. *Developmental Cognitive Neuroscience, 5,* 106–118.

Koopmans-van Beinum, F. J., Clement, C. J., & van den-Dikkenberg-Pot, I. (2001). Babbling and the lack of auditory speech perception: A matter of coordination? *Developmental Science, 4*(1), 61–70.

Korczak, D., Madigan, S., & Colasanto, M. (2017). Children's physical activity and depression: A meta-analysis. *Pediatrics, 139*(4).

Kornbluh, M., & Neal, J. W. (2016). Examining the many dimensions of children's popularity: Interactions between aggression, prosocial behaviors, and gender. *Journal of Social and Personal Relationships, 33*(1), 62–80.

Korner, A. F., & Constantinou, J. C. (2001). The neurobehavioral assessment of the preterm infant: Reliability and developmental and clinical validity. In L. T. Singer & P. S. Zeskind (Eds.), *Biobehavioral assessment of the infant* (pp. 381–397). New York: Guilford Press.

Kornienko, O., Santos, C. E., Martin, C. L., & Granger, K. L. (2016). Peer influence on gender identity development in adolescence. *Developmental Psychology, 52*(10), 1578.

Korotchikova, I., Stevenson, N. J., Livingstone, V., Ryan, C. A., & Boylan, G. B. (2016). Sleep–wake cycle of the healthy term newborn infant in the immediate postnatal period. *Clinical Neurophysiology: Official Journal of the International Federation of Clinical Neurophysiology, 127*(4), 2095–2101.

Korten, I., Ramsey, K., & Latzin, P. (2017). Air pollution during pregnancy and lung development in the child. *Paediatric Respiratory Reviews, 21,* 38–46.

Kosciw, J. G., Diaz, E. M., COLAGE, Family Equality Council, & Gay, Lesbian, and Straight Education Network. (2008). *Involved, invisible, ignored: The experiences of lesbian, gay, bisexual and transgender parents and their children in our nation's K–12 schools.* New York: GLSEN.

Koyama, R., Takahashi, Y., & Mori, K. (2006). Assessing the cuteness of children: Significant factors and gender differences. *Social Behavior and Personality, 34,* 1087–1100.

Koziel, S., & Jankowska, E. A. (2002). Effect of low versus normal birthweight on menarche in 14-year-old Polish girls. *Journal of Paediatrics and Child Health, 38*(3), 268–271.

Kramer, K. L. (2014). Why what juveniles do matters in the evolution of cooperative breeding. *Human Nature, 25*(1), 49–65.

Kramer, K. L., & Greaves, R. D. (2011). Juvenile subsistence effort, activity levels, and growth patterns: Middle childhood among Pumé foragers. *Human Nature, 22*(3), 303–326.

Krapohl, E., & Plomin, R. (2016). Genetic link between family socioeconomic status and children's educational achievement estimated from genome-wide SNPs. *Molecular Psychiatry, 21,* 437–443.

Krasnogorski, N. I. (1907/1967). The formation of artificial conditioned reflexes in young children. In Y. Brackbill & G. G. Thompson (Eds.), *Behavior in infancy and early childhood: A book of readings.* New York: Free Press.

Kreutzer, M. A., Leonard, S. C., & Flavell, J. H. (1975). An interview study of children's knowledge about memory. *Monographs of the Society for Research in Child Development, 40*(1, Serial No. 159).

Kroger, J., Martinussen, M., & Marcia, J. E. (2010). Identity status change during adolescence and young adulthood: A meta-analysis. *Journal of Adolescence, 33,* 683–698.

Kroll, J. F., Dussias, P. E., Bice, K., & Perrotti, L. (2015). Bilingualism, mind, and brain. *Annual Review of Linguistics, 1,* 377–394.

Kroll, L. R. (2017). Early childhood curriculum development: The role of play in building self-regulatory capacity in young children. *Early Child Development and Care, 187*(5–6), 854–868.

Kronenberger, W. G., Colson, B. G., Henning, S. C., & Pisoni, D. B. (2014). Executive functioning and speech-language skills following long-term use of cochlear implants. *Journal of Deaf Studies and Deaf Education, 19,* 456–470.

Kruger, A. C., & Konner, M. (2010). Who responds to crying? Maternal care and allocare among the !Kung. *Human Nature, 21,* 309–329.

Kuhl, P. K. (2015, November). How babies learn language. *Scientific American.* Retrieved from www.scientificamerican.com/article/how-babies-learn-language/

Kuhl, P. K., Stevens, E., Hayashi, A., Deguchi, T., Kiritani, S., & Iverson, P. (2006). Infants show a facilitation effect for native language phonetic perception between 6 and 12 months. *Developmental Science, 9*(2), F13–F21.

Kulis, S., Napoli, M., & Marsiglia, F. (2002). Ethnic pride, biculturalism, and drug use norms of urban American Indian adolescents. *Social Work Research, 26,* 101–112.

Kuo, Y.-L., Liao, H.-F., Chen, P.-C., Hsieh, W.-S., & Hwang, A.-W. (2008). The influence of wakeful prone positioning on motor development during the early life. *Developmental and Behavioral Pediatrics, 29,* 367–376.

Kupersmidt, J. B., Coie, J. D., & Howell, J. C. (2004). Resilience in children exposed to negative peer influences. In K. I. Maton, C. J. Schellenbach, B. J. Leadbeater, & A. L. Solarz (Eds.), *Investing in children, youth, families, and communities: Strengths-based research and policy* (pp. 251–268). Washington, DC: American Psychological Association.

Kurtz-Costes, B., DeFreitas, S., Halle, T., & Kinlaw, C. (2011). Gender and racial favouritism in black and white preschool girls. *British Journal of Developmental Psychology, 29*(2), 270–287.

Kusiako, T., Ronsmans, C., & Van der Paal, L. (2000). Perinatal mortality attributable to complications of childbirth in Matlab, Bangladesh. *Bulletin of the World Health Organization, 78*(5), 621–627.

Kuther, T., & Higgins-D'Alessandro, A. (2000). Bridging the gap between moral reasoning and adolescent engagement in risky behavior. *Journal of Adolescence, 23,* 409–422.

Kuti, O., Adeyemi, A. B., & Owolabi, A. T. (2007). Breast-feeding pattern and onset of menstruation among Yoruba mothers of south-west Nigeria. *European J. of Contraception and Reproductive Healthcare, 12*(4), 335–339.

Kuttler, A., & La Greca, A. (2004). Linkages among adolescent girls' romantic relationships, best friendships, and peer networks. *Journal of Adolescence, 27,* 395–414.

Kuyken, W., Weare, K., Ukoumunne, O. C., Vicary, R., Motton, N., Burnett, R., et al. (2013). Effectiveness of the mindfulness in schools programme: Non-randomised controlled feasibility study. *The British Journal of Psychiatry, 203*(2), 126.

Laberge, L., Petit, D., Simard, C., Vitaro, F., Tremblay, R., & Montplaisir, J. (2001). Development of sleep patterns in early adolescence. *Journal of Sleep Research, 10,* 59–67.

Ladd, G. W. (1999). Peer relationships and social competence during early and middle childhood. *Annual Review of Psychology, 50,* 333–359.

Ladd, G. W., & Dinella, L. M. (2009). Continuity and change in early school engagement: Predictive of children's achievement trajectories from first to eighth grade? *Journal of Educational Psychology, 101,* 190–206.

Ladd, G. W., & Troop-Gordon, W. (2003). The role of chronic peer difficulties in the development of children's psychological adjustment problems. *Child Development, 74,* 1344–1367.

LaFontana, K. M., & Cillessen, A. H. N. (2010). Developmental changes in the priority of perceived status in childhood and adolescence. *Social Development, 19,* 130–147.

LaFromboise, T., Hoyt, D., Oliver, L., & Whitbeck, L. (2006). Family, community, and school influences on resilience among American Indian adolescents in the upper Midwest. *Journal of Community Psychology, 34,* 193–209.

Lagattuta, K. H., Nucci, L., & Bosacki, S. L. (2010). Bridging theory of mind and the personal domain: Children's reasoning about resistance to parental control. *Child Development, 81,* 616–635.

Lahey, B. B., Schwab-Stone, M., Goodman, S. H., Waldman, I. D., Canino, G., Rathouz, P. J., et al. (2000). Age and gender differences in oppositional behavior and conduct problems: A cross-sectional household study of middle childhood and adolescence. *Journal of Abnormal Psychology, 109,* 488–503.

Laible, D., Carlo, G., Davis, A. N., & Karahuta, E. (2016). Maternal sensitivity and effortful control in early childhood as predictors of adolescents' adjustment: The mediating roles of peer group affiliation and social behaviors. *Developmental Psychology, 52*(6), 922.

Lalonde, K., & Werner, L. A. (2016). Infant auditory and audiovisual speech discrimination. *Journal of the Acoustical Society of America, 140*(4), 3447.

Lamarche, V., Brendgen, M., Boivin, M., Vitaro, F., Dionne, G., & Pérusse, D. (2007). Do friends' characteristics moderate the prospective links between peer victimization and reactive and proactive aggression? *Journal of Abnormal Child Psychology, 35*(4), 665–680.

Lamb, M. E. (2010). How do fathers influence children's development? Let me count the ways. In M. E. Lamb (Ed.), *The role of the father in child development* (5th ed., pp. 1–26). New York: John Wiley & Sons.

Lamb, M. E., & Ahnert, L. (2006). Nonparental child care: Context, concepts, correlates, and consequences. In K. A. Renninger, I. E. Sigel, W. Damon, & R. M. Lerner (Eds.), *Handbook of child psychology: Vol. 4. Child psychology in practice* (6th ed., pp. 950–1016). Hoboken, NJ: John Wiley & Sons.

Lambert, B. L., & Bauer, C. R. (2012). Developmental and behavioral consequences of prenatal cocaine exposure: A review. *Official Journal of the California Perinatal Association, 32*(11), 819–828.

Lan, X., Legare, C. H., Ponitz, C. C., Li, S., & Morrison, F. J. (2011). Investigating the links between the subcomponents of executive function and academic achievement: A cross-cultural analysis of Chinese and American preschoolers. *Journal of Experimental Child Psychology, 108*(3), 677–692.

Lancaster, B., Gadaire, D., Holman, K., & LeBlanc, L. (2015). Association between diabetes treatment adherence and parent–child agreement regarding treatment responsibilities. *Families Systems & Health, 33*(2), 120–125.

Lancy, D., & Grove, M. (2010). The role of adults in children's learning. In D. Lancy, J. Bock, & S. Gaskins (Eds.), *The anthropology of learning in childhood* (pp. 145–180). Lanham, MD: AltaMira Press.

Landale, N. S., Oropesa, R. S., & Noah, A. J. (2014). Immigration and the family circumstances of Mexican-origin children: A binational longitudinal analysis. *Journal of Marriage and Family, 76*(1), 24–36.

Lander, K., Chuang, L., & Wickham, L. (2006). Recognizing face identity from natural and morphed smiles. *The Quarterly Journal of Experimental Psychology, 59,* 801–808.

Lane, H. (1976). *The wild boy of Aveyron.* Cambridge, MA: Harvard University Press.

Lane, J. D., Harris, P. L., Gelman, S. A., & Wellman, H. M. (2014). More than meets the eye: Young children's trust in claims that defy their perceptions. *Developmental Psychology, 50*(3), 865–871.

Langlois, J. H., Kalakanis, L., Rubenstein, A. J., Larson, A., Hallam, M., & Smoot, M. (2000). Maxims or myths of beauty? A meta analysis and theoretical review. *Psychological Bulletin, 126,* 390–423.

Langlois, J. H., Ritter, J. M., Casey, R. J., & Sawin, D. B. (1995). Infant attractiveness predicts maternal behaviors and attitudes. *Developmental Psychology, 31,* 464–472.

Langnes, T. F., & Fasting, K. (2016). Identity constructions among breakdancers. *International Review for the Sociology of Sport, 51*(3), 349–364.

Lansford, J. E., Bornstein, M. H., Deater-Deckard, K., Dodge, K. A., Al-Hassan, S. M., Bacchini, D., et al. (2016). How international research on parenting advances understanding of child development. *Child Development Perspectives, 10*(3), 202–207.

Lansford, J. E., Cappa, C., Putnick, D. L., Bornstein, M. H., Deater-Deckard, K., & Bradley, R. H. (2017). Change over time in parents' beliefs about and reported use of corporal punishment in eight countries with and without legal bans. *Child Abuse & Neglect, 71,* 44–55.

Lansford, J. E., Godwin, J., Uribe Tirado, L. M., Zelli, A., Al-Hassan, S. M., Bacchini, D., et al. (2015). Individual, family, and culture level contributions to child physical abuse and neglect: A longitudinal study in nine countries. *Development and Psychopathology, 27*(4 Pt. 2), 1417.

Lansford, J. E., Skinner, A. T., Sorbring, E., Giunta, L. D., Deater-Deckard, K., Dodge, K. A., et al. (2012). Boys' and girls' relational and physical aggression in nine countries. *Aggressive Behavior, 38*(4), 298–308.

Lansing, J. S., & Cox, M. P. (2011). The domain of the replicators: Selection, neutrality, and cultural evolution. *Current Anthropology, 52*(1), 105–125.

Larsen, B. (1996). Closeness and conflict in adolescent peer relationships: Interdependence with friends and romantic partners. In W. Bukowski, A. Newcomb, & W. Hartup (Eds.), *The company they keep: Friendship in childhood and adolescence.* New York: Cambridge University Press.

Larson, N., Neumark-Sztainer, D., Hannan, P. J., & Story, M. (2007). Family meals during adolescence are associated with higher diet quality and healthful meal patterns during young adulthood. *Journal of the American Dietetic Association,* 107, 1502–1510.

Larson, R., Moneta, G., Richards, M., & Wilson, S. (2002). Continuity, stability, and change in daily emotional experience across adolescence. *Child Development, 73,* 1151–1165.

Larson, R., & Richards, M. (1991). Daily companionship in late childhood and early adolescence: Changing developmental contexts. *Child Development, 62,* 284–300.

Larson, R. W. (2007). From "I" to "we": Development of the capacity for teamwork in youth programs. In R. K. Silbereisen & R. M. Lerner (Eds.). *Approaches to positive youth development* (pp. 277–292). London: Sage.

Larson, R. W., & Tran, S. P. (2014). Invited commentary: Positive youth development and human complexity. *Journal of Youth and Adolescence, 43*(6), 1012–1017.

Laski, E. V., & Siegler, R. S. (2014). Learning from number board games: You learn what you encode. *Developmental Psychology, 50*(3), 853–864.

Laughlin, J., Luerssen, T. G., Dias, M. S., Committee on Practice and Ambulatory Medicine, Section on Neurological Surgery, & The Committee on Practice and Ambulatory Medicine, Section on Neurological Surgery. (2011). Prevention and management of positional skull deformities in infants. *Pediatrics, 128*(6), 1236–1241.

Laupa, M., Turiel, E., & Cowan, P. (1995). Obedience to authority in children and adults. In M. Killen & D. Hart (Eds.), *Morality in everyday life: Developmental perspectives* (pp. 131–165). Cambridge, England: Cambridge University Press.

Lave, J., & Wenger, E. (1991). *Situated learning: Legitimate peripheral practice.* New York: Cambridge University Press.

Lavezzi, A. M., Corna, M., Mingrone, R., & Matturri, L. (2010). Study of the human hypoglossal nucleus: Normal development and morpho-functional alterations in sudden unexplained late fetal and infant death. *Brain & Development, 32,* 275–284.

Lavin, T., Franklin, P., & Preen, D. B. (2016). Association between caesarean delivery and childhood asthma in India and Vietnam. *Paediatric and Perinatal Epidemiology, 31*(1), 47–54.

Lawlor, D. A., Davey Smith, G., Clark, H., & Leon, D. A. (2006). The associations of birthweight, gestational age and childhood BMI with type 2 diabetes: Findings from the Aberdeen Children of the 1950s cohort. *Diabetologia, 49,* 2614–2617.

Lawrence, J. A., & Valsiner, J. (2003, December). Making personal sense: An account of basic internalization and externalization processes. *Theory & Psychology, 13*(6), 723–752.

Lazar, L., Lebenthal, Y., Yackobovitch-Gavan, M., Shalitin, S., de Vries, L., Phillip, M., & Meyerovitch, J. (2015). Treated and untreated women with idiopathic precocious puberty: BMI evolution, metabolic outcome, and general health between third and fifth decades. *The Journal of Clinical Endocrinology & Metabolism, 100*(4), 1445–1451.

Leakey, M. D., & Hay, R. L. (1979). Pliocene footprints in the laetoli beds at Laetoli, northern Tanzania. *Nature, 278,* 317–323.

Learmonth, A. E., Cuevas, K., & Rovee-Collier, C. (2015). Deconstructing the reactivation of imitation in young infants. *Developmental Psychobiology, 57*(4), 497–505.

Lebron, C., Stoutenberg, M., Janowsky, M., Asfour, L., Huang, S., & Prado, G. (2017). The role of physical activity and sedentary behavior in substance use and risky sex behaviors in Hispanic adolescents. *The Journal of Early Adolescence, 37*(7), 910–924.

Lecanuet, J.-P., & Jacquet, A.-Y. (2002). Fetal responsiveness to maternal passive swinging in low heart rate variability state: Effects of stimulation direction and duration. *Developmental Psychobiology, 40*(1), 57–67.

Lecanuet, J.-P., & Schaal, B. (1996). Fetal sensory competencies. *European Journal of Obstetrics, Gynecology, and Reproductive Biology, 68,* 1–23.

LeCorre, M., Li, P., Huang, B., Jia, G., & Carey, S. (2016). Numerical morphology supports early number word learning: Evidence from a comparison of young mandarin and English learners. *Cognitive Psychology, 88,* 162–186.

LeCuyer, E. A., & Swanson, D. P. (2017). A within-group analysis of African American mothers' authoritarian attitudes, limit-setting and children's self-regulation. *Journal of Child and Family Studies, 26*(3), 833–842.

LeDoux, J. (2012). Rethinking the emotional brain. *Neuron, 73,* 653–676.

Lee, C. D. (2010). Every shut eye ain't sleep: Modeling the scientific from the everyday as cultural process. In C. Milbrath & C. Lightfoot (Eds.), *Art and human development* (pp. 139–166). New York: Psychology Press.

Lee, C. D. (2017). Integrating research on how people learn and learning across settings as a window of opportunity to address inequality in educational processes and outcomes. *Review of Research in Education, 41*(1), 88–111.

Lee, C. D., Rosenfeld, E., Mendenhall, R., Rivers, A., & Tynes, B. (2004). Cultural modeling as a frame for narrative analysis. In C. Daiute & C. Lightfoot (Eds.), *Narrative analysis: Studying the development of individuals in society.* Thousand Oaks, CA: Sage.

Lee, H. C., Green, C., Hintz, S. R., Tyson, J. E., Parikh, N. A., Langer, J., & Gould, J. B. (2010). Prediction of death for extremely premature infants in a population-based cohort. *Pediatrics, 126,* 644–650.

Lee, H. S., Yoon, J. S., & Hwang, J. S. (2016). Luteinizing hormone secretion during gonadotropin-releasing hormone stimulation tests in obese girls with central precocious puberty. *Journal of Clinical Research in Pediatric Endocrinology, 8*(4), 392.

Lee, S., & Tsai, S. (2017). Experimental intervention research on students with specific poor comprehension: A systematic review of treatment outcomes. *Reading and Writing, 30*(4), 917–943.

Lees, A. (2016). Roles of urban indigenous community members in collaborative field-based teacher preparation. *Journal of Teacher Education, 67*(5), 363–378.

Lefeber, Y., & Voorhoeve, H. W. A. (1998). *Indigenous customs in childbirth and child care.* Assen, Netherlands: Von Gocum.

Legare, C. H., Gelman, S. A., & Wellman, H. M. (2010). Inconsistency with prior knowledge triggers children's causal explanatory reasoning. *Child Development, 81,* 929–944.

Legare, C. H., Schult, C. A., Impola, M., & Souza, A. L. (2016). Young children revise explanations in response to new evidence. *Cognitive Development, 39,* 45–56.

Lehmann, M. (2015). Rehearsal development as development of iterative recall processes. *Frontiers in Psychology, 6,* 308.

Lemerise, E., & Arsenio, W. (2000). An integrated model of emotion processes and cognition in social information processing. *Child Development, 71,* 107–118.

Lengua, L. J., Moran, L., Zalewski, M., Ruberry, E., Kiff, C., & Thompson, S. (2015). Relations of growth in effortful control to family income, cumulative risk, and adjustment in preschool-age children. *Journal of Abnormal Child Psychology, 43*(4), 705–720.

Lenneberg, E. H. (1967). *Biological foundations of language.* Hoboken, NJ: Wiley.

Lenoir-Wijnkoop, I., van der Beek, E. M., Garssen, J., Nuijten, M. J. C., & Uauy, R. D. (2015). Health economic modeling to assess short-term costs of maternal overweight, gestational diabetes, and related macrosomia—A pilot evaluation. *Frontiers in Pharmacology, 6,* 103.

Lenroot, R. K., & Giedd, J. N. (2011). Annual Research Review: Developmental considerations of gene by environment interactions. *The Journal of Child Psychology and Psychiatry and Allied Disciplines, 52*(4), 429–441.

Lenroot, R., & Giedd, J. (2006). Brain development in children and adolescents: Insights from anatomical magnetic resonance imaging. *Neuroscience and Biobehaviorial Reviews, 30,* 718–729.

Lenroot, R., & Giedd, J. (2010). Sex differences in the adolescent brain. *Brain and Cognition, 72,* 46–55.

Leoni, L. (1964). *Tico and the golden wings.* New York: Pantheon.

Lerner, J., Phelps, E., Forman, Y., & Bowers, E. (2009). Positive youth development. In R. Lerner & R. Steinberg (Eds.), *Handbook of Adolescent Psychology.* New York: John Wiley & Sons.

Lerner, R. M., Almerigi, J. B., Theokas, C., & Lerner, J. V. (2005). Positive youth development: A view of the issues. *The Journal of Early Adolescence, 25,* 110–116.

Lerner, R. M., Lerner, J., Bowers, E., Lewin-Bizan, S., Gestsdottir, S., & Urban, J. (2011). Thriving in childhood and adolescence: The role of self-regulating processes. *New Directions for Child and Adolescent Development, 133,* 1–97.

Leroy, F., Glasel, H., Dubois, J., Hertz-Pannier, L., Thirion, B., Mangin, J.-F., & Dehaene-Lambertz, G. (2011). Early maturation of the linguistic dorsal pathway in human infants. *Journal of Neuroscience, 31*(4), 1500–1506.

Lesane-Brown, C. L. (2006). A review of race socialization within Black families. *Developmental Review, 26,* 400–426.

Leslie, A. M. (2002). Pretense and representation revisited. In N. L. Stein, P. J. Bauer, & M. Rabinowitz (Eds.), *Representation, memory, and development: Essays in honor of Jean Mandler* (pp. 103–114). Mahwah, NJ: Lawrence Erlbaum Associates.

Lester, B. M., Boukydis, C. Z., Garcia-Coll, C. T., Hole, W., & Peucker, M. (1992). Infantile colic: Acoustic cry characteristics, maternal perception of cry, and temperament. *Infant Behavior & Development, 15,* 15–26.

Lester, N., Garcia, D., Lundström, S., Brändström, S., Råstam, M., Kerekes, N., et al. (2016). The genetic and environmental structure of the character sub-scales of the temperament and character inventory in adolescence. *Annals of General Psychiatry, 15*(1), 10.

Leventhal, T., & Brooks-Gunn, J. (2011). Changes in neighborhood poverty from 1990 to 2000 and youth's problem behaviors. *Developmental Psychology, 47*(6), 1680–1698.

LeVine, R. A. (1988). Human parental care: Universal goals, cultural strategies, individual behavior. *New Directions for Child Development, 40,* 3–12.

LeVine, R. A., Dixon, S., LeVine, S., Richman, A., Leiderman, P. H., Keefer, C. H., & Brazelton, T. B. (1994). *Child care and culture: Lessons from Africa.* New York: Cambridge University Press.

LeVine, R. A., LeVine, S. E., & Schnell, B. (2001). "Improve the women": Mass schooling, female literacy, and worldwide social change. *Harvard Educational Review, 71*(1), 1–50.

Levy, B. S., Wilkinson, F. S., & Marine, W. M. (1971). Reducing neonatal mortality rate with nurse-midwives. *American Journal of Obstetrics and Gynecology, 109*(2), e10–e18.

Levy, E. (1989). Monologue as development of the text-forming function of language. In K. Nelson (Ed.), *Narratives from the crib.* Cambridge, MA: Harvard University Press.

Lewin, D., Wang, G., Chen, Y., Skora, E., Hoehn, J., Baylor, A., & Wang, J. (2017). Variable school start times and middle school student's sleep health and academic performance. *Journal of Adolescent Health, 61*(2), 205–211.

Lewis, M. (2005). Shared intentions without a self. *Behavioral and Brain Sciences, 28*(5), 707–708.

Lewkowicz, D. J. (2010). Infant perception of audio-visual speech synchrony. *Developmental Psychology, 46,* 66–77.

Lewontin, R. (2001). *The triple helix: Gene, organism, and environment.* Cambridge, MA: Harvard University Press.

Li, H., Boguszewski, K., & Lillard, A. (2015). Can that really happen? Children's knowledge about the reality status of fantastical events in television. *Journal of Experimental Child Psychology, 139,* 99–114.

Li, Y., Xie, H., & Shi, J. (2012). Chinese and American children's perceptions of popularity determinants: Cultural differences and behavioral correlates. *International Journal of Behavioral Development, 36*(6), 420–429.

Liang, Z., Wu, L., Fan, L., & Zhao, Q. (2014). Ambient air pollution and birth defects in Haikou City, Hainan Province. *BMC Pediatrics, 14*(1), 283–283.

Liben, L., & Bigler, R. (2002). The developmental course of gender differentiation. *Monographs for the Society for Research in Child Development, 67,* 1–147.

Libertus, K., Joh, A. S., & Needham, A. W. (2016). Motor training at 3 months affects object exploration 12 months later. *Developmental Science, 19*(6), 1058–1066.

Lickliter, R. (2007). The dynamics of development and evolution: Insights from behavioral embryology. *Developmental Psychobiology, 49,* 749–757.

Lickliter, R. (2013). *The origins of variation: Evolutionary insights from developmental science.* San Diego, CA: Elsevier.

Lickliter, R. (2017). Developmental evolution. *Wiley Interdisciplinary Reviews: Cognitive Science, 8*(1–2), e1422.

Liebal, K., Behne, T., Carpenter, M., & Tomasello, M. (2009). Infants use shared experience to interpret pointing gestures. *Developmental Science, 12,* 264–271.

Lillard, A. (2006). The socialization of theory of mind: Cultural and social class differences in behavior explanation. In A. Antonietti, O. Sempio-Liverta, & A. Marchetti (Eds.), *Theory of mind and language in developmental contexts* (pp. 65–76). New York: Springer Science.

Lin, Y., & Seo, D. (2017). Cumulative family risks across income levels predict deterioration of children's general health during childhood and adolescence. *PLOS ONE, 12*(5)

Lindberg, L. D., Maddow-Zimet, I., & Boonstra, H. (2016). Changes in adolescents' receipt of sex education, 2006–2013. *Journal of Adolescent Health, 58*(6), 621–627.

Litt, D. M., Stock, M. L., & Gibbons, F. X. (2015). Adolescent alcohol use: Social comparison orientation moderates the impact of friend and sibling behaviour. *British Journal of Health Psychology, 20*(3), 514–533.

Liu, C. H., Yang, Y., Fang, S., Snidman, N., & Tronick, E. (2013). Maternal regulating behaviors through face-to-face play in first- and second-generation Chinese American and European American mothers of infants. *Research in Human Development, 10*(4), 289–307.

Liu, S., Quinn, P. C., Wheeler, A., Xiao, N., Ge, L., & Lee, K. (2011). Similarity and difference in the processing of same- and other-race faces as revealed by eye tracking in 4- to 9-month-olds. *Journal of Experimental Child Psychology, 108*(1), 180–189.

Locke, J. L., & Bogin, B. (2006). Language and life history: A new perspective on the development and evolution of human language. *Behavioral and Brain Sciences, 29,* 259–325.

Lonsdorf, E. V. (2007). The role of behavioral research in the conservation of chimpanzees and gorillas. *Journal of Applied Animal Welfare Science, 10,* 71–78.

Lopez, G. (2001). The value of hard work: Lessons on parent involvement from an (im)migrant household. *Harvard Educational Review, 71,* 416–437.

Lorenz, J. M. (2001). The outcome of extreme prematurity. *Seminars in Perinatology* (Philadelphia), *25*(5), 348–359.

Love, J., Harrison, L., Sagi-Schwartz, A., van IJzendoorn, M., Ross, C., Ungerer, J., et al. (2003). Child care quality matters: How conclusions may vary with context. *Child Development, 74,* 1021–1033.

Low, J., & Hollis, S. (2003, March). The eyes have it: Development of children's generative thinking. *International Journal of Behavioral Development, 27*(2), 97–108.

Lu, J., Jones, A., & Morgan, G. (2016). The impact of input quality on early sign development in native and non-native language learners. *Journal of Child Language, 43*(3), 537.

Luciana, M. (2010). Adolescent brain development: Current themes and future directions: Introduction to the special issue. *Brain and Cognition, 72,* 1–5.

Lucić, L. (2016). Developmental affordances of war-torn landscapes: Growing up in Sarajevo under siege. *Human Development, 59*(2–3), 81–106.

Lucifora, C., & Tonello, M. (2015). Cheating and social interactions. Evidence from a randomized experiment in a national evaluation program. *Journal of Economic Behavior & Organization, 115,* 45.

Lucy, J. A. (2016). Recent advances in the study of linguistic relativity in historical context: A critical assessment. *Language Learning, 66*(3), 487–515.

Luder, M., Pittet, I., Berchtold, A., Akré, C., Michaud, P., & Surís, J. (2011). Associations between online pornography and sexual behavior among adolescents: Myth or reality? *Archives of Sexual Behavior, 40*(5), 1027–1035.

Lumeng, J. C., Kaciroti, N., Retzloff, L., Rosenblum, K., & Miller, A. L. (2017). Longitudinal associations between maternal feeding and overweight in low-income toddlers. *Appetite, 113,* 23–29.

Lund, I. O., Fischer, G., Welle-Strand, G. K., O'Grady, K. E., Debelak, K., Morrone, W. R., & Jones, H. E. (2013). A comparison of buprenorphine + naloxone to buprenorphine and methadone in the treatment of opioid dependence during pregnancy: Maternal and neonatal outcomes. *Substance Abuse, 7,* 61–74.

Lundqvist, C., & Sabel, K.-G. (2000). Brief report: The Brazelton Neonatal Behavioral Assessment Scale detects differences among newborn infants of optimal health. *Journal of Pediatric Psychology, 25,* 577–582.

Luo, Y., & Baillargeon, R. (2005). Can a self-propelled box have a goal? Psychological reasoning in 5-month-olds. *Psychological Science, 16,* 601–608.

Luria, A. R. (1973). *The waking brain.* New York: Basic Books.

Luria, A. R. (1976). *Cognitive development: Its cultural and social foundations* (M. Lopez-Morillas & L. Solotaroff, Trans.). London: Harvard University Press.

Luria, A. R. (1981). *Language and cognition.* New York: Wiley.

Lussier, P., Corrado, R., & Tzoumakis, S. (2012). Gender differences in physical aggression and associated developmental correlates in a sample of Canadian preschoolers. *Behavioral Sciences and the Law, 30*(5), 643–671.

Luster, T., & Haddow, J. L. (2005). Adolescent mothers and their children: An ecological perspective. In T. Luster & L. Okagaki (Eds.), *Parenting: An ecological perspective. Monographs in parenting* (2nd ed., pp. 73–101). Mahwah, NJ: Lawrence Erlbaum Associates.

Luthar, S., & Becker, B. (2002). Privileged but pressured? A study of affluent youth. *Child Development, 73,* 1593–1610.

Lutz, A., Slagter, H. A., Dunne, J. D., & Davidson, R. J. (2008). Attention regulation and monitoring in meditation. *Trends in Cognitive Sciences, 12*(4), 163–169.

Lutz, C. (1987). Goals, events, and understanding Ifaluk emotion theory. In D. Holland & N. Quinn (Eds.), *Cultural models in language and thought.* Cambridge, England: Cambridge University Press.

Luyckx, K., Goossens, L., Soenens, B., Beyers, W., & Vansteenkiste, M. (2005). Identity statuses based on 4 rather than 2 identity dimensions: Extending and refining Marcia's Paradigm. *Journal of Youth and Adolescence, 34,* 605–618.

Lynch, M. (2015). Guys and dolls: A qualitative study of teachers' views of gendered play in kindergarten. *Early Child Development and Care, 185*(5), 679–693.

Lynch, S. A., & Warner, L. (2012). A new theoretical perspective of cognitive abilities. *Childhood Education, 88*(6), 347–353.

Lynne, S., Graber, J. A., Nichols, T., Brooks-Gunn, J., & Botvin, G. (2007). Links between pubertal timing, peer influences, and externalizing behaviors among urban students followed through middle school. *Journal of Adolescent Health, 40,* 181.e7–181.e13.

Lyon, T. D., Carrick, N., & Quas, J. A. (2010). Young children's competency to take the oath: Effects of task, maltreatment, and age. *Law and Human Behavior, 34,* 141–149.

Lyra, M. C. D. P. (2007). Modeling the dynamics of meaning construction: Appropriation of the home environment. *Culture & Psychology, 13,* 179–188.

Ma, M., Malcolm, L. R., Diaz-Albertini, K., Klinoff, V. A., Leeder, E., Barrientos, S., & Kibler, J. L. (2014). Latino cultural values as protective factors against sexual risks among adolescents. *Journal of Adolescence, 37*(8), 1215–1225.

Macare, C., Bates, T. C., Heath, A. C., Martin, N. G., & Ettinger, U. (2012). Substantial genetic overlap between schizotypy and neuroticism: A twin study. *Behavior Genetics, 42*(5), 732–742.

MacCallum, F., & Golombok, S. (2004). Children raised in fatherless families from infancy: A follow-up of children of lesbian and single heterosexual mothers at early adolescence. *Journal of Psychology and Psychiatry, 45,* 1407–1419.

Maccoby, E. E. (1998). *The two sexes.* Cambridge, MA: Harvard University Press.

Maccoby, E. E. (2004). Aggression in the context of gender development. In M. Putallaz & K. Bierman (Eds.), *Aggression, antisocial behavior, and violence among girls.* New York: Guilford Press.

Maccoby, E. E. (2007). Historical overview of socialization research and theory. In J. E. Grusec & P. D. Hastings (Eds.), *Handbook of socialization: Theory and research* (pp. 13–41). New York: Guilford Press.

MacDorman, M. F., Declercq, E., & Mathews, T. J. (2013). Recent trends in out-of-hospital births in the United States. *Journal of Midwifery & Women's Health, 58,* 494–501.

MacDorman, M., Mathews, M., & Declercq, E. (2014). Trends in out-of-hospital births in the United States, 1990–2012. *NCHS Data Brief,* no. 144. Retrieved from https://www.cdc.gov/nchs/data/databriefs/db144.pdf

MacDorman, M. F., & Singh, G. K. (1998). Midwifery care, social and medical risk factors, and birth outcomes in the USA. *Journal of Epidemiology & Community Health, 52*(5), 310–317. BMJ Group. Retrieved from http://eutils.ncbi.nlm.nih.gov/entrez/eutils/elink.fcgi?dbfrom=-pubmed&id=9764282&retmode=ref&cmd=prlinks

Mace, S. E. (2016). Global threats to child safety. *Pediatric Clinics of North America, 63*(1), 19.

Macfarlane, A. (1977). *The psychology of childbirth.* Cambridge, MA: Harvard University Press.

Mackintosh, N. J. (2011). *IQ and human intelligence.* Oxford, UK: Oxford University Press.

Macones, G. A. (Ed.). (2015). *Management of labor and delivery* (2nd ed.). Chichester, UK: John Wiley & Sons.

Mageo, J. (2013). Toward a cultural psychodynamics of attachment: Samoa and U.S. comparisons. In N. Quinn & J. M. Mageo (Eds.), *Attachment reconsidered: Cultural perspectives on a Western theory.* New York: Palgrave Macmillan.

Magolda, M. (2008). The evolution of self-authorship. In M. Khine (Ed.), *Knowing, knowledge and beliefs: Epistemological studies across diverse cultures* (pp. 45–64). New York: Springer Science 1 Business Media.

Maguen, S., Floyd, F., Bakeman, R., & Armistead, L. (2002). Developmental milestones and disclosure of sexual orientation among gay, lesbian, and bisexual youths. *Applied Developmental Psychology, 23,* 219–233.

Mah, V. K., & Ford-Jones, E. L. (2012). Spotlight on middle childhood: Rejuvenating the "forgotten years." *Paediatrics & Child Health, 17*(2), 81.

Mahdi, A. (2003). *Teen life in the Middle East.* Westport, Connecticut: Greenwood Press.

Mahy, C., Moses, L., & Pfeifer, J. (2014). How and where: Theory-of-mind in the brain. *Developmental Cognitive Neuroscience, 9,* 68–81.

Main, M., & Solomon, J. (1990). Procedures for identifying infants as disorganized/disoriented during the Ainsworth strange situation. In M. Greenberg, D. Cicchetti, & E. M. Cummings (Eds.), *Attachment in the preschool years: Theory, research, and intervention* (pp. 121–160). Chicago, IL: University of Chicago Press.

Majnemer, A., & Barr, R. G. (2005). Influence of supine sleep positioning on early motor milestone acquisition. *Developmental Medicine & Child Neurology, 47*(6), 370–376.

Malina, R. M., & Bouchard, C. (1991). *Growth, maturation and physical activity.* Champaign, IL: Human Kinetics Books.

Malloy, L. C., & Quas, J. A. (2009). Children's suggestibility: Areas of consensus and controversy. In K. Kuehnle & M. Connell (Eds.), *The evaluation of child sexual abuse allegations: A comprehensive guide to assessment and testimony* (pp. 267–297). Hoboken, NJ: John Wiley & Sons.

Man, K., Kaplan, J., Damasio, H., & Damasio, A. (2013). Neural convergence and divergence in the mammalian cerebral cortex: From experimental neuroanatomy to functional neuroimaging. *Journal of Comparative Neurology, 521*(18), 4097–4111.

Mandler, J. M. (2004). *The foundations of mind: Origins of conceptual thought.* Oxford, England: Oxford University Press.

Mandler, J. M. (2006). Actions organize the infant's world. In K. Hirsh-Pasek & R. M. Golinkoff (Eds.), *Action meets word: How children learn verbs.* New York: Oxford University Press.

Mandler, J. M. (2012). On the spatial foundations of the conceptual system and its enrichment. *Cognitive Science, 36*(3), 421–451.

Mandler, J. M., & McDonough, L. (1996). Drinking and driving don't mix: Inductive generalization in infancy. *Cognition, 59,* 307–335.

Mann, F., Patterson, M., Grotzinger, A., Kretsch, N., Tackett, J., Tucker-Drob, E., & Harden, K. (2016). Sensation seeking, peer deviance, and genetic influences on adolescent delinquency: Evidence for person–environment correlation and interaction. *Journal of Abnormal Psychology, 125*(5), 679–691.

Marceau, K., Laurent, H. K., Neiderhiser, J. M., Reiss, D., Shaw, D. S., Natsuaki, M. N., et al. (2015). Combined influences of genes, prenatal environment, cortisol, and parenting on the development of children's internalizing versus externalizing problems. *Behavior Genetics, 45*(3), 268.

Marcia, J. E. (1966). Development and validation of ego identity status. *Journal of Personality and Social Psychology, 3,* 551–558.

Marcia, J. E. (2002). Identity and psychosocial development in adulthood. *Identity, 2*(1), 7–28.

Marcovitch, S., Clearfield, M. W., Swingler, M., Calkins, S. D., & Bell, M. A. (2016). Attentional predictors of 5-month-olds' performance on a looking A-not-B task. *Infant and Child Development, 25*(4), 233–246.

Mares, M., & Sivakumar, G. (2014). "Vámonos means go, but that's made up for the show": Reality confusions and learning from educational TV. *Developmental Psychology, 50*(11), 2498–2511.

Maric, J., Dunjic, B., Stojiljkovic, D., Britvic, D., & Jasovic-Gasic, M. (2010). Prenatal stress during the 1999 bombing associated with lower birth weight: A study of 3,815 births from Belgrade. *Archives of Women's Mental Health, 13,* 83–89.

Marinelli, M., Sunyer, J., Alvarez-Pedrerol, M., Iniguez, C., Torrent, M., Vioque, J., et al. (2014). Hours of television viewing and sleep duration in children: A multicenter birth cohort study. *JAMA Pediatrics, 168,* 458–464.

Mark, K., Desai, A., & Terplan, M. (2016). Marijuana use and pregnancy: Prevalence, associated characteristics, and birth outcomes. *Archives of Women's Mental Health, 19*(1), 105–111.

Markovits, H. (2014). On the road toward formal reasoning: Reasoning with factual causal and contrary-to-fact causal premises during early adolescence. *Journal of Experimental Child Psychology, 128,* 37–51.

Markovits, H., & Barrouillet, P. (2002). The development of conditional reasoning: A mental model account. *Developmental Review, 22,* 5–36.

Markovits, H., & Lortie-Forgues, H. (2011). Conditional reasoning with false premises facilitates the transition between familiar and abstract reasoning. *Child Development, 82,* 646–660.

Marks, A. K., Patton, F., & Coll, C. G. (2011). Being bicultural: A mixed-methods study of adolescents' implicitly and explicitly measured multiethnic identities. *Developmental Psychology, 47*(1), 270.

Markström, A., & Simonsson, M. (2011). Constructions of girls in preschool parent–teacher conferences. *International Journal of Early Childhood, 43*(1), 23–41.

Markstrom, C. A. (2011). Identity formation of American Indian adolescents: Local, national, and global considerations. *Journal of Research on Adolescence, 21*(2), 519–535.

Marraudino, M., Miceli, D., Farinetti, A., Ponti, G., Panzica, G., & Gotti, S. (2017). Kisspeptin innervation of the hypothalamic paraventricular nucleus: Sexual dimorphism and effect of estrous cycle in female mice. *Journal of Anatomy, 230*(6), 775–786.

Marshall, P. J., & Kenney, J. W. (2009). Biological perspectives on the effects of early psychosocial experience. *Developmental Review, 29,* 96–119.

Marshall, P. J., & Meltzoff, A. N. (2014). Neural mirroring mechanisms and imitation in human infants. *Philosophical Transactions of the Royal Society of London. Series B, Biological Sciences, 369*(1644), 20130620.

Marshall, P. J., Saby, J. N., & Meltzoff, A. N. (2013). Infant brain responses to object weight: Exploring goal-directed actions and self-experience. *Infancy, 18*(6), 942–960.

Martin, A., Peperkamp, S., & Dupoux, E. (2013). Learning phonemes with a proto-lexicon. *Cognitive Science, 37*(1), 103–124.

Martin, C. H., & Halverson, C. F. (1981). A schematic processing model of sextyping and stereotyping in children. *Child Development, 52,* 1119–1134.

Martin, C. L., & Ruble, D. N. (2010). Patterns of gender development. *Annual Review of Psychology, 61,* 353–381.

Martin, J., Hamilton, B., & Osterman, M. (2015). Births in the United States, 2015. *HCHS Data Brief,* no. 258. Retrieved from https://www.cdc.gov/nchs/products/databriefs/db258.htm

Martin, J., Sokol, B. W., & Elfers, T. (2008). Taking and coordinating perspectives: From prereflective interactivity, through reflective intersubjectivity, to metareflective sociality. *Human Development, 51,* 294–317.

Martin, J. A., Hamilton, B. E., Sutton, P. D., Ventura, S. J., Menacker, F., Kirmeyer, S., et al. (2009). Births: Final data for 2006, *National vital statistics reports*: *Vol. 57*. Hyattsville, MD: National Center for Health Statistics.

Martin, J. A., Kung, H. C., Mathews, T. J., Hoyert, D. L., Strobino, D. M., Guyer, B., et al. (2008). Annual summary of vital statistics: 2006. *Pediatrics, 121,* 788–801.

Martin, K. (1996). *Puberty, sexuality and the self: Boys and girls at adolescence.* New York: Routledge.

Martin, K. A., & Kazyak, E. (2009). Hetero-romantic love and heterosexiness in children's G-rated films. *Gender and Society, 23*(3), 315–336.

Martinez, D. C., Morales, P. Z., & Aldana, U. S. (2017). Leveraging students' communicative repertoires as a tool for equitable learning. *Review of Research in Education, 41*(1), 477–499.

Martinez, G., Copen, C. E., & Abma, J. C. (2011). Teenagers in the United States: Sexual activity, contraceptive use, and childbearing, 2006–2010 National Survey of Family Growth. National Center for Health Statistics. *Vital Health Statistics, 23*(31), 1–35.

Martínez, M. L., Pérez, J. C., & Cumsille, P. (2014). Chilean adolescents' and parents' views on autonomy development. *Youth & Society, 46*(2), 176–200.

Martino, W., & Pallotta-Chiarolli, M. (2003). *So what's a boy? Addressing issues of masculinity in education.* London: Open University Press.

Martins, N., & Wilson, B. J. (2012). Mean on the screen: Social aggression in programs popular with children. *Journal of Communication, 62*(6), 991–1009.

Marufu, T. C., Ahankari, A., Coleman, T., & Lewis, S. (2015). Maternal smoking and the risk of still birth: Systematic review and meta-analysis. *BMC Public Health, 15*(1), 1552.

Marusic, F., Zaucer, R., Plesnicar, V., Razborsek, T., Sullivan, J., & Barner, D. (2016). Does grammatical structure accelerate number word learning? Evidence from learners of dual and non-dual dialects of Slovenian. *PLOS ONE, 11*(8), e0159208.

Masapollo, M., Polka, L., & Ménard, L. (2016). When infants talk, infants listen: Pre-babbling infants prefer listening to speech with infant vocal properties. *Developmental Science, 19*(2), 318–328.

Mascalzoni, E., Regolin, L., Vallortigara, G., & Simion, F. (2013). The cradle of causal reasoning: Newborns' preference for physical causality. *Developmental Science, 16*(3), 327–335.

Mascolo, M., Fischer, K., & Li, J. (2003). Dynamic development of component systems of emotions: Pride, shame and guilt in China and the United States. In R. Davidson, K. Scherer, & H. Goldsmith (Eds.), *Handbook of affective sciences.* Oxford, England: Oxford University Press.

Maslow, C. B., Caramanica, K., Li, J., Stellman, S. D., & Brackbill, R. M. (2016). Reproductive outcomes following maternal exposure to the events of September 11, 2001, at the World Trade Center, in New York City. *American Journal of Public Health, 106*(10), 1796–1803.

Mather, M. (2009). *Children in immigrant families chart new path.* Population Reference Bureau Reports on America. Retrieved from http://www.prb.org/pdf09/immigrantchildren.pdf

Mathys, C., Hyde, L. W., Shaw, D. S., & Born, M. (2013). Deviancy and normative training processes in experimental groups of delinquent and nondelinquent male adolescents. *Aggressive Behavior, 39*(1), 30–44.

Matsubayashi, T., & Ueda, M. (2015). Relative age in school and suicide among young individuals in Japan: A regression discontinuity approach. *PLOS ONE, 10*(8), e0135349.

Mattebo, M., Tydén, T., Häggström-Nordin, E., Nilsson, K., & Larsson, M. (2016). Pornography consumption among adolescent girls in Sweden. *The European Journal of Contraception & Reproductive Health Care, 21*(4), 295.

Matusov, E. (2015). Comprehension: A dialogic authorial approach. *Culture & Psychology, 21*(3), 392–416.

Matusov, E., Smith, M., Soslau, E., Marjanovic-Shane, A., & Von Duyke, K. (2016). Dialogic education for and from authorial agency. *Dialogic Pedagogy: An International Online Journal, 4.*

Matute, E., Montiel, T., Pinto, N., Rosselli, M., Ardila, A., & Zarabozo, D. (2012). Comparing cognitive performance in illiterate and literate children. *International Review of Education, 58*(1), 109–127.

Maurer, D. (2016). How the baby learns to see: Donald O. Hebb Award Lecture, Canadian Society for Brain, Behaviour, and Cognitive Science, Ottawa, June 2015. *Canadian Journal of Experimental Psychology/Revue Canadienne De Psychologie Expérimentale, 70*(3), 195–200.

Maynard, A. E. (2008). What we thought we knew and how we came to know it: Four decades of cross-cultural research from a Piagetian point of view. *Human Development, 51,* 56–65.

Maynard, A. E., & Greenfield, P. M. (2003). Implicit cognitive development in cultural tools and children: Lessons from Maya Mexico. *Cognitive Development, 18,* 489–510.

McAdams, D. P. (2015). Three lines of personality development: A conceptual itinerary. *European Psychologist, 20*(4), 252–264.

McCabe, D. (1999). Academic dishonesty among high school students. *Adolescence, 34,* 681–687.

McCarthy, A., Hughes, R., Tilling, K., Davies, D., Smith, G. D., & Ben-Shlomo, Y. (2007). Birth weight; postnatal, infant, and childhood growth; and obesity in young adulthood: Evidence from the Barry Caerphilly Growth Study. *American Journal of Clinical Nutrition, 86,* 907–913.

McCarty, M. E., Clifton, R. K., Ashmead, D. H., Lee, P., & Goubet, N. (2001). How infants use vision for grasping objects. *Child Development, 72,* 973–987.

McCormick, M. P., Cappella, E., Hughes, D. L., & Gallagher, E. K. (2015). Feasible, rigorous, and relevant: Validation of a measure of friendship homophily for diverse classrooms. *The Journal of Early Adolescence, 35*(5–6), 817–851.

McDade, T. (2003). Life history theory and the immune system: Steps toward a human ecological immunology. *Yearbook of Physical Anthropology, 46,* 100–125.

McDonald, K. L., Malti, T., Killen, M., & Rubin, K. H. (2014). Best friends' discussions of social dilemmas. *Journal of Youth and Adolescence, 43*(2), 233–244.

McDonald, L., Wardle, J., Llewellyn, C. H., Johnson, L., Jaarsveld, C. H. M., Syrad, H., & Fisher, A. (2015). Sleep and nighttime energy consumption in early childhood: A population-based cohort study. *Pediatric Obesity, 10*(6), 454–460.

McDonald, P. G., te Marvelde, L., Kazem, A. J. N., & Wright, J. (2008). Helping as a signal and the effect of a potential audience during provisioning visits in a cooperative bird. *Animal Behaviour, 75,* 1319–1330.

McElwain, N. L., & Booth-LaForce, C. (2006). Maternal sensitivity to infant distress and nondistress as predictors of infant-mother attachment security. *Journal of Family Psychology, 20*(2), 247–255.

McFarlane, J., Nava, A., Gilroy, H., & Maddoux, J. (2016). Child brides, forced marriage, and partner violence in America: Tip of an iceberg revealed. *Obstetrics & Gynecology, 127*(4), 706–713.

McGillion, M., Herbert, J. S., Pine, J., Vihman, M., dePaolis, R., Keren-Portnoy, T., & Matthews, D. (2017). What paves the way to conventional language? The predictive value of babble, pointing, and socioeconomic status. *Child Development, 88*(1), 156–166.

McGloin, J. M., & Widom, C. S. (2001). Resilience among abuse and neglected children grown up. *Development and Psychopathology, 13*(4), 1021–1038.

McHale, S. M., Whiteman, S. D., Kim, J. Y., & Crouter, A. C. (2007). Characteristics and correlates of sibling relationships in two-parent African American families. *Journal of Family Psychology, 21,* 227–235.

McIntosh, P. (1988). *White privilege and male privilege: A personal account of coming to see correspondences through work in women's studies.* Wellesley, MA: Wellesley College, Center for Research on Women.

McKay, M. T. (2015). Parental rules, parent and peer attachment, and adolescent drinking behaviors. *Substance use & Misuse, 50*(2), 184–188.

McKenna, J. J. (1996). Sudden infant death syndrome in cross-cultural perspective: Is infant-parent cosleeping protective? *Annual Review of Anthropology, 25,* 201–216.

McLean, K. C., Wood, B., & Breen, A. V. (2013). Reflecting on a difficult life narrative construction in vulnerable adolescents. *Journal of Adolescent Research, 28*(4), 431–452.

McLeod, N. M. H., Arana-Urioste, M. L., & Saeed, N. R. (2004, March). Birth prevalence of cleft lip and palate in Sucre, Bolivia. *The Cleft Palate—Craniofacial Journal, 41*(2), 195–198.

McNeill, D. (1966). Developmental psycholinguistics. In S. Smith & G. A. Miller (Eds.), *The genesis of language: A psycholinguistic approach.* Cambridge, MA: The MIT Press.

McPhee, C. (1970). Children and music in Bali. In J. Belo (Ed.), *Traditional Balinese culture* (pp. 212–239). New York: Columbia University Press.

McQuade, J. D., Breaux, R. P., Gómez, A. F., Zakarian, R. J., & Weatherly, J. (2016). Biased self-perceived social competence and engagement in subtypes of aggression: Examination of peer rejection, social dominance goals, and sex of the child as moderators. *Aggressive Behavior, 42*(5), 498–509.

McQueen, A., Cress, C., & Tothy, A. (2012). Using a tablet computer during pediatric procedures: A case series and review of the "apps." *Pediatric Emergency Care, 28*(7), 712–714.

Mead, M. (1928). *Coming of age in Samoa: A psychological study of primitive youth for Western civilisation.* New York: W. Morrow & Co.

Meehan, C., & Hawks, S. (2013). Cooperative breeding and attachment among the Aka foragers. In N. Quinn & J. M. Mageo (Eds.), *Attachment reconsidered: Cultural perspectives on a Western theory.* New York: Palgrave Macmillan.

Meeus, W. H. J. (2003). Parental and peer support, identity development and psychological well-being in adolescence. *Psychology: The Journal of the Hellenic Psychological Society, 10*(2–3), 192–201.

Meeus, W. H. J., & de Wied, M. (2007). Relationships with parents and identity in adolescence: A review of 25 years of research. In M. Watzlawik & A. Born Aristi (Eds.), *Capturing identity: Quantitative and qualitative methods* (pp. 131–147). Lanham, MD: University Press of America.

Meier, A., & Allen, G. (2009). Romantic relationships from adolescence to young adulthood: Evidence from the National Longitudinal Study of Adolescent Health. *The Sociological Quarterly, 50,* 308–335.

Meléndez, L. (2005). Parental beliefs and practices around early self-regulation: The impact of culture and immigration. *Infants & Young Children, 18,* 136–146.

Melinder, A., Alexander, K., Cho, Y. I., Goodman, G. S., Thoresen, C., Lonnum, K., & Magnussen, S. (2010). Children's eyewitness memory: A comparison of two interviewing strategies as realized by forensic professionals. *Journal of Experimental Child Psychology, 105*(3), 156.

Melot, A.-M., & Houde, O. (1998). Categorization and theories of mind: The case of the appearance/reality distinction. *Cahiers de Psychologie Cognitive/Current Psychology of Cognition, 17*(1), 71–93.

Meltz, B. (2004, January 29). Nurturing an adopted child. *Boston Globe,* p. H1.

Meltzoff, A., & Borton, R. (1979). Intermodal matching by human neonates. *Nature, 282,* 403–404.

Meltzoff, A., & Decety, J. (2003). What imitation tells us about social cognition: A rapprochement between developmental psychology and cognitive neuroscience. *The Royal Society, 358,* 491–500.

Meltzoff, A. N. (1988). Imitation of televised models by infants. *Child Development, 59,* 1221–1229.

Meltzoff, A. N. (2007). The "like me" framework for recognizing and becoming an intentional agent. *Acta Psychologica. Special Issue: Becoming an Intentional Agent, 124*(1), 26–43.

Mennella, J. A. (2014). Ontogeny of taste preferences: Basic biology and implications for health. *The American Journal of Clinical Nutrition, 99*(3), 704S–711S.

Mennella, J., & Beauchamp, G. (2005). Understanding the origin of flavor preferences. *Chemical Senses, 30*(Suppl. 1), 242–243.

Mennella, J., Jagnow, C., & Beauchamp, G. (2001). Prenatal and postnatal flavor learning by human infants. *Pediatrics, 107,* 88–94.

Mennitti, L. V., Oliveira, J. L., Morais, C. A., Estadella, D., Oyama, L. M., Oller do Nascimento, C. M., & Pisani, L. P. (2015). Type of fatty acids in maternal diets during pregnancy and/or lactation and metabolic consequences of the offspring. *The Journal of Nutritional Biochemistry, 26*(2), 99–111.

Menzies, L., Goddings, A., Whitaker, K. J., Blakemore, S., & Viner, R. M. (2015). The effects of puberty on white matter development in boys. *Developmental Cognitive Neuroscience, 11,* 116–128.

Meristo, M., Morgan, G., Geraci, A., Iozzi, L., Hjelmquist, E., Surian, L., et al. (2012). Belief attribution in deaf and hearing infants. *Developmental Science, 15*(5), 633–640.

Merrill, N., & Fivush, R. (2016). Intergenerational narratives and identity across development. *Developmental Review, 40,* 72–92.

Mesman, J., van IJzendoorn, M. H., & Bakermans-Kranenburg, M. J. (2009). The many faces of the Still-Face Paradigm: A review and meta-analysis. *Developmental Review, 29,* 120–162.

Mesoudi, A. (2016). Cultural evolution: A review of theory, findings and controversies. *Evolutionary Biology, 43*(4), 481–497.

Metz, S. M., Frank, J. L., Reibel, D., Cantrell, T., Sanders, R., & Broderick, P. C. (2013). The effectiveness of the learning to BREATHE program on adolescent emotion regulation. *Research in Human Development, 10*(3), 252–272.

Meyers, S. (2001). *Everywhere babies.* San Diego, CA: Harcourt.

Micalizzi, L., Wang, M., & Saudino, K. J. (2017). Difficult temperament and negative parenting in early childhood: A genetically informed cross-lagged analysis. *Developmental Science, 20*(2).

Migliano, A. B., Vinicius, L., & Lahr, M. M. (2007). Life history trade-offs explain the evolution of human pygmies. *Proceedings of the National Academy of Sciences of the United States of America, 104,* 20216–20219.

Miller, C. A., & Golden, N. H. (2010). An introduction to eating disorders: Clinical presentation, epidemiology, and prognosis. *Nutrition in Clinical Practice, 25,* 110–115.

Miller, J. G., & Kinsbourne, M. (2012). Culture and neuroscience in developmental psychology: Contributions and challenges. *Child Development Perspectives, 6*(1), 35–41.

Miller, J. G., & Schaberg, L. (2003). Cultural perspectives on personality and social psychology. In T. Millon, & M. J. Lerner (Eds.), *Handbook of psychology: Vol. 5. Personality and social psychology* (pp. 31–56). New York: Wiley.

Miller, J. L., Macedonia, C., & Sonies, B. C. (2006). Sex differences in prenatal oral-motor function and development. *Developmental Medicine and Child Neurology, 48,* 465–470.

Miller, P. J., Fung, H., & Mintz, J. (1996). Self-construction through narrative practices: A Chinese and American comparison of early socialization. *Ethos, 24,* 1–44.

Mills, C. M., & Keil, F. C. (2004, January). Knowing the limits of one's understanding: The development of an awareness of an illusion of explanatory depth. *Journal of Experimental Child Psychology, 87,* 1–32.

Milnitsky-Sapiro, C., Turiel, E., & Nucci, L. (2006). Brazilian adolescents' conceptions of autonomy and parental authority. *Cognitive Development, 21*(3), 317–331.

Mintz, S. (2004). *Huck's raft: A history of American childhood.* Cambridge, MA: Cambridge University Press.

Mireault, G. C., Crockenberg, S. C., Sparrow, J. E., Cousineau, K., Pettinato, C., & Woodard, K. (2015). Laughing matters: Infant humor in the context of parental affect. *Journal of Experimental Child Psychology, 136,* 30–41.

Mishra, R. C. (2014). Piagetian studies of cognitive development in India. *Psychological Studies, 59*(3), 207–222.

Mitchell, E. (1985). The dynamics of family interaction around home video games. *Marriage & Family Review. Special Issue: Personal computers and the family, 8,* 121–135.

Mitchell, K., Ybarra, M., & Korchmaros, J. (2014). Sexual harassment among adolescents of different sexual orientations and gender identities. *Child Abuse & Neglect, 38*(2), 280–295.

Modell, J., & Elder, G. H. (2002). Children develop in history: So what's new? In W. Hartup & R. A. Weinberg (Eds.), *Child psychology in retrospect and prospect: In celebration of the 75th anniversary of the Institute of Child Development. The Minnesota symposia on child psychology: Vol. 32* (pp. 173–205). Mahwah, NJ: Lawrence Erlbaum Associates.

Moffitt, T. E. (2007). A review of research on the taxonomy of life-course persistent versus adolescence-limited antisocial behavior. In D. J. Flannery, A. T. Vazsonyi, & I. D. Waldman (Eds.), *The Cambridge handbook of violent behavior and aggression* (pp. 49–74). New York: Cambridge University Press.

Moffitt, T. E., Caspi, A., Rutter, M., & Silva, P. A. (2002, November). Review of sex differences in antisocial behaviour: Conduct disorder, delinquency and violence in the Dunedin Longitudinal Study. *Psychological Medicine, 32*(8), 1475–1476.

Moisala, M., Salmela, V., Hietajärvi, L., Salo, E., Carlson, S., Salonen, O., et al. (2016). Media multitasking is associated with distractibility and increased prefrontal activity in adolescents and young adults. *Neuroimage, 134,* 113–121.

Molina, J. C., Spear, N. E., Spear, L. P., Mennella, J. A., & Lewis, M. J. (2007). The International Society for Developmental Psychobiology 39th annual meeting symposium: Alcohol and development: Beyond fetal alcohol syndrome. *Developmental Psychobiology, 49*(3), 227–242.

Mondloch, C. J., & Desjarlais, M. (2010). The function and specificity of sensitivity to cues to facial identity: An individual-differences approach. *Perception, 39,* 819–829.

Monk-Turner, E., Heiserman, M., Johnson, C., Cotton, V., & Jackson, M. (2010). The portrayal of racial minorities on prime time television: A replication of the Mastro and Greenberg study a decade later. *Studies in Popular Culture, 32.*

Montgomery, E. (2011). Trauma, exile and mental health in young refugees. *Acta Psychiatrica Scandinavica, 124*(440), 1–46.

Montroy, J. J., Bowles, R. P., Skibbe, L. E., McClelland, M. M., & Morrison, F. J. (2016). The development of self-regulation across early childhood. *Developmental Psychology, 52*(11), 1744–1762.

Moon, C., Lagercrantz, H., & Kuhl, P. K. (2013). Language experienced in utero affects vowel perception after birth: A two-country study. *Acta Paediatrica, 102,* 156–160.

Moon, C., Zernzach, R. C., & Kuhl, P. K. (2015). Mothers say "baby" and their newborns do not choose to listen: A behavioral preference study to compare with ERP results. *Frontiers in Human Neuroscience, 9,* 153.

Moore, K., Persaud, T., & Torchia, M. (2015). *The developing human* (10th ed.). Philadelphia, PA: Elsevier.

Moore, K. L., & Persaud, T. V. N. (1993). *The developing human: Clinically oriented embryology* (5th ed.). Philadelphia, PA: Saunders.

Moran, L. (2016). Constructions of race: Symbolic ethnic capital and the performance of youth identity in multicultural Australia. *Ethnic and Racial Studies, 39*(4), 708–726.

Morelli, C. (2017). The river echoes with laughter: A child-centred analysis of social change in Amazonia. *Journal of the Royal Anthropological Institute, 23*(1), 137.

Morgan, G., & Woll, B. (Eds.). (2002). *Directions in sign language acquisition.* Philadelphia, PA: John Benjamins.

Morgan, G., Meristo, M., Mann, W., Hjelmquist, E., Surian, L., Siegal, M., et al. (2014). Mental state language and quality of conversational experience in deaf and hearing children. *Cognitive Development, 29*(1), 41–49.

Morgan, J. (1999). *When chickenheads come home to roost.* New York: Simon & Schuster.

Morgan, R. E. (2013). Does consumption of high-fructose corn syrup beverages cause obesity in children? *Pediatric Obesity, 8*(4), 249.

Morokuma, S., Doria, V., Ierullo, A., Kinukawa, N., Fukushima, K., Nakano, H., et al. (2008). Developmental change in foetal response to repeated low-intensity sound. *Developmental Science, 11,* 47–52.

Morris, A. S., Robinson, L. R., Hays-Grudo, J., Claussen, A. H., Hartwig, S. A., & Treat, A. E. (2017). Targeting parenting in early childhood: A public health approach to improve outcomes for children living in poverty. *Child Development, 88*(2), 388.

Morris, B., Croker, S., Zimmerman, C., Gill, D., & Romig, C. (2013). Gaming science: The "gamification" of scientific thinking. *Frontiers in Psychology, 4,* 607.

Morrison, L., Sieving, R., Pettingell, S., Hellerstedt, W., McMorris, B., & Bearinger, L. (2016). Protective factors, risk indicators, and contraceptive consistency among college women. *Journal of Obstetric Gynecologic and Neonatal Nursing, 45*(2), 155–165.

Morrongiello, B. A., Fenwick, K. D., Hillier, L., & Chance, G. (1994). Sound localization in newborn human infants. *Developmental Psychobiology, 27*(8), 519–538.

Morrow, C., Hidinger, A., & Wilkinson-Faulk, D. (2010). Reducing neonatal pain during routine heel lance procedures. *MCN, The American Journal of Maternal/Child Nursing, 35*(6), 346–354.

Morrow, C. E., Bandstra, E. S., Anthony, J. C., Ofir, A. Y., Xue, L., & Reyes, M. B. (2003). Influence of prenatal cocaine exposure on early language development: Longitudinal findings from four months to three years of age. *Journal of Developmental and Behavioral Pediatrics, 24*(1), 39–50.

Morton, S. M. B. (2006). Maternal nutrition and fetal growth and development. In P. Gluckman & M. Hanson (Eds.), *Developmental origins of health and disease* (pp. 98–129). New York: Cambridge University Press.

Mosco, N., & Atzaba-Poria, N. (2016). In search of "the Bedouin adaptive adult": Socialization goals of mothers and fathers from the Bedouin society of the Negev. *Journal of Cross-Cultural Psychology, 47*(1), 54–71.

Moshman, D. (1999). *Adolescent psychological development: Rationality, morality and identity.* Mahwah, NJ: Lawrence Erlbaum Associates.

Moshman, D. (2011). *Adolescent rationality and development.* New York: Psychology Press.

Moshman, D. (2013). *Adolescent rationality*. San Diego, CA: Elsevier Academic Press Inc.

Motti-Stefanidi, F., Masten, A., & Asendorpf, J. B. (2015). School engagement trajectories of immigrant youth: Risks and longitudinal interplay with academic success. *International Journal of Behavioral Development, 39*(1), 32–42.

Mou, Y., & vanMarle, K. (2014). Two core systems of numerical representation in infants. *Developmental Review, 34*(1), 1.

Moua, M. Y., & Lamborn, S. D. (2010). Hmong American adolescents' perceptions of ethnic socialization practices. *Journal of Adolescent Research, 25*(3), 416–440.

Moussa, S., El Kholy, M., Enaba, D., Salem, K., Ali, A., Nasreldin, M., et al. (2015). Impact of political violence on the mental health of school children in Egypt. *Journal of Mental Health, 24*(5), 289–293.

Muhlhausler, B. S., Gugusheff, J. R., Ong, Z. Y., & Vithayathil, M. A. (2013). Nutritional approaches to breaking the intergenerational cycle of obesity. *Canadian Journal of Physiology and Pharmacology, 91*(6), 421.

Müller, U. (2009). Infancy. In U. Müller (Ed.), *The Cambridge companion to Piaget* (pp. 200–228). New York: Cambridge University Press.

Müller, U., Liebermann-Finestone, D. P., Carpendale, J. I. M., Hammond, S. I., & Bibok, M. B. (2012). Knowing minds, controlling actions: The developmental relations between theory of mind and executive function from 2 to 4 years of age. *Journal of Experimental Child Psychology, 111*(2), 331–348.

Munakata, Y., Casey, B., & Diamond, A. (2004). Developmental cognitive neuroscience: Progress and potential. *Trends in Cognitive Sciences, 8,* 122–128.

Munroe, R. L., & Romney, A. K. (2006). Gender and age differences in same-sex aggregation and social behavior: A four-culture study. *Journal of Cross-Cultural Psychology, 37*(1), 3–19.

Murphy, K. M., Rodrigues, K., Costigan, J., & Annan, J. (2017). Raising children in conflict: An integrative model of parenting in war. *Peace & Conflict, 23*(1), 46.

Murray, C. (2016). *Global burden of disease study.* Retrieved from http://ghdx.healthdata.org

Musgrave, S., Morgan, D., Lonsdorf, E., Mundry, R., & Sanz, C. (2016). Tool transfers are a form of teaching among chimpanzees. *Scientific Reports, 6,* 34783.

Mustanski, B., Viken, R. J., Kaprio, J., Pulkkinen, L., & Rose, R. J. (2004). Genetic and environmental influences on pubertal development: Longitudinal data from 12–14-year-old twins. *Developmental Psychology, 40,* 1188–1198.

Musu-Gillette, L., Zhang, A., Wang, K., Zhang, J., & Oudekerk, B. A. (2017). *Indicators of school crime and safety: 2016* (NCES 2017-064/NCJ 250650). Washington, DC: National Center for Education Statistics, U.S. Department of Education, and Bureau of Justice Statistics, Office of Justice Programs, U.S. Department of Justice.

Nabors, L., Bartz, J., Kichler, J., Sievers, R., Elkins, R., & Pangallo, J. (2013). Play as a mechanism of working through medical trauma for children with medical illnesses and their siblings. *Issues in Comprehensive Pediatric Nursing, 36*(3), 212–224.

Nabors, L., & Liddle, M. (2017). Perceptions of hospitalization by children with chronic illnesses and siblings. *Journal of Child and Family Studies, 26*(6), 1681.

Nadel, J. (2002). Imitation and imitation recognition: Functional use in preverbal infants and nonverbal children with autism. In A. Meltzoff & W. Prinz (Eds.), *The imitative mind: Development, evolution, and brain bases.* Cambridge, England: Cambridge University Press.

Nader, P., O'Brien, M., Houts, R., Bradley, R., Belsky, J., Crosnoe, R., et al. (2006). Identifying risk for obesity in early childhood. *Pediatrics, 118,* 594–601.

Narayan, C. R., & McDermott, L. C. (2016). Speech rate and pitch characteristics of infant-directed speech: Longitudinal and cross-linguistic observations. *The Journal of the Acoustical Society of America, 139*(3), 1272–1281.

Narula, H. S., & Carlson, H. E. (2007). Gynecomastia. *Endocrinology and Metabolism Clinics of North America, 36*(2), 497–519.

Nasir, N. (2005). Individual cognitive structuring and the sociocultural context: Strategy shifts in the game of dominoes. *Journal of the Learning Sciences, 14,* 5–34.

National Center for Education Statistics. (2013). *Table 202.60. Percentage distribution of quality rating of child care arrangements of children at about 4 years of age, by type of arrangement and selected child and family characteristics: 2005–06.* Retrieved from https://nces.ed.gov/programs/digest/d14/tables/dt14_202.60.asp?currentDyes

National Heart, Lung, and Blood Institute. (2016). *What are the signs and symptoms of sickle cell disease?* Retrieved from https://www.nhlbi.nih.gov/health/health-topics/topics/sca/signs

National Institute on Deafness and Other Communication Disorders. (2012). *Aphasia.* Retrieved from http://www.nidcd.nih.gov/health/voice/pages/aphasia.aspx#types

National Society of Genetic Counselors. (2017). *Who are genetic counselors?* Retrieved from http://www.nsgc.org/page/whoaregcs

Natsiopoulou, T., & Bletsou, M. (2011). Greek preschoolers' use of electronic media and their preferences for media or books. *International Journal of Caring Sciences, 4*(2), 97–104.

Navarro, V. M., & Tena-Sempere, M. (2011). Neuroendocrine control by kisspeptins: Role in metabolic regulation of fertility. *Nature Reviews Endocrinology, 8*(1), 40–53.

Neal, J. W., Durbin, C. E., Gornik, A. E., & Lo, S. L. (2017). Codevelopment of preschoolers' temperament traits and social play networks over an entire school year. *Journal of Personality and Social Psychology,* doi: 10.1037/pspp0000135

Neal, J. W., Neal, Z. P., & Cappella, E. (2014). I know who my friends are, but do you? Predictors of self-reported and peer-inferred relationships. *Child Development, 85*(4), 1366–1372.

Needham, A., & Baillargeon, R. (1993). Intuitions about support in 4.5-month-old infants. *Cognition, 47*(2), 121–148.

Needham, A., Barrett, T., & Peterman, K. (2002). A pick-me-up for infants' exploratory skills: Early stimulated experiences reaching for objects using "sticky mittens" enhances young infants' object exploration skills. *Infant Behavior and Development, 25,* 279–295.

Neef, N. E., Müller, B., Liebig, J., Schaadt, G., Grigutsch, M., Gunter, T. C., et al. (2017). Dyslexia risk gene relates to representation of sound in the auditory brainstem. *Developmental Cognitive Neuroscience, 24,* 63–71.

Nehring, I., Kostka, T., von Kries, R., & Rehfuess, E. A. (2015). Impacts of in utero and early infant taste experiences on later taste acceptance: A systematic review. *The Journal of Nutrition, 145*(6), 1271–1279.

Nelson, A. M. (2017). Risks and benefits of swaddling healthy infants: An integrative review. *MCN, The American Journal of Maternal/Child Nursing,* doi: 10.1097/NMC.0000000000000344

Nelson, C. A., Zeanah, C. H., Fox, N. A. (2007). The effects of early deprivation on brain-behavioral development: The Bucharest Early Intervention Project. In D. Romer & E. F. Walker (Eds.), *Adolescent psychopathology Adolescent psychopathology and the developing brain: Integrating brain and prevention science* (pp. 85–91). New York: Oxford University Press.

Nelson, K. (1981). Social cognition in a script framework. In J. H. Flavell & L. Ross (Eds.), *Social cognitive development.* Cambridge, MA: Cambridge University Press.

Nelson, K. (2003). Co-constructing the cultural person through narratives in early childhood. In C. Daiute & C. Lightfoot (Eds.), *Narrative analysis: Studying the development of individuals in society.* New York: Sage Press.

Nelson, K. (2009). Narrative practices and folk psychology: A perspective from developmental psychology. *Journal of Consciousness Studies, 16,* 69–93.

Nelson, K. (2014). A matter of meaning: Reflections on forty years of *JCL. Journal of Child Language, 41*(Suppl. 1), 93.

Nelson, K. (2015). Quantitative and qualitative research in psychological science. *Biological Theory, 10*(3), 263–272.

Nelson, K., & Shaw, L. (2002). Developing a socially shared symbolic system. In E. Amsel & J. Byrnes (Eds.), *Language, literacy, and cognitive development.* Mahwah, NJ: Lawrence Erlbaum Associates.

Nelson, K., Skwerer, D. P., Goldman, S., Henseler, S., Presler, N., & Walkenfeld, F. F. (2003). Entering a community of minds: An experimental approach to "theory of mind." *Human Development, 46,* 24–46.

Nesi, J., & Prinstein, M. J. (2015). Using social media for social comparison and feedback-seeking: Gender and popularity moderate associations with depressive symptoms. *Journal of Abnormal Child Psychology, 43*(8), 1427–1438.

Netter, F. H. (1965). *The CIBA collection of medical illustrations.* Summit, NJ: CIBA Pharmaceutical Products.

Neville, H. J. (2005). Development and plasticity of human cognition. In U. Mayr, E. Awh, & S. W. Keele (Eds.), *Developing individuality in the human brain: A tribute to Michael I. Posner. Decade of behavior* (pp. 209–235). Washington, DC: American Psychological Association.

Newberger, D. (2000). Down syndrome: Prenatal risk assessment and diagnosis. *American Family Physician, 15,* 825–837.

Newcomb, A. F., Bukowski, W. M., & Pattee, L. (1993). Children's peer relations: A meta-analytic review of popular, rejected, controversial and average sociometric status. *Psychological Bulletin, 113,* 99–128.

Newell, M. L., Coovadia, H., Cortina-Borja, M., Rollins, N., Gaillard, P., & Dabis, F. (2004). Ghent International AIDS Society (IAS) Working Group on HIV Infection in Women and Children. Mortality of infected and uninfected infants born to HIV-infected mothers in Africa: A pooled analysis. *Lancet, 364,* 1236–1243.

Newheiser, A., Dunham, Y., Merrill, A., Hoosain, L., & Olson, K. R. (2014). Preference for high status predicts implicit outgroup bias among children from low-status groups. *Developmental Psychology, 50*(4), 1081–1090.

Newport, E. L., Bavelier, D., & Neville, H. J. (2001). Critical thinking about critical periods: Perspectives on a critical period for language acquisition. In E. Dupoux (Ed.), *Language, brain, and cognitive development: Essays in honor of Jacques Mehler* (pp. 481–502). Cambridge, MA: The MIT Press.

Nguyen, D., Smith, L. M., Lagasse, L. L., Derauf, C., Grant, P., Shah, R., et al. (2010). Intrauterine growth of infants exposed to prenatal methamphetamine: Results from the infant development, environment, and lifestyle study. *The Journal of Pediatrics, 157,* 337–339. Retrieved from http://www.ncbi.nlm.nih.gov/pubmed/16951010

NICHD Early Child Care Research Network. (2003c). Does quality of care affect child outcomes at age 4? *Developmental Psychology, 39,* 451–469.

Nicholls, D., Chater, R., & Lask, B. (2000). Children into DSM don't go: A comparison of classification systems for eating disorders in childhood and early adolescence. *The International Journal of Eating Disorders, 28*(3), 317–324.

Nicolopoulou, A., Cortina, K. S., Ilgaz, H., Cates, C. B., & de Sá, A. B. (2015). Using a narrative- and play-based activity to promote low-income preschoolers' oral language, emergent literacy, and social competence. *Early Childhood Research Quarterly, 31,* 147–162.

Nigg, J. T. (2016). Where do epigenetics and developmental origins take the field of developmental psychopathology? *Journal of Abnormal Child Psychology, 44*(3), 405–419.

Nijhuis, J. G., Prechtl, H. F. R., Martin, C. B., & Bots, R. S. G. M. (1982). Are there behavioral states in the human foetus? *Early Human Development, 6,* 177–195.

Nilsson, M., & Ferholt, B. (2014). Vygotsky's theories of play, imagination and creativity in current practice: Gunilla Lindqvist's "creative pedagogy of play" in U.S. kindergartens and Swedish Reggio-Emilia inspired preschools. *Perspectiva, 32*(3), 919–950.

Noble, K. G., Houston, S. M., Kan, E., & Sowell, E. R. (2012). Neural correlates of socioeconomic status in the developing human brain. *Developmental Science, 15*(4), 516–527.

Nolan, L., Grigorenko, A., & Thorstensson, A. (2005). Balance control: Sex and age difference in 9- to 16-year-olds. *Developmental Medicine and Child Neurology, 47,* 449–454.

Nomaguchi, K., Johnson, W. L., Minter, M. D., & Aldrich, L. (2017). Clarifying the association between mother–father relationship aggression and parenting. *Journal of Marriage and Family, 79*(1), 161–178.

Nord, M., Coleman-Jensen, A., Andrews, M., & Carlson, S. (2010). *Household food security in the United States, 2009* (Economic Research Report No. 108): United States Department of Agriculture.

Nour, N. M. (2009). Child marriage: A silent health and human rights issue. *Reviews in Obstetrics & Gynecology, 2*(1), 51–56.

Novelli, L., D'atri, A., Marzano, C., Finotti, E., Ferrara, M., Bruni, O., & De Gennaro, L. (2016). Mapping changes in cortical activity during sleep in the first 4 years of life. *Journal of Sleep Research, 25*(4), 381–389.

Novin, S., Banerjee, R., Dadkhah, A., & Rieffe, C. (2009). Self-reported use of emotional display rules in the Netherlands and Iran: Evidence for sociocultural influence. *Social Development, 18*(2), 397–411.

Nsamenang, A. (2006). Human ontogenesis: An indigenous African view on development and intelligence. *International Journal of Psychology. Special Issue: The indigenous psychologies, 41*(4), 293–297.

Nucci, L. (2004). The promise and limitations of the moral self construct. In C. Lightfoot, C. LaLonde, & M. Chandler (Eds.), *Changing conceptions of psychological life.* Mahwah, NJ: Lawrence Erlbaum Associates.

Nucci, L. (2016). Recovering the role of reasoning in moral education to address inequity and social justice. *Journal of Moral Education, 45*(3), 291–307.

Nucci, L., Creane, M. W., & Powers, D. W. (2015). Integrating moral and social development within middle school social studies: A social cognitive domain approach. *Journal of Moral Education, 44*(4), 479–496.

Nunes, T., & Bryant, P. (2009). Children's reading and spelling: Beyond the first steps. In T. Nunes & P. Bryant (Eds.), *Children's reading and spelling: Beyond the first steps.* Malden, MA: Wiley-Blackwell.

Nunes, T., Bryant, P., & Barros, R. (2012). The development of word recognition and its significance for comprehension and fluency. *Journal of Educational Psychology, 104*(4), 959–973.

Nyiti, R. M. (1976). The development of conservation in the Meru children of Tanzania. *Child Development, 47,* 1122–1129.

Nyiti, R. M. (1982). The validity of "cultural differences explanations" for cross-cultural variation in Piagetian cognitive development. In D. A. Wagner & H. W. Stevenson (Eds.), *Cultural perspectives on child development.* San Francisco, CA: W. H. Freeman.

O'Brien, M., Peyton, V., Mistry, R., Hruda, L., Jacobs, A., Caldera, Y., et al. (2000). Gender-role cognition in three-year-old boys and girls. *Sex Roles, 42,* 1007–1025.

Odden, H. (2009). Interactions of temperament and culture: The organization of diversity in Samoan infancy. *Ethos, 37*(2), 161–180.

Ogbu, J. U. (1997). Understanding the school performance of urban blacks: Some essential background knowledge. In H. J. Walberg & O. Reyes (Eds.), *Children and youth: Interdisciplinary perspectives* (pp. 190–222). Thousand Oaks, CA: Sage.

O'Driscoll, T., Payne, L., Kelly, L., Cromarty, H., Pierre-Hansen, N. S., & Terry, C. (2011). Traditional first nations birthing practices: Interviews with elders in northwestern Ontario. *Journal of Obstetrics and Gynaecology Canada, 33*(1), 24–29.

Okami, P., Weisner, T., & Olmstead, R. (2002). Outcome correlates of parent-child bedsharing: An eighteen-year longitudinal study. *Journal of Developmental and Behavioral Pediatrics, 23,* 244–253.

Okigbo, C. C., Kabiru, C. W., Mumah, J. N., Mojola, S. A., & Beguy, D. (2015). Influence of parental factors on adolescents' transition to first sexual intercourse in Nairobi, Kenya: A longitudinal study. *Reproductive Health, 12*(1), 73.

Okonofua, F. (2013). Prevention of child marriage and teenage pregnancy in Africa: Need for more research and innovation. *African Journal of Reproductive Health, 17*(4), 9–13.

Olds, D. L. (2006). The nurse-family partnership: An evidence-based preventive intervention. *Infant Mental Health Journal, 27*(1), 5–25.

O'Leary, A. P., & Sloutsky, V. M. (2016). Carving metacognition at its joints: Protracted development of component processes. *Child Development, 88*(3), 1015–1032.

Oliner, S. B., & Oliner, P. (1988). *The altruistic personality: Rescuers of Jews in Nazi Germany.* New York: Macmillan.

Olsen, B. R., Reginato, A. M., & Wang, W. (2000). Bone development. *Annual Review of Cell and Developmental Biology, 16,* 191–220.

Olson, K. (2007, February 18). Her autistic brothers. *New York Times Magazine,* 42–47.

Ong, A. D., Fuller-Rowell, T. E., & Phinney, J. S. (2010). Measurement of ethnic identity: Recurrent and emergent issues. *Identity, 10,* 39–49.

Oostenbroek, J., Suddendorf, T., Nielsen, M., Redshaw, J., Kennedy-Costantini, S., Davis, J., et al. (2016). Comprehensive longitudinal study challenges the existence of neonatal imitation in humans. *Current Biology, 26*(10), 1334–1338.

Opfer, J. E., & Gelman, S. A. (2001). Children's and adults' models for predicting teleological action: The development of a biology-based model. *Child Development, 72*(5), 1367–1381.

Orioli, I. M., & Castilla, E. E. (2000). New associations between prenatal exposure to drugs and malformations. *American Journal of Human Genetics, 67*(4, Suppl. 2), 175.

Orlandi, S., Garcia, C., Bandini, A., Donzelli, G., & Manfredi, C. (2016). Application of pattern recognition techniques to the classification of full-term and preterm infant cry. *Journal of Voice, 30*(6), 656–663.

Ornstein, P. A., & Haden, C. (2009). Developments in the study of memory development. In M. Courage & N. Cowan (Eds.), *The development of memory in infancy and childhood.* Hove, UK: Psychology Press.

Ornstein, P. A., Haden, C., & Hendrick, A. (2004). Learning to remember: Social-communicative exchanges and the development of children's memory skills. *Developmental Review, 24,* 374–395.

Ornstein, P. A., & Light, L. L. (2010). Memory development across the life span. In P. A. Ornstein & L. L. Light (Eds.), *The handbook of life-span development: Vol. 1. Cognition, biology, and methods.* Hoboken, NJ: John Wiley & Sons.

Ornstein, P. A., Shapiro, L. R., Clubb, P. A., Follmer, A., & Baker-Ward, L. (1997). The influence of prior knowledge on children's memory for salient medical experiences. In N. Stein, P. A. Ornstein, B. Tversky, & C. J. Brainerd (Eds.), *Memory for everyday and emotional events* (pp. 83–112).

Oster, H. (2005). The repertoire of infant facial expressions: An ontogenetic perspective. In J. Nadel & D. Muir (Eds.), *Emotional development.* Oxford, England: Oxford University Press.

Osterman, M., & Martin, J. (2011). Epidural and spinal anesthesia use during labor: 27-state reporting area, 2008. *National Vital Statistics Report.* Retrieved from https://www.cdc.gov/nchs/data/nvsr/nvsr59/nvsr59_05.pdf

Osterman, M., & Martin, J. (2014). *Declines in induction of labor by gestational age.* Retrieved from https://www.cdc.gov/nchs/data/databriefs/db155.pdf

Ostlund, B. D., Measelle, J. R., Laurent, H. K., Conradt, E., & Ablow, J. C. (2017). Shaping emotion regulation: Attunement, symptomatology, and stress recovery within mother–infant dyads. *Developmental Psychobiology, 59*(1), 15–25.

Ostrov, J., Gentile, D., & Crick, N. (2006). Media exposure, aggression and prosocial behavior during early childhood: A longitudinal study. *Social Development, 15,* 612–627.

O'Sullivan, L. F., Meyer-Bahlburg, H. F. L., & McKeague, I. W. (2006). The development of the sexual self-concept inventory for early adolescent girls. *Psychology of Women Quarterly, 30*(2), 139–149.

Ott, M. Q., Corliss, H. L., Wypij, D., Rosario, M., & Austin, S. B. (2011). Stability and change in self-reported sexual orientation identity in young people: Application of mobility metrics. *Archives of Sexual Behavior, 40*(3), 519–532.

Otto, H., & Keller, H. (Eds.). (2014). *Different faces of attachment: Cultural variations on a universal human need.* New York: Cambridge University Press.

Otto, H., & Keller, H. (2015). Good child is a calm child: Mothers' social status, maternal conceptions of proper demeanor, and stranger anxiety in one-year old Cameroonian Nso children. *Psychological Topics, 24*(1), 1–25.

Out, D., Pieper, S., Bakermans-Kranenburg, M. J., & van IJzendoorn, M. H. (2010). Physiological reactivity to infant crying: A behavioral genetic study. *Genes, Brain & Behavior, 9,* 868–876.

Oyeku, S., Raphael, J., Cassell, C., & Hulihan, M. (2016). Developing a unified approach for sickle cell disease. *American Journal of Preventive Medicine, 51*(1).

Oyserman, D., Bybee, D., & Terry, K. (2006). Possible selves and academic outcomes: How and when possible selves impel action. *Journal of Personality and Social Psychology, 91*(1), 188–204.

Özçalışkan, Ş. (2007). Metaphors we move by: Children's developing understanding of metaphorical motion in typologically distinct languages. *Metaphor and Symbol, 22*(2), 147.

Paasch-Anderson, J., & Lamborn, S. D. (2014). African American adolescents' perceptions of ethnic socialization and racial socialization as distinct processes. *Journal of Adolescent Research, 29*(2), 159–185.

Padilla, A. (2006). Bicultural social development. *Hispanic Journal of Behavioral Sciences, 28,* 467–497.

Padula, A. M., Yang, W., Carmichael, S. L., Tager, I. B., Lurmann, F., Hammond, S. K., & Shaw, G. M. (2015). Air pollution, neighbourhood socioeconomic factors, and neural tube defects in the San Joaquin Valley of California. *Paediatric and Perinatal Epidemiology, 29*(6), 536–545.

Pagani, L., Levesque-Seck, F., & Fitzpatrick, C. (2016). Prospective associations between televiewing at toddlerhood and later self-reported social impairment at middle school in a Canadian longitudinal cohort born in 1997/1998. *Psychological Medicine, 46*(16), 3329–3337.

Page-Goertz, S., McCamman, S., & Westdahl, C. (2001). Breastfeeding promotion. Top tips for motivating women to breastfeed their infants. *AWHONN Lifelines, 5*(1), 41–43.

Pak, S. (2010). The growth status of North Korean refugee children and adolescents from 6 to 19 years of age. *Economics and Human Biology, 8,* 385–395.

Palermo, F., Mikulski, A. M., & Conejo, L. D. (2017). Self-regulation abilities and Spanish-speaking preschoolers' vocabulary and letter-word skills in Spanish and English. *Early Education and Development, 28*(2), 207–223.

Paley, V. G. (1981). *Wally's stories.* Cambridge, MA: Harvard University Press.

Paley, V. G. (1984). *Boys & girls: Superheroes in the doll corner.* Chicago, IL: The University of Chicago Press.

Palincsar, A. S., Spiro, R. J., Kucan, L., Magnusson, S. J., Collins, B., Hapgood, S., et al. (2007). Designing a hypermedia environment to support comprehension instruction. In D. S. McNamara (Ed.), *Reading comprehension strategies: Theories, interventions, and technologies* (pp. 441–462). Mahwah, NJ: Lawrence Erlbaum Associates.

Pan, B. A., & Snow, C. E. (1999). The development of conversational and discourse skills. In M. Barrett (Ed.), *The development of language* (pp. 229–250). Hove, England: Psychology Press.

Panksepp, J. (2010). The evolutionary sources of jealousy: Cross-species approaches to fundamental issues. In S. Hart & M. Legerstee (Eds.), *Handbook of jealousy: Theory, research, and multidisciplinary approaches* (pp. 101–120). Hoboken, NJ: Wiley-Blackwell.

Panksepp, J., & Smith-Pasqualini, M. (2005). The search for fundamental brain/mind sources of affective experience. In J. Nadel & D. Muir (Eds.), *Emotional Development.* Oxford, England: Oxford University Press.

Papagiannopoulou, E. A., & Lagopoulos, J. (2017). P300 event-related potentials in children with dyslexia. *Annals of Dyslexia, 67*(1), 99.

Parent, A.-S., Teilmann, G., Juul, A., Skakkebaek, N. E., Toppari, J., & Bourguignon, J.-P. (2003). The timing of normal puberty and the age limits of sexual precocity: Variations around the world, secular trends, and changes after migration. *Endocrine Reviews, 24,* 668–693.

Parke, R. D., O'Neil, R., Spitzer, S., Isley, S., Welsh, M., Wang, S., et al. (1997). A longitudinal assessment of sociometric stability and the behavioral correlates of children's social acceptance. *Merrill-Palmer Quarterly, 43,* 635–662.

Parker, S. E., Mai, C. T., Canfield, M. A., Rickard, R., Wang, Y., Meyer, R. E., et al. (2010). Updated national birth prevalence estimates for selected birth defects in the United States, 2004–2006. *Birth Defects Research Part A: Clinical and Molecular Teratology, 88,* 1008–1016.

Parker, S. T. (2005). Piaget's legacy in cognitive constructivism, niche construction, and phenotype development and evolution. In S. T. Parker, J. Langer, & C. Milbrath (Eds.), *Biology and knowledge revisited: From neurogenesis to psychogenesis.* Mahwah, NJ: Lawrence Erlbaum Associates.

Parker, S. T., & McKinney, M. L. (1999). *Origins of intelligence: The evolution of cognitive development in monkeys, apes, and humans.* Baltimore, MD: Johns Hopkins University Press.

Parolin, M., & Simonelli, A. (2016). Attachment theory and maternal drug addiction: The contribution to parenting interventions. *Frontiers in Psychiatry, 7,* 152.

Parsons, T. (1963). Youth in the context of American society. In E. Erikson (Ed.), *Youth: Change and challenge.* New York: Basic Books.

Partanen, E., Kujala, T., Näätäanen, R., Liitola, A., Sambeth, A., & Huotilainen, M. (2013). Learning-induced neural plasticity of speech processing before birth. *Proceedings of the National Academy of Sciences, 110,* 15145–15150.

Pascuzzo, K., Cyr, C., & Moss, E. (2013). Longitudinal association between adolescent attachment, adult romantic attachment, and emotion regulation strategies. *Attachment & Human Development, 15*(1), 83–103.

Pasterski, V., Acerini, C., Dunger, D., Ong, K., Hughes, I., Thankamony, A., & Hines, M. (2015). Postnatal penile growth concurrent with mini-puberty predicts later sex-typed play behavior: Evidence for neurobehavioral effects of the postnatal androgen surge in typically developing boys. *Hormones and Behavior, 69,* 98–105.

Patrick, H., Anderman, L. H., & Ryan, A. M. (2002). Social motivation and the classroom social environment. In C. Midgley (Ed.), *Goals, goal structures, and patterns of adaptive learning* (pp. 85–108). Mahwah, NJ: Lawrence Erlbaum Associates.

Patrick, R. B., & Gibbs, J. C. (2012). Inductive discipline, parental expression of disappointed expectations, and moral identity in adolescence. *Journal of Youth and Adolescence, 41*(8), 973–983.

Patterson, C. J., & Riskind, R. G. (2010). To be a parent: Issues in family formation among gay and lesbian adults. *Journal of GLBT Family Studies, 6,* 326–340.

Patterson, G. R., DeBaryshe, B. D., & Ramsey, E. (1989). A developmental perspective on antisocial behavior. *American Psychologist, 44*(2), 329–335.

Pattiselanno, K., Dijkstra, J., Steglich, C., Vollebergh, W., & Veenstra, R. (2015). Structure matters: The role of clique hierarchy in the relationship between adolescent social status and aggression and prosociality. *Journal of Youth and Adolescence, 44*(12), 2257–2274.

Paulus, M., & Fikkert, P. (2014). Conflicting social cues: Fourteen- and 24-month-old infants' reliance on gaze and pointing cues in word learning. *Journal of Cognition and Development, 15*(1), 432.

Pavlov, I. P. (1927). *Conditioned reflexes.* Oxford, England: Oxford University Press.

Pawloski, L. R., Ruchiwit, M., & Pakapong, Y. (2008). A cross-sectional examination of growth indicators from Thai adolescent girls: Evidence of obesity among Thai youth? *Annals of Human Biology, 35,* 378–385.

Peck, S., Brodish, A., Malanchuk, O., Banerjee, M., & Eccles, J. (2014). Racial/ethnic socialization and identity development in black families: The role of parent and youth reports. *Developmental Psychology, 50*(7), 1897–1909.

Pedersen, S., Vitaro, F., Barker, E. D., & Borge, A. I. H. (2007). The timing of middle-childhood peer rejection and friendship: Linking early behavior to early-adolescent adjustment. *Child Development, 78,* 1037–1051.

Peeters, M., Cillessen, A. H. N., & Scholte, R. H. (2010). Clueless or powerful? identifying subtypes of bullies in adolescence. *Journal of Youth and Adolescence, 39*(9), 1041.

Pelaez, M., Field, T., Pickens, J., & Hart, S. (2008). Disengaged and authoritarian parenting behavior of depressed mothers with their toddlers. *Infant Behavior & Development, 31*(1), 145–148.

Pellegrini, A. D., & Long, J. (2002). A longitudinal study of bullying, dominance, and victimization during the transition from primary through secondary school. *British Journal of Developmental Psychology, 20,* 259–280.

Pellegrini, A. D., & Long, J. D. (2003). A sexual selection theory longitudinal analysis of sexual segregation and integration in early adolescence. *Journal of Experimental Child Psychology, 85*(3), 257–278.

Pellegrini, A. D., Long, J. D., Solberg, D., Roseth, C., & Dupuis, D. (2010). Bullying and social status during school transitions. In S. R. Jimerson, S. M. Swearer, & D. L. Espelage (Eds.), *Handbook of bullying in schools: An international perspective* (pp. 199–210). New York: Routledge/Taylor & Francis Group.

Pellicano, E. (2010). Preview. The development of core cognitive skills in autism: A 3-year prospective study. *Child Development, 81,* 1400–1416.

Peltonen, K., Qouta, S., El Sarraj, E., & Punamäki, R. (2010). Military trauma and social development: The moderating and mediating roles of peer and sibling relations in mental health. *International Journal of Behavioral Development, 34*(6), 554–563.

Péneau, S., Rouchaud, A., Rolland-Cachera, M. F., Arnault, N., Hercberg, S., Castetbon, K. (2011). Body size and growth from birth to 2 years and risk of overweight at 7–9 years. *International Journal of Pediatric Obesity, 6,* 162–169.

Peper, J. S., Brouwer, R. M., Schnack, H. G., Van Baal, G. C. M., Van Leeuwen, M., Van Den Berg, S. M., et al. (2008). Cerebral white matter in early puberty is associated with luteinizing hormone concentrations. *Psychoneuroendocrinology, 33,* 909–915.

Perry, W. G. (1970). *Forms of intellectual and ethical development in the college years: A scheme.* New York: Holt, Rinehart, and Winston.

Peter, C. R., Tasker, T. B., & Horn, S. S. (2016). Adolescents' beliefs about harm, wrongness, and school policies as predictors of sexual and gender-based harassment. *Psychology of Sexual Orientation and Gender Diversity, 3*(4), 426–431.

Peter, J., & Valkenburg, P. M. (2010). Processes underlying the effects of adolescents' use of sexually explicit internet material: The role of perceived realism. *Communication Research, 37*(3), 375–399.

Peters, S., Peper, J. S., Van Duijvenvoorde, A. C. K., Braams, B. R., & Crone, E. A. (2017). Amygdala–orbitofrontal connectivity predicts alcohol use two years later: A longitudinal neuroimaging study on alcohol use in adolescence. *Developmental Science, 20*(4).

Peterson, C. (2005). Mind and body: Concepts of human cognition, physiology and false belief in children with autism or typical development. *Journal of Autism and Developmental Disorders, 35,* 487–497.

Peterson, C., & McCabe, A. (2004). Echoing our parents: Parental influences on children's narration. In M. W. Pratt & B. H. Fiese (Eds.), *Family stories and the life course, Across time and generations* (pp. 27–54). Mahwah, NJ: Lawrence Erlbaum Associates.

Petitto, L.-A. (2009). New discoveries from the bilingual brain and mind across the life span: Implications for education. *Mind, Brain, and Education, 3,* 185–197.

Pfeffer, C. (2012). Normative resistance and inventive pragmatism. *Gender & Society* 19: 456–479.

Phinney, J. S. (2008). Ethnic identity exploration in emerging adulthood. In D. L. Browning (Ed.), *Adolescent identities: A collection of readings. Relational perspectives book series* (pp. 47–66). New York: The Analytic Press/Taylor & Francis Group.

Phinney, J. S. (2010). Understanding development in cultural contexts: How do we deal with the complexity? *Human Development, 53,* 33–38.

Phinney, J. S., & Baldelomar, O. A. (2011). Identity development in multiple cultural contexts. In J. S. Phinney & O. A. Baldelomar (Eds.), *Bridging cultural and developmental approaches to psychology: New syntheses in theory, research, and policy* (pp. 161–186). New York: Oxford University Press.

Phinney, J. S., & Devich-Navarro, M. (1997). Variations in bicultural identification among African American and Mexican American adolescents. *Journal of Research on Adolescence, 7*(1), 3–32.

Phinney, J. S., & Ong, A. D. (2002). Adolescent–parent disagreements and life satisfaction in families from Vietnamese- and European-American backgrounds. *International Journal of Behavioral Development, 26*(6), 556–561.

Phinney, J. S., & Ong, A. D. (2007). Conceptualization and measurement of ethnic identity: Current status and future directions. *Journal of Counseling Psychology, 54*(3), 271–281.

Piaget, J., & Inhelder, B. (1973). *Memory and intelligence.* New York: Basic Books.

Piaget, J. (1926). *The language and thought of the child.* New York: Meridian Books.

Piaget, J. (1929/1979). *The child's conception of the world.* New York: Harcourt Brace.

Piaget, J. (1930). *The child's conception of physical causality.* New York: Harcourt Brace.

Piaget, J. (1932/1965). *The moral judgment of the child.* New York: Free Press. (Original work published 1932)

Piaget, J. (1952a). *The child's conception of number.* New York: W. W. Norton.

Piaget, J. (1952b). *The origins of intelligence in children.* New York: International Universities Press.

Piaget, J. (1954). *The construction of reality in the child.* New York: Basic Books.

Piaget, J. (1965/1995). *Sociological studies.* New York: Routledge.

Piaget, J. (1966/1974). Need and significance of cross-cultural studies in genetic psychology. In J. W. Berry & P. R. Dasen (Eds.), *Culture and cognition: Readings in cross-cultural psychology.* London: Methuen.

Piaget, J. (1973). *The psychology of intelligence.* Totowa, NJ: Littlefield & Adams.

Piaget, J. (1977). *The development of thought: Equilibration of cognitive structure.* New York: Viking.

Piaget, J., & Inhelder, B. (1956). *The child's conception of space.* London: Routledge & Kegan Paul.

Piaget, J., & Inhelder, B. (1969). *The psychology of the child.* New York: Basic Books.

Piazza, C., Cantiani, C., Akalin-Acar, Z., Miyakoshi, M., Benasich, A. A., Reni, G., et al. (2016). ICA-derived cortical responses indexing rapid multi-feature auditory processing in six-month-old infants. *Neuroimage, 133,* 75–87.

Pick, A. D. (1997). Perceptual learning, categorizing, and cognitive development. In C. Dent-Read & P. Zukow-Golding (Eds.), *Evolving explanations of development: Ecological approaches to organism environment systems* (pp. 335–370). Washington, DC: American Psychological Association.

Pickles, A., Hill, J., Breen, G., Quinn, J., Abbott, K., Jones, H., & Sharp, H. (2013). Evidence for interplay between genes and parenting on infant temperament in the first year of life: Monoamine oxidase A polymorphism moderates effects of maternal sensitivity on infant anger proneness. *Journal of Child Psychology and Psychiatry, 54*(12), 1308–1317.

Pieloch, K. A., McCullough, M. B., & Marks, A. K. (2016). Resilience of children with refugee statuses: A research review. *Canadian Psychology, 57*(4), 330.

Pietschnig, J., & Voracek, M. (2015). One century of global IQ gains: A formal meta-analysis of the Flynn effect (1909–2013). *Perspectives on Psychological Science, 10*(3), 282–306.

Pike, A., & Oliver, B. (2017). Child behavior and sibling relationship quality: A cross-lagged analysis. *Journal of Family Psychology, 31*(2), 250–255.

Piña-Watson, B., Dornhecker, M., & Salinas, S. R. (2015). The impact of bicultural stress on Mexican American adolescents' depressive symptoms and suicidal ideation: Gender matters. *Hispanic Journal of Behavioral Sciences, 37*(3), 342–364.

Pinelli, J., & Symington, A. (2001). Non-nutritive sucking for the promotion of physiologic stability and nutrition in preterm infants. *Cochrane Database of Systematic Reviews, 3,* CD001071.

Pingault, J., Tremblay, R. E., Vitaro, F., Japel, C., Boivin, M., & Côté, S. M. (2015). Early nonparental care and social behavior in elementary school: Support for a social group adaptation hypothesis. *Child Development, 86*(5), 1469–1488.

Pinker, S. (1994). *The language instinct: How the mind creates language.* New York: Harper Collins.

Pinker, S. (2002). *The blank slate: The modern denial of human nature.* New York: Viking.

Pinker, S. (2007). *The stuff of thought: Language as a window into human nature.* New York: Viking.

Pinquart, M. (2017). Associations of parenting dimensions and styles with externalizing problems of children and adolescents: An updated meta-analysis. *Developmental Psychology, 53*(5), 873.

Pinquart, M., & Teubert, D. (2010). Effects of parenting education with expectant and new parents: A meta-analysis. *Journal of Family Psychology, 24,* 316–327.

Pinto, D., Pagnamenta, A., Klei, L., Anney, R., & Merico, D. (2010). Functional impact of global rare copy number variation in autism spectrum disorders. *Nature, 466,* 368–372.

Piochon, C., Kano, M., & Hansel, C. (2016). LTD-like molecular pathways in developmental synaptic pruning. *Nature Neuroscience, 19*(10), 1299–1310.

Placa, V. L., & Corlyon, J. (2016). Unpacking the relationship between parenting and poverty: Theory, evidence and policy. *Social Policy and Society, 15*(1), 11.

Planalp, E. M., Van Hulle, C., Lemery-Chalfant, K., & Goldsmith, H. H. (2017). Genetic and environmental contributions to the development of positive affect in infancy. *Emotion, 17*(3), 412–420.

Plomin, R. (2014). Genotype–environment correlation in the era of DNA. *Behavior Genetics, 44*(6), 629–638.

Plumert, J. M., Kearney, J. K., Cremer, J. F., Recker, K. M., & Strutt, J. (2011). Changes in children's perception-action tuning over short time scales: Bicycling across traffic-filled intersections in a virtual environment. *Journal of Experimental Child Psychology, 108,* 322–337.

Pnevmatikos, D. (2002). Conceptual changes in religious concepts of elementary schoolchildren: The case of the house where God lives. *Educational Psychology, 22*(1), 93–112.

Polivy, J., & Herman, C. P. (2004). Sociocultural idealization of thin female body shapes: An introduction to the special issue on body image and eating disorders. *Journal of Social and Clinical Psychology, 23*(1), 1–6.

Pollitt, E. (2001). Statistical and psychobiological significance in developmental research. *American Journal of Clinical Nutrition, 74*(3), 281–282.

Pollock, D. (1999). *Telling bodies performing birth: Everyday narratives of childbirth.* New York: Columbia University Press.

Pomery, E. A., Gibbons, F. X., Gerrard, M., Cleveland, M. J., Brody, G. H., & Wills, T. A. (2005). Families and risk: Prospective analyses of familial and social influences on adolescent substance use. *Journal of Family Psychology, 19*(4), 560–570.

Pons, F., Bosch, L., & Lewkowicz, D. J. (2015). Bilingualism modulates infants' selective attention to the mouth of a talking face. *Psychological Science, 26*(4), 490–498.

Pontius, K., Aretz, M., Griebel, C., Jacobs, C., LaRock, K., & members of the OT-PT Baby Team. (2001). Back to sleep—Tummy time to play. *Newsletter of the Children's Hospital, 4*(4), 1–3.

Ponzo, M., & Scoppa, V. (2014). The long-lasting effects of school entry age: Evidence from Italian students. *Journal of Policy Modeling, 36*(3), 578–599.

Poole, D., & Lindsay, D. (2001). Children's eyewitness reports after exposure to misinformation from parents. *Journal of Experimental Psychology: Applied, 7,* 27–50.

Popp, D., Laursen, B., Kerr, M., Stattin, H., & Burk, W. K. (2008). Modeling homophily over time with an actor-partner interdependence model. *Developmental Psychology, 44,* 1028–1039.

Porter, R., & Winberg, J. (1999). Unique salience of maternal breast odors for newborn infants. *Neuroscience and Biobehavioral Reviews, 23,* 439–449.

Portes, A., & Rumbaut, R. (2001). *Legacies: The story of the second generation.* Berkeley: University of California Press.

Posada, G., Trumbell, J., Noblega, M., Plata, S., Peña, P., Carbonell, O. A., & Lu, T. (2016). Maternal sensitivity and child secure base use in early childhood: Studies in different cultural contexts. *Child Development, 87*(1), 297–311.

Posner, M. I., Rothbart, M. K., Sheese, B. E., & Voelker, P. (2014). Developing attention: Behavioral and brain mechanisms. *Advances in Neuroscience, 2014,* 1–9.

Posner, M. I., Rothbart, M. K., & Voelker, P. (2016). Developing brain networks of attention. *Current Opinion in Pediatrics, 28*(6), 720–724.

Potijk, M. R., Kerstjens, J. M., Bos, A. F., Reijneveld, S. A., & de Winter, A. F. (2013). Developmental delay in moderately preterm-born children with low socioeconomic status: Risks multiply. *The Journal of Pediatrics, 163*(5), 1289–1295.

Poulin, F., & Chan, A. (2010). Friendship stability and change in childhood and adolescence. *Developmental Review, 30,* 257–272.

Poulin, F., & Pedersen, S. (2007). Developmental changes in gender composition of friendship networks in adolescent girls and boys. *Developmental Psychology, 43*(6), 1484–1496.

Poulin-Dubois, D., & Forbes, J. (2006). Word, intention, and action: A two-tiered model of action word learning. In K. Hirsh-Pasek & R. M. Golinkoff (Eds.), *Action meets word: How children learn verbs* (pp. 262–285). New York: Oxford University Press.

Poulsen, P., Esteller, M., Vaag, A., & Fraga, M. F. (2007). The epigenetic basis of twin discordance in age-related diseases. *Pediatric Research, 61,* 38R–42R.

Prado, E. L., & Dewey, K. G. (2014). Nutrition and brain development in early life. *Nutrition Reviews, 72*(4), 267–284.

Pratt, M. W., & Fiese, B. H. (Eds.). (2004). *Family stories and the life course: Across time and generations.* Mahwah, NJ: Lawrence Erlbaum Associates.

Preisser, D. A., Hodson, B. W., & Paden, E. P. (1988). Developmental phonology: 18–29 months. *Journal of Speech and Hearing Disorders, 53,* 125–130.

Prentice, A. M., & Jebb, S. A. (2003). Fast foods, energy density and obesity: A possible mechanistic link. *Obesity Review, 4*(4), 187–194.

Pressley, M., & Hilden, K. (2006). Cognitive strategies. In D. Kuhn, R. S. Siegler, W. Damon, & R. M. Lerner (Eds.), *Handbook of child psychology: Vol. 2. Cognition, perception, and language* (6th ed., pp. 511–556). Hoboken, NJ: John Wiley & Sons.

Preyer, W. (1888). *The mind of the child.* New York: D. Appleton & Co.

Preyer, W. T. (1890). *The mind of the child . . . observations concerning the mental development of the human being in the first years of life.* New York: Appleton.

Price, A. L., & Marzani-Nissen, G. R. (2012). Bipolar disorders: A review. *American Family Physician, 85*(5), 483.

Price, S., Price, C., & McKenry, P. (2010). *Families and change coping with stressful events and transitions* (4th ed.). Thousand Oaks, CA: Sage Publications.

Prinstein, M. J., Cheah, C. S. L., & Guyer, A. E. (2005). Peer victimization, cue interpretation, and internalizing symptoms: Preliminary concurrent and longitudinal findings for children and adolescents. *Journal of Clinical Child & Adolescent Psychology, 34*(1), 11–24.

Propper, C., & Moore, G. A. (2006). The influence of parenting on infant emotionality: A multi-level psychobiological perspective. *Developmental Review, 26*(4), 427–460.

Provençal, N., Booij, L., & Tremblay, R. (2015). The developmental origins of chronic physical aggression: Biological pathways triggered by early life adversity. *Journal of Experimental Biology, 218*(1), 123–133.

Provenzi, L., Giusti, L., Fumagalli, M., Tasca, H., Ciceri, F., Menozzi, G., et al. (2016). Pain-related stress in the neonatal intensive care unit and salivary cortisol reactivity to socio-emotional stress in 3-month-old very preterm infants. *Psychoneuroendocrinology, 72,* 161–165.

Pruden, S., Hirsh-Pasek, K., Golinkoff, R., & Hennon, E. (2006). The birth of words; Ten-month-olds learn words through perceptual salience. *Child Development, 77,* 266.

Pujol, J., Soriano-Mas, C., Ortiz, H., Sebastián-Gallés, N., Losilla, J., M., & Deus, J. (2006). Myelination of language-related areas in the developing brain. *Neurology, 66,* 339–343.

Pullen Sansfaçon, A., Robichaud, M., & Dumais-Michaud, A. (2015). The experience of parents who support their children's gender variance. *Journal of LGBT Youth, 12*(1), 39–63.

Puzzanchera, C., & Adams, B. (2011). Juvenile arrests 2009. *Juvenile Offenders and Victims: National Report Series Bulletin, December 2011.* Office of Juvenile Justice and Delinquency Prevention. Retrieved from http://ojjdp.gov/publications/PubAbstract.asp?pubi=258483

Qiu, A., Tuan, T. A., Ong, M. L., Li, Y., Chen, H., Rifkin-Graboi, A., et al. (2015). COMT haplotypes modulate associations of antenatal maternal anxiety and neonatal cortical morphology. *American Journal of Psychiatry, 172*(2), 163–172.

Quast, A., Hesse, V., Hain, J., Wermke, P., & Wermke, K. (2016). Baby babbling at five months linked to sex hormone levels in early infancy. *Infant Behavior and Development, 44,* 1–10.

Quevedo, K., Waters, T. E. A., Scott, H., Roisman, G. I., Shaw, D. S., & Forbes, E. E. (2017). Brain activity and infant attachment history in young men during loss and reward processing. *Development and Psychopathology, 29*(2), 465.

Quinn, N., & Mageo, J. M. (Eds.). (2013). *Attachment reconsidered: Cultural perspectives on a Western theory.* New York: Palgrave Macmillan.

Quinn, P. C. (2002). Early categorization. In U. Goswami (Ed.), *Blackwell handbook of childhood cognitive development* (pp. 85–101). Oxford, England: Blackwell Publishing.

Quinn, P. C., & Eimas, P. D. (1996). Perceptual organization and categorization in young infants. In C. Rovee-Collier & L. P. Lipsitt (Eds.), *Advances in infancy research: Vol. 10* (pp. 1–36). Norwood, NJ: Ablex.

Quinn, P. C., Eimas, P. D., & Rosenkrantz, S. L. (1993). Evidence for representations of perceptually similar natural categories by 3-month-old and 4-month-old infants. *Perception, 22,* 463–475.

Quinn, P. C., Westerlund, A., & Nelson, C. A. (2006) Neural markers of categorization in 6-month-old infants. *Psychological Science, 17*(1), 59–66.

Raby, K. L., Steele, R. D., Carlson, E. A., & Sroufe, L. A. (2015). Continuities and changes in infant attachment patterns across two generations. *Attachment & Human Development, 17*(4), 414–428.

Racz, S. J., McMahon, R. J., & Luthar, S. S. (2011). Risky behavior in affluent youth: Examining the co-occurrence and consequences of multiple problem behaviors. *Journal of Child and Family Studies, 20,* 120–128.

Radesky, J. S., Schumacher, J., & Zuckerman, B. (2015). Mobile and interactive media use by young children: The good, the bad, and the unknown. *Pediatrics, 135*(1), 1–3.

Radke, K. M., Ruf, M., Dohrmann, K., Schauer, M., Meyer, A., & Elbert, T. (2011). Transgenerational impact of intimate partner violence on methylation in the promoter of the glucocorticoid receptor. *Translational Psychiatry, 21,* 1–6.

Radmacher, K., & Azmitia, M. (2006). Are there gendered pathways to intimacy in early adolescents' and emerging adults' friendships? *Journal of Adolescent Research, 21*(4), 415–448.

Raeburn, P. (2005, August 14). A second womb. *New York Times Magazine,* p. 37.

Raes, F., Griffith, J. W., Van der Gucht, K., & Williams, J. M. G. (2014). School-based prevention and reduction of depression in adolescents: A cluster-randomized controlled trial of a mindfulness group program. *Mindfulness, 5*(5), 477–486.

Ragnarsdottir, L., Kristjansson, A., Thorisdottir, I., Allegrante, J., Valdimarsdottir, H., Gestsdottir, S., & Sigfusdottir, I. (2017). Cumulative risk over the early life course and its relation to academic achievement in childhood and early adolescence. *Preventive Medicine, 96,* 36–41.

Rahilly, E. P. (2015). The gender binary meets the gender-variant child: Parents' negotiations with childhood gender variance. *Gender & Society, 29*(3), 338–361.

Raikes, H., Luze, G., Brooks-Gunn, J., Raikes, H. A., Pan, B. A., Tamis-LeMonda, C. S, et al. (2006). Mother–child bookreading in low income families: Correlates and outcomes during the first three years of life. *Child Development, 77,* 924–953.

Rakison, D. H., & Krogh, L. (2012). Does causal action facilitate causal perception in infants younger than 6 months of age? *Developmental Science, 15*(1), 43–53.

Rao, N., Sun, J., & Zhang, L. (2014). Learning to learn in early childhood: Home and preschool influences in Chinese societies. In C. Stringher & R. Deakin Crick (Eds.), *Learning to learn for all: Theory, practice and international research: A multidisciplinary and lifelong perspective* (pp. 127–144). Abingdon, UK: Taylor & Francis.

Rathbun, A., & Zhang, A. (2016). *Primary early care and education arrangements and achievement at kindergarten entry* (NCES 2016-070). Washington, DC: National Center for Education Statistics, U.S. Department of Education.

Rattaz, C., Goubet, N., & Bullinger, A. (2005). The calming effect of a familiar odor on full-term newborns. *Journal of Developmental & Behavioral Pediatrics, 26*(2), 86–92.

Rauch, F., & Schoenau, E. (2001). Changes in bone density during childhood and adolescence: An approach based on bone's biological organization. *Journal of Bone and Mineral Research, 16,* 597–604.

Read, M. (1960/1968). *Children of their fathers: Growing up among the Ngoni of Malawi.* New York: Holt, Rinehart & Winston.

Read, M. (1983). *Children of their fathers: Growing up among the Ngoni of Malawi.* New York: Irvington.

Reddy, V. (2005). Feeling shy and showing-off: Self-conscious emotions must regulate self-awareness. In J. Nadel & D. Muir (Eds.), *Emotional development* (pp. 183–204). Oxford, England: Oxford University Press.

Redford, J., Desrochers, D., & Hoyer, K. (2017). *The years before school: Children's nonparental care arrangements from 2001 to 2012.* Retrieved from https://nces.ed.gov/pubs2017/2017096.pdf

Reese, B. M., Haydon, A. A., Herring, A. H., & Halpern, C. T. (2013). The association between sequences of sexual initiation and the likelihood of teenage pregnancy. *Journal of Adolescent Health, 52*(2), 228–233.

Refshauge, A. D., Stigsdotter, U. K., Lamm, B., & Thorleifsdottir, K. (2015). Evidence-based playground design: Lessons learned from theory to practice. *Landscape Research, 40*(2), 226–246.

Reichel-Dolmatoff, G., & Reichel-Dolmatoff, A. (1961). *The people of Aritama.* London: Routledge & Kegan Paul.

Reinecke, L. (2017). *The Routledge handbook of media use and well-being: International perspectives on theory and research on positive media effects.* New York: Routledge.

Reissland, N., Francis, B., Aydin, E., Mason, J., & Schaal, B. (2014). The development of anticipation in the fetus: A longitudinal account of human fetal mouth movements in reaction to and anticipation of touch. *Developmental Psychobiology, 56,* 955–963.

Renz-Polster, H., & Buist, A. S. (2002). Being born by cesarean section increases the risk of asthma and hay fever as a child. *Journal of Investigative Medicine, 50,* 29a.

Repacholi, B. M., Meltzoff, A. N., & Olsen, B. (2008). Infants' understanding of the link between visual perception and emotion: "If she can't see me doing it, she won't get angry." *Developmental Psychology, 44,* 561–574.

Rest, J., Narvaez, D., Bebeau, M. I. J., & Thoma, S. J. (1999). *Postconventional moral thinking: A neo-Kohlbergian approach.* Mahwah, NJ: Lawrence Erlbaum Associates.

Reynolds, G. D., & Richards, J. E. (2007). Infant heart rate: A developmental psychophysiological perspective. In L. A. Schmidt & S. J. Segalowitz (Eds.), *Developmental psychophysiology* (pp. 106–117). New York: Cambridge Press.

Rhein, D., Oldehinkel, M., Beckmann, C. F., Oosterlaan, J., Heslenfeld, D., Hartman, C. A., et al. (2016). Aberrant local striatal functional connectivity in attention-deficit/hyperactivity disorder. *Journal of Child Psychology and Psychiatry, 57*(6), 697–705.

Ribot, K. M., & Hoff, E. (2014). "¿Cómo estas?" "I'm good." conversational code-switching is related to profiles of expressive and receptive proficiency in Spanish–English bilingual toddlers. *International Journal of Behavioral Development, 38*(4), 333–341.

Richardson, J., & Scott, K. (2002). Rap music and its violent progency: America's culture of violence in context. *The Journal of Negro Education, 71*(3), 175–192.

Richardson, K., & Norgate, S. H. (2006). A critical analysis of IQ studies of adopted children. *Human Development, 49,* 319–335.

Richardson, T., & Murray, J. (2017). Are young children's utterances affected by characteristics of their learning environments? A multiple case study. *Early Child Development and Care, 187*(3–4), 457–468.

Richerson, P., & Boyd, R. (2005). *Not by genes alone: How culture transformed human evolution.* Chicago, IL: University of Chicago Press.

Richmond, J., & Nelson, C. A. (2007, September). Accounting for change in declarative memory: A cognitive neuroscience perspective. *Developmental Review, 27*(3), 349–373.

Rideout, V., Roberts, D. F., & Foehr., U. G. (2005). *Generation M: Media in the lives of 8–18 year-olds.* Menlo Park, CA: Kaiser Family Foundation.

Rideout, V. J., Foehr, U. G., & Roberts, D. F. (2010). *Generation M2: Media in the lives of 8- to 18-year-olds.* Menlo Park, CA: Kaiser Family Foundation.

Ridgers, N., Knowles, Z., & Sayers, J. (2012). Encouraging play in the natural environment: A child-focused case study of forest school. *Children's Geographies, 10*(1), 49–65.

Riina, E., Martin, A., & Brooks-Gunn, J. (2014). Parent-to-child physical aggression, neighborhood cohesion, and development of children's internalizing and externalizing. *Journal of Applied Developmental Psychology, 35*(6), 468–477.

Riquelme, E., & Montero, I. (2013). Improving emotional competence through mediated reading: Short term effects of a children's literature program. *Mind, Culture, and Activity, 20*(3), 226–239.

Ritz, B., Wilhelm, M., & Zhao Y. (2006). Air pollution and infant death in southern California, 1989–2000. *Pediatrics, 118,* 493–502.

Rivera-Mulia, J., Buckley, Q., Sasaki, T., Zimmerman, J., Didier, R., Nazor, K., et al. (2015). Dynamic changes in replication timing and gene expression during lineage specification of human pluripotent stem cells. *Genome Research, 25*(8), 1091–1103.

Rizzolatti, G. (2014). Imitation: Mechanisms and importance for human culture. *Rendiconti Lincei, 25*(3), 285–289.

Roa, J., García-Galiano, D., Castellano, J. M., Gaytan, F., Pinilla, L., & Tena-Sempere, M. (2010). Metabolic control of puberty onset: New players, new mechanisms. *Molecular and Cellular Endocrinology, 324,* 87–94.

Robertson, C. L., & Duckett, L. (2007). Mothering during war and postwar in Bosnia. *Journal of Family Nursing, 13*(4), 461–483.

Robinson, S. R., & Kleven, G. A. (2005). Learning to move before birth. In B. Hopkins & S. P. Johnson (Eds.), *Prenatal development of postnatal functions (Advances in infancy research)* (pp. 131–175). Westport, CT: Praeger Publishers/Greenwood Publishing Group.

Rochat, P. (2009) *Others in mind—Social origins of self-consciousness.* New York: Cambridge University Press.

Rochat, P. (2015). Self-conscious roots of human normativity. *Phenomenology and the Cognitive Sciences, 14*(4), 741–753.

Rochat, P., & Striano, T. (2002). Who's in the mirror? Self-other discrimination in specular images by four- and nine-month-old infants. *Child Development, 73,* 35–46.

Roche, C., & Kupermine, G. P. (2012). Acculturative stress and school belonging among Latino youth. *Hispanic Journal of Behavioral Sciences, 34*(1), 61–76.

Rodkin, P. C., Farmer, T. W., Pearl, R., & Van Acker, R. (2000). Heterogeneity of popular boys: Antisocial and prosocial configurations. *Developmental Psychology, 36*(1), 14–24.

Rodriguez, J., Umaña-Taylor, A., Smith, E. P., & Johnson, D. J. (2009). Cultural processes in parenting and youth outcomes: Examining a model of racial-ethnic socialization and identity in diverse populations. *Cultural Diversity and Ethnic Minority Psychology, 15*(2), 106–111.

Roembke, T. C., Wasserman, E. A., & McMurray, B. (2016). Learning in rich networks involves both positive and negative associations. *Journal of Experimental Psychology: General, 145*(8), 1062–1074.

Roeser, W. R., & Zelazo, P. D. (2012). Contemplative science, education and child development: Introduction to the special section. *Child Development Perspectives, 6*(2), 143–145.

Roffman, I., Savage-Rumbaugh, S., Rubert-Pugh, E., Stadler, A., Ronen, A., & Nevo, E. (2015). Preparation and use of varied natural tools for extractive foraging by bonobos (*Pan paniscus*). *American Journal of Physical Anthropology, 158*(1), 78–91.

Rogoff, B. (2003). *The cultural nature of human development.* Oxford, England: Oxford University Press.

Rogoff, B., Correa-Chávez, M., & Navichoc-Cotuc, M. (2005). A Cultural/Historical View of Schooling in Human Development. In D. B. Pillemer & S. H. White (Eds.), *Developmental Psychology and the Social Changes of Our Time* (pp. 225–263). New York: Cambridge University Press.

Rogoff, B., Moore, L., Najafi, B., Dexter, A., Correa-Chávez, M., & Solís, J. (2007). Children's development of cultural repertoires through participation in everyday routines and practices. In J. E. Grusec & P. D. Hastings (Eds.), *Handbook of socialization: Theory and research* (pp. 490–515). New York: Guilford Press.

Rogoff, B., Najafi, B., & Mejía-Arauz, R. (2014). Constellations of cultural practices across generations: Indigenous American heritage and learning by observing and pitching in. *Human Development, 57*(2–3), 82–95.

Rogoff, B., & Waddell, K. J. (1982). Memory for information organized in a scene by children from two cultures. *Child Development, 53,* 1224–1228.

Rohlfing, K. J., Longo, M. R., & Bertenthal, B. I. (2012). Dynamic pointing triggers shifts of visual attention in young infants. *Developmental Science, 15*(3), 426–435.

Romer, D., & Hennessy, M. (2007). A biosocial-affect model of adolescent sensation seeking: The role of affect evaluation and peer-group influence in adolescent drug use. *Prevention Science, 8,* 89–101.

Romito, P., & Beltramini, L. (2015). Factors associated with exposure to violent or degrading pornography among high school students. *The Journal of School Nursing, 31*(4), 280–290.

Rosario, M., Schrimshaw, E. W., Hunter, J., & Braun, L. (2006). Sexual identity development among gay, lesbian, and bisexual youths: Consistency and change over time. *Journal of Sex Research, 43*(1), 46.

Rose, A. J., & Asher, S. R. (2017). The social tasks of friendship: Do boys and girls excel in different tasks? *Child Development Perspectives, 11*(1), 3–8.

Rose, A. J., Schwartz-Mette, R. A., Smith, R. L., Asher, S. R., Swenson, L. P., Carlson, W., & Waller, E. M. (2012). How girls and boys expect disclosure about problems will make them feel: Implications for friendships. *Child Development, 83*(3), 844–863.

Rose, A. J., Swenson, L., & Carlson, W. (2004). Friendships of aggressive youth: Considering the influence of being disliked and of being perceived popular. *Journal of Experimental Child Psychology, 88,* 25–45.

Rose, L. T., & Fischer, K. W. (2009). Dynamic development: A neo-Piagetian approach. In L. T. Rose & K. W. Fischer (Eds.), *The Cambridge companion to Piaget* (pp. 400–421). New York: Cambridge University Press.

Rose, S. A., Feldman, J. F., & Jankowski, J. J. (2004). Infant visual recognition memory. *Developmental Review, 24,* 74–100.

Roseberry, S., Hirsh-Pasek, K., & Golinkoff, R. M. (2014). Skype me! Socially contingent interactions help toddlers learn language. *Child Development, 85*(3), 956–970.

Rosenfeld, R. (2015). The evolution of body size. *Journal of Clinical Research in Pediatric Endocrinology,* 7(1).

Rosenstein, D., & Oster, H. (1988). Differential facial responses to four basic tastes in newborns. *Child Development, 59,* 1555–1568.

Rosenzweig, M. R. (1984). Experience, memory, and the brain. *American Psychologist, 39,* 365–376.

Roseth, C. J., Pellegrini, A. D., Dupuis, D. N., Bohn, C. M., Hickey, M. C., Hilk, C. L., & Peshkam, A. (2011). Preschoolers' bistrategic resource control, reconciliation, and peer regard. *Social Development, 20*(1), 185–211.

Ross, M. G., & Nyland, M. J. M. (1998). Development of ingestive behavior. *American Journal of Physiology, 43,* 879–893.

Rostad, K., Yott, J., & Poulin-Dubois, D. (2012). Development of categorization in infancy: Advancing forward to the animate/inanimate level. *Infant Behavior & Development, 35*(3), 584–595.

Rostosky, S. S., Galliher, R. V., Welsh, D. P., & Kawaguchi, M. C. (2000). Sexual behaviors and relationship qualities in late adolescent couples. *Journal of Adolescence, 23*(5), 583.

Roth, M., & Parker, J. (2001). Affective and behavioral responses to friends who neglect their friends for dating partners: Influences of gender, jealousy and perspective. *Journal of Adolescence, 24,* 281–296.

Rothbart, M. K. (2007). Temperament, development, and personality. *Current Directions in Psychological Science, 16*(4), 207–212.

Rothbart, M. K., & Bates, J. E. (2006). Temperament. In W. Damon & N. Eisenberg (Eds.), *Handbook of child psychology: Vol. 3. Emotional and personality development* (6th ed., pp. 99–166). New York: Wiley.

Rothman, E. F., & Adhia, A. (2016). Adolescent pornography use and dating violence among a sample of primarily black and Hispanic, urban-residing, underage youth. *Behavioral Sciences, 6*(1), 1.

Rousseau, P. V., Matton, F., Lecuyer, R., & Lahaye, W. (2017). The Moro reaction: More than a reflex, a ritualized behavior of nonverbal communication. *Infant Behavior and Development, 46,* 169–177.

Rovee-Collier, C., & Giles, A. (2010). Why a neuromaturational model of memory fails: Exuberant learning in early infancy. *Behavioural Processes, 83,* 197–206.

Rovee-Collier, C., Mitchell, K., & Hsu-Yang, V. (2013). Effortlessly strengthening infant memory: Associative potentiation of new learning. *Scandinavian Journal of Psychology, 54*(1), 4–9.

Rubin, K. H., Bukowski, W. M., & Laursen, B. P. (2009). *Handbook of peer interactions, relationships, and groups.* New York: Guilford Press.

Rubin, K. H., Bukowski, W. M., & Parker, J. G. (2006). Peer interactions, relationships, and groups. In N. Eisenberg, W. Damon, & R. M. Lerner (Eds.), *Handbook of child psychology: Vol. 3. Social, emotional, and personality development* (6th ed., pp. 571–645). New York: Wiley.

Rubin, K. H., Wojslawowicz, J. C., Rose-Krasnor, L., Booth-LaForce, C., & Burgess, K. B. (2006). The best friendships of shy/withdrawn children: Prevalence, stability, and relationship quality. *Journal of Abnormal Child Psychology, 34*(2), 143–157.

Rubin, Z. (1980). *Children's friendships.* Cambridge, MA: Harvard University Press.

Ruble, D. N., & Martin, C. L. (1998). Gender development. In W. Damon & N. Eisenberg (Eds.), *Handbook of child development: Social, emotional, and personality development: Vol. 5* (pp. 933–1016). New York: Wiley.

Ruble, D. N., & Martin, C. L. (2002). Conceptualizing, measuring and evaluating the developmental course of gender differentiation. *Monographs of the Society for Research in Child Development, 67,* 148–166.

Rudolph, K. D. (2008). Developmental influences on interpersonal stress generation in depressed youth. *Journal of Abnormal Psychology, 117,* 673–679.

Rudolph, K. D., Hammen, C., Burge, D., Lindberg, N., Herzberg, D., & Daley, S. E. (2000). Toward an interpersonal life-stress model of depression: The developmental context of stress generation. *Development and Psychopathology, 12*(2), 215–234.

Ruffman, T., Slade, L., & Redman, J. (2005). Young infants' expectations about hidden objects. *Cognition, 97,* 35–43.

Rumbaugh, D. M., & Washburn, D. A. (2003). *Intelligence of apes and other rational beings.* New Haven, CT: Yale University Press.

Rumbaugh, D. M., Savage-Rumbaugh, E. S., & Sevcik, R. A. (1994). Biobehavioral roots of language: A comparative perspective on chimpanzee, child, and culture. In R. W. Wrangham, W. C. McGrew, F. B. M. de Waal, & P. G. Helthe (Eds.), *Chimpanzee cultures.* Cambridge, MA: Harvard University Press.

Russell, S., & Joyner, K. (2001). Adolescent sexual orientation and suicide risk: Evidence from a national study. *American Journal of Public Health, 91,* 1276–1281.

Rust, J., Golombok, S., Hines, M., & Johnston, K. (2000). The role of brothers and sisters in the gender development of preschool children. *Journal of Experimental Child Psychology, 77,* 292–303.

Ryan, R. R., Martin, A., & Brooks-Gunn, J. (2006). Is one good parent good enough? Patterns of mother and father parenting and child cognitive outcomes at 24 and 36 months. *Parenting: Science and Practice, 6,* 211–228.

Rychtarikova, J., Gourbin, C., Sipek, A., & Wunsch, G. (2013). Impact of parental ages and other characteristics at childbearing on congenital anomalies: Results for the Czech Republic, 2000–2007. *Demographic Research, 28,* 137–176.

Saarni, C. (2007). The development of emotional competence: Pathways for helping children to become emotionally intelligent. In R. Bar-On, J. G. Maree, & M. J. Elias (Eds.), *Educating people to be emotionally intelligent* (pp. 15–35). Westport, CT: Praeger Publishers/Greenwood Publishing Group.

Saarni, C. (2011). Emotional competence and effective negotiation: The integration of emotion understanding, regulation, and communication. In C. Saarni (Ed.), *Psychological and political strategies for peace negotiation: A cognitive approach* (pp. 55–74). New York: Springer.

Saarni, C., Campos, J. J., Camras, L. A., & Witherington, D. (2006). Emotional development: Action, communication, and understanding. In N. Eisenberg, W. Damon, & R. M. Lerner (Eds.), *Handbook of child psychology: Vol. 3. Social, emotional, and personality development* (6th ed., pp. 226–299). Hoboken, NJ: John Wiley & Sons.

Sabbagh, M. A., Xu, F., Carlson, S. M., Moses, L. J., & Lee, K. (2006). The development of executive functioning and theory of mind: A comparison of Chinese and U.S. preschoolers. *Psychological Science, 17,* 74–81.

Sachdeva, S., Singh, P., & Medin, D. (2011). Culture and the quest for universal principles in moral reasoning. *International Journal of Psychology, 46*(3), 161–176.

Sai, F. Z. (2005). The role of the mother's voice in developing mother's face preference: Evidence for intermodal perception at birth. *Infant and Child Development, 14,* 29–50.

Salaria, S., Chana, G., Caldara, F., Feltrin, E., Altieri, M., Faggioni, F., et al. (2006). Everall microarray analysis of cultured human brain aggregates following cortisol exposure: Implications for cellular functions relevant to mood disorders. *Neurobiology of Disease, 23,* 630–636.

Sales, J. M., Merrill, N. A., & Fivush, R. (2013). Does making meaning make it better? Narrative meaning making and well-being in at-risk African-American adolescent females. *Memory, 21*(1), 97–110.

Salmivalli, C., Sainio, M., & Hodges, E. (2013). Electronic victimization: Correlates, antecedents, and consequences among elementary and middle school students. *Journal of Clinical Child and Adolescent Psychology, 42*(4), 442–453.

Salzarulo, P., & Ficca, G. (Eds.). (2002). *Advances in consciousness research: Vol. 38. Awakening and sleep-wake cycle across development.* Amsterdam: John Benjamins.

Samarova, V., Shilo, G., & Diamond, G. M. (2014). Changes in youths' perceived parental acceptance of their sexual minority status over time. *Journal of Research on Adolescence, 24*(4), 681–688.

Samek, D. R., McGue, M., Keyes, M., & Iacono, W. G. (2015). Sibling facilitation mediates the association between older and younger sibling alcohol use in late adolescence. *Journal of Research on Adolescence, 25*(4), 638–651.

Sameroff, A. J. (1983). Developmental systems: Contexts and evolutions. In P. H. Mussen (Ed.), *Handbook of child psychology: Vol. 1. History, theory and methods.* New York: Wiley.

Samuelson, L. K., & McMurray, B. (2017). What does it take to learn a word? *Wiley Interdisciplinary Reviews: Cognitive Science, 8*(1–2), e1421.

San Antonio, D. M. (2004). Adolescent lives in transition: How social class influences the adjustment to middle school. Albany, NY: State University of New York Press,

Sandberg, A., & Samuelsson, I. P. (2003). Preschool teachers' play experiences then and now. *Early Childhood Research and Practice, 5,* 1–19.

Santarossa, S., & Woodruff, S. J. (2017). Social media: Exploring the relationship of social networking sites on body image, self-esteem, and eating disorders. *Social Media + Society, 3*(2).

Sarmah, S., Muralidharan, P., & Marrs, J. A. (2016). Common congenital anomalies: Environmental causes and prevention with folic acid containing multivitamins. *Birth Defects Research Part C: Embryo Today: Reviews, 108*(3), 274–286.

Sarnecka, B., & Gelman, S. (2004). Six does not just mean a lot: Preschoolers see number words as specific. *Cognition, 92,* 329–352.

Sarnecka, B., Kamenskaya, V. G., Yamana, Y., Ogura, T., & Yudovina, J. B. (2007). From grammatical number to exact numbers: Early meanings of "one," "two," and "three" in English, Russian, and Japanese. *Cognitive Psychology, 55,* 136–168.

Sasaki, A., de Vega, W. C., St-Cyr, S., Pan, P., & McGowan, P. O. (2013). Perinatal high fat diet alters glucocorticoid signaling and anxiety behavior in adulthood. *Neuroscience, 240,* 1–12.

Sato, Y., Sogabe, Y., & Mazuka, R. (2010). Discrimination of phonemic vowel length by Japanese infants. *Developmental Psychology, 46,* 106–119.

Savabieasfahani, M., Ali, S. S., Bacho, R., Savabi, O., & Alsabbak, M. (2016). Prenatal metal exposure in the Middle East: Imprint of war in deciduous teeth of children. *Environmental Monitoring and Assessment, 188*(9), 1–9.

Savage, J. (2007). *Teenage: The creation of youth culture.* New York: Viking.

Savage-Rumbaugh, E. S. (1993). How does evolution design a brain capable of learning language? *Monographs of the Society for Research in Child Development, 58,* 243–252.

Saveliev, S. V. (2010). Natural selection in brain evolution of early hominids. *Paleontological Journal, 44*(12), 1589–1597.

Savin-Williams, R. C. (2001). A critique of research on sexual-minority youths. *Journal of Adolescence, 24,* 5–13.

Savin-Williams, R. C. (2017). *Mostly straight: Sexual fluidity among men.* Cambridge, MA: Harvard University Press.

Savin-Williams, R. C., & Diamond, L. (2004). Sex. In R. M. Lerner & L. Steinberg (Eds.), *Handbook of adolescent psychology* (2nd ed.). Hoboken, NJ: John Wiley & Sons.

Savin-Williams, R. C., & Diamond, L. M. (2000). Sexual identity trajectories among sexual-minority youths: Gender comparisons. *Archives of Sexual Behavior, 29*(6), 607–627.

Savin-Williams, R. C., & Joyner, K. (2014). The dubious assessment of gay, lesbian, and bisexual adolescents of add health. *Archives of Sexual Behavior, 43*(3), 413–422.

Savin-Williams, R. C., & Ream, G. L. (2007). Prevalence and stability of sexual orientation components during adolescence and young adulthood. *Archives of Sexual Behavior, 36,* 385–394.

Saxe, G. B. (2014). *Cultural development of mathematical ideas: Papua New Guinea studies.* New York: Cambridge University Press.

Saxon, T. F., Gollapalli, A., Mitchell, M. W., & Stanko, S. (2002). Demand feeding or schedule feeding: Infant growth from birth to 6 months. *Journal of Reproductive and Infant Psychology, 20*(2), 89–100.

Schachner, A., & Hannon, E. E. (2011). Infant-directed speech drives social preferences in 5-month-old infants. *Developmental Psychology, 47,* 19–25.

Schalet, A. (2011). *Not under my roof: Parents, teens, and the culture of sex.* Chicago, IL: University of Chicago Press.

Scherf, K. S., Sweeney, J. A., & Luna, B. (2006, July). Brain basis of developmental change in visuospatial working memory. *Journal of Cognitive Neuroscience, 18*(7), 1045–1058.

Scheuermann, B. (2002). *Autism: Teaching does make a difference.* Belmont, CA: Wadsworth Thomson Learning.

Schick, B. (2006). Acquiring a visually motivated language: Evidence from diverse learners. In B. Schick, M. Marschark, & P. Spencer (Eds.), *Advances in the sign language development of deaf children.* New York: Oxford University Press.

Schick, B., de Villiers, P., de Villiers, J., & Hoffmeister, R. (2007). Language and theory of mind: A study of deaf children. *Child Development, 78*(2), 376–396.

Schick, V. R., Calabrese, S. K., Rima, B. N., & Zucker, A. N. (2010). Genital appearance dissatisfaction: Implications for women's genital image self-consciousness, sexual esteem, sexual satisfaction, and sexual risk. *Psychology of Women Quarterly, 34*(3), 394–404.

Schiebener, J., García-Arias, M., García-Villamisar, D., Cabanyes-Truffino, J., & Brand, M. (2015). Developmental changes in decision making under risk: The role of executive functions and reasoning abilities in 8- to 19-year-old decision makers. *Child Neuropsychology, 21*(6), 759–778.

Schlagmüller, M., & Schneider, W. (2002). The development of organizational strategies in children: Evidence from a microgenetic longitudinal study. *Journal of Experimental Child Psychology, 81*(3), 298–319.

Schmidt, M. F. H., Butler, L. P., Heinz, J., & Tomasello, M. (2016). Young children see a single action and infer a social norm: Promiscuous normativity in 3-year-olds. *Psychological Science, 27*(10), 1360–1370.

Schmitt, J. E., Neale, M. C., Fassassi, B., Perez, J., Lenroot, R. K., Wells, E. M., & Giedd, J. N. (2014). The dynamic role of genetics on cortical patterning during childhood and adolescence. *Proceedings of the National Academy of Sciences of the United States of America, 111*(18), 6774–6779.

Schneider, B. H. (2000). *Friends and enemies: Peer relations in childhood.* New York: Oxford University Press.

Schneider, B. H., del Pilar Soteras de Toro, M., Woodburn, S., Fulop, M., Cervino, C., Bernstein, S., et al. (2006). Cross-cultural differences in competition among children and adolescents. In X. Chen, D.C. French, & B. H. Schneider (Eds.), *Peer relationships in cultural context. Cambridge studies in social and emotional development* (pp. 310–338). New York: Cambridge University Press.

Schneider, B. H., Woodburn, S., del Pilar Soteras del Toro, M., & Udvari, S. J. (2005, April). Cultural and gender differences in the implications of competition for early adolescent friendship. *Merrill-Palmer Quarterly, 51*(2), 163–191.

Schneider, W. (2011). Memory development in childhood. In Usha Goswami (Ed.), *The Wiley-Blackwell handbook of childhood cognitive development* (2nd ed.). New York: Wiley-Blackwell.

Schneider, W., Knopf, M., & Sodian, B. (2009). Verbal memory development from early childhood to early adulthood. In W. Schneider & M. Bullock (Eds.), *Human development from early childhood to early adulthood: Findings from a 20 year longitudinal study.* New York: Psychology Press.

Schoenmaker, C., Juffer, F., Van IJzendoorn, M. H., Linting, M., van der Voort, A., & Bakermans-Kranenburg, M. J. (2015). From maternal sensitivity in infancy to adult attachment representations: A longitudinal adoption study with secure base scripts. *Attachment & Human Development, 17*(3), 241–256.

Schoenwolf, G., Bleyl, S., Brauer, P., & Francis-West, P. (2015). *Larsen's human embryology* (5th ed.). Philadelphia, PA: Elsevier.

Scholes, R. J. (1998). The case against phonemic awareness. *Journal of Research in Reading, 21*(3), 177–218.

Schore, A. (2016). *Affect regulation and the origin of the self: The neurobiology of emotional development.* New York: Taylor & Francis.

Schroeder, J. H., Desrocher, M., Bebko, J. M., & Cappadocia, M. C. (2010). The neurobiology of autism: Theoretical applications. *Research in Autism Spectrum Disorders, 4,* 555–564.

Schroeder, M., Drefs, M., & Cormier, D. (2017). The messiness of LD identification: Contributions of diagnostic criteria and clinical judgment. *Canadian Psychology, 58*(3), 218–227.

Schuetze, P., Eiden, R. D., & Danielewicz, S. (2009). The association between prenatal cocaine exposure and physiological regulation at 13 months of age. *Journal of Child Psychology and Psychiatry, 50,* 1401–1409.

Schuetze, P., Eiden, R. D., & Edwards, E. P. (2009). A longitudinal examination of physiological regulation in cocaine-exposed infants across the first 7 months of life. *Infancy, 14,* 19–43.

Schuler, M. E., & Nair, P. (1999). Frequency of maternal cocaine use during pregnancy and infant neurobehavioral outcome. *Journal of Pediatric Psychology, 24*(6), 511–514.

Schwartz, D., Lansford, J. E., Dodge, K. A., Pettit, G. S., & Bates, J. E. (2015). Peer victimization during middle childhood as a lead indicator of internalizing problems and diagnostic outcomes in late adolescence. *Journal of Clinical Child & Adolescent Psychology, 44*(3), 393–404.

Schwartz, S. J., Syed, M., Yip, T., Knight, G. P., Umaña-Taylor, A. J., Rivas-Drake, D., et al. (2014). Methodological issues in ethnic and racial identity research with ethnic minority populations: Theoretical precision, measurement issues, and research designs. *Child Development, 85*(1), 58–76.

Schwartz, S. J., Unger, J. B., Baezconde-Garbanati, L., Benet-Martínez, V., Meca, A., Zamboanga, B. L., et al. (2015). Longitudinal trajectories of bicultural identity integration in recently immigrated Hispanic adolescents: Links with mental health and family functioning. *International Journal of Psychology, 50*(6), 440–450.

Scott, R., & Baillargeon, R. (2017). Early false-belief understanding. *Trends in Cognitive Sciences, 21*(4), 237–249.

Scott, R. M., Richman, J. C., & Baillargeon, R. (2015). Infants understand deceptive intentions to implant false beliefs about identity: New evidence for early mentalistic reasoning. *Cognitive Psychology, 82,* 32–56.

Seabra, A. C., Seabra, A. F., Mendonca, D. M., Brustad, R., Maia, J. A., Fonseca, A. M., & Malina, R. M. (2013). Psychosocial correlates of physical activity in school children aged 8–10 years. *European Journal of Public Health, 23*(5), 794–798.

Sedgh, G., Finer, L. B., Bankole, A., Eilers, M. A., & Singh, S. (2015). Adolescent pregnancy, birth, and abortion rates across countries: Levels and recent trends. *Journal of Adolescent Health, 56*(2), 223–230.

Segal, N. L., & Johnson, W. (2009). Twin studies of general mental ability. In Y. Kim (Ed.), *Handbook of behavior genetics* (pp. 81–99). New York: Springer.

Segall, M. H., Dasen, P., Berry, J. W., & Poortinga, Y. (1999). *Human behavior in global perspective: An introduction to cross-cultural psychology* (2nd ed.). Needham Heights, MA: Allyn & Bacon.

Selemon, L. D. (2013). A role for synaptic plasticity in the adolescent development of executive function. *Translational Psychiatry, 3,* e238.

Selman, R., Levitt, M., & Schultz, L. (1997). The friendship framework: Tools for the assessment of psychosocial development. In R. Selman, C. Watts, & L. Schultz (Eds.), *Fostering friendship: Pair therapy for treatment and prevention.* New York: Aldine de Gruyter.

Senghas, A. (2011). The emergence of two functions for spatial devices in Nicaraguan sign language. *Human Development, 53,* 287–302.

Senghas, R., Senghas, A., & Pyers, J. (2005). The emergence of Nicaraguan sign language: Questions of development, acquisition, and evolution. In S. T. Parker, J. Langer, & C. Milbrath (Eds.), *Biology and knowledge revisited: From neurogenesis to psychogenesis* (pp. 287–306). Mahwah, NJ: Lawrence Erlbaum Associates.

Senn, T. E., Espy, K. A., & Kaufmann, P. M. (2004). Using path analysis to understand executive function organization in preschool children. *Developmental Neuropsychology, 26,* 445–464.

Senna, I., Addabbo, M., Bolognini, N., Longhi, E., Macchi Cassia, V., & Turati, C. (2017). Infants' visual recognition of pincer grip emerges between 9 and 12 months of age. *Infancy, 22*(3), 389–402.

Sentse, M., Dijkstra, J. K., Salmivalli, C., & Cillessen, A. H. N. (2013). The dynamics of friendships and victimization in adolescence: A longitudinal social network perspective. *Aggressive Behavior, 39*(3), 229–238.

Serpell, R. (2000). Intelligence and culture. In R. J. Sternberg and E. L. Grigorenko (Eds.), *Handbook of intelligence.* New York: Cambridge University Press.

Serpell, R., & Haynes, B. P. (2004). The cultural practice of intelligence testing: Problems of international export. In R. J. Sternberg & E. L. Grigorenko (Eds.), *Culture and competence: Contexts of life success* (pp. 163–185). Washington, DC: American Psychological Association.

Ševčíková, A., Daneback, K., & Institutionen för socialt arbete, Samhällsvetenskapliga fakulteten, Faculty of Social Sciences, Gothenburg University. (2014). Online pornography use in adolescence: Age and gender differences. *European Journal of Developmental Psychology, 11*(6), 674–686.

Shafique, S., Sellen, D. W., Lou, W., Jalal, C. S., Jolly, S. P., & Zlotkin, S. H. (2016). Mineral- and vitamin-enhanced micronutrient powder reduces stunting in full-term low-birth-weight infants receiving nutrition, health, and hygiene education: A 2 × 2 factorial, cluster-randomized trial in Bangladesh. *American Journal of Clinical Nutrition, 103*(5), 1357–1369.

Shager, H. M., Schindler, H. S., Magnuson, K. A., Duncan, G. J., Yoshikawa, H., & Hart, C. M. D. (2013). Can research design explain variation in Head Start research results? A meta-analysis of cognitive and achievement outcomes. *Educational Evaluation and Policy Analysis, 35*(1), 76–95.

Shanty, N. O. (2016). Investigating students' development of learning integer concept and integer addition. *Journal on Mathematics Education,* 7(2), 57–72.

Shapira, A., & Madsen, M. C. (1969). Cooperative and competitive behavior of kibbutz and urban children in Israel. *Child Development, 4,* 609–617.

Sharkey, H. J. (2012). Language and conflict: The political history of Arabisation in Sudan and Algeria. *Studies in Ethnicity and Nationalism, 12*(3), 427–449.

Shatz, M. (1978). Children's comprehension of question-directives. *Journal of Child Language, 5,* 39–46.

Shaw, D., Sitnick, S., Brennan, L., Choe, D., Dishion, T., Wilson, M., & Gardner, F. (2016). The long-term effectiveness of the family check-up on school-age conduct problems: Moderation by neighborhood deprivation. *Development and Psychopathology, 28*(4), 1471–1486.

Shaw, P., Greenstein, D., Lerch, J., Clasen, L., Lenroot, R., Gogtay, N., et al. (2006, March). Intellectual ability and cortical development in children and adolescents. *Nature, 440*(7084), 676–679.

Shaw, P., Kabani, N. J., Lerch, J. P., Eckstrand, K., & Lenroot, R. (2008). Neurodevelopmental trajectories of the human cerebral cortex. *Journal of Neuroscience, 28,* 432–443.

Shearer, A., Herres, J., Kodish, T., Squitieri, H., James, K., Russon, J., et al. (2016). Differences in mental health symptoms across lesbian, gay, bisexual, and questioning youth in primary care settings. *The Journal of Adolescent Health, 59*(1), 38–43.

Sheinkopf, S. J., Righi, G., Marsit, C. J., & Lester, B. M. (2016). Methylation of the glucocorticoid receptor (NR3C1) in placenta is associated with infant cry acoustics. *Frontiers in Behavioral Neuroscience, 10,* 100.

Shen, S., Emlen, S. T., Koenig, W. D., Rubenstein, D. R., & Hosken, D. (2017). The ecology of cooperative breeding behaviour. *Ecology Letters, 20*(6), 708–720.

Sherif, M., & Sherif, C. W. (1956). *An outline of social psychology.* New York: Harper & Row.

Sherman, L., Rice, K., & Cassidy, J. (2015). Infant capacities related to building internal working models of attachment figures: A theoretical and empirical review. *Developmental Review, 37,* 109–141.

Sheskin, M., Bloom, P., & Wynn, K. (2014). Anti-equality: Social comparison in young children. *Cognition, 130*(2), 152–156.

Shetgiri, R., Lin, H., & Flores, G. (2012). Identifying children at risk for being bullies in the United States. *Academic Pediatrics, 12*(6), 509–522.

Shin, Y. (2007). Peer relationships, social behaviors, academic performance and loneliness in Korean primary school children. *School Psychology International, 28*(2), 220–236.

Shing, Y.L., Werkle-Bergner, M., Li, S.C., & Lindenberger, U. (2008). Associative and strategic components of episodic memory: A lifespan dissociation. *Journal of Experimental Psychology: General, 137,* 495–513.

Shinskey, J. L., & Jachens, L. J. (2014). Picturing objects in infancy. *Child Development, 85*(5), 1813–1820.

Shinskey, J., & Munakata, Y. (2005). Familiarity breeds searching: Infants reverse their novelty preferences when reaching for hidden objects. *Psychological Science, 16,* 596–600.

Shinskey, J., & Munakata, Y. (2010). Something old, something new: A developmental transition from familiarity to novelty preferences with hidden objects. *Developmental Science, 13*(2), 378–384.

Shonkoff, J., & Fisher, P. (2013). Rethinking evidence-based practice and two-generation programs to create the future of early childhood policy. *Development and Psychopathology, 25*(4), 1635–1653.

Shonkoff, J., & Phillips, D. (Eds.). (2000). *From neurons to neighborhoods: The science of early childhood development.* Washington, DC: National Academy Press.

Shonkoff, J. P., Boyce, W. T., McEwen, B. S. (2009). Neuroscience, molecular biology, and the childhood roots of health disparities: Building a new framework for health promotion and disease prevention. *Journal of the American Medical Association, 301,* 2252–2259.

Shonkoff, J. P., Garner, A. S., Siegel, B. S., Dobbins, M. I., Earls, M. F., Garner, A. S., et al. (2012). The lifelong effects of early childhood adversity and toxic stress. *Pediatrics, 129*(1), e232–e246.

Shostak, M. (1981). *Nissa: The life and words of a !Kung Woman.* Cambridge, MA: Harvard University Press.

Shuler, C. (2012). *iLearn II: An analysis of the education category of the iTunes App Store.* New York :The Joan Ganz Cooney Center at Sesame Workshop. Retrieved from http://www.joanganzcooneycenter.org/publication/ilearn-ii-an-analysis-of-the-education-category-on-apples-app-store/

Shulman, E. P., Harden, K. P., Chein, J. M., & Steinberg, L. (2016). The development of impulse control and sensation-seeking in adolescence: Independent or interdependent processes? *Journal of Research on Adolescence, 26*(1), 37–44.

Shulman, S., & Seiffge-Krenke, I. (2001). Adolescent romance: Between experience and relationships. *Journal of Adolescence, 24,* 417–428.

Shweder, R. A., Goodnow, J. J., Hatano, G., LeVine, R. A., Markus, H. R., & Miller, P. J. (2006). The cultural psychology of development: One mind, many mentalities. In R. M. Lerner & W. Damon (Eds.), *Handbook of child psychology: Vol. 1. Theoretical models of human development* (6th ed., pp. 716–792). Hoboken, NJ: John Wiley & Sons.

Shweder, R. A., Mahapatpa, M., & Miller, J. G. (1987). Culture and moral development. In J. Kagan & S. Lamb (Eds.), *The emergence of morality in young children.* Chicago, IL: University of Chicago Press.

Shweder, R. A., Minow, M., & Markus, H. R. (Eds.). (2002). *Engaging cultural differences: The multicultural challenge in liberal democracies.* New York: Russell Sage Foundation.

Siegel, L. S. (2008, January–March). Morphological awareness skills of English language learners and children with dyslexia. *Topics in Language Disorders, 28*(1), 15–27.

Siegel, L. S. (2017). Adding math disabilities into the dialogue on language and literacy. *Perspectives on Language and Literacy, 43*(1), 5.

Siegler, R. S. (2005). Children's learning. *American Psychologist, 60,* 769–778.

Siegler, R. S., & Opfer, J. (2003). The development of numerical estimation: Evidence for multiple representations of numerical quantity. *Psychological Science, 14*(3), 237–243.

Silbereisen, R. K., & Kracke, B. (1997). Self-reported maturational timing and adaptation in adolescence. In J. Schulenberg, J. L. Maggs, & K. Hurrelmann (Eds.), *Health risks and developmental transitions during adolescence* (pp. 85–109). New York: Cambridge University Press.

Silva, L. M., Jansen, P. W., Steegers, E. A., Jaddoe, V. W., Arends, L. R., Tiemeier, H., et al. (2010). Mother's educational level and fetal growth: The genesis of health inequalities. *International Journal of Epidemiology, 39,* 1250–1261.

Silverman, M. H., Jedd, K., & Luciana, M. (2015). Neural networks involved in adolescent reward processing: An activation likelihood estimation meta-analysis of functional neuroimaging studies. *Neuroimage, 122,* 427–439.

Simmering, V., & Wood, C. (2017). The development of real-time stability supports visual working memory performance: Young children's feature binding can be improved through perceptual structure. *Developmental Psychology, 53*(8), 1474–1493.

Simmons, R. (2002). *Odd girl out: The hidden culture of aggression in girls.* New York: Harcourt.

Simpkins, S. D., Fredricks, J. A., Davis-Kean, P. E., & Eccles, J. S. (2006). Healthy mind, healthy habits: The influence of activity involvement in middle childhood. In A. C. Huston & M. N. Ripke (Eds.), *Developmental contexts in middle childhood: Bridges to adolescence and adulthood. Cambridge studies in social and emotional development* (pp. 283–302). New York: Cambridge University Press.

Simpson, E. A., Murray, L., Paukner, A., & Ferrari, P. F. (2014). The mirror neuron system as revealed through neonatal imitation: Presence from birth, predictive power and evidence of plasticity. *Philosophical Transactions of the Royal Society of London. Series B, Biological Sciences, 369*(1644), 20130289.

Simpson, J. A., Collins, W. A., Tran, S., & Haydon, K. C. (2007). Attachment and the experience and expression of emotions in romantic relationships: A developmental perspective. *Journal of Personality and Social Psychology, 92,* 355–367.

Sinclair, D. C., & Dangerfield, P. (1998). *Human growth after birth.* New York: Oxford University Press.

Singh, G. P., Chowdhury, T., Bindu, B., & Schaller, B. (2016). Sudden infant death syndrome—Role of trigeminocardiac reflex: A review. *Frontiers in Neurology, 7,* doi: 10.3389/fneur.2016.00221

Singh-Manoux, A. (2000). Culture and gender issues in adolescence: Evidence from studies on emotion. *Psicothema, 12*(Suppl. 1), 93–100.

Singleton, J. (Ed.). (1998). *Learning in likely places: Varieties of apprenticeship in Japan.* New York: Cambridge University Press.

Sizun, J., & Westrup, B. (2004). Early developmental care for preterm neonates: A call for more research. *Archives of Disease in Childhood: Fetal and Neonatal Edition, 89,* 384–388.

Skinner, B. F. (1938). *The behavior of organisms.* New York: Appleton-Century-Crofts.

Slater, S. J., Ewing, R., Powell, L. M., Chaloupka, F. J., & Johnston, L. D. (2010). The association between community physical activity settings and youth physical activity, obesity, and body mass index. *Journal of Adolescent Health, 47,* 496–503.

Slaughter, V., Itakura, S., Kutsuki, A., & Siegal, M. (2011). Learning to count begins in infancy: Evidence from 18 month olds' visual preferences. *Proceedings: Biological Sciences, 278*(1720), 2979–2984.

Slobin, D. (2005). From ontogenesis to phylogenesis: What can child language tell us about language evolution? In S. T. Parker, J. Langer, & C. Milbrath (Eds.), *Biology and knowledge revisited: From neurogenesis to psychogenesis* (pp. 287–306). Mahwah, NJ: Lawrence Erlbaum Associates.

Smetana, J. G. (2006). Social-cognitive domain theory: Consistencies and variations in children's moral and social judgments. In M. Killen & J. G. Smetana (Eds.), *Handbook of moral development* (pp. 119–153). Mahwah, NJ: Lawrence Erlbaum Associates.

Smetana, J. G. (2008). Conflicting views of conflict. *Monographs of the Society for Research in Child Development, 73,* 161–168.

Smetana, J. G., & Gettman, D. C. (2006, November). Autonomy and relatedness with parents and romantic development in African American adolescents. *Developmental Psychology, 42*(6), 1347–1351.

Smith, G. I., & Mittendorfer, B. (2016). Sexual dimorphism in skeletal muscle protein turnover. *Journal of Applied Physiology, 120*(6), 674–682.

Smith, J. F., & Skrbiš, Z. (2017). A social inequality of motivation? The relationship between beliefs about academic success and young people's educational attainment. *British Educational Research Journal, 43*(3), 441–465.

Smith, J. J., Eather, N., Morgan, P. J., Plotnikoff, R. C., Faigenbaum, A. D., & Lubans, D. R. (2014). The health benefits of muscular fitness for children and adolescents: A systematic review and meta-analysis. *Sports Medicine, 44*(9), 1209–1223.

Smith, K. (2002). *Who's minding the kids? Child care arrangements: Spring 1997.* Current Population Reports, P70–86, U.S. Census Bureau. Washington, DC: U.S. Government Printing Office.

Smith-Greenaway, E. (2013). Mothers' reading skills and child survival in Nigeria: Examining the relevance of mothers' decision-making power. *Social Science & Medicine, 97,* 152–160.

Smuts, A. B., & Smuts, R. W. (2006). *Science in the service of children, 1893–1935.* New Haven, CT: Yale University Press.

Smyser, C. D., Inder, T. E., Shimony, J. S., Hill, J. E., Degnan, A. J., et al. (2010). Longitudinal analysis of neural network development in preterm infants. *Cerebral Cortex,* 2852–2862.

Snowden, J. M., Tilden, E. L., Snyder, J., Quigley, B., Caughey, A. B., & Cheng, Y. W. (2015). Planned out-of-hospital birth and birth outcomes. *New England Journal of Medicine, 373*(27), 2642.

Society for Adolescent Health and Medicine. (2013). Recommendations for promoting the health and well-being of lesbian, gay, bisexual, and transgender adolescents: A position paper of the Society for Adolescent Health and Medicine. *Journal of Adolescent Health, 52*(4), 506–510.

Sokol, B. W., & Chandler, M. J. (2004). A bridge too far: On the relations between moral and secular reasoning. In J. I. M. Carpendale & U. Müller (Eds.), *Social interaction and the development of knowledge* (pp. 155–174). Mahwah, NJ: Lawrence Erlbaum Associates.

Solomon, S., & Knafo, A. (2007). Value similarity in adolescent friendships. In T. C. Rhodes (Ed.), *Focus on adolescent behavior research* (pp. 133–155). Hauppauge, NY: Nova Science Publishers.

Somerset, D. A., Moore, A., Whittle, M. J., Martin, W., & Kilby, M. D. (2006). An audit of outcome in intravascular transfusions using the intrahepatic portion of the fetal umbilical vein compared to cordocentesis. *Fetal Diagnosis and Therapy, 21*(3), 272–276.

Somerville, L. H., Jones, R. M., & Casey, B. J. (2010). A time of change: Behavioral and neural correlates of adolescent sensitivity to appetitive and aversive environmental cues. *Brain and Cognition, 72,* 124–133.

Son, S. C., & Peterson, M. F. (2017). Marital status, home environments, and family strain: Complex effects on preschool children's school readiness skills. *Infant and Child Development, 26*(2), e1967.

Song, Y., Ma, J., Wang, H., Wang, Z., Lau, P. W. C., Agardh, A., et al. (2016). Age at spermarche: 15-year trend and its association with body mass index in Chinese school-aged boys. *Pediatric Obesity, 11*(5), 369–374.

Sosa, A. V. (2016). Association of the type of toy used during play with the quantity and quality of parent–infant communication. *JAMA Pediatrics, 170*(2), 132–137.

Southgate, V., Chevallier, C., & Csibra, G. (2010). Seventeen-month-olds appeal to false beliefs to interpret others' referential communication. *Developmental Science, 13*(6), 907.

Sowislo, J., & Orth, U. (2013). Does low self-esteem predict depression and anxiety? A meta-analysis of longitudinal studies. *Psychological Bulletin, 139*(1), 213–240.

Spear, L. P. (2007). The developing brain and adolescent-typical behavior patterns: An evolutionary approach. In D. Romer & E. F. Walker (Eds.), *Adolescent psychopathology and the developing brain: Integrating brain and prevention science* (pp. 9–30). New York: Oxford University Press.

Spear, L. P. (2009). *The behavioral neuroscience of adolescence.* New York: W. W. Norton & Co.

Spelke, E. S., Breinlinger, K., Macomber, J., & Jacobson, K. (1992). Origins of knowledge. *Psychological Review, 99*(4), 605–632.

Spencer, M. B. (1988). Self-concept development. *New Directions for Child Development, 42,* 59–72.

Spencer, M. B. (2006). Revisiting the 1990 special issue on minority children: An editorial perspective 15 years later. *Child Development, 77,* 1149–1154.

Spinath, F. M., Bleidorn, W., Briley, D. A., & Tucker-Drob, E. M. (2017). Comparing the developmental genetics of cognition and personality over the life span. *Journal of Personality, 85*(1), 51.

Spinelli, J., Collins-Praino, L., Van Den Heuvel, C., & Byard, R. W. (2017). Evolution and significance of the triple risk model in sudden infant death syndrome. *Journal of Paediatrics and Child Health, 53*(2), 112–115.

Sreeramareddy, C. T., Joshi, H. S., Sreekumaran, B. V., Giri, S., & Chuni, N. (2006). Home delivery and newborn care practices among women in western Nepal: A questionnaire survey. *BMC Pregnancy and Childbirth, 6,* 27.

Sroufe, L. A., & Fleeson, J. (1986). Attachment and the construction of relationships. In W. W. Hartup & Z. Rubin (Eds.), *Relationships and development.* Mahwah, NJ: Lawrence Erlbaum Associates.

Sroufe, L. A., Egeland, B., Carlson, E., & Collins, W. A. (2005). Placing early attachment experiences in developmental context. In K. E. Grossmann, K. Grossmann, & E. Waters (Eds.), *Attachment from infancy to adulthood: The major longitudinal studies* (pp. 48–70). New York: Guilford Publications.

St. James-Roberts, I., Alvarez, M., Csipke, E., Abramsky, T., Goodwin, J., & Sorgenfrei, E. (2006). Infant crying and sleeping in London, Copenhagen, and when parents adopt a "proximal" form of care. *Pediatrics, 117,* 1146–1155.

Stattin, H., Kerr, M., & Tilton-Weaver, L. (2015). *Parental monitoring: A critical examination of the research.* New York: Columbia University Press.

Stauffer, S. (2008). Trauma and disorganized attachment in refugee children: Integrating theories and exploring treatment options. *Refugee Survey Quarterly, 27,* 150–163.

Stearns, P. (2010). *Childhood in world history* (2nd ed.). London: Routledge.

Steele, R. G., Nesbitt-Daly, J. S., Daniel, R. C., & Forehand, R. (2005, December). Factor structure of the Parenting Scale in a low-income African American sample. *Journal of Child and Family Studies, 14*(4), 535–549.

Steensma, T. D., & Cohen-Kettenis, P. T. (2015). More than two developmental pathways in children with gender dysphoria? *Journal of the American Academy of Child and Adolescent Psychiatry, 54*(2), 147–148.

Steiger, A., Allemand, M., Robins, R., & Fend, H. (2014). Low and decreasing self-esteem during adolescence predict adult depression two decades later. *Journal of Personality and Social Psychology, 106*(2), 325–338.

Stein, A., Thompson, A., & Waters, A. (2005). Childhood growth and chronic disease: Evidence from countries undergoing the nutrition transition. *Maternal and Child Nutrition, 3,* 177–184.

Steinberg, L. (2005, February). Cognitive and affective development in adolescence. *Trends in Cognitive Sciences, 9*(2), 69–74.

Steinberg, L. (2008, March). A social neuroscience perspective on adolescent risk-taking. *Developmental Review, 28*(1), 78–106.

Steinberg, L., & Duncan, P. (2002). Work group IV: Increasing the capacity of parents, families, and adults living with adolescents to improve adolescent health outcomes. *Journal of Adolescent Health, 31*(Suppl. 6), 261–263.

Steinberg, L., Silk, J. S. (2002). Parenting adolescents. In M. H. Bornstein (Ed.) *Handbook of parenting: Vol. 1. Children and parenting* (2nd ed., pp. 103–133). Mahwah, NJ: Lawrence Erlbaum Associates.

Steiner, M., Attarbaschi, A., Konig, M., Nebral, K., Gadner, H., Haas, O. A., et al. (2005). Equal frequency of TEL/AML1 rearrangements in children with acute lymphoblastic leukemia with and without Down syndrome. *Journal of Pediatric Hematology/Oncology, 22*(1), 11–16.

Steiner, R. J., Liddon, N., & Dittus, P. (2017). Associations between parent-adolescent communication about sex and provider counseling about HIV among adolescents: Findings from the 2011–2013 national survey of family growth. *Journal of Adolescent Health, 60*(2), S2–S3.

Stenberg, G. (2017). Does contingency in adults' responding influence 12-month-old infants' social referencing? *Infant Behavior & Development, 46,* 67–79.

Stennes, L. M., Burch, M. M., Sen, M. G., & Bauer, P. J. (2005). A longitudinal study of gendered vocabulary and communicative action in young children. *Developmental Psychology, 41,* 75–88.

Sterelny, K. (2016). Cumulative cultural evolution and the origins of language. *Biological Theory, 11*(3), 173–186.

Stern, D. N. (2002). *The first relationship: Infant and mother.* Cambridge, MA: Harvard University Press.

Stern, W. (1910). Abstracts of lectures on the psychology of testimony and on the study of individuality. *American Journal of Psychology, 21,* 273–282.

Stern, W. (1912). *Psychologische methoden der intelligenz-prufung.* Leipzig: Barth.

Sternberg, R. (1985). *Beyond IQ: A triarchic theory of human intelligence.* New York: Cambridge University Press.

Sternberg, R. J. (1990). *Metaphors of mind: Conceptions of the nature of intelligence.* New York: Cambridge University Press.

Sternberg, R. J. (2007, January). A systems model of leadership: WICS. *American Psychologist. Special Issue: Leadership, 62*(1), 34–42.

Sternberg, R. J., & Grigorenko, E. L. (2008). Ability testing across cultures. In L. A. Suzuki & J. G. Ponterotto (Eds.), *Handbook of multicultural assessment: Clinical, psychological, and educational applications* (pp. 449–470). San Francisco, CA: Jossey-Bass.

Sternberg, S. (2011). Modular processes in mind and brain. *Cognitive Neuropsychology, 28*(3–4), 156–208.

Stevenson, H. W., Stigler, J. W., Lee, S., Lucker, G. W., Kitamura, S., & Hsu, C. (1985). Cognitive performance and academic achievement of Japanese, Chinese, and American children. *Child Development, 56,* 718–734.

Stevenson, R. (1977). *The fetus and newly born infant: Influence of the prenatal environment* (2nd ed.). St. Louis, MO: Mosby.

Stice, E., Marti, C. N., Shaw, H., & Jaconis, M. (2009). An 8-year longitudinal study of the natural history of threshold, subthreshold, and partial eating disorders from a community sample of adolescents. *Journal of Abnormal Psychology, 118,* 587–597.

Stipek, D. (2001). Pathways to constructive lives: The importance of early school success. In A. C. Bower & D. J. Stipek (Eds.), *Constructive & destructive behavior: Implications for family, school, & society* (pp. 291–315). Washington, DC: American Psychological Association.

Stojković, I. (2013). Pubertal timing and self-esteem in adolescents: The mediating role of body-image and social relations. *European Journal of Developmental Psychology, 10*(3), 359–377.

Stoltz, H. E., Barber, B. K., & Olsen, J. A. (2005). Toward disentangling fathering and mothering: An assessment of relative importance. *Journal of Marriage and Family, 67,* 1076–1092.

Stone, J. L., & Church, J. (1957). *Childhood and adolescence: A psychology of the growing person.* New York: Random House.

Storvoll, E. E., & Wichstrom, L. (2002, April). Do the risk factors associated with conduct problems in adolescents vary according to gender? *Journal of Adolescence, 25*(2), 182–202.

Strathearn, L., Gray, P. H., O'Callaghan, M. J., & Wood, D. O. (2001). Childhood neglect and cognitive development in extremely low birth weight infants: A prospective study. *Pediatrics, 108*(1), 142–151.

Straus, M. (2009). *Differences in corporal punishment in 32 nations and its relation to national differences in IQ.* Paper presented at the 14th International Conference on Violence, Abuse, and Trauma.

Strayer, F. F. (1991). The development of agonistic and affiliative structures in preschool play groups. In J. Silverberg & P. Gray (Eds.), *To fight or not to fight: Violence and peacefulness in humans and other primates.* Oxford, England: Oxford University Press.

Streri, A., Coulon, M., Marie, J., & Yeung, H. H. (2016). Developmental change in infants' detection of visual faces that match auditory vowels. *Infancy, 21*(2), 177–198.

Striano, T., & Rochat, P. (2000). Emergence of selective social referencing in infancy. *Infancy, 1*(2), 253–264.

Striano, T., Stahl, D., & Cleveland, A. (2009). Taking a closer look at social and cognitive skills: A weekly longitudinal assessment between 7 and 10 months of age. *European Journal of Developmental Psychology, 1,* 567–591.

Striepe, M., & Tolman, D. (2003). Mom, Dad, I'm straight: The coming out of gender ideologies in adolescent sexual-identity development. *Journal of Clinical Child and Adolescent Psychology, 32,* 523–530.

Stronach, E. P., Toth, S. L., Rogosch, F., & Cicchetti, D. (2013). Preventive interventions and sustained attachment security in maltreated children. *Development and Psychopathology, 25*(4 Pt. 1), 919.

Stross, B. (1973). Acquisition of botanical terminology by Tzeltal children. In M. S. Edmonson (Ed.), *Meaning in Mayan languages* (pp. 107–142). The Hague: Mouton

Štulhofer, A., Buško, V., & Schmidt, G. (2012). Adolescent exposure to pornography and relationship intimacy in young adulthood. *Psychology & Sexuality, 3*(2), 95–107.

Stump, G. S., Husman, J., & Corby, M. (2014). Engineering students' intelligence beliefs and learning. *Journal of Engineering Education, 103*(3), 369–387.

Stunkard, A. J., Sorenson, T. I., Hanis, C., Teasdale, T. W., Chakraborty, R., Schull, W. J., & Schulsinger, F. (1986). An adoption study of human obesity. *New England Journal of Medicine, 314,* 193–198.

Su, Q., Zhang, H., Zhang, Y., Zhang, H., Ding, D., Zeng, J., et al. (2015). Maternal stress in gestation: Birth outcomes and stress-related hormone response of the neonates. *Pediatrics and Neonatology, 56*(6), 376–381.

Suarez, J. J., Isakova, T., Anderson, C. A. M., Boulware, L. E., Wolf, M., & Scialla, J. J. (2015). Food access, chronic kidney disease, and hypertension in the U.S. *American Journal of Preventive Medicine, 49*(6), 912–920.

Suárez-Orozco, C., Bang, H. J., & Onaga, M. (2010). Contributions to variations in academic trajectories amongst recent immigrant youth. *International Journal of Behavioral Development, 34,* 500–510.

Suárez-Orozco, C., Gaytán, F. X., Bang, H. J., Pakes, J., O'Connor, E., & Rhodes, J. (2010). Academic trajectories of newcomer immigrant youth. *Developmental Psychology, 46*(3), 602–618.

Suárez-Orozco, C., Suárez-Orozco, M. M., & Todorova, I. (2008). *Learning a new land: Immigrant students in American society.* Cambridge, MA: Harvard University Press.

Subrahmanyam, K., & Greenfield, P. (2008). Online communication and adolescent relationships. *The Future of Children, 18,* 119–146.

Subrahmanyam, K., & Renukarya, B. (2015). Digital games and learning: Identifying pathways of influence. *Educational Psychologist, 50*(4), 335–348.

Subrahmanyam, K., & Šmahel, D. (2011). Digital youth: The role of media in development. New York: Springer.

Suchert, V., Hanewinkel, R., & Isensee, B. (2016). Longitudinal relationships of fitness, physical activity, and weight status with academic achievement in adolescents. *Journal of School Health, 86*(10), 734–741.

Sugiura, M., Miyauchi, C., Kotozaki, Y., Akimoto, Y., Nozawa, T., Yomogida, Y., et al. (2015). Neural mechanism for mirrored self-face recognition. *Cerebral Cortex, 25*(9), 2806–2814.

Sukys, S., Lisinskiene, A., & Tilindiene, I. (2015). adolescents' participation in sport activities and attachment to parents and peers. *Social Behavior and Personality, 43*(9), 1507–1518.

Sullivan, A. L., & Simonson, G. R. (2016). A systematic review of school-based social-emotional interventions for refugee and war-traumatized youth. *Review of Educational Research, 86*(2), 503.

Sullivan, H. S. (1953). *The interpersonal theory of psychiatry.* New York: W. W. Norton.

Sullivan, J. A. (2000). Introduction to the musculoskeletal system. In J. A. Sullivan & S. J. Anderson (Eds.), *Care of the Young Athlete* (pp. 243–258). Rosemont, IL: American Academy of Orthopaedic Surgeons and American Academy of Pediatrics.

Sullivan, J. A., Anderson, S. J. (Eds.). (2000). *Care of the young athlete.* Rosemont, IL: American Academy of Orthopaedic Surgeons and American Academy of Pediatrics.

Summerfield, D. (1999). A critique of seven assumptions behind psychological trauma programmes in war-affected areas. *Social Science and Medicine, 48,* 1449–1462.

Sun, Y., & Li, Y. (2008). Stable postdivorce family structures during late adolescence and socioeconomic consequences in adulthood. *Journal of Marriage and Family 70,* 129–143.

Sun, Y., Liu, J., Liu, Y., Yan, S., Hu, J., Xu, G., & Tao, F. (2016). Longitudinal pattern of early maturation on morning cortisol and depressive symptoms: Sex-specific effects. *Psychoneuroendocrinology, 71,* 58–63.

Suomi, S. (1995). Influences of attachment theory on ethological studies of biobehavioral development in nonhuman primates. In S. Goldberg, R. Muir, & J. Kerr (Eds.), *Attachment theory: Social, developmental, and clinical perspectives* (pp. 185–202). Mahwah, NJ: Analytic Press.

Suomi, S. J. (2000). A biobehavioral perspective on developmental psychopathology: Excessive aggression and serotonergic dysfunction in monkeys. In A. Sameroff, M. Lewis, & S. M. Miller (Eds.), *Handbook of developmental psychopathology* (2nd ed., pp. 237–256). Dordrecht, Netherlands: Kluwer Academic.

Super, C. M. (1976). Environmental effects on motor development: A case of African infant precocity. *Developmental Medicine and Child Neurology, 18,* 561–567.

Super, C. M., & Harkness, S. (1972). The infant's niche in rural Kenya and metropolitan America. In L. Adler (Ed.), *Issues in cross-cultural research.* New York: Academic Press.

Super, C. M., & Harkness, S. (2002). Culture structures the environment for development. *Human Development, 45,* 270–274.

Surana, V., Dabas, A., Khadgawat, R., Marwaha, R., Sreenivas, V., Ganie, M., et al. (2017). Pubertal onset in apparently healthy Indian boys and impact of obesity. *Indian Journal of Endocrinology and Metabolism, 21*(3), 434–438.

Susman, E. J. (2006). Psychobiology of persistent antisocial behavior: Stress, early vulnerabilities and the attenuation hypothesis. *Neuroscience & Biobehavioral Reviews, 30*(3), 376–389.

Susman, E. J., Schmeelk, K. H., Ponirakis, A., & Gariepy, J. L. (2001). Maternal prenatal, postpartum, and concurrent stressors and temperament in 3-year-olds: A person and variable analysis. *Development and Psychopathology, 13*(3), 629–652.

Suzuki, K., Minai, J., & Yamagata Z. (2007). Maternal negative attitudes towards pregnancy as an independent risk factor for low birthweight. *Journal of Obstetrics and Gynaecology Research 33,* 438–444.

Swain, J. E., Kim, P., Spicer, J., Ho, S. S., Dayton, C. J., Elmadih, A., & Abel, K. M. (2014). Approaching the biology of human parental attachment: Brain imaging, oxytocin and coordinated assessments of mothers and fathers. *Brain Research, 1580,* 78–101.

Swanson, J. A. (2016). Trends in literature about emerging adulthood: Review of empirical studies. *Emerging Adulthood, 4*(6), 391–402.

Sweeting, H., & West, P. (2003). Sex differences in health at ages 11, 13 and 15. *Social Science & Medicine, 56,* 31–39.

Sweeting, H., Young, R., West, P., & Der, G. (2006). Peer victimization and depression in early-mid adolescence: A longitudinal study. *The British Journal of Educational Psychology, 76*(Pt. 3), 577–594.

Symington, A., & Pinelli, J. (2003). Developmental care for promoting development and preventing morbidity in preterm infants. *Cochrane Database of Systematic Reviews, 4,* CD001814.

Syrad, H., Johnson, L., Wardle, J., & Llewellyn, C. H. (2016). Appetitive traits and food intake patterns in early life. *The American Journal of Clinical Nutrition, 103*(1), 231–235.

Tabacchi, G., Giammanco, S., La Guardia, M., & Giammanco, M. (2007). A review of the literature and a new classification of the early determinants of childhood obesity: From pregnancy to the first years of life. *Nutrition Research, 27,* 587–604.

Tager-Flusberg, H. (2007, December). Evaluating the theory-of-mind hypothesis of autism. *Current Directions in Psychological Science, 16*(6), 311–315.

Takei, W. (2001). How do deaf infants attain first signs? *Developmental Science, 4*(1), 71–78.

Tan, L., & Martin, G. (2015). Taming the adolescent mind: A randomised controlled trial examining clinical efficacy of an adolescent mindfulness-based group programme. *Child and Adolescent Mental Health, 20*(1), 49–55.

Tani, C. R., Chavez, E. L., & Deffenbacher, J. L. (2001). Peer isolation and drug use among while non-Hispanic and Mexican American adolescents. *Adolescence, 36,* 127–139.

Tanner, J. M. (1978). *Fetus into man: Physical growth from conception to maturity.* Cambridge, MA: Harvard University Press.

Tanner, J. M. (1990). *Fetus into man: Physical growth from conception to maturity* (Rev. ed.). Cambridge, MA: Harvard University Press.

Tarchi, C., & Pinto, G. (2016). Reciprocal teaching: Analyzing interactive dynamics in the co-construction of a text's meaning. *The Journal of Educational Research, 109*(5), 518–530.

Tardif, T., Fletcher, P., Liang, W., Zhang, Z., Kaciroti, N., & Marchman, V. A. (2008). Baby's first 10 words. *Developmental Psychology, 44*(4), 929–938.

Taylor, C. A., Manganello, J. A., Lee, S. J., & Rice, J. C. (2010). Mothers' spanking of 3-year-old children and subsequent risk of children's aggressive behavior. *Pediatrics, 125,* 1057–1065.

Taylor, G., Hipp, D., Moser, A., Dickerson, K., & Gerhardstein, P. (2014). The development of contour processing: Evidence from physiology and psychophysics. *Frontiers in Psychology, 5,* 719.

Taylor, P., Passel, J., Fry, R., Morin, R., Wang, W., Velasco, G., & Dockterman, D (2010). *The return of the multi-generational family household: A social and demographic trends report.* Washington, DC: Pew Research Center.

Taylor, P. D., McConnell, J., Khan, I. Y., Holemans, K., Lawrence, K. M., Asare-Anane, H., et al. (2005). Impaired glucose homeostasis and mitochondrial abnormalities in offspring of rats fed a fat-rich diet in pregnancy. *American Journal of Physiology: Regulatory, Integrative and Comparative Physiology, 288,* 134–139.

Taylor, Z. E., Eisenberg, N., Spinrad, T. L., Eggum, N. D., & Sulik, M. J. (2013). The relations of ego-resiliency and emotion socialization to the development of empathy and prosocial behavior across early childhood. *Emotion, 13*(5), 822–831.

Temming, L., Cahill, A., & Riley, L. (2016). Clinical management of medications in pregnancy and lactations. *American Journal of Obstetrics and Gynecology, 214*(6), 698–702.

Temple, C. M., & Sanfilippo, P. M. (2003). Executive skills in Klinefelter's syndrome. *Neuropsychologia, 41,* 1547–1559.

Tenenbaum, H. R., Callanan, M., Alba-Speyer, C., & Sandoval, L. (2002). The role of educational background, activity, and past experiences in Mexican-descent families' science conversations. *Hispanic Journal of Behavioral Sciences, 24*(2), 225–248.

Tereno, S., Madigan, S., Lyons-Ruth, K., Plamondon, A., Atkinson, L., Guedeney, N., et al. (2017). Assessing a change mechanism in a randomized home-visiting trial: Reducing disrupted maternal communication decreases infant disorganization. *Development and Psychopathology, 29*(2), 637.

Terplan, M., Smith, E. J., Kozloski, M. J., & Pollack, H. A. (2009). Methamphetamine use among pregnant women. *Obstetrics and Gynecology, 113,* 1285–1291.

Tharp, R. G. (2005). Research in diversity and education: Process and structure in synthesizing knowledge. *Journal of Education for Students Placed at Risk, 10,* 355–361.

Thelen, E. (2002). Self-organization in developmental processes: Can systems approaches work? In M. H. Johnson & Y. Munakata (Eds.), *Brain development and cognition: A reader* (2nd ed., pp. 336–374). Malden, MA: Blackwell Publishing.

Thelen, E., Fisher, D. M., & Ridley-Johnson, R. (2002). The relationship between physical growth and a newborn reflex. *Infant Behavior and Development, 25*(1), 72–85.

Thelen, E., Schoener, G., Scheier, C., & Smith, L. B. (2001). The dynamics of embodiment: A field theory of infant perseverative reaching. *Behavioral and Brain Sciences, 24*(1), 1–86.

Thelen, E., & Smith, L. B. (1998). Dynamic systems theory. In W. Damon & R. M. Lerner (Eds.), *Handbook of child psychology: Vol. 12* (5th ed., pp. 563–634). New York: Wiley.

Thoma, B. C., & Huebner, D. M. (2014). Parental monitoring, parent–adolescent communication about sex, and sexual risk among young men who have sex with men. *AIDS and Behavior, 18*(8), 1604–1614.

Thoman, E. B., & Whitney, M. P. (1989). Sleep states of infants monitored in the home: Individual differences, developmental trends, and origins of diurnal cyclicity. *Infant Behavior & Development, 12,* 59–75.

Thomas, J., Letourneau, N., Campbell, T., Tomfohr-Madsen, L., Giesbrecht, G. F., & APrON Study Team. (2017). Developmental origins of infant emotion regulation: Mediation by temperamental negativity and moderation by maternal sensitivity. *Developmental Psychology, 53*(4), 611–628.

Thompson, C. A., & Siegler, R. S. (2010). Linear numerical–magnitude representations aid children's memory for numbers. *Psychological Science, 21,* 1274–1281.

Thompson, R. A., & Newton, E. K. (2010). Emotion in early conscience. In R. A. Thompson & E. K. Newton (Eds.), *Emotions, aggression, and morality in children: Bridging development and psychopathology* (pp. 13–31). Washington, DC: American Psychological Association.

Thompson, R., & Einstein, F. (2010). Epigenetic basis for fetal origins of age-related disease. *Journal of Women's Health, 19,* 581–587.

Thorn, B., Tadler, C., Huret, N., Trippe, C., Ayo, E., Mendelson, M., et al. (2015). *WIC participant and program characteristics, 2014.* Alexandria, VA: U.S. Department of Agriculture, Food and Nutrition Service.

Thorne, B. (1993). *Gender play: Girls and boys in school.* New Brunswick, NJ: Rutgers University Press.

Thrasher, F. (1927). *The gang: A study of 1,313 gangs in Chicago.* Chicago: University of Chicago Press.

Tills, O., Rundle, S. D., & Spicer, J. I. (2013). Variance in developmental event timing is greatest at low biological levels: Implications for heterochrony. *Biological Journal of the Linnean Society, 110*(3), 581–590.

Tither, J. M., & Ellis, B. J. (2008). Impact of fathers on daughters' age at menarche: A genetically and environmentally controlled sibling study. *Developmental Psychology, 44*(5), 1409–1420.

Tokunaga, R. S. (2010). Following you home from school: A critical review and synthesis of research on cyberbullying victimization. *Computers in Human Behavior, 26,* 277–287.

Tollenaar, M. S., Beijers, R., Jansen, J., Riksen-Walraven, J. M. A., & Weerth, C. D. (2012). Solitary sleeping in young infants is associated with heightened cortisol reactivity to a bathing session but not to a vaccination. *Psychoneuroendocrinology, 37*(2), 167–177.

Tolman, D. L., & McClelland, S. I. (2011). Normative sexuality development in adolescence: A decade in review, 2000–2009. *Journal of Research on Adolescence, 21*(1), 242–255.

Tomasello, M. (2000). First steps toward a usage-based theory of language acquisition. *Cognitive Linguistics. Special Issue: Language Acquisition 11*(1–2), 61–82.

Tomasello, M. (2011). Language development. In U. Goswami (Ed.), *The Wiley-Blackwell handbook of childhood cognitive development* (2nd ed., pp. 239–257). Malden, MA: Blackwell.

Tomasello, M., & Hermann, E. (2010). Ape and human cognition: What's the difference? *Current Directions in Psychology Science, 19,* 3–8.

Toppari, J., & Juul, A. (2010). Trends in puberty timing in humans and environmental modifiers. *Molecular and Cellular Endocrinology, 324,* 39–44.

Torday, J. S., & Miller, W. B. (2016). Phenotype as agent for epigenetic inheritance. *Biology, 5*(3), 30.

Treit, S., Chen, Z., Rasmussen, C., & Beaulieu, C. (2014). White matter correlates of cognitive inhibition during development: A diffusion tensor imaging study. *Neuroscience, 276,* 87–97.

Tremblay, R., Nagin, D., Séguin, J., Zoccolillo, M., Zelazo, P., Boivin, M., et al. (2005). Physical aggression during early childhood: Trajectories and predictors. *Canadian Child and Adolescent Psychiatry Review, 14*(1), 3–9.

Trevarthen, C. (1998). The concept and foundations of infant intersubjectivity. In S. Braten (Ed.), *Intersubjective communication and emotion in early ontogeny* (pp. 15–46). New York: Cambridge University Press.

Trevarthen, C. (2015). Infant semiosis: The psycho-biology of action and shared experience from birth. *Cognitive Development, 36,* 130–141.

Troiden, R. R. (1993). The formation of homosexual identities. In L. D. Garnets & D. C. Kimmel (Eds.), *Psychological perspectives on lesbian and gay male experiences* (pp. 191–217). New York: Columbia University Press.

Tsai, K. M., Telzer, E. H., Gonzales, N. A., & Fuligni, A. J. (2015). Parental cultural socialization of Mexican-American adolescents' family obligation values and behaviors. *Child Development, 86*(4), 1241–1252.

Tso, W., Rao, N., Jiang, F., Li, A., Lee, S., Ho, F., et al. (2016). Sleep duration and school readiness of Chinese preschool children. *Journal of Pediatrics, 169,* 266–271.

Tuchmann-Duplessis, H. (1975). *Drug effects on the fetus.* Acton, MA: Publishing Science Group.

Tudge, J., Odero, D., Piccinini, C., Doucet, F., Sperb, T., & Lopes, R. (2006). A window into different cultural worlds: Young children's everyday activities in the United States, Brazil, and Kenya. *Child Development, 77,* 1446–1469.

Tulving, E., & Craik, F. I. M. (Eds.). (2000). *The Oxford handbook of memory.* London: Oxford University Press.

Turati, C., Di Giorgio, E., Bardi, L., & Simion, F. (2010). Holistic face processing in newborns, 3-month-old infants, and adults: Evidence from the composite face effect. *Child Development, 81,* 1894–1905.

Turiel, E. (1983). *The development of social knowledge: Morality and convention.* Cambridge, England: Cambridge University Press.

Turiel, E. (2002). *The culture of morality.* Cambridge, England: Cambridge University Press.

Turiel, E. (2006). The development of morality. In N. Eisenberg, W. Damon, & R. M. Lerner (Eds.), *Handbook of child psychology: Vol. 3. Social, emotional, and personality development* (6th ed., pp. 789–857). Hoboken, NJ: John Wiley & Sons.

Turiel, E. (2008a). The development of children's orientations toward moral, social, and personal orders: More than a sequence in development. *Human Development, 51*(1), 21.

Turiel, E. (2008b). Thought about actions in social domains: Morality, social conventions, and social interactions. *Cognitive Development, 23*(1), 136–154.

Turiel, E. (2010). Domain specificity in social interactions, social thought, and social development. *Child Development, 81,* 720–726.

Turnpenny, P., & Ellard, L. (2012). *Emery's elements of medical genetics* (14th ed.). New York: Churchill Livingstone.

Twenge, J. M., & Nolen-Hoeksema, S. (2002, November). Age, gender, race, socioeconomic status, and birth cohort difference on the children's depression inventory: A meta-analysis. *Journal of Abnormal Psychology, 111*(4), 578–588.

U.S. Census Bureau. (2011). *Statistical abstract of the United States: 2012: Historical Statistics* (131st ed.). Washington, DC: U.S. Department of Commerce.

U.S. Department of Health & Human Services. (2009). *Child maltreatment 2007.* Washington, DC: U.S. Government Printing Office.

U.S. Department of Health and Human Services, Health Resources and Services Administration, Maternal and Child Health Bureau. (2013). *Child Health USA 2013.* Rockville, MD: U.S. Department of Health and Human Services.

U.S. Department of Health and Human Services. (2017). *Child maltreatment 2015.* Retrieved from https://www.acf.hhs.gov/cb/resource/child-maltreatment-2015

Uink, B. N., Modecki, K. L., & Barber, B. L. (2017). Disadvantaged youth report less negative emotion to minor stressors when with peers: An experience sampling study. *International Journal of Behavioral Development, 41*(1), 41–51.

Umaña-Taylor, A. J., Quintana, S. M., Lee, R. M., Cross, W. E., Rivas-Drake, D., Schwartz, S. J., et al. (2014). Ethnic and racial identity during adolescence and into young adulthood: An integrated conceptualization. *Child Development, 85*(1), 21–39.

UNAIDS. (2016a). *Fact sheet: Latest statistics on the status of the AIDS epidemic.* Retrieved from http://www.unaids.org/en/resources/fact-sheet

UNAIDS. (2016b). *Global AIDS update.* Retrieved from http://www.unaids.org/sites/default/files/media_asset/global-AIDS-update-2016_en.pdf

Underwood, M. (2002). Aggression among boys and girls. In P. Smith & C. Hart (Eds.), *Blackwell handbook of childhood social development.* Malden, MA: Blackwell Publishing.

UNESCO. (2015). *EFA Global Monitoring Report: Education for All 2000–2015: Achievements and Challenges.* Paris: UNESCO Publishing.

UNESCO Institute for Statistics. (2017). *Gross enrolment ratio, pre-primary, both sexes.* Retrieved from http://data.worldbank.org/indicator/SE.PRE.ENRR?end=2016&start=1970&view=chart

UNICEF. (2009). *Tracking progress on child and maternal nutrition: A survival and development priority.* Atlanta, GA: Center for Disease Control.

UNICEF. (2014). *Ending child marriage: Progress and prospects.* Retrieved from http://www.unicef.org/media/media_82282.html

UNICEF. (2015). *Levels & trends in child mortality: Report 2015.* Retrieved from https://data.unicef.org/wp-content/uploads/2015/12/IGME-report-2015-child-mortality-final_236.pdf

United Nations Department of Economic and Social Affairs Population Division. (2017). *World Population Prospects: The 2017 Revision, Key Findings and Advance Tables.* Working Paper No. ESA/P/WP/248.

United Nations General Security Council. (2011). *Children and armed conflict.* Retrieved from http://www.un.org/children/conflict/_documents/S2011250.pdf

United Nations High Commission for Refugees. (2016). *Global trends: Forced displacement in 2015.* https://s3.amazonaws.com/unhcrsharedmedia/2016/2016-06-20-global-trends/2016-06-14-Global-Trends-2015.pdf

United Nations Population Fund. (2015). *Migration.* Retrieved from http://www.unfpa.org/migration

United Nations Population Fund. (2016). *State of the world population 2016.* Retrieved from http://www.unfpa.org/sites/default/files/sowp/downloads/The_State_of_World_Population_2016_-_English.pdf

Updegraff, K. A., Perez-Brena, N. J., Baril, M. E., McHale, S. M., & Umaña-Taylor, A. J. (2012). Mexican-origin mothers' and fathers' involvement in adolescents' peer relationships: A pattern-analytic approach. *Journal of Marriage and Family, 74*(5), 1069–1083.

Urberg, K. A., Degirmencioglu, S. M., & Tolson, J. M. (1998). Adolescent friendship selection and termination: The role of similarity. *Journal of Social & Personal Relationships, 15*(5), 703–710.

Urlacher, S. S., Blackwell, A. D., Liebert, M. A., Madimenos, F. C., Cepon-Robins, T. J., Gildner, T. E., et al. (2016). Physical growth of the Shuar: Height, weight, and BMI references for an indigenous Amazonian population. *American Journal of Human Biology, 28*(1), 16–30.

Ursache, A., & Noble, K. G. (2016). Socioeconomic status, white matter, and executive function in children. *Brain and Behavior, 6*(10).

Uzefovsky, F., Döring, A. K., & Knafo-Noam, A. (2016). Values in middle childhood: Social and genetic contributions. *Social Development, 25*(3), 482–502.

Uzgiris, I. C., & Hunt, J. (1975). *Assessment in infancy: Ordinal scales of psychological development.* Champaign: University of Illinois Press.

Valian, V. (1999). Input and language acquisition. In W. C. Ritchie & T. K. Bhatia (Eds.), *Handbook of child language acquisition* (pp. 497–530). San Diego, CA: Academic Press.

Valkenburg, P. M., & Peter, J. (2007). Online communication and adolescent well-being: Testing the stimulation versus the displacement hypothesis. *Journal of Computer-Mediated Communication, 12*(4), article 2.

Valkenburg, P. M., & Peter, J. (2008). Adolescents' identity experiments on the Internet: Consequences for social competence and self-concept unity. *Communication Research, 35*(2), 208–231.

Valkenburg, P. M., & Peter, J. (2013). The differential susceptibility to media effects model. *Journal of Communication, 63*(2), 221–243.

Valkenburg, P., Schouten, A., & Peter, J. (2005). Adolescents' identity experiments on the Internet. *New Media & Society, 7*(3), 383–402.

Valsiner, J. (2005). Transformations and flexible forms: Where qualitative psychology begins. *Qualitative Research in Psychology, 4*(4), 39–57.

Valsiner, J. (2007). *Culture in minds and societies.* New York: Sage.

Valsiner, J. (2015a). The place for synthesis: Vygotsky's analysis of affective generalization. *History of the Human Sciences, 28*(2), 93–102.

Valsiner, J. (2015b). Where are you, *Culture & Psychology*? Making of an interdisciplinary field. *Culture & Psychology, 21*(4), 419–428.

Valsiner, J., & van der Veer, R. (2014). Encountering the border: Vygotsky's zona blizaishego razvitya and its implications for theory of development. In A. Yasnitsky, R. van der Veer, & M. Ferrari (Eds.), *The Cambridge handbook of cultural-historical psychology.* New York: Cambridge University Press.

Valsiner, J., van Oers, B., Wardekker, W., Elbers, E., & van der Veer, R. (2009). Contextualizing learning: How activity theories can change our conventional research practices in the study of development. *Human Development, 52,* 69–76.

Van Campen, K. S., & Romero, A. J. (2012). How are self-efficacy and family involvement associated with less sexual risk taking among ethnic minority adolescents? *Family Relations, 61*(4), 548–558.

Van den Veyver, I. B. (2016). *Recent advances in prenatal genetic screening and testing.* Retrieved from https://f1000research.com/articles/5-2591/v1

van der Steen, S. L., Riedijk, S. R., Verhagen-Visser, J., Govaerts, L. C. P., Srebniak, M. I., van Opstal, D., et al. (2016). The psychological impact of prenatal diagnosis and disclosure of susceptibility loci: First impressions of parents' experiences. *Journal of Genetic Counseling, 25*(6), 1227–1234.

van der Willik, E. M., Vrijkotte, T. G. M., Altenburg, T. M., Gademan, M. G. J., & Kist-van Holthe, J. (2015). Exclusively breastfed overweight infants are at the same risk of childhood overweight as formula fed overweight infants. *Archives of Disease in Childhood, 100*(10), 932–937.

Van IJzendoorn, M., & Sagi-Schwartz, A. (2008). Cross-cultural patterns of attachment: Universal and contextual dimensions. In J. Cassidy & P. Shaver (Eds.), *Handbook of attachment: Theory, research, and clinical applications* (2nd ed., pp. 880–1020). New York: Guilford Press.

Van Leijenhorst, L., Gunther Moor, B., Op De Macks, Z. A., Rombouts, S. A. R. B., Westenberg, P. M., & Crone, E. A. (2010). Adolescent risky decision-making: Neurocognitive development of reward and control regions. *NeuroImage, 51,* 345–355.

Van Mierlo, J., & Van den Bulck, J. (2004). Benchmarking the cultivation approach to video game effects: A comparison of the correlates of TV viewing and game play. *Journal of Adolescence, 27,* 97–111.

van Oosten, J. M. F., Peter, J., & Valkenburg, P. M. (2015). The influence of sexual music videos on adolescents' misogynistic beliefs: The role of video content, gender, and affective engagement. *Communication Research, 42*(7), 986–1008.

van Roekel, G. H., Scholte, R. H. J., Engels, R. C. M. E., Goossens, L., & Verhagen, M. (2015). Loneliness in the daily lives of adolescents: An experience sampling study examining the effects of social contexts. *Journal of Early Adolescence, 35*(7), 905–930.

Van Ryzin, M. J., & Dishion, T. J. (2013). From antisocial behavior to violence: A model for the amplifying role of coercive joining in adolescent friendships. *Journal of Child Psychology and Psychiatry, 54*(6), 661–669.

van Schalkwyk, G. I., Ortiz-Lopez, M., Volkmar, F. R., & Silverman, W. K. (2016). Social media use improves friendship quality in adolescents with autism spectrum disorder. *Journal of the American Academy of Child & Adolescent Psychiatry, 55*(10), S100.

Van Wagner, V., Epoo, B., Nastapoka, J., & Harney, E. (2007). Reclaiming birth, health, and community: Midwifery in the Inuit villages of Nunavik, Canada. *Journal of Midwifery and Women's Health, 52*(4), 384–391.

van Wieringen, A., & Wouters, J. (2015). What can we expect of normally-developing children implanted at a young age with respect to their auditory, linguistic and cognitive skills? *Hearing Research, 322,* 171–179.

VanDeventer, S. S., & White, J. A. (2002). Expert behavior in children's video game play. *Simulation & Gaming, 33*(1), 28–48.

Vanfraussen, K., Ponjaert-Kristoffersen, I., & Brewaeys, A. (2002). What does it mean for youngsters to grow up in a lesbian family created by means of donor insemination. *Journal of Reproductive and Infant Psychology, 20,* 237–252.

Vara, A. S., Pang, E. W., Vidal, J., Anagnostou, E., & Taylor, M. J. (2014). Neural mechanisms of inhibitory control continue to mature in adolescence. *Developmental Cognitive Neuroscience, 10,* 129–139.

Vargesson, N. (2015). Thalidomide-induced teratogenesis: History and mechanisms. *Birth Defects Research Part C: Embryo Today: Reviews, 105*(2), 140–156.

Vasquez, O. (2002). *La classe magica.* Mahwah, NJ: Lawrence Erlbaum Associates.

Vasquez-Salgado, Y., Greenfield, P. M., & Burgos-Cienfuegos, R. (2015). Exploring home–school value conflicts: Implications for academic achievement and well-being among Latino first-generation college students. *Journal of Adolescent Research, 30*(3), 271–305.

Vavatzanidis, N. K., Mürbe, D., Friederici, A. D., & Hahne, A. (2016). The perception of stress pattern in young cochlear implanted children: An EEG study. *Frontiers in Neuroscience, 10,* 68.

Veronese, G., Pepe, A., Jaradah, A., Al Muranak, F., & Hamdouna, H. (2017). Modelling life satisfaction and adjustment to trauma in children exposed to ongoing military violence: An exploratory study in Palestine. *Child Abuse & Neglect, 63,* 61–72.

Vespa, J., Lewis, J., & Kreider, R. (2013). *America's families and living arrangements: 2012. Current population report.* Washington, DC: U.S. Census Bureau.

Vicedo, M. (2013). The nature and nurture of love: From imprinting to attachment in Cold War America. Chicago, IL: University of Chicago Press.

Viddal, K. R., Berg-Nielsen, T. S., Wan, M. W., Green, J., Hygen, B. W., & Wichstrøm, L. (2015). Secure attachment promotes the development of effortful control in boys. *Attachment & Human Development, 17*(3), 319–335.

Viding, E., Jones, A. P., Frick, P. J., Moffitt, T. E., & Plomin, R. (2008, January). Heritability of antisocial behaviour at 9: Do callous unemotional traits matter? *Developmental Science, 11*(1), 17–22.

Vinden, P. (1999). Children's understanding of mind and emotion: A multi-culture study. *Cognition & Emotion, 13,* 19–48.

Vinden, P. G. (2002). Understanding minds and evidence for belief: A study of Mofu children in Cameroon. *International Journal of Behavioral Development, 26*(5), 445–452.

Violato, C., & Wiley, A. (1990). Images of adolescence in English literature: The middle ages to the modern period. *Adolescence, 25,* 253–264.

Visootsak, J., & Graham, J. M. (2006). Klinefelter syndrome and other sex chromosomal aneuploidies. *Orphanet Journal of Rare Diseases, 1,* 42.

Voegtline, K. M., Costigan, K. A., Pater, H. A., & DiPietro, J. A. (2013). Near-term fetal responses to maternal spoken voice. *Infant Behavior and Development, 36,* 526–533.

Vogan, V. M., Morgan, B. R., Powell, T. L., Smith, M. L., & Taylor, M. J. (2016). The neurodevelopmental differences of increasing verbal working memory demand in children and adults. *Developmental Cognitive Neuroscience, 17,* 19–27.

Volterra, V., Iverson, J., & Castrataro, M. (2006). The development of gesture in hearing and deaf children. In B. Schick, M. Marschark, & P. Spencer (Eds.), *Advances in the sign language development of deaf children* (pp. 46–70). New York: Oxford University Press.

von Hofsten, C. (1982). Eye–hand coordination in the newborn. *Developmental Psychology, 18*(3), 450–461.

von Hofsten, C. (1984). Developmental changes in the organization of prereaching movements. *Developmental Psychology, 20*(3), 378–388.

von Hofsten, C. (2001). On the early development of action, perception, and cognition. In F. Lacerda, C. von Hofsten, & M. Heimann (Eds.), *Emerging cognitive abilities in early infancy* (pp. 73–89). Mahwah, NJ: Lawrence Erlbaum Associates.

von Koss Torkildsen, J., Friis Hansen, H. F., Svangstu, J. M., Smith, L., Simonsen, H. G., Moen, I., & Lindgren, M. (2009). Brain dynamics of word familiarization in 20-month-olds: Effects of productive vocabulary size. *Brain and Language, 108,* 73–88.

von Soest, T. Wichstrøm, L., & Kvalem, I. L. (2016). The development of global and domain-specific self-esteem from age 13 to 31. *Journal of Personality and Social Psychology, 110*(4), 592.

Votruba-Drzal, E., Miller, P., & Coley, R. L. (2016). Poverty, urbanicity, and children's development of early academic skills. *Child Development Perspectives, 10*(1), 3–9.

Vurpillot, E. (1968). The development of scanning strategies and their relation to visual differentiation. *Journal of Experimental Child Psychology, 6,* 632–650.

Vygotsky, L. S. (1934/1986). *Thought and language.* Cambridge, MA: MIT Press.

Vygotsky, L. S. (1978). *Mind in society.* Cambridge, MA: Harvard University Press.

Wachs, T. D., & Bates, J. E. (2001). *Temperament.* In G. Bremmer & A. Fogel (Eds.), *Blackwell handbook of infant development: Vol. 12. Handbooks of developmental psychology* (pp. 465–501). Malden, MA: Blackwell Publishing.

Waddington, C. H. (1957). *The Strategy of the Genes.* London: Geo Allen & Unwin.

Wagner, D. A. (1974). The development of short-term and incidental memory: A cross cultural study. *Child Development, 48,* 389–396.

Wagner, S., Cepeda, I., Krieger, D., Maggi, S., D'Angiulli, A., Weinberg, J., & Grunau, R. (2016). Higher cortisol is associated with poorer executive functioning in preschool children: The role of parenting stress, parent coping and quality of daycare. *Child Neuropsychology, 22*(7), 853–869.

Wahlstrom, K. L. (2002). Accommodating the sleep patterns of adolescents within current educational structures: An uncharted path. In M. Carskadon (Ed.), *Adolescent sleep patterns: Biological, social, and psychological influences* (pp. 172–197). New York: Cambridge University Press.

Wainright, J. L., & Patterson, C. J. (2008). Peer relations among adolescents with female same-sex parents. *Developmental Psychology, 44,* 117–126.

Wainryb, C. (1995). Reasoning about social conflicts in different cultures: Druze and Jewish children in Israel. *Child Development, 66*(2), 390–401.

Wainryb, C. (2010). Resilience and risk: How teens experience their violent world, and what they learn—and lose—in the process. *Journal of Applied Developmental, 31,* 410–412.

Wakai, R. T., & Lutter, W. J. (2016). Slow rhythms and sleep spindles in early infancy. *Neuroscience Letters, 630,* 164–168.

Walker, L. J., Hennig, K., & Krettenauer, T. (2000). Parent and peer contexts for children's moral reasoning development. *Child Development, 71,* 1033–1048.

Walker, R., Hill, K., Burger, O., & Hurtado, M. (2006). Life in the slow lane revised: Ontogenetic separation between chimpanzees and humans. *American Journal of Physical Anthropology, 129,* 577–583.

Walker, S., Irving, K., & Berthelsen, D. (2002). Gender influences on preschool children's social problem-solving strategies. *The Journal of Genetic Psychology,* 163, 197–209.

Waller, R., Dishion, T., Shaw, D., Gardner, F., Wilson, M., & Hyde, L. (2016). Does early childhood callous-unemotional behavior uniquely predict behavior problems or callous-unemotional behavior in late childhood? *Developmental Psychology, 52*(11), 1805–1819.

Walton, M. (2013). The "wages of Burman-ness": Ethnicity and Burman privilege in contemporary Myanmar. *Journal of Contemporary Asia, 43*(1), 1–27.

Wang, M. V., Lekhal, R., Aarø, L. E., & Schjølberg, S. (2014). Co-occurring development of early childhood communication and motor skills: Results from a population-based longitudinal study. *Child: Care, Health and Development, 40*(1), 77–84.

Wang, S., Zhang, Y., & Baillargeon, R. (2016). Young infants view physically possible support events as unexpected: New evidence for rule learning. *Cognition, 157,* 100–105.

Wang, S.-H., & Baillargeon, R. (2008). Can infants be "taught" to attend to a new physical variable in an event category? The case of height in covering events. *Cognitive Psychology, 56,* 284–326.

Wang, S.-H, Baillargeon, R., & Brueckner, L. (2004). Young infants' reasoning about hidden objects: Evidence from violation-of-expectation tasks with test trials only. *Cognition, 93,* 167–198.

Ward, T. C. S. (2015). Reasons for mother–infant bed-sharing: A systematic narrative synthesis of the literature and implications for future research. *Maternal and Child Health Journal, 19*(3), 675–690.

Warren, K. L., & Peterson, C. (2014). Exploring parent–child discussions of crime and their influence on children's memory. *Behavioral Sciences and the Law, 32*(6), 686–701.

Waters, T. E. A., Bosmans, G., Vandevivere, E., Dujardin, A., & Waters, H. S. (2015). Secure base representations in middle childhood across two western cultures: Associations with parental attachment representations and maternal reports of behavior problems. *Developmental Psychology, 51*(8), 1013–1025.

Watson, J. B. (1930). *Behaviorism.* Chicago, IL: University of Chicago Press.

Waxman, S., & Leddon, E. (2011). Early word-learning and conceptual development: Everything had a name, and each name gave birth to a new thought. In U. Goswami (Ed.), *The Wiley-Blackwell handbook of childhood cognitive development* (2nd ed., pp. 180–209). Malden, MA: Blackwell.

Way, N. (2013). Boys' friendships during adolescence: Intimacy, desire, and loss. *Journal of Research on Adolescence, 23*(2), 201–213.

Way, N., & Greene, M. L. (2006). Trajectories of perceived friendship quality during adolescence: The patterns and contextual predictors. *Journal of Research on Adolescence, 16*(2), 293–320.

Way, N., & Pahl, K. (2001). Individual and contextual predictors of perceived friendship quality among ethnic minority, low-income adolescents. *Journal of Research on Adolescence, 11*(4), 325–349.

Webb, P. (2016). Sabotaging success: Examining academic dis-identification among African American male adolescents. *Race, Gender & Class, 23*(1/2), 172–182.

Weinstock, M. (2015). Changing epistemologies under conditions of social change in two Arab communities in Israel. *International Journal of Psychology, 50*(1), 29–36.

Weisfeld, G. E., & Janisse, H. C. (2005). Some functional aspects of human adolescence. In B. J. Ellis & D. F. Bjorklund (Eds.), *Origins of the social mind: Evolutionary psychology and child development* (pp. 189–218). New York: Guilford Press.

Weisgram, E. S. (2016). The cognitive construction of gender stereotypes: Evidence for the dual pathways model of gender differentiation. *Sex Roles, 75*(7–8), 301–313.

Weisner, T. S. (2014). The socialization of trust: Plural caregiving and diverse pathways in human development across cultures. In H. Otto and H. Keller (Eds.), *Different faces of attachment: Cultural variations on a universal human need* (pp. 263–277). New York: Cambridge University Press.

Weisz, A. N., & Black, B. M. (2003). Gender and moral reasoning: African American youths respond to dating dilemmas. *Journal of Human Behavior in the Social Environment, 6*(3), 17–34.

Weitoft, G., Hern, A., Haglunk, B., & Rosen, M. (2003). Mortality, severe morbidity, and injury in children living with single parents in Sweden: A population-based study. *Lancet, 361,* 289–295.

Wellings, K., Martine, C., Slaymaker, E., Singh, S., Hodges, Z., Patel, D., et al. (2006). Sexual behaviour in context: A global perspective. *Lance, 368,* 1706–1728.

Wellman, F. (2011). Developing a theory of mind. In U. Goswami (Ed.), *The Wiley-Blackwell handbook of childhood cognitive development* (2nd ed.). Malden, MA: Blackwell.

Wellman, H. M., Hickling, A. K., & Schult, C. A. (1997). Young children's psychological, physical, and biological explanations. In H. M. Wellman & K. Inagaki (Eds.), *The emergence of core domains of thought: Children's reasoning about physical, psychological, and biological phenomena* (pp. 7– 26). San Francisco, CA: Jossey-Bass.

Wells, G. (2007). The mediating role of discoursing in activity. *Mind, Culture, and Activity, 14*(3), 160–177.

Wendell, A. D. (2013). Overview and epidemiology of substance abuse in pregnancy. *Clinical Obstetrics and Gynecology, 56*(1): 91–96.

Wentzel, K. R., & Asher, S. R. (1995). The academic level of neglected, rejected, popular, and controversial children. *Child Development, 66,* 754–763.

Werker, J. F., Yeung, H. H., & Yoshida, K. A. (2012). How do infants become experts at native-speech perception? *Current Directions in Psychological Science, 21*(4), 221–226.

Wetherill, R., & Tapert, S. F. (2013). Adolescent brain development, substance use, and psychotherapeutic change. *Psychology of Addictive Behaviors: Journal of the Society of Psychologists in Addictive Behaviors, 27*(2), 393–402.

Whitaker, R. C., Wright, J. A., Pepe, M. S., Seidel, K. D., & Dietz, W. H. (1997). Predicting obesity in young adulthood from childhood and parental obesity. *New England Journal of Medicine, 337,* 869–873.

White, R. E., & Carlson, S. M. (2016). What would batman do? Self-distancing improves executive function in young children. *Developmental Science, 19*(3), 419–426.

White, R. M. B., Liu, Y., Gonzales, N. A., Knight, G. P., & Tein, J. (2016). Neighborhood qualification of the association between parenting and problem behavior trajectories among Mexican-origin father–adolescent dyads. *Journal of Research on Adolescence, 26*(4), 927–946.

White, S. H. (1991). Three visions of educational psychology. In L. Tolchinsky-Landsmann (Ed.), *Culture, schooling and psychological development* (pp. 1–38). Norwood, NJ: Ablex.

White, S. H. (1996). The relationship of developmental psychology to social policy. In E. F. Zigler & S. L. Kagan (Eds.), *Children, families, and government: Preparing for the twenty-first century* (pp. 409–426). New York: Cambridge University Press.

Whitehouse, A., Maybery, M. T., Hart, R., & Sloboda, D. M. (2010). Free testosterone levels in umbilical-cord blood predict infant head circumference in females. *Developmental Medicine and Child Neurology, 52,* 73–77.

Whiteman, S. D., McHale, S. M., & Crouter, A. C. (2007, November). Competing processes of sibling influence: Observational learning and sibling deidentification. *Social Development, 16*(4), 642–661.

Whiting, B. B., & Whiting, J. W. M. (1975). *Children of six cultures: A psycho-cultural analysis.* Cambridge, MA: Harvard University Press.

Whiting, J. W. M., Burbank, V. K., and Ratner. M. S., (1986). The duration of maidenhood across cultures. In J. B. Lancaster & B. A. Hamburg (Eds.), *School Age Pregnancy and Parenthood* (pp. 273–302). New York: Aldine.

Whiting, J. W. M., & Child, I. L. (1953). *Child training and personality.* New Haven, CT: Yale University Press.

Whiting, S. J., Vatanparast, H., Baxter-Jones, A., Faulkner, R. A, Mirwald, R., & Bailey, D. A. (2004, March). Factors that affect bone mineral accrual in the adolescent growth spurt. *The Journal of Nutrition, 134*(3), 696S–700S.

Whittle, S., Yücel, M., Fornito, A., Barrett, A., Wood, S. J., Lubman, D. I., et al. (2008). Neuroanatomical correlates of temperament in early adolescents. *Journal of the American Academy of Child & Adolescent Psychiatry, 47,* 682–693.

Wicklund, C., & Trepanier, A. (2014). Adapting genetic counseling training to the genomic era: More an evolution than a revolution. *Journal of Genetic Counseling, 23*(4), 452–454.

Wideman, L., Calkins, S. D., Janssen, J. A., Lovelady, C. A., Dollar, J. M., Keane, S. P., et al. (2016). Rationale, design and methods for the RIGHT track health study: Pathways from childhood self-regulation to cardiovascular risk in adolescence. *BMC Public Health, 16*(1), 459.

Widome, R., Neumark-Sztainer, D., Hannan, P. J., Haines, J., & Story, M. (2009). Eating when there is not enough to eat: Eating behaviors and perceptions of food among food-insecure youths. *American Journal of Public Health, 99*(5), 822–828.

Wiesner, M., Silbereisen, R. K., & Weichold, K. (2008). Effects of deviant peer association on adolescent alcohol consumption: A growth mixture modeling analysis. *Journal of Youth and Adolescence, 37*(5), 537–551.

Wilcox, A. J., Baird, D. D., & Weinberg, C. R. (1999). Time of implantation of the conceptus and loss of pregnancy. *New England Journal of Medicine, 340,* 1796–1799.

Wilkinson, N., Paikan, A., Gredebäck, G., Rea, F., Metta, G., et al. (2014). Staring us in the face? An embodied theory of innate face preference. *Developmental Science, 17*(6), 809–825.

Williams, J. F., Smith, V. C., & Committee on Substance Abuse. (2015). Fetal alcohol spectrum disorders. *Pediatrics, 136*(5), e1395–e1406.

Wilson, B. J., Smith, S. L., Potter, W. J., Kunkel, D., Linz, D., Colvin, C. M., et al. (2002, March). Violence in children's television programming: Assessing the risks. *Journal of Communication, 52*(1), 5–35.

Wilson, E. O. (1975). *Sociobiology: The new synthesis.* Cambridge, MA: Harvard University Press.

Wilson, S., & Gore, J. (2013). An attachment model of university connectedness. *Journal of Experimental Education, 81*(2), 178–198.

Wilson, S. M., Olver, R. E., & Walters, D. V. (2007). Developmental regulation of lumenal lung fluid and electrolyte transport. *Respiratory Physiology and Neurobiology, 159*(3), 247–255.

Wit, J. M. (2015). Idiopathic short stature. *Journal of Clinical Research in Pediatric Endocrinology, 7*(1).

Witecy, B., & Penke, M. (2017). Language comprehension in children, adolescents, and adults with Down syndrome. *Research in Developmental Disabilities, 62,* 184–196.

Witherington, D., & Lickliter, R. (2016). Integrating development and evolution in psychological science: Evolutionary developmental psychology, developmental systems, and explanatory pluralism. *Human Development, 59*(4), 200–234.

Wittman, A. B., & Wall, L. L. (2007). The evolutionary origins of obstructed labor: Bipedalism, encephalization, and the human obstetric dilemma. *Obstetrical & Gynecological Survey, 62*(11), 739–748.

Wohlfahrt-Veje, C., Mouritsen, A., Hagen, C. P., Tinggaard, J., Mieritz, M. G., Boas, M., et al. (2016). Pubertal onset in boys and girls is influenced by pubertal timing of both parents. *Journal of Clinical Endocrinology & Metabolism, 101*(7), 2667–2674.

Wojcik, E. H., & Saffran, J. R. (2015). Toddlers encode similarities among novel words from meaningful sentences. *Cognition, 138,* 10–20.

Wolak, J., Mitchell, K., & Finkelhor, D. (2007). Unwanted and wanted exposure to online pornography in a national sample of youth internet users. *Pediatrics, 119*(2), 247–257.

Wolff, P. H. (1967). The role of biological rhythms in early psychological development. *Bulletin of the Menninger Clinic, 31*(4), 197.

Wolfenstein, M. (1953). Trends in infant care. *American Journal of Orthopsychiatry, 23,* 120–130.

Wolff, P. H. (1966). The causes, controls, and organization of behavior in the neonate. *Psychological Issues, 5,* 1–105.

Wood, S. H. (2003). Should women be given a choice about fetal assessment in labor? *The American Journal of Maternal/Child Nursing, 28*(5), 292–298.

Wood, S., McNeil, D., Yee, W., Siever, J., & Rose, S. (2014). Neighbourhood socio-economic status and spontaneous premature birth in Alberta. *Canadian Journal of Public Health, 105*(5), e383.

Woolley, J. D., & McInnis, M. (2015). The development of children's concepts of invisibility. *Cognitive Development, 34,* 63–75.

World Health Organization. (2006). WHO child growth standards based on length/height, weight and age. *Acta Paediatrica, 95*(Suppl. 450), 76–85.

World Health Organization. (2010). *Marketing of food and nonalcoholic beverages to children.* Resolution of the Sixty-third World Health Assembly, adopted 21 May 2010, (WHA 63). Retrieved from http://whqlibdoc.who.int/publications/2010/9789241500210_eng.pdf

World Health Organization. (2016). *Congenital anomalies.* Retrieved from www.who.int/mediacentre/factsheets/fs370/en/

World Health Organization. (2016). *Infant and young child feeding.* Retrieved from http://www.who.int/mediacentre/factsheets/fs342/en/

World Health Organization. (2017). *Global Accelerated Action for the Health of Adolescents (AA-HA!): Guidance to support country implementation. Summary.* Geneva: World Health Organization.

World Health Organization/UNAIDS/UNICEF. (2016). *WHO-UNAIDS HIV vaccine initiative.* Retrieved from http://www.who.int/immunization/research/forums_and_initiatives/HIV_vaccine_initiative/en/

Wörmann, V., Holodynski, M., Kärtner, J., & Keller, H. (2012). A cross-cultural comparison of the development of the social smile. A longitudinal study of maternal and infant imitation in 6- and 12-week-old infants. *Infant Behavior & Development, 35,* 335–347.

Wright, K., Poulin-Dubois, D., & Kelley, E. (2015). The animate–inanimate distinction in preschool children. *British Journal of Developmental Psychology, 33*(1), 73–91.

Wright, T. E., Schuetter, R., & Sauvage, L. (2014). Methamphetamines and birth outcomes. *Obstetrics & Gynecology, 123*(Suppl. 1), 178S–178S.

Wu, P., Robinson, C. C., Yang, C., Hart, C. H., & Olsen, S. F. (2002). Similarities and differences in mothers' parenting of preschoolers in China and the United States. *International Journal of Behavioral Development, 26,* 481–491.

Wu, Q. (2017). Effects of social capital in multiple contexts on the psychosocial adjustment of Chinese migrant children. *Youth & Society, 49*(2), 150–179.

Wu, Y., Reece, E. A., Zhong, J., Dong, D., Shen, W., Harman, C. R., & Yang, P. (2016). Type 2 diabetes mellitus induces congenital heart defects in murine embryos by increasing oxidative stress, endoplasmic reticulum stress, and apoptosis. *American Journal of Obstetrics and Gynecology, 215*(3), 366.e1–366.e10.

Wynn, K. (1992). Addition and subtraction by human infants. *Nature, 358,* 749–750.

Wynne-Edwards, K. E., Edwards, H. E., & Hancock, T. M. (2013). The human fetus preferentially secretes corticosterone, rather than cortisol, in response to intra-partum stressors. *PLOS ONE, 8*(6), e63684.

Xia, Z., Hancock, R., & Hoeft, F. (2017). Neurobiological bases of reading disorder part I: Etiological investigations. *Language and Linguistics Compass, 11*(4), e12239.

Xiong, X., Harville, E. W., Mattison, D. R., Elkind-Hirsch, K., Pridjian, G., & Buekens, P. (2008). Exposure to Hurricane Katrina, post-traumatic stress disorder and birth outcomes. *American Journal of Medical Science, 336,* 111–115.

Yahirun, J. J., Perreira, K. M., & Fuligni, A. J. (2015). Family obligation across contexts: Hispanic youth in North Carolina and southern California. *Journal of Family Issues, 36*(10), 1296–1323.

Yahyaoui, A., Methni, M. E., Gaultier, S., & Lakhdar-Yahyaoui, D. B. H. (2013). Acculturative processes and adolescent sexuality: A comparative study of 115 immigrant adolescents from cultures influenced by Islam and 115 French adolescents from cultures influenced by Christianity. *International Journal of Intercultural Relations, 37*(1), 28–47.

Yajnik, C. S. (2014). Transmission of obesity-adiposity and related disorders from the mother to the baby. *Annals of Nutrition and Metabolism, 64*(Suppl. 1), 8–17.

Yanai, J., Steingart, R. A., Snapir, N., Gvaryahu, G., Rozenboim, I., & Katz, A. (2000). The relationship between neural alterations and behavioral deficits after prenatal exposure to heroin. *Annals of the New York Academy of Sciences, 914*(1), 402–411.

Yang, C., & Hahn, H. (2002). Cosleeping in young Korean children. *Journal of Developmental & Behavioral Pediatrics, 23,* 151–157.

Yang, I., Corwin, E. J., Brennan, P. A., Jordan, S., Murphy, J. R., & Dunlop, A. (2016). The infant microbiome: Implications for infant health and neurocognitive development. *Nursing Research, 65*(1), 76–88.

Yang, Q., Carter, H., Mulinare, J., Berry, R., Friedman, J., & Erickson, J. (2007). Race-ethnicity differences in folic acid intake in women of childbearing age in the United States after folic acid fortification: Findings from the National Health and Nutrition Examination Survey, 2001–2002. *American Journal of Clinical Nutrition, 85,* 1409–1416.

Yanuarti, H. P., Rusmil, K., & Effendi, S. H. (2014). Environment as a risk factor in delayed development in premature, low-birthweight and mild asphyxia children. *Pediatrics International, 56*(5), 720–725.

Yau, J., & Smetana, J. (2003). Conceptions of moral, social-conventional, and personal events among Chinese preschoolers in Hong Kong. *Child Development, 74*(3), 647–658.

Yeh, Z., Lin, Y., Liu, S., & Fang, C. (2017). Social awareness and its relationship with emotion recognition and theory of mind in patients with borderline personality disorder. *Journal of Social and Clinical Psychology, 36*(1), 22.

Yektaei-Karin, E., Moshfegh, A., Lundahl, J., Berggren, V., Hansson, L., Marchini, G., et al. (2007). The stress of birth enhances in vitro spontaneous and IL-8-induced neutrophil chemotaxis in the human newborn. *Pediatric Allergy and Immunology, 18*(8), 643–651.

Yerkes, R. M. (Ed.). (1921). *Psychological examining in the United States Army. Memoirs of the National Academy of Sciences, 15,* 1–890.

Yinan, H. (2007). Infant born with birth defects every thirty seconds. *China Daily* Retrieved from http://www.chinadaily.com.cn/china/2007-10/30/content_6215074.htm

Ying-Xiu, Z., & Shu-Rong, W. (2008). Distribution of body mass index and the prevalence changes of overweight and obesity among adolescents in Shandong, China from 1985 to 2005. *Annals of Human Biology, 35*(5), 547–555.

Ylisaukko-oja, T., Alarcón, M., Cantor, R. M., Auranen, M., Vanhala, R., Kempas, E., et al. (2006). Search for autism loci by combined analysis of Autism Genetic Resource Exchange and Finnish families. *Annals of Neurology, 59*(1), 145–155.

Yoo, H. C., Steger, M. F., & Lee, R. M. (2010). Validation of the subtle and blatant racism scale for Asian American college students (SABR-A^2). *Cultural Diversity and Ethnic Minority Psychology, 16*(3), 323.

Yoon, E., Chang, C. T., Kim, S., Clawson, A., Cleary, S. E., Hansen, M., et al. (2013). A meta-analysis of acculturation/enculturation and mental health. *Journal of Counseling Psychology, 60*(1), 15–30.

Yoon, E., Hacker, J., Hewitt, A., Abrams, M., & Cleary, S. (2012). Social connectedness, discrimination, and social status as mediators of acculturation/enculturation and well-being. *Journal of Counseling Psychology, 59*(1), 86–96.

Yoon, E., Langrehr, K., & Ong, L. (2011). Content analysis of acculturation research in counseling and counseling psychology: A 22-year review. *Journal of Counseling Psychology, 58,* 83–96.

Yorifuji, T., Kashima, S., Higa Diez, M., Kado, Y., Sanada, S., & Doi, H. (2016). Prenatal exposure to traffic-related air pollution and child behavioral development milestone delays in Japan. *Epidemiology, 27*(1), 57–65.

Yorifuji, T., Tsuda, T., Inoue, S., Takao, S., & Harada, M. (2011). Long-term exposure to methylmercury and psychiatric symptoms in residents of Minamata, Japan. *Environment International, 37,* 907–913.

Yoshida, K. A., Iversen, J. R., Patel, A. D., Mazuka, R., Nito, H., Gervain, J, & Werker, J. F. (2010). The development of perceptual grouping biases in infancy: A Japanese-English cross-linguistic study. *Cognition,* 356–361.

Yoshikawa, H., Rosman, E., & Hsueh, J. (2001). Variation in teenage mothers' experiences of child care and other components of welfare reform: Selection processes and developmental outcomes. *Child Development, 72,* 299–317.

Young, M., Denny, G., Penhollow, T., Palacios, R., & Morris, D. (2015). Hiding the word: Examining the relationship between a new measure of religiosity and sexual behavior. *Journal of Religion and Health, 54*(3), 922–942.

Yow, W. Q., Li, X., Lam, S., Gliga, T., Chong, Y. S., Kwek, K., & Broekman, B. F. P. (2017). A bilingual advantage in 54-month-olds' use of referential cues in fast mapping. *Developmental Science, 20*(1), e12482.

Zaccarella, E., Meyer, L., Makuuchi, M., & Friederici, A. D. (2015). Building by syntax: The neural basis of minimal linguistic structures. *Cerebral Cortex, 27*(1), 411–421.

Zafeiriou, D. I., Tsikoulas, I. G., Kremenopoulos, G. M., & Kontopoulos, E. E. (1999). Moro reflex profile in high-risk infants at the first year of life. *Brain and Development, 21*(3), 216–217.

Zaff, J. F., Malanchuk, O., & Eccles, J. S. (2008). Predicting positive citizenship from adolescence to young adulthood: The effects of a civic context. *Applied Developmental Science, 12*(1), 38–53.

Zahn-Waxler, C., & Polanichka, N. (2004). All things interpersonal: Socialization and female aggression. In M. Putallaz & K. Bierman (Eds.), *Aggression, antisocial behavior, and violence among girls.* New York: Guilford Press.

Zakaria, E., & Syamaun, M. (2017). The effect of realistic mathematics education approach on students' achievement and attitudes towards mathematics. *Mathematics Education Trends and Research, 2017*(1), 32–40.

Zampini, L., Fasolo, M., & D'Odorico, L. (2012). Characteristics of maternal input to children with Down syndrome: A comparison with vocabulary size and chronological age-matched groups. *First Language, 32*(3), 324–342.

Zash, R., Souda, S., Leidner, J., Ribaudo, H., Binda, K., Moyo, S., et al. (2016). HIV-exposed children account for more than half of 24-month mortality in Botswana. *BMC Pediatrics, 16*(1), 103.

Zeanah, C. H., & Gleason, M. M. (2015). Annual research review: Attachment disorders in early childhood—Clinical presentation, causes, correlates, and treatment. *Journal of Child Psychology and Psychiatry, 56*(3), 207–222.

Zeanah, C. H., Egger, H. L., Smyke, A. T., Nelson, C. A., & Fox, N. A. (2009). Institutional rearing and psychiatric disorders in Romanian preschool children. *The American Journal of Psychiatry, 166,* 777–785.

Zeanah, C. H., Gunnar, M. R., McCall, R. B., Kreppner, J. M., & Fox, N. A. (2011). Sensitive periods. *Monographs of the Society for Research in Child Development, 76,* 147–162.

Zelazo, P. D., & Müller, U. (2011). Executive function in typical and atypical development In U. Goswami (Ed.), *The Wiley-Blackwell handbook of childhood cognitive development* (2nd ed., pp. 574–603). New York: Wiley-Blackwell.

Zelazo, P. R. (1983). The development of walking: New findings and old assumptions. *Journal of Motor Behavior, 15,* 99–137.

Zeng, F.-G., Tang, Q., and Lu, T. (2014). Abnormal pitch perception produced by cochlear implant stimulation. *PLOS ONE, 9,* e88662.

Zero to Three. (2010). *How to choose quality child care.* Retrieved from https://www.zerotothree.org/resources/84-how-to-choose-quality-child-care#chapter-58

Zeskind, P., McMurray, M., Lippard, E., Grewen, K., Garber, K., & Johns, J. (2014). Translational analysis of effects of prenatal cocaine exposure on human infant cries and rat pup ultrasonic vocalizations. *PLOS ONE, 9*(10), e110349.

Zhang, L., & Rao, N. (2017). Effortful control and academic achievement in rural China. *Early Education and Development, 28*(5), 541–558.

Zielinski, D. S., & Bradshaw, C. P. (2006, February). Ecological influences on the sequelae of child maltreatment: A review of the literature. *Child Maltreatment: Journal of the American Professional Society on the Abuse of Children, 11*(1), 49–62.

Zielinski, D. S., Eckenrode, J., & Olds, D. L. (2009). Nurse home visitation and the prevention of child maltreatment: Impact on the timing of official reports. *Development and Psychopathology, 21,* 441–453.

Zigler, E., & Styfco, S. J. (2010). The hidden history of Head Start. In E. Zigler & S. J. Styfco (Eds.), *The hidden history of Head Start.* New York: Oxford University Press.

Zimmer-Gembeck, M. J., & French, J. (2016). Associations of sexual subjectivity with global and sexual well-being: A new measure for young males and comparison to females. *Archives of Sexual Behavior, 45*(2), 315–327.

Zirkel, P. A. (2017). RTI and other approaches to SLD identification under the IDEA: A legal update. *Learning Disability Quarterly, 40*(3), 165–173.

Zosh, J. M., Verdine, B. N., Filipowicz, A., Golinkoff, R. M., Hirsh-Pasek, K., & Newcombe, N. S. (2015). Talking shape: Parental language with electronic versus traditional shape sorters: Traditional toys promote parent spatial talk. *Mind, Brain, and Education, 9*(3), 136–144.

Zsirai, L., Csákány, G. M., Vargha, P., Fülöp, V., & Tabák, Á. G. (2016). Breech presentation: Its predictors and consequences. An analysis of the Hungarian Tauffer Obstetric Database (1996–2011). *Acta Obstetricia et Gynecologica Scandinavica, 95*(3), 347–354.

Zsolnai, A., Lesznyák, M., & Kasik, L. (2012). Pre-school children's aggressive and pro-social behaviours in stressful situations. *Early Child Development and Care, 182*(11), 1503–1522.

Zuberi, A., & Teixeira, S. (2017). Child health in low-income neighborhoods: The unexpected relationship with neighborhood disorder and other aspects of distress. *Journal of Community Psychology, 45*(4), 459–472.

Zuilkowski, S. S., Collet, K., Jambai, M., Akinsulure-Smith, A. M., & Betancourt, T. S. (2016). Youth and resilience in postconflict settings: An intervention for war-affected youth in Sierra Leone. *Human Development, 59*(2–3), 64–80.

NAME INDEX

Note: Page numbers followed by f indicate figures; those followed by t indicate tables.

SUBJECT INDEX

Note: Page numbers followed by f indicate figures, and those followed by t indicate tables.